Multicultural

D0074462

WE

ARE

EVERYWHERE

D0074461

WE

ARE

EVERYWHERE

A Historical Sourcebook of Gay and Lesbian Politics

Edited by

MARK BLASIUS and SHANE PHELAN

Routledge

New York   London

Published in 1997 by

Routledge
29 West 35th Street
New York, NY 10001

Published in Great Britain by

Routledge
11 New Fetter Lane
London EC4P 4EE

Library of Congress Cataloging-in-Publication Data
We are everywhere: a historical sourcebook of gay and lesbian politics /
edited by Mark Blasius and Shane Phelan.
      p.   cm.
    Includes bibliographical references.
    ISBN 0-415-90858-2 (Hb)
    ISBN 0-415-90859-0 (Pb)
    1. Homosexuality—Political aspects. 2. Homosexuality—History.
3. Gay liberation movement—History. 4. Gay men—Political activity. 5. Lesbians—Political
activity. 6. Political science—Philosophy. I. Blasius, Mark II. Phelan, Shane.
HQ76.W33 1995   95-2434
305.9'0664—dc20   CIP

British Library Cataloging-in-Publication Data is available from the British Library

CONTENTS

B. THE EMERGENCE OF A GAY AND LESBIAN POLITICAL CULTURE IN GERMANY

1. THE SCIENTIFIC–HUMANITARIAN COMMITTEE

2. CULTURAL CRITIQUE: THE COMMUNITY OF THE SPECIAL

3. LEGAL REFORM: KURT HILLER AND THE ACTION COMMITTEE

4. COMBINING POLITICAL AND CULTURAL WORK: THE LEAGUE FOR HUMAN RIGHTS

C. BRITAIN AND FRANCE

D. FROM LIBERALISM TO THE NEW SOCIAL RELATIONS OF SOVIET SOCIALISM

E. SUBCULTURE, CENSORSHIP, AND CIVIL RIGHTS IN THE UNITED STATES

PART III: THE HOMOPHILE MOVEMENT 1950-1969

A. CONTEXT

B. THE MATTACHINE SOCIETY

C. ONE

D. DAUGHTERS OF BILITIS

PART IV: GAY LIBERATION AND LESBIAN-FEMINISM

PART V: THE GAY AND LESBIAN POLITICS OF AIDS

PART VI: THE PRESENT MOMENT AND THE FUTURE OF DESIRE

ACKNOWLEDGMENTS

Many people have helped to make this project a reality. Colleagues, friends, and reviewers have suggested materials; we would especially like to thank Maria Diaz, Ron Goldberg, Jeffrey Merrick, Michel Cressole, Hert Hekma, Patrick Cardon, Richard Parker, David Robinson, David Nimmons, Gene Rice, Albert Dichy, Daniel Defert, Michael Denneny, Maurice Woodard, Julie Dorf, Jorge Cortines, Brian Wolbaum, N' Tanya Lee, Dan Schluter, Vivek Batra, Larry-Bob, Javid Syed, Jonathan Ned Katz, Leonard Harris, Odell Mays II, Bob Bailey, Wayne Dynes, Karla Jay, Edmund White, David Thomas, and several anonymous reviewers. The staffs of the International Gay and Lesbian archives in Los Angeles and the Sophia Smith Archives of Smith College worked to locate material from the 1950s and 1960s; those of the International Gay and Lesbian Human Rights Commission helped with non-Western material. Valerie Hegstrom Oakey read Spanish-language work; Michael West and Nancy Erber translated from French. Michael Lombardi-Nash translated Benkert; Hubert Kennedy translated Ulrichs and gave advice about him. We are gratified by the incredible outpouring of support from them and many other scholars in the history of homosexuality.

Among scholars, Laura Engelstein and James Steakley deserve special mention and thanks. Jim worked together with Mark criticizing and revising the material on the German movement; he also translated much of it. Laura made suggestions on which Russian and Soviet pieces to include and, all in the line of duty, ended up translating and writing introductions for them. Their work here demonstrates why politics needs fine scholarship, and they each exemplify the kind of conscience those of us in academic life should have.

Anne Frost and Mary Morell discussed the project with Shane and helped gain permissions for writing from *The Ladder*. Edmundo Urrutia served as research assistant. Cecelia Cancellaro, our editor at Routledge, encouraged and prodded us; Maura Burnett and Claudia Gorelick worked to smooth the smooth the rough edges of all the relationships involved; Dave Auburn took responsibility for the final stages of production.

In the fall of 1991 we began work on this book. Cecelia invited Mark to do a reader. Mark discussed the idea with his gym buddy Michael Denneny and decided upon a history of primary documents—political speech—of the lesbian and gay movement. He then asked Shane to do it with him. At the time we began it was an exciting idea; five years later it is exhausting but gratifying. Shane thanks Kaile Goodman, Ann Nihlen, and Diane Robin for their support and patience during this time. Mark thanks the many political colleagues who helped find the documents reprinted here, and his housemates at 161 Ocean Walk, Fire Island Pines, for their tolerance during the first summer of work on this book. Mark's work was supported in part by a CUNY faculty research grant.

Most of all we would like to thank everyone who made this book possible by writing before us, until recently always in situations of social hostility and political invisibility, and today in the medical calamity that is AIDS. Indeed, a number of the authors whose works are included here died while this book was being prepared for publication. Without all of them, and all of you now here to read and write and speak, we could not do this work; not only because we reprint here words that went before, but because those words helped to make a gay and lesbian world where our own lives and ideas can become meaningful and have political import. We thank you for your courage, your persistence, and your vision.

INTRODUCTION

Across the U.S. and around the world, gays and lesbians are challenging social presumptions that have kept them invisible or marginalized. From Chicago to Sri Lanka, people are claiming an identity that most were "taught to despise," in Michelle Cliff's memorable phrase. This identity is built on the sexual and emotional desire we feel for members of the same sex. In some places we face a social climate of overt hostility, and are then labelled "unnatural" or "sinful"; in others we encounter simple ignorance or refusal to accord significance to our desires. As we claim this identity, we face opponents who claim that our desires are pathological, that we are a product of secular humanism, Western decadence, capitalism, or Communism, and that our struggle is unimportant or divisive in the context of other struggles, such as those for national independence or women's equality. Our resistance to oppression and our attempts to untangle the relations between sexuality, identity, culture, and citizenship are the subject of this book.

We Are Everywhere provides a record of the issues and ideas surrounding the politics of homosexuality. It is not, strictly speaking, a history of lesbian and gay politics; it is, rather, a largely chronological presentation of the ways in which people whose primary sexual attraction is to others of the same sex have understood their social and political position. Our goals are to provide readers with some tools to grasp our contemporary situation, to understand who we are by looking at how we came to be who we are; and to involve readers in the activity of theorizing in order to better inform their political action. We do this by presenting historically and theoretically important statements representing the diversity of lesbian and gay politics.

Same-sex love is a phenomenon common to almost every culture, one occurring throughout recorded history. The ways in which people have understood this attraction, however, have varied widely. For some cultures, such a love is natural and desirable. In ancient Greece, love for boys was seen as evidence of virility, and the relation between boys and men was crucial for the development of boys into men. The distinction was not between homosexual and heterosexual, but between passive and active; while boys could be the object of male affection and desire, the beloved, as they grew into men they were required to assume the posture of the lover instead. We see such distinctions today in many Islamic and Latin American societies. In Islamic Africa, for example, both men and women may have same-sex relationships, but these relationships are typically between wealthy older patrons and poorer, younger companions.

In some places and times, the attraction to another man or another woman has been interpreted as evidence that the person is not really a man or a woman, but is a hybrid or placed inside that body; the North American *berdache* may be the most prominent example. In Hawaii, *moe-aikane* (men who have sex with other men) and *mahus* (men who dress as women) are largely accepted in their families and social groups.

In other societies, most notably Jewish and modern Christian-dominated ones, love between men or between women is prohibited, and those who persist in it are stigmatized. This fear and hatred has provided much of the context for European and North American lesbian and gay politics.

Thus, while we will often use the word "homosexuality," it must be understood that this is an inevitably inadequate category to encompass the variety of desires, identities, and lives that we have lived. Each tradition has its own approach to same-sex love, and that tradition inflects both the sexual understandings and the political reasoning of its participants.

In Europe and Euro-America, the politics of homosexuality is currently shaped by the heritage of Christianity and by medical views of sexuality. The medical discussion of sexuality, begun in the nineteenth century, produced "types" or categories of people that had not previously existed as such. The "homosexual" is quite different from the "sodomite," who was the target of legal persecution. Unable to understand sex in nonheterosexual terms, doctors insisted that gay men were not simply men who performed certain acts with other men. For example, the "sexual invert" was portrayed as effeminate, embodying the stereotypical qualities of women. This of course raised problems for the other partner: was he a "normal" man who had been seduced or had been unable to find a heterosexual outlet? Many doctors divided couples in just such a way. The analogous treatment was made of lesbians, dividing masculine "true inverts" from "normal" (because stereotypically feminine) women who had "gone wrong."

This new designation worked, ironically, to provide a common identity for the men and women who were now labelled. Given a common (although derogatory) understanding of themselves, as well as the increasing flow of information that made them aware that others like them existed, homosexual women and men began to seek each other out not simply for sex, but to build a common life. As they did, they drew on the political language of the modern West—individual rights, equality, citizenship—to justify their choices and claim equal membership in their communities. Imperialism linked Europe and North America with the rest of world, and as a result, the languages of prohibition, medical discourse, and political liberalism spread throughout the world. The modern gay or lesbian political identity is a Western invention, however adapted or transformed it may be to and by other cultures.

This is the context for most of our readings. Readings on international struggles reflect the ways in which the fight for equality and freedom is being fought around the globe. Although the modern homosexual identity is a European product, international struggles for homosexual rights do not always simply replicate European or American understandings of sexuality. We cannot claim that this volume offers a complete picture of worldwide struggles; fortunately, the "pink books" of the International Lesbian and Gay Association, the recent collection edited by Stephen Likosky, entitled *Coming Out*, and recent volumes on gay and lesbian life in Southern Asia, South Africa, and Latin America contribute to this project.

Lesbians are notably absent from the early sections of the book, as they are from early European history. The relative dearth of writing by and about lesbians reflects the different positions of men and women in society. The treatment of women as household property, apparent in European and American law into the twentieth century, meant that women's desires were ignored by men. The denial of education to women meant that writings by women were fewer than by men, in this area as in others. The belief that women had no autonomous sexuality, but simply responded to men (if, indeed, they experienced sexual pleasure at all) reduced male curiosity about women's desire. As capitalism fostered the growth of cities and of greater individual autonomy, women as well as men began to explore their own sexuality in greater numbers. Medical discourse incited discussion of women's sexuality, inviting women to think about and thus act upon their own desires. Mass education increased women's ability to write about their ideas and their lives. Feminism spread the radical idea that women could make their own lives independently of men. Even as psychoanalytic discourse increased the policing of women's friendships and loves, these other movements encouraged women's sexual autonomy. Thus the twentieth century inaugurated discussion by and about lesbians.

This book is divided into six roughly chronological sections. Part I provides treatments of homosexuality by philosophers of the eighteenth and early nineteenth centuries, and concludes with new translations of pamphlets from the French Revolution. Part II covers the emergence of a distinctively homosexual political concern corresponding to the identities we call "lesbian" and "gay." This begins in Europe in the eighteenth century, and lasts until the violent repressions of Stalinism, fascism, and the Holocaust. Part III deals with the reemergence and reinvention of homosexual politics and identities in the 1950s and 1960s, culminating in the Stonewall Riot of 1969 and the advent of lesbian-feminism. Part IV documents gay liberation, lesbian-feminism, and the rise of organized political battles through the 1970s. This period, and the theories of liberation that it generated, was interrupted and transformed by the AIDS epidemic; the politics of AIDS and its transformation of lesbian and gay political discourse is the topic of Part V. Part VI follows the course of contemporary debates. The late 1980s witnessed several shifts—the disparagement of lesbian-feminism, "queer" politics and theory, the beginnings of academic respectability for lesbian and gay studies, and gradually greater attention given to the voices and concerns of people of color, as well as sharpened attacks from the religious fundamentalism and battles over inclusion in mainstream institutions such as the military.

We are both political theorists by training, both teaching in universities. We are both white, of middle-class backgrounds. We are a lesbian and a gay man, from different geographical locations, with different political affinities and experience. We have disagreed with one another as often as we have agreed about many of the key questions posed in the book: Can we speak of "the lesbian and gay movement," or only of several movements by lesbians and gays collaborating for expedience in the achievement of particular political ends? To what extent are we fighting for the same things, and to what extent are our agendas divergent or opposed? Who are our allies, and what are the dangers we face? We have not attempted to agree on or resolve these issues, for part of the excitement of our project has been knowing that we would bring to others the debates that have challenged us. We have tried to present a comprehensive range of positions on the major issues, to open channels for debate rather than to present a monolithic picture of a movement or to bias the reader in one direction or another. Space limitations prevent us from including much of the wonderful writing on gay and lesbian politics that has been produced worldwide. Some pertinent 'classic' writings that are widely available elsewhere have been excluded. Limitations on our time and resources have probably resulted in some significant perspectives not being represented here. Our choices of material and the circumstances of inclusion may paint a picture of the past and present with which some may disagree. However we welcome readers' comments and suggestions; we hope that you will share your experience and knowledge with us and, in later editions, with other readers. We invite you to join the conversation that has provided the material for *We Are Everywhere*, to write yourselves into future collections such as this.

I

PRE-HISTORY
OF A GAY AND LESBIAN
MOVEMENT

Three of the selections that follow are exemplary of Enlightenment efforts at legal reform. What the fourth author, Blackstone, calls the "crime not fit to be named" was, in England, "buggery" or sex between men; sex between women was not even codified there, rendering it legally nonexistent (the buggery statute was not interpreted as criminalizing sex between women). However, according to Louis Crompton, "[i]n Europe before the French revolution . . . notably in such countries as France, Spain, Italy, Germany, and Switzerland, lesbian acts were regarded as legally equivalent to acts of male sodomy and were, like them, punishable by the death penalty. On occasion, executions of women were carried out."[1] Indeed, Crompton's research documents more than four hundred executions for homosexuality of European women and men by beheading, drowning, burning, and hanging, not to mention punishments short of death such as torture and mutilation. Although these punishments ceased with the French Revolution and the Napoleonic Code, hangings continued in England until 1835. In the United States executions continued at least until 1743, and the death penalty remained in the law (of South Carolina) until 1873. (In at least one state, Pennsylvania, the law was "liberalized" in the eighteenth century to life imprisonment for whites, death for blacks.) Therefore, even though the examples used in the following involve male (usually pederastic) homosexuality, legal sanctions were applied to women as well.

Charles-Louis Secondat, Baron de La Brède et de Montesquieu (1689–1755) was a French nobleman who, as a critic of the monarchy, compared different political and legal systems to discover the best alternative to it. He argued that the "crime against nature," like witchcraft and heresy, should not be "punished with fire," particularly because this crime could be prevented by altering social customs (such as eliminating sex segregation in schooling). This is exemplary of Enlightenment discourse—that it is better to prevent sodomy than to punish it.

Voltaire (François Marie Arouet) (1694–1778), the celebrated *philosophe* and mentor of the French revolution, answered Montesquieu that Greek pederasty was not "infamous," and was not really love in the sexual sense at all—it was rather what today we call platonic love, the friendship and guidance of an older man given to a younger man. To be sure, he said, there were abuses of this in Greece, as there were among the clergy of his day. However, Voltaire was ambivalent about homosexuality; he saw religious intolerance of it as mere superstition, and viewed male homosexuality, at least, as natural: the stronger sex drive of males, the scarcity of available females when pubescent males were reared separately and in need of sexual outlet, and the fact that such young males can resemble females means that homosexuality can occur naturally, and human laws cannot contradict what is natural.

Voltaire was influenced by Italian criminologist Cesare Bonesana, Marchese di Beccaria (1738–1794), who goes one step further in adding that *punishment* of such a crime, which usually goes unpunished (because it is difficult to prove), acts as an *incentive* to commit it (by publicizing it, as well as exciting our desire for a "forbidden fruit"). He, too, recommends social engineering to prevent the occurrence of homosexuality. (We include his discussion of adultery because he alludes in it to sexual expression as a natural need, worthy of understanding, rather than an antisocial passion demanding punishment.)

Finally, the "pre-Enlightened" approach of Sir William Blackstone (1723–1780, solicitor to the British Crown) is included here to contrast with Bentham's approach a generation later. (Bentham will also specifically address the ideas of Montesquieu, Voltaire, and Beccaria.) Although the crime's very mention by the law is a "disgrace to human nature," it is an offense not only because of Biblical prohibition, but because it is against one's personal security. The problem for the law is that the crime has so "dark a nature," it is so easily charged, and innocence is so difficult to prove, that false accusation deserves almost the same punishment as the crime itself; death. Blackstone's ideas were approvingly cited in U.S. Supreme Court Chief Justice Burger's opinion upholding the criminalization of sodomy in *Bowers v. Hardwick* (1986).

1. Louis Crompton, "The Myth of Lesbian Impunity: Capital Laws from 1270 to 1791," *Journal of Homosexuality*, Vol. 6 (1/2), Fall/Winter 1980–1981, p. 11.

OF THE CRIME AGAINST NATURE

from *The Spirit of the Laws* (1754)

Charles-Louis de Secondat, Baron de La Brède et de Montesquieu
trans. *Thomas Nugent*

XII, 6.—*Of the Crime against Nature*

God forbid that I should have the least inclination to diminish the public horror against a crime which religion, morality, and civil government equally condemn. It ought to be proscribed, were it only for its communicating to one sex the weaknesses of the other, and for leading people by a scandalous prostitution of their youth to an ignominious old age. What I shall say concerning it will in no way diminish its infamy, being levelled only against the tyranny that may abuse the very horror we ought to have against the vice.

As a natural circumstance of this crime is secrecy, there are frequent instances of its having been punished by legislators upon the deposition of a child. This was opening a very wide door to calumny. "Justinian," says Procopius, "published a law against this crime; he ordered an inquiry to be made not only against those who were guilty of it, after the enacting of that law, but even before. The deposition of a single witness, sometimes of a child, sometimes of a slave, was sufficient, especially against such as were rich, and against those of the green faction."

It is very odd that these three crimes, witchcraft, heresy, and that against nature, of which the first might easily be proved not to exist; the second to be susceptible of an infinite number of distinctions, interpretations, and limitations; the third to be often obscure and uncertain—it is very odd, I say, that these three crimes should amongst us be punished with fire.

I may venture to affirm that the crime against nature will never make any great progress in society unless people are prompted to it by some particular custom, as among the Greeks, where the youth of that country performed all their exercises naked; as amongst us, where domestic education is disused; as amongst the Asiatics, where particular persons have a great number of women whom they despise, while others can have none at all. Let there be no customs preparatory to this crime; let it, like every other violation of morals, be severely proscribed by the civil magistrate; and nature will soon defend or resume her rights. Nature, that fond, that indulgent parent, has strewed her pleasures with a bounteous hand, and while she fills us with delights she prepares us, by means of our issue, in whom we see ourselves, as it were, reproduced—she prepares us, I say, for future satisfactions of a more exquisite kind than those very delights.

CRIMES DIFFICULT TO PROVE
from *On Crimes and Punishments* (1764)

Cesare Bonesana, Marchese di Beccaria
trans. David Young

Crimes Difficult To Prove

. . . It will appear strange to anyone who fails to consider that reason has almost never been the lawgiver of nations that the most atrocious or the most obscure of crimes—in other words, those that are most unlikely—are the ones proved by conjecture and by the weakest and most equivocal evidence; as though the law and the judge were not interested in seeking the truth, but in establishing the fact of a crime; as though the danger of condemning an innocent man were not all the greater as the probability of his innocence surpasses the likelihood of his guilt. Most men lack that vigor which is equally necessary for great crimes and great virtues; thus, it seems that the former always coexist with the latter in those nations that sustain themselves by the activity of their governments and by passions working together for the public good, rather than in countries that depend on their size or the invariable excellence of their laws. In the latter sort of nation, weakened passions seem better suited to the maintenance rather than to the improvement of the form of government. From this, one can draw an important conclusion: that great crimes in a nation are not always a proof of its decline.

There are some crimes that are both frequent in society and difficult to prove, and, in such cases, the difficulty of establishing guilt takes the place of the probability of innocence. In cases of this nature, the danger arising from impunity is less significant, because the frequency with which the crimes occur has no relationship to escaping punishment. Therefore, the time allotted for judicial inquiry and the statutory delay in granting immunity against prosecution should both be curtailed. Yet adultery and pederasty, which are crimes difficult to prove, are the ones that, according to accepted principles, admit of tyrannical presumptions, of *quasi-proofs* and *semi-proofs* (as if a man could be *semi-innocent* or *half-guilty*, which is to say, *semi-punishable* and *half–acquittable*; these are the crimes, too, in which torture exercises its cruel sway over the person of the accused, over the witnesses, and even over the whole family of a poor wretch, according to the coldly iniquitous teaching of certain learned men who set themselves up as the rule and precept for judges.

Adultery is a crime that, politically considered, derives its strength and orientation from two causes: variable human laws and that very strong attraction which impels one sex toward the other. The latter is similar in many respects to the force of gravity which moves the universe; for, like gravity, it diminishes with distance, and, if the one influences all the movements of bodies, so the other, throughout its duration, influences almost all movement of the spirit. The two differ in this, that gravity reaches a state of equilibrium with obstructions, while sexual attraction generally gathers strength and vigor with the growth of the very obstacles opposed to it.

If I were to speak to nations still deprived of the light of religion, I would say that there is yet another considerable difference between adultery and other crimes. Adultery arises from the abuse of a need that is constant and universal throughout the human race, a need that is anterior to society and, indeed, on which society itself was founded, whereas other crimes tending to the destruction of society originate more from the promptings of momentary passion than from natural need. For someone who knows history and human nature, the intensity of such a need always appears to be constant in a given climate. If such is the case, laws and customs that seek to diminish the total sum would be useless and even pernicious, for the effect would be to burden some peoples with the needs of others in addition to their own. On the contrary, truly wise laws and customs, following the gentle slope of the plain, as it were, would divide and distribute the total river into a number of equal portions sufficient to prevent both drought and flooding everywhere. Conjugal fidelity always depends on the number and freedom of marriages. Where hereditary prejudices hold sway over marriages, where such unions are arranged or broken by familial authority, secret love affairs undo their bonds in spite of common morality, whose business is to inveigh against the effects while condoning the causes. Such reflections, however, are useless for someone who, imbued with true religion, has more sublime motives that correct the force of natural impulses. A crime of this sort is an act so quickly committed and so mysterious, so covered by the very veil with which the law has shrouded it (a necessary veil, but one so delicate as to increase rather than diminish the desirability of what it covers), the opportunities for it are so easy, and the consequences are so equivocal, that the legislator will find it easier to prevent rather than correct this offense. As a general rule, with every crime which because of its very nature, goes unpunished most of the time, the punishment becomes an incentive. It is characteristic of our imagination that difficulties, if they are not insurmountable or too great for the mental laziness of particular persons, excite the imagination more vividly and magnify the object of our desires. Difficulties are like so many barriers that prevent our errant and fickle imagination from deserting that particular object. Constrained to examine every aspect, our imagination fastens more securely on the pleasant part, toward which our mind is drawn quite naturally, whereas it flees and withdraws from the painful and harmful.

Pederasty, so severely punished by the laws and so easily subjected to the torments that conquer innocence, is founded less upon the needs of the isolated and free man than upon the passions of the sociable and enslaved man. It draws its strength not so much from a surfeit of pleasures as from the sort of education that begins by making men useless to themselves in order to make them useful to others. It is the result of those institutions where hotblooded youth is confined and where there is an insurmountable barrier to every other sort of relationship; all developing natural vigor is wasted in a way that is useless to humanity and that brings on premature old age . . .

I do not pretend to diminish the horror which these crimes deserve. Having called attention to their origins, however, I believe that I am entitled to draw a general conclusion: namely, that a punishment for a crime cannot be deemed truly just (which is to say, necessary) unless the laws have adopted the best possible means, in the given circumstances of a nation, to prevent that crime.

THE LOVE CALLED "SOCRATIC"

from the *Philosophical Dictionary* (1764)

Voltaire (François-Marie Arouet)
trans. Donald Webster Cory

The Love Called "Socratic"

How can it be that a vice, one which would destroy the human race if it became general, an infamous assault upon Nature, can nevertheless be so natural? It looks like the last degree of thought-out corruption, and, at the same time, it is the usual possession of those who haven't had the time to be corrupted yet. It has entered hearts still new, that haven't known either ambition, nor fraud, nor the thirst of riches; it is a blind youth that, by a poorly straightened out instinct, throws itself into the confusion upon leaving childhood.

The attraction of the two sexes for each other is welcomed; but regardless of whatever has been said about the women of Africa and Southern Asia, this attraction is usually much stronger in men than in women; it is a law that nature has established for all animals. It is always the male that attracts the female.

The young males of our species, reared together, feeling this force that nature begins to develop in them and not finding the natural object of their instinct, throw themselves upon that which resembles it. A young boy will often, by the freshness of his complexion, by the intensity of his coloration and by the sweetness of his eyes, resemble a beautiful girl for the space of two or three years; if he is loved, it is because nature is misunderstood: on becoming attached to the one who has these beauties, one renders homage to sex, and when age has made this resemblance vanish, the error ceases.

It is well known that this mistake of nature is much more common in mild climates than among the snows of the North, for the blood runs hotter there and the occasion arises more frequently: also, that which is taken merely a weakness in young Alcibiade is a disgusting abomination in a Dutch sailor and in a Muscovite soldier. I cannot accept the claim that the Greeks permitted license. Some quote Solon because he said, in two bad verses:

> *You shall cherish a beautiful boy*
> *As long as he remains beardless*

But really was Solon the legislator when he wrote this? He was still young, and, once the rake had become the sage, he did not include such an infamy in the laws of his republic. This is like accusing Theodore de Bége of having practiced pederasty in his church because, in his youth, he had written poems for young Candide, and that he had said: "*Applecton hunc et illam.*"

Some also abuse Plutarch's text, when, reading his chatter in the "Dialogue of Love," he has the protagonist state that women are not worthy of true love; but another character upholds the side of women, as he should.

Montesquieu is quite wrong. It is true that, with whatever certainty history can offer, Socratic love was not an infamous love at all: it is this word *Love* that has confused people. Those who were called *the lovers of a young man,* were precisely those who, among us, are the companions of our princes the elite; these people attended to the education of a distinguished child, partaking of the same education, the same military life: warring and holy institutions, in which some abuses entered, turning it into nocturnal feasts and orgies. The regiment of lovers instituted by Laïnes was an invincible army of young warriors dedicated by the oath to give their lives for one another; and this is the most beautiful thing that ancient discipline had to offer.

Sextus Empericus and others have said that pederasty was recommended by the laws of Persia. Let them quote the text of the law, let them exhibit the Persian Code, and, if they do exhibit them, I still will not believe it, I shall say that it is not true, because it is impossible. No, it is not human nature to make a law that contradicts and outrages Nature, a law that would make the human race disappear if it were followed to the letter. How many people have taken shameful but tolerated behavior in a country to be the law of the country! Sextus Empiricus, who doubted everything, should have doubted this jurisprudence. Were he alive today, and were he to see two or three young Jesuits take advantage of a few students, would he have the right to say that this was permitted by the laws of Ignatius Loyola?

Love of boys was so common in Rome that they didn't bother to punish it. Octavius Augustus, this debauched murderer, who dared exile Ovid, was pleased to have Virgil sing to Alexis and for Horace to compose little odes for Ligunius; but the ancient law, which prohibited pederasty, survived all along. Emperor Philip reactivated it and expelled from Rome the little boys who were guilty. In conclusion, I do not believe that there has ever been an organized nation which has made laws against morals.

---

from

COMMENTARIES ON THE LAWS OF ENGLAND
Book IV, Chapter 15 (1769)

Sir William Blackstone

IV. What has been observed, especially with regard to the manner of proof, which ought to be the more clear in proportion as the crime is more detestable, may be applied to another offense, of a still deeper malignity ; the *infamous crime against nature*, committed either with man or beast. A crime, which ought to be strictly and impartially proved, and then strictly and impartially punished. But it is an offense of so dark a nature, so easily charged, and the negative so difficult to be proved, that the accusation should be clearly made out: for, if false, it deserves punishment inferior only to that of the crime itself.

I will not act so disagreeable part, to my readers as well as myself, as to dwell any longer upon a subject, the very mention of which is a disgrace to human nature. It will be more eligible to imitate in this respect the delicacy of our English law, which treats it, in it's [sic] very indictments, as a crime not fit to be named; "*peccatum illud horribile, inter christianos non nominandum.*"[1] A taciturnity observed likewise by the edict of Constantius and Constans:

"*ubi soelus est id, quod non proficit scire, jubemus insurgere leges, armari jura gladio ultare, ut exquisitis poenis subdantur infames, que sunt, vel qui futuri sunt, rei.*"[2] Which leads me to add a word concerning it's [sic] punishment.

This is the voice of nature and of reason, and the express law of God, determined to be capital. Of which we have a signal instance, long before the Jewish dispensation, by the destruction of two cities by fire from heaven: so that this is an universal, not merely a provincial, precept. And our antient law in some degree initiated this punishment, by commanding such miscreants to be burnt to death; though Fleta says they should be buried alive: either of which punishments was indifferently used for this crime among the antient Goths. But now the general punishment of all felonies is the same, namely, by hanging: and this offense (being in the times of popery only subject to ecclesiastical censures) was made single felony by the statute 25 Hen.VIII. c. 6. and felony without benefit of clergy by statute 5 Eliz. c. 17. And the rule of law herein is, that, if both are arrived at years of discretion, *agentes et consentients par poena plectanture.*[3]

1. [*that horrible sin not to be named among Christians.—Eds*]

2. [*when the crime is that which it does not help us to know, then we command the laws to rise up and justice to arm itself with an avenging sword so that the evil ones—who are and will be the accused—may be subjected to choice punishments.—Eds*]

3. [*Those who act and consent with one another are equally at fault.—Eds*]

An important British figure of the late enlightenment movement called philosophic radicalism, Jeremy Bentham (1748–1832) wrote over three hundred manuscript pages on homosexuality; none were published during his lifetime, and most are still unpublished. Trained as a lawyer, he spent his life working out a system of jurisprudence to both codify and reform existing laws according to the principle of "utilitarianism," and advised the crowned heads of Europe as well as the nascent French and U.S. republics on such codification and reform. Utilitarianism, simply, is the philosophy that laws and government policies should promote the greatest good for the greatest number of people. In this context, legal prohibition of sexual behavior should be considered only when the behavior has a "tendency to subtract anything from the aggregate sum of human happiness" and when the social benefits of such a prohibition outweigh the costs to the individual and society. The selections reproduced here may be read as an exemplification of this philosophical doctrine.

Bentham argues against the received opinion of his time, referring to Blackstone, Montesquieu, and Voltaire as well as current interpretations of biblical scripture. In "Offences Against Taste" (1814–16), he describes sexuality (in one of the first uses of this term in the English language) as a human sense equivalent to the five other senses. While this sense has the "effect" of preservation of the species, that is not its "object"; the object is happiness, and laws concerning sexuality should be governed by utilitarian principles.

In "Paederasty" (written about 1785), Bentham argues that by utilitarian principles, intercourse between two persons of the same sex should not be a punishable offense. By the time he writes "Offences Against Taste," this has expanded into the belief that sexual freedom may present a positive social good.

Bentham is also notable for his recognition of the gendered double standard that prevailed at the time (and continues today). Describing the "hand of the law" in sexual matters, he notes that female-female sex is largely ignored while all the anger of the public is focussed on male homosexuality.

Although he was an advocate of sexual freedom, Bentham's language reflects his admitted fear that his advocacy of legal reform would lead to suspicions that he was a sodomite. At the time he was writing, the punishment in England for sodomy was hanging, so his concerns were justified. His language, therefore, is often oblique, taking a cautious stance toward the subject matter that he is, at the same time, attempting to redeem. [*Marks in brackets are those of the editors, or of Bentham himself, when indicated J.B.*]

JEREMY BENTHAM

from

OFFENCES AGAINST ONE'S SELF: PAEDERASTY

(ca. 1785)

Jeremy Bentham

To what class of offenses shall we refer these irregularities of the venereal appetite which are stiled unnatural? When hidden from the public eye there could be no colour for placing them any where else: could they find a place any where it would be here. I have been tormenting myself for years to find if possible a sufficient ground for treating them with the severity with which they are treated at this time of day by all European nations: but upon the principle of utility I can find none.

Offenses of impurity—their varieties

The abominations that come under this head have this property in common, in this respect, that they consist in procuring certain sensation by means of an improper object. The impropriety then may consist either in making use of an object

1. Of the proper species but at an improper time: for instance, after death.
2. Of an object of the proper species and sex, and at a proper time, but in an improper part.
3. Of an object of the proper species but the wrong sex. This is distinguished from the rest by the name of pederasty.
4. Of a wrong species.
5. In procuring this sensation by one's self without the help of any other sensitive object.

Pederasty makes the greatest figure

The third being that which makes the most figure in the world it will be proper to give that the principal share of our attention. In settling the nature and tendency of this offense we shall for the most part have settled the nature and tendency of all the other offenses that come under this disgusting catalogue.

Whether they produce any primary mischief

1. As to any primary mischief, it is evident that it produces no pain in anyone. On the contrary it produces pleasure, and that a pleasure which, by their perverted taste, is by this supposition preferred to that pleasure which is in general reputed the greatest. The partners are both willing. If either of them be unwilling, the act is not that which we have here in view: it is an offense totally different in its nature of effects: it is a personal injury; it is a kind of rape.

As a secondary mischief whether they produce any alarm in the community

2. As to any secondary mischief, it produces not any pain of apprehension. For what is there in it for anybody to be afraid of? By the supposition, those only are the objects of it who choose to be so, who find a pleasure, for so it seems they do, in being so.

Whether any danger

3. As to any danger exclusive of pain, the danger, if any, must consist in the tendency of the example. But what is the tendency of this example? To dispose others to engage in the same practices: but this practise for anything that has yet appeared produces no pain of any kind to any one.

Reasons that have commonly been assigned

Hitherto we have found no reason for punishing it at all: much less for punishing it with the degree of severity with which it has been commonly punished. Let us see what force there is in the reasons that have been commonly assigned for punishing it.

The whole tribe of writers on English law, who none of them knows any more what they mean by the word "peace" than they do by many other of the expressions that are most familiar to them, reckon this among offenses against the peace. It is accordingly treated in all respects as an offense against the peace. They likewise reckon forgery, coining, and all sorts of frauds among offenses against the peace. According to the same writers it is doubted whether adultery be not a breach of the peace . . . it is certain however that whenever a gallant accepts an invitation of another man's wife he does it with force and arms. This needs no comment.

Whether against the security of the individual

Sir W. Blackstone is more particular.

According to him it is not only an offense against the peace, but it is of that division of offenses against the peace which are offenses against security. According to the same writer, if a man is guilty of this kind of filthiness, for instance, with a cow, as some men have been known to be, it is an offense against somebody's security. He does not say whose security, for the law makes no distinction in its ordinances, so neither does this lawyer or any other English lawyer in his comments make any distinction between this kind of filthiness when committed with the consent of the patient and the same kind of filthiness when committed against his consent and by violence. It is just as if a man were to make no distinction between concubinage and rape.

Whether it debilitates—Montesquieu

The reason that Montesquieu gives for reprobating it is the weakness which he seems to suppose it to have a tendency to bring upon those who practise it. (*Esp. des Loix*, L.12,ch6, "Il faudroit le proscrire quand il ne feroit que donner à un sexe les faibleses de l'autre et préparer à un vieillesse infâme par une jeunesse honteuse." "It ought to be proscribed were it only for its giving to the one sex the weaknesses of the other and paving the way by a scandalous youth for an infamous old age." J.B.) This, if it be true in fact, is a reason of a very different complexion from any of the preceding and it is on the ground of this reason as being the most plausible one that I have ranked the offense under its present head. As far as it is true in fact, the act ought to be regarded in the first place as coming within the list of offenses against one's self, of offenses of imprudence: in the next place, as an offense against the state, as an offense the tendency of which is to diminish the public force.

If however it tends to weaken a man it is not any single act that can in any sensible degree have that effect. It can only be the habit: the act thus will become obnoxious as evidencing the existence, in probability, of the habit. This enervating tendency, be it what it may, if it is to be taken as a ground for treating the practise in question with a degree of severity which is not bestowed upon the regular way of gratifying the venereal appetite, must be greater in the former case than in the latter. Is it so? If the affirmative can be shown it must be either by arguments a priori drawn from considerations of the nature of the human frame or from experience. Are there any such arguments from physiology? I have never heard of any: I can think of none.

What says history?

What says historical experience? The result of this can be measured only upon a large scale or upon a very general survey. Among the modern nations it is comparatively but rare. In modern Rome it is perhaps not very uncommon; in Paris probably not quite so common; in London still less frequent; in Edinburgh or Amsterdam you scarce hear of it two or three times in a century. In Athens and in ancient Rome in the most flourishing period of the history of those capitals, regular intercourse between the sexes was scarcely much more common. It was upon the same footing throughout Greece: everybody practiced it; nobody was ashamed of it. They might be ashamed of what they looked upon as an excess in it, or they might be ashamed of it as a weakness, as propensity that had a tendency to distract men from more worthy and important occupations, just as a man with us might be ashamed of excess or weakness in his love for women. In itself one may be sure they were not ashamed of it . Agesilaus, upon somebody's taking notice of the care he took to avoid taking any familiarities with a youth who passed for being handsome acknowledges it, indeed, but upon what ground? Not on account of the turpitude but the danger. Xenophon in his retreat of the ten thousand gives an anecdote of himself in which he mentions himself as particularly addicted to this practise without seeming to entertain the least suspicion that any apology was necessary. In his account of Socrates's conversation he introduces that philosopher censuring or rather making merry with a young man for his attachment to the same practise. But in what light does he consider it? As a weakness unbecoming to a philosopher, not as a turpitude or a crime unbecoming to a man. It is not because an object of the one sex more than one of the other is improper game: but on account of the time that must be spent and the humiliation submitted to in the pursuit.

What is remarkable is that there is scarce a striking character in antiquity, not on that in other respects men are in use to cite as virtuous, of whom it does not appear by on circumstance or another, that he was infected with this inconceivable propensity. It makes a conspicuous figure in the very opening of Thucydides's history, and by an odd accident it was to the spirit of two young men kindled and supported by this passion that Athens according to that historian stood indebted on a trying occasion for the recovery of its liberty. The firmness and spirit of the Theban band—the band of lovers as it was called—is famous in history; and the principle by which the union among the members of it was commonly supposed to be cemented is well known. (Plutarch, *in vita Pelopidae. Esp. des Loix*, L. 4,ch. 8. J.B.). Many moderns and among others Mr. Voltaire, dispute the fact, but that intelligent philosopher sufficiently intimates the ground of his incredulity—if he does not believe it, it is because he likes not to believe it. What the antients called love in such a case was what we call Platonic, that is, was not love but friendship. But the Greeks know the difference between love and friendship as well as we—they had distinct terms to signify them by: it seems reasonable therefore to suppose that when they say love they meant love, and that when they say friendship only they mean friendship only. And with regard to Xenophon and his master, Socrates, and his fellow-scholar Plato, it seems more reasonable to believe them to have been addicted to this taste when they or any of them tell us so in express terms than to trust to the interpretation, however ingenious and however well-intended, of any men who write at this time of day, when they tell us it was no such thing. Not to insist upon Agesilaus and Xenophon, it appears by one circumstance or another that Themistocles, Aristrides, Epaminondus, Alcibiades, Alexander and perhaps the greatest number of the heroes of Greece were infected with this taste. Not that the historians are at the pains of informing us so expressly, for it was not extraordinary enough to make it worthwhile, but it comes out collaterally in the course of the transactions they have occasion to relate.

It were hardly worth while after this to take up much time in proving the same thing with regard to the Romans, in naming distinguished persons of consequence whom history has mentioned as partakers in this abomination, or in bringing passages to shew that the same depraved taste prevailed generally among the people. Not to mention notorious profligates such as the Antonies, the Clodius's the Pisos, the Gabinius's of the age, Cicero, if we may believe either his enemy Sallust or his admirer Pliny neither avoided this propensity nor thought proper to dissemble it . . . that austere philosopher, after writing books to prove that pleasure was no good and that pain was no evil and that virtue could make a man happy upon the rack, that affectionate husband, in the midst of all his tenderness for his wife Terentia, could play at blind man's bluff with his secretary (i.e. Marcus Tullius Tiro. Pliny, *Letters*, VII, 4 *Ed.*) for pipes and make verses upon this notable exploit of gallantry.

With regard to the people in general it may be presumed that if the Gods amused themselves in this way—if Apollo loved Hyacinthus, if Hercules could be in a frenzy for the loss of Hylas, and the father of Gods and men could solace himself with Ganymede, it was neither an odious nor an infrequent thing for mortal men to do so. The Gods we make, it has been well and often said, we make always after our own image. In times much anterior to those of Cicero and in which according to the common prejudice the morals of the people are supposed to have been proportionately more pure, when certain festivals were suppressed on account of their furnishing opportunities for debauchery, irregularities of this kind were observed according to Livy to be more abundant than ordinary intrigues. This circumstance would scarcely perhaps have been thought worth mentioning, had not the idea of excess in this, as it is apt to do on all occasions, struck the imagination of the historian as well as of the magistrate whose administration he is recording

This much will probably be thought enough: if more proofs were necessary, it were easy to collect materials enough to fill a huge, a tedious and a very disgusting volume.

It appears then that this propensity was universally predominant among the antient Greeks and Romans, among the military as much as any. The antient Greeks and Romans, however, are commonly reputed as a much stouter as well as a much braver people than the stoutest and bravest of any of the modern nations of Europe. They appear to have been stouter at least in a very considerable degree than the French in whom this propensity is not very common and still more than the Scotch in whom it is still less common, and this although the climate even for Greece was a great deal warmer and in that respect more enervating than that of modern Scotland.

If then this practise was in those antient warm countries attended with any enervating effects, they were much more than counteracted by the superiority of [illegible] in the exertions which were then required by the military education over and above those which are now called forth by ordinary labor. But if there be any ground derived from history for attributing to it any such enervating effects it is more than I can find.

Whether it enervates the patient more than the agent

Montesquieu however seems to make a distinction—he seems to suppose these enervating effects to be exerted principally upon the person who is the patient in such a business. This distinction does not seem very satisfactory in any point of view. Is there any reason for supposing it to be a fixed one? Between persons of the same age actuated by the same incomprehensible desires would not the parts they took in the business be convertible? Would not the patient be the agent in his turn? If it were not so, the person on whom he supposes these effects to be the greatest is precisely the person with regard to whom it is most difficult to conceive whence those consequences should result. In the one case there is exhaustion which when carried to excess may be followed by debility: in the other case there is no such thing.

What says history?

In regard to this point too in particular, what says history? As the two parts that a man may take in this business are so naturally convertible however frequently he may have taken a passive part, it will not ordinarily appear. According to the notions of the antients there was something degrading in the passive part which was not in the active. It was ministering to the pleasure, for so we are obliged to call it, of another without participation, it was making one's self the property of another man, it was playing the woman's part: it was therefore unmanly. (*Paedicabo vos et irrumabo, Antoni* [*sic*] *pathice et cinaede Furi.* [*Carm.* 16] Catullus. *J.B.*)[1] On the other hand, to take the active part was to make use of another for one's pleasure, it was making another man one's property, it was preserving the manly, the commanding character. Accordingly, Solon in his laws prohibits slaves from bearing an active part where the passive is borne by a freeman. In the few instances in which we happen to hear of a person's taking the passive part there is nothing to favour the above-mentioned hypothesis. The beautiful Alcibiades, who in his youth, says Cornilius Nepos, after the manner of the Greeks, was beloved by many, was not remarkable either for weakness or for cowardice: at least, [blank] did not find it so. The Clodius whom Cicero scoffs at for his servile obsequiousness to the appetite of Curio was one of the most daring and turbulent spirits in all Rome. Julius Caesar was looked upon as a man of tolerable courage in his day, notwithstanding the complaisance he showed in his youth to the King of Bithynia, Nicomedes. Aristotle, the inquisitive and observing Aristotle, whose physiological disquisitions are looked upon as some of the best of his works—Aristotle, who if there had been anything in this notion had every opportunity and inducement to notice and confirm it—gives no intimation of any such thing. On the contrary he sits down very soberly to distribute the male half of the species under two classes: one class having a natural propensity, he says, to bear a passive part in such a business, as the other have to take an active part. (*Probl.* Sect. 4 art 27: The former of these propensities he attributes to a peculiarity of organization analogous to that of women. The whole passage is abundantly obscure and shows in how imperfect a state of anatomical knowledge was his time. *J.B.*). This observation it must be confessed is not much more satisfactory than that other of the same philosopher when he speaks of two sorts of men—the one born to be masters, the other to be slaves. If however there had appeared any reason for supposing this practise, either with regard to the passive or the active part of it, to have had any remarkable effects in the way of debilitation upon those who were addicted to it, he would have already said so much upon the subject without taking notice of that circumstance.

Whether it hurts population?

A notion more obvious, but perhaps not much better founded than the former is that of its being prejudicial to population. Mr. Voltaire appears inclined in one part of his works to give some countenance to this opinion. He speaks of it as a vice which would be destructive to the human race if it were general. "How did it come about that a vice which would destroy mankind if it were general, that an infamous outrage against nature…?" (*Questions sur l'Encyclop.* "Amour Socratique." *J.B.*)

A little further on, speaking of Sextus Empiricus who would have us believe that this practise was "recommended" in Persia by the laws, he insists that the effect of such a law would be to annihilate the human race if it were literally observed. "No," says he, "it is not in human nature to make a law that contradicts and outrages nature, a law that would annihilate mankind if it were observed to the letter." This consequence however is far enough from being a necessary one. For a law of the purport he represents to be observed, it is sufficient that this unprolific kind of energy be practised; it is not necessary that it should be practised to the exclusion of that which is prolific. Now that there should ever be wanting such a measure of the regular and ordinary inclination of desire for the proper object as is necessary for keeping up the numbers of mankind upon their present footing is a notion that stands warranted by nothing that I can find in history. To consider the matter a priori, if we consult Mr. Hume and Dr. Smith, we shall find that it is not the strength of the inclination of the one sex for the other that is the measure of the numbers of mankind, but the quantity of subsistence which they can find or raise upon a given spot. With regard to the mere object of population, if we consider the time of gestation in the female sex we shall find that much less than a hundredth part of the activity a man is capable of exerting in this way is sufficient to produce all the effect that can be produced by ever so much more. Population therefore cannot suffer till the inclination of the male sex for the female be considerably less than a hundredth part as strong as for their own. Is there the least probability that [this] should ever be the case? I must confess I see not any thing that should lead us to suppose it. Before this can happen the nature of the human composition must receive a total change and that propensity which is commonly regarded as the only one of the two that is natural must have become altogether an unnatural one.

I have already observed that I can find nothing in history to countenance the notion I am examining. On the contrary the country in which the prevalence of this practise is most conspicuous happens to have been remarkable for its populousness. The bent of popular prejudice has been to exaggerate this populousness: but after all deductions [are] made, still it will appear to have been remarkable. It was such as not-withstanding the drain of continual wars in a country parcelled out into paltry states as to be all of it frontier, gave occasion to the continued necessity of emigration.

This reason however well grounded soever it were in itself could not with any degree of consistency be urged in a country where celibacy was permitted, much less where it was encouraged. The proposition which (as will be shewn more fully by and by) is not at all true with respect to paederasty, I mean that were it to prevail universally it would put an end to the human race, is most evidently and strictly true with regard to celibacy. If then merely out of regard to population it were right that paederasts should be burnt alive monks ought to be roasted alive by a slow fire. If a paederast, according to the monkish canonist Bermondus, destroys the whole human race Bermondus destroyed I don't know how many thousand times over. The crime of Bermondus is I don't know how many times worse than paederasty . . .

Whether it robs women

A more serious imputation for punishing this practise [is] that the effect of it is to produce in the male sex an indifference to the female, and thereby defraud the latter of their rights. This, as far as it holds good in point of fact, it in truth a serious imputation. The interest of the female part of the species claim just as much attention, and not a whit more, on the part of the legislator, as those of the male. A complaint of this sort, it is true, would not come with a very good grace from a modest woman; but should the women be stopped from making complaint in such a use it is the business of the men to make it for them. This then as far as it holds good in point of fact is in truth a very serious imputation: how far does it will be proper to inquire.

In the first place the female sex is always able and commonly disposed to receive a greater quantity of venereal tribute than the male sex is able to bestow. If then the state of manners be such in any country as lift the exertion of this faculty entirely unrestrained, it is evident that (except in particular cases when no object of the female sex happen to be within each) any effort of this kind that was exerted by a male upon a male would be so much lost to the community of females . . .

It appears then that if the female sex are losers by the prevalence of this practise it can only be on this supposition—that the force with which it tends to divert men from entering into connection with the other sex is greater than the force with which the censure of the world tends to prevent those connections by its operation on the women.

In countries where, as in Otaheite, no restraint is laid on the gratification of the amorous appetite, whatever part of the activity of that appetite in the male sex were exercised upon the same sex were be so much loss in point of enjoyment to the female. But in countries where it is kept under restraint, as in Europe, for example, this is not by any means the case. As long as things are upon that footing there are many cases in which the women can be no sufferers for the want of sollicitation on the part of the men. If the institution of the marriage contract be a beneficial one, and if it be expedient that the observance of it should be maintained inviolate, we must in the first place deduct from the number of the women who would be sufferers by the prevalence of this taste all married women whose husbands were not infected with it. In the next place, upon the supposition that a state of prostitution is not a happier site than a state of virginity, we must deduct all those women who by means of this prevalence would have escaped being debauched. The women who would be sufferers by it *ab initio* are those only who, were it not for the prevalence of it, would have got husbands. (I say *ab initio* for when a woman has been once reduced to take up the trade of prostitution, she also would be of the number of those who are sufferers by the prevalence of this taste, in case the effect of it were to deprive her of any quantity of this commerce beyond that which she would rather be without. It is not in this business as in most other businesses, where the quantity of the object in demand is in proportion to the demand. The occupations with respect to which that rule holds good are those only which are engaged in through character, reflection, and upon choice. But in this profession scarce any woman engages for the[se] purposes. The motive that induces a woman to engage in it is not any such circumstance as the consideration of the probability of getting custom. She has no intention of engaging in it when she takes the step that eventually proves a means of her engaging in it. The immediate cause of her engaging in it is the accident of a discovery which deprives her of every other source of livelihood. Upon the supposition then that a given number have been debauched there would be the same number ready to comply with sollicitation whenever so little was offered as whenever so much was offered. It is a conceivable case therefore that upon the increased prevalence of this taste there might be the same numbers of women debauched as at present, and yet all the prostitutes in the place might be starving for want of customers. *J.B.*)

The question then is reduced to this. What are the number of women who by the prevalence of this taste would, it is probable, be prevented from getting husbands? These and these only are they who would be sufferers by it. Upon the following considerations it does not seem likely that the prejudice sustained by the sex in this way could ever rise to any considerable amount. Were the prevalence of this taste to rise to ever so great a heighth the most considerable part of the motives to marriage would remain entire. In the first place, the desire of having children, in the next place the desire of forming alliances between families, thirdly the convenience of having a domestic companion whose company will continue to be agreeable throughout life, fourthly the convenience of gratifying the appetite in question at any time when the want occurs and without the expense and trouble of concealing it or the danger of a discovery.

Were a man's taste even so far corrupted as make him prefer the embraces of a person of his own sex to those of a female, a connection of that preposterous kind would therefore be far enough from answering to him the purposes of a marriage. A connection with a woman may by accident be followed with disgust, but a connection of the other kind, a man must know, will for certain come in time to be followed by disgust. All the documents we have from the antients relative to this matter, and we have a great abundance, agree in this, that it is only for a very few years of his life that a male continues an object of desire even to those in whom the infection of this taste is at the strongest. The very name it went by among the Greeks may stand instead of all other proofs, of which the works of Lucian and Martial alone will furnish any abundance that can be required. Among the Greeks it was called Paederastia, the love of boys, not Andereastia, the love of men. Among the Romans the act was called Paedicare because the object of it was a boy. There was no particular name for those who have past the short period beyond which no man hoped to be an object of desire to his own sex. They were called *exoleti*. No male therefore who has passed this short period of life could expect to find in this way any reciprocity of affection; he must be as odious to the boy from the beginning as in a short time the boy would be to him. The objects of this kind of sensuality would therefore come only in the place of common prostitutes; they could never even to a person of this depraved taste answer the purposes of a virtuous woman.

What says history?

Upon this footing stands the question when considered a priori; the evidence of facts seems to be still more conclusive on the same side. There seems no reason to doubt, as I have already observed but that population went on altogether fast and that the men were altogether as well inclined to marriage among that Grecian in whom this vitious propensity was most prevalent as in any modern people in whom it is least prevalent. In Rome, indeed, about the time of the extinction of liberty we find great complaints of the decline of population: but the state of it does not appear to have been at all dependent on or at all influenced by the measures that were taken from time to time to restrain the love of boys: it was with the Romans, as with us, what kept a man from marriage was not the preferring boys to women but the preferring the convenience of a transient connection to the expense and hazard of a lasting one. (See *Pilati, Traité des Loix Civiles*, ch. Du marriage. *J.B.*)

How is it at Otaheite?

To judge how far the regular intercourse between the sexes is probably affected by this contraband intercourse in countries where, as in Europe, the gratification of the venereal appetite is kept upon a footing of restraint, it may help us a good deal if we observe in what degree it is affected by the latter in countries where the gratification of that appetite is under no restraint. If in those countries paederasty prevailed to so considerable a degree as to occasion a visible diminution of the regard that was shewn to women, this phenomenon, unless it could be accounted for from other causes, would afford a strong argument to prove that prevalence of it might have the effect of diminishing the regard that might otherwise be paid to them in other countries and that the prevalence of it in those countries was owing not to the comparative difficulty of getting women but to a comparative indifference, such as might turn to the prejudice of the women in any state of things: and in short that what was transferred to boys was so much clear loss to women. But the fact is that in Otaheite it does not appear that this propensity is at all prevalent.

If it were more frequent than the regular connection in what sense could it be termed unnatural?

The nature of the question admits of great latitude of opinion: for my own part I must confess I can not bring myself to entertain so high a notion of the alluringness of this preposterous propensity as some men appear to entertain. I can not suppose it to [be] possible it should ever get to such a heighth as that the interests of the female part of the species should be materially affected by it: or that it could ever happen that were they to contend upon equal ground the eccentric and unnatural propensity should ever get the better of the regular and natural one. Could we for a moment suppose this to be the case, I would wish it to be considered what meaning a man would have to annex to the expression, when he bestows on the propensity under consideration the epithet of unnatural. If contrary to all appearance the case really were that if all men are left perfectly free to choose, as many men would make choice of their own sex as of the opposite one, I see not what reason there would be for applying the word natural to the one rather than to the other. All the difference would be that the one was both natural and necessary where as the other was natural but not necessary. If the mere circumstance of its not being necessary were sufficient to warrant the terming it unnatural it might as well be said that the taste a man has for music is unnatural.

My wonder is how any man who is at all acquainted with the most amiable part of the species should ever entertain any serious apprehensions of their yielding the ascendant to such unworthy rivals.

Among the antients—whether it excluded not the regular taste

A circumstance that contributes considerably to the alarms entertained by some people on this score is the common prejudice which supposes that the one propensity is exclusive of the other. This notion is for the most part founded on prejudice as may be seen in the works of a multitude of antient authors in which we continually see the same person at one time stepping aside in pursuit of this eccentric kind of pleasure but at other times diverting his inclination to the proper object. Horace, in speaking of the means of satisfying the venereal appetite, proposes to himself as a matter of indifference a prostitute of either sex: and the same poet, who forgetting himself now and then says a little here and there about boys, says a great deal everywhere about women. The same observation will hold good with respect to every other personage of antiquity who either by his own account or that of another is represented to us as being infected with this taste. It is so in all the poets who in any of their works have occasion to say anything about themselves. Some few appear to have had no appetite about boys, as is the case for instance with Ovid, who takes express notice of it and gives a reason for it. But it is a neverfailing rule wherever you see anything about boys, you see a great deal more about women. Virgil has one Alexis, but he has Galateas in abundance. Let us be unjust to no man: not even to a paederast. In all antiquity there is not a single instance of an author nor scarce an explicit account of any other man who was addicted exclusively to this taste. Even in modern times the real women haters are to be found not so much among paederasts, as among monks and catholic priests, such of them, be they more or fewer, who think and act in consistency with their profession.

Reason why it might be expected so to do

I say even in modern times; for there is one circumstance which should make this taste where it does prevail much more likely to be exclusively present than it was formally. I mean the severity with which it is treated by the laws and contempt and abhorrence with which regarded by the generality of the people. If we may so call it, the persecution they meet with from all quarters, whether deservedly or not, has the effect in this instance which persecution has and must have more or less in all instances, the effect of rendering those persons who are objects of it more attached than they would otherwise be to the practise it proscribes. It renders them the more attached to one another, sympathy of itself having a powerful tendency, independent of all other motives to attach a man to his own companions in misfortune. This sympathy has at the same time a powerful tendency to beget a proportionable antipathy even towards all such persons as appear to be involuntary, much more to such as appear to be voluntary, authors of such misfortune. When a man is made to suffer it is enough on all other occasions to beget in him a prejudice against those by whose means or even for whose sake he is made to suffer. . . . The reason which there may be in point of utility or on any other account for treating these people with such severity makes no difference in the sentiments which such severity is calculated to inspire; for whatever reason there may be, they, one may be certain, do not see it. In spite of such powerful incentives it does not appear that the effect of this propensity is in general even under the present system to inspire in those who are infected with it an aversion or even an indifference to the other sex: a proof of how powerful the force of nature is and how little reason the sex whose dominion is supported by the influence of pleasure have for being apprehensive of any permanent alienation in the affections of those fugitive vassals, were no harsh measure taken to drive them into rebellion . . .

As it excludes not the regular taste, it is not liable to disturb marriage

This circumstance, however, which in one set of circumstances tends to the exculpation of the practise in question, in another situation of things, and, in another point of view, operated to the commination [sic] of it. I have already given the considerations which seem to render it probable that this propensity does not in any considerable degree stand in the way of marriage: on that occasion we took it for granted for the time that if it did not hinder a man from engaging in matrimonial connection, it was of no prejudice to the other sex at all. When a man was once lodged within the pale of matrimony, we took no notice of any danger there might be of his deviating afterwards into such extravagances. This however is an event which, from the two propensities not appearing to be exclusive of one another, we have reason a priori to suppose not to be in itself absolutely improbable, and which from occasional observation, but particularly from antient history, we find not to be uncommon. The wretches who are prosecuted for this offense often turn out to be married men. The poet Martial, we find, has a wife with whom he is every now and then jarring on the score of the complaints she makes of his being unfaithful to her in this way. It is to be considered however that it is [not] to the amount of the whole sum of the infidelities the husband is guilty of in this way that a wife is a sufferer by this propensity but only to the surplus, whatever it may be, over and above what, were it not for this propensity, the same man would be guilty of in the natural was. A woman would not be a sufferer by this propensity any further than as it betrays her husband into an act of infidelity to which he would not have been betrayed by the allurements of any female rival. Supposing the degree of infidelity in both cases to be equal, there seems reason to think that a woman would not be so much hurt by an infidelity of this sort as by an infidelity into which her husband had been betrayed by a person of her own sex. An attachment of the former kind could not be lasting, that is confined for any length of time to the same individual; of the other she might not be satisfied but that it might be lasting. It is for the same reason that a woman's affection would not be so much wounded, however her pride might, by her husband's intriguing with a servant wench or other woman of a condition very much her inferior as by his intriguing with a woman of a condition near about the level of her own. It is indeed a general observation that in all cases of rivalry the jealousy is the greater the nearer in all respects the condition of the rival is to your own . . .

This at least would seem likely to have been the case in times in which the propensity was not held in the abhorrence in which it is held at present, and where consequently the wife would [not] have as at present to add to her other motives of concern the infamy with which under the present system it is one effect of such behavior to cast upon any man who is guilty of it.

Causes of this taste

I have already intimated how little reason there seems to be to apprehend that the preference of the improper to the proper object should ever be constant or general. A very extraordinary circumstance it undoubtedly is that it should be ever have arrived at the heighth at which we find it to have arrived. The circumstance is already an extraordinary one as it is: it would be much more so if it were common under equal importunities for the improper object to meet with a decided preference. But such an incident there is every reason, as I have already observed for not looking upon as likely to become otherwise than rare. Its prevalence, wherever it prevails to a considerable degree, seems always to be owing to some circumstance relative to the education of youth. It is the constraint in which the venereal appetite is kept under the system of manners established in all civilized nations that seems to be the principal cause of its deviating every now and then into these improper channels. When the desire is importunate and no proper object is at hand it will sometimes unavoidably seek relief in an improper way. In the antient as well as the modern plans of education young persons of the male sex are kept as much as possible together: they are kept as much at a distance as possible from the female. They are in a way to use all sorts of familiarities with each other: they are kept as much as possible from using any sorts of familiarities with females. Among the antients they used to be brought together in circumstances favourable to the giving birth to such desires by the custom of exercising themselves naked. (See *Esp.des Loix*, L.8, ch.11 Plut. *Morals. J.B.*) On the present plan they are often forced together under circumstances still more favourable to it by the custom of lying naked together in feather beds, implements of indulgence and incentives to the venereal appetite with which the antients were unacquainted. When a propensity of this sort is once acquired it is easier to conceive how it should continue than how it should be at first acquired. It is no such great wonder if the sensation be regarded as if it were naturally connected with the object, whatever it be, by means of which it came to be first experienced. That this practise is the result not of indifference to the proper object but of the difficulty of coming at the proper object, the offspring not of wantonness but of necessity, the consequence of the want of opportunity with the proper object, and the abundance of opportunity with such as are improper is a notion that seems warranted by the joint opinions of Montesquieu and Voltaire. "The crime against nature," says the former, "will never make any great progress in society unless people are prompted to it by some particular custom, as among the Greeks, where the youths of that country performed all their exercises naked; as amongst us, where domestic education is disused; as amongst the Asiatics, where particular persons have a great number of women whom they despise, while others can have none at all." (*Esp. des Loix*, L. 12, ch 6. *J.B.*)

"When the young males of our species," says Voltaire, "brought up together, feel the force which nature begins to unfold in them, and fail to find the natural object of their instinct, they fall back on what resembles it. Often, for two or three years, a young man resembles a beautiful girl, with the freshness of his complexion, the brilliance of his coloring, and the sweetness of his eyes; if he is loved, it's because nature makes a mistake; homage is paid to the fair sex by attachment to one who owns its beauties, and when the years have made this resemblance disappear, the mistake ends.

And this is the way:
Pluck the brief Spring, the first flowers of youth.
[Ovid, Metamorphoses, X, 84–85. Ed]

"It is well known that this mistake of nature is much more common in mild climates than in the icy north, because the blood is more inflamed there and opportunity more frequent; also, what seems only a weakness in young Alcibiades is a disgusting abomination in a Dutch sailor or a Muscovite soldier."

"Pederasty," says Beccaria, "so severely punished by law and so freely subjected to tortures which triumph over innocence, is based less on man's needs when he lives in freedom and on his own, than on his when he lives with others in slavery. It draws its strength, not so much from a surfeit of every other pleasure, as from that education which begins by making men useless to themselves in order to make them useful to others. In those institutions packed with hot-blooded youth natural vigour, as it develops, is faced with insurmountable obstacles to every other kind of relationship and wears itself out in an activity useless to humanity, and which brings on premature old age."

Whether, if it robbed women, it ought at all events to be punished?

The result of the whole is that there appears not any great reason to conclude that, by the utmost increase of which this vice is susceptible, the female part of the species could be sufferers to any very material amount. If however there was any danger of their being sufferers to any amount at all this would of itself be ample reason for wishing to restrain the practise. It would not however follow absolutely that it were right to make use of punishment for that purpose, much less that it were right to employ any of those very severe punishments which are commonly in use. It will not be right to employ any punishment, 1) if the mischief resulting from the punishment be equal or superior to the mischief of the offence, nor 2) if there be any means of compassing the same end without the expense of punishment. Punishment, says M. Beccaria, is never just so long as any means remain untried by which the end of punishment may be accomplished at a cheaper rate . . .

But on the ground of antipathy

In this case, in short, as in so many other cases the disposition to punish seems to have had no other ground than the antipathy with which persons who had punishment at their disposal regarded the offender. The circumstances from which this antipathy may have taken its rise may be worth inquiring to. One is the physical antipathy to the offence. This circumstance indeed, were we to think and act consistently, would of itself be nothing to the purpose. The act is to the highest degree odious and disgusting, that is, not to the man who does it, for he does it only because it gives him pleasure, but to one who thinks [?] of it. Be it so, but what is that to him? He has the same reason for doing it that I have for avoiding it. A man loves carrion—this is very extraordinary—much good may it do him. But what is this to me so long as I can indulge myself with fresh meat? But such reasoning, however just, few persons have calmness to attend to. This propensity is much stronger than it is to be wished it were to confound physical impurity with moral. (I pass without examination from the literal use of the word impurity [to] the figuritive. J.B.). From a man's possessing a thorough aversion to a practise himself, the transition is but too natural to his wishing to see all others punished who give into it. Any pretence, however slight, which promises to warrant him in giving way to this intolerant propensity is eagerly embraced. Look the world over, we shall find that differences in point of taste and opinion are grounds of animosity as frequent and as violent as any opposition in point of interest. To disagree with our taste [and] to oppose our opinions is to wound our sympathetic feelings and to affront our pride. James the 1st of England, a man [more] remarkable for weakness than for cruelty, conceived a violent antipathy against certain persons who were called Anabaptists on account of their differing from him in regard to certain speculative points of religion. As the circumstances of the times were favourable to [the] gratification of antipathy arising from such causes, he found means to give himself the satisfaction of committing one of them to the flames. The same king happened to have an antipathy to the use of tobacco. But as the circumstances of the times did not afford the same pretenses nor the same facility for burning tobacco–smokers as for burning Anabaptists, he was forced to content himself with writing a flaming book against it. The same king, if he be the author of that first article of the works which bear his name, and which indeed were owned by him, reckons this practise among the few offences which no Sovereign ever ought to pardon. This must needs seem rather extraordinary to those who have a notion that a pardon in this case is what he himself, had he been a subject, might have stood in need of.

Philosophical pride

This transition from the idea of physical to that of moral antipathy is the more ready when the idea of pleasure, especially of intense pleasure, is connected with that of the act by which the antipathy is excited. Philosophical pride, to say nothing at present of superstition, has hitherto employed itself with effect in setting people a-quarreling with whatever is pleasurable even to themselves, and envy will always be disposing them to quarrel with what appears to be pleasurable to others. In the notions of a certain class of moralists we ought, not for any reason they are disposed to give for it, but merely because we ought, to set ourselves against every thing that recommends itself to us under the form of pleasure. Objects, it is true, the nature of which it is to afford us the highest pleasures we are susceptible of are apt in certain circumstances to occasion us still greater pains. But that is not the grievance: for if it were, the censure which is bestowed on the use of any such object would be proportioned to the probability that could be shewn in each case of its producing such greater pains. But this is not the case: it is not the pain that angers them but the pleasure.

Religion

We need not consider at any length [the length] to which the rigor of such philosophy may be carried when reinforced by notions of religion. Such as we are ourselves, such and in many respects worse it is common for us to make God to be: for fear blackens every object that it looks upon. It is almost as common for men to conceive of God as a being of worse than human malevolence in their hearts, as to stile him a being of infinite benevolence with their lips. This act is one amongst others which some men and luckily not we ourselves have a strong propensity to commit. In some persons it produces it seems, for there is no disputing it, a pleasure: there needs no more to prove that it is God's pleasure they should abstain from it. For it is God's pleasure that in the present life we should give up all manner of pleasure, whether it stands in the way of another's happiness or not, which is the sure sign and earnest of the pleasure he will take in bestowing on us all imaginable happiness hereafter that is, in a life of the futurity of which he has given us no other proofs than these.

This is so true that, according the notion of these moralists and these religionists, that is, of the bulk of moralists and religionists who write, pleasures that are allowed of, are never allowed of for their own sake but for the sake of something else which though termed an advantage or a good presents not to any one so obviously and to them perhaps not at all, idea of pleasure. When the advantage ceases the pleasure is condemned. Eating and drinking by good luck are necessary for the preservation of the individual: therefore eating and drinking are tolerated, and so is the pleasure that attends the courses of these functions in so far as it is necessary to that end; but if you eat or if you drink otherwise than or beyond what is thus necessary, if you eat or drink for the sake of pleasure, says the philosopher, "It is shameful;" says the religionist, "It is sinful." The gratification of the venereal appetite is also by good luck necessary to the preservation of the species: therefore it is tolerated in as far as it is necessary to that end, not otherwise. Accordingly it has been a question seriously debated whether a man ought to permit himself the partaking of this enjoyment with this wife when from age or any other circumstance there is no hope of children: and it has often been decided in the negative. For the same reason or some other which is not apparent, for a man to enjoy his wife at unseasonable times in certain systems of laws has been made a capital offence. Under the above restriction however it has been tolerated. It has been tolerated, but as the pleasure appeared great, with great reluctance and at any rate not encouraged; it has been permitted not as a good but as a lesser evil. It has indeed been discouraged and great rewards offered in a future life for those who will forego it in the present.

Hatred of pleasure

Nero I think it was, or some other of the Roman tyrants, who is said to have offered a reward to any one who should discover a new pleasure. That is, in fact, no more than what is done by those who offer rewards for new poems, for new mechanical contrivances, for improvements in agriculture and in the arts; which are all but so many means of producing new pleasures, or what comes to the same thing, of producing a greater quantity of the old ones. The object however that in these cases is advertised for is not advertised for under the name of pleasure, so that the ears of these moralists are not offended with that detested sound. In the case above mentioned, from the character of the person who offered the reward it is natural enough to presume that the sort of pleasure he had in view in offering it was sensual and probably venereal, in which way no new discoveries would be endured. It is an observation of Helvetius and, I believe, of Mr. Voltaire's, that if a person were born with a particular source of enjoyment, in addition to the 5 or 6 senses we have at present, he would be hunted out of the world as a monster not fit to live. Accordingly nothing is more frequent than for those who could bear with tolerable composure the acts of tyranny by which all Rome was filled with terror and desolation to lose all patience when they come to the account of those miserable devices of lasciviousness which had no other effect than that of giving surfeit and disgust to the contemptible inventor.

How far the antipathy is a just ground

Meanwhile the antipathy, whatever it may arise from, produces in persons how many soever they be in whom it manifests itself, a particular kind of pain as often as the object by which the antipathy is excited presents itself to their thoughts. This pain, whenever it appears, is unquestionably to be placed to the account of the mischief of the offence, and this is the one reason for the punishing of it. More than this—upon the view of any pain which these obnoxious persons are made to suffer, a pleasure results to those by whom the antipathy is entertained, and this pleasure affords an additional reason for the punishing of it. There remain however two reasons against punishing it. The antipathy in question (and the appetite of malevolence that results from it) as far as it is not warranted by the essential mischievousness of the offence is grounded only in prejudice. It may therefore be assuaged and reduced to such a measure as to be no longer painful only in bringing to view the considerations which show it to be ill-grounded. The case is that of the accidental existence of an antipathy which [would have] no foundation [if] the principle of utility were to be admitted as a sufficient reason for gratifying it by the punishment of the object; in a word, if the propensity to punish were admitted in this or any case as a sufficient ground for punishing, one should never know where to stop. Upon monarchical principles, the Sovereign would be in the right to punish any man he did not like; upon popular principles, every man, or at least the majority of each community, would be in the right to punish every man upon no better reason.

The antipathy itself a punishment

Besides this, the antipathy in question, so long as it subsists, draws with it in course, and without having recourse to the political magistrate, a very galling punishment, and this punishment is the heavier the greater number of persons is by whom the antipathy is entertained and the more intense it is in each person: it increases therefore in proportion to the demand there is for punishment on this ground. Although the punishing it by the hands of the magistrate were not productive of the ill consequences just stated, it would seem hard to punish it in this way upon the ground of that circumstance which necessarily occasions it to be punished another way; its being already punished beyond what is enough is but an indifferent reason to give for punishing it more.

Punishment however not an incentive

Some writers have mentioned as an objection to the punishing of practices of the obscene kind, that the punishment is a means of putting men in mind to make experiment of the practise: the investigation of the offence and publicity of the punishment being the means of conveying the practise to the notice of a multitude of persons who otherwise would never have thought of any such thing. From the circumstance of its being punished they learn of its being practised, from the circumstance of its being practised they conclude that there is a pleasure in it; from the circumstance of its being punished so severely they conclude that the pleasure is a great one, since it overcomes the dread of so great a punishment. That this must often happen is not to be denied, and in so far as it does happen and occasions the offence to be repeated it weighs against the benefit of the punishment. This is indeed the most popular argument of any that can urged against the punishment of such practices; but it does not appear to be well-grounded. It proves nothing unless the punishment tends as strongly in the one way to spread the practise as it does in the other to repress it. This, however, does not appear to be the case. We should not suppose it a priori for at the same time that it brings to view the idea of the offence it brings to view in connection with that idea the idea not only of punishment but of infamy; not only of the punishment which should prevent men's committing it in the face of the public, but of the infamy which should prevent their discovering any inclination to commit it to the nearest and most trusty of their friends. It does not appear to be the case in point of experience. In former times, when it was not punished, it prevailed to a very great degree; in modern times in the very same countries since it has been punished it has prevailed in a much less degree. Besides this, the mischief produced by the punishment in this way may be lessened in a considerable degree by making the trial and all the other proceedings private, which may be done without any danger of abuse by means of the expedient suggested in the book relative to procedure.

Danger of false prosecutions greater in this case than others

A very serious objection, however, to the punishment of this offence is the opening it makes for false and malicious prosecutions. This danger in every case weighs something against the reasons for applying punishment, but in this case it weighs much more considerably than perhaps in any other. Almost every other offence affords some particular test of guilt, the absence of which constitutes so many criterions of innocence. The evidence of persons will be in some way or other confirmed by the evidence of things: in the ordinary offences against property the circumstance of the articles being missing or seen in undue place, in offences against persons the marks of violence upon the person. In these and, in short, in all other or almost all other cases where the offence has really been committed, some circumstances will take place relative to the appearance of things, and will therefore be expected to be proved. In any offences which have hatred for their motive the progress of the quarrel will afford a number of characteristic circumstances to fix the imputation upon the person who is guilty. In the case of rape, for instance, where committed on a virgin, particular characteristic appearances will not fail to have been produced, and even where the object has been a married woman or a person of the same sex marks of violence will have been produced by the resistance. But when a filthiness of this sort is committed between two persons, both willing, no such circumstances need have been exhibited; no proof therefore of such circumstances will be required. Whenever, therefore, two men are together, a third person may alledge himself to have seen them thus employing themselves without fear of having the truth of his story disproved. With regard to a bare proposal of this sort the danger is still greater; one man any charge it upon any other man without the least danger of being detected. For a man to bring a charge of this sort against any other man without the possibility of its being disproved there needs no more than for them to have been alone together for a few moments.

Used as an instrument of extortion

The mischief is often very severely felt. In England the severity of the punishment and what is supported by it, the moral antipathy to the offence, is frequently made use of as a means of extorting money. It is the most terrible weapon that a robber can take in hand; and a number of robberies that one hears of, which probably are much fewer than the ones which one does not hear of, are committed by this means. If a man has resolution and the incidental circumstances are favourable, he may stand the brunt and meet his accuser in the face of justice; but the danger to his reputation will at any rate be considerable. Men of timid natures have often been almost ruined in their fortunes ere they can summon up resolution to commit their reputations to the hazard of a trial. A man's innocence can never be his security; knowing this it must be an undaunted man to whom it can give confidence; a well-seasoned perjurer will have finally the advantage over him. Whether a man be thought to have actually been guilty of this practise or only to be disposed to it, his reputation suffers equal ruin.

After so much has been said on the abomination of paederasty, little need be said of the other irregularities of the venereal appetite. If it be problematical whether it be expedient upon the whole to punish the former, it seems next to certain that there can be no use in punishing any of the latter.

Between women

Where women contrive to procure themselves the sensation by means of women, the ordinary course of nature is as much departed from as when the like abomination is practiced by men with men. The former offence however is not as generally punished as the latter. It appears to have been punished in France but the law knows nothing of it in England. (*Code pénal*, Tit. 35, p.238 *J.B.*)

Whether worse between men and women than between men

It seems to be more common for men to apply themselves to a wrong part in women and in this case grave authors have found more enormity than when the sex as well as the part of the object is mistaken, those who go after the principle of the affront, which they say in affairs of any such sort is to God Almighty, assure us that the former contrivance is a more insolent affront than the latter. (See *Fort. Rep. qua supra. J.B.*) The affront should be the same if from necessity or caprice a person of the female sex should make use of a wrong part in one of the male. If there be one idea more ridiculous than another, it is that of a legislator who, when a man and a woman are agreed about a business of this sort, thrusts himself in between them, examining situations, regulating times and prescribing modes and postures. The grave physician who, as soon as he saw Governor Sancho take a fancy to a dish, ordered it away is the model, though but an imperfect one, of such a legislator.

Thus far his business goes on smoothly: he may hang or burn the parties according as he fancies without difficulty. But he will probably be a little at a loss when he comes to inquire with the Jesuit Sanchez (*De Matrimonio*) how the case stands when the man for example, having to do with a woman, begins in one part and consummates in another; thinks of one person or of one part while he is employing himself with another; begins with a woman and leaves her in the lurch. Without calling in the principle of utility such questions may be multiplied and remain undecided for evermore; consult the principle of utility, and such questions never will be started . . .

1. [*I'll fuck your ass and suck you off Antonius Furius, you fag and queer.—Eds*]

from

OFFENCES AGAINST TASTE

(1814-16)

Jeremy Bentham

Physical Division of the Subject

Any act having for its object the immediate gratification of the sexual appetite may be termed *an act of sexuality*.

Till of late years the number of senses had been fixed at five; of late years a sense correspondent to and put in excercise by the act of sexuality has been added to the number.

In no other instance other than the act of sexuality has excercise of any act of sensuality been considered as being naturally subjected to any restrictive rule other than that rule of probity, by which injury to third persons is interdicted, and that rule of individual prudence by which *excess* in interdicted, *i.e.* that degree in which the act has for its consequence a quantity of pain, whether concomitant or subsequent, more than equivalent to the pleasure. In this instance alone has excess been considered as subjected to restrictive rules, other than the two just mentioned ones . . .

Advantages from Proposed Liberty

Benefit to morality in general, viz. benefit to genuine morality from the exclusion put on false and spurious morality.

Seldom can spurious morality be attended to, but genuine morality experiences proportionable neglect. That human character in general is chequered is a proposition to which few men will refuse their assent. At the same time a sort of exception, generally overlooked among religionists, is that, perfect conformity to the rule of right being unattainable, deviations from it in a more or less considerable number of instances are not incompatible with such a degree of excellence as it lies in a man's power to attain to. Yielding to transgression in this or that shape, he may, with the less danger, give way to it in this or that other shape. Thus by abstention in a shape in which, gratification being innoxious, abstention is of no use, he is led into gratification in this or that shape in which it is really noxious.

[The only sources from which the sum of happiness can receive increase.]

1. The bringing within each man's reach a pleasure in a quantity greater than that in which it would otherwise be within his reach:

2. The removing of obstacles which error and prejudice have hitherto, with such fatal success, opposed to his making use of those which have been lying within his reach.

By the removal of that cloud of prejudice by which this part of the field of morals has to this time been obscured, what calculation shall comprehend the mass of pleasure that may be brought into existence, the value of the service that may be rendered to mankind, in a word, the mass of good that may be done? By this thought it is that the hand by which these papers have been penned, has been enabled to go through the labour which they required, to endure the disgust with which the subject was found encompassed.

B

THE FRENCH REVOLUTION: SEXUAL LIBERATION AND POLITICAL SPEECH

The impact of the French Revolution on the legal status of homosexuality and the political situation of gays and lesbians cannot be underestimated. With it, France moved from the last public burning for homosexual acts in 1784 to decriminalization of homosexuality with the constitution of 1791. Indeed, not only did the polemics surrounding the adoption of the constitution tend to place homosexuality on an equal level with heterosexuality, but the subsequent Napoleonic code decriminalized homosexual activity, thus affecting the penal codes of all continental Europe to this day.

The three revolutionary pamphlets excerpted here represent the beginnings of distinctively political speech by lesbians and gay men. While writings by and about self-identified lesbians and gay men date to before these pamphlets, they mark the first time lesbians and gay men organized as such to address a national government. The radical difference between these and the earlier Enlightenment texts is that, while the former proposed a combination of social engineering and decriminalization under the principle that it is better to prevent homosexuality than to punish it, these texts argue both that there is no such thing as "unnatural behavior" (the idea of "nature" having been understood as a religious prescription masquerading as a scientific statement), and that every citizen has a right to her or his own body (an idea which will be picked up in later gay rights discourse as "self-ownership" and sexual privacy). In the penal code adopted in 1791, sodomy was not mentioned, and later law enforcers had to be reminded by judges that sodomy was not prohibited under the new code. Whether and how these pamphlets contributed to this absence of prohibition is a matter for further historical research.

Political pamphleteering was a form of political participation, through noncensored publication, by a formerly politically uninvolved populace. Many of the postrevolutionary pamphlets were pornographic, using explicit sexual discourse to draw parallels between sexual debauchery and political conspiracy and corruption among the aristocracy and clergy. In these pamphlets there was often a concern with prostitution that reflected a fear about the role of women in the new republic and their possible entrance into the public sphere; many pamphlets' allusions to the sexual life of Marie Antoinette are emblematic of this concern. Homosexuality was in the paradoxical position of being at once the basis for criticism of the hypocrisy of the clergy and aristocracy, while at the same time having to be defended in order now to give, on behalf of universal equality and human rights, what had once been the privilege of a few to all citizens. It is in this context that the excerpts from the three pamphlets should be read. The pamphlets are either anonymously written or signed with apocryphal names.

"Les Petits Bougres" (1790) is a plea for the right to use one's own body as property (as the right to one's property was secured by the revolution). Therefore what to do with one's genitals, as one's property, is of no concern of the state. It still strikes an apologetic tone, however, by stating that lovers of the ass would return to the cunt if prostitutes were regularly examined and their cunts were made the width of assholes. At the time, "bougres" meant "buggers," deriving from adherents of heresies of Bulgarian origin; the term later became identified with sodomites.

"The Children of Sodom" (1790) used the figure of Charles, Marquis de Villette (1734–1793), a homosexual friend of Voltaire who was nicknamed Corydon (a name that Gide will later take up in his pro–gay tract) to satirically argue for sexual freedom. Villette was portrayed at the time as a militant battling prejudice against homosexuality, and was involved in drawing up the constitution of 1791. In the text, arguments from nature, history, and necessity legitimate individual sexual liberty.

"Liberty, or Miss Raucourt" (1791) proclaims the legitimacy and universality of lesbians' sexuality paralleling that of buggers and berdaches (men, usually youths, who were penetrated). This appeared during a time in which lesbianism was considered exceptional, since most women who had sex with other women ("tribades") were considered bisexual, unable to stifle what was believed to be a natural inclination of women to men. "Mademoiselle Raucourt" was in fact the stage name of a well–known actress, Françoise-Marie-Antoinette-Joseph Saucerotte (1753–1815, although different accounts give different dates) who, while enjoying the protection of Marie Antoinette, supposedly dressed as a man when sexually involved with women and as a woman when sexually involved with a man. However, it was also said that she "married" a female singer and only had sex with men for cash or favours. She was supposedly a central figure in the Secte Anandryne, a lesbian sex sorority. Although we do not know its author, this pamphlet is modeled on a prior address of Raucourt's to members of the Secte in which she explained and justified lesbian love. Here we see the tension between, on the one hand, portrayals of lesbianism as an aristocratic vice and prostitution as patriotic necessity, and on the other hand, an individualistic philosophy of sexual freedom. In the end, this pamphlet seems a critique of the political and sexual liberty emblematized by Raucourt. Name spellings were not fully regularized in the eighteenth century; thus her name is spelled "Raucour" and "Raucourt" at the same time. We now write her name as Raucourt.

LES PETITS BOUGRES AU MANÈGE,

OR

THE LITTLE BUGGER-GO-ROUND

(1790)

Anonymous
trans. Michael West

Individual liberty, decreed by our very noble and very respectable representatives, is assuredly not a reasonable being; and, according to this principle, I may dispose of my property, such as it is, according to my taste and my fantasies. Thus, my cock and my balls belong to me, and so I may put them in stew or in broth, or, to speak clearly, whether I put them in a cunt or an asshole is of no business to anyone else, especially whores. These vile prostitutes, who have the audacity to gossip about us, are in fact no more than dykes who lend themselves with no difficulty to all means of lewd fantasies that any lecherous rich old man might have. Sucking, getting fucked in the ass, having their tits fucked, getting fucked between their thighs, under their armpits, it's all the same to them, as long as you stick gold in front of their eyes, and no assignats,[1] either. Paper money has no value among our princesses of corrupted blood. Even the jack-off girls on the Place Louis XV themselves wouldn't give a damn about a hundred-pound assignat; they wouldn't even dare touch it, because they'd swear their hands would be paralyzed.

I'm no great dialectician, but after I've fucked someone in the ass, my judgment is as excellent, my mind is as enlightened, as that of any deputy to the National Assembly. I may therefore conclude from everything that I have just proven that our whores, madams, jack-off artists, and all the rest must be declared incompetent.

A decree handed down in their favor is null and void when the judges are incompetent and suspect; I can prove it.

A tribune is competent when the instruction in a case has been handed down by the sovereign power; therefore, to dispute the right to know according to these authorities would be the height of foolishness. But any time the tribune assumes this right unto itself, its decrees are null and void in their entirety, and this is the situation of the National Assembly. Unless one says that the prostitutes' request has principal bearing on public morality, the national legislators have not the right to be involved. In this hypothesis I will allow myself to ask whether those who are charged with maintaining the public morality are dispensed with maintaining their own. I wonder whether the cream of the aristocracy has proven the purity of its own, by judging itself guilty of rape and kidnapping, of forcing a woman to yield her favors with a pistol at her throat. I ask whether democracy's orator has given proof of the quality of his life and his morals in kidnapping a wife from her husband, in publicly cuckolding the idiot bookseller on ——Street, etc., etc., etc. Besides, is it any improvement to morality to brand buggers and cock-suckers? No, the error is too coarse, and the success is more than uncertain. This truth needs no proof; everyone understands it. I'll allow myself to say that branding buggers is the only sure way to allow prostitutes to leave their mark on the entire earth.

Any judge who consorts with one of his lawyers is suspect. This principle is incontestable, and therefore inadmissible, the proof of suspicion being easy enough to establish. In their request to the national legislators, the whores and their gang admit to having fucked the deputies more times than they have pubic hairs on their asses, and that they have very often had their share of the eighteen livres that the government grants them.[2] When two individuals share everything in common, their complicity is beyond doubt. And when one of the two is the judge of the other, one cannot help but conclude that the judge must be suspect. Therefore, given the fact that the Assembly is incompetent and suspect, the decree it has issued in favor of fucking is null and void.

People will perhaps object that all these reasons hardly justify the abominable predilection shared by you and your ilk for turd fishing.[3] Fucking is very evil, you will say, when it goes against the directives of nature, and thus sodomy is the limit of depravity. This preference of ours for which you reproach us is justified in countless examples throughout time, however. I could cite the example of Socrates, who used to fuck Alcibiades in front of and with the full knowledge of everyone, despite the fact that Greek women were and still are beautiful enough to inspire men's desires and to give them erections. Several Roman emperors had titulary [male] cocksuckers, even though they could have enjoyed the most beautiful women in all of Rome. All the people of the Middle East are passionate ass-fuckers, even though their harems contain marvels of feminine grace and beauty. The residents of Sodom themselves had wives who would have given hard-ons to paintings, and yet they fucked each other in the ass with all the more pleasure. Don't tell me about torrents of flaming sulfur engulfing the city as punishment for their crime; this is an old tale from the imagination of someone's empty dream, which our sanctimonious churchgoers have adopted for their own interests. Here is the truth, such as it has been handed down in the splendors of ass-fucking. The High Priest [of Sodom], one of the proudest buggers that the Earth has ever produced, wanted to celebrate the Feast of Fertility[4] and ordered his cook, himself an expert in buggery, to prepare a sumptuous feast to which he had invited all of his minions. A young kitchen boy, a fifteen-year-old blond lad, as beautiful as Cupid with an ass like Ganymede's, was busy in a corner of the kitchen, washing dishes. The cook, burning with desire and with a hard-on like a monk's, was devouring the lad with his eyes, and hurried to finish what he was doing so that he could satisfy his burning desires. Finally, the cook finished his menial chore. The meat was turning on a spit in front of a raging fire in the chimney. The impatient bugger grabs his young Ganymede and undertakes Herculean labors to shove his massive cock into the young man's narrow asshole. Meanwhile, the fire became so hot that the chimney caught fire. The bugger, having totally given himself over to pleasure, didn't even notice. The fire made rapid progress and quickly consumed the whole city of Sodom. You will excuse the digression, but it was necessary. The examples which I have just cited would suffice in justifying us, since, with no motive other than the satisfaction of a curious preference, the majority of ancient and modern people have had a furious desire to ass-fuck. In our case, it is less a preference than a necessity that forces us into this habit.

Beautiful women are very rare in Paris, big cunts are very common, and disease is even more common still. If you fuck a common woman you eventually get disgusted, and there's very little pleasure involved. If you happen to fuck a great big cunt you get lost, you wander around for an hour, you break your back, and finally lose your hard-on completely without ever coming. If by chance you happen across a beautiful woman, which is quite rare, she is doubtless a whore, and then the fear of catching some disease poisons any possibility of pleasure. None of these disadvantages presents itself in the case of men: a nice narrow passage, hard, white buttocks, an infinite willingness to please, everything invites you to satisfy yourself. One can, it is true, get a case of gonorrhea, but since this disease is fairly rare, the risk is not daunting.

At any rate, my brothers and I are in agreement, and I hereby declare in my name and theirs, that we are prepared to renounce our inclination for ass, under the following conditions.

A general inspection of all the prostitutes in Paris will be undertaken, and all those who are contaminated or suspected of being contaminated with the pox will be imprisoned in Bicêtres.[5] Furthermore, all cunts that are larger than normal will be sewn up so that they are no wider than two inches in diameter, and all those whose two slits are no longer but one will be declared disabled and incapable of making their clients come. And if they reject this reconciliation, let them retire from prostitution; if they insist on continuing the way they are, let them be paid only in assignats.

Signed, M. de V——, authorized Procurer of the Sodomitical Society

1. Paper currency of dubious value printed during the Revolution.—Trans.

2. "The whores and their gang" is a reference to the members of the Chamber of Deputies; their salary was eighteen livres.—Eds.

3. A somewhat colorful expression for anal intercourse. The expression in French is la pêche des étrons à la ligne. —Trans.

4. In French, les Lupercales, an annual Roman feast in honor of Lupercus, the wolf-god, god of Fertility.—Trans.

5. A prison on the outskirts of Paris.—Trans.

THE CHILDREN OF SODOM
BEFORE THE NATIONAL ASSEMBLY
OR
DELEGATION OF THE ORDER OF THE CUFF
BEFORE THE REPRESENTATIVES OF ALL OTHER ORDERS
OF ALL SIXTY DISTRICTS OF PARIS AND VERSAILLES

(1790)

Charles, Marquis de Villette, High Commander of the Order
trans. *Michael West*

> *Preferences are in Nature;*
> *The best one is one's own.*
> —*Chevalier de Florain*

The Children of Sodom before the National Assembly

Following the example of the Greeks and Romans, around whom everyone rallied at the very mention of the words Country and Freedom, hardly had the question been broached of convening the Etats-Généraux for the first time in two hundred years when the cry went out for a general meeting of the entire French empire. Shortly thereafter, the nobility, the clergy, and the commons met to elect their representatives to the Etats-Généraux, and soon no one spoke of anything but electors and elected officials. In the same way that monkeys spontaneously imitate humans in the middle of intersections and along the wharves, that is, everywhere, we now see nothing but Assemblies and hear nothing but motions being proposed and debated. Young tailors took over the lawns of the Louvre, and servants abandoned the dance halls and antechambers to hold forth in their own way.

The cuckolds of the capital, because of their great number, chose the Plain of Sablons to hold their meeting, and their diaries, made public, became the object of universal admiration.

Prostitutes organized themselves into squadrons. Those at the Palais-Royal, jealous of the protection of their patron the Prince, refused to budge and communicated with citizens; other prostitutes in different neighborhoods held forth at the Porcherons and at the Nouvelle-France, while those with no specific locale except the streets met at the Place Louis XV in the middle of the piles of stones waiting to be used in the construction of the Louis XVI Bridge (named for Louis XV's grandson). This latter group was by no means the least numerous.

In the middle of all this turmoil, the famous Order of the Cuff had remained inactive. From time to time the group had met at the Tuileries, in the Alley of Sighs, in the Cloister of Chartreux, and at the home of Father Viennet, the most zealous partisan of buggery, not to discuss the various motions being currently debated, but to bring about the burning of Paris through their great efforts at buggery, just as the residents of Sodom had managed to burn down their city through the same operation.

But the Supreme Being, having grown less inflexible regarding similar trifles, and no longer burning down cities for such petty crimes, sent to Earth a healthy Philosophy who was confronted by prejudice, and the Buggers adopted as their motto that of Chevalier Florain, and said:

Preferences are in Nature;
The best one is one's own.

...The speech of le Duc de Noailles:

Gentlemen,

Anti-physics,[1] which its detractors have referred to derisively as buggery, and which the ignorance of several centuries has portrayed as an illicit game of lewdness, and which jurisconsults call bestiality,[2] will henceforth become a science studied and taught in all classes of society.

Thanks to philosophers, the times have indeed changed; we will no longer be treated to the shame of watching Italy march alone in glory towards its own perfection in this science: because nature has endowed all of us with the necessary knowledge, in order to know the primary and essential elements, it is up to us to employ the wisest and most thoroughly considered means to hasten progress in the country in which we live; and to arrive at this end, gentlemen, the most important operation is to eliminate, down to their very roots, those biases which have tried since the beginning of time to destroy us, and have created among our Order martyrs whom we will mourn forever.[3]

The barbarism of criminal laws has robbed us of Urbain Grandier, Duchaufour, and thousands upon thousands of others; jealousy has separated us many a time; liberty reunites us; let us make noble use of it; let us instruct the entire Earth that great men have been for the most part Anti-physicians, and that this famous and illustrious Order is on a par with those of Malta and the Holy Spirit.

Let us instruct future centuries to venerate the memories of those unfortunate ones who succumbed under the efforts of feminine tyranny, and to see their tragic ends only as assassinations . . . As for myself, gentlemen, I will admit without vanity, penetrated by the ineffable charms that the pleasure of being associated with this Order have procured for me, that I have always been its most zealous defender.[4] Religion, armed with its political whip, has pretended in vain to punish us, to have revealed the sweetest of its mysteries: and yet, has not its Legislator himself,[5] motivated by the most tender affection for his younger cousin, led us all, such as we are, down the path of knowledge? Has he not shown us the primary elements of this preference, which fools have called monstrous and bizarre, but whose divine essence we have recognized.

Do not accuse me, gentlemen, of displaying vainglory if I recall here all that I have done for the Order, and how many creatures I have brought into it. Yes, everywhere I have declared myself the precursor of the rebels fighting the sentimental laws of our institution. I have conquered my domestic staff and its surroundings; I have buggered my vassals as much as I have been able to; I have sodomized my wife, my niece, and I have thrust my kingpin all the way up my groom; in a word I have made buggers of everyone around me; here is the proof of my devotion. To this I have added the proof that concubinage was no more natural than Anti-physics, and since every man is free to do what he chooses, he must be free to more or less explore this matter. I am sure, gentlemen, that all the members of this august Assembly will not agree completely on all the points and principles that I have just established, but following my reasoning we have only to make them into laws in order to make them known and respected in the land of the Franks, and probably have them adopted into the Constitution by the National Assembly, where we already figure prominently, in order to append it to the one they are currently trying to retrieve from the heart of darkness." ...

Article One:

The Assembly of Buggers, Sodomites and Lesbians, to which has been added by special favor the Chatelaines of the Slipper, Lesbians and Butt-lickers, who have taken the oath before us to do whatever necessary, and to present the Knights of our Order with whatever the Knights wish to be revealed, has decreed during its convention that, according to the report made to it by the Verification Committee on the scope and fortune of the Rights of Man, every Knight of the Cuff will be permitted to dispose of his person, passively or actively as he pleases, either in the Avenues of Sodom, known as the Feuillants, in the Garden of Friendship, under the auspices of the Count of Rouhaut, in the Panthéon and in the Lodge of the Nine Sisters, even in the paths of the Luxembourg Gardens, despite what the legal owner says, and without hindrance by any other person.

Article Two:

Any person creating an obstruction, that is, any born enemy of the prerogatives outlined in Article One, will be declared infamous and be barred from the Catalog that will be published at the end of these articles, so that he will be expelled from our Order and pursued like the Cubs in the Masonic Lodges.

Article Three:

Every Knight of the Cuff finding himself bound by the laws of marriage shall be free to renounce his obligation in order to join the opposition party; likewise all members of the opposition shall be free to embrace the Knights of the Cuff.

Article Four:

Henceforth Bicêtres, Avènes, and in general all places reserved for the treatment of anti-social diseases shall be reserved also for the treatment of all persons afflicted with the unfortunate disease of Anti-physics; we decree this only regretfully, given that Anti-physics is only one result of the inconveniences resulting to those who give up the Ass for the Cunt.

Article Five:

All Doctors and Surgeons, certified or otherwise, assassins licensed by the Medical School, will be bound to find a cure for Cristaline [gonnorhea—eds.], under penalty of extraordinary prosecution, by all authorized means, possible or not, as prescribed in Article Two, as an obstruction, and contrary to the strengthening of the Order.

Article Six:

A manuscript saved from the burning of Sodom will be sent immediately to press and published without interruption. The manuscript is entitled "Elementary Treatise on Anti-physics, or Theoretical Abstract of that Obsession, for the use of Pretenders and Young Bardaches." Four of the most senior members of the Order will be charged with its publication, namely: Bareau de Girac, Bishop of Rennes; Bourdeilles, Bishop of Soissons; the Count of Montrevel, Field Marshal; and the Marquis de Visé, Lieutenant-General of the King's Armies.

Article Seven (Last):

The Order will be divided into a civil branch, a legislative branch and a military branch; and in the same way that one can be a Bugger and a Citizen, and that the matters of Ass do not and cannot prevent one from being dearly concerned with matter of State, a list of the principal commanders, legislators, and burghers of the Order will be drawn up before the end of the present meeting, and presented to the National Assembly with the intention of presenting our respects to the Assembly and to secure its sanction.

These seven articles receiving unanimous approval, there remained only the matter of giving them the widest publicity possible. As a result, and according to the report given on ass-fucking, for and against, it was decreed that the diligence of the Duc de Noailles, President of the Order, would ensure the printing, publication, and distribution of the articles throughout the streets and intersections of the good city of Paris, notably on the gates of the Tuileries, those of the Luxembourg Gardens, and that furthermore permission would be granted to all booksellers to freely print the articles, including Lord Pain, would-be bookseller of the Palais-Royal, number 145, to print, distribute, and sell the articles door-to-door. At the same time all Investigators, Inspectors, Moles, Spies, Bums and other riffraff on the payroll of the new police force will be prevented from disturbing them in any way from the execution of their activities, under the penalty of being dragged out onto the very Terrace of the Feuillants.

Signed,

De Noailles, President, Father Aubert, Vice-Pres., Duviquet, Secretary

1. "Anti-physical" was a common way of describing men who had sex with men, supposedly being contrary to the natural or physical order of things.—Eds.

2. Quite inappropriately named such by idiots wearing cornets, hereditary enemies of our taste; because Bordaloue, Lully, Dalembert, La Harpe, Thomas, etc., who were not and aren't yet idiots are nevertheless Buggers (author's note.)

3. Cf. the Martyrology of Buggery and the public execution of Paschal, burned at the stake in the Place de Grève, for having attempted willingly or by force to rob a shoe-shine boy of his virginity (author's note.)

4. Ah, it's true, all true, so very true! (author's note.)

5. The dying Jesus, who suffered the same fate as our brother Paschal, death on the bed of honor, used to say to St. John: "Come, my son; come, my beloved, rest your head on my chest." Can we doubt the true essence of these tender expressions? (author's note.)

LIBERTY, OR MISS RAUCOUR

(1791)

Anonymous
trans. Michael West

to the whole sect of women without men
assembled in the foyer of the Comédie Française

Published in Cunt-lick
also found in the wings of all theaters
even at Audinos

song on frontispiece (facing):

To the tune of *We'd Count the Diamonds:*

In order to celebrate you, beautiful Raucourt,
If only I had the power
To change my sex and pleasure
Twenty times a day!
Yes, in order to tell you
How dear you are to me,
I'd like to be a man to love you,
And a woman to make you happy.

. . . As Frenchwomen, as active citizens, you must take part in everything that interests the entire nation of which we are members; but once this duty is fulfilled, let us not forget our cunts and clits; we would be lacking in our duty towards ourselves, we would deserve the worse case of the pox, if by some unforeseeable motive we neglected to take precautions to protect ourselves or to conserve our ability to suck anything we wished. Already I can see a mournful sadness on your foreheads; already the clap has taken its most ravaging toll. Graces are disappearing, pale violets are taking the place of roses and lilies which formerly shone on your faces; you're trembling, your juices retreat deeper into your bodies; however, you're still unaware of what danger threatens you! As for myself, although I am familiar with fear, I never think of it without my pubic hair standing on end, without my clit suddenly retracting, without my very ample cunt suddenly shrinking prodigiously. No, particular news never had a more surprising or more sudden effect than this; but let us arm ourselves with a heroic strength, let us forget for a moment that we are women—it won't be a very painful effort—and let us try to get used to acting like men, let us have courage. Here's the story.

Through a request worthy of those women who presented it, and which ought to have been met with stitches for their ample solution of continuity, the prostitutes, that public plague that lightning should strike dead, obtained from the fucking committee, composed of the worst fuck-offs the world has ever produced, a decree ordering all ass-fuckers and cock-suckers to adorn their hats with a dick nestled in pubic hair in the shape of a plume, as a sign of condemnation by which they might be recognized and pointed out, unless they either abandon their furious ass-fucking or make a public confession of prostitution. The sodomites realized that they were being singled out for scorn and revulsion, and so they met immediately in the Luxembourg Gardens, presided over by the brave ass-fucker Villette, and they named dedicated sodomites as commissars and a procurer, in order to fuck the fleeing prostitutes and defend themselves in an affair that was compromising their taste for ass as well as their social esteem. Up to this point we didn't give a fuck; our cunts and clits didn't have anything to do with it. But yesterday, as I was fucking Miss Lange without having closed my door, while I was trying furiously to make myself come with my heels, the Chevalier Half-cunt, a proven fucker who tickled me many a time with his balls when I was at the Théâtre Français, came into my room with a terrified look on his face, looking like a man who'd just been castrated; and without noticing that I was just about to come, he says, taking me rudely by the arm, "I have just come from the Viscountess Split-cunt where, while you've been amusing yourself fucking around, they are devising a plot against the sect of women without men that is capable of completely destroying it. My friendship for you and my gratitude for previous services rendered obliged me to warn you of this; just as soon as I was jacked off I came right over to give you this important news. Now that I've done my duty, come if you have the courage and prepare to defend yourself."

At these words the cum coagulated inside my balls and I lost my hard-on,[1] and Miss L—— who had already come in gushes, suddenly felt the source of her cum dry up completely. I'll readily admit that the chevalier's words had a more terrible effect on me than the destruction of the entire universe; the most horrific case of the pox would have frightened me less; I fell into a stupor that caused everyone to panic for my life. In vain people tried smelling salts and spirits, they deluged me with perfume and Eau des Carmes, even essence of cum was useless. It was only by jacking me off and sucking me that Miss Lange was finally able to revive me. Regaining consciousness, my first gesture was to put my hand to my cunt to reassure myself I was still alive. I believed that I'd dreamt the Chevalier Half-cunt's words, but Miss Lange assured me I was mistaken. I tortured my imagination to uncover the motives behind the prostitutes' odious plot, I thought carefully about our own behavior towards the whole vile bunch, and I could find nothing, neither in our cunts nor in our assholes, which would merit such hostility. Finally, after reflecting long enough, cum was beginning to circulate again when I hit on a brilliant idea. Here it is.

As long as our pecuniary needs or our preference for ordinary fucking have required us to make use of balls and cocks, we have been involved with innumerable inconveniences which have been inseparable from the job of prostitution. But since the product of our cunts has placed us out of the reach of poverty, and since we have appropriated the goods of a number of jerks dressed like men, who have fallen prey to our charms and our artifices, and since our mutual preference for clit has made us give up on using dildos, whores and others accustomed to sharing chancres, pox, and all the rest with us, finding themselves entrusted all alone to ply the trade of the partisans of St. Cosmo, have formulated the horrible project of relegating us to the class of common prostitutes, by denouncing us to the committee on fucking as making illicit use of our talents and all of the parts comprising our organs of pleasure. If their success against us is to be judged by that of their campaign against the sodomites, I dare predict that we are fucked, and fucked without being paid. The decree of the committee on fucking, the resemblance of our case with that of the buggers and cocksuckers, the advantage of the whores with judges who fuck them free of charge, all of this should make us fear of being ruined by a ruling in which we have no hope of seducing those who will decide the case.

We must immediately, then, seize all possible means of deflecting this storm which threatens to break not over our heads but rather over our cunts and over our clits, in a word over everything that produces the pleasure of fucking and coming. Remember that fucking is just like quarreling: the first one to fuck you in the ass is the first one to come, and so the first lawyer to get a good jab in is most likely to win the case. Let us ally ourselves strategically, then, with the Children of Sodom; let us create with them a league bonded together by cum; let us get ourselves fucked in the ass if necessary; we should not be unduly picky as to the means; all are acceptable when they lead to the right end; as proof I cite the poet who says *"dolus an virtus quis in hoste requirat,"* and this poet was no jerk. Let our forces joined with those of the sodomites be the undoing of the awful hussies, those damned bitches who have puffed themselves up with a fleeting success, having triumphed for a mere instant, only to return more shamefaced and confused to the quagmire of their bordellos. Indeed, my dear cunt-spirators [*con-soeurs*], either these intimidated fuckers will give up on their hopelessly fucked project or they will try to see it through: if they give it up, we won't give a fuck about them, and our fears will disappear; if they're stupid enough to persist, they will inevitably capitulate before our forces, which have been joined by those of the sodomites, even if we have to sell the hairs of our cunts to make moustaches for the grenadiers of the Blue Army. Thus, in any event, my motion seems reasonable, and I ask the honorable Assembly to express its opinion in its usually honest way.

A lovable whore, a charming actress named Adeline, stood up and said: "I am a fucker to the depths of my soul, everybody knows it and I'm proud of it: I love men, and I've got women hanging off my ass. I'd rather have a long, fat cock that fills, at least partly, the vast opening of my cunt, that shakes me vigorously and makes me come abundantly, than a tiny, short clit that gets lost in my hole and only tickles me, making me come only in a few drops. This is the first reason why I do not share Mlle Raucour's opinions. Secondly, I wouldn't give the hair off my asshole for the sect of women without men.

"I don't know whether this supposed plot on the part of prostitutes really exists or not; even if it were true, I wouldn't be any more motivated to act against them; as fuckers, our interests are the same; and unless you take me for a fool, you'd better not hope that I'll supply dildos to fuck myself with: as an active citizen, which they will not disagree with, I must contribute to the pleasures of fuckers who have so often contributed to my own pleasure; and to obligate you to perform public prostitution is to do a favor for those who prefer big cunts, it's doing them a great big favor, in fact, one that they've earned by virtue of their money and their health; after all, how many fortunes have our cunts influenced? How many cases of the clap have we circulated? I can personally vouch for a bunch of degenerates currently wallowing in the pallets of Bicêtres, of filthy laundry we've made for them; and yet you would rather announce your preference for clits! And you're not ashamed to make the most revolting and dismal use of your toys and accessories, a use that would have disgusted Parisian women, Aspasians and even Messalines[2] themselves! Oh, give up instead your preferences for clit and go back to your worship of cock, the only thing worthy of your attractions and your charms. May a deluge of sperm dumped on your cunts as a cleansing wash clean them of all the innumerable impurities which have sullied them. Appease Priapus with the expiatory sacrifice, and I dare promise you that you'll come with more pleasure than ever. I dare promise you tireless fuckers, cum everywhere, and money, maybe not a lot, but more assignats than you could ever want. Some people have enough of them that they're not stingy with them.

"Believe me, abandon the children of Sodom to their unhappy fate, they're not worthy of your compassion; the shame of nature they violate in every way, may they be infected with the clap to the marrow of their bones! I hope my observations will have the effect I desire on you. If they do not, I will have at least done for cock and balls what my preference and my taste required of me, and I will console myself by fucking every which way as long as there's a drop of cum left inside me."

"I did not presume," replied Miss de Raucour, "to convince Miss Adeline of my ideas. With her she-wolf temperament and her insatiable cupidity, it would be difficult for her to adopt practices in direct conflict with her two favorite passions, fucking and making money. But since I didn't say anything in my speech that would have offended her sensibility, I nevertheless expected her to temper her responses somewhat, that she should have some accommodation for this preference to which we have given ourselves without reservation, and to which we are as attached as strongly as balls are to a dick. Whatever Miss Adeline says, despite the fact that cum made her flushed as she vomited her diatribe against us, I am persuaded, my dear cunt-spirators, that there is not one among us, no matter how much of a whore she has been in the past, who would prefer to have her cunt sewn up rather than go back to cock, which has spoiled your figures. Don't believe that our preference for clit is something new; it wasn't just yesterday that women got the idea to fuck without men, we have examples from all countries and all times. Those warrior women about whom history has so many marvelous things to say; those famous Amazons who lived along the banks of the Thanaïs had cunts as hot as ours; and yet they only fucked men once a year and then only to perpetuate the race, the rest of the time they fucked each other. Roman women excluded men from their Saturnalia only so that they could enjoy the same innocent frolics for which we're criticized. The wild women of Canada, whose husbands abandon them for seven or eight months while they are hunting, compensate for the lack of cock by stimulating the clitoris. And if you need more recent and more respectable examples, I could always cite . . . but let's not tempt fate by touching the Holy Ark, lest a sudden paralysis be a fitting punishment for such a crime."

1. *The original French text reads: "A ces mots le foutre se coagule dans mes couilles, je débande . . . " Like her partner, Mlle Raucour is given masculine characteristics to the point that vocabulary such as foutre is used to describe vaginal fluids and je débande refers to her loss of arousal.* —Trans.

2. *"Aspasians" refers to Aspasia, a fifth-century B.C. Greek woman famous for her beauty and wit, whose influence on Pericles was satirized in Attic comedy. This reference was probably meant to criticize the influence of women in politics. "Messalines" derives from the name of the mother of Roman emperor Claudius I, who was notorious for her debauchery. The name was a popularly used expression for a sexually voracious but also dangerous woman, and was often used to refer to Marie Antoinette.* —Eds.

MARQUIS DE SADE

We conclude our texts from the French revolutionary period with extracts by the Marquis de Sade (1740–1814), who is infamous for his infliction of pain as a component of sexual stimulation (hence the origin of the word "sadism"). In his own life, Sade was often arrested for kidnapping and rape in connection with sexual theatrics that usually involved blasphemy combined with what was then considered sexual perversion. Many of de Sade's biographers viewed him as primarily homosexual, and some have viewed him as a founder of a "homosexual liberation" tradition. For de Sade homosexuality was natural, because humans have an innate "polymorphous perversity" (as we would say today); sexuality in the service of reproduction is a by-product of this polymorphous erotic capacity. For de Sade, "the sodomite and the lesbian" serve rather than violate nature by redeeming sexuality for its own sake. Today, people draw upon Sade's intimation of blurring the distinction between pain and pleasure to create sexual ecstasy as well as erotic "scenes."

The first part of Sade's text is from the fifth dialogue of *Philosophy in the Bedroom* (1795), a novel. The second extract is excerpted from a small pamphlet inserted into the novel which one of the characters, Dolmancé, claims to have bought at the Palais Égalité. It is entitled "Yet Another Effort Frenchmen, If You Would Become True Republicans," and brings into focus the moral logic of the new republican order the novel is supposed to represent. In this section on "Manners," de Sade states, new governments require new manners, and after the revolutionary destruction of the old regime, the French need to invent a moral system that would prevent the reestablishment of dictatorial government. This is de Sade's contribution to that effort which includes sexual morality; we include only his discussion of sodomy in this context. We also excerpt his discussion of murder, because it dramatically elucidates his naturalistic philosophy and theory of sexuality: nature encompasses both good and evil and the will to be only good must necessarily result in evil. Yet, no matter how one might want to embrace liberatory discourse about sexuality today, the philosophy upon which Sade based it shows his limits in his analysis of murder.

from

PHILOSOPHY IN THE BEDROOM

(1795)

Dialogue the Fifth
(between Dolmancé, Le Chevalier, Augustin, Eugénie, Madame de Saint-Ange)

Comte Donatien-Alphonse-François, Marquis de Sade

. . . Nature has not got two voices, you know, one of them condemning all day what the other commands, and it is very certain that it is nowhere but from her organ that those men who are infatuated with this mania receive the impressions that drive them to it. They who wish to denigrate the taste or proscribe its practice declare it is harmful to population; how dull-witted they are, these imbeciles who think of nothing but the multiplication of their kind, and who detect nothing but the crime in anything that conduces to a different end. Is it really so firmly established that Nature has so great a need for this over-crowding as they would like to have us believe? Is it very certain that one is guilty of an outrage whenever one abstains from this stupid propagation? To convince ourselves, let us for an instant scrutinize both her operations and her laws. Were it that Nature did naught but create, and never destroy, I might be able to believe, with those tedious sophists, that the sublimest of all actions would be incessantly to labor at production, and following that, I should grant, with them, that the refusal to reproduce would be, would perforce have to be, a crime; however, does not the most fleeting glance at natural operations reveal that destructions are just as necessary to her plan as are creations? That the one and the other of these functions are interconnected and enmeshed so intimately that for either to operate without the other would be impossible? That nothing would be born, nothing would be regenerated without destructions? Destruction, hence, like creation, is one of Nature's mandates.

This principle acknowledged, how may I offend Nature by refusing to create that which, supposing there to be some evil in it, would appear infinitely less evil, no question about it, than the act of destruction, which latter is numbered among her laws, as I have but a moment ago proven. If on the one hand I admit the penchant Nature has given me to fabricate these losses and ruins, I must examine, on the other hand, to see whether they are not necessary to her and whether I do not conform with her will when I destroy; thus considered, where then, I ask you, is the crime? But, the fools and the populators continue to object—and they are naught but one—this procreative sperm cannot have been placed in your loins for any purpose other than reproduction: to misuse it is an offense. I have just proven the contrary, since this misuse would not even be equivalent to destruction, and since destruction, far more serious than misuse, would not itself be criminal. Secondly, it is false that Nature intends this spermatic liquid to be employed only and entirely for reproduction; were this true, she would not permit its spillage under any circumstance save those appropriate to that end. But experience shows that the contrary may happen, since we lose it both when and where we wish. Secondly, she would forbid the occurrence of those losses save in coitus, losses which, however, do take place, both when we dream and when we summon remembrances; were Nature miserly about this so precious sap, 'twould never but be into the vessel of reproduction she would tolerate its flow; assuredly, she would not wish this voluptuousness, wherewith at such moments she crowns us, to be felt by us when we divert our tribute; for it would not be reasonable to suppose she could consent to give us pleasures at the very moment we heaped insults upon her. Let us go further; were women not born save to produce—which most surely would be the case were this production so dear to Nature— would it happen that, throughout the whole length of a woman's life, there are no more than seven years, all the arithmetic performed, during which she is in a state capable of conceiving and giving birth? What! Nature avidly seeks propagation, does she; and everything which does not tend to this end offends her, does it! And out of a hundred years of life the sex destined to produce cannot do so during more than seven years! Nature wishes for propagation only, and the semen she accords man to serve in these reproducings is lost, wasted, misused wherever and as often as it pleases man! He takes the same pleasures in this loss as in useful employment of his seed, and never the least inconvenience! . . .

Let us cease, good friends, let us cease to believe in such absurdities: they cause good sense to shudder. Ah! far from outraging Nature, on the contrary—and let us be well persuaded of it—the sodomite and Lesbian serve her by stubbornly abstaining from a conjunction whose resultant progeniture can be nothing but irksome to her. Let us make no mistake about it, this propagation was never one of her laws, nothing she ever demanded of us, but at the very most something she tolerated; I have told you so. Why! what difference would it make to her were the race of men entirely to be extinguished upon earth, annihilated! She laughs at our pride when we persuade ourselves all would be over and done with were this misfortune to occur! Why, she would simply fail to notice it. Do you fancy races have not already become extinct? Buffon counts several of them perished, and Nature, struck dumb by a so precious loss, doesn't so much as murmur! The entire species might be wiped out and the air would not be the less pure for it, nor the Star less brilliant, nor the universe's march less exact. What idiocy it is to think that our kind is so useful to the world that he who might not labor to propagate it or he who might disturb this propagation would necessarily become a criminal! Let's bring this blindness to a stop and may the example of more reasonable peoples serve to persuade us of our errors. There is not one corner of the earth where the alleged crime of sodomy has not had shrines and votaries. The Greeks, who made of it, so to speak, a virtue, raised a statue unto Venus Callipygea; Rome sent to Athens for law, and returned with this divine taste.

And under the emperors, behold the progress it made! Sheltered by the Roman eagle, it spread from one end of the earth to the other; with the Empire's collapse, it took refuge near the diadem, it followed the arts in Italy, it is handed down to those of us who govern ourselves aright. We discover a hemisphere, we find sodomy in it. Cook casts anchor in a new world: sodomy reigns there. Had our balloons reached the moon, it would have been discovered there as well. Delicious preference, child of Nature and of pleasure, thou must be everywhere men are to be found, and wherever thou shalt be known, there shall they erect altars to thee! O my friends, can there be an extravagance to equal that of imagining that a man must be a monster deserving to lose his life because he has preferred enjoyment of the asshole to that of the cunt, because a young man with whom he finds two pleasures, those of being at once lover and mistress, has appeared to him preferable to a young girl, who promises him but half as much! He shall be a villain, a monster, for having wished to play the role of a sex not his own! Indeed! Why then has Nature created him susceptible of this pleasure?

Let us inspect his conformation; you will observe radical differences between it and that of other men who have not been blessed with this predilection for the behind; his buttocks will be fairer, plumper; never a hair will shade the altar of pleasure, whose interior, lined with a more delicate, more sensual, more sensitive membrane, will be found positively of the same variety as the interior of a woman's vagina; this man's character, once again unlike that of others, will be softer, more pliant, subtler; in him you will find almost all the vices and all the virtues native to women; you will recognize even their weaknesses there; all will have feminine manias and sometimes feminine habits and traits. Would it then be possible that Nature, having thuswise assimilated them into women, could be irritated by what they have of women's tastes? Is it not evident that this is a category of men different from the other, a class Nature has created in order to diminish or minimize propagation, whose overgreat extent would infallibly be prejudicial to her? . . . Ah, dear Eugénie, did you but know how delicate is one's enjoyment when a heavy prick fills the behind, when, driven to the balls, it flutters there, palpitating; and then, withdrawn to the foreskin, it hesitates, and returns, plunges in again, up to the hair! No, no, in the wide world there is no pleasure to rival this one: 'tis the delight of philosophers, that of heroes, it would be that of the gods were not the parts used in his heavenly conjugation the only gods we on earth should reverence! . . .

Yet Another Effort, Frenchmen If You Would Become Republicans
MANNERS

After having made it clear that theism is in no wise suitable to a republican government, it seems to me necessary to prove that French manners are equally unsuitable to it. This article is the more crucial, for the laws to be promulgated will issue from manners, and will mirror them.

Frenchmen, you are too intelligent to fail to sense that new government will require new manners. That the citizens of a free State conduct themselves like a despotic king's slaves is unthinkable: the differences of their interests, of their duties, of their relations amongst one another essentially determine an entirely different manner of behaving in the world; a crowd of minor faults and of little social indelicacies, thought of as very fundamental indeed under the rule of kings whose expectations rose in keeping with the need they felt to impose curbs in order to appear respectable and unapproachable to their subjects, are due to become as nothing with us; other crimes with which we are acquainted under the names of regicide and sacrilege, in a system where kings and religion will be unknown, in the same way must be annihilated in a republican State. In according freedom of conscience and of the press, consider, citizens—for it is practically the same thing—whether freedom of action must not be granted too: excepting direct clashes with the underlying principles of government, there remain to you it is impossible to say how many fewer crimes to punish, because in fact there are very few criminal actions in a society whose foundations are liberty and equality. Matters well weighed and things closely inspected, only that is really criminal which rejects the law; for Nature, equally dictating vices and virtues to us, in reason of our constitution, yet more philosophically, in reason of the need Nature has of the one and the other, what she inspires in us would become a very reliable gauge by which to adjust exactly what is good and bad. But, the better to develop my thoughts upon so important a question, we will classify the different acts in man's life that until the present it has pleased us to call criminal, and we will next square them to the true obligations of a republican.

In every age, the duties of man have been considered under the following three categories:
1. Those his conscience and his credulity impose upon him, with what regards a supreme being;
2. Those he is obliged to fulfill toward his brethren;
3. Finally, those that relate only to himself . . .

The transgressions we are considering in this second class of man's duties toward his fellows include actions for whose undertaking libertinage may be the cause; among those which are pointed to as particularly incompatible with approved behavior are *prostitution, incest, rape,* and *sodomy.* We surely must not for one moment doubt that all those known as moral crimes, that is to say, all acts of the sort to which those we have just cited belong, are of total inconsequence under a government whose sole duty consists in preserving, by whatever may be the means, the form essential to its continuance: there you have a republican government's unique morality. Well, the republic being permanently menaced from the outside by the despots surrounding it, the means to its preservation cannot be imagined as *moral means,* for the republic will preserve itself only by war, and nothing is less moral than war. I ask how one will be able to demonstrate that in a state rendered *immoral* by its obligations, it is essential that the individual be *moral?* I will go further: it is a very good thing he is not. The Greek lawgivers perfectly appreciated the capital necessity of corrupting the member-citizens in order that, their *moral dissolution* coming into conflict with the establishment and its values, there would result the *insurrection* that is always indispensable to a political system of perfect happiness which, like republican government, must necessarily excite the hatred and envy of all its foreign neighbors. Insurrection, thought these sage legislators, is not at all a *moral* condition; however, it has got to be a republic's permanent condition. Hence it would be no less absurd than dangerous to require that those who are to insure the perpetual *immoral* subversion of the established order themselves be *moral* beings: for the state of a moral man is one of tranquillity and peace, the state of an *immoral* man is one of perpetual unrest that pushes him to, and identifies him with, the necessary insurrection in which the republican must always keep the government of which he is a member . . .

But sodomy, that alleged crime which will draw the fire of heaven upon cities addicted to it, is sodomy not a monstrous deviation whose punishment could not be severe enough? Ah, sorrowful it is to have to reproach our ancestors for the judiciary murders in which, upon this head, they dared indulge themselves. We wonder that savagery could ever reach the point where you condemn to death an unhappy person all of whose crime amounts to not sharing your tastes. One shudders to think that scarce forty years ago the legislators' absurd thinking had not evolved beyond this point. Console yourselves, citizens; such absurdities are to cease: the intelligence of your lawmakers will answer for it. Thoroughly enlightened upon this weakness occurring in a few men, people deeply sense today that such error cannot be criminal, and that Nature, who places such slight importance upon the essence that flows in our loins, can scarcely be vexed by our choice when we are pleased to vent it into this or that avenue.

What single crime can exist here? For no one will wish to maintain that all the parts of the body do not resemble each other, that there are some which are pure, and others defiled; but, as it is unthinkable such nonsense be advanced seriously, the only possible crime would consist in the waste of semen. Well, is it likely that this semen is so precious to Nature that its loss is necessarily criminal? Were that so, would she every day institute those losses? and is it not to authorize them to permit them in dreams, to permit them in the act of taking one's pleasure with a pregnant woman? Is it possible to imagine Nature having allowed us the possibility of committing a crime that would outrage her? Is it possible that she consent to the destruction by man of her own pleasures, and to his thereby becoming stronger than she? It is unheard of—into what an abyss of folly one is hurled when, in reasoning, one abandons the aid of reason's torch! Let us abide in our unshakable assurance that it is as easy to enjoy a woman in one manner as in another, that it makes absolutely no difference whether one enjoys a girl or a boy, and as soon as it is clearly understood that no inclinations or tastes can exist in us save the ones we have from Nature, that she is too wise and too consistent to have given us any which could ever offend her.

The penchant for sodomy is the result of physical formation, to which we contribute nothing and which we cannot alter. At the most tender age, some children reveal that penchant, and it is never corrected in them. Sometimes it is the fruit of satiety; but even in this case, is it less Nature's doing? Regardless of how it is viewed, it is her work, and, in every instance, what she inspires must be respected by men. If, were one to take an exact inventory, it should come out that this taste is infinitely more affecting than the other, that the pleasures resulting from it are far more lively, and that for this reason its exponents are a thousand times more numerous than its enemies, would it not then be possible to conclude that, far from affronting Nature, this vice serves her intentions, and that she is less delighted by our procreation than we so foolishly believe? Why, as we travel about the world, how many peoples do we not see holding women in contempt! Many are the men who strictly avoid employing them for anything but the having of the child necessary to replace them. The communal aspect of life in republics always renders this vice more frequent in that form of society; but it is not dangerous. Would the Greek legislators have introduced it into their republics had they thought it so? Quite the contrary; they deemed it necessary to a warlike race. Plutarch speaks with enthusiasm of the battalion of lovers: for many a year they alone defended Greece's freedom. The vice reigned amongst comrades-in-arms, and cemented their unity. The greatest of men lean toward sodomy. At the time it was discovered, the whole of America was found inhabited by people of this taste. In Louisiana, amongst the Illinois, Indians in feminine garb prostituted themselves as courtesans. The blacks of Benguéla publicly keep men; nearly all the seraglios of Algiers are today exclusively filled with young boys. Not content to tolerate love for young boys, the Thebans made it mandatory; the philosopher of Chaeronea prescribed sodomy as the surest way to a youth's affection.

We know to what extent it prevailed in Rome, where they had public places in which young boys, costumed as girls, and girls as boys, prostituted themselves. In their letters, Martial, Catullus, Tibullus, Horace, and Virgil wrote to men as though to their mistresses; and we read in Plutarch[1] that women must in no way figure in men's love. The Amasians of Crete used to abduct boys, and their initiation was distinguished by the most singular ceremonies. When they were taken with love for one, they notified the parents upon what day the ravisher wished to carry him off; the youth put up some resistance if his lover failed to please him; in the contrary case, they went off together, and the seducer restored him to his family as soon as he had made use of him; for in this passion as in that for women, one always has too much when one has had enough. Strabo informs us that on this very island, seraglios were peopled with boys only; they were prostituted openly.

Is one more authority required to prove how useful this vice is in a republic? Let us lend an ear to Jerome the Peripatetic: "The love of youths," says he, "spread throughout all of Greece, for it instilled in us strength and courage, and thus stood us in good stead when we drove the tyrants out; conspiracies were formed amongst lovers, and they were readier to endure torture than denounce their accomplices; such patriots sacrificed everything to the State's prosperity; it was beheld as a certain thing, that these attachments steadied the republic, women were declaimed against, and to entertain connections with such creatures was a frailty reserved to despots." Pederasty has always been the vice of warrior races. From Caesar we learn that the Gauls were to an extraordinary degree given to it. The wars fought to sustain the republic brought about the separation of the two sexes, and hence the propagation of the vice, and when its consequences, so useful to the State, were recognized, religion speedily blessed it. That the Romans sanctified the amours of Jupiter and Ganymede is well known. Sextus Empiricus assures us that this caprice was compulsory amongst the Persians. At last, the women, jealous and contemned, offered to render their husbands the same service they received from young boys; some few men made the experiment, and returned to their former habits, finding the illusion impossible. The Turks, greatly inclined toward this depravity Mohammed consecrated in the Koran, were nevertheless convinced that a very young virgin could well enough be substituted for a youth, and rarely did they grow to womanhood without having passed through the experience. Sextus Quintus and Sanchez allowed this debauch; the latter even undertook to show it was of use to procreation, and that a child created after this preliminary exercise was infinitely better constituted thanks to it. Finally, women found restitution by turning to each other. This latter fantasy doubtless has no more disadvantages than the other, since nothing comes of the refusal to reproduce, and since the means of those who have a bent for reproduction are powerful enough for reproduction's adversaries never to be able to harm population. Amongst the Greeks, this female perversion was also supported by policy: the result of it was that, finding each other sufficient, women sought less communication with men and their detrimental influence in the republic's affairs was thus held to a minimum. Lucian informs us of what progress this license promoted, and it is not without interest we see it exemplified in Sappho.

In fine, these are perfectly inoffensive manias; were women to carry them even further, were they to go to the point of caressing monsters and animals, as the example of every race teaches us, no ill could possibly result therefrom, because corruption of manners, often of prime utility to a government, cannot in any sense harm it, and we must demand enough wisdom and enough prudence of our legislators to be entirely sure that no law will emanate from them that would repress perversions which, being determined by constitution and being inseparable from physical structure, cannot render the person in whom they are present any more guilty than the person Nature created deformed.

In the second category of man's crimes against his brethren, there is left to us only murder to examine, and then we will move on to man's duties toward himself. Of all the offenses man may commit against his fellows, murder is without question the cruelest, since it deprives man of the single asset he has received from Nature, and its loss is irreparable. Nevertheless, at this stage several questions arise, leaving aside the wrong murder does him who becomes its victim.

1. As regards the laws of Nature only, is this act really criminal?
2. Is it criminal with what regards the laws of politics?
3. Is it harmful to society?
4. What must be a republican government's attitude toward it?
5. Finally, must murder be repressed by murder?

Each of these questions will be treated separately; the subject is important enough to warrant thorough consideration; our ideas touching murder may surprise for their boldness. But what does that matter? Have we not acquired the right to say anything? The time has come for the ventilation of great verities; men today will not be content with less. The time has come for error to disappear; that blindfold must fall beside the heads of kings. From Nature's point of view, is murder a crime? That is the first question posed.

It is probable that we are going to humiliate man's pride by lowering him again to the rank of all of Nature's other creatures, but the philosopher does not flatter small human vanities; ever in burning pursuit of truth, he discerns it behind stupid notions of pride, lays it bare, elaborates upon it, and intrepidly shows it to the astonished world.

What is man? and what difference is there between him and other plants, between him and all the other animals of the world? None, obviously. Fortuitously placed, like them, upon this globe, he is born like them; like them, he reproduces, rises, and falls; like them he arrives at old age and sinks like them into nothingness at the close of the life span Nature assigns each species of animal, in accordance with its organic construction. Since the parallels are so exact that the inquiring eye of philosophy is absolutely unable to perceive any grounds for discrimination, there is then just as much evil in killing animals as men, or just as little, and whatever be the distinctions we make, they will be found to stem from our pride's prejudices, than which, unhappily, nothing is more absurd. Let us all the same press on to the question. You cannot deny it is one and the same, to destroy a man or a beast; but is not the destruction of all living animals decidedly an evil, as the Pythagoreans believed, and as they who dwell on the banks of Ganges yet believe? Before answering that, we remind the reader that we are examining the question only in terms of Nature and in relation to her; later on, we will envisage it with reference to men.

Now then, what value can Nature set upon individuals whose making costs her neither the least trouble nor the slightest concern? The worker values his work according to the labor it entails and the time spent creating it. Does man cost Nature anything? And, under the supposition that he does, does he cost her more than an ape or an elephant? I go further: what are the regenerative materials used by Nature? Of what are composed the beings which come into life? Do not the three elements of which they are formed result from the prior destruction of other bodies? If all individuals were possessed of eternal life, would it not become impossible for Nature to create any new ones? If Nature denies eternity to beings, it follows that their destruction is one of her laws. Now, once we observe that destruction is so useful to her that she absolutely cannot dispense with it, and that she cannot achieve her creations without drawing from the store of destruction which death prepares for her, from this moment onward the idea of annihilation which we attach to death ceases to be real; there is no more veritable annihilation; what we call the end of the living animal is no longer a true finis, but a simple transformation, a transmutation of matter, what every modern philosopher acknowledges as one of Nature's fundamental laws. According to these irrefutable principles, death is hence no more than a change of form, an imperceptible passage from one existence into another, and that is what Pythagoras called metempsychosis.

These truths once admitted, I ask whether it can ever be proposed that destruction is a crime? Will you dare tell me, with the design of preserving your absurd illusions, that transmutation is destruction? No, surely not; for, to prove that, it would be necessary to demonstrate matter inert for an instant, for a moment in repose. Well, you will never detect any such moment. Little animals are formed immediately a large animal expires, and these little animals' lives are simply one of the necessary effects determined by the large animal's temporary sleep. Given this, will you dare suggest that one pleases Nature more than another? To support that contention, you would have to prove what cannot be proven: that elongated or square are more useful, more agreeable to Nature than oval or triangular shapes; you would have to prove that, with what regards Nature's sublime scheme, a sluggard who fattens in idleness is more useful than the horse, whose service is of such importance, or than a steer, whose body is so precious that there is no part of it which is not useful; you would have to say that the venomous serpent is more necessary than the faithful dog.

Now, as not one of these systems can be upheld, one must hence consent unreservedly to acknowledge our inability to annihilate Nature's works; in light of the certainty that the only thing we do when we give ourselves over to destroying is merely to effect an alteration in forms which does not extinguish life, it becomes beyond human powers to prove that there may exist anything criminal in the alleged destruction of a creature, of whatever age, sex, or species you may suppose it. Led still further in our series of inferences proceeding one from the other, we affirm that the act you commit in juggling the forms of Nature's different productions is of advantage to her, since thereby you supply her the primary material for her reconstructions, tasks which would be compromised were you to desist from destroying.

Well, let *her* do the destroying, they tell you; one ought to let her do it, of course, but they are Nature's impulses man follows when he indulges in homicide; it is Nature who advises him, and the man who destroys his fellow is to Nature what are the plague and famine, like them sent by her hand which employs every possible means more speedily to obtain of destruction this primary matter, itself absolutely essential to her works.

Let us deign for a moment to illumine our spirit by philosophy's sacred flame; what other than Nature's voice suggests to us personal hatreds, revenges, wars, in a word, all those causes of perpetual murder? Now, if she incites us to murderous acts, she has need of them; that once grasped, how may we suppose ourselves guilty in her regard when we do nothing more than obey her intentions?

But that is more than what is needed to convince any enlightened reader, that for murder ever to be an outrage to Nature is impossible.

Is it a political crime? We must avow, on the contrary, that it is, unhappily, merely one of policy's and politics' greatest instruments. Is it not by dint of murders that France is free today? Needless to say, here we are referring to the murders occasioned by war, not to the atrocities committed by plotters and rebels; the latter, destined to the public's execration, have only to be recollected to arouse forever general horror and indignation. What study, what science, has greater need of murder's support than that which tends only to deceive, whose sole end is the expansion of one nation at another's expense? Are wars, the unique fruit of this political barbarism, anything but the means whereby a nation is nourished, whereby it is strengthened, whereby it is buttressed? And what is war if not the science of destruction? A strange blindness in man, who publicly teaches the art of killing, who rewards the most accomplished killer, and who punishes him who for some particular reason does away with his enemy! Is it not high time errors so savage be repaired?

Is murder then a crime against society? But how could that reasonably be imagined? What difference does it make to this murderous society, whether it have one member more, or less? Will its laws, its manners, its customs be vitiated? Has an individual's death ever had any influence upon the general mass? And after the loss of the greatest battle, what am I saying? after the obliteration of half the world—or, if one wishes, of the entire world—would the little number of survivors, should there be any, notice even the faintest difference in things? No, alas. Nor would Nature notice any either, and the stupid pride of man, who believes everything created for him, would be dashed indeed, after the total extinction of the human species, were it to be seen that nothing in Nature had changed, and that the stars' flight had not for that been retarded. Let us continue.

What must the attitude of a warlike and republican state be toward murder?

Dangerous it should certainly be, either to cast discredit upon the act, or to punish it. Republican mettle calls for a touch of ferocity: if he grows soft, if his energy slackens in him, the republican will be subjugated in a trice. A most unusual thought comes to mind at this point, but if it is audacious it is also true, and I will mention it. A nation that begins by governing itself as a republic will only be sustained by virtues because, in order to attain the most, one must always start with the least. But an already old and decayed nation which courageously casts off the yoke of its monarchical government in order to adopt a republican one, will only be maintained by many crimes; for it is criminal already, and if it were to wish to pass from crime to virtue, that is to say, from a violent to a pacific, benign condition, it should fall into an inertia whose result would soon be its certain ruin. What happens to the tree you would transplant from a soil full of vigor to a dry and sandy plain? All intellectual ideas are so greatly subordinate to Nature's physical aspect that the comparisons supplied us by agriculture will never deceive us in morals . . .

It cannot be denied that it is extraordinarily necessary, extremely politic to erect a dike against overpopulation in a republican system; for entirely contrary reasons, the birth rate must be encouraged in a monarchy; there, the tyrants being rich only through the number of their slaves, they assuredly have to have men; but do not doubt for a minute that populousness is a genuine vice in a republican government. However, it is not necessary to butcher people to restrain it, as our modern decemvirs used to say; it is but a question of not leaving it the means of extending beyond the limits its happiness prescribes. Beware of too great a multiplication in a race whose every member is sovereign, and be certain that revolutions are never but the effect of a too numerous population. If, for the State's splendor, you accord your warriors the right to destroy men, for the preservation of that same State grant also unto each individual the right to give himself over as much as he pleases, since this he may do without offending Nature, to ridding himself of the children he is unable to feed, or to whom the government cannot look for assistance; in the same way, grant him the right to rid himself, at his own risk and peril, of all enemies capable of harming him, because the result of all these acts, in themselves of perfect inconsequence, will be to keep your population at a moderate size, and never large enough to overthrow your regime. Let the monarchists say a State is great only by reason of its extreme population: this State will forever be poor, if its population surpasses the means by which it can subsist, and it will flourish always if, kept trimly within its proper limits, it can make traffic of its superfluity. Do you not prune the tree when it has overmany branches? and do not too many shoots weaken the trunk? Any system which deviates from these principles is an extravagance whose abuses would conduct us directly to the total subversion of the edifice we have just raised with so much trouble; but it is not at the moment the man reaches maturity one must destroy him in order to reduce population. It is unjust to cut short the days of a well-shaped person; it is not unjust, I say, to prevent the arrival in the world of a being who will certainly be useless to it. The human species must be purged from the cradle; what you foresee as useless to society is what must be stricken out of it; there you have the only reasonable means to the diminishment of a population, whose excessive size is, as we have just proven, the source of certain trouble.

The time has come to sum up.

Must murder be repressed by murder? Surely not. Let us never impose any other penalty upon the murderer than the one he may risk from the vengeance of the friends or family of him he has killed. "I grant you pardon," said Louis XV to Charolais who, to divert himself, had just killed a man; "but I also pardon whoever will kill you." All the bases of the law against murderers may be found in that sublime motto.[2]

Briefly, murder is a horror, but an often necessary horror, never criminal, which it is essential to tolerate in a republican State. I have made it clear the entire universe has given an example of it; but ought it be considered a deed to be punished by death? They who respond to the following dilemma will have answered the question:

Is it or is it not a crime?

If it is not, why make laws for its punishment? And if it is, by what barbarous logic do you, to punish it, duplicate it by another crime?

1. *The Moralities: "On Love."*

2. *The Salic Law only punished murder by exacting a simple fine, and as the guilty one easily found ways to avoid payment, Childebert, king of Austrasia, decreed, in a writ published at Cologne, the death penalty, not against the murderer, but against him who would shirk the murderer's fine. Ripuarian Law similarly ordained no more against this act than a fine proportionate to the individual killed. A priest was extremely costly: a leaden tunic, cut to his measurements, was tailored for the assassin, and he was obliged to produce the equivalent of this tunic's weight in gold; in default of which the guilty one and his family remained slaves of the Church.*

II

THE
BEGINNINGS
OF A
GAY AND LESBIAN
MOVEMENT

A

THE THIRD SEX THEORY
AND THE
CREATION OF POLITICAL SUBJECTS

Karl Heinrich Ulrichs (1825–1895) was a German attorney who, in his twen-
ties, left his government job in the Kingdom of Hanover to devote the rest of his life
to theoretical elaboration of and political activism on behalf of what he called the
third sex. He was motivated by his own erotic experience, his coming out to his
family at an early age, and the mistreatment of himself and others like him that was
sanctioned by German law. Basing his ideas on embryological theory that posited
a rudimentary hermaphroditism and bisexual potential, as well as on historical and
cross-cultural evidence of the prevalence of same-sex erotic love despite persecution, Ulrichs named male same-sexers *"Urnings"* or "Uranians" (lesbians were called
"Uraniads"). The word derives from Plato's *Symposium,* where two different kinds
of love are described, and are said to be ruled by two different goddesses of love—
Aphrodite, daughter of Uranus, and Aphrodite, daughter of Zeus and Dione. The
second Aphrodite rules those who love the opposite sex. Ulrichs called these type
of people "Dionings," and thus coined predecessors to the terms "homosexual" and
"heterosexual." He called people who who loved both males and females *"Uranodi-
onings,"* a precursor to the term "bisexual."

Urnings were, in terms of personality, hermaphrodites—they were typically either
biological males who were psychically females (drawn erotically to other biological males), or biological females who were psychically males (drawn erotically to
other biological females). Toward the male pole from the middle is what Ulrichs
called the *"Mannling"* (*"Mannlingin"*) for a more masculine *Urning,* and toward the
female pole from the middle is the *"Weibling"* (*"Weiblingin"*), a more feminine *Urning.* The third sex theory is rather complicated owing to Ulrichs's neologisms
describing his categorization of sexual "types." The typologies were produced
from Ulrich's own observations, and he also hypothesized that there was one *Urning* in every five hundred males in Germany. At the time the figure was criticized
as too high, today people might say it is too low. The complexities of the theory
are reiterated in Ulrichs's final summary, *Critical Arrow* (1879) reprinted here.

Ulrichs's theory of the third sex represents the assimilation of homosexuality into
the nineteenth century Western gender structure, with its assumption of reproductive sexuality. It foreshadows Kinsey's range of sexual behaviors, from exclusive heterosexuality to exclusive homosexuality. For Ulrichs, sexuality remains
inextricable from reproduction and gender roles; so, for example, a male *Urning*
is defined negatively as someone with a female soul in a male body, and not a
"true" male (one who would be sexually attracted to women). This left Ulrichs's
third sex open to pathologization, as was almost immediately done by the proponents of "degeneration theory" such as Krafft-Ebing. Although Ulrichs theorizes
that *Urnings* primarily loved *Dionings* (usually younger ones), his ideas represent
an important transition point between same-sex love understood paederastically
and/or as occurring between a "homosexual" and a "nonhomosexual," and later
observations and understandings about erotic love between two homosexual
adults. Finally, although it was a theory developed about men and applied by analogy to women, it was the first supposedly scientific treatment that grouped
women-loving women and men-loving men together as a class, thus opening the
door to political understandings and goals.

We include a brief excerpt from a petition to the legislatures of Austria and northern Germany, entitled *Araxes* (1870). The title refers to a bridge built by Alexander the Great over the Araxes river in Armenia that was destroyed during a flood.

Ulrichs here meant an allusion to the destruction of any obstacle in the path of equal rights for *Urnings*.

Following German unification under Bismarck, male homosexuality was criminalized in 1871 through Paragraph 175 of the Imperial Penal Code, which follows. Efforts to prevent the codification of, and later to overturn Paragraph 175 led Ulrichs and others to establish gay and lesbian organizations such as the Scientific-Humanitarian Committee. Lesbian sexuality was not criminalized under the law, but lesbians did join with male homosexuals for legal reform and social tolerance.

PARAGRAPH 175
OF THE GERMAN IMPERIAL PENAL CODE

(1871)

trans. James Steakley

Unnatural vice committed by two persons of the male sex or by people with animals is to be punished by imprisonment; the verdict may also include the loss of civil rights.

---

from

ARAXES

APPEAL FOR THE LIBERATION OF THE URNING'S NATURE FROM PENAL LAW.
TO THE IMPERIAL ASSEMBLIES OF NORTH GERMANY AND AUSTRIA

(1870)

Karl Heinrich Ulrichs
trans. James Steakley

I. The Man-Loving Urning's Sexual Nature and the Lawmaker's Proper Sphere

Members of the North German Reichstag! You are being called upon to sanction anew a penal law inherited from your fathers. It is so-called "unnatural vice between persons of the male sex" which once again is supposed to be stamped as a crime.

Living in North Germany at present are approximately 20,000 adult urnings, i.e., individuals of male physical build who feel sexual love exclusively for men or youths. At issue is thus a numerous, distinct class of people whose sexual actions are to receive this stamp.

But indeed, not just humanitarianism, no, sheer justice requires that prior to the decision the following be tested:

whether these people are *capable of acting any differently* than they do? or whether they might be subject to an *entirely different law of nature* than actual men?

Such a test will lead to a surprising result.

That an actual man would feel sexual love for a man is impossible. The urning is not a true man. He is a mixture of man and woman. He is man only in terms of body build. The love drive inherent to him, on the other hand, is that of a female being. Accordingly, it must be directed toward the male sex, while sexual contact with women elicits female dread in him. His sexual nature is in fact so organized. Toward sexual contact with a woman he feels an unextinguishable aversion, one which has all the characteristics of a *horror naturalis*. Sexual love he feels only for the male sex. *He cannot act differently.* He did not give himself this love direction. And he cannot eliminate it, either.

Accordingly, his sexual nature is organized entirely differently than that of an actual man, who is permeated with the love drive of a male directed toward women and who feels male dread at sexual contact with a man. The urning is subject to an entirely different law of nature.

How and why nature has called such intermixed beings into existence is a riddle not yet solved. On the other hand, that it does act in this way, that it is *nature* which gives the urning his sexual love, is now beyond dispute. The cause of urning love has been complacently attributed to all sorts of other causes (to self-abuse, etc.). All these hypotheses are false.

In all of creation, no other living creature endowed with sexual feeling is required to engage in life-long suppression of this powerful drive, causing it to consume itself in cruel self-martyrdom. Rather, at the stage of sexual maturity, its periodic satisfaction is a clear-cut natural need, necessary to maintain the health of body and soul. Nature requires this, demanding its tribute just as unrelentingly from the urning as from the actual man. For the urning, carrying out sexual acts with a woman would simply be unnatural vice.

It is nonsensical to seek to judge the urning's acts of sexual love torn out of their context within his hermaphroditic sexual nature, of which they are simply an effect.

To prove all of these statements I submit:

   a) the content of my scientific studies *Inclusa, Formatrix, Prometheus,* and
      particularly *Memnon,*
   b) the findings of a scientific panel that could be convened.

The urning, too, is a human being. He, too, therefore has *natural human rights.* His sexual direction is justified by virtue of natural rights. The lawmaker has no right to place himself *above* nature, no right to persecute the creator in the beings it created, no right to martyr living creatures for being subject to the drive which nature gave them.

The urning is also a citizen of the state. He, too, therefore has civil rights: and correspondingly, the state has duties to fulfill vis-à-vis him as well. It does not have the right to let itself be guided by arbitrariness or blind, persecutory zeal. *The state is not entitled to treat the urning as a man without rights, as it has up to now.*

The lawmaker does, to be sure, have the right to confine the expressions of the urning's love drive within the same boundaries that it is entitled to draw for all citizens. The lawmaker may accordingly forbid the urning three things:

   a) seduction of immature boys,
   b) violations of justice (through coercion, threat, etc., abuse of unconscious people, etc.),
   c) public violation of the sense of decency.

But to forbid absolutely the expressions of the love drive when they take place among adults,

with the free consent of both parties,

without any public violation of the sense of decency:

this lies beyond the lawmaker's purview. He lacks any legal basis for doing so. He is prevented from doing so by natural law and the principles of the rule of law. He is prevented from doing so by the law of justice, which forbids measuring with two different standards. As long as the urning respects the restrictions a, b, c, the lawmaker *must* not forbid him to follow the justified law of nature to which he is subject.

Urning love within these restrictions is no real crime anywhere. It lacks any of the characteristics of such a crime. It is not even misconduct or malfeasance, for it is quite simply the fulfillment of a law of nature. It is to be counted among the various *imaginary* crimes which, to the shame of civilized humanity, have besmirched Europe's law books. To punish it is therefore an act of injustice carried out with official sanction.

That the urnings have the misfortune to constitute a weak minority cannot in any way diminish their human rights and their civil rights. Under the rule of law, justice must prevail for minorities as well.

And even if the lawmaker has violated this principle for centuries now, from the queen of Peru to the Incas of Peru, and from the Hermunduras to the latest barbarism of the Citizens' Council and Senate of the Free City of Bremen: natural law and the law of justice are not subject to any statute of limitations.

Ever to wipe out the urning's love drive: this hope ought to be abandoned by the lawmaker from the very outset. Even the flaming funeral pyres of earlier centuries, on which urnings were burnt at the stake to make a sweet odor unto the Lord, could not succeed in doing so. Even to gag him and tie him up is in vain. To fight against nature is pointless. Against it, even the omnipotence of state power outfitted with the apparatus of all its coercive devices is too weak. The state is capable of *regulating* the urning's love drive. The urnings' own feeling of morality, their sense of reason, and their conscience offer the lawmaker their unreserved cooperation for *this* goal.

---

from

CRITICAL ARROW

(1879)

Karl Heinrich Ulrichs
trans. Hubert Kennedy

Finally, I wish to report the result of my latest observations on the phenomenon in human nature, which I call Urningtum.

a. The typical manifestation of Urningtum is the Weibling. I call Weibling that Urning whose soul and body are inspired by femininity, i.e., bear a female impression. Whoever wishes to study the nature of Urningtum must begin with the nature of Weiblings. The Weibling is a total mixture of male and female, in which the female element is even predominant, a thoroughly hermaphroditically organized being. Despite his male sexual organs, he is more woman than man. He is a woman with male sexual organs. He is a neutral sex. He is a neuter. He is the hermaphrodite of the ancients.

b. There is a gradually and regularly proceeding transition, i.e., a progression of transitional individuals, from Weibling through the various phases of intermediate Urnings on to the Mannling. I call Mannling that Urning whose soul and body are inspired by masculinity, i.e., bear a male impression.

c. There is also, however, a gradually and regularly proceeding transition, i.e., a progression of transitional individuals, from Weibling through the various phases of intermediate Urning and Mannling, and on through further transitional phases all the way to the true man, i.e., born woman-loving.

d. The sexual varieties, which exist among true men, are only a continuation of the phases of the entire transition.

e. There is an entirely equal transition in Urningintum, namely from the masculine-inspired, woman-loving Mannlingin, the typical manifestation of Urningintum, through the phases of the intermediate Urningin and the Weiblingin, on to the man-loving, true woman.

f. Such a transition does not exist between Weibling and woman, between Mannlingin and man, nor between man and woman altogether.

Other observers have already perceived bits of feminine elements in Urnings. Thus, e.g., Casper, Tardieu, Stark. Yet they did not know what to make of them. Stark even tried to evaluate them from a pathological standpoint, while, as it appears to me, they precisely speak in favor of the physiological.

I mean, the assumption of any kind of sickness is not compatible with that series of stages. There can be perceived in it nothing other than a purely natural phenomenon, which bears the stamp of health on its forehead, a physiological phenomenon, a fact of the natural law, which is based on an inner necessity of nature, in particular on the laws of the embryonic development of the individual. Nature creates transitions in so many of her fields.

My scientific opponents are mostly doctors of the insane. Thus, e.g., Westphal, Krafft-Ebing, Stark. They have made their observations on Urnings, who were in institutions for the insane. They appear never to have seen mentally healthy Urnings. The rest followed the published views of doctors for the insane.

Speaking in favor of "inborn by a natural law" is also, it appears to me, that occurrence of sexual acts between male beetles. My opponents must separate this phenomenon from the field of natural history. They must insert it into the doctrine of animal sicknesses, into the section of animal psychiatry for mentally ill beetles.

Documentation of the creation of the political subject "homosexual" would not be complete without reference to the inventor of the term itself, Karoly Maria Benkert (Kertbeny) (1824–1882). A journalist who claimed not to be homosexual himself, he used the name Benkert until in 1847 the Viennese authorities allowed him to use his Hungarian noble name of Karoly Maria Kertbeny. Although he first used the terms "homosexuality" and "heterosexuality" in a letter to Ulrichs in 1868, the selection that follows represents the first time "homosexual" enters into public discourse. It enters through this letter to the Prussian Minister of Justice (1869), in which Benkert argues that homosexuality should be decriminalized not only, following Ulrichs, because it is innate, but more because the modern constitutional state should not interfere with the right of all human beings to engage in sexual relations, which is a matter of personal privacy. The letter is divided into three portions. In the first, the social conditions for recognition of homosexuality and its decriminalization are described. In the second, his theory of homosexuality and heterosexuality (what he here calls "normalsexuality"), as well as his theory of what we today call "bisexuality," is elaborated. Finally, he discusses how the sexual theories upon which the law is founded (and which he criticizes through his own theory) are untenable in practice, and he concludes with an eighteen-point summary of his argument for reform.

KAROLY MARIA
BENKERT

from

AN OPEN LETTER TO THE PRUSSIAN MINISTER OF JUSTICE

(1869)

Karoly Maria (Kertbeny) Benkert
trans. Michael Lombardi-Nash, Ph.D.

Paragraph 143 of the Prussian Penal Code of
April 14, 1851, and its Preservation as Paragraph 152
in the Draft of a Penal Code for the
North German Confederation

Public Address in a Special Branch of Science to His Excellency Dr. Leonhardt
Royal Prussian Minister of State and Justice

From time immemorial and among all peoples which can be included as the upholders of culture there have been people who always have been dissatisfied with tradition, filled with ideal conceptions which gravitate towards the possibility of better and purer conditions among people either here and now or in the hereafter. To attain the former, people devised the theory of crime and punishment, both of which, however, only could be conclusions of social contracts, thus, never having more justification than those of a means of discipline; and in regard to the hereafter, people gave certain personal ideas to the dark feelings people have for the need of a belief, conferred upon these the attributes of infinite wisdom and justice and declared everything else, including intellectual opposition in any degree, as sinful. In this way, ever since the highly intellectual times of the Greek culture and the thoroughly realistic ones of the Romans, European people have sacrificed millions upon millions of their brothers to the senseless doctrines of religious, moral, legal, social and political fanaticism, and have tried to suppress every germ of sound thinking.

Fortunately, however, the victory of sound thinking is an unchanging law of nature; people certainly can prevent it at times but cannot suppress it for long periods of time; its principles finally come to power, enforcing its natural laws with total sovereignty.

Thus, in this manner has our humanity rightfully become more and more emancipated from unsound, intellectually confused idealistic doctrines and has been made more perfect by the concrete views of nature, by the political responsibilities of social contract and by the tolerance of the many diverse religious faiths.

This stimulation, itself, leads to a revision of each and every view to date and forces us again to think through every question and no longer to regard a thing in an idealistic and doctrinal manner, as matters should be, but rather to view each matter in an empirical way as it is according to its special nature.

Therefore, it is now the task of humanity to make the most of this understanding so that we submit to the inevitable, to recognize it as a natural law, and just in this way we will be able to overcome its disagreeable effects on us, indeed, perhaps even gain some advantages from it . . .

This often hardly noticed and still continuing aftereffect of the injected poison of the confused concept in the battle with the categorical imperative of logic [*i.e.,* absurdity—Eds.] is no longer noticed in any area except in the legislature concerning the question of sexuality of society. Modern society has developed totally different relationships and needs from those ever thought possible in earlier times. Especially the rapid increase in population of European cities—in cities with 8,656 to thirty thousand inhabitants, together 75 million individuals, thus, more than a quarter of the total population of Europe—with their hourly expanding political as well as social democratization, with their greater and greater bombastic claim for freedom, easier burdens, greater services, more lucrative realization of labor, more comfortable means of enjoying life and with their eagerness for instant profit, and, on the other hand, the wealth of individuals which continues to increase, and the limitless means to every luxury and the most ghastly contrast between rich and poor; finally the ever increasing awareness of equality under the law—all these factors imperiously push the state no longer to play the role of the guardian, which is, anyhow, a thankless and irritating role, but rather limits it in every way to the principle of the constitutional state which has been gained finally, and only then does it care about society and its activities when the rights of others are injured or brought into question by one's own actions. Inalienable rights begin, however, always with the people themselves, and the most direct one of the people's rights is one's own life, with which one may do as one pleases, fully free from start to finish as long as the rights of other individuals, of society or of the state are not injured by these actions, whatever the advantage or disadvantage may be . . .

Why should people refrain from doing what brings in the greatest profit—even if it is sexual and is easy to succeed in—and even to take personal pleasure in it? Does not the porter sell his muscular strength, the night watchman his sleep, the singer her voice, the actress her charming appearance, indeed, and what is more, the physician and soldier their lives, and with this I will make no further comparisons. Therefore, after people have reached greater awareness of this, a young woman or a widow will hardly ever hesitate to enjoy her life, if not directly for money then for other advantages. Totally unreflected misery, and especially partial necessity, which is lacking luxury at the same time, also shows itself unceremoniously in the whirl of "the good life." In 1867, Berlin alone had 352,914 male and 349,127 female inhabitants. However, among these there were 111,300 men and 111,142 women who were married. Thus, almost two thirds of the total population was single, widowed or divorced, and it appears to be natural that the vice squad has directly booked 11,855 prostitutes, however, has had 12,000 others under observation, while, besides, 20,000 female domestic servants, workers, store clerks, etc. who evade every kind of control, can be assumed to be living together in a temporary or lasting relationship . . . This open or hidden prostitution has such a command over the public life of Berlin, especially at certain hours and on certain strips—not to mention other cities for the time being—so that the quiet walker is easily offended. However, walkers are more often exposed to the most shameless propositions concerning the so-called most unnatural ones . . .

. . . legitimate marriage is made so extremely difficult for so many reasons in the modern states that hardly a third of the inhabitants are able to enter into it . . . What a blatant contradiction: These extraordinary difficulties exist amid the increasingly barbaric punishments for so-called unnatural spurting of even one drop of semen dissipated fruitlessly between two male individuals, which however, goes unpunished when applied between man and wife, two women and finally and especially, masturbation alone, thus every form of vice including the most unnatural ones.

Then, we have the frightful spreading of venereal diseases and of their treatment, both of which are ignored by the government and the legislature, and even by the principles of the constitutional state, but the care of which has been left to the individual. And this scourge, which has raged among the people of Europe for four hundred years, and is such a frequent infection that you can hardly find two male adults in a hundred who have never in their life been a party to this epidemic without having any important consequences—even more ghastly are the effects of this venereal disease in its secondary and tertiary stages with regard to procreation, so that we physicians can state without exaggeration that actually one third of all inherited diseases have their roots in the parents or grandparents, and in practically every case the explanation for the puzzling development of general or especially complex diseases in many individuals can only be found in dispositions which are brought about by secondary causes. Thus, in 1866 in France, among 325,000 recruits—hence those people in the prime of their youth—there were 109,000 unfit for service, possibly because of the secondary and tertiary stages of venereal diseases of their parents. Such statistical evidence is lacking for Germany. For this reason, is it not rather excusable if daily a more significant number of epicureans, out of fear of such consequences, prefer the so-called most unnatural ways of gratification rather than the so-called natural ones with women, which to this day are known to be the ones the possibility of infection lies with?

Finally, just as the danger of infection increases, and for that reason the so-called natural fornication becomes a bogey to people with tender feelings, the more those so-called unnatural ones in the male sex become mental images of crime, however, normal marriage is made extremely difficult and is mostly only possible at maturity. Thus the more do you see the reason for the overwhelming practice of onanism, the lonely self-abuse, in all classes, among all races, at any age in our society and government, threatening humanity with the possibility of total extinction. We know that practically every male as well as every female of school age has been seized alike from childhood on by this truly wicked mania, which, in comparison, is the most evil so-called natural and unnatural fornication from which they have to be directly, physically as well as morally protected. This self-abuse, which is as dangerous to the health as it is objectionable, may be summarized thus: its initiative is not physical sensuality called forth by another living being but the effect of heightened fantasy; it attacks, therefore, not only the body but at the same time all one's spiritual might, and for that reason is dangerous to the brain and spinal cord and throat, chest and lungs. Even more detrimental is solitary self-abuse practiced in an arbitrary manner whereby want of moderation can ensue; anyone affected by it needs no special occasion or person, and can, therefore, practice it at any moment, and persons with terribly shattered nerves can do it at any place, even in the midst of a large crowd and without the touching of the body, just by the impulse of the fantasy. For that reason it usually increases daily to become a mania until its victim is destroyed as a result of the excess. In spite of this, not all die of the consequences, even if a great proportion do. However, not an insignificant number have a chronic drive to masturbate. They devote themselves to it their entire lives, even in matrimony, into which circumstances or advantages force onanists, and many reach a great and apparent very healthy age after their bodies have long accustomed themselves to this truly unnatural excitement. But the one thing that all secretive male and female self-abusers have in common is the total insusceptibility to the sensual excitement by others, the possibility of erection only by one's own fantasy, self-abuse without witnesses. Accordingly, secretive onanists are never ever capable of enjoying marriage or procreation—because the spermatozoids have disappeared from their semen and the same becomes watery—or even the so-called natural fornication between man and wife or even the so-called unnatural one of one's own sex. These are, therefore, true physical eunuchs. Yet it is even more bleak that secretive onanists become mental eunuchs, too, hermaphrodites of the mind. Secretive self-abusers also lose the warmth of feeling with the warmth of the blood. Their feelings become cold, unsociable, heartless, abstract, they are hard in their decisions and view of the world, filled with physical as well as moral loathing for reciprocal satisfaction of the sex drive; and whenever you meet a cool, remorseless, ironically hard-hearted person, you can be sure that person is a secretive self-abuser. And we, by our confusion of ideas on the natural and the unnatural, along with the help of the fear of infection, have caused more than one third of the male as well as the female sex to devote themselves to self-abuse, often for life! . . .

Any prostitute or any female being for that matter can seduce a boy over 14 years, plunder him, abuse him by doing the most unnatural acts, make him ill by infection, perhaps making him an invalid forever, and go unpunished, and there is no judge for such a crime, for such acts of sexual intercourse between the opposite sexes, acts which in their significance are not in full view at all. But woe to both as soon as a man even tries any kind of lewd behavior with a youth or another man, even with his consent, and undertaken out of the sight of the public! Those who know the facts of life not only from books or the twaddle of old maids also know that there is hardly one prostitute who has not taken part in one form of unnatural intercourse, as it is called; that there are thousands of civil-minded men who—partly out of refinement, partly out of fear of infection—devote themselves to so-called unnatural acts with the other sex, indeed, they practice cunnilingus, anilingus, fellatio, urination, pedophilia and masturbation with their own wives, or have these done to them, as, on the other side, women, even ones in the higher classes and mostly out of refinement, directly provoke so-called unnatural coitus, no less with other female beings, obtaining so-called unnatural refinement as "tribades". And all these persons not only go unpunished for all of these most certain so-called unnatural acts which are dispassionate and loathsome, but many of these men are in no way embarrassed to publicly confess such preferences, laughing and smirking while relating their story, without raising moral indignation or even disgust for that matter. Indeed, how many seemingly highly respected men in the community devote themselves to secretive passions in such a manner as the unnatural refinement with women; and often the only ones that know are their doctors or their closest friends; yet even if it were well known in the town, they would neither lose honor or self-esteem, because they are threatened by no punishment . . .

And in the face of a society such as ours is today, especially in the large and medium cities—and Prussia alone has no less than 1,212 cities of more than one hundred thousand to less than six thousand inhabitants—do they still want to maintain the medieval views concerning sexual excesses, do they want to allow the same acts of the great majority of opposite-sexual (*gegengeschlechtlich*) natures to go totally unpunished, but to punish the relationships of the very small minority of homosexual natures as true hardened and brutal criminals and even to declare them as dishonorable? This is not only unjust, it is an unpardonable absurdity of our present standpoint on the view of the world . . .

Such a revolting injustice, which is an absurdity at the same time, cannot be allowed to go unchallenged in our day . . .

Prussia has maintained its penal code which became effective on the 14th of April 1851, and Austria, its own, which became effective on the 27th of May 1852.

The former threatens "unnatural fornication between people and animals, as well as between persons of the male sex with 6 months to 4 years imprisonment with easy labor, as well as the loss of civil rights at the same time, even if temporarily" the latter refers to fornication between "woman and woman"; because it punished fornication according to the text: "a) with animals, b) with persons of the same sex," with imprisonment with hard labor from one to five years. According to the principles of the Prussian penal code such acts are simple transgressions, according to the Austrian one, actual crimes! . . .

Already in 1847 the draft of the "Motives for a Prussian Penal Code" set forth Paragraph 143 as law: "because such behavior is a demonstration of especial degeneration and degradation of the person, and is so dangerous to morality."

This argument seems above all, perhaps unconsciously, to have been reminiscent of the Byzantine Emporor Theodosius, whose code dictated death by fire, yet who still maintained serfdom in the most inhumane and animalistic manner!

In any case, however, the argument does reveal its founders either to have lied to themselves about the true condition of today's society or wanted to lie to the world for the benefit of their precious prudery.

Above all, all three conclusions of this argument really take care of every kind of sexual excess, actually even more so of the ones that are totally allowed, and, moreover, on the whole, of numerous other pretensions and actions not at all of a sexual nature.

If the same deed is performed between man and wife or woman and woman, does this not presuppose the same "degeneration and degradation" of people as if it is performed between one man and another? How can you possibly rationalize such a great difference, that the same act goes totally unpunished for the majority; for the minority it is considered as an abominable and disgraceful crime? . . . How did this so-so legislation ever come into being except as a consequence of the overuse of morality by men who, moreover, as the stronger sex, domineer over and make unreasonable demands on other men, because this act is dictated to be especially "degenerate" and "degrading" only between one man and another, not also between a man and a woman or two women?

You can see there is no end to this vicious circle, which can only be blocked by the alternative, that either every form of mutual fornication be punished equally or that no category be subject to punishment, except in cases where the rights of others are injured. The first notion would be acceptable to every morally minded person. However, it cannot be carried out practically for numerous reasons, as enough experience has taught; so the only thing remaining is the second, more just and rational alternative, which is the one of the constitutional state. Those arguments of the reasons for punishment of 1851 betray a certain amount of naivety with respect to the historical facts, a direct ignorance of the anthropological and, in general, of the scientific questions, and finally, moreover, an obvious ignorance of the true nature of the matter, what the subject was about, its true relationship to society and to the individual, and of its character with regards to health.

The word "degenerate" no doubt referred to those individuals who are affected by such homosexual passions and sought to satisfy them actively with other people; on the other hand, in the case of passive persons, it is presupposed that they, for their own part, find absolutely no satisfaction by this, who, therefore, abandon themselves to the most despicable interests and, in addition, always exclusively only in such a revolting manner and, at the same time—as is the accepted tradition—in such a manner most dangerous to one's health, that it unconditionally deserves to be called the "degradation of the person". This is not the place here to cram in the scientific details of the study of sexuality. Its conclusions are, in short: besides the normalsexual drives of all humanity and of animals, nature, in its sovereign frame of mind, appears to have given a homosexual drive to certain male and female individuals at birth. Nature also gave them a sexual constraint which has a physical and mental effect, that even with the best intentions, prevents a normal/sexual response. This presupposes a direct horror for the opposite sex; and it also makes those who are constrained by this passion incapable of withdrawing from the influence which particular individuals of the same sex have over them. The Greeks called such female homosexualists, as you know, "tribades," and such are also many times, in certain cases physically abnormally built; these kinds of homosexualists were usually called "paederasts" by the Greeks because this drive was mostly directed to young mature men among the southern tribes. On the other hand, in northern climates a noteworthy and enigmatic scientific result has been yielded, and should be mentioned in a more suitable place. Now, it is obvious to thinkers educated in anthropology that those who are constrained by such drives either meet with individuals of their own nature, and, therefore, there is absolutely nothing at all to justify objecting to such reciprocal inclinations, because both are lacking normalsexuality by nature, and, therefore, it would be asking too much of them to live their whole life long in absolute chastity, and to submit their existence to a penalty because, through no fault of their own, nature organized them with this very constraint. Or, however, such homosexualists turn their inclinations to normalsexuals; and if the modern constitutional state makes a concession to the latter, in principle, in all cases in which no rights of others are injured by it, that they are allowed to do with their bodies as they please, then it will not be necessary to differentiate between acts, whether the same are natural or would-be unnatural, if they are practiced by the opposite sex or the same sex. In any case, however, to a certain degree the reciprocity of gratification more or less must be presupposed between both individuals, because the gratification exists, indeed, in the nature of the thing, even if it may be far more satisfactory for the normalsexuals with the opposite sex. This is all the more obvious when you soberly picture to yourself what can possibly happen between two individuals of the same sex. Usually only two conclusions: either emission (*emissio*) of semen or taking in (*immissio*) of semen. Both acts are not only also possible between man and woman, they occur among the opposite sexes daily, far much more than the non-observer of realism wants to believe! The all-decisive difference between the acts between the opposite sex and those between the same sex is, however, that the former, in almost every case, winds up with real or imitated coitus, on the other hand, among the latter, the imitation of coitus occurs at the most ten percent actively or passively, thus, the so ill-reputed ejaculation (emission) which occurs among nine-tenths of all homosexuals, is reached rather by self-abuse, and even the thought of going further is abhorrent to them. . . . Therefore, the would-be unnatural imitation of coitus is not the erector of the drive of one man for another; at the most it occurs at times among these as well as among normalsexual passion, and, indeed, only among especially unrefined and vulgar individuals. The fact is that, beyond a doubt, if the activity of the union was the impulse among homosexuals, indeed, that no other male individual was needed by them for their gratification, they could also be satisfied by a woman, which,for them, moreover, as already noted, would be doubly harmless and fully guiltless. However, they are not only incapable of the same act with women, indeed, not even of an erection in the presence of one; but rather actually nine-tenths of homosexuals do not seek this conclusion during same-sex pleasure; on the contrary, they have a physical aversion to it, while they give themselves up all the more passionately to mutual self-abuse. Therefore, it becomes evident to the anthropological observer that the male (das Männliche) itself, as opposed to the female (das Weibliche), whose habitual atmosphere as well as peculiar genital erector is the actual motor of this passion, and that at best there are certain ones among the fallen who are forced to do the physical imitation of coitus. This fact explains, on the one hand, why certain apologists have so often wanted to try to explain the homosexual impulse being due to a special sense for beauty, namely for the plastic arts, because not only is the manly body as an end in itself certainly esthetically more beautiful than the more sensually tempting one of the woman, which is, however, only a means to an end; it explains also, on the other hand, why, in fact, the homosexual impulse mostly turns towards undeniably bodily and physically beautiful persons, also often even finding its fullest satisfaction in such purely platonic relationships, even more often simply seeking it by self-abuse, and only in relatively very few cases falling into the uncouth imitation of coitus. However, the characteristics of normalsexuality are exactly the opposite. This totally sexual impulse cannot maintain itself in the purely platonic at all, and soon finds its way to the touching of the body. Mutual self-abuse takes place in the normalsexual's case, at best, out of precaution and for that reason appears to him as unnatural. In most cases, therefore, touching between the opposite sexes with every drop of passion leads directly to coitus, and the need for this conclusion is self-explanatory, that the stimulus is excited to the same less by especially esthetic beauty than mostly only by attractive sensuality, which is often even connected to ugliness and uncleanliness. Accordingly, we see that it is rather easy to bring a man into a sensual relationship with any woman, even more, a woman with almost any man, a relationship which almost always leads to a conclusion by coitus; however, on the other hand, because homosexuals daily move in the midst of thousands of their own sex without ever attracting attention to their special orientation, they turn simply to some particular ones, and, to be sure, seldom to ugly ones. All this must lead us to the generalized logical conclusion that homosexuals are naturally constrained, for no matter how hard they strive, they can turn to no woman—or the woman to a man—nor adolescent children—indeed, not even to each and every male individual, because virility is the foundation for their impulse. Rather, in their passion they are dependent upon certain sensual causes, and are capable of no erection at all as soon as these are lacking. Out of this, also, the most characteristic thing is explained, that homosexuals almost never give themselves up to solitary self-abuse, no matter how much they are driven to mutual self-abuse, simply because their impulse is not excited by fantasy nor by a superfluous disease on their body, but rather by certain personalities which, from mature boyhood to manhood, represent the full features of virility in every detail of its habit, in opposition to the feminine. In this constraint also, at the same time, is the full guarantee that even in cases of the most unlimited freedom of these special beings who are always present only in small numbers, morality in general will not be put in jeopardy at all; indeed, on the contrary. For, in the first place, homosexual impulses are not optional, not some refinement—as thoughtless tradition so often maintains—but rather congenital. Therefore, this excludes the thought that homosexuals in time, can be made to join the ranks of the majority, which has been born with the stronger drive, normalsexualism—the majority who at most temporarily give way to such demands, then time and again follow the stronger nature. And in the second place is the lesser danger concerning the question of procreation. For this task is lost to homosexuals simply by their very nature: and normalsexuals can likewise never change forever. And even if they do at times allow themselves to enjoy the lesser pleasure, the "eternal feminine" will attract them more strongly at the very next opportunity . . .

To the sober anthropologist, the normal sexuality of both the man and the woman appears totally different and unequally more dangerous to society in its lack of constraint of the ability to degenerate. Both incite their nature in an opposite-sexual manner, yielding to both the would-be natural and the unnatural coitus. They also are capable of surrendering themselves actively or passively to same-sex debauchery. Normalsexuals no less take part in secretive self-abuse at times if a more appropriate means of satisfying the sexual drive is lacking; and just as infrequently is it to their taste, if they do not practice any amount of self-discipline, to violate immature children of the male sex however, especially of the female sex, to pander to incest, indeed, as far as to abuse animals, even to brutalize corpses. And the specialty of "blood sucking" occurs only among normalsexuals; indeed, even some animals take part in, this, those who can satisfy their sexual desire only by sucking blood, causing injury by torture. For normalsexuals by nature are totally unrestrained in their ability to become excited; whereas homosexuals, just as with monosexuals, whose secretive self-abuse has become a chronic need, are impotent and, at best, partially constrained.

The belief that homosexuals, following their nature, commit crimes, is one of the most wicked confusions of ideas. Originating with religious ideas, and continuing for thousands of years, it has so long prevented the knowledge that would have made clear those riddles of nature. The exact opposite is the truth . . .

Footnote to II.

Since it was at first mentioned that homosexuals are not at all capable of erections by the opposite sex, the historical list, however, points to several names whose bearers were married and were even the fathers of several children, then this appears to be a contradiction . . . Here let us only make note that the general characteristic of this drive points to the congenital antipathy in the face of the opposite sex, which cannot be deviated, where men entered into marriages with the opposite sex because they were totally unclear about the nature of their drive and never had the opportunity to gratify it, or because conventional reasons forced them to do it. On the average there are, especially for the man, highly unhappy and fruitless ones; or, at the beginning, his youth, as a result of its potency, mechanically overcame the impulse, and even though he may have enjoyed his wife and have become a father, until that time when he would finally succeed in reaching the correct course of his dark impulse, from then on there is little possibility for him to return to normal sexuality, just as it is for he who out of instinct never experienced a woman from his youth onward. And such noteworthy examples which speak for the congenital factors more than all the other symptoms, which can be suppressed, indeed, for long periods of time by relationships, but which never let themselves be totally choked, are, in fact, coming more often to the attention of anthropologists and physicians, even if they are never a decisive majority. However, on the other hand, there also really are natures, even if they are now little known, who have in themselves both drives at the same time, the one towards the feminine and the one towards the, at least, boyish masculine . . .

In all these cases, they are in no way true homosexualists but rather are normal sexuals who are highly blinded by their passions for their addiction to refinement. This anthropological riddle of nature, nevertheless, has been intentionally ignored by scientific researchers for centuries, and people have simply kept their terribly ignorant traditions on its nature and know nothing at all about its exceptions and nuances . . . One thing remains the same, that the great majority of homosexuals are incapable in the face of women, the majority of them having nothing at all to do with women, but rather always and irrepressibly turning towards their own sex from the beginning of puberty . . .

If the first two letters have yielded the proof and grounds that, even at the beginning of our century, the law in all the civilized countries has made epoch-making breakthroughs in that sexual intercourse cannot be punished as long as it injures none of the rights of another, just as the state does not punish other acts of immorality and bad manners, . . . and that, while the legislation of France, Bavaria, Württemberg and Hanover punish so-called unnatural fornication between men only when the rights of others are injured, the Prussian penal code of the 14th of April, 1850, not only preserves the strict threat of punishment but also— to use the mildest term—so oddly subjectively motivates it—then the present letter will attempt to genetically prove how these legal ideas in practice immediately turn out to be impracticable . . .

. . . [I]n 1853, Dr. Casper, now deceased, joined the medical council and, through his many examples taken from extensive experience which he especially published in his *Quarterly for Forensic Medicine* (*Vierteljahrsschrift für gerichtsärztliche Medizin*), proved that, on the one hand, the great majority of so-called sodomites are simply mutual onanists for the greater part of their lives, thus innocent anyway in the sense of the decision of the Superior Court; that, however, on the other hand, even the majority of those who are most suspected of active or passive imitation of coitus will show hardly any trace on their bodies if the parties are not caught in the act, and the conscientious physician used in the trial cannot absolutely provide proof that this act had occurred between the two. By this means it was proven that the concession of the Supreme Court decision was to the advantage of at least nine-tenths of suspected homosexuals, and made them guiltless, but could protect them in no way from charges and investigations. For, as long as any act of homosexuality, as long as it injures none of the rights of others, is still threatened with punishment, and it cannot be previously determined, especially concerning malicious denunciation, which kind of act actually has been made (whether it was an innocent one or one of those threatened by punishment), then nothing remains but to call the accused or suspect into account, to subject him to what may become a lengthy investigation; which, alone, can already be enough to ruin one's business, or, in any case, to bring one's good reputation to an end. Then everything weighs upon chance or the mood of the physicians giving testimony, who cling to certain traditional physical symptoms in their expert opinions; thus whether the innocent person may be pronounced guilty, or the truly guilty person would be acquitted on account of some play in nature or some totally harmless reason, i.e. the incidental symptoms of having taken an enema—a funnel-shaped sphincter muscle—while the other, in spite of his submitting to this excess, shows no physical trace of it . . .

. . . [A]ll in all, that terrifying confusion of ideas on the question of sexuality has reigned for a thousand years. It originated with the national views of the theocratic Jewish peoples, "that not one single drop of semen be ejaculated wantonly, so that another Jew can be added to the family to fight against its enemies," whereby also polygamy as well as having concubines was allowed, incest between relations (Onan) was directly forbidden, onanism and sodomy were declared punishable by death; then followed the craziness of original sin, of the crime of uncleanliness in historical Christianity—not through the teachings of Christ—which led the Church Fathers and anchorites to self-mutilation—which brought about the doctrine of virginity and all physical pleasures as temptations of the devil and signs of heresy, which led to the practice of celibacy and the categorization of mortal and venial sins by hierarchical Christianity; then the Reformation succeeded in its counterattack, which sanctioned legitimate matrimony alone, yet greatly detested all other excesses as "unnatural," and yet the teaching of original sin, the pact with the devil and witchcraft were reversed—therefore, after this kind of confusion of ideas had been fanatically pursued for thousands of years, and then, like a chameleon, was changed into new phases of orthodox blindness to devour millions of innocent victims,—it was reserved for the nineteenth century, for the last sixty-nine years, to escape this horrible curse and to restore the frightful, exaggerated bugbear again to its normal natural truth. Thus, little by little the following views of basic truths as well as the results of practical experience have made breakthroughs concerning fornication, including the so-called crime against nature:

1. The modern constitutional state, which has only to protect rights, having no other secondary tasks which other organizations in society exist for and are called upon for, has no reason to become involved with the question of sex where the rights of others are not injured.

2. Since the modern constitutional state is built upon the consequence of this principle, under the condition that, as long as the rights of others are not injured, it does not become involved with any kind of so-called natural or so-called unnatural fornication, and does not threaten with punishment coitus, any kind of sexual love, solitary onanism or so-called sodomy between man and woman as well as between one woman and another woman, therefore, logically and legally, it cannot make an exception of sodomy (*sodomia generis* and *sodomia sexus*) between one man and another man.

3. Even less where, in all questions of sexuality, the greater freedom of modern society is so extensive, that the majority generally does as it pleases; in relation to it, the state has only to confine itself to the protection of the rights of others.

4. Even less, because history has taught us that homosexualism is and always has been present beside normalsexualism among all races and in all climates, and cannot be suppressed even by the most brutal persecutions.

5. Furthermore, for this reason as well as because of the essence of this drive, its inclinations as well as its antipathies, it is evident that it is rooted in a changeable riddle of nature, thus, is not voluntary or simple refinement, but rather can only be an inborn drive and, therefore, cannot be suppressed.

6. This hypothesis is supported by the historical fact that so many important and noble characters of our history in general are either suspected of being or are known for sure to be of this partial drive, which, were it not an inborn one, and consequently one that could be suppressed, would not occur among such important men, with their intellectual understanding and physical capabilities, or in the case of wealthy and powerful people, whose free choice of pleasure is unlimited.

7. In the face of this undeniable fact, we either have to call our ideas of culture into question, that we should consider these same historical people, whose intellect we esteem and honor to such a degree, as fit for imprisonment for their dishonorable acts, or we must find two kinds of law, one for the intellectual and socially powerful, and another for the rest of humanity.

8. However, it would never occur to us to enumerate the hundreds of representatives of cultural as well as political history who were capable of crimes such as rape, murder, theft,

forgery and treason; therefore, here there is every reason to believe in criminality, not in our own inborn sense of justice.

9. If "there is a debasement and a degradation of the person" in excess, fornication, bad manners, as in any intemperance and inordinate desire, then that is surely meant for every act of lewdness; however, from such a standpoint, at least, the one and the same act is to be excused from punishment when practiced between a man and a woman or a woman and a woman, while at the same time, it is an abominable crime when practiced between a man and a man!

10. Moreover, the evidence in the latest findings on this crime, which has long been condemned to an unheard-of degree has proven that almost nine-tenths of all homosexualists simply submit to mutual self-abuse only, which cannot possibly be threatened by punishment, because such punishment is an infringement of the inalienable rights of each individual, and when practiced between the opposite sexes is not punished.

11. In the case of the unfortunate spreading that solitary onanism has won in our times, especially as a result of the horrible teachings of prudery, and in the case of the extreme destructiveness of this egoistic cowardice for the physical and mental health and frame of mind, mutual masturbation is still a better escape and can be considered more humanistic, because it is motivated not by fantasy alone—for that reason its effects on the body and mind are less dangerous; for, when there is human reciprocity, those cold feelings which result from the solitary outpumping of the warmth of life do not occur.

12. For all these reasons, therefore, the decision of the Royal Superior Court of July 1, 1853, was that mutual onanism between men is innocent.

13. Accordingly, Paragraph 143 would make sense only against would-be fornication against nature between man and animal and against direct imitation of coitus between male individuals.

14. In practice we have learned that, in the way our culture is conditioned, fornication between man and animal occurs very seldomly, that it never becomes a passion, but rather is practiced always only either because of the lack of persons of the opposite sex or out of boredom and playfulness during hours of loneliness and besides, always by persons who have such a primitive sense of self-awareness that they are not at all expected to know the penal code.

15. On the other hand, we have learned, through experience with regards to sodomy proper between one man and another man, that it is very difficult and rare to prove this very act in court unless the participants are caught in the state of being flagrant, and that it is even more difficult forensically to detect and to show physical symptoms positively originating from this behavior; consequently, the conscientious court physician must almost always abstain from rendering a definite opinion.

16. For all that, the result is the flagrant contradiction between practice and theory, that thousands, indeed, hundreds of thousands carry out acts in secret—daily—hourly—which presently are threatened by punishment, which punishment, however, they can easily evade by their position, their wealth, the comfort of their private lives and by hundreds of other methods, while one particular individual becomes the victim of denunciation or incidental bad luck and the martyr and scapegoat of the secured majority, is ruined at his place of work just by the inquest, gets into trouble with his family, is socially dishonored, even if he is acquitted, and in addition if he were by chance found guilty, would have to suffer a terribly painful and humiliating punishment that would not be deserving of the crime.

17. Yet the decision of the Royal Supreme Court does not prevent this sad possibility at all, because closed investigations are hardly ever established, whether the allowable mutual

self-abuse or the still-punishable form of sodomy (*sodomia sexus*) is under discussion or not. Because such a severe penalty is given for the latter, its possibilities cannot be left uninvestigated. A case of anonymous denunciation will suffice to make it perfectly clear that Paragraph 143 does not only affect homosexuals, who usually only practice mutual masturbation, but also totally innocent normalsexuals who would be submitted to investigations that would bring them totally to shame and dishonor, and would be called in to answer to allegations of acts—so-called natural as well as would-be unnatural ones—which are practiced by everyone without being punished; and all who do this carry their heads high in this feeling of security, sometimes even sit on the jury in the case of such an unlucky person, dictate severe punishment for him, strip him of his honor, because the former practice the same act, but not with persons of the same sex!

18. This shocking nonsense is raised to a higher form of indignation when we recognize the injustices in our times and in our own society:

a) in which matrimony is possible for hardly one-third of the population;

b) where the specter of overpopulation keeps us constantly worried, yet, however, the fruitless squandering of a drop of semen is considered a crime;

c) which has already been tormented for hundreds of years by the terrible scourge of venereal disease—not only the health of the individual is greatly endangered but also all the generations that follow—without there being a penal code against this social vampire to prevent it from spreading, or science to the present day knowing of any cure, and without us, in our cowardice and prudery, making use of rational means to put a stop to this terrible spreading;

d) on the other hand, the fear of this epidemic by normalsexuals and, besides this, the terrible spreading of the physically and mentally disabling solitary self-abuse caused by the penal code that stamps homosexualism as a crime are to blame for and are the reason that perhaps one-third of adult males and females of our society have fallen into this truly physically as well as mentally enervating vice;

e) whereas by being more considerate than biased, furthermore, our social conditions have already long ago overcome the misery and economic difficulties in our cities, and whereas we are daily growing aware of our rights in general to existence and happiness in the face of the daily challenge for luxury that prevails, millions of people unhesitatingly prostitute their bodies and give in to the most dangerous, filthiest, most exhaustive, most distressing and, according to old notions, also the most disgraceful demands for payment; so that the sale of the body for mutual pleasure cannot be a crime;

f) Finally, these days an innocent weak woman can be seduced, made pregnant, made ill, brought to a miserable death, have her entire future poisoned or be subjected to every kind of inhumanity without the state taking the least bit of interest, even if her rights have been infringed upon, it is absolutely ridiculous that the male sex, which by nature is physically and morally stronger, has to be protected so highly from his own kind, stamping most of the harmless lewdness as horrible crimes by such strict means of punishment and dishonor, while the same state powers totally ignore the same male individuals when, without hardly any exceptions, they fall into secretive self-abuse as fully immature school boys, who could be seduced by a woman, weakened, made ill, infected and be made to practice so-called natural as well as would-be unnatural fornication, without having to worry about any threat of punishment, yet in the case of the same act practiced between two male persons, both parties are subject to severe punishment, not only the seducer, but also the one seduced!

Already, in the course of this century, each and every one of these logical reasons and the sense of justice concerning these disgraceful contradictions have moved the legislators of France, Bavaria, Belgium, Württemberg, Hanover and now even Austria to fully establish equality between so-called natural fornication and would-be unnatural fornication, i.e., only to threaten with punishment in those cases in which the rights of another were injured.

Fifty-six years of practice in Bavaria, thirty years in Württemberg and twenty-six years in Hanover have provided the evidence, yet, for all that, the moral situation is by no means made worse by this tolerance.

Therefore, it would by all means be expected, after the legislative unification of the greater part of Germany having been reached by the events of 1866—and Prussia having come to the summit, which calls itself the "State of Intelligence," whose penal code of 1851 is already paralyzed, moreover, in the main by Paragraph 143 through the decision of the Royal Superior Court, and where the practice [i.e., homosexuality] has already been making its appearance more moderately than the theory shows—that finally the memory of the medieval law will be blotted out just like the earlier witch trials, and the penal code book for the North German Confederation will be totally void of this defect of injustice. And that would be hoped for more from a Prussian minister of justice who, earlier as the Minister of Justice of Hanover, accomplished this judicial reform right in his home state and knows its practical results!

WALT WHITMAN

Walt Whitman's (1819–1892) poetry and prose exemplify a characteristically American secular religiosity and democratic individualist ethos of the young republic that continue today. Of course, the important questions for our purposes are "Did he or didn't he?" (have sex with men), and how is his sexual behavior related to his political views, questions for which we may never have definitive answers. He fathered children and also had a longtime companion, Peter Doyle. His poetry in particular is richly homoerotic. One set of poems, "Calamus," within the larger collection called *Leaves of Grass*, evokes homoerotic bonding ("we two boys together clinging"), admires the male physique and visage, and, calling Manhattan a "city of orgies," literally describes what gay men today call "cruising," where "your frequent and swift flash of eyes offering me love, offering response to my own—these repay me, lovers, continual lovers, only repay me." Indeed, the British philosopher of sexual politics, Edward Carpenter, wrote in 1924 about Whitman's writings on the loves of men toward each other and the loves of women toward each other: "thousands of people date from their reading of them a new era in their lives."

Whitman's philosophy is that democracy is held together not only by laws, but more fundamentally, by individual character and a new kind of friendship. This friendship is comradeship based upon "adhesiveness" (which also is the wellspring of social reform). Adhesiveness is a phrenological term coined in the nineteenth century, in contrast to "amativeness" (sexual love yielding reproduction between males and females). The American phrenologist Orson Fowler defined it as "friendship, sociability, fondness for society; susceptibility of forming attachments; inclination to love and desire to be loved; propensity to associate together in families and neighborhoods." Sexual love was not ruled out in adhesiveness, however. Here is an 1836 description of an adhesive relationship: "when one visited the other, they slept in the same bed, sat continuously alongside of each other at table, spoke in affectionate whispers, and were, in short, miserable when separated.[1]" Phrenologists also wrote of women with small amativeness, and large adhesiveness who spent most of their time in affectionate relations with other women. In Whitman's writings and life we see the inklings of a conscious choice of same-sex companionship rather than opposite-sex marriage as a basis for personal life.

Adhesiveness/amativeness became an early parallel of the homosexual/heterosexual distinction. Romantic passionate friendships might or might not have involved sexual relations—specific individual cases must be examined, but by the mid-nineteenth century, such friendships were widely socially recognized. By the 1870s, however, psychiatrists merged the concept of adhesiveness with pederasty and uranianism, and distinguished this from amativeness. The former became homosexuality or sexual inversion, a psychopathology. This new stigma is perhaps why Whitman reacted as he did when questioned whether what he wrote about in "Calamus" and the selections excerpted here was "sexual."

Whitman corresponded extensively with John Addington Symonds, who pressed him to know if the adhesiveness and comradely love about which Whitman wrote meant sexual love. In private conversations recorded by Horace Traubel and reported by Jonathan Ned Katz, Whitman responded: "Perhaps 'Calamus' means more or less than what I thought myself . . . I maybe do not know all my own meanings." Then, in 1890, Whitman received a letter in which Symonds asked him directly if Whitman's "manly love" refers to "the intimate and physical [and sexual] love of comrades and lovers." Whitman denied it, defending himself in part by saying that the difference between him and Symonds was one of "restraint." Symonds' analysis of Whitman is included in this volume.

We have excerpted here only the portion of *Democratic Vistas* that gives a flavor of Whitman's political theory based upon erotic love. Also included is a revised edition of his 1876 Preface to *Leaves of Grass* in which he addresses his intentions in writing the Calamus poems, and what he thought were the implications of comradely love based on adhesiveness for the new democratic society of the U.S.

1. Michael Lynch, "Here Is Adhesiveness: From Friendship to Homosexuality," *Victorian Studies* 29 (Autumn 1985), p. 84.

from

DEMOCRATIC VISTAS

(1871)

Walt Whitman

. . . Let us survey America's works, poems, philosophies, fulfilling prophecies, and giving form and decision to best ideals. Much that is now undream'd of, we might then perhaps see establish'd, luxuriantly cropping forth, richness, vigor of letters and of artistic expression, in whose products character will be a main requirement, and not merely erudition or elegance.

Intense and loving comradeship, the personal and passionate attachment of man to man—which, hard to define, underlies the lessons and ideals of the profound saviours of every land and age, and which seems to promise, when thoroughly develop'd, cultivated and recognized in manners and literature, the most substantial hope and safety of the future of these States, will then be fully express'd . . .[1]

. . . Offsetting the material civilization of our race, our nationality, its wealth, territories, factories, population, products, trade, and military and naval strength, and breathing breath of life into all these, and more, must be its moral civilization—the formulation, expression, and aidancy whereof, is the very highest height of literature. The climax of this loftiest range of civilization, rising above all the gorgeous shows and results of wealth, intellect, power, and art, as such—above even theology and religious fervor—is to be its development, from the eternal bases, and the fit expression, of absolute Conscience, moral soundness, Justice. Even in religious fervor there is a touch of animal heat. But moral conscientiousness, crystalline, without flaw, not Godlike only, entirely human, awes and enchants forever. Great is emotional love, even in the order of the rational universe. But, if we must make gradations, I am clear there is something greater. Power, love, veneration, products, genius, esthetics, tried by subtlest comparisons, analyses, and in serenest moods, somewhere fail, somehow become vain. Then noiseless, with flowing steps, the lord, the sun, the last ideal comes. By the names right, justice, truth, we suggest, but do not describe it. To the world of men it remains a dream, an idea as they call it. But no dream is it to the wise—but the proudest, almost only solid, lasting thing of all. Its analogy in the material universe is what holds together this world, and every object upon it, and carries its dynamics on forever sure and safe. Its lack, and the persistent shirking of it, as in life, sociology, literature, politics, business, and even sermonizing, these times, or any times, still leaves the abysm, the mortal flaw and smutch, mocking civilization to-day, with all its unquestion'd triumphs, and all the civilization so far known . . . [2]

1. It is to the development, identification, and general prevalence of that fervid comradeship, (the adhesive love, at least rivaling the amative love hitherto possessing imaginative literature, if not going beyond it,) that I look for the counterbalance and offset of our materialistic and vulgar American democracy, and for the spiritualization thereof. Many will say it is a dream, and will not follow my inferences: but I confidently expect a time when there will be seen, running like a half-hid warp through all the myriad audible and visible worldly interests of America, threads of manly friendship, fond and loving, pure and sweet, strong and life-long, carried to degrees hitherto unknown—not only giving tone to individual character, and making it unprecedently emotional, muscular, heroic, and refined, but having the deepest relations to general politics. I say democracy infers such loving comradeship, as its most inevitable twin or counterpart, without which it will be incomplete, in vain, and incapable of perpetuating itself.

2. I am reminded as I write that out of this very conscience, or idea of conscience, of intense moral right, and in its name and strain'd construction, the worst fanaticisms, wars, persecutions, murders, etc., have yet, in all lands, in the past, been broach'd, and have come to their devilish fruition. Much is to be said—but I may say here, and in response, that side by side with the unflagging stimulation of the elements of religion and conscience must henceforth move with equal sway, science, absolute reason, and the general proportionate development of the whole man. These scientific facts, deductions, are divine too—precious counted parts of moral civilization, and, with physical health, indispensable to it, to prevent fanaticism. For abstract religion, I perceive, is easily led astray, ever credulous, and is capable of devouring, remorseless, like fire and flame. Conscience, too, isolated from all else, and from the emotional nature, may but attain the beauty and purity of glacial, snowy ice. We want, for these States, for the general character, a cheerful, religious fervor, endued with the ever-present modifications of the human emotions, friendship, benevolence, with a fair field for scientific inquiry, the right of individual judgment, and always the cooling influences of material Nature.

from

LEAVES OF GRASS

Preface (1876)

Walt Whitman

... For some reason—not explainable or definite to my own mind, yet secretly pleasing and satisfactory to it—I have not hesitated to embody in, and run through the volume, two altogether distinct veins, or strata—politics for one, and for the other, the pensive thought of immortality. Thus, too, the prose and poetic, the dual forms of the present book. The volume, therefore, after its minor episodes, probably divides into these two, at first sight far diverse, veins of topic and treatment. Three points, in especial, have become very dear to me, and all through I seek to make them again and again, in many forms and repetitions, as will be seen: 1. That the true growth-characteristics of the democracy of the New World are henceforth to radiate in superior literary, artistic and religious expressions, far more than in its republican forms, universal suffrage, and frequent elections, (though these are unspeakably important.) 2. That the vital political mission of the United States is, to practically solve and settle the problem of two sets of rights—the fusion, thorough compatibility and junction of individual State prerogatives, with the indispensable necessity of centrality and Oneness—the national identity power—the sovereign Union, relentless, permanently comprising all, and over all, and in that never yielding an inch: then 3d. Do we not, amid a general malaria of fogs and vapors, our day, unmistakably see two pillars of promise, with grandest, indestructible indications—one, that the morbid facts of American politics and society everywhere are but passing incidents and flanges of our unbounded impetus of growth? weeds, annuals, of the rank, rich soil—not central, enduring, perennial things? The other, that all the hitherto experience of the States, their first century, has been but preparation, adolescence—and that this Union is only now and henceforth, (*i.e.* since the secession war,) to enter on its full democratic career?

Of the whole, poems and prose, (not attending at all to chronological order, and with original dates and passing allusions in the heat and impression of the hour, left shuffled in, and undisturb'd,) the chants of "Leaves of Grass," my former volume, yet serve as the indispensable deep soil, or bast-out of which, and out of which only, could come the roots and stems more definitely indicated by these later pages (While that volume radiates physiology alone, the present one, though of the like origin in the main, more palpable doubtless shows the pathology which was pretty sure to come in time from the other.)

In that former and main volume, composed in the flush of my health and strength, from the age of 30 to 50 years, I dwelt on birth and life, clothing my ideas in pictures, days transactions of my time, to give them positive place, identity—saturating them with that vehemence of pride and audacity of freedom necessary to loosen the mind of still-to-be form'd America from the accumulated folds, the superstitions, and all the long, tenacious and stifling anti-democratic authorities of the Asiatic and European past—my enclosing purport being to express, above all artificial regulation and aid, the eternal bodily composite, cumulative, natural character of one's self.

*Since I have been ill, (1873–74–75,) mostly without serious pain, and with plenty of time and frequent inclination to judge my poems, (never composed with eye on the book-market, nor for fame, nor for any pecuniary profit) I have felt temporary depression more than once, for fear that in "Leaves of Grass" the *moral* parts were not sufficiently pronounc'd. But in my clearest and calmest moods I have realized that as those "Leaves," all and several surely prepare the way for, and necessitate morals, and are adjusted to them just the same as Nature does and is, they are what, consistently with my plan they must and probably should be. (In a certain sense, while the Moral is the purport and last intelligence of all Nature, there is absolutely nothing of the moral in the works, or laws, or shows of Nature. Those only lead inevitably to it—begin and necessitate it.)

Then I meant "Leaves of Grass," as publish'd, to be the Poem of average Identity, (of *yours*, whoever you are, now reading these lines.) A man is not greatest as victor in war, nor inventor or explorer, nor even in science, of his intellectual or artistic capacity, or exemplar in some vast benevolence. To the highest democratic view, man is most acceptable in living well the practical life and lot which happens to him as ordinary farmer, sea-farer, mechanic, clerk, laborer, or driver—upon and from which position as a central basis or pedestal, while performing its labors, and his duties as citizen, son, husband, father and employ'd person, he preserves his physique, ascends, developing, radiating himself in other regions—and especially where and when, (greatest of all, and nobler than the proudest mere genius or magnate in any field,) he fully realizes the conscience, the spiritual, the divine faculty cultivated well, exemplified in all his deeds and words, through life, uncompromising to the end—a flight loftier than any of Homer's or Shakespeare's broader than all poems and bibles—namely, Nature's own, and in the midst of it, Yourself, your own Identity, body and soul. (All serves, helps—but in the centre of all, absorbing all, giving, for your purpose, the only meaning and vitality to all, master or mistress of all, under the law, stands Yourself.) To sing the Song of that law of average Identity, and of Yourself, consistent with the divine law of the universal, is a main intention of those "Leaves of Grass".

Something more may be added—for, while I am about it, I would make a full confession. I also sent out "Leaves of Grass" to arouse and set flowing in men's and women's hearts, young and old, endless streams of living, pulsating love and friendship, directly from them to myself, now and ever. To this terrible, irrepressible yearning, (surely more or less down underneath in most human souls)—this never-satisfied appetite for sympathy, and this boundless offering of sympathy—this universal democratic comradeship—this old eternal, yet ever-new interchange of adhesiveness, so fitly emblematic of America—I have given in that book, undisguisedly, declaredly, the openest expression. Besides, important as they are in my purpose as emotional expressions for humanity, the special meaning of the "Calamus" cluster of "Leaves of Grass," (and more or less running through the book, and cropping out in "Drum-Taps,") mainly resides in its political significance. In my opinion, it is by a fervent, accepted development of comradeship, the beautiful and sane affection of man for man, latent in all the young fellows, north and south, east and west—it is by this, I say, and by what goes directly and indirectly along with it, that the United States of the future, (I cannot too often repeat), are to be most effectually welded together, intercalated, anneal'd into a living union.

Then, for enclosing clue of all, it is imperatively and ever to be borne in mind that "Leaves of Grass" entire is not to be construed as an intellectual scholastic effort or poem mainly, but more as a radical utterance out of the Emotions and the Physique—an utterance adjusted to, perhaps born of, democracy and the Modern—in its very nature regardless of the old conventions, and, under the great laws, following only its own impulses.

SIR RICHARD FRANCIS BURTON

Richard von Krafft-Ebing's *Psychopathia Sexualis* was the standard reference for the new psychiatric field of sexual psychopathology; after its publication in 1886, it was republished in enlarged, revised editions twelve times during his lifetime. Although he originally pathologized Ulrichs's conceptualization of homosexuality as primarily engaged in by third-sexed *Urnings*, as a result of the influence of Magnus Hirschfeld, Krafft-Ebing changed in 1901 to view homosexuality as a natural variant of the sex drive.

Krafft-Ebing wrote in the tradition of "degeneracy" theorists who believed that humans descended from a unitary source, that while racial differences and hierarchies existed, each race had a normal type, that deviations from this norm were degenerate, that degeneration is inherited, cannot be reversed, and if left unchecked, would lead to extinction. Early theorists focused on an acquired degeneracy; Tissot, for example, thought that masturbation led to insanity. Later theorists focused upon the psychophysiological determinants of "wrong lovers" that paralleled the theory of the "born criminal" of the mid-nineteenth century. At the same time, sexual psychopathology developed an elaborate classificatory scheme for perversions (defined by Krafft-Ebing as "every expression of the sex drive that does not correspond to the purposes of nature, *i.e.*, reproduction"), and government policies were concerned with regulating population growth and policing newly urbanized populations.

Degeneracy theory was not the only connection between racism and homophobia. Another connection was the slaughter of indigenous peoples on the basis of their "unnatural vices." Sodomy was considered an indication of an uncivilized state in the peoples met by Renaissance European travelers and reported in their writings; male homosexuality as well as lesbian behavior, hermaphroditism, and cross-dressing were observed, and recorded, and condemned. However, gay writers such as Edward Carpenter and more open-minded anthropologists began to document same-sex love among non-European peoples in a less judgmental manner.

One early such treatment that drew political implications was that of Sir Richard Francis Burton (1821–1890), a British anthropologist and explorer. Although married, he had a lifetime interest in homosexuality. The work excerpted here is from the Appendix to his translation of *The Thousand and One Nights*, a book considered scandalous at the time for its depiction of Asian eroticism. In the Terminal Essay's section on pederasty, Burton writes about what he calls the "Sotadic Zone" (presumably named after Sotades, a third century Hellenic poet who invented verse that was pornographic when read backwards.) This zone seemingly embraces Southern Europe and most of the non-European world except for southern, central and non–coastal Africa, and South Asia. Drawing upon historical, lexicographical, and anthropological sources, Burton describes the prevalence of male and female homosexuality within the zone. However, he also suggests that it is widespread in European capitals as manifested in drag, anonymous and public sex venues, and bars.

Although often writing disparagingly of homosexuality, Burton's writing was popular among advocates for acceptance. While his rhetorical strategy portrays the prevalence of homosexuality as central to the cultures of "others," he then acknowledges its existence among Europeans as well. He argues against censorship of homosexuality in European speech and writing, since such speech and writing are "no offense . . . to the wise . . . and no encouragement to the loose."

from the Terminal Essay

THE BOOK OF THE THOUSAND NIGHTS AND A NIGHT

(1886)

Sir Richard Francis Burton

PEDERASTY

The "*execrabilis familia pathicorum*"[1] first came before me by a chance of earlier life. In 1845, when Sir Charles Napier had conquered and annexed Sind, despite a fraction (mostly venal) which sought favour with the now defunct "Court of Directors to the Honourable East India Company," the veteran began to consider his conquest with a curious eye. It was reported to him that Karachi, a townlet of some two thousand souls and distant not more than a mile from camp, supported no less than three lupanars or bordels, in which not women but boys and eunuchs, the former demanding nearly a double price, lay for hire. Being then the only British officer who could speak Sindi, I was asked indirectly to make enquiries and to report upon the subject; and I undertook the task on express condition that my report should not be forwarded to the Bombay Government, from whom supporters of the Conqueror's policy could expect scant favour, mercy or justice. Accompanied by a *Munshi*, Mirza Mohammed Hosayn of Shiraz, and habited as a merchant, Mirza Abdullah the Bushiri passed many an evening in the townlet, visited all the porneia and obtained the fullest details which were duly despatched to Government House. But the "Devil's Brother" presently quitted Sind leaving in his office my unfortunate official: this found its way with sundry other reports to Bombay and produced the expected result. A friend in the Secretariat informed me that my summary dismissal from the service had been formally proposed by one of Sir Charles Napier's successors, whose decease compels me *parcere sepulto*. But this excess of outraged modesty was not allowed.

Subsequent enquiries in many and distant countries enabled me to arrive at the following conclusions:

1. There exists what I shall call a "Sotadic Zone," bounded westwards by the northern shore of the Mediterranean (N. Lat. 43°) and by the southern (N. Lat. 30°). Thus, the depth would be 780 to 800 miles including meridional France, the Iberian Peninsula, Italy and Greece, with the coast regions of Africa from Morocco to Egypt.

2. Running eastward the Sotadic Zone narrows, embracing Asia Minor, Mesopotamia and Chaldea, Afghanistan, Sind, the Punjab and Kashmir.

3. In Indo-China, the belt begins to broaden, enfolding China, Japan and Turkistan.

4. It then embraces the South Sea Islands and the New World where, at the time of its discovery, Sotadic love was, with some exceptions, an established racial institution.

5. Within the Sotadic Zone, the vice is popular and endemic, held at the worst to be a mere peccadillo, whilst the races to the North and South of the limits here defined, practise it only sporadically amid the opprobrium of their fellows who, as a rule, are physically incapable of performing the operation and look upon it with the liveliest disgust.

Before entering into topographical details concerning pederasty, which I hold to be geographical and climatic, not racial, I must offer a few considerations of its cause and origin. We must not forget that the love of boys has its noble, sentimental side. The Platonists and pupils of the academy, followed by the Sufis or Moslem Gnostics, held such affection, pure and ardent, to be the *beau idéal* which united in man's soul the creature with the Creator. Professing to regard youths as the most cleanly and beautiful objects in this phenomenal world, they declared that by loving and extolling the *chef-d'œuvre*, corporeal and intellectual, of the Demiurgus, disinterestedly and without any admixture of carnal sensuality, they are paying the most fervent adoration to the *Causa causans*. They add that such affection, passing as it does the love of women, is far less selfish than fondness for and admiration of the other sex which, however innocent, always suggest sexuality; and Easterns add that the devotion of the moth to the taper is purer and more fervent than the Bulbul's love for the rose. Amongst the Greeks of the best ages the system of boy favourites was advocated on considerations of morals and politics. The lover undertook the education of the beloved through precept and example, while the two were conjoined by a tie stricter than the fraternal. Hieronymus, the Peripatetic, strongly advocated it because the vigorous disposition of youth and the confidence engendered by their association often led to the overthrow of tyrannies. Socrates declared that "a most valiant army might be composed of boys and their lovers; for that of all men they would be most ashamed to desert one another." And even Virgil, despite the foul flavour of Formosum pastor Corydon, could write:

Nisus amore pio pueri.[2]

The only physical cause for the practice which suggests itself to me (that must be owned to be purely conjectural) is that within the Sotadic Zone there is a blending of the masculine and feminine temperaments, a crasis which elsewhere occurs only sporadically. Hence the male *féminisme* whereby the man becomes *patiens* as well as *agens*, and the woman a tribade, a votary of mascula Sappho, Queen of Frictrices or Rubbers. Prof. Mantegazza claims to have discovered the cause of this pathologic love, this perversion of the erotic sense, one of the marvellous list of amorous vagaries which deserve, not prosecution but the pitiful care of the physician and the study of the psychologist. According to him, the nerves of the rectum and the genitalia, in all cases closely connected, are abnormally so in the pathic who obtains, by intromission, the venereal orgasm which is usually sought through the sexual organs. So amongst women, there are tribads who can procure no pleasure except by foreign objects introduced *a posteriori*. Hence his threefold distribution of sodomy; 1 Peripheric or anatomical, caused by an unusual distribution of the nerves and their hyperesthesia; 2 luxurious, when love *a tergo* is preferred on account of the narrowness of the passage; and 3 the psychical. But this is evidently superficial: the question is what causes this neuropathy, this abnormal distribution and condition of the nerves?

As Prince Bismarck finds a moral difference between the male and female races of history, so I suspect a mixed physical temperament effected by the manifold subtle influences massed together in the word climate. Something of the kind is necessary to explain the fact of this pathological love extending over the greater portion of the habitable world, without any apparent connection of race or media, from the polished Greek to the cannibal Tupi of the Brazil. Walt Whitman speaks of the ashen grey faces of onanists: the faded colours, the puffy features and the unwholesome complexion of the professed pederast with his peculiar cachetic expression, indescribable but once seen never forgotten which stamps the breed, and Dr. G. Adolph is justified in declaring "*Alle Gewohnneits-paederasten erkennen sich einander schnell, oft met einen Blick.*" This has nothing in common with the *féminisme* which betrays itself in the pathic by womanly gait, regard and gesture: it is a something *sui generis*;

and the same may be said of the colour and look of the young priest who honestly refrains from women and their substitutes. Dr. Tardieu, in his well known work "*Étude medico-légale sur les attentats aux mœurs,*" and Dr. Adolph note a peculiar infundibuliform disposition of the "after" and a smoothness and want of folds even before any abuse has taken place, together with special forms of the male organs in confirmed pederasts. But these observations have been rejected by Caspar, Hoffman, Brouardel and Dr. J. H. Henry Coutagne ("Notes sur la sodomie", Lyon 1880), and it is a medical question whose discussion would here be out of place . . .

. . . Pederasty is forbidden by the Koran. In chapter iv, 20 we read: "And if two (men) among you commit the crime, then punish them both," the penalty being some hurt or damage by public reproach, insult or scourging. There are four distinct references to Lot and the Sodomites in chapters vii, 78; xi 77–84; xvi 160–174 and xxix 28–35. In the first the prophet commissioned to the people says, "Proceed ye to a fulsome act wherein no creature hath foregone ye? Verily ye come to men in lieu of women lustfully." We have then an account of the rain which made an end of the wicked and this judgment on the Cities of the Plain is repeated with more detail in the second reference. Here the angels, generally supposed to be three, Gabriel, Michael and Raphael, appeared to Lot as beautiful youths, a sore temptation to the sinners and the godly man's arm was straitened concerning his visitors because he felt unable to protect them from the erotic vagaries of his fellow townsmen. Therefore, he shut his doors and from behind them argued the matter: presently the riotous assembly attempted to climb the wall when Gabriel, seeing the distress of his host, smote them on the face with one of his wings and blinded them so that all moved off crying for aid and saying that Lot had magicians in his house. Hereupon the "cities" which, if they ever existed, must have been Fellah villages, were uplifted: Gabriel thrust his wing under them and raised them so high that the inhabitants of the lower heaven (the lunar sphere) could hear the dogs barking and the cocks crowing. Then came the rain of stones: these were clay pellets baked in hell fire, streaked white and red, or having some mark to distinguish them from the ordinary and each bearing the name of its destination like the missiles which destroyed the host of Abrahat al-Ashram. Lastly the "Cities" were turned upside down and cast upon earth. These circumstantial unfacts are repeated at full length in the other two chapters; but rather as an instance of Allah's power than as a warning against pederasty, which Mohammed seems to have regarded with philosophic indifference. The general opinion of his followers is that it should be punished like fornication unless the offenders made a public act of penitence. But here, as in adultery, the law is somewhat too clement and will not convict unless four credible witnesses swear to have seen *rem in re*. I have noticed the vicious opinion that the Ghilmán or Wuldán, the beautiful boys of Paradise, the counterparts of the Houris, will be lawful catamites to the True Believers in a future state of happiness; the idea is nowhere countenanced in Al-Islam; and, although I have often heard debauchees refer to it, the learned look upon the assertion as scandalous.

As in Morocco so the vice prevails throughout the old regencies of Algiers, Tunis and Tripoli and all the cities of the South Mediterranean seaboard, whilst it is unknown to the Nubians, the Berbers and the wilder tribes dwelling inland. Proceeding Eastward we reach Egypt, that classical region of all abominations which, marvellous to relate, flourished in closest contact with men leading the purest of lives, models of moderation and morality, of religion and virtue. Amongst the ancient Copts *le vice* was part and portion of the ritual and was represented by two male partridges alternately copulating . . .

We find the earliest written notices of the vice in the mythical destruction of the Pentapolis, Sodom, Gomorrah (Õ 'Aámirah, the cultivated country), Adama, Zeboïm and

Zoar or Bela. The legend has been amply embroidered by the Rabbis who make the Sodomites do everything à l'envers: e.g., if a man were wounded he was fined for bloodshed and was compelled to fee the offender; and if one cut off the ear of a neighbor's ass he was condemned to keep the animal till the ear grew again.

The Jewish doctors declare the people to have been a race of sharpers with rogues for magistrates, and thus they justify the judgment which they read literally. But the traveller cannot accept it. I have carefully examined the lands at the North and at the South of that most beautiful lake, the so called Dead Sea, whose tranquil loveliness, backed by the grand plateau of Moab, is an object of admiration to all save patients suffering from the strange disease "Holy Land on the Brain." But I found no trace of craters in the neighborhood, no signs of vulcanism, no remains of "meteoric stones": the asphalt which named the water is a mineralised vegetable washed out of the limestones, and the sulphur and salt are brought down by the Jordan into a lake without issue. I must therefore look upon the history as a myth which may have served a double purpose. The first would be to deter the Jew from the Malthusian practices of his pagan predecessors, upon whom obloquy was thus cast, so far resembling the scandalous and absurd legend which explained the names of the children of Lot by Pheiné and Thamma as "Moab" (Mu-ab) the water or semen of the father, and "Ammon" as mother's son, that is, bastard. The fable would also account for the abnormal fissure containing the lower Jordan and the Dead Sea, which the late Sir R. I. Murchison used wrong headedly to call a "Volcano of Depression": this geological feature, that cuts off the river basin from its natural outlet the Gulf of Eloth (Akabah), must date from myriads of years before there were "Cities of the Plains." But the main object of the ancient lawgiver, Osarsiph, Moses or the Moseidæ, was doubtless to discountenance a perversion prejudicial to the increase of population. And he speaks with no uncertain voice, "Whoso lieth with a beast shall surely be put to death." If a man lie with mankind as he lieth with a woman, both of them have committed an abomination: they shall surely be put to death; their blood shall be upon them. Again, "there shall be no whore of the daughters of Israel nor a sodomite of the sons of Israel."

The old commentators on the Sodom-myth are most unsatisfactory, e.g., Parkhurst, Kadesh. "From hence we may observe the peculiar propriety of this punishment of Sodom and of the neighbouring cities. By their sodomitical impurities they meant to acknowledge the Heavens as the cause of fruitfulness independently upon, and in opposition to Jehovah; therefore Jehovah, by raining upon them not genial showers but brimstone from heaven, not only destroyed the inhabitants, but also changed all that country, which was before as the garden of God, into brimstone and salt that is not sown nor beareth, neither any grass groweth therein."

It must be owned that to this Pentapolis was dealt very hard measure for religiously and diligently practising a popular rite which a host of cities even in the present day, as Naples and Shiraz, to mention no others, affect for simple luxury and affect with impunity. The myth may probably reduce itself to very small proportions, a few Fellah villages destroyed by a storm, like that which drove Brennus from Delphi . . .

The cities of Afghanistan and Sind are thoroughly saturated with Persian vice, and the people sing

Kadr-i-kus Aughán dánad, kadr-i-kunrá Kábuli:
The worth of coynte the Afghan knows: Cabul prefers the other chose!

The Afghans are commercial travellers on a large scale and each caravan is accompanied by a number of boys and lads almost in woman's attire with kohl'd eyes and rouged cheeks, long tresses and henna'd fingers and toes, riding luxuriously in Kajáwas or camel-panniers: they are called Kúchi-safari, or travelling wives, and the husbands trudge patiently by their sides. In Afghanistan also a frantic debauchery broke out amongst the women when they found incubi who were not pederasts; and the scandal was not the most insignificant cause of the general rising at Cabul (Nov. 1841), and the slaughter of Macnaghten, Burnes and other British officers.

Resuming our way Eastward we find the Sikhs and the Moslems of the Panjab much addicted to *Le Vice*, although the Himalayan tribes to the north and those lying south, the Rájputs and Marathás, ignore it. The same may be said of the Kashmirians who add another Kappa to the tria Kakista, Kappadocians, Kretans, and Kilicians: the proverb says,

> *Agar kaht-i-mardum uftad, az ín sih jins kam gírí;*
> *Eki Afghán, dovvuin Sindí, siyyum badjins-i-Kashmírí:*
> *Though of men there be famine yet shun these three—*
> *Afghan, Sindi and rascally Kashmírí.*

M. Louis Daville describes the infamies of Lahore and Lakhnau where he found men dressed as women, with flowing locks under crowns of flowers, imitating the feminine walk and gestures, voice and fashion of speech, and ogling their admirers with all the coquetry of bayadères...

Beyond India, I have stated, the Sotadic Zone begins to broaden out embracing all China, Turkistan and Japan. The Chinese, as far as we know them in the great cities, are omnivorous and omnifutuentes: they are the chosen people of debauchery and their systematic bestiality with ducks, goats, and other animals is equalled only by their pederasty...

Passing over to America, we find that the Sotadic Zone contains the whole hemisphere from Behring's Strait to Magellan's Strait. This prevalence of "mollities" astonishes the anthropologist, who is apt to consider pederasty the growth of luxury and the especial product of great and civilised cities, unnecessary and therefore unknown to simple savagery where the births of both sexes are about equal and female infanticide is not practised. In many parts of the New World, this perversion was accompanied by another depravity of taste, confirmed cannibalism. The forests and campos abounded in game from the deer to the pheasant-like penelope, and the seas and rivers produced an unfailing supply of excellent fish and shell-fish; yet the Brazilian Tupis preferred the meat of man to every other food.

A glance at Mr. Bancroft proves the abnormal development of sodomy amongst the savages and barbarians of the New World. Even his half-frozen Hyperboreans "possess all the passions which are supposed to develop most freely under a milder temperature." The voluptuousness and polygamy of the North American Indians, under a temperature of almost perpetual winter is far greater than that of the most sensual tropical nations...

Outside the Sotadic Zone, I have said, *le vice* is sporadic, not endemic: yet the physical and moral effect of great cities where puberty, they say, is induced earlier than in country sites, has been the same in most lands, causing modesty to decay and pederasty to flourish. The Badawi Arab is wholly pure of *le vice*; yet San'á the capital of Al-Yaman and other centres of population have long been and still are thoroughly infected. History tells us of Zú Shanátir, tyrant of "Arabia Felix," in A.D. 478, who used to entice young men into his palace and cause them after use to be cast out of the windows: this unkindly ruler was at last poinarded by the youth Zerash, known from his long ringlets as "Zú Nowás." The Negro race is mostly untainted by sodomy and tribadism. Yet Joan dos Sanctos found in Cacango of West Africa certain "*Chibudi, which are men attyred like women and behaue themselves womanly, ashamed to be called men; are also married to men, and esteem that unnaturale damnation an honor.*" . . .

In our modern capitals, London, Berlin and Paris, for instance, the vice seems subject to periodical outbreaks. For many years, also, England sent her pederasts to Italy, and especially to Naples whence originated the term "*Il vizio Inglese.*" It would be invidious to detail the scandals which of late years have startled the public in London and Dublin: for these the curious will consult the police reports. Berlin, despite her strong flavour of Phariseeism, Puritanism and Chauvinism in religion, manners and morals, is not a whit better than her neighbours. Dr. Gaspar, a well known authority on the subject, adduces many interesting cases especially an old Count Cajus and his six accomplices. Amongst his many correspondents, one suggested to him that not only Plato and Julius Caesar but also Winckelmann and Platen belonged to the society; and he found it flourishing in Palermo, the Louvre, the Scottish Highlands and St. Petersburg, to name only a few places. Frederick the Great is said to have addressed these words to his nephew, "*Je puis vous assurer, par mon expérience personelle, que ce plaisir est peu agréable à cultiver.*" This suggests the popular anecdote of Voltaire and the Englishman who agreed upon an "experience" and found it far from satisfactory. A few days afterwards the latter informed the Sage of Ferney that he had tried it again and provoked the exclamation, "Once a philosopher: twice a sodomite!". . .

Under Louis Philippe, the conquest of Algiers had evil results, according to the Marquis de Boissy. He complained without *ambages* of *mœurs Arabes* in French regiments, and declared that the result of the African wars was an *éffrayable débordement pédérastique*, even as the *vérole* resulted from the Italian campaigns of that age of passion, the sixteenth century. From the military the *fléau* spread to civilian society and the vice took such expansion and intensity, that it may be said to have been democratised in cities and large towns; at least we gather from the *Dossier des Agissements des Pédérastes*. A general gathering of *La Sainte Congrégation des glorieux Pédérastes* was held in the old Petite Rue des Marais where, after the theatre, many resorted under pretext of making water. They ranged themselves along the walls of a vast garden and exposed their podices: bourgeois, richards and nobles came with full purses, touched the part which most attracted them and were duly followed by it. At the Allée des Veuves, the crowd was dangerous from 7 to 8 p.m.: no policeman or *ronde de nuit* dared venture in it; cords were stretched from tree to tree and armed guards drove away strangers amongst whom, they say, was once Victor Hugo. This nuisance was at length suppressed by the municipal administration.

The Empire did not improve morals. Balls of sodomites were held at No. 8 Place de la Madeleine where, on Jan. 2, 1864, some one hundred and fifty men met, all so well dressed as women that even the landlord did not recognise them. There was also a club for sotadic debauchery called Cent Gardes and the Dragons de l'Impératrice. They copied the imperial toilette and kept it in the general wardrobe: hence *faire l'Impératrice* meant to be used carnally. The site, a splendid hotel in the Allée des Veuves, was discovered by the Procureur–Général who registered all the names; but, as these belonged to not a few senators and dignitaries, the Emperor wisely quashed proceedings . . .

Those who have read through these ten volumes will agree with me that the proportion of offensive matter bears a very small ratio to the mass of the work. In an age saturated with cant and hypocrisy, here and there a venal pen will mourn over the "pornography" of *The Nights*, dwell upon the "Ethics of Dirt" and the "Garbage of the Brothel"; and will lament the "wanton dissemination (!) of ancient and filthy fiction." This self-constituted *Censor morum* reads Aristophanes and Plato, Horace and Virgil, perhaps even Martial and Petronius, because "veiled in the decent obscurity of a learned language;" he allows men *Latinè loqui* less important in plain English. To be consistent, he must begin by bowdlerising not only the classics, with which boys' and youths' minds and memories are soaked and saturated at schools and colleges, but also Boccaccio and Chaucer, Shakespeare and Rabelais; Burton, Sterne, Swift and a long list of works which are yearly reprinted and republished without a word of protest. Lastly, why does not this inconsistent Puritan purge the Old Testament of its allusions to human ordure and the pudenda, to carnal copulation and impudent whoredom, to adultery and fornication, to onanism, sodomy and bestiality? But this he will not do, the whited sepulchre! To the interested critic of the *Edinburgh Review* (No. 335 of July, 1886), I return my warmest thanks for his direct and deliberate falsehoods: lies are one-legged and short-lived, and venom evaporates. It appears to be that when I show to such men, so "respectable" and so impure, a landscape of magnificent prospects whose vistas are adorned with every charm of nature and art, they point their unclean noses at a little heap of muck here and there lying in a field corner.

1. *Accursed family of fags—Eds.*

2. *Depending on the loyal love of a boy—Eds.*

JOHN ADDINGTON SYMONDS

John Addington Symonds (1840–1893) was a wealthy physician and well-known British man of letters who, with Edward Carpenter, became one of the early theorists of the homosexual rights movement in England. Although married with four daughters, he recognized his homosexuality early in life and spent most of his life trying to come to terms with it. He influenced intellectuals on both sides of the Atlantic, including Whitman, Henry James, Charles Pierce, Havelock Ellis, Edward Carpenter, and many ethnologists, classicists, and clergy.

Symonds was a lifelong fan of Whitman and corresponded with him regularly between 1871 and 1890. His homoerotic interpretation of Whitman's work is included in the document excerpted here. In 1873 he wrote *A Problem in Greek Ethics*. It was published ten years later in a ten-copy edition privately circulated among friends of whom he asked that they be discreet in discussing it. Its purpose was to show male homosexuality as a normal part of Ancient Greek life, a demonstration which he thought indispensible to interpreting homosexuality of his time in light of the assertions of psychopathologists. He later collaborated with sexologist Havelock Ellis on a book about sexual inversion.

The essay excerpted here, *A Problem in Modern Ethics* was published in 1891; fifty copies were issued, but his family made him remove his name from the English edition. In it, he summarizes the views of sexologists and criminologists such as Moreau, Tarnowsky, Ulrichs, Krafft-Ebing, Caspar and Lombroso, and argues against the medical model of homosexuality as psychopathology and for a sexual ethics of male homosexuality. Sexual relations among men were positive for participants and for society because of the deep comradeship they created, because they were complementary with (and in no way prejudicial against) male-female relations, and, while cutting across social strata and abolishing class distinction derived from prejudice and education, they furthered the advance of social equality and even socialism. This last theme is one that Edward Carpenter and twentieth century gay thinkers would address in some detail.

from

A PROBLEM IN MODERN ETHICS
(1891)

John Addington Symonds

Introduction

There is a passion, or a perversion of appetite, which, like all human passions, has played a considerable part in the world's history for good or evil; but which has hardly yet received the philosophical attention and the scientific investigation it deserves. The reason for this may be that in all Christian societies the passion under consideration has been condemned to pariahdom. Consequently, philosophy and science have not considered it dignified to make it the subject of special enquiry.

Only the Greek race, to whom we owe the inheritance of our ideas, succeeded in raising it to the level of chivalrous enthusiasm. Nevertheless, we find it present everywhere and in all periods of history. We cannot take up the religious books, the legal codes, the annals, the descriptions of the manners of any nation, whether large or small, powerful or feeble, civilized or savage, without finding it in one form or other. Sometimes it assumes the calm and dignified attitude of conscious merit, as in Sparta, Athens, Thebes. Sometimes it skulks in holes and corners, hiding an abashed head and shrinking from the light of day, as in the capitals of modern Europe. It confronts us on the steppes of Asia, where hordes of nomads drink the milk of mares; in the bivouac of Keltish warriors lying wrapped in wolves' skins round their camp-fires; upon the sands of Arabia where the Bedouin raise desert dust in flying squadrons. We discern it among the palm groves of the South Sea Islands; in the card houses and temple gardens of Japan; under Eskimos' snow-huts; beneath the sultry vegetation of Peru; beside the streams of Shiraz and the waters of the Ganges; in the cold clear air of Scandinavian winters. It throbs in our huge cities. The pulse of it can be felt in London, Paris, Berlin, Vienna, no less than in Constantinople, Naples, Teheran, and Moscow. It finds a home in Alpine valleys, Albanian ravines, Californian canyons, and gorges of Caucasian mountains. It once sat, clothed in imperial purple, on the throne of the Roman Cæsars, crowned with the tiara on the chair of St. Peter. It has flaunted the heraldries of France and England, in coronation ceremonies at Rheims and Westminster. The royal palaces of Madrid and Aranjuez could tell their tales of it. So do the ruined courtyards of Granada and the castle-keep of Avignon. It shone with clear radiance in the gymnasium of Hellas, and nerved the dying heroes of Greek freedom for their last forlorn hope upon the plains of Chæronea. Endowed with inextinguishable life, in spite of all that has been done to suppress it, this passion survives at large and penetrates society, makes itself felt in every quarter of the globe where men are brought into communion with men.

Yet no one dares to speak of it; or if they do, they bate their breath, and preface their remarks with maledictions.

Those who read these lines will hardly doubt what passion it is that I am hinting at. *Quod semper ubique et ab omnibus*[1]—surely it deserves a name. Yet I can hardly find a name which will not seem to soil this paper. The accomplished languages of Europe in the nineteenth century supply no term for this persistent feature of human psychology, without importing some implication of disgust, disgrace, vituperation. Science, however, has recently—within the last twenty years in fact—invented a convenient phrase, which does not prejudice the matter under consideration. It is called "inverted sexual instinct;" and with this neutral nomenclature this investigator has good reason to be satisfied.

Inverted sexuality, the sexual instinct diverted from its normal channel, directed (in the case of males) to males, forms the topic of the following discourse. The study will be confined to modern times, and to those nations which regard the phenomenon with religious detestation. This renders the enquiry peculiarly difficult, and exposes the enquirer, unless he be a professed expert in diseases of the mind and nervous centres, to almost certain misconstruction. Still, there is no valid reason why the task of statement and analysis should not be undertaken. Indeed, one might rather wonder why candid and curious observers of humanity have not attempted to fathom a problem which faces them at every turn in their historical researches and in daily life. Doubtless, their neglect is due to natural or acquired repugnance, to feelings of disgust and hatred, derived from immemorial tradition, and destructive of the sympathies which animate a really zealous pioneer. Nevertheless, what is human is alien to no human being. What the law punishes, but what, in spite of law, persists and energizes, ought to arrest attention. We are, all of us, responsible to some extent for the maintenance and enforcement of our laws. We are as evolutionary science teaches, interested in the facts of anthropology, however repellant some of these may be to our own feelings. We cannot evade the conditions of atavism and heredity. Every family runs the risk of producing a boy or a girl, whose life will be embittered by inverted sexuality, but who in all other respects will be no worse or better than the normal members of the home. Surely, then, it is our duty and our interest to learn what we can about its nature, and to arrive through comprehension at some rational method of dealing with it . . .

Vulgar Errors

. . . It is the common belief that all subjects of sexual inversion have originally loved women, but that, through monstrous debauchery and superfluity of naughtiness, tiring of normal pleasure, they have wilfully turned their appetites into other channels. This is true about a certain number. But the sequel of this essay will prove that it does not mean by far the larger proportion of cases, in whom such instincts are inborn, and a considerable percentage in whom they are also inconvertible. Medical jurists and physicists have recently agreed to accept this as a fact.

It is the common belief that a male who loves his own sex must be despicable, degraded, depraved, vicious, and incapable of humane or generous sentiments. If Greek history did not contradict this supposition, a little patient enquiry into contemporary manners would suffice to remove it. But people will not take this trouble about a matter, which, like Gibbon, they "touch with reluctance and despatch with impatience." Those who are obliged to do so find to their surprise that "among the men who are subject to this deplorable vice, there are even quite intelligent, talented, and highly-placed persons, of excellent and even noble character." The vulgar expect to discover the objects of their outraged animosity in the scum of humanity. But these may be met with every day in drawing-rooms, law-courts, banks, universities, mess-rooms; on the bench, the throne, the chair of the professor; under the blouse of the workman, the cassock of the priest, the epaulettes of the officer, the smock-frock of the ploughman, the wig of the barrister, the mantle of the peer, the costume of the actor, the tights of the athlete, the gown of the academician.

It is the common belief that one, and only one, unmentionable act is what the lovers seek as the source of their unnatural gratification, and that this produces spinal disease, epilepsy, consumption, dropsy, and the like. Nothing can be more mistaken, as the scientifically reported cases of avowed and adult sinners amply demonstrate. Neither do they invariably or even usually prefer the *aversa Venus;* nor, when this happens, do they exhibit peculiar signs of suffering in health. Excess in any venereal pleasure will produce diseases of nervous exhaustion and imperfect nutrition. But the indulgence of inverted sexual instincts within due limits, cannot be proved to be especially pernicious. Were it so, the Dorians and Athenians, including Sophocles, Pindar, Æschines, Epaminondas, all the Spartan kings and generals, the Theban legion, Pheidias, Plato, would have been one nation of rickety, phthisical, dropsical paralytics. The grain of truth contained in this vulgar error is that, under the prevalent laws and hostilities of modern society, the inverted passion has to be indulged furtively, spasmodically, hysterically; that the repression of it through fear and shame frequently leads to habits of self-abuse; and that its unconquerable solicitations sometimes convert it from a healthy outlet of the sexual nature into a morbid monomania. It is also true that professional male prostitutes, like their female counterparts, suffer from local and constitutional disorders.

It is common belief that boys under age are specially liable to corruption. This error need not be confuted here. Anyone who chooses to read the cases recorded by Casper-Liman, Casper in his *Novellen*, Krafft-Ebing, and Ulrichs, or to follow the developments of the present treatise, or to watch the manners of London after dark, will be convicted of its absurdity. Young boys are less exposed to dangers from the abnormal than young girls from normal voluptuaries.

It is common belief that all subjects from inverted instinct carry their lusts written in their faces; that they are pale, languid, scented, effeminate, painted, timid, and oblique in expression. This vulgar error rests upon imperfect observation. A certain class of such people are undoubtedly feminine. From their earliest youth they have shown marked inclination for the habits and the dress of women; and when they are adult, they do everything in their power to obliterate their manhood. It is equally true that such unsexed males possess a strong attraction for some abnormal individuals. But it is a gross mistake to suppose that all the tribe betray these attributes. The majority differ in no detail of their outward appearance, physique, or dress, from normal men. They are athletic, masculine in habits, frank in manner, passing through society year after year without arousing a suspicion of their inner temperament. Were it not so, society would long ago have had its eyes opened to the amount of perverted sexuality it harbours.

The upshot of this discourse on vulgar errors is that popular opinion is made up of a number of contradictory misconceptions and confusions. Moreover, it has been taken for granted that "to investigate the depraved instincts of humanity is unprofitable and disgusting." Consequently the subject has been imperfectly studied; and individuals belonging to radically different species are confounded in one vague sentiment of reprobation. Assuming that they are all abominable, society is contented to punish them indiscriminately. The depraved debauchee who abuses boys receives the same treatment as the young man who loves a comrade. The male prostitute who earns his money by extortion is scarcely more condemned than a man of birth and breeding who has been seen walking with soldiers ...

Literature — Medico-Forensic

... The leading writers on forensic medicine at the present time in Europe are Casper (edited by Liman) for Germany, Tardieu for France, and Taylor for England. Taylor is so reticent upon the subject of unnatural crime that his handbook on *The principles and practice of medical jurisprudence* does not demand minute examination. However, it may be remarked that he believes false accusations to be even commoner in this matter than in the case of rape, since they are only too frequently made the means of blackmailing. For this reason he leaves the investigation of such crimes to the lawyers.

Both Casper and Tardieu discuss the topic of sexual inversion with antipathy. But there are notable points of difference in the method and in the conclusions of the two authors. Tardieu, perhaps because he is a Frenchman, educated in the school of Paris, which we have learned to know from Carlier, assumes that all subjects of the passion are criminal or vicious. He draws no psychological distinction between pederast and pederast. He finds no other name for them, and looks upon the whole class as voluntarily degraded beings, who, for the gratification of monstrous desires, have unsexed themselves. A large part of his work is devoted to describing what he believes to be the signs of active and passive immorality in the bodies of persons addicted to these habits. It is evident that imagination has acted powerfully in the formation of his theories. But this is not the place to discuss their details.

Casper and Liman approach the subject with almost equal disgust, but with more regard for scientific truth than Tardieu. They point out that the term pederast is wholly inadequate to describe the several classes of male persons afflicted with sexual inversion. They clearly expect, in course of time, a general mitigation of the penalties in force against such individuals. According to them, the penal laws of North Germany on the occasion of their last revision, would probably have been altered, had not the jurists felt that the popular belief in the criminality of pederasts ought to be considered. Consequently, a large number of irresponsible persons, in the opinion of experts like Casper and Liman, are still exposed to punishment by laws enacted under the influence of vulgar errors.

These writers are not concerned with the framing of codes, nor again with the psychological diagnosis of accused persons. It is their business to lay down rules whereby a medical authority, consulted in a doubtful case, may form his own view as to the guilt or innocence of the accused. Their attention is therefore mainly directed to the detection of signs upon the bodies of incriminated individuals.

This question of physical diagnosis leads them into a severe critique of Tardieu. Their polemic attacks each of the points which he attempted to establish. I must content myself by referring to the passage of their work which deals with this important topic. Suffice it here to say that they reject all signs as worse than doubtful, except a certain deformation of one part of the body, which may possibly be taken as the proof of habitual prostitution, when it occurs in quite young persons. Of course they admit that wounds, violent abrasions of the skin, in certain places, and some syphilitic affections strongly favour the presumption of a criminal act. Finally, after insisting on the insecurity of Tardieu's alleged signs, and pointing out the responsibility assumed by physicians who base a judgment on them, the two Germans sum up their conclusions in the following words: "It is extremely remarkable that while Tardieu mentions 206 cases, and communicates a select list of 19, which to him exhibit these peculiar conformations of the organs, he can only produce one single instance where the formation seemed indubitable. Let any one peruse his 19 cases, and he will be horrified at the unhesitating condemnations pronounced by Tardieu." The two notes of exclamation which close this sentence in the original are fully justified. It is indeed horrifying to think that a person, implicated in some foul accusation, may have his doom fixed by a doctrinaire like Tardieu. Antipathy and ignorance in judges and the public, combined with erroneous canons of evidence in the expert, cannot fail to lead in such cases to some serious miscarriage of justice.

Passing from the problem of diagnosis and the polemic against Tardieu, it must be remarked that Casper was the first writer of this class to lay down the distinction between inborn and acquired perversion of the sexual instinct. The law does not recognize this distinction. If a criminal act be proved, the psychological condition of the agent is legally indifferent—unless it can be shown that he was clearly mad and irresponsible, in which case he may be consigned to a lunatic asylum instead of the jail. But Casper and Liman, having studied the question of sexual maladies in general, and given due weight to the works of Ulrichs, call attention to the broad differences which exist between persons in whom abnormal appetites are innate and those in whom they are acquired . . .

Medicojuristic science made a considerable step when Casper adopted this distinction of two types of sexual inversion. But, as is always the case in the analysis of hitherto neglected phenomena, his classification falls far short of the necessities of the problem. While treating of acquired sexual inversion, he only thinks of debauchees. He does not seem to have considered a deeper question—deeper in its bearing upon the way in which society will have to deal with the whole problem—the question of how far these instincts are capable of being communicated by contagion to persons in their fullest exercise of sexual vigour. Taste, fashion, preference, as factors in the dissemination of anomalous passions, he has left out of his account. It is also, but this is a minor matter, singular that he should have restricted his observations on the freemasonry among pederasts to those in whom the instinct is acquired. That exists quite as much or even more among those in whom it is congenital.

However, the upshot of the whole matter is that the best book on medical jurisprudence now extant repudiates the enormities of Tardieu's method, and lays it down for proved that "the majority of persons who are subject" to sexual inversion come into the world, or issue from the cradle, with their inclination clearly marked.

Literature — Medicine

Medical writers upon this subject are comparatively numerous in French and German literature, and they have been multiplying rapidly lately. The phenomenon of sexual inversion is usually regarded in these books from the point of view of psychopathic or neuropathic derangement, inherited from morbid ancestors, and developed in the patient by early habits of self-abuse.

What is the exact distinction between "psychopathic" and "neuropathic" I do not know. The former term seems intelligible in the theologian's mouth, the latter in a physician's. But I cannot understand both being used together to indicate different kinds of pathologic diathesis. What is the soul, what are the nerves? We have probably to take the two terms as indicating two ways of considering the same phenomenon; the one subjective, the other objective; "psychopathic" pointing to the derangement as observed in the mind emotions of its subject; "neuropathic" to the derangement as observed in anomalies of the nervous system . . .

Des aberrations du sens; génésique, par le Dr. Paul Moreau, 4th edition, 1887

Moreau starts with the proposition that there is a sixth sense, "le sens génital," which, like other senses, can be injured psychically and physically without the mental functions, whether affective or intellectual, suffering thereby. His book is therefore a treatise on the diseases of the sexual sense. These diseases are by no means of recent origin, he says. They have always and everywhere existed . . .

It is not necessary to follow Moreau in his otherwise interesting account of the various manifestations of sexual disease. The greater part of these have no relation to the subject of my work. But what he says in passing about "pederasts, sodomites, sapphists," has to be resumed. He reckons them among "a class of individuals who cannot and ought not to be confounded either with men enjoying the fullness of their intellectual faculties, or yet with madmen properly so called. They form an intermediate class, a mixed class, constituting a real link of union between reason and madness, the nature and existence of which can most frequently be explained only by one word: heredity." It is surprising, after this announcement, to discover that what he has to say about sexual inversion is limited to Europe and its moral system, "having nothing to do with the morals of other countries where pederasty is accepted and admitted." Literally, then, he regards sexual inversion in modern Christian Europe as a form of hereditary neuropathy, a link between reason and madness; but in ancient Greece, in modern Persia and Turkey, he regards the same psychological anomaly from the point of view, not of disease, but of custom. In other words, an Englishman or a Frenchman who loves the male sex must be diagnosed as tainted with disease; while Sophocles, Pindar, Phedias, Epaminondas, Plato are credited with yielding to an instinct with was healthy in their times because society accepted it. The inefficiency of this distinction in a treatise of analytical science ought to be indicated. The bare fact that ancient Greece tolerated, and that modern Europe refuses to tolerate sexual inversion, can have nothing to do with the etiology, the pathology, the psychological definition of the phenomenon in its essence. What has to be faced is that a certain type of passion flourished under the light of day and bore good fruits for society in Hellas; that the same type of passion flourishes in the shade and is the source of misery and shame in Europe. The passion has not altered; but the way of regarding it morally and legally is changed. A scientific investigator ought not to take changes of public opinion into account when he is analysing a psychological peculiarity . . .

His conclusion therefore is that the aberrations of the sexual sense, including its inversion, are matters for the physician rather than the judge, for therapeutics rather than punishment, and that representatives of the medical faculty ought to sit upon the bench as advisers or assessors when persons accused of outrages against decency come to trial.

As the final result of this analysis, Moreau classifies sexual inversion with erotomania, nymphomania, satyriasis, bestiality, rape, profanation of corpses, etc., as the symptom of a grave lesion of the procreative sense. He seeks to save its victims from the prison by delivering them over to the asylum. His moral sentiments are so revolted that he does not even entertain the question whether their instincts are natural and healthy though abnormal. Lastly, he refuses to face the aspects of this psychological anomaly which are forced upon the student of ancient Hellas. He does not even take into account the fact, patent to experienced observers, that simple folk not unfrequently display no greater disgust for the abnormalities of sexual appetite than they do for its normal manifestations.

Die krankhaften Erscheinungen des Geschlechtssinnes.
B. Tarnowsky. Berlin, Hirschwald, 1886.

This is avowedly an attempt to distinguish the morbid kinds of sexual perversion from the merely vicious, and to enforce the necessity of treating the former not as criminal but as pathologic. "The forensic physician discerns corruption, oversatiated sensuality, deep-rooted vice, perverse will, etc., where the clinical observer recognizes with certainty a morbid condition of the patient marked by typical steps of development and termination. Where the one wishes to punish immorality, the other pleads for the necessity of methodical therapeutic treatment."

The author is a Russian, whose practice in St. Petersburg has brought him into close professional relations with the male prostitutes and habitual pederasts of that capital.

Therefore he is able to speak with authority, on the ground of a quite exceptional knowledge of the moral and physical disturbances connected with sodomy. I cannot but think that the very peculiarities of his experience have led him to form incomplete theories . . .

Psychopathia Sexualis, mit besonderer Berücksichtigung der
Conträren Sexualempfindung
Von Dr. R. v. Krafft-Ebing. Stuttgart, Enke, 1889.

Krafft-Ebing took the problem of sexual inversion up, when it had been already investigated by a number of pioneers and predecessors. They mapped the ground out, and established a kind of psychical chart. We have seen the medical system growing in the works of Moreau and Tarnowsky. If anything, Krafft-Ebing's treatment suffers from too much subdivision and parade of classification. However, it is only by following the author in his differentiation of the several species that we can form a conception of his general theory, and of the extent of the observations upon which this is based. He starts with (A) Sexual inversion as an acquired morbid phenomenon. Then he reviews (B) Sexual inversion as an inborn morbid phenomenon.

(A). "Sexual feeling and sexual instinct," he begins, "remain latent, except in obscure foreshadowings and impulses, until the time when the organs of procreation come to be developed. The exciting or efficient cause is sexual abuse, and more particularly onanism. The etiological centre of gravity has to be sought in hereditary disease; *and I think it questionable whether an untainted individual is capable of homosexual feelings at all."*

Krafft-Ebing's theory seems then to be that all cases of acquired sexual inversion may be ascribed in the first place to morbid predispositions inherited by the patient (*Belastung*), and in the second place to onanism as the exciting cause of the latent neuropathic ailment.

He excludes the hypothesis of a physiological and healthy deflection from the normal rule of sex. "I think it questionable," he says, whether the untainted individual (*das unbelastete Individuum*) is capable of homosexual feelings at all." The importance of this sentence will be apparent when we come to deal with Krafft-Ebing's account of congenital sexual inversion, which he establishes upon a large induction of cases observed in his own practice.

For the present, we have the right to assume that Krafft-Ebing regards sexual inversion, whether "acquired" or "congenital," as a form of inherited neuropathy (Belastung). In cases where it seems to be "acquired", he lays stress upon the habit of self-pollution.

This is how he states his theory of onanism as an exciting cause of inherited neuropathy, resulting in sexual inversion. The habit of self-abuse prepares the patient for abnormal appetites by weakening his nervous force, degrading his sexual imagination, and inducing hypersensibility in his sexual apparatus. Partial impotence is not unfrequently exhibited. In consequence of this sophistication of his nature, the victim of inherited neuropathy and onanism feels shy with women, and finds it convenient to frequent persons of his own sex. In other words, it is supposed to be easier for an individual thus broken down at the centres of his nervous life to defy the law and to demand sexual gratification from men than to consort with venal women in a brothel.

Krafft-Ebing assumes that males who have been born with neuropathic ailments of an indefinite kind will masturbate, destroy their virility, and then embark upon a course of vice which offers incalculable dangers, inconceivable difficulties, and inexpressible repugnances. That is the theory. But whence, if not from some overwhelming appetite, do the demoralized victims of self-abuse derive courage for facing the obstacles which a career of sexual inversion carries with it in our civilization? One would have thought that such people, if they could not approach a prostitute in a brothel, would have been unable to solicit a healthy man upon the streets. The theory seems to be constructed in order to elude the fact that the persons designated are driven by a natural impulse into paths far more beset with difficulties than those of normal libertines . . .

The invocation of heredity in problems of this kind is always hazardous. We only throw the difficulty of explanation further back. At what point of the world's history was the morbid taste acquired? If none but tainted individuals are capable of homosexual feelings, how did these feelings first come into existence? On the supposition that neuropathy forms a necessary condition of abnormal instinct, is it generic neuropathy or a specific type of that disorder? If generic, can valid reasons be adduced for regarding nervous malady in any of its aspects (hysteria in the mother, insanity in the father) as the cause of so peculiarly differentiated an affection of the sexual appetite? If specific, that is if the ancestors of the patient must have been afflicted with sexual inversion, in what way did they acquire it, supposing all untainted individuals to be incapable of the feeling?

At this moment of history there is probably no individual in Europe who has not inherited some portion of a neuropathic strain. If that be granted, everybody is liable to sexual inversion, and the principle of heredity becomes purely theoretical.

That sexual inversion may be and actually is transmitted, like any other quality, appears to be proved by the history of well-known families both in England and in Germany. That it is not unfrequently exhibited by persons who have a bad ancestral record, may be taken for demonstrated. In certain cases we are justified then in regarding it as the sign or concomitant of nervous maladies. But the evidence of ancient Greece and Rome, of what Burton calls the "sotadic races" at the present time, of European schools and prisons, ought to make us hesitate before we commit ourselves to Krafft-Ebing's theory that hereditary affliction is a necessary predisposing cause . . .

(B). Ultimately, Krafft-Ebing attacks the problems of what he calls "the innate morbid phenomenon" of sexual inversion.

Casper, continues Krafft-Ebing, thoroughly diagnosed the phenomenon. Griesinger referred it to hereditary affliction. Westphal defined it as "a congenital inversion of the sexual feeling, together with a consciousness of its morbidity." Ulrichs explained it by the presence of a feminine soul in a male body, and gave the name *Urning* to its subjects. Gley suggested that a female brain was combined with masculine glands of sex. Magnan hypothesized a woman's brain in a man's body.

Krafft-Ebing asserts that hardly any of these Urnings are conscious of morbidity. They look upon themselves as unfortunate mainly because law and social prejudice stand in the way of their natural indulgence. He also takes for proof, together with all the authorities he cites, that the abnormal sexual appetite is constitutional and inborn.

Krafft-Ebing, as might have been expected, refers the phenomenon to functional degeneration dependent upon neuropathic conditions in the patient, which are mainly derived from hereditary affliction . . .

Sexual inversion, in persons of the third main-species, has reached its final development. Descending, if we follow Krafft-Ebing's categories, from acquired to innate inversion, dividing the latter into psychopathic hermaphrodites and Urnings, then subdividing Urnings into those who retain their masculine habit and those who develop a habit analogous to that of females, we come in this last class to the most striking phenomenon of inverted sex. Here the soul which is doomed to love a man, and is nevertheless imprisoned in a male body, strives to convert that body to feminine uses so entirely that the marks of sex, except in the determined organs of sex, shall be obliterated. And sometimes it appears that the singular operation of nature, with which we are occupied in this Essay, goes even further. The inverted bias given to the sexual appetite, as part of the spiritual nature of the man, can never quite transmute male organs into female organs of procreation. But it modifies the bony structure of the body, the form of face, the fleshly and muscular integuments, to such an obvious extent that Krafft-Ebing thinks himself justified in placing a separate class of androgynous being (with their gynandrous correspondents) at the end of the extraordinary process.

At this point it will be well to present a scheme of his analysis under the form of a table.

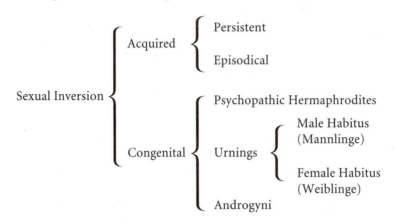

What is the rational explanation of the facts presented to us by the analysis which I have formulated in this table, cannot as yet be thoroughly determined. We do not know enough about the law of sex in human beings to advance a theory. Krafft-Ebing and writers of his school are at present inclined to refer them all to diseases of the nervous centres, inherited, congenital, excited by early habits of self-abuse. The inadequacy of this method I have already attempted to set forth; and I have also called attention to the fact that it does not sufficiently account for phenomena known to us through history and through every-day experience . . .

Cesare Lombroso. "Der Verbrecher in Anthropologischer, Aerztlicher und Juristischer Beziehung."

This famous book, which has contributed so much to a revolution of opinion regarding crime and its punishment in Italy, contains a searching inquiry into the psychological nature, physical peculiarities, habits, and previous history of criminals. It is, in fact, a study of the criminal temperament. Lombroso deals in the main, as is natural, with murder, theft, rape, cruelty, and their allied species. But he includes sexual inversion in the category of crimes, and regards the abnormal appetites as signs of that morbid condition into which he eventually resolves the criminal impulse.

Wishing to base his doctrine on a sound foundation, Lombroso begins with what may be termed the embryology of crime. He finds unnatural vices frequent among horses, donkeys, cattle, insects, fowls, dogs, ants. The phenomenon, he says, is usually observable in cases where the male animal has been excluded from intercourse with females. Having established his general position that what we call crimes of violence, robbery, murder, cruelty, blood-thirstiness, cannibalism, unnatural lust, etc., exist among the brutes—in fact that most of these crimes form the rule and not the exception in their lives—he passes on to the consideration of the savage man . . .

Lombroso arrives then at the conclusion that what civilised humanity punishes as a crime, is the law of nature in brutes, and persists as a normal condition among savages, and displays itself in the habits and instincts of children. The moral instinct itself is therefore slowly elaborated out of crime in the course of generations by whole races, and in the course of infancy and adolescence in the individual. The habitual criminal, who remains a criminal in his maturity, in whom crime is inborn and ineradicable, who cannot develop a moral sense, he explains at first by atavism. A large section of his volume is devoted to anthropometrical observations . . .

Having started with the hypothesis of atavism, and adopted the term "born criminal," he later on identifies "innate crime" with "moral insanity," and illustrates both by the phenomena of epilepsy.

Be this as it may, whether we regard offenders against law and ethic as "born criminals," or as "morally insane," or whether we transcend the distinction implied in these two terms, Lombroso maintains that there is no good in trying to deal with them by punishment. They ought to be treated by life-long sequestration in asylums and rigidly forbidden to perpetuate the species. That is the conclusion to which the whole of his long argument is carried. He contends that the prevalent juristic conception of crime rests upon ignorance of nature, brute life, savagery, and the gradual emergence of morality. So radical a revolution in ideas, which gives new meaning to the words sin and conscience, which removes moral responsibility, and which substitutes the anthropologist and the physician for the judge and jury, cannot be carried out even by its fervent apostle, without some want of severe logic. Thus we find Lombroso frequently drawing distinctions between "habitual" or "born" criminals and what he calls "occasional" criminals, without explaining the phenomenon of "occasional crime" and saying how he thinks this ought to be regarded by society. Moreover, he almost wholly ignores the possibility of correcting criminal tendencies by appeal to reason, by establishing habits of self-restraint, and by the employment of such means as hypnotic suggestion . . .

The final word upon Lombroso's book is this: Having started with the natural history of crime, as a prime constituent in nature and humanity, which only becomes crime through the development of social morality, and which survives atavistically in persons ill adapted to their civilized environment, he suddenly turns round and identifies the crime thus analysed with morbid nerve-conditions, malformations, and moral insanity. Logically, it is impossible to effect this coalition of two radically different conceptions. If crime was not crime but nature in the earlier stages, and only appeared as crime under the conditions of advancing culture, its manifestation as a survival in certain individuals ought to be referred to nature, and cannot be relegated to the category of physical or mental disease. Savages are savages, but not lunatics or epileptics . . .

This is powerfully yet temperately written. It confirms what I have attempted to establish while criticizing the medical hypothesis; and raises the further question whether the phenomenon of sexual inversion ought not to be approached from the point of view of embryology rather than of psychical pathology. In other words, is not the true Urning to be regarded as a person born with sexual instincts improperly correlated to his sexual organs? This he can be without any inherited or latent morbidity; and the nervous anomalies discovered in him when he falls at last beneath the observation of physicians, may be not the evidence of an originally tainted constitution, but the consequence of unnatural conditions to which he has been exposed from the age of puberty.

Literature — Historical, Anthropological

. . . In England an essay appended to the last volume of Sir Richard Burton's *Arabian Nights* made a considerable stir upon its first appearance. The author endeavoured to coordinate a large amount of miscellaneous matter, and to frame a general theory regarding the origin and prevalence of homosexual passions. However, his erudition is incomplete; and though he possesses a copious store of anthropological details, he is not at the proper point of view for discussing the topic philosophically. For example, he takes for granted that "Pederasty," as he calls it, is everywhere and always what the vulgar think it. He seems to have no notion of the complicated psychology of Urnings, revealed to us by their recently published confessions in French and German medical and legal works. Still his views deserve consideration.

Burton regards the phenomenon as "geographical and climatic, not racial. . . . The only physical cause for the practice which suggests itself to me, and that must be owned to be purely conjectural, is that within the Sotadic Zone there is a blending of the masculine and feminine temperament, a crasis which elsewhere occurs only sporadically." So far as it goes, this suggestion rests upon ground admitted to be empirically sound by the medical writers we have already examined, and vehemently declared to be indisputable as a fact of physiology by Ulrichs, whom I shall presently introduce to my readers. But Burton makes no effort to account for the occurrence of this combination of masculine and feminine temperaments in the Sotadic Zone at large, and for its sporadic appearance in other regions. Would it not be more philosophical to conjecture that the temperament, if that exists at all, takes place universally; but that the consequences are only tolerated in certain parts of the globe, which he defines as the Sotadic Zone? Ancient Greece and Rome permitted them. Modern Greece and Italy have excluded them to the same extent as Northern European nations. North and South America, before the Conquest, saw no harm in them. Since its colonization by Europeans, they have been discountenanced. The phenomenon cannot therefore be regarded as specifically geographical climatic. Besides, there is one fact mentioned by Burton which ought to make him doubt his geographical theory. He says that, after the conquest of Algiers, the French troops were infected to an enormous extent by the habits they had acquired there, and from them it spread so far and wide into civilian society that "the vice may be said to have been democratized in cities and large towns." This surely proves that north of the Sotadic Zone males are neither physically incapable of the acts involved in abnormal passion, nor gifted with an insuperable disgust for them. Law, and the public opinion generated by law and religious teaching, have been deterrent causes in those regions. The problem is therefore not geographical and climatic, but social. Again, may it not be suggested that the absence of "the vice" among the Negroes and Negroid races of South Africa, noticed by Burton, is the result of their excellent customs of sexual initiation and education at the age of puberty—customs which it is the shame of modern civilization to have left unimitated?

However this may be, Burton regards the instinct as natural, not *contre nature*, and says that its patients "deserve, not prosecution but the pitiful care of the physician and the study of the psychologist." . . .

After perusing what physicians, historians, and anthropologists have to say about sexual inversion, there is good reason for us to feel uneasy as to the present condition of our laws. And yet it might be argued that anomalous desires are not always maladies, not always congenital, not always psychical passions. In some cases they must surely be vices deliberately adopted out of lustfulness, wanton curiosity, and seeking after sensual refinements. The difficult question still remains then—how to repress vice, without acting unjustly toward the naturally abnormal, the unfortunate, and the irresponsible . . .

Literature — Idealistic

To speak of Walt Whitman at all in connection with . . . sexual inversion seems paradoxical. At the outset it must be definitely stated that he has nothing to do with anomalous, abnormal, vicious, or diseased forms of the emotion which males entertain for males. Yet no man in the modern world has expressed so strong a conviction that "mainly attachment," "athletic love," "the high towering love of comrades," is a main factor in human life, a virtue upon which society will have to rest, and a passion equal in its permanence and intensity to sexual affection.

He assumes, without raising the question, that the love of man for man coexists with the love of man for woman in one and the same individual. The relation of the two modes of feeling is clearly stated in this poem:

> Fast-anchored, eternal, O love! O woman I love;
> O bride! O wife! More resistless than I can tell you, the thought of you!
> Then separate, as disembodied, or another born,
> Ethereal, the last athletic reality, my consolation;
> I ascend—I float in the regions of your love, O man,
> O sharer of my roving life.

Neuropathic Urnings are not hinted at in any passage of his works. As his friend and commentator Mr. Burroughs puts it: "The sentiment is primitive, athletic, taking form in all manner of large and homely out-of-door images, and springs, as anyone may see, directly from the heart and experience of the poet."

This being so, Whitman never suggests that comradeship may occasion the development of physical desires. But then he does not in set terms condemn these desires, or warn his disciples against them. To a Western boy he says:

> "If you be not silently selected by lovers, and do not silently select lovers,
> Of what use is it that you seek to become eleve of mine?"

Like Plato, in the Phedrus, Whitman describes an enthusiastic type of masculine emotion, leaving its private details to the moral sense and special inclination of the person concerned.

The language of "Calamus" (that section of *Leaves of Grass* which is devoted to the gospel of comradeship) has a passionate glow, a warmth of emotional tone, beyond anything to which the modern world is used in the celebration of the love of friends. It recalls to our mind the early Greek enthusiasm—that fellowship in arms which flourished among Dorian tribes, and made a chivalry for prehistoric Hellas. Nor does the poet himself appear to be unconscious that there are dangers and difficulties involved in the highly-pitched emotions he is praising. The whole tenor of two mysterious compositions, entitled "Whoever you are, Holding me now in Hand," and "Trickle, Drops," suggests an underlying sense of spiritual conflict. The following poem, again, is sufficiently significant and typical to call for literal transcription:

> Earth, my likeness!
> Though you look so impressive, ample and spheric here,
> I now suspect that is not all;
> I now suspect there is something fierce in you, eligible to burst forth;
> For an athletic is enamoured of me—and I of him,
> But toward him there is something fierce and terrible in me, eligible to burst forth,
> I dare not tell it in words—not even in these songs.

The reality of Whitman's feeling, the intense delight which he derives from the personal presence and physical contact of a beloved man, find expression in "A Glimpse," "Recorders ages hence," "When I heard at the Close of Day," "I saw in Louisiana a Live-Oak growing," "Long I thought that Knowledge alone would content me," "O Tan-faced Prairie-Boy," and "Vigil Strange I kept on the Field one Night."

It is clear then that, in his treatment of comradeship, or the impassioned love of man for man, Whitman has struck a key-note, to the emotional intensity of which the modern world is unaccustomed. It therefore becomes of much importance to discover the poet-prophet's *Stimmung*—his radical instinct with regard to the moral quality of the feeling he encourages. Studying his works by their own light, and by the light of their author's character, interpreting each part by reference to the whole and in the spirit of the whole, an impartial critic will, I think, be drawn to the conclusion that what he calls the "adhesiveness" of comradeship is meant to have no interblending with the "amativeness" of sexual love. Personally, it is undeniable that Whitman possesses a specially keen sense of the fine restraint and continence, the cleanliness and chastity, that are inseparable from the perfectly virile and physically complete nature of healthy manhood. Still we may predicate the same ground-qualities in the early Dorians, those martial founders of the institution of Greek Love; and it is notorious to students of Greek civilization that the lofty sentiment of their chivalry was intertwined with singular anomalies in its historical development.

To remove all doubt about Whitman's own intentions when he composed "Calamus," and promulgated his doctrine of impassioned comradeship, I wrote to him, frankly posing the questions which perplexed my mind. The answer I received, dated Camden, New Jersey, U.S.A., August 19, 1890, and which he permits me to make use of, puts the matter beyond all debate, and confirms the conclusions to which I had been led by criticism. He writes as follows: "About the questions on 'Calamus,' etc., they quite daze me. *Leaves of Grass* is only to be rightly construed by and within its own atmosphere and essential character—all its pages and pieces so coming strictly under. That the Calamus part has ever allowed the possibility of such construction as mentioned is terrible. I am fain to hope the pages themselves are not to be even mentioned for such gratuitous and quite at the time undreamed and unwished possibility of morbid inferences—which are disavowed by me and seem damnable."

No one who knows anything about Walt Whitman will for a moment doubt his candour and sincerity. Therefore the man who wrote "Calamus" and preached the gospel of comradeship, entertains feelings at least as hostile to sexual inversion as any law abiding humdrum Anglo-Saxon could desire. It is obvious that he has not even taken the phenomena of abnormal instinct into account. Else he must have foreseen that, human nature being what it is, we cannot expect to eliminate all sensual alloy from emotions raised to a high pitch of passionate intensity, and that permanent elements within the midst of our society will imperil the absolute purity of the ideal he attempts to establish.

However, these considerations do not affect the spiritual nature of that ideal. After acknowledging, what Whitman has omitted to perceive, that there are inevitable points of contact between sexual inversion and his doctrine of comradeship, the question now remains whether he has not suggested the way whereby abnormal instincts may be moralized and raised to higher value. In other words, are those instincts provided in "Calamus" with the means of their salvation from the filth and mire of brutal appetite? It is difficult to answer this question; for the issue involved is nothing less momentous than the possibility of evoking a new chivalrous enthusiasm, analogous to that of primitive Hellenic society, from emotions which are at present classified among the turpitudes of human nature.

Let us look a little closer at the expression which Whitman has given to his own feelings about friendship. The first thing that strikes us is the mystic emblem he has chosen for masculine love. That is the water-plant, or scented rush, called Calamus, which springs in wild places, "in paths, untrodden, in the growth by margins of pond-waters." He has chosen these "emblematic and capricious blades" because of their shyness, their aromatic perfume, their aloofness from the patent life of the world. He calls them "sweet leaves, pink-tongued roots, timid leaves," "scented herbage of my breast." Finally, he says:

Here my last words, and the most baffling,
Here the frailest leaves of me, and yet my strongest-lasting,
Here I shade down and hide my thoughts—I do not expose them,
And yet they expose me more than all my other poems.

The manliness of the emotion, which is thus so shyly, mystically indicated, appears in the magnificent address to soldiers at the close of the great war: "Over the Carnage rose Prophetic a Voice." Its tenderness emerges in the elegy on a slain comrade:

Vigil for boy of responding kisses, (never again on earth responding:)
Vigil for comrade swiftly slain—vigil I never forget, how as day brightened,
I rose from the chill ground, and folded my soldier well in his blanket,
And buried him where he fell.

Its pathos and clinging intensity transpire through the last lines of the following piece, which may have been suggested by the legends of David and Jonathan, Achilles and Patroclus, Orestes and Pylades:

When I peruse the conquered fame of heroes, and the victories of
mighty generals,
I do not envy the generals,
Nor the president in his Presidency, nor the rich in his great house;
But when I read of the brotherhood of lovers, how it was with them,
How through life, through dangers, odium, unchanging, long and long,
Through youth, and through middle and old age, how unfaltering, how affectionate
and faithful they were,
Then I am pensive—I hastily put down the book, and walk away, filled with the bit-
terest envy.

But Whitman does not conceive of comradeship as a merely personal possession, delightful to the friends it links in bonds of amity. He regards it essentially as a social and political virtue. This human emotion is destined to cement society and to render common-wealths inviolable. Reading some of his poems, we are carried back to ancient Greece—to Plato's Symposium, to Philip gazing on the Sacred Band of Thebans after the fight at Chaeronea.

I dream'd in a dream, I saw a city invincible to the attacks of the whole of the rest of
the earth:
I dream'd that was the new City of Friends;
Nothing was greater there than the quality of robust love—it led the rest;
It was seen every hour in the actions of the men of that city,
And in all their looks and words.

And again:

I believe the main purport of these States is to found a superb friendship, exalté, previously unknown,
Because I perceive it waits, and has been always waiting, latent in all men.

And once again:

Come, I will make the continent indissoluble;
I will make the most splendid race the sun ever yet shone upon;
I will make divine magnetic lands,
                                    With the love of comrades,
                                    With the life-long love of comrades.
I will plant companionship thick as trees all along the shores of America, and along
the shores of the great lakes, and all over the prairies;
I will make inseparable cities, with their arms about each other's necks;
                                    By the love of comrades,

By the manly love of comrades.
For you these from me, O Democracy, to serve you ma femme!
For you, for you I am thrilling these songs.

In the company of Walt Whitman we are very far away from Gibbon and Carlier, from Tardieux and Casper-Liman, from Krafft-Ebing and Ulrichs. What indeed has this "superb friendship, exalté, previously unknown," which "waits, and has been always waiting, latent in all men," that "something fierce in me, eligible to burst forth," "ethereal comradeship," "the last athletic reality"—what has all this in common with the painful topic of the preceding sections of my essay?

It has this in common with it. Whitman recognises among the sacred emotions and social virtues, destined to regenerate political life and to cement nations, an intense, jealous, throbbing, sensitive, expectant love of man for man: a love which yearns in absence, droops under the sense of neglect, revives at the return of the beloved: a love that finds honest delight in hand touching, meeting lips, hours of privacy, close personal contact. He proclaims this love to be not only a daily fact in the present, but also a saving and ennobling aspiration. While he expressly repudiates, disowns, and brands as "damnable" all "morbid inferences" which may be drawn by malevolence or vicious cunning from this doctrine, he is prepared to extend the gospel of comradeship to the whole human race. He expects democracy, the new social and political medium, the new religious ideal of mankind, to develop and extend "that fervid comradeship," and by its means to counterbalance and to spiritualize what is vulgar and materialistic in the modern world. "Democracy," he maintains, "infers such loving comradeship, as its most inevitable twin or counterpart, without which it will be incomplete, in vain, and incapable of perpetuating itself."

If this be not a dream, if he is right in believing that "threads of manly friendship, fond and loving, pure and sweet, strong and life-long, carried to degrees hitherto unknown," will penetrate the organism of society, "not only giving tone to individual character, and making it unprecedentedly emotional, muscular, heroic, and refined, but having deepest relations to general politics"—then are we perhaps justified in foreseeing here the advent of an enthusiasm which shall rehabilitate those outcast instincts, by giving them a spiritual atmosphere, an environment of recognized and healthy emotions, wherein to expand at liberty and purge away the grossness and the madness of their pariahdom?

This prospect, like all ideals, until they are realized in experience, may seem fantastically visionary. Moreover, the substance of human nature is so mixed that it would perhaps be fanatical to expect from Whitman's chivalry of "adhesiveness" a more immaculate purity than was attained by the medieval chivalry of "amativeness." Still that medieval chivalry, the great emotional product of feudalism, though it fell short of its own aspiration, bequeathed incalculable good to modern society by refining and clarifying the crudest of male appetites. In like manner, the democratic chivalry, announced by Whitman, may be destined to absorb, control, and elevate those darker, more mysterious, apparently abnormal appetites, which we have seen to be widely diffused and ineradicable in the ground-work of human nature.

Returning from the dream, the vision of a future possibility, it will at any rate be conceded that Whitman has founded comradeship, the enthusiasm which binds man to man in fervent love, upon a natural basis. Eliminating classical associations of corruption, ignoring the perplexed questions of a guilty passion doomed by law and popular antipathy to failure, he begins anew with sound and primitive humanity. There he discovers "a superb friendship, exalté, previously unknown." He perceives that "it waits, and has been always waiting, latent in all men." His method of treatment, fearless and uncowed by any thought of evil, his touch upon the matter, chaste and wholesome and aspiring, reveal the possibility of restoring in all innocence to human life a portion of its alienated or unclaimed moral birthright. The aberrations we have been discussing in this treatise are perhaps the morbid symptoms of suppression, of hypertrophy, of ignorant misregulation, in a genuine emotion capable of being raised to good by sympathetic treatment.

It were well to close upon this note. The half, as the Greeks said, is more than the whole; and the time has not yet come to raise the question whether the love of man for man shall be elevated through a hitherto unapprehended chivalry to nobler powers, even as the barbarous love of man for woman once was. This question at the present moment is deficient in actuality. The world cannot be invited to entertain it.

Epilogue

The conclusions to which I am led by this enquiry into sexual inversion are that its several manifestations may be classified under the following categories: 1 Forced abstinence from intercourse with females, or *faute de mieux;* 2 Wantonness and curious seeking after novel pleasure; 3 Pronounced morbidity; 4 Inborn instinctive preference for the male and indifference to the female sex; 5 Epochs of history when the habit has become established and endemic in whole nations.

Under the first category, we group the phenomena presented by schools, prisons, convents, ships, garrisons in solitary stations, nomadic tribes of marauding conquerors. Under the second belong those individuals who amuse themselves with experiments in sensual pleasure, men jaded with ordinary sexual indulgence, and indifferent voluptuaries. It is possible that something morbid or abnormal usually marks this class.

Under the third we assign clear cases of hereditary malady, in which a want of self control is prominent, together with sufferers from nervous lesion, wounds, epilepsy, senile brain softening, in so far as these physical disturbances are complicated with abnormal passions.

The fourth includes the whole class of Urnings, who have been hitherto ignored by medical investigators, and on whose numerical importance Ulrichs has perhaps laid exaggerated stress. These individuals behave precisely like persons of normal sexual proclivities, display no signs of insanity, and have no morbid constitutional diathesis to account for their peculiarity.

Under the existing conditions of European society, these four categories exist sporadically. That is to say, the members of them are found scattered through all communities, but are nowhere recognized except by the penal code and the medical profession. In the fifth category, we are brought face to face with the problem offered by ancient Hellas, by Persia, by Afghan, by the peoples of what Burton calls the Sotadic Zone. However we may account for the origin of sexual inversion, the instinct has through usage, tradition, and social toleration, passed here into the nature of the race; so that the four previous categories are confounded, or, if distinguished, are only separable in the same way as the vicious and morbid affections of the ordinary sexual appetite may be differentiated from its healthier manifestations.

Returning to the first four categories, which alone have any importance for a modern European, we perceive that only one of them, the third, (pronounced morbidity) is positively morbid, and only one, the second, (wantonness and curious seeking after novel pleasure) is, *ipso facto,* vicious. The first is immoral in the same sense as all incontinence (forced abstinence from intercourse with females), including self-abuse, fornication, and so forth, practised *faute de mieux,* is immoral; but it cannot be called either morbid or positively vicious, because the habit in question springs up under extrasocial circumstances. The members of the fourth category are abnormal through their constitution. Whether we refer that abnormality to atavism, or to some hitherto unapprehended deviation from the rule in their sexual conformation, there is no proof that they are the subjects of disease. At the same time it is certain that they are not deliberately vicious.

The treatment of sexual inversion by society and legislation follows the view taken of its origin and nature. Ever since the age of Justinian, it has been regarded as an unqualified crime against God, the order of the world, and the state. This opinion, which has been incorporated in the codes of all the Occidental races, sprang originally from the conviction that sterile passions are injurious to the tribe by checking propagation. Religion adopted this view, and, through the legend of Sodom and Gomorrah, taught that God was ready to punish whole nations with violent destruction if they practised "the unmentionable vice." Advancing civilization, at the same time, sought in every way to limit and regulate the sexual appetite; and while doing so, it naturally excluded those forms which were not agreeable to the majority, which possessed no obvious utility, and which *prima facie* seemed to violate the cardinal laws of human nature.

Social feeling, moulded by religion, by legislation, by civility, and by the persistent antipathies of the majority, regards sexual inversion with immitigable abhorrence. It does not distinguish between the categories I have indicated, but includes all species under the common condemnation of crime.

Meanwhile, of late years, we have come to perceive that the phenomena presented by sexual inversion cannot be so roughly dealt with. Two great nations, the French and the Italians, by the "Code Napoleon" and the "Codice Penale" of 1889, remove these phenomena from the category of crime into that of immorality at worst. That is to say, they place the intercourse of males with males upon the same legal ground as the normal sex relation. They punish violence, protect minors, and provide for the maintenance of public decency. Within these limitations, they recognize the right of adults to deal as they choose with their persons.

The new school of anthropologists and psychological physicians study sexual inversion partly on the lines of historical evolution, and partly from the point of view of disease. Mixing up atavism and heredity with nervous malady in the individual, they wish to substitute medical treatment for punishment, lifelong sequestration in asylums for terms of imprisonment differing in duration according to the offence.

Neither society nor science entertains the notion that those instincts which the laws of France and Italy tolerate, under certain restrictions, can be simply natural in a certain percentage of male persons. Up to the present time the Urning has not been considered as a sport of nature in her attempt to differentiate the sexes. Ulrichs is the only European who has maintained this view in a long series of polemical and imperfectly scientific works. Yet facts brought daily beneath the notice of open-eyed observers prove that Ulrichs is justified in his main contention. Society lies under the spell of ancient terrorism and coagulated errors. Science is either wilfully hypocritical or radically misinformed.

Walt Whitman, in America, regards what he calls "manly love" as destined to be a leading virtue of democratic nations, and the source of a new chivalry. But he does not define what he means by "manly love." And he emphatically disavows any "morbid inferences" from his doctrine as "damnable."

This is how the matter stands now. The one thing which seems clear is that sexual inversion is no subject for legislation, and that the example of France and Italy might well be followed by other nations. The problem ought to be left to the physician, the moralist, the educator, and finally to the operation of social opinion.

Suggestions on the Subject of Sexual Inversion in Relation to Law and Education

I

§ The laws in force against what are called unnatural offences derive from an edict of Justinian, A.D. 538. The Emperor treated these offences as criminal, on the ground that they brought plagues, famines, earthquakes, and the destruction of whole cities, together with their inhabitants, upon the nations who tolerated them.

II

§ A belief that sexual inversion is a crime against God, nature, and the state pervades all subsequent legislation on the subject. This belief rests on (1) theological conceptions derived from the Scriptures; (2) a dread of decreasing the population; (3) the antipathy of the majority for the tastes of the minority; (4) the vulgar error that antiphysical desires are invariably voluntary, and the result either of inordinate lust or of satiated appetites.

III

§ Scientific investigation has proved in recent years that a very large porportion of persons in whom abnormal sexual inclinations are manifested, possess them from their earliest childhood, that they cannot divert them into normal channels, and that they are powerless to get rid of them. In these cases then, legislation is interfering with the liberty of individuals, under a certain misconception regarding the nature of their offence.

IV

§ Those who support the present laws are therefore bound to prove that the coercion, punishment, and defamation of such persons are justified either (1) by any injury which these persons suffer in health of body or mind, or (2) by any serious danger arising from them to the social organism.

V

§ Experience, confirmed by scientific observation, proves that the temperate indulgence of abnormal sexuality is no more injurious to the individual than a similar indulgence of normal sexuality.

VI

§ In the present state of overpopulation, it is not to be apprehended that a small minority of men exercising sterile and abnormal sexual inclinations should seriously injure society by limiting the increase of the human race.

VII

§ Legislation does not interfere with various forms of sterile intercourse between men and women: (1) prostitution, (2) cohabitation in marriage during the period of pregnancy, (3) artificial precautions against impregnation, and (4) some abnormal modes of congress with the consent of the female. It is therefore in an illogical position, when it interferes with the action of those who are naturally sterile, on the ground of maintaining the numerical standard of the population.

VIII

§ The danger that unnatural vices, if tolerated by the law, would increase until whole nations acquired them, does not seem to be formidable. The position of women in our civilization renders sexual relations among us occidentals different from those of any country—ancient

Greece and Rome, modern Turkey and Persia—where antiphysical habits have hitherto become endemic.

IX

§ In modern France, since the promulgation of the Code Napoleon, sexual inversion has been tolerated under the same restrictions as normal sexuality. That is to say, violence and outrages to public decency are punished, and minors are protected, but adults are allowed to dispose as they like of their own persons. The experience of nearly a century shows that in France, where sexual inversion is not criminal *per se*, there has been no extension of it through society. Competent observers, like agents of police, declare that London, in spite of our penal legislation, is no less notorious for abnormal vice than Paris.

X

§ Italy, by the Penal Code of 1889, adopted the principles of the Code Napoleon on this point. It would be interesting to know what led to this alteration of the Italian law. But it cannot be supposed that the results of the Code Napoleon in France were not fully considered.

XI

§ The severity of the English statutes render them almost incapable of being put in force. In consequence of this, the law is not unfrequently evaded, and crimes are winked at.

XII

§ At the same time our laws encourage blackmailing upon false accusation; and the presumed evasion of their execution places from time to time a vile weapon in the hands of unscrupulous politicians, to attack the Government in office. Examples: the Dublin Castle Scandals of 1884, the Cleveland Street Scandals of 1889.

XIII

§ Those who hold that our penal laws are required by the interests of society, must turn their attention to the higher education. This still rests on the study of the Greek and Latin classics, a literature impregnated with *paiderastia*. It is carried on at public schools, where young men are kept apart from females, and where homosexual vices are frequent. The best minds of our youth are therefore exposed to the influences of a paiderastic literature, at the same time that they acquire the knowledge and experience of unnatural practices. Nor is any trouble taken to correct these adverse influences by physiological instruction in the laws of sex.

XIV

§ The points suggested for consideration are whether England is still justified in restricting the freedom of adult persons, and rendering certain abnormal forms of sexuality criminal, by any real dangers to society: after it has been shown 1 that abnormal inclinations are congenital, natural, and ineradicable in a large percentage of individuals; 2 that we tolerate sterile intercourse of various types between the two sexes; 3 that our legislation has not suppressed the immorality in question; 4 that the operation of the Code Napoleon for nearly a century has not increased this immorality in France; 5 that Italy, with the experience of the Code Napoleon to guide her, adopted its principles in 1889; 6 that the English penalties are rarely inflicted to their full extent; 7 that their existence encourages blackmailing, and their nonenforcement gives occasion for base political agitation; 8 that our higher education is in open contradiction to the spirit of our laws.

1. *That which is everywhere, from everyone, and for all time—Eds.*

Although Oscar Wilde (1856–1900) is one of the most famous of gay men, he is included here not for his explicitly political speech, which was not about homosexuality, but because of the shock effect of his trial and conviction. The event was, in a sense, a "shot heard 'round the world," causing panic among homosexuals, and serving as an incentive to redouble their efforts for legal and social equality, and it became an incitement among moral crusaders, particularly in England in the first quarter of the twentieth century. The trial gave a public face to homosexuality, albeit one of negative stereotype and pathological deviance.

Wilde was accused by the father of his younger lover, Lord Alfred Douglas, of "posing as a sodomite." Wilde sued for libel, but the trial, during which his life and works were publicly examined, backfired and he was eventually prosecuted for buggery. He was found guilty and sentenced to two years of hard labor in prison. We include here a portion of the trial transcript, including Wilde's last statement in court as well as his sentencing hearing.

from

THE TRIAL OF OSCAR WILDE

(1895)

Is it not clear that the love described relates to natural love and unnatural love?—No.

What is the "Love that dare not speak its name"?—"The Love that dare not speak its name" in this century is such a great affection of an elder for a younger man as there was between David and Jonathan, such as Plato made the very basis of his philosophy, and such as you find in the sonnets of Michelangelo and Shakespeare. It is that deep, spiritual affection that is as pure as it is perfect. It dictates and pervades great works of art like those of Shakespeare and Michelangelo, and those two letters of mine, such as they are. It is in this century misunderstood, so much misunderstood that it may be described as the "Love that dare not speak its name," and on account of it I am placed where I am now. It is beautiful, it is fine, it is the noblest form of affection. There is nothing unnatural about it. It is intellectual, and it repeatedly exists between an elder and a younger man, when the elder man has intellect, and the younger man has all the joy, hope and glamour of life before him. That it should be so the world does not understand. The world mocks at it and sometimes puts one in the pillory for it. (Loud applause, mingled with some hisses.)

Mr. JUSTICE CHARLES—If there is the slightest manifestation of feeling I shall have the Court cleared. There must be complete silence preserved.

Cross-examination continued—Then there is no reason why it should be called "Shame"?—Ah, that, you will see, is the mockery of the other love, love which is jealous of friendship and says to it, "You should not interfere."

You were staying at the Savoy Hotel with Lord Alfred Douglas at the beginning of March, 1893?—Yes.

And after that you went into rooms?—Yes.

I understand you to say that the evidence given in this case by the witnesses called in support of the prosecution is absolutely untrue?—Entirely.

Entirely untrue?—Yes.

Did you hear the evidence of the servants from the Savoy?—It is absolutely untrue.

Had you a quarrel with Lord Alfred Douglas in that week?—No; we never did quarrel—perhaps a little difference. Sometimes he said things that pained me and sometimes I said things that pained him.

Had he that week said unkind things?—I always made a point of forgetting whenever he said anything unkind.

I wish to call your attention to the style of your correspondence with Lord Alfred Douglas?—I am ready. I am never ashamed of the style of my writings.

You are fortunate, or shall I say shameless? (Laughter.) I refer to passages in two letters in particular?—Kindly quote them.

In letter number one you use the expression "Your slim gilt soul," and you refer to Lord Alfred's "red rose-leaf lips." The second letter contains the words, "You are the divine thing I want," and describes Lord Alfred's letter as being "delightful, red and yellow wine to me." Do you think that an ordinarily constituted being would address such expressions to a younger man?—I am not happily, I think, an ordinarily constituted being.

It is agreeable to be able to agree with you, Mr. Wilde? (Laughter.)—There is nothing, I assure you, in either letter of which I need be ashamed. The first letter is really a prose poem, and the second more of a literary answer to one Lord Alfred had sent me.

In reference to the incidents alleged against you at the Savoy Hotel, are you prepared to contradict the evidence of the hotel servants?—It is entirely untrue. Can I answer for what hotel servants say years after I have left the hotel? It is childish. I am not responsible for hotel servants. I have stayed at the hotel and been there constantly since.

There is no possibility of mistake? There was no woman with you?—Certainly not.

You had the opportunity of seeing the plea of justification in the Queensberry case, and you saw the different names?—Yes.

At the hearing of that case before Mr. Justice Henn Collins, except the hall porter and yourself no other witness was called?—No.

You had seen Taylor within a few days of the trial?—Yes.

He was not called?—No. He was subpoenaed by the other side. I knew that he was here.

And you knew that while the counsel for Lord Queensberry was addressing the jury, the case was interrupted, a verdict of "Not Guilty" was agreed to, and the jury found that the justification was proved and the libel published for the public benefit?—I was not in Court.

But you knew it?—No, I did not. I knew my counsel had considered it would be impossible to get a verdict on the question as far as the literature went, and it was not for me to dispute their superior wisdom. I was not in Court, nor have I read any account of that trial.

Sentence

(Taylor was placed in the dock beside Wilde.)

Sir EDWARD CLARKE—I have to suggest to your lordship that you will not pass sentence until the next sessions. There is a demurrer on record which has to be argued, and I submit that it would be well to postpone passing sentence in order that that argument may be considered.

Mr. GRAIN—I do not know how far that will affect the case of Mr. Taylor, but I think it would affect him equally. Therefore, if I may re-echo the observation of Sir Edward Clarke, I would make the same application.

The SOLICITOR-GENERAL—I oppose the application. The matter has been argued and decided. It relates to certain counts not included in this indictment; and passing sentence now can in no way affect any argument that may be raised at any future time.

Sir EDWARD CLARKE—The conspiracy counts are contained in the indictment.

Mr. JUSTICE WILLS—But there is a verdict of Not Guilty on them. What is the contention?

Sir EDWARD CLARKE—That the indictment was bad, there being a different mode of trial. In a case of conspiracy the defendants are not capable of being witnesses, but in the other they are capable of giving evidence and they plead to that indictment alone. The demurrer is just as arguable, whatever has taken place since.

Mr. GILL—That question was argued before Mr. Justice Charles, and he held the indictment to be perfectly good.

The SOLICITOR-GENERAL—Sentence can be passed without prejudicing the argument before the Court of Crown Cases Reserved.

Mr. JUSTICE WILLS—Of the correctness of the indictment I have myself no doubt. But, in any case, my passing sentence will not interfere with the arguing of the point raised, and I think it my duty to pass sentence at once. It is not a matter about which I entertain any doubt; and to pass sentence now will in no sense prejudice the result of the inquiry. I think it may be well to complete the proceedings here on other counts.

(To the prisoners)—Oscar Wilde and Alfred Taylor, the crime of which you have been convicted is so bad that one has to put stern restraint upon one's self to prevent one's self from describing, in language which I would rather not use, the sentiments which must rise to the breast of every man of honour who has heard the details of these two terrible trials. That the jury have arrived at a correct verdict in this case I cannot persuade myself to entertain the shadow of a doubt; and I hope, at all events, that those who sometimes imagine that a judge is half-hearted in the cause of decency and morality because he takes care no prejudice shall enter into the case, may see that that is consistent at least with the utmost sense of indignation at the horrible charges brought home to both of you.

It is no use for me to address you. People who can do these things must be dead to all sense of shame, and one cannot hope to produce any effect upon them. It is the worst case I have ever tried. That you, Taylor, kept a kind of male brothel it is impossible to doubt. And that you, Wilde, have been the centre of a circle of extensive corruption of the most hideous kind among young men, it is equally impossible to doubt.

I shall, under such circumstances, be expected to pass the severest sentence that the law allows. In my judgment it is totally inadequate for such a case as this. The sentence of the Court is that each of you be imprisoned and kept to hard labour for two years.

[Some cries of "Oh! Oh!" and "Shame" were heard in Court.]

OSCAR WILDE—And I? May I say nothing, my lord?

[His lordship made no reply beyond a wave of the hand to the warders, who hurried the prisoners out of sight.]

The JURY were discharged.

The Court adjourned.

EDWARD CARPENTER

Edward Carpenter (1844–1929) was one of the preeminent figures in the "liberationist" strain of gay political thought. His work theorized the situation of women together with homosexuals with regard to sexual oppression, analyzing how homoerotics leads to intermingling between different social strata and cultural backgrounds thus paving the way for socialism and universalism. He posited sexual expression within an ethical and scientific realm, thereby countering with an ethos of self-actualization, the reaction of religious inspired moral purity campaigns after the Oscar Wilde conviction.

Carpenter was, like his elder, Symonds, an admirer of Whitman, and visited him in 1877. He was inspired by U.S. transcendentalist Henry David Thoreau to support the English socialist movement led by William Morris. Carpenter's thought reflects an anti-commercial, back-to-nature, spiritually informed discarding of the remnants of the old society in preparation for a new one, what he called "exfoliation." Indeed, he was trained for the clergy at upper-class Cambridge Divinity School, traveled to India, where he learned first hand the Hindu and Buddhist philosophy that informed his thought, and rather than remaining in the Church of England, devoted his energies to organizing and lecturing on socialism, feminism, prison reform, and gay liberation. His lover, George Merrill, was of working-class background; although they may both have had other erotic relationships, they lived together for thirty years.

The excerpt here is a compilation of Carpenter's essays written and published separately between 1894 and 1899; they were finally published together in 1908. His conceptualization of the "intermediate sex" takes off from the third-sex theory. He coins the term "homogenic" rather than "homosexual" because of the latter's half-Greek, half-Latin derivation. Homogenic love, referenced in his writings to the *berdache*, shaman, and *samurai*, points the way, through sexuality, toward a free society. [*Author's notes have been deleted from this excerpt—Eds.*]

from

THE INTERMEDIATE SEX

(1894–1907)

Edward Carpenter

There are transitional forms between the metals and non-metals; between chemical combinations and simple mixtures, between animals and plants, between phanerogams and cryptogams, and between mammals and birds . . . The improbability may henceforth be taken for granted of finding in Nature a sharp cleavage between all that is masculine on the one side and all that is feminine on the other; or that any living being is so simple in this respect that it can be put wholly on one side, or wholly on the other, of the line.

—O. Weininger

1. Introductory

The subject dealt with in this book is one of great, and one may say growing, importance.

Whether it is that the present period is one of large increase in the numbers of men and women of an intermediate or mixed temperament, or whether it merely is that it is a period in which more than usual attention happens to be accorded to them, the fact certainly remains that the subject has great actuality and is pressing upon us from all sides. It is recognised that anyhow the number of persons occupying an intermediate position between the two sexes is very great, that they play a considerable part in general society, and that they necessarily present and embody many problems which, both for their own sakes and that of society, demand solution. The literature of the question has in consequence already grown to be very extensive, especially on the Continent, and includes a great quantity of scientific works, medical treatises, literary essays, romances, historical novels, poetry, etc. And it is now generally admitted that some knowledge and enlightened understanding of the subject is greatly needed for the use of certain classes—as, for instance, medical men, teachers, parents, magistrates, judges, and the like.

That there are distinctions and gradations of Soul-material in relation to Sex—that the inner psychical affections and affinities shade off and graduate, in a vast number of instances, most subtly from male to female, and not always in obvious correspondence with the outer bodily sex—is a thing evident enough to anyone who considers the subject; nor could any good purpose well be served by ignoring this fact—even if it were possible to do so. It is easy of course (as some do) to classify all these mixed or intermediate types as *bad*. It is also easy (as some do) to argue that just because they combine opposite qualities they are likely to be *good* and valuable. But the subtleties and complexities of Nature cannot be despatched in this off-hand manner. The great probability is that, as in any other class of human beings, there will be among these too, good and bad, high and low, worthy and unworthy—some perhaps exhibiting through their double temperament a rare and beautiful flower of humanity, others a perverse and tangled ruin.

Before the facts of Nature we have to preserve a certain humility and reverence; nor rush in with our preconceived and obstinate assumptions. Though these gradations of human type have always, and among all peoples, been more or less known and recognised, yet their frequency today, or even the concentration of attention on them, may be the indication of some important change actually in progress. We do *not* know, in fact, what possible evolutions are to come, or what new forms, of permanent place and value, are being already slowly differentiated from the surrounding mass of humanity. It may be that, as at some past period of evolution the worker-bee was without doubt differentiated from the two ordinary bee-sexes, so at the present time certain new types of human kind may be emerging, which will have an important part to play in the societies of the future—even though for the moment their appearance is attended by a good deal of confusion and misapprehension. It may be so; or it may not. We do not know; and the best attitude we can adopt is one of sincere and dispassionate observation of facts.

Of course wherever this subject touches on the domain of love we may expect difficult queries to arise. Yet it is here probably that the noblest work of the intermediate sex or sexes will be accomplished, as well as the greatest errors committed. It seems almost a law of Nature that new and important movements should be misunderstood and vilified—even though afterwards they may be widely approved or admitted to honour. Such movements are always envisaged first from whatever aspect they may possibly present, of ludicrous or contemptible. The early Christians, in the eyes of Romans, were chiefly known as the perpetrators of obscure rites and crimes in the darkness of the catacombs. Modern Socialism was for a long time supposed to be an affair of daggers and dynamite; and even now there are thousands of good people ignorant enough to believe that it simply means 'divide up all around, and each take his threepenny bit.' Vegetarians were supposed to be a feeble and brainless set of cabbage-eaters. The Women's movement, so vast in its scope and importance, was nothing but an absurd attempt to make women 'the apes of men'. An so on without end; the accusation in each case being some tag or last fag-end of fact, caught up by ignorance, and coloured by prejudice. So commonplace is it to misunderstand, so easy to misrepresent.

That the Uranian temperament, especially in regard to its affectional side, is not without faults must naturally be allowed; but that it has been grossly and absurdly misunderstood is certain. With a good deal of experience in the matter, I think one may safely say that the defect of the male Uranian, or Urning, is *not* sensuality—but rather *sentimentality*. The lower, more ordinary types of Urning are often terribly sentimental; the superior types strangely, almost incredibly emotional; but neither *as a rule* (though of course there must be exceptions) are so sensual as the average normal man.

This immense capacity of emotional love represents of course a great driving force. Whether in the individual or in society, love is eminently creative. It is their great genius for attachment which gives to the best Uranian types their penetrating influence and activity, and which often makes them beloved and accepted far and wide even by those who know nothing of their inner mind. How many so-called philanthropists of the best kind (we need not mention names) have been inspired by the Uranian temperament, the world will probably never know. And in all walks of life the great number and influence of folk of this disposition, and the distinguished place they already occupy, is only realised by those who are more or less behind the scenes. It is probably also that it is this genius for emotional love which gives to the Uranians their remarkable *youthfulness*.

Anyhow, with their extraordinary gift for, and experience in, affairs of the heart—from the double point of view, both of the man and of the woman—it is not difficult to see that these people have a special work to do as reconcilers and interpreters of the two sexes to each other. Of this I have spoken at more length below (chaps. 2 and 5). It is probable that the superior Urnings will become, in affairs of the heart, to a large extent the teachers of future society; and if so that their influence will tend to the realisation and expression of an attachment less exclusively sensual than the average of today, and to the diffusion of this in all directions.

While at any rate not presuming to speak with authority on so difficult a subject, I plead for the necessity of a patient consideration of it, for the due recognition of the types of character concerned, and for some endeavour to give them their fitting place and sphere of usefulness in the general scheme of society.

One thing by way of introductory explanation. The word Love is commonly used in so general and almost indiscriminate a fashion as to denote sometimes physical instincts and acts, and sometimes the most intimate and profound feelings; and in this way a good deal of misunderstanding is caused. In this book (unless there be exceptions in the Appendix) the word is used to denote the inner devotion of one person to another; and when anything else is meant—as, for instance, sexual relations and actions—this is clearly stated and expressed.

2. The Intermediate Sex

Urning men and women, on whose book of life Nature has written her new word which sounds so strange to us, bear such storm and stress within them, such ferment and fluctuation, so much complex material having its outlet only towards the future; their individualities are so rich and many-sided, and withal so little understood, that it is impossible to characterise them adequately in a few sentences.
—Otto de Joux

In late years (and since the arrival of the New Woman amongst us) many things in the relation of men and women to each other have altered, or at any rate become clearer. The growing sense of equality in habits and customs—university studies, art, music, politics, the bicycle, etc.—all these things have brought about a *rapprochement* between the sexes. If the modern woman is a little more masculine in some ways than her predecessor, the modern man (it is to be hoped), while by no means effeminate, is a little more sensitive in temperament and artistic in feeling than the original John Bull. It is beginning to be recognised that the sexes do not or should not normally form two groups hopelessly isolated in habit and feeling from each other, but that they rather represent the two poles of *one* group—which is the human race; so that while certainly the extreme specimens at either pole are vastly divergent, there are great numbers in the middle region who (though differing corporeally as men and women) are by emotion and temperament very near to each other. We all know women with a strong dash of the masculine temperament, and we all know men whose almost feminine sensibility and intuition seem to belie their bodily form. Nature, it might appear, in mixing the elements which go to compose each individual, does not always keep her two groups of ingredients—which represent the two sexes—properly apart, but often throws them crosswise in a somewhat baffling manner, now this way and now that; yet wisely, we must think—for if a severe distinction of elements were always maintained the two sexes would soon drift into far latitudes and absolutely cease to understand each other. As it is, there are some remarkable and (we think) indispensable types of character in whom there is such a union or balance of the feminine and masculine qualities that these people become to a great extent the interpreters of men and women to each other.

There is another point which has become clearer of late. For as people are beginning to see that the sexes form in a certain sense a continuous group, so they are beginning to see that Love and Friendship—which have been so often set apart from each other as things distinct—are in reality closely related and shade imperceptibly into each other. Women are beginning to demand that Marriage shall mean Friendship as well as Passion; that a comrade-like Equality shall be included in the word Love; and it is recognised that from the one extreme of a 'Platonic' friendship (generally between persons of the same sex) up to the other extreme of passionate love (generally between persons of opposite sex) no hard and fast line can at any point be drawn effectively separating the different kinds of attachment. We know, in fact, of Friendships so romantic in sentiment that they verge into love; we know of Loves so intellectual and spiritual that they hardly dwell in the sphere of Passion.

A moment's thought will show that the general conceptions indicated above—if anywhere near the truth—point to an immense diversity of human temperament and character in matters relating to sex and love; but though such diversity has probably always existed, it has only in comparatively recent times become a subject of study.

More than thirty years ago, however, an Austrian writer, K.H. Ulrichs, drew attention in a series of pamphlets (*Memnon, Ara Spei, Inclusa*, etc.) to the existence of a class of people who strongly illustrate the above remarks, and with whom specially this paper is concerned. He pointed out that there were people born in such a position—as it were on the dividing line between the sexes—that while belonging distinctly to one sex as far as their bodies are concerned they may be said to belong *mentally* and *emotionally* to the other; that there were men, for instance, who might be described as of feminine soul enclosed in a male body (*anima muliebris in corpore virili inclusa*), or in other cases, women whose definition would be just the reverse. And he maintained that this doubleness of nature was to a great extent proved by the special direction of their love-sentiment. For in such cases, as indeed might be expected, the (apparently) masculine person instead of forming a love-union with a female tended to contract romantic friendships with one of his own sex; while the apparently feminine would, instead of marrying in the usual way, devote herself to the love of another feminine.

People of this kind (i.e., having this special variation of the love-sentiment) he called Urnings; and though we are not obliged to accept his theory about the crosswise connection between 'soul' and 'body', since at best these words are somewhat vague and indefinite; yet his work was important because it was one of the first attempts, in modern times, to recognise the existence of what might be called an Intermediate sex, and to give at any rate *some* explanation of it.

Since that time the subject has been widely studied and written about by scientific men and others, especially on the Continent (though in England it is still comparatively unknown), and by means of an extended observation of present-day cases, as well as the indirect testimony of the history and literature of times past, quite a body of general conclusions has been arrived at—of which I propose in the following pages to give some slight account.

Contrary to the general impression, one of the first points that emerges from this study is that 'Urnings,' or Uranians, are by no means so very rare; but that they form, beneath the surface of society, a large class. It remains difficult, however, to get an exact statement of their numbers; and this for more than one reason: partly because, owing to the want of any general understanding of their case, these folk tend to conceal their true feelings from all but their own kind, and indeed often deliberately act in such a manner as to lead the world astray—(whence it arises that a normal man living in a certain society will often refuse to believe that there is a single Urning in the circle of his acquaintance, while one of the latter, or one that understands the nature, living in the same society, can count perhaps a score or more)—and partly because it is indubitable that the numbers do vary very greatly, not only in different countries but even in different classes in the same country. The consequence of all this being that we have estimates differing very widely from each other. Dr Grabowsky, a well-known writer in Germany, quotes figures (which we think must be exaggerated) as high as one man in every 22, while Dr Albert Moll (*Die Conträre Sexualempfindung*, chap. 3) gives estimates varying from 1 in every 50 to as low as 1 in every 500. These figures apply to such as are exclusively of the said nature, i.e., to those whose deepest feelings of love and friendship go out only to persons of their own sex. Of course, if in addition are included those double-natured people (of whom there is a great number) who experience the normal attachment, with the homogenic tendency in less or greater degree superadded, the estimates must be greatly higher.

In the second place it emerges (also contrary to the general impression) that men and women of the exclusively Uranian type are by no means necessarily morbid in any way— unless, indeed, their peculiar temperament be pronounced in itself morbid. Formerly it was assumed as a matter of course, that the type was merely a result of disease and degeneration; but now with the examination of the actual facts it appears that, on the contrary, many are fine, healthy specimens of their sex, muscular and well-developed in body, of powerful brain, high standard of conduct, and with nothing abnormal or morbid of any kind observable in their physical structure or constitution. This is of course not true of all, and there still remain a certain number of cases of weakly type to support the neuropathic view. Yet it is very noticeable that this view is much less insisted on by the later writers than by the earlier. It is also worth noticing that it is now acknowledged that even in the most healthy cases the special affectional temperament of the 'Intermediate' is, as a rule, ineradicable; so much so that when (as in not a few instances) such men and women, from social or other considerations, have forced themselves to marry and even have children, they have still not been able to overcome their own bias, or the leaning after all of their life-attachment to some friend of their own sex.

This subject, though obviously one of considerable interest and importance, has been hitherto, as I have pointed out, but little discussed in this country, partly owing to a certain amount of doubt and distrust which has, not unnaturally perhaps, surrounded it. And certainly if the men and women born with the tendency in question were only exceedingly rare, though it would not be fair on that account to ignore them, yet it would hardly be necessary to dwell at great length on their case. But as the class is really, on any computation, numerous, it becomes a duty for society not only to understand them but to help them to understand themselves.

For there is no doubt that in any cases people of this kind suffer a great deal from their own temperament—and yet, after all, it is possible that they may have an important part to play in the evolution of the race. Anyone who realises what Love is, the dedication of the heart, so profound, so absorbing, so mysterious, so imperative, and always just in the noblest natures so strong, cannot fail to see how difficult, how tragic even, must often be the fate of those whose deepest feelings are destined from the earliest days to be a riddle and a stumbling-block, unexplained to themselves, passed over in silence by others. To call people of such temperament 'morbid', and so forth, is of no use. Such a term is, in fact, absurdly inapplicable to many, who are among the most active, the most amiable and accepted members of society; besides, it forms no solution of the problem in question, and only amounts to marking down for disparagement a fellow-creature who has already considerable difficulties to contend with. Says Dr Moll. 'Anyone who has seen many Urnings will probably admit that they form a by no means enervated human group; on the contrary, one finds powerful, healthy-looking folk among them', but in the very next sentence he says that they 'suffer severely' from the way they are regarded; and in the manifesto of a considerable community of such people in Germany occur these words, 'The rays of sunshine in the night of our existence are so rare, that we are responsive and deeply grateful for the least movement, for every single voice that speaks in our favour in the forum of mankind.'

In dealing with this class of folk, then, while I do not deny that they present a difficult problem, I think that just for that very reason their case needs discussion. It would be a great mistake to suppose that their attachments are necessarily sexual, or connected with sexual acts. On the contrary (as abundant evidence shows), they are often purely emotional in their character; and to confuse Uranians (as is so often done) with libertines having no law but curiosity in self-indulgence is to do them a great wrong. At the same time, it is evident that their special temperament may sometimes cause them difficulty in regard to their sexual relations. Into this subject we need not just now enter. But we may point out how hard it is, especially for the young among them, that a veil of complete silence should be drawn over the subject, leading to the most painful misunderstandings, and perversions and confusions of mind; and that there should be no hint of guidance; nor any recognition of the solitary and really serious inner struggles they may have to face! If the problem is a difficult one—as it undoubtedly is—the fate of those people is already hard who have to meet it in their own persons, without their suffering in addition from the refusal of society to give them any help . . .

3. The Homogenic Attachment

. . . Though much in relation to the homogenic attachment is obscure, and though it may have its special pitfalls and temptations—making it quite necessary to guard against a too great latitude on the physical side; yet on its ethical and social sides it is pregnant with meaning and has received at various times in history abundant justification. It certainly does not seem impossible to suppose that as the ordinary love has a special function in the propagation of the race, so the other has its special function in social and heroic work, and in the generation—not of bodily children—but of those children of the mind, the philosophical conceptions and ideals which transform our lives and those of society. J. Addington Symonds, in his privately printed pamphlet, *A Problem in Greek Ethics* (now published in a German translation), endeavours to reconstruct as it were the genesis of comrade-love among the Dorians in early Greek times. Thus: 'Without sufficiency of women, without the sanctities of established domestic life, inspired by the memories of Achilles and venerating their ancestor Herakles, the Dorian warriors had special opportunity for elevating comradeship to the rank of an enthusiasm. The incidents of emigration into a foreign country— perils of the sea, passages of rivers and mountains, assaults of fortresses and cities, landings on a hostile shore, night-vigils by the side of blazing beacons, foragings for food, picquet service in the front of watchful foes—involved adventures capable of shedding the lustre of romance on friendship. These circumstances, by bringing the virtues of sympathy with the weak, tenderness for the beautiful, protection for the young, together with corresponding qualities of gratitude, self-devotion, and admiring attachment into play, may have tended to cement unions between man and man no less firm than that of marriage. On such connections a wise captain would have relied for giving strength to his battalions, and for keeping alive the flames of enterprise and daring.' The author then goes on to suggest that though in such relations as those indicated the physical probably had some share, yet it did not at that time overbalance the emotional and spiritual elements, or lead to the corruption and effeminacy of a later age.

At Sparta the lover was called *eispnêlos*, the inspirer, and the younger beloved *aïtes*, the hearer. This alone would show the partly educational aspects in which comradeship was conceived; and a hundred passages from classic literature might be quoted to prove how deeply it had entered into the Greek mind that this love was the cradle of social chivalry and heroic life. Finally it seems to have been Plato's favourite doctrine that the relation if properly conducted led up to the disclosure of true philosophy in the mind, to the divine vision or mania, and to the remembrance or rekindling within the soul of all the forms of celestial beauty. He speaks of this kind of love as causing a 'generation in the beautiful' within the souls of the lovers. The image of the beloved one passing into the mind of the lover and upward through its deepest recesses reaches and unites itself to the essential forms of divine beauty there long hidden—the originals as it were of all creation—and stirring them to life excites a kind of generative descent of noble thoughts and impulses, which henceforward modify the whole cast of thought and life of the one so affected.

If there is any truth—even only a grain or two—in these speculations, it is easy to see that the love with which we are specially dealing is a very important factor in society, and that its neglect, or its repression, or its vulgar misapprehension, may be matters of considerable danger or damage to the common-weal. It is easy to see that while on the one hand marriage is of indispensable importance to the State as providing the workshop as it were for the breeding and rearing of children, another form of union is almost equally indispensable to supply the basis for social activities of other kinds. Every one is conscious that without a close affectional tie of some kind his life is not complete, his powers are crippled, and his energies are inadequately spent. Yet it is not to be expected (though it may of course happen) that the man or woman who have dedicated themselves to each other and to family life should leave the care of their children and the work they have to do at home in order to perform social duties of a remote and less obvious, though may be more arduous, character. Nor is it to be expected that a man or woman single-handed, without the counsel of a helpmate in the hour of difficulty, or his or her love in the hour of need, should feel equal to these wider activities. If—to refer once more to classic story—the love of Harmodius had been for a wife and children at home, he would probably not have cared, and it would hardly have been his business, to slay the tyrant. And unless on the other hand each of the friends had had the love of his comrade to support him, the two could hardly have nerved themselves to this audacious and ever-memorable exploit. So it is difficult to believe that anything can supply the force and liberate the energies required for social and mental activities of the most necessary kind so well as a comrade-union which yet leaves the two lovers free from the responsibilities and impediments of family life.

For if the slaughter of tyrants is not the chief social duty nowadays, we have with us hydra-headed monsters at least as numerous as the tyrants of old, and more difficult to deal with, and requiring no little courage to encounter. And beyond the extirpation of evils we have solid work waiting to be done in the patient and life-long building up of new forms of society, new orders of thought, and new institutions of human solidarity—all of which in their genesis must meet with opposition, ridicule, hatred, and even violence. Such campaigns as these—though different in kind from those of the Dorian mountaineers described above—will call for equal hardihood and courage, and will stand in need of a comradeship as true and valiant. And it may indeed be doubted whether the higher heroic and spiritual life of a nation is ever quite possible without the sanction of this attachment in its institutions, adding a new range and scope to the possibilities of love.

Walt Whitman, the inaugurator, it may almost be said, of a new world of democratic ideals and literature, and—as one of the best of our critics has remarked—the most Greek in spirit and in performance of modern writers, insists continually on this social function of 'intense and loving comradeship, the personal and passionate attachment of man to man.' 'I will make,' he says, 'the most splendid race the sun ever shone upon, I will make divine magnetic lands ... I will make inseparable cities with their arms about each others' necks, by the love of comrades.' And again, in *Democratic Vistas*, 'It is to the development, identification, and general prevalence of that fervid comradeship (the adhesive love at least rivaling the amative love hitherto possessing imaginative literature, if not going beyond it), that I look for the counterbalance and offset of materialistic and vulgar American Democracy, and for the spiritualisation thereof ... I say Democracy infers such loving comradeship, as its most inevitable twin or counterpart, without which it will be incomplete, in vain, and incapable of perpetuating itself.'

Yet Whitman could not have spoken, as he did, with a kind of authority on this subject, if he had not been fully aware that through the masses of the people this attachment was already alive and working—though doubtless in a somewhat suppressed and un-self-conscious form—and if he had not had ample knowledge of its effects and influence in himself and others around him. Like all great artists he could but give form and light to that which already existed dim and inchoate in the heart of the people. To those who have dived at all below the surface in this direction it will be familiar enough that the homogenic passion ramifies widely through all modern society, and that among the masses of the people as among the classes, even below the stolid surface and reserve of British manners, letters pass and enduring attachments are formed, differing in no very obvious respect from those correspondences which persons of the opposite sex knit with each other under similar circumstances; but that hitherto while this relation has occasionally, in its grosser forms and abuses, come into public notice through the police reports, etc., its more sane and spiritual manifestations—though really a moving force in the body politic—have remained unrecognised.

It is hardly needful in these days when social questions loom so large upon us to emphasise the importance of a bond which by the most passionate and lasting compulsion may draw members of the different classes together, and (as it often seems to do) none the less strongly because they are members of different classes. A moment's consideration must convince us that such a comradeship may, as Whitman says, have 'deepest relations to general politics'. It is noticeable, too, in this deepest relation to politics that the movement among women towards their own liberation and emancipation, which is taking place all over the civilised world, has been accompanied by a marked development of the homogenic passion among the female sex. It may be said that a certain strain in the relations between the opposite sexes which has come about owing to a growing consciousness among women that they have been oppressed and unfairly treated by men, and a growing unwillingness to ally themselves unequally in marriage—that this strain has caused the womenkind to draw more closely together and to cement alliances of their own. But whatever the cause may be it is pretty certain that such comrade-alliances—and of quite devoted kind—are becoming increasingly common, and especially perhaps among the more cultured classes of women, who are working out the great cause of their sex's liberation; nor is it difficult to see the importance of such alliances in such a campaign. In the United States where the battle of women's independence is also being fought, the tendency mentioned is as strongly marked.

A few words may here be said about the legal aspect of this important question. It has to be remarked that the present state of the Law, both in Germany and Britain—arising as it does partly out of some of the misapprehensions above alluded to, and partly out of the sheer unwillingness of legislators to discuss the question—is really impracticable. While the Law rightly seeks to prevent acts of violence or public scandal, it may be argued that it is going beyond its province when it attempts to regulate the private and voluntary relations of adult persons to each other. The homogenic affection is a valuable social force, and in some cases a necessary element of noble human character—yet the Act of 1885 makes almost any familiarity in such cases the possible basis of a criminal charge. The Law has no doubt had substantial ground for previous statutes on this subject—dealing with a certain gross act; but in so severely condemning the least familiarity between male persons we think it has gone too far. It has undertaken a censorship over private morals (entirely apart from social results) which is beyond its province, and which—even if it were its province—it could not possibly fulfill; it has opened wider than ever before the door to a real, most serious social evil and crime—that of blackmailing; and it has thrown a shadow over even the simplest and most ordinary expressions of an attachment which may, as we have seen, be of great value in the national life.

That the homosexual feeling, like the heterosexual, may lead to public abuses of liberty and decency; that it needs a strict self-control; and that much teaching and instruction on the subject is needed; we of course do not deny. But as, in the case of persons of opposite sex, the law limits itself on the whole to a maintenance of public order, the protection of the weak from violence and insult, and of the young from their inexperience; so we think it should be here. The much-needed teaching and the true morality on the subject must be given—as it can only be given—by the spread of proper education and ideas, and not by the clumsy bludgeon of the statute-book.

Having thus shown the importance of the homogenic or comrade-attachment, in some form, in national life, it would seem high time now that the modern peoples should recognise this in their institutions, and endeavour at least in their public opinion and systems of education to understand this factor and give it its proper place. The undoubted evils which exist in relation to it, for instance in our public schools as well as in our public life, owe their experience largely to the fact that the whole subject is left in the gutter so to speak—in darkness and concealment. No one offers a clue of better things, nor to point a way out of the wilderness; and by this very non-recognition the passion is perverted into its least satisfactory channels. All love, one would say, must have its responsibilities, else it is liable to degenerate, and to dissipate itself in mere sentiment or sensuality. The normal marriage between man and woman leads up to the foundation of the household and the family; the love between parents and children implies duties and cares on both sides. The homogenic attachment left unrecognised, easily loses some of its best quality and becomes an ephemeral or corrupt thing. Yet, as we have seen, and as I am pointing out in the following chapter, it may, when occurring between an elder and younger, prove to be an immense educational force; while, as between equals, it may be turned to social and heroic uses, such as can hardly be demanded or expected from the ordinary marriage. It would seem high time, I say, that public opinion should recognise these facts; and so give to this attachment the sanction and dignity which arise from public recognition, as well as the definite form and outline which would flow from the existence of an accepted ideal or standard in the matter. It is often said how necessary for the morality of the ordinary marriage is some public recognition of the relation, and some accepted standard of conduct in it. May not, to a lesser degree, something of the same kind (as suggested in the next chapter) be true of the homogenic attachment? It has had its place as a recognised and guarded institution in the elder and more primitive societies; and it seems quite probable that a similar place will be accorded to it in the societies of the future.

4. Affection in Education

The place of Affection, and the need of it, as an educative force in school-life, is a subject which is beginning to attract a good deal of attention. Hitherto Education has been concentrated on intellectual (and physical) development; but the affections have been left to take care of themselves. Now it is beginning to be seen that the affections have an immense deal to say in the building up of the brain and the body. Their evolution and organisation in some degree is probably going to become an important part of school management.

School friendships of course exist; and almost every one remembers that they filled a large place in the outlook of his early years; but he remembers, too, that they were not recognised in any way, and that in consequence the main part of their force and value was wasted. Yet it is evident that the first unfolding of a strong attachment in boyhood or girlhood must have a profound influence; while if it occurs between and elder and a younger school-mate, or—as sometimes happens—between the young thing and its teacher, its importance in the educational sense can hardly be overrated . . .

It is not necessary, however, to quote authorities on such a subject as this. Any one who has had experience of schoolboys knows well enough that they are capable of forming these romantic and devoted attachments, and that their alliances are often of the kind especially referred to as having a bearing on education—i.e., between an elder and a younger. They are genuine attractions, free as a rule, and at their inception, from secondary motives. They are not formed by the elder one for any personal ends. More often, indeed, I think they are begun by the younger, who naively allows his admiration of the elder one to become visible. But they are absorbing and intense, and on either side their influence is deeply felt and long remembered.

That such attachments *may* be of the very greatest value is self-evident. The younger boy looks on the other as a hero, loves to be with him, thrills with pleasure at his words of praise or kindness, imitates, makes him his pattern and standard, learns exercises and games, contracts habits, or picks up information from him. The elder one, touched, becomes protector and helper; the unselfish side of his nature is drawn out, and he develops a real affection and tenderness towards the younger. He takes all sorts of trouble to initiate his *protégé* in field sports or studies; is proud of the latter's success; and leads him on perhaps later to share his own ideals of life and thought and work . . .

We have then in education generally, it seems to me (and whether of boys or of girls), two great currents to deal with, which cannot be ignored, and which certainly ought to be candidly recognised and given their right direction. One of these currents is that of friendship. The other is that of the young thing's natural curiosity about sex. The latter is of course, or should be, a perfectly legitimate interest. A boy at puberty naturally wants to know—and ought to know—what is taking place, and what the uses and functions of his body are. He does not go very deep into things; a small amount of information will probably satisfy him; but the curiosity is there, and it is pretty certain that the boy, if he is a boy of any sense or character, *will* in some shape or another get to satisfy it.

The process is really a *mental* one. Desire—except in some abnormal cases—has not manifested itself strongly; and there is often perhaps generally, an actual repugnance at first to anything like sexual practices; but the wish for information exists and is, I say, legitimate enough. In almost all human societies except, curiously, the modern nations, there have been institutions for the initiation of the youth of either sex into these matters, and these initiations have generally been associated, in the opening blossom of the young mind, with inculcation of the ideals of manhood and womanhood, courage, hardihood, and the duties of the citizen or the soldier.

But what does the modern school do? It shuts a trap-door down on the whole matter. There is a hush; a grim silence. Legitimate curiosity soon becomes illegitimate of its kind; and a furtive desire creeps in, where there was no desire before. The method of the gutter prevails. In the absence of any recognition of schoolboy needs, contraband information is smuggled from one to another; chaff and 'smut' take the place of sensible and decent explanations; unhealthy practices follow; the sacredness of sex goes its way, never to return, and the school is filled with premature and morbid talk and thought about a subject which should, by rights, only just be rising over the mental horizon.

The meeting of these two currents, of ideal attachment and sexual desire, constitutes a rather critical period, even when it takes place in the normal way—i.e., later on, and at the matrimonial age. Under the most favourable conditions a certain conflict occurs in the mind at their first encounter. But in the modern school this conflict, precipitated far too soon, and accompanied by an artificial suppression of the nobler current and a premature hastening of the baser one, ends in simple disaster to the former. Masters wage war against incontinence, and are right to do so. But how do they wage it? As said, by grim silence and fury, by driving the abscess deeper, by covering the drain over, *and* by confusing when it comes before them—both in their own minds and those of the boys—a real attachment with that which they condemn.

Not long ago the headmaster of a large public school coming suddenly out of his study chanced upon two boys embracing each other in the corridor. Possibly, and even probably, it was the simple and natural expression of an unsophisticated attachment. Certainly, it was nothing that in itself could be said to be either right or wrong. What did he do? He haled the two boys into his study, gave them a long lecture on the nefariousness of their conduct, with copious hints that he knew *what such things meant*, and *what they led to*, and ended by punishing both condignly. Could anything be more foolish? If their friendship was clean and natural, the master was only trying to make them feel that it was unclean and unnatural, and that a lovely and honourable thing was disgraceful; if the act was—which at least is improbable—a mere signal of lust—even then the best thing would have been to assume that it was honourable, and by talking to the boys, either together or separately, to try and inspire them with a better ideal; while if, between these positions, the master really thought the affection though honourable would lead to things undesirable, then, plainly, to punish the two was only to cement their love for each other, to give them a strong reason for concealing it, and to hasten its onward course. Yet every one knows that this is the *kind* of way in which the subject is treated in schools. It is the method of despair. And masters (perhaps not unnaturally) finding that they have not the time which would be needed for personal dealing with each boy, nor the forces at their command by which they might hope to introduce new ideals of life and conduct into their little community, and feeling thus utterly unable to cope with the situation, allow themselves to drift into a policy of mere silence with regard to it, tempered by outbreaks of ungoverned and unreasoning severity.

I venture to think that schoolmasters will never successfully solve the difficulty until they boldly recognise the two needs in question, and proceed candidly to give them their proper satisfaction.

The need of information—the legitimate curiosity—of boys (and girls) must be met, (1) partly by classes on physiology, (2) partly by private talks and confidences between elder and younger, based on friendship. With regard to (1) classes of this kind are already, happily, being carried on at a few advanced schools, and with good results. And though such classes can only go rather generally into the facts of motherhood and generation they cannot fail, if well managed, to impress the young minds, and give them a far grander and more reverent conception of the matter than they usually gain.

But (2) although some rudimentary teaching on sex lessons in physiology may be given in classes, it is obvious that further instruction and indeed any real help in the conduct of life and morals can only come through very close and tender confidences between the elder and the younger, such as exist where there is a strong friendship to begin with. It is obvious that effective help *can* only come in this way, and that this is the only way in which it is desirable that it should come. The elder friend in this case would, one might say, naturally be, and in many instances may be, the parent, mother or father—who ought certainly to be able to impress on the clinging child the sacredness of the relation. And it is much to be hoped that parents will see their way to take this part more freely in the future. But for some unexplained reason there is certainly often a gulf of reserve between the (British) parent and child; and the boy who is much at school comes more under the influence of his elder companions than his parents. If, therefore, boys and youths cannot be trusted and encouraged to form decent and loving friendships with each other, and with their elders or juniors—in which many delicate questions could be discussed and the tradition of sensible and manly conduct with regard to sex handed down—we are indeed in a bad plight and involved in a vicious circle from which escape seems difficult.

And so (we think) the need of attachment must also be met by full recognition of it, and the granting of it expression within all reasonable limits; by the dissemination of a good ideal of friendship and the enlistment of it on the side of manliness and temperance. Is it too much to hope that schools will in time recognise comradeship as a regular institution—considerably more important, say, than 'fagging'—an institution having its definite place in the school life, in the games and in the studies, with its own duties, responsibilities, privileges, etc., and serving to ramify through the little community, hold it together, and inspire its members with the two qualities of heroism and tenderness, which together form the basis of all great character? . . .

The remarks in this paper have chiefly had reference to boys' schools; but they apply in the main to girls' schools, where much the same troubles prevail—with this difference, that in girls' schools friendships instead of being repressed are rather encouraged by public opinion; only unfortunately they are for the most part friendships of a weak and sentimental turn, and not very healthy either in themselves or in the habits they lead to. Here too, in girls' schools, the whole subject wants facing out, friendship wants setting on a more solid and less sentimental basis; and on the subject of sex, so infinitely important to women, there needs to be sensible and consistent teaching, both public and private. Possibly the co-education of boys and girls may be of use in making boys less ashamed of their feelings, and girls more healthy in the expression of them.

At any rate the more the matter is thought of, the clearer I believe will it appear that a healthy affection must in the end be the basis of education and that the recognition of this will form the only way out of the modern school-difficulty. It is true that such a change would revolutionise our school-life; but it will have to come, all the same, and no doubt will come *pari passu* with other changes that are taking place in society at large.

5. The Place of the Uranian in Society

Whatever differing views there may be on the many problems which the Intermediate sexes present—and however difficult of solution some of the questions involved—there is one thing which appears to me incontestable: namely that a vast number of intermediates do actually perform most valuable social work, and that they do so partly on account and by reason of their special temperament.

This fact is not generally recognised as it ought to be, for the simple reason that the Uranian himself is not recognised, and indeed (as we have already said) tends to conceal his temperament from the public. There is no doubt that if it became widely known *who are* the Uranians, the world would be astonished to find so many of its great or leading men among them.

I have thought it might be useful to indicate some of the lines along which valuable work is being performed, or has been performed, by people of this disposition; and in doing this I do not of course mean to disguise or conceal the fact that there are numbers of merely frivolous, or feeble or even vicious homosexuals, who practically do no useful work for society at all—*just as there are of normal people*. The existence of those who do no valuable work does not alter the fact of the existence of others whose work is of great importance. And I wish also to make it clearly understood that I use the word Uranians to indicate simply those whose lives and activities are inspired by a genuine friendship or love for their own sex, without venturing to specify their individual and particular habits or relations towards those whom they love (which relations in most cases we have no means of knowing). Some Intermediates of light and leading—doubtless not a few—are physically very reserved and continent; others are sensual in some degree or other. The point is that they are all men, or women, whose most powerful motive comes from the dedication to their own kind, and is bound up with it in some way. And if it seems strange and anomalous that in such cases work of considerable importance to society is being done by people whose affections and dispositions society itself would blame, this is after all no more than has happened a thousand times before in the history of the world.

As I have already hinted, the Uranian temperament (probably from the very fact of its dual nature and swift and constant interaction between its masculine and feminine elements) is exceedingly sensitive and emotional; and there is no doubt that, going with this, a large number of the artist class, musical, literary or pictorial, belong to this description. That delicate and subtle sympathy with every wave and phase of feeling which makes the artist possible is also very characteristic of the Uranian (the male type), and makes it easy or natural for the Uranian man to become an artist . . .

Of Literature in this connection, and of the great writers of the world whose work has been partly inspired by the Uranian love, I have myself already spoken. It may further be said that those of the modern artist-writers and poets who have done the greatest service in the way of interpreting and reconstructing *Greek* life and ideals—men like Winckelmann, Goethe, Addington Symonds, Walter Pater—have had a marked strain of this temperament in them. And this has been a service of great value, and one which the world could ill have afforded to lose.

The painters and sculptors, especially of the renaissance period in Italy, yield not a few examples of men whose work has been similarly inspired—as in the cases of Michel Angelo, Leonardo, Bazzi, Cellini, and others. As to music, this is certainly the art which in its subtlety and tenderness—and perhaps in a certain inclination to *indulge* in emotion—lies nearest to the Urning nature. There are few in fact of this nature who have not some gift in the direction of music—though, unless we cite Tschaikovsky, it does not appear that any thorough-going Uranian has attained to the highest eminence in this art.

Another direction along which the temperament very naturally finds an outlet is the important social work of Education. The capacity that a man has, in cases, of devoting himself to the welfare of boys or youths, is clearly a thing which ought not to go wasted—and which may be most precious and valuable. It is incontestable that a great number of men (and women) are drawn into the teaching profession by this sentiment—and the work they do is, in many cases, beyond estimation. Fortunate the boy who meets with such a helper in early life! I know a man—a rising and vigorous thinker and writer—who tells me that he owes almost everything mentally to such a friend of his boyhood, who took the greatest interest in him, saw him almost every day for many years, and indeed cleared up for him not only things mental but things moral, giving him the affection and guidance his young heart needed. And I have myself known and watched not a few such teachers, in public schools and in private schools, and seen something of the work and of the real inspiration they have been to boys under them. Hampered as they have been by the readiness of the world to misinterpret, they still have been able to do most precious service. Of course here and there a case occurs in which privilege is abused; but even then the judgment of the world is often unreasonably severe. A poor boy once told me with tears in his eyes of the work a man had done for him. This man had saved the boy from drunken parents, taken him from the slums, and by means of a club helped him out into the world. Many other boys he had rescued, it appeared, in the same way—scores and scores of them. But on some occasion or other he got into trouble, and was accused of improper familiarities. No excuse, or record of a useful life, was of the least avail. Every trumpery slander was believed, every mean motive imputed, and he had to throw up his position and settle elsewhere, his lifework shattered, never to be resumed.

The capacity for sincere affection which causes an elder man to care so deeply for the welfare of a youth or boy, is met and responded to by a similar capacity in the young thing of devotion to an elder man. This fact is not always recognised; but I have known cases of boys and even young men who would feel the most romantic attachments to quite mature men, sometimes as much as forty or fifty years of age, and only for them—passing by their own contemporaries of either sex, and caring only to win a return affection from these others. This may seem strange, but it is true. And the fact not only makes one understand what riddles there are slumbering in the breasts of our children, but how greatly important it is that we should try to read them—since here, in such cases as these, the finding of an answering heart in an elder man would probably be the younger one's salvation.

How much of the enormous amount of philanthropic work done in the present day—by women among needy or destitute girls of all sorts, or by men among like classes of boys—

is inspired by the same feeling, it would be hard to say; but it must be a very considerable proportion. I think myself that the best philanthropic work—just because it is the most personal, the most loving, and the least merely formal and self-righteous—has a strong fibre of the Uranian heart running through it; and if it should be said that work of this very personal kind is more liable to dangers and difficulties on that account, it is only what is true of the best in almost all departments.

Eros is a great leveller. Perhaps the true Democracy rests, more firmly than anywhere else, on a sentiment which easily passes the bounds of class and caste, and unites in the closest affection the most estranged ranks of society. It is noticeable how often Uranians of good position and breeding are drawn to rougher types, as of manual workers, and frequently very permanent alliances grow up in this way, which although not publicly acknowledged have a decided influence on social institutions, customs and political tendencies—and which would have a good deal more influence could they be given a little more scope and recognition. There are cases that I have known (although the ordinary commercial world might hardly believe it) of employers who have managed to attach their workmen, or many of them, very personally to themselves, and whose object in running their businesses was at least as much to provide their employees with a living as themselves; while the latter, feeling this, have responded with their best output. It is possible that something like the guilds and fraternities of the middle ages might thus be reconstructed, but on a more intimate and personal basis than in those days; and indeed there are not wanting signs that such a reconstruction is actually taking place.

The *Letters of Love and Labour* written by Samuel M. Jones of Toledo, Ohio, to his workmen in the engineering firm of which he was master, are very interesting in this connection. They breathe a spirit of extraordinary personal affection towards, and confidence in, the employees, which was heartily responded to by the latter; and the whole business was carried on, with considerable success, on the principle of a close and friendly co-operation all around.

These things indeed suggest to one that it is possible that the Uranian spirit may lead to something like a general enthusiasm of Humanity, and that the Uranian people may be destined to form the advance guard of that great movement which will one day transform the common life by substituting the bond of personal affection and compassion for the monetary, legal and other external ties which now control and confine society. Such a part of course we cannot expect the Uranians to play unless the capacity for their kind of attachment also exists—though in a germinal and undeveloped state—in the breast of mankind at large. And modern thought and investigation are clearly tending that way—to confirm that it does so exist . . .

To proceed. The Uranian, though generally high-strung and sensitive, is by no means always dreamy. He is sometimes extraordinarily and unexpectedly practical; and such a man may, and often does, command a positive enthusiasm among his subordinates in a business organisation. The same is true of military organisation. As a rule the Uranian temperament (in the male) is not militant. War with its horrors and savagery is somewhat alien to the type. But here again there are exceptions; and in all times there have been great generals (like Alexander, Caesar, Charles XII of Sweden, or Frederick II of Prussia—not to speak of more modern examples) with a powerful strain in them of the homogenic nature, and a wonderful capacity for organisation and command, which combined with their personal interest in, or attachment to, their troops, and the answering enthusiasm so elicited, have made their armies well-nigh invincible.

The existence of this great practical ability in some Uranians cannot be denied; and it points to the important work they may some day have to do in social reconstruction. At the same time I think it is noticeable that *politics* (at any rate in the modern sense of the word, as concerned mainly with party questions and party government) is not as a rule congenial to them. The personal and affectional element is perhaps too remote or absent. Mere 'views' and 'questions' and party strife are alien to the Uranian man, as they are on the whole to the ordinary woman.

If politics, however, are not particularly congenial, it is yet remarkable how many royal personages have been decidedly homogenic in temperament. Taking the Kings of England from the Norman Conquest to the present day, we may count about thirty. And three of these, namely, William Rufus, Edward II, and James I were homosexual in a marked degree—might fairly be classed as Urnings—while some others, like William III had a strong admixture of the same temperament. Three out of thirty reveals a high ratio—ten per cent— and considering that sovereigns do not generally choose themselves, but come into their position by accident of birth, the ratio is certainly remarkable. Does it suggest that the general percentage in the world at large is equally high, but that it remains unnoticed, except in the fierce light that beats upon thrones? Or is there some other explanation with regard to the special liability of royalty to inversion? Hereditary degeneracy has sometimes been suggested. But it is difficult to explain the matter even on this theory; for though the epithet 'degenerate' might possibly apply to James I, it would certainly not be applicable to William Rufus and William III, who, in their different ways, were both men of great courage and personal force—while Edward II was by no means wanting in ability.

But while the Uranian temperament has, in cases, specially fitted its possessors to become distinguished in art or education or war or administration, and enabled them to do valuable work in these fields, it remains perhaps true that above all it has fitted them, and fits them, for distinction and service in affairs of the heart.

It is hard to imagine human beings more skilled in these matters than are the Intermediates. For indeed no one else can possibly respond to and understand, as they do, all the fluctuations and interactions of the masculine and feminine in human life. The pretensive coyness and passivity of women, the rude invasiveness of men, lust, brutality, secret tears, the bleeding heart; renunciation, motherhood, finesse, romance, angelic devotion—all these things lie slumbering in the Uranian soul, ready on occasion for expression; and if they are not always expressed are always there for purposes of divination or interpretation. There are few situations, in fact, in courtship or marriage which the Uranian does not instinctively understand; and it is strange to see how even an unlettered person of this type will often read Love's manuscript easily in cases where the normal man or woman is groping over it like a child in the dark. (Not of course that this means to imply any superiority of *character* in the former; but merely that with his double outlook he necessarily discerns things which the other misses.)

That the Uranians do stand out as helpers and guides, not only in matters of Education, but in affairs of love and marriage, is tolerably patent to all who know them. It is a common experience for them to be consulted now by the man, now by the woman, whose matrimonial conditions are uncongenial or disastrous—not generally because the consultants in the least perceive the Uranian nature, but because they instinctively feel that here is a strong sympathy with and understanding of their side of the question. In this way it is often the fate of the Uranian, himself unrecognised, to bring about happier times and a better comprehension of each other among those with whom he may have to deal. Also he often becomes the confidant of young things of either sex, who are caught in the tangles of love or passion, and know not where to turn for assistance.

I say that I think perhaps of all the services the Uranian may render to society it will be found some day that in this direction of solving the problems of affection and of the heart he will do the greatest service. If the day is coming as we have suggested—when Love is at last to take its rightful place as the binding and directing force of society (instead of the Cash-nexus), and society is to be transmuted in consequence to a higher form, then undoubtedly the superior types of Uranians—prepared for this service by long experience and devotion, as well as by much suffering—will have an important part to play in the transformation. For that the Urnings in their own lives put Love before everything else—postponing to it the other motives like money-making, business success, fame, which occupy so much space in most people's careers—is a fact which is patent to everyone who knows them. This may be saying little or nothing in favour of those of a poor and frivolous sort; but in the case of those others who see the god in his true light, the fact that they serve him in singleness of heart and so unremittingly raises them at once into the position of the natural leaders of mankind.

From this fact—i.e. that these folk think so much of affairs of the heart—and from the fact that their alliances and friendships are formed and carried on beneath the surface of society, as it were, and therefore to some extent beyond the inquisitions and supervisions of Mrs. Grundy, some interesting conclusions flow.

For one thing, the question is constantly arising as to how Society would shape itself if *free*: what form, in matters of Love and Marriage, it would take, if the present restrictions and sanctions were removed or greatly altered. At present in these matters, the Law, the Church, and a strong pressure of public opinion interfere, compelling the observance of certain forms; and it becomes difficult to say how much of the existing order is due to the spontaneous instinct and common sense of human nature, and how much to mere outside compulsion and interference: how far, for instance, Monogamy is natural or artificial; to what degree marriages would be permanent if the Law did not make them so; what is the rational view of Divorce; whether jealousy is a necessary accompaniment of Love; and so forth. These are questions which are being constantly discussed, without finality; or not infrequently with quite pessimistic conclusions.

Now in the Urning societies a certain freedom (though not complete, of course) exists. Underneath the surface of general Society, and consequently unaffected to any great degree by its laws and customs, alliances are formed and maintained, or modified or broken, more in accord with inner need than with outer pressure. Thus it happens that in these societies there are such opportunities to note and observe human grouping under conditions of freedom, as do not occur in the ordinary world. And the results are both interesting and encouraging. As a rule I think it may be said that the alliances are remarkably permanent. Instead of the wild 'general post' which so many good people seem to expect in the event of law being relaxed, one finds (except of course in a few individual cases) that common sense and fidelity and a strong tendency to permanence prevail. In the ordinary world so far has doubt gone that many to-day disbelieve in life-long free marriage. Yet among the Uranians such a thing is, one may almost say, common and well known; and there are certainly few among them who do not believe in its possibility.

Great have been the debates, in all times and places, concerning jealousy; and as to how far jealousy is natural and instinctive and universal, and how far it is the product of social opinion and the property sense, and so on. In ordinary marriage what may be called social and proprietary jealousy is undoubtedly a very great factor. But this kind of jealousy hardly appears or operates in the Urning societies. Thus we have an opportunity in these latter of observing conditions where only the natural and instinctive jealousy exists. This of course is present among the Urnings—sometimes rampant and violent, sometimes quiescent and vanishing almost to *nil*. It seems to depend almost entirely upon the individual; and we certainly learn that jealousy though frequent and widespread, is not an absolutely necessary accompaniment of love. There are cases of Uranians (whether men or women) who, though permanently allied, do not object to lesser friendships on either side—and there are cases of very decided objection. And we may conclude that something the same would be true (is true) of the ordinary Marriage, the property considerations and the property jealousy being once removed. The tendency anyhow to establish a dual relation more or less fixed, is seen to be very strong among the Intermediates, and may be concluded to be equally strong among the more normal folk.

Again with regard to Prostitution. That there are a few natural-born prostitutes is seen in the Urning-societies; but prostitution in that world does not take the important place which it does in the normal world, partly because the law-bound compulsory marriage does not exist there, and partly because prostitution naturally has little chance and cannot compete in a world where alliances are free and there is an open field for friendship. Hence we may see that freedom of alliance and of marriage in the ordinary world will probably lead to the great diminution or even disappearance of Prostitution.

In these and other ways the experience of the Uranian world forming itself freely and not subject to outside laws and institutions comes as a guide—and really a hopeful guide—towards the future. I would say however that in making these remarks about certain conclusions which we are able to gather from some spontaneous and comparatively unrestricted associations, I do not at all mean to argue *against* institutions and forms. I think that the Uranian love undoubtedly suffers from want of a recognition and a standard. And though it may at present be better off than if subject to a foolish and meddlesome regulation; yet in the future it will have its more or less fixed standards and ideals, like the normal love. If one considers for a moment how the ordinary relations of the sexes would suffer were there no generally acknowledged codes of honour and conduct with regard to them, one then indeed sees that reasonable forms and institutions are a help, and one may almost wonder that the Urning circles are so well-conducted on the whole as they are.

I have said that the Urning men in their own lives put love before money-making, business success, fame, and other motives which rule the normal man. I am sure that it is also true of them as a whole that they put love before lust. I do not feel *sure* that this can be said of the normal man, at any rate in the present stage of evolution. It is doubtful whether on the whole the merely physical attraction is not the stronger motive with the latter type. Unwilling as the world at large is to credit what I am about to say, and great as are the current misunderstandings on the subject, I believe it is true that the Uranian men are superior to the normal men in this respect—in respect for their love-feeling—which is gentler, more sympathetic, more considerate, more a matter of the heart and less one of mere physical satisfaction than that of ordinary men. All this flows naturally from the presence of the feminine element in them, and its blending with the rest of their nature. It should be expected *a priori*, and it can be noticed at once by those who have any acquaintance with the Urning world. Much of the current misunderstanding with regard to the character and habits of the Urning arises from his confusion with the ordinary *roué* who, though of normal temperament, contracts homosexual habits out of curiosity and so forth—but this is a point which I have touched on before, and which ought now to be sufficiently clear. If it be once allowed that the love-nature of the Uranian is of a sincere and essentially humane and kindly type then the importance of the Uranian's place in Society, and of the social work he may be able to do, must certainly also be acknowledged.

B

THE EMERGENCE OF A GAY AND LESBIAN POLITICAL CULTURE IN GERMANY

[Introduction and headnotes for this section were written with the assistance of James Steakley.]

Distinctly homosexual lifestyles and even incipient identities began emerging in the urban centers of Germany (and indeed most of Western Europe) well before the twentieth century, as documented by legal and medical records as well as the testimony of homosexuals themselves. Following the Protestant Reformation and the Thirty Years War, the medieval prohibition on male and female sodomy that had been enforced throughout the Holy Roman Empire was gradually superseded by a wide range of statutes promulgated by particular German states. When these states were eventually united by Bismarck in 1871, all of Germany (excluding Austria) was once again under a single law: Paragraph 175 of the Imperial Penal Code criminalized homosexual acts between men, but not between women. Karl Heinrich Ulrichs courageously tried to halt the ratification of Paragraph 175, but his gay contemporaries were too timid to support his one-man campaign. By the turn of the century, however, and during the entire first third of the twentieth century, Germany differed from all other countries by virtue of its gay and lesbian political movement and comprehensive cultural formation.

Why Germany? To begin with, Germany's status as a "belated" nation in comparison with other Western European countries evoked a compensatory eagerness to embrace modernization, at least on the part of bourgeois liberals. The tempo of transformation invigorated both the nation's intellectual elite and its powerful socialist movement, who saw themselves as the cutting edge of social and political progress; and even the conservative imperial regime was likewise determined to propel Germany to world leadership in commerce and culture. Dire social dislocation resulting from rapid urbanization spawned an innovative middle-class "life reform movement," which provided an oppositional context in which the homosexual emancipation movement could crystallize. In addition, the uneven but largely successful course of Jewish emancipation in the nineteenth century served as a model for the acceptance of other minorities, and a notable number of gay leaders were of Jewish ancestry. Finally, in an increasingly secular age, Germany attached exceptional prestige to science, which enjoyed the special patronage of Kaiser Wilhelm II; striking advances were made in the natural and social sciences.

As a result, the 1890s witnessed a remarkable production of knowledge in the domain of sexuality, including theories that medicalized homosexuality as well as other research that investigated its dynamics from a sociological perspective. Published case histories not only reflected but actually stimulated a growing self-awareness on the part of homosexuals, which was also manifest in lesbian and homosexual literature that proliferated around the turn of the century. In 1895, the Berlin police discontinued closing homosexual bars, and an urban subculture could fully emerge. By 1897, these developments had reached a momentum that allowed for the founding of the first gay rights organization in the world, the Scientific-Humanitarian Committee, in Berlin. Although lesbian sexuality was not criminalized under Paragraph 175, lesbians too were subject to social discrimination, and some were actively involved in the Committee's work. A major setback occurred in 1907, when two members of the Kaiser's entourage were smeared as homosexuals, resulting in a campaign for moral rearmament and the bolstering of military-patriarchal values that even led to Reichstag deliberations on criminalizing lesbianism.

Following German defeat in World War I, the Weimar Republic provided an unprecedentedly favorable setting for lesbian and gay politics and culture, instituting not just women's suffrage but also freedoms of speech, press, and assembly. Thus Germany became an international beacon for lesbian and gay political culture much as the U.S. is today. In Berlin alone, for example, thirty lesbian and gay and periodicals were published, inspiring similar but short-lived efforts in Paris and Chicago. In 1929, socialist and communist Reichstag delegates voted to reform Paragraph 175, but this proposal was scathingly denounced by the burgeoning Nazi party, which repudiated Weimar culture as decadent and promised to wipe out homosexuality.

On coming to power, Hitler moved quickly to ban all public manifestations of homosexuality and to toughen Paragraph 175; the criminalization of lesbianism was once again debated. The Nazis arrested 90,000 homosexuals and bisexuals, consigning some 10,000 of them to concentration camps, where their uniforms were marked with pink triangles; thousands of others were only able to avoid internment by submitting to castration. Thus this century has witnessed unprecedented tolerance of homosexuality as well as drastic persecution in Germany. Although the prewar gay movement was stamped out in Germany by the fascist dictatorship, the flame was kept alive in Switzerland through the Swiss Friendship League.

During the postwar Adenauer era in West Germany, gay male organizations and periodicals emerged cautiously, but the Nazi version of Paragraph 175 remained on the books until the Social Democrats came to power in 1969. (By contrast, East Germany struck down the Nazi law in 1949, and Paragraph 175 was reformed in 1968 and entirely repealed in 1988; homosexual organizations and periodicals were nonetheless banned in East Germany, and not until the 1980s could lesbian and gay discussion groups meet under the protection of the Lutheran Church.) Inspired by German law reform as well as the 1969 Stonewall Rebellion, German gay liberationists challenged the continued enforcement of Paragraph 175 and, beginning in the 1980s, responded to the AIDS epidemic. At the initiative of the Green party, West Germany granted belated restitution to pink-triangle survivors in 1988. Unification in 1990 brought the application of West German law in the former East Germany, but a two-year moratorium was declared in the cases of Paragraph 175 and Paragraph 218 (covering abortion). In a split outcome, Paragraph 218 now applies to united Germany, while Paragraph 175 was formally repealed in March 1994.

Here we present four strands conceptualizing lesbian and gay politics and culture in pre-Hitler Germany. The first is that of the Scientific-Humanitarian Committee, founded and emblematized by the Jewish physician Magnus Hirschfeld (1868–1935). The Committee was established in 1897 with the express aim of abolishing Paragraph 175 by using on-going scientific research to change both public opinion and how gays and lesbians understood themselves. Second, we present the cultural critique of the Community of the Special, founded in 1902 and guided until the Nazi takeover by the Berlin schoolteacher Adolf Brand (1874–1945). The Community's philosophy was a heady brew of individualist anarchism, Nietzschean antifeminism, glorification of pedophilia, and homosexual elitism, all of which inspired Brand to clash repeatedly with both the German government and his rivals within the gay movement. As a third strand we reprint two texts authored by Kurt Hiller (1885–1972), who was active in Hirschfeld's Committee but restive under the authority of the movement's great "patriarch" and sought to advance alternative models of organization and leadership. Fourth, grassroots organizations that aimed to combine social activities with legal reform emerged after World War I and were consolidated in 1922 as the League for Human Rights by the entrepreneur Friedrich Radszuweit (1876–1932), who achieved prominence as the publisher of a number of lesbian and gay periodicals. Radszuweit criticized Hirschfeld's Committee for its scientific-medical slant and Brand's Community for its cultural snobbery and male chauvinism, but he seriously underestimated the homophobia of the Nazis and hoped to win them for the cause of gay liberation.

1. See James Steakley, "Sodomy in Enlightenment Prussia: From Execution to Suicide," in *The Pursuit of Sodomy: Male Homosexuality in Renaissance and Enlightenment Europe*, ed. Kent Gerard and Gert Hekma (New York: Haworth, 1989), pp. 163–175.

2. See James W. Jones, *"We of the Third Sex": Literary Representations of Homosexuality in Wilhelmine Germany* (New York: Peter Lang, 1990).

This is the first and most influential of the early gay rights organizations. We present three representative documents 1) The Committee's 1897 petition to the Reichstag for abolition of Paragraph 175; 2) a 1903 pamphlet published by the Committee entitled "What the People Should Know about the Third Sex," here presented in a translation entitled "The Social Problem of Sexual Inversion," adapted and distributed by the British Society for the Study of Sex Psychology in 1915; 3) an address by Anna Rueling to a conference held by the Committee in 1904. Rueling criticized feminists and their organizations for not assisting homosexual organizations and thereby not helping to eliminate the invisibility of both lesbians and their issues, which she regarded as legitimate feminist concerns. (Indeed, revisions of Paragraph 175 to criminalize lesbianism, although never enacted, were discussed in 1909, 1921, and 1935.) Rueling's argument, however, reflects the legacy of Richard von Krafft-Ebing's medicalization of homosexuality in his *Psychopathia sexuais* (1886). In spite of her denial that there is a hierarchy among the three sexes, her hypostatization of biologically masculine, feminine, and androgynous personalities led her to tacit endorsement of the choice by heterosexual women to enter marriage rather than pursue a career.

THE SCIENTIFIC-HUMANITARIAN COMMITTEE

PETITION TO THE REICHSTAG

(1897)

The Scientific Humanitarian Committee
(written by Magnus Hirschfeld)

To the Judiciary of the German Reich

1. As early as 1869 men like Langenbeck and Virchow had been asked for their expert opinion about the possible punishment of homosexual intercourse by the Austrian and German Ministries of Health. Both certified that such activities were in no way different from other sexual relationships which, to date, had never been threatened by court proceedings, be it masturbation, or love between women, or love between men, as well as intercourse between men and women.

2. The abolition of similar punishments in France, Italy, Holland and many other countries had never lowered moral standards.

3. Another important reason for the abolition is the following: scientific research undertaken during the last twenty years in Germany, England and France, which studied in depth the question of homosexuality, has confirmed what the first scientists who considered this subject had asserted without exception, that this way of love is constitutional. One of the reasons given was that homosexuality has occurred at all times, all over the world.

4. The experts pointed out that it is practically proved that the real cause of homosexu-

ality, which at first glance looks like an enigma of nature, is due to development of the bisexual nature of man. The human foetus, during its first three months, is a bisexual organism. Therefore no moral guilt can possibly be attributed to homosexual sentiments.

5. One must also consider that homosexuality urges a person to active expression just as much as, if not more than, heterosexuality.

6. The experts remind the Judiciary that, according to the investigations of all specialists, the *coitus analis* and *oralis* occurs comparatively rarely in homosexuals. In any case, it is not practised among them more often than among 'normal' people.

7. One must also be aware that men and women who have lived a homosexual life at any time, from classic antiquity to our own days, have produced many people of the highest mental quality.

8. Furthermore, Paragraph 175 has not helped to 'cure' homosexuals, but on the contrary has made many courageous and useful human beings desperate and guilty. And in some cases this law was and is responsible for madness and suicide, even when the court sentence is only one day in prison, which is the most lenient punishment in the German Reich for this 'action'. And cases of suicide have even occurred when a court case was only threatened.

9. We must also be aware that this law has given rise to an enormous amount of blackmail, and encouraged the vice of male prostitution.

These explanations, given under the name of people whose expertise as well as their sense of truth, justice and humanity is unquestionable, insist that the present form of Paragraph 175 is contrary to progressive scientific knowledge.

They demand, therefore, that the Judiciary should as soon as possible change this Paragraph in the same way as those countries we have named, and that homosexual actions should be treated in the same way as those between people of the opposite sex, and are punishable only:

a) when force by one partner is exercised against the other,

b) when either person is under the age of sixteen,

c) when their activities offend public decency (when Paragraph 183 of the Reichstrafgesetzbuch is rightly applied).

Apart from the demands made by these two eminent expert witnesses, which alone would be sufficient to show the senselessness of keeping Paragraph 175 in its present form, many representatives of jurisprudence followed the same course, but added further arguments:

1. Paragraph 175 contradicts the demands of a just society, which allows punishment only for unlawful actions. If two consenting adults have a secret sexual affair the rights of a third person are not involved.

2. Inquiries about sexual matters mostly lead to unpleasant situations which one should prevent. According to the *Théorie du code pénal*, Vol. VI, p. 110, Chauveau and Faustin Hélie give as a reason for the abolition of punishment of homosexuals: 'Smutty and scandalous investigations should be avoided as they are an interference in family life, and the cause of much worry and annoyance.'

3. One must take into account the great difficulties of weighing up whether a person has violated the law against homosexuality. Many legal experts have rightly pointed out that a law is worthless if only very few of those who come into conflict with it are apprehended.

4. Paragraph 175 lacks clarity to such an extent that members of the legal profession have different ideas as to what is punishable and what is not. In Germany, punishment is not only meted out in cases of anal intercourse, but also when people

embrace and rub their bodies one against the other; mutual masturbation, however, is not seen as a sexual offence.

'Such an unhappy state of affairs,' says von Krafft-Ebing in *Der Konträrsexuelle vor dem Strafrichter* (p. 16), 'forces the judge to make most painful statements about a case, for example, whether "frictions" have taken place or not. The only witness for the case is generally the person who was passively involved, or a blackmailer, or a male prostitute, or a scoundrel who doesn't care if he commits perjury as otherwise he might get into trouble for calumny.'

5. We must especially point out that any punishment of homosexuality itself is an error of judgement. Those who made this law were scientific ignoramuses. One can say that it is highly probable that this law would never have been made if the fact that homosexuality is inborn had been known to the legislators.

The same holds good for the so-called 'sense of justice of the people', which has been the only motivation for not abolishing Paragraph 175. Therefore, Paragraph 175 is kept on in spite of three wrong preconditions concerning the public:

a) It has not been enlightened about the fact that there are people who can only feel sexually and emotionally for their own sex,

b) It has the wrong idea that homosexuality means anal intercourse,

c) It believes that homosexuals seduce immature juveniles, whereas the fact is that pedicatio and love for juvenile individuals is just as rare in 'inverts' as in 'normal' people.

6. Sexual relations between two men or two women, which most often have no particular consequences, should rather be uninteresting to other people. They should consider that it is morally untenable not to prosecute extra-marital intercourse between men and women, which can lead to venereal infection, illegitimate births and prostitution. Neither do they consider that a young girl has the same power to hold off a seducer as a young man.

7. Paragraph 175 chases hundreds of people away from countries which punish homosexuality into other lands where they are free. The Fatherland is therefore deprived of many spiritual and material values which they might have contributed.

The thought that they are branded as criminals without being guilty drives homosexual people into the deepest despair. Many of them who never damaged anybody or anything, and didn't even 'sin' against Paragraph 175, have committed suicide.

8. Lastly, Paragraph 175 makes it very difficult to fight homosexuality, as people who are that way are afraid to undergo treatment for their condition. They fear to make confessions about themselves to a doctor, as that might lead to prosecution by the law.

THE SOCIAL PROBLEM OF SEXUAL INVERSION
(1903)

The Scientific Humanitarian Committee

English Introduction
[Issued by the British Society for the Study of Sexual [sic] Psychology, to members of the Educational, Medical, and Legal Professions.]

The following translation is from a pamphlet published in Germany ten years ago [1901]. It marks only the preliminary stage in the practical application to social ends of a scientific enquiry which has been pursued in that country for many years with thoroughness and ardour.

The subject is difficult to deal with. But ignorance both as to the cause and the extent of this too-long-hidden problem which permeates society will not make the problem itself less complex or render its just solution more probable.

Where German science has led, and where the appeal for a clearer understanding of the social problem presented has been backed by thousands of distinguished Germans of all classes and callings, those who are anxious for English medical opinion also to find thoughtful expression, may stand without fear of misconstruction.

That any courage should be needed in a demand for facts to be recognized and scientifically investigated, is in itself a sufficient condemnation of the obscurantist attitude which prevails so largely among us in regard to this question.

Investigation will almost certainly show that the problem, as it actually exists in this country, is of no less dimensions than in Germany. If, then, it exists in so large a proportion to the whole population, it will certainly not cease to exist because we disregard it, or debar its discussion. And if, as seems probable, there are some tens or even hundreds of thousands of homosexuals in English society to-day, there they will be in at least equal numbers to-morrow. Homosexuals are being born and bred in our midst in large numbers. They become members of a society which understands nothing of their nature and does nothing to explain it to them or to make the burden of it tolerable when they arrive at the dangerous age of puberty.

Where so large a problem exists it becomes an urgent duty to cope with it. Society cannot solve it by ignoring it. If the aim of society is to be the extermination of these thousands of homo-sexuals, society must organise its policy on a practical basis: if its aim is to alter their nature without exterminating them, to that end also it must devise a means: if its aim is to allow homosexuals to remain themselves without hurt to society, then also organisation of some practical kind will be necessary. But without knowledge no good can be done, no solution found. For knowledge we require investigation and the awakening of scientific interest. In the following Digest of the German pamphlet we put before English readers the conclusions that have been reached as a result of scientific investigation in Germany. We do not necessarily endorse all the opinions here set forth.

The German pamphlet circles round a demand for the alteration of the Law—paragraph 175 in the German Statute Book. We do not think the time has yet arrived in England for a similar demand to be made; because before the Law can be amended, it is clear that the subject with which it deals must be better understood; and our object is primarily discussion and elucidation of the subject. Still the main object which we and the writers of this pamphlet have in view is the same; namely the consideration, without fear or prejudice, of homosexual phenomena as set forth by the scientists; and the harmonising of our social and juridical practice, as far as possible, with scientific recommendations and conclusions.

The Pamphlet (Digest)
What is known of the Intermediate Sex

Everyone interested in public affairs must have heard of the recent petition, signed by a number of the best-known and most distinguished men in Germany, and having for its object the repeal of a penal law aimed at a not inconsiderable class of persons who, otherwise normal, are peculiarly constituted as regards their sexual tendencies—a class of persons whose nature and peculiarities have, until comparatively recent years, escaped scientific enquiry.

The object of this pamphlet is to enlighten the thoughtful public on the subject of this "Intermediate sex", in the hope of removing a widespread prejudice and inducing a sane judgment. We are following, in so doing, the private advice which Dr. M. Hirschfeld, the president of the "Humanitarian-Science" committee, received from an important quarter: "Try to enlighten public opinion, so that the action of the Government in dealing with these clauses may not be misunderstood."

Whoever reads these pages conscientiously and without prejudice cannot fail to see that their object is not the advocacy of any form of vice, but the removal of a form of injustice which presses heavily upon a certain type of human being.

May this little pamphlet help to render unnecessary the fear expressed by Ernst von Wildenbruch, one of the earliest signatories to the petition. He wrote as follows: "I hasten to reply to your request for my signature. It is a serious request, for I cannot disguise from myself that the signatories to your petition for the repeal of these penalties will expose themselves to the danger of slander and misrepresentation from the stupid and evil-minded. Nevertheless, it seems to me impossible not to comply with your request."

Everyone should be aware that the physical and mental characteristics which are considered essentially masculine are found, occasionally, in woman; and that the essentially feminine characteristics are found, occasionally, in men. There are, for instance, men with a feminine pelvis, with a feminine formation of breast and vocal organs, with feminine growth of hair and lack of beard, with the delicate skin and rounded figure which are characteristically womanly. Hence, one comes across men whose manners and movements are womanly; whose handwriting resembles a woman's, who have the tastes and mental outlook of a woman, who number among their traits a womanly modesty and gentleness.

There are even men—though this is rarer—whose resemblance to women is actually organic.

In the same way, we find women who, in body as well as in mind, bear the stamp of masculinity. Still more frequent are the "intermediates" of both sexes; that is to say, persons in whom the exchange of characteristics, though clearly marked, is by no means complete.

This exchange of characteristics is not only found amongst humans of every race; it is common also to the animal kingdom, in every species of animal where the division into sexes exists. It is to be traced to the fact that the sexes arose from a common origin by a varying process of growth—a process which sometimes fails to reach the average and sometimes overshoots it.

Of this the simplest proof is that each human being carries about with him for as long as he lives certain traces of the sex to which he does not belong. Such traces, to give one example among many, are to be found in the survival on the breast of a man, of the nipple, a purely feminine organ.

Sexual desire which has its root not, as is commonly supposed, in the external organs, but in the brain, is either masculine—and therefore aroused by a woman—or feminine and aroused by a man. Should it, however—in the same way as other characteristics—have undergone this process of exchange, and be, though implanted in a masculine body, essentially feminine in character, it will be impossible for such a man, however masculine in other respects, not to be attracted to his own sex rather than the other. In the same way, a woman in whom the sexual tendency is masculine will feel the impulse of love towards those of her own sex.

Nor must it be supposed that any organic operation on such persons can change or exterminate this attraction. To do so effectually it would be necessary to remove the seat of the instinct, that is to say the brain.

In scientific parlance such persons are described as homosexual, popularly they are known by other terms; in Roman days a man of this type was called *homo mollis*. By some scientists the name "urning" or "uranian" has been employed.

God, or Nature, has brought into being not only normal men and women but uranians; and Professor O. Schulze has rightly declared that it is really too ridiculous to imagine that the processes of nature can be abolished, or even appreciably restrained, by pen and paper enactments. All parents ought to realize that one of their own children may possibly be a uranian—and understand, further, that the penal clause in question (paragraph 175) may chance to threaten their nearest and dearest. Amongst those who have openly opposed the repeal of the law is a clergyman who is quite unaware of the fact—of which we have absolute proof—that one of his sons is a uranian.

About 750 headmasters and teachers in the higher schools have signed the petition; and one of them, who had recently lost a son, accompanied his signature with the following words:

"Even at the time of the Krupp case, I was still in ignorance of the facts we are now considering, and I believed in the necessity of retaining clause 175. It was only after the death of a promising lad—a lad whose mind was set on the best and highest, and who was driven to suicide by his discovery of his own tendencies—that my eyes were opened to the truth. A father, who has known what it is to suffer, thanks your Society for its work in the cause of Humanity."

There is many a mother who fails to understand why her boy, in spite of so much that she knows to be good in him, seems to have no pleasure in life and one day makes an end of himself; or who wonders why it is that her daughter turns from one suitor after another. Often enough such parents would grasp the situation had they only learnt what we are here trying to teach them; and, being possessed of such knowledge, they would take it into account in settling questions of education, profession and marriage. They would realize that, for these particular children, marriage and the founding of a family would be a sin against nature—a torment to themselves and a danger to their descendants, who are especially liable to nervous and mental trouble.

There are certain primitive races who shew far more understanding and justice than we do in their treatment of uranians, who reserve for them certain callings as for example, the care of the sick.

The public ought not to be ignorant that the number of the in-born homosexuals (in Germany probably between half a million and a million) if insignificant in comparison with the number of the normal, is yet far too formidable for any State to attempt to get rid of by confinement in prisons, asylums or institutions; nor is it possible for any State to render practical the alternatives of suicide, wholesale emigration, or the suppression of one of the strongest natural impulses—an impulse concerning whose workings the world of science is by no means in agreement.

There are uranians in the highest as in the lowest ranks of society; among the roughest as among the most cultured, in capitals as in villages, among the most moral as among the most vicious.

Anyone who has studied the problem knows that, in a thousand uranians, hardly one is suspected; in fifty thousand hardly one detected; and knows, further, that Bebel was right when he said in the Reichstag (Jan. 13, 1898): "If the offences against paragraph 175—offences committed by thousands of persons from the highest to the lowest—were really brought to light, there would be a scandal such as the world has never known."

It ought to be understood that the attraction towards those of the same sex is not, as is commonly believed, the result of satiety, self-abuse, evil example, viciousness, or fear of propagation; Dr. Hirschfeld, in his observation of more than 1800 cases, has failed to establish any of these causes. On the contrary, in most cases, efforts have been made to overcome the desire. Its victims know the dangers to which they are exposed, the disgrace that threatens them; but the tendency is stronger than the will.

Professor von Krafft-Ebing, of Vienna, the greatest authority on the subject, says: "At times the homo-sexual passion is so strong that it is impossible to control it." It may be added that there is much popular misconception as to the manner in which this desire attains its fulfillment.

But even those in whom the desire produces no active results feel the existing law as a burden and a reproach, since it strikes at the finest side of them, their capacity for love. Love for a member of the same sex can be just as pure and noble as love for a member of the other—the only difference between the two sentiments being one of direction, and not of kind. Like normal love, it can be an inspiration; there are numerous examples of great men of whose tendencies there cannot be the slightest doubt—for instance, Socrates, Michelangelo, Frederick the Great, Hans Andersen. The verses written by Frederick the Great to "Cesarion", as he called the young Count Kaiserlingk, give documentary evidence of this fact as regards himself.

Every normal being should try to imagine himself in the position of a uranian, a difficult but not an unprofitable task. His inner life resembles that of a man unjustly condemned, a man who does penance for a crime that he has not committed; he knows that he is guiltless of his own desires, that nature has played a trick on him and that, try as he may, he cannot think or feel except as she has ordered. This unhappy plight, which he has had no hand in bringing about, is the cause of contempt and loathing in the minds of those of his fellow men who fail to grasp that his nature is not theirs.

The authors of paragraph 175 assumed—and its administrators and people in general assume likewise—that the persons at whom it is aimed are men like themselves who, of their own free will, divert their natural desires towards women into unnatural desires towards men. They cannot see that the uranian is as strongly drawn towards his own sex as those who sit in judgment on him are drawn towards the other; that, to him, intercourse with women is unnatural, and that he is forced, whether he will or not, to feel the attraction which draws him to men. The same argument applies, of course, where the uranian is a woman.

The uranian is all too often unhappy, not merely on account of his passion itself, but because of the persecution, the social condemnation and loss of honour which threaten him for an impulse which the normal man can obey without reproach.

It is this lack of understanding which fills him with bitterness. One has only to think of the scorn which would be heaped on a lad, who, without attempting to act upon them should put his feelings into words.

No, this clause to which we object does not protect the natural and inborn instincts. It attacks them; for the law fails to recognise what Nature has already done. If the law is to stand, we must declare Nature herself unnatural. It is impossible that we shall continue to brand as criminals, men and women who often blend in their characters the best traits of the two sexes.

As it is impossible to extirpate the Intermediate sex, society and the State must do their best to tolerate it. As a matter of fact, that is what they have to do now, since only a comparatively small number of uranians are removed by suicide or by imprisonment in gaols, hospitals or asylums.

We are attributing to the Law a power it does not possess when we imagine that it can have any real influence upon an instinct implanted by Nature. Penalties cannot suppress that instinct, immunity from penalty cannot produce it; the repeal of a law against it does not increase it; the existence of a law against it does not diminish it. Bavaria and Hanover where, from the War of Liberation to the introduction of the Imperial Penal Code (1815–73) the offence was not illegal, afford absolute proof of this statement.

The idea that an entire people can be enervated by the existence of the homosexual temperament is an idea without foundation. Such temperaments have existed amongst primitive nations and were frequent, not only in Greece and Rome, but in other countries—as well during their rise to power as during their decay.

On the contrary, the uranian, unfitted though he be to found a family, can, after his own fashion, be of service to the community—has, in spite of his unfortunate position, often been of service. He should not be regarded as an anti-social being: he should have his place alloted to him. And, since we require a young woman to protect herself from seduction, we can certainly require the same of a young man, without enacting special legislation for his protection.

Every uranian owes a duty to himself: self-realisation is his right, of that which has come to him by birth he must make the best. To that which he feels to be honourable he must give honourable form, and seek for its honourable recognition from the State. He should not be ashamed of his promptings, but should devote his energies to ennobling them and to directing them as far as possible to the service of his kind.

But if he owes so much to others, the State and society owe him a like recognition in return. They must not deny in blind prejudice that those natural and inborn feelings can be put to social use, so as to be recognized and honoured.

But if society refuses to recognise the uranian, how can he be rightly placed, or attain to the full stature of his nature?

We repeat expressly that we disclaim any desire to dispute the precepts of the Christian moral law; that is an ideal of which all men, however normal, fall short. What we *do* desire to fight is the practice of stamping as criminals and visiting with legal penalties, one section alone, which upon its own lines of advance has not yet attained to the ideal.

WHAT INTEREST DOES THE WOMEN'S MOVEMENT HAVE IN THE HOMOSEXUAL QUESTION?

(1904)

Anna Rueling

The women's movement is necessary to the history of civilization. Homosexuality is a necessity in terms of natural history, representing the bridge, the natural and obvious link between men and women. This, now, is a scientific fact against which ignorance and intolerance struggle in vain. Nevertheless, some will ask why I mention the history of civilization and natural history in one breath, two fields which upon cursory examination seem to be diametrically opposed. There is a basis for this broader view.

In general, when homosexuality is discussed, one thinks only of the Uranian men and overlooks the many homosexual women who exist and about whom much less is said because—I would almost like to say "unfortunately"—they don't have to fight an unjust penal code which resulted from false moral views. Women are not threatened with painful trials and imprisonment when they follow their inborn drive for love. But the mental stress that Uranian women endure is just as great, or greater, than the burden under which Uranian men suffer. To the world which bases its judgment on outward appearances, these women are much more obvious than even the most effeminate man. Only too often, misdirected morality exposes them to scorn and mockery.

Uranian women, even if they are not discussed, are important for our entire social structure because they influence it in many ways. Upon consideration of the facts, one must conclude that homosexuality and the women's movement are not opposed to each other, but rather that they are destined to help each other find justice and recognition and to abolish the injustice against which they now struggle.

The homosexual movement fights for the rights of all homosexuals, men as well as women. The Scientific-Humanitarian Committee is distinguished from the other movement groups which have or should have an interest in this struggle, in that it has dedicated itself enthusiastically to the Uranian woman as well as the Uranian man.

The women's movement strives for long-neglected women's rights; it is fighting especially for the greatest possible independence for women and their legal equality with men both in and out of marriage. The latter is of particular importance, first of all because of present economic conditions, and second, because the statistically proven surplus of women in the population of our country means that a large number of women simply cannot get married. Since only 10 percent of these women inherit sufficient means to live, the other 90 percent are forced to enter the labor market to earn their living in some sort of occupation. The position and participation of homosexual women in the women's movement and the movement's attempts to solve these problems are significant and deserve extensive, universal attention.

One must distinguish between two facets of the homosexual woman, her general personality and her sexual proclivity. Her overall personality is of primary importance; of secondary importance is the direction of her sex drive, which must be considered in all its complexity before it can be completely understood, since the physical love drive is generally an overflow, a natural result of psychological qualities, i.e., in people with primarily masculine characteristics, it naturally directs itself toward women and vice versa, regardless of the actual physical sex of the person. The homosexual woman possesses many qualities, inclinations, and capacities which we ordinarily consider masculine. She particularly deviates from the feminine norm in her emotional life. While emotion is almost always—exceptions prove the rule—the predominant and deciding trait in the heterosexual woman, clear reason rules the Uranian woman. She is, like the average man, more objective, energetic, and goal oriented than the feminine woman; her thoughts and feelings are those of a man; she does not imitate man, she is inherently similar to him, and this is the important point that the foes of the so-called "man-woman" always ignore because they never really bother to study the homosexual phenomenon. It is very easy to condemn something one does not understand, just as easy as it is difficult to correct a preconceived and wrong opinion or to allow a false notion to be changed by enlightenment.

I want to mention here that there exist both an absolute and a merely psychological homosexuality. Masculine characteristics do not necessarily result in a sexual drive toward the female sex, for each homosexual woman possesses more or less feminine characteristics, which, with the immensely diverse gradations in the transition between the sexes, can at times be expressed in a sexual drive toward a man. Of course, in these cases the drive usually exerts itself toward a very feminine man, as the natural complement to the woman with a strongly masculine soul. To support my statement, let me cite the cases of George Sand and Daniel Stern, both of whom loved men who were of the most feminine type, Frederick Chopin and Franz Liszt. Clara Schumann, the great artist, was also married to a man with strongly feminine inclinations, Robert Schumann. It appears, by the way, as though in the women I described as psychologically homosexual, the sexual drive was never very strongly developed; George Sand and Daniel Stern loved their artists far more with their souls than with their senses. To a certain extent I am therefore inclined to refer to "unsexual" natures when I speak of psychologically homosexual women.

Since the homosexual woman with her masculine proclivities will never suitably complement a masculine man, it is clear that the Uranian woman is not suited for marriage. Uranian women usually are aware of this fact, at least subconsciously, and accordingly refuse to go to the altar. But often they must deal with parents, cousins, aunts, and all the other dear friends and relatives, who tell them day in and day out about the necessity of marriage, and with this wise advice make life hell for them. Thanks to the poor education we provide for young girls, Uranian women often stumble blindly into marriage, without clear views and concepts of sexuality and sex life. As long as so-called "society" views spinsterhood as something unpleasant, even inferior, Uranian women will all too often allow outer circumstances to drive them into marriages in which they will neither give nor receive happiness. Aren't such marriages far more immoral than the love pact of two people who are drawn to each other by a powerful force?

The women's movement wants to reform marriage. It wants to bring about legal changes so that present conditions will cease to exist, so that discord and injustice, arbitrariness and slavish subjection, will disappear from the family, so that future generations will be healthier and stronger.

In connection with these attempts to reform, the women's movement must not forget the degree to which absurd attitudes toward homosexual women are responsible for tragic marriages. I specifically say "the degree to which" because naturally I do not attribute total blame to those absurd attitudes. But because even part of the blame lies there, the women's movement cannot dismiss its responsibility for informing society by spoken and written work how pernicious it is to force homosexual women into marriage. First of all, it is bad for the two people involved. The man is simply deceived because, apart from its ideal meaning, marriage is a mutual contract in which both parties assume rights and duties. However, a homosexual woman can fulfill her duties toward the man only with aversion or, at best, with indifference. A forced sexual union is doubtless a torture for both parties, and no decent, thoughtful man can see anything desirable in it, or find the happiness for which he was looking in a marriage with a Uranian woman. It often happens that the decent man then avoids sexual intercourse at home for the sake of the woman and looks for satisfaction of his sex drive in the arms of his mistress or with prostitutes. Because feminists care about the moral fiber and health of our people, they must wholeheartedly combat the pressures used to force homosexuals to marry. The women's movement can spread enlightenment which will enable society to see that the marriage of homosexuals is a triple crime; it is a crime against the state, against society itself, and against an unborn generation, for experience teaches us that the offspring of Uranians are seldom healthy and strong. The unhappy creatures who are conceived and born without love, or even desire, represent a large percentage of the mentally disturbed, retarded, epileptics, tuberculars, and degenerates of all kinds. Morbid sexual drives such as sadism and masochism are often the legacy from Uranians who procreated against their nature. The state and society should have an urgent interest in preventing Uranians from marrying, since it is the state and society who bear the burden of the care of these sick and weak beings who are unable to make any contribution in return.

It seems to me that an essentially practical point for heterosexual women to remember is that if homosexuals would remain single without damage to their social status, there would be more husbands available for those women whose natural inclinations are satisfied by the role of wife, housekeeper, and mother. Unfortunately, we still lack valid statistics regarding the number of homosexual women, but according to my intense work in this area, I believe that the statistics which resulted from Dr. Hirschfeld's studies of male homosexuality can be applied also to women. Therefore, there are approximately as many Uranian women as single women in Germany. To be more precise: say there are two million unmarried women and two million homosexual women; among these probably around 50 percent (one million) of the single women are Uranians, and around 50 percent (one million) of female homosexuals are married. They married because of social pressure, and thus blocked marriage for one million single heterosexual women. The conclusion is obvious. If more Uranian women remained single, more heterosexual women would have the opportunity to marry, which of course does not mean that this is a universal remedy against spinsterhood because there are many social conditions which are causing men to have increasing animosity toward marriage—a subject that is not relevant to our discussion here.

If the women's movement would focus on homosexuality as it relates to the marriage question, the original conception of marriage as a union between a man and woman who love each other might again come into its own. Today's too frequent marriages for money or "sensible" matches are in direct contrast to the ethical demand that people marry only for love.

I have observed that many homosexual women marry because they recognize their natural inclinations too late, and as a result they create unhappiness for themselves and others. Here too the women's movement can help, since it is very concerned with the education of the young; it can point out the importance of explaining the nature of homosexuality rationally and sensibly to older children and young people in whom homosexual tendencies have been detected by loving parents and honest, understanding friends. In this way, immense tortures and misery caused by attempts to force homosexual children into heterosexual paths could be prevented. There is no danger that effeminate heterosexual children might be considered homosexual and therefore made into homosexuals because such education would only be given after a consultation with a physician who is knowledgeable in this area. Also, experience proves that neither seduction nor anything else can transform a heterosexual into a homosexual or vice versa. Of course, a heterosexual individual can be seduced into homosexual acts, but this is a result of curiosity, craving for personal pleasure, or the need to obtain a substitute for unavailable normal intercourse. For example, the latter instance is prevalent amongst sailors, whose natural sexual drives do not change and will prevail under normal conditions.

Now, I personally want to reiterate a point frequently made by Dr. Hirschfeld, and that is that homosexuals do not belong exclusively to any particular social class; that is, homosexuality does not occur more frequently in the upper class than the lower class, or vice versa. No father or mother—not even those among you—can safely assume that there is no Uranian child among his or her offspring. There is a strange belief prevalent in the middle class that homosexuality does not exist in their circles, and from this group comes the greatest opposition to Uranian liberation. I myself remember that once in my parents' home when homosexuality became a topic of conversation, my father declared with conviction: "This sort of thing can't happen in my family!" The facts prove the opposite! Nothing else need be said!

To return to the marriage question, I would like to note that a homosexual woman almost never becomes what can be described as a "spinster." And this remarkable fact makes Uranian women more easily recognized, especially in their later years. If one looks at an unmarried homosexual woman between the age of thirty and fifty, none of the ridiculed characteristics attributed to the average single heterosexual woman can be found. This is interesting because it proves that sensible and moderate satisfaction of the sex drive also keeps women full of life, fresh and active, while absolute sexual abstinence easily causes those unpleasant qualities we find in the spinster, such as meanness, hysteria, irritability, etc.

In order to obtain for homosexuals and all women generally the opportunity to live according to their natures, it is necessary to actively aid the women's movement's efforts to expand educational opportunities and new professions for women. But what about the ancient argument of sexual superiority? I believe that with a little good will the dispute can be settled after examination of nature's intent in creating man and woman and the transitions between the two. One must conclude that it is wrong to value one sex more highly than the other—to speak of a first-class sex, man, a second-class sex, woman, and a third-class sex, the Uranian. The sexes are not of different value, they are merely of different kind. Because of this, it is clear that men, women, and Uranians are not equally suited for all professions. This is a fact the women's movement cannot change, nor does it want to.

The feminine woman has been designed by nature to become first of all wife and mother. And she has a right to be proud of this natural destiny because there is no more honorable occupation than that of mother. Naturally, the woman who is wife, or mother, or both, does not need to forget the rest of the world because of this occupation. Rather, she should participate in all aspects of public life according to her capabilities. This is one of the most attractive goals of the women's movement.

Nature has assigned different functions to the normal man (that is, the completely virile man) than to the woman. It is undeniable that the man is physically more suited for a rugged life's struggle than a woman, so that occupations are open to him that are automatically closed to a woman, for example that of the soldier and all those jobs requiring hard physical labor.

Of course, outside of such extremes there are many professions that can be practiced equally well by men or by women, depending on their individual capabilities. One of the weakest points in the logic of the opponents of the women's movement is found in their penchant for lumping all women together under the rubric "woman," failing to note that there are no two completely identical beings, and further that professional attitudes depend upon the combined masculine and feminine qualities a person possesses. Therefore we can differentiate between a feminine personality in which feminine characteristics dominate; a masculine one, in which the masculine characteristics dominate; and finally, a feminine-masculine or a masculine-feminine personality with equally masculine and feminine qualities. When nature created the different sexes, she certainly did not intend for there to be one sphere for woman—the home—and another for man—the world. Rather, the intention was for each person to fill the role appropriate to his or her own traits and abilities.

The combinations of masculine and feminine characteristics vary so much from one person to another that all children, whether masculine or feminine, should be educated for independence in the name of simple justice. This will enable the adults to decide for themselves whether their nature suits them for the home or the world, marriage or no marriage. There must be free choice available to enable women to make their own decisions to pursue an artistic or learned profession, or to feel that they are not strong enough to do so. It is the sacred responsibility of parents to avoid stereotyped upbringing for their children and to see that each is educated according to his or her individual characteristics. Of course the schools now follow established patterns, but in the future they must provide equal education for both boys and girls and discard the notion that girls have less intellectual capacity than boys.

One need not fear that equal education for boys and girls will cause increasing competition in the professions—particularly in academia, as our opponents claim. It is true that homosexual women are specially suited for the sciences because they have those qualities lacking in feminine women: greater objectivity, energy, and perseverance. Naturally, this observation does not preclude the fact that there are extremely capable heterosexual women who are doctors, lawyers, etc. Nevertheless, I must maintain that under favorable conditions most heterosexual women choose marriage. They seek a broader, more comprehensive education in order to be esteemed companions for their husbands, not just sensual love-objects, and to be wives who are respected by their husbands as intellectual equals, and accordingly granted equal rights and responsibilities in the marriage.

Therefore, men, women, and homosexuals all benefit from a more equitable upbringing and education. Men will gain rational, sensitive companions for their lives; women will gradually gain a more worthy and legally protected position; and the Uranians will be free to dedicate themselves to their chosen professions.

Just as homosexual men often prefer professions that have a feminine quality, such as women's fashions, nursing, cooking, or being servants, homosexual women also lean toward certain professions. Thus there are many homosexual women in the medical, judicial, and agricultural professions, as well as in the creative arts.

There are those who, like Weininger, maintain that all well-known, significant, or famous women in history, literature, science, or other fields were homosexual. With my earlier statements in mind, it should be unnecessary for me to emphasize my belief that this concept cannot be substantiated, for not only history but our own observations daily prove its fallacy. On the other hand, one cannot and should not deny that many noted women were indeed homosexually inclined—I'll mention only Sappho, Christine of Sweden, Sonja Kowalewska, Rosa Bonheur. However, it would be inaccurate to include Elizabeth of England and Katharine the Great of Russia among the Uranians; while the latter was probably bisexual—her many male and female "friendships" definitely point in that direction—she was definitely not purely homosexual.

Contrary to the belief of the anti-feminists that women are inferior and that only those with strong masculine characteristics are to be valued, I believe that women in general are equal to men. I am convinced, however, that the homosexual woman is particularly capable of playing a leading role in the international women's rights movement for equality. And indeed, from the beginning of the women's movement until the present day, a significant number of homosexual women assumed the leadership in the numerous struggles and, through their energy, awakened the naturally indifferent and submissive average women to an awareness of their human dignity and rights. I am unable and unwilling to name names because as long as many consider homosexuality criminal and unnatural, at best sick, ladies I could call homosexual might feel insulted. Above all, decency and duty forbid indiscretion, and neither the noble love of a Uranian suffragette nor the feelings of a heterosexual need be aired in a public forum. But anyone with the slightest bit of familiarity with homosexual traits who has been following the women's movement at all or who knows any of its leading women personally or by pictures, will find the Uranians among the suffragettes and recognize that Uranians are often noble and fine.

Considering the contributions made to the women's movement by homosexual women for decades, it is amazing that the large and influential organizations of the movement have never lifted a finger to improve the civil rights and social standing of their numerous Uranian members. It is amazing that they have done nothing, absolutely nothing, to protect many of their best-known and most deserving leaders from ridicule and scorn by enlightening the general public about the true nature of Uranianism. They could, for example, point out that homosexual proclivities express themselves often unconsciously and unintentionally in appearance, speech, deportment, movement, dress, etc., exposing the Uranian unjustly to the heartless mockery of coarse, ignorant people. Of course not all homosexual women show masculine exteriors that harmonize with their inner selves. There are many Uranian women with completely feminine appearance which they accentuate with very feminine behavior in order to escape being detected as homosexuals. This is a comedy which is bitter and painful to those who must participate.

I understand the reason for the reluctance of the women's movement to deal with this problem, although it deals very frankly with other purely sexual matters. It stems from its fear that the movement could suffer in the eyes of the still blind and ignorant masses if it took up the homosexual question by energetically supporting the human rights of Uranians. I'll frankly admit that this fear was justified during the early days of the women's movement when it had to carefully avoid losing converts, and this fear was a credible excuse for temporarily ignoring the homosexual question. Today, however, when the movement is advancing unimpeded, when no bureaucratic wisdom, no philistinism, can block its triumphant march, this failure to deal with an important question is an injustice, an injustice which the women's movement inflicts on itself. Of course, the so-called "moderate" faction of the movement will not rouse itself to support the homosexuals simply because action along this line does not appeal to them. Someday victory will be won under the banner of radicalism. It is the radicals we expect to break the spell and openly and honestly confess: Yes, there are many Uranians among us, and we are indebted to them for their energy and work, which have brought us many great successes. Not that I want all questions of the women's movement dealt with from the homosexual standpoint; it is not my wish to credit the Uranians with all or even the largest share of accomplishments—that would be just as silly as it is wrong to ignore them.

Without a doubt, the women's movement has greater and more important assignments to complete than homosexual liberation, but it can only handle the more important tasks if it does not neglect the less significant ones. Therefore, the women's movement should not place special emphasis on the homosexual question; it is not necessary to preach about the injustices done to the Uranians from every rooftop—this would only harm the movement—I understand this aspect well; it need only speak objectively about the homosexual question when addressing the sexual, official, economic, and purely human relationships of the sexes to each other. That it can do, and in so doing, it can slowly and quietly bring about enlightenment.

I am now getting to a topic with which the women's movement has been specially concerned in recent years—prostitution. From an ethical standpoint, one can think of it as one wishes; in any case, it will have to be dealt with for a long time to come. Personally, I regard prostitution as an unfortunate but necessary evil which will be impossible to eradicate as long as there are human passions, but which, if we are fortunate, we can lessen—a goal worth striving for.

An important fact that has been completely ignored by the women's movement's struggle against the increase of prostitution and its destructive companion, venereal disease, is that 20 percent of all prostitutes are homosexual. At first this may seem odd because of the contradiction between homosexuality and constant sexual intercourse with the male. This situation has been explained to me more than once by a "girl of the streets" who told me that she considered her sad trade as business—completely divorced from her sexual drive, which was satisfied by her woman lover. Adverse domestic and economic conditions had driven these girls into the street.

When the women's movement succeeds in creating a situation in which occupants are open equally to all people according to their individual talents and capabilities, homosexual prostitutes would disappear, and a large percentage of the heterosexual girls who now turn to prostitution because of bad social conditions, could support themselves better and with more human dignity. They would prepare themselves for a profession early in life because they would be brought up to be independent. A girl who learns to deal with life at an early age will not be as apt to end up in the street as a girl who lives thoughtlessly with no understanding of the simplest and most natural aspects of life. In a certain sense, the struggle of the homosexual woman for social acceptance is also a struggle against prostitution, although I must emphasize the fact that this struggle could only result in a lessening of prostitution, not its eradication.

One must not forget that justice for Uranians in general would mean that a great number of homosexual men who are driven to prostitutes by their fear of detection would no longer find this necessary. This, of course, would result in a reduction of venereal disease, which though small would be valuable, for each single case in which syphilis or other venereal infection is avoided is a victory for the health of the people and the coming generation on whom rests the well-being and greatness of our fatherland.

The women's movement fights for the right of individuality and self-determination. It must admit that the alienating ban that society still places on Uranians suppresses this right; and therefore its responsibility is to join the homosexuals in their struggles, just as it actively assists unwed mothers, working women, and many others as they fight for freedom and right, battling against old, false, traditional concepts of a morality which is in actuality an immorality of the worst kind.

Just as woman is battling to win back the ancient human right which was taken from her by raw force, the Uranians have an innate, natural right to their love, which is as noble and pure as heterosexual love when the persons involved are good. There are good people among homosexuals just as there are among the so-called "normals."

I want most of all to avoid the appearance of having overestimated the Uranians. I can assure you, ladies and gentlemen, that I have not. I recognize the faults and weaknesses of homosexuals too well, but I also know their good points and therefore can say: The Uranians are neither better nor worse than heterosexuals—they are not of different value, only of different kind.

In summary, I want to emphasize once more that the Uranian woman has played an important part in all aspects of our great women's movement. With her androgynous characteristics, she was often the one who initiated action because she felt most strongly the many, many injustices and hardships with which laws, society, and archaic customs treat women. Without the active support of the Uranian women, the women's movement would not be where it is today—this is an undisputable fact.

The women's movement and the homosexual rights movement have long traveled a dark path filled with innumerable obstacles. Now the light is gradually being turned on in human hearts, and it is becoming brighter for us. Not that the difficult fight for the rights of women and Uranians is over; we are still in the middle of strife in both instances, and many a heated battle will be fought, many a victim will fall because of false morality or an unfortunate law, before both movements attain their goal—individual liberation. Much sooner, both movements will reach the point when they will recognize that they have many mutual interests, when they will peacefully join hands in order to join forces in battle where it is necessary.

And if at first we find serious and difficult hours in store for us, we must not give up in cowardice, but must move courageously through the hostile forces, onward to the victory which is assured us. For the sun of understanding and truth has risen in the east, and no power of darkness can alter its radiant course—slowly it will rise higher and higher! Not today or tomorrow, but in the not too distant future, the women's movement and Uranians will raise their flags of victory!

Per aspera ad astra!

2

CULTURAL CRITIQUE: THE COMMUNITY OF THE SPECIAL

In 1896, the Berlin schoolteacher Adolf Brand (1874–1945) founded a journal entitled *Der Eigene,* a term meaning at once "the special" or "the exceptional" as well as "the self-owner." Inspired initially by a combination of individualist anarchism and libertarianism inspired by the philosophers Max Stirner and Friedrich Nietzsche, Brand shifted his editorial focus in 1899 and made *Der Eigene* a purely homophile journal with the subtitle *A Periodical for Masculine Culture, Art, and Literature.* With significant interruptions due to censorship, this first homosexual periodical of the world appeared as a monthly, an annual, and at times a weekly until 1932. Brand also published numerous pamphlets and brochures, prose and poetry anthologies, photo collections of male nudes, and two other homophile journals, *Freundschaft und Freiheit* (1921) and *Eros* (1929–31).

In 1902, Brand joined Benedict Friedländer and Wilhelm Jansen in founding the *Gemeinschaft der Eigenen,* or Community of the Special (or Self-Owners) with membership drawn largely from readers of the journal. Members also received a *Wochenbericht* (1904–05), *Korrespondenzblatt* (1905–06), *Extrapost* (1911–12), and *Flugschriften* (1906–25). Informed by the German "life reform movement," which sought to remedy the ills of urbanism by a return to a healthy lifestyle in nature (including nudism, organic food, and exercise), the Community had three guiding principles.

First, it repudiated the "third-sex" notion of homosexuality first advanced by Ulrichs and continued by Hirschfeld. In doing so, it simultaneously criticized Hirschfeld's alleged personal effeminacy, discredited his medical model as tantamount to conceding the biological inferiority of practicing homosexuals, and glorified masculine culture while relegating heterosexuality to purely procreative ends. Indeed, it ridiculed both exclusive heterosexuality and exclusive homosexuality while glorifying the notion of a bisexual elite. Second, this elite ethos was traced back historically to the erotic friendships among youths and between youths and mature men in ancient Greece—a form of social intercourse that had been stamped out by Christian asceticism. The Committee's antifeminism was expressed in its advocacy of separate spheres for men and women, with politics a masculine reserve while females served purely domestic roles. Friedländer, who like Brand was married, called for a combination of heterosexual marriage and extramarital relations with teenage boys, anticipating in some respects today's political discussions of pedophilia. Influenced by the widespread turn-of-the-century concern about national/racial degeneracy, the Committee held the preponderance of "feminine" values in modern Western culture to be the root cause. Third, the Community emphasized male bonding, especially among youth and between men and boys, and was therefore delighted by the development of the *Wandervogel,* a contemporaneous youth movement that advocated hiking and camping. The *Wandervogel* was interpreted by the influential Hans Blüher (1888–1952) as fundamentally homoerotic; with some changes, it survived until the onset of Nazism and compulsory membership in the Hitler Youth.

Some members of Hirschfeld's Committee, such as Friedländer, seceded in 1904 and became active opponents. While the Committee sought cooperation with other groups, such as the Social Democrats and the feminists, the Community proudly abjured any such contacts and remained exclusively male. While the Committee favored internationalism, the Community was nationalistic. The Committee's nonpartisan approach to politics was derived from what it regarded as its purely scientific research into the nature of human sexuality; the Community repudiated any form of parliamentary politics and cultivated aestheticism. Brand and his following lashed out at Hirschfeld in explicitly anti-Semitic terms and took an ambivalent approach to the rise of Nazism, pleased by its emphasis upon masculinity but concerned about its homophobia. Forced to stop publishing during the Third Reich, Brand lived with his family in Berlin until the final year of World War II, when he was killed in an aerial bombardment.

We present here three texts representing the Community's principles: 1) Friedländer's statement of secession from Hirschfeld's Committee; 2) a programmatic statement by Adolf Brand; and 3) an excerpt from "Seven Propositions" that shows the Community's cultural politics and forays into partisan politics.

from

MEMOIR FOR THE FRIENDS AND CONTRIBUTORS OF THE SCIENTIFIC-HUMANITARIAN COMMITTEE IN THE NAME OF THE SECESSION OF THE SCIENTIFIC-HUMANITARIAN COMMITTEE

(1907)

Benedict Friedländer

I. Scientific Points of Difference

... The importance of our separation for the whole emancipation movement ... lies chiefly in the area of theory: The path is open for a less dogmatic, more impartial, and more correct evaluation of same-sex love. Let it be sharply emphasized here that we lay far less weight on a scientific theory than Herr Hirschfeld and see the question much more from the standpoint of natural rights as one of personal freedom.

The forces that heretofore have been placed in the service of the Urning-farce, partly from genuine conviction, partly on the grounds of a deceptive opportunism, and mostly in the absence of something better, have already become free in part and are partly becoming free in a progressive measure. Already three years ago I declared that the exclusive or preponderate medical leadership of a movement that in the final analysis amounts to a demand for personal and social freedom has to be understood as in itself an abnormality and only a transitional stage, if perhaps necessary at the beginning. This intermezzo has now, with the separation and new foundation of a different kind of organization, reached its definitive end, or at least made a great step toward that end.

Not a few of Hirschfeld's contributors hold to the "intermediate" theory less from conviction than in the belief that the doctrine of the "intermediate nature" of same-sex love is especially suited to the fight for the repeal of §175.

I myself have heard from persons who stand close to Herr Hirschfeld that other scientific theories are less fruitful for public discussion, perhaps even harmful. Now, it is an old experience that science cannot flourish where respect is paid to opportunistic motives. One asks less for the criteria of truth or probability of a theory than for the agitation effect to be expected. Genuine science, or better said perhaps—since the word science has been sullied by too many—an honest searching for truth asks less for the agitation effect and has no diplomatically pliant motives. It is true that it is mostly exposed to stronger hostility than one with concern for the ruling prejudices and the unjust power of a stew of the correct and incorrect. If one fixes his eyes on a longer period of time, then the victory is on the side of impartial science. Those contributors should think about this, who themselves hold the Ulrichs-theory represented by Herr Hirschfeld to be basically false but yet support it with clinking coins because they suppose it to be indispensable for agitation ...

The Secession protests not only against the organizational and financial troubles of the old Committee, but also against its beggarly theory—a theory that is shabbily borrowed and is used to beg for pity. Although we too—to emphasize it immediately—neither make propaganda for same-sex love, at least not for its more material, sexual side, nor "glorify" it, but rather only want to research and spread the truth about it, we still intend to take a road that is more direct, perhaps somewhat steeper, but at any rate shorter than that of the old Committee. And since this is in part a matter of temperament, it has already been shown and will in the future more clearly appear that our conception can from the beginning count on sympathy in the circles of the more virile friends of male youth—no matter whether they have "sexual" intercourse or not, since that is for the unbiased a relatively secondary matter and at any rate a purely private affair; whereas the extremely feminine "homosexuals" will, on the whole, feel more comfortable in Hirschfeld's camp . . .

Now, just what is the science of the Scientific Committee?

Not only Hirschfeld but the medical writers all together have spread about, with small divergences and insignificant additions, the contents of the twelve brochures of the jurist K. H. Ulrichs. Ulrichs was a sincere, courageous, and original man. With his appearance, which for that time was truly pioneering, he had seemingly little success. A generation later, when the question was no longer so un-discussable, there came eager medical doctors, armored with their authority, who believed that they had tracked down a new field of activity for theory and practice. And their scent did not deceive them. Ulrichs was shouted down at the meeting of jurists in Munich in 1867 and died alone in 1895 in Aquila in Abruzzi; the medical men who followed him had, each in his own way, pretty fair success with money, esteem, or both. One satisfied himself with commercial speculation on the need for sexual excitement of the public, who bought numerous editions of his so-called *Psychopathia sexualis*; others, for a fee, through hypnotism and suggestion therapy, took away love for a friend and turned it into love for a woman; still others carried on successful agitation activities . . .

In truth the medical writers on homosexuality presented to the public, partly in thick volumes, partly in tract format, everything that the Hannoverian *Amtsassessor* had brought into the world, supplied with the stamp of medical authority almost without any criticism, partly translated into the jargon of medical quackery, and decorated with so-called "case histories."

For the knowledgeable, these latecomers betray themselves as such principally through the fact that they even copy the errors and tastelessness of the original—exactly the way that the plagiarist is most surely betrayed by taking over typographical errors. Thus the dependence of the medical literature on the truths and errors of Ulrichs is seen externally by the fact that the silly, ungrammatical, and tasteless word "Urning," invented by Ulrichs in an evil hour, has by now, along with its derivations, come into circulation with the serious aspect of a "scientific" technical term. It's supposed to have come from Urania; having been amputated, however, it rather recalls urn or Urner Lake in Switzerland—or whatever—than the heavenly goddess.

Essentially, however—in spite of a few partial predecessors, which cannot be discussed here—Ulrichs is the inventor of the theory, celebrated in propaganda and subsidized by thousands, of the "sexual intermediate," the theory of the poor female soul that languishes in a male body, and of the "third sex."

Certainly there are "sexual intermediates." Earlier they were called hermaphrodites. They are the rare malformations, which may be estimated to make up—at most—a small fraction per thousand. Of those who are aware of their same-sex feelings, however, there are whole percents; if one counts together the totally and partially homosexual, then on the basis of statistical inquiries one reaches a full six percent; and if one does not limit the concept of same-sex love to crude external factors, one would attain still larger numbers. This monstrous difference alone in the orders of size of objectively perceived hermaphrodites and those with same-sex feelings makes the theory of sexual intermediates extremely unlikely.

A glance at the non- and pre-Christian cultures is sufficient to prove the complete untenability of the theory. In ancient Hellas in particular most of the generals, artists, and thinkers would have to have been hermaphrodites. Every people from whose initiative in all higher human endeavors every later European culture fed must have consisted in great part of sick, hybrid individuals, and indeed especially before and at their golden age. For it is directly the older Hellenic literature in which by "love" only the love of youths is understood, while the love of woman became more apparent only with the emergence of the relatively emancipated woman toward the period of decline. The ancient Hellenic cult of youth, therefore, has been a suppressed and avoided stumbling-block. That custom was indeed much, much too universal to have been able to be borne by the assumed 1.5 percent of "homosexuals"! Rather, it was obvious that that state of affairs rested predominantly on the very much larger number of so-called "bisexuals" and the idea at least suggested itself that a certain degree of "bisexuality" was still more widespread than the modern statistic shows and only with us could be artificially brought to shrivel up through effective suggestion from youth on against everything that even remotely reminded one of homosexuality.

All that was discussed in detail by me three years ago in my *Renaissance des Eros Uranios*. Until then there was little talk of bisexuals in the Urning camp, since it was unsuited to theory and agitation, and it was only my writing and also, perhaps, the results of statistics that forced the champions of the theory of intermediates to concern themselves a bit more with bisexuality. The state of Hellenic customs, the great number of bisexuals, and the considerations connected with them appeared critical, that is, since they could give the opponents a ready assumption that a repeal of §175 would bring with it the Hellenic customs and social condition, against which there exists a nearly insurmountable prejudice, principally borne by the interests of womanhood.

The answer to that reflection would not be difficult; a glance at the countries without §175 proves—one may complain about it or rejoice over it—that such a result in no way comes about, since custom is much stronger than law. Custom is Argus-eyed and affects the slightest approbations; the law must be limited to sharply definable, coarse events and of these sees only a downright vanishing fraction. On the other hand, close observation of society in Germany shows that an approximation to the Hellenic cult of the adolescent is very well possible in not entirely small circles in spite of §175. In this sense the Hellenic condition just depends much less on any such paragraph as on custom, which in this case predominantly rests on the social position of women. As long as women, by operating merely with social weapons through their social omnipresence, are able to proscribe and make difficult the love of youths, which they hate as a kind of unfair competition, then that condition is impossible to a wide extent, with or without §175. But as soon as a nation or individual groups have got rid of the European valuation of woman, then, with or without §175, the formation of a Hellenic social condition or an approximation to it is the inevitable consequence . . .

Recently the most productive of the medical doctors who have been writing about things sexual have wanted to separate Hellenic paederasty, sanctified by national custom, as a "pseudo-homosexuality" connected with bisexuality from "genuine" homosexuality. That this national custom was based in a much higher degree on bisexuality than on pure homosexuality is correct of course, as has been said, and this was long ago emphasized by us and others. But since it is still a matter of true love among those truly of the same sex, it is simply incomprehensible what should be "pseudo" about it . . .

In spite of its lack of originality the medical literature has doubtless been extremely useful. The medical authority that spoke of "observations of illness" was allowed expressions otherwise made difficult by the touch-me-not stamp of prudery and suppressive laws. Only through the intercession of several doctors, no matter whether through selflessness or self-interest, could wider circles be educated about the mere presence of same-sex love and the fact be made the object of universal knowledge, that there is really a large number of purely "homosexually" inclined men—something asserted till now by only a few and doubted by others. And only thereby has that movement come about that is constantly drawing in wider circles and can surely no longer be stopped by any power. Far be it from us to underestimate the significance of the medical agitation.

Through its undivided dominance, however, the movement has fallen into a fateful one-sidedness that, if allowed to continue undisturbed, must in the end do more damage than the whole medical propaganda has otherwise done good. For one would finally get rid of §175 on the basis of purely juridical considerations, just as the analogous penal clauses in other countries have passed away without medical help.

The mere circumstance that the larger public always sees only doctors at the head of the movement must further the error that it is a question of a sickness or at least a pathology. With sicknesses one can have pity, of course, and act "humanely" toward the sick, and even seek to "cure" them; the equal rights of those alleged to be physically inferior will never be recognized.

Now, it is true that the more progressive among the medical men have expressly dropped the doctrine of the sickness of same-sex love: they also had to do it, for otherwise their clients would have run away from them.

But a remainder of the error is left and can only disappear along with the false "intermediate stage" theory. An admixture of feminine characteristics, that is, an approximation to an at least physical hermaphrodite, such as the Ulrichs theory teaches as an explanation of same-sex love, must of course always give the appearance that all men who have complete or partial same-sex feelings are to be considered to be not quite whole and afflicted with an incompleteness. As long as the love for a male being is presented as a specific and exclusively feminine characteristic—something that applies to non-social creatures, to be sure, but not to highly social human beings—it will not help to deny sickness: there remains an unavoidable image of a partial hermaphrodite, that is, a kind of psychic malformation. Here too one cannot claim respect, but only at most beg for pity and at best tolerance.

The medical direction has occupied itself all too exclusively with the coarser and crudest side of the question and at most only touched on the psychic and cultural part of the question. That amounts to the same thing as wanting to concentrate one's point of view exclusively on the possibly, but not necessarily occurring physiological-animal sexual acts in the case of man-woman love in life, art, and literature. Granted, the grotesque penal clause, in the case of man-man love, concerns only the sexual act and it only under certain limitations.

But number §175 is also not the main point. Certainly the legal monster creates a great amount of undeserved misery, in that it yearly sends to prison like thieves and swindlers 500–600 men and youths who have never caused the least harm to anyone. For the whole of the nation, however, the decisive disadvantage is the impediment to friendship and bonds between men that comes from that superstition and the clause that belongs to it. That prejudice weighs, namely, on all men and youths who feel themselves more or less drawn to one another, but who mistrust their natural instinct because they have been taught to view the possible extremes, which could happen, as a horrible vice and, strangely, even as a "punishable act."

Thus the tabu of same-sex love among men contributes very essentially to the improper absolute rule of woman-love, to the suppression of male friendship, and thereby to a feminization of the whole culture. A comparison of the appreciation which that friendship enjoyed in classic antiquity—without regard for the foolish and indiscreet question of whether it came to "sexual" acts or not!—with our condition makes that all too clear. At that time there was still no one who seriously talked that nonsense about the equal intellect and equal rights of women. In the case of the whole white race it has come to a fateful exaggeration of the family principle—that most primitive form of socialization, which human beings share even with the beasts of prey—which breaks up states and eats away the national unity. The other, world-enriching love, which is reserved to the social species, which Walt Whitman called "love of comrades," and which is most closely connected with so-called homosexuality, has on the contrary withdrawn entirely into the background.

Poor Whitman! What hope you had for the love of comrades for your United States! And you forgot that over there by you the prevailing "lady-economy" will never allow the love of comrades, which reaches beyond feminine show and family life.[1]

Of these cultural-scientific connections, which indeed give more offence to our enemies, but because of their truth also represent a much greater moral force than talk about Urnings, there is basically nothing said in the medical literature.

Still, that would also have been asking too much for the beginner. The public is even less ready for the last and highest branch of the homosexual question than it is for the physical foundation; it was perhaps an indeed regrettable, but necessary precept of wisdom to keep silent about it in the agitation in the beginning. But it certainly should have been exceptionally emphasized that man-man love is capable of the same spiritualization and emotional depth as man-woman love. . . . But what is one to say when the principal spokesman, Herr Hirschfeld himself, in a half-literary, half-popular scientific form talks about "Berlin's third sex" and leads the reader into a sort of "thieves' den" milieu, as if that belonged to the essence of the matter! In my *Renaissance* I rather warned against forming a judgment in the matter from the doings of this "third sex" in the well-known bars, since one gets to see there only some of the symptoms of degeneration caused by the pressure of modern morality.

Through such presentations the cause advocated will, without need and against the truth, be degraded and harmed. Certainly the seamy side may sometimes be shown and the sad consequences of the unhealthy pressure that—with and without a penal clause—weighs on Hellenic love in Christian Europe; that should have been done in a passing way by another party and not by the spokesman in the liberation movement. There are really enough bright sides to the love of friends! Let us just not hide the fact that most really intimate and passionate young friendships, even those that later predominantly incline toward women, are permeated by the spirit of Eros Uranios—no matter whether it thereby comes to sexual trifles or not! Let us just understand that no one can be a good educator who does not love his pupils! And let us not lie to ourselves that in love the so-called "spiritual" element can ever be completely detached from its physiological foundation. It is an eternal verity: Only a good paederast can be a complete pedagogue. Here the word "paederast" is not to be understood, of course, in the meaning that medieval slander imposed on it by confounding the similar sounding words *paiderastia* and *pedicatio* . . .[2]

At the time I was writing my earlier booklet I did not yet know the work of Heinrich Schurtz . . .[3] What I discovered by the physiological-analytical path, namely the presence of a "physiological friendship," or, as Schurtz says, "sympathy" between persons of the same sex and the necessity of that affect for the sociability of our species, Schurtz had already discovered before me on the synthetic path of a cultural comparison of numerous examples, even though he explained and evaluated it somewhat differently. The diversity of the paths that Schurtz and I took guarantees my complete independence, and the similarity of the results found by us guarantees the essential correctness of our doctrines. These, however, unanimously attest that an instinctive, i.e., physiological sympathy between man and man is a normal basic character-istic of our species and is necessary for sociability, indeed is more important than the family principle, which in Christian Europe is exaggerated, at the cost of male friendship, to the dis-advantage of national unity. That Schurtz expressly distinguishes what he calls "sympathy" of men and especially of youths from sexuality does not change the matter. One needs only to read the descriptions in Schurtz of the men's unions and men's houses, in short the life togeth-er of the men and especially of the mature male youths of many primitive people, to gain the well-founded conviction that in those men's clubs and men's houses—even when women could enter—Venus Urania must not be less secret than, say, in our boarding schools and cadet institutes, all the more since those primitive people, at least before their Christianization, could not have had any kind of superstitious prejudice against lust.

The curious idea, that a pleasant feeling and its mutual arousal is in itself a wrong, a "sin," really goes back historically to the priesthood of the early Middle Ages and is therefore at present, even if in weakened form, limited to Christian and, with a somewhat different stamp, Buddhist cultural circles. The physiological analysis further shows that sexuality is altogether not a simple and inseparable instinct, but rather the result of a series of elemen-tary sensitivities. That, however, Schurtz' alleged entirely asexual "sympathy" between youths has some of these tropisms in common with undoubted sexuality, consequently is connect-ed with it in its root, and therefore is distinguished only by mixture, degree, and nuance, but by no means completely, nor can be distinguished in any imaginable way—this I believe I have proved on the basis of sound science and strict logic . . . [4]

To sum up precisely: the Urning theory proceeds from the false premise that love for a male being is an exclusively female characteristic, a "secondary female sex characteristic." That indeed holds true for the non-social species, but is false for the social species, for whose unity a physiological force of attraction also between those of the same sex is necessary. This is taught by a thoughtful consideration of every social species; it is proved by the trivial uni-versal fact that mere family instinct, that is man-woman love and parent-love, by no means leads to socialization, as we may see in the case of beasts of prey. Schurtz and I, independent of one another and on diverse paths, found the analog for the human being. This "physio-logical friendship," as I called it, or "sympathy," as Schurtz says, necessarily has several tro-pistic roots in common with sexuality and so is not a completely different kind of thing alto-gether; it therefore, as the observation of all peoples and all periods teaches, also very easily leads to the practice of sexual acts. That in some of the relatively few extreme cases of homo-sexuality there is also present a genuine sort of hermaphroditism—that is, for a minority of the most extreme constitutions the theory of intermediates is at least approximately cor-rect—is very well possible and even, from various grounds, not unlikely. But it certainly won't do to attribute such an extremely frequent phenomenon as homosexuality and bisex-uality to such a rare phenomenon as a partial hermaphroditism. It really is more obvious to think about the fact that, in the case of a human being as a social creature, there normally exist physiological-tropistic forces of attraction also between those of the same sex, which, since these cannot be entirely separated from sexual attraction, easily lead to sexual feelings and acts. By this means, and only thereby, does the great frequency and universal extent of bisexuality and homosexuality precisely in our species become comprehensible . . .

The connection between love of friends and men's unions is obvious besides. Dühring,[5] in his latest work *Waffen, Kapital, Arbeit,* expresses the view that paederasty is originally a dowry of militarism. I hold that to be not precisely false, but indeed too narrowly conceived. It appears everywhere to a certain extent and sometimes, in noble form, develops to a salu-tary people's custom, wherever men's unions exercise a greater influence, no matter whether these men's unions have a military character or not. But the connection is reciprocal. Just as the restraint of men's unions and the social omnipresence of women reduce paederasty, so too, the other way around, through an excessive tabu of paederasty the formation of a purely male society is made difficult, since this is then suspect and unpopular. A general revision of the highly important cultural-historical and cultural-technical chapter on "Men's unions and paederasty" is a scientific desideratum . . .

Thus the Urning theory by no means has remained without contradiction. Not only the experts on Hellenic antiquity, not only the cultural historians, and not only the poets with their more emotional expressions, but also the presentations of natural science as well have entered a repeated and searching protest. Every contradiction, however, remains as good as without any practical effect—at most that the science of the medical men, which is held to be competent in the question, has found occasion to go more closely into what in jargon is called bisexuality and which consists of the union of the ability for woman-love with that of *Lieblingminne*.

That the Urning theory, in spite of multiple disclosures of its untenability, could still be widely held and only occasionally, such as through the recognition of so-called "pseudo-homosexuality," suffer some limitations, has a very simple basis in the economic fact that the Urning theory acts toward the others somewhat the way a subsidized steamship line acts toward one not subsidized. A theory that in contrast to competing views is supported yearly with so and so many thousand marks through the free distribution of its books and tracts to the leaders of public opinion is as good as assured of the final victory in our busy and commercial age. In the year 1905 alone, besides the *Jahrbuch*, Urning publications to the value of 4000 marks (!) were distributed gratis to "newspapers, periodicals, experts, authorities, libraries, etc." (see *Jahrbuch* 8, page 939)! That, of course, is the private matter of those who give their money for it—what we are emphasizing here is the consideration that, under these circumstances, scientific truths can be established even less than is usually the case. Henry George, I believe, says or quotes somewhere—I don't recall the author—that even the law of gravity would be disputed if important interests stood in the way of its recognition. It can be asserted, the other way around, that one can make successful propaganda for any true or false theory, if one spends the money necessary for it. The connoisseur who observes the budding of a new "author" will at times be reminded of the rise of a new wine firm, which knows how, through clever advertising, travelers, and correspondents, to introduce itself "in the best circles," even when its wine is watered. If it may be shown in a certain case, therefore, that a theory has grown large through systematic advertising, reminding one of a commercial enterprise, that indeed does not prove that the theory must be false; it does prove that its victory over competing theories is not really due to its correctness. But those sums are available, on the one hand, because many believe that the Urning theory will lead quickest to the repeal of §§175, and partly just because the only influential organization is based on Ulrichs's theory. If our new organization succeeds in uniting a large part of the opposing elements under one banner, then that will probably change in a short time, all the more so since we do not at all wish to establish any special biological theory of paederasty—not even that which I personally hold to be correct. For the needs of agitation it is completely sufficient to point to the numerous instances of exclusive homosexuals and the still greater number of so-called bisexuals. A learned scientific discussion may here and there arouse interest; for all practical questions, in particular for the repeal of the penal clause, purely moral and juridical considerations are sufficient, according to which it is extremely immoral to act as guardian of the sexual lives of others by trailing and spying and is a juridical absurdity to punish acts by which every harm is lacking. But that is the subject of the following section.

II. Our Program

It now only remains to briefly explain our program. From a scientific view, regarding the theoretical judgment of same-sex love we reject the Ulrichs-theory of intermediates for the reasons set forth above. Thus we shall not speak of "Urnings," nor of the "third sex," nor yet of "sexual intermediates."

We are further of the opinion that through the exclusively medical treatment of a general human matter a basic error has been made. The object of the doctor is sicknesses; therefore he is inclined, because of his profession, to classify everything possible under the concept of sickness or pathology. We are of the view that the scientist who does not have a one-sided medical training, the physiologist and anthropologist, is by profession at least as competent an expert to scientifically judge the question of same-sex love as the medical man, whose general scientific education is mostly poorly cultivated. We are of this opinion for the reason that at any rate most cases of same-sex love are not in the least pathological, but are rather completely normal. Only in the extreme cases—as, after all, in all extremes!—may one raise the question of pathology.

Otherwise, however, we shall establish no special medical or scientific theory at all. We are rather of the opinion that the last word on the nature, significance, and goal of same-sex love either has not yet been spoken at all, or that it will last a long time before in fact a definite conception will have banished all competing conceptions from the field by the inner force of its truth. For this question is burdened with grave material interests. We believe, however, that we also do not need a theory admitted to be absolutely correct. Sufficient for us is the fact of the presence and frequency of same-sex love, in connection with the axiomatic principle of the demand for personal freedom in all cases where no rights are injured.

We likewise believe that comparative cultural history must be called upon for a judgement in the question. In particular, we place value on the proof that male friendship and every more intimate relationship among men, in short all men's unions in the ethnological sense, is affected and made difficult by the excessive tabu of sexual forms of male friendship. This especially holds true of the pedagogically quite irreplaceable deep personal relationship between mature men and youths.

As for the worst in our question, that is, §175 itself, we shall fight it from purely juridical and moral viewpoints. For whereas the medical theory is controversial and in part really quite vacuous, the juridical and moral consideration is clear, simple, and convincing:

Two responsible people, freely consenting and without harm to a third or even merely to themselves, produce for each other a pleasant feeling. Then comes the state—if by exception it once learns of it—and locks up the culprits, as if they had done something wrong!

On the basis of §175, every year 500–600 men who have made no one suffer in the least, nor have done harm to anyone, are "sentenced" to prison, exactly as if they had swindled or stolen!

That is as absurd as any tabu of wild primitive peoples. Truly no biological or pathological theory is needed here, and an actual refutation of the justification for §175 or even a begging for pity is more superfluous than a corresponding attitude to the clause against heretics would be. One rather asks in such cases how the nonsense came about historically. From history there follows automatically not only the refutation, but also the path to combating it in practice.

Now, it turns out that §175 is only a partial symptom of a wider superstition and fraud. We mean the ascetic madness spread by the Christian priests of the early Middle Ages, according to which everything sexual was suspicious, and a feeling of lust—without regard to the question of harming a third—was posed as sinful in itself. That was partly superstition and partly fraud. Just as doctors live from healing sicknesses, those medieval priests lived from the forgiveness of sins. Thus, just as the doctor is dependent on the presence of the real or imagined sick person, so too the medieval priest was dependent on the presence of people who held themselves, with or without reason, to be "sinners." Now, the amount of genuine wrong, that is, the sum of all unjust harm between one person and another, did not suffice for the needs of the all too massive and pretentious budding priesthood of the Middle Ages; it therefore made the attempt to produce in all people, even the best, a sort of hypochondriac madness of sinfulness—and that succeeded most surely by pretending that something was sinful which every healthy man has need of from time to time or at least bears an intensive desire for. Hence the propagation of the ascetic spirit, borrowed in part from Buddhism. Man-woman love could not entirely be made tabu; the priests had to be satisfied with making its admissibility dependent on their sanction. Same-sex love, however, whose necessity is not so obvious as man-woman love, could be posed absolutely as sinful.

In fact, it turns out that even today the most vehement and numerous adversaries are to be found in those circles where the medieval doctrine, to be sure strongly changed and weakened, still very audibly resounds: in the orthodox circles of the Protestant and Catholic churches. The circumstance that many churchmen of both confessions are notable exceptions and stand up for the equal rights of same-sex love should not mislead us in judging the average. Thus we shall fight against §175, as far as we treat it at all, as a juridical and moral monstrosity and emphasize its origin from the ascetic fraud overcome by the modern Weltanschauung.

It is precisely this sincerer, stronger, and more manly change in direction that the representatives of the Urning theory have made an accusation and pose as dubious; they fear it will heighten the resistance and animosity of the opponents. We reply, first, that our view obviously has truth on its side and, further, that the opposition in the two orthodox camps can probably not become stronger than it already is; further, that it is our change in direction that makes the so-called homosexual movement recognizable at all as a part of the modern freedom movement and therefore must awake sympathy in all liberally thinking people.

Open attacks on the ascetic fraud of the medieval priesthood and its painful consequences in a weakened form up to the present are indeed no longer something really unheard of today; the whole modern sexual freedom movement, of which the homosexual movement is only a part, proceeds, consciously or unconsciously, from a protest against the ascetic morality of the Middle Ages.

Just take a glance, for example, at the movement for so called "protection of mothers" and the attacks of emancipation-hungry womanhood on the existing form of marriage and sexual morality: one will see that those women today are truly more honest, more courageous, and more manly, so to speak, than the men—at least those men whom Herr Hirschfeld has gathered around him! The "mother-protectors" openly and frankly demand the right to sexual satisfaction for the female sex, even outside of marriage, by the most daring disregard of tradition and morality, yes, in our opinion even of justified morality . . .

Neither to glorify, nor to detract on the basis of inadequate theories or one-sided presentations of the nature of prostitution—that will be our precept.

Since we renounce in principle making propaganda for homosexual activity, viewing sexual matters rather as a private affair, and fight against §175 on purely juridical grounds, and since that which we positively advocate is nothing other than male friendships and men's unions—our propaganda will be strictly legal and much safer from police intervention than that of Hirschfeld, which on the basis of its medical theory is forced to go into all kinds of sexual details openly in public.

1. *See my booklet* Männliche und weibliche Kultur *(Leipzig, Deutscher Kampf-Verlag, 1906), in which the masculine culture of Japan and the effeminate condition of North America are contrasted as extreme opposites to one another.*

2. *Unfortunately, in my* Renaissance *I too still used the word "paederasty" in a false sense. The slander that the word suffers under should be a spur to honest people to win back for it the good, old, platonic meaning through consistent correct use. Then the factually veiled and formally hideous linguistic monsters, such as "homosexuality" and others, will little by little become superfluous.*

3. *[Heinrich Schurtz was a German ethnologist. Friedländer is referring here to his study* Altersklassen und Männerbünde *(Age-Groups and Male Societies), published in 1902. In this book Schurtz expounded his theory about the two basic human instincts, the "Geschlechtstrieb" (sex instinct) and the "Gesellungstrieb" (social instinct). Whereas the sex instinct was the foundation of the female-dominated family, the social drive, which was, according to Schurtz, reserved only for men, was the prerequisite for more developed social forms, such as political organizations and the state. Harry Oosterhuis]*

4. *See* Renaissance des Eros Uranios *and especially the "Entwurf zu einer reizphysiologischen Analyse der erotischen Anziehung,"* Jahrbuch für sexuelle Zwischenstufen, *1905.*

5. *[Eugen Dühring was a German political theorist of socialism. His views were criticized by Friedrich Engels in his* Anti-Dühring. *Harry Oosterhuis]*

SEVEN PROPOSITIONS

(1908)

Benedict Friedländer

1. The white race is becoming ever sicker under the curse of Christianity, which is foreign to it and mostly harmful: That is the genuinely bad "Jewish influence," an opinion that has been proven true, especially through the conditions in North America.

2. The people's strength rests in the final analysis predominantly on the unity, the social spirit, and the close union of fellow countrymen. Love of the fatherland is much less love for the land of one's father than for one's fellow countrymen. Since in a population of millions no one can know everyone, everything depends on group associations. Kernel and source of this social love, on which everything else rests, is physiological friendship, especially among young men as the flourishing bearers of the strongest life-force. Prejudice and laws against so-called homosexuality (on whose material forms there may be diverse judgments) are therefore so extremely harmful, since they work against the systematic cultivation of this physiological friendship . . .

Physiological male friendship, not the family, is the foundation of the human community, exactly as in the bee commonwealth physiological friendship is among the females. The beasts of prey also have family instincts. The family instincts are necessary for propagation, but without the addition of physiological friendship never lead to the construction of the state, as every tiger or vulture family proves. The family is necessary, but it is not true that it is the foundation of the state or any larger human society.

3. Every normal youth is more or less capable of physiological friendship; one must only cultivate it, instead of suppressing it. A certain degree of "homosexuality" is consequently quite generally distributed and in addition is necessary for the existence of nations.

4. The erotic and social pretension of women is the enemy; with it is also often bound the tricks of a caste of priests or other deceivers, which cunningly uses the influence of the superstitious sex with its smaller and simpler brain. A nation subject to these influences must degenerate in a way that is ochlocratic, gynecocratic, and klepto-cratic, and get the worst of it in the competition of nations. On the opposite of all this rested the greatness of the Hellenes in their best, pre-Periclean period, in their victory over the Persians, and on this rests—two and a half centuries later—Japan's victory over Russia. This is one of the few clearly recognizable basic laws of the history of nations. The victories at Marathon and Mukden, at Salamis and Tsushima may be traced back to the same causes.

5. Among people there are a number of men whose family instinct has in varying degrees been weakened to the benefit of physiological friendship and the general social instinct; these men are, if they are otherwise capable, the born educators of youth, legislators, and military leaders of their people. They are of more benefit to the human community than if they were to procreate dozens of children. For those who can see, history is full of proof of this. Woe to the nation that does away with those men.

6. The condemnation of lust is a completely transparent trick of the medieval priests. Naturally one has to respect here as everywhere the rights of others, to be moderate for the sake of justice and for one's own sake.

7. The continuing misunderstanding of these truths must harm the entire white race to the benefit of the yellow. Behind the 40 million Japanese stand 400 million Chinese. It is questionable whether an effective spreading of these truths is still possible and thereby can halt the relative decline of the white race. No time has ever lacked seers, but they were not listened to.

Panta rhei [all things are in flux], to what goal and in which direction? That is the insoluble problem of the world.

Written 14 June 1908.

from

WHAT WE WANT

(1925)

Adolph Brand

Let the friend be the festival of the earth to you!
—Nietzsche

1. Men of the Renaissance

The G.D.E. (*Gemeinschaft der Eigenen* = Community of Self-Owners) addresses only people who know that the deepest experience that the earth bestows is not to be sought in animal lust, but rather in the inexpressible delight and bliss of the old heavenly gods, which transfigured every desire through beauty, and for whom the joy of one person in another was the sanctity of life itself. People who know that this is altogether the unique and mighty difference between sensuality and love; whether the chaos of elementary feelings of pleasure, which at the time of puberty gain power in us, makes a person into a god or an animal— whether it raises him up to the light of self-ruling grace and freedom, or throws him down into the dull, gloomy night of inextricable chains and self-imposed tyranny. For love is the elevated and sacred, voluntary offering of eternal beauty, goodness, and honor for the joy and happiness of the other. Giving vent to unbridled sensuality, however, is common robbery and murder on all mankind. Therefore the task falls on us to master and gain control of it, to make it noble and transfigure it, and to bring it into the wholesome and beneficial domain of human knowledge and human art.

2. Freedom and Love

The G.D.E. teaches that the right of self-determination over body and soul is the most important basis of all freedom—and that sexuality and love are the deeply interlaced roots and the golden crown of our being, from which human work and creation draw their inexhaustible and eternal strengths. The G.D.E. advocates the right of personal freedom and the sovereignty of the individual to the ultimate consequence. It promotes in every area of human feeling and human collaboration the free play of strength, the abolition of every monopoly, and unlimited free competition, since it is the only thing that guarantees again and again the establishment of healthy relationships and that holds the whole of life's blood in an eternal, salutary circulation. For this reason it also strives for a radical improvement in morality, without force or hypocrisy, and a beautiful harmony precisely in the human relationships that are most intimate and important for life, and it seeks to do this only by again awakening, beside the sense of female beauty, also the sense for male beauty, and by again setting friend-love beside woman-love as having completely equal rights in the intercourse of the sexes among themselves, such as, before the victory of Pauline Christianity and its view so inimical to life, was always the case in ancient Greece, in ancient Rome, and in ancient Germany to the advantage of all mankind . . .

4. Sexual Culture

The G.D.E. is of the opinion that sexuality is obviously just as necessary as eating and drinking—but it believes that a person of intellect and culture will always strive to accomplish the most important function of life as much as possible at a beautifully set table and in pleasant company—and that the satisfaction of the sexual drive requires at least the same careful cultivation and refinement. If the G.D.E. occupies itself with these sexual things, then we do it at any rate, not to create for some libertine or other a license for sexual excesses or to recommend that immature persons follow the so often misused doctrine of free love, but rather to show people that it is unworthy of them to live as wild animals and to suggest to them, precisely also in these things, how to keep a beautiful measure in every enjoyment of life.

5. Bisexuality

The G.D.E. stands on the point of view of a bisexual tendency of all people, which we have inherited from father and mother, and which is the primary form for all varieties of love. It therefore views the presence of a more or less strong inclination to both sexes as an elementary and healthy instinct of the individual. It is likewise able to see in every case only a source of strength in the natural and wise satisfaction of this inclination to the other or to the same sex. The G.D.E. is convinced that only this bisexual tendency of all people and its recognition in every individual can yield the new and powerful foundation on which a mutual understanding in sexual questions is still possible at all, and on which alone the fight for the equal rights of love of friends in addition to woman-love can lead to victory.

6. Seduction of Girls

The G.D.E. is convinced that the seduction of decent young girls, without wishing to marry them, is a great meanness and a severe wrong, which harms not only the seduced girl and her family, but also the illegitimate child and the whole community, and which, therefore, a young man, if he has understanding, heart, and character, will allow himself to commit under no circumstances. The G.D.E. naturally advocates full equal rights for the unmarried mother and her illegitimate child along with the married mother and her legitimate child.

7. Prostitution

The G.D.E. fights just as decidedly against the common sale of love as a focus of people's contamination and of corruption, which has increased to such a terrible extent only through the false morality of society, and which only through a new morality, through an absolute openness and honesty in the discussion of all sexual things can be successfully overcome. The G.D.E. sees in the irresponsible sexual intercourse with prostitutes, male and female, a disastrous lack of a sense of social responsibility, a danger to the population, and a self-abuse that every nobly thinking man should be too proud to engage in. It condemns the phrase "necessary evil," used by the men-about-town of all camps of sexual variety and addiction to pleasure, as unscrupulous and a sin against humanity, since every practice of prostitution is a spiritual rape of youth by the abuse of money. The G.D.E. shows the young man the right path and right means, with whose help he can avoid the evil without any difficulty.

8. Onanism

The G.D.E. would like to protect every young man just as much from the unhealthy consequences of sexual satisfaction carried out in solitude. For this can very easily become a sexual excess and a sexual vice, if, in the case of strong sexuality and lack of every control, the addiction to sensual excitement drives him to a continued repetition of the sexual act.

But the G.D.E. tells parents, teachers, and doctors that only the excess of the pleasure is harmful, whereas kept to a judicious and prudent measure the matter absolutely cannot be harmful. It is rather a much worse offence to completely forbid sexual self-satisfaction to young people under the threat of foolish punishments. For it is clear right off to every physiologist and psychologist that such a prohibition cannot be kept, since the sexual drive in the young person is of course an elementary one, which absolutely requires practice and satisfaction. And since forbidden fruit are doubly enticing, instead of promoting self-control and voluntary renunciation, the attraction of acts not permitted only powerfully contributes to the attainment of sexual self-satisfaction under all circumstances and by all means. Namely, secretly, in hiding, and concealed. And only through this forced secrecy and solitude, which is lacking in every trust, every good advice, and every help of another person, does self-satisfaction, which otherwise means something quite natural and healthy, become a sexual excess and a sexual vice, which must naturally be harmful to the young person. Done moderately it would be on the contrary quite without danger. The G.D.E. also suggests in this matter the right path and the right means to achieve healthy proportions without difficulty.

9. Friendship

The G.D.E. sees in the friendship of youth the sure and uniquely possible path, as well as the proven and reliable means, to overcome the horrors of prostitution and finally get out of the sexual misery of our time. It sees it as its most important task to protect girls and women from infection and to avert the poisoning and polluting of their blood in the interest of the health of their children and for the blessing of coming generations, and to make the contamination of the family impossible. And it therefore shows every young man that he, through a close union with a friend, can calm the dark pressure of his blood, extend his youth, and keep body and spirit fresh and pure. It teaches him about the fact that the natural and moderate satisfaction of boys and lads among themselves is no sin, but rather a sensible expedient of nature, which is the transition to sexual intercourse, and which one should not stupidly hinder and suppress, as the madness of medical charlatans and sanctimoniousness of today's schools does. The G.D.E. rather demands that one should give to this first self-help of nature in the time of beginning puberty all imaginable care and respect, and that one must guard against destroying the secret charm of such a harmless joy of life through senseless prohibitions and interferences. The G.D.E. even pursues the goal: that the general cultivation of such intimate services of friendship become the concern of public welfare and that it must become an affair of school and state to foster in every direction this close union and these first proofs of friendship of boys and youths among themselves, since they are the first proud stages of awakening manhood toward the quiet sanctuaries of genuine love. The G.D.E. advises the young man to have sexual intercourse with no woman before marriage, but rather until then to seek his highest joy of human contact, his moral strength, his bodily release, his spiritual calm, and his inner peace in the intimate intercourse with a friend. With a friend who means his ideal, who understands him; who joins in his adventures and shares his studies with him; who wins influence over him in every way, who emotionally and bodily gives him all, who furthers him as a comrade and enriches him as a human being; and who is ready with desire and love, for the sake of his beauty, his character, and his personality, to render him every imaginable service. The G.D.E. is convinced that such a cultivation of friendship and mutual affirmation of body and soul are absolutely necessary, and that it not only lies in the interest of the spiritual and bodily improvement of our race, but also assures us for all time the thriving and flourishing of an always cheerful and happy youth.

10. Marriage

The G.D.E. suggests to all young men to marry only when a really great, noble love binds them to the girl of their choice and when they find also in a woman, in a new and different noble form, that which only their friend gave them so long in the value and beauty of life. A basic condition for this is that both partners, man and woman, are truly mature for marriage, bodily, emotionally, and economically, so that the children that result from their union also will be the most vigorous, beautiful, noble, and intelligent children possible, so that they never need be ashamed of this fruit of their bodies. Man and woman should be, therefore, both at the same time equally spotless in body and soul, so that their love will be for them an inexhaustible source of strength and blessing for their work and an immeasurable treasure for the enrichment and refinement of their lives on the whole. The G.D.E. is convinced that the position of woman and the institution of marriage will only win through the competition of friendship and that through the latter a sublimation of the polygamous inclination and of the insatiable addiction to variety on the part of the man will be possible to such a high degree that in the future a wife will only seldom have to fear the unfaithfulness of her husband. Infidelity and infection of the family from crude, sensuous lust may in the future be something quite unknown, as soon as the husband can also go to his friend to seek a halt to the raging of his blood with the comrade of his youth.

11. Nudism

The G.D.E. holds it to be obvious that only beautiful and noble persons should mate through love, and that no young man should marry before he has seen his beloved in the nude, just as he also sees the comrades of his youth and the companions of his games nude. . . . Therefore the G.D.E., in the interest of racial improvement, sexual health, and advancement in general, calls for the promotion of a noble nudism, further the generous support of the whole open-air movement in the German Empire, as well as the encouragement of every sport establishment that does not degrade people to machines in a revolting way, but rather elevates the pleasure of every individual and the joy of our whole people in bodily strength and beauty. Our demand for careful sexual selection before marriage would then doubtless no longer resound unheard. A large establishment for swimming, open-air and sun bathing in natural nudity is to be opened next year by the G.D.E. itself.[1]

12. Population Politics

The G.D.E. judges all population politics as unscrupulous and generally dangerous that starts from the premise of bringing as many children into the world as possible by every means, so as to furnish again for the military and capitalism massive and cheap cannon fodder. The G.D.E. shows young people that the procreation of children is not at all the goal of love—and not even the goal of sexual intercourse. At the very least it is not a question of the quantity of the rising generation but rather its quality. For we already have enough sick and stunted people, imbeciles and idiots. It must be impressed upon every young man, and he be told at the same time, that he is an infamous scoundrel if he misuses his wife and if through merely animal satisfaction he makes the mother of his children into a child-bearing machine, instead of thinking in the first place of easing and beautifying her home, of enriching her inner life, as well as transfiguring and blessing her small world.

13. The Rebirth of the Love of Friends

The G.D.E. advocates above all the moral and social rebirth of the love of friends, the recognition of its natural right to exist in public and private life, just as it existed, promoting art and freedom, in the time of its highest regard in ancient Greece. The G.D.E. wishes to cultivate in word and picture, through art and sport, a cult of youthful beauty, such as was the custom in the golden age of antiquity. And it wishes to become a mighty union of all those for whom the friend is the festival of the earth!

14. The Social Significance of the Love of Friends

The G.D.E. wishes that man once again take delight in man, in the interest of freedom, fatherland, and culture. It therefore promotes a close joining of man to youth and of youth to man, so that through respect and mutual trust, and not least through the offering of the one to the other, through the care of the older for the younger, through assistance in his education and progress, as well as through the promotion of his whole personality—to educate each individual to loyalty, to voluntary subordination, to civil virtue, to a noble ambition, free from all social climbing, to a noble courage constantly ready to act, and to a sacrificing willingness and joy in working for the national cause! In a word: to make the love of friends great and mature again, to fulfill serious social and national tasks! And it will risk everything so that finally in our manly youth a new spirit will again rise up, such as was present in the time of our classic authors, which will show Germany the path to the heights and inner greatness!

15. The International Significance of the Love of Friends

The G.D.E. is an international union of all those for whom the friend is the festival of the earth! The G.D.E. knows that no international collaboration is still possible today under disregard and surrender of national plans and national necessities of life.

Therefore it fights for the conviction that, after the madness of war, the right to self-determination of all races, nations, and religions must be for us the unassailable foundation to successfully work together for the reconstruction of the world. For it is of the opinion that all races, nations, and religions are extremely valuable for the many-colored diversity and beauty of human life, and that it is not the equality of all people that is the salvation of the world, but rather only their absolutely individual inequality in nature and ability that creates the wonderful harmony of life, as well as its primal strength and eternal charm.

The G.D.E. is the only union that has the courage to openly express this truth. But it is also the only one that establishes from race to race, from nation to nation, and from leader to leader the connection necessary for life, which builds from land to land and from continent to continent the golden roads and bridges, which serves the understanding and cultural work of all nations, through the ideal of friendship, which holds us together.

The G.D.E. wants to bring every nation to the knowledge that the love for a friend is the natural regulator, which should hinder every overpopulation on both sides of national borders, and which is able everywhere to contribute that the rising generation of a nation does not grow without limit and that every imperialistic hunger for power in the world at the cost of neighbor states ceases.

The G.D.E. makes it clear to everyone that the love for a friend does not come from animal desire nor serve animal purposes, but rather that it springs from the divine spirit and divine drive to create, which has allotted it the great task of renouncing bodily creation and progeny in favor of pursuing intellectual creation—not to work, that is, in a family way but in a social way, and to see its most distinguished duty to provide education, art, freedom, and well-being, not only for the welfare and blessing of our fatherland, but also for the good of the whole world!

The G.D.E. shows people that the deepest meaning and kernel of friendship and the love of friends is not in receiving, but in giving. The voluntary offering, the conscious enrichment and making happy of the other from the overflowing treasure of one's own strength! The pleasure of incessantly lavishing one's own personality, of the highest joy of life and the highest value of life not only in all close relationships from person to person, but also in all the wider and widest connections from nation to nation!

The G.D.E. wishes, therefore, to make the love of friends into a cultural factor of the first rank, which does not proceed from robbery and murder, nor promote hatred and eternal revenge, but rather which assures the sociability of the whole world and the mutual help of all nations! Which repudiates war and likewise class struggle as a means of arranging a stage of development, which now belongs to the past and which has been just as unworthy of mankind as of men. Yes, the love of friends should become a cultural factor that gathers around us the quiet heroism of all nations, which sees its only fame and its only greatness in honorable cultural work that no longer concerns the state but humanity.

The G.D.E. is to be an international fraternity and fellowship of all men who generously and clear-sightedly serve only a liberal socialism, which is not programmatic, but individual—not regulative, but naturally determined—not dogmatic, but earth-born—and which nowhere strives for political power. Which pursues no leveling mania, which rejects every dictatorship and fights every use of force. Which in all establishments and organizations leaves the leadership and administration of things only to competent experts, to whom every reasonable worker subordinates himself on his own initiative. And which places only those leaders at the head of the nation who are born leaders and great personalities. Which does not forbid private property, but rather makes everyone an owner. And whose most important and vivid goal in the sense of our great German classics is the dismantling of the state and its dissolution into purely private administrative bodies and work groups.

The G.D.E. calls this international fraternity and fellowship of its members to the common struggle against the spirit of unnaturalness and senselessness that surrounds us and which until now has constantly hindered all nations from deciding to reach out their hands to work in common for peace and culture, since the meaning and sun of life, the love of friendship is lacking. It expects from each of its representatives in the whole world that they be inspired by no other goal than to help in the elimination of human need and human misery in the service and for the blessing of their own countrymen. To perform deeds of noble-mindedness and works of exemplary friendship and sacrifice, to bring about a flourishing welfare for all, in which the rest of the world can also find a lively part, for the glory of all those who bear a human countenance!

The G.D.E. wishes to be a fellowship of voluntary fighters and a fraternity of all leaders, for whom the friend is the festival of the earth. Leaders who do not wait for payment or recognition before fulfilling their ideals, but rather for whom the simple joy in every work that benefits others is their most powerful stimulus, their highest reward, their greatest satisfaction, and also—together with their friend—their most precious happiness in life.

16. The Equal Right of the Love of Friends

The G.D.E. claims for the artist and writer the unconditional right to celebrate the love for a friend just as highly as the love for woman, and through word and picture to represent and glorify love of friends and the beauty of youths, with all their peaks and abysses, just as is usual for woman-love and the beauty of girls, as well as to procure for them everywhere in the world the highest appreciation and recognition.

17. State and Philistine

The G.D.E. shows that the mendacity of the state and the hypocrisy of the Philistines are our worst enemies, since they stamp as a vice the most harmless and the highest pleasure of life, the joy of man in man, and since it is precisely they who have no respect for all the wonders and blessed secrets of love.

18. Repeal of the Laws

The G.D.E. therefore advocates the repeal of all laws that are inimical to life and natural rights, which again and again hinder us from being human, and which pour poison and gall into every cup of joy. It demands of the current government and legislature in particular the repeal of §175, since it benefits only male prostitution and blackmail and since it is a constant crime of the state against the right of personal freedom. It likewise demands that ¶184 finally be set aside,[2] since the guardianship that it presents is a lasting offence to all adult persons, who are able to protect themselves from smut in word and picture all by themselves, and who under no circumstances need either the state or the church as censor for their untroubled delight in reading a book or for their untroubled pleasure in a work of art. Especially since art and literature are only afflicted and unbearably hindered in their free creation when the narrow-mindedness of subordinate officials and stubborn bigots persecute their works and can forbid entirely at their discretion the creations of their souls and dreams. And thirdly, the G.D.E. also demands that ¶218 of the penal code likewise fall,[3] since it is a woman's affair and hers alone to do with her body and its fruit whatever she will. For she is clear about what she is doing. And of course she has to bear all alone the consequences of an operation. The G.D.E. expressly emphasizes, however, that it demands the repeal of all these laws solely in the interest of personal freedom. It would not in any way think of calling good all those acts that today still remain under punishment. Every sexual excess and every sexual dissolution is of course decidedly to be advised against. For they are at least ugly, or sins, as the church says. But so long as no third party is harmed through such sins, the state has no right to intervene with monetary fines or imprisonment. The reformation of such sins is rather to be left exclusively to religious and moral education.

19. Work in Quiet

The G.D.E. rejects in principle every noisy agitation and therefore sees as its most distinguished task to pave the way for its ideals through quiet action from person to person, in the manner of the Freemasons' lodges, as well as through purely artistic, scientific, and athletic offerings and events, but above all, through the creation of a great and firmly united organization, to strive for the closest joining of all those like-minded, who acknowledge the above principles.

20. No Politics

The G.D.E. receives in its ranks men of all political creeds. It is not a political union and lets itself be taken in tow by no political party. For, in the interest of its cultural work, it dares not let itself plunge into the whirlpool of party wrangling, since it needs the liberal and sensible thinkers of all parties.

1. [Brand planned to establish such a facility for the members of his society in the countryside near Berlin. Because of lack of money, however, the plan was never realized. Harry Oosterhuis]

2. [Brand refers to the article in the German penal code that penalized the creation and distribution of so-called obscene writings and images. Harry Oosterhuis]

3. [By this article abortion was made punishable. Harry Oosterhuis]

3

LEGAL REFORM: KURT HILLER AND THE ACTION COMMITTEE

Kurt Hiller (1885–1972) was the intellectually gifted descendant of a notable Jewish family that had already achieved prominence in socialist politics by the late nineteenth century. Following his law studies, Hiller moved to Berlin in 1908, joined the Scientific-Humanitarian Committee, and quickly rose to its board of directors; he would eventually serve as its co-chair during the late years of the Weimar Republic, when Magnus Hirschfeld had left Germany. Throughout his life but particularly at the time of the 1918 revolution following German defeat in World War I, Hiller played a major role in German cultural life beyond the homosexual rights movement as an essayist, political commentator, and founder of so-called Activist Expressionism. Trained as a lawyer and influenced by anarchist and Nietzschean concepts of individualism, Hiller was deeply committed to the absolute freedom to control one's own body, including the right to practice homosexuality, undergo abortion, use addictive drugs, and commit suicide. While Hirschfeld was a lifelong Social Democrat who was confident about the prospects for sexual reform under socialism and hailed Bolshevik Russia's repeal of sodomy and abortion laws, Hiller was highly ambivalent about both socialism and democracy, and he sharply criticized the Stalinist regime for recriminalizing sodomy and abortion in 1934.

We present here two texts that document Hiller's views on the aims and methods of the homosexual rights movement during the early years of the Weimar Republic: 1) the appeal he drafted in 1921 for an Action Committee for the Repeal of Paragraph 175 (*Aktionsausschuß für die Beseitigung des § 175*) that aimed to forge a coalition among the Scientific-Humanitarian Committee, the Community of the Special, and the German Friendship League; 2) a 1923 essay in which Hiller called for a young dictator to govern the homosexual movement. Both texts reveal Hiller's acerbic writing style and sense of activist urgency; the second also reveals an impatience with democratic process and a fascination with a heroic style of leadership that many Germans shared and which contributed to the rise of Nazism.

Hiller was the sole leader of the pre-Hitler homosexual gay rights movement to be briefly interned in a Nazi concentration camp, but also the only one who survived the Third Reich and was able to play a role in the postwar West German gay movement.

DECLARATION OF THE ACTION COMMITTEE FOR THE REPEAL OF PARAGRAPH 175

(1921)

Kurt Hiller
trans. James Steakley

To All the Homosexuals of Germany

goes the call to be mindful of your high duty to work with utmost energy for the liberation of your people, to fight for full human and civil liberty for every member of your group in the present and the future.

For decades to come, perhaps for an entire age, the die is now being cast for all those whom an inscrutable decree of nature leads to pour out their deepest fervor to people of the same sex. What nature impels them to do is defamed as "unnatural" by ignorance and intellectually lazy vindictiveness. Because your nature, homosexuals, is "against nature," society is allowed to outlaw you—the same society which can go peddling the ideal demand of "protecting minorities" in all the back alleys of politics. Because your forthright, honest existence violates supposed "laws" of existence, the state is allowed to oppress you by means of penal justice. Because, as is stated in the "rationale" for the latest "draft" of Messers Joel, Ebermayer, Cormann, and Bumke, "offenses of this sort appear reprehensible to the healthy feeling of the people," they are "offenses."

You know, homosexuals, what the reasons and motives of your enemies portend; you know too that your leaders and advisers have been tirelessly at work for decades to dispel the prejudices, to spread the truth, to win for you due justice (and these efforts have not been entirely without success). Yet ultimately you must secure justice by struggling yourselves, for ultimately it will be yours only as the fruit of your own labors. The liberation of homosexuals can only be the work of homosexuals themselves.

Your task is twofold. On the one hand, what counts is to spread knowledge in your social circles, not obtrusively, but courageously; on the other hand: to endow the men you trust with the financial means they require to carry out the liberation struggle with the perspective of succeeding. This struggle is truly difficult; it is not without prospect of success. A significant number of important German thinkers and artists, researchers and doctors, jurists and statesmen, cultural leaders and writers of the most diverse outlooks, movements, and parties, in many cases persons of international repute, have signed our petition and thus shown the entire world that they join our demand to modify penal law so that "sexual acts between persons of the same sex, just like those between persons of different sexes, will be punishable only if carried out by means of coercion, with persons under the age of sixteen, or in a manner that creates a public nuisance."

This support of our cause by a considerable part of the nation's intellectual leadership obligates us to persevere in our good struggle against all forms of enmity and resistance. Help us continue! We must distribute the petition far more widely than heretofore; we must systematically work on the press; we must arrange educational and publicity lectures in the most important cities. In short, we have to deploy a propaganda apparatus in a manner that, especially under present conditions, cannot be mounted without considerable financial means. If we dispense with this apparatus, if we dispense with exploiting and extending the successes already achieved, the chances of our victory shrink to a very critical extent.

Do not believe, homosexuals, that we enjoy appealing to your sense of sacrifice and laying claim to your help over and over again. But what alternative do we have? Tell us what else we can do. And finally: by helping us, you are helping yourselves.

This trust you must have, and this trust you can have. If we fall short, recall us from office. If you choose to leave us in place, then make it possible for us to carry out our mission fully.

(signed)
The Action Committee for the Repeal of §175
Dr. Magnus Hirschfeld, physician; Dr. Theodor Ahrens, lawyer; Adolf Brand; Max H. Danielsen; Peter Hamecher; Dr. Kurt Hiller, lawyer; Dr. K.F. Jordan, professor; Hans Kahnert; Dr. Walther Niemann, lawyer; Georg Plock; Dr. Ernst Emil Schweitzer, lawyer; Dr. Arthur Weil, physician.

from

ON THE STATE OF THE STRUGGLE:
BRASH THOUGHTS

(1923)

Kurt Hiller
trans. James Steakley

Within the German Reich live a few hundred thousand people of the male sex who, for mysterious reasons, are impelled by their love-drive toward men just as irresistibly and tempestuously as the majority is toward woman. For these men, any ensuing, consensual fulfillment of their nature is forbidden by society and the law under pain of outlawry and prison sentence, thereby assigning them the obligation of lifelong abstinence or lifelong masturbation. This barbaric suppression of a minority in Germany—one which, to be sure, amounts to no more than a minority anywhere in the world—is not receiving the attention of those whose profession otherwise leads them to expose and seek to halt abuses: cultural pundits, political journalists, parliamentarians. They refuse to lift a finger to challenge an evil that here, in the guise of a law, torments and destroys people whose only fault lies in having been created by God as they are, whose only crime is living in accordance with their nature without inflicting harm upon anyone. No one lifts a finger; no one gets worked up about it. Prudish, as conservatives always and revolutionaries often are, they regard this entire issue as touchy and embarrassing, or at least pretend to see it so. At any rate they treat it as an issue about which it is better to keep silent than to talk, a matter which clean people do their utmost not to come in contact with, one which they won't trouble the public with—at least in such serious, difficult times as these . . . [Hiller then discusses the reason for delay in penal reform and abolition of Paragraph 175. He continues:]

At least there's a positive side to the delay of reform. Time has been won. Our propaganda can blare out once again; there is time to draw a breath for one final, powerful blast.

If the movement misses this opportunity, all will be lost for a generation to come and the immeasurable work of researchers and militants will have been essentially for naught.

If the movement misses this opportunity . . . but for it not to miss it, a new verve has to come into the movement! At this critical moment I do not wish to criticize. It would lead nowhere. Those who can see, know; and one cannot open the eyes of the blind. A jackass does not become more intelligent through teaching, and a loafer does not become more diligent through urging; a base intriguer does not become a nobleman through sermonizing. What matters is: we must purge the jackasses, loafers, and base intriguers from our ranks. Along with the wheeler-dealers and the fun-seekers and the pompous blowhards. The hour is too serious for those who feel any responsibility to show the least personal consideration; every pest who presses forward must be ruthlessly exposed as a pest. And at this moment not just a scoundrel qualifies as a pest; perhaps to an even greater degree, a pest is the regular guy who, by chance or ambition, has found his way into leadership circles and there, by dint of of stupidity or timidity or neutrality or hysteria or pedantry or whatever sort of a conventional virtue, is a constant hindrance, a steady brake. The movement, I openly acknowledge, finally needs the most rigorous centralization and a dictator. This dictator need not be an academic (how petty academics often are!); he only needs to have cultivation, that is, exact knowledge about certain fundamentals in the fields of science and society; a clear recognition of the movement's ethical-political core, its aims, and its methods; steadfastness in advancing the radicalism of our principled demand; and simultaneously cool insight into what can actually be achieved at any given moment, the current possibilities. Above all he must be an unerring judge of people and, for the rest, a straightforward fellow: forthright, tenacious, pure-willed, tough-willed. Such personalities do exist; there are such happy mixtures of passion and intelligence. Age is no hindrance if it is combined with fire, youth no hindrance if combined with wisdom. I am no opponent of people over fifty; but would it be a misfortune if a youth finally stepped to the top of our cultural-political movement? Not every youngster wrestling with intellectual things is a mystical muddle-head or an avant-garde clown. The dictator whom I envision certainly could not and should not do everything himself; his chief activity would consist precisely in systematically keeping the right people doing their work systematically. By virtue of understanding people, he would find the right person for every task. The amateurishness from which the movement has suffered up to the present day must be brought to an end. It won't do that the tailor does the work of the cobbler, that the chimney sweep does the work of the smithy. As we know, a person can be a terrific guy and a simply awful musician—he can be an epoch-making scientist and a miserable organizer of political campaigns. Or an outstanding organizer, but a wretched speaker. Or a brilliant speaker, yet incapable of writing a publishable line. Or an outstanding columnist, but totally clumsy when it comes to negotiating with a politician diplomatically. Or a superb diplomat, but appallingly devoid of taste. Or an aesthete, fine as they come, cultured to the nth degree, but totally lost when it comes to legal questions. Or a lawyer, cagey as a racketeer . . . but as shallow as a racketeer. Or a profound philosopher of love . . . and a profound ignoramus concerning what goes on in the real world.

People who can handle and understand what the movement must collectively think, handle, and understand don't exist. At least I am not acquainted with a universal talent of this sort. I do know that certain (meritorious) specialized talents within the movement—for reasons I do not wish to explore—have repeatedly tried to cripple and shut out certain other specialized talents: a situation with the consequence that in areas in which the aforementioned meritorious specialized talents were especially untalented, they achieved nothing at all or the very opposite of what they set out to do. It is counterproductive when someone, no matter how great he may be, tries to control everything instead of delegating some tasks to those who can handle them far better. It is counterproductive, indeed it is almost a crime. One of the most illustrious personalities in the cultural-political arena of our era, a woman, Dr. Helene Stöcker, came up with the concept of "mutual superiority." Within our movement such "mutual superiority" needs to be recognized, acknowledged, and put into practice far more frequently than up to now. The universal genius is lacking: therefore fresh, fruitful cooperation of special talents needs to be organized; the organizer of this cooperation I would term "the dictator."

The particulars of what needs to be done I will reserve for a future presentation. One can't say everything at once. Our courage in the struggle must constantly be bolstered by the fact that an impressive number of impressive luminaries of German intellectual life have supported our demand with their signatures; we must not allow our courage to be weakened by the difficult times. Should a child in some dark corner be sexually abused, no one would dare propose that the rapist ought to go unpunished because the youngster's torment is meaningless in comparison with the hardships being visited upon our fatherland as a whole by brutal French imperialism. "The state cannot be troubled right now with such trivial and low-priority matters." No one would come up with such a crazy thought! If anyone did and expressed it, every sensible person, regardless of political affiliation, would reply: Poincaré and the military occupation of the Ruhr and our national emergency have nothing to do with the fact that society must mobilize its agencies to respond vigorously to the case of a child-rape.

Applying this case to our movement, we are confronted with the rape of an entire social class–one as innocent as that child. It's just that here the rapist, rather than being an individual fiend, is the state itself. There is no such thing as a point in time unsuited for intervention against the rape of innocents. And no point in time would be more suitable to bring about justice in Germany than the present, when justice in Germany is being trampled underfoot.

4

COMBINING POLITICAL AND CULTURAL WORK: THE LEAGUE FOR HUMAN RIGHTS

Friedrich Radszuweit (1876-1932) was an entrepreneur who moved to Berlin in 1922 and within a matter of months rose to prominence as a gay leader by responding to the emergence of a large number of grassroots gay organizations that had emerged in Berlin and elsewhere beginning in 1919. These organizations drew primarily on the lower middle-class public that frequented gay and lesbian bars and showed scant interest in political activism, Magnus Hirschfeld's medical theories, or the cultural airs of Adolf Brand. By 1921, these organizations had been loosely united in an umbrella organization called the *Deutscher Freundschaftsverband*, or German Friendship League, by the activist Max Danielsen. In 1922, Radszuweit usurped leadership and renamed the organization *Bund für Menschenrecht*, or League for Human Rights, but he basically continued the established approach of combining a wide range of social activities with an effort to make gay men and lesbians aware of their own political interests. To this end, he published two periodicals aimed specifically at lesbians, *Die Freundin* (1924-33) and *Ledige Frauen* (1926-29), and three periodicals for gay men, *Blätter für Menschenrecht* (1923-33), *Das Freundschaftsblatt* (1924-33), and *Die Insel* (1925-33); censors at times banned these periodicals for a year or more for carrying personal ads and publishing nude photographs. Affiliation with the League of Human Rights entitled members to a free subscription to a journal of their choice and free legal counsel if they were prosecuted under Paragraph 175. This was apparently a successful formula, for the League of Human Rights claimed a membership in the tens of thousands (figures that were probably inflated) and eventually even asserted that it was Germany's sole homosexual emancipation organization. Ever mindful of respectability, Radszuweit entirely repudiated the pedophile slant of Brand's Community and rebuked Hirschfeld's Committee for proposing an age of consent of sixteen. Following Friedrich Radszuweit's death in 1932, leadership was assumed by his son, Martin Radszuweit.

The League distributed material agitating for the repeal of Paragraph 175 to politicians and newspapers, negotiated with the police in various cities, and polled political parties prior to elections.

We present here two documents representing the work of the League for Human Rights: 1) a 1931 text in which Radszuweit attempted to pin the blame for the Nazi party's homophobic pronouncements on Magnus Hirschfeld (who by then had already left Germany); and 2) Radszuweit's 1931 remarks on the emergence of homosexuality as a political issue.

The first document has a somewhat anti-Semitic tone which Radszuweit would elsewhere make even more pointed, arguing that Hirschfeld was unsuited for leadership
because of his Jewish ancestry. The second document, although it mentions no names,
was a thinly veiled response to the exposure of the homosexuality of Ernst Röhm, the
head of the Nazi Party's paramilitary SA, by Germany's leftwing political parties in
1931. Röhm was in fact a member in good standing of the League for Human Rights,
and Radszuweit naively imagined that Rïhm would be able to ameliorate Nazi homophobia, indeed even that the Nazis issued homophobic pronouncements solely in order
to garner votes from moral conservatives. Germany's Social Democrats and Communists, on the other hand, hoped that exposing Röhm as a homosexual would discredit
the Nazis as hypocrites and moral degenerates; but in doing so they opportunistically
compromised their commitment to gay rights. Following the Nazi accession to power,
Röhm was killed on orders from Hitler on June 30, 1934, the "Night of the Long
Knives," which signaled a drastic intensification of homosexual persecution: Hitler falsely stated on July 1 that he had not known of Röhm's homosexuality until then and that
he was now more determined than ever to rid Germany of the homosexual menace.

PENAL LAW REFORM

(1931)

Friedrich Radszuweit
trans. James Steakley

The Penal Justice Committee of the Reichstag has convened under the chairmanship of Prof.
Dr. D. Kahl and is again at work on the draft as passed by the Penal Justice Committee of the
previous Reichstag.

Following on the Reichstag's call for the creation of a joint parliament with Austria, the
Austrian National Council has also declared that it is absolutely necessary for the Austrian
Penal Justice Committee to convene and energetically continue deliberating on the draft of
a joint penal code with Germany.

These steps awaken the hope that a new penal code may be passed in a short time. All
signs indicate that those committee members who contributed to the passage of the previous draft will once again do their utmost to accept the draft in its reformed language. We are
particularly interested in the elimination of Paragraph 175, and we firmly hope that this
measure will prevail. In their newspapers and public pronouncements, the opposition parties have been calling in at times very ugly terms for the retention of Paragraph 175. When
the time comes for the decisive vote, they will need to consider whether they want to continue to force nearly two million German citizens under the provisions of a special law. We
do not believe that even the National Socialists intend to act against homosexuals in the rigorous way that they proclaimed before the elections of September 1930. Any regular reader
of the National Socialist newspapers, especially the *Völkischer Beobachter*, will occasionally
find fairly reasonable articles on homosexuality. Reading between the lines, it is clear that the
Völkischer Beobachter does not aim to damn homosexuals universally nor to make them
social pariahs, but instead by and large is striking out only at the Jews (especially Magnus
Hirschfeld), who use the most coarse language to drag human sexuality into public view in

such an ugly way. Some time ago I read an article in the *Völkischer Beobachter* about the difference between Krafft-Ebing's and Magnus Hirschfeld's scientific research. This article reviewed Hirschfeld's book, *The Sexual History of the World War,* and it remarked that this book was tantamount to an abomination ("*Schweinerei*"). The reviewer made a very fine distinction between Hirschfeld and Krafft-Ebing by emphasizing that, in his books, the latter employed Latin terms for almost everything that had to do with grossly sensual and purely sexual matters, whereas Hirschfeld's book was entirely different and described these matters in such ugly and coarse language that morality was smothered, and anyone would feel his sense of decency violated. Morality and decency are, to be sure, terms that each of us uses according to his own view of life and his upbringing. It is of course generally known that precisely the educated circles of our people do not hold the lower class's sense of decency and morality to be as high as their own. And various court trials dealing with sexual matters have shown that the judiciary also regards the morality and decency of the lowest classes as inferior to that of educated circles.

We do not wish to quarrel and pass judgment on morality and so-called decency here; we simply want to note that everything changes over the course of time. Notions about morality are different today than they were a century ago. This is acknowledged even by the political right-wingers, and therefore we can only reiterate one thing: general concepts of morality cannot be applied to the most deeply human quality of people, their sexual activity. Not, that is, as long as those involved behave decently and do not in any way create a public nuisance. The great majority of homosexual men in Germany would not think of making a public display of their sex lives, and would never even have thought of creating a homosexual movement if the lawmakers had not been so unreasonable and sought to maintain the disgraceful Paragraph 175, and if society would finally move toward not constantly speaking of homosexuality as a vice or an illness. The homosexual men of Germany take the standpoint that one need not talk about these things at all, and that it is nobody's business when two people, of their own free will and with mutual consent, satisfy their sexual urges in the privacy of their own chamber.

PARAGRAPH 175
AS THE FOCUS OF POLITICAL STRUGGLE

(1931)

Friedrich Radszuweit
trans. *James Steakley*

Paragraph 175 of the Penal Code has unexpectedly moved to the very center of political polemics, with political adversaries assailing each other by yanking into public view the private relationships or, more accurately, sexual orientation of the individual. In our journal

Das Freundschaftsblatt we have repeatedly called upon the political opponents to use more decent weapons than precisely this Paragraph 175 to combat those of different views.

The April 30, 1931, issue of *Das Freundschaftsblatt* featured a lead article by me under the headline "Hitler and Paragraph 175" which has drawn very many letters. Regretfully, I have to state that all of these letters were written in such a partisan spirit that they are unsuited for publication. Fellow homosexuals on the political left demand that I stop concealing and start revealing the names of so-called Nazi leaders who are homosexual. Fellow homosexuals on the political right, on the other hand, express their satisfaction that I have remained nonpartisan by not publishing the names of the homosexuals among Hitler's following. I regard the latter view as the sole correct one. The League for Human Rights, Inc., is a completely nonpolitical organization, and for this reason the leadership and I as League chairman must scrupulously see to it that the names and addresses entrusted to us are always kept secret. Any communist who plays a leadership role in his party rightly expects us not to disclose his name, but he must also grant this to the so-called Nazi leader. And the Nazi leader can also expect us to keep his identity just as secret as anybody else's.

Only by remaining completely nonpartisan with regard to politics can we continue to safeguard our organization from a split, and only in this way can our members, who are spread among all political parties, continue to carry out indirect propaganda within their parties for the repeal of Paragraph 175.

We do know that our fellow homosexuals in the Hitler camp are carrying out indirect propaganda for our goals, and we also know that on many levels they have achieved success: the Nazis are beginning to think differently about homosexuality than was previously the case.

The Hitler following, too, has no interest in seeing Paragraph 175 repeatedly drawn into debate as the subject of polemics. It is regrettable that the political parties still have not decided to leave the individual's sexual orientation out of the game. Sadly, the pattern of characterizing homosexuality as a political shortcoming initiated by the Eulenburg trials is still with us. We are constantly reminded of that time, when Maximilian Harden, editor of *Die Zukunft*, dragged the homosexual orientation of Prince Eulenburg, Moltke, etc. into public view in order to polemicize against the ruling caste (and Dr. Magnus Hirschfeld also played a role on those trials). When we recognize that things have remained *the same* up to the present day, it becomes clear how backwards the political parties are with regard to the issue of sexual orientation.

Precisely those parties that pride themselves on their commitment to freedom and equality are often the worst when it comes to eliminating a political adversary with the weapon of his homosexual orientation.

We owe it to Dr. Magnus Hirschfeld that Paragraph 175 and the homosexual orientation are still being dragged into today's political debates as a medical question. It would not be appropriate in this short article to go into the whole topic in detail. I will turn to this in a future article in order to show our fellow homosexuals how wrong it was to take up the homosexual question from a medical angle, which led to its being regarded as something sick, and how wrong it was to combat Paragraph 175 of the Penal Code from a medical angle.

PARAGRAPH 175

of the German Penal Code (Nazi Version)

(Jan. 28, 1935)

175:

1. A male who indulges in unnatural vice with another male or who allows himself to participate in such activities will be punished with jail.

2. If one of the participants is under the age of twenty-one, and if the crime has not been grave, the court may dispense with the jail sentence.

175(a): A jail sentence of up to ten years or, if mitigating circumstances can be established, a jail sentence of no less than three years will be imposed on

1. any male who by force or by threat of violence and danger to life and limb compels another man to indulge in criminally indecent activities, or allows himself to participate in such activities;

2. any male who forces another male to indulge with him in criminally indecent activities by using the subordinate position of the other man, whether it be at work or elsewhere, or who allows himself to participate in such activities;

3. any male who indulges professionally and for profit in criminally indecent activities with other males, or allows himself to be used for such activities or who offers himself for same.

175(b): Criminally indecent activities by males with animals are to be punished by jail; in addition, the court may deprive the subject of his civil rights.

C

BRITAIN AND FRANCE
1910-1930

In 1914 Hirschfeld visited London to speak at a medical conference. His work was well known among British homosexuals, including Edward Carpenter, and there were discussions about starting a British chapter of the Scientific-Humanitarian Committee. Instead, in 1914, a separate organization, the British Society for the Study of Sex Psychology was founded with Carpenter as its first president. Women were involved from the start, and the concept of homosexual oppression was framed not in isolation from but as integrally related to wider issues of sexuality in society, including women's rights, birth control and eugenics, divorce law reform, sexual problems in marriage, sex hormones in determining personality, and childhood sex education. Its goal was self-education of its members as well as public education; monthly lectures, many open to the public, were offered into the 1920s, and pamphlets about the above topics were published and distributed (including "The Social Problem of Sexual Inversion," printed in this volume). Here we present a 1914 statement of the society's policy and principles. The anonymity of the speaker/authors perhaps reflects the hostility faced by those who spoke on behalf of "inverts."

THE BRITISH SOCIETY FOR THE STUDY OF SEX PSYCHOLOGY

(1914)

Policy and Principles

The British Society of Sex Psychology has been established for the consideration of problems and questions connected with sexual psychology from their medical, juridical, and sociological aspects.

This statement, which forms the foreword to the Rules of the Society, indicates the double-sided problem with which we have to deal. On the one side is sex-psychology, a subject of scientific investigation which has only of recent years become wide and far-reaching; on the other side social custom, based often upon preconceptions immemorially old, by which problems, arising from unknown causes, have of necessity been unscientifically treated. And since on the scientific side—in all that concerns cause and effect—we have to recognise, as students, that humanity is still very ignorant in regard to these matters, it follows necessarily that, on the practical side, in law, in medicine, and in education, humanity has been acting ignorantly, or, at least, experimentally. As a result society is faced to-day by sex-problems of the gravest character, apparently as far from solution as ever—patent symptoms of wrong social conditions which, by common agreement, demand a new mind and mode of approach. The admitted evil of prostitution, male and female; the attendant and wide-spread existence of blackmail which takes criminal advantage of the law as it now stands; the lack of proper safeguards for consent in sex-relations, free from all compulsion social, economic, or physical; the unsatisfactory conditions of marriage and divorce; the failure to deal equitably and soundly with the spread of venereal disease; the almost total absence of sex-training from education; all these things are a cause of weakness and deterioration to the national life. And here, where science is most needed for right and effective treatment, science, so far as popular acceptance is concerned, is most lacking. We need, far more than we have it to-day, the co-operation of all classes of society—experts willing to state and explain, laymen willing to learn. We need a general understanding that a huge unsolved problem of double aspect, intimate in its effect upon the lives of all, stands at our doors: on the one hand human nature waiting to be investigated; on the other failures in our social treatment of it needing to be exposed. The work of the Society will be to focus the conscience of the community on both sides of the problem.

Many branches of the sex-problem will occupy the Society's attention: the study of some of them has been hindered—at times made even impossible—by the weight of moral judgment passed upon their outward manifestations; while other manifestations, because their significance in relation to the whole question of sex was not appreciated, have been treated as though socially unimportant, and no moral judgment whatever has been passed on them. In some cases, that is to say, ignorance and moral judgment have gone together to decide how certain problems should be treated; in other cases ignorance combined with social indifference has allowed them to be left to their own solution of natural decrease or increase. And when we consider instances of these two treatments side by side, it can hardly be said that an alliance of ignorance and moral judgment has produced better results than a fortuitous leaving of the problem to take care of itself.

It is not the business of our Society to say that moral judgments ought not to be formed, or that they may not have a very valuable place in the solution of our social problems, and the strengthening of those materials of life which are the real basis of a nation's wealth; but it is very much the business of the Society to insist that moral judgments founded on ignorance are more than likely to produce bad results, to insist also they must ever be open to revision in the light of fuller knowledge.

In the middle ages society assumed that ecclesiastical authority was the safe repository of natural science; and as a result it persecuted and endeavoured to exterminate those who held that the world and the solar system were of an altogether different construction from that described by theologians. The results of that assumption seem laughable to us now; but they were no laughing matter when the moral judgments arising therefrom were enforced by the civil arm.

We are faced to-day by a very similar position. The official mind wherever it is found (as inadequately equipped for the task as were the censors of Bruno and Galileo) makes assumption to-day of knowledge about human phenomena, and of the right to pass judgment thereon, as arrogant as were claimed in the 16th and 17th century with regard to astronomy, and shows an equal readiness to condemn on moral grounds those who are determined to question and to investigate even its most cherished conclusions.

All of us probably have some moral judgments, stubbornly or strongly founded; yet it is a sign not of strength but of weakness if we will not allow their investigation. In the face of problems like those with which our Society has set out to deal, such free allowance is almost the first requisite for membership. We must recognise, what perhaps, is never easy to recognise in its entirety, that point of contemporary blindness which most affects the social mind of our own day: it is no longer a refusal to believe that the world is round or less stationary than the sun; it is rather a reluctance to admit that human nature is a much more open problem than has ever yet been allowed by our moralists and theologians of the past. Human nature is the unknown land which the pressure of our social problem is now forcing us to explore. We believe that in regard to it too many previous explorers have made false maps, unverified in the localities they treat of, and have set up sham landmarks, which have failed to make safe our course.

With this statement of our general standpoint, we issue, as our first publication, and as one individual illustration of that for which we aim, a paper which was read by one of our members at the Society's Inaugural Meeting held on July 12th, 1914. The views which it sets forward on certain points are in no way binding upon the Society; but the claim there made for a free investigation of all sex-problems however difficult, and however prejudged by the popular mind, is one which must command the sympathy of all who wish to become members.

General Aims

The British Society for the study of Sex-Psychology welcomes you to-night to the fact of its existence, and we hope you are here to welcome it. As a Society which intends activity over a wide field, so soon as the sinews of war are given to us, we might define ourselves in many ways. But perhaps our standpoint is most comprehensively defined when I say that we are a note of interrogation. We intend to question things that have not been questioned before. We intend to enquire into them—to examine the authorities who have laid down the law about them—often, we believe,—always, it may be—on very insufficient grounds; and we mean to push our enquiry on the basis of men and women working fearlessly and frankly together over territory that is really common to both, but which, hitherto, has been ridiculously cut up, separated and divided.

A notice warning us of "Ancient Lights,"—but really meaning "ancient darkness" has long stood between us and all chance of profitable building upon the land of our inheritance. That notice has got to come down. Convention must be no bar; for behind all conventions lie germinal forces infinitely older, infinitely more venerable, which conventions, formed on narrow and incomplete premises, tend only to hide. Convention may often have right and truth in its keeping; it may cover truths whose meaning and value have become obscured by time, it may contain some snippets of justice and good sense. But those snippets will be in proportion to the knowledge and understanding on which the convention formed itself and was afterwards kept going—and not in proportion to the ignorance, original, or acquired through long habit. Ignorance, refusal to discuss, to review, to re-consider, has never solved anything, and never will.

And so we have set out to deal—or to ask society to deal—with a vast amount of neglected material lying at our very doors, possessing life, but for that very reason the more liable, if neglected, to breed corruption and decay. Dirt has been defined as "matter misplaced." Corruption we might define, I think, as living matter neglected, or misused through ignorance. The ignorant handling of living matter clears up nothing and protects nothing. And I am inclined to think that a refusal to examine things down to their very foundations is often the cowardly defence of ignorance which does not want to be found out, or to have its settled conclusions disturbed. You cannot make matter non-existent. Living, or dead, whether use it or abuse it, it is there, responding to the use or the abuse; but in neither case diminishing in amount, only altering its quality, assuming other aspects for good or ill.

The most important material with which society has to deal is human nature: and sometimes one is tempted to think that it is of human nature that society is most afraid. And so, if anything we say to-night frightens some of you, it will be because you are afraid of human nature—or of fuller knowledge concerning it. But all the fear in the world will not rid you of it; nor will any driving of it to live out of sight make the material of your problem any less in amount. Are we to treat human nature as the early Victorian lady treated telegrams?—the lady, I mean, who, whenever one of those modern portents came to the door, rushed upstairs with it and hid it at the back of the top-shelf of her linen cupboard, as though by such action she could wipe out facts or avert catastrophe.

Let me put before you, then, quite briefly what attitude the Society intends to assume toward the subjects it has to consider. First and foremost, it will maintain that we must never be afraid to investigate. Secondly, that we must never assume that phenomena, which have not yet been investigated, are unimportant or negligible merely because science happens to have neglected them, or because society happens to dislike them. And thirdly that we must not pass judgment or condemnation on anything that has obviously missed a thorough scientific investigation, or which still presents to the instruments of science a nebulous aspect.

It may be that our most difficult line of work—the line of work which will require most courage on our part, and most patient countenance from our members—will be insistent investigation, combined (so far as we as a society are concerned) with a suspension of judgment, in regard to those things which we are investigating; and a single-minded determination to supply full material to others for their better judgment, while refraining ourselves from passing any judgment whatever.

That, I think, is very important. We may hold strong views individually about the right or the wrong of things: but here, within our Society, we are only social analysts. That which is unanalysed, we say, cannot be rightly treated. And if we are to collect the human documents which will be required for supplying the necessary material, and the necessary impulse for sound and expert treatment, to doctors, lawyers, and teachers, we must not ourselves adopt the condemnatory attitude, or pronounce moral judgments. We may individually feel that the phenomena we investigate have to be curbed and controlled for the good of society: but our duty, as an examining body, will be merely to supply others with material for a fuller and a sounder judgment, and for a far more expert treatment, than they at present possess. We, as a Society, are here to set going the machinery of investigation, to arouse interest, and to fight that careless and cowardly attitude—shameful to the sociologist and the scientist—which avoids enquiry in certain directions because the subject is unpopular, or difficult, or painful, or—for any other insufficient reason—a "forbidden" one. Is it not rather appalling that to a great International Medical Congress on sex-questions, to be held this autumn, only one official representative goes from this country, while other countries are sending doctors by the score.

Because sex-questions are pornographically attractive, are they therefore to be neglected by those who have a clean-minded longing for their solution? We have to-day become painfully aware that the social problem in nearly every department has overtaken the organizing efforts of our experts and administrators: partly because those experts have so small and unorganized a public to appeal to in the presentation of their conclusions. Part of our work, therefore, carried on mainly by lectures and by the issue of pamphlets, original and translated—will be to organise understanding in the lay mind on a larger scale, to make people more receptive to scientific proof, and more conscious of their social responsibility; so that, at the back of the experts, when they pronounce judgment, will be a greater weight of public opinion—more available for organised expression—ready and willing to move others in the direction pointed by science.

We laymen and women—many of us not experts ourselves—have become aware of a stupendous ignorance lying all around us in relation to sex-questions, and also, I fear I must add, of a self-indulgent indifference. The man who has got his own individual sex-interests sufficiently well suited and provided for, inclines to be indifferent to the fact that sex-questions generally are in a horribly muddled condition. And yet those conditions are to-day involving us and the whole of society in their evil consequences. We have to recognise, for instance, that the least scientific, the most haphazard branch of our training and education of the young, or of our social organisation, is that of sex. It is the most unsolved problem, because the most burked. Because many of its manifestations are evil, we have shunned speaking of them. Because we have not to hand the solution of Prostitution—and are nowhere near it—therefore, prostitution being so ugly and evil, we have burked the task of making its facts known and understood by society in general; and especially have we burked an honest statement of the huge and tenacious hold it almost necessarily has on society as at present constituted. But do not think, when I say that, that I am saying one word in its defence. Society breeds prostitution: that is what is the matter. But society does not like to be told so.

Our platform reformers, on the other hand, go into the question as though determined to be ideally blind. By being so, or pretending to be so, they can make a popular appearance. Because temperance and continence are ideals of self-discipline to which some have attained, and which many pretend to, nothing half-way between that and the present worst is acceptable to our moral extremists. A ready-made morality, put up for public show on platforms, stands between us and honesty. It is the most difficult thing in the world to get honest talk upon sex-questions on public platforms. I know, for I have tried, and have failed again and again to satisfy both my own conscience and my audience. Unless you take the idealist line you will probably be abused and told that you "advocate vice."

It is the same with Inversion. We have faced that problem with a petulant and a disgusted ignorance, priding ourselves on a refusal to consider it at all. And meanwhile, Inversion goes on breeding apace, taking the most deplorable outlet in underground conditions. Yet if we say that the surreptitious combination of invert-prostitution and blackmail which at present exists is the worst solution of a case that cries out for medical investigation, we are at once threatened with the charge of "advocating vice." If we say that the law deals ignorantly and even dangerously with that barred and tabooed subject, we are liable to assault from moralists who would die rather than examine into the origin and causes of that mysterious phenomenon of human nature.

Closely related to this comes the question of Sexual Ignorance in girls and boys. At school we drill into the minds of youth the meaning of the dead languages, and shut from them the meaning of the living language of the blood. We never say of the former "it is unnatural that they should know these things": but we do sometimes say it of the latter. Yet in this case the knowledge is inevitable; and the mind does not stay a clean vacuum till suddenly full knowledge comes to tenant it. Ignorance breeds quite as quickly and much more riotously and licentiously than knowledge.

The neglected mind may become diseased just as much as the neglected body and I think the unimaginative hardly realise the terrible mental strain it is—especially to sensitive natures in youth—to come upon shock after shock of something unexplained, but ingrained and unavoidable, the weight of which for ever increases through the early years of development and puberty; and all taking place within a forbidden area, secretively cut off from that frank expression of life which is the normal code of youth. You thrust upon the mind of the growing child two incompatible courses of conduct, frankness and secretiveness, self-confidence and self-distrust; and during that crude stage of development—when self-realisation is going on at a gallop—you leave to boy or girl the solution, almost unaided—in the darkness of their own thoughts—of the most difficult problem of life: a problem of which grown society has itself made a most hideous mess. And perhaps it is because we have no good solution to show, in the broad face of society, that we shamefacedly conceal the very existence of these things from the young until too late when we discover that the mischief has already been done.

Here again it will be part of our work to invite more courage and honesty in parents and teachers, and to give documentary reason for regarding ignorance as the most dangerous solution. Youth is really our test in these matters. For when you come to examine you will find that practically all our sex problems have their germ in early youth. And that being so we are bound to enquire of society—"At what stage do you think it wise and humane and remedial to treat these troubles on the criminal and punitive lines?" If you do not think it wise and humane so to treat them in the very young, at what stage of human life does it become right and just to do so without regard to attendant conditions—without, that is to say, calling in medical science to aid? Is it ever wise, at any stage, abruptly to hand over this class of problem to the tender mercies of the law alone? Can the law alone solve them, or act curatively or beneficently towards them? Ought we not always to have medical assessors in such cases to assist the law; ought not our sanatoria to be as open to them as our prisons?

For in truth many of these problems are of a nature that the law cannot deal with: they lie too much outside the logic of its purpose. In a wise State you must permit many things that you do not approve, because the law is not the right means for treating them. Where the law merely effects a transference of activities and not a cure—driving below the surface things which still go on—it is certainly useless, and probably harmful. You cannot bring a thing into form by one-sided pressure: you can only impress an aspect to flatter the popular eye, and make it seem that the law has power which it has not.

Certain forms of marital indulgence, for instance, though bad for man, for woman, and above all for the race, cannot be suppressed by law. But to assert that legal repression is not the right means of approach—that such interference may do harm not good—is not to approve the practices referred to. It is only to assert that root causes must be got at, first by clear understanding of their origin, and then by remedies directed to origin rather than symptom. Many of us may regard the imposition of marital relations on bearing motherhood as an unnatural act. Yet it is probably a normal practice in this country both with and without the wife's consent. But that is a matter in which the law can only interfere safely by securing to the wife conditions of freedom and of choice by endowed motherhood, or by otherwise making more secure her economic status, not by putting its legal veto upon the practice. I could raise other points intimately sexual and extremely usual, but perhaps they can better be dealt with in papers of a special rather than of a general character. Only do, please, rid us of the imputation that we advocate all those things which we say the law cannot properly touch.

Indeed, I doubt whether we shall ever definitely advocate any cut and dried method for dealing with unsolved problems—except the method of fearless investigation, for the increase and dissemination of knowledge. We shall publish—it is quite likely—side by side in the same pamphlet, opposite conclusions formed by opposing schools. Our aim will be much nearer satisfaction when we have thus put the thinking public in possession of two points of view—however opposite—than by merely leaving them ignorant of the grounds on which either is based.

Another section of our enquiry is Disease: not necessarily venereal. It is fairly evident that many of the sexual phenomena we have to deal with will be found to have a connection in disease. But others, it is equally likely, may have a connection in growth, in re-adjustment of life to new ends; and may, in fact, deserve to be classed rather as growing-pains than as ailments. That being so, disease necessarily comes within the scope of our enquiry. If you find certain phenomena in obstinately healthy bodies—in children born of good stock and of clean up-bringing—well, there is something on which we need medical pronouncement to guide us to clearer conclusions, and to class for us what should and what should not be treated as disease.

In this connection you will see that one of our branches of enquiry is Aberration of various kinds. That warp from the normal, or the cult of the unusual, which manifests through special and localised attractions in the amative relations, and which goes by the name of Fetishism, may, if properly studied be explanatory of much which now seems dark and forbidding. In a good many of its forms it may strike those who are not subject to it as rather ridiculous, or at any rate trivial. But in other forms or developments it is not trivial at all; and it is very closely related in its origin to things we are bound very seriously to consider and get to the root of. Certain forms of fetishism have indeed become so normal, and are so harmless, that we do not recognise them at all. The bulk of us may be subject to them without knowing it, and so, accepting the symptom merely as a social habit or as a racial characteristic, may be wholly unaware that we are innocuously connected to something which, of precisely similar origin but of different manifestation, arouses our wraths or our scorn.

Are the less usual—the so-called less normal instances of fetish-attraction necessarily more insane than those which we ourselves harbour and practice? If not, then should not a knowledge of our susceptibility to fetishism lead us to have more charity and understanding toward others, in whom it takes a more unfortunate—possibly even a dangerous form. And even in cases which must obviously be controlled, because they infringe on the liberty and well-being of others—such for instance as that terrible by-product of fetishism, the instinct which finds its sexual satisfaction in blood—even there it is well for us to remember that, however repugnant the aspect, at root there may be a relation of origin between this and forms of eroticism the most harmless that we could name.

I speak but as a layman on these subjects, having no claim to expert knowledge. And I own frankly that I am mainly drawn to this Society by that principle of its constitution which admits to the discussion of these subjects men and women upon an equal footing. It is because we believe that nothing concerning sex can be rightly dealt with apart from the full equation—men and women thinking and working together for a common understanding—that no sex-problem has ever yet been rightly dealt with by one sex deciding and acting alone, and that in consequence of decisions so formed and so acted on society is suffering to-day—it is because we hold this to be fundamentally true that we ask you to give countenance and aid to our new Society, whose main aim is the co-education of grown men and women in matters which vitally concern both sexes alike.

STELLA BROWNE

One of the prime movers in the British Society for the Study of Sex Psychology, the only official organization for English homosexuals in the early twentieth century, was Stella Browne. She was a feminist, and an advocate of birth control and abortion rights. Her views on lesbianism are a classic case of the double-bind produced by the medical model.

In the first paper excerpted here, presented before the Society in 1915, her defense of lesbianism is mediated through the Krafft-Ebingesque conceptualization of "innate morbidity" and the logic that "artificial" homosexuality of women is a result of sexually repressive social arrangements to which women are exposed. The removal of this repression would result in fulfillment in "normal heterosexuality." (The same logic is used to conceptualize masturbation, "inflicting pain" or "suffering pain," and fetishism as abnormal instincts which are allowed to develop under repression but would not do so in a sexually free society.)

The second paper excerpted below was also read before the society and then published in a New York sexology journal in 1923. Its methodology is the interpretation of case studies; in another part of the paper she states "they would probably be much more illuminating had they been recorded by an observer who was herself entirely or predominantly homosexual." This excerpt is from her "comments and conclusions" section.

from

THE SEXUAL VARIETY AND VARIABILITY AMONG WOMEN AND THEIR BEARING UPON SOCIAL RECONSTRUCTION

(1915)

F. W. Stella Browne

Perhaps I had better preface what I have to say, by stating my point of view on some essential subjects.

I do not think that any intelligent, humane and self-respecting attitude towards sex is generally possible, without great economic changes; and a responsible education in the laws of sex, and a much wider co-operation and companionship between men and women, wholly apart from erotic relations, are equally necessary.

I am utterly opposed to the 'double standard'; but I believe the 'double standard' is an integral part of a certain social order: to repudiate that standard, while upholding and accepting the social order, seems to me absurd.

Finally: I do not accept traditional platitudes: especially not that doctrine of the uncleanness of sex, insisted on by the Christian—or as it should be called, the Pauline—superstition.

Now what are the assumptions underlying the conventional view of women's sexuality?

  1. The denial, first of all, of any strong, spontaneous, discriminating,—note these qualifications—sex impulse in women.

2. The division of women into two arbitrary classes, corresponding to no psychological or ethical individual differences: as
   (a) The prospective or actual private sex property of one man.
   (b) The public sex property of all and sundry.
3. The over-rating, which amounts sometimes to a sadistic fetishism, of one manifestation of sex and one characteristic.

Hence the belief that the majority of women, those not belonging to the prostitute class, feel neither curiosity, nor desire on these matters, while they are maidens. And that when their sexual life has begun, its physical side is quite subordinate, and merely a *response* to their husbands.

Also that no woman who has any principle or any fastidiousness, can be physically attracted to more than one man; in the words of the thousand-fold repeated cliché: 'Woman is instinctively monogamous, while man is polygamous.' . . .

The sexual emotion in women is not, taking it broadly, weaker than in men. But it has an enormously wider range of variation; and much greater diffusion, both in desire and pleasure, all through women's organisms. And thirdly, arising from these two characteristics of variability and diffusion, it is extremely liable to aberrations and perversions, which, I believe, under constant social and religious repression of normal satisfaction, have often developed to a pathological extent, while sometimes remaining almost entirely subconscious.

The variability of the sexual emotion in women is absolutely basic and primary. It can never be expressed or satisfied by either patriarchal marriage or prostitution. It is found in the same woman as between different times, and in different individuals. This is the cause of much cant and bitterness between women, for there is a considerable and pretty steady percentage of cold natures, who may yet be very efficient and able and very attractive to men. These cold women generally have a perfect mania for *prohibition* as a solution for all ills. But surely, we do not want the new world to be built up only by women who have long ago forgotten what sex means, or who have never experienced strong sexual emotions, and regard them as a sign of grossness or decadence.

I think no one who knows the 'personnel' of many social reform movements, can doubt that this is a very real danger. Persons of cold temperament have special aptitudes for much valuable work: they have their peculiar excellences, their precious achievements. But they must not alone make the laws for more ardent natures.

And the greatest drawback of the sexually frigid woman is the ease with which her coldness adapts itself to venality and vulgarity, whether conventionally sanctioned or not.

It is this variety and variability of the sexual impulse among women, which would militate against any real promiscuity, if women were all economically secure and free to follow their own instincts, and to control their maternal function by the knowledge of contraceptives (a most important part of women's real emancipation). Most people are apt to under-rate the real strength of desire, and at the same time, to exaggerate its indiscriminate facility. I submit that, though few women are absolutely monandrous, still fewer are really promiscuous. And I believe that much of the promiscuity of men is either a reaction from conditions of life and work, which a sane social order will abolish, or a response to organised commercial exploitation, and therefore an artificial product. In a social order where women were not tempted for bread and butter, and any of the 'jam' of life, to exploit the desires of men, it would soon become apparent that the sexual instinct is selective. The most ardent natures, if they are not insane or suffering from prolonged sexual starvation, have their cool quiescent times; and I think no woman who has had the inestimable happiness and interest of real friendship with men, can doubt that it may exist without any conscious sexual desire.

Much of the unhealthiness of sexual conditions at present, is due to the habit of segregating the sexes in childhood and partly in latter life, and making them into 'alien enemies' to one another. Some measure of co-education and a much wider professional and administrative co-operation will clarify our views, and induce a more generous and human tone.

. . . The education of women together with the complexity of their emotional life, and their special physiology, help to stimulate sexual aberrations to a degree which is not generally realised; but it is none the less important and injurious. I wish particularly to make this point clear. Of course, normal sexuality includes the beginnings of most abnormal instincts. The pleasure in either inflicting a certain degree of pain on the beloved one, or suffering a certain degree of pain from them, is almost inextricably a part of desire. So are certain forms of fetishism . . . We are learning to recognise congenital inversion as a vital and very often valuable factor in civilisation, subject of course, to the same restraints as to public order and propriety, freedom of consent, and the protection of the immature, as normal heterosexual desire. Also a certain amount of self-excitement, and solitary enjoyment, seems inevitable in any strongly developed sexual life, and is indisputably much safer, and more consonant with humanity and refinement, than the so-called safety-valve of prostitution. The black shadow of the Christian superstition has perpetuated needless ignorance and suffering here.

In short, sex is complex, and in humanity, largely mental and imaginative. Certain minor and occasional aberrations are part of the complete life. But the system of silence and repression, often reacts on women's organism in a thoroughly abnormal manner, and a completely *artificial* (this is the point) perversion may be established, and if it is established early enough, may be quite unconscious for years. And the more sensitive and diffident and amenable to ideas of modesty the girl is, the more easily may this process be developed.

Any direct external stimulation is much rarer among young girls than among boys of the same age and class. The actual physiology of women, as well as the sense of modesty and the fear of shocking and offending, will generally prevent this, either alone or with other girls, though here again there are many exceptions. But day-dreaming, the production of a high degree of excitement, and sometimes of the actual climax of enjoyment, by means of vague yet delightful imaginings, is the most exquisite pleasure and deepest secret of many imaginative and sensitive girls, and may even begin before puberty. The development of the heterosexual relation, either in marriage or with a lover, may supersede those experiences, and they remain a beautiful but temporary episode, or recur at intervals of loneliness between normal erotic activity. But in these days of suppressed desires and delayed marriages, it is more and more probable that the habit will become a necessity, and it may lead to a great difficulty in forming normal connections or even to an aversion thereto. I would even say that after twenty-five, the woman who has neither husband nor lover and is not under-vitalised and sexually deficient, is suffering mentally and bodily—often without knowing why she suffers; nervous, irritated, anaemic, always tired, or ruthlessly and feverishly fussing over trifles; or else she has other consolations, which make her so-called 'chastity' a pernicious sham.

Artificial or substitute homosexuality—as distinct from true inversion—is very widely diffused among women, as a result of the repression of normal gratification and the segregation of the sexes, which still largely obtains. It appears, I think, later in life than onanism; in the later twenties or thirties rather than in the teens. Sometimes its only direct manifestations are quite noncommittal and platonic; but even this incomplete and timid homosexuality can always be distinguished from true affectionate friendship between women, by its jealous, exacting and extravagant tone. Of course, when one of the partners in such an attachment is a real or congenital invert, it is at once much more serious and much more physical. The psychology of homogenic women has been much less studied than that of inverted men. Probably there are many varieties and subtleties of emotional fibre among them. Some very great authorities have believed that the inverted woman is more often bisexual—less exclusively attracted to other women—than the inverted man. This view needs very careful confirmation, but if true, it would prove the greater plasticity of women's sex-impulse. It has also been stated that the invert, man or woman, is drawn towards the normal types of their own sex. These and other points, should be elucidated by the Society's work. Certainly, the heterosexual woman of passionate but shy and sensitive nature, is often responsive to the inverted woman's advances, especially if she is erotically ignorant and inexperienced. Also many women of quite normally directed (heterosexual) inclinations, realise in mature life, when they have experienced passion, that the devoted admiration and friendship they felt for certain girl friends, had a real, though perfectly unconscious, spark of desire in its exaltation and intensity; an unmistakable, indefinable note, which was absolutely lacking in many equally sincere and lasting friendships.

Neither artificial homosexuality nor prolonged auto-erotism—to use Havelock Ellis' masterly phrase—prove *innate* morbidity. Careful observation and many confidences from members of my own sex, have convinced me that our maintenance of outworn traditions is manufacturing habitual auto-erotists and perverts, out of women who would instinctively prefer the love of a man, who would bring them sympathy and comprehension as well as desire. I repudiate all wish to slight or depreciate the love-life of the real homosexual; but it cannot be advisable to force the growth of that habit in heterosexual people. And remember, there are other very dangerous and degrading perversions which may develop under repression. I know of a case in which a sudden, inexplicable, but apparently quite irresistible, lust of cruelty developed in a woman of the most actively kind and tender heart, but highly emotional and nervous, and sexually unsatisfied. As for the indirect psychic effects of involuntary and prolonged abstinence, surely Freud's researches can leave no doubt in the minds of thinking people. Here again, I know *personally* of a case of a fixed idea, which for three years developed recurrent spasms of maniacal terror.

Again, I ask, why all this waste of women, and of life?

---

from

STUDIES IN FEMININE INVERSION

(1923)

F. W. Stella Browne

... This problem of feminine inversion is very pressing and immediate, taking into consideration the fact that in the near future, for at least a generation, the circumstances of women's lives and work will tend, even more than at present, to favour the frigid [sexually repressed] and next to the frigid, the inverted types. Even at present, the social and affectional side of the invert's nature has often fuller opportunity of satisfaction than the heterosexual woman's, but often at the cost of adequate and definite physical expression. And how decisive for vigor, sanity and serenity of body and mind, for efficiency, for happiness, for the mastery of life, and the understanding of one's fellow-creatures—just this definite physical expression is! The lack of it, "normal" and "abnormal," is at the root of most of what is most trivial and unsatisfactory in women's intellectual output, as well as of their besetting vice of cruelty. How can anyone be finely or greatly creative, if one's supreme moral law is a negation! Not to *live*, not to *do*, not even to try to understand . . .

I am sure that much of the towering spiritual arrogance which is found, e.g., in many high places in the Suffrage movement, and among the unco' guid generally, is really unconscious inversion.

I think it is perhaps not wholly uncalled-for, to underline very strongly my opinion that the homo-sexual impulse *is not in any way superior* to the normal; it has a fully equal right to existence and expression, it is no worse, no lower; *but no better.*

By all means let the invert—let all of us—have as many and varied "channels of sublimation" as possible; and far more than are at present available. But, to be honest, are we not too much inclined to make "sublimation" an excuse for refusing to tackle fundamentals? The tragedy of the repressed invert is apt to be not only one of emotional frustration, but complete dislocation of mental values.

Moreover, our present social arrangements, founded as they are on the repression and degradation of the normal erotic impulse, artificially stimulate inversion and have thus forfeited all right to condemn it. There is a huge, persistent, indirect pressure on women of strong passions and fine brains to find an emotional outlet with other women. A woman who is unwilling to accept either marriage—under present laws—or prostitution, and at the same time refuses to limit her sexual life to auto-erotic manifestations, will find she has to struggle against the whole social order for what is nevertheless her most precious personal right. The right sort of woman faces the struggle and counts the cost well worth while; but it is impossible to avoid seeing that she risks the most painful experiences, and spends an incalculable amount of time and energy on things that should be matters of course. Under these conditions, some women who *are not innately or predominantly homosexual* do form more or less explicitly erotic relations with other women, yet these are makeshifts and essentially substitutes, which cannot replace the vital contact, mental and bodily, with congenial men.

No one who has observed the repressed inverted impulse flaring into sex-antagonism, or masked as the devotion of daughter or cousin, or the solicitude of teacher or nurse, or perverted into the cheap, malignant cant of conventional moral indignation, can deny its force. Let us recognise this force, as frankly as we recognise and reverence the love between men and women. When Paris was devouring and disputing over Willy and Colette Willy's wonderful Claudine stories, another gifted woman writer, who had also touched on the subject of inversion, defended not only the artistic conception and treatment of the stories (they need no defence, and remain one of the joys and achievements of modern French writing), but also their ethical content: Mme. Rachilde wrote "*une amoureuse d'amour n'est pas une vicieuse*" [a woman in love with love is not depraved].

After all: every strong passion, every deep affection, has its own endless possibilities, of pain, change, loss, incompatibility, satiety, jealousy, incompleteness: why add wholly extraneous difficulties and burdens? Harmony may be incompatible with freedom; we do not yet know, for few of us know either. But both truth and the most essential human dignity are incompatible with things as they are.

Unlike the mainstream of the German lesbian and gay movement, the French one in the early part of the twentieth century derived its inspiration from art rather than science. While the relatively authoritarian political culture of Germany (with its Paragraph 175), conditioned an oppositional political movement for reform, the law of France at the same time was characterized by sexual liberalism (sodomy had been decriminalized in the constitution of 1793, and had remained so since then). It was the fabric of everyday life in France that was conservative; *pudeur* or modesty was its reigning principle. As André Gide wrote, "we have the courage of our opinions, but never of our behavior." As a result, French gay and lesbian thought took culture as its object, but not in the reactionary mode of the Community of the Self-Owners. Rather, French gays and lesbians of the period focused upon transforming the heterosexism of their society through living their lives in ways that derived from their homosexuality, as in the development of specifically lesbian forms of relationships; this transformation was then reflected in art, literature, and other forms of cultural production, rather than directly in the policies of the government.

Natalie Clifford Barney (1876-1972) was a wealthy American lesbian living in Paris; her lovers included Renée Vivien and American painter Romaine Brooks. She maintained a salon, a regular meeting place of a network of prominent writers and artists, many of whom were lesbians from different parts of the world living in Paris at the time. As a wealthy lesbian, she wrote about the independence of women and their relationships as such with each other. The selection printed here, published in 1910, sums up her view of homosexual love as offering "a perilous advantage." While it is not explicitly political, "being other than normal" implies an ethos that can inform political action. Thus, with her contemporary, André Gide, Barney freed thought about homosexuality from the trappings of medicalization by psychiatry and its concern with normal and abnormal expression of an instinct, and moved toward thinking about homosexuality in ethical terms, as an art of living. Although she was part Jewish, Barney spent World War II in Italy in sympathy with the fascists. She advocated pacifism, an unpopular position, during World War I.

We also include a selection from the first French gay journal, "*Inversions*," which was published from 1924-1926. It was shut down by the police and later revived as "*L'Amitié*"; it again ceased publication after the government charged it with compromising public morality, or *pudeur*. Later French gay thinkers, notably Guy Hocquenghem and Michel Foucault, would call this *la loi de la pudeur*, implying unofficial, but no less powerful suppression of homosexuality. Many articles in the journal were translations of German articles—an indication of the relationship between the French and German gay and lesbian movements of the day.

PREDESTINED FOR FREE CHOICE

(1910)

Natalie Clifford Barney

One does not always recognize oneself in one's acts, any more than one recognizes oneself in one's parents. My ancestors covered the range from Celts to Latins, Jews to Puritans—and doubtless more besides. But these contrasts, instead of creating a civil war inside me, bequeathed me an excellent sense of balance.

My great grand-parents, seeking refuge in America from France, Holland and England, participated in the formation of the United States and our War of Independence.[1]

Interpreting this spirit of independence in my own way, I returned to my maternal origins, and France has become my country of choice.

Paris has always seemed to me to be the only city in which one can live as one sees fit. Despite the baleful progress inflicted from the outside, she continues to respect, and even encourage, personality. In France, thought, food and love have remained a matter of individual choice where each person follows their own inclination, instead of that of their neighbors. Which is probably why the country is so difficult to govern, and so easy to live in.

I was predestined for free choice, for, contrary to the warnings given back home in the United States of "what is and is not done," I have always done as I pleased. What's more, does it not require deep concentration to catch hold of the messages of our interior being, and thus experience the mysteries of self-initiation?

One cannot, after all, judge an existence except in terms of what it has made of us, and what we have made of it. If life is to be the expression, and not the suppression, of self, have I not roundly fulfilled and succeeded in mine?

I love my life. Principally because I have been able to keep it free, in order freely to give it. Guided by love—the kind which forces us to surpass ourselves—I have loved my fellow man, and particularly my fellow woman, with passion. That such feelings and dispositions may be seen as blameworthy or too intense, has never bothered me. That was the direction in which I developed.

That right-thinking people, making light of our precious relationships here below, have had other affinities, other predilections than mine, seems to me as strange as my singular life and attachments must appear to them. Is it natural, though, to despise love in favour of heavenly, or earthly, ambition? Love is certainly a great expense of self.

Which is doubtless why so many people find it so hard to accept or practise! Whether they scheme for honor and fame, get into cut-throat rivalry with their colleagues over career promotion (for one needs to make a living—living off others), whether they amass great fortunes or contract profitable marriages, all these attempts at "making it" have the same result: one loses oneself on the way. Consequently, almost no one lives their own true life, almost no one pays attention to the one thing which, to my mind, is essential: love. Love, the perfect median between heaven and earth—for it spiritualizes the material and materializes the spiritual in the form of our own being, blessed with both body and soul which only love can reunite.

Do not let us imagine, however, that the lover's calling is an unmixed delight: it is, rather, a continual tension in which one tries to guide and guard the one we love, exercising all one's perspicacity and charm to ensure her continued happiness. For it to last, love should be composed of all our other loves. I am, perhaps, love's mystic, though this has never deterred me from the thrill of its practice. But should we not abandon the trappings of love before they abandon us?

Being other than normal is a perilous advantage. And does one not need a more tempered courage to live one's life than to sacrifice oneself to some duty or other?

Living in the eye of love is an adventure for which few are suited. It's a very trying environment; most of those who attempt it are in danger of burning up with fever or starvation. Few constitutions survive. As for me, the striving, the pain and the mystery are more than just my native land. It is only there that I feel I am in my element . . .

My life is truly my own, without pretence, and so, consequently, is my work: my writing is simply the result, the accompaniment. I offer them as such.

If too little of the love I am claiming is found in this book, it is because I have spent it more profitably elsewhere. There remain only fragments here. And when I leave my natural element, I go armed as an amazon.

How can I complete this moral, or immoral, portrait?

Born to young, good-looking, healthy parents, I have never had a serious illness.

My childhood? "Extraordinary," like everyone else's but unlike everyone else, I am not set on recounting it in detail.

I am more conscious of my adolescence as a "sad, sweet little page."

If my education was nil, it is because:

"My only books were women's looks . . . "

My love affairs? Many.

My friendships? Loyal and faithful.

My youth? It continues, like for the elderly Goethe: how many first loves meet up with our last loves! How many chosen affinities find each other again then!

I have examined many hearts, comparing them with my own.

"How many beauties, how much candor have aroused my feeble heart which, till it beat its last, will remain the heart of a lover."

My last heart beat, which I neither long for nor fear.

Without hatred for those who are different from me, nor for those who would be my enemy, my sensibility is such that I cannot witness suffering without suffering myself.

Naturally intuitive, I am able to interpret even the silence of children. I believe I have never approached another being without doing them some good.

My joys are quite unselfish, for I experience them only through the one I love.

To love like that is to play only for the other, stirring up wonder, demanding from life more than it gives, for it is a raw, intractable material which must be continually reworked if it is to yield more than our paradise lost.

It seems that all my journeys have been with, or toward, someone who was dear to me, and that all my letters and poems were inspired by love, or by loving friendship.

Would Renée Vivien have found her way without me?

Would Rémy de Gourmont's life have been renewed without his Amazon?

As for the portraits which follow, those who would condemn them as indiscreet, should bear in mind that all art, all artistic expression, is an indiscretion we commit against ourselves.

Discretion about the past, which is really passed, is no better than oblivion. Silence too can be indiscreet. And would it not be the height of cowardice to allow our dead to die?

If, in the course of these confessions, which are open to the heavens, I have pushed certain memories to the extremes of confidence, I hope I have never overstepped the line where indiscretion is the privilege of tact.

1. *Some of their deeds and exploits are featured in the preface to my* Adventures of the Mind.

selections from

INVERSIONS

(1925)

trans. Nancy Erber Cadet

The first issue of *Inversions* was published on November 15, 1924. It contained a quotation by Goethe on the front cover, "it [inversion] is in Nature, even though it is against Nature." The lead article was a statement by the editor, entitled "On the Threshold," which described *Inversions* unequivocally as "a journal *for* homosexuality, not . . . *about* homosexuality." As "the only publication [in France] devoted entirely to the defense of homosexuality," *Inversions* would serve two goals, they stated. One was to educate "public opinion," which was biased against homosexuals. "We know the general attitude toward homosexuals. We believe it springs entirely from ignorance and prejudice and that is what we want to fight against." Another mission was to increase homosexuals' access to public speech and self-knowledge and the editors urged readers to send in personal stories and observations. "Aside from a few exceptional cases where homosexuals motivated by a profound need for self-awareness or self-justification have tried to analyze themselves and their lives, few of us have investigated sexual inversion in depth."

Addressing medico-psychiatric categories of sexual deviance, the editors noted: "The different sensations and emotions that inverts have cause them to be classified as abnormal. It is therefore logical that by the same token heterosexuals should be seen as abnormal from the inverts' point of view. Unfortunately, this is not the case. All too often homosexuals will think of themselves as abnormal, as inferior, will try to normalize themselves and suppress their desires. For them, it's a death sentence. We want to shout out to inverts that they are normal and healthy beings, that they have the right to live their lives fully, that they don't have to adhere to a morality created by heterosexuals, to normalize their perceptions and feelings, to repress their desires, to stifle their passions. Celebrating that love which is as beautiful and noble as all others . . . we want to unite all those who suffer from isolation, and make *Inversions* the voice of all their 'brothers-in-love' [comrades in arms]." Rejecting the association of sexual inversion with deviance or mental incapacity, *Inversions* would also feature articles on "homosexuals in the fields of literature, the arts, philosophy and science . . . recognized as geniuses."

Having addressed such topics as "The Homosexual Question in Germany," "The Trial of Oscar Wilde," and the reception of Gide's *Corydon* and published personal accounts like "The Awakening of a Uranian Heart," an announcement appeared in the fourth issue, dated March 1, 1925, introducing a "survey of the readership." The announcement read:

"The Public Prosecutor of the Seine region has begun an investigation of the journal *Inversions* on the charge of offenses against decency. *Inversions* has put the following questions to well-known members of the literary, scientific and political world and will publish their responses in future issues.

Has the journal *Inversions* offended your decency?

In your opinion, does the charge against this journal constitute a limitation of freedom of the press or freedom of thought?

What is your opinion about homosexuality and homosexuals?"

Among the responses printed in the next issue of the journal, now re-titled Friendship, [L'Amitié] were those of Havelock Ellis and Camille Spiess. Ellis replied briefly: "1. No. 2. Yes. 3. Along with Moll, Hirschfeld, Freud and other authorities, I maintain that some of the most eminent men [*sic*] of our time and other times have been inverts." Spiess, an Anthroposophist and doctor of natural science, noted that the charges filed against *Inversions* constituted "a serious infringement on human dignity, the freedom of the press and of thought" and observed that "from a physiological point of view, uranian love is superior."

On October 13, 1926, Gustave Beyria, the publisher of *Inversions* was brought to trial on the charge of "offenses against decency"; Gaston Lestrade, the journal's editor, was charged as his accomplice. During the trial, the statement of purpose from the first issue of *Inversions* was quoted at length. Beyria was sentenced to ten months in prison and a two hundred franc fine and Lestrade to six months in prison and a hundred franc fine.

At the trial, "the District Attorney stood up and requested that the judge order the trial held in closed court, given the nature of the subject matter. After deliberations, the chief judge ruled that 'since the publicity given to arguments in the case could be dangerous to public order and decency,' the trial would be held behind closed doors." He cited article 81 of the 1848 constitution.

Beyria and Lestrade's offenses were "having founded on 15 November 1924 a monthly magazine called *Inversions* and after a few issues, adopted the title *Friendship*. The journal was currently for sale at newspaper stands for 1.50 francs. The very first lines of the journal informed its readers as to the spirit in which it was conceived and its goals: '*Inversions* is not a journal *about* homosexuality but a journal *for* homosexuality . . . We want to shout out to inverts that they are normal, healthy people, that they have the right to live their lives fully . . .'"

Beyria's and Lestrade's attorneys argued in their defense that "the journal under examination is very proper in its form; one couldn't find a single word in it which would offend decency" and cited the amendments to relevant statutes (laws of August 2, 1882, March 16, 1898 and April 7, 1908), which had added "obscenity to the more general notion of offense against decency." In turn, the prosecutor replied that "considering that virtually every page of this publication is a cynical apology for pederasty, a systematic appeal to homosexual passions and an incessant provocation to the most unhealthy curiosity . . . the articles in the journal are not only an offense against morality and a form of propaganda which, because of its neo-Malthusian [*i.e.* pro-birth control] slant might have dire effects on the future of the race [*sic*], the obscenity is less in the words themselves or the subject matter than in the general philosophy of the publication. In addition, there are the personal ads . . . 'Would like to meet a young man between 20–30 years old who likes literature and long walks' . . . 'Berlin reader wants to correspond with *Inversions* reader in Paris.' Considering that in these veiled but sufficiently clear terms the journal is a means for homosexuals from various countries to meet, the journal is a vehicle for propaganda favoring the further development of pederasty . . . This licentious provocation, this incitement to the most repulsive of vices is the worst and most dangerous offense to decency. Of course, we must ensure freedom of thought and safeguard the greatest independence of all intellectual productions, even if this means allowing strong and frank language in print, but one cannot compare a work of literature or a serious scientific study to the journal which has been charged, which has no other goal than the glorification of homosexuality and the solicitation of new recruits to pederasty . . . "

The verdict was appealed unsuccessfully to the Paris Superior Court in a hearing held on March 31, 1927.

Press reactions to *Inversions*:

Among the reactions to the journal were a series of statements attacking Gide and other gay writers, in addition to *Inversions*, published in the small journal, *Illusions,* by Pierre Lazareff in November 1924. Satirical articles appeared in the illustrated journal *Fantasio*, which had a long history of homo- and lesbophobia and in *The Lantern*, a right-wing paper. In the November 15, 1924 issue, *Fantasio*'s headline read "Let's be French, For God's Sake, Long Live Women!" and criticized unnamed celebrities in the arts, theater and science for "having cast aside all shame . . . making a show of their vice . . . This year alone we can count five important novels dedicated to the glory of this heresy . . . *Fantasio* protests against this particular journal [*Inversions*], and it is not alone in this. France has always been, throughout history, the land of beautiful women . . . perhaps a country outwardly frivolous but still not one infected by that *AngloSaxon gangrene*. And all French women will join us in this protest." *The Lantern* noted ominously on November 19, 1924 that "the title of this journal alone is worthy of the German propaganda machine."

Press reactions to the trial:

There was little comment or protest in the press, other than a brief mention in the "Trials" column of the daily newspaper *Le Temps* on March 21, 1926, announcing the verdict.

D

FROM LIBERALISM TO THE NEW SOCIAL RELATIONS OF SOVIET SOCIALISM

[Introduction by Laura Engelstein]

Reflecting the latest in Western medicine, law, and social science, Russian professionals in the late tsarist period expressed a range of attitudes toward homosexual activity. Physicians, psychiatrists, and legal experts, as well as artists and intellectuals, insofar as they addressed the question at all, usually denounced homosexual activity as abnormal or immoral. A few defended same-sex love as deviant but harmless. For example, the internationally renowned physician Veniamin M. Tarnovskii condemned homosexual practices on standard medical grounds, while his colleague (and perhaps relative), the gynecologist Ippolit M. Tarnovskii, considered homosexual relationships a matter of personal taste. The liberal lawyer Vladimir D. Nabokov, a member of the Provisional Government in 1917 and father of the famous novelist, attacked the anti-sodomy laws as violations of privacy and individual rights (neither guaranteed by imperial law). Whether hostile or sympathetic to this form of sexual desire, Russian professionals replicated a discourse fashioned in the West.

It is to the world of turn-of-the-century poets and philosophers, busy exploring the realm of erotic experience in search of spiritual renewal, that one must turn for a more peculiarly Russian vision of sexual desire, in all its various guises. Vasilii V. Rozanov (1856–1919), the maverick Christian philosopher and gifted prose stylist, was among their number. His treatise, *People of the Moonlight* (1911), excerpted here is unique among contemporary Russian texts in its sustained attention to the question of alternative sexual practices. It is also characterized by the hallmark of Rozanov's thinking—self-contradiction. On the one hand, he affirms the "naturalness" of same-sex love. On the other, he condemns the aversion to procreative sex as the root of Christian asceticism, which he considers spiritually destructive and "unnatural."

The title of this work derives from the contrast between two principles of sexual attraction. Heterosexual love is represented by "the bright and scorching sun, which drives the grass from the earth, which drives the sweet sap from the tree trunks, which causes flowers to bloom, which causes the pistils of flowers to be pollinated, and the stamens and pericarp of flowers to be filled with nectar . . . The sun is marriage (coitus), the sun is fact and reality."

The moon, by contrast, represents "eternal 'promise,' reverie, languor, expectation, hope: the exact opposite of the real. The moon forbids people to 'love very much,' 'to be intimate.' . . . It is monastic love, strolls of enamoured nuns in a field, nuns who are sad and silent, who have no idea what to do with their love, who have as yet found no 'object' for it. It is unhappy or criminal love, abnormal love, ending in nothing, love to which fatal bounds are set."

Such love derives from a sentimentalism that is idealistic and uncompromising and leads to political extremes. And yet, Rozanov also describes it as "highly spiritualistic."

Both Rozanov's appreciation and his critique of homosexual desire were rooted in a cast of mind completely at odds with the scientific terms in which nineteenth-century Western societies thought about sex. Rozanov rejected the categories of normal and abnormal applied by medical experts to the wide and ever fluctuating variety of human desire and sexual performance. As a philosophical conservative, he considered nature too protean a force to be bound by rationally conceivable rules. Yet Rozanov also believed that procreation was a fundamental principle of the natural order and that nonprocreative love was therefore "abnormal." Champion of idiosyncrasy in any form, he respected the nonconformity of those who refused to reproduce. Yet his purpose was not to promote the happiness of sexual rebels or vindicate their choice but to challenge the spiritual foundation of Christianity. While the Old Testament celebrated the joys and virtue of procreative family life, the New Testament denigrated marriage and raised celibacy to a spiritual ideal, thus, Rozanov believed, undermining the vitality of the faith. Insofar as homosexuality, too, excluded marriage and procreation, it was neither admirable nor desirable, though understandable as the particular contour of individual lives.

Rozanov's brand of spiritual empathy should not be mistaken for toleration as we now understand it. His appreciation for sexual diversity had nothing to do with the principles of individual rights or personal integrity we associate with modern liberalism. Quite the opposite. His refusal of standard categories, whether scientific, legal, or theological, reflected a studied refusal of systematic thinking altogether. In this he was deliberately and quintessentially, but never ideologically, conservative. A proud enemy of Enlightenment rationality, Rozanov exalted unpredictability and uncertainty, whether in the form of erratic or perverse desire, changeable appetites, ambiguities of gender, or logical contradiction. A practitioner of modernist prose, he despised modern life. Hostile to political ideology, he hailed the Revolution of 1905 as an outburst of primal force. His complex attitude toward the Jews is closely connected to his interest in and celebration of sexual expression. While he often praised the Jewish people as exemplars of Old Testament family virtues and libidinous vitality, he just as often denounced them in the crudest anti-Semitic terms, as blood-sucking exploiters of the Russian people, money-mad conspirators determined to control the Christian world, and, most odiously, as perpetrators of ritual blood murders. Yet the reason he feared and hated them was the same reason he admired them: their alleged sexual prowess gave them the kind of power ascetic Christians supposedly lacked.

In short, one cannot extract from Rozanov a consistent position on any subject. Whatever present-day gay liberationists may seek in appropriating his work for their own purposes, he was no simple partisan of homosexuals or gender ambiguity. Ultimately, he embraced the patriarchal ideal of reproductive heterosexuality, in which wives bore children and husbands ruled the roost. He was particularly harsh on women who adopted careers or displayed masculine propensities. Yet his penchant for intellectual perversity and his boldness in exploring the psychological terrain led him to understand the complexities of human sexual experience, both in terms of gender identity and object choice. His fearless self-exploration and the literary talent that allowed the uncensored flow of emotion and ideas to emerge in print make him to this day a fascinating (if also repulsive) figure.

One must, however, give Rozanov his due for intellectual courage, given the formal status of homosexual love under tsarist law, which made sodomy between consenting adult men (defined as anal intercourse) a criminal offense. With the gradual softening of the penal regime, however, penalties for sodomy also diminished with the years: before the abolition of most forms of corporal punishment in 1863, a man of nonprivileged social estate convicted of this crime would be sentenced to the lash; all culprits were deprived of civil rights and sent to Siberia. Exile remained the penalty until 1900, when it was replaced by a term of 4 to 5 years' forced labor. Anal intercourse with another man achieved by force or coercion, or practiced on a minor or mentally defective partner, incurred loss of civil rights and exile at hard labor for 10 to 12 years. Sex between women was not a crime. When the Bolsheviks came to power in October 1917, they abrogated all tsarist laws. The first Soviet criminal code, enacted in 1922, did not penalize sex between consenting adult men. Men (and even women) were nevertheless sometimes tried for alleged homosexual activity. Such disregard of legal process reflected a deliberate repudiation of so-called bourgeois principles in the law.

As for Soviet psychiatry, it was not of one voice on the subject of homosexuality. The author of the 1930 encyclopedia article excerpted here refrains from moral judgment, even in the guise of scientific theory. The writings of Sigmund Freud and of Magnus Hirschfeld, the renowned champion of homosexual rights in Germany, both mentioned in the text, were available in Russia before 1917 and continued to be discussed until any positive reference to Freud or publication of his work were banned in 1930. Not all Soviet psychiatrists even in the 1920s showed Sereiskii's scientific neutrality, moreover; the eminent Vladimir Bekhterev, for example, testified for the prosecution at a trial of alleged sodomites in 1922. In December 1933 the Communist Party recriminalized sex between consenting adult males; the statute introduced in early 1934 applied a penalty of 3 to 5 years' incarceration. It did not mention sex between women. The turn from tolerance (at least in theory) to prosecution in the case of male homosexuality was part of a general about-face in regulating private and sexual life: the easy divorce introduced in 1918 became more difficult, and abortion, legalized in 1920, once again became a crime.

As the 1952 Encyclopedia entry and the excerpted speeches of Gorky and Krylenko demonstrate, under Stalin homosexuality came to be associated with upper-class and bourgeois "decadence." This association was later invoked in Cuba, as documents in section IV will show.

Sources: Laura Engelstein, *The Keys to Happiness: Sex and the Search for Modernity in Fin-de-Siècle Russia* (Ithaca: Cornell University Press, 1992); idem, "Lesbian Vignettes: A Russian Triptych from the 1890s," *Signs* 15:4 (1990); idem, "Soviet Policy Toward Male Homosexuality: Its Origins and Historical Roots," *Journal of Homosexuality* 29:3–4 (1995); Wendy Z. Goldman, *Women, the State, and Revolution: Soviet Family Policy and Social Life, 1917–1936* (Cambridge: Cambridge University Press, 1993).

from

PEOPLE OF THE MOONLIGHT

(1911)

V.V. Rozanov

THE THIRD SEX
Sex as a Progression of Decreasing and Increasing Quantities

Sex would be a completely clear, or a fairly clear, phenomenon if it merely consisted in the periodic coupling of a male and a female in order to produce a new person: in that case it would be the same as the elements oxygen and hydrogen forming "in combination" a third and "new being"—water. But oxygen and hydrogen do not know "counterflows": and if suddenly we saw not a particle of oxygen combining eagerly (as always in chemical affinity) with a particle of hydrogen to produce a drop of water but, on the contrary, a particle of hydrogen—some exceptional one—suddenly starting, also "with eagerness," to climb on a particle of hydrogen similar to itself, avoiding with disgust the particle of oxygen complementing it, we would say: "It is a miracle! It is alive! It is individually different! It is a person!!" The individual began where it was suddenly said to the law of nature: "Stop! I won't let you function here." And the one who refused to let it function was also the first "spirit"—*not* "nature," *not* "mechanics." And so the "individual" appeared in the world in that place where for the first time there was a violation of the law—a violation of it as uniformity and constancy, as the norm and the "ordinary," as the "natural" and the "generally-expected."

Then these "counteractions" in the "cauldron" would be clear to us as the process in which the foundation was laid in the world, "from the beginning of time," for a principle so important as the *person, personality*, individualism, the principle of the self, a principle universally-significant for the cosmos, universally-necessary for the world . . .

. . . Without individuality, the world would have no sparkle: "clouds" of people, nations, and generations would pass by . . . And, in a word, without individuality, there would be no spirit or genius . . .

But I have digressed somewhat in the cosmological direction, away from the search for the primordial kernel that is the basis of "celibate" phenomena. The universal "I don't want to" of the male in regard to the female and of the female in regard to the male has been studied only recently; only in the nineteenth century did people begin to collect facts on this subject. And these facts lead to the indisputable conclusion that "sex" is not, so to say, a "constant" in us, in mankind, in man, but that it belongs to the order of phenomena or quantities that Newtonian-Leibnitzian mathematics and the philosophy of mathematics called "flowing quantities" or "fluxions" (Newton) . . .

In general, it is thus: we are 1) males and 2) females. But around this "it is thus" is also "it is not thus": opposition, counterflow, "fluxion" (Newton), the "I" rejecting every "non-I." And, in a word—*life*, the principle of life; the *individual*, the principle of individuality . . .

The assumption that sex is a constant and not in the least "flowing" gave rise to the expectation that every male will want a female and that every female will want a male—an expectation so universal that it even turned into a demand: "every male *will* want his own female" and "every female *will* want her own male" . . . Of course, "be fruitful and multiply" includes all this. But it will always remain a mystery why, considering the universal commandment to be fruitful and multiply, given to all nature, one person, Adam, was created entirely alone. Our amazement will increase even more if we note that Eve, the "mother of life" (in Hebrew—the"mother of lives," egg-bearing, viviparous "*ad infinitum*"), later emerged from Adam: i.e. Eve was concealed in Adam's essence, and it was she who set him dreaming about a "life's companion" . . . Adam, "created in the image and likeness of God," was, in his concealed completeness, Adam-Eve, both male and (*in potentia*) female; the two then divided, and this was the creation of Eve, with whom, as we know, the creation of new creatures came to an end. "There will be nothing more that is new." Eve was the last innovation in the world, the very last.

Only because of the general expectation that "every male will want a female," and so on, did the expectation also arise that the very pairing of males and females will flow with the regularity of the rotation of the sun and the moon, or according to the model of oxygen uniting with hydrogen, *without exception*. But everything that lives, beginning with the grammar of languages, has "exceptions": and sex, i.e. the principle of *life*, would simply not be *alive* if it did not have "exceptions"—and, of course, all the more so the more alive, vital, viable, and life-giving it is . . . Not everyone knows that one meets in the animal kingdom all, or almost all, the "deviations" that one meets in man—but less frequently. One can say that in the case of man it is impossible to find two pairs of males and females who copulate in exactly the same way. "There are as many kinds of handwriting as there are people," or vice versa; and it would be completely preposterous even to expect that if man is so individualized in such an insignificant, uninteresting, and unnecessary thing as handwriting that he would not be individualized in copulation as well. Of course, there are as many individuals with individualized ways in sex life as there are people . . .

Having unjustly encroached on a field not belonging to it, the moral law divided methods of copulation into "normal," i.e. expected, and "abnormal," i.e. "undesired"—the "undesired" not being desired by those who do not desire them and being in the highest degree desired by those who do desire them and who in that case practice them . . .

. . . And there is no better way to hide the "peculiar" than to subscribe to the "general rule" and to condemn everything that is "peculiar." From the aggregate of these circumstances and conditions, there came the unusual firmness—one might say the stability—of the moral law in the field of sex, a field which in fact not only has always been unstable, but one might say has never for a minute at any point in it ceased to be in flux. It has been an endless ocean, with majestic currents in it, with tempests, whirlpools, the insweep and back-sweep of the water at each individual cliff . . . The "stability" of the law ran parallel to the complete instability of what it referred to; and, as a matter of fact, this was the only inner law to come from the very essence of the element involved . . . Family virtues have been praised also by homosexuals; masturbators also have written about the harm of masturbation; and hermits living in the wilderness and copulating with the birds of the field and the beasts of the forest have been unable to tolerate a man having sexual relations with more than three women in his lifetime, or a woman with more than three men, also in her lifetime (the inadmissibility of a fourth marriage with Christians, i.e. as demanded by the "saints" of Christianity). All this is not so "indifferent." Of course, everyone conceals things—and therefore no one suffers very much from the "general rule"; but there are cases when people are found out, when what was concealed becomes known: and then stones are hurled at the "apostate" to force him from doing what absolutely no one has a "tendency to." Nevertheless, sex is precisely an ocean: and a "whirlpool" will never appear in it where one has not been "ordered to appear"; its endless currents will not cease, and they will not intermingle, nor will they expand or contract, and everything will remain "as is" and as it has been predetermined, even in case the rule disappears under the pressure of the fact that it has meddled in an area that is essentially not its own . . .

Here everything belongs to observation and nothing to correction.

What is "one's own" with each person manifests itself first and foremost in strength, in intensity. We have here a series of degrees that can easily be expressed by a series of natural numbers:

. . . +7 +6 +5 +4 +3 +2 +1 ±0 −1 −2 −3 −4 −5 −6 −7 . . .

The greatest intensity so far as the possibility of giving satisfaction and the constant desire for receiving satisfaction are concerned denotes the highest degree of sexuality—of the male in satisfying the female lying opposite him and of the female the male opposite her. The most "male" male is the one who copulates with a woman most often, most willingly and most vigorously, while the most "female" female is the one who submits to the male the most languidly, tenderly, and submissively. Under the influence of all sorts of superstitions, fears, and particularly assumptions and gossip, there developed in mankind a completely false idea of the image of the "true male" and "true female", i.e. mankind—nations and individual people—quite wrongly complicated the greatest sexual strength by giving it secondary, supplementary features, and moreover, not only mental but even physical ones. As generally imagined by novelists, playwrights, the petty bourgeoisie, and "society," it is something huge, noisy, loud-voiced, and with brazen and offensive manners. "He" and "she" "thump along," they roar, they give no one any peace; they are embarrassing and disturbing to all. The "smart alec" and the "boisterous woman" are those against whom mothers and fathers supposedly should guard their daughters and hide their growing sons. Such people are said to "seduce," "pervert," rape and corrupt. But it would be a sad kind of posterity to come from these empty, clattering "barrels"; the fact is that the human race, "being fruitful and multiplying," is not at all like that : it is lively, energetic, indefatigable, and inexhaustible.

True strength does not "clatter and thump." True strength instead floats along like the fog, it creeps along. The master of the steppe is not the buffalo bellowing on the plains, but the jaguar hiding in the tall grass. In this regard, Russian and Chinese folk wisdom has expressed a kind of semi-fear and semi-conjecture. For example, the Russians say: "Still waters run deep." And I happened to read that the Chinese have a saying that goes: "If a woman resembles an angel, beware, and know that she has in her the devil." In both cases, the old people who thought up these sayings, were, in a way, warning the young, pointing out to them that they should assume that beneath the surface lies something quite the opposite. These sayings were not, of course, thought up solely in regard to sex: but they hardly would have been composed in this general form if sex life, sex images and types, which play such a prominent role in the life of every nation, community, and private person, ran sharply counter to these sayings. Obviously not! Both the Chinese and the Russians pointed out that sexual passion does not "roar in the fields," but rather steals along in the bushes; that it is something "quiet" in appearance, sometimes even "angelic"—at least in the case of women. But at this point we must enter into a small discussion.

From the very first it is evident that the most "male" male must look completely different from the most "female" female. All his accompanying secondary characteristics must be completely different from hers—precisely because he is her opposite, because he is her other pole. Very masculine men often have a very thick beard: but is it possible we must conclude from this that the most perfect woman must also have a beard, or at least the small moustache that sometimes appears on a woman's lip? Yet the assumption that the most "female" female must be "boisterous" is exactly the same as the assumption that Joan of Arc, Desdemona, Ophelia, and Tatyana had a small moustache. Of course, this is stupid, and so much so that now that we have mentioned it we need not even pause to refute it.

No, the male and the female are *opposites*, and that is all! Hence all conclusions, all philosophy and truth. The greater the contrast between man and woman the stronger the sex in them! I.e. the less masculine a woman the more of a female she is, and the less feminine a man the more of a male he is. Pallas Athena, a "warrioress" and "sage," is not married; she is not a mother, and, in general, there is very little of the female about her. She has no age, she knew no childhood, she will never be a grandmother. Parallel to this masculine woman is the exclusively feminine Ganymede, who will never be a husband, a father, a grandfather. It is clear that in their opposition the most "male" male and the most "female" female are:

1) the hero, the doer
2) the family woman, the housewife

The one will be:

1) active, enterprising, inventive, bold, daring. Perhaps he really does "stamp" and "thump." The other will be:
2) quiet, tender, gentle, silent, or at least not very talkative.

The "Eternal Feminine" is the prototype of the one.

The "creator of worlds" is the prototype of the other.

There is a kind of secret, inexpressible, and as yet unresearched correlation (as a matter of fact, not only a correlation but a complete identity) between the typical characteristics of the genitalia of both sexes and their soul in its ideal form, its perfection. And the words about the union of souls in marriage, i.e. in the sex act, are to a startling degree true. With these persons the souls do indeed unite when they are joined, when they are coupled together in sexual union. But how different their souls are (and because of this they complement each other). The male soul in its ideal form is firm, straightforward, strong, aggressive, forward moving, pressing, overpowering; but, after all, that is practically a verbal photograph of what a man shyly covers with his hands when naked. Now let us turn to the woman: the ideal of her character, behavior, life, and the whole outline of her soul, in general, is tenderness, softness, yieldingness, and pliancy. But these are merely the characteristics of her genitalia. We express what is expected of and desired in a man, in his soul, in his biography, by means of the very same words, terms, and concepts that his wife uses in her own mind to express what is "expected and desired" of his sex organ; and reciprocally, when a husband describes with delight and rapture the "soul" and "character" of his wife, he uses, he cannot help using, the same words he uses mentally when, separated from her or after not having seen her for a long time, he pictures to himself the sexual region of her body. Note also the following subtle peculiarity. In a woman's psyche, there is no harshness or hardness; it is not outlined sharply and clearly. On the contrary, it spreads like the fog, it covers an indefinitely vast area—in fact you do not even know where its boundaries lie. But, after all, these all are predicates of the moist and fragrant tissues of her sex organ and her sex region in general. A man will never fill the whole house with a pleasant aroma: his psychology, his ways, his actions, are loud, but they do not "spread." He is a tree, but without fragrance; she is a flower, ever fragrant, spreading her fragrance far and wide. Like souls, like organs! From this essentially cosmogonic constitution (*not* just earthly), they are fruitful, they produce a line of descendants, they create *ad infinitum* "in their own image and likeness." A soul from a soul, as in the case of a spark from a flame: this is procreation . . .

. . . One must only keep this numeration in mind:

$\dots +8 \ +7 \ +6 \ +5 \ +4 \ +3 \ +2 \ +1 \ \pm 0 \ -1 \ -2 \ -3 \ -4 \ -5 \ -6 \ -7 \ -8 \dots$

The "sainte prostituée" is the +8+7+6. . . And the closer we come to the lower numbers, to the +3+2+1, the harsher is the timbre of the voice, the sterner the look, the cruder the manners, the greater the "brazenness," as seminarians would say. There appear those typical "priests' daughters," who enter into marriage with a sack filled with a fixed dowry, and who all their lives are happy merely putting together "a dowry to add to their own dowry"—not a very pleasant life for the priest and the deacon, but it is "not bad," "one can put up with it." And finally there comes the "±0." Note both the "+" and "−" signs. Such women are not dead, although they absolutely never "have the desire." There is something of the "+" in them: but it is bound up with something of the "−." Thus, there is no *unilinear* attraction in them to the "male": it is as if there were two arrows here, their tips pointing in different directions: the one toward the "male" and the other . . .? The law of progression, as well as the fact that everything here takes place between two sexes only, shows that the second arrow can be pointed toward nothing but the female. The female seeks a female; consequently, in this type of female, there simultaneously exists the male. But for the time being, he is so weak— scarcely born—that he is completely bound up with the remnants of the female, who is dying away. The female, however, is also bound up with the "male," who has been born here once again. A woman of this type is "neither this nor that." Her voice is terribly harsh, her manners are "partly masculine"; she smokes, inhales, spits, and speaks in a deep voice. Her hair grows poorly, it is ugly, she cuts it short: "her braid won't braid." She is more of a boy than a girl. Where is the "Eternal Feminine" here?

> She sat there pensively alone,
> And God knows what plunged her young soul
> Into this melancholy reverie!

No, you would not say that about such a girl: she takes courses, goes to rallies, argues, curses, reads, translates, compiles. She is a "bluestocking" with a touch of the politician, or a politician with pretensions to erudition. "God forbid a man taking a girl like this as his wife": and men instinctively do not marry them (although they do marry girls who are plain or ugly, even those who are a real fright). If, "contrary to expectations," she gave birth to a child, she would not even know how to take out her breast and feed it. "She is not a Madonna but a drill sergeant." And she needs no husband at all. She would be bored with one; she could not keep from running off to participate in community affairs, in the work of various organizations, in sham "charity," mainly in things involving noise, running around, fuss and bustle. The man, the "warrior and citizen" (the arrow of the male), is already partly aroused in her. The only thing lacking is a little moustache. As a matter of fact, she does not even know how to wear a dress in a truly feminine way: she puts it on wrong, awkwardly; somehow she makes everything too short, so that it lacks the long, beautiful lines that excite men. And men do not like these women. But other women are beginning to like them: "What a great *guy* that Masha is!"

And finally everything passes over to the purely minus quantities: "she" is agitated in the presence of those of her own sex, she casts passionate glances, she gets excited, she feels hot all over in the presence of women and girls. Their braids, their hands, their necks . . . and, alas, their invisible breasts, and, alas, alas, their completely hidden parts, the whole of a woman's "secret"—everything, inexplicably excites them, makes them yearn, the more so, to the point of torment and suffering, because all this is to be hidden from them forever, hidden precisely from *them*, and revealed only to a man, to a husband. The torments of Tantalus: it is so close, it is always around, it can even be seen if a woman is careless when undressing or when bathing; but one cannot get a good look at it without dying then and there of shame. There is a universal barrier in the very arrangement of things, in the plan of the world. "So near, and yet so far!" The torments of Tantalus: the realization of one's desires being put off endlessly; it is impossible, it will never be!

Tears, depression, dreams. Daydreams. Poetry, much poetry. Philosophy—lengthy philosophy! And, by the way, she has a certain talent for it. This "drill sergeant in a skirt" easily masters both Marx and Kuno Fischer—and, in general, she is superior to the "weaker sex" mentally, spiritually, ideologically, verbally, and even in so far as a capacity for work is concerned.

This law can, of course, be applied to the male as well. How does it manifest itself here?

Whereas women like this often have a slight moustache, the men often have a sparse beard. All this has to do not with things physical, but mainly with those relating to the spirit, disposition, manners and morals, the heart, but partly to things physical as well.

The northern Normans, as described by Ilovaisky, probably provide us best of all with a vivid picture of the primordial male—the "+8 +7" of the male progression: "In time of peace, when at war with no one, they would ride out to the fields; closing their eyes tightly, they would rush forward and slash the air with their swords, as if striking down their enemies. And in battle they would throw themselves fearlessly into the very slaughter; they would slash at the enemy, inflict wounds, and would perish themselves, expecting death to cross over to Valhalla, which they also imagined to be filled with heroes, fighting eternally." An indomitably energy—as with the Turks, who astounded Europe with their bravery and their wars. Probably the early wars of the Romans and the everlasting "internecine struggle" of the early Hellenes are also based on this very same type of male who, because of his burning ardor, does not know what to do with himself—so he rushes here and there, into battles, adventures, travels (Odysseus and the period of Henry the Navigator.) All this is the primordial, crude upturning of the stones of culture. A volcano upturns the earth, seemingly disfiguring it, splitting it open, breaking it up: but, as a matter of fact, this is already the beginning of culture. A small island is more "cultural" than a continent; a "tiny land" always receives God's first ray. And the breaking up, the smashing of something or other in general, is the first step toward culture.

But it is one thing to break up an inert mass and another to start to polish the pieces. Breaking up and polishing are different phases of a single process, and they require quite different qualities.

And it is here, in the universal need for polishing, that the role of "+2 +1 ±0" and the "−1 −2 and so on" of sex comes to the fore.

The beard begins to be shorter and sparser, the ardor to decrease, and the disposition, up to now harsh, crude, and unbearable to one's neighbor, begins to acquire a gentleness that makes proximity to it comfortable and even pleasant. "Neighbors" appear both in the territorial and the moral sense; "kinship" appears, in the spiritual and figurative sense, not only in the consanguineous one. All this is in proportion as the male shifts from the higher degrees—the "+8 and +7"—to the middle and very low ones—the "+3 +2 +1." In these middle stages, marriage occurs because of the attachment of the one to the *other*, the satisfaction of the one by the other. And finally there appears the mysterious "±0," the complete lack of desire for sex, the lack of "I want to" . . . There is no desire for it at all. The peace and quiet of existence are not disturbed. Such a man will never challenge another to a duel, he will never take offence—and least of all will he give offence. Socrates, who said that it was easier for him to suffer an insult than to inflict one on someone else, falls into this category. So does the conciliatory: "Father, forgive them, for they know not what they do." In general, there comes to the fore the principle of forgiveness, meekness, the conciliatory "nonresistance to evil." Platon Karatayev, in Tolstoy's *War and Peace*, is here too, right along with Socrates; so is Spinoza, peacefully writing his treatises and observing the life of spiders. They all are spokesmen of the conciliatory "I don't want to," "I don't feel like it" . . . There is in these people an extremely great decrease in energy, almost to the point where it no longer exists (Amiel, Marcus Aurelius). There are long periods of daydreaming, endless daydreaming. The whole of existence here is lacy and weblike; it is as if the sun never played here, as if all this had barely been born and existed in some dark and unilluminated corner of the world. The mystery of the world . . . In the character of these people, there is much that is lunar, tender, and pensive; much that is useless for life, for action. But there is much that is surprisingly fruitful for culture, for civilization. It is precisely a cobweb, it is precisely lace, with long threads running from it and attaching themselves to everything else. In the nature of these people, there is also something melancholic, despite all the serenity and calm of their appearance and life; moreover, it is a melancholy that is unconscious and without cause. "World sorrow," "Weltschmerz," has its roots here in this mysterious "I don't want to" of the organism. Here the sciences and philosophy blossom. And finally the "±0," breaks down into the "+0" and "−0": the former dies away—after all, there was nothing in it anyway. And there remains the "−0," which quickly changes to "−1," "−2," "−3," and so on.

In the lower, primary degrees, the "−0," "−1," we observe this in the form those well-known dual friendships—not in the form of a noisy comradeship of many friends, who go in for all sorts of amusements and "undertakings," but always in the form of a quiet, noiseless friendship of just *two*. If you look closely, you will see that they are always opposites—so far as their spirit, way of life, character, and even physical characteristics are concerned: and the one seems to complement the other. There is mutual "complementation," and from this comes the harmony and union of their lives. One might say that life is crammed with these wandering and stationary dyads (a linking of two), who, in general, always make a pretty picture, attracting the attention of everybody by their silence, their modest behavior, by the fact that they disturb no one and are obviously pleased with their quiet contentment, pleased with their life. Gogol was the first to give us such a dyad in those two well-known neighbors, Ivan Ivanovich and Ivan Nikiforovich. But spiteful Gogol made them quarrel: usually, however, they do not quarrel, and the one buries the other. Why *should* they quarrel? One sees this also in the works of Turgenev: he has portrayed a whole series of such dyads—"Khor and Kalinych," "Chertopkhanov and Nedopyuskin," to a certain extent Rudin and Lezhnyov (fire and water) in *Rudin*—and, I think, several more, many more. Most often the one is the protector, the other, the protected; the one is harsh, cruel, coarse, brusque, the other gentle, mild, complaisant. They are like a man and wife, a man and a woman. But this is nothing yet. In Dostoevsky, we find all this expressed in the idyll "An Honest Thief," where a weak, spineless, and, moreover, a hard-drinking man is taken under the protection of a sober, quiet, and amiable tailor. Rephrasing the observation of the early Christians, according to which "the very virtues of the pagans are but beautiful *vices*," we can say that "the very vices of these dyads are somehow innocent." . . .

Fluctuating Intensities in Sex: The Greatest Intensity of the Sex Impulse

Man, coming from the sex act and composed of passionate sex particles, is a sexual creature in his entire "I," in both his whole and his parts, passionately breathing sex and only sex, in battle, in the desert, in the hermit life, in asceticism, in business—but in its purest and holiest form, in its most normal form, the family . . .

Moderate Degrees of the Sex Impulse

We must remember that we attach ourselves to everything in this world through our semen; just as we use everything in this world for our semen. However, in order not to become too rigorous in this regard, we must not lose sight of the fact that, although a husband and wife do not have sex often when the wife is pregnant, they do go on caressing each other all the time—and also that there is nothing in nature without purpose. Man grows weak and cold when his "goblet" is not full: so let it always be full, i.e. let there be coitus when one's inner wine and genius are on the point of running over the edge. But all else in the man which is attractive to the woman-wife, and all else in the woman which is attractive to the man-husband, should continue to have its place and retain its rights too. On the remaining six days, one's daily work must, none the less, have its reward in the form of charm, tenderness, kisses, kind looks, touches, caresses, and most of all, of course, in the form of words, in conversation. And the child carried in the womb can receive its plenitude of gifts only when the husband fondles and caresses his wife's genitals, so that the feeling of pleasure and sweet agitation in her womb never cease, so that the womb never grows numb . . . One can say that just as the mother feeds the child milk when it leaves the womb and thus gives it its body from her milk so before its birth does she even more directly, "from gut to gut," feed its entire being, its blood, its bones, its nerves, and the metaphysics inherent in all this (the second, spiritual half of every particle of the body) through her coitus and, in general, through the spasms of her womb. And since the husband participates in all this, one can even go on and say that during these nine months they have nourished the child together; and, moreover, they have nourished it with particles of their inner being, something incomparably more precious, significant, and powerful than milk, that comparatively rational and earthly substance. A whole person will never come from milk, but one does come from semen; milk does not grow, it does not grow up, but a tiny drop of semen does grow into a complete person and lives in him all his life. Thus has nature arranged its aims and means. The semi-impotent, semi-homosexual idea (because of its disgust for coitus), according to which coitus is bound to weaken a pregnant woman's strength when this strength is needed by the child, should be read the other way around: when the mother is in great need of strength to carry her fetus, the husband should give it to her through coitus. For who but out-and-out liars and hypocrites does not know that if a woman wants sex beforehand, if she is predisposed to it, she will get strength from it, she will get new freshness from it, she will even blossom from it. Who has not known girls who were anemic, pale, nervous, and chlorotic until they were married? So why should anyone take it into his head to subject a pregnant woman to the likes of all that? Actually, a woman of thirty who must go without sex when she is used to it suffers more and is even more unhappy than a girl of seventeen before she has had any sex at all. It is a well-known fact that widows suffer from a lack of sex even more than young unmarried girls; and every pregnant woman who no longer receives the caresses of her husband is really a "grass widow" for nine whole months[1] . . .

Female-Males and Their Teaching

A person with a "+1 +2 +3," and so on, attraction to sex, of course, feels that the sex act is 1) healthy 2) moral 3) useful 4) noble 5) beautiful. And mothers and fathers of the purest girls are furious when they find their daughter has married a sexually inadequate man; they demand the dissolution of such a "foul and loathsome" marriage so that the girl can marry again, this time a man who is sexually adequate, one who will be able to deflower and impregnate her. And as I have noticed on two occasions, when the daughter has her first child, the grandfathers very touchingly carry photographs of the baby around with them (in one case the child was photographed naked). Spiritual homosexuals, on the other hand, cannot even imagine the sex act as anything but shameful, silly, obscene, dirty, and, on a religious plane, sinful, disagreeable to God, and immoral. The obdurate tone with which complete physical homosexuals say "I am a girl" when physicians and judges call them by the male name given them at baptism is identical with the obduracy that manifests itself in semi-homosexuals in their feeling that the sex act is vile and their complete confidence that the whole world is in sympathy with them, that all people feel the same as they. And that is understandable. All the aversion that a normal person (with a "+1" of sex) feels for so-called perverted sexual relations, imagined or real—a man with a man or a woman with a woman—all this same horror and mystical fear is felt by a person with a "±" attraction to sex when he thinks of natural sexual relations, i.e. the usual method of coitus and of marriage in general: "You can't imagine anyone not loathing it," "you can't believe that anyone would do it without a feeling of sin!" No one can jump over his own blood: and what is a homosexual act for us is a normal one for them. Homosexuality is a "perversion" to us: but conversely, "our way" is a perversion to the homosexual. In countless pieces of writing, both secular and philosophical, but mainly religious, they try to convince us, they assure us, they swear that it is "vile," although everyone else says that it is "good"; they assure us that "no one feels that it is *good*," that "everyone is ashamed of it," when, of course, no one is ashamed of it (the open family status, the open way in which daughters are given in marriage, the open way in which parents find wives for their sons). And then too they say over and over that God forbade it, that He "does not want it," even though "be fruitful and multiply" is on the very first page of the Bible. "We think of ourselves as virgins," say these fellows with long, girlish hair; and there is not a single voice, at least in sacred literature, that tends to destroy this harmony, this unanimity—from which one can conclude that all sacred literature flows from this source, that it owes its origin to it alone, and, in a word, that the "essence of the spiritual" is at the same time the "essence of the homosexual." I am not saying that all writers of sacred literature are sincere in asserting this, since they reproduce just as we, and, generally speaking, the clergy *cannot* belong to this rare category: but even if one of them does not inwardly agree with this homosexual taste, he is obliged by law and tradition to repeat it anyway: "decency demands" that the spiritual homosexual not be betrayed, that not a single word be said in favor of the biblical, natural, and universal method of copulation and the sensation of that copulation. "*We too* dislike it," say archpriests with ten children and deacons with eight. "We too are ashamed—we feel how unnatural and sinful it is," says the dean of a cathedral, searching quickly and eagerly for a husband for his daughter . . .

The Shifting of Sex from Positive to Negative Inclinations

Ideas opposing birth cannot come into being without instincts opposing birth; and such are met with—and moreover they are unquestionably met with—only at that point in flowing sex where it passes from the inclination to harmonize with the opposite sex (union, matrimony) to the inclination to unite with one's own sex. At this point of transition there appears, for just a moment, the complete rejection of sex. Sex—both one's own and the opposite—is felt to be completely unnecessary, superfluous, accessory; something to which no psychology or thoughts inside one respond. This extremely placid state can be compared with the state of childhood and early adolescence; or more precisely, childhood and early adolescence are a phase in the life of every person when he crosses that zone we called spiritual homosexuality[2] in order to enter either that vast field of union with the opposite sex or that small but deep, acerb, and very old lake of union with one's own sex. Dr. Forel (*The Sex Question*, p. 282) gives the results of a survey of 3,916 men, in which it turned out that 94.6% of them felt attracted to the opposite sex, 3.9% felt attracted to both sexes all or part of the time, and 1.5% felt attracted to their own sex only. Science has given this last category the name "urnings." The usual theory that they are people "with a male body and a female brain and soul" is more name and description than explanation. Apparently the explanation of this phenomenon lies in a complete theory of sex, which we now lack and which would explain not only this anomaly but others as well. However, it is perfectly obvious that the study of urnings and particularly of their profession of faith offers extremely important material for working out, or, better put, for discovering this theory and this explanation.

Just as there is positive and negative electricity, just as there are positive and negative quantities in mathematics with "0" between them, just as there is movement forward and backward and a point of rest, so is the phenomenon of sex (which is "woven" during conception from the two sexes—the maternal, i.e. female, and the paternal, i.e. male) definitely male-female in every organism at every moment of its life; and because of this, it is flowing, vibrant, and radiant. Moreover, no individual remains completely identical with himself throughout his life, and not all individuals are alike. The sex in us wavers, fluctuates, vibrates, radiates. At one time the maternal side predominates, at another, the paternal, at another, both sides are in harmony (childhood), and at still another, one of them becomes subordinate, disappears, or dies (the time of normal sexual activity, when a person seeks to replenish himself with the side dying away in him). The craving of old men for sex, which sometimes manifests itself in fits of folly and various offenses, amounts to the "gulping down" of life and its sources by a person on the point of dying: it is that gulp of air a drowning man takes when he rises to the surface for a second time. These are extremely pitiful and scarcely punishable cases which everyone must simply guard himself and others against. It is *dementia non individui, sed generis humani* [an insanity not of individuals, but of the human species].

Let us, however, pull all this aside. We are not constructing a theory of sex here. But in order to show the reader that sex is precisely flowing and moreover that it flows from positive to negative quantities, we must point out the case of a mature man, a patient of Krafft-Ebing's and himself a physician, who was transformed into a woman . . . [Here, Rosanov quotes from a case study of Krafft-Ebing—Eds.]

"*General feeling*: I feel like a woman in a man's form; and even though I am often aware of the man's form, it is always in a feminine way. Thus, for example, I feel as if the penis is a clitoris; as if the urethra is a urethra and vaginal orifice, which always feels a little wet, even when it is actually dry; and as if the scrotum is *labia majora*. In short, I always feel as if I have a vulva. And the only one who can know what this means is one who feels this same way or who has at one time felt so. But the skin all over my body feels feminine; it receives all impressions—whether of touch, of warmth, or even of hostility—as a woman's would; and I have the sensations of a woman. I cannot go about with bare hands, as I am troubled by both heat and cold. When summer is over and we men can no longer carry shade-umbrellas, I have to endure great pain in the skin of my face until shade-umbrellas can be used again. On awakening in the morning, I am confused for a few moments, as if I were seeking myself; then the imperative feeling of being a woman awakens. I experience the sensation of having a vulva. And I always greet the day with a soft or a loud sigh; for again I dread the game I must play the whole day long . . .

"Marriage then, except during coitus, where the man has to feel himself a woman, is like two women living together, one of whom considers herself disguised as a male. If the periodical menstrual symptoms fail to occur, then come feelings of pregnancy or of sexual satiety, which a man never experiences, but which take possession of the whole being, just as the feeling of femininity does, and which are disgusting in themselves; therefore, I gladly welcome the regular menstrual symptoms again. When I have erotic dreams or ideas, I see myself in the form of a woman surrounded by erect penises. Since my anus feels feminine, it would not be difficult to become a passive pederast. Only positive religious command prevents it, as all other deterrent ideas could be surmounted. Since such conditions are as loathsome as they would be to anyone, I have a desire to be sexless, or to make myself sexless. If I had been single, I would long ago have separated myself from my testes, scrotum, and penis.

"Of what use is female pleasure if one does not conceive? What good comes from the excitation of female love if one has only a wife for gratification, even though copulation is felt as if it were with a man? What a terrible feeling of shame is caused by feminine perspiration! How the feeling for a dress and jewelry degrades a man! Even in his changed form, even when he can no longer recall the masculine sexual feeling, he would not want to be forced to feel like a woman. He still knows very well that up to now he did not always feel sexually; that he was merely a human being uninfluenced by sex. Now, suddenly, he has to consider his former individuality as a mask and constantly feel like a woman, only having a change when, every four weeks, he has his menstrual period, and in the intervals his insatiable female desire. If only he could awake without immediately being forced to feel like a woman! Finally, he longs for a moment in which he might lift his mask; but that moment never comes. He can only find amelioration of his misery when he can put on some bit of female attire or finery, an undergarment and suchlike; for he cannot go about as a woman. To be forced to fulfill all the duties of one's profession, while feeling oneself to be a woman dressed as a man, and to see no end of it, is by no means a trifle. Religion alone saves one from a great lapse, but it does not prevent the pain when temptation strikes the man who feels as a woman; and so it must be felt and put up with! Nor does religion prevent the pain that comes when a respectable man who enjoys an unusual degree of public confidence and who has authority must go about with a vulva—imaginary though it be; nor when a man, on leaving his arduous daily work, feels compelled to examine the attire of the first lady he meets and criticize her with feminine eyes, and to read her thoughts in her face; nor when he finds a fashion magazine to be just as interesting as a scientific book (I felt this as a child); nor when he must conceal his condition from his wife, whose thoughts, the moment he feels like a woman, he can read in her face, as it becomes perfectly clear to her that he has changed in body and soul. Think of the misery caused by trying to overcome feminine gentleness! Often, of course, when I am away from home alone, it is possible for a time to live more like a woman; for example, to wear woman's clothes, especially at night, to keep gloves on, or to wear a veil or a mask in my room, so that in this way there is respite from excessive libido. But when the feminine feeling has once gained an entrance, it imperatively demands recognition. It is often satisfied by a moderate concession, such as the wearing of a bracelet above the cuff; but it imperatively demands some concession. My only happiness is to see myself dressed as a woman without a feeling of shame; indeed when my face is veiled or masked, I prefer it so, and find it quite natural. Like every one of fashion's fools, I have a taste for the prevailing mode, so greatly am I transformed. To get accustomed to the thought of feeling only like a woman, and only to remember the previous manner of thought to a certain extent in contrast with it, and, at the same time, to express one's self as a man, requires a long time and an infinite amount of persistence . . .

. . . The touch of a woman seems homogeneous to me; sex with my wife seems possible to me because she is somewhat masculine and has a firm skin. And yet all this is more of a lesbian love.

"Besides, I always feel passive. Often at night, when I cannot sleep for excitement, I finally manage to do so by spreading my thighs, as in the case of a woman lying with man, or by lying on my side; but an arm or the bedclothing must not touch my breasts or I get no sleep; nor must there be any pressure on the abdomen. I sleep best in a chemise and nightgown and with gloves on, for my hands get cold easily. Also I am comfortable in female drawers and petticoats, because they do not touch my genitals. I liked womens' dresses best when crinolines were worn. Dresses do not bother the feminine-feeling man, for he, like every woman, feels them as belonging to his person, and not as something foreign . . .

"A schooltime male friend of mine felt like a girl from the very beginning and was attracted to males. His sister felt like a male and was attracted to females, but when her uterus demanded its right, and she saw herself as a loving woman in spite of her masculinity, she cut the matter short and drowned herself.

"Since my complete effemination, I have observed the following changes in myself:
1. A constant feeling of being a woman from head to foot.
2. A constant feeling of having female genitals.
3. A periodicity of the monthly menstrual symptoms.
4. A regular occurrence of female desire, though not directed to any particular man.
5. A passive female feeling in coitus.
6. Afterward, a feeling of impregnation.
7. A female feeling when thinking of coitus.
8. At the sight of women, a feeling of being one of them, of having a feminine interest in them.
9. At the sight of men, a feminine interest in them.
10. At the sight of children, a similar feeling.
11. A changed disposition and much greater patience.
12. A final feeling of resignation to my fate, for which I have nothing to thank but positive religion; without it, I should have long ago committed suicide."

Krafft-Ebing writes that three years later this same man sent him a new *status praesens* of his way of thinking and his feelings. Essentially, it corresponded to the earlier one. The man felt himself physically and mentally a woman; but his intellectual powers remained intact, thus guarding him from paranoia. Virtually no substantial changes had taken place in this doctor's condition, and he went on practicing until 1900.

The Self-denial of Sex

The frequent statement of ordinary physicians and obstetricians: "I'd cut off my reproductive organs once they were no longer needed" offers so complete an explanation of those primordial and original cases of self-castration that one needs add nothing more, one needs search for nothing more, than the story of the Hungarian physician told above. Evidently, that and similar phenomena in flowing sex have been the cause of all cases of self-castration, both ancient and modern. Simultaneously, one cannot help feeling that such a bearer of a living miracle in himself, a person who can feel in himself what he can neither see nor touch, and who can see and touch what he cannot feel, must be deeply shaken,agitated, and filled with everlasting fear. And like everyone in such a situation, he cannot help turning to Him Who has eternally been for mankind both a support and consolation; he cannot help turning in this predominantly metaphysical condition to the Primary Source of all metaphysics, of all that is inscrutable.

Such instances of turning to God in the part of those who are in some way or other anomalous in sex, anomalous to greater or lesser degree, of those who cannot lead a normal family life, who cannot marry in the normal way, have formed the whole of asceticism, both ancient and modern, both pagan and Christian. However, whereas in other religions it occupied only a tiny corner, it constituted only a tiny floret, in Christianity it is all, except for a few additions that are merely tolerated and regarded with indulgence, additions that are semi legitimate, and, as a matter of fact, so far as Christianity's strict inner idea is concerned, illegitimate.

There are original phenomena, and there are phenomena that are imitative. The latter can come from example, from teaching; but the former always come from a person's nature. "I cannot do otherwise!"—this is the cry of nature underlying the silent biography of a saint, as well as doctrine and propaganda. [Rozanov then recounts such a Christian story, that of Saint Moses the Hungarian, and concludes:]

Everything in this story strikingly coincides with attempts reported by biologists to couple a "female-male" with a woman. There is in such a person an insuperable feeling of disgust—like that aroused in us ordinary and normal people at the thought of an *actus sodomiticus*. And one cannot help noting for the benefit of legislators, physicians, and parents that attempts to force these people of the "third sex" to marry are tantamount to horrible and criminal attempts to turn them into sodomites. For to them, our method of coitus is "sodomy," it is "filth," it is "impossible."

"A quite young girl, who I knew was a lesbian and who suspected I knew but who never revealed or tried to keep it from me, once said, hanging her head: 'For me to marry would be tantamount to my going mad—not, however, in my mind, but in my whole being.'"

... If the formation and the life of the sperm and the formation and the life of the egg give to each of their bearers, in the one case a man and in the other a woman, a psychology of such enormous richness, complexity, and individuality, then we cannot even imagine how strange and unusual will be the psychology that results from this "Everlasting and Indestructible Virginity"—where we have a person about whom we cannot say "this is a man," and we cannot say "this is a woman," and the person himself does not know what he is; and, as a matter of fact, none of this even exists in the person. Instead there is something belonging to a third category, a third type of person. We might call it the "*third sex*" if we did not have a person who is simultaneously male and female, one in whom the sexes are strangely intermingled and fragmented. At any rate, a third psychology will definitely appear—one neither male nor female.

What will it be like?

There never will be children. There never will be a home, a "household"—other than in the sense of lodgings, a stopping place, a den, quarters, a cell, a cave, a tent. There will be only a small grape, but no vine—and the space needed by a grape is quite different from the space needed by a vine. Thus, the type of social life will to a great extent be destroyed—destroyed not at its everyday-life roots, but at its psychological roots, i.e. roots that run much deeper. This kind of destruction is so severe that nothing will ever grow again on its site. And just as badly destroyed will be the *type of history*. Its head will remain, but severed from the body. The *future* is not necessary to one who will have no descendants—the future is complete, it is universal. The subsequent fate of mankind will be regarded not from the standpoint of the interests of mankind but the interests of this group of loners, their spiritual union (for want of a union of kinship), their spiritual continuity and bond. This group of people will live and develop among mankind, but it will be against mankind, it will deny its very roots. And finally, in every tribe and people, this group will have no connecting lateral ties in the form of deeply cherished relatives. "What are brothers and sisters to me? Important to me are disciples"—this is the typical voice, the typical feeling, of every such loner and of them all.

There is no tribe, no clan, no nation. There is no future. There is no need of progress. What then is left, and particularly what is left for very great abilities, for great enthusiasm of the spirit, for that vivacity of spirit, which always distinguishes the child and early adolescent (double-sexed—see above) from the corpulent husband and the tired wife? . . .

The aroma of European civilization, its completely secular aspects, even those that are atheistic and anti-Christian, came part and parcel from the cell of the monk. It is the monk's boundless subjectivism, his aimless reveries, his presentiments, expectations, anxieties, fears, embarrassments, indecision, all of which intersect in dialogues of the drawing-room and in literature. The timid eyes, the mysterious smile, the weak body—all, absolutely all, comes from the monk's cell—all that which very much denies, all that which buried so very deeply Agamemnon, Odysseus, that shouter Demosthenes, and the self-satisfied Roman patricians. The very vices of antiquity, once they passed over to the new world with the very same names, received a new coloring; the very virtues of the ancient world became permeated with a different smell in the new world. The patriotism of Guizot or Michelet has nothing in common with the patriotism of Herodotus or Thucydides. And Byron's love of glory is completely different from Cicero's. Everything became more nervous, more sickly, more delicate, more fragile. And all this comes from the unsteady legs of the (true) monk, his thin neck, long hair, and effeminate voice.

The *soul* is wrong! The soul is *new*. What kind is it? Sterile. Stemless, flexible, creeping over the ground or soaring beyond the clouds. In negative situations—devious, crafty, sly, spiteful, vindictive, womanish. Masculinity, that bony, hard principle, snapped in two when the ancient world died. Femininity, the "Eternal Feminine," increased greatly and permeated even the souls of men. Mannishness decreased greatly in Europe in comparison with the classical world, where women were braver and more manly than Christian men. The "Christian man"—somehow that is even awkward to say. One feels like asking sarcastically: "What sort of a *man* is he?" One feels like asking it about Rousseau, Tolstoy, Dostoevsky, about a whole multitude of people who did brilliant creative work to the taste of Christian Europe. The coincidence of the "feminine in the masculine" with the basic tone of European civilization is so striking that one needs know nothing more in order to say: "Yes, basically this civilization sprang neither from the head of Zeus nor from the loins of Aphrodite but developed as a reflection of the nature of Pallas and Ganymede."

We have digressed from our subject and shall now return to it again. Our theme is not civilization but, more narrowly, the Church. When the Lutherans rejected monasticism, they lost all *metaphysics* along with it: for monasticism alone makes up the whole of the metaphysics of Christianity. All else is rational, explainable, and ordinary. The only thing completely unexplainable, whether from the standpoint of support in the Old Testament or from the standpoint of understanding and reason, is monasticism . . . The "special" aspect of the Church begins with the monk, be he disheveled, be he malicious, be he completely ignorant. It makes no difference: he bears in himself that metaphysical kernel which stuns us with its newness and strangeness, which we marvel at, and before which, as before any wonder, we can bow down. The "wondrousness" of it lies in its deep transcendental isolation from us all, its complete dissimilarity to us all, by virtue of which—depending on our disposition and preparation—we call it a "demon" or a "god" (among the common people), standing above or below man, but, in any case, *apart* from him. This isolation and this "wondrousness" has to do with an original or imitative, a true or feigned, loss of a liking for woman, a loss of an *interest* in woman, which, in the imitative and nonoriginal group, manifests itself in hostility towards woman, in running away from her, in fear of her . . .

"You shall not marry, you shall not have a family! It is not necessary!"

This is not just "something or other" of Christianity, it is its *all*. Just as it was possible to reduce hundreds of Old-Testament instructions to two: "Love God and thy neighbor, for in this is the whole law and the prophets," so is it possible to reduce all New-Testament instructions, parables, images, similes, promises, and rules to one: "Do not be attracted to woman.". . .

. . . Therefore, so long as the principle of sterility is adhered to, even if not a single person can be found who lives according to it, the whole Church will also be preserved: another will come, a new one will come, he will come sometime, and he will live according to that principle—and then the Church's main idea, its main task, its great theme, its great cause will all be restored at once. There will be restored that special spirit which does not exist in thousands, not even in millions, of happy families. It exists nowhere, except in the cell of the monk, in the monk himself.

1. On page seventy-eight, after completing his explanation of the side effects of coitus on the whole network of organs of a woman's body and, among other things, on the nourishing and functioning of her intestines, Professor Rohleder omits, through an innocent lack of medical knowledge, the most important, the effect on the blood. He then says something we all know to be true: "All this explains the well-known fact that very often girls who are pale and weak before the marriage change to the point of nonrecognition a few weeks after: they turn into blossoming women, exuding health, whereas, earlier, all methods of treatment, even the most diverse, did nothing to change their pitiful appearance and thinness." Statements such as the one in the text earlier, advising continence during pregnancy, are typical of the muck, the opium and carrion, that moralists advise a pregnant woman to take "as medicine" (Tolstoy, in The Kreutzer Sonata, and a whole throng of scribblers after him).

2. Schopenhauer's utterly dim-witted assumption that homosexuality was created by Nature itself in order to produce a strong line of descendants and is, therefore, met with in early adolescence, when the seed has not yet "ripened," and in decrepit old age, when it has partly "rotted," is disproved: 1) by the fact that the essence of homosexuality consists in the "devouring"—granted by old men—of the seed of precisely those in the full bloom of youth, from which the very best children could be born; and 2) by the fact that active homosexuality, except in cases where a person has been corrupted by another—which are not very frequent—is innate and embraces a person's life from beginning to end. Actually, this hypothesis of the famous philosopher's so fails to correspond to all the facts that there is no need even to refute it.

from the

GREAT SOVIET ENCYCLOPEDIA

(1930, 1952)

with fragments of speeches by Maxim Gorky (1934) and N. V. Krylenko (1936)

trans. Laura Engelstein

Bol'shaia sovetskaia entsiklopediia, 1930: vol. 17

HOMOSEXUALITY [*Gomoseksualizm*]—unnatural sexual attraction to persons of one's own sex (the opposite of the normal—heterosexuality). According to M[agnus] Hirschfeld, about 2 percent of people (more commonly men) suffer from H. H. occurs in all races and social classes and in various professions; homosexuals have included many outstanding people (Socrates, Michelangelo, Leonardo da Vinci, and others) . . . [Sigmund] Freud sees H. as a transitional "phase" in early childhood. It is important to know that homosexual tendencies do not exclude heterosexual ones (so-called bisexuality). Certain homosexuals alternate periodically between the two tendencies and may experience prolonged phases of heterosexuality . . . As for sexual perversions, they are no more frequent among homosexuals than among heterosexuals: among men the most common is masochism; among women, especially those who play the active role, sadistic tendencies predominate. H. is often accompanied by transvestism . . . In most cases H. is probably genetically determined; environmental conditions may encourage the emergence of the anomaly in general and may even determine its form (fetishism and others) . . .

Homosexuals are sometimes indifferent to their anomaly, but most suffer from the impossibility of leading a normal sexual life. They experience feelings of sexual inferiority, of insecurity, especially in relation to sex, of not being understood, and of loneliness and isolation. About 60 percent of homosexuals attempt suicide.

The prognosis for H. is relatively poor. Only a very few cases have been cured, and then usually among those with bisexual tendencies. The most important task is prophylaxis: correct sexual upbringing and coeducational primary schooling. In cases in which external factors play a significant part, psychotherapy can be successful, especially psychoanalysis, hypnosis, and athletics . . .

Searching for sexual satisfaction among those of their own sex forces them [homosexuals] to violate the so-called social norms of behavior. Abroad, as well as in prerevolutionary Russia, such violations of the general rules of behavior were penalized by special "moral legislation." In addition to the fact that these laws, directed against a biological deviation, are absurd in themselves and have no tangible results, they also have an extremely harmful psychological effect on homosexuals . . . [By contrast,] Soviet law does not recognize so-called crimes against morality. Our legislation, based on the principle of social defense, punishes only those cases in which the object of the homosexual's sexual interest is under age.

From this it is clear that the Soviet evaluation of the peculiarities and distinctive features of homosexuals completely diverges from that prevalent in the West. In acknowledging the homosexual's mistaken development, society does not and cannot blame these peculiarities on those who have them. This in itself goes a long way toward bringing down the wall that naturally separates homosexuals from society and forces them to retreat into themselves. In stressing the causes of this anomaly, our society goes beyond prophylactic and curative measures to create the indispensable conditions under which the everyday interactions of homosexuals will be as normal as possible and their usual sense of estrangement will be resorbed in the new collective.

article signed: *M. Sereinski*

Bol'shaia sovetskaia entsiklopediia. 2d ed.: 1952: vol. 12

. . . In capitalist society H. is a widespread phenomenon. Suffice it to mention the existence of professional homosexual prostitution in capitalist countries. Drunkenness and early childhood sexual impressions play a large role in the development of H., whose origins reflect the social conditions of everyday life. The vast majority of people with H. tendencies overcome these perversions as soon as social circumstances become favorable. The only exceptions are psychopathic, mentally retarded, and psychotic personalities (schizophrenics and others) . . . The external conditions that evoke H. make a greater impression in the presence of these psychological anomalies. Many homosexuals suffer from the inability to live a normal sexual life, from insecurity (especially sexual), and the feeling of isolation.

Soviet society, with its healthy morality, considers H., as a sexual perversion, shameful and criminal. Soviet criminal law penalizes H. except in cases where H. is only one manifestation of congenital psychological disturbance . . . In bourgeois countries, where H. expresses the moral disintegration of the ruling classes, H. is virtually never punished.

Excerpt from 1934 speech by Maxim Gorky:

In the land where the proletariat governs courageously [*muzhestvenno*; can also be translated as "manfully"] and successfully, homosexuality, with its corrupting effect on the young, is considered a social crime punishable under the law. By contrast, in [Germany,] the "cultivated land" of the great philosophers, scholars, and musicians, it is practiced freely and with impunity. There is already a sarcastic saying: "Destroy homosexuality and fascism will disappear."

Excerpt from 1936 speech to the party Central Executive Committee
by Commissar of Justice Nikolai Krylenko:

The laboring masses believe in normal relations between the sexes and are building their society on healthy principles. In this environment there is no place for such effete gentlemen. Who provides the main clientele for such affairs? The laboring masses? No! The déclassé riff-raff, whether from the dregs of society or the remnants of the exploiting classes. With nowhere to turn, they take up pederasty. In their company, in foul secret dens, another kind of work also takes place, using this pretext—counterrevolutionary work. These are the people who destabilize the new social relations we are trying to establish among people and between men and women in the laboring masses. And therefore these are the gentlemen we prosecute in court and deprive of five years' freedom.

E

SUBCULTURE, CENSORSHIP, AND CIVIL RIGHTS IN THE UNITED STATES

The United States was something of a latecomer to gay and lesbian activism. Obscenity laws banned virtually any depiction, and certainly any defense, of homosexuality. *The Well of Loneliness* by Radcliffe Hall (1880-1943), a novel featuring a classic "invert" and ending in tragedy but nonetheless making a plea for acceptance, was the subject of intense debate.

Criticized for being too apologetic by many intellectual gays and lesbians, it was nonetheless too much for the authorities. Abandoned by its British publisher, it was printed in Paris; exported to Britain, it was seized by customs. When it was brought to the U.S. it was seized by the police in New York and its publisher, Donald Friede, was charged with obscenity. Our first document is the record of the judge's reasons for conviction. His judgment was reversed on appeal.

The first documented gay organization in the U.S., the Chicago Society for Human Rights, was founded by Henry Gerber in 1924. According to its charter, its goal was to

" . . . *protect the interests of people who by reasons of mental and physical abnormalities are abused and hindered in the legal pursuit of happiness which is guaranteed them by the Declaration of Independence, and to combat the public prejudices against them by dissemination of facts according to modern science among intellectuals of mature age. The Society stands only for law and order; it is in harmony with any and all general laws insofar as they protect the rights of others, and does in no manner recommend any acts of violation of present laws nor advocate any matter inimical to the public welfare."*

The society began publishing a journal, *Friendship and Freedom*. Members were harassed and arrested by the Chicago police, and then prosecuted for founding a "strange sex cult" that "urged men to leave their wives and children." They were ultimately freed, based upon a technicality, but continuing harassment of its members resulted in the society's demise a year later.

In 1932, Gerber, writing under the pseudonym of "Parisex," published a response to a homophobic article by W.Béran Wolfe, M.D. in a periodical, *The Modern Thinker*. It is reproduced here.

PEOPLE V. FRIEDE

City Magistrate's Court of New York City (1929)

BUSHEL, **City Magistrate.** Friede and another person are charged with having violated the New York Penal Law by their possession and sale of a book entitled "The Well of Loneliness." Evidence proving possession and sale of the book by Friede had been introduced and is not controverted by him.

This court in a prosecution of this character is not the trier of the fact. Its judicial province is limited to a determination of the question as to whether as matter of law it can be said that the book which forms the basis of the charge in question is not violative of the statute. The evidence before me, however, is the same as that which would be presented to the tribunal vested with the power of deciding the facts as well as the law.

The book here involved is a novel dealing with the childhood and early womanhood of a female invert. In broad outline the story shows how these unnatural tendencies manifested themselves from early childhood; the queer attraction of the child to the maid in the household, her affairs with one Angela Crossby, a normally sexed, but unhappily married, woman, causing further dissension between the latter and her husband, her jealousy of another man who later debauched this married woman, and her despair, in being supplanted by him in Angela's affections, are vividly portrayed. The book culminates with an extended elaboration upon her intimate relations with a normal young girl, who becomes a helpless subject of her perverted influence and passion, and pictures the struggle for this girl's affections between this invert and a man from whose normal advances she herself had previously recoiled, because of her own perverted nature. Her sex experiences are set forth in some detail and also her visits to various resorts frequented by male and female inverts.

The author has treated these incidents not without some restraint; nor is it disputed that the book has literary merit. To quote the people's brief: "It is a well written, carefully constructed piece of fiction, and contains no unclean words." Yet the narrative does not veer from its central theme, and the emotional and literary setting in which they are found give the incidents described therein great force and poignancy. The unnatural and depraved relationships portrayed are sought to be idealized and extolled. The characters in the book who indulge in these vices are described in attractive terms, and it is maintained throughout that they be accepted on the same plane as persons normally constituted, and that their perverse and inverted love is as worthy as the affection between normal beings and should be considered just as sacred by society.

The book can have no moral value, since it seeks to justify the right of a pervert to prey upon normal members of a community, and to uphold such relationship as noble and lofty. Although it pleads for tolerance on the part of society of those possessed of and inflicted with perverted traits and tendencies, it does not argue for repression or moderation of insidious impulses. An idea of the moral tone which the book assumes may be gained from the attitude taken by its principal character towards her mother, pictured as a hard, cruel, and pitiless woman, because of the abhorrence she displays to unnatural lust, and to whom, because of that reaction, the former says: "But what I will never forgive is your daring to try and make me ashamed of my love. I'm not ashamed of it; there's no shame in me."

The theme of the novel is not only antisocial and offensive to public morals and decency, but the method in which it is developed, in its highly emotional way attracting and focusing attention upon perverted ideas and unnatural vices, and seeking to justify and idealize them, is strongly calculated to corrupt and debase those members of the community who would be susceptible to its immoral influence.

Although the book in evidence is prefaced by a laudatory commentary by Havelock Ellis, yet it is he who, in his scientific treatise on the subject, states: "We are bound to protect the helpless members of society against the invert." The court is charged with that precise duty here. The test of an obscene book laid down in *Regina* v. *Hicklin*, is "whether the tendency of the matter charged as obscenity is to deprave or corrupt those whose minds are open to such immoral influences, and who might come into contact with it." Although not sole and exclusive, this test is one which has been frequently applied. It may be accepted as a basis for judicial decision here.

Its application and soundness are assailed by learned counsel for Friede, who argue that it seeks to gauge the mental and moral capacity of the community by that of its dullest-witted and most fallible members. This contention overlooks the fact that those who are subject to perverted influences, and in whom that abnormality may be called into activity, and who might be aroused to lustful and lecherous practices are not limited to the young and immature, the moron, the mentally weak, or the intellectually impoverished, but may be found among those of mature age and of high intellectual development and professional attainment.

Men may differ in their conceptions as to the propriety of placing any restrictions upon a literary work or absolute freedom of expression and interchange of ideas. This conflict between liberty and restraint is not new to the law. However, the Legislature has spoken on that subject in the enactment of the law in question. Even if the courts were not (as a matter of fact they are) in accord with the public policy it declares, they would not be free to disregard it, because it may be founded upon conceptions of morality with which they disagree. Moreover, the Legislature has not sought to set up a literary censorship, or attempted to confine thought and discussion in a strait jacket of inflexible legal definition, but has imposed upon the courts the duty of protecting the weaker members of society from corrupt, depraving, and lecherous influences, although exerted through the guise and medium of literature, drama or art. The public policy so declared was reaffirmed by the Legislature by its recent amendment to the Penal Law, making it a misdemeanor to prepare, advertise, or present any drama, play, etc., dealing with the subject of sex degeneracy or sex perversion.

Defendants' counsel urge that the book is to be judged by the mores of the day. The community, through this recent legislation, has evinced a public policy even more hostile to the presentation and circulation of matter treating of sexual depravity. The argument, therefore, that the mores have so changed as to fully justify the distribution of a book exalting sex perversion is without force . . .

The defendants' brief refers the court to eminent men of letters, critics, artists, and publishers who have praised "The Well of Loneliness." Were the issue before the court the book's value from a literary standpoint, the opinions of those mentioned might, of course, carry great weight. However, the book's literary merits are not challenged, and the court may not conjecture as to the loss that its condemnation may entail to our general literature, when it is plainly subversive of public morals and public decency, which the statute is designed to safeguard. Moreover, it has been held that the opinions of experts are inadmissible.

I am convinced that "The Well of Loneliness" tends to debauch public morals, that its subject-matter is offensive to public decency, and that it is calculated to deprave and corrupt minds open to its immoral influences and who might come in contact with it, and applying the rules and recognized standards of interpretation as laid down by our courts, I refuse to hold as matter of law that the book in question is not violative of the statute. Accordingly, and under the stipulation entered into in this case, that the testimony taken upon the summons shall be the testimony taken upon the complaint, if one is ordered, I hereby order a complaint against these defendants.

IN DEFENSE OF HOMOSEXUALITY
(1932)

Parisex (Henry Gerber)

The following essay is one of the numerous replies received attacking The Riddle of Homosexuality, *by W. Béran Wolfe, which appeared in the April issue, for its "severe" position with reference to sexual inversion.*

After reading the article by W. Béran Wolfe, M.D., in the April issue of *The Modern Thinker*, one cannot but deeply sympathize with the inverts for being the world's eternal scapegoats. In the early Middle Ages the Papacy stipulated that "sodomers, heretics and sorcerers be burned." When the legal control of the population slipped from the hands of Mother Church into that of the legislatures and politicians, better times came for the homosexuals in that their sexual "crimes" were considered less heinous. After Napoleon had written his liberal code, homosexuals were no longer molested by the law in Latin countries, but in the Anglo-Saxon world, in England and the United States, persecution of them is still in vogue, and as recently as the year 1915 the legislature of the State of California passed a new law, extending the scope of the term of sodomy. Today a more lenient attitude is being shown to homosexuals by the law. On October 16, 1929, the German committee of the Reichstag, discussing the new German legal code, proposed to abolish punishment for homosexual acts *per se*, between *men*, and in Russia, of course, the medieval persecution of homosexuals was repudiated with religious superstitions.

Now, that the inverts have almost escaped the stake and the prison, the psychoanalysts threaten them with the new danger of the psychiatric torture chamber. It is not to be wondered that a priest, a legislator and a psychoanalyst should be interested only in their dogmas. The priest is as much convinced of his sin theory as the legislator is sure that prison is the cure of crime, and the psychoanalyst, not a bit less, is certain that his therapy will bring back the erring homosexual to the normal fold. But he is strangely silent on the method.

Of course, the chief fallacy of psychiatry and similar trades is that it puts the cart before the horse. If we may believe the psychoanalysts, it is not modern machine civilization, at great variance with nature, that is conducive to neuroses, but civilization itself is the norm, and anything else, even nature, is perverse and neurotic. Nature, which has struggled along valiantly these million years, is now being told by the Freuds, the Adlers, the Jungs, and their slavish followers, that its manifold sex urges are abnormal, and that civilization, that recent upstart, is the only norm of life; that if one reverted to good old mother nature he would quickly be accused of no less a crime than seeking to flee from reality. As if it needed homosexuality, impotence and other "neuroses" nowadays to drive a man crazy! Are not the long lines of unemployed, the starving, those cheated out of their lives' savings by the leaders of society and those married and unable to feed their brood, enough reasons for mental, physical and moral breakdowns?

And what about the homosexual fleeing from reality? Thousands of priests, nuns, monks, choose celibacy to avoid "normal sex life." Psychoanalysts undoubtedly include them too in their long list of "neurotics"; still there is no law compelling anyone to marry. As to social responsibilities of homosexuals, I am not aware of their having been exempted in the late war, neither do I see on the tax blanks where the unmarried homosexuals pay less than the heterosexual who is not fleeing from reality; nor do I know of any place of employment where the homosexual is not required to work as hard for his pennies as the heterosexual worker. Is it perhaps an exception to the psychoanalyst's rule of neurotic symptoms for those avoiding "normal sex life" that the psychoanalytic studios are filled with married women but shunned by the "neurotic" homosexuals?

And is not the psychiatrist again putting the cart before the horse in saying that homosexuality is a symptom of a neurotic style of life? Would it not sound more natural to say that the homosexual is made neurotic because his style of life is beset by thousands of dangers? What heterosexual would not turn highly neurotic were his mode of love marked "criminal," and were he liable to be pulled into prison every time he wanted to satisfy his sex urge—not to speak of the dangers of being at all times exposed to blackmail by heterosexuals who prey upon him, and the ostracism of society? Were he not clever in pretending to be "normal," he would lose his place of employment quickly. This constant insecurity and danger from all sides would drive anyone into any number of neuroses. That the average homosexual even in spite of a thousand dangers does not want to be "cured" and wants nothing but to be left alone by hypocritical meddlers, and feels comparatively happy in his love, is evidence enough that his condition cannot be merely acquired.

If it were so easy to "cure" a homosexual, the homosexuals would flock to the psychiatrists, and instead of having to ask the authorities to establish free clinics for homosexuals, the landscape would be dotted with such hospitals. The surgeon removing the "queer" complex would find his practice as profitable as that of taking out tonsils and appendices. While Dr. Wolfe unhesitatingly affirms the question whether homosexuality can be cured, how, where, and for how much this can be done, the deponent sayeth not. I doubt if there ever was a cure of a genuine homosexual. Such cures have been reported once and then, but they are as temporary as the famous experiments of Dr. Steinach and the monkey gland transplantations. It stands to reason that a homosexual cannot be cured (and the doctor cautiously adds: provided the homosexual *wants* to be cured) because if he showed any interest in women he would simply not be a homosexual. The few cures reported were brought about by alleged heterosexual suggestions to the "patient," but Hirschfeld points out very clearly the absurdity of suggesting to a homosexual to get married. There are thousands of homosexuals who are married, upon the advice of doctors, and unless they were strongly bisexually inclined, not even marriage has cured them. The homosexual man does not shun women because he wants to flee from the reality of normal sex life, but because he himself is physically a woman and his normal sex life is directed to the other sex, another man, the only person to attract him. According to the physical formula, opposite poles attract each other, while like poles repel each other.

It is highly improbable that an intelligent homosexual could be "cured" by suggesting to him the blessings of monogamy, an institution which, according to Russell, Calverton, Schmalhausen, Lindsey and other modern writers resembles a ship full of leaks, ready to sink at any moment. Few homosexuals are stupid enough to forget the scandalous divorce courts, the ever increasing desertions, and marital unhappiness in general, to decide to jump from the frying pan into the fire. Too much pessimism, of course, is uncalled for, but anyone acquainted with the real life of homosexuals or heterosexuals will have to admit that many heterosexuals lead a happy life, but also that homosexuals live in happy, blissful unions, especially in Europe, where homosexuals are unmolested as long as they mind their own business, and are not, as in England and in the United States, driven to the underworld of perversions and crime for satisfaction of their very real craving for love.

Nowadays, when commissioners of health and other medical authorities sell their names to advertise the gadgets of clever business concerns, one would not find it so much out of place, if (presumed Dr. Wolfe were broadcasting his article on homosexuality) the radio announcer would after the closing words of the good doctor enunciate: This program comes to you through the courtesy of John Doe, manufacturer of baby carriages. As a matter of fact, one finds the law against invert sex acts and other sex taboos labeled in some state penal codes as: *Laws for the Protection of the Christian Institution of Marriage.*

But the contradictions in his article alone disprove the various statements of Dr. Wolfe. Let me point out only the most glaring ones. He says on page 99: "Analytic investigation of the invert's total personality demonstrates *practically without exception* a basic misanthropy of the invert." On page 96 he says: "Today homosexual 'joints', homosexual 'drags', homosexual plays, and homosexual clubs are known in every large American city," and again on page 99: "Homosexuality is unique in that the homosexual neurotics form communities and thus develop a certain social feeling." They are then not misanthropes without exception, but rather as gregarious as the heterosexuals who also may be found congregating in ball rooms, clubs and "joints." One cannot really blame the parisexual if he is not very much in love with heterosexuals who exploit and persecute him and make his life miserable.

The fact that scientific information concerning the nature of homosexuality is almost unobtainable is not due to the ignorance of the medical profession but to the public policy of suppressing anything truthful about homosexuals. The truth about homosexuals is suppressed in the same degree as the knowledge of birth control, for homosexuality, of course, is but one of the many natural forms of birth control.

It is ridiculous to assume that the whole Greek nation was neurotic because homosexuality was practiced there with the sanction of the state. Homosexuality even exists among the primitive tribes and among animals, though this fact also has been suppressed. It must be more than a neurosis if a certain natural trait persists throughout all ages and still carries on after the most cruel and fatal persecution of those so inclined. It is not very clear how one could "easily" escape the reality of normal sex life by merely adopting a sex mode the very practice of which is punished with penitentiary terms, with social ruin and the danger of blackmail from all directions. But many heterosexuals are also in jails, socially ruined by jealous competitors and blackmailed by greedy women. It is so much easier to conform to conventionality and marry. The politicians have always believed that they could put over their various panaceas to make the world perfect according to their beliefs. They have sponsored their sacred institution of monogamy by propaganda in all fields of public education, and not enough with this, have surrounded holy wedlock with vicious taboos, punishing the violators with penitentiary terms; they have passed the 18th Amendment to stop people from drinking, but we see in reality only about 50% of the population married, and getting plenty of booze to drink. One cannot enforce a law against natural cravings. Taboos always result in bootleggers of love or drink. The very fact that it takes so many laws to enforce monogamy at once labels it only an ideal but not a natural institution. One never hears of laws compelling people to eat! Sex and drink are very closely related. Where sex laws are lenient, as in Latin countries, people drink more modestly, but the Protestant countries are notorious for hard drinking and drunkenness. Drinking is another "neurosis," an effort to escape the bitter reality of the "responsibilities of normal sex life." But intoxication is not *per se* punished.

The Bible story on which the persecution of the homosexuals is based even now, is also full of contradictions, for it tells of the willingness of Yahwe to save the wicked city if there were only five righteous among the citizens (that is, those not given to sodomy). But not even five could be found. The men and women, both young and old (*Genesis:* all the people from every quarter), surrounded Lot. One wonders by which methods the children of the homosexuals were produced!

Dr. Wolfe states that a too great desire for complete security characterizes all inverts. Page the premier of France! 50,000,000 cannot be neurotic! In these days of insecurity, general unemployment and racketeering, one does not need to be a homosexual to feel the need for more security in employment, house and home. All the other symptoms of neurosis which the doctor here enumerates are too general to be blamed merely upon homosexuals. The inferiority complex? We wonder how many people in very high ranks of life are homosexual without being suspected? And they might be considered the very acmes of superiority and excellent character. Schopenhauer said that those who look for the devil with horns and claws and clanging bells are always fooled. Conventional opinion looks for homosexuals only in the gutters. It is not fair to hold up a homosexual in the gutter to the scorn of the normal world and maintain that all homosexuals practically without an exception are like him. Heterosexuals do not point to their weakest member for the benefit of the homosexuals. There are hundreds of homosexuals among the pillars of society and no one knows of their being homosexual, except perhaps a cute little boy prostitute in Paris.

We cannot all be bank presidents and millionaires, but the percentage of homosexuals among the lowly workers is not greater than that of the number of heterosexuals. Homosexuals often occupy well-paid positions as secretaries and bank clerks and not rarely hold positions of trust. Especially in hospitals they are considered more valuable than heterosexual men.

The writer knows several elderly homosexuals of wealth who spend part of their incomes for the support of unfortunate children deserted by their parents and interned in orphan asylums.

If homosexuals were stupid enough openly to make converts to their aberrations they would not be at liberty very long, for the public policy demands a stern suppression of homosexuality.

"Homosexuality often becomes criminal because of their aggressive acts against society," says Dr. Wolfe. It would be interesting to look up the statistical figures of crimes. Thus it might surprise Dr. Wolfe that the average annual convictions for sodomy in the State of New York are only about 15, while the number of cases of rape, adultery, and other sexual delinquencies of heterosexuals reaches many hundred cases. It must be remembered also that the sodomy law in the State of New York likewise punishes heterosexual men and women convicted of committing certain sexual perversions. The statement of Dr. Wolfe that homosexual sex acts are a penitentiary offence is not a fact. There are certain extreme sex acts which are punished by law, but it makes no difference at all whether the perpetrators are homosexuals or heterosexuals. Many homosexual sex acts are not punished at all, neither is homosexuality *per se*. The inability of our legislators properly to evaluate social phenomena is significant. While two grown-up persons who in private with mutual agreement perform a certain harmless sex act, may be sent to prison for twenty years (or life as in the State of Georgia), a syphilitic may freely spread his loathsome disease to wife and children without the law lifting a finger. Our sex laws are still based on the ignorance of Christian sex morality.

While we must congratulate Dr. Wolfe on his courageous stand in the matter of punishing homosexuals, we do not believe that homosexuals would want to be freed from the jails in turn to be put in lunatic asylums. But, no doubt, there are many psychologists looking for jobs and they are as desirous of getting onto the public payrolls as other vendors of nostrums.

If homosexuals were permitted to let loose one-tenth as much propaganda about homosexuality as the heterosexuals (the stage, radio, film, literature, theatre, and especially the vaudeville, reek with a nauseating display of female legs and whatnot—while homosexual propaganda is entirely out of question) we wonder if there would not be much more homosexual "neuroses" present. Even today the works of Havelock Ellis on sex are banned from the mails because he does not moralize on inversion. It is well known that a great number of homosexuals are only attracted by masculine men of normal inclinations, and if they tried to convert all men to homosexuality, they would defeat their own purpose.

To make an analogy of homosexuality with epilepsy is highly arbitrary insofar as Dr. Wolfe himself has stated in his article (page 99) that homosexuality is not a disease in itself. It is, of course, just as ridiculous to state that homosexuals have a greater number of truly great men among their ranks as it would be to maintain that a man could not be a genius because of his being homosexual. Many inverts are driven to introversion by the hostile attitude of society and thus often turn to study and literature instead of watching ball games, prize fights and other pastimes of the heterosexuals.

After considering Dr. Wolfe's thesis one is somewhat in doubt whether he is interested in homosexuality or whether he is interested in squaring it with the Adlerian individual psychology, of which he is so obviously an advocate. It must seem to a layman intelligence that the latter case is the true one. There is a matter of finality about his findings and his "remedy" that, to the body of scientists who realize the complexity of this field and who admit that they are only at the beginning of the solution, must appear engagingly naïve. One is suspicious of anyone who approaches an intricate phase of life with a definite theory, for the simple reason that he is apt to find something that will not tally with his original theoretical pre-possessions, and his pride of theory is very apt to prevent him from sacrificing the theory.

Once more we are told that inversion is not a matter of biology or physiology, but is acquired by social conditions and determined by "early childhood experiences." We are shown the proof of this by the statement that homosexuals as children, "in the vast majority" of cases, occupy an ordinal position in the family—that is, they are almost always the oldest or youngest child, that also the father dies early (in the boy's case) and that the resulting coddling of the boy by its mother ultimately makes the boy homosexual. Suppose this is true: How then will psychiatric therapy of the "individual homosexual" effect a cure? Supposing such a cure possible, supposing further that each homosexual could be prevailed upon to submit to this cure (which is preposterous) the fact would still remain that in every generation there would be another crop of homosexuals, simply because boys still continued to be first and last children, losing their fathers and mothers early in life. If it is true that the "ordinal family position" occupied by the incipient homosexual is a basic cause of homosexuality, how can curing the individual results of such family conditions abolish the root of the condition? According to this view the only possible way to exterminate homosexuality is to alter social conditions, to see that no married couple has a first or a last child, and that neither the father nor mother die while the child is yet young.

The making of the homosexual, we are further assured, does not, however, cease in the family conditions. Increasing maturity intensifies his difficulties. Still more hellish is the fact that segregation of the sexes aggravates the situation. Segregation in schools—and, it might be added, the army, navy, labor and prison camps; this may be true, somewhat, but how will individual therapy solve it? By arranging society so that no army, navy, prison and labor camps and schools will be necessary, it would seem.

Next he introduces the factor of masturbation as a formative element in the making of homosexuality. The idea seems to be that masturbation is peculiar to homosexuals. But every heterosexual who reads that passage will know that this is absurdly false. Havelock Ellis shows that 60% of theological students practice it. Dr. Max Huhner says that any man who denies it is a liar. There can be no actual statistics about the extent of masturbation, but McCabe states that most of the estimates given vary between 90 and 99% of the adult community. Thus, were the practice of masturbation an indication of homosexuality, we would find 95% of the population homosexual rather than an alleged 5%.

That social conditions, environment, may be a factor in homosexuality is no doubt true, but it is not *the* factor. Is character, anyone's character, a matter of physical constitution, or is it a product of environment? It seems absurd to stress one of those factors. Both are necessary, and it is yet impossible to say which is the more important and formative. They both act on and supplement each other. A good seed planted in poor soil will result in little. A poor seed planted in the richest soil will similarly result in little. Who can say at what point physical structure ends and environment begins? Who can say whether the excellence of a fruit is due to the inherent qualities of the seed, or the qualities of the soil that nourished it? Dr. Wolfe says it is all a matter of soil.

He is so intent on improving the mental health of society by condemning the homosexual, so busy listing the evil and vicious aspects of inversion, that he nowhere asks the question: Is it possible that homosexuality, in the final analysis, does contribute something of value to society? Yes, he points out that though Wilde, da Vinci, and others (to name but a few) were homosexuals, "this is hardly a valid argument for being homosexual." As though becoming a homosexual were a matter of choice! He fails to account for those homosexual geniuses, and takes arbitrary refuge in holding up to scorn and contempt the prostitutes, the "seducers," making it appear further that these boy prostitutes are innocent victims. This thin trick should fool nobody. Prostitution is a large and perpetual element in heterosexuality, and no doubt many people believe that heterosexual women prostitutes are seduced into their profession, which leaves room for much doubt. A large per cent of girl prostitutes are so by choice, nothing else. And while social conditions are such that prostitution must be even more closely associated with homosexuality, homosexuality offers therefore opportunities of exploitation through blackmail, etc., that are not possible to such a large extent among heterosexual prostitutes. But such argument by Dr. Wolfe is arbitrary. Would he cast any such reflection on heterosexual great men by some one who detracted from their greatness by pointing out the heterosexual seducers and prostitutes? Arbitrary indeed.

He does not ask anywhere whether homosexuality might not have a social value. On the face of it, there must be some social gain in homosexuality. Homosexuality has existed from the beginning of time, in all sorts of social regimes and conditions. It is a *constant* human quality. It survives, almost if at all, undiminished since the dawn of history. Why? There has to be a reason somewhere, and that reason must be one of utility, of human value, else it could not survive. If the homosexuality of geniuses does not prove that homosexuality is a higher order, it certainly does prove that homosexuality is not exclusively an affliction of gutter snipes, maniacs, and thugs. Can anyone say definitely that homosexuality has not in the past contributed valuable things to society—unsuspected things perhaps—or that homosexuality, by its strange duality of character, may not fill an important function in the future of society?

Dr. Wolfe is at pains to list the defects and weaknesses of the homosexual temperament, but none of the fine and worthy qualities: the artistic nature of the homosexual man, his sensitive spirit, his rhythmic emotions, his "hardihood of intellect and body," or his capacities for friendship. I find myself in sympathy with the statement of Edward Carpenter, in his intelligent and human book, *Love's Coming of Age:* "It may be said to give them both (women and men of homosexual inclination) through their double nature, command of life in all its phases, and a certain free-masonry of the secrets of the two sexes which may well favor their function as reconcilers and interpreters." There are the great artists of the world, wholly or partially homosexual, Michaelangelo, Shakespeare, Alexander, Julius Caesar, Christine, Sappho, and the rest. Whether or not homosexuality has been a large factor in genius, it has been closely associated with it, and that significant fact has not yet been explained away. And further, who will say that an element of homosexuality is not today woven into the temperament of our artists and creators and interpreters? And that it will not continue to be in the future? The extermination of homosexuality, even if it were possible, might result in a very jagged hole in the fabric of society and its culture; might, in fact, be a costly experiment.

But there is a yet more complex problem attached to this therapeutic cure of homosexuality. Dr. Wolfe gives the impression that homosexuality centers around actual sexual intercourse, that it is exclusively absorbed with intercourse and the act itself. But there are all shades and degrees of homosexuality, from Platonic, spiritual attachments down to the sexual. Where is the psychiatrist to draw the line here? Will he cure the homosexual who is literally sexual, and permit to exist all the varying shades of attachment between similar sexes, attachments that verge close to the sexual border and are yet beyond it? There is no hard and fast distinction between friendship and love—friendship can and does deepen into love. Therapeutic methods, developed to their ultimate capacities, would, it seems, cast suspicion on friendships existing between members of the same sex, however non-homosexual those friendships might really be. Such a state of affairs might inconvenience many people, including heterosexuals; including also Dr. Wolfe, of course.

While Dr. Wolfe upbraids the apologists of homosexuality as liable to forget the far greater number of dilapidated homosexuals who are brought into police courts, he is strangely silent on the fact that normal heterosexuals also clutter up police stations. And why harp on the very few homosexuals who find satisfaction for their pathological craving to deal with the young boys, when the papers are at present full of the details of atrocious killings of little girls by mentally deranged heterosexual men? The cinemas in which homosexuals often seek contact with their kind are closed to minors, and the homosexuals who prefer the very young boys are as rare as the heterosexual "cradle snatchers." These shows are full of heterosexual prostitutes who as rugged individualists have long ago caught up with the ready market for young men, and they, like their heterosexual sisters of the street, are not as innocent as Dr. Wolfe might think. The youth of 16 or 17 is no longer ignorant of masturbation and other onanistic acts, and to blame the seduction of all boys on the homosexuals is a bit exaggerated. There is much work for the police to save the youth of today from heterosexual seduction and venereal infection, and the pot should not call the kettle black.

One who knows the world and life will not have to look far for "neurotic" camouflage to find the motive of the average young bachelor who is not willing to take up the "normal" mode of sex life, i.e. monogamy. In a society where monogamy is a contract in many ways disadvantageous to men and which is on all sides admitted to be a tottering institution, one need not accuse the hard-beset man of trying to "flee from reality." He is merely wisely avoiding trouble. There are too many plain reasons for his preferring to remain single to need dragging the red herring of neurosis across the road. Are all the men in the army and navy, who constitute the first line of defense of our nation, and who are unable to find "normal sex life" with its social obligations, therefore neurotics?

If the theory of Weininger is faulty, so is the theory of Adler, for while there are admittedly a great number of neurotics among the homosexuals, whose lives are made miserable by heterosexual persecution, there are also a great number of homosexuals who go through life every bit as "normal", healthy, and morally of value to society. The theory of Adler plainly does not fit here. Dr. Hirschfeld has examined thousands of homosexuals and his reports do not bring out the general theory of Dr. Adler and of psychoanalysis, which science Dr. Jastrow calls the "most amazing vagary in the history of Twentieth Century thought." Even psychoanalysts do not agree among themselves as to the cause of homosexuality. Dr. Wilhelm Stekel, while he also holds to the neurosis theory, at least admits that a person is by nature, normally, bisexual, and that a person who represses his heterosexuality is just as neurotic as a homosexual who represses or attempts to repress his sexual part of nature.

After all, it is highly futile for Dr. Wolfe to worry about neurotic homosexuals when the world itself, led and ruled by the strong heterosexual "normal" men is in such chaotic condition, and knows not where to turn.

It is quite possible that if called upon, the homosexuals in this country would put up the money to send Dr. Wolfe to Washington to examine these great big "normal" men, who guide the destinies of millions, to find their "neurosis" and to cure it.

HARLEM RENAISSANCE

What is called the Harlem Renaissance resulted from the migration of African-Americans from the rural south to urban areas of the northern U.S. due to employment opportunities deriving in part from that country's entry into World War I. Comprised of returning soldiers, entrepreneurs, teachers, intellectuals, artists, writers, and performers, Harlem, on Manhattan island in New York City, became the largest such self-contained urban Black community. Calling themselves the "New Negroes," residents expected and demanded full and equal participation in American cultural, social, and political life. Homosexuality was integral to, and to some degree an accepted part of, the new cultural life of Harlem. This spawned a lesbian and gay subculture centered in private parties and social clubs, drag balls both for gay men and butch/femme lesbian, speakeasies, and rent parties. The more renowned participants included writers Countee Cullen, Langston Hughes, and Wallace Thurman; singers Gladys Bently, Bessie Smith, Ma Rainey, and Ethel Waters; philosopher Alain Locke; and visual artist Richard Barthe.

There were, to be sure, difficulties with social acceptance that included police harassment, segregation, and psychiatric incarceration; and the economic problems that culminated in the 1929 stock market crash marked the beginning of the period's decline. However, according to Ira Jeffries, a lesbian inhabitant of Harlem, the gay and lesbian subculture included softball leagues (with black and white participants), boat rides, picnics, cocktail sips, and a public bar scene that lasted until the 1960's when "certain" white businessmen wanted to tap into it and make money (the clubs closed or burned down and the scene moved downtown). During the Harlem Renaissance, Bruce Nugent wrote what appears to be the first defense of homoerotic love published by an African-American; it appeared in *Fire* magazine as a long poem under the title "Smoke, Lilies,and Jade." While nothing else so outspoken has yet been discovered, evidence of this homoerotic subculture and its interpersonal networks is preserved in letters, diaries, and novels written by the participants and its observers, and in the undercover police report included here.

Across the country, the same growth was occurring in other cities, including San Francisco. Even before the massive migrations of World War II that made San Francisco such a popular destination for gays and lesbians, a consciousness and a subculture was taking shape; and again, we find African-Americans active participants in that development. Our selection from the *Spokesman*, an African-American San-Francisco Bay-area weekly newspaper uncovered for us by the late historian of the Harlem Renaissance Eric Garber, demonstrates an understanding of the parallels between racial and sexual oppression.

New York City Police Report

COMMERCIALIZED AMUSEMENT

(1928)

Gen. Div.
Feb. 24, 1928
A, B, 5, 7

COMMERCIALIZED AMUSEMENT
12:30 TO 1:10 AM $4

Manhattan Casino, 8th Ave. & 155th Street

About 12:30A.M. we visited this place and found approximately 5,000 people, colored and white, men attired in women's clothes, and vice versa. The affair, we were informed, was a "Fag (fairy) Masquerade Ball." This is an annual affair where the white and colored fairies assemble together with their friends, this being attended also by a certain respectable element who go here to see the sights.

While here, remaining about three-quarters of an hour, a certain amount of intoxication was observed. On three occasions it was seen where both men and women were intoxicated to the extent of being unable to walk unaided, and were taken from the hall by their friends. There was also a large number of uniformed patrolmen seen both outside, and in the hall proper as well as plainsclothesmen. Noticing that to remain here would be unproductive, we shortly departed.

Prior to leaving B and 5 questioned some casuals in the place as to where women could be met, but could learn nothing.

Read and found correct

(initials) J.K. & J.S.

H.K.

PREJUDICE AGAINST HOMOSEXUALS

(November 3, 1932)

The San Francisco *Spokesman*

In Berkeley a fortnight ago, a group of young men entertained themselves. Some wore female attire; some danced and talked as women do. All acted naturally and without restraint. They enjoyed the occasion and returned to their homes, their loved ones, or their work.

This ordinary occurrence in the lives of human beings is still affording child-minded members of the community much amusement. Men and women, apparently intelligent and kind, are using the incident as a subject for parlor conversation, referring to the young men as though they were visitors to the earth from some strange and unknown land.

Perhaps these "normal" people do not know that EVERY MAN AND WOMAN IS POTENTIALLY HOMOSEXUAL. Perhaps they have not stopped to consider that a different kind of environment may have closed the "normal" channel of sex expression, and made THEM sexually different. Keep a dozen male canaries in a cage for a long enough time, and they will become homosexual. Most other animals—including human beings—will react the same way. The riddle of homosexuality is yet far from being explained, but intelligent people know that only by chance have they themselves escaped the penalty of being DIFFERENT from the great majority—just as intelligent white people know that it was accident alone which saved them from being Negroes!

Because of the stupidity and malevolence of "normal" men and women, a DIFFERENT color of skin than white is a badge of inferiority, the possessor of which may be outraged or outlawed as the whim of the "normal" person decides. Because of this same stupidity and malevolence of "normal" men and women, a DIFFERENT form of sexual expression than with persons of opposite sexes is symbolic of a "curse of God", the victim of which may be jeered, hooted, and shunned as the self-righteousness of "normal" people permits. Both of these attitudes stink of bigotry and the deep-seated brutality of human nature.

Both race prejudice and the prejudice against homosexuals are bolstered and maintained by social taboo and law. Both prejudices make life in this world a living hell for men and women whose only crime is that of being DIFFERENT from the majority.

This is no plea for sympathy for the homosexual. To sympathize with a person because he or she happens to be homosexual is as little appreciated and as much insulting as to sympathize with a Negro for being black. What Negroes and homosexuals both desire is to be regarded as human beings with the rights and liberties of human beings, including the right to be let alone, to enjoy life in the way most agreeable and pleasant, to live secure from interference and insult.

It is idle for Negroes to preach against race prejudice as long as they themselves practice another kind of prejudice.

THE POLITICS OF
COMING OUT

During the next historical period with the formation of the U.S. homophile organizations Mattachine, Daughters of Bilitis, and One, "coming out" becomes the preeminent political act. In this essay published in the August 1944 issue of *Politics*, Robert Duncan argues against a ghettoized gay sensibility of oppression for the socially transformative act of "coming out" (although he doesn't call it that) which he does in the course of the essay. A well known poet of his time who was discharged from the military during World War II for coming out, Duncan's perspective is evocative of the "prerevolutionary" sensibility that one finds immediately before (or pre-Stonewall), in works such as the play and film *The Boys in the Band*, which challenge gay men to leave camp closetry and change their position in society.

THE HOMOSEXUAL IN SOCIETY

(1944)

Robert Duncan

Something in James Agee's recent approach to the Negro pseudo-folk (*Partisan Review*, Spring 1944) is the background of the notes which I propose in discussing yet another group whose only salvation is in the struggle of all humanity for freedom and individual integrity; who have suffered in modern society persecution, excommunication; and whose "intellectuals," whose most articulate members, have been willing to desert that primary struggle, to beg, to gain at the price, if need be, of any sort of prostitution, privilege for themselves, however ephemeral; who have been willing, rather than to struggle toward self-recognition, to sell their product, to convert their deepest feelings into marketable oddities and sentimentalities.

Although in private conversation, at every table, at every editorial board, one *knows* that a great body of modern art is cheated by what almost amounts to a homosexual cult; although hostile critics have opened fire in a constant attack as rabid as the attack of Southern senators upon "niggers"; critics who might possibly view the homosexual with a more humane eye seem agreed that it is better that nothing be said. Pressed to the point, they may either, as in the case of such an undeniable homosexual as Hart Crane, contend that they are great despite their "perversion"[*]—much as my mother used to say how much better a poet Poe would have been had he not taken dope; or where it is possible they have attempted to deny the role of the homosexual in modern art, the usual reply to unprincipled critics like Craven and Benton in painting being to assert that modern artists have not been homosexual. (Much as PM goes to great length to prove that none of the Communist leaders have been Jews—as if, if *all* the leaders were Jews, it would be that that would make the party suspect.)

But one cannot, in face of the approach taken to their own problem by homosexuals, place any weight of criticism upon the liberal body of critics. For there are Negroes who have joined openly in the struggle for human freedom, made articulate that their struggle against racial prejudice is part of the struggle for all; while there are Jews who have sought no special privilege of recognition for themselves as Jews, but have fought for *human* recognition and rights. But there is in the modern scene no homosexual who has been willing to take in his own persecution a battlefront toward human freedom. Almost co-incident with the first declarations for homosexual rights was the growth of a cult of homosexual superiority to the human race; the cultivation of a secret language, the *camp*, a tone and a vocabulary that is loaded with contempt for the human. They have gone beyond, let us say, Christianity, in excluding the pagan world.

Outside the ghetto the word "goy" disappears, wavers and dwindles in the Jew's vocabulary. But in what one would believe the most radical, the most enlightened "queer" circles the word "jam" remains, designating all who are not homosexual, filled with an unwavering hostility and fear, gathering an incredible force of exclusion and blindness. It is hard (for all the sympathy which I can bring to bear) to say that this cult plays any other than an evil role in society.

But names cannot be named. I cannot, like Agee, name the nasty little midgets, the entrepreneurs of this vicious market, the pimps of this special product. There are critics whose cynical, back-biting joke upon their audience is no other than this secret special superiority; there are poets whose nostalgic picture of special worth in suffering, sensitivity and magical quality is no other than this intermediate "sixth sense"; there are new cult leaders whose special divinity, whose supernatural and visionary claim is no other than this mystery of sex. The law has declared homosexuality secret, non-human, unnatural (and why not then supernatural?). The law itself sees in it a crime, not in the sense that murder, thievery, seduction of children or rape is seen as a crime—but in an occult sense. In the recent Lonergan case it was clear that murder was a *human* crime, but homosexuality was non-human. It was not a crime against man but a crime against "the way of nature," as defined in the Christian religion, a crime against "God."** It was lit up and given an awful and lurid attraction such as witchcraft (I can think of no other immediate example) was given in its time. Like early witches, the homosexual propagandists have rejected any struggle toward recognition in social equality and, far from seeking to undermine the popular superstition, have accepted the charge of Demonism. Sensing the fear in society that is generated in ignorance of their nature, they have sought not to bring about an understanding, to assert their equality and their common aims with mankind, but they have sought to profit by that fear and ignorance, to become witch doctors in the modern chaos.

To go about this they have had to cover with mystery, to obscure, the work of all these who have viewed homosexuality as but one of the many facets, one of the many eyes through which the human being may see and who, admitting through which eye they saw, have had primarily in mind as they wrote (as Melville, Proust, or Crane had) mankind and its liberation. For these great early artists their humanity was the source, the sole source, of their work. Thus in *Remembrance of Things Past* Charlus is not seen as the special disintegration of a homosexual but as a human being in disintegration, and the forces that lead to that disintegration, the forces of pride, self-humiliation in love, jealousy, are not special forces but common to all men and women. Thus in Melville, though in *Billy Budd* it is clear that the conflict is homosexual, the forces that make for that conflict, the guilt in passion, the hostility rising from subconscious sources, and the sudden recognition of these forces as it comes to Vere in that story; these are forces which are universal, which rise in other contexts, which in Melville's work have risen in other contexts.

It is, however, the body of Crane that has been most ravaged by these modern ghouls and, once ravaged, stuck up cult-wise in the mystic light of their special cemetery literature. The live body of Crane is there, inviolate; but in the window display of modern poetry, of so many special critics and devotees, is a painted mummy, deep sea green. One may tiptoe by, as the visitors to Lenin's tomb tiptoe by and, once outside, find themselves in a world in his name that has celebrated the defeat of all that he was devoted to. One need only point out in all the homosexual imagery of Crane, in the longing and vision of love, the absence, for instance, of the "English" specialty, the private world of boys' schools and isolate sufferings that has been converted into the poet's intangible "nobility," into the private*** sensibility that colors so much of modern writing. Where the Zionists of homosexuality have laid claim to a Palestine of their own, asserting in their miseries their nationality, Crane's suffering, his rebellion, and his love are sources of poetry for him not because they are what make him different from, superior to, mankind, but because he saw in them his link with mankind; he saw in them his sharing in universal human experience.

What can one do in the face of this, both those critics and artists, not homosexuals, who, however, are primarily concerned with all inhumanities, all forces of convention and law that impose a tyranny upon man, and those critics and artists who, as homosexuals, must face in their own lives both the hostility of society in that they are "queer" and the hostility of the homosexual cult of superiority in that they are human?

For the first group the starting point is clear, that they must recognize homosexuals as equals and as equals allow them neither more nor less than can be allowed any human being. For the second group the starting point is more difficult; the problem is more treacherous.

In the face of the hostility of society which I risk in making even the acknowledgement explicitly in this statement, in the face of the "crime" of my own feelings, in the past I publicized those feelings as private and made no stand for their recognition but tried to sell them disguised, for instance, as conflicts rising from mystical sources. I colored and perverted simple and direct emotions and realizations into a mysterious realm, a mysterious relation to society. Faced by the inhumanities of society I did not seek a solution in humanity but turned to a second out-cast society as inhumane as the first. I joined those who, while they allowed for my sexual nature, allowed for so little of the moral, the sensible and creative direction which all of living should reflect. They offered a family, outrageous as it was, a community in which one was not condemned for one's homosexuality, but it was necessary there for one to desert one's humanity for which one would be suspect, "out of key." In drawing rooms and in little magazines I celebrated the cult with a sense of sanctuary such as a Medieval Jew must have found in the ghetto; my voice taking on the modulations which tell of the capitulation to snobbery and the removal from the "common sort"; my poetry exhibiting the objects made divine and tyrannical as the Catholic church has made bones of saints, and bread and wine, tyrannical.

After an evening at one of those salons where the whole atmosphere was one of suggestion and celebration, I returned recently experiencing again the after-shock, the desolate feeling of wrongness, remembering in my own voice and gestures the rehearsal of unfeeling.

Alone, not only I, but, I felt, the others who had appeared as I did so mocking, so superior to feeling, had known, knew still, those troubled emotions, the deep and integral longings that we as human beings feel, holding us from violate action by the powerful sense of humanity that is their source, longings that lead us to love, to envision a creative life. "Towards something far," as Hart Crane wrote, "now farther away than ever."

Among those who should understand those emotions which society condemned, one found that the group language did not allow for any feeling at all other than this self-ridicule, this gaiety (it is significant that the homosexual's word for his own kind is "gay"), a wave surging forward, breaking into laughter and then receding, leaving a wake of disillusionment, a disbelief that extended to one-self, to life itself. What then, disowning this career, can one turn to?

What I think can be asserted as a starting point is that only one devotion can be held by a human being as a creative life and expression, and that is a devotion to human freedom, toward the liberation of human love, human conflicts, human aspirations. To do this one must disown *all* the special groups (nations, religions, sexes, races) that would claim allegiance. To hold this devotion every written word, every spoken word, every action, every purpose, must be examined and considered. The old fears, the old specialties will be there, mocking and tempting; the old protective associations will be there, offering for a surrender of one's humanity congratulations upon one's special nature and value. It must be always recognized that the others, those who have surrendered their humanity, are not less than oneself. It must be always remembered that one's own honesty, one's battle against the inhumanity of his own group (be it against patriotism, against bigotry, against, in this specific case, the homosexual cult) is a battle that cannot be won in the immediate scene. The forces of inhumanity are overwhelming, but only one's continued opposition can make any other order possible, can give an added strength for all those who desire freedom and equality to break at last those fetters that seem now so unbreakable.

*Critics of Crane, for instance, consider that his homosexuality is the cause of his inability to adjust to society. Another school feels that inability to adjust to society causes homosexuality. What seems fairly obvious is that what society frustrated in Crane was his effort to write poetry and to write what he wanted to in the way he wanted to. He might well have adjusted his homosexual desires within society as many have done by "living a lie." It was his desire for truth that society condemned.

**"Just as certain judges assume and are more inclined to pardon murder in inverts and treason in Jews for reasons derived from original sin and racial predestination." Sodome et Gomorrhe, Proust.

***By private I in no sense mean personal.

James Baldwin (1924–1987) was an openly gay Black American writer who lived in France most of his adult life. Interviews with him revealed that one of the reasons for his moving to and remaining in France was that he felt more comfortable living an openly homosexual or bisexual life there. His writings ranged from the topics of the Black civil rights movement to interracial heterosexual relationships, and his novel *Giovanni's Room* is considered an early classic of gay male literature. (Indeed, he is considered one of the greatest of U.S. writers.) The essay reproduced here was published in the Moroccan journal *Zero* in 1949. Besides its content, it is notable for the courage it took to publish it at the time (just prior to Baldwin's commercial success with *Go Tell It On the Mountain*.) We can also see in here the way that Baldwin predates some of the 1970's feminist arguments about the relationship between homophobia and sexism.

JAMES BALDWIN

from

PRESERVATION OF INNOCENCE

(1949)

James Baldwin

The problem of the homosexual, so vociferously involved with good and evil, the unnatural as opposed to the natural, has its roots in the nature of man and woman and their relationship to one another. While at one time we speak of nature and at another of the nature of man, we speak on both occasions of something of which we know very little, and we make the tacit admission that they are not one and the same. Between nature and man there is a difference; there is, indeed, perpetual war. It develops when we think about it, that not only is a natural state perversely indefinable outside of the womb or before the grave, but that it is *not* on the whole a state which is altogether desirable. It is just as well that we cook our food and are not baffled by water-closets and do not copulate in the public thoroughfare. People who have not learned this are not admired as natural but are feared as primitive or incarcerated as insane.

We spend vast amounts of our time and emotional energy in learning how not to be natural and in eluding the trap of our own nature and it therefore becomes very difficult to know exactly what is meant when we speak of the unnatural. It is not possible to have it both ways, to use nature at one time as the final arbiter of human conduct and at another to oppose her as angrily as we do. As we are being inaccurate, perhaps desperately defensive and making, inversely, a most damaging admission when we describe as inhuman, some reprehensible act committed by a human being, so we become hopelessly involved in paradox when we describe as unnatural something which is found in nature. A cat torturing a mouse to death is not described as inhuman for we assume that it is being perfectly natural; nor is a table condemned as being unnatural for we know that is has nothing to do with nature. What we really seem to be saying when we speak of the inhuman is that we cannot bear to be confronted with that fathomless baseness shared by all humanity and when we speak of the unnatural that we cannot imagine what vexations nature will dream up next.

We have, in short, whenever nature is invoked to support our human divisions, every right to be suspicious, nature having betrayed only the most perplexing and untrustworthy interest in man and none whatever in his institutions. We resent this indifference and we are frightened by it; we resist it; we ceaselessly assert the miracle of our existence against this implacable power. Yet we know nothing of birth or death except that we remain powerless when faced by either. Much as we resent or threaten or cajole nature, she refuses absolutely to relent; she may at any moment throw down the trump card she never fails to have hidden and leave us bankrupt. In time, her ally and her rather too explicit witness, suns rise and set and the face of the earth changes; at length the limbs stiffen and the light goes out of her eyes.

> *And nothing 'gainst time's scythe may make defense*
> *Save breed to brave him when he takes thee hence.*

We arrive at the oldest, the most insistent and the most vehement charge faced by the homosexual: he is unnatural because he has turned from his life-giving function to a union which is sterile. This may, in itself, be considered a heavy, even an unforgivable crime, but since it is not so considered when involving other people, the unmarried or the poverty-stricken or the feeble, and since his existence did not always invoke that hysteria with which he now contends, we are safe in suggesting that his present untouchability owes its motive power to several other sources. Let me suggest that his present debasement and our obsession with him corresponds to the debasement of the relationship between the sexes; and that his ambiguous and terrible position in our society reflects the ambiguities and terrors which time has deposited on that relationship as the sea piles seaweed and wreckage along the shore.

For, after all, I take it that no one can be seriously disturbed about the birth-rate: when the race commits suicide, it will not be in Sodom. Nor can we continue to shout unnatural whenever we are confronted by a phenomenon as old as mankind, a phenomenon, more-over, which nature has maliciously repeated in all of her domain. If we are going to be nat-ural then this is a part of nature; if we refuse to accept this, then we have rejected nature and must find other criterion.

Instantly the Deity springs to mind, in much the same manner. I suspect, that He sprang into being on the cold, black day when we discovered that nature cared nothing for us. His advent, which alone had the power to save us from nature and ourselves, also created a self-awareness and, therefore, tensions and terrors and responsibilities with which we had not coped before. It marked the death of innocence; it set up the duality of good-and-evil; and now Sin and Redemption, those mighty bells, began that crying which will not cease until, by another act of creation, we transcend our old morality. Before we were banished from Eden and the curse was uttered, "I will put enmity between thee and the woman," the homosexual did not exist; nor, properly speaking, did the heterosexual. We were all in a state of nature.

We are forced to consider this tension between God and nature and are thus confront-ed with the nature of God because He is man's most intense creation and it is not in the sight of nature that the homosexual is condemned, but in the sight of God. This argues a pro-found and dangerous failure of concept, since an incalculable number of the world's humans are thereby condemned to something less than life; and we may not, of course, do this with-out limiting ourselves. Life, it is true, is a process of decisions and alternatives, the conscious awareness and acceptance of limitations. Experience, nevertheless, to say nothing of history, seems clearly to indicate that it is not possible to banish or to falsify any human need with-out ourselves undergoing falsification and loss. And what of murder? A human characteris-tic, surely. Must we embrace the murderer? But the question must be put another way: is it possible not to embrace him? For he is in us and of us. We may not be free until we under-stand him.

The nature of man and woman and their relationship to one another fills seas of con-jecture and an immense proportion of the myth, legend, and literature of the world is devot-ed to this subject. It has caused, we gather, on the evidence presented by any library, no lit-tle discomfort. It is observable that the more we imagine we have discovered, the less we know and that, moreover, the necessity to discover and the effort and self-consciousness involved in this necessity makes their relationship more and more complex.

Men and women seem to function as imperfect and sometimes unwilling mirrors for one another; a falsification or distortion of the nature of the one is immediately reflected in the nature of the other. A division between them can only betray a division within the soul of each. Matters are not helped if we thereupon decide that men must recapture their status as men and that women must embrace their function as women; not only does the resulting rigidity of attitude put to death any possible communion, but, having once listed the bald physical facts, no one is prepared to go further and decide, of our multiple human attributes, which are masculine and which are feminine. Directly we say that women have finer and more delicate sensibilities we are reminded that she is insistently, mythically, and even historically treacherous. If we are so rash as to say that men have greater endurance, we are reminded of the procession of men who have long gone to their long home while women walked about the streets—mourning, we are told, but no doubt, gossiping and shopping at the same time.

We can pick up no novel, no drama, no poem; we may examine no fable nor any myth without stumbling on this merciless paradox in the nature of the sexes. This is a paradox which experience alone is able to illuminate and this experience is not communicable in any language that we know. The recognition of this complexity is the signal of maturity; it marks the death of the child and the birth of the man.

III

THE
HOMOPHILE
MOVEMENT
1950–1969

A

CONTEXT

A mythology has grown around the Stonewall riots. In this myth, Stonewall was the beginning of gay and lesbian political activism and culture. In fact, the groundwork for that historical event was laid by decades of hard work. We cannot make sense of later movements without understanding both European movements discussed previously and the "homophile" movement of the 1950s and 1960s. The label "homophile" is an example of the sexual repression of the period: in their desire to draw attention away from the sexual aspect of their identities, politically active gays and lesbians often used this more euphemistic word.

In 1950, gays and lesbians were completely isolated by the dominant U.S. society. Even the American Civil Liberties Union proclaimed in 1957 that laws against consensual gay and lesbian sex and entrapment procedures used against gay men were not within the province of the ACLU. Not only were homosexuals pariahs in the military and other government jobs; discovery by one's employer virtually guaranteed dismissal. It was the official opinion of the American Psychiatric Association that homosexuality was an illness in and of itself. With a widespread social consensus that homosexuality was abnormal, gays and lesbians had to choose between being sinners, being criminals, and being sick (a choice still too common). The renewed conservatism—social, sexual, political—of the United States in the 1950s made any homosexual organizing a difficult and risky endeavor.

Nonetheless, the 1950s saw the birth of the first sustained homophile organizations in the United States. The Mattachine Society, the Daughters of Bilitis, and ONE were the largest and most vocal organizations of the 1950s, and were all based in California. By the late 1960s there were chapters of Mattachine and DOB across the country, as well as other groups. NACHO (the North American Conference of Homophile Organizations) and regional counterparts provided venues for discussing common goals and emerging differences.

Through these organizations, gay and lesbian writing began to flourish. The *Mattachine Review*, *The Ladder*, *ONE Magazine*, and others provided outlets for budding and established writers to discuss gay and lesbian topics. The terrible fear of discovery gradually eased as the 1960s drew to a close, but never enough to vitiate the tremendous courage of those who wrote and subscribed to these magazines. The range of issues and opinions expressed in them belies the later conception of those who wrote as staid and narrow. Discussions of bisexuality, butch/femme, pedophilia, and gay and lesbian culture, including sexual culture and its institutions, and other contemporary issues are in their pages. By the time Stonewall occurred, the groundwork had been laid for a full political and cultural movement.

Nonetheless, the homophile period is notably different from post-Stonewall activism. The participants in these organizations were by and large white and of middle-class backgrounds. There was substantial (though not complete) agreement that assimilation was the desired goal, and that accommodation to heterosexual society was the way to achieve that. Both the Daughters of Bilitis and Mattachine urged their members to dress neatly and "appropriately" for meetings, especially for meetings with "experts" such as clergy, government officials, or doctors. With the exception of leaders such as Harry Hay, they did not wish to challenge prevailing gender norms or cultural mores. There were extensive debates in *The Ladder* about whether or not picketing would alienate heterosexuals. Clearly, the homophile movement was tame by contemporary standards.

This early period also witnessed the birth of what would soon become lesbian-feminism. "The homophile movement" had always been composed of largely sex-segregated groups, though women were welcome in Mattachine and ONE. By the late 1960s, however, with the rise of feminist consciousness in general, lesbians would become radicalized not only as homosexuals but as women. Just as the Stonewall Riots would not have marked the birth of a movement without the organizing and growing consciousness of the years before, so lesbian-feminism would draw on the experience of both new lesbians and DOB veterans.

Many governments have equated homosexuality with corruption and danger, as have some reactionary social movements. Just as the post-Cold War Right in the United States has shifted from using communism to homosexuality as its primary organizing fear, the early Cold War saw an equation of "perversion" with treason. The late 1940's and 1950's, heyday of Joseph McCarthy's persecution of communists and "subversives," also witnessed the terror of "sex perverts" in government. Relying on the homophobic medical opinions of the time and on legal bans on homosexual activity, McCarthyites constructed a vision of the pervert who, as the victim of blackmail, would betray his or her country.

The report of the Senate Investigations Subcommittee of the Committee on Expenditures in the Executive Departments represents the sum of these fears and their consequences—the persecution and expulsion of gays and lesbians from their jobs and the possibility of future employment, public embarrassment, and continual harassment by police. This document speaks as vividly as any can of the situation of homosexuals in the United States in the 1950s, making their growing resistance during this period doubly heroic.

THE UNITED STATES
SENATE

from
United States Senate

EMPLOYMENT OF HOMOSEXUALS AND OTHER SEX PERVERTS IN THE U.S. GOVERNMENT

(1950)

Mr. Hoey submitted the following

INTERIM REPORT
[Pursuant to S. Res. 280, 81st Cong.]
Made to the Committee on Expenditures in the Executive Departments by its Subcommittee on Investigations

Introduction

The Senate Investigations Subcommittee of the Committee on Expenditures in the Executive Departments was directed, under authority of Senate Resolution 280 (81st Cong., 2d sess., adopted June 7, 1950), (see Appendix I), to make an investigation into the employment by the Government of homosexuals and other sex perverts. This resolution was the result of preliminary inquiries made earlier this year by a subcommittee of the Senate District of Columbia Subcommittee on Appropriations composed of Senator Hill of Alabama and Senator Wherry of Nebraska. The reports and testimony of that subcommittee were of considerable value to the Investigations Subcommittee in the conduct of this inquiry.

An investigation on a Government-wide scale of homosexuality and other sex perversion is unprecedented. Furthermore, reliable, factual information on the subject of homosexuality and sex perversion is somewhat limited. In the past, studies in this field, for the most part, were confined to scientific studies by medical experts and sociologists. The criminal courts and the police have had considerable experience in the handling of sex perverts as law violators, but the subject as a personnel problem until very recently has received little attention from Government administrators and personnel officers.

The primary objective of the subcommittee in this inquiry was to determine the extent of the employment of homosexuals and other sex perverts in Government; to consider reasons why their employment by the Government is undesirable; and to examine into the efficacy of the methods used in dealing with the problem. Because of the complex nature of the subject under investigation it was apparent that this investigation could not be confined to a mere personnel inquiry. Therefore, the subcommittee considered not only the security risk and other aspects of the employment of homosexuals, including the rules and procedures followed by Government agencies in handling these cases, but inquiries were also made into the basic medical, psychiatric, sociological and legal phases of the problem. A number of eminent physicians and psychiatrists, who are recognized authorities on this subject, were consulted and some of these authorities testified before the subcommittee in executive session. In addition, numerous medical and sociological studies were reviewed. Information was also sought and obtained from law-enforcement officers, prosecutors, and other persons dealing with the legal and sociological aspects of the problem in 10 of the larger cities in the country.

The subcommittee, being well aware of the strong moral and social taboos attached to homosexuality and other forms of sex perversion, made every effort to protect individuals from unnecessary public ridicule and to prevent this inquiry from becoming a public spectacle. In carrying out this policy it was determined at the outset that all testimony would be taken by the subcommittee in executive session. Accordingly, all witnesses appearing before the subcommittee testified in executive hearings. In the conduct of this investigation the subcommittee tried to avoid the circus atmosphere which could attend an inquiry of this type and sought to make a thorough factual study of the problem at hand in an unbiased, objective manner.

It was determined that even among the experts there existed considerable difference of opinion concerning the many facets of homosexuality and other forms of sex perversion. Even the terms "sex pervert" and "homosexual" are given different connotations by the medical and psychiatric experts. For the purpose of this report the subcommittee has defined sex perverts as "those who engage in unnatural sexual acts" and homosexuals are perverts who may be broadly defined as "persons of either sex who as adults engage in sexual activities with persons of the same sex." In this inquiry the subcommittee is not concerned with so-called latent sex perverts, namely, those persons who knowingly or unknowingly have tendencies or inclinations toward homosexuality or other types of sex perversion, but who, by the exercise of self-restraint or for other reasons do not indulge in overt acts of perversion. This investigation is concerned only with those who engage in overt acts of homosexuality or other sex perversion.

The subcommittee found that most authorities agree on certain basic facts concerning sex perversion and it is felt that these facts should be considered in any discussion of the problem. Most authorities believe that sex deviation results from psychological rather than physical causes, and in many cases there are no outward characteristics or physical traits that are positive as identifying marks of sex perversion. Contrary to a common belief, all homosexual males do not have feminine mannerisms, nor do all female homosexuals display masculine characteristics in their dress or actions. The fact is that many male homosexuals are very masculine in their physical appearance and general demeanor, and many female homosexuals have every appearance of femininity in their outward behavior.

Generally speaking, the overt homosexual of both sexes can be divided into two general types; the active, aggressive or male type, and the submissive, passive or female type. The passive type of male homosexual, who often is effeminate in his mannerisms and appearance, is attracted to the masculine type of man and is friendly and congenial with women. On the other hand the active male homosexual often has a dislike for women. He exhibits no traces of femininity in his speech or mannerisms which would disclose his homosexuality. This active type is almost exclusively attracted to the passive type of homosexual or to young men or boys who are not necessarily homosexual but who are effeminate in general appearance or behavior. The active and passive type of female homosexual follow the same general patterns as their male counterparts. It is also a known fact that some perverts are bisexual. This type engages in normal heterosexual relationships as well as homosexual activities. These bisexual individuals are often married and have children, and except for their perverted activities they appear to lead normal lives.

Psychiatric physicians generally agree that indulgence in sexually perverted practices indicates a personality which has failed to reach sexual maturity. The authorities agree that most sex deviates respond to psychiatric treatment and can be cured if they have a genuine desire to be cured. However, many overt homosexuals have no real desire to abandon their way of life and in such cases cures are difficult, if not impossible. The subcommittee sincerely believes that persons afflicted with sexual desires which result in their engaging in overt acts of perversion should be considered as proper cases for medical and psychiatric treatment. However, sex perverts, like all other persons who by their overt acts violate moral codes and laws and the accepted standards of conduct, must be treated as transgressors and dealt with accordingly.

Sex Perverts as Government Employees

Those charged with the responsibility of operating the agencies of Government must insist that Government employees meet acceptable standards of personal conduct. In the opinion of this subcommittee homosexuals and other sex perverts are not proper persons to be employed in Government for two reasons; first, they are generally unsuitable, and second, they constitute security risks.

General Unsuitability of Sex Perverts

Overt acts of sex perversion, including acts of homosexuality, constitute a crime under our Federal, State, and municipal statutes and persons who commit such acts are law violators. Aside from the criminality and immorality involved in sex perversion such behavior is so contrary to the the normal accepted standards of social behavior that persons who engage in such activity are looked upon as outcasts by society generally. The social stigma attached to sex perversion is so great that many perverts go to great lengths to conceal their perverted tendencies. This situation is evidenced by the fact that perverts are frequently victimized by blackmailers who threaten to expose their sexual deviations . . .

Law enforcement officers have informed the subcommittee that there are gangs of blackmailers who make a regular practice of preying upon the homosexual. The modus operandi in these homosexual blackmail cases usually follow the same general pattern. The victim, who is a homosexual, has managed to conceal his perverted activities and usually enjoys a good reputation in his community. The blackmailers, by one means or another, discover that the victim is addicted to homosexuality and under the threat of disclosure they extort money from him. These blackmailers often impersonate police officers in carrying out their blackmail schemes. Many cases have come to the attention of the police where highly respected individuals have paid out large sums of money to blackmailers over a long period of time rather than risk the disclosure of their homosexual activities. The police believe that this type of blackmail racket is much more extensive than is generally known, because they have found that most of the victims are very hesitant to bring the matter to the attention of the authorities.

In further considering the general suitability of perverts as Government employees, it is generally believed that those who engage in overt acts of perversion lack the emotional stability of normal persons. In addition there is an abundance of evidence to sustain the conclusion that indulgence in acts of sex perversion weakens the moral fiber of an individual to a degree that he is not suitable for a position of responsibility.

Most of the authorities agree and our investigation has shown that the presence of a sex pervert in a Government agency tends to have a corrosive influence upon his fellow employees. These perverts will frequently attempt to entice normal individuals to engage in perverted practices. This is particularly true in the case of young and impressionable people who might come under the influence of a pervert. Government officials have the responsibility of keeping this type of corrosive influence out of the agencies under their control. It is particularly important that the thousands of young men and women who are brought into Federal jobs not be subjected to that type of influence while in the service of the Government. One homosexual can pollute a Government office.

Another point to be considered in determining whether a sex pervert is suitable for Government employment is his tendency to gather other perverts about him. Eminent psychiatrists have informed the subcommittee that the homosexual is likely to seek his own kind because the pressures of society are such that he feels uncomfortable unless he is with his own kind. Due to this situation the homosexual tends to surround himself with other homosexuals, not only in his social, but in his business life. Under these circumstances if a homosexual attains a position in Government where he can influence the hiring of personnel, it is almost inevitable that he will attempt to place other homosexuals in Government jobs.

Sex Perverts as Security Risks

. . . The lack of emotional stability which is found in most sex perverts and the weakness of their moral fiber, makes them susceptible to the blandishments of the foreign espionage agent. It is the experience of intelligence experts that perverts are vulnerable to interrogation by a skilled questioner and they seldom refuse to talk about themselves. Furthermore, most perverts tend to congregate at the same restaurants, night clubs, and bars, which places can be identified with comparative ease in any community, making it possible for a recruiting agent to develop clandestine relationships which can be used for espionage purposes.

. . . The pervert is easy prey to the blackmailer. It follows that if blackmailers can extort money from a homosexual under the threat of disclosure, espionage agents can use the same type of pressure to extort confidential information or other material they might be seeking. A classic case of this type involved one Captain Raedl who became chief of the Austrian counterintelligence service in 1912. He succeeded in building up an excellent intelligence net in Russia and had done considerable damage to the espionage net which the Russians had set up in Austria. However, Russian agents soon discovered that Raedl was a homosexual and shortly thereafter they managed to catch him in an act of perversion as the result of a trap they had set for that purpose. Under the threat of exposure Raedl agreed to furnish and he did furnish the Russians with Austrian military secrets. He also doctored or destroyed the intelligence reports which his own Austrian agents were sending from Russia with the result that the Austrian and German General Staffs, at the outbreak of World War I in 1914, were completely misinformed as to the Russian's mobilization intentions. On the other hand, the Russians had obtained from Raedl the war plans of the Austrians and that part of the German plans which had been made available to the Austrian Government. Shortly after the outbreak of the war Captain Raedl's traitorous acts were discovered by his own Government and he committed suicide.

Other cases have been brought to the attention of the subcommittee where Nazi and Communist agents have attempted to obtain information from employees of our Government by threatening to expose their abnormal sex activities. It is an accepted fact among intelligence agencies that espionage organizations the world over consider sex perverts who are in possession of or have access to confidential material to be prime targets where pressure can be exerted. In virtually every case despite protestations by the perverts that they would never succumb to blackmail, invariably they express considerable concern over the fact that their condition might become known to their friends, associates, or the public at large. The present danger of this security problem is well illustrated by the following excerpt from the testimony of D. Milton Ladd, Assistant to the Director of the Federal Bureau of Investigation, who appeared before this subcommittee in executive session:

> The Communists, without principles or scruples, have a program of seeking its possession
> information of unquestionable reliability that orders have been issued by high Russian
> intelligence officials to their agents to secure details of the private lives of Government offi-
> cials, their weaknesses, their associates, and in fact every bit of information regarding
> them, hoping to find a chink in their armor and a weakness upon
> which they might capitalize at the appropriate time . . .

The subcommittee in pointing out the unsuitability of perverts for Government employment is not unaware of the fact that there are other patterns of human behavior which also should be considered in passing upon the general suitability or security-risk status of Government employees. There is little doubt that habitual drunkards, persons who have engaged in criminal activities, and those who indulge in other types of infamous or scandalous personal conduct are also unsuitable for Government employment and constitute security risks. However, the subcommittee, in the present investigation, has properly confined itself to the problem of sex perverts.

Extent of Sex Perversion in Government

It is not possible to determine accurately the number of homosexuals and other sex perverts in the Government service. The only known perverts are those whose activities have been brought to the attention of the authorities as the result of an arrest or where some other specific information has resulted in the disclosure of their perversion.

Not even the experts are in agreement as to the incidence of homosexuality and other sex perversion among the general population and to attempt to arrive at an estimated figure as to the number of perverts in the Federal Government would be sheer speculation and serve no useful purpose. While most authorities agree that the incidence of sex perversion follows a rather constant pattern throughout our entire social structure, regardless of education, wealth, or social position, it clearly does not follow that the same relative number of perverts should be found in the Federal service as are found outside of the Government. In this regard we must consider the fact that homosexuals and other persons with arrest records or other known indications of unsavory character are largely eliminated from a great many Federal positions in such agencies as the Atomic Energy Commission, the Federal Bureau of Investigation, the State Department, certain branches of the Treasury, and other sensitive jobs where all applicants are thoroughly investigated prior to employment. Furthermore, some check is made of all Government employees prior to or soon after their appointment and this would tend to eliminate many undesirables.

In considering the extent of homosexuality in the Government, the subcommittee has confined itself, as far as it has been reasonably possible, to those cases where specific information has led to the conclusion that a person is a pervert, or at least a likely suspect. It is realized that there are bound to be some unknown perverts in Government, because in any organization as large as the Federal Government it is logical to assume that there will be perverts whose clandestine activities may never be discovered. However, it is expected that the number of perverts in Government can be kept to a minimum if the problem is handled properly.

The subcommittee has attempted to arrive at some idea as to the extent of sex perversion among Government employees by obtaining information from the personnel records of all Government agencies and the police records in the District of Columbia. Due to the manner in which personnel records are maintained it was found that any effort to obtain statistics from these records prior to January 1, 1947, would necessarily involve a prohibitive cost and that the fragmentary information obtained from such records prior to that date would be of little or no value to this investigation . . .

An examination of the statistical data gathered from the civilian agencies of Government . . . indicates that from January 1, 1947 through October 31, 1950, 574 cases have been handled in these agencies. Of that number 207 have been dismissed from the Government service and 213 have resigned. In 85 cases it was determined that charges and the persons involved were retained. In addition investigation is pending in 69 cases in which no final determination has been made as yet.

Handling of the Sex Perversion Problem in Government
The Rules of Government Regarding the Employment of Sex Perverts

The regulations of the Civil Service Commission for many years have provided that criminal, infamous, dishonest, immoral or notoriously disgraceful conduct, which includes homosexuality or other types of sex perversion, are sufficient grounds for denying appointment to a Government position or for the removal of a person from the Federal service. Furthermore, under the civil service regulations (Ch. S1–21, Federal Personnel Manual), specific procedures have been set up under which unsuitable Federal employees who are subject to the civil service regulations shall be removed from the Government. These civil service regulations are applicable to over 90 percent of the civilians employed in the Federal Government and the remaining civilian employees who are not subject to the rules of the Civil Service Commission are covered by agency regulations which are similar to those of the Commission. In addition to the rules and regulations of the Civil Service Commission, the armed services have promulgated and adopted their own regulations for the handling of this problem among military personnel. As was previously pointed out in this report, the armed services have traditionally taken a firm and agressive [*sic*] attitude toward the problem, but until early this year, each service was handling the problem in its own way. In December 1949, the Department of Defense effected standard procedures for the handling and disposition of homosexual cases among military personnel. Since that time each of the services has issued regulations based upon these procedures and the problem is now being handled uniformly in all of the military services.

Methods Used to Prevent Sex Perverts from Obtaining Government Employment and to Remove Them from Government Jobs

In reviewing the methods and procedures in the handling of the problem of sex perversion in the Government, two factors must be considered. First, consideration must be given to preventing such persons from obtaining Government employment and, second, the methods used in detecting and removing perverts who are already in the Government service should be examined. Under present procedures all applicants for Government positions are screened by the Civil Service Commission soon after their appointment. While these applicants are not subject to a so-called full field investigation, their fingerprints are checked against the files of the FBI to determine whether they have a prior arrest record, and other name checks are also made. As a result of this screening process, the Civil Service Commission is notified in the event the applicant has a police record of sex perversion; and, if such a record does exist, further investigation is conducted to determine the complete facts. A spot check of the records of the Civil Service Commission indicates that between January 1, 1947, and August 1, 1950, approximately 1,700 applicants for Federal positions were denied employment because they had a record of homosexuality or other sex perversion.

On the other hand, the subcommittee has found that many civilian agencies of government have taken an entirely unrealistic view of the problem of sex perversion and have not taken adequate steps to get these people out of government. Known perverts and persons suspected of such activities have been retained in some Government agencies, or they have been allowed to leave one agency and obtain employment in another, notwithstanding the regulations of the Civil Service Commission and the rules of the agencies themselves. There are several reasons why this situation existed. In many cases the fault stemmed from the fact that personnel officers and other officials were acting in outright disregard of existing rules, and they handled the problem in accordance with their individual feelings or personal judgments in the matter. To further confuse the problem, there was considerable ignorance and wide difference of opinion among Government officials as to how personnel cases involving sex perverts should be handled. Some officials undoubtedly condoned the employment of homosexuals for one reason or another. This was particularly true in those instances where the perverted activities of the employee were carried on in such a manner as not to create public scandal or notoriety. Those who adopted that view based their conclusions on the false premise that what a Government employee did outside of the office on his own time, particularly if his actions did not involve his fellow employees or his work, was his own business. That conclusion may be true with regard to the normal behavior of employees in most types of Government work, but it does not apply to sex perversion or any other types of criminal activity or similar misconduct.

There also appears to have been a tendency in many Government agencies to adopt a head-in-the-sand attitude toward the problem of sex perversion. Some agencies tried to avoid the problem either by making no real effort to investigate charges of homosexuality or by failing to take firm and positive steps to get known perverts out of Government and keep them out. In other cases some agencies did get rid of perverts, but in an apparent effort to conceal the fact that they had such persons in their employ, they eased out these perverts by one means or another in as quiet a manner as possible and circumvented the established rules with respect to the removal or dismissal of unsuitable personnel from Government positions. As a result of this situation a sex pervert would be forced out of one department and in many instances he would promptly obtain employment in another public agency. Such cases occurred because the pervert was usually allowed to resign and the real reason for his resignation was not noted in his regular personnel file, nor was the Civil Service Commission notified of the actual reason for the resignation. In order to prevent exactly that type of abuse, the civil service regulations, for a number of years, have provided that when an employee resigns or is dismissed from an agency the real reason must be noted in his personnel file and the Civil Service Commission must also be notified. This acts as a double check in that the regular personnel file must be forwarded to any new agency to which the employee might transfer and the derogatory information is also carried in the central files of the Civil Service Commission . . .

As has been previously stated, the regulations of the Civil Service Commission provide that certain procedures must be followed by Government agencies in removing sex perverts or other undesirable civil service employees from the Government. In essence the regulations provide that the employee must be informed in writing of the charges against him: that he must be allowed a reasonable time to file an answer; and that if the employee answers the charges, his answers must be considered by the agency and he must be furnished with a written decision in his case. While this procedure gives the employee an opportunity to know and answer the charges against him, the subcommittee is convinced that unless the persons who actually administer these procedures are in possession of sufficient facts upon which to draw up the charges and to make their final decisions, the public interest will not be protected adequately.

The Necessity of Thoroughly Investigating Cases of Sex Perversion in Government

Rules, regulations and procedures are of little value in dealing with sex perverts in Government unless full and complete facts, which can only be established by a thorough investigation, are available for the review of the agencies in each specific case. The only effective way to handle sex perversion cases in a Government agency is to make sure that every reasonable complaint is thoroughly investigated. Many of these cases first come to the attention of a Government agency as the result of an arrest on a morals charge. In such a case the investigation should not be confined to a mere review of the arrest record. While it is not deemed advisable to set forth in this report a detailed outline of the investigation that should be made in sex perversion cases, there are certain investigative steps that should be followed out in these cases. In this regard the subcommittee has found that many persons in and out of Government believe that evidence tending to prove or disprove homosexuality or other types of sex perversion is difficult, if not impossible to obtain. That is not a fact. On the contrary the subcommittee has found that in most of these cases concrete information can be adequately developed by experienced investigators using accepted investigative techniques. Examinations by medical psychiatrists experienced in this field can be helpful but there is evidence that such tests are by no means conclusive. Some psychiatrists have been successful in detecting homosexuality and other forms of sex perversion by means of psychiatric tests, but they have been most successful in those cases where information concerning the patient's life and activities has been made available to them as a result of collateral investigations . . .

Failure to Obtain Police Records

In view of the fact that the police departments in the District of Columbia and elsewhere fingerprint persons arrested for sex perversion and forward these prints to the FBI, the present system of channeling this arrest information on Government employees from the FBI through the Civil Service Commission to the employing agency means that Government agencies are notified promptly when a Government employee is arrested here or in other parts of the country for perverted sex activities. Under these circumstances the agency will have an opportunity to make an immediate investigation and will be in a position to take the necessary administrative action in each individual case.

Lack of Review Procedures

In view of the very serious consequences of dismissal from the Government based on charges of sex perversion, the subcommittee is of the opinion that reasonable safeguards should be set up for the protection of the individuals involved in these cases. Under present procedures certain categories of Federal employees have a right to appeal to the Civil-Service Commission in the event they are dismissed from an agency as sex perverts or for any other reason. However, no present machinery exists by which persons without veterans' preference or civil service status can appeal dismissals from the department or agencies of Government. The subcommittee believes that every person dismissed from the Government as a sex pervert should have the right to appeal the findings of the employing agency and these appeals should be handled in a uniform manner.

On the other hand, under the Federal employees loyalty program, any person who is found to be disloyal by an agency loyalty board has the right to appeal to the Loyalty Review Board. This Review Board has the power to review the entire case. It is believed that the ends of justice would be better served by setting up a similar type of review in cases involving the removal of sex perverts from the Federal Government. However, should any such review machinery be set up it is further recommended that the Review Board be given the authority to subpoena witnesses and records, which powers the Loyalty Review Board does not have at present. It might be stated parenthetically at this point that homosexual or other sex perversion cases are not handled under the Federal employees loyalty program. The agency loyalty boards and the Loyalty Review Board are authorized to consider only that evidence bearing on an employee's loyalty; these boards have no power to act upon charges of sex perversion or other matters reflecting upon a person's suitability for Federal employment.

Considering the fact that each agency and department of Government is primarily responsible for the hiring and firing of its own personnel this subcommittee does not propose to set forth or recommend any detailed blueprint for the handling of the problem of sex perversion in Government. However, our investigation has disclosed certain shortcomings in the present methods of handling the problem and it is believed that the following recommendations should be considered in the future handling of this problem:

1. All reasonable complaints of sex perversion should be thoroughly investigated by qualified investigators. Those agencies without trained investigative staffs should request investigations by the Civil Service Commission, or some other investigative agency.
2. The present rules and procedures of the Civil Service Commission, concerning the employment and discharge of sex perverts should be enforced and carried out by all agencies of Government.
3. Consideration should be given to the establishment of a board of review outside of the employing agency so that all persons who are ordered dismissed on charges of sex perversion may appeal the findings of the employing agency.

Handling of Sex Perversion Cases by the Legislative Branch

Generally speaking the subcommittee found that the same shortcomings and delinquencies existed in the handling of this problem by the legislative branch as were found in the executive branch of Government. As the result of this situation there were cases where legislative employees who had been arrested on charges of sex perversion were able to remain in their jobs. However, since the initiation of this investigation all known perverts in the legislative agencies have either been removed or the cases are being given active consideration. With the exception of the General Accounting Office and the Government Printing Office, which come under the general provisions of the Civil Service Commission although they are in the legislative branch of the Government, the legislative branch has adopted no definite procedures for the handling of sex perversion cases.

Employees of the Library of Congress, the Botanical Gardens, and the employees of both Houses of Congress, are subject to the general jurisdiction of the Senate Committee on Rules and Administration or the Committee on House Administration. Arrangements have been made to have the Department of Justice furnish these committees with information coming to the attention of the FBI concerning the arrest of legislative employees in these departments in order that investigations can be made in each case and proper administrative action taken. It is expected that this arrangement will make it possible for these two congressional committees to handle properly any future cases of sex perversion which might be discovered in these legislative departments . . .

Conclusion

There is no place in the United States Government for persons who violate the laws or the accepted standards of morality, or who otherwise bring disrepute to the Federal service by infamous or scandalous personal conduct. Such persons are not suitable for Government positions and in the case of doubt the American people are entitled to have errors of judgment on the part of their officials, if there must be errors, resolved on the side of caution. It is the opinion of this subcommittee that those who engage in acts of homosexuality and other perverted sex activities are unsuitable for employment in the Federal Government. This conclusion is based upon the fact that persons who indulge in such degraded activity are committing not only illegal and immoral acts, but they also constitute security risks in positions of public trust.

The subcommittee found that in the past many Government officials failed to take a realistic view of the problem of sex perversion in Government with the result that a number of sex perverts were not discovered or removed from Government jobs, and in still other instances they were quietly eased out of one department and promptly found employment in another agency. This situation undoubtedly stemmed from the fact that there was a general disinclination on the part of many Government officials to face squarely the problem of sex perversion among Federal employees and as a result they did not take the proper steps to solve the problem. The rules of the Civil Service Commission and the regulations of the agencies themselves prohibit the employment of sex perverts and these rules have been in effect for many years. Had the existing rules and regulations been enforced many of the perverts who were forced out of Government in recent months would have been long since removed from the Federal service.

It is quite apparent that as a direct result of this investigation officials throughout the Government have become much more alert to the problem of the employment of sex perverts in Government and in recent months they have removed a substantial number of these undesirables from public positions. This is evidenced by the fact that action has been taken in 382 sex perversion cases involving civilian employees of Government in the past 7 months, whereas action was taken in only 192 similar cases in the previous 3-year period from January 1, 1947, to April 1, 1950. However, it appears to the subcommittee that some Government officials are not-yet fully aware of the inherent dangers involved in the employment of sex perverts. It is the considered opinion of the subcommittee that Government officials have the responsibility of exercising a high degree of diligence in the handling of the problem of sex perversion, and it is urged that they follow the recommendations of this subcommittee in that regard.

While this subcommittee is convinced that it is in the public interest to get sex perverts out of Government and keep them out, this program should be carried out in a manner consistent with the traditional American concepts of justice and fair play. In order to accomplish this end every reasonable complaint of perverted sex activities on the part of Government employees should be thoroughly investigated and dismissals should be ordered only after a complete review of the facts and in accordance with the present civil-service procedures. These procedures provide that the employee be informed of the charges against him and be given a reasonable time to answer. Furthermore, in view of the very serious consequence of dismissal from the Government on charges of sex perversion, it is believed that consideration should be given to establishing a board of review or similar appeal machinery whereby all persons who are dismissed from the Government on these charges may, if they so desire, have their cases reviewed by higher authority outside of the employing agency. No such appeal machinery exists at the present time.

Although 457 persons who were arrested by police authorities in sex perversion cases in the District of Columbia during the past 4 years indicated that they were employees of the Government at the time of their arrest, information concerning the great majority of these arrests did not come to the attention of the Civil Service Commission or the other agencies of Government until April of this year. This deplorable situation resulted from the lack of proper liaison between the law-enforcement agencies and the departments of Government. The subcommittee is gratified to report that this situation has now been corrected. Since April information concerning Government employees arrested on charges of sex perversion in the District of Columbia and elsewhere has been promptly reported from the FBI to the Civil Service Commission and the employing agencies of Government in order that appropriate action may be taken in each case.

The subcommittee also found that the existing criminal laws in the District of Columbia with regard to acts of sex perversion are inadequate and the subcommittee has drawn up proposed amendments to the District Criminal Code which should materially strengthen these laws. It was also discovered that most of the homosexuals apprehended by the police in the District of Columbia were booked on charges of disorderly conduct. In most cases they were never brought to trial but were allowed to make forfeitures of small cash collateral at police stations. This slipshod method of disposing of these cases with little or no review by the prosecutive or judicial authorities was corrected after the subcommittee brought this situation to the attention of the judges of the municipal court in August 1950.

Since the initiation of this investigation considerable progress has been made in removing homosexuals and similar undesirable employees from positions in the Government. However, it should be borne in mind that the public interest cannot be adequately protected unless responsible officials adopt and maintain a realistic and vigilant attitude toward the problem of sex perverts in the Government. To pussyfoot or to take half measures will allow some known perverts to remain in Government and can result in the dismissal of innocent persons.

In view of the importance of preventing the employment of sex perverts in Government the subcommittee plans to reexamine the situation from time to time to determine if its present recommendations are being followed and to ascertain whether it may be necessary to take other steps to protect the public interest.

THE WOLFENDEN
REPORT

The Wolfenden Report reflects a simultaneous increase in concern by modern governments about homosexuality (with homosexuals as "security risks" becoming scapegoats for "the enemy within") during the cold war and a recognition of a decline in effectiveness of legal proscription in regulating sexual morality. In the construction of a distinction between public decency, which was the law's prerogative to monitor, and private morality, which was to be monitored by the extralegal or supplement to law of religion, family, educational and medical institutions and public opinion via peer pressure (toward preventing or diminishing homosexuality). The report's apparent support for increased individual freedom in the private sphere became a recipe for increased regulation of sexual behavior. Sexuality became officially recognized as something that should be regulated, but that would now be accomplished by more effective means throughout society. What gays and lesbians have called "the closet" is exemplary of this strategy of regulation where, in England, although homosexuality in the "private" domain of one's bedroom was not regulated by law, any "public" expression that implied homosexual conduct, such as holding hands or kissing in public was, and still is, illegal. The legacy of this liberal framework for regulating sexuality remains today, for example in the "don't ask, don't tell" policy regarding gays and lesbians in the U.S. military, and in political struggles over the nature of sexual consent, especially with respect to the age at which such consent can be expressed.

from

THE WOLFENDEN REPORT

from *Part Two, Homosexual Offenses* (1957)

The U.K. Parliamentary Committee on Homosexuality and Prostitution

CHAPTER III
Homosexuality

18. It is important to make a clear distinction between "homosexual offenses" and "homosexuality." . . . homosexuality is a sexual propensity for persons of one's own sex. Homosexuality, then, is a state or condition, and as such does not, and cannot, come within the purview of the criminal law.

19. This definition of homosexuality involves the adoption of some criteria for its recognition. As in other psychological fields, an inference that the propensity exists may be derived from either subjective or objective data, that is, either from what is felt or from what is done by the persons concerned. Either method may lead to fallacious results. In the first place, introspection is neither exhaustive nor infallible; an individual may quite genuinely not be aware of either the existence or the strength of his motivations and propensities, and there is a natural reluctance to acknowledge, even to oneself, a preference which is socially condemned, or to admit to acts that are illegal and liable to a heavy penalty. Rationalization and self-deception can be carried to great lengths, and in certain circumstances lying is also to be expected. Secondly, some of those whose main sexual propensity is for persons of the opposite sex indulge, for a variety of reasons, in homosexual acts. It is known, for example,

that some men who are placed in special circumstances that prohibit contact with the opposite sex (for instance, in prisoner-of-war camps or prisons) indulge in homosexual acts, though they revert to heterosexual behavior when opportunity affords; and it is clear from our evidence that some men who are not predominantly homosexual lend themselves to homosexual practices for financial or other gain. Conversely, many homosexual persons have heterosexual intercourse with or without homosexual fantasies. Furthermore, a homosexual tendency may not be manifested exclusively, or even at all, in sexual fields of behavior, as we explain in paragraph 23 below.

20. There is the further problem how widely the description "homosexual" should be applied. According to the psycho-analytic school, a homosexual component (sometimes conscious, often not) exists in everybody; and if this is correct, homosexuality in this sense is universal. Without going so far as to accept this view *in toto*, it is possible to realize that the issue of latent homosexuality, which we discuss more fully in paragraph 24 below, is relevant to any assessment of the frequency of occurrence of the condition of homosexuality. However, for the purposes of the main body of our report, and in connection with our recommendations, we are strictly speaking concerned only with those who, for whatever reason, commit homosexual offenses.

21. In spite of difficulties such as those we have mentioned in the preceding paragraphs, there is a general measure of agreement on two propositions: (i) that there exists in certain persons a homosexual propensity which varies quantitatively in different individuals and can also vary quantitatively in the same individual at different epochs of life; (ii) that this propensity can affect behavior in a number of ways, some of which are not obviously sexual; although exactly how much and in what ways may be matters for disagreement and dispute.

22. The first of these propositions means that homosexuality as a propensity is not an "all or none" condition, and this view has been abundantly confirmed by the evidence submitted to us. All gradations can exist from apparently exclusive homosexuality without any conscious capacity for arousal by heterosexual stimuli to apparently exclusive heterosexuality, though in the latter case there may be transient and minor homosexual inclinations, for instance in adolescence. According to the psycho-analytic school, all individuals pass through a homosexual phase. Be this as it may, we would agree that a transient homosexual phase in development is very common and should usually cause neither surprise nor concern.

It is interesting that the late Dr. Kinsey, in his study entitled "The Sexual Behavior of the Human Male," formulated this homosexual-heterosexual continuum on a 7-point scale, with a rating of 6 for sexual arousal and activity with other males only, 3 for arousals and acts equally with either sex, 0 for exclusive heterosexuality, and intermediate ratings accordingly. The recognition of the existence of this continuum is, in our opinion, important for two reasons. First, it leads to the conclusion that homosexuals cannot reasonably be regarded as quite separate from the rest of mankind. Secondly, as will be discussed later, it has some relevance in connection with claims made for the success of various forms of treatment.

23. As regards the second proposition, we have already pointed out that a distinction should be drawn between the condition of homosexuality (which relates to the direction of sexual preference) and the acts or behavior resulting from this preference. It is possible to draw a further distinction between behavior which is overtly sexual and behavior, not overtly sexual, from which a latent homosexuality can be inferred.

It must not be thought that the existence of the homosexual propensity necessarily leads to homosexual behavior of an overtly sexual kind. Even where it does, this behavior does not necessarily amount to a homosexual offense; for instance, solitary masturbation with homosexual fantasies is probably the most common homosexual act, many persons, though they are aware of the existence within themselves of the propensity, and though they may be conscious of sexual arousal in the presence of homosexual stimuli, successfully control their urges towards overtly homosexual acts with others, either because of their ethical standards or from fear of social or penal consequences, so that their homosexual condition never manifests itself in overtly sexual behavior. There are others who, though aware of the existence within themselves of the propensity, are helped by a happy family life, a satisfying vocation, or a well-balanced social life to live happily without any urge to indulge in homosexual acts. Our evidence suggests however that complete continence in the homosexual is relatively uncommon—as, indeed, it is in the heterosexual—and that even where the individual is by disposition continent, self-control may break down temporarily under the influence of factors like alcohol, emotional distress or mental or physical disorder or disease.

24. Moreover, it is clear that homosexuals differ one from another in the extent to which they are aware of the existence within themselves of the propensity. Some are, indeed, quite unaware of it, and where this is so the homosexuality is technically described as latent, its existence being inferred from the individual's behavior in spheres not obviously sexual. Although there is room for dispute as to the extent and variety of behavior of this kind which may legitimately be included in the making of this inference, there is general agreement that the existence of a latent homosexuality is an inference validly to be drawn in certain cases. Sometimes, for example, a doctor can infer a homosexual component which accounts for the condition of a patient who has consulted him because of some symptom, discomfort or difficulty, though the patient himself is completely unaware of the existence within himself of any homosexual inclinations. There are other cases in which the existence of a latent homosexuality may be inferred from an individual's outlook or judgment; for instance, a persistent and indignant preoccupation with the subject of homosexuality has been taken to suggest in some cases the existence of repressed homosexuality. Thirdly, among those who work with notable success in occupations which call for service to others, there are some in whom a latent homosexuality provides the motivation for activities of the greatest value to society. Examples of this are to be found among teachers, clergy, nurses and those who are interested in youth movements and the care of the aged.

25. We believe that there would be a wide measure of agreement on the general account of homosexuality and its manifestations that we have given above. On the other hand, the general position which we have tried to summarize permits the drawings of many different inferences, not all of them in our opinion justified. Especially is this so in connection with the concept of "disease." There is a tendency, noticeably increasing in strength over recent years, to label homosexuality as a "disease" or "illness." This may be no more than a particular manifestation of a general tendency discernible in modern society by which, as one leading sociologist puts it, "the concept of illness expands continually at the expense of the concept of moral failure." There are two important practical consequences which are often thought to follow from regarding homosexuality as an illness. The first is that those in whom the condition exists are sick persons and should therefore be regarded as medical problems and consequently as primarily a medical responsibility. The second is that sickness implies irresponsibility, or at least diminished responsibility. Hence it becomes important in this connection to examine the criteria of "disease," and also to examine the claim that these consequences follow.

26. We are informed that there is no legal definition of "disease" or "disease of the mind"; that there is no precise medical definition of disease which covers all its varieties; that health and ill health are relative terms which merge into each other, the "abnormal" being often a matter of degree or of what is accepted as the permissible range of normal variation;

and that doctors are often called upon to deal not only with recognizable diseases, but also with problems of attitude and with anomalies of character and instinct.

The traditional view seems to be that for a condition to be recognized as a disease, three criteria must be satisfied, namely (i) the presence of abnormal symptoms, which are caused by (ii) a demonstrable pathological condition, in turn caused by (iii) some factor called "the cause," each link in this causal chain being understood as something necessarily antecedent to the next. An example would be the invasion of the body by diphtheria bacilli, leading to pathological changes, leading to the symptoms of diphtheria.

While we have found this traditional view a convenient basis for our consideration of the question whether or not homosexuality is a disease, it must be recognized that the three criteria, as formulated above, are oversimplified, and that each needs some modification. Moreover, there are conditions now recognized as diseases though they do not satisfy all three criteria. Our evidence suggests, however, that homosexuality does not satisfy any of them unless the terms in which they are defined are expanded beyond what could reasonably be regarded as legitimate.

27. In relation, first, to the presence of abnormal symptoms, it is nowadays recognized that many people behave in an unusual, extraordinary or socially unacceptable way, but it seems to us that it would be rash to assume that unorthodox or aberrant behavior is necessarily symptomatic of disease if it is the only symptom that can be demonstrated. To make this assumption would be to underestimate the very wide range of "normal" human behavior, and abundant evidence is available that what is socially acceptable or ethically permissible has varied and still varies considerably in different cultures. From the medical standpoint, the existence of significant abnormality can seldom be diagnosed from the mere exhibition of unusual behavior, be this criminal or not, the diagnosis depending on the presence of associated symptoms. Further, a particular form of behavior, taken by itself, can seem to be within the range of the normal but may nevertheless be symptomatic of abnormality, the abnormality consisting in (i) the intensity and duration of the symptoms, (ii) their combination together, and (iii) the circumstances in which they arise. Certain mental diseases, for example, can be diagnosed by the mere association of symptoms to form a recognized psychiatric syndrome, an example of this being schizophrenia, which has no known or generally accepted physical pathology. On the criterion of symptoms, however, homosexuality cannot legitimately be regarded as a disease, because in many cases it is the only symptom and is compatible with full mental health in other respects. In some cases, associated psychiatric abnormalities do occur, and it seems to us that if, as has been suggested, they occur with greater frequency in the homosexual, this may be because they are products of the strain and conflict brought about by the homosexual condition and not because they are causal factors. It has been suggested to us that associated psychiatric abnormalities are less prominent, or even absent, in countries where the homosexual is regarded with more tolerance.

28. As regards the second criterion, namely, the presence of a demonstrable pathological condition, some, though not all, cases of mental illness are accompanied by a demonstrable physical pathology. We have heard no convincing evidence that this has yet been demonstrated in relation to homosexuality. Biochemical and endocrine studies so far carried out in this field have, it appears, proved negative, and investigations of body build and the like have also so far proved inconclusive. We are aware that studies carried out on sets of twins suggest that certain genes lay down a potentiality which will lead to homosexuality in the person who possesses them, but even if this were established (and the results of these studies have not commanded universal acceptance), a genetic predisposition would not necessarily amount to a pathological condition, since it may be no more than a natural biological variation compa-

rable with variations in stature, hair pigmentation, handedness and so on.

In the absence of a physical pathology, psychopathological theories have been constructed to explain the symptoms of various forms of abnormal behavior or mental illness. These theories range from rather primitive formulations like a repressed complex or a mental "abscess" to elaborate systems. They are theoretical constructions to explain observed facts, not the facts themselves, and similar theories have been constructed to explain "normal" behavior. These theoretical constructions differ from school to school. The alleged psychopathological causes adduced for homosexuality have, however, also been found to occur in others besides the homosexual.

29. As regards the third criterion, that is, the "cause," there is never a single cause for normal behavior, abnormal behavior or mental illness. The causes are always multiple. Even the invasion of the body by diphtheria bacilli does not of itself lead to the disease of diphtheria, as is shown by the existence of "carriers" of live diphtheria bacilli. To speak, as some do, of some single factor such as seduction in youth as the "cause" of homosexuality is unrealistic unless other factors are taken into account. Besides genetic predisposition, a number of such factors have been suggested, for instance, unbalanced family relationships, faulty sex education, or lack of opportunity for heterosexual contacts in youth. In the present state of our knowledge, none of these can be held to bear a specific causal relationship to any recognized psychopathology or physical pathology; and to assert a direct and specific causal relationship between these factors and the homosexual condition is to ignore the fact that they have all, including seduction, been observed to occur in persons who become entirely heterosexual in their disposition.

30. Besides the notion of homosexuality as a disease, there have been alternative hypotheses offered by others of our expert witnesses. Some have preferred to regard it as a state of arrested development. Some, particularly among the biologists, regard it as simply a natural deviation. Others, again, regard it as a universal potentiality which can develop in response to a variety of factors.

We do not consider ourselves qualified to pronounce on controversial and scientific problems of this kind, but we feel bound to say that the evidence put before us has not established to our satisfaction the proposition that homosexuality is a disease. Medical witnesses have, however, stressed the point, and it is an important one, that in some cases homosexual offenses do occur as symptoms in the course of recognized mental or physical illness, for example, senile dementia. We have the impression, too, that those whose homosexual offenses stem from some mental illness or defect behave in a way which increases their chances of being caught.

31. Even if it could be established that homosexuality were a disease, it is clear that many individuals, however their state is reached, present social rather than medical problems and must be dealt with by social, including penological, methods. This is especially relevant when the claim that homosexuality is an illness is taken to imply that its treatment should be a medical responsibility. Much more important than the academic question whether homosexuality is a disease is the practical question whether a doctor should carry out any part or all of the treatment. Psychiatrists deal regularly with problems of personality which are not regarded as diseases, and conversely the treatment of cases of recognized psychiatric illness may not be strictly medical but may best be carried out by non-medical supervision or environmental change. Examples would be certain cases of senile dementia or chronic schizophrenia which can best be managed at home. In fact, the treatment of behavior disorders, even when medically supervised, is rarely confined to psychotherapy or to treatment of a strictly medical kind. This is not to deny that expert advice should be sought in very many

homosexual cases. We shall have something more to say on these matters in connection with the treatment of offenders.

32. The claim that homosexuality is an illness carries the further implication that the sufferer cannot help it and therefore carries a diminished responsibility for his actions. Even if it were accepted that homosexuality could properly be described as a "disease," we should not accept this corollary. There are no *prima facie* grounds for supposing that because a particular person's sexual propensity happens to lie in the direction of persons of his or her own sex it is any less controllable than that of those whose propensity is for persons of the opposite sex. We are informed that patients in mental hospitals, with few exceptions, show clearly by their behavior that they can and do exercise a high degree of responsibility and self-control; for example, only a small minority need to be kept in locked wards. The existence of varying degrees of self-control is a matter of daily experience—the extent to which coughing can be controlled is an example—and the capacity for self-control can vary with the personality structure or with temporary physical or emotional conditions. The question which is important for us here is whether the individual suffers from a condition which causes diminished responsibility. This is a different question from the question whether he was responsible in the past for the causes or origins of his present condition. That is an interesting inquiry and may be of relevance in other connections; but our concern is with the behavior which flows from the individual's present condition and with the extent to which he is responsible for that behavior, whatever may have been the causes of the condition from which it springs. Just as expert opinion can give valuable assistance in deciding on the appropriate ways of dealing with a convicted person, so can it help in assessing the additional factors that may affect his present responsibility.

33. Some psychiatrists have made the point that homosexual behavior in some cases may be "compulsive," that is, irresistible, but there seems to be no good reason to suppose that at least in the majority of cases homosexual acts are any more or any less resistible than heterosexual acts, and other evidence would be required to sustain such a view in any individual case. Even if immunity from penal sanctions on such grounds were claimed or granted, nevertheless preventive measures would have to be taken for the sake of society at large, in much the same way as it is necessary to withhold a driving license from a person who is subject to epileptic fits. This is particularly true of the offender who is a very bad risk for recurrence, but is not certifiable either as insane or as a mental defective.

34. When questions of treatment or disposal of offenders are being considered, the assessment of prognosis is very important, and expert advice may need to be sought on such questions as whether the factors that in the view of the doctors lead to diminished control, that is, diminished "responsibility," are capable of modification, or what environmental changes should be advocated or ordered to reduce the chances of a recurrence. Thus it is just as reasonable for a doctor to recommend that a paedophiliac should give up school-mastering as it would be to recommend to another patient never to return to a hot climate.

35. Some writers on the subject, and some of our witnesses, have drawn a distinction between the "invert" and the "pervert." We have not found this distinction very useful. It suggests that it is possible to distinguish between two men who commit the same offense, the one as the result of his constitution, the other from a perverse and deliberate choice, with the further suggestion that the former is in some sense less culpable than the latter. To make this distinction as a matter of definition seems to prejudge a very difficult question.

Similarly, we have avoided the use of the terms "natural" and "unnatural" in relation to sexual behavior, for they depend for their force upon certain explicit theological or philosophical interpretations, and without these interpretations their use imports an approving or a condemnatory note into a discussion where dispassionate thought and statement should not be hindered by adherence to particular preconceptions.

36. Homosexuality is not, in spite of widely held belief to the contrary, peculiar to members of particular professions or social classes; nor, as is sometimes supposed, is it peculiar to the *intelligentsia*. Our evidence shows that it exists among all callings and at all levels of society; and that among homosexuals will be found not only those possessing a high degree of intelligence, but also the dullest oafs.

Some homosexuals, it is true, choose to follow occupations which afford opportunities for contact with those of their own sex, and it is not unnatural that those who feel themselves to be "misfits" in society should gravitate towards occupations offering an atmosphere of tolerance or understanding, with the result that some occupations may appear to attract more homosexuals than do others. Again, the arrest of a prominent national or local figure has greater news value than the arrest of (say) a laborer for a similar offense, and in consequence the Press naturally finds room for a report of the one where it might not find room for a report of the other. Factors such as these may well account to some extent for the prevalent misconceptions . . .

CHAPTER IV
The Extent of the Problem

44. Some of us have a definite impression, derived from what we have observed or read, and by inference from the tenor of evidence submitted to us, that there has been an increase in the amount of homosexual behavior. Others of us prefer, in the absence of conclusive evidence, not to commit themselves to expressing even a general impression.

45. Those who have the impression of a growth in homosexual practices find it supported by at least three wider considerations. First, in the general loosening of former moral standards, it would not be surprising to find that leniency towards sexual irregularities in general included also an increased tolerance of homosexual behavior and that greater tolerance had encouraged the practice. Secondly, the conditions of war time, with broken families and prolonged separation of the sexes, may well have occasioned homosexual behavior which in some cases has been carried over into peace time. Thirdly, it is likely that the emotional insecurity, community instability and weakening of the family, inherent in the social changes of our civilization, have been factors contributing to an increase in homosexual behavior.

Most of us think it improbable that the increase in the number of offenses recorded as known to the police can be explained entirely by greater police activity, though we all think it very unlikely that homosexual behavior has increased proportionately to the dramatic rise in the number of offenses recorded as known to the police.

46. Our medical evidence seems to show three things: first, that in general practice male homosexuals form a very small fraction of the doctor's patients; secondly, that in psychiatric practice male homosexuality is a primary problem in a very small proportion of the cases seen; and thirdly, that only a very small percentage of homosexuals consult doctors about their condition. It is almost impossible to compare the incidence of homosexual behavior with the incidence of other forms of sexual irregularity, most of which are outside the purview of the criminal law and are therefore not recorded in criminal statistics; our impression is that of the total amount of irregular sexual conduct, homosexual behavior provides only a very small proportion. It cannot, however, be ignored. The male population of Great Britain over the age of fifteen numbers nearly eighteen million, which are the lowest figures relating to incidence that have come to our notice, are at all applicable to this country, the incidence of homosexuality and homosexual behavior must be

large enough to present a serious problem.

47. Our conclusion is that homosexual behavior is practiced by a small minority of the population, and should be seen in proper perspective, neither ignored nor given a disproportionate amount of public attention. Especially are we concerned that the principles we have enunciated above on the function of the law should apply to those involved in homosexual behavior no more and no less than to other persons . . .

CHAPTER V

The Present Law and Practice

48. It is against the foregoing background that we have reviewed the existing provisions of the law in relation to homosexual behavior between male persons. We have found that with the great majority of these provisions we are in complete agreement. We believe that it is part of the function of the law to safeguard those who need protection by reason of their youth or some mental defect, and we do not wish to see any change in the law that would weaken this protection. Men who commit offenses against such persons should be treated as criminal offenders. Whatever may be the causes of their disposition or the proper treatment for it, the law must assume that the responsibility for the overt acts remains theirs, except where there are circumstances which it accepts as exempting from accountability. Offenses of this kind are particularly reprehensible when the men who commit them are in positions of special responsibility or trust. We have been made aware that where a man is involved in an offense with a boy or youth the invitation to the commission of the act sometimes comes from him rather than from the man. But we believe that even when this is so that fact does not serve to exculpate the man.

49. It is also part of the function of the law to preserve public order and decency. We therefore hold that when homosexual behavior between males takes place in public it should continue to be dealt with by the criminal law. Not all the elements in the apprehension of offenders, or in their trial, seem to us to be satisfactory, and on these points we comment later. But so far as the law itself is concerned we should not wish to see any major change in relation to this type of offense.

50. Besides the two categories of offense we have just mentioned, namely, offenses committed by adults with juveniles and offenses committed in public places, there is a third class of offense to which we have had to give long and careful consideration. It is that of homosexual acts committed between adults in private . . .

52. . . . We have reached the conclusion that legislation which covers acts in the third category we have mentioned goes beyond the proper sphere of the law's concern. We do not think that it is proper for the law to concern itself with what a man does in private unless it can be shown to be so contrary to the public good that the law ought to intervene in its function as the guardian of that public good.

53. In considering whether homosexual acts between consenting adults in private should cease to be criminal offenses we have examined the more serious arguments in favor of retaining them as such. We now set out these arguments and our reasons for disagreement with them. In favor of retaining the present law, it has been contended that homosexual behavior between adult males, in private no less than in public, is contrary to the public good on the grounds that—

(i) it menaces the health of society;

(ii) it has damaging effects on family life;

(iii) a man who indulges in these practices with another man may turn his attention to boys.

54. As regards the first of these arguments, it is held that conduct of this kind is a cause of the demoralization and decay of civilizations, and that therefore, unless we wish to see our nation degenerate and decay, such conduct must be stopped, by every possible means. We have found no evidence to support this view, and we cannot feel it right to frame the laws which should govern this country in the present age by reference to hypothetical explanations of the history of other peoples in ages distant in time and different in circumstances from our own. In so far as the basis of this argument can be precisely formulated, it is often no more than the expression of revulsion against what is regarded as unnatural, sinful or disgusting. Many people feel this revulsion, for one or more of these reasons. But moral conviction or instinctive feeling, however strong, is not a valid basis for overriding the individual's privacy and for bringing within the ambit of the criminal law private sexual behavior of this kind. It is held also that if such men are employed in certain professions or certain branches of the public service their private habits may render them liable to threats of blackmail or to other pressures which may make them "bad security risks." If this is true, it is true also of some other categories of person: for example, drunkards, gamblers and those who become involved in compromising situations of a heterosexual kind; and while it may be a valid ground for excluding from certain forms of employment men who indulge in homosexual behavior, it does not, in our view, constitute a sufficient reason for making their private sexual behavior an offense in itself.

55. The second contention, that homosexual behavior between males has a damaging effect on family life, may well be true. Indeed, we have had evidence that it often is; cases in which homosexual behavior on the part of the husband has broken up a marriage are by no means rare, and there are also cases in which a man in whom the homosexual component is relatively weak nevertheless derives such satisfaction from homosexual outlets that he does not enter upon a marriage which might have been successfully and happily consummated. We deplore this damage to what we regard as the basic unit of society; but cases are also frequently encountered in which a marriage has been broken up by homosexual behavior on the part of the wife, and no doubt some women, too, derive sufficient satisfaction from homosexual outlets to prevent their marrying. We have had no reasons shown to us which would lead us to believe that homosexual behavior between males inflicts any greater damage on family life than adultery, fornication or lesbian behavior. These practices are all reprehensible from the point of view of harm to the family, but it is difficult to see why on this ground male homosexual behavior alone among them should be a criminal offense. This argument is not to be taken as saying that society should condone or approve male homosexual behavior. But where adultery, fornication and lesbian behavior are not criminal offenses there seems to us to be no valid ground, on the basis of damage to the family, for so regarding homosexual behavior between men. Moreover, it has to be recognized that the mere existence of the condition of homosexuality in one of the partners can result in an unsatisfactory marriage, so that for a homosexual to marry simply for the sake of conformity with the accepted structure of society or in the hope of curing his condition may result in disaster.

56. We have given anxious consideration to the third argument, that an adult male who has sought as his partner another adult male may turn from such a relationship and seek as his partner a boy or succession of boys. We should certainly not wish to countenance any proposal which might tend to increase offenses against minors. Indeed, if we thought that any recommendation for a change in the law would increase the danger to minors we should not make it. But in this matter we have been much influenced by our expert witnesses. They are in no doubt that whatever may be the origins of the homosexual condition, there are two recognizably different categories among adult male homosexuals. There are those who seek

as partners other adult males, and there are paedophiliacs, that is to say men who seek as partners boys who have not reached puberty.

57. We are authoritatively informed that a man who has homosexual relations with an adult partner seldom turns to boys, and vice versa, though it is apparent from the police reports we have seen and from other evidence submitted to us that such cases do happen . . . But paedophiliacs, together with the comparatively few who are indiscriminate, will continue to be liable to the sanctions of criminal law, exactly as they are now. And the others would be very unlikely to change their practices and turn to boys simply because their present practices were made legal. It would be paradoxical if the making legal of an act at present illegal were to turn men towards another kind of act which is, and would remain, contrary to the law. Indeed, it has been put to us that to remove homosexual behavior between adult males from the listed crimes may serve to protect minors; with the law as it is there may be some men who would prefer an adult partner but who at present turn their attention to boys because they consider that this course is less likely to lay them open to prosecution or to blackmail than if they sought other adults as their partners. If the law were changed in the way we suggest, it is at least possible that such men would prefer to seek relations with older persons which would not render them liable to prosecution. In this connection, information we have received from the police authorities in the Netherlands suggests that practicing homosexuals in that country are to some extent turning from those practices which are punishable under the criminal law to other practices which are not. Our evidence, in short, indicates that the fear that the legalization of homosexual acts between adults will lead to similar acts with boys has not enough substance to justify the treatment of adult homosexual behavior in private as a criminal offense, and suggests that it would be more likely that such a change in the law would protect boys rather than endanger them.

58. In addition, an argument of a more general character in favor of retaining the present law has been put to us by some of our witnesses. It is that to change the law in such a way that homosexual acts between consenting adults in private ceased to be criminal offenses must suggest to the average citizen a degree of toleration by the Legislature of homosexual behavior, and that such a change would "open the floodgates" and result in unbridled license. It is true that a change of this sort would amount to a limited degree of such toleration, but we do not share the fears of our witnesses that the change would have the effect they expect. This expectation seems to us to exaggerate the effect of the law on human behavior. It may well be true that the present law deters from homosexual acts some who would otherwise commit them, and to that extent an increase in homosexual behavior can be expected. But it is no less true that if the amount of homosexual behavior has, in fact, increased in recent years, then the law has failed to act as an effective deterrent. It seems to us that the law itself probably makes little difference to the amount of homosexual behavior which actually occurs; whatever the law may be there will always be strong social forces opposed to homosexual behavior. It is highly improbable that the man to whom homosexual behavior is repugnant would find it any less repugnant because the law permitted it in certain circumstances; so that even if, as has been suggested to us, homosexuals tend to proselytize, there is no valid reason for supposing that any considerable number of conversions would follow the change in the law.

59. . . . In only very few European countries does the criminal law now take cognizance of homosexual behavior between consenting parties in private. It is not possible to make any useful statistical comparison between the situation in countries where the law tolerates such behavior and that in countries where all male homosexuals acts are punishable, if only because in the former the acts do not reflect themselves in criminal statistics. We have, how-

ever, caused inquiry to be made in Sweden, where homosexual acts between consenting adults in private ceased to be criminal offenses in consequence of an amendment of the law in 1944. We asked particularly whether the amendment of the law had had any discernible effect on the prevalence of homosexual practices, and on this point the authorities were able to say no more than that very little was known about the prevalence of such practices either before or after the change in the law. We think it reasonable to assume that if the change in the law had produced any appreciable increase in homosexual behavior or any large-scale proselytizing, these would have become apparent to the authorities . . .

61. . . .We have outlined the arguments against a change in the law, and we recognize their weight. We believe, however, that they have been met by the counter-arguments we have already advanced. There remains one additional counter-argument which we believe to be decisive, namely, the importance which society and the law ought to give to individual freedom of choice and action in matters of private morality. Unless a deliberate attempt is to be made by society, acting through the agency of the law, to equate the sphere of crime with that of sin, there must remain a realm of private morality and immorality which is, in brief and crude terms, not the law's business. To say this is not to condone or encourage private immorality. On the contrary, to emphasize the personal and private nature of moral or immoral conduct is to emphasize the personal and private responsibility of the individual for his own actions, and that is a responsibility which a mature agent can properly be expected to carry for himself without the threat of punishment from the law.

62. . . .We accordingly recommend that homosexual behavior between consenting adults in private should no longer be a criminal offense.

63. This proposal immediately raises three questions: What is meant by "consenting"; What is meant by "in private"; What is meant by "adult"?

So far as concerns the first of these, we should expect that the question whether or not there has been "consent" in a particular case would be decided by the same criteria as apply to heterosexual acts between adults. We should expect, for example, that a "consent" which had been obtained by fraud or threats of violence would be no defense to a criminal charge; and that a criminal charge would also lie where drugs had been used to render the partner incapable of giving or withholding consent, or where the partner was incapable for some other reason (for example, mental defect) of giving a valid consent.

We are aware that the quality of the consent may vary; consent may amount to anything from an eager response to a grudging submission. We are aware, too, that money, gifts or hospitality are sometimes used to induce consent. But these considerations apply equally to heterosexual relationships, and we find in them no ground for differentiating, so far as the behavior of adults is concerned, between homosexual and heterosexual relationships.

64. . . .Our words "in private" are not intended to provide a legal definition. Many heterosexual acts are not criminal if committed in private but are punishable if committed in circumstances which outrage public decency, and we should expect the same criteria to apply to homosexual acts. It is our intention that the law should continue to regard as criminal any indecent act committed in a place where members of the public may be likely to see and be offended by it, but where there is no possibility of public offense of this nature it becomes a matter of the private responsibility of the persons concerned and as such, in our opinion, is outside the proper purview of the criminal law. It will be for the courts to decide, in cases of doubt, whether or not public decency has been outraged, and we cannot see that there would be any greater difficulty about establishing this in the case of homosexual acts than there is at present in the case of heterosexual acts.

65. The question of the age at which a man is to be regarded as "adult" is much more

difficult. A wide range of ages has been covered by proposals made in the evidence which has been offered to us by our witnesses. On the analogy of heterosexual behavior there is a case for making the age sixteen, for heterosexual acts committed by consenting partners over that age in private are not criminal. At the other end of the scale an age as high as thirty was suggested. Within these two extremes, the ages most frequently suggested to us have been eighteen and twenty-one.

66. It seems to us that there are four sets of considerations which should govern the decision on this point. The first is connected with the need to protect young and immature persons; the second is connected with the age at which the pattern of a man's sexual development can be said to be fixed; the third is connected with the meaning of the word "adult" in the sense of "responsible for his own actions"; and the fourth is connected with the consequences which would follow from the fixing of any particular age. Unfortunately, these various considerations may not all lead to the same answer.

67. So far as concerns the first set of considerations, we have made it clear throughout our report that we recognize the need for protecting the young and immature. But this argument can be pressed too far; there comes a time when a young man can properly be expected to "stand on his own feet" in this as in other matters, and we find it hard to believe that he needs to be protected from would-be seducers more carefully than a girl does. It could indeed be argued that in a simply physical sense he is better able to look after himself than she is. On this view, there would be some ground for making sixteen the age of "adulthood," since sexual intercourse with a willing girl of this age is not unlawful.

68. We have given special attention to the evidence which has been given to us in connection with the second set of considerations—those which relate the notion of "adulthood" to a recognizable age in the fixation of a young man's sexual pattern—for we should not wish to see legalized any forms of behavior which would swing towards a permanent habit of homosexual behavior a young man who without such encouragement would still be capable of developing a normal habit of heterosexual adult life. On this point we have been offered many and conflicting opinions which agree however in admitting the difficulty of equating stabilization of sexual pattern with a precise chronological age. Our medical witnesses were unanimously of the view that the main sexual pattern is laid down in the early years of life, and the majority of them held that it was usually fixed, in main outline, by the age of sixteen. Many held that it was fixed much earlier. On this ground again, then, it would seem that sixteen would be an appropriate age.

69. We now turn to the third set of considerations, that is, the age at which a person may be regarded as sufficiently adult to take decisions about his private conduct and to carry the responsibility for their consequences. In other fields of behavior the law recognizes the age of twenty-one as being appropriate for decisions of this kind: for example, this is the age at which a man is deemed to be capable of entering into legal contracts, including (in England and Wales) the contract of marriage, on his own responsibility. Apart altogether from legal or medical technicalities, we believe that it would be generally accepted, as a matter of ordinary usage, that "adult" means, broadly speaking, "of the age of twenty-one or more"; and we believe that it is, as a matter of common sense, reasonable to accept this as designating the age at which a man is regarded as being maturely responsible for his actions.

70. To suggest that the age of adulthood for the purposes we have in mind should be twenty-one leads us to the fourth set of considerations we have mentioned, namely, the consequences which would follow from the decision about any particular age. To fix the age at twenty-one (or indeed at any age above seventeen) raises particular difficulties in this connection, for it involves leaving liable to prosecution a young man of almost twenty-one for actions

which in a few days' time he could perform without breaking the law. This difficulty would admittedly arise whatever age was decided upon, for it would always be the case that an action would be illegal a few days below that age and legal above it. But this difficulty would present itself in a less acute form if the age were fixed at eighteen, which is the other age most frequently suggested to us. For whereas it would be difficult to regard a young man of nearly twenty-one charged with a homosexual offense as a suitable subject for "care or protection" under the provisions of the Children and Young Persons Acts, it would not be entirely inappropriate so to regard a youth under eighteen. If the age of adulthood for the purposes of our amendment were fixed at eighteen, and if the "care or protection" provisions were extended to cover young persons up to that age, there would be a means of dealing with homosexual behavior by those under that age without invoking the penal sanctions of the criminal law.

71. There must obviously be an element of arbitrariness in any decision on this point; but all things considered the legal age of contractual responsibility seems to us to afford the best criterion for the definition of adulthood in this respect. While there are some grounds for fixing the age as low as sixteen, it is obvious that however "mature" a boy of that age may be as regards physical development or psycho-sexual make-up, and whatever analogies may be drawn from the law relating to offenses against young girls, a boy is incapable, at the age of sixteen, of forming a mature judgment about actions of a kind which might have the effect of setting him apart from the rest of society. The young man between eighteen and twenty-one may be expected to be rather more mature in this respect. We have, however, encountered several cases in which young men have been induced by means of gifts of money or hospitality to indulge in homosexual behavior with older men, and we have felt obliged to have regard to the large numbers of young men who leave their homes at or about the age of eighteen and, either for their employment or their education or to fulfill their national service obligations, are then for the first time launched into the world in circumstances which render them particularly vulnerable to advances of this sort. It is arguable that such men should be expected, as one of the conditions of their being considered sufficiently grown-up to leave home, to be able to look after themselves in this respect also, the more so if they are being trained for responsibility in the services or in civil life. Some of us feel, on various grounds, that the age of adulthood should be fixed at twenty-one, not because we think that to fix the age at eighteen would result in any greater readiness on the part of young men between eighteen and twenty-one to lend themselves to homosexual practices than exists at present, but because to fix it at eighteen would lay them open to attentions and pressures of an undesirable kind from which the adoption of the later age would help to protect them, and from which they ought, in view of their special vulnerability, to be protected. We therefore recommend that for the purpose of the amendment of the law which we have proposed, the age at which a man is deemed to be an adult should be twenty-one . . .

75. Since it is a defense to a first charge of sexual intercourse with a girl under sixteen that the man, if he is under the age of twenty-four, had reasonable cause for believing that the girl was over sixteen, we have considered whether a similar defense should be available to a man, up to the age to be specified, who had committed a homosexual act with a young man under twenty-one in the belief that he was above that age. We do not believe that it should. This defense applies only in the special case we have mentioned; it applies only to offenders within an age-range specified on no very clear grounds, and we see no valid reason for importing into the homosexual field a provision designed to deal with a particular heterosexual offense . . .

Buggery (Sodomy)

78. As the law at present stands, it singles out buggery from other homosexual offenses

and prescribes a maximum penalty of life imprisonment . . . the offense of buggery is, in practice, punished more severely than other forms of homosexual behavior even when committed in similar circumstances, and we have accordingly considered whether any justification exists, from the point of view either of the offender or the offense itself, for the imposition of heavier penalties in respect of this particular form of behavior.

79. As regards the offender, some of our witnesses, more particularly our judicial and police witnesses, have suggested to us that those who commit buggery possess poorer personalities and tend to be more generally antisocial than those whose homosexual behavior takes other forms. It was also suggested to us that they are more inclined to repeat their offenses; and a few of our medical witnesses held that those who indulged in buggery responded less satisfactorily to treatment than other homosexual offenders.

80. We have found no convincing evidence to support these suggestions. It has to be borne in mind that there are many homosexuals whose behavior never comes to the notice of the police or the courts, and it is probable that the police and the courts see only the worst cases; the more antisocial type of person is more likely to attract the attention of the police than the discreet person with a well-developed social sense. Moreover, those of our medical witnesses who thought that those who indulged in buggery responded less well to treatment than other homosexual offenders were doctors who saw a high proportion of persons on a criminal charge, so that here again the sample would tend to be representative of the more antisocial types.

81. From information supplied to us by the Prison Commissioners it would appear that there is no significant difference in social, occupational or educational level as between those who had been convicted of buggery and those whose offenses took other forms. This was confirmed by the evidence of our medical witnesses who, almost unanimously, found no significant difference from other practicing homosexuals in personality, social or economic success, stability or social worth. The information supplied by the Prison Commissioners also indicates that the proportion of male prostitutes is no higher among those convicted of buggery than among those convicted of other homosexual offenses. Moreover, medical evidence, while granting that individuals did differ in their preferences, suggested that the majority of practicing homosexuals indulged at some time or other in all types of homosexual acts, both actively and passively, and the police reports we have seen tend to confirm this.

82. The suggestion that those who indulge in buggery are more inclined to repeat their offenses is not borne out by our statistical evidence . . . offenders convicted of buggery are in a similar category, as regards the numbers of their previous offenses, homosexual or otherwise, to those convicted of other homosexual offenses, and include a larger proportion of first offenders than some other classes of offenders. In so far, therefore, as the frequency of conviction can be taken as an index of persistence in crime, these figures suggest that persons who commit buggery are no more prone to repeat their offenses than those convicted of other homosexual offenses. They also show that they are less prone to repeat them than some other classes of offenders.

83. On the question of treatability, the evidence submitted to us by the Prison Commissioners indicated that there was no significant difference, as between those convicted of buggery and those convicted of other homosexual offenses, in the proportions found suitable for treatment, accepted for treatment or benefiting from treatment, and our medical evidence on the whole confirms this view.

84. If, therefore, the question of the maximum penalty were to be considered simply in relation to its deterrent effect on the particular offender or to the possibility of successful treatment, there would be no clear case for attaching to buggery a penalty heavier than that

applicable to other homosexual offenses.

85. As regards the offense itself, the risk of physical injury to the passive partner, especially if young, has been mentioned to us as a justification for attaching a specially heavy penalty to buggery. Our evidence suggests that cases in which physical injury results from the act of buggery are very rare. Moreover, there are other forms of homosexual behavior which are no less likely to result in physical damage; and since the general law provides for the punishment of acts causing bodily harm, there is no apparent justification for attaching a special penalty to buggery on the ground that it might cause physical injury. It seems probable, too, that a homosexual act which caused bodily harm would amount in most cases to an "indecent assault," and the present maximum penalty of ten years' imprisonment for indecent assault allows sufficiently for any case in which physical injury is caused.

86. There remains the possibility of emotional or psychological damage, whether in the sense of producing homosexual deviation or in the sense of producing more general damage of an emotional or moral kind. In the first sense, this possibility arises only in relation to offenses with boys or youths, since the direction of sexual preference is usually fixed at an early age. Homosexual behavior between adults is not likely to affect the direction of the sexual preference of the participants, so that the question does not arise in relation to homosexual behavior between adults even in those cases where we propose that this should remain amenable to the criminal law. As regards offenses with young persons, it will be apparent from what we say elsewhere that we are not convinced that homosexual behavior is a decisive factor in the production of the homosexual condition; and even in those cases where seduction in youth can legitimately be regarded as one of the factors in producing the condition, our medical evidence suggests that this result is dependent more on the make-up of the individual boy or youth than on the nature of the physical act to which he was subjected. On the question of more general emotional or moral damage, our medical witnesses regarded this as depending more on the surrounding circumstances, including the kind of approach made and the emotional relationships between the partners, than on the specific nature of the homosexual act committed.

87. There is therefore no convincing case for attaching a heavier penalty to buggery on the ground that it may result in greater physical, emotional or moral harm to the victim than other forms of homosexual behavior.

88. Other arguments of a more general kind have, however, been adduced in favor of the retention of buggery as a separate offense. It is urged that there is a long and weighty tradition in our law that this, the "abominable crime" (as earlier statutes call it), is in its nature distinct from other forms of indecent assault or gross indecency; that there is in the minds of many people a stronger instinctive revulsion from this particular form of behavior than from any other; that it is particularly objectionable because it involves coition and thus simulates more nearly than any other homosexual act the normal act of heterosexual intercourse; that it may sometimes approximate in the homosexual field to rape in the heterosexual; and that it therefore ought to remain a distinct offense with a maximum penalty equivalent to that for rape.

89. We believe that there is some case for retaining buggery as a separate offense: and there may even be a case for retaining the present maximum penalty of life imprisonment for really serious cases (for example, those in which repeated convictions have failed to deter a man from committing offenses against young boys, or cases in which serious physical injury is caused in circumstances approximating to rape), though cases of this sort would fall into the category of indecent assault, and we think that the maximum penalty of ten years' imprisonment which we propose for indecent assault should normally suffice for even

the most serious cases. But it is ludicrous that two consenting parties should be liable to imprisonment for life simply because the act of indecency takes a particular form, while they would be liable to only two years' imprisonment if the act took some other form which may be no less repulsive to ordinary people; and if the law were to be changed in the sense we propose in paragraph 62 above, it would be even more ludicrous that two young men just under twenty-one should be liable to imprisonment for life for an act they could perform with impunity a little later on, or that two men over twenty-one should be liable to imprisonment for life because they happened to be found committing in public an act which, if committed in private, would not be criminal at all.

90. We appreciate that in determining the appropriate sentence the courts have regard to the circumstances of the particular case, and in practice it is most unlikely that the courts would ever contemplate imposing life imprisonment for offenses committed between consenting parties, whether in private or in public. But . . . the courts inflict heavier sentences for buggery than they do for gross indecency even where the offenses are committed between consenting parties; and as long as the law provides the maximum penalty of life imprisonment for buggery without any regard to the circumstances in which the offense is committed, this is likely to be the case. We feel, therefore, that although it may be appropriate that the law should distinguish in some way between buggery and other homosexual acts, and although there may be a case for retaining the present maximum penalty for buggery in certain circumstances, the law ought, in defining the offenses, and in prescribing the penalties to be attached thereto, to have regard to their gravity as measured by the circumstances surrounding their commission, and not merely to the nature of the physical act. An offense by a man with a boy or youth, for example, is a more serious matter than a similar offense with a partner of comparable age; and an act committed with an unwilling partner is more serious than one carried out by mutual consent. There is no new principle involved here: sexual intercourse with a girl under 13 is punishable with life imprisonment, while sexual intercourse with a girl over 13 but under 16 carries only two years' imprisonment; breaking and entering a dwelling house with intent to commit a felony is punishable with life imprisonment if committed by night, but with seven years' imprisonment if committed in the day time; and so on.

91. We recognize that it would not be practicable to provide in this way for every conceivable set of circumstances in which a homosexual act could take place, but it is possible to devise a few broad categories, each carrying a maximum penalty within which the courts would be able to pass sentences commensurate with the gravity of the particular offense. We accordingly recommend that the following offenses should be recognized, and we suggest the maximum penalties for them:

Offense / **Suggested maximum penalty**
(a) Buggery with a boy under the age of sixteen / **Life imprisonment** (as at present)
(b) Indecent assault. (This would embrace all acts of buggery or gross indecency committed against the will of the partner, whatever his age; it would also cover, except for the special case mentioned in the footnote to paragraph 114 below, all acts of gross indecency committed with boys under sixteen.) / **Ten years' imprisonment** (as at present in England and Wales)
(c) Buggery or gross indecency committed by a man over twenty-one with a person of or above the age of sixteen but below the age of twenty-one, in circumstances not amounting to an indecent assault. / **Five years' imprisonment**
(d) Buggery or gross indecency committed in any other circumstances (that is, by a person under twenty-one with a consenting partner of or above the age of sixteen; or by any persons in public in circumstances which do not attract the higher penalties; or the special case mentioned in the footnote to paragraph 114). / **Two years' imprisonment**

93. It has not escaped us that the offense of buggery as known to the present law comprises some acts which are not homosexual offenses and which are accordingly outside our terms of reference . . . We assume, however, that if our recommendations are adopted, the Legislature will make corresponding adjustments, if it deems them necessary, in the penalties attaching to buggery in its other forms.

94. In English law, buggery is classified as a felony. A person who knows that a felony has been committed himself commits a criminal offense, known as misprision of felony, if he fails to reveal it to the proper authorities. In practice, prosecutions for misprision of felony are extremely rare; there is, indeed, now some doubt about what the ingredients of the offense are. But it has been suggested to us that a doctor who fails to report to the proper authorities an act of buggery disclosed to him by a patient is technically liable to such prosecution, and that this fact may make some homosexuals reluctant to confide in a doctor. We think that anything which tends to discourage a homosexual from seeking medical advice is to be deprecated. Further, it is important that doctors called upon to furnish medical reports for the information of the courts should enjoy the full confidence of the person under examination if an accurate prognosis is to be made. This is not likely to be the case if the person being examined feels, rightly or wrongly, that the doctor is under an obligation to reveal to the court every act of buggery disclosed in the course of the examination. We accordingly recommend that buggery, if it is retained as a separate offense, should be reclassified as a misdemeanor.

Indecent Assault

95. An indecent assault has been defined by the courts as "an assault accompanied by circumstances of indecency on the part of the person assaulting towards the person alleged to have been assaulted." The law applies irrespective of the person by whom the assault was committed, but our terms of reference apply only to assault by persons of the same sex as the victim. It is a defense to a charge of indecent assault that the person alleged to have been assaulted consented to what was done to him, but a child under sixteen cannot, in law, give any such consent, nor can a mental defective. Where, therefore, the victim is under sixteen, or is mentally defective, an act which could not in the ordinary sense of the word be regarded as an assault becomes one in law simply by reason of the victim's incapacity to give "consent" to what is done to him. Accordingly, an act amounting in law to an indecent assault does not necessarily involve any violence towards the "victim"; indeed, we have evidence that offenders frequently approach their victims with gentleness, and there is no doubt, too, that in many cases the child is a willing party to, and in some cases even the instigator of, the act which takes place. For example, only 43 per cent of the 524 boys under sixteen involved in the sexual offenses covered by the Cambridge survey showed any resentment or offered any objection to the misconduct of the offenders.

96. In many cases, too, the misbehavior which constitutes the "assault" is of a relatively minor character; frequently it amounts to no more than placing the hands on or under the clothing of the victim and handling, or attempting to handle, the private parts; in some cases it may amount to nothing more than horseplay. The Cambridge survey shows that of 624 male victims of sexual offenses only 21 (3.4 per cent) received any physical injury. Seventeen of these received slight injuries only, and four received considerably bodily injury requiring medical attention. Unfortunately we have no figures distinguishing between cases in which the offender was charged with indecent assault and those in which he was charged with another offense, for example, buggery or gross indecency. If, as is likely, the cases in which the victim received some physical injury were cases in which the act of buggery had been perpetrated, it follows that the proportion of cases in which injury is caused by indecent

assaults not involving buggery is even smaller.

97. One consequence of homosexual behavior with young persons can, however, be serious and detrimental. Even where no resistance is offered or no physical harm ensues, there may be considerable damage to the moral and emotional development of the victim. For example, a boy or youth who is induced by means of gifts, whether in money or in kind, to participate in homosexual behavior, may come to regard such behavior as a source of easy money or as a means of enjoying material comforts or other pleasures beyond those which he could expect by decent behavior, and we have encountered cases where this has happened. Indeed, it is our opinion that this sort of corruption is a more likely consequence than the possible conversion of the victim to a condition of homosexuality.

98. It is a view widely held, and one which found favor among our police and legal witnesses, that seduction in youth is the decisive factor in the production of homosexuality as a condition, and we are aware that this view has done much to alarm parents and teachers. We have found no convincing evidence in support of this contention. Our medical witnesses unanimously hold that seduction has little effect in inducing a settled pattern of homosexual behavior, and we have been given no grounds from other sources which contradict their judgment. Moreover, it has been suggested to us that the fact of being seduced often does less harm to the victim than the publicity which attends the criminal proceedings against the offender and the distress which undue alarm sometimes leads parents to show . . .

Indecent Assaults by Females on Females

103. Since an indecent assault by one female on another could take the form of a homosexual act, we have included indecent assaults on females by females in the lists of homosexual offenses . . . We have, however, found no case in which a female has been convicted of an act with another female which exhibits the libidinous features that characterize sexual acts between males. We are aware that the criminal statistics occasionally show females as having been convicted of indecent assaults on females; but on inquiry we find that this is due in the main to the practice of including in the figures relating to any particular offense not only those convicted of the offense itself, but also those convicted of aiding and abetting the commission of the offense. Thus, a woman convicted of aiding and abetting a man to commit an indecent assault on a female would be shown in the statistics as having herself committed such an assault.

Gross Indecency between Males

104. It is an offense for a male person (a) to commit an act of gross indecency with another male person, whether in public or in private; or (b) to be a party to the commission of such an act; or (c) to procure the commission of such an act. "Gross indecency" is not defined by statute. It appears, however, to cover any act involving sexual indecency between two male persons. If two male persons acting in concert behave in an indecent manner the offense is committed even though there has been no actual physical contact.

105. From the police reports we have seen and the other evidence we have received it appears that the offense usually takes one of three forms; either there is mutual masturbation; or there is some form of intercrural contact; or oral-genital contact (with or without emission) takes place. Occasionally the offense may take a more recondite form; techniques in heterosexual relations vary considerably, and the same is true of homosexual relations.

106. Buggery and attempted buggery have long been criminal offenses, wherever and with whomsoever committed; but, in England and Wales at least, other acts of gross indecency committed in private between consenting parties first became criminal offenses in

1885. Section 11 of the Criminal Law Amendment Act of that year contained the provisions now re-enacted in Section 13 of the Sexual Offenses Act, 1956.

These provisions have been criticized by various witnesses on three grounds: (*a*) that they introduced an entirely new principle into English law in that they took cognizance of the private acts of consentient parties, (*b*) that they were inserted into a Bill introduced for totally different purposes without adequate consideration by Parliament; and (*c*) that they created a particularly fruitful field for blackmail.

107. The first of these criticisms is without foundation. The Act of 1885 merely extended to homosexual indecencies other than buggery the law which previously applied to buggery. Buggery had for over three hundred years been a criminal offense whether committed in public or in private, and whether by consenting parties or not.

108. The second criticism is valid. . . .

Blackmail

109. The third criticism was . . . one that found more frequent expression among our witnesses.

111. We would certainly not go so far as some of our witnesses have done and suggest that the opportunities for blackmail inherent in the present law would be sufficient ground for changing it. We have found it hard to decide whether the blackmailer's primary weapon is the threat of disclosure to the police, with the attendant legal consequences, or the threat of disclosure to the victim's relatives, employer or friends, with the attendant social consequences. It may well be that the latter is the more effective weapon; but it may yet be true that it would lose much of its edge if the social consequences were not associated with (or, indeed, dependent upon) the present legal position. At the least, it is clear that even if this is no more than one among other fields of blackmailing activity, the present law does afford to the blackmailer opportunities which the law might well be expected to diminish . . .

Persistent Soliciting or Importuning

116. It is an offence, punishable with six months' imprisonment on summary conviction or with two years' imprisonment on indictment, for a male person persistently to solicit or importune in a public place for immoral purposes. "Immoral purposes" is not defined, but where it is clear from the circumstances that the "immoral purposes" in contemplation involve homosexual behaviour the offence may be regarded as a "homosexual offence.". . .

120. Of 425 convictions at magistrates' courts in England and Wales during 1954, 323 related to offences committed in London. Outside London, the highest figures were 49 at Birmingham and 20 at Portsmouth. It seems, therefore, that the problem is almost confined to London and a few other large towns; and our evidence shows that it is largely concentrated on certain public conveniences. We have been surprised to find how widely known among homosexuals, even those who come from distant parts of the world, the location of these conveniences has proved to be. Occasionally, men are detected in the streets importuning male passers-by; the men so detected are usually male prostitutes. But for the most part, those convicted of importuning are in no sense male prostitutes; they are simply homosexuals seeking a partner for subsequent homosexual behaviour.

121. This particular offence necessarily calls for the employment of plain-clothes police if it is to be successfully detected and prevented from becoming a public nuisance; and it is evident that the figures of convictions, both for importuning and for indecencies committed in such places as public lavatories, must to some extent reflect police activity. It has been suggested by more than one of our witnesses that in carrying out their duty in connection

with offences of this nature police officers act as *agents provocateurs*. We have paid special attention to this matter in our examination of the Commissioner of Police and other senior police officers, and we are satisfied that they do everything they can to ensure that their officers do not act in a deliberately provocative manner. We also made a special point of examining some of the constables engaged in this work. Those whom we saw were ordinary police constables, normally employed on uniformed duty but occasionally employed in pairs, for a four weeks' spell of duty on this work, between substantial periods on other duties. We feel bound to record that we were on the whole favourably impressed by the account they gave us of the way in which they carried out their unpleasant task. It must, in our view, be accepted that in the detection of some offences—and this is one of them—a police officer legitimately resorts to a degree of subterfuge in the course of his duty. But it would be open to the gravest objection if this were allowed to reach a point at which a police officer deliberately provoked an act; for it is essential that the police should be above suspicion, and we believe that if there is to be an error in the one direction or the other it would be better that a case of this comparatively trivial crime should occasionally escape the courts than that the police as a whole should come under suspicion.

122. Some of our witnesses have suggested that the offence with which a person is charged does not always correspond with the actual behaviour of the offender. We have seen one case, and have heard of others, in which the facts would seem to sustain a charge of gross indecency, or attempting to procure the commission of an act of gross indecency, rather than a charge of importuning, though the offender was charged with the latter offence. It has been suggested that the police sometimes advise persons found committing acts of gross indecency in public lavatories to plead guilty at the magistrates' court to importuning in order to avoid going for trial before a jury on a charge of gross indecency. How often this happens we cannot say; the statements of persons who plead guilty to offences which they subsequently deny must be treated with a certain amount of reserve. But if our recommendation that gross indecency should be triable summarily is accepted, there would be no encouragement to the offender to enter a false plea of guilty to importuning in order to avoid going for trial in respect of an act of gross indecency which had been committed, and no temptation to the police to frame a charge with a view to enabling the magistrates' courts to dispose of a case they could not otherwise properly deal with.

123. As a general rule, a person charged in England and Wales with an offence for which he is liable to imprisonment for more than three months may claim to be tried by a jury. Male persons charged with importuning are, however, excluded from the benefit of this rule. We see no reason why a person charged with this offence should not enjoy the general right. On the contrary, we see every reason why he should. Frequently, conviction of this offence has serious consequences quite apart from any punishment which may be imposed. Moreover, behaviour which seems to establish a *prima facie* case of importuning and so leads up to an arrest may occasionally be attributable to innocent causes; and in cases such as this, where actions are susceptible of different interpretations, it is clearly right that the defendant should be entitled to have the issue put to a jury. We recommend accordingly.

124. We call attention to the fact that the possible penalties for this offence are substantially greater than those which we have recommended in relation to solicitation by females for the purposes of prostitution (paragraph 275 below). The very fact that the law can impose severe penalties is, however, a considerable factor in producing the present situation that the amount of male importuning in the streets is negligible and that consequently male importuning is not nearly so offensive or such an affront to public decency as are the street activities of female prostitutes. Having regard to the modifications we have recommended in

the law relating to homosexual offences, we do not think that it would be expedient at the present time to reduce in any way the penalties attaching to homosexual importuning. It is important that the limited modification of the law which we propose should not be interpreted as an indication that the law can be indifferent to other forms of homosexual behaviour, or as a general licence to adult homosexuals to behave as they please . . .

General

127. Apart from such exceptions as are mentioned in this report, the general criminal law and procedure apply to homosexual offences as to other offences. Persons charged with homosexual offences are brought to trial and tried in the same way as other offenders; and the various methods by which the courts can deal with persons charged with criminal offences generally are equally available in respect of persons charged with homosexual offences. So, too, an attempt to commit a homosexual offence is itself a criminal offence, just as is an attempt to commit any other offence; and compounding or aiding or abetting a homosexual offence, or conspiring or inciting to commit a homosexual offence, is an offence in the same way as compounding or aiding or abetting, or conspiring or inciting to commit, any other offence . . .

CHAPTER VII
Preventive Measures and Research

213. Our terms of reference are confined, strictly speaking, to the criminal law and the treatment of persons convicted of offences against that law. The law is, however, concerned with the prevention of crime no less than with its detection and punishment, and we have felt that it would not be proper to conclude our enquiry without giving some consideration to possible preventive measures.

214. Clearly, one of the most effective ways of reducing crime would be to eliminate its causes, if these could be identified and dealt with. Most homosexual behaviour is no doubt due to the existence of the homosexual propensity, in a greater or less degree, in one or both of the participants. As we have said earlier, various hypotheses have been put before us about the nature and origins of this propensity. But there is still a great deal of work to be done before any of the proffered explanations can be regarded as established, or any inferences from them accepted as wholly reliable. We have no doubt that properly co-ordinated research into the aetiology of homosexuality would have profitable results.

215. Secondly, there is much to be learnt about the various methods of treatment, their suitability to various kinds of patients, their varying chances of success, and the criteria by which that success is to be judged. Whether or not it is possible to establish the nature or origins of homosexuality, it is evident that psychiatric treatment has beneficial results in some cases. As we have said elsewhere, this treatment does not always involve psychotherapy, neither does it necessarily lead to any discernible change in the direction of sexual preference. But reliable information showing what type of person was likely to benefit, and in what way, from a particular form of treatment, would clearly be of great value as a preventive measure.

216. We therefore recommend that the appropriate body or bodies be invited to propose a programme of research into the aetiology of homosexuality and the effects of various forms of treatment. The actual carrying out of such research would necessarily be in the hands of those directly concerned with the treatment of the homosexual, since it is only from observations carried out over long periods by doctors treating individual cases that results can be established. These should include both prison doctors and psychiatrists working outside the prisons. The organisation of the research suggests the establishment, on the

pattern familiar to the Medical Research Council, of a research unit which would include, for example, psychiatrists, geneticists, endocrinologists, psychologists, criminologists and statisticians. This unit could well be based on some establishment (for example, a University Department) experienced in socio-medical research and having access to prisons, psychiatric clinics and other centres where homosexuals are undergoing treatment. We hope that such work will form part of a wider study of forensic psychiatry, not confined to homosexuality, for which this country has fewer facilities than some others. Research of this kind would also increase the two-way flow between the prison medical service and outside psychiatrists, which, as we have said earlier, we consider to be desirable.

217. Researches of the kind we have proposed will necessarily take a long time. We have, however, had suggested to us several other measures which might be taken to diminish the incidence of homosexual offences. Some of them are general and wide in their application, such as the desirability of a healthy home background; medical guidance of parents and children; sensible education in matters of sex, not only for children but for teachers, youth leaders and those who advise students. Particularly, it is urged that medical students should be given more information about homosexuality in their courses, and that clergy and probation officers should be better equipped to deal with the problems about which they are often consulted.

218. The Press might do much towards the education of public opinion, by ensuring that reports of court cases concerning homosexual offences were treated in the same way as that in which matrimonial cases have been treated for some years past; for there is little doubt that the influence of detailed reports of such cases is considerable and almost wholly bad. We have, incidentally, encountered several cases in which men have got into touch with homosexual offenders whose convictions were reported in the Press, with the result that further homosexual offences were committed.

219. It has been suggested, especially, that more care should be taken by those responsible for the appointment of teachers, youth leaders and others in similar positions of trust, to ensure that men known to be, or suspected of being, of homosexual tendencies, should be debarred from such employment. In regard to teachers, we are aware, and approve, of the steps taken by the Ministry of Education and the Scottish Education Department to ensure that men guilty of homosexual offences are not allowed to continue in the teaching profession. But it appears that headmasters of private schools are sometimes lax in taking up references in respect of teachers whom they propose to employ, and it occasionally happens that a teacher who has been dismissed, or asked to resign, from one post because of misconduct with boys under his charge subsequently finds employment in another school, where his misconduct is repeated. As far as youth organisations are concerned, these vary so much in their nature and structure that it is not possible to devise watertight measures. But we hope that the Criminal Record Office would be ready to supply, to responsible officers of the Headquarters of recognised youth organisations, information about the convictions of persons who seek positions of trust in those organisations.

220. On a point of detail, it has been put to us that the number of lavatory offences would be substantially reduced if all public lavatories were well lighted; but the facts do not seem to support this suggestion, since some of the lavatories at which most of the offences take place are particularly well lit. Our own opinion is that if uniformed police officers in the course of their duties on the beat keep a vigilant eye on public lavatories, that is more likely to discourage potential offenders than anything else. We have been informed that in some places in Scotland there are in force bye-laws making it an offence to stay for more than a certain time in a public lavatory; and it is for consideration whether the wider adoption of some similar bye-law might further discourage the improper use of such places.

221. The preventive measures we have mentioned above are not, in our view, such as to call for legislation, but we put them forward for consideration by the appropriate bodies.

AMERICAN CIVIL
LIBERTIES UNION

Even democratic societies cannot mandate understanding and equality for all. Governments are only as open as their citizens' understandings allow, and these understandings vary over time and place. The following article demonstrates this point. The American Civil Liberties Union, consistently the strongest U. S. voice for personal liberties since its founding, turned its back on gays and lesbians during the Cold War period. In an era of constant police harassment, the ACLU bowed to the belief that homosexuality raised issues of public health and morals rather than questions of personal and sexual freedom. Although some local chapters were more supportive, the national board of directors did not reverse the policy articulated here until ten years later, after several U. S. Supreme Court rulings affirmed sexual privacy in marriage. The ACLU today has an active Lesbian and Gay Rights Project, both at the national level and in the states.

HOMOSEXUALITY AND CIVIL LIBERTIES

(1957)

Policy Statement adopted by the Union's Board of Directors
January 7, 1957

The American Civil Liberties Union is occasionally called upon to defend the civil liberties of homosexuals. It is not within the province of the Union to evaluate the social validity of laws aimed at the suppression or elimination of homosexuals. We recognize that overt acts of homosexuality constitute a common law felony and that there is no constitutional prohibition against such state and local laws on this subject as are deemed by such states or communities to be socially necessary or beneficial. Any challenge to laws that prohibit and punish public acts of homosexuality or overt acts of solicitation for the purpose of committing a homosexual act is beyond the province of the Union.

In examining some of the cases that have come to our attention, however, we are aware that homosexuals, like members of other socially heretical or deviant groups, are more vulnerable than others to official persecution, denial of due process in prosecution, and entrapment. As in the whole field of due process, these are matters of proper concern for the Union, and we will support the defense of such cases that come to our attention.

Some local laws require registration when they enter the community of persons who have been convicted of a homosexual act. Such registration laws, like others requiring registration of persons convicted of other offenses, are in our opinion unconstitutional. We will support efforts for their repeal or proper legal challenge of them.

The ACLU has previously decided that homosexuality is a valid consideration in evaluating the security risk factor in sensitive positions. We affirm, as does Executive Order 10450 and all security regulations made thereunder, that homosexuality is a factor properly to be considered only where there is evidence of other acts which come within valid security criteria.

DONALD WEBSTER CORY

The 1950s were not a good time to be different in the United States, especially with respect to gender roles and sexual expression. The end of World War II and the beginning of the Cold War produced strong conservative social and political agendas. The early 1950s were dominated by the hearings of the House Un-American Activities Committee (HUAC), chaired by Sen. Joseph McCarthy of Wisconsin. The 1950 Senate hearings on "homosexuals and other sex perverts" in government positions were part of this atmosphere of fear and repression.

It was at this unlikely time that *The Homosexual in America: A Subjective Approach* was published. Writing under the pseudonym of "Donald Webster Cory," its author argued that homosexuals were an oppressed minority analogous to racial and religious groups. Cory's brief for equality was presented in what many would now consider degrading or self-hating terms, yet his personal feelings and experiences are still shared by many gays and lesbians today. Cory works to challenge his presumably heterosexual audience not only through sympathy, however, but also through classic liberal arguments for the privacy of sexual acts and the injustice of discrimination on the basis of "personal characteristics" over which one has no control and which do not affect one's public life. While tame by today's standards, in 1951 this was a radical step; as the first full-length discussion of homosexual politics in the United States, its very publication was an act of heroism.

THE SOCIETY WE ENVISAGE

Chapter 21 of *The Homosexual In America: A Subjective Approach* (1951)

Donald Webster Cory

What does the homosexual want? He cries out against the injustice of society, yet offers no alternative. He finds the discrimination and the calumnies a manifestation of the grossest intolerance, but he fails to offer the world at large a pattern for a better social organization in which he could be integrated.

This is not at all surprising, for the development of such a plan would, by its very nature, imply freedom of discussion. It is only from the exchange of opinion in a free press and by all other methods of communication that a subject of this type, wrought with so many unknowns and paradoxes, can reach adequate solution.

What does the homosexual want? The question cannot be answered because each person can speak only for himself, and his reply will be prejudiced by his religious and ethical background, by his philosophy of life, and by the degree of happiness he has been able to achieve. The actress whose predilections are almost public knowledge and are no impediment to her stardom and public acceptance is hardly likely to feel the same need for social reorganization as the lonely, the wretched, and the frustrated. A deeply religious Roman Catholic priest who professes that there is no justification for any sexual pleasure outside of the sacrament of marriage can hardly share aspirations for social change with two men who are living together in a happy physical and spiritual union.

The homosexual society, such as it is and to the extent that it exists at all, reflects differences of opinion on the social solution of this question just as does any other group of people on any problem confronting them. There is no single, quasi-official, universally accepted version of the social organization envisaged by homosexuals, any more than there could be a single opinion of college professors on loyalty oaths, of university students on the accomplishments of education, of physicians on socialized medicine.

But the homosexual viewpoint is less well developed than that of the other groups on other questions because of the virtual impossibility of having an exchange of opinion through the usual channels of thought expression. First, the facts themselves on which an opinion must be based are difficult to obtain and, once found, are difficult to communicate to others. There are very few reliable statistics, and even the words of experts are usually based on the most atypical homosexuals, namely those who fall into the hands of the law or who are seeking help from a psychiatrist.

Even were the facts more readily available, an expression of opinion requires a free and open debate, and American society is hardly more advanced in this respect that the totalitarian lands. There is, of course, no interference with the effort to discuss the subject by word of mouth, provided the discussion remains within the homosexual group. It is almost impossible to have, except in a few and rare circles, a full interchange of opinion between people of all sexual temperaments in which each viewpoint is defended ably and each argument refuted honestly.

Homosexuals have had little opportunity for the development of a well-defined outlook. Within the homosexual group, there is little uniformity of opinion, and perhaps even less so than would be found in another minority group. One person can therefore do little more than express his personal viewpoint, reflecting only what he himself envisions for the homosexual group in the supposedly Utopian situation, but in this reflection there are distilled the arguments, viewpoints, contradictions, and philosophies of many others with whom discussions have been held over a period of many years.

There is probably only one thing on which homosexuals would in general agree with regard to the attitude of society, and that is that the present situation is unjust and that change is necessary. The injustice is not so much before the bar, nor in the effort to obtain employment, but is found above all in the general social attitude in the heterosexual society. No one can prevent an individual from expressing hostility toward another, provided he stays within the law and neither libels nor physically harms his enemy, but when the hostile attitude is officially sponsored by all possible means among the entire population, it is no longer the private affair of a single person.

The homosexual, first and foremost, wants recognition of the fact that he is doing no one any harm. He wants to live and let live, to punish and be punished when there are transgressions, and to go out of the ordinary and everyday pursuits of life, unhindered either by law or by an unwritten hostility which is even more effectual than the written law.

This is a far-reaching program, requiring the modification of attitudes over a period of generations, and it is only natural that it must fall upon those most concerned with this problem—the inverts—to take the initiative in remolding public opinion.

However, the invert is not alone in feeling that the present situation is unsatisfactory. The dominant group in our society tacitly understands and is ready to concede that it has no proposal for bettering a situation which is obviously unjust. It would like—in a manner similar to the attitude of many white persons on the color question—to "wish" the problem out of existence. It dreams of a world in which the problem does not exist, hopes that the problem will not reach the lives of individuals personally related to oneself, and just does not think, talk, or write about it. But its dreams are in vain.

The dominant society cannot offer a cure for homosexuality. It urges in a weak, ineffectual, and ignorant manner that willpower be cured, but willpower solves nothing. It talks of suppression and sublimation, while its own scientists scoff at such a proposal. It damns in the harshest of terms in the hope that damnation will be a deterrent, but again there is failure. It passes laws that make felons of homosexuals, but ignores its own laws and admits that it cannot put homosexuals behind bars. It concedes that homosexuals must earn a living and banishes them from employment. And, as society always does when it is in a blind alley, tied by tradition and folkways to a system which is unreasonable and which does not answer the needs of the people, it uses silence as the answer. It hides its head in the sand and pretends that the problem does not exist, and forbids discussion, save in professional circles.

But the problem does exist, and it will be discussed. Furthermore, it is not a problem created by the homosexuals. A sociologist writing on racial minorities—and again the parallel is inescapable—has stated that there are no minority problems. There are only majority problems. There is no Negro problem except that created by whites; and Jewish problem except that created by Gentiles. To which I add and no homosexual problem except that created by the heterosexual society.

There would be no economic dilemma for the invert were he not excluded from practically all jobs unless he hides his identity. There would be no blackmail problem for the homosexual except that he cannot live happily after exposure, because the world which has learned of his temperament will inflict severe sanctions. There would be no ethical problem of being a lawbreaker except that the laws have been codified in such manner that he cannot be a homosexual without at least aspiring to break them. And thus the problems of the homosexual could be enumerated, and it could be seen that they are majority problems—not minority ones!

Even the psychological aspects of the homosexual's dilemma primarily involve adjustment to a hostile world. There would be no need for the invert to feel guilty, to suffer remorse, to be forced to suppress hatred toward his love-object, if society did not condemn so bitterly. He would not be faced with the paradoxical problem of attempting on the one hand to be proud of himself and on the other to deny his temperament, if it were not so difficult to live in a world that demanded such denial.

It is a majority problem, but only the minority is interested in solving it. The fundamental dilemma is that it must rest primarily upon the homosexuals, being the most interested party, to take the initiative in bringing about change, but until such change is effected, anyone taking such initiative is open to pillory and contumelious scorn.

The homosexual is thus locked in his present position. If he does not rise up and demand his rights, he will never get them, but unless he gets those rights, he cannot be expected to expose himself to the martyrdom that would come if he should rise up and demand them. It is a vicious circle, and what the homosexual is seeking, first and foremost, is an answer to this dilemma.

It is an answer that I contend can be found and one which happens, by the most fortunate of coincidences, to be identical with the need of society at large and with the historic task of the democratic form of our generation. The answer is to be found in the liberalization of our newspapers, radio, and theater, so that homosexuality can be discussed as freely as any other subject and within the confines that circumscribe any other type of discussion. Already a beginning has been made in the very large interest shown in the subject by novelists, and in the occasional portrayal of homosexuality on the stage. A few popular magazines in the United States have at least mentioned it. In the larger cities serious articles have appeared even in the newspapers, and in one case an entire series of articles, written in a penetrating and not unsympathetic manner and without any evasion of terms, appeared in a New York newspaper.

This discussion may prove to be an opening wedge. There will be more articles, books, and further utilization of other means of thought communication, and out of this will come the interchange of opinion, the conflict and the controversy, which alone can establish truth.

And all of this is good for society, good particularly in this era, when no greater threat to the democratic way of life and to everything that has evolved in modern civilization, both Western and Eastern, appears than the suppression of all differences of opinion, the repression of all controversy. At this moment in history, when the forces of totalitarianism seek to extend the conspiracy of silence and the distortions of truth to all phases of life—to science and politics and human relations—the homosexuals (including even those few who are mistakenly in the camp of the totalitarians) are seeking to extend freedom of the individual, of speech, press, and thought to an entirely new realm. While others wish to narrow the confines of allowable differences of opinion and permissible discussion, the homosexual seeks to broaden them. This is not because he is a greater lover of liberty, but because he is fortunately placed in that historic position where his liberties have been denied and he seeks to regain them.

Thus, as the first answer to the society we homosexuals envisage, we seek freedom of thought and expression on this question. This involves not only the right to publish books and magazines without interference from the police, but the right to employ the main channels of communication, the leading newspapers, magazines, and the air for the expression of a viewpoint in the spirit and traditions of American freedoms. It may be the right of one editor or publisher to express his own viewpoint, as he does on things political, and to exclude the opposition from his press, but when his outlook coincides with that of all of the major editors, and when those who differ fear to open their pages because of reprisals by church, government, or advertisers, then there is a totalitarian control of the press by a particular group and hence a denial of freedom to the other. This is indubitably the situation so far as the rights of homosexuals are concerned today.

If the day of free and open discussion arrives, and if, during the course of such discussion, the struggle for it, and as a consequence of it, the social stigma attached to being a homosexual begins to be lifted there will automatically come about a happier milieu in which the individual can live, love, thrive, and work. Part of that happier relationship will be found in the dropping of the disguise.

Many homosexuals consider that their greatest fortune, their only saving grace, has been the invisibility of the cross which they have had to bear. The ease with which they were able to hide their temperaments from the closest friends and business associates, from their parents, wives, and children, made it possible to partake of the full benefits and material and spiritual advantages life offers to the heterosexual. Many such people—and I include myself—have constantly striven to perfect their technique of concealment.

Actually, the inherent tragedy—not the saving grace—of homosexuality is found in the ease of concealment. If the homosexual were as readily recognizable as are members of certain other minority groups, the social condemnation could not possibly exist. Stereotype thinking on the part of the majority would, in the first instance collapse of its own absurdity if all of us who are gay were known for what we are. Secondly, our achievements in society and our contributions to all phases of culture and social advancement would become well-known, and not merely the arsenal of argument in the knowledge of a few. The laws against homosexuality could not be sustained if it were flagrantly apparent that millions of human beings in all walks of life were affected. Blackmail, naturally enough, would be non-existent as a problem facing the invert.

It is a chimera, but worthy of speculation. If only all of the inverts the millions in all lands, could simultaneously rise up in our full strength! For the fact is that we homosexuals are defeated by the self-perpetuation of the folkways which inflict severe punishment on those who protest against these folkways. Again, the circle is vicious.

We need freedom of expression to achieve freedom of inversion, but only the free invert is in a position to demand and to further freedom of expression. And what are we to do in the meantime?

A few individuals, well-placed because of their position in society, their economic freedom, their universally acknowledged attainments, can speak up and further their cause. Others can, with discretion, spread enlightenment to a few intimate and trustworthy friends. And all others can utilize their knowledge or talents by disseminating truthful information and by bringing the subject before the public, but behind the veil of pseudonymity.

But once there is freedom of expression and once the invert is fully accepted and is an object neither of calumny nor sneer, an object neither to scorn nor to pity, how will he fit into our social and family life? Is it proposed that society recognize and sanction marriages in which both "bride" and "groom" are of the same sex and in which the two parties to such a union have the same rights and obligations as in any other marriage?

Most of the problems concomitant with being homosexual would be automatically solved if there were no discriminatory attitudes on the part of society. Many homosexuals would marry and have children, attracted by the family life which such a prospect offers, but there would be no shame of the homosexuality, no concealment from wife or from offspring. Others would form unions with males, as they do today, but without social ostracism; they would bring their friends to social functions and might adopt an orphan child or a nephew of an overcrowded and overburdened family. Others would live the lives of bachelors, perhaps have many loves or few, and as the years pass would probably show less interest in the pursuit of the sexual object than in cultural activities.

In all such matters the homosexual's life would parallel that of the heterosexual. Some people require a mate; others do not. Some pursue sex relentlessly; others organize a life in which the physical gratification of their impulses plays a rather minor role.

What the homosexual wants is freedom—not only freedom of expression, but also sexual freedom. By sexual freedom is meant the right of any person to gratify his urges when and how he sees fit, without fear of social consequences, so long as he does not use the force of either violence, threat, or superior age; so long as he does not inflict bodily harm or disease upon another person; so long as the other person is of sound mind and agrees to the activity. This means that both on the statute books and in the realm of public opinion all sexual activity is accepted as equally correct, right, and proper so long as it is entered into voluntarily by the parties involved they are perfectly sane and above a reasonable age of consent, free of communicable disease, and no duress or misrepresentation is employed.

This is, for our society, a radical proposal. It has been expounded in the remarkable works of Guyon,* among others, and its full exposition would be beyond the realm of this book. But it is radical only to expound and defend this theory, for sexual freedom is actually being practiced on a very wide scale in modern life, despite its being condemned by school, church, newspapers, and government. Adultery, fellatio between husband and wife, homosexuality, premarital fornication—all are so common that it is rare to find the individual who has not indulged in one or several of these forms of sexual activity quite frequently.

However, on the law books these are punishable acts, and in the realm of public opinion even more so. The result is that modern civilization adopts a hypocritical attitude and attempts to force an extreme feeling of shame upon the individuals who live what to them is a normal and natural life.

The homosexual often feels that the source of his difficulty lies in the fact that he is born into a hostile world, and this hostility is inherent, he believes, in that he lives in a heterosexual society. He is in my opinion, entirely wrong in this concept. The root of the homosexual difficulty is that he lives, not in a heterosexual world but in an anti-sexual world.

The anti-sexual nature of modern civilization is apparent wherever one turns. In the description of the virgin birth, the term "immaculate conception" is used, and thus an inference is made that all conceptions that take place by means of sexual intercourse are not immaculate and are therefore unclean. Any humor pertaining to sex is called a "dirty joke." It is "lewd" to fail to conceal the sexual organs, and the strongest epithets in the English language—and in many other languages—are synonymous with having sexual intercourse. Even the more progressive educators teach the children about birds and flowers and something about the physiology of sex, but skirt the fact that the higher animals, and particularly man, indulge in sex for the pure joy of the thing. In modern anti-sexual society, the heterosexual is tolerated only because he is necessary for the propagation of the species, but the virgin and the chaste are glorified as pristine purity. If we homosexuals lived in a predominantly heterosexual and not an anti-sexual society—as witness the American Indians and the South Sea Islanders—we would not be in constant conflict with our fellowmen nor with ourselves.

Some will object that there is a basic contradiction. Have I not, throughout this book, decried the attitudes of the heterosexual society, of the heterosexual-dominated society? Is the reader now to be informed that that heterosexual society is non-existent? The fact is that it is only apparently a heterosexual society. The anti-sexual culture pretends that it is heterosexual, in order the better to suppress all sex for pleasure!

The heterosexual's conflicts in our society are also deep; sexual maladjustment is by no means the sole property of the homosexual in modern life. But the lesser stigma attached to adultery and premarital relationships, the ease of concealment of fellatio when it takes place with the opposite sex, and, finally, society's acceptance (albeit reluctantly) of sex in the conjugal relationships—these facts place the heterosexual in a preferred position in the anti-sexual setup.

The homosexual then, to summarize, desires freedom of expression, aspires to recognition of his temperament without discriminatory attitudes or punishment, and will find all of this possible only when he is able to proclaim his true nature. Such a program will be possible only in a culture that proclaims sexual freedom—the right of adults to enter into any voluntary sexual arrangement with each other without fear of reprisal by society. At the same time the embracing of such a guiding policy of sexual freedom will hasten the liberation of the homosexual from concealment and from silence.

The homosexual, thus, has two historic missions to perform. Whether he is a democrat or a totalitarian by political conviction, he is historically forced to enter the struggle for the widening of freedom of expression. And, whether his religious and ethical convictions are those of the continent or the libertarian, he is historically compelled to enlist in the legions fighting for liberalization of the sexual mores of modern civilization.

It is interesting and heartening to note that in the two greatest totalitarian regimes of our century veritable reigns of terror against homosexuality were instituted, despite the collaboration of certain homosexuals in the establishment of these regimes. The purge of Roehm by Hitler can be understood only in this light—that no free, deviating, unassimilable viewpoint was tolerable in Nazi Germany, no matter how obsequious it might be to the Hitler regime.

After the Russian Revolution, the laws against homosexuality were repealed. These Tsarist laws were denounced as the remnants of the bourgeois concept of sex, and a new era of sexual freedom was foreseen. In the years that followed, as the totalitarian stranglehold on all channels of thought expression was strengthened, the old bourgeois and Tsarist laws were restored. Abortion was illegalized, divorce made increasingly difficult to obtain, and the law restoring homosexuality to a crime, placing it in the same category as other social crimes, was signed by Kalinin in March, 1934. This is a significant date, for it was the period of the heightened struggle against the Old Bolsheviks, the last great effort of the Stalin regime to bring about a complete system of thought and action control. "The mass arrests of homosexuals," writes Wilhelm Reich, "led to a panic . . . It is said that there were numerous suicides in the army."** Since that time, there have been several reports that homosexuals have been involved in anti-Stalinist conspiracies.

Today, Russia is much more backward than the rest of Europe and America in its attitudes toward the sexual non-conformist, just as it is in the attitude toward all non-conformists. There is no room except for orthodoxy, and that includes things sexual as much as things political. In the socialist state the homosexual lives in dread. Even the few channels open to him in the United States are closed in Russia. With medieval severity he can be seized and pilloried.

How can one account for Russian and Nazi cruelty on this question? Only in this way—that in a totalitarian state, there was no room for a group of people who, by their very sexual temperaments, could never be assimilated, must always remain apart with their own ways of life, their own outlooks, their own philosophies.

And it is this inherent lack of assimilability that is the greatest historic value of homosexuality. Any minority which does not commit anti-social acts, which is not destructive of the life, property, or culture of the majority or of other minority groups, is a pillar of democratic strength. So long as there are such minorities in our culture, whether of a sexual or religious or ethnic character, there will be many broths in the melting pot, many and variegated waves in the seas. No force will be able to weave these groups into a single totalitarian unity which is the unanimity of the graveyard.

Thus on three scores, homosexuality—fortunately but unwittingly—must inevitably play a progressive role in the scheme of things. It will broaden the base for freedom of thought and communication, will be a banner-bearer in the struggle for liberalization of our sexual conventions, and will be a pillar of strength in the defense of our threatened democracy.

*René Guyon, The Ethics of Sexual Acts (New York: Alfred A. Knopf, 1934 and 1948) and Sexual Freedom (New York: Alfred A. Knopf, 1950).

**Wilhelm Reich, The Sexual Revolution (New York: Orgone Institute Press 1945), p. 209.

B

THE MATTACHINE SOCIETY

In Europe in the Middle Ages, the Mattachines were societies of men who played the fool or the jester in dance, and in doing provided veiled political satire. The Mattachine dance spread throughout Europe and into Latin America (including New Mexico).

The Mattachine Society was founded in Los Angeles in 1950 by Harry Hay and Rudi Gernreich. They were soon joined by Bob Hull, Dale Jennings, and Chuck Rowland. Harry Hay held a vision of gay men as akin to jesters, embodying the rejected but crucially important elements of their societies. The Mattachine founders fostered and led discussion groups on homosexuality, recruiting apt students for their organization. They formed committees, such as the Citizens' Committee to Outlaw Entrapment, that worked to stop persecution of gays. They had research committees, speakers' committees, and many other projects. Eventually Mattachine chapters sprang up in several other cities.

Mattachine was, in part, the product of Hay's Communist-taught organizational skills. The following statements show the radicalism that the founders envisioned for their society, as well as the seriousness of the commitment made by members. It also reveals Hay's vision of gays as a minority group, assigned through birth, with its own culture beneath heterosexual persecution. He would spend the rest of his life developing that vision of social/sexual oppression and the possibilities for liberation. The original statement of purpose and membership pledge, formulated in 1951, reflects these views.

1. TO UNIFY:—While there are undoubtedly individual homosexuals who number many of their own people among their friends, thousands of homosexuals live out their lives bewildered, unhappy, alone,—isolated from their own kind and unable to adjust to the dominant culture. Even those who may have many homosexual friends are still cut off from the deep satisfactions man's gregarious nature can achieve *only* when he is consciously part of a larger unified whole. A major purpose of the Mattachine Society is to provide a concensus (sic) of principle around which all of our people can rally and from which they can derive a feeling of "belonging."

2. TO EDUCATE:—The total of information available on the subject of homosexuality is woefully meagre and utterly inconclusive. The Society organizes all available material, and conducts extensive researches itself—psychological, physiological, anthropological, and sociological—for the purpose of informing all interested homosexuals, and for the purpose of informing and enlightening the public at large.

The Mattachine Society holds it possible and desirable that a highly ethical homosexual culture emerge, as a consequence of its work, paralleling the emerging cultures of our fellow minorities . . . the Negro, Mexican, and Jewish Peoples. The Society believes homosexuals can lead well-adjusted, wholesome, and socially productive lives once ignorance, and prejudice, against them is successfully combatted, and once homosexuals themselves feel they have a dignified and useful role to play in society. The Society, to these ends, is in the process of developing a homosexual ethic . . . disciplined, moral, and socially responsible.

3. TO LEAD:—It is not sufficient for an oppressed minority such as the homosexuals merely to be conscious of belonging to a minority collective when, as is the situation at the present time, that collective is neither socially organic nor objective in its directions and activities,—although this minimum is in fact a great step forward. It is necessary that the more far-reaching and socially conscious homosexuals provide leadership to the whole mass of social deviants if the first two missions, (the unification and the education of the homosexual minority), are to be accomplished. Further, once unification and education have progressed, it becomes imperative (to

consolidate these gains) for the Corporation to push forward into the realm of political action to erase from our law books the discriminatory and oppressive legislation presently directed against the homosexual minority.

The Society, founded upon the highest ethical and social principles, serves as an example for homosexuals to follow, and provides a dignified standard upon which the rest of society may base a more intelligent and accurate picture of the nature of homosexuality than currently obtains in the public mind. The Society provides the instrument necessary to work with like-minded and socially valuable organizations, and supplies the means for the assistance of our people who are victimized daily as a result of our oppression. Only a Society, providing an enlightened leadership, can rouse the homosexuals . . . one of the largest minorities in America today . . . to take the actions necessary to elevate themselves from the social ostracism an unsympathetic culture has perpetrated upon them.

MEMBERSHIP PLEDGE

While it is my conviction that homosexuality in our society is not a virtue but rather a handicap, I believe that I can live a well-oriented and socially productive life. I further believe the social ostracism and legal persecution of homosexuals can be minimized or eliminated through the Mattachine Society which is organized to influence the conduct of homosexuals themselves, and to formulate and develop a social, positive, body of ethic for the homosexual. I shall live and work to the end that, through these principles, I myself shall become a better person, and through my work and my self-improvement the Mattachine Society shall be that much more enabled to aid an enlightened society to accept my people as useful and valuable citizens.

The Missions and Purposes of the Mattachine Society have been explained to me in detail, and I understand and accept them as my own. In order to further these missions and purposes, I take the following pledge without reservation or qualifications:

I PLEDGE MYSELF -

(1) always to keep the interests of the Mattachine Society uppermost in my mind and to conduct myself in a way that will reflect credit upon myself and the organization;

(2) in every possible way, to respect the rights of all racial, religious, and national minorities, since I realize that I also am a member of a persecuted minority;

(3) to try to observe the generally accepted social rules of dignity and propriety at all times . . . in my conduct, attire, and speech;

(4) to strive in every possible way to interest other responsible people in the Mattachine Society and to recruit members for the organization with regard to their race, color, or creed;

(5) to participate actively and seriously in the work, responsibilities, and functions of the Society;

(6) unconditionally, to guard the anonymity of all members of the Mattachine Society, of sponsoring organization and affiliates; and, in the event I ever leave the organization for any reason whatsoever, I pledge myself to guard the anonymity of the membership, sponsoring organizations and affiliates, throughout my entire life.

I have read this pledge carefully and thoughtfully, and I understand it completely. In the presence of these members of the Mattachine Society, I do, here, and now, of my own free will and volition, and after careful thought and reason, solemnly swear to uphold this pledge which admits me to membership in the Organization.

Both statements were written in April, 1951 and ratified July 20, 1951.

In 1953, the original founders were forced out of Mattachine by a group led by Ken Burns, who then became chairman of the new board of directors. This group was upset by whisperings about Communist affiliations, some suggesting that a loyalty oath be a requirement for membership. They were also concerned about a questionnaire that had been sent to political candidates, fearing that political involvement would harm the group. Under this new leadership, Mattachine abandoned political activity and became a forum for legal and medical "experts" who, by using members for their research and giving lectures on their findings, would presumably "legitimize" homosexuality.

Fearing greater persecution if they resisted oppression, the next generation pursued accommodation with the dominant, heterosexual culture rather than the creation of their own "highly ethical homosexual culture." The assimilationists also fundamentally disagreed with the "minority group" concept, arguing that homosexuals were just like "everyone else" in everything other than private sexual activity.

The reliance on science and the insistence on finding the "cause" of homosexuality, the refusal to "condone" "sex variation," and the refusal of group identity all demonstrates how profoundly the "new" Mattachine has diverged from its founders' vision. This is, however, the Mattachine that would open a space for (male) homosexuals to find one another and discuss their common problems. As such it was much more revolutionary than either the Stonewall generation or its founders believed.

In 1955 the Society began to publish *The Mattachine Review*, a monthly magazine with news, historical and cultural articles, and opinion pieces. Although a far cry from the early group's activism, the *Review* documented a wide range of activity and debate that was ignored by the post-Stonewall movement. Articles (always worded very cautiously) appeared on veterans' rights, police persecution, and state repression as well as medical, legal and religious perspectives on homosexuality. The following articles we hope will convey a sense of the lively discourse as well as the fear that coexisted in the pages of the *Review*.

THE HOMOSEXUAL FACES A CHALLENGE

A speech to the 3rd Annual Convention of The Mattachine Society, published in the *Mattachine Review* (1956)

Ken Burns

... Let us look for a few moments at some of the problems which face the homosexual and cause him to be set apart or feel that he is set apart, from society and his family. In reviewing these problems it is not my desire to emphasize differences in principle, but rather to emphasize differences of approach which I feel have done much to continue this segregation of man. And, let me add, these problems are not subject to the homosexual alone. They are, as well, the problems of society—every individual in it—for each of us is interdependent on the other in this complex civilization in which we live. Our social order is based on the principle that each of us shall be our brother's keeper. It is tragic that this has not been universally accepted and practiced not only by Mr. Average Citizen, but by those in authority as well.

But to get back to the problems which the Mattachine Society must meet. One which has seemed to me at times to be definitely over-rated because of the unusual amount of emphasis placed on it is the problem of the law. I sometimes wonder if some homosexuals don't desire a carte blanche to carry on their activities "anywhere, anytime, anybody." This is regarded as a right. To those individuals I would say, "Come down from your marble pillar and begin to live. This Utopia is neither constructive nor productive." We do not enact laws just to have laws—there is a reason—good or bad—behind each law. Laws are made for the protection of man, and, when these laws are broken, the consequences must be expected and accepted. This is not to say, however, that we must agree with the suitability of the law. We must test it on the basis of whether the law accomplishes the purpose for which it became statute. Has it impelled those for whom it was intended to act differently? Does it serve the principles of society and our social order?

In the case of the homosexual, it would seem that law has had little or no effect on his activities. Yet, to prove that all law accomplishes that for which it was designed—and incidentally, to prove that all human problems can be solved by law—it is the custom for some enforcement agencies to hide behind their authority using techniques of harassment, blackmail, and entrapment and to assume the role of judge and jury in the interpretation and application of law. Some are no better than male prostitutes themselves in their role of agent provocateurs. Society seems to have taken theory, or the explanation of some phenomenon which exists in someone's mind and which has not yet been demonstrated by scientific measurement, and made it into law which is a summary of the truth supported by facts which no one can dispute, and expressed in terms of a sound working principle which can safely be used as a guide. The basic theory seems not to prevent trouble but to punish it. Is it a case of reforming or getting even? Yes, it would seem that the law, dealing with homosexual practices has had much more effect on the activities of some law enforcement officers and those in the legal field.

The Report of the American Law Institute has pointed the way toward legal reform, and we concur in its decisions. Those who are not yet mature enough to adequately decide for themselves and those who are compelled by force to submit must be protected, as must public decency. This is as it should and must be in an orderly society. What consenting adults do in private, however, is their own business as long as they don't injure themselves or others. Maybe you don't agree with what they do; maybe they don't agree with what you do. If that is so, then it is a matter of education, not law. These are principles fundamental to our democracy.

The Mattachine Society is prepared to sit down with legislators, law enforcement officers, judges and others in the legal field to work out an objective program to meet the legal problems affecting homosexuality and to constructively administer to the causes and not the symptoms of the problem. We do not say that our judgement is sound and the judgement of others unwise. We do say, however, that "if you want to build a bridge, go to an engineer": if you have a problem with homosexuals go to an organization that can help you. This offer is also open to others interested in the homosexual.

Let us look for a moment at the religious or spiritual problem of the homosexual. In my opinion this is a subject which needs more emphasis. All of us have a spiritual side to our nature. This cannot be divorced from the material, for only through the spiritual does the material have meaning and value. Some would deny this, but I believe they do so as a defense against the teachings—or what they believe to be the teachings—of particular faiths. We have only to look around us and within us to discern a force, a spirit, God—call this what you will. There is a plan in this great universe and you and I—every single person and thing—is an integral part of that plan.

There are those who profess to minister to us on behalf of God, however, who would deny the homosexual any part in this universal plan. "The church is no place for this filth, he is anathema," they would say. I submit to you that the church if it truly be the representative of God, must be always open to the creatures of God no matter what they may think, say, or do. God is not exclusive. He does not create only to reject and forget. Neither does he create scapegoats. These are the results of fearful men who because of this fear are unable to comprehend love—not only love of their fellow-man, but love of God, also.

The results of this rejection by ministers has caused them to deviate from their role as leaders toward a fuller spiritual life for everyone. Both religion and homosexuality are emotional subjects and they have been played to the hilt in creating and maintaining strife among groups. Sodom and Gomorrah have been twisted all out of proportion to their original intent and meaning. But don't waste your time getting a martyr complex over it; just read Dr. Bailey's "Homosexuality and the Western Christian Tradition." It is high time that all of us got back on the path toward a richer and more satisfying life. A life in which we will welcome all people, leaving it to God to judge their intentions.

We have seen that the law cannot legislate morals. Morals are the result of ethical values. These values are the result of tradition and education to a large extent. These interpretations must be constantly reexamined in order to give meaning to this modern day. We have advanced measurably since the middle ages and our philosophy of life must be vitalized if the brotherhood of man is to be accomplished. We must mean what we say and practice what we preach.

Now, what about the medical problem of the homosexual. Generally, this is a field which has been most progressive in its attitudes. Psychiatry especially has made great strides forward in its analysis and comprehension of homosexuality. Medical people, schooled as they are in the objective approach to research, however, would be the first subject. They have only scratched the surface. Most of the questions still remain to be answered accurately through recognized research methods.

But what is being done by the medical profession to determine the answers and thereby partially, at least release the homosexual from this dark age of ignorance of a problem affecting untold millions throughout the world? I know of no concerted effort being made by any professional group to conduct research into the psychic, physical, or social reaches of homosexuality. True, some individuals have conducted research into various phases of the subject and this is certainly a beginning. But, there has been no attempt to correlate these findings and exhibit them into the entire picture of the individual. We are composed of arms, legs, a trunk and a head. Yet, there is a correlation and interdependence of these members. Without this, there is little meaning. The problems involved are, of course, much more complex than I can describe. I doubt if man will ever be able to truly understand and evaluate either himself, another individual, or mankind. This is always the constant challenge which has urged man on to greater feats.

If professional people, most particularly those in the medical profession, determine to undertake the task of meeting and solving this unknown—homosexuality and its many facets—this nation would literally experience a rebirth. One person is born every second of the day and night in the U.S. Of those that survive every 5th person may become homosexually inclined temporarily, and every 10th person permanently. There are few things which are termed problems which have greater incidence. And as long as we continue in this twilight of comparative inactivity it shall continue to be so. But, does it have to be? The homosexual is accused of attempting to create a homosexual society. Yet it is the homosexual himself who cries out for help in controlling this continuous cycle by constructive means. Castigating homosexuals now living is sheer stupidity. The solution of the problems of persons yet to be born who will become homosexual—who are maybe even destined to be homosexual—lies in preventive means.

This brings us to the problem the homosexual encounters in his home, with his family and those who are nearest and dearest to him. Love and companionship contribute much to our inner security and much to our outward attitudes. They are essential to life and its adjustments. They are so important that individuals feel forced to lie and lead double existences to keep them. These most precious things—so fleeting and elusive they seem at times. We seem to be inadequate to their meaning and potential—and perhaps we are.

If the homosexual cannot receive love and compassion from those who have given him his existence, if he cannot share his innermost secrets with those whom he trusts the most, then where must he turn? The family who has taught him to come to them when needed—yes, the very family who may have contributed a great deal to his present state—this is the family that cannot face this common problem. Unwilling and inadequate to the task, they must turn their backs to avoid embarrassment. This is truly a time of inner conflict for all concerned. Yet, what to do, what to do?

Fortunately, some families have faced the situation and do everything possible to understand. People who love for the joy they receive rather than hate that which life contains. Others, however, resign themselves only to hate. They must punish themselves to remove this stain. Tragic!

Yes, tragic indeed that the future mothers and fathers of this nation are destined to this same experience. Uneducated in homosexuality except as it may apply to the Rhesus monkey. It may be of unequaled pleasure to the monkey to know that such an interest is taken in him, but I think the human being might have some sexual existence, and study and understanding of this might be as appropriate.

Society has often spoken out to control the "homosexual menace." Yet today it cannot recognize and evaluate homosexuality. Until it can do this, society must grope blindly in the dark—continually knocking the periphery and never getting at the core. A good example of this and its consequences is the problem the homosexual faces in employment.

Business, taking its lead from the federal government to a large extent, has denied employment to homosexuals. This has been found expedient because they are "security risks." I would remind you of the hundreds of thousands of homosexuals who served this country and still serve it well. I know no homosexual who would not lay down his life for the security of all the people in this nation and the ideals on which this nation was built. We, perhaps more than most, know the value of security But what is this "risk." Is it the risk of homosexuals because of their acts? Or is it the risk of blackmailing which some homosexuals may be subject to? Is it because some are more talkative, less adequately adjusted, or more willing to submit to blackmail than all other individuals?

The federal government more and more, has spoken out against unequal rights for groups. Yet, here are individuals given the status of a group to be judged and condemned as a group. This nation was founded on individual rights, individual freedoms and individual responsibility. The destiny of the individual was to be protected. We have strayed far when every man does not recognize this devaluation of the individual—his cherished heritage to be judged on his own merits. The federal government has afforded sanctuary to those who would make all men the same. It has encouraged the blackmailer and given protection to his practices. It has pronounced a sentence of "guilty until proven innocent" on the homosexual.

Compliance with this has permeated every branch of the government and seeped down into private enterprise, sometimes at the direction of the government. Today, the homosexual is the victim—the scapegoat. Tomorrow, unless we are vigilant and unless this practice is ended, we may see further inroads into the basic freedom of the individual.

Now we come to perhaps the greatest problem of all—the homosexual's relationship with himself and his surroundings. We can never adequately solve the problems which face us without first facing and seeking solutions to the problems within us. Pressures from without are often the reaction to pressures within. We must blame ourselves for much of our plight. When will the homosexual ever realize that social reform, to be effective, must be preceded by personal reform? People who are non-homosexual usually get their knowledge of homosexuality by the education given them by homosexuals. And what an education it has been at times.

In his efforts to be recognized, the homosexual has channeled his actions into super-colossal productions to demonstrate and accentuate differences. The result has been an ever widening chasm based on a premise that there is a difference. If we are to publicly act different than accepted standards we must be certain that our differences will be recognized as superior. There are some who would say that homosexuals are superior, "the chosen of God." But I say, "show me the facts. I am not interested in your egotism. Look beyond your self-interest and emotions. You are different only in that way you think you are different. Stop being afraid of yourself and use fear as an aid to growth and not as a form of escape." Yes, it is time that all of us took an 'agonizing reappraisal' of our personal and social relationships. Do we truly contribute welfare of others? There is no place for complacency in the answer. None of us are so good that we can't be better.

It would seem that all homosexuals would desire to compare their thinking with others on a basis of mutual trust, benefit from this exchange, and make up their own minds a lot of effort to learn to think out fear of judgements by others. But this takes time and patience. It takes a lot of effort to learn to think objectively—to control that which we have created. It takes a little guts to stand up for what is right and for the common good. It is difficult to live 24 hours a day dedicated to constructive ends in which all may benefit.

I do not mean to infer that what I have said is the official position of the Mattachine Society; I have spoken only for myself, nor do I wish to give you the impression that I am bitter or have a chip on my shoulder. I am not fighting against the situation which exists. Rather, I am fighting for all of us to undertake the responsibility of being citizens in a nation which still gives us the right to disagree. Uniformity is not demanded of us—but unity of all of our people is required to meet and solve the problems of our environment. There need be no fear, for all of us together are adequate and equal to the problems. I am reminded of Justice Holmes statement: "The inevitable comes to pass through effort." Greater effort is needed on the part of all of us if we are to guarantee that future generations shall live in a [gap in original—Eds.]

All who join the ranks of this crusade can feel justly proud. We must never falter in the principles on which Mattachine was organized. We must continue to serve, to face the world boldly, unafraid, with faith in the future and say, "This I believe. This I have done."

AN OPEN LETTER TO SENATOR DIRKSEN

from the *Mattachine Review* (1955)

Anonymous

To: *Senator Everett M. Dirksen, Senate of the United States, Washington, D.C.*

Dear Senator Dirksen:

Because I have admired you and applauded your career as a great Republican from a State which has meant much to me, I trouble to write you this letter. I write, not only for myself however, but as a self-appointed spokesman for a large group of misunderstood and maligned people, a group to which you referred in your speech before the Republican women on September 22.

We are citizens of this country, we carry the blood and traditions of many great countries and races, and we share the American Dream; that is, we share it until it is discovered that we are homosexual.

Your reference to homosexuals, and the manner in which you classified us, does not perhaps distinguish you from other high Government authorities. But because your speech was made close to home, and was quoted in the local press, it is to you I write my words of protest.

Government employees are being fired as security risks when it is discovered that they are homosexual. Speaking for myself, while I am not a government employee, I cannot be bought, frightened, or blackmailed into revealing information the confidential nature of which I am morally charged with protecting. Speaking for the millions of other homosexuals, the same can be said for them as individuals in the same proportions that it can be said for heterosexuals.

In short, Senator, homosexuals are not homosexual 24 hours a day 365 days a year. We are not distinguishable from heterosexual people in any visible way. It has been established by psychological research at the Langley-Porter Clinic in San Francisco, and at the University of California at Los Angeles that we are no more unreliable, unstable or dangerous than heterosexuals, except as individual products of our circumstances of birth, early training and youthful experiences in a worldly world would lead or cause us to be. The most prejudiced person must surely, if subconsciously realize that the same is true of heterosexual people.

I know of my own personal knowledge, Senator Dirksen, that the government of the United States, in the executive, the legislative, and the judicial branches is heavily staffed with wonderful men and women who are homosexual. I know of my own personal knowledge that the United States Army, the Air Force, the Navy and the Marine Corps are heavily staffed, from Generals and Admirals to privates and ordinary seamen, with homosexual people. It was hinted at in the Army-McCarthy investigations, and I suspect suppressed for political reasons.

Thousands of graves in France, many many thousand more graves on South Pacific Islands and beneath the seas, contain the sad remains of men who were brave soldiers, airmen, sailors and marines *first* and homosexuals second. They were no less brave, they did no less to win the war for democracy, than did their heterosexual compatriots. But the democracy for which they did fight and die, and still fight and still die, and will yet fight and yet die, denies them and us our rights as individuals, and classifies us with "wreckers, destroyers, security risks, blabber-mouths, drunks, traitors and saboteurs."

There are all of those things *among* us, true, but there are also all of those things among the heterosexual population of these wonderful United States. Our hearts do not beat less fast at the excitement of a political rally such as the one for Eisenhower at which you spoke so sonorously on September 22 because we are homosexual. Our tears do not flow less freely that yours at the loss of husbands, sons and brothers in warfare with Communism because we are homosexual. Our hearts are not less full of pride and honor at the sight of massed American flags because we are homosexual. We do not work less hard for America, or love her less, or support the Republican administration and policies less whole-heartedly because we are homosexual.

I personally have worked long and hard for good government generally and the Republican Party specifically. I am widely known as a devoted and dedicated Republican, and the fact that I am homosexual has nothing to do with it. Yet I cannot, by law, be employed by the government I serve and love if it is known that I am homosexual.

God has granted you a distinguished political career, for which He is to be thanked. But He has denied you the compassion which is the hallmark of a truly great man. Cannot you and the many other intelligent men in high public office retain your prestige and serve your constituency without public reference to the private tragedies of millions of people? For make no mistake, Senator, homosexuality is a tragedy; not inherently, perhaps, but because the unenlightened have made it so. To earn a living we integrate with the heterosexual population by donning a false garment of heterosexuality ourselves. We must conceal and dissimulate because it is unlawful to be what we are. Yet we cannot be otherwise. Is it American and democratic to cause a man to deny what God has made him? I am sure you'll agree it is not.

We know we cannot change or even materially influence public and political opinion about homosexuality. But within your lifetime, Senator, if it has not already done so, there will come to your attention a slow but steady trend toward public acceptance of a condition which is as old as mankind and has existed in all times and in all places.

Being a politician, I suppose, carries a certain obligation to work for personal popularity by public denunciation of that which one believes to be publicly unpopular. Only keep this in mind—homosexuals vote too, in greater numbers than you can possibly know. Their homosexuality does not cause them to espouse any ology or ism which is out of keeping with their individual training, growth and experiences. You cannot know, this, of course, if you are heterosexual.

Open your mind and heart, Senator, like the distinguished American you are, and if you truly believe in the principles of democracy and personal liberty, do not again, publicly or privately, class homosexuals as you did before the Republican women. Many of those women have homosexual sons and daughters. Some of them know it and some of them don't but one of God's noblest creatures is a mother who has been able to accept and understand the fact of her children's homosexuality. If one whose heart is as close to it it as the mother of a homosexual can understand it, our request that people in your position try to understand it does not seem unreasonable.

Special privilege we do not want and would not accept. Equal rights under the law we want and will fight for. Please don't make our fight, already a heart-breaking one, more difficult.

Sincerely yours,
(Name Withheld)

ON THE BISEXUALITY OF MAN

from the *Mattachine Review* (1955)

Ward Summer

First of all, let us remember that man is not classified as heterosexual, homosexual or bisexual by the biological scientist. He is classified in the animal kingdom, as a primate, homo sapiens. In other words, he is a human being before he is anything else. He is possessed of an immortal soul, he belongs to this or that culture or subculture, he lives in such and such a time, he belongs to one economic class or another, he is young or middle-aged or old, and he is motivated by certain instincts or drives. The point of all this is simply that a man is no more essentially a homosexual than he is essentially 35 years old or a citizen of the United States of America. He is only a creature who bleeds when he is cut, and who must breathe oxygen in order to live.

Remembering that man is **man** before anything else, it will soon be seen that if his manner of sexual gratification is habitually different from the majority, it is merely an individual idiosyncrasy. It does not in the least touch upon his basic nature. As André Gide has shown in his rather unusual book, *Corydon,* the lower animals have been observed engaging in homosexual activities. No one in his right mind would feel that the basic nature of the lower animals had been changed by these activities. They are still the same animals. The fact is, any sexual activity is acceptable to the animal. He appears to care little about the "means" of gratification. Whatever is easiest is most acceptable. Usually, normal coitus is easiest for them, but were it not for that, the whole business of procreation would be nothing more than a haphazard, accidental thing. This attitude permeates the entire life-stream. Flowers pollinate their neighbors in a most promiscuous disregard for their sex. And any sexual activity at all, hit-or-miss, is also natural for man. This can be observed in primitive, or uncivilized societies where, outside of certain bizarre taboos, anything is permitted. It is only that man, in our culture, with his great intellectualization, has the ability (and uses it) to repress in himself anything he chooses.

In our modern society, it is the custom of the majority to repress in themselves all elements of homosexuality. Among the homosexuals, it is the heterosexual element that is repressed. It is obvious that the bisexual, who is supposedly unrepressed, must necessarily be a freer individual in that he is in touch with more of himself than the others.

People repress sides of their personalities because of fear. The heterosexual represses his homosexuality because of fear of social condemnation. The homosexual represses his heterosexuality because of fear of the opposite sex, or because of rebellion born of fear of society. There has been a great deal of talk of late about children and adolescents going through a "homosexual phase." This so-called infantile stage of development is nothing more than natural bisexuality. The pubertal or adolescent child is actually as interested in the one sex as in the other—it is all hero worship. Some homosexuals have even admitted going through a "heterosexual" stage as children. If their development had been arrested at that age, would they now be normal individuals? The implications are that homosexuality is childish. I maintain that it is no more childish than heterosexuality. Either orientation is one-sided. The bisexual alone is natural—as is demonstrated by children and animals. (I don't mean to imply that this is an argument for promiscuity. Psychopathic sexual excess is another problem altogether and has no place in this discussion.)

Certainly it **IS** childish to ignore our responsibilities. And society might at least have some reason to criticize the bisexual if he limited himself to homosexual activities and ignored his familial duties. We must accept our responsibilities, although society is not necessarily a valid judge as to what those responsibilities are. At any rate, for society to condemn the homosexual on the same grounds (and what other grounds could it have?) is not merely presumptuous, it is pointless. The homosexual does not have the choice that the bisexual has. His actions are determined by subconscious needs over which he has no control. By the same token, the heterosexual need not feel that he is superior to the former, inasmuch as his actions are likewise governed by unconscious needs. That he is admittedly happier and luckier in many respects, is beside the point. He is still helpless.

Society must protect itself from the individual just as the individual who is maladjusted must protect himself from society. The latter, to be sure, is an amorphous abstract concept only but its fears are none the less as great and as irrational as those of the individual. What society must learn is that the race will continue regardless of the actions of isolated individuals. Somehow, babies will continue to be born (adding to the over-population problem of the world, by the way) and there will always be families to protect and instruct them.

What the individual must learn is that if he limits himself to one sex or the other, he is limiting HIMSELF. The homosexual is missing out, perhaps, on the joys of family life and parenthood. The heterosexual, on the other hand, who has difficulty finding a compatible spouse, is isolated from the opposite sex, is sterile, etc., is ignoring the fact that **ANY** permanent relationship between two compatible people of either sex can be a very happy and productive experience.

Most important of all, sexual matters are **PERSONAL**. It is the individual, in the final analysis, who must determine what his life is going to be. He must be allowed the exercise of his own free will. He should know and accept all parts of himself, the open as well as the hidden. He should become an integrated whole. But regardless of this, whether he sleeps with a man or with a woman is no one's business to condemn.

Sodomy became a crime in the U.S. military only in 1919. Homosexuals were officially banned from the U.S. military in 1943. With the official ban and consequent purges of gays and lesbians, many men lost their pride and their chances for a livelihood as their discharges were branded "dishonorable." The homoerotic experience of the military, together with the anti-homosexual policies that ruined lives, radicalized many young men (and later many women). As the following article from the *Mattachine Review* demonstrates, this persecution was an early and constant concern of American gay men.

THE MILITARY

THE HOMOSEXUAL VETERAN

from the *Mattachine Review* (1955)

MacKinneth Fingal

Uncle Sam Keeps Hacking Away the Rights and Benefits of THE HOMOSEXUAL VETERAN

As of October 28, 1954, the homosexual veteran whom the incompetent psychiatrist didn't detect, or who was too shy and fearful to tell his true story to the psychiatrist, or who rendered faithful, competent service to his country but nevertheless "got caught" and so suffered an "undesirable" or "dishonorable" discharge, will find himself definitely denied the benefits flowing to heterosexual veterans from two of our Federal laws.

Public Law No. 2, 73rd Congress, approved by the president on March 20, 1933, provides a pension (now called "compensation") for:

Any person who served in the active military or naval service and who is disabled as a result of disease or injury incurred in line of duty in such service.[1]

Another important section of the Law provides:

Sec. 6. In addition to the pensions provided, . . . Administrator of Veteran's Affairs is hereby authorized under such limitations as may be prescribed by the President . . . to furnish to veterans of any war domiciliary care where they are suffering with permanent disabilities, tuberculosis or neuropsychotic ailments and medical and hospital treatment for diseases and injuries.

The other statute which discriminates against the homosexual veteran is Public Law 346, the "Servicemen's Readjustment Act of 1944," which was an act "To Provide Federal Government aid for the readjustment in civilian life of returning World War II veterans."[2] It is said that this law was conceived by the Congress as a "necessary and constructive aid to returning veterans in their readjustment to civilian life."[3] The statute is rather lengthy, consisting of 15 chapters, the most important of which are as follows:

Chapter I—"Hospitalization, Claims, and Procedures"
Chapter II—"Aid by Veterans' Organizations"
Chapter IV—"Education of Veterans"
Chapter V—"General Provisions for Loans" (i.e., for "homes, farms, and business property")
Chapter VI—"Employment of Veterans"
Chapter VII—"Readjustment Allowances for Former Members of the Armed Forces Who are Unemployed."

But the most important section or paragraph of P.L. 346 is Section 1503:

A discharge or release from active service under conditions other than dishonorable shall be a prerequisite to entitlement to veterans' benefits provided by this Act or Public Law Numbered 2, Seventy-third Congress, as amended.

Congress makes laws and Federal agencies make rules and regulations pursuant thereto. In this case the Veterans Administration, under authority of the aforementioned laws, has recently been paring benefits.

As far back as 1938 the legislative intent of Public Law No. 2, 73rd Congress, was spelled out, but the word "homosexual" was not there:

Sec. 2.1064. Character of discharge under Public Law, No. 2, 73rd Congress. To be entitled to compensation or pension under Public, No. 2, 73rd Congress, the period of active service upon which claim is based must have been terminated by an honorable discharge. A 'bad conduct discharge,' and 'undesirable discharge,' separation 'for the good of the service,' and ordinary discharge (unless under honorable conditions) or other form of discharge not specifically an honorable discharge, or held by the Service Department to have been granted 'under honorable conditions' will not meet the service requirements of Public No. 2, 73d Congress, and all regulations issued thereunder. An officer who resigned from the service under honorable conditions will be considered as having been honorably discharged.[4]

By 1946, however, the language of the Veteran's Administration had got stronger, so that we find the following:

Sec. 2.1064(c). The acceptance of an undesirable or blue discharge to escape trial by general courtmartial will, by the terms of section 1503, Public No. 2, 73d Congress, as amended, and Public No. 346, 78th Congress, as it will be considered the discharge was under dishonorable conditions.

(d). An undesirable or blue discharge issued because of homosexual acts or tendencies generally will be considered as under dishonorable conditions and a bar to entitlement under Public No. 2, 73d Congress, as amended, and Public No. 346, 78th Congress. **However, the facts in a particular case may warrant a different conclusion, in which event the case should be submitted to central office for the attention and consideration of the director of the service concerned.**[5] (Emphasis supplied)

In 1947, we find the same thing, except that the last few words of Section (d) were changed to read: ". . . submitted to the director, claims service, branch office, for attention and consideration."[6]

The year 1949 saw no changes from 1947, and 1951–52 saw only another slight change in the final phrases of Section (d): ". . . submitted to the director, claims service, district office, in field death cases, to the director, veterans claims service, central office, in field living cases, or to the director of the service concerned in central office cases, for attention and consideration."[7]

Until lately it seemed as though no changes would occur in these two important sections during 1954 or 1955. The homosexual veteran was seemingly "on the fence," for Section (d) was a little ambiguous and not too cruel, what with that second sentence:

However, the facts in a particular case may warrant a different conclusion, in which event the case should be submitted . . . for . . . attention and consideration . . .

Somebody, though, got impatient all of a sudden and decided to do some trimming. On October 28, there were found hidden amongst the vast and intricate mass of rules, regulations, notices, orders, etc., which continually issue from Washington, Sections (c) and (d) again. And this time Section (d) got a haircut, or at least a good shave. It consisted of but **ONE** sentence:

Sec. 3.64 (d). An undesirable discharge issued because of homosexual acts or tendencies generally will be considered as under dishonorable conditions and a bar to entitlement under Public

No. 2, 73d Congress, as amended, and Public Law 346, 78th Congress, as amended . . .[8]

The homosexual veteran seems doomed now. Meanwhile Section (c) is still perched up there above Section (d), with the same shaggy hair, beard, glowering look and everything.

1. *48 Stat. 8, Sec. 1(a)*

2. *58 Stat. 284.*

3. *38 U. S. C. A., pxxxviii*

4. *38 CFR 1939 (1st ed. of CFR, in effect 6-1-38).*

5. *38 CFR (1946 Supp.).*

6. *Ibid., (1947 Supp.).*

7. *38 CFR 3.64(d) (1951 Cumulative Pocket Supp., "for use during 1952").*

8. *19 F. R. 6918 (10-28-54).*

A HOMOSEXUAL LOOKS AT THE CHILD MOLESTER

from the *Mattachine Review* (1956)

James (Barr) Fugate

Our local headlines carried the story even before the facts of the case were known to the police and I heard myself saying with so many others, "Oh no! No! Not that again!" The story was like a nightmare that couldn't have happened, but I knew it had.

In addition to the horror felt by the average reader there was a keener edge to the sorrow that I as a confessed homosexual felt, an edge that would cut deeper for I knew what I must face in the days to come, the grim looks of doubt, contempt, hatred, directed at me as another "pervert." Though people who know me seem to accept and trust me as a member of our community with equal rights, responsibilities and privileges, still they do not always differentiate between the terms used so loosely in the newspapers. To the average person the terms **homosexual, pervert, degenerate** and **sex fiend** all mean the same thing. To them, as a confessed homosexual I am a potential child molester, perhaps even a killer. To the average newsman I am a future headline. To the police I am one of the known deviates in the area to be rounded up after every sex crime and held until I can prove my innocence. (If I can't I may stand trial, and conceivably even be executed for a murder I did not commit, and all because I cannot live a lie by pretending to a heterosexuality that I do not feel as do so many homosexuals today.) To the average parent I am a menace to warn their children against: "Never talk to strange men, and never, never get into a car with anyone you don't know! As for James down the street, always speak to him kindly, but don't ever be friendly with him. He can't help being what he is."

Credit and character references mean nothing here. Acts of kindness and generosity, a clean record with the police are cancelled out. Responsibility and trust held for years are forgotten. And in the light of what happened in Chicago these parents, neighbors and police cannot be blamed for taking all possible precautions to insure their children's safety. Truly, those of my stamp have inherited the furious winds of ignorance, suppression of knowledge, censorship and other such evils whether we deserve them or not. Yet the question that haunts the parents, haunts the homosexual too. What can we do to stop this hideous slaughter?

A week after the Chicago murders a radio commentator widely known for his radical views called for newer, stronger laws against all sex deviates. He criticized the Kefauver committee, the "mealy mouthed protectors of minority rights," the existing laws, the parents themselves for not condemning immediately all sex deviates without so much as a hearing. His solution was simple: "Round 'em up and operate on their brains! We must protect the majority!"

This attitude is no stranger to the Might Makes Right school of politics. Yet if one stops to think a moment it becomes clear that such a legal panacea might do as much harm as good. For instance, to apply this same reasoning to the companion headlines beside those of the Chicago tragedy which told of a young father who, while drunk, beat his infant daughter to death because she had cried to go to the bathroom, shall the law then round up and robotize all young fathers who get drunk in order to protect all infant daughters in this country? Or, by the same standard, because of a 15-year-old son who shot his father to prevent his mother's taking a beating, shall we force all 15-year-old boys with fathers who occasionally beat their mothers to undergo brain surgery that will reduce them to helpless automatons the rest of their lives? Obviously one cannot judge a barrel of apples by a few rotten ones.

To educate, to discuss freely, to study without prejudice is to protect and to arm equally against actual danger and possible error. But who will dare come forward these days and proclaim strongly as two-inch headlines that all deviates are not sex killers, or even potential killers? Most people would laugh at the suggestion that all malaria victims are Typhoid Marys. No one would seriously think of recommending lobotomy to arthritis or polio sufferers as a cure. Yet how many of these same people listen to the radicals who are ready to compound existing miseries by loosing vigilante bands on new witch hunts of comparative innocents?

Obviously there are degrees of sex deviation the same as there are degrees of everything else. In homosexuality a complete range of behavior patterns can be cited by any practicing psychiatrist from the intellectually platonic ties of the chaste to the most savage and sadistic rites of the most bestial. Who is to say all are sex killers when those who study the infinite subtleties of personality will not?

Stronger laws are not the answer to sexual deviation. Law never stopped a disease, nor was a seriously disturbed mental patient ever legislated into healthy and normal behavior. But if enough money were legislated to make available adequate treatment for all who needed it, many sex crimes could be prevented in the years to come. Stronger laws means stronger social stigmas, which in turn breed more individual fears and hiding and frustrations driven underground to ferment until they explode into more Chicago tragedies. Give the deviate a chance to come out in the open and declare himself by exposing his troubles to a competent doctor, rather than suppress and compound them in prison, and chances for his recovery will multiply rapidly.

Certainly laws must be made and enforced to protect children and preserve public decency. Intelligent people, homo and heterosexual alike, agree on this. But there must be common sense and humanitarian consideration in the law too. Yet the age-old argument arises anew: shall our laws aim at collecting an eye for an eye, or shall there be an attempt at understanding and helping through study and knowledge? Vengeance is an ever narrowing circle of fears and hatreds. Charity can be compared to an investment in peace and security. The isolationist, the advocate of any Master Race theory, is perhaps as dangerous in the eyes of history as any pervert or group of deviates, for where one's crimes [are of] passion, the others are guilty of crimes of intellect—or more properly, the lack of it.

Let us look, for instance, at the pervert who has committed a heinous crime against a child. Why did he do what he did? How could he have been prevented from doing it? What were the original causes that made him a killer?

In the first place, it is generally agreed that homosexuality is a product of environment problems, not hereditary weaknesses. Probably nine out of ten sexual inverts have been allowed (or even forced) to become so because of parental ignorance. The mother who devours the son as an infant, the father who rejects him as a teen-ager, the teacher who is not allowed to answer his questions because of conventionally false modesty and prudery, the shortage of doctors, (or their expensive fees), which makes consultation and counseling financially impossible when the time is ripe for it, all have contributed to the sex crime that makes headlines and causes such violent rage in the minds of the readers and radio commentators. The actual murderer is perhaps no more to blame for what he has done than is a can of inflammable cleaning fluid left carelessly in a room where children play. (Yet are we to outlaw cleaning fluids simply because they are sometimes dangerous?)

Chances are the invert (or pervert, as you wish,) has made many attempts to adjust to society. If nothing more, since misery loves company, he has probably tried to find and make friends with others in society that suffer the same torments that are his. But because the homosexual is a criminal in the eyes of the law, where is he forced to go to find those of his own kind so that he may not be jailed in a possible raid? In short, when he cannot fraternize with others of his nature, he is forced to do his hunting for companions on the streets where jungle law is too often in evidence. There he may be preyed upon by thugs and blackmailers who find him a foolproof mark because he dares not go to the police no matter what is done to him. Eventually, in his turn, he comes to prey on those who are weaker than himself—unfortunately, this sometimes means children. Thus, crimes are committed and headlines are made. How can these things be prevented? The answer seems to be in laws which treat the invert justly, but fairly, and medicine to treat him or confine him as individually necessary. Recently there have been two healthy steps taken in this direction.

In a special report on Sanity, *Newsweek* magazine, (October 24, 1955) highlighted the need for a greater government-supported mental health program by spelling the situation out in figures that will make anyone stop and think. For instance, the report points out that there are less than 600 mental hospitals in this country of 160 millions, just half of what is needed! Only 1/20th of our doctors are psychiatrists: 12,000 are needed immediately against an increase of only 250 per year! Were every person needing psychiatric care to apply for it today, existing psychiatrists would have about 2500 patients each!

Is it any wonder that newspapers can feature almost a complete catalogue of crimes daily on their front pages? How many murders of all varieties might never have been committed if there had been some place for the criminal to go for medical aid before it was too late? Information such as this disseminated over wide areas of the population will eventually make available the funds needed to help those who need help. Until then we can expect more headlines.

Still more encouraging, and striking at the very root of the stigmata that prevents so many sexual inverts from identifying themselves and seeking aid openly, last summer in

Philadelphia the American Law Institute in adopting its Model Penal Code decided that acts of adultery and sodomy must not be considered criminal so long as they are practiced privately and without force between consenting adults. This does not mean that laws preserving public decency are to be altered or laws punishing those who molest children are to be any less strict. Under this new Penal Code, the invert would be encouraged to acknowledge his sexual status in the very beginning without fear of being blackmailed the rest of his life for his honesty. He would be free to associate with those of his own stamp and thus find an outlet for those frustrations and feelings of isolation that can become so dangerous when they are bottled up for long periods. In addition to this, thousands of homosexuals might hope to lead the lives of normal men if psychiatric treatment is administered early enough, and at prices they can afford to pay.

All this is a far cry from those who demand blood, law, brain surgery and prison brutality to stop the perverts. Which will it be for us as the leader of nations—the enlightened ways of civilization, or a legal reversion to the instincts of a pack of beasts? Homosexuals are not potential killers any more than heterosexuals. A few are driven to kill, but the percentage seems much smaller than the percentage of heterosexuals who are involved in crimes of passion. Homosexuals have contributed as generously to the progress of mankind, and especially to his cultures, as any other group. At various times they have written his books and music, painted his pictures, made his laws, spread his religions, doctored his sick, farmed his land, fought his wars as has everyone else. Because of those few who have become killers, are we to deprive the country and the world of the talents and services of an entire group? The answer is up to us; and, thank God, there is still time to decide this most important question fairly.

SEXUAL FREEDOM: WHY IT IS FEARED

from the *Mattachine Review* (1962)

Robert Anton Wilson

Those who believe in, and seriously advocate and practice, sexual freedom are, and always have been, a minority. If there is one generalization that truly applies to the *majority* of men and women in all civilizations, everywhere, it is that they fear sexual freedom more than anything else, more than death itself, even. This is the crucial mystery of human nature and, quite properly, it has been the area of most intense investigation by depth psychologists from Freud and Reich to Marcuse and Brown.

A. S. Neill, the founder of the Summerhill school, was once asked where in the civilized world a man could practice homosexuality without fear of legal persecution. Neill replied that he knew of no such place, adding that he didn't even know of a place where a man could practice heterosexuality without being persecuted for it. Homosexuals, Dr. Albert Ellis wrote, think that they suffer because they live in an anti-homosexual culture, but the truth is, he added, we *all* suffer because we live in an *anti-sexual* culture.

Eschewing depth psychology for the moment and taking a deliberately superficial view, why does the "man in the street" fear sexual freedom? That is, what reason would he himself give for the irrational taboos to which he submits and tries to inflict upon others? The answer is a truism. "Sexual freedom," the man in the street will tell you, "leads to anarchy and the collapse of Order."

Instead of automatically denying this (as most advocates of sexual freedom do), let us consider it for a moment. The architect of modern anarchism, Michael Bakunin, wrote in his *God and the State* that without "God," the State is impossible. He instances as proof the Republics of France and the United States, both of which were founded by free-thinkers and atheists, but which both embraced the "God" idea very rapidly when the practical details of governing had to be faced. Wilhelm Reich's *Sexual Revolution* and *Mass Psychology of Fascism* document that pro-State attitudes and authoritarianism are usually joined with dogmatic religion and anti-sex fears, whereas anti-State and libertarian attitudes are generally coupled with free thought and pro-sex affirmation. Adorno's classic *Authoritarian Personality* gives reams of statistical proof of the Reichian thesis. A governor, we can safely say, has less problems in enforcing obedience if his subjects are mystical, religious and frightened of sex.

The reason for this is easy to understand. *Sex denial is very close to being absolutely impossible*, and—as the subtle Jesuits new long before Freud—even when the would-be ascetic thinks he has "triumphed" over the flesh, it sneaks up on him from a new direction and takes him by surprise. Thus, *the inevitable consequence of sex denial is guilt*: that special guilt which comes of continual failure to accomplish that which you consider "good." (This continual failure is the "dark night of the soul" lamented by medieval monks). Now, a guilt-ridden man is an easy man to manipulate and force to your own will, because self-respect is the prerequisite of independence and rebellion, and the guilt-ridden person can have no self-respect. Modern advertising revolves around this central fact as a great safe lock pivots on a single jewel: from "B.O." and "97 pound weakling" to the soap that makes you feel "*clean all over*," advertising has inculcated self-doubts and guilts in order to persuade that the sponsor's panacea will cure these very doubts which the sponsor himself through his ad agency has created!

What does "government" mean, after all? Control of Mr. A by Mr. B—or, in other words, the subordination of one man's will to another's. We have been taught that society cannot exist without government and that this subordination of wills is existentially necessary and unchangeable; hence, we accept it. But anthropology presents a different picture. As the anthropologist Kathleen Gough has written, "The State as a social form has existed for about one-two-hundredth part of man's history . . . it may be one of the shortest-lived forms of human society."[*] What we call anarchy—i.e., voluntary association—has been man's dominant pattern for 199/200ths of his history. It should be no surprise that, as Rattray Taylor shows in *Sex in History*, these pre-State societies were not sexually repressed and did not fear sexual freedom to the utmost extent.

Enforced conformity of human beings—the subjugation of society to the will of the State—leads to generalized stress upon the total organism of each. Modern psychosomatic medicine makes abundantly clear that all life (protoplasm) consists of electro-colloidal equilibrium between gel (total dispersion) and sol (total contraction), and every stress produces contraction, as is seen in exaggerated form in the typical withdrawal of the snail and turtle, a human infant visibly cringing with fear, etc. It is this (usually microscopic) contraction of the physical body that we experience psychically as "anxiety." When it becomes chronic, this contraction effects the large muscles and creates that "hunched, bowed" look which actors employ when portraying a timid and beaten man. The tendency toward this "posture of defeat" is visible in all State-dominated societies, as it was conspicuously absent in the bold carriage of the State-less Polynesians and American Indians when first contacted.

But the chronic anxiety which is the subjective aspect of this physical "shrinking biopathy" leads to a *defensive* attitude and a philosophy of *control*. Government per se consists of this compulsion to control in its most highly developed form, and war represents the most coercive and ultimate form of control. No government lasts more than a generation without plunging its subjects into war; even the government founded by the pacifist Gandhi has plunged its subjects into war *eight times* in the generation since his death. Four wars per century is the average ratio for a long-lasting government.

Geldings, any farmer will tell you, are easier to control than stallions. The first governments, which were frankly slave-States, inculcated sexual repression for precisely this reason. Besides creating loads of guilt and self-doubt in the slaves, thus making them easier to intimidate for the reasons previously explained, sexual repression is itself a contraction of the large muscles. You cannot banish a wish from consciousness, as Groddeck demonstrates in *The Book of the It*, without contracting your abdominal muscles. Sexual repression in particular means what Neill calls "the stiff stomach disease," because the only way the genitals can be stopped from lively activity is by deadening them through abdominal armoring. It is Wilhelm Reich who deserves credit for seeing the ultimate implications of this. Reich pointed out that loosening of the chronic muscle contractions which characterize submissive "civilized" man must be a process of *physical* pain and *psychic* anxiety. We are not able to understand the two great mysteries of social behavior: why sexual repression is accepted and why government is accepted, when the first diminishes joy and the second is leading obviously to the destruction of the species. *Submissiveness is anchored in the body.* The anti-sexual training of infants, children and adolescents creates muscular tensions which cause pain whenever rebellion is attempted. This is [why] homosexuals and sexually free heterosexuals are so conspicuously "neurotic": besides the condemnation of society, they suffer also the "condemnation" of their own muscles pushing them toward conformity and submission.

Freud's famous pessimism is rooted in understanding of the psychic side of this process which I have described physically. "Man is his own prisoner," was Freud's final, gloomy conclusion. But recent thinkers have been less sure of this. Reich's *Sexual Revolution*, Brown's *Life Against Death* and Marcuse's *Eros and Civilization* all look forward toward a "civilization without repression," and all three tend to recognize that this would have to be a State-less civilization.

Before the murder of Mangus Colorado and the betrayal of Cochise, Apache society represented an approximation of such a free culture. Until marriage, all were sexually free to enjoy themselves as they wished (the same freedom returned when a marriage was dissolved) and if the chief's wishes were not acceptable to anyone he was at liberty to enter another Apache tribe or start one of his own if he had enough followers. (Geronimo did just this when Cochise made his treaty with the U.S. government.) The tribe, thus, was held together by what anarchists call *voluntary association* and did not contain an authoritarian State apparatus.

In a technilogically [*sic*] more advanced society the same principle can be carried out. Proudhon's famous formula for anarchism, "the dissolution of the State into the economic organism," means, basically, the substitution of voluntary contractual organizations for the involuntary coercive authority of the State. In such a system, whatever voluntary associations a man joined would be truly an expression of his will (otherwise, he would not join them). Such a State-less civilization could be sexually free as the State-less bands, tribes and chiefdoms of pre-history; *repression would have no social function*, as there would be no need of creating guilt and submissiveness in the population.

Such a picture is not as "utopian" as it may seem—and "utopianism" is not something to despise nowadays, when the very survival of mankind is, as Norman Brown has noted, a "utopian dream." Cybernation has created—as Norbert Weiner predicted it would, and as writers like Kathleen Gough and Henri [*sic*] Marcuse are beginning to note with mixed joy and fear—the possibility of a society of abundance in which there will be very little need for work. Traditional humanity is at the end of its tether, due to the two great achievements of modern science, nuclear energy and cybernation. If we as individuals manage to survive the first, our culture certainly cannot survive the second. When it is no longer necessary for the masses of men to toil "by the sweat of their brows" for bread, one of the chief props for social repression will fall. Large-scale unemployment up to the level of massive starvation has, it is true, occurred in the past, and the ruling class has managed to remain in their saddles; but the large-scale unemployment to which we are now heading will make all previous "depressions" seem minor by comparison, and there will be no hope of relief ever coming—there will be no way to create new jobs. Undoubtedly, the ruling classes will allow the starvation to reach epic proportions; and, undoubtedly, the muscularly repressed masses, conditioned to submission and self-denial, will accept it—except for a few rebels, as always; but, eventually, perhaps when cannibalism sets in, the whole edifice of culture based on repression will come tumbling down and, like Humpty Dumpty, nobody will be able to put it together again. Those now alive may live to see this.

The unrepressed man of the future—if there is a future—will look back at our age and wonder how we survived without all landing in the madhouse. That so many of us do land in madhouses will be accepted as the natural consequence of repressed civilization.

*The Decline of the State, by Kathleen Gough, Correspondence Publishing Company, 1962.

SEX OFFENSES: AN OBSOLETE CONCEPT

from *Forbidden Sexual Behavior and Morality*, the *Mattachine Review* (1962)

R. E. L. Masters

Scientific knowledge of human sexuality has increased immeasurably in the last century—especially in the last half century, under the impetus given the study of both normal and aberrant sexual phenomena by the work of the truly great Sigmund Freud, his colleagues and followers, and laborers in the fruitful vineyard of psychoanalysis generally.

However, and as many persons still do not seem to recognize, the knowledge of the phenomena of sex acquired in recent times has by no means been provided exclusively by psychoanalysts. Psychoanalysis is identified in the public mind with investigations of sexuality, particularly of deviant sexuality, and it is true that psychoanalysis provided the decisive *élan vital* for such thorough going investigations as we have seen in the last fifty years; but that should not be taken to mean that other sciences and areas of scholarship have not by now made their own extensive, significant, and influential contributions.

Psychology and psychiatry, along with anthropology, sociology, various non-psychiatric branches of medicine, and law, have all made—along with still other disciplines—important studies and findings in the erotic realm. The result is that there now exists a vast body of knowledge in the area of human sexuality which is not yet complete or very well integrated, but still valuable and illuminating.

In view of this, it is not only distressing (*tragic* is doubtless the more appropriate word), but also most curious, to find that sex legislation in this country continues to be based upon unscientific, supernaturalistic religio-ethical notions and no longer existing practicalities current at the time of Moses. The phenomenon is particularly curious when one is aware that within the legal profession—which is not as reactionary, stupid, and ill-informed (perhaps only less prolifically literary) in these matters as sexologists often assume—there is a widespread and perhaps almost general recognition of the inadequacy and inequity of contemporary legislation dealing with sexual behavior and powerful sentiment in behalf of statutory revisions to conform more nearly with the realities of the present-day situation where sexual knowledge, beliefs, and behavior are concerned.

Even though attorneys, judges, and professors of jurisprudence are not lacking in appreciation of the irrationality, barbarism, and absurdity of the American sex statutes, the ground for criticism remains that the statutes continue to exist. Moreover, impetus to reforms that may be called effective has come not, in the main, from those concerned professionally with the law and with law-making and legal reform, who might have been expected to provide such leadership, but from workers in the sciences who have had not only to provide the requisite knowledge, but have tackled the almost overwhelming job of re-educating the public in sexological matters as well. Some will feel, indeed, that the very fact that the legal profession is *not* lacking in an understanding of the inequities of contemporary sex legislation places that profession in an even worse light than would be the case were its members merely ignorant.

The American Law Institute's proposed *Model Penal Code*, which seeks to bring United States legislation more nearly into line with the comparatively enlightened French *Code penal*, is an example of just this kind of juristic awareness on the one hand and impotence on the other. Modern jurists recognize the principle that sexual acts between adults, which are private and take place by mutual consent, should be excluded from statutory consideration; but apart from drawing up recommendations, to be perused and praised by fellow attorneys and academicians of other disciplines, they do little to implement their own findings—the best method of implementation being, of course, the introduction *and wholehearted backing* of genuinely remedial legislation.

In defense of the ineffectuality and velleity characteristic of attorneys and legislators where sex laws are concerned, it is argued that the public will not support any liberalization of the statutes, and corrective legislation is not introduced and/or supported because, as Morris Ploscowe has put it, "of the fear that a vote for repeal would be branded as a vote for immorality." Whether the legal profession, and the legislative representatives of the people, are here offering a valid defense is for the reader to decide. However, we have recently seen expressed, most notably in the U.S. Supreme Court's desegregation decisions, the philosophy that it is up to legal and legislative leaders to lead, and this whether the masses of the people wish to be led or not—the prerequisite being that the direction taken should be towards, and not away from, a position consistent with contemporary notions of what is moral, just, and socially realistic.

Whether they would wipe most of the sex "offenses" from the statute books altogether, or punish masturbators by burning them alive and strewing their odious ashes to the winds, the typical attorney and judge are likely to be painfully aware of the need for *uniform* sex legislation which will end once and forever the idiocy that what is no offense at all, or only a misdemeanor, in one jurisdiction, is a heinous crime warranting the most severe retribution in another, and perhaps adjoining, jurisdiction.

For example, fornication is punished in Virginia with a twenty-dollar fine while the same offense committed in Arizona may result in a three-year prison term. Two other states, North Dakota and Rhode Island, penalize fornicators and fornicatresses with thirty-day jail sentences (North Dakota) and ten-dollar fines (Rhode Island).

Homosexuality, a misdemeanor in New York when the relationship is between consenting adults, can send both parties to prison for the rest of their lives in Nevada.

Penalties for prostitution may vary, in the various states, from fines or brief jail sentences to five-year prison terms.

Age of consent ranges from twelve years in some states to the ludicrous extreme of twenty-one years in another. Intercourse with an underage female may or may not be rape, depending on where it occurs, when the girl in question is a sexually mature prostitute who has actively solicited the intercourse.

And so on.

To suppose that such a travesty upon judicial logic and common sense as this hodgepodge of conflicting legislation represents is the will of the people, is probably to underestimate the intelligence of the public—a feat rarely accomplished by lawmakers or anyone else outside of the film and television industries. Legislators in a position to do something about sex laws, and the legal profession generally, have been too long fearful of the noisy pressures of a minority which no longer speaks for the people—if it ever did.

To propose and support remedial sex legislation of a liberalized variety is to incite a highly vociferous and vicious rabble of fundamentalist preachers and other neurotics, psychotics, and demagogues who are always looking for just such an opportunity to win headlines for themselves and inflame the emotions of their followers. But the political power of such spokesmen for the illiterate rabble—who readily accuse of seeking to legitimize vice any spokesman for the liberal sex-legalistic viewpoint—is certainly disproportionate to their public influence generally. Against them, though lawmakers seem never to have noticed, is thrown not only the politically negligible weight of the intellectual and scientific communities, but also the weight of the larger and more powerful churches, which are the bitter foes of radical fundamentalism and which have, in many cases, already gone on record as being aware that contemporary restraints of a legal kind upon human sexuality are unrealistic and generally unenforceable. Unfortunately, since they no longer believe it quite proper to lift their voices, the larger and more intelligent religious groups are often drowned out by the hysterical screams and shouts and strident screechings of the fanatics. However, that does not at all mean that the rabble-rousers and their followers control anything like a majority of the votes, as seems often to be assumed.

What it does mean, and this has long been true, is that a minority of anachronistic (and atavistic) ethical and theological cultists, by dint of sheer lung power and uninhibited vituperation, have imposed upon the majority of non-fundamentalists a dictatorship of the ignorant in the area of official sexual morality as reflected in antisexual legislation. The majority of Americans have for some time now been prepared for statutory revisions, but are often cowed, as are so many legislators, judges, and attorneys, by the outcries of the demagogues, so that they are hesitant to make their views publicly known. One can thus only ponder with sadness and wonder a situation wherein a noisy minority is permitted to endure as the arbiter of official sexual morality by a majority which could overturn the minority rule at any time, if only it could find the necessary courage and initiative to undertake the effort.

The foregoing should not be taken to imply of course that the majority of Americans—especially the majority of church-going Americans—are in favor of condoning sexual promiscuity or other transgressions against the old Biblical codes. Rather, what is suggested is that a probable significant majority of spokesmen for the more responsible religious and juristic viewpoints are now prepared to make the distinction, which should have been made long ago, between sins on the one hand, and crimes on the other; and that if this leadership were vigorously exerted, a sizable majority of all Americans would almost certainly go along with some sane legislative changes, especially in the direction of uniformity, but even in the direction of liberalization consistent with reality.

What is needed, obviously—though doubtless it will be necessary in the beginning to settle for something less—is to eliminate the whole notion of "sex crimes," placing actual crimes against persons, such as rape and child-molesting, under other more appropriate headings, and eliminating from statutory consideration altogether such matters as (adult) homosexuality and the various sexual practices of men and women, such as fellation, cunnilingus, and anal intercourse, presently punishable as felonies even when occurring between husband and wife.

It is too often impossible to obtain justice where behavior labeled "sex offense" is concerned. The whole area of sex is so beclouded by emotions, superstitions, and puerilities as to preclude the possibility of rational approach. While placing rape, child-molesting, and other offenses against persons under other headings would not eliminate prejudice altogether, at least it would be helpful in procuring a somewhat more dispassionate climate both of general opinion and in the courtroom.

In addition to abolishing the concept of "sex crimes" as a special class of offenses unto themselves, great care should be taken to avoid terminology which, by its very nature, generates emotionality and thus makes impossible the objectivity essential to reasoned consideration of the facts in any given case if justice is to result.

Such terminology as "crimes against nature," which is not only emotion-generating but scientifically inaccurate as well, should be barred from all statutes and from the courtroom deliberations. Similarly, any semantical revision should prohibit the use of such words as "pervert," "perverted," "sex fiend," and others which, it is clear, tend to interpose blind emotivity between the facts and the reasoning processes of those who must try to evaluate them.

The abolition of the whole concept of "sex offenses" may seem to some too sweeping a measure, but it is demonstrably evident that nothing less will now suffice to eradicate the evils arising out of superstition, misconception, and hysteria engendered by the sex offender witch hunt of recent times. The alternative is to persist in the repugnant practice of scapegoat prosecutions and wholesale hypocrisy where a few unfortunates too often suffer, cast up as offerings to the prejudice of our forbears, in order that society may seem to prohibit what is generally practiced or may be permitted to be practiced without the slightest detriment to the social structure.

FRANKLIN KAMENY

Subscribers to lesbian and gay magazines endured constant threats of exposure. Many in the 1950s feared any association with any "deviant" group. Both the *Mattachine Review* and *The Ladder* published articles seeking to assure subscribers that they were safe. Cautious readers of the *Review* were justified in their fears when, in 1963, Rep. John Dowdy of Texas introduced into Congress a bill to revoke the registration and fund-raising permit of The Mattachine Society of Washington. In the course of hearings for the bill, Frank Kameny, founder and then-president of the Mattachine Society of Washington, was pressured to reveal the names of members. Fortunately, by 1963, the National Capital Area Civil Liberties Union had decided to concern themselves with the issue, and a lawyer from the group testified to the bill's unconstitutionality.

Founded in 1961 by Frank Kameny and Jack Nichols, Mattachine of Washington was much more radical than the West Coast (then based in San Francisco) society. A physicist by training, Kameny had lost his government job in 1957 after a "lewd conduct" arrest was uncovered. He envisioned a civil rights movement and direct action tactics along with education and community service. He pushed his organization to work on issues of government persecution.

Kameny was not interested in listening to heterosexual professionals tell homosexuals about homosexuality. He clearly separated the question of the "causes" or "nature" of homosexuality, and argued that the goal of the homophile movement should be equality and justice, not tolerance based on pity. He firmly denied that homosexuality was a disease and challenged not only the evidence of those who insisted on the pathology of homosexuality, but the motives for studying homosexuality at all.

LETTER TO THE MEMBERS OF THE U.S. HOUSE OF REPRESENTATIVES
(1962)

Franklin Kameny

The Mattachine Society of Washington,
Washington, D.C., August 28, 1962.

Hon. _____,
House of Representatives, Washington, D.C.

DEAR _____,: Enclosed, for your interest and information, is a formal statement of the purposes of the Mattachine Society of Washington, a newly formed organization, devoted to the improvement of the status of our country's 15 million homosexuals.

Included, also, is a copy of our news release, which was submitted to the Washington newspapers and others, and to the various press services.

The question of homosexuality, and the prejudice against it, both personal and official, is a serious one, involving, as it does more than 1 out of every 10 American citizens, including roughly a quarter-million in, each, the Federal civil service, the Armed Forces, and security-sensitive positions in private industry, and at least 10 percent of your constituents.

We feel that the Government's approach is archaic, unrealistic, and inconsistent with basic American principles. We feel, in addition, that it is inexcusably and unnecessarily wasteful of trained manpower and of the taxpayers' money.

We realize that this area presents you with many potential problems, some of them quite subtle and touchy ones of politics and public relations, and that they are not always subject to easy solution, but policies of repression, persecution, and exclusion will not prove to be workable ones in the case of this minority, any more than they have, throughout history, in the case of other minorities. This is a problem which must be worked with, constructively, not worked against, destructively, as is now the case. A fresh approach by the Federal Government is badly needed.

We welcome any comments which you may have on this subject.

We will be pleased to meet with you personally, at your convenience, to discuss these and related matters.

Thank you for your consideration of our position.

Sincerely yours,

FRANKLIN E. KAMENY
President

Excerpts of the Constitution of the Mattachine Society of Washington

Article II. Purpose:

SEC. 1. It is the purpose of this organization to act by any lawful means:

(a) To secure for homosexuals the right to life, liberty, and the pursuit of happiness, as proclaimed for all men by the Declaration of Independence; and to secure for homosexuals the basic rights and liberties established by the word and the spirit of the Constitution of the United States;

(b) To equalize the status and position of the homosexual with those of the heterosexual by achieving equality under law, equality of opportunity, equality in the society of his fellow men, and by eliminating adverse prejudice, both private and official;

(c) To secure for the homosexual the right, as a human being, to develop and achieve his full potential and dignity, and the right, as a citizen, to make his maximum contribution to the society in which he lives;

(d) To inform and enlighten the public about homosexuals and homosexuality;

(e) To assist, protect, and counsel the homosexual in need.

Sec. 2. It is not a purpose of this organization to act as a social group, or as an agency for personal introductions.

Sec. 3. This organization will cooperate with other minority organizations which are striving for the realization of full civil rights and liberties for all.

Mattachine Society of Washington

The formation of a new social action group in the Greater Washington, D.C., area is announced. This group, the Mattachine Society of Washington, is dedicated to improving the status of the homosexual in our society, in the interest both of that minority group and of the Nation. The society discusses and acts upon all problems relating to the homosexual, both general and specific.

Guest speakers will address the group from time to time on a variety of relevant subjects. The society is also setting up a professional referral service—doctors, lawyers, clergymen, etc.—for the homosexual in need.

The organization feels that the homosexual today is where the Negro was in the 1920's, except that the Negro has had, at worst, the mere indifference of his Government and, at best, its active assistance, whereas the homosexual has always had to contend with the active hostility of his Government. For this reason, it is time that a strong initiative be taken to obtain for the homosexual minority—a minority in no way different, as such, from other of our national minority groups—the same rights, provided in the Constitution and the Declaration of Independence, as are guaranteed to all citizens. These include the rights to the pursuit of happiness, and to equality of opportunity; the right, as human beings, to develop and achieve their full potential and dignity; and the right, as citizens, to be allowed to make their maximum contribution to the society in which they live—rights which Federal policy and practice now deny them.

The society feels that prejudice directed against an individual, for no cause other than an unconventional sexual preference, is unwarranted, and that harsh, discriminatory action taken on the basis of such prejudice, with its incident waste of useful talent and manpower, is not consistent with the national welfare. It is felt that personal and popular prejudice cannot be eliminated as long as official prejudice exists and is indulged.

For this reason, the society's primary effort will be directed to four main areas: First, the clearly improper, discriminatory policies of the U.S. Civil Service Commission, policies which are plainly unconstitutional, and which operate against the best interests of the country, in that they act to deprive the Nation of the services of many clearly well-qualified citizens who have much to offer. That these policies are quite needless is demonstrated by the fact that, despite them, there are at least 200,000 homosexuals in the Federal service, and have been for many years, with no ill effects.

Second, the Armed Forces' needless and harshly administered policies of exclusion. The present practice of giving less than fully honorable discharges to homosexuals is unnecessarily vicious. In view of the fact that the Armed Forces also presently include at least a quarter-million homosexuals in all ranks, without ill effects, and that over a million served well and honorably in World War II, present policy seems open to serious question.

Third, the illogical policies of our security-clearance system for civilian and military Government personnel, and for those in private industry, under which all homosexuals, as a group, are regarded as security risks, without consideration of the merits of each individual case. Despite the continuing presence of some quarter-million homosexuals with security-clearance, at all levels, and within the cognizance of all agencies, the number of breaches of security resulting from homosexuality is virtually, if not actually, nil. Examination will show that present policies foster just that susceptibility to blackmail against which these policies are supposed to protect.

Fourth, the area of local law, both its provisions and its administration and enforcement. The society feels that the example of the State of Illinois should be followed, in legalizing private relations on the part of consenting adults, but that, in any case, action must be taken against existing, often flagrant and shocking abuses and violations of due process and of proper rights, liberties, and freedoms in this area.

The organization seeks a reassessment and reconsideration of present, totally unrealistic Federal policy and practice, law and regulation, on homosexuality. A New Frontier approach to official policies and practices which relegate over 15 million Americans to second-class citizenship is long overdue and badly needed. The Government, hitherto, has attempted to sweep this problem under the rug and, ostrichlike, has refused to face the situation or to deal with it in a logical fashion.

The Mattachine Society of Washington is confident that all intelligent, informed, public-spirited citizens will join them in their efforts to achieve a fresh and reasonable approach to this problem.

C

ONE

Of the three major U.S. homophile organizations founded in the 1950s, ONE was undoubtedly the most contentious and radical. Upon the assimilationist takeover of Mattachine, some early members went to ONE, and from there they not only offered a different perspective on homophile issues, but also criticized Mattachine.

In contrast to the apologetic tone of both the Mattachine Society and the Daughters of Bilitis, the activists at ONE argued that homosexuality was a positive, life-affirming option. Foreshadowing gay liberationist themes, they suggested that homosexuals were rebellious and creative by nature. David Freeman argued for the existence of a homosexual culture and suggested that it has much to offer "mainstream" cultures.

ONE magazine, begun in 1954, provided the following statement of beliefs and purpose:

ONE does not claim that homosexuals are better or worse than anyone else, that they are special in any but one sense. And in that one sense ONE claims positively that homosexuals do not have the civil rights assured all other citizens. ONE is devoted to correcting this.

ONE means to stimulate thought, criticism, research, literary and artistic production in an effort to bring the public to understand deviants and deviants to understand themselves as the two sides are brought together as one.

ONE advocates in no way any illegal acts, condones none in the past, incites none in the future. This magazine is not and does not wish to be merely an erotic publication.

ONE is frankly at odds with present unjust laws pertinent to deviation and with present authorities who abuse their offices in unjust treatment of deviants.

ONE is backed by no political or social group, leans toward none, is wholly and completely unfinanced. ONE has no paid employees yet and its growth is dependent entirely upon its readers.

ONE sponsored an annual mid-winter institute on gay and lesbian issues, which members of many different groups attended. This was the site of some of the most contentious battles, around issues such as "homosexual rights" among others. Founded in Los Angeles in 1952, the ONE Institute continues to operate today in conjunction with the International Gay and Lesbian Archives. The following articles show some of the range and the distinctive politics of ONE.

TO BE ACCUSED, IS TO BE GUILTY

from *ONE Magazine* (1953)

Dale Jennings

Today when I reported at the office of the Jury Commissioner for jury duty, I was given a long questionnaire. It included the surprising question: "Have you ever been arrested?" Though I need not have answered, I checked yes and added: "Should not this word have been *convicted?* Innocent persons can be and are arrested." I wonder when I'll be called.

The asking of this actually stupid question reminded me immediately of the attitude of many who heard of my case. The general feeling ran something like: "But *nice* people just don't get arrested!" although it usually came out in these words: "*How* could you have let this happen to you!" Homosexuals asked me hundreds of questions about where I first met the officer, what I said to him, why I let him into the house and exactly what happened there. Of course, none of these data were homosexually to the point. Even if I had done all the things which the prosecution claimed—repeating over and over: "... a gesture no normal person would make even ONCE"—I would have been guilty of no unusual act, only an illegal one in this society. Yet even the most confirmed homosexuals seemed to have forgotten this as they sympathetically grilled me to determine the merits of the case and whether it should be supported, and held long debates on whether I was "guilty" or not. They had accepted society's evaluation of themselves.

But if they only debated, how my heterosexual friends sweat blood wrestling with incredulity! This just couldn't be so! Innocent people just *don't* get into such a situation! *For to be accused is to be guilty.* These, of course, ceased to be friends by mutual consent. Others were outraged at such obvious framing and became even stauncher supporters than many homosexuals involved. They realized that this could happen to anyone.

There is a certain smugness in many of our own number regarding arrest—which I myself shared until that badge loomed in my face and the handcuffs locked my wrists together. We homosexuals have said in effect: "I never expose myself to danger. I never speak to strangers, go to questionable places or do anything that might give me away. Those who do, ask for it and deserve what they get." This assumes that everyone is arrested in "questionable" places by total strangers under even stranger circumstances and that they made the dangerous gesture themselves. It assumes that they know everything to be known about their friends, that their names, addresses and phone numbers could never fall into the wrong hands because *their* friends are never arrested either, and that no police officer could ever break into their social circle. It assumes that there are no homosexual or bisexual police, that officers can always be spotted and that they never use illegal means to make an arrest. Finally, it assumes that these admirably careful persons never make a culpable gesture, have no mannerisms that could be construed as deviate, are totally unknown in homosexual circles, and that there are certain places where certain behavior is safe and acceptable—in spite of the fact that *all* homosexual acts are legally criminal and socially taboo.

For this reason, many of my own harassed minority would have nothing to do with the case of a person who was so foolish as to let himself get arrested. It would certainly never happen to them. Making the most elating and at the same time depressing remark during the campaign, a friend of mine said: "To me, you are unquestionably guilty of the charges, but I shall fight it with you because the law and not the act is unnatural." To be innocent and yet not be able to convince even your own firm constituents, carries a peculiar agony that perhaps explains the tone of indignation in this account.

However the circumstances were certainly typical and the design so familiar that I blame no one for disbelief. I was looking for a movie to fill in an empty evening. I found later that people with this pastime in mind are never as discriminating as I claimed to be. Two movies that I passed were uninviting and, on the way to a third up the street, I was unwise enough to use a public rest room in a park. This, too, was a mistake: respectable people don't use these civic conveniences under any circumstances. Having done nothing that the city architect didn't have in mind when he designed the place, I left—followed by a big, rough looking character who appeared out of nowhere. He caught up with with me, struck up a one-sided conversation, walked to the third movie with me (which I'd already seen, darn it) and then followed me over a mile home. Thinking he had robbery in mind, I walked fast, took detours and said goodbye at each corner. Later I wondered how obvious I must have appeared to him to cause this persistence, until he remarked to another officer in the patrol car that things had been very dull this week: "It's all I can do to keep up the old quota."

Arriving home, and in front of a witness, I said another goodbye and unlocked the door: he pushed on by and entered uninvited. What followed would have been a nightmare even if he hadn't turned out to be vice squad. Sure now that this big character was a thug, I—as the prosecutor described it—"flitted wildly" from room to room wondering how to get rid of this person sprawled in the divan making sexual gestures and proposals. I was almost relieved when he strolled into the back bedroom because now I could call the police. What I'd have said to them, I don't know and what he'd have done if he'd heard, was up to luck. Then he called twice, "Come in here!" His voice was loud and commanding. He'd taken his jacket off, was sprawled on the bed and his shirt was unbuttoned half way down. During the tense conversation there, he asked me what kind of work I did, how much I made, and what the rent here was. Then he slapped the bed and said, "Sit down." Now he insisted that I was homosexual and urged me to "let down my hair." He'd been in the Navy and "all us guys played around." I told him repeatedly that he had the wrong guy; he got angrier each time I said it. At last he grabbed my hand and tried to force it down the front of his trousers. I jumped up and away. Then there was the badge and he was snapping the handcuffs on with the remark, "Maybe you'll talk better with my partner outside."

The partner wasn't there. We walked all the way back to the park before finding him. Wearing handcuffs in public is an interesting experience. I was forced to sit with him in the rear seat of a car on a dark street for almost an hour, while he and the two officers in the front seat questioned me. It was a peculiarly effective type of grilling. They laughed a lot among themselves then, in a sudden silence, one would ask, "How long you been this way?" I sat on my hands and wondered what would happen each time I refused to answer. Yes, I was scared stiff. Then more laughter and shop talk and another sudden question. Some of them were about my work and pay. At last the driver started the car up; we went hardly more than ten miles an hour. Having expected the usual beating before, now I was positive it was coming out in the country somewhere. They drove over a mile past Lincoln Heights then slowly doubled back. During this time, they repeatedly made jokes about police brutality, laughingly asked me if they'd been brutal and each of the three instructed me to plead guilty and everything would be all right. He had approached me at five to nine in the park, I was booked at eleven-thirty and not allowed to send out a message till three the next morning.

The trial was a surprise. The attorney, engaged by the Mattachine Foundation, made a brilliant opening statement to the jury in which he pointed out that homosexuality and lasciviousness are not identical after stating that his client was admittedly homosexual, that no fine line separates the variations of sexual inclinations and the only true pervert in the court room was the arresting officer. He asked, however, that the jury feel no prejudice merely because I'd been arrested: these two officers weren't necessarily guilty of the charges of beating another prisoner merely because they were so accused; it would take a trial to do that and theirs was coming the next day. The jury deliberated for forty hours and asked to be dismissed when one of their number said he'd hold out for guilty till hell froze over. The rest voted straight acquittal. Later the city moved for dismissal of the case and it was granted. The officers, in their trial, were found innocent although one was later suspended by the Chief of Police for the same charges.

Actually I have had very little to do with this victory. Yes, I gave my name and publicly declared myself to be a homosexual, but the moment I was arrested my name was no longer "good" and this incident will stand on record for all to see for the rest of my life. In a situation where to be accused is to be guilty, a person's good name is worthless and meaningless. Further, without the interest of the Citizens' Committee to Outlaw Entrapment and their support which gathered funds from all over the country, I would have been forced to resort to the mild enthusiasm of the Public Defender. Chances are I'd have been found guilty and now be either still gathering funds to pay the fine or writing this in jail.

Yet I am not abjectly grateful. All of the hundreds who helped push this case to a successful conclusion, were not interested in me personally. They were being intelligently practical and helping establish a precedent that will perhaps help themselves if the time comes. In this sense, a bond of brotherhood is not mere blind generosity. It is unification for self-protection. Were all homosexuals and bisexuals to unite militantly, unjust laws and corruption would crumble in short order and we, as a nation, could go on to meet the really important problems which face us. Were heterosexuals to realize that these violations of our rights threaten theirs equally, a vast reform might even come within our lifetime. This is no more a dream than trying to win a case after admitting homosexuality.

DAVID FREEMAN

In *Epistemology of the Closet* Eve Sedgwick contrasts what she labels "universalizing" discourses about sexuality to "minoritizing" ones. While universalizing discourses establish the shared attributes or situation of diverse people, such as the claim that everyone is born bisexual, minoritizing ones serve to mark off particular groups as different and enable them to claim a particular unique position. Minoritizing claims are recently seen in the work of writers such as Judy Grahn who seek to discover a hidden history of cultural continuity for gays and lesbians.

Debate over whether gays and lesbians have their own culture has a surprisingly lost history. Harry Hay, the founder of Mattachine, believed that gays were a "people" hidden by coercion within the heterosexual population. In the pages of ONE, Jeff Winters argued against such a view, making a universalizing argument. David Freeman, in 1953 the corresponding secretary of the Mattachine Foundation, replies in the following piece that a homosexual culture in ways analogous to racial and ethnic cultures exists and that it can enrich American culture.

THE HOMOSEXUAL CULTURE

from *ONE Magazine* (1953)

David Freeman

In a recent issue of ONE, Jeff Winters suggested that homosexuality is too omnipresent to warrant labeling every living (and dead) individual as being in or out of the category. He also questioned the present insistence that "homosexuals" constitute a minority. As tempest-maker, Mr. Winters has been highly successful in stimulating diverse opinion, itself often tempestuous. This stormy petrel has stirred the following petrol on troubled waters—which may itself be a typhoon in disguise. The decision, of course, is yours.

Webster defines "culture" in a variety of ways. Among the definitions it lists are these:

"The complex distinctive attainments, beliefs, traditions, etc., constituting the background of a racial, religious or social group . . .

"The trait complex manifested by a tribe or a separate unit of mankind . . .

"The enlightenment and refinement of taste acquired by intellectual and aesthetic training; the intellectual content of civilization; state of being cultivated."

It is the last of these that Jeff Winters use in his article, and his tone would indicate he is unaware of the others.

When the Mattachine Foundation (for it is obviously the organization to which Mr. Winters mysteriously alludes) speaks of homosexual culture it has in mind the first of these definitions. And this is the definition, in reputable use by anthropologists and students of all the social sciences, which I have in mind in what follows.

What, exactly, do we mean when we talk about homosexual culture? Simply this: the manner of speaking and thinking, the beliefs, traditions and attainments of the homosexual minority. While it would be absurd to claim that this culture is a highly developed or "cultivated" one, it is equally inaccurate to protest its non existence. The very fact of ONE'S existence and Mr. Winter's article, however misguided, are evidences of this culture. Were there no homosexual culture there would be no need for, no interest in, such a magazine as ONE. Not all cultural groups are aware of their existence as such, and until the development of the Mattachine movement there was little consciousness of the existence of our homosexual culture. The Mattachine movement, incidentally, is another manifestation of this culture and an expression of its impact on the dominant, heterosexual culture.

The existence of a culture implies, of course, that there are individuals who participate in it. In the case of the homosexual culture this does, indeed, rule out Mr. Winter's "big quarterbacks," "brawniest laborer," and "rugged athletes" who have wives and children, the truck drivers who have an occasional homosexual experience and even prisoners who turn to homosexual relations for sexual outlet and continue them for many years even though they are basically heterosexual and will again be so in fact upon their return to society. The homosexual culture does not even represent all the individuals whose sole sexual outlet is and always has been found with members of their own sex.

As Mr. Winters correctly points out, "This leaves the exclusively homosexual who is not only abnormal but in a distinctly small minority." For the manifestations of homosexual culture we look to this small minority numbering possibly a million and a half in the United

States. Mr. Winter's lamentations notwithstanding, if ONE succeeds in reaching all the members of this minority it will have one of the *large* periodical circulations in the country, and his fear that this minority could not support a publication is not well taken. The homosexual minority will support a publication in its interest but not one in disguise. It is not the size of a cultural group which determines its influence. The Jewish minority, for example, has always been small but highly influential throughout the world.

Obviously a culture exists only so long as people participate in it. Some participate to a great extent; others only occasionally. The percentage of Negroes participating in the Negro-American culture is relatively large; the percentage of Jews participating in the Jewish culture relatively small. It is, however, the participants in a culture which keep it alive and influential.

Consider the homosexual culture (and I mean here the pure, 100% homosexual culture which is somewhat hypothetical) in which perhaps only a few of the 1,500,000 "absolute" American homosexuals participate. Who are these participants? What do they do? They are the homosexuals who visit the homosexual bars, who walk or talk or gesticulate in the universally-recognized, homosexual manner. They are the homosexuals who admit (at least to themselves) they are, indeed, homosexual and that their lives, plans, hopes and prospects must, accordingly, be different. A small minority of this small minority recognizes the existence of an emergent, homosexual culture—a way of life, a striving and a hope for a world in which they will not be hounded, degraded, ostracized. And some of them look toward the development of a homosexual ethic.

The author of "Homosexuals Are Not People" seems to regard the words "homosexual ethic" as almost unclean if not idiotic. The problems of the homosexual ethic are too broad to be discussed at length here and should be the subject of a separate essay, but I should like to say merely that the words refer to the establishment, through conscious understanding of homosexuality by homosexuals themselves, of a code of behavior or morals by which the homosexual minority may operate. Our moral code obviously cannot be the same as the heterosexual one, since it is not based on the necessity of reproduction and the family, but there is no reason our present chaos of social and sexual contact cannot be resolved into a workable pattern. This would not have to be a set of fixed rules set down by a church or government, and in fact it could not of course be such. But as we come to understand ourselves and each other better there can and will emerge, by a kind of common consent, a standard of conduct to which we can at least aspire.

As for Mr. Winter's bisexuals, thousands of them participate in the homosexual culture, and they are, to all intents, homosexuals, an occasional heterosexual notwithstanding. Some predominantly homosexual individuals may have occasional heterosexual relations. This scarcely makes them heterosexual as long as they are *basically* homosexual in thought, desire, orientation and culture.

Mr. Winters asks, "Are those who drink coffee a minority?" Of course not, for the drinking of coffee happens to be a particularly American cultural attribute. If we could imagine, however, a group of people in the United States to whom the drinking of coffee had a profound religious or social significance and determined, to a large extent, their way of looking at life and the world, this group would be a minority. But there are also Englishmen, Germans, Frenchmen and Turks who drink coffee. They are not participating in American culture when doing so. In fact, not all Americans who drink coffee are participating in our dominant culture when so doing. White, Protestant bisexuals and heterosexuals participate in the homosexual culture at some time and to some extent. They also participate in the Negro, Jewish and Mexican-American culture at some time and to some extent. But this does not make them homosexuals, Negroes, Jews or Mexican-Americans.

Most homosexuals in this country as a matter of fact, do participate in the homosexual culture and also in the dominant, heterosexual culture and in any other culture from which they sprang or in which their lives involve them. A Mexican-American homosexual, for example, would participate in the homosexual culture, the dominant American culture and the Mexican-American culture. He would also participate in the Mexican-American, homosexual culture. He would use English at work and Spanish at home. He would make homosexual, sexual contacts in both languages and in both cultural areas. He would swish (if he were so inclined) in both English and Spanish or be butch within the framework of all three cultures as he felt the situation demanded.

The argument that the bisexual is the real problem of homosexuality is analogous to and about as sensible as saying that the Negro who can pass as white is the *real* problem or the argument that the "Jew" whom no one can recognize as a Jew and who is a practicing Catholic is the real problem of the Jewish people! The fact that homosexuality, in one degree or another, is common to all of mankind is wildly irrelevant. Of course it is, but manifestations of American-Negro culture are also common to nearly all Americans. Most of us dance to swing-time or jive; most of us use Negro expressions every day whether we are conscious of them or not. Millions of us (if we are descendants of grand- or great-grandparents born in this country) have some Negro blood in our veins even though we have blond hair, blue eyes and freckles.

"Homosexuality, in one degree or another, is common to all." Undoubtedly true, Mr. Winters, but so what? Homosexuality will require attention long after legal and religious prejudice against it has been abolished if the homosexual culture develops a self-conscious effort to guide and direct itself in the interests of all of society. Before Hitler anti-Semitism had virtually disappeared in Germany. Did this mean that Jewish culture had vanished there? True, the German-Jewish culture had undergone many transformations since the Eighteenth Century and was probably more German than Jewish, but it was still Jewish and did still exist. It was, moreover, still a factor in the whole, social life of Germany, for Jewish culture had enriched German culture out of all proportion to the number of Jews in Germany. And it is this enrichment that the homosexual minority seeks to contribute to American culture. Homosexuality, Mr. Winters, is about as irrelevant as Christianity.

The uproar over the conservative takeover of Mattachine could not be gleaned from the pages of the *Review*. The victors presented themselves as reasonable, the furor inspired by a few hotheads. The "hotheads" moved to ONE, and in the pages of ONE Magazine they continued the battle.

JEFF WINTERS

The article below documents the concerns of those who were left when Mattachine was sanitized. The author, Jeff Winters, argues that a Mattachine that does not address the injustices faced by homosexuals can only be "a club of perverts," and that such a posture leaves them open to more, rather than less, interference and attack. This is a characteristic note of ONE, in contrast to both the later Mattachine and the DOB. Whether ONE's members engaged in more effective politics than those of the DOB or Mattachine is perhaps in doubt, but they certainly find a more sympathetic audience today.

A FRANK LOOK AT THE MATTACHINE: CAN HOMOSEXUALS ORGANIZE?

from *ONE Magazine* (1954)

Jeff Winters

What is the Mattachine?

It is revealing that no member of the Mattachine Society can answer this question to the satisfaction of most of the other members. At the third annual convention last November, the loudest and longest debates were on this very question. And in asking themselves *Why have we banded together?* members came up with answers so contradictory that the founders rolled over in their premature graves. No one seems to know.

The original intention of the Mattachine was three-fold: its originators intended that it should be an organized means of bringing about specific changes in laws effecting homosexuals, of informing the public about homosexuality and of developing a cultural pattern for the homosexual. The founders themselves did not agree on this last idea that homosexuals have a special cultural heritage but they were unanimous in their other aims of fighting cases, speaking out against unfair laws, illegal police practices and prejudice, and in educating both the public and the homosexual on the subject of sexual deviation. These original purposes were gathered together under the name, Mattachine Foundation, which derives from a traditional word for the Fool and Jester who spoke out the truth in the face of brutal authority no matter what the consequences.

Fairies for Freedom!

The Foundation grew with staggering speed. Before the founders realized it, the Mattachine was internationally known. Its leaflets circled the globe and were printed in many languages. Thousands of letters rolled in. Then came the now legendary case which the Foundation fought, financed and won. The defendant said in court, *"I am homosexual but I am not guilty of the charges."* A unique plea and it opened a unique trial. When the jury was nearing acquittal, the city moved to dismiss and it was granted. The Foundation had won an historic victory.

The Foundation made mistakes, too. When its officers paid an attorney to file incorporation papers, they considered the job done and thought no more about it for a whole year. This ignorance proved their undoing. A local columnist "exposed" the Mattachine as unlisted among California corporations. He further revealed the attorney as one of those deplorable traitors who availed himself of the Fifth Amendment when a touring committee invited him to publicly hang himself. This could only mean that the Mattachine was the hub of an atom-stealing ring financed by the Soviet. This columnist, upholding the American tradition of freedom of the press, refused to print an answer to his accusations nor would he speak to anyone asking for an interview.

How Clean Can a House Get?

The attack was effective in the most unexpected quarter. The public, familiar with this columnist's tactics, forgot the whole thing. Not so the "loyal" members of the Mattachine. A mighty rumble came from these followers of Chauvin. At the second annual convention, a bloc insisted on loyalty oaths for all officers and the taking of a political stand. These patriots spoke with passion. The founders, feeling they had perhaps served their purpose in bringing the Mattachine into existence, resigned so that these promising young zealots might march on to greater victories. The new order, a little shocked at the victory, took over and cleaned house from cellar to weather vane.

During the next year the Mattachine was completely re-designed. Literally hundreds of new by-laws were adopted, new offices created and an intricate administrative pattern set up. In the streamlining, discussion groups dropped off, chapters seceded and membership shrank. No other cases were taken up due to rigid new requirements but there was some research done although not for publication. Two dozen pints of plasma were donated to the Red Cross and some magazines taken to a hospital. It is true that a whole year passed with nothing spectacular accomplished under this new regime, however this could be looked upon as a period of adjustment and preparation.

That Third Convention

It was short-sighted to think that the new officers had merely wanted to get rid of the old order so that they could forge ahead. No one ever points the patriotic finger just once. It's habit forming. The new order began to worry about whether they'd gotten *all* the reds out. They squinted at each other suspiciously. And they became insomniac worrying about the old order sneaking back in. They changed the Mattachine Foundation to the Mattachine Society and made regular announcements that the two had *nothing* to do with one another. Feeling no better, they insisted that this magazine publish the fact that the Mattachine Society and ONE had nothing to do with one another either. It was a bit insulting but the editors complied. But the old worry remained.

Then came the shocking third annual convention. It was at this meet that a proposal was passed to remove the words "homosexual," "ethic" and "culture" from the statement of purposes. The reason given was that the words might invite trouble. It was decided to handle no more homosexual cases—only heterosexual. The public mustn't think that the Society was selfishly interested only in deviates. The policy was accepted that no organized pressure be put on law-makers because it might antagonize them. A person reportedly close to the state legislature insisted that organized pressure never works anyway. And if the homosexual tried to better his lot, the public wouldn't like it at *all*. Let's not. It was considered at this convention that all homosexuals who got themselves arrested really deserve it when you get right down to it. Everybody knows that. When an eloquent speaker tried to challenge these decisions, his credentials were found to be lacking and he was denied the right to speak thereafter. When he objected, he was threatened with having criminal charges placed against him as inciting the public to illegal acts. It was a very confused convention.

The appalling implications of this psychotic threat were apparently seen by no one in authority. In spite of the fact that one man was ready to destroy the entire Mattachine and movement to satisfy his personal irritation, his apology was graciously accepted and his words stricken from the record. It was agreed that everyone should forget the whole thing happened and be friends. He was neither expelled nor reprimanded. Many continue to respect him and those who don't, are afraid to speak out because of his assumed influence in the state legislature. He remains in the Society and continues to shape policy.

It was shortly after this fiasco that someone had a wonderful idea for improving the lot of the homosexual and firmly cementing relations between him and the public. He proposed seriously that the Mattachine open a private bar where everyone could come and drink like mad and let down hair after hair. An attorney was fetched and much discussion put into the project before it was dropped as too expensive for the present.

As of today, this is the Mattachine Society.

Why Try to Organize a Bunch of Queers Anyway?

It is erroneous to assume that all those who are inclined toward members of their own gender constitute a concrete minority. There are many degrees of both homo- and hetero-sexuality. Actually neither of these words has a valid meaning. To attempt to label everyone either one or the other would require much bigotry or foolishness. Those of homosexual experience have no more in common than have "normal" persons. It would be pointless to give every man who sleeps with women a certain label and declare that he belongs to a special category. He and society would exclaim, "So what!" The label would mean nothing in view of the fact that he shares this habit with an infinite variety of other males. To describe a person as heterosexual is to say nothing about him which conveys meaning. To say he drinks water conveys nothing and to label him homosexual describes nothing about his age, mind, physique or talents. He, too, comes in a variety of sizes, shapes and qualities. Homosexuals do not and cannot share a culture.

But there is one thing that homosexuals do share most definitely. That is the denial of their civil rights. They are victimized by society more than any other single group. The legal and religious prejudice against them is as ancient as man himself. But when this prejudice goes, homosexuals will cease to be a group. They are not different. All but a tiny few cannot be detected by proper means. They're just people. The only reason that they should and must organize is to fight cases of entrapment, lobby against unjust laws and to educate. This is not a fight for special favors, nor for a special place in society. Homosexuals demand only that which is their due as citizens. For this, there must be a militant organization. No such organization now exists.

Quo Vadis, Mattachine Society?

Till now the Mattachine has not been attacked by authority because it was entirely legal in function and purpose. It declared its status and proclaimed its aims. The present Society however invites certain destruction by denial of all those things for which the Mattachine was founded. With no aims and no concrete accomplishments to point to—and worse, with a denial *that it is what it is*. It can only be legally classified as a club of perverts who have gotten together to perform unnatural acts. If they don't fight for social respect and their legal rights, if they don't educate and champion their own, there is no reason that they should gather together unless it be for lewd purposes. The fact that it even toyed with the idea of a private bar where its members could gather *"with their own kind"* and commit unconventional, if not unlawful acts, is most revealing—and damning.

Prognosis Negative?

There are innumerable fine things which an organization of homosexuals can do for themselves and for society. The field of potential projects is endless. The Mattachine Foundation nibbled at its edges. The Mattachine Society not only refuses to even nibble but denies blandly, that there is anything to be done that is of any great consequence. It seems to see no reason for its own existence. And the reason for this is not stupidity. The present leaders of the Society are not giddy, unthinking fools. They are plainly afraid.

From the trembling president on down to the least officer, they are terrified. In spite of the fact that the job before them is fine and good and tragically urgent, they live in constant terror. Most of the leaders are desperately sorry they got into the damned thing in the first place. It is true that they should be afraid. They certainly could be falsely charged and thrown into jail, but this very possibility is the strongest proof that they *must* fight whether they want to or not. You can't run from corruption and remain uncorrupt.

The Mattachine's name (which the Society has retained in an involuntary tribute to the old Foundation's accomplishments) referred to those who stand up against misused power and speak out the truth in spite of direst consequences. The Society should perhaps shed the name too, if it means to be only a social club ignoring its reason for existence. Perhaps it should also admit that it is just a refuge for fairies who have hair which they must take down—who must behave in a manner they know is objectionable to society.

Now Hear This

The only way that the Mattachine Society can save itself from gradual dissolution or spontaneous combustion on the front pages of the daily press, is to initiate a series of projects concretely beneficial to both society and the homosexual. The deviate must see not only from the Society's' intentions but from its record that here is an outfit worth giving time and money to. Membership will continue to drop off (there are now approximately fifty members) as long as the individual gets nothing for attending long meetings except a new phone number now and then. The Mattachine must prove itself worthy of the bother.

Finally the leadership must stop being afraid. They think they're doing wrong and, in their legal ignorance, tremble like bunnies. They are not! They, in demanding rights and respect for the homosexual, are performing an historic job, a magnificent job. They must either give over the reins to braver, more capable hands—or stand up and fight. There is no other choice.

PREAMBLE TO CONSTITUTION CHANGED OVER OBJECTION OF SOME MEMBERS

from *The Mattachine Newsletter* (1953)

The preamble to the Constitution of the Mattachine Society was changed by a vote of the convention on November 15 at Los Angeles.

Gone from it are the words, "A highly ethical homosexual culture." Such reference, members and delegates believed, was incorrect, because the Society's aims were primarily directed toward full integration of the sex variant, and not the establishment of any special "culture."

Further, members believed that reference to "homosexual" in the preamble was "ill-advised" and incorrect, because the Society is not an organization of homosexuals, but rather a group interested in the problems of the homosexual and the sex variant. Statements were also made in which delegates told of difficulties they had experienced because of the implication of the words questioned when presented to persons whose aid was sought in connection with the Society's program.

The particular wording if the preamble was felt to be a handicap to the Society and prevented certain institutions and agencies from supporting the organization freely.

As adopted, here is the new preamble to the Constitution of the Mattachine Society:

"We, the members of the Mattachine Society, believing in sexual equality, in full awareness of our social obligations as members of the human community, hold it necessary that the priceless integrity and freedom of the individual be forever maintained in our society; and, whereas the present laws of many lands are discriminatory; and, whereas we are resolved that all people shall find this equality and, whereas we desire to spread knowledge of the aims and aspirations of this Society through mutual education of its membership and of society, We therefor hereby resolve . . . "

Other significant accomplishments of the convention included adoption of several important resolutions, a set of by-laws for out of state chapters and for the Society itself, and changes in allocation of funds from chapters.

Previously, 10% of chapter funds went to coordinating council and 40% to area councils. The new formula calls for 40% to remain in chapter treasury, and 30% to go each to each coordinating council and area council.

A specific resolution passed gave the coordinating council clear authority to operate the Society between conventions, but gave the convention itself the power to review and pass upon all actions of the council.

LYN PEDERSEN

Consistent with the minoritizing approach, the article presented here argues that homosexuals are different from heterosexuals not just in their choice of sexual partner but in their entire view of life. Jim Kepner, writing under the name of "Lyn Pederson," distinguishes between the "natural" rebellion and creativity of homosexuals and the "anti-social" forms these take under conditions of repression. This piece manifests the tensions in 1950s white America between the drive to conform and the transcendent image of rebellion against conformity. Rebellion is associated with autonomy and maturity, but this rebellion is contained through the rejection of "anti-social" responses such as hating those who oppress or being "flagrant" about our sexuality. What would he make of Queer Nation?

THE IMPORTANCE OF BEING DIFFERENT

from *ONE Magazine* (1954)

Lyn Pederson (Jim Kepner)

> *When in Rome, do as you damn please.*
> *– John Arnold.*

Homosexuals have some problems heterosexuals don't have. Agreed?

That's as far as we go. Once we try to list or analyze the problems, or suggest remedies, and agreement vanishes. The Mattachine Society, nee Foundation, and ONE magazine hope to tackle said problems, but the means remain in dispute. And there is no little disagreement on the ends.

Are homosexuals in any important way different from other people? If so, ought that difference be cultivated, or hidden under a bushel, or extirpated altogether?

For myself, I must say with the French legislator, who had something quite different on his mind, "Vive la différence!"

While the magazine has been relatively clear in its policy, the Mattachine Society has become almost schizoid on the question of whether we're different, whether to admit it and what to do about it.

What can a Society accomplish if half of it feels its object is to convince the world we're just like everyone else and the other half feels homosexuals are variants in the full sense of the term and have every right to be? What can that Society do but tie itself in knots of protective coloration? What can it it do but publish statements one day contradicting those it published the day before, and seldom even knowing a contradiction is involved?

Are homosexuals different?

That is, does the one difference which we all know about, make any other difference in their attitudes, habits, etc.? Is it possible to make any generalizations about homosexuals except that they are drawn to their own sex? Recalling that generalizations need only apply directly to *most* members of a group, I think several valid ones could be made, the sum and substance of which would be that homosexuals are different in more ways than they often know. But I am concerned with one particular point.

Homosexuals are natural rebels.

In our society, only freak conditions or cowardice or total ignorance of his own nature would permit a homosexual any alternative. A rare homosexual is protected by a thoroughly sympathetic family, which performs for him the function that the family performs for members of most other minority groups, that of providing, early in life when it counts, the spirit of group solidarity. Unfortunately for the rest of us, that "mystic bond. . ." of wishful thinking ". . . that makes all men one," is less cohesive than the family bond, which for us, is likely to be the first thing shattered.

Leaving ignorance aside, for overt homosexuals, their chief problem is whether to do as society demands or whether to follow their own inclinations. For most, this is a moral crisis. The homosexuals find themselves impelled by wild and mysterious desires to cross the line which all the authorities have set between what they call Right and what they call Wrong.

In such crises, people react variously, and on different levels of consciousness. For many, the tabu will stifle the desire, and perhaps even disguise its nature. But for most, the rule must be broken, and the act must be given context. Either the sin must be repented, or the break somehow justified. The penitents need not concern us here, except to comment that repentance can only satisfy those who merely "go astray" occasionally.

Most homosexuals become inured to breaking the rules. They must somehow reject what they learned as children and still hear repeated about them. But when people break rules and know they have done so, and are not sorry, they usually are forced to decide that the rule is either irrelevant or wrong. Here, a new factor enters. They put their own judgement above the rules, which represent society's judgment, in short, they become rebels.

Therefore, homosexuals are natural rebels. Born or made, they are constitutionally incapable of being sincere conformists. They may try desperately, as many in fact do, to conform in little things, to put on the show of being just like everyone else; but in the basic "facts of life" they are inescapably different, and through all the veneer of normality with which they may seek to cover themselves, they must suspect that this one essential difference colors their outlook on all other matters.

Because he is clanless, set apart, a lone individual searching for others of his kind (if he even suspects their existence) he must come to judge the world, its morals, customs and beliefs by his own nature, or else, in contrition reject and despise his own nature.

Some make the judgments easily, unaware that they've done any such thing. They'll drop their religion or its practice, casually, say the-hell-with-the-law, and go blindly on thinking of themselves as conformists.

Some will limit their non-conformity to sex and its most inescapable consequences, such as telling a "white lie" now and then, or on the other hand, shocking an acquaintance with the sudden truth.

But most people require a certain consistency, superficial at least, in their attitudes. The rejection of some of the rules leaves gaping holes in the concept of orderly society. Anyone much motivated by consistency must begin examining other parts of the social picture with a jaundiced eye. And if one reads any of history, he is likely to come by the opinion that the world owes as much to the rule-breakers as to the rule-keepers. He will then become a rebel in principle. He will seek his own standards of good and true and beautiful and just, or may even reject standards entirely. Liberty will become his aim and cause: conformity his enemy.

This, I say, is the natural course for homosexuals. But few follow it. Some become merely anti-social, flaunting the laws, hating the cops, flagrantly trying to shock people for the fun it gives, and likely quite intolerant of any variant habits they don't happen to be personally addicted to. This is the homosexual society sees, the stereotype. It is an unnatural course because it is primarily unconscious.

The more common, and more unnatural course, is motivated by protective coloration. These become so enwrapped in the desire to make the world believe they are no different that they succeed at least in making themselves believe it. This attitude provides, as I see it, the greatest pitfall for any group that would seek to help homosexuals.

It is this sort that would turn a homosexual organization into a refuge for cowards. It is this sort that would so fear the specter of non-conformity, and the red tag that goes with it these days, that they would bend backwards with dishonest but popular slogans about "upholding the law," "sanctity of home, church and state," "loyalty to the American way of life," and such, even though they may admit in private that they don't mean a word of it.

It is this sort who will Puritanically attack the "swishes and fairies" insisting that they wouldn't think of associating with such trash, except *perhaps* for the very noble purpose of reforming them, teaching them to behave decently.

This sort will view the job of a Mattachine Society or a ONE Magazine as primarily a "public relations" job, the object being nothing more or less than to convince society at large that homosexuals are not different at all.

And finally, this sort will attempt to excommunicate any homosexual who belies their thesis that we aren't different. Neither rebels nor swishes, nor any others who fall short of their slightly personalized standards of respectability will be welcome in their society.

Which brings us back to the starting point.

We are all agreed that homosexuals have problems. And some seem now convinced that such agencies as ONE and the Mattachine can do something. But agreement stops there.

Will we be called pollyannas or paranoids? Is our aim to pacify or to fight? Will we concentrate on activities that ignore the variance and demonstrate that we're just like any other civic group, putting the best face on things, with covert attempts to sidle up to judges and police chiefs?

Or will we leave room for disagreement, but with the basic group energies attacking the present laws and customs as unjust, developing ourselves as free individuals and joining a broad defense of liberty against the dead hand of conformity?

There is room in one organization for both views, but at the sacrifice of coordinated purpose. Only by allowing the free action of individual groups within the structure of an elastic society can such diverse philosophies work together. But such schizophrenia is hard to handle. With other minorities, racial and religious, similar dichotomies have forced into existence a variety of opposing organizations, each with its own clearcut program. For homosexuals as well, this must probably come, in time.

It should barely be necessary to state that I am interested in defending my right to be as different as I damn please. And somewhere, I've picked up the notion that I can't protect my own rights in that quarter without fighting for everyone else's.

In the pages of ONE we may read the words of those (mostly men) who continued early Mattachine commitment to "ethical homosexual culture." As part of this, they argued that homosexuality was nothing to be ashamed of or apologetic about. While the later Mattachine minimized its members' differences from the mainstream of white America, ONE printed many pieces that contended that homosexuals were in fact privileged in their exemption from heterosexual life. The following article, written by Dorr Legg under the pseudonym of "Hollister Barnes," is one such piece. Note the assumption that lesbians are free from childbirth and rearing, an assumption that is certainly no longer true (if it ever was).

HOLLISTER BARNES

I AM GLAD I AM A HOMOSEXUAL

from *ONE Magazine* (1958)

Hollister Barnes (Dorr Legg)

"I am proud of being a homosexual." This powerfully affirmative statement, made by a speaker at the Constitutional Convention of the Mattachine Society, in April, 1953, acted as an electrifying catalyst. Some few applauded its forth-rightness. Others, whether consciously or not, rallied together defensively as a bloc. As the Convention proceeded the views of this bloc gradually took the lead and a Constitution generally expressive of their thinking was adopted. Thus, two radically opposite attitudes towards homosexuality were thrown into bold relief. During the years since then this divergence has become even more clearly marked. Time has not exerted the softening and mellowing influence so often ascribed to it. On the contrary, each year finds views a little more stoutly maintained, the focus less fuzzy than before. What are these opposing views?

The term *asexual* might be used a bit sardonically as characterizing the attitude, if not the behavior, of the majority of homophiles. They tend to agree with popular opinion—that homosexuality is wrong; that it is sinful; that it is shameful; to be vigorously curbed by self-denial, sublimation, or other methods (even masturbation). They seem to feel that homosexuals should at all costs present a public appearance of conformity and "normalcy," of asexuality, if necessary. The homosexual, and his organizations, should cooperate to the fullest extent with "public authorities," according to this view. Above all things, the individual is held to be obligated to be an all-around "good guy." "Act square," is the motto. "It's only sensible," they say.

Is it fair to term this group *asexuals?* It is fair in that this is the public impression they strive to convey, save for the pitiful cases which, at the behest of family, minister or psychiatrist, strive desperately to contort themselves into simulacra of heterosexuality, by marrying. Strangely enough, as their public behavior by no means accords with their private conduct, in the majority of cases their behavior might more justly be termed amoral than asexual.

Sociologists and those dealing in mental health problems never tire of telling us of the dangers both to the individual and to his society whenever preaching and the practice are found to be at too great variance.

The admitted homosexuals are a smaller group, comprised mainly of those claiming to be more intellectually sophisticated, and of the flaming queens. This group, in whatever terms, express pride in its homosexuality, finding nothing either sinful or shameful in it. They feel that homosexual men and women should be in every way as free to practice their sexual preferences as are other segments of the population; that they should enjoy the same legal and social privileges as others, no more, but also, no less. They feel themselves under no obligations whatever to conform to the particular social standards of any particular community; that instead of their adjusting to popular mores, the mores should be adjusted to their own wishes. The demands of rationalism and basic human freedoms admit of no other interpretation, they state.

This group feels that habitually to think one thing and act another breeds nothing but hypocrisy in a society and schizophrenia in the individual. They say, "I am homosexual. I am proud of it. I shall live my life according to the dictates of its nature, and neither social pressures nor legal prohibitions (which are probably without any moral 'legality' anyway) will turn me from this resolve. If society does not wish to accept me, or to understand me that is not my problem, for, to paraphrase Louis, The Sun King's, "L'etat, c'est moi," "I am Society."

This rugged individualism has an almost anarchistic quality that is yet as American as the "hot dog." It is in the spirit of that old Colonial flag, emblazoned with a rattlesnake and the motto, "Don't tread on me." This is the individualism of the queen, flaunting make-up and a bracelet or two the face of an amused or embarrassed public, and of the intellectual, saying, "I am proud of being a homosexual," then throwing this declaration into the very teeth of public opinion.

Are such persons really serious in their views? Do they mean what they say, or are their words but a form of compensation for hurts and insults they may have endured? That we should ask such questions shows the very depth of the infection we have suffered through centuries of religious and other propaganda. If we can somehow manage to render ourselves quite objective, lifting ourselves, as it were, out of the epoch in which we live, we begin to wonder if it is not we who have been guilty of absurdities, we who are not to be taken seriously.

In this objective vein we would be forced to inquire of what the homosexual is deprived, by virtue of his homosexuality, in either realms domestic or public, moral or ethical. Is he, for instance, debarred from expressing any of the classic Seven Virtues? Is he more prone than his brothers to succumbing to the Seven Deadly Sins? Is he subject to particular bodily deformities? Is his IQ inherently deficient? Or, is he barred from "normal" sexual pleasures?

Ask any homosexual about this point. Try to offer him "normal" sexual pleasures, so-called, as a substitute and see how many takers there will be. But, says the moralist, you quite mistake the true purpose of sex, for sexual pleasures are but the means to an end, a noble end—the perpetuation of the race. This poor, shopworn argument has been around for countless centuries, despite its lack of support from philosophical, biological or other evidence! Who, for instance, can be so sure that the race should be perpetuated at all? Or in its present form? Is it not entirely likely that by arranging race-perpetuation a bit better than the "sexual pleasure" principle has done it that we might make some headway with the problem of juvenile delinquency? We just might happen also to end up with far fewer monsters, dwarfs, cretins, morons and all the picturesque horde who may delight in a Hogarth but are pretty much a social luxury. Or are we being too Utopian?

But surely, continues our moralist, you must grant that in domestic and in public life the homosexual is at a hopeless disadvantage. Is this so certain? I, for one, am glad I am homosexual, glad to be spared the deadly monotonies of marital wranglings or, worse, still, the marshmallow puffiness of marital bliss. I consider myself fortunate in having seen through the deadly deceptions of the procreative cycle—devouring energies, talents, ambition and individual achievement, all in the name of that great communal juggernaut, The Family, before which church and state so abjectly debase themselves.

How darkly vicious this may all seem to us one day, this myth which sanctions the most incredible interweaving of clashing and disparate personalities by means of the semen and the blood-stream. How cleanly healthy we all may feel when at least some of us shall have purged our thinking of such ritualistic tribal vestiges. How much nearer may we find ourselves to the moral freedom which is the right of each of us. The prospect gives one the courage to pull through life's duller stretches.

That there are some domestic and public disadvantages the homosexual must endure is not denied, but these are the unhealthy manifestations of a society so sick, a culture so unsure of itself that it shrinks in horror from some of the greatest and basically elemental forces of man and nature, while striving feverishly at an impossible repression. Is it proposed that the honest man, the upright women, shall lend themselves to the furtherance of such sickness, such unhealthiness, such weakness? Should they not rather strive to lead their blind fellows out of this nasty-minded neuroticism?

If it is claimed that the root of the whole matter can be found in the realm of ethics or morality, I would ask in what respects this is so. Because homosexual relations are vile and unnatural, answers the moralist. I would meet the moralist on his own ground by quoting Scripture. "If God be for us, who can be against us?" Or, if God be so much in favor of heterosexuality as you claim, is He not to be trusted to rid the universe of things "vile and unnatural?" Further, If God is so against homosexuality as you claim, how comes it that century after century homosexuals are born, and that some of the most shining stars in the human firmament have been homosexual? Without these great men and women the world in which we live today would indeed be a sad, drab place—less moral. Who doubts this knows neither religion, history, nor art.

Like other homosexuals who have self-respect and a natural pride, I am proud of being a human being, quite as capable as any of my fellows of doing good work, to the extent of my individual abilities. In addition, I feel sure that my particular way of life has given me certain insights into human problems and character that most heterosexuals apparently lack.

Under the present social and cultural system the homosexual automatically finds himself a member of a world-wide freemasonry which cuts across educational and financial levels with utter impartiality. If Marxists were not so sociologically naive as they are they would have to admit that here exists the only truly classless society. From this vantage point the homosexual discovers in himself a sympathy for the poor and oppressed of all kinds denied to all but the saints. Being utterly untouched by their interests and concerns he has an unerring eye for the follies and foibles of his heterosexual brothers and sisters, so unerring in fact that he often finds himself cast in the role of sympathetic adviser and confidant of husband, wife, child and parent. Indeed, it well may be that the only valid and objective consideration of marital problems must come from the homosexual, heterosexuals being too strongly biased to evaluate themselves wisely.

The male homosexual is both relieved and glad to discover that, unlike the heterosexual who is forever seeking "completion" and fulfillment in his supposed opposite—a woman, he seeks his fulfillment in the very highest development of his own maleness, in love for another male. The lesbian also is relieved and glad not to have to attempt two readjustments of her selfhood, 1st, to some male; 2nd, to her children, "fruit of her womb," which, in most cases lead her with fatal accuracy to the Curse of Eve, "in sorrow thou shalt bring forth children." She learns, and what a happy release it is, that it is possible for her to find fulfillment otherwise, to heighten her womanliness through love and sexual union with another woman.

Do these concepts seem shocking, or startling? If so, the reader should prepare himself to continue being shocked, for ideas such as these are present today in the minds of many homosexuals. They will be expressing them more and more vigorously as time goes on. Their day is on the march. They are actively, resiliently proud of their homosexuality, glad for it. Society is going to have to accustom itself to many new pressures, new demands from the homosexual. A large and vigorous group of citizens, millions of them, are refusing to put up any longer with outworn shibboleths, contumely and social degradation.

Like the rest of my brothers and sisters I am glad to be a homosexual, proud of it. Let no one think we don't mean business, or intend to enforce our rights.

D

DAUGHTERS OF BILITIS

The Daughters of Bilitis (DOB), the first lesbian organization in the U.S., began in September of 1955 in San Francisco. The group's name came from Pierre Louys's *Songs of Bilitis*, a book of poetry written by a man, purporting to describe love among Sappho's school. The name had other advantages, however: as Del Martin and Phyllis Lyon described it, the DOB sounded like "any other women's lodge," and so would be safe. Formed as a social and discussion group, DOB had monthly parties and also meetings to discuss issues facing them as lesbians—often referred to as "Gab 'n Javas," for the huge amounts of coffee consumed. An early split along class lines left DOB largely a middle-class, white organization, firmly anchored in the homophile way of doing things. This location is evident in the statement of purposes reprinted below.

The *Ladder*, DOB's monthly magazine, began publication in 1956, with Barbara Gittings its first editor. Immediately, they encountered the same fear as that expressed by would-be Mattachine Review subscribers. The second issue included an article entitled "Your Name is Safe!" While some of the same arguments were used to soothe readers—for example, that subscription did not label one a lesbian—the editors specifically cited the Supreme Court's decision in *U.S. v. Rumely* (345 U.S. 41) upholding the right to refuse to reveal to Congress the names of subscribers or purchasers of publications. They knew exactly how serious their situation was.

The following articles show the homophile face of DOB. The first piece, describing "the philosophy of DOB," is a very polite assertion of the worth of "the homosexual" as a human being, mingled with criticisms of self-pity and hostility. The aim of DOB is clearly integration and "adjustment"—of both lesbians and heterosexual society. Soothing public fears (and those of many lesbians), the author of the second essay moves very gradually to a critique of existing laws and an endorsement of the Model Penal Code. She reveals the extent to which DOB, while always a lesbian organization, worked with and for men; lesbians were not generally subject to entrapment, and indeed in most states lesbian sex was not a crime. Many lesbians were jailed, but often the offense was "male impersonation" or "disorderly conduct" rather than a "sex crime." In 1959, this author clearly identified as a "homosexual" as well as a "lesbian." As we will see, the rise of feminism will strain this identification to the breaking point. Frustration with gay men who couldn't or wouldn't recognize the special problems of lesbians; questions of alliance with groups whose membership overlaps with that of lesbian ones, were all addressed in the pages of The Ladder. Also present were racism and classism, as white women compartmentalized Black women's lives into sex and race and authors urged their readers to educate "non-professional, non-college" women about the realities of their lives.

From the beginning, the Daughters of Bilitis was formed to address the "special needs" of lesbians. With the rise of second-wave feminism, *The Ladder* became a forum for lesbians' frustration with both male homophile groups such as Mattachine and with lesbian invisibility in society at large. While never abandoning a lesbian focus, it eventually redefined itself as "an all-women's rights magazine" in 1971.

STATEMENT OF PURPOSE

Daughters of Bilitis (1955)

A WOMEN'S ORGANIZATION FOR THE PURPOSE OF PROMOTING THE INTEGRA-TION OF THE HOMOSEXUAL INTO SOCIETY BY:

1. Education of the variant, with particular emphasis on the psychological, physiological and sociological aspects, to enable her to understand herself and make her adjustment to society in all its social, civic and economic implications—this to be accomplished by establishing and maintaining as complete a library as possible of both fiction and non-fiction literature on the sex deviant theme; by sponsoring public discussions on pertinent subjects to be conducted by leading members of the legal, psychiatric, religious and other professions; by advocating a mode of behavior and dress acceptable to society.

2. Education of the public at large through acceptance first of the individual, leading to an eventual breakdown of erroneous taboos and prejudices; through public discussion meetings aforementioned; through dissemination of educational literature on the homosexual theme.

3. Participation in research projects by duly authorized and responsible psychologists, sociologists and other such experts directed towards further knowledge of the homosexual.

4. Investigation of the penal code as it pertains to the homosexual, proposal of changes to provide an equitable handling of cases involving this minority group, and promotion of these changes through due process of law in the state legislatures.

WHAT ABOUT THE DOB?

from *The Ladder* (1959)

Anonymous

What About the DOB?

The Daughters of Bilitis, Inc., is a non-profit organization which was founded prior to election in 1955 and incorporated under the laws of the State of California in 1957. Established as a women's organization for the purpose of promoting the integration of the homosexual into society, it has also been qualified under Federal law by the Bureau of Internal Revenue as a non-profit corporation with contributions deductible on income tax returns.

"Organized Homosexuals?"

The DOB membership is comprised of women interested in the problems of the homosexual in our society—some mothers, some heterosexual women and of course, Lesbians themselves. The Lesbian who joins would tend to be the thoughtful, public spirited, responsible type, for the organization places particular emphasis on helping her to understand herself and her relationship to society. If this means "organized homosexuals", then it is an organization for social, not anti-social, ends.

Clandestine organization?

Clandestine means "secret, hidden or underhanded". Those who would question the existence of our organizations would seem to infer the "underhanded" definition. They base the accusation upon the fact that the organizations have declared quite openly that with the exception of national officers, the anonymity of members and subscribers would be protected. This would seem to be very logical under the circumstances in which we live in this society. Ignorance breeds fear and hostility and until education in this field relieves the necessity, concealment of identity is only practical. Just as many authors who have broached a controversial subject have chosen to use a pseudonym, many members do likewise. This matter is left entirely up to the individual.

Threat to Public Morality?

DOB sponsors open meetings which have had as guest speakers professional persons in the fields of psychology, sociology, religion, philosophy, law and anthropology. The organization publishes a monthly magazine which is regarded as a sounding board for *various* points of view on the homophile and related subjects. DOB members have cooperated in research projects conducted by the Kinsey Institute for Sex Research and by others in the psychological field. The September LADDER was devoted in its entirety to a sociological survey conducted by members of the organization itself. This data was gathered primarily for use by professional persons to better understand and handle the Lesbian problem. The organization also holds regular group therapy sessions to enable the Lesbian to understand herself.

How can such a program threaten the public? The DOB and similar organizations might conceivably stimulate public thinking and discussion as to what its moral views *actually are* with regard to various aspects of sex. Free discussion of any issue, including this one, with the presentation of *all* sides of the question, should be a contribution, not a threat, to the public good.

Child Molesters?

DOB is an organization of adult women. The rule—"no minors allowed"—is strictly adhered to. It has already been stated that many of our members have a homosexual orientation and by token of their sexual preference, which does not conform to the pattern of the majority, may be called sex deviates. The sex deviate is *anyone* varying in *any* manner from the *legal* method of sexual gratification and by such definition would even include many socially accepted married couples. At the New York convention of the Mattachine Society in 1958, Dr. Theodore Weiss, senior psychiatrist at Bellevue Hospital, stated that only a small percentage of sexual deviates are child molesters and there is "no evidence to show that this crime is perpetrated more by homosexuals than heterosexuals".

Revision of Sex Laws?

The law in relation to the homosexual must necessarily be a part of any study of homosexuality. DOB's concern with laws can be best expressed by the following excerpt from an "Open Letter to Assemblyman John A. O'Connell, chairman of the California Assembly Interim Subcommittee on Constitutional Rights," which appeared in THE LADDER for

September, 1958:

> It is generally conceded by the experts in the field that the *cause* of homosexuality is still an unknown quantity, that it is a process of development and *not a matter of choice*, that the incidence cannot be controlled by legislation, that the fear and insecurity imposed upon the homosexual by prejudiced and outmoded laws hamper the rapist in his efforts to help the individual make his adjustment to himself and society, and finally that legal prohibitions benefit no one but the blackmailers.

Steps to remedy such unjust and passe laws have been taken recently in England. The Wolfenden Committee recommended to Parliament that English law be changed so that homosexual behavior between consenting adults in private no longer be considered a criminal offense. The Church of England has approved the report and . . . the English Methodist Church went on record to urge the passage of the Wolfenden recommendations, stating that the law should not interfere with private homosexual conduct "unless that conduct is clearly detrimental to the public good in an extraordinary degree."

In our own country the American Law Institute has spent years of work in drafting a model penal code which would modify the antiquated statutes now on the books. It is certainly to be hoped that special study be given to this document of modern legal thought before any revisions to California laws are considered.

We believe that the practical solution to the problem is to judge sex activity on the grounds of whether or not society is harmed. Homosexual activity between consenting adults in private is not harmful to society. However, there must necessarily be protection given the public against offenders where assault, force or violence is involved; in the cases of molesting children whether they be homosexual or heterosexual in nature, and against indecent public behavior. We are not asking for license, but rather a realistic approach to an ever-growing problem.

We would ask the committee to give consideration too to the laws requiring persons who have been convicted of a homosexual act to register with the police as sexual psychopaths on entering the community. This law, besides being unfair, is in our opinion unconstitutional.

We also call your attention to the tactics of certain law enforcement agencies where the use of decoys is employed to entice individuals into engaging in an overt homosexual act leading to arrest. It would seem to us that the first duty of the police is to *prevent*, not to punish crime—certainly not to incite or create crime for the sole purpose of its prosecution and punishment.

. . . We sincerely hope that out of your investigations will come definite action toward long needed remedial legislation for an equitable, realistic and enforceable penal code.

"Enlightened Attitude?"

It has been inferred that an "enlightened" administrative attitude is synonymous with lenience toward crime. This is as ridiculous as saying an "enlightened attitude" toward mental health causes mental illness. Whether or not the city administration and/or police are aware of it, the organizations are in effect acting as a policing force. DOB has tried to channel the homosexual's activities into a constructive program of benefit, both to the individual and to the public at large. The "gay bar" is no longer the only place where homosexuals may gather. DOB promotes nothing that is criminal and discourages any acts offending public decency.

DOB pleads guilty only to the attempt to provide enlightenment ("give the light of truth and knowledge to; free from prejudice, ignorance, etc."—Dictionary definition) on the very controversial subject of homosexuality.

THE HOMOSEXUAL VOTE

editorial from *The Ladder* (1962)

Dorothy L. (Del) Martin

In recent years there have been attempts to determine the strength of the homosexual vote in San Francisco . . .

The homosexual minority is unlike any other minority group. Homosexuals cannot be bound together by tradition as in the case of Jews. They cannot be readily identified as can the negroes. Homosexuals do not have a common ground in the areas of religion, politics or economics. Homosexuals are from all ethnic groups, of all religions, from every economic and educational level. They are Catholics, protestants, Jews, agnostics, atheists, metaphysicians. They are republicans, democrats and socialists; they are liberals and conservatives. they are union workers and business management; they are professional and unskilled. And these various influences will have more to do with how they vote than their sexuality.

It is agreed by many that the only issue that may draw homosexuals together in a common vote might be in the area of civil liberties and repeal of our outmoded sex laws. Even in the 1959 mayoralty election when assessor Russell Wolden accused incumbent George Christopher of "harboring organized homosexuals" in San Francisco—when homosexuality itself was an issue in the campaign—how could the homosexual vote wisely? To vote for Wolden was to vote for a scandalmonger who, having made capital of a group, would have to follow through with some trumped-up prosecution. To vote for Christopher, who wouldn't even utter that nasty word, was to vote for a man smarting from the accusations, who, in aspiring for future political office, would be out to prosecute the homosexual in every way possible to clear his so-called record. Either way the homosexual could not possibly win—and hasn't. It was interesting to note that some 9000 citizens went to the polls in this particular election and voted, but abstained as far as the post for mayor was concerned.

Homosexuals were once again the political pawn. But despite the age-old tactics at election time of unenlightened candidates—"Let's clean up the gay bars" and "Let's get rid of the queers"—there has been a growing concern by the public in general, evidenced by published letters in the daily newspapers, that the police department could better serve the public's interest than in entrapment of homosexuals.

At a recent DOB gab 'n java it was agreed by those present that they would not vote for a candidate simply because he was a homosexual, or was sympathetic toward the problem; their vote would be cast strictly on his qualifications as a candidate. They would have a tendency, they admitted, to expect more of such a candidate—that is, an even higher standard—because he would be representing them as a minority group. It was further stated that facetious campaigns to determine what they felt to be a nonexistent homosexual voting bloc were harmful to the group in general, since they imply that the homosexual is an irresponsible citizen who finds sport in plaguing the politicos.

There are issues which come up in elections from time to time which do affect the homosexual. And these issues should be dealt with knowledgeably and with responsibility by the leaders of the homophile movement. But to stir up cries for a homosexual vote without an issue to vote on is to make mockery of a very precious franchise.

THE PHILOSOPHY OF DOB: THE EVOLUTION OF AN IDEA

from *The Ladder* (1963)

Anonymous

In approaching this subject it must be clearly understood at the outset that DOB is all things to all persons who come in contact with the organization. Just as in the case where a speaker, who having delivered a lecture on a given subject, finds that of the 25 people in his audience there are 25 different versions of what he said, so it is with DOB. To each member DOB is something different—it may be a social outlet, a means of meeting others who share the same problem; it may be an opportunity for self expression, a means of finding oneself in a seemingly hostile world; it may be a chance for public service, a means of bridging the gap of misunderstanding between the homosexual and the heterosexual. To the outsider DOB may pose a threat, either personally or to society in general; to the outsider, too, who has no direct contact with the organization and who reads about DOB in newspapers or in books there could be many misconceptions about the group and what it represents.

This article, then, is an attempt to clarify the philosophy of DOB as a member of the San Francisco Chapter might view it. Because this chapter was the first it has necessarily witnessed more clearly "the evolution of an idea". The original idea came into being in the fall of 1955 when eight women got together to organize a social club which was to provide a means for Lesbians to meet one another without resorting to the gay bar. It was conceived as a self-help organization providing the members with the security of a group where they could discuss their problems freely and openly. From these discussions grew the need for more knowledge, for more understanding of self and society; and out of this need a library of books both non-fiction and fiction, was established. Out of the need for contact outside the immediate group the public discussion meetings came into being. Out of the need for further communication with those beyond the local area came publication of THE LADDER and the formation of other chapters.

Thus DOB has become an ever changing process of growth for the individual and for the group. It is not a crusade necessarily, for the emphasis to date has not been placed upon society per se, but rather on the Lesbian herself—to help the individual in making her adjustment to self and society, first through the acceptance and the security of the group, then to gain knowledge of herself and her relationship to society, and finally to move on into the world at large as a more, secure, self-assured and productive citizen.

While others go on beating their heads against the wall trying to convince a hostile public, while others continue to wrestle with the problems of cause and cure, DOB quietly deals with that which *is*. Homosexuality *is*, and neither law nor threat nor name calling nor scorn has been able to alter that fact. Society is gradually becoming aware of this fact, but has been slow in coming to terms—in the areas of human rights and dignity, of personal security and employment, and of research and knowledge. Consequently the initiative, the catalytic [*sic*]agent to get society to recognize and deal with the problem, must come from such organizations as DOB.

To bring understanding between society and the homosexual is a two-fold problem. On the one hand, the homosexual must recognize himself as a human being, as an individual with many attributes to be fostered and cherished and *contributed* to the welfare of *all* humanity. For the homosexual to foster the hurts, to meet prejudice with whining, to openly antagonize the public or to cower in the fear and guilt of misconception is to commit homo-cide.

On the other hand, unjust discrimination against any large group of citizens not only stifles the potential of these individuals but also denies society the benefit of that group's creative productivity. Society must come to realize that the stereotyped image of the homosexual is but a half-truth and that condemnation and imprisonment for simply *being* is not about to solve anything. Ignorance and misconception can best be tackled through research; yet researchers are also stymied in their search for *truth* by the stigma attached to the mere subject of homosexuality. For society to ignore the problem by continuance of the out-moded methods of closing the "gay" bars, thus abridging the constitutional rights of the homosexual by denying him the right to congregate in a public place; of denying employment to the homosexual when his inclinations are discovered; of casting aspersions upon anyone who would help or do research on the homosexual is also to commit socio-cide.

If homosexuality is a disease, as some claim, certainly it is not contagious; nor need it be crippling. While it is true that if there were less public pressure there would be less crippling effects, it is also true that the homosexual's "affliction" stems more from Self—self-pity, self-consciousness, self-abasement. If this Self were redirected toward another Self—self-awareness, self-knowledge, self-observation—then the homosexual would find that much of the rejection he feels is self-imposed.

Granted *The Ladder* has placed emphasis on the Lesbian as a Lesbian. But is this the whole truth about the Lesbian? Is she a Lesbian first, last and always? Or is she a woman of many roles, of many personalities and identities? For those of us who have worked for many years in the homophile movement there has evolved the concept of the homosexual as a human being with both male and female attributes with all the props of understanding for acting out the many roles of human life. But all too often the homosexual role (which is only part of the whole being) bogs down in the limitations of the "gay" world. This is the world where the Lesbian in her first awareness of her self as different tends to accentuate her masculine qualities, while denying all that is feminine (or heterosexual). This is the stage of discovery of new vistas and denial or rebellion against the old patterns. This is the world of non-conformity and creativity—BUT this is also the world of conflict which leads to fear, guilt, hostility and misery because we are all products of our previous conditioning and habit patterns.

To identify wholly with the sexuality of one's being, which is what the homosexual so often does, is to close off and limit one's perception of himself and the world he lives in. There is a difference between the concept of non-conformity and immersion in being "different". The homosexual who cries, "I am different—you don't understand me, you ridicule and despise me because I'm different" is setting into motion an act and re-act pattern of self-pity, doubt, guilt and fear—a mode of behavior which will continue in his life until he realizes, "Yes, I'm different. So what? I wouldn't be an individual if I were not".

How often have we heard the homosexual decry the dual role which society has foisted upon him? But how often has the homosexual considered the many roles the heterosexual is also forced to play? How often can the heterosexual speak out his true thoughts and emotions? Is not the heterosexual also beleaguered by family, teacher, boss—yes, even the police? Society demands from heterosexual and homosexual alike—consideration for others and decorum in public.

Many of the injustices suffered by the homosexual have been self-provoked because of his inability to see him self as a *human being*. This is the common denominator, and recognizing this, the homosexual need not feel apart from, but rather a part of—society. For it is not always society which isolates the homosexual; it can also be the homosexual's view of himself which may isolate him.

This then is part of the work of DOB—to help the individual homosexual to realize his worth as a human being, to turn the wasted energies of hostility toward more productive goals, to bring understanding to and about the homosexual.

Yes, this is part of the work, for the job cannot be completed until society also learns to separate the real fears, the real threats, from the self-imposed fears. Through the use of mass communications media, through the various organizations in the homophile movement, from professional spokesmen, the public is gradually coming to learn that the homosexual per se is not harmful to society. And it is on this basis that society must learn to view its outmoded sex laws. Sexual activity between consenting adults in private is not harmful to society, and for the first time in the U.S.A. the State of Illinois this year so stated in its revised penal code. This is a beginning, a break through of the barrier.

DOB is a democratically run organization with an informed membership. Policy is determined by the membership at large. To date DOB has been more conservative than any of the other organizations, more introspective and less extroverted, because its members believe that the homosexual can be integrated into society through understanding—by understanding self, by understanding society, by offering and *giving* understanding. It is felt that much more can be accomplished for the common good of the homosexual *and* society in this manner than by the beating of the drums—and the gums. It is felt that discussion and the exchange of ideas will do more to change the lot of the homosexual than ranting and raving.

But this concept is sometimes misconstrued as fence straddling. Do not be misled. Where there is infringement of the homosexuals' civil rights, when freedom of the press is threatened, when a homosexual loses the opportunity to earn a livelihood, DOB will not only take a firm stand, but will act boldly and aggressively to alleviate or correct the situation. True, we will mediate, discuss and arbitrate wherever possible, but we will also stand our ground when we feel there is unjust discrimination.

DOB was founded in fear, but has traded that fear for knowledge and understanding. Our only demand is that we continue to learn, continue to grow—knowing that the constant, ever changing, ever developing absorption of the past experiences into present day philosophy may be good only for today and today's problems and that tomorrow holds perhaps a different aspect to be considered. Freedom is an activity, not a state—it consists in working for goals that are beyond ourselves.

DOES RESEARCH INTO HOMOSEXUALITY MATTER?

(1965)

Franklin Kameny

PART I
On Some Aspects of Militancy in the Homophile Movement

As little as two years ago, "militancy" was something of a dirty word in the homophile movement. Long inculcation in attitudes of cringing meekness had taken its toll among homosexuals, combined with a feeling, still widely prevalent, that reasonable, logical, gentlemanly and ladylike persuasion and presentation of reasonable, logical argument, could not fail to win over those who would deny us our equality and our right to be homosexual and to live as homosexuals without disadvantage. There was—and is—a feeling that given any fair chance to undertake dialogue with such opponents, we would be able to impress them with the basic rightness of our position and bring them into agreement with it.

Unfortunately, by this approach alone we will not prevail, because most people operate not rationally but emotionally on questions of sex in general, and homosexuality in particular, just as they do on racial questions.

It is thus necessary for us to adopt a *strongly* positive approach, a *militant* one. It is for us to take the initiative, the offensive—not the defensive—in matters affecting us. It is time that we began to move from endless talk (directed, in the last analysis, by us to ourselves) to firm, vigorous action.

We ARE right; those who oppose us are both factually and morally wrong. We are the true authorities on homosexuality, whether we are accepted as such or not. We must DEMAND our rights, boldly, not beg cringingly for mere privileges, and not be satisfied with crumbs tossed to us. I have been deeply gratified to note in the past year a growing spirit of militancy on the part of an increasing number of members of the homophile organizations.

We would be foolish not to recognize what the Negro rights movement has shown us is sadly so: that mere persuasion, information and education are not going to gain for us in actual practice the rights and equality which are ours in principle.

I have been pleased to see a trend away from weak, wishy-washy compromise positions in our movement, toward ones of strong affirmation of what it is that we believe and want, followed by a drive to take whatever action is needed to obtain our rights. I do not of course favor uncontrolled, unplanned, ill-considered lashing out. Due and careful consideration must always be given to tact and tactics. Within the bounds dictated by such considerations, however, we must be prepared to take firm, positive, definite action—action initiated by us, not merely responding to the initiatives of others. The homophile movement increasingly is adopting this philosophy.

PART II
On the Homophile Movement and Homosexuality as a Disease

Among the topics to which we are led by the preceding, is that of our approach to the question of homosexuality as a sickness. This is one of the most important issues—probably THE most important single issue—facing our movement today.

It is a question upon which, by rationalization after rationalization, members of the homophile movement have backed away from taking a position. It is a question upon which a clear, definite, unambiguous, no-nonsense stand MUST be taken, must be taken promptly, and must be taken by US, publicly.

There are some who say that WE will not be accepted as authorities, regardless of what we say, or how we say it, or what evidence we present, and that therefore we must take no positions on these matters but must wait for the accepted authorities to come around to our position—if they do. This makes of us a mere passive battlefield across which conflicting "authorities" fight their intellectual battles. I, for one, am not prepared to play a passive role in such controversy, letting others dispose of me as they see fit. I intend to play an active role in the determination of my own fate.

As a scientist by training and by profession, I feel fully and formally competent to judge good and poor scientific work when I see them—and fully qualified to express my conclusions.

In looking over the literature alleging homosexuality as a sickness, one sees, first, abysmally poor sampling technique, leading to clearly biased, atypical samplings, which are then taken as representative of the entire homosexual community. Obviously all persons coming to a psychiatrist's office are going to have problems of one sort or another, are going to be disturbed or maladjusted or pathological, in some sense, or they wouldn't be there. To characterize ALL homosexuals as sick, on the basis of such a sampling—as Bieber, Bergler, and others have done—is clearly invalid, and is bad science.

Dr. Daniel Cappon, in his recent appalling book *Toward an Understanding of Homosexuality* (perhaps better named "Away from an Understanding of Homosexuality" or "Toward a Misunderstanding of Homosexuality") acknowledges at least this non-representative sampling and actually shows some faint signs of suggesting that perhaps there are two classes of homosexuals: patients and non-patients.

Notwithstanding Dr. Bieber's cavalier dismissal of it, Dr. Evelyn Hooker's work involving non-clinical homosexual subjects, with its very careful sampling technique and its conclusions of non-sickness, still remains convincing.

One sees secondly, in the literature alleging homosexuality as sickness, a violation of basic laws of logic by the drawing of "conclusions" which were inserted as assumptions. Dr. Bieber does this (and by implication, attributes it to his entire profession) in his statement: "All psychoanalytic theories ASSUME that homosexuality is psychopathological." Dr. Cappon says: ". . . homosexuality, BY DEFINITION, is not healthy. . . ." (Emphasis supplied in both quotations.) Obviously, if one assumes homosexuality as pathological or defines it as unhealthy at the outset, one will discover that homosexuals are sick. The "conclusions," however, can carry no weight outside the self-contained, rather useless logical structure erected upon the assumption or definition. The assumptions must be proven; the definitions must be validated. They have not been.

I am able to speak as a professional scientist when I say that we search in vain for any evidence, acceptable under proper scientific standards, that homosexuality is a sickness or disorder, or that homosexuals per se are disturbed.

On the basis of a disguised moralistic judgement (sometimes not at all disguised, as with Dr. Cappon), mixed both with a teleological approach to sexual matters, and with a classification as sickness of any departure from conformity to the statistical societal norms (on this basis, Dr. Cappon seems to come close to defining left-handedness as sickness), homosexuality has been DEFINED as pathological. We have been *defined* into sickness.

In logic, the entire burden of proof in this matter rests with those who would call us sick. We do not have to prove health. They have not shouldered their burden or proof of sickness; therefore we are not sick. These are things which it is our duty to point out, and, having pointed them out, to take strong public positions on them.

Then there are those who say that the label appended really doesn't matter. Let the homosexual be defined as sick, they say, but just get it granted that even if sick, he can function effectively and should therefore be judged only on his individual record and qualifications, and it is that state of being-judged-as-an-individual, regardless of labels, toward which we must work. This unfortunately is a woefully impractical, unrealistic, ivory-tower approach. Homosexuality is looked upon as a psychological question. If it is sickness or disease or illness, it becomes then a mental illness. Properly or improperly, people ARE prejudiced against the mentally ill. Rightly or wrongly, employers will NOT hire them. Morally or immorally, the mentally ill are NOT judged as individuals, but are made pariahs. If we allow the label of sickness to stand, we will then have *two* battles to fight—that to combat prejudice against homosexuals per se, and that to combat prejudice against the mentally ill—and we will be pariahs and outcasts twice over. One such battle is quite enough—

Finally, as a matter of adopting a unified, coherent, self-consistent philosophy, we MUST argue from a positive position of health. We cannot declare our equality and ask for acceptance and for judgement as whole persons, from a position of sickness. More than that, we argue for our RIGHT to be homosexuals, to remain homosexuals, and to live as homosexuals. In my view and by my moral standards, such an argument is immoral if we are not prepared, at the same time, to take a positive position that homosexuality is not pathological. If homosexuality indeed IS a sickness, then we have no right to remain homosexuals; we have the moral obligation to seek cure, and that only.

When we tell the various arms of organized society that part of our basic position is the request for acceptance *as homosexuals,* freed from constant pressure for conversion to heterosexuality, we are met with the argument of sickness. This occurred recently at a meeting between Washington Mattachine members and eleven representatives of all three major faiths, at which we asked for such acceptance of the homosexual into the religious community. Our entire position, our entire raison d'etre for such meetings, falls to the ground unless we are prepared to couple our requests with an affirmative, definitive assertion of health—as we in Washington did in that instance.

I feel, therefore, that in the light of fact and logic, the question of sickness is a settled one and will remain so until and unless valid evidence can be brought forth to demonstrate pathology. Further, I feel that for purposes of strategy, we must say this and say it clearly and with no possible room for equivocation or ambiguity.

PART III
On Research and the Homophile Movement

Movements tend to get themselves tied up with certain ideas and concepts, which in time assume the status of revealed and revered truth and cease being subjected to continuing, searching re-examination in the light of changed conditions. As an habitual skeptic, heretic, and iconoclast, I wish here to examine critically if briefly the value and importance to the homophile movement of research into homosexuality, of our commitment to it, and of the role, if any, which such research should play in the movement and in the activities of the homophile organizations.

I recognize that, with the deference granted to science in our culture, it is very respectable and self-reassuring and impressive to call one's group a research organization or to say that the group's purpose is research. However, at the outset one fact should be faced directly. For all their pledges of allegiance to the value of research, for all their designation of themselves as research organizations, for all their much-vaunted support and sponsorship of research, NO American homophile organization that I know of has thus far done any effective or meaningful research, has sponsored any research, has supported or participated in any truly significant research. (With the single exception of Dr. Evelyn Hooker's study, and while I grant that to be a major and important exception, the participation involved nothing more than supplying candidates for experimentation.) The homophile movement's loss from its failure to contribute to research has been not from that failure, but from the diversion into talking ("maundering" might be a better term) about research—diversion of effort, time, and energy better expended elsewhere.

For purposes of this discussion, we can divide the objectives of relevant research into two loosely delineated classes: research into the origins and causes of homosexuality, and research into collateral aspects of the homosexual and his life and his community.

Almost always, when the homosexual speaks of research on homosexuality, he means the former class in one aspect or another: "What is the nature of homosexuality?" "What are its causes?" "Why am I a homosexual?" "Is homosexuality a sickness?" "Can the homosexual be changed?" Objectionably, "How can homosexuality be prevented?" etc.

A consideration of the rationale behind the homosexual's interest in such questions will quickly show that they are symptomatic of a thinly-veiled defensive feeling of inferiority, of uncertainty, of inequality, of insecurity—and most important, of lack of comfortable self-acceptance.

I have never heard of a single instance of a heterosexual, whatever problems he may have been facing, inquiring about the nature and origins of heterosexuality, or asking why he was a heterosexual, or considering these matters important, I fail to see why we should make similar inquiry in regard to homosexuality or consider the answers to these questions as being of any great moment to us. The Negro is not engrossed in questions about the origins of his skin color, nor the Jew in questions of the possibility of his conversion to Christianity.

Such questions are of academic, intellectual, scientific interest, but they nor NOT—or ought not to be—burning ones for the homophile movement. Despite oft-made statements to the contrary, there is NO great need for research into homosexuality, and our movement is in no important way dependent upon such research or upon its findings.

If we start out—I do, on the basis presented in Part II above—with the premises (1) that the homosexual and his homosexuality are fully and unqualifiedly on par with, and the equal of, the heterosexual and his heterosexuality; and (2) (since others have raised the question) that homosexuality is not an illness—then all these questions recede into unimportance.

We start off with the fact of the homosexual and his homosexuality and his right to remain as he is, and proceed to do all that is possible to make for him—as a homosexual (similarly, in other contexts, as a Negro and as a Jew)—as happy a life, useful to self and to society, as is possible.

Research in these areas therefore is not, in any fundamental sense, particularly needed or particularly important. There is no driving or compelling urgency for us to concern ourselves with it. Those who do allege sickness have created THEIR need for THEIR research; let THEM do it.

In the collateral areas mentioned, well planned and executed research on carefully chosen projects can be of importance, particularly where it will serve to dispel modern folklore. Evelyn Hooker's research (referred to above) showing no difference outside their homosexuality itself, in its narrowest, denotive sense, between homosexuals and heterosexuals, is one case in point. A study in the Netherlands by a Dr. Tolsma, which showed that the seduction of young boys by homosexuals had no effect upon their adult sexual orientation, is another.

The study now under way by the Mattachine Society of Washington to obtain the first meaningful information on the actual susceptibility of homosexuals to blackmail, will probably be a third.

These are all useful projects. Dr. Hooker's has turned out to be one of our major bulwarks against the barrage of propaganda currently being loosed against us by the agents of organized psychiatry. (However, as I pointed out above, this is a bulwark not needed, in strict logic.) I shall in fact probably be using the results of all three of these collateral research projects from time to time in my presentations of our case. But these studies are not of the vital importance which could properly lead many of our homophile groups to characterize themselves as research organizations (only one of these projects actually involved a homophile organization to any significant degree) or to divert into research resources better expended elsewhere.

Research does not play the important role in our movement which much lip-service attributes to it. It plays a very useful and occasionally valuable supporting role, but not more than that.

More important than the preceding, however, is the matter of this emphasis upon research, in terms of the evolution of our movement. In the earlier days of the modern homophile movement, allegiance to the alleged importance of research was reasonable. As the philosophy of the movement has formed, crystallized, and matured, and more important, as our society itself has changed—and it has changed enormously in the past fifteen years and even in the past two—the directions and emphases in our movement have changed too. As indicated in Part I of this article, the mainstream has shifted toward a more activist mode of operation.

Continued placing of primary or strong emphasis within our movement upon research will only result in the movement's loss of the lead which it is taking in the shaping, formation, and formulation of society's attitudes and policies toward homosexuality and the homosexual.

Thus, while as a scientist I will never derogate the value of research for its own sake in order to provide additional knowledge, as an active member of the homophile movement my position must be quite different. It is time for us to move away from the comfortably detached respectability of research into the often less pleasant rough-and-tumble of political and social activism.

With the notion of a homosexual "culture" follow questions about the ways in which that culture is or should be manifested. Those who have argued for a culture have made analogies between homosexuals and racial, ethnic, and religious groups to argue for politics based on that shared position and ethos. Those who deny the cultural aspect, who present sexuality as not giving rise to any larger differences, generally promote a politics of equal rights and assimilations.

LEO EBREO

Leo Ebreo's article uses the analogy between Judaism and homosexuality to argue for an increased pride in a distinctive identity, but one that opens connections between homosexuals and others, rather than isolating us. Though written in 1965, the arguments presented here continue to be important in lesbian and gay politics.

A HOMOSEXUAL GHETTO?

from *The Ladder* (1965)

Leo Ebreo

When I was younger—about sixteen—I was an active Zionist. I believed that the best thing for American Jews, in fact *all* Jews, to do would be to go to Israel and live in a kibbutz (collective). I belonged to a Zionist "movement" and tried to get the Jews I knew to join. I expected of course that few would want to emigrate, but I thought that most would be interested in helping Israel and the Zionist movement.

This was not the case. I was met, very often, by an extraordinary hostility. It was not until years later, reading works on Jewish self-hatred, Negro self-hatred, that I could realize that I had frightened some already-frightened people.

For this fright I have still no cure. The rational arguments which I gave my Jewish friends then, I would give them now.

These arguments (both the ones they gave me and my replies) came back to me recently when I began working in the homophile movement and speaking to homosexual friends about it. When I attempted to draw some parallel between the Jew's struggle for his rights and the homosexual's struggle for his, I was often stopped short with the explanation that there could be no parallel because one was a "religious problem" and the other a "sexual problem." I tried, without success, to show how much the Negro's struggle paralleled that of the Jew, even though the Negro "problem" was a "race problem" and not a "religious problem."

As I have said, I have no rational arguments against the surrender to fear, and the rejection of self that lies behind it. This essay is not written for those who have surrendered to fear, but for the others, the fighters.

I think we need to constantly reaffirm our perspective in the fight for homophile rights, to realize that we are part of a broad, general movement towards a better, freer, happier world.

This struggle of ours for complete acceptance will probably continue throughout our lifetime, as will the struggle of the Negro and the Jew. Oceans of hatred, unreason, rejection, craven fear will continue to come from the "other" world (of the white, the gentile, the heterosexual), will continue to infect many individuals within these oppressed minorities.

And in this light, I think my parallel Zionist experience will show us both the currents of the Opposition from within our own ranks, and the answers which we must make. The objections my Jewish friends raised were as follows:

(1) "I'm not that Jewish! Being Jewish isn't that important to me." (2) "I don't want to go to Israel." (3) "*You* are making the situation bad for *us*. There isn't any great problem. Discretion is the password. You are being offensive. You are putting us in a GHETTO, or would if we allowed you."

The answers I gave then come back to me now:

1. "I'm not that Jewish." What does "that" mean? Orthodoxy? Many Zionists are not *that* orthodox. To be Jewish does not mean a series of outward observances. It means being part of a people, recognizing their history, trying to find within that historical experience your lesson, your place.

2. "I don't want to go to Israel." Perhaps not. Perhaps not now when conditions for Jewish life are good in the United States (as they were once in Germany). But don't you want

Israel to exist? Some place which will represent the Jews, to which they can go if oppressed? What other nation would try Eichmann? And if an Israel had existed in the time of Nazi Germany, could not the Jews have gone there? And, with an Israel to represent them, might there not have been some action taken to prevent the extermination of the Jews in Europe?

3. "You are making the situation bad for *us* . . . You are putting us in a ghetto." Nonsense. Israel is not a ghetto. It is a place where the Jew is, if anything, more normal than in other countries, a place where he is a farmer, seaman, shepherd, rather than furrier and candy store owner.

Of course, the Jews who offered me these arguments were not convinced by my replies. They had a certain picture in their minds of what being "Jewish" was—a curious, narrow, ill-informed vision defined by an old man (always old) with a long white beard and a yamulka and a long black coat, a Yiddish accent, the boredom of prayer mumbled and half-heard on certain holy days in a synagogue. The reality of Jewish existence, history, aspirations was unknown to them. Small wonder then that they could not imagine the reality of Israel, its youth, vitality, the variety of its peoples.

So they hung back—often, too often, proud of not being "too Jewish," changing their names to less Jewish-sounding ones, the girls having their noses shortened surgically.

And yet, as the years passed, I saw them grow more confident, less apologetic of their Judaism, because, in spite of themselves, they were proud of Israel, that nation whose growth they had at first resented.

And so, I think, it will be with those homosexual friends of mine who are now fearful, even resentful, of the homophile organizations. Their reactions now parallel, almost word for word, those of the Jews:

1. "I'm not that homosexual!" Here too, the image the outside world pictures is used by those raising this objection. One doesn't have to fit the stereotype to be *that* homosexual.

(Yet to a certain extent we must work with the outside world's definition of the homosexual.) The German Jews were the most assimilated, often not knowing Yiddish, often not religious, often converted to Christianity. Still they were exterminated. Similarly, too often the one who suffers from persecution of homosexuals is the respectable married man, like Jenkins, who makes a single slip. No one trying to defend Jenkins (and there were few who did, to our eternal shame) noted that he wasn't *that* homosexual.

2. "I don't want to be a member of a homophile organization." My full sympathies. Neither do I. But I do belong, just as I belong to the UJA, to the NAACP. Being in the Zionist movement, like being in the homophile movement, was to some extent a burden to me. It is a trial to pay dues, to attend meetings, to hear lectures, and—most of all—to have to deal with so many people and with their many, many faults. (St. Theresa, the Jewess of Avila, said that people were a great trial to her. That was the 16th century, and people are still a great trial.) But don't you want the homophile movement to exist? Don't you want to see some organization represent homosexuals, stand up for their rights?

Fighting though I was for the state of Israel, I was still—and am still—a confirmed internationalist. But to arrive at that place in history, these intermediate steps are necessary. It is not a certain good—an absolute good—that there be a state of Israel, with borders, army, taxes, ministries. But until there are no French, German, Russian, American nationalities, I think it unwise to eliminate the Jewish nationality, which all these nations have at times acknowledged (before its official creation) by discriminating against it.

The question you must ask yourself is not whether you "like" to join or at least support a homophile organization (or a civil rights organization), but whether it is *needed*. And the homophile movement is needed, as Israel is needed, *at this point in history*.

3. "Your homophile organizations make our situation worse . . . Discretion is the pass-

word. You are being offensive. You are putting homosexuals in a ghetto." Here again we are dealing often with homosexual fear and self-hatred and self-rejection.

This very word—GHETTO—has been used to me by homosexuals outside the movement. The homosexual who says this has accepted the negative picture of the homosexual drawn by the outside world. And, just as the American Jew may imagine a nation of candy store keepers with Yiddish accents and skull-caps, so the "assimilated" homosexual, from his troglodyte perspective, may imagine an assembly of campy ballet dancers and hair dressers.

There is already something of a ghetto pattern for homosexuals, because of the pressures put on them to confine themselves to certain vocations where they are "expected" and to isolate themselves.

But the aim of the homophile organizations, like that of the NAACP, the UJA, is not for further ghettoization but for *integration*, for *equality*.

However, there is a radical difference between the situation of the homosexual and that of the Negro and Jew in relation to their organizations. The Negro can rarely "pass." The Jew might be able to, but he is under many pressures, especially family upbringing and sometimes family presence, not to. The homosexual, on the other hand, can usually "pass" easily and does not have the family pressure as an inducement to declare himself. If anything, there is another pressure, to "pass" for the sake of family appearances.

Thus the individual homosexual may claim that membership in a homophile organization, rather than enabling him to normalize his situation, might endanger the assimilation, the equality he can achieve with just a bit of "discretion" and silence. This argument has a certain cogency. Its limitation is that it is a solution for the *individual* homosexual.

It is the "solution" (or, to be charitable, the "path") taken by the average homosexual, especially the one outside a major city, or who is not in touch with the gay community. And this is not a solution, a path, which is to be avoided. For certain people, in positions in the government, in schools, there may be no choice but secrecy at this time.

But the price can be a terrible one. It is, as I have said, an individual solution. Often, too often, it results in an isolation for the individual, sometimes a world of pathetic furtive sexuality or public lavatory sex—shameful, inadequate, ridiculous, dangerous. Even when the hidden homosexual has a mate, the union still has a peculiar isolate character, being secret, disguised. Thus the homosexual who "passes" is often in a ghetto composed of one person, sometimes of two. An individual solution perhaps, but hardly a permanent one, or a good one.

Those of us who are active in the homophile movement feel ourselves working for those outside and fearful of joining. We are working for a day when our organizations will be strong enough, active enough, to protect the rights of those in public employment (such as teachers), in the armed services, in government. The homosexual who is accepted as a homosexual will be a fuller, better person than the furtive imitation-heterosexual who has found his individual "solution."

The aim of the homophile organizations is not to draw a small circle and place the homosexual within it. The very term "homosexual" (only 68 years old if we are to believe the Oxford English Dictionary) may not be used with such frequency in the Larger Society which we are working to create. We *are* drawing a circle—but a LARGE circle, to draw the large society of which we are a part, in. We are asking to be accepted. This acceptance which the homosexual minority needs, wants, can only be gotten when it is *asked* for—if need be, DEMONSTRATED for through groups like ECHO [East Coast Homophile Organizations –an umbrella for homophile groups, formed in 1963—Eds.] and their picket lines.

The drive to eliminate discrimination against homosexuals (sex fascism) is a direct parallel to the drive to eliminate discrimination against Negroes (race fascism). These minority movements are not attempts to overthrow the white race, or to destroy the institution of the family, but to allow a fuller growth of human potential, breaking down the barriers against a strange race or sexuality. When the Negro, the Jew, the homosexual, is known and a neighbor, he will cease to be a bogey.

We are working towards that world in which there will be respect for, enjoyment of, the differences in nationality, race, sexuality, when the homosexual impulse is seen as part of the continuum of love which leads some persons to be husbands and wives, others to be parents, others to be lovers of their fellow men and women, and still others to be celibate and devote themselves to humanity or deity.

In that world there will also be greater variety. Our stratified ideas of masculinity and femininity will long have been altered. (Have you noticed that men's greeting cards have either a gun and mallard ducks, or a fishing rod and trout?)

It is this world, where the barriers of nation, sex, race have been broken, this larger, non-ghettoized world, that minority groups are organizing to work toward. And it is this picture of the larger world of the future that we must hold up when we are accused, by the very existence of homophile organizations at this point in history, of wanting to ghettoize homosexuals.

"Knock, and it shall be opened unto you."

LESBIANS AND FEMINISM

The existence of lesbians before 1970 has been made invisible in two ways. The first way is through the revisionist story in which Stonewall marks the first moment of resistance or radicalism; this move erases all pre-Stonewall queers. The other invisibility concerns the growth of lesbian-feminism within Daughters of Bilitis. In the minds of many heterosexual women, feminism was a contest between heterosexual women and men; lesbians were not welcome in groups such as the National Organization for Women until much later. In spite of such hostility, however, lesbians were always in the forefront of struggles for women.

The following series of articles document the rise of feminist analysis within DOB. Collectively, these articles show how far the homophile organizations did indeed go—and how much we have still to do.

WHAT CONCRETE STEPS CAN BE TAKEN TO FURTHER THE HOMOPHILE MOVEMENT?

an address printed in *The Ladder* (1966)

Shirley Willer, President, DOB

To an extent it is difficult for me to discuss what the homophile movement should be doing. I have some very clear ideas about what the Lesbian should be doing but the problems of the male homosexual and the female homosexual differ considerably.

Most perceptive authorities have stated that the basic problems in relations between the sexes arise from the completely artificial dichotomies of role and appearance ascribed to each sex by society. From the median beds wherein we lie, few persons, homosexual or heterosexual, arise whole and healthy individuals.

The social conformist is wracked by anxieties in his ambivalent clinging to the social artifacts which require his denunciation of his nature. The social non-conformist is driven to propound his personal revelation as being above reproach and beyond question. In such a society Lesbian interest is more closely linked with the women's civil rights movement than the homosexual civil liberties movement.

The particular problems of the male homosexual include police harassment, unequal law enforcement, legal proscription of sexual practices and for a relatively few the problem of disproportionate penalties for acts of questionable taste such as evolve from solicitations, wash-room sex acts and transsexual attire.

In contrast, few women are subject to police harassment and the instances of arrest of Lesbians for solicitation, wash-room sex or transsexual attire are so infrequent as to constitute little threat to the Lesbian community beyond the circle of the immediately involved. The rare occurrences serve to remind the Lesbian that such things are possible, but also that they rarely happen.

The problems of importance to the Lesbian are job security, career advancement and family relationships.

The important difference between the male and female homosexual is that the Lesbian is discriminated against not only because she is a Lesbian, but because she is a woman. Although the Lesbian occupies a "privileged" place among homosexuals, she occupies an under-privileged place in the world.

It is difficult for a woman to be accepted as a leader in any community or civic organization and the woman who does succeed in breaking down the barriers in recognition is usually greeted with a mixture of astonishment and sympathetic amusement. There are few women who desire to emulate Carrie Nation, chained to a fire hydrant and swinging a battle-axe—but the few women who achieve community, professional or civic leadership are compared to that image, sometimes rightfully so, since despite legal recognition of feminine equality, the road to public recognition for each woman leads across the battlefield.

Lesbians have agreed (with reservations) to join in common cause with the male homosexual—her role in society has been one of mediator between the male homosexual and society. The recent DOB Convention was such a gesture. The reason we were able to get the public officials there was because we are women, because we offered no threat. However, they did not bargain for what they got. They did not expect to be challenged on the issues of male homosexuality. In these ways we show our willingness to assist the male homosexual in seeking to alleviate the problems our society has inflicted on him.

There has been little evidence however, that the male homosexual has any intention of making common cause with us. We suspect that should the male homosexual achieve his particular objectives in regard to his homosexuality he might possibly become a more adamant foe of women's rights than the heterosexual male has ever been. (I would guess that a preponderance of male homosexuals would believe their ultimate goal achieved if the laws relating to sodomy were removed and a male homosexual were appointed chief of police.)

This background may help you understand why, although the Lesbian joins the male homosexual in areas of immediate and common concern, she is at the same time preparing for a longer struggle, waged on a broader base with the widest possible participation of the rank and file Lesbian. It shows why, to the Lesbian leader, diffusion and consensus are as important as leadership and direction. Demonstrations which define the homosexual as a unique minority defeat the very cause for which the homosexual strives—TO BE CONSIDERED AN INTEGRAL PART OF SOCIETY. The homosexual must show that he is, in fact, NOT a unique "social problem." That concept is too widely held to require endorsement from homophile organizations. Demonstrations that emphasize the uniqueness of the homosexual may provide an outlet for some homosexuals' hostilities, but having acted out his revolt, he loses a part of the drive that might have been available for more constructive approaches to problem solving.

The basic objectives of the homophile organizations must continue to be open to new avenues of in-depth communication. Its energies must not be channelized—its attempts must be repetitive—its approaches must be as diverse as imagination will allow. To put this more specifically, THE MORE WAYS WE CAN GET MORE PEOPLE INVOLVED IN THE GREATEST VARIETY OF APPROACHES TO THE WIDEST POSSIBLE CONFIGURATION OF THE PROBLEMS RELATED TO HOMOSEXUALITY, THE MORE LIKELY WE ARE TO ACHIEVE SOME MEASURE OF SUCCESS.

I can name a few dozen of the concrete steps your organizations should be taking. I do not doubt that you have tried them. Then, I say continue these and add more and more and more.

The argument that concentration is more productive than diversity is false when applied to homophile organizations. You cannot "retool" the talents of your membership to meet a current market. The only thing you may do is warehouse talent which could be of use to the common cause. Because this is a fact, one also hears the notion that instead of re-tooling the members, we should retool the organizations and perhaps, eventually, each person will find the organization of his level and interest.

Accordingly, proceeding from our statement of wish to offer a few constructive steps—steps we do not like to call concrete, but in full knowledge of the shifts of time and structure, we believe to be firm and tread-worthy.

1. To affirm as a goal of such a conference: to be as concerned about women's civil rights as male homosexuals' civil liberties.

2. To suggest that homosexual men attempt to appreciate the value of women as PEOPLE in the movement, respect abilities as individuals, not seek them out as simple "show-pieces."

3. That those philosophical factors of homosexuality which engage both sexes be basic to our concepts of reform.

4. That the number of one sex not be a determinate factor in decisions of policy, but that a consideration of all arguments be heard and that CONSENSUS be the goal of the conference. Insofar as we do find trust and value in the male-oriented homophile organizations, we will find common ground upon which to work.

THE LESBIAN'S OTHER IDENTITY

(1968)

Dorothy L. (Del) Martin

In speaking to public audiences about the Lesbian, DOB spokeswomen have often alluded to the fact that she is first a human being, a woman second, and incidentally a Lesbian. DOB's program over the years, however, has lent itself almost exclusively to the Lesbian role—the problems these women face in employment, for instance, as Lesbians. But don't they also face employment discrimination just on the basis of being women? And wouldn't it also serve the purpose of DOB to join with other women's organizations in fighting against sex discrimination as it relates to women?

The National Organization for Women has launched an active campaign throughout the country to combat some of these inequities. Candidates for political office have been queried on their stand in relation to the equal rights amendment for women to the U.S. Constitution, proper enforcement of prohibitions against sex discrimination in employment under Title VII of the Civil Rights Act of 1964, the fundamental human right of a woman to control her own reproductive life with the repeal of laws penalizing abortion as violating that right, and a Bill of Rights for Women ensuring equal opportunity to participate in employment and government without conflict with motherhood.

NOW has called for a nationwide boycott against the Colgate-Palmolive Company to protest that company's long-standing job discrimination against female employees. For years, Colgate has maintained a separate list of jobs that women may work at—at less pay. The company's system of seniority lists also is discriminating, since women may not "bump" a man with less seniority to win one of the men-only jobs. This has resulted in the layoff of women with 20 to 25 years seniority.

Would it not serve DOB's membership to join NOW in exerting pressure through boycotting all Colgate products? If the one in 10 estimate for the incidence of homosexuality is applied, certainly many Lesbians are affected by such discriminating company policies. The products involved are Ajax cleansers, Baggies, Colgate and Palmolive toiletries, Dermassage lotion, Fab, Halo shampoo, Handi-Wipes, Sterno, Vel soaps, Lustre-Creme, Wildroot and 007 men's toiletries.

NOW has also been fighting for an end to the air lines' discrimination against stewardesses because of age and marital status. And more recently NOW has taken on the United Air Lines for their "Executive Flight—For Men Only." In New York a suit has been brought against a hotel for refusing to serve women at the bar.

Volunteer, "spare time" attorneys for NOW have also brought suit against various companies to test state "protective" laws which in effect bar women from certain jobs and promotions because of restrictions on hours and lifting. NOW maintains that protective legislation should apply equally to men and women employees.

Because of an all-out campaign including a nationwide demonstration last December, NOW can take much of the credit for the Equal Employment Opportunities Commission's recent decision to enforce the desegregation of help wanted ads, thereby forcing the newspapers to list jobs alphabetically, by category only. This should be of help to Lesbians who are qualified in what has heretofore been considered men's jobs such as engineers, draftsmen, machinists, truck drivers, etc. While it will not immediately put a stop to all sex discrimination in jobs, it will put employers on the spot and force them to reevaluate their positions.

Some of NOW's chapters are also working for equalization of housing and curfew regulations at colleges; against discrimination in press clubs, city golf courses and church administration; for paid maternity leave, income tax deduction for child care expenses, and for child care centers on the same basis as parks, libraries and public schools. The latter would most certainly be of benefit to the working mother who also happens to be a Lesbian.

"For women, as for black people, self determination cannot be real without economic and political power. As long as women face the barriers of sex discrimination in employment and are restricted to the menial, lowest paying jobs in industry, as long as women are subtly discouraged or explicitly barred from the education and training that would enable them to achieve a decision-making role in society, as long as no major politician or political party takes women seriously enough to give attention to 51% of the voters in terms of concrete legislative programs, and not just token appointments and lip service, 'woman power' is a putdown slogan," says Betty Friedan, author of *The Feminine Mystique* and national president of NOW, in reply to "a recent silly suggestion by a major women's magazine" for "woman power" as a means of ending violence in this country.

By the same token let us not forget that discrimination exists in the homophile movement—in those organizations who claim to be "open" to both men and women, but whose activities and public relations emphasis are clearly male dominated and male oriented. DOB has fought long and hard for "equality" in the homophile community and its movement.

DOB needs to maintain its alliance with other organizations in the homophile movement—and properly so. But DOB also needs to broaden its identity and make another alliance treaty with such women's organizations as NOW.

The National Organization for Women's national headquarters is located at 1424 16th St. N.W., Washington, D.C. 20036. National membership is $7.50 per year for individuals and $10 for couples. One Lesbian couple has already been accepted under the "couple" rate . . .

OF WHAT USE IS NACHO?

(1969)

Rita Laporte

I am not a joiner. I never was. My twelve year membership in DOB is the exception that proves the rule. I love DOB because it is for women and run by women. It is the only organization I know of that is fighting for the rights of Lesbians. Within DOB I need not make the usual obeisance to the male, homosexual or heterosexual, nor need I expect one day to be taking orders from a male boss (something I will do only for pay).

As most women are not aware of their status as slaves, so some Lesbians do not understand the subtle ways in which homosexuals attempt to undermine Lesbians. From the moment of birth men are taught their "superiority" and women, their "inferiority." It takes time and experience to pierce this heavy veil of conditioning. Most men are not vicious about it; they simply take it so much for granted. Some quotations from a prime mover of NACHO will make this clear: (in connection with a request for DOB's endorsement of a statement on rights for homosexuals that made no mention whatsoever of Lesbians, and to which omission I took exception, he writes) "... these male homosexuals just won't give you a break, will they? Well, I think it's more oversight than evil intent—not that that's good. I just never gave the omission of lesbians . . . a thought. It's so easy to forget about women when you're living in a man's world—and it is indeed a man's world isn't it? Always has been and I dare say always will be—in the nature of things, you know . . . After all, somebody has to assume authority and it might just as well be the male."

It is NOT in the nature of things, it has NOT always been so, and it need NOT continue to be so. In the distant past matriarchies flourished. What humanity needs now, and time is running out, is TOTAL EQUALITY between the sexes. In the meantime and as long as I am President of DOB I will fight to keep us independent and to remind the men that we will not be forgotten, not for a moment.

It needs to be said over and over again that the real gap within humanity is that between men and women, not that between homosexual and heterosexual. When all homosexuals, male and female, have their rights as homosexuals, we Lesbians will have all the rights that *women* have. To be sure, this is a step in the right direction. We will no longer need to fear being fired from our lowly, boring, and ill-paid jobs by virtue of our Lesbianism. We will be fired, or at least not promoted, simply because we are women. A male homosexual couple will be an economic power indeed. And the Lesbian couple?

Heterosexual women are hampered in gaining their rights because each one is married to a man. Divide and conquer. The Lesbian does not have this handicap. This is our unique strength, a strength that can benefit all women. Yet there are some of us who want to throw this away, to dissipate this force by, in effect, a sort of group "marriage," by allowing DOB to become an adjunct, a "wife," to the male homophile community, i.e., NACHO. Other than disbanding I cannot think of a better way in which to disappear.

Let us not be fooled. It is a fact that men, whether gay or straight, have more need of women than women, of men. Homosexuals are constantly trying to entice Lesbians to join their organizations. I have no objection to Lesbians who wish to devote their energies to the cause of the male homosexual (and incidentally what crumbs we pick up as the men get their rights) but I do not want to see DOB do this. The men will come to us and we will be glad to help them when it is to our mutual advantage to do so. In time some of them will learn that while Lesbians cannot be pushed around like other women of their acquaintance, that we are very nice people when treated as equals.

Over the years DOB has built an enviable reputation and a fine image with the public. We are an old homophile organization, we are National, and for thirteen years we have published THE LADDER. The male homosexuals have not been able to do this and there is an underground element of jealousy. In this year, 1969, the Year of the Lesbian, DOB is growing up and spreading its influence with renewed vigor. A recent review of THE LADDER in the LIBRARY JOURNAL (April 15, 1969) says in part that, "The official publication of THE DAUGHTERS OF BILITIS, INC. is . . . serious in purpose, and contentwise seems a bit more mature than its Hollywood fellow." The same article says of Gene Damon's and Lee Stuart's bibliography, THE LESBIAN IN LITERATURE, " . . . it is a model of its kind." This Journal goes to all libraries excepting some of the smallest. Random House has contracted for a book, to be published in October of this year in both hard- and paperback, on the Women's Liberation or Women's Rights movement. No less a writer than our LADDER Editor has been invited to submit an article on DOB and Lesbianism. This book will reach a far, far larger audience than any previous book that has mentioned DOB.

In the coming months 1005 Market Street will be deluged with requests for the bibliography and subscriptions to THE LADDER. More slowly, as Lesbians discover our publications in their local libraries and buy or borrow the Random House book, inquiries about membership in DOB will snowball. More members will lead to more and bigger chapters. DOB can and will become a mighty organization, a force to reckon with working for Lesbians everywhere. All of our energies are needed in our work, our battle.

LESBIANISM AND FEMINISM
(1969)

Wilda Chase

For some time now attempts have been made to establish dialogue between organized feminists and organized lesbians in the New York area. These attempts, unfortunately, have usually been one-sided. Most women's groups expressly welcome the participation of lesbians. Most lesbians, however, seem not to understand that feminist issues are relevant to *them*. Not only does participation in the Movement advance the interests of lesbians as *women*, but also a mutually profitable liaison—and this is very important!—with groups of women who are not lesbians is a very good means of gaining acceptance of the lesbian as a citizen of the community, and of achieving recognition of lesbianism as a valid lifestyle.

There are many different groups in the woman's movement. Some of them are mainly action-oriented; others are mainly theory-oriented study groups or self-exploratory therapy groups. Some are conservative, others are radical. They are constantly splintering as new areas of interest and consciousness arises. They all "do their thing," yet they maintain a united front on basic issues.

It is with great effort and pain that these women dissect, examine, and define what women *are*, and what they are *meant* to be. No area of women's experience is out of bounds, and the issues are constantly being refined and clarified. We have made great progress during the past year, and our numbers are steadily increasing.

Recently a Women's Liberation encounter group—a therapy-oriented group group—appeared as guests at an open discussion meeting at the DOB. They explained how their group was formed in response to the ever-recurring confessions of women in the Movement that they feel "damaged" through their relationships with men, that their sense of *self* is diminished. They feel that the time has come for women to admit that they are being (have always been) short-changed in their relationships with men, and that their best course is to *give one another* the recognition and encouragement for the personal growth and fulfill-ment they are denied by men. Some of them feel intense hate and anger toward men for their refusal (or, as some believe, their natural incapacity) to return to women the self-recognition they *take* from women as a natural right. The most highly "evolved" groups are composed of girls and women who have broken off all diplomatic relations with the enemy. Much talk is going around about the possibility of forming communes, living arrangements which would combine privacy with community and provide an atmosphere of tender concern in which the members could help one another to recapture their lost or damaged self-hood. We have not yet been able to provide facilities for communal living, but the idea is vigorously alive and the possibility for creative living that it promises is irresistibly attractive.

It is ironic that feminists have always been accused of being lesbians. They are far from it. In fact, their *heterosexuality* is their problem, such a crippling problem that they seek extreme measures to protect themselves against it. Most of those in the vanguard of the Movement are sworn to celibacy or asexuality, determining to invest their creative energies in more meaningful pursuits. They commonly share the view that sexual relationships with men—as men now are—are against the interests of women and that women should find other solutions to their human need to love and be loved, to be affectionately related to oth-ers. Most of the women, however, still cling to the fond hope that men will somehow reach a "higher level of consciousness;" that is, humanize themselves, sometime in the future, and that it will then be possible for women to re-establish relationships with men that will reaf-firm rather than sabotage their human dignity.

Radical feminists, those whose persistent efforts to face the truth about men have led them to sever all relations with them, have courageously advanced the proposition that les-bianism is a valid alternative for women. Convinced that heterosexuality, as it now stands, is a sickness, they are willing to consider the possibility that lesbianism is a healthier solution. One member of the visiting encounter group said, "In some crazy way, you people are ahead of us." She was referring to the lesbian's sense of *self*, which develops without reference to men and is less likely to be damaged. The lesbian's situation, it was noted, gives her a better chance to grow up with a healthy respect for herself as a *primary* human being rather than a *secondary* one, i.e., an appendage to a male. Most feminists admit that deeply ingrained inhibitions will always prevent them from seeking a truly passionate (lesbian) friendship with another woman. Yet they admire and respect such relationships, and strive to achieve the social advantages of truly loving contact with one another, without overt sexual involve-ment. They admit impediments. Their conditioning led them to feel that men are the "real" people and that women are somehow contemptible and not worth cultivating. They are now beginning to realize that they can really *enjoy* the company of other women. They are mak-ing rapid progress in discovering in themselves and in one another, rich potentialities for true person-hood. They are learning, with some bitterness, that their ideas of what it means to be a woman, and that men define women *as they use them*, not as they *are*, and that women can only be damaged in the process. They are learning that they can feel more cre-atively, humanly involved with women than they ever could with men, which not only increases their respect for women, but hones a sharper edge still on their contempt for men.

Lesbians do have definite advantages over heterosexual women. Their less intimate con-tact with men gives them a margin of protection against the grossest forms of damage. They should guard against complacency, however. Like all female citizens who grow up and live in a male-dominated world, lesbians also have identity problems. They, too, are self-alienated to some degree. Furthermore, their political consciousness is much lower than that of the women in the Movement. In referring to the lesbian's generally superior sense of self-identity, one member of the encounter group remarked, "You people have more to offer us at this time than we have to offer you." That's doubtful. Lesbians may be psychically healthier than feminists, but their political IQ is generally disgracefully low. They have a lot to learn. They do have a vague notion that equal employment opportunity, equal educational opportunity, etc. somehow apply to them. But that is usually as far as they can go. One DOB member of the encounter meeting conceded that the abortion laws perhaps *should* be repealed. "It *is* possible—god forbid—that I could be raped," she said. That much occurred to her. She did not ask the larger question of why women should tolerate having male legislators make laws controlling the use of women's bodies. She could not go further and ask herself why women should obey *any* laws made by men. She did not raise the possibility of women's congresses enacting their own laws and living with total disregard for what the irrelevant males do with their repulsive and irrelevant lives. She failed to state that women are a captive people ruled by foreigners; that women must fight a war, if necessary, to achieve the right of self-government and self-determination that men take for granted as their natural right; that a male candidate cannot "represent" the interests of women constituents: indeed, they always ignore the women voters who have helped put them into office. She never mentioned that the Equal Rights Amendment to the Constitution, officially recognizing women as "persons," has never been passed, that every time the issue is raised it is laughed off the floor by male senators, who cannot distinguish between a female human being and a public toilet. She made no comment about a recent statement of the Equal Employment Opportunity Commission that the demands put forward by women for full economic rights clash with like demands made by males of minority groups and that, instead of seeking economic reforms which would provide economic independence for *all* citizens, the EEOC brazenly admitted that they intend to give priority to males and leave the females to shift for themselves. No DOB member observed that many fields traditionally dominated by women, such as library work, are being invaded by men, and—get this!—they move in at the top and seize the management positions. There are even males who go into nursing these days and climb right on the backs of the women and establish themselves as "nurse supervisors!" No DOB member complained about the decreasing numbers of women who obtain advanced degrees, of the gross inequities in the handing out of scholarships, fellowships and grants to female students, of the closed doors to executive training programs, of unequal pay for equal work, of invisible walls to advancement in the sciences and other prestige fields, of quota systems limiting the number of female students in professional schools, of the absence of women as department heads of universities, of the *presence* of male directors in girls' schools, of the impertinence of males writing for women's magazines, of the downright obscenity of males writing for women's magazines, of the downright obscenity of males writing on *feminist* issues! Most of these problems sound vaguely familiar to lesbians, but they don't get *angry* like the feminists do. Lesbians seem to lack that quality of divine rage, of righteous indignation that makes a good feminist.

There *was* one complaint that aroused some of the DOB members to mild expressions of indignation. The issue concerned the physical violence against female citizens which is daily growing at an alarming rate. One girl reported that six girls in her neighborhood had been raped, with no concern shown by the police until a man was killed—then, more police were detailed to the neighborhood. One DOB member called attention to the fact that female citizens live under the constant threat of violence, that the mere *existence* of males results in an oppressive atmosphere for female citizens, a condition which restricts their activities and experiences and cannot but undermine their efforts to develop themselves to their fullest human possibilities.

It seems that, with a little prompting, even lesbians can get angry. Mention was made of the constant harassment to which female citizens are subjected in the innocent act of walking down the street. This problem, called verbal rape in the Movement, has long been under discussion. Feminists, more aware of the psychological damage caused by men's unrelenting assaults upon the female's human dignity, regard this harassment as a chauvinistic act in which the male reaffirms his self-sovereignty as one who *acts*, and defines the female as an *object*, that which is *acted upon*. Verbal rape is a small but insidiously subtle part of the total process of conditioning by means of which passive-masochistic (self-defeating) tendencies are built inside the female citizens, tendencies then ascribed to her *nature*.

It was encouraging to hear even lesbians admit that being forced constantly to the defensive by males is not the healthiest environmental condition for a person's self-development.

Feminism irrelevant to lesbians? Snap out of it, sisters, and get with it! *Demand* your rights to your whole human dignity. *Demand* living conditions which will enable you to be fully, creatively *yourself*, not just a shadow of yourself. It is a characteristic of life that it pays no higher a price than you ask of it. Don't learn too late that you have priced yourself lower than life was prepared to pay.

IF THAT'S ALL THERE IS

(1970)

Dorothy L. (Del) Martin

Assemblyman Willie Brown, author of twice-defeated California legislation to repeal those laws regulating sexual activity between consenting adults, at the SIR Political Action Dinner at California Hall delivered a message of unity—unity of all oppressed peoples, unity of all minority groups, unity *within* the homophile community.

The greatest political force to effect change, he said, could come from a coalition of racial and ethnic minorities, the homophile community, the student and women's liberation movements. The occasion followed the closing session of the North American Conference of Homophile Organizations, which had displayed vividly our divisions rather than our unity, and Brown cautioned that whatever differences each of us had within our own communities should be kept within our own families.

It was an unfortunate analogy. Families usually include women, and they usually include youth—both of whom are integral parts of the homophile community, both of whom were ignored in the grand gesture of unity that closed the festivities. Willie's message went unheeded.

After fifteen years of working for the homophile movement—of mediating, counselling, appeasing, of working for coalition and unity—I am facing a very real identity crisis. Like NACHO I have been torn apart. I am bereft. For I have during this week of struggle between the men and the women, the conservatives and the Gay Liberationists, been forced to the realization that I have no brothers in the homophile movement.

Oh yes, when six of my sisters from the Daughters of Bilitis, Nova Organization and Gay Women's Liberation stood with me to confront the NACHO meeting on August 26th (the day of the National Women's Strike) [1970] about the relevance of the homophile movement to the women within it, the delegates passed a resolution in support of the women's liberation movement. They rationalized that all of their organizations were open to women, but the women didn't join in numbers and they just didn't know what else they could do to relate to their Lesbian sisters. We suggested that their programs and their publications were not inclusive of or relevant to women. They decried the segregationist organizations which we represented, but would not address themselves to the underlying reason for the existence of separate women's organizations—that the female homosexual faces sex discrimination not only in the heterosexual world, but within the homophile community.

And so, like my sister, Robin Morgan, I have come to the conclusion that I must say, "Good Bye to All That." Goodbye to the wasteful, meaningless verbiage of empty resolutions made by hollow men of self-proclaimed privilege. They neither speak for us nor to us. They acknowledged us on our "day" and then ditched us that very same night in their "male only" sanctuaries. It's the system, and there was not one among them with guts enough to put a stop to it. And, too late, they shall find that the joke is really on them.

Goodbye, my alienated brothers. Goodbye to the male chauvinists of the homophile movement who are so wrapped up in the "cause" they espouse that they have lost sight of the people for whom the cause came into being. Goodbye to the bulwark of the Mattachine grandfathers, self-styled monarchs of a youth cult which is no longer theirs. As they cling to their old ideas and their old values in a time that calls for radical change, I must bid them farewell. There is so much to be done, and I have neither the stomach nor the inclination to stand by and watch them self destruct.

Goodbye to co-ed organizations like SIR. The Political Action Dinner, we were told, was a "community" project. The Society for Individual Rights supposedly had finally learned that politics isn't a loner's game and called out the forces of coalition in the gay community. The Daughters of Bilitis responded, came to the first planning committee meetings and were, as usual, overlooked as plans progressed. Better it should be a SIR blow job. And it was.

Goodbye to all that. The finale at the head table said it all. It was no oversight. It was a demonstration of where the head is at—not just one man's head, for he was representative of the vast majority of those men present. Women are invisible. There is only one credential for acceptance in the homophile "brotherhood"—the handle Mayor Alioto couldn't find on Women's Day.

Goodbye, not just to SIR, but all those homophile organizations across the country with an open door policy for women. It's only window dressing for the public, and in the small towns of suburbia, for mutual protection. It doesn't really mean anything and smacks of paternalism. Goodbye, too, (temporarily, I trust) to my sisters who demean themselves by accepting "women's status" in these groups—making and serving the coffee, doing the secretarial work, soothing the brows of the policy makers who tell them, "We're doing it all for you, too." Don't believe it, sisters, for you are only an afterthought that never took place.

Goodbye to *Vector*. Goodbye to the "Police Beat"—the defense of wash room sex and pornographic movies. That was never my bag anyway. Goodbye to the Women's Page and the NACHO delegate who admitted that's how he regarded my column, professing all the while, of course, that he considered it most worthwhile reading. He meant it as a compliment. Goodbye to my editor, George Mendanhall, who has tried to understand and who is seeking to cement relations between the men and women of the community. He can't go it alone. So I say, "Go ahead, George. Let it all hang out. It's all they have, and *that* needs to be exposed."

Goodbye to all the "representative" homophile publications that look more like magazines for male nudist colonies. Goodbye to the biased male point of view. The editors say they have encouraged women to contribute, but they don't. Nor will they until the format is changed, policy broadened and their material taken seriously.

Goodbye to the gay bars that discriminate against women. Goodbye to those that "allow" them in only if they dress up in skirts, while the men slop around in their "queer" costumes. Gay Liberationists are right when they observe that gay bars ghettoize the homophile community. They are, after all, our chief base for socialization, for meeting *people* of our own kind. But there is no time or place for forming friendships, for exchanging ideas, for camaraderie—only for dispensing of drinks and sex partners.

Goodbye to the Hallowe'en Balls, the drag shows and parties. It was fun, while it lasted. But the humor has gone out of the game. The exaggerations of the switching (or swishing) of sex roles has become the norm in the public eye. While we were laughing at ourselves we became the laughing stock and lost the personhood we were seeking. It is time to stop mimicking the heterosexual society we've been trying to escape. It is time to get our heads together to find out *who we really are*.

Goodbye to NACHO. It never really happened. It was a non-organization consisting only of reams of purple dittoed rules and regulations that no one had the time nor stamina to read and big-mouthed, self-appointed and anointed homophile leaders—the steeple without the people.

Goodbye to Gay Liberation, too. They applauded the Lesbians who wished to establish common cause with them and the other men at the NACHO meeting. But somehow we are left with the feeling their applause was for the disruption of the meeting, not its purpose. There is reason for the splits within their own movement, why there is a women's caucus in GLF in New York and why there is a Gay Women's Liberation in the San Francisco Bay Area. Like the tired old men they berate they have not come to grips with the gut issues. Until they do, *their* revolution cannot be ours. Their liberation would only further enslave us.

Goodbye to the various Councils on Religion and the Homosexual. Like the institutions they sprang from they are bastions of male prestige—male evangelists from two disparate worlds. There is no place for women in the Christian and homophile brotherhoods. Be warned, my sisters, CRH spells only purgatory for you.

Goodbye to the male homophile community. "Gay is good," but not good enough—so long as it is limited to white males only. We joined with you in what we mistakenly thought was a common cause. A few of you tried, we admit. But you are still too few, and even you fall short of the mark. You, too, are victims of our culture. Fifteen years of masochism is enough. None of us is getting any younger or any closer to where it's really at. So, regretfully, I must say goodbye to you, too. It's been nice and all that, but I have work to do. My friends neither look up to me nor down at me. They face me as equals, and we interact reciprocally with respect and love.

There is no hate in this goodbye—only the bitter sting of disappointment. Momentarily I am pregnant with rage at your blindness and your deafness—the psychosomatic symptoms of narcissism and egocentricity. But my rage will pass. Most of it has been spent already. For I realize you were programmed by society for your role of supremacy. But somehow I expected more of you. I had hoped that you were my brothers and would grow up, to recognize that freedom is not self contained. You cannot be free until you free me—*and all women*—until you become aware that, in all the roles and games you play, *you* are always "IT."

Believe it or not, there is love, too, in this farewell—just as there has always been. How could anyone hold a grudge against helpless beings who are compelled to grope for their very existence? But I must leave you—for your good as well as mine. I refuse to be your scapegoat. By removing the target, you may no longer mock me. Besides, I must go where the action is—where there is still hope, where there is possibility for personal and collective growth. It is a revelation to find acceptance, equality, love and friendship—everything we sought in the homophile community—not there, but in the women's movement.

I will not be your "nigger" any longer. Nor was I ever your mother. Those were stultifying roles you laid on me, and I shall no longer concern myself with your toilet training. You're in the big leagues now, and we're both playing for big stakes. They didn't turn out to be the same.

As I bid you adieu, I leave each of you to your own device. Take care of it, stroke it gently, mouth it and fondle it. As the center of your consciousness, it's really all you have.

The question of butch and femme has been a difficult one for lesbians as long as lesbians have been noticed. The medical profession labeled butch lesbians as "true" lesbians, "inverts" who suffered from a refusal to adjust to femininity. Femmes often **RITA LAPORTE** escaped notice entirely unless they chose to associate openly with butches. The women of DOB faced a quandary when confronting butch/femme relations, for the butch seemed to justify heterosexual stereotypes and thereby threaten the claim that lesbians were just like heterosexuals. DOB urged its members to dress in a "ladylike" manner when meeting non-lesbians, especially those in power, and generally shrank from the topic of butch/femme, thus abandoning the (largely working-class) lesbians for whom butch and femme were basic elements of their identities.

In 1971 Rita Laporte, a former national president of DOB, wrote the following article. She strongly defends butches against censure based in fear and challenges us to celebrate lesbians' freedom to build relationships on models other than heterosexual monogamy. At the same time, she defends monogamous lesbian relationships against those who claim that monogamy is necessarily oppressive.

THE BUTCH/FEMME QUESTION

from *The Ladder* (1971)

Rita Laporte

Whenever a group of Lesbians gathers together over a period of time, this question invariably comes up and, for some of us, it has become probably the most boring question of all time. Nevertheless, the question is very much alive today, has in fact become more pertinent again in view of women's liberation. The answers given to the question range from: it is a pseudo-question, a matter of aping heterosexual relationships, to the conviction that it is a delightful reality. Why is it that this question is still so much alive today and no nearer solution among Lesbians themselves?

Lesbians are born into the heterosexual world of sex stereotypes just as are heterosexuals. As they mature and gradually surmount the first big hurdle, that of acknowledging and accepting their nature, they are, for the most part, quite without Lesbian models on the one hand, while imbued with heterosexual stereotyping, on the other. Some Lesbians fall in with that stereotyping easily and thoughtlessly, imagining themselves to be essentially male; others toss it out completely, settling for an oversimplified female to female relationship. Many of us, however, have experienced a real meaning to that miserable, slang phrase, butch/femme. But this is hardly the end of it. The anti-butch/femme contingent tries to make our lives miserable by making fun of what to them is a ridiculous copy-cat existence. Many young Lesbians therefore find that their own kind can be as vicious as heterosexual society.

Among those Lesbians who try to think sanely and without rancor about the problem, little progress has been made because they uncritically accept heterosexual male psychologists' pronouncements. One strange theory is that masculine Lesbians, i.e. butches, are really men born into a female body and that feminine Lesbians, i.e., femmes, learn or are conditioned to fall in love with butches rather than heterosexual males. We have all been thoroughly conditioned to think the adjectives, male and masculine, are interchangeable, as are female and feminine. This is a mental straightjacket under which not only Lesbians but all of society suffers. Before going further into this matter, let us look more closely at the butch/femme phenomenon with a sociologist's eye. This is the eye of the heterosexual male, who sees himself as the center of humanity as once he saw the earth the center of the universe. (There may be other "centers" equally valid, e.g., women, Lesbians, etc.)

Most Lesbians live in great isolation, whether alone or married to a woman, but there are many small pockets of Lesbians, usually gathered together around a big city gay or Lesbian bar, that may be designated Lesbian subcultures. The "bar scene" tends to have considerable consistency from city to city. It's habitués come for the most part from the lower socio-economic stratum and it is here that the butch/femme phenomenon is played out in its crudest form. It is here also that most of the "research" on Lesbianism takes place for the 90% or so of Lesbians who do not care for this milieu are invisible to the researchers. It is here that one encounters a genuine copying of heterosexual sex roles. The butches are not simply more masculine women, they imitate males at their worst. No male has spoken more derogatorily of his "chicks" than some of these butches. And the femmes manage to outdo the sexiest of sex bunnies. An elaborate game is played where, if a strange butch happens to smile or say hello to another's chick, she is apt to get slugged in the best barroom brawl tradition. Chicks are strictly property. Being small of stature myself, I would prefer the relative safety of a waterfront sailor's bar to the toughest of Lesbian bars. But fortunately most Lesbian bars offer no such danger, but they do exhibit much of the less brutal male-female, dominance-submission behavior, exactly that kind of behavior feminists loathe.

Many, if not most, Lesbians, including those belonging to the upper socio-economic stratum, do at one time frequent these bars, knowing nowhere else to meet with their own kind, or what they hope will be their own kind. Many of these Lesbians are appalled by what they see and sense the unnaturalness of it. In their revulsion they throw the baby out with the bath water, throw out the whole butch/femme phenomenon. What they are left with is: "We are all women, aren't we? therefore we are all feminine and must not deny our femininity." Yet many Lesbians know a middle ground, though it may have taken them many years to find it, to accept it, and to be thoroughly comfortable about it. This is the true butch/femme phenomenon.

I would like to digress here for a moment to point out a common error of sociology: to discover what should be, just find out what is. This sort of thinking is particularly misleading where Lesbianism is concerned. We Lesbians have a very difficult time of it for we have no models other than the, for us, irrelevant heterosexual models. Even if heterosexual sex roles *were* right for all heterosexual women, they could hardly be right for Lesbians. And this brings us back to the straightjackets of female equals feminine and male equals masculine. Since many Lesbians, about 50%, are simply not "feminine" as interpreted by heterosexual society, that leaves them nothing to be except "masculine" which means "male."

As yet there is no reliable sociological study on the behavior of Lesbians, let alone their inner life. A study that is based upon a true, statistical sampling does not exist because most Lesbians hide too well for such a study to be possible. But, even if such a study were possible, what would it prove? Such a study would include all those confused Lesbians who were trying either to imitate heterosexual behavior patterns or to deny them altogether. It is quite probable that the reality of Lesbianism is known only to a minority, and that minority consisting of Lesbians over 30. Truth is hardly a matter of a vote. The Lesbian can arrive at her own truth, if she ever does, only by much soul searching and experience of life. It is not easy for any human being to achieve an authentic inner life. Women's liberation has taught many a heterosexual woman this, but one still finds studies that "prove" the female to be passive and all those other attributes that add up to a creature no one would care to be, least of all the Lesbian.

How are we Lesbians to escape or resolve the butch/femme controversy? Let us once and for all separate female from feminine and male from masculine. All Lesbians are female, but most assuredly not all Lesbians are feminine, no matter how one defines that elusive word. It might be wise to discard altogether the words, masculine and feminine, for heterosexual men have so loaded them in their own favor. All sorts of desirable qualities such as courage, strength, ambition, leadership, aggressiveness, and mental brilliance are said to be masculine, which means attributes pertaining to the male only. The Lesbian is living proof that these qualities can just as well belong to the female, that they are, in short, human qualities. And yet the persistence of the butch/femme controversy points to a residue of meaning to the words, feminine and masculine. The words have a real, relational meaning. They refer to qualities that exert a mutual attraction, analogous to the attraction between the north and south poles of magnets, to use an inanimate example. Here we get down to the bedrock level of experience, the level not covered by sociological investigation. A butch, however "feminine" she may appear to the general public, feels something she is inclined to label "masculine" and that impels her toward a more feminine Lesbian. She may form a strong *friendship* with another butch or a femme, for she is not confused between "falling in love" with a woman and forming a deep friendship with a woman. A femme will find herself attracted to the more masculine appearing woman (again, it may be a woman who "passes" as "feminine" to society at large, but whose masculinity is sensed by the femme).

A danger here is that the reader will think there are two and only two kinds of Lesbians, the butch and the femme. This is merely a shorthand way of labeling. The qualities, femininity and masculinity, are distributed in varying proportions in all Lesbians (in all human beings, but we are here dealing only with Lesbians). A butch is simply a Lesbian who finds herself attracted to and complemented by a Lesbian more feminine than she, whether this butch be very or only slightly more masculine than feminine. Fortunately for all of us, there are all kinds of us. Some femmes prefer a very masculine butch, many do not. No doubt there are some women, confused and brainwashed by heterosexual sex roles, who think they want the butch chauvinist Lesbian, the Lesbian who outmales a male. I say "no doubt" for every kind of human being exists, but in my experience femmes have soon turned away from such types.

Having hypothesized the four separate qualities or traits: femaleness, maleness, femininity, and masculinity, I am left with the problem of defining them. This is an almost impossible task, in view of centuries of cultural overlay and eons of wishful thinking on the part of men. I can define femaleness and maleness only as those aspects of personality that derive from the biology and physiology that distinguish the sexes. But what these aspects are is largely unknown, though I suspect they pertain to differences in the sexuality of female and male. My personal definition of maleness is a negative one—a quality that precludes any erotic feeling. Whatever may be learned eventually about these two qualities, it is not germane to this discussion as all Lesbians are female. And whatever femaleness is, it is a constant when considering Lesbians.

A tougher problem is defining femininity and masculinity. It would indeed simplify matters if butch/femme were no more than the limitation of male/female. Then we could dispense with those two traits as nothing more than cultural convention. The scientific principal of parsimony, that the simplest theory is the best, will seldom work where human nature is concerned. Human nature is more complicated than we are able to conceive in theoretical terms. Since femmes and butches are meaningful categories, so are the adjectives, feminine and masculine. This is so despite the fact that much if not most of what is today designated masculine or feminine is neither, is simply human. Take aggression, for example. The male loves to think that this is a virtue of his alone and, in its cruder aspects perhaps, such as war and street fighting, it is. But there is a wealth of aggressiveness in the female else how would there be any women's liberation movement? Or take grief. Though the male is not supposed to cry, which is very similar to enforcing a taboo against laughing when something is funny, he can feel grief and should be permitted to cry since this is a human expression of feeling.

Let me begin with my assumption that masculinity and femininity are essences of some sort that have ontological reality. But a mental essence cannot be seen; it is a concept, rather like the concept of an electron, that has an explanatory value. Masculinity can be felt or observed only as it expresses itself through the body, in behavior, however subtle. We posit something we call intelligence, but we can become aware of it only in a live, awake, and acting person. No one could determine the intelligence of someone in a catatonic state. Measuring intelligence is full of pitfalls for it can be measured only in and through a particular culture. We have the same problem with femininity and masculinity. No one can express these qualities in a cultureless vacuum. A child of decided masculine nature, whether male or female makes no difference, will tend to express this nature by engaging in activities that the culture, however arbitrarily, has designated 'masculine.' The little tomboy, if her immediate cultural environment (parents and kindergarten) is not too restrictive, will play husband to another little girl's wife and mother role. These girls may or may not be Lesbians, but the little butch is apt to persist longer than the little heterosexual tomboy because her inner masculinity insists more strongly that she flaunt convention. We all have, not only a generalized urge to live, but to live as our inner nature directs. Too often cultural straightjackets distort us beyond recognition, as would be apparent if we could see into souls. We all know now that Helen Keller was a very intelligent woman, but the average person would not have thought so, seeing her as a young child. The means for her expressing her intelligence were blocked until her teacher opened up the way through touch. Few of us are blocked in this physical manner, but all women are blocked in cultural ways. But, just as Helen Keller found a way around her terrible physical handicaps, some women find ways to pierce through the heavy veil of cultural distortion. Butches and femmes who have found each other in love and marriage are such women, however much they hide their true selves from society.

Those Lesbians who persist in denying any meaning to butch/femme are simply those who either have no experience of this attraction or who are denying it in their fear of being accused of copying heterosexuals. In either case their denials mean nothing, for those of us who know the delight in finding our true mate, one who is like us and yet different, stand witness to the reality of butch/femme. As for copying heterosexuals: as someone has said, there is no worse butch/femme relationship than the male/female one of the heterosexual world. But, though all heterosexual relationships are butch/femme, they vary tremendously. We cannot out of hand condemn all heterosexual relationships. What is so bad about most of them is not their butch/femme quality but their *in*equality. It is the dominance/submission or master/slave quality of the relationship that is outrageous. A Lesbian marriage that tries to imitate this aspect of the heterosexual marriage is equally rotten. There is nothing inherently wrong with a division of labor in a marriage, so long as it is freely chosen and the labor of the wife is as worthy as the labor of the husband. While most heterosexuals are hopelessly caught up in a sliding scale of values imposed on the everyday activities of living—what the male does is important, what the female does amounts to little or nothing, we Lesbians need pay no attention to this. Housework is a bore and nothing more. It is neither femme nor butch activity. What wrecks heterosexual marriages is not so much the kind of work the woman is expected to do, but the underlying implication that she must do it because she is the inferior. The butch/femme Lesbian marriage that has no place for male or butch chauvinism, that in no way attempts to copy male/female relationships, that is a positive union of two authentic women, one more masculine and one more feminine, is a model of marital happiness that heterosexuals would do well to study.

This is what Lesbians should try to do in the difficult search for their own truth. They should neither copy heterosexual life nor react against it. They must find their own way, unconcerned about how much or how little it turns out to resemble aspects of heterosexual life. We cannot say out of hand that everything heterosexual is bad. We may find that some heterosexual pronouncements about life and love are happy ones. This should hardly be cause for surprise in view of the fact that heterosexuals are human too. We Lesbians, unlike male homosexuals, know that the basic heterosexual distortion is the myth of male supremacy. In theory Lesbians should be free of this and growing up Lesbian should be easy. Perhaps it would be if Lesbians grew up with each other in a Lesbian world. But Lesbians, unlike heterosexual women, grow up in total psychological isolation from each other. All we see is the heterosexual world and we must cope alone with our inner emotions as they gradually make their way into consciousness. Many of us fall by the wayside, some going through life in a completely heterosexual fashion, others finding only partial and unhappy solutions, and numbers of us finding fulfillment in a marriage of two persons who complete each other in equality *and* difference. What are some of the hazards awaiting the growing Lesbian?

Let us begin with the "tomboy." She is not as damned as the "sissy" boy, destined to become a more feminine homosexual, for females are not so important, and, anyway, she will outgrow it. I was a tomboy and will never forget, when in my 20's and upon meeting a grownup who had known me as a child, being complimented upon turning into a fine, i.e., 'feminine', woman. I was at the time playing the heterosexual to the hilt, dressed in a skirt, wearing lipstick, and acting like a lady rather in the fashion of an accomplished drag queen. That "compliment" had the flavor of an insult, though it was meant well and it did at least compliment my acting ability. I cannot say that all tomboys are butch Lesbians, but many are. There is a wide range of butchiness to begin with and the outward aspects of butchiness are variably modified by upbringing. The more "privileged" tomboy is apt to be far more pressured into learning to "act like a lady" than her freer, less "privileged", sister. The story of a friend of mine illustrates how tomboys or butch Lesbians are born, not made.

There are today a number of young women who, in the course of "consciousness raising" sessions in women's liberation, have come to realize they are Lesbians (have "come out", as the expression goes) or are wondering whether they might be. These are women who have, at least before joining women's liberation, experimented with heterosexual sex relations. In their new-found Lesbianism they proclaim that butch/femme must go. They are hopelessly confusing the heterosexual relationship per se with its almost universal tendency to be a master/slave relationship and then to transfer this reprehensible aspect of heterosexuality over into Lesbianism. This ignores the fact that there are heterosexual marriages wherein the male/female attraction does not entail any master/slave, dominance/submission, superior/inferior connotations (albeit such marriages are hard to find). For the real Lesbian, however, even such a fine heterosexual relationship is out of the question. Her inner nature makes impossible the enjoyment of sexual relations with any man. It does not follow that a polarity of attraction, whether male/female or butch/femme, must go. What these women seem to be seeking is "friendship plus sex" or an eroticized friendship. This is a far cry from a true marriage between a feminine and a masculine Lesbian.

The heterosexual, in her limited view of human relationships, imagines that it is biological sexual differentiation that determines the attraction of erotic love, that, if one woman is so attracted to another woman, it must be an attraction of same to same—hence the word, homo-(Greek for same) sexual. But human beings are a good deal more complex and blindness to the very real difference, which might be called a psychosexual one, between butch and femme cannot make it go away. The persistent need to do so proves only that many Lesbians are still infected with heterosexual stereotyping, still confuse heterosexuality per se with female oppression . . . Let us now ignore the heterosexual world and its problems and try to look at the Lesbian world as if it were the only one, or, like the sociologist, place the Lesbian at the "center."

This woman, during her childhood, would have made me look like a sissy. In her late teens she fell into the error of thinking herself to be essentially male, having, like all of us, only the models of male and female sex roles to go by. She dressed like a man and held her own with the 'malest' of them. This woman, unlike me, grew up virtually free of parental control and, while I went into a phase of trying desperately to be properly 'feminine', that is, typical female, she erred in the opposite direction. Then, around the age of 17, she came under the guidance of an older Lesbian who pointed out to her the folly of her course. My friend tossed away her male costume and tried to be a woman. A few years later, dressed in a feminine suit, nylons and girdle, a frilly blouse, and a coquettish hat, she sat on a park bench waiting for a friend. Some minutes later a policeman tapped her on the shoulder and said, "Don't you know you can be arrested for impersonating a woman?" Amusing as this story is, it contains considerable truth. My friend was impersonating. When I met this woman she was in her 30's, she dressed comfortably, made no fuss one way or the other about being female, and was simply butch.

The essence of butchiness is interior, psychological, emotional—a form of psychosexuality as fundamental as heterosexual male, heterosexual female, or femme. Some butches are easily recognizable by outward manner and gesture by even the most naive heterosexual, but most have picked up from the prevailing culture outward behavior that makes "passing" easy. Only the experienced eye of another Lesbian can spot the little telltale gestures. A factor of consequence in this matter of behavior is the butch's own attitude toward herself. If early on she has fully accepted herself, she ceases to be concerned with every little gesture that might give her away. She presents a naturalness that offends no one despite her being thought of as a masculine woman. In contrast, the butch who fears herself, who is overly sensitive to the ridicule generally heaped upon the masculine woman, may suffer the torments of hell. Day in and day out she tries to disguise her inner masculinity, she may even manage to hide it from herself. To others she appears strange and unnatural. Though she has thoroughly accepted her Lesbianism, she knows not what to do with this tender masculinity hidden within her. In some instances this leads to her taking the role of the femme. This is a curious inversion of her true self, one that points out the reciprocity or mirror-image aspect of butch/femme. For the qualities of butch and femme are not opaque to each other—the butch senses the nature of the femme by what it is she seeks in another, and vice versa. An analogy might be the right and left hands. These two hands, though the same in most ways, are also the exact reversals of each other.

An interesting side light in this connection is the masculine, apparently heterosexual, woman. There are some very masculine women who have never questioned their heterosexuality. And then something happens to such a woman that puts the fear of God into her—perhaps a Lesbian, taking this woman's "Lesbianism" for granted, assumes she is butch and says something to that effect. Overnight, such a threatened masculine woman may discard her masculine clothes, get her hair redone, and appear all frilly-feminine and unnatural looking. Many will insist that such a woman *is* heterosexual. No, this is an extreme case of denying one's self. So long as this woman was convinced of her heterosexuality, she was unaware of her masculinity. It is often easier to spot a Lesbian who does not know she is one, for in this state of ignorance of herself she does not know how to hide the truth. The Lesbian who knows herself also knows how to conceal it. This is sometimes carried to amusing extremes, as when Lesbians go to meet their Lesbian friends arriving from out of town and mingle with heterosexual women who are also meeting their women friends. The women who kiss each other are heterosexual. We have covered three possible errors butches may fall into: imitating men, denying their masculinity, or playing femme. These are errors in addition to the basic one of denying the reality of butch/femme altogether. What errors await the young femme?

She too is aware that there is supposed to be something unnatural about a masculine woman. If she is drawn to the masculine quality in a woman, that must mean she is *really* drawn to, or should be drawn to, a male, but she knows this cannot be. The least she can do, she thinks, is to try to feminize the butch of her choice. She is not denying her own masculinity, but her butch's masculinity. Another form this may take is that the femme denies and fears her femininity, since femininity in our culture is synonymous with inferiority. She early made up her mind, however unconsciously, that she would not be subjected to the feminine role (and rightly so as defined by heterosexuals) and now cannot accept herself as femme in the Lesbian relationship. She has it too firmly rooted in her mind that feminine (heterosexual type) equals passive and inferior. "PASSIVE?" Whether or not the words "passive" and "active" apply properly to heterosexuals, they do not describe the butch/femme Lesbian relationship. That so-called passivity can be most active and that so-called activity becomes indistinguishable from passivity. One might say the butch is actively passive and the femme is passively active and make of that what you will.

More common than the butch who has accepted a femme role is the femme who fancies herself butch. This is not simply a denial of femininity. It is more often sheer confusion. If one is attracted to a woman, one must be masculine or man-like. And too, since femmes are indistinguishable from heterosexual women, the young Lesbian is not aware of any difference and imagines that all women (except Lesbians) want someone masculine or as male-like as possible. Like society in general, she has swallowed uncritically the notion that all Lesbians are mannish. This leads some femmes into pathetic role playing. It is written all over them that they are desperately acting a role, wearing a facade that is hopelessly out of place. And it happens that a loving Lesbian couple may consist of a butch playing femme and a femme playing butch. Each is acting out in herself what she desires in the other. This is not necessarily as bad as it sounds for, if they truly love each other and their relationship is a truly equal one, that they have their "roles" upside down is not fatal. But it is hard on each one as a complete person.

I look back with amusement to my early days in the Lesbian world when it seemed to me that there was a terrible excess of butches. How unfair that there should be only one femme for every five or more butches. In later years, again to my amusement, it began to look the other way around. So many butches were afraid to stand up and be counted that those of us who did . . . well. But all is well—nature provides. There is a butch for every femme and a femme for every butch.

To summarize so far: Put schematically, growing up Lesbian means first to come to know and accept one's attraction for women; then to understand and to know experiencially the butch/femme reality; and lastly to know whether one is butch or femme. I question whether one could know butch/femme if one grew up entirely alone. This knowledge grows out of one's relations to others, particularly in a love relation. What one comes to understand is that a butch is as real, as ontological, a being as a heterosexual male. And so is a femme as real a being as a heterosexual woman. Just as a woman is not some kind of inferior man, or male manqué, as Aristotle, St. Thomas Aquinas and Freud would have it, so a butch is no imitation male nor is a femme a woman whose emotions have strayed in illness from their proper object, a male. We have, then, as fully equal and authentic types of human beings: femmes, butches, heterosexual women, and heterosexual men.[*] When I finally arrived at this simple existential truth that I, as a butch, am as fully valid as anyone else, a tremendous load was lifted from me.

We have shown that femmes and butches do indeed exist in their own right and not as distorted Lesbians caught up in aping heterosexuals. I cannot say that all Lesbians fall into these two categories nor is the answer to this of much importance. Ultimately every individual must try to find her true inner self however restrictive her society. But it helps to know what others have found to be their truth. It helps to know that the variety of authentic women is greater than heterosexual society would have us believe. I would like now to discuss more in detail the nature of the butch/femme relationships, as opposed to butches and femmes separately.

Since human beings are not disembodied spirits, they tend to express feelings growing out of their inner nature in outward behavior. Culture provides behavior molds and without culture a specimen of homo sapiens would not be human. A cultureless human being is a contradiction in terms, for our humanness can develop only in some cultural context. On the other hand, culture is confining and the more primitive the culture, the more confining it is. Ancient Greek culture was the most liberating culture for men that history has so far known because it provided fully for homosexual as well as heterosexual relationships. But its terrible restrictiveness on women was its limitation and the cause of the death of Greek civilization. Our American culture today is providing a slightly better milieu for heterosexual women, but it lags behind Greek culture in its frantic heterosexuality. Our culture provides no place and no molds or patterns for Lesbians. This is both a drawback, to put it mildly, and an advantage. Lesbians must work out their own patterns of behavior, a very difficult undertaking, but we can do this in total freedom once we have set aside heterosexual models as irrelevant. It is a bit ironic that the total condemnation of Lesbianism by a world that also proceeds as though we did not exist should, at the same time, provides us with total freedom, but so it is.

"The institution we call marriage can't hold two full human beings—it was only designed for one and a half." So says sociologist Andrew Hacker. He was, of course, referring to heterosexual marriage. The Lesbian butch/femme marriage can and usually does hold two full human beings. And this is not because it is a friendship arrangement wherein each partner respects the other as a person and agrees to play at sex from time to time, where each goes her own way but provides warmth and affection for the other, where both carefully divide the chores so that neither one gets stuck doing more of the menial. There is nothing wrong with such friendships. Anyone who has achieved so fine a relationship is fortunate indeed. But such a relationship is not a marriage. Nor can one say that a marriage, based on love and entered into for life on a monogamous basis is for everyone. What is so terrible today, among Lesbians and among women's liberationists, is the attempt to deny the beauty and authenticity of such lifelong, monogamous Lesbian marriages. Those of us who seek such a love or who have found it are supposed to be uptight, ensnared in the Judeo-Christian mythology of the "sanctity" of marriage (perverted from the heterosexual reality), unliberated spirits afraid of our sexuality. It is good that many women today are thinking about and experimenting with new patterns of living and loving. It is very bad that they are assuming that all old patterns of living and loving are wrong. The mutual love of a butch and femme is a very old pattern, and for some of us, the happiest.

A 'whole person' is yet not whole. Each of us seeks someone or some idea or God to complete us. The phrase 'whole person' does not mean an individual who has need of nothing and no one. Each of us needs more than herself, though we do not all need or want the same thing. A butch needs and seeks a femme for her completion. A heterosexual woman needs and seeks a man, but, because of the oppression of women, finds that she must become that half person in the heterosexual marriage of one and a half. In her rage at so horrible a fate, she thinks that making her husband do the dishes while she tinkers with the car will somehow change things. Such solutions attack only the behavior, the symptoms, and not the basic disease. In a typical butch/femme relationship the butch will work on the car while the femme washes the dishes. Why does this in no way strain the relationship? Because neither the butch nor the femme has attached any inferior-superior significance to these activities. They are both chores necessary to the maintenance of the household. The butch does express her masculinity in car-mending activity, since that activity has a masculine connotation in our society and we all need to express ourselves in behavior. However, it may happen that the butch does not even drive, let alone know anything about a car. It may be the femme who has a knack with things mechanical. Sensible grownups will not quibble over who does what, for one's masculinity or femininity may be expressed in thousands of bits of behavior. Each Lesbian couple is free to decide upon its division of labor. Behavior itself is of secondary importance. If the butch has delusions of superiority, no amount of activity juggling will change anything.

There is something immature about heterosexual marriages and those butch/femme marriages that imitate them. How can there be a fulfilling love between a master and a slave, however subtle these distinctions may be? I think all of us can understand the pleasure there is in lording it over someone else. We can all fall into this human (not male or female) foible. But it is a far smaller pleasure that the joy of love, and one cannot have both at the same time with the same person. But love, the kind I am speaking of here, is not easy and there is no reason why it should be right for everyone. Any time one embarks upon a particular course, one at the same time foregoes many other courses. The truly monogamous Lesbian, butch or femme, is so not out of a morality picked up from the church or elsewhere, but out of a deep desire to dedicate herself to one particular other person. She simply does not enjoy promiscuity, or changing partners. Like the monotheist, who prefers one God to many, she prefers to be faithful to one person for life. And this in no way restricts her in friendship.

On the contrary, being happily married, her freedom to choose friends is unlimited. She can choose as a friend someone she could not stand to be married to. She need not worry about whether she should proceed to a sexual liaison of temporary or more permanent character, for her whole sexual life revolves around the person she loves. She may or may not have made this decision consciously, but in either case it frees her. She is made whole by her love, her marriage, and this wholeness gives her the freedom to grow into the fullness of her humanity. The femme is made whole in union with the butch she loves as the butch is made whole by her femme, a wholeness no amount of friendship can give them. I do not know how to put into words the difference between this Lesbian love and a friendship that includes sex. There is a kind of feeling between a butch and a femme in love with each other that is neither purely erotic nor purely friendly, though these feelings are present too. There is a total and liberating kind of possession, each of the other and each by the other.

Also included are male homosexuals, but I do not care to go into their problems with butch and femme, itself an interesting morass of confusion with the culturally assumed inferiority of women.

ANITA CORNWELL   By 1972, its last year of publication, *The Ladder* had begun to reflect the changes in the lesbian and gay movements; the impact of Vietnam, feminism, civil rights and Black Power struggles were all manifest in its pages. The following article by Anita Cornwell refers to this complexity as she tries to untangle her position as a Black lesbian in a largely white movement. The question she raises, and the answers she suggests, remain with us in the 1990s.

FROM A SOUL SISTER'S NOTEBOOK
(1972)

Anita Cornwell

Since joining the Movement, I find myself associating mainly with white women. Most of the time I forget there is a racial gap between us, but I sometimes feel that such may not be the case with many of them.

That is not a sneaky way of saying racism exists within the Movement—which it does, of course, yet not nearly as much as one would expect considering the nature of our society—but rather that I do miss my black Sisters and yearn for the day when they will embrace the Movement more whole-heartedly.

Still, I know why they have not, the main reason being that age-old sickness, racism and sexism, and the damage it has done to all of us.

What really got me onto this train of thought though, was neither sexism nor racism, per se, but Lesbianism. I was somewhat shocked recently when I realized that most of the white Lesbians I know seem to feel more oppressed *as Lesbians* than I do.

At first I thought it was because I am older than most of them, that since I had been oppressed longer, I noticed it less. Normally, I guess I would have assumed it was because I am black. But, really, one does grow weary of making *that* assumption.

One of the absolute certainties of life in this country is the almost endless parade of dilemmas you find crossing your path daily. Not that you take such a rational, detached attitude while trying to grapple with one, however.

As a case in point, when George Jackson, the Soledad Brother, was killed, I happened to be in Kent, Connecticut, at a Conference for Gay Women. I had gone there in a caravan of three cars consisting of ten women, two of us black. About 125 Sisters attended the Conference, and at most I can recall only about twelve black women being present.

Which means that at any given time, one could look in all directions and see only white faces.

Then, as I lay in our tent on Sunday morning, I heard one white Sister saying to another, "There's a story on the front page of the Sunday Times that says George Jackson was killed in prison . . ."

I lay there, not unmindful of the fact that I was a fairly great distance from home, from any public transportation apparently as we were out on a large farm, that I had come in a white woman's car, and was at that moment lying in another white woman's tent. *And their white Brothers had killed my black Brother!*

Their Brothers were pigs, I thought then, and I think so now. But what of my Brother? A pig too, in all probability, as most black men are no different from white men as far as sexism is concerned.

But they didn't shoot him because he was a pig. They got him because he was black. I am black, too, and as James Baldwin is reputed to have said to Angela Davis, "If they get you in the morning, they will certainly come for me in the night."

So what does one do at such a time? Do you get drunk at eight o'clock in the morning although you're already on the verge of ulcers, and you don't want a drink anyway? Do you go on a rampage, ripping white Sisters apart merely because they are white like your oppressors who are coming for you also? Or do you shove the problem into the vast, overstuffed room located somewhere in the deep recesses of the mind and slam the door?

I lay there a while longer, then finally realizing that divine inspiration was not forthcoming, I turned to stare at the canvas wall of the tent and told myself I would deal with the situation after breakfast.

Yet many hours later, when I saw the black headline regarding Jackson's death, I quickly averted my eyes, unable to even look at the newspaper, let alone cope with the dilemma it had dropped in my lap. I still haven't, for that matter.

Then, several months afterwards, I heard a bleating voice on the radio describing how Angela Davis' health had deteriorated in prison (because of poor medical care and other environmental stresses) before they let her out on bail. And again I had to swallow my impotent rage because I knew she would not have been treated in such fashion had her skin not been the color of mine.

But why travel far across the country? Why not consider the black Sisters in my own front yard who are raped, beaten or/and murdered with monotonous regularity and whose violators are *never* apprehended because our white law insists that black women do not exist, nor poor white women either for that matter?

Thus year after year, the hidden chamber is crammed with repressed fury, but you dare not stop to wonder what would happen if the walls should suddenly give way. You simply keep on hoping that with a little luck, the reckoning will not come today.

Yet there is always tomorrow which haunts the mind like a half-forgotten nightmare.

I suppose that is why I was so surprised when I first heard some of my Gay white Sisters complaining about Castro's oppression of homosexuals in Cuba. Not that I don't think they should complain. Indeed, I am just as pissed off as they are!

But why didn't I or the other black Lesbians I know get more uptight over the oppression of Gay people? Don't we feel just as threatened by a Castro as we do by the cop on the corner? Weren't we just as concerned as our white Lesbian Sisters that "society" forbids us to hold hands or kiss in public?

Inevitably, one comes up with the indisputable truth that oppression is oppression no matter what the ideology behind it. And just as there is no such thing as a little bit of pregnancy, ditto with oppression. So why should one be concerned about which label is attached to one's oppression? Does it make any difference?

Then a tiny door of the vast room opened just a crack, and a few of the outrages I have faced on a daily basis because of my color floated through my mind. I had to admit, yes, there is a difference, it matters like hell. Because as someone has said, "When things go wrong, all blacks are black, and all whites are whitey."

That things stay wrong in this nation, can be readily seen by even a casual reading of the morning paper. And the moment I or any other black forget we *are* black, it may be our last. For when the shooting starts *any* black is fair game. The bullets don't give a damn whether I sleep with woman or man, their only aim is to put me to sleep forever.

FRANKLIN KAMENY

As President of the Mattachine Society of Washington (D.C.), Frank Kameny fought discrimination by the federal government throughout the 1960s (and continues to do so today). It was Mattachine-Washington picketing that forced the Civil Service Commission to meet with gays and lesbians for the first time. On September 8, 1965, five members of The Mattachine Society of Washington (two women and three men) met with two representatives from the Commissioners. Although the Commission retained its policy for several more years, the meeting forced a formal justification of its exclusionary policies. In 1980, the Office of Personnel Management issued a directive banning discrimination on the basis of sexual orientation.

The following essay, published in 1969, was a contribution to a debate about homosexuality within the United Church of Christ. Here Kameny reiterates one of his favorite themes. He has consistently argued that research into the causes of homosexuality is counter to the interests of lesbians and gays, both because it distracts attention from the fight for rights and because researchers have presumed heterosexuality to be "normal" and thus not in need of explanation. He also attacks existing research on lesbians and gays for their bias, a bias which gave scientific credence to view of homosexuals as sick and unhappy. Kameny adopts the view of gays and lesbians as a minority group and urges homosexuals to be proud and confident.

GAY IS GOOD

(1969)

Franklin Kameny

More, probably, than any other significant sociological phenomenon in our society, homosexuality remains immersed in a sea of persistent misimpressions, myths, folklore, and legends.

In significant part, this arises because the subject is usually discussed by people who are only onlookers with a sketchy knowledge and an often-biased viewpoint based upon highly nonrepresentative samplings of the group of which they speak, and from which samplings they then make improper and unwarranted generalizations—people like clergymen, psychiatrists and psychoanalysts, doctors, lawyers, policemen, and those in various social and counseling services, whose sampling is preselected for a high incidence of emotional and social maladjustment and problems.

As a result, discussions of homosexuality tend to sink quickly into a morass of psychiatry, criminal law, moral theology, emotional disturbance, "abnormality," "deviance," and the like, most if not all of which is irrelevant or only peripherally relevant to the average, ordinary, guilt-free, unanguished, reasonably untroubled, basically happy homosexual, whose major problems in regard to his homosexuality are not emotional problems but much more likely to be employment problems not of his own making.

Such discussions, too, are always saturated with a pervasive, pernicious, insidious—and deeply destructive—negativism, often quite unrecognized as such, which literally saturates every approach to the matter and colors initial assumptions and approaches, logic and reasoning, and final conclusions. This negativism is based upon unquestioned assumptions that homosexuality is undesirable, or less desirable than heterosexuality; that it is inferior to heterosexuality; that it is a second-rate condition, to be put up with at worst, and to be changed at best.

Increasingly, homosexuals are becoming impatient with the place of their traditional role as that of a mere passive, silent battlefield, across which conflicting "authorities" parade and fight out their questionable views, prejudices, and theories. Increasingly, homosexuals are insisting upon a role in which they are not seen as mere specimens to be examined and discussed, but as active, informed participants in the consideration of their condition and in the disposition of their fate.

This short essay will be an attempt to discuss a few aspects of homosexuality from the viewpoint of one of those most concerned, most knowledgeable and, unfortunately, least consulted—the homosexuals themselves.[1]

Therefore the approach taken here will be a positive one: that homosexuality is not an inferior state; that it is neither an affliction to be cured nor a weakness to be resisted; that it is not less desirable for the homosexual than heterosexuality is for the heterosexual; that the homosexual is a first-class human being and first-class citizen, entitled, by right, to all of the privileges and prerogatives of his citizenship, and to all of the God-given dignity of his humanity—as the homosexual that he is and has a moral right to continue to be; that homosexuality is nothing to be ashamed of, nothing to be apologetic about, nothing to bemoan, but something around which the homosexual can and should build part of a rewarding and productive life and something which he can and should enjoy to its fullest, just as heterosexuality is for the heterosexual.

We might commence with some examples of the negativism mentioned, with commentary where appropriate. A full listing would be almost endless; a few illustrations will suffice to indicate the pattern.

The overt negativism of the a priori, untested assumption, by psychoanalysts—used as their conceptual starting point—that all adult homosexuality is pathological.[2]

The widely touted assertion is that homosexuality is indicative of immaturity. This arises, in part, from a misinterpretation by Freud and others, of a cultural artifact growing out of the barriers placed, in past years, in the way of comfortable relationships between young people of both genders, and in part upon circular reasoning which unwarrantedly uses heterosexuality as part of the definition of maturity. The negative effects of this unfounded assertion of immaturity are insidious, pernicious, and extensive, in terms both of general attitudes toward the homosexual and of the homosexual's self-image.

The condemnation of certain family patterns, not because they are intrinsically bad, but because—supposedly—they produce homosexual children. Thus although there is no actual evidence which will withstand careful examination, the very widespread, widely accepted assertion that the pattern of a strong, dominant, affectionate mother, and a submissive, distant father produces homosexuals is used as a basis for condemnation of this harmless, very common departure from the traditional familial mold.

The almost universal characterization of homosexuality as something purely physical and lustful, devoid of elements of love and affection. In our anti-sexual society, this is a particularly strong condemnation. So deep lying is this concept of homosexuality that a supposedly authoritative psychoanalyst of some note said, "The idea may be at least theoretically entertained that a homosexual adult love relationship can exist."[3] For the many homosexual couples living in lasting, stable, mature, deeply affectionate love relationships, such a statement is patronizing and offensive (and somewhat ludicrous), and is indicative of the shallow, misinformed approach commonly found. In point of fact, homosexuality is far more a matter of love and affection than it is commonly considered to be; and heterosexuality is far more a matter of physical lust than our culture, with its over-romanticized approach, admits it to be. Actually, homosexuality and heterosexuality differ but little, if at all, in this respect.

The almost universal tendency, in consideration of the possible nature of and origins of homosexuality, to examine a variety of "problems" or pathological alternatives—defective family background, glandular imbalance, etc.—but never even to consider the possibility that homosexuality is nothing other than a non-pathological preference, not different in kind or origins from heterosexuality. Obviously, if no non-pathological alternatives are even considered, homosexuality *will* be found to be pathological, or to result from a disturbed or defective background.

The rather patronizing attitude, often expressed by the most well-meaning and seemingly enlightened, which says something to the effect that "these poor, afflicted people should not be punished for the weakness from which they suffer." But of course, as indicated elsewhere, homosexuality is no affliction, no weakness, and nothing being suffered from.

The attitude of many that the way to improve the status of the homosexual is through "reform" of the homosexual. One does not eliminate irrational and unfounded prejudice by reforming the victims of that prejudice; one reforms the prejudiced. Many of these same people, while piously disclaiming any desire to change the practicing homosexuals to heterosexuality, will subscribe, in the name of freedom of choice, to the idea that "of course those who *wish* to change should be assisted to do so," without realizing that the majority of those who wish to change are doing so in surrender to the prejudice around them (quite as much as are those Negroes who try to "pass" as white) either because life has been made uncomfortable for them or because they have been persuaded ("brainwashed" might be a better word) into a false feeling that they and their homosexuality are inferior to heterosexuals and heterosexuality. The immorality of surrender to prejudice ranks second only to the immorality of prejudice itself.

The nonobjective terminology, saturated with subjective, negative value judgments, used with great frequency by the medical profession in discussing treatment of homosexuals, in which change from homosexuality to or toward heterosexuality is characterized as "improvement," "recovery," "successful" therapy, etc. The homosexual is considered "helped" not by assistance in adjustment to his homosexuality—probably the only legitimate goal, when therapy is needed—but by the extent to which he is enabled—or pressured—into entering into heterosexual relationships.

The oft-repeated statement that "of course" all homosexuals would convert to heterosexuality if only they could. Quite aside from the factual inaccuracy of the statement—surveys have shown that most homosexuals would not change—never do we see anyone coming to grips with the basic question of *why* the homosexual should change to heterosexuality, even if he could. Obviously, if the disadvantages, disabilities, and penalties which the homosexual faces are a result of society's prejudices—and of course they are, in their entirety—then suggesting that the homosexual improve his lot by submission to those prejudices, at cost of his personal integrity, is fundamentally immoral. One does not propose to solve the problems of anti-Semitism by conversion of Jews to Christianity, much as that might improve the life of many individual Jews. The homosexual has a right to remain a homosexual, and in fact, a moral obligation to do so, in order to resist immoral prejudice and discrimination, no matter how possible, practical, and easy a change to heterosexuality might be.

The endlessly reiterated theme of psychiatrists, psychoanalysts, and others that homosexuality is a fear of relating to, and an inability to relate to, members of the opposite sex, or a fear of women. This is no more true, of course, than to say that *hetero*-sexuality arises from fear of relating to, or an inability to relate to, members of the same sex, or a fear of men. (Both are true in some instances, of course.) This theme makes of homosexuality something negative, whereas, as the majority of homosexuals are very well aware, homosexuality is as positive an attraction toward members of the same sex as heterosexuality is toward those of the opposite sex.

The casual use of terms such as "queer" by sensitive people of a liberal turn of mind, who would never think of using equivalent, no more offensive terms such as "nigger," "kike," "wop," etc. It is quite clear that whatever the users of those terms may claim on an intellectual basis, they are quite willing, at an emotional level, to deal with homosexuals as something less than full human beings with the same right to human dignity as others.

Application of the pejorative term "compulsive" to a strong, continuing, or exclusive preference for homosexual relationships, when the same term is not applied to identical preferences for heterosexual relationships. The statement is usually made that persistence in such a preference despite strong societal disapproval and sanctions must indicate pathology. The invalidity of such reasoning can be seen easily enough by applying it to the case of Jews in an anti-Semitic context, or Protestants or Catholics or others in any of the many countries or societies intolerant of their religious persuasion. Obviously an individual does not have to be compulsive or otherwise pathological in order to persist in refusing to subordinate his own individuality to societal conformity.

Statements frequently made, alleging—incorrectly—an increase in the incidence of homosexuality. Rarely are these phrased objectively. Almost always we see such negative phrases as "an *alarming* increase in homosexuality."

The much more subtle negativism seen in "assurances" by well-meaning people that changing the law to legalize private, adult, homosexual acts is not going to lead to an increase in homosexuality—with the obvious implication that "of course" homosexuality is undesirable and that, therefore, while we should not make criminals out of homosexuals, we should not do anything which might increase their number.

The incredible callousness and blunted sensitivity of others who cavalierly dismiss homosexuals from full membership in the human race by saying—falsely, as it turns out, and with an utter disregard for the effects of arrest and imprisonment upon people—that the criminal laws against certain private, adult, consensual homosexual acts must be maintained to provide an incentive for change to heterosexuality. At the very least, there seems to be a severe loss of both perspective and sense of proportion here.

Sex education classes in the schools in which homosexuality is almost universally portrayed as something undesirable, and the homosexual as someone to be shunned. Few people planning such courses, with an exaggerated and ill-conceived regard for what they consider to be the welfare of heterosexual students, ever stop to consider what they are doing to the students in those classes who are homosexuals and who are listening to themselves being described as unacceptable, less-than-human lepers. Apparently the psychological welfare of homosexual students is not important.

The attitudes and policies of our federal government which, by attempted exclusion of homosexuals from civil service employment, from eligibility for security clearances and for inclusion in the armed services (quite ineffectively, let it be said; the actual percentage of homosexuals in each of the three areas is not significantly different from the percentage in the populace at large) upon grounds which, when examined beneath the sometimes superficially persuasive legalistic verbiage with which they are disguised, are seen to be little more than concessions to the unpopularity of homosexuals. Unfortunately, federal policies set the tone and tenor for attitudes and policies on the part of private employers and private citizens generally. Consequently, had the homosexual the visibility of the Negro, there would be some fifteen million unemployed homosexuals in America. One effect of these governmental policies is the surrounding of homosexuals, in the minds of the larger community, with an aura of unreliability, irresponsibility, and disloyalty, quite unwarranted by facts.

Endless Theorizing about the Causes of Homosexuality

While objective inquiry into the causes of homosexuality and the processes leading to it may be a valid scientific exercise of minor intellectual value or importance, the inquiries *actually* made are not at all objective. It quickly becomes apparent that what is being asked is *not* the objective "What causes homosexuality?" but "What goes wrong to cause homosexuality?" or "What can be done to prevent homosexuality?" or "What can be done to change homosexuals into heterosexuals?" These are clearly nonobjective questions, laden with a negative value judgment upon homosexuality. There is exactly as much reason, but no more, to inquire about the causes of *homo*sexuality as there is to inquire about the causes of *hetero*sexuality. Yet we see no inquiries made as to what family environment causes a heterosexual to become so; as to what relationships among father, mother, and child lead to heterosexuality, etc. These are equally valid questions of no lesser importance. They are rarely, if ever, asked. We will never learn what causes homosexuality until we have found a valid answer to the question, What causes heterosexuality? or What are the processes through which a person becomes a heterosexual? No one even bothers to ask these questions.

Like members of other minority groups, homosexuals are interested in their rights, freedom, and basic human dignity, as homosexuals, and are little if at all properly concerned with how they got to be that way. We did not see the late Dr. Martin Luther King devoting much of his attention to futile debates about which gene on which chromosome causes a black skin. There is no more reason for debates with respect to the cause of homosexuality.

The universal "raising of hackles" at any slightest suggestion or imputation of so-called proselytism on behalf of homosexuality. It must be kept in mind that the homosexual has long been the object of one of the most intensive, evangelical, crusading efforts at proselytism that history has ever seen, directed at converting him to heterosexuality. In fairness, one would expect that what is sauce for the goose would be sauce for the gander. In actual fact, of course, the whole question is academic, since changes but very rarely, if ever, occur in either direction.

The Portrayals of Homosexuals and Homosexuality in Current Movies

Rarely if ever do we see homosexuals shown as sensitive, admirable, affectionate, likable human beings, and homosexuality as something enjoyable, satisfying, and rewarding, and as an expression of love and affection. Homosexuals are far from perfect, and homosexuality is certainly not all sweetness, love, and light; but of course exactly the same is true, in precisely equal measure, of heterosexuals and heterosexuality. But we see all sides and aspects of heterosexuality portrayed. We see only caricatures, portraying the sordid, the sad, the unpleasant, and the ridiculous—the negative—side of homosexuality.

Finally, the contempt, ridicule, derision, scorn, despisal, denigration, and belittlement of himself and of his condition, the assault upon his right to his very existence as a homosexual, which the homosexual faces at every turn, continuingly and everywhere, often vicious, totally non-supportive, totally unrelieved, except within his own community.

It is possible to go on citing such examples at considerably greater length, but the point has been made clearly. The homosexual is faced at every turn with a relentless barrage of assaults upon his self-esteem and his dignity. While any one of the items listed, taken by itself, might be considered small, trivial, and insignificant, when taken together they add up to a concentrated and rather virulent dose of psychological poison. It is certainly not unexpected, therefore, that many homosexuals suffer from damaged self-image, lack of self-confidence, diminished self-esteem, unwillingness to come forward as homosexuals.

A rereading of the examples cited above will show that a significant number flow from the basic attitude of the medical profession—particularly psychiatry and psychoanalysis —that homosexuality is a sickness or disorder, or a symptom of a sickness or disorder. This essay is neither the place for an extended exposition of the pros and cons of theories alleging the pathology of homosexuality nor for an exploration in depth of the grave failings of medicine, psychiatry, and psychoanalysis vis-à-vis homosexuality. Suffice it to say that the intellectual burden of an adequate demonstration of the pathology of homosexuality obviously rests upon those making the allegations of pathology, and that they have not shouldered their burden.

In past years, that which was considered objectionable was condemned by the "high priests" as sinful. Later, the lawyers took over, and the key to condemnation became criminality. Nowadays, sin is not fashionable anymore, and the criminal law on sexual matters is held in disrepute and is well-nigh universally disregarded; so our latter-day high priests, the psychiatrists and psychoanalysts, perpetuate the traditional condemnation by terming homosexuality a sickness. The basis for the designation in all three contexts is neither fact nor logic, but a subjective negative attitude—prejudice, in short—often well concealed, but no less discreditable for being classified under morality or law, or being misclassified under science.

An examination of the extensive professional literature upon homosexuality shows that the conclusion that homosexuality is a sickness founders upon three major bases, which should be considered very briefly in order to dispose of the entire theory.

First, we find slovenly definitions of terms such as pathology, sickness, neurosis, disturbance, etc. When any effort is made to define these terms, the definitions usually amount to little more than mere nonconformity. As discussed above, if the individual persists in his nonconformity, his actions are then *compulsive*—one of the psychiatrists' "dirty words," saved for the ultimate in condemnation.

Second, and most important, we find a total failure to attend properly to even the most elementary and basic techniques of experimental and observational science. In particular, we see massive tomes written and extensive "research" projects undertaken, based completely upon patients who have come to a psychiatrist's office, and totally without the use of control groups so basic to the validity of any scientific investigation. One can imagine the judgments as to the psychic health of the *hetero*sexual population which would be drawn by a psychiatrist who, through some strange set of circumstances, saw only those heterosexuals who came to him as patients.

Third, we find assumptions of pathology inserted at the outset, only to be drawn out as conclusions. One of the more flagrant examples of this was quoted near the beginning of this chapter.

Basically, what we find is an almost unparalleled example of shoddy, slovenly, slipshod, just plain bad science—and that is said with no little indignation and sense of offense by this author as a scientist by profession, training, and background. In short, homosexuality has been *defined* into sickness by subjective, personal, social, moral, cultural, and religious value judgments, cloaked and camouflaged in the language of science. Therefore, *in the continuing absence of valid scientific evidence to the contrary, homosexuality per se cannot properly be considered a sickness, illness, disturbance, disorder, or pathology of any kind, nor a symptom of any of these, but must be considered as a preference, orientation, or propensity, not different in kind from heterosexuality, and fully on par with it.*

With this whole matter of sickness out of the way, it is possible to take consideration of the entire subject off the psychoanalyst's couch and out of the psychiatrist's office, and to place it into proper perspective so it can be dealt with constructively.

Thus homosexuality is not a psychiatric or medical problem in emotional disturbance or disorder, and psychiatrists, psychoanalysts, and doctors are not the authorities on the subject; it is a *sociological* problem in entrenched prejudice and discrimination directed against a minority group.

In their entirety, the problems of the homosexual as such are—or stem directly from—problems of prejudice and discrimination directed against this minority by the hostile majority around them.

It has been said that there is no Negro problem, that there is really a white problem. It can as accurately be said that there is no homosexual problem, that there is really a heterosexual problem.

It will stand repetition to note that despite common misconceptions, the average homosexual is a reasonably well-adjusted, reasonably happy person, whose problems, if he has any at all in regard to his homosexuality, are much more likely to be employment problems than emotional problems. Medicine, psychiatry, psychoanalysis, etc., are as irrelevant to a constructive consideration of the problems of the average homosexual or to dealing with homosexuality itself, as they are to a parallel consideration of the problems of the average heterosexual, or to dealing with heterosexuality itself.

Once the sickness fantasy has been disposed of, it is possible to draw the necessary parallels to demonstrate that homosexuals are simply another of the minority groups which make up our nation, not different, as such, from religious, ethnic, so-called racial, and other minorities, with problems best appreciated and solved along exactly the same lines as the problems of those other minorities—by seeking to change attitudes and practices *not* of the minority itself, but of those of the majority who discriminate in word and in deed. After all, there is very little fundamental difference in basic essence between the corporation which will not hire Jews or Negroes, and the U.S. Civil Service Commission which will not hire homosexuals.

This classification of homosexuals as a minority group is one which is often met with singular resistance, upon rather specious grounds. Since it is basic to a positive and constructive approach to the question, it is not out of order to explore it briefly.

When we examine the groups which we consider as minorities, we find a thoroughly mixed bag, seeming upon first impression to have nothing in common: Jews and Catholics; Italians, Irish, and Poles; Negroes, Chinese, and Indians; etc. With considerable justification, as will be seen shortly, we may even class women as a minority group, although they hold a numerical majority. What do all of these groups, in terms of their minority status, have in common? Upon examination, we find four characteristics which can be used to define a sociological minority group.

1. **A defining characteristic** or set of closely related characteristics. This can be skin color, mode of religious observance, country of ancestral origin, gender, etc. The characteristic can be inherent or inborn (e.g., skin color or gender) or environmentally determined (e.g., religion). It can be unalterable (e.g., skin color) or alterable (e.g., religion). Its origin and permanence are not of importance. What is important is how the larger society responds or reacts to it.

2. **Prejudice and discrimination.** Because of the defining characteristic, but not in logical consequences of it, members of the minority group are subjected to adverse prejudice and discrimination. Because, for example, of the color of a Negro's skin, but not in logical consequence of it, he is made the object of adverse prejudice and discrimination.

3. **Depersonalization, dehumanization, stereotyping, group culpability.** Let a white, Anglo-Saxon, heterosexual Protestant commit a crime, make himself offensive, or make himself foolish, and he alone, personally and individually, bears the consequences of his actions. Let a member of a minority group do the same, and the culpability is generalized to "all Negroes are ...," "all Jews are ...," etc. Stereotypes are formed, and the member of the minority is not judged and dealt with as an individual upon his own merits and demerits, strengths and weaknesses, but as a stereotype that has no relationship to more than a very small number of the real people involved. (Very few Negroes are stupid, dirty, and lazy; very few Jews have certain objectionable personality traits; very few homosexuals are effeminate. There are whites, Christians, and heterosexuals who have all of those traits.) Thus there develops a process of depersonalization and dehumanization which is part of the minority condition.

4. **Internalization, group identity.** In response to the attitudes and actions of the surrounding majority, the minority group internalizes its feelings. There develop attitudes of "we" and "they," ingroups, subcultures, "ghettos," etc. The minority characteristic becomes the very definition of the person, both in his own eyes and in those of the majority. There are few characteristics of a man which are of lesser importance than the color of his skin. Yet

the Negro looks upon himself first as a black—and only later in terms of the truly significant and meaningful facets of his being. This, of course, is part of the human breakage caused by the minority condition.

Even casual consideration will show that all of the diverse and disparate groups which we consider as sociological minority groups meet the four criteria just set forth. Consideration will show that the homosexual also meets these criteria. Thus once homosexuality has been removed from the category of a pathological state it can be brought into company with other minority conditions, and need not stand out as something warranting totally unique treatment, but as merely one more problem in irrational and immoral prejudice.

The effects upon the homosexual of the kind of unmitigated, unrelenting negativism discussed are severe. As stated, they include damaged self-image, lowered self-esteem, doubts and uncertainties as to personal worth, an attitude of self-deprecation, and a false and unwarranted sense of an inferiority and undesirability of the homosexual condition—in short, all the complex forms of damage to personality which accompany membership in a minority.

For many years, and continuingly, the effect of these attitudes resulted in an almost universal covertness and secrecy upon the part of homosexuals. More recently, however, there has developed a growing militancy and rebellion by homosexuals against the position into which they are placed.

There has always been a minority of homosexuals—far fewer than commonly believed—who desired to convert to heterosexuality, if possible. It has been pointed out that this desire is, of course, the consequence of the same kind of brainwashing which has resulted in the efforts by many Negroes to "pass" as white; the related usage, by many, of hair-straightening devices; etc. The response by the Negro is understandable in a society in which black is equated with all that is bad, evil, immoral, undesirable, dirty, and ugly, and white with all that is good, pure, moral, desirable, clean, and beautiful. In an effort to counter these feelings, the Negro community has had some measure of success through the adoption of the slogan "Black is beautiful."

In a parallel effort to replace negative feelings upon the part of the homosexual—or at the least, a kind of grudging, wishy-washy acceptance of his homosexuality as something that perhaps is not so bad, if nothing better is possible—with the positive feelings of pride, self-esteem, self-confidence, and self-worth so necessary to true human dignity, the North American Conference of Homophile Organizations (at the suggestion of this writer) has adopted the slogan which is the theme of this essay: "Gay is good."

"Good" has a number of meanings. Homosexuality is good in terms of all of them. One of these meanings, not touched upon thus far, but particularly relevant to the book of which this is a chapter, is the moral one—"good" meaning right as opposed to wrong.

As already indicated, emotionally, homosexuality, no less than heterosexuality, is an expression of love and affection. Physically, no less than heterosexuality, homosexuality is a source of pleasure, enjoyment, and satisfaction. It has no discernible undesirable consequences, either to the participants or to society. It is obvious that affectionally and sexually satisfied persons are far better able to live with others and to contribute, productively and constructively, to society than those who are unsatisfied, dissatisfied, and frustrated.

In passing judgment upon the morality of homosexuality, there is a continuing tendency—overt in Catholicism, more subdued and indirect but nonetheless real and forceful in Protestantism—to invoke outmoded and outworn concepts of so-called natural law. Ever more, people these days are unwilling to allow abstract and questionable principles and interpretations of such natural law, or the harsh and unyielding, joyless and unreasonable prohibitions imposed by the mores of bygone eras and the voices of ancient societies, or chance words and phrases, written long ago and invoked in the form of a mindless resort to authority, or the how-many-angels-can-dance-upon-the-head-of-a-pin type of theology, so truly irrelevant to real life, to interfere with the living of a life personally rewarding and satisfying to self and to others, harmful neither to self, to others, nor to society, and fully in keeping with the most basic spirit and concepts of a Christianity interpreted as a joyful religion of love. And they are right, of course.

By any thoughtful and reasonably applied, meaningful criteria—as distinguished from many of the inflexible, doctrinaire, authoritarian applications of words and phrases arising from particular cultural contexts but used as absolutes, totally divorced from those contexts, which are increasingly being properly rejected by modern men, taught to think for themselves—homosexuality can only be considered to be as fully and affirmatively moral as heterosexuality. It thus follows that *homosexuality, both by inclination and by overt act, is not only not immoral, but is moral in a real and positive sense, and is good and right and desirable, both personally and societally.*

All of the preceding serves merely to support the assertion made near the outset of this brief essay that homosexuality is no disease, no misfortune, no sin, no weakness, no affliction; nothing about which to despair, to be apologetic, or to be ashamed; no second-rate state to be minimized as much as possible, and to be changed if feasible. Homosexuality is a first-class condition, in no way inferior to or less desirable for the homosexual than is heterosexuality for the heterosexual. It is a condition which can and should be lived and enjoyed to its fullest by the homosexual, exultantly and exuberantly, and around which a life satisfying and rewarding to self, and productive and useful to society can and should be built—exactly as for and by the heterosexual—and in the building of which the homosexual should expect as a matter of course the full assistance of the entire society in which he lives, with all of its resources, arms, and agencies, exactly as does the heterosexual. For after all, does society have any other reason for existence than to enable each individual member to live a life more personally rewarding and more satisfying than he could achieve without society?

I will close this personal statement by addressing myself, briefly, first to the larger heterosexual community and then to my fellow homosexuals.

To the heterosexual community, I say that we are full human beings—children of God, no less than you—with the same feelings, needs, sensitivities, desires, and aspirations. We are not the monsters that so many of you have been led to believe we are. We differ not at all from you except in our choice of those whom we love and with whom we relate intimately—in those ways, in their narrowest sense, but in no other ways.

We ask you to accept us as the homosexuals that we are, just as you accept others who differ from the majority. But we ask for acceptance as full equals, not as poor unfortunate creatures in need of compassion and some crumbs of sympathy.

We ask for nothing that is really more than or different from what everyone else asks—and what in our culture everyone is brought up to expect as a matter of course: our basic rights and equality as citizens; our human dignity; acceptance of us and judgment of us, each upon his own individual merits and by criteria reasonably relevant to the context of the judgment; the right as human beings to achieve our full potential and dignity, and the right as citizens to make our maximum contribution to the society in which we live; recognition that our right to the pursuit of our happiness is as inalienable as the right of all others to the pursuit of theirs; and the right to love whom we wish, how we wish—all while being true to ourselves as the homosexuals that we are and that we have an absolute moral right to be.

We recognize the changes in traditional attitudes which are needed to accept us in this way, and the difficulties inherent in the making of such changes; but we are increasingly firm in our justified insistence that such changes be made, and quickly, because they are essential to the fundamental prerogatives of citizenship and of humanity, of justice and of morality—and of Christianity in its truest and most meaningful sense.

At my suggestion the North American Conference of Homophile Organizations, in 1968, adopted substantially the following statement:

> *The homosexual, in our pluralistic society, has the moral right to be a homosexual. Being a homosexual, he has the moral right to live his homosexuality fully, freely, and openly, and to be so and to do so free of arrogant and insolent pressures to convert to the prevailing heterosexuality, and free of penalty, disability, or disadvantage of any kind, public or private, official or unofficial, for his nonconformity.*

> *By analogy and by parallel, the homosexual has the same moral rights as do the Catholic and the Jew, in our pluralistic society, to be Catholics and Jews, and being so to live their Catholicism and Judaism fully, freely, and openly, and to be so and to do so free of arrogant and insolent pressures to convert to the prevailing Protestant Christianity, and free of penalty, disability, or disadvantage of any kind, public or private, official or unofficial, for their nonconformity.*

That statement contains within itself nothing more than or different from what every minority group wants, and what every American is correctly brought up to believe is his, by right.

Finally, to those of my fellow homosexuals who may read this, I say that it is time to open the closet door and let in the fresh air and the sunshine; it is time to doff and to discard the secrecy, the disguise, and the camouflage; it is time to hold up your heads and to look the world squarely in the eye as the homosexuals that you are, confident of your equality, confident in the knowledge that as objects of prejudice and victims of discrimination you are right and they are wrong, and confident of the rightness of what you are and of the goodness of what you do; it is time to live your homosexuality fully, joyously, openly, and proudly, assured that morally, socially, physically, psychologically, emotionally, and in every other way: *Gay is good*. It is.

1. *It must be kept in mind, of course, that homosexuals are no more a homogeneous group than any other minority; that they have in common only their affectional and sexual preference in its narrowest denotive sense; and that therefore, while the author does informally express here the feelings of very large and growing numbers of his fellow homosexuals, in any formal sense, he is expressing the viewpoint of only one individual homosexual.*

2. *For example: "All psychoanalytic theories assume that adult homosexuality is psychopathologic," (Italics added) Irving Bieber, et al., Homosexuality (New York: Vintage), p18.*

3. *Clara Thompson, "Changing Concepts of Homosexuality in Psychoanalysis."*

IV

GAY LIBERATION
AND
LESBIAN-FEMINISM

We date the birth of contemporary lesbian and gay politics at 1969, the year of the Stonewall riots in New York City. We choose this date not because of Stonewall, however, but because 1969 is the year of the formation in New York of the Gay Liberation Front. With a name suggested by Martha Shelley, GLF represented the union of New Left politics with homosexual oppression. For our purposes, "gay liberation" is important as the name for a distinctive moment and analysis of lesbian and gay oppression that blended New Left politics with the attempt to build a gay counterculture. Gay liberationists generally agreed on the oppressive nature of capitalism and drew connections to repressive sexuality as well as to racism and imperialism. They suggested that full expression of sexuality, especially homosexual desire, would undermine existing structures of power and privilege. The different angles and dimensions of this perspective are represented here in the selections by Wittman, Red Butterfly, Shelley, Third World Gay Revolution, the Black Panthers, Gay Liberation Party, Hocquenghem, and Mieli. Most of these writers are strongly influenced by Marxism and the New Left, but they go on to develop analyses specifically addressing the relations between capitalism, imperialism, and sexual repression. From New York, "gay liberation" spread in 1970–71 throughout the U.S., Great Britain, Australia, Canada, and Western Europe. By the mid-1970s, gay liberation waned with the general decline of leftist activism. Although gay politics would continue to grow, it would become increasingly dominated by reformist voices.

Toby Marotta, in his book *The Politics of Homosexuality*, made a useful distinction between "radicals" and "revolutionaries" in GLF. In his terms "radicals" were those who focused on cultural change, while the primary concern of "revolutionaries" was political and economic. The disagreement between these two groups about aims and needs persists into the present. GLF, and gay liberation in general, was in the United States a "radical" movement virtually from the beginning. We might hypothesize that this is related to the lack of a strong socialist movement in the U.S.; the "radicals" could talk about the crimes of capitalism, but their real energies were focused on the American quest for personal liberty. In other countries the balance has not always gone to the individualist impulse; as Mario Mieli and Guy Hocquenghem demonstrate, gay liberation could indeed remain strongly wedded to a political left tradition. And for some, the blend of political and cultural analysis is what continues to give the unique acuity of gay liberationist thought. While gay liberation as a movement has died, there are still remnants of those earlier arguments present in the work of many contemporary writers. Dennis Altman, John Preston, and Pat Califia are among these more recent voices.

Gay liberation embodied another, related but distinct, conflict. Although most in GLF were thoroughly suspicious of any formal institutions, some wanted to intervene in mainstream politics. That minority left to form the Gay Activists Alliance, the predecessor of the National Gay and Lesbian Task Force in the U.S. Their politics may be distrusted by some, but many of the greatest concrete gains for lesbian and gay people have come as a result of their actions. Politicians such as Harvey Milk provide inspiring examples of how to "get into the system" and use power both for issues of sexuality and for larger matters of social justice.

Although many women were active in early gay liberation, their early euphoria was replaced with a growing disappointment. Their gay "brothers" who had proclaimed that sexism was the property of heterosexuals often proved to be no less misogynist or patronizing than any others. Lesbian-feminism grew out of this disillusionment as well as the rejection of lesbians by most feminist groups in the 1960s. Lesbians were chased out of the National Organization for Women and asked to remain in the closet "for the greater good" of women. As a distinctive analysis, lesbian-feminism combined the radical feminist claim that sex oppression was the original prototype for all other oppressions with the analysis of heterosexuality as the vehicle for sex oppression. First fully articulated in "the Woman-Identified Woman," this position developed over time to account more fully for racial and class oppression. Indeed, many lesbian-feminists came to reject the early privileging of sex oppression, insisting that we examine and challenge each as co-equal. Charlotte Bunch, Robin Morgan, Audre Lorde, Marilyn Frye, and Irena Klepfisz are only a few of the many lesbian-feminist writers of the 1970s and 1980s. Through journals such as *Sinister Wisdom* and *Lesbian Ethics* lesbian-feminism continues to develop and grow. Although few women seem to accept the most stringent claims about the priority of sex oppression and the love of women for one another, lesbian-feminist critiques of existing institutions remain invaluable. Many women came out in lesbian-feminist communities and became politicized through those communities. Lesbian-feminists such as Audre Lorde and Adrienne Rich are among the greatest contributors, not only to the lesbian and gay movements, but to the literature of the late 20th century.

Through the 1970s, lesbian-feminist writers had increasingly moved to view lesbianism not as primarily a matter of sexual desire, but rather saw it as a matter of loving women in a range of ways. "Political lesbians" were women who identified as lesbians out of feminist solidarity with and love for women even though they might have had no sexual experience with or desire for women. On the other hand, lesbians who identified as butch or femme were treated as pre-feminist relics. This movement was given fullest voice in Adrienne Rich's 1980 article, "Compulsory Heterosexuality and Lesbian Existence." Rich argued for a "lesbian continuum" that ranged from 1950s bar dykes to Chinese marriage resisters to nuns. All were bound by their rejection of compulsory heterosexuality and their love for women. As powerful as this view was, it came under fire by many women who found the historical specificity of lesbian struggles erased. They argued that it was not just "resistance" that got them beaten up, taunted, and fired from jobs; it was their sexual desire for women, and especially the self-presentation of butches, that threatened patriarchy.

In the 1980s lesbian-feminism came under fire for dogmatism and a narrow view of lesbianism. There were two major issues in these critiques: race and sex. Lesbian-feminism's confident division between men and women was less tenable for women of color, who felt the need to work with men of color against racism even as they challenged their sexism. Writers such as Audre Lorde and Gloria Anzaldúa refused to deny their connection to their brothers or (as the reading from Lorde demonstrates) straight sisters. In the "lesbian sex wars," women who had been ignored or derided in lesbian-feminist circles, especially women doing S/M or women in butch/femme relationships, began to speak up. Led by lesbians such as Pat Califia, Joan Nestle, Cherrie Moraga, and Gayle Rubin, the "sex radicals" set out to reclaim a value for their sexual practices as potentially valuable and transformative. In so doing, they reopened alliances with gay men that had lain dormant. Finding more support among gay men than among lesbian-feminists, S/M lesbians were among the first to move past the segregated seventies. As AIDS became an issue in the 1980s, these alliances would expand to reshape the terrain of homosexuality in the U.S.

The predominance of U.S. writers in this section is reflective of the explosion of U.S. writing and activism in the period. This should not be taken to mean, however, that other countries lacked gay and/or lesbian movements. In Canada, the journal *Body Politic* has offered a valuable left perspective on lesbian and gay politics for over twenty years. In Britain, *Gay Left* offered some of the earliest and best liberationist writing. Our selections here aim at presenting the range of ideas rather than representing all the spheres and locations of debate.

CARL WITTMAN AND
THE RED BUTTERFLY

We open our history of gay liberation with Carl Wittman's "A Gay Manifesto." Written in San Francisco, the manifesto points to many of the differences that gay liberation had with its homophile contemporaries. It is important to remember that in 1969 the homophile organizations were still active and represented the dominant face of homosexuality. One of the aims of gay liberation was to replace that face with a radical, confrontative vision.

One aspect of the shift from homophile to liberationist politics is the refusal of a "ghetto" for homosexuals. Although ghettos can feel comfortable, Wittman argues that ghettos keep us marginalized and ineffective. The challenge of gay liberation is the call to spread homosexuality throughout society, to fight sexual repression. Doing that requires that everyone examine their own behavior and motives. Thus gay liberation is much more than the demand for "our own space"; it is a demand for the transformation of all of society. For Wittman this includes the end of "male chauvinism," marriage, roles, and racism. Also important in this document is Wittman's mention of the sexual rigidity of political radicals; as the Cuban documents demonstrate, this is not an isolated problem but a continuing theme in heterosexual leftist movements.

Red Butterfly's comment on Wittman's "Manifesto" is included for the cogency of the issue of "coming out" and for their insistence on connecting sexual oppression to economic inequality and domination. In gay liberation, and increasingly today, many argue that coming out is in itself a political act. Coming out lessens our invisibility and also removes the personal constriction that goes with hiding. Red Butterfly suggests that coming out is valuable but it is not inherently liberatory. Personal "liberation" can only occur to the extent that it leads beyond the comforts of the ghetto to changes in social structures that have made "liberation" an imperative for gay men and lesbians.

A GAY MANIFESTO

(1969-1970)

Carl Wittman

San Francisco is a refugee camp for homosexuals. We have fled here from every part of the nation, and like refugees elsewhere, we came not because it is so great here, but because it was so bad there. By the tens of thousands, we fled small towns where to be ourselves would endanger our jobs and any hope of a decent life; we have fled from blackmailing cops, from families who disowned or 'tolerated' us; we have been drummed out of the armed services, thrown out of schools, fired from jobs, beaten by punks and policemen.

And we have formed a ghetto, out of self-protection. It is a ghetto rather than a free territory because it is still theirs. Straight cops patrol us, straight legislators govern us. Straight employers keep us in line, straight money exploits us. We have pretended everything is OK, because we haven't been able to see how to change it—we've been afraid.

In the past year there has been an awakening of gay liberation ideas and energy. How it began we don't know; maybe we were inspired by black people and their freedom movement; we learned how to stop pretending from the hip revolution. Amerika in all its ugliness

380   GAY LIBERATION AND LESBIAN-FEMINISM

has surfaced with the war and our national leaders. And we are revulsed by the quality of our ghetto life.

Where once there was frustration, alienation, and cynicism, there are new characteristics among us. We are full of love for each other and are showing it; we are full of anger at what has been done to us. And as we recall all the self-censorship and repression for so many years, a reservoir of tears pours out of our eyes. And we are euphoric, high, with the initial flourish of a movement.

We want to make ourselves clear: our first job is to free ourselves; that means clearing our heads of the garbage that's been poured into them. This article is an attempt at raising a number of issues and presenting some ideas to replace the old ones. It is primarily for ourselves, a starting point of discussion. If straight people of good will find it useful in understanding what liberation is about, so much the better.

It should also be clear that these are the views of one person, and are determined not only by my homosexuality, but my being white, male, middle class. It is my individual consciousness. Our group consciousness will evolve as we get ourselves together—we are only at the beginning.

I. On Orientation

1. *What homosexuality is:* Nature leaves undefined the object of sexual desire. The gender of that object is imposed socially. Humans originally made homosexuality taboo because they needed every bit of energy to produce and raise children: survival of species was a priority. With overpopulation and technological change, that taboo continued only to exploit us and enslave us.

As kids we refused to capitulate to demands that we ignore our feelings toward each other. Somewhere we found the strength to resist being indoctrinated, and we should count that among our assets. We have to realize that our loving each other is a good thing, not an unfortunate thing, and that we have a lot to teach straights about sex, love, strength, and resistance.

Homosexuality is *not* a lot of things. It is not a makeshift in the absence of the opposite sex; it is not hatred or rejection of the opposite sex; it is not genetic; it is not the result of broken homes except inasmuch as we could see the sham of American marriage. *Homosexuality is the capacity to love someone of the same sex.*

2. *Bisexuality:* Bisexuality is good; it is the capacity to love people of either sex. The reason so few of us are bisexual is because society made such a big stink about homosexuality that we got forced into seeing ourselves as either straight or non-straight. Also, many gays got turned off to the ways men are supposed to act with women and vice-versa, which is pretty fucked-up. Gays will begin to turn on to women when 1) it's something that we do because we want to, and not because we should, and 2) when women's liberation changes the nature of heterosexual relationships.

We continue to call ourselves homosexual, not bisexual, even if we do make it with the opposite sex also, because saying "Oh, I'm Bi" is a cop out for a gay. We get told it's OK to sleep with guys as long as we sleep with women, too, and that's still putting homosexuality down. We'll be gay until everyone has forgotten that it's an issue. Then we'll begin to be complete.

3. *Heterosexuality:* Exclusive heterosexuality is fucked up. It reflects a few people of the same sex, it's anti-homosexual, and it is fraught with frustration. Heterosexual sex is fucked up, too; ask women's liberation about what straight guys are like in bed. Sex is aggression for the male chauvinist; sex is obligation for traditional woman. And among the young, the modern, the hip, it's only a subtle version of the same. For us to become heterosexual in the sense that our straight brothers and sisters are is not a cure, it is a disease.

II. On Women

1. *Lesbianism*: It's been a male-dominated society for too long, and that has warped both men and women. So gay women are going to see things differently from gay men; they are going to feel put down as women, too. Their liberation is tied up with both gay liberation and women's liberation.

This paper speaks from the gay male viewpoint. And although some of the ideas in it may be equally relevant to gay women, it would be arrogant to presume this to be a manifesto for lesbians.

We look forward to the emergence of a lesbian-liberation voice. The existence of a lesbian caucus within the New York Gay Liberation Front has been very helpful in challenging male chauvinism among gay guys, and anti-gay feelings among women's lib.

2. *Male Chauvinism*: All men are infected with male chauvinism—we were brought up that way. It means we assume that women play subordinate roles and are less human than ourselves. (At an early gay liberation meeting one guy said, "Why don't we invite women's liberation—they can bring sandwiches and coffee.") It is no wonder that so few gay women have become active in our groups.

Male chauvinism, however, is not central to us. We can junk it much more easily than straight men can. For we understand oppression. We have largely opted out of a system which oppresses women daily—our egos are not built on putting women down and having them build us up. Also, living in a mostly male world we have become used to playing different roles, doing our own shit-work. And finally, we have a common enemy: the big male chauvinists are also the big anti-gays.

But we need to purge male chauvinism, both in behavior and in thought among us. Chick equals nigger equals queer. Think it over.

3. *Women's liberation*: They are assuming their equality and dignity and in doing so are challenging the same things we are: the roles, the exploitation of minorities by capitalism, the arrogant smugness of straight white male middle-class Amerika. They are our sisters in struggle.

Problems and differences will become clearer when we begin to work together. One major problem is our own male chauvinism. Another is uptightness and hostility to homosexuality that many women have—that is the straight in them. A third problem is differing views on sex: sex for them has meant oppression, while for us it has been a symbol of our freedom. We must come to know and understand each other's style, jargon and humor.

III. On Roles

1. *Mimicry of straight society*: We are children of straight society. We still think straight: that is part of our oppression. One of the worst of straight concepts is inequality. Straight (also white, English, male, capitalist) thinking views things in terms of order and comparison. A is before B, B is after A; one is below two is below three; there is no room for equality. This idea gets extended to male/female, on top/on bottom, spouse/not spouse, heterosexual/homosexual; boss/worker, white/black and rich/poor. Our social institutions cause and reflect this verbal hierarchy. This is Amerika.

We've lived in these institutions all our lives. Naturally we mimic the roles. For too long we mimicked these roles to protect ourselves—a survival mechanism. Now we are becoming free enough to shed the roles which we've picked up from the institutions which have imprisoned us.

"Stop mimicking straights, stop censoring ourselves."

2. *Marriage*: Marriage is a prime example of a straight institution fraught with role play-

ing. Traditional marriage is a rotten, oppressive institution. Those of us who have been in heterosexual marriages too often have blamed our gayness on the breakup of the marriage. No. They broke up because marriage is a contract which smothers both people, denies needs, and places impossible demands on both people. And we had the strength, again, to refuse to capitulate to the roles which were demanded of us.

Gay people must stop gauging their self respect by how well they mimic straight marriages. Gay marriages will have the same problems as straight ones except in burlesque. For the usual legitimacy and pressures which keep straight marriages together are absent, e.g. kids, what parents think, what neighbors say.

To accept that happiness comes through finding a groovy spouse and settling down, showing the world that "we're just the same as you" is avoiding the real issues, and is an expression of self-hatred.

3. *Alternatives to Marriage*: People want to get married for lots of good reasons, although marriage won't often meet those needs or desires. We're all looking for security, a flow of love, and a feeling of belonging and being needed.

These needs can be met through a number of social relationships and living situations. Things we want to get away from are: 1. exclusiveness, propertied attitudes toward each other, a mutual pact against the rest of the world; 2. promises about the future, which we have no right to make and which prevent us from, or make us feel guilty about, growing; 3. inflexible roles, roles which do not reflect us at the moment but are inherited through mimicry and inability to define equalitarian relationships.

We have to define for ourselves a new pluralistic, role free social structure for ourselves. It must contain both the freedom and physical space for people to live alone, live together for a while, live together for a long time, either as couples or in larger numbers; and the ability to flow easily from one of these states to another as our needs change.

Liberation for gay people is defining for ourselves how and with whom we live, instead of measuring our relationship in comparison to straight ones, with straight values.

4. *Gay 'stereotypes'*: The straights' image of the gay world is defined largely by those of us who have violated straight roles. There is a tendency among 'homophile' groups to deplore gays who play visible roles—the queens and the nellies. As liberated gays, we must take a clear stand. 1. Gays who stand out have become our first martyrs. They came out and withstood disapproval before the rest of us did. 2. If they have suffered from being open, it is straight society whom we must indict, not the queen.

5. *Closet queens*: This phase is becoming analogous to "Uncle Tom." To pretend to be straight sexually, or to pretend to be straight socially, is probably the most harmful pattern of behavior in the ghetto. The married guy who makes it on the side secretly; the guy who will go to bed once but who won't develop any gay relationships; the pretender at work or school who changes the gender of the friend he's talking about; the guy who'll suck cock in the bushes but who won't go to bed.

If we are liberated we are open with our sexuality. Closet queenery must end. *Come out.*

But: In saying come out, we have to have our heads clear about a few things: 1) closet queens are our brothers, and must be defended against attacks by straight people; 2) the fear of coming out is not paranoia; the stakes are high: loss of family ties, loss of job, loss of straight friends—these are all reminders that the oppression is not just in our heads. It's real. Each of us must make the steps toward openness at our own speed and on our own impulses. Being open is the foundation of freedom: it has to be built solidly. 3) "Closet queen" is a broad term covering a multitude of forms of defense, self-hatred, lack of strength, and habit. We are all closet queens in some ways, and all of us had to come out—very few of us were 'flagrant' at the age of seven! We must afford our brothers and sisters the same patience we afforded ourselves. And while their closet queenery is part of our oppression, it's more a part of theirs. They alone can decide when and how.

IV. On Oppression

It is important to catalog and understand the different facets of our oppression. There is no future in arguing about degrees of oppression. A lot of 'movement' types come on with a line of shit about homosexuals not being oppressed as much as blacks or Vietnamese or workers or women. We don't happen to fit into their ideas of class or caste. Bull! When people feel oppressed, they act on that feeling. We feel oppressed. Talk about the priority of black liberation or ending imperialism over and above gay liberation is just anti-gay propaganda.

1. *Physical attacks*: We are attacked, beaten, castrated and left dead time and time again. There are half a dozen known unsolved slayings in San Francisco parks in the last few years.

"Punks," often of minority groups who look around for someone under them socially, feel encouraged to beat up on "queens" and cops look the other way. That used to be called lynching.

Cops in most cities have harassed our meeting places: bars and baths and parks. They set up entrapment squads. A Berkeley brother was slain by a cop in April when he tried to split after finding out that the trick who was making advances to him was a cop. Cities set up 'pervert' registration, which if nothing else scares our brothers deeper into the closet.

One of the most vicious slurs on us is the blame for prison 'gang rapes'. These rapes are invariably done by people who consider themselves straight. The victims of these rapes are us and straights who can't defend themselves. The press campaign to link prison rapes with homosexuality is an attempt to make straights fear and despise us, so they can oppress us more. It's typical of the fucked-up straight mind to think that homosexual sex involves tying a guy down and fucking him. That's aggression, not sex. If that's what sex is for a lot of straight people, that's a problem they have to solve, not us.

2. *Psychological warfare*: Right from the beginning we have been subjected to a barrage of straight propaganda. Since our parents don't know any homosexuals, we grow up thinking that we're alone and different and perverted. Our school friends identify 'queer' with any non-conformist or bad behavior. Our elementary school teachers tell us not to talk to strangers or accept rides. Television, billboards and magazines put forth a false idealization of male/female relationships, and make us wish we were different, wish we were 'in'. In family living class we're taught how we're supposed to turn out. And all along, the best we hear if anything about homosexuality is that it's an unfortunate problem.

3. *Self-oppression*: As gay liberation grows, we will find our uptight brothers and sisters, particularly those who are making a buck off our ghetto, coming on strong to defend the status quo. This is self-oppression: 'don't rock the boat'; 'things in SF are OK'; 'gay people just aren't together'; 'I'm not oppressed'. These lines are right out of the mouths of the straight establishment. A large part of our oppression would end if we would stop putting ourselves and our pride down.

4. *Institutional*: Discrimination against gays is blatant, if we open our eyes. Homosexual relationships are illegal, and even if these laws are not regularly enforced, they encourage and enforce closet queenery. The bulk of the social work/psychiatric field looks upon homosexuality as a problem, and treats us as sick. Employers let it be known that our skills are acceptable only as long as our sexuality is hidden. Big business and government are particularly notorious offenders.

The discrimination in the draft and armed services is a pillar of the general attitude toward gays. If we are willing to label ourselves publicly not only as homosexual but as sick, then we qualify for deferment; and if we're not 'discreet' (dishonest) we get drummed out of the service. Hell, no, we won't go, of course not, but we can't let the army fuck us over this way either.

V. On Sex

1. *What sex is*: It is both creative expression and communication: good when it is either, and better when it is both. Sex can also be aggression, and usually is when those involved do not see each other as equals; and it can also be perfunctory, when we are distracted or pre-occupied. These uses spoil what is good about it.

I like to think of good sex in terms of playing the violin: with both people on one level seeing the other body as an object capable of creating beauty when they play it well; and on a second level the players communicating through their mutual production and appreciation of beauty. As in good music, you get totally into it—and coming back out of that state of consciousness is like finishing a work of art or coming back from an episode of an acid or mescaline trip. And to press the analogy further: the variety of music is infinite and varied, depending on the capabilities of the players, both as subjects and as objects. Solos, duets, quartets (symphonies, even, if you happen to dig Romantic music!) are possible. The variations in gender, response, and bodies are like different instruments. And perhaps what we have called sexual 'orientation' probably just means that we have not yet learned to turn on to the total range of musical expression.

2. *Objectification*: In this scheme, people are sexual objects, but they are also subjects, and are human beings who appreciate themselves as object and subject. This use of human bodies as objects is legitimate (not harmful) only when it is reciprocal. If one person is always object and the other subject, it stifles the human being in both of them. Objectification must also be open and frank. By silence we often assume or let the other person assume that sex means commitments: if it does, ok: but if not, say it. (Of course, it's not all that simple: our capabilities for manipulation are unfathomed—all we can do is try.)

Gay liberation people must understand that women have been treated exclusively and dishonestly as sexual objects. A major part of their liberation is to play down sexual objectification and to develop other aspects of themselves which have been smothered so long. We respect this. We also understand that a few liberated women will be appalled or disgusted at the open and prominent place that we put sex in our lives; and while this is a natural response from their experience, they must learn what it means for us.

For us, sexual objectification is a focus of our quest for freedom. It is precisely that which we are not supposed to share with each other. Learning how to be open and good with each other sexually is part of our liberation. And one obvious distinction: objectification of sex for us is something we choose to do among ourselves, while for women it is imposed by their oppressors.

3. *On positions and roles*: Much of our sexuality has been perverted through mimicry of straights, and warped from self-hatred. These sexual perversions are basically anti-gay:

"I like to make it with straight guys"

"I'm not gay, but I like to be 'done'"

"I like to fuck, but don't want to be fucked"

"I don't like to be touched above the neck"

This is role playing at its worst: we must transcend these roles. We strive for democratic, mutual, reciprocal sex. This does not mean that we are all mirror images of each other in bed, but that we break away from roles which enclave us. We already do better in bed than straights do, and we can be better to each other than we have been.

4. *Chickens and Studs*: Face it, nice bodies and young bodies are attributes, they're groovy. They are inspiration for art, for spiritual elevation, for good sex. The problem arises only in the inability to relate to people of the same age, or people who don't fit the plastic stereotypes of a good body. At that point, objectification eclipses people, and expresses self-hatred: "I hate gay people, and I don't like myself, but if a stud (or chicken) wants to make it with me, I can pretend I'm someone other than me."

A note on exploitation of children: kids can take care of themselves, and are sexual beings way earlier than we'd like to admit. Those of us who began cruising in early adolescence know this, and we were doing the cruising, not being debauched by dirty old men. Scandals such as the one in Boise, Idaho—blaming a "ring" of homosexuals for perverting their youth—are the fabrications of press and police and politicians. And as for child molesting, the overwhelming amount is done by straight guys to little girls: it is not particularly a gay problem, and is caused by the frustrations resulting from anti-sex puritanism.

5. *Perversion*: We've been called perverts enough to be suspect of any usage of the word. Still many of us shrink from the idea of certain kinds of sex: with animals, sado/masochism, dirty sex (involving piss or shit). Right off, even before we take the time to learn any more, there are some things to get straight:

1. We shouldn't be apologetic to straights about gays whose sex lives we don't understand or share;
2. It's not particularly a gay issue, except that gay people probably are less hung up about sexual experimentation.
3. Let's get perspective: even if we were to get into the game of deciding what's good for someone else, the harm done in these 'perversions' is undoubtedly less dangerous or unhealthy than is tobacco or alcohol.
4. While they can be reflections of neurotic or self-hating patterns, they may also be enactments of spiritual or important phenomena: e.g. sex with animals may be the beginning of interspecies communication: some dolphin-human breakthroughs have been made on the sexual level; e.g. one guy who says he digs shit during sex occasionally says it's not the taste or texture, but a symbol that he's so far into sex that those things no longer bug him; e.g. sado/masochism, when consensual, can be described as a highly artistic endeavor, a ballet the constraints of which are the threshold of pain and pleasure.

VI. On Our Ghetto

We are refugees from Amerika. So we came to the ghetto—and as other ghettos, it has its negative and positive aspects. Refugee camps are better than what preceded them, or people never would have come. But they are still enslaving, if only that we are limited to being ourselves there and only there.

Ghettos breed self-hatred. We stagnate here, accepting the status quo. The status quo is rotten. We are all warped by our oppression, and in the isolation of the ghetto we blame ourselves rather than our oppressors.

Ghettos breed exploitation: Landlords find they can charge exorbitant rents and get away with it, because of the limited area which is safe to live in openly. Mafia control of bars and baths in NYC is only one example of outside money controlling our institutions for their profit. In San Francisco the Tavern Guild favors maintaining the ghetto, for it is through ghetto culture that they make a buck. We crowd their bars not because of their merit but because of the absence of any other social institutions. The Guild has refused to let us collect defense funds or pass out gay liberation literature in their bars—need we ask why?

Police or con men who shake down the straight gay in return for not revealing him; the bookstores and movie makers who keep raising prices because they are the only outlet for pornography; heads of 'modeling' agencies and other pimps who exploit both the hustlers and the johns—these are the parasites who flourish in the ghetto.

SAN FRANCISCO—*Ghetto or Free Territory*: Our ghetto certainly is more beautiful and larger and more diverse than most ghettos, and is certainly freer than the rest of Amerika. That's why we're here. But it isn't ours. Capitalists make money off us, cops patrol us, government tolerates us as long as we shut up, and daily we work for pay and taxes to those who oppress us.

To be a free territory, we must govern ourselves, set up our own institutions, defend ourselves, and use our own energies to improve our lives. The emergence of gay liberation communes, and our own paper is a good start. The talk about a gay liberation coffee shop-dance hall should be acted upon. Rural retreats, political action offices, food cooperatives, a free school, unalienating bars and after hours places—they must be developed if we are to have even the shadow of a free territory.

VII. On Coalition

Right now the bulk of our work has to be among ourselves—self educating, fending off attacks, and building free territory. Thus basically we have to have a gay/straight vision of the world until the oppression of gays is ended.

But not every straight is our enemy. Many of us have mixed identities, and have ties with other liberation movements: women, blacks, other minority groups: we may also have taken on an identity which is vital to us: ecology, dope, ideology. And face it: we can't change Amerika alone:

Who do we look to for coalition?

1. *Women's Liberation*: summarizing earlier statements, 1) they are our closest ally; we must try hard to get together with them; 2) a lesbian caucus is probably the best way to attack gay guys' male chauvinism, and challenge the straightness of women's liberation; 3) as males we must be sensitive to their developing identities as women, and respect that; if we know what our freedom is about, they certainly know what's best for them.

2. *Black liberation*: This is tenuous right now because of the uptightness and supermasculinity of many black men (which is understandable). Despite that, we must support their movement, particularly when they are under attack from the establishment; we must show them that we mean business; and we must figure out which our common enemies are: police, city hall, capitalism

3. *Chicanos*: Basically the same problem as with blacks: trying to overcome mutual animosity and fear, and finding ways to support them. The extra problem of super up-tightness and machismo among Latin cultures, and the traditional pattern of Mexicans beating up "queers", can be overcome: we're both oppressed, and by the same people at the top.

4. *White radicals and ideologues*: We're not, as a group, Marxist or communist. We haven't figured out what kind of political/economic system is good for us as gays. Neither capitalist or socialist countries have treated us as anything other than non grata so far.

But we know we are radical, in that we know the system that we're under now is a direct source of oppression, and it's not a question of getting our share of the pie. The pie is rotten.

We can look forward to coalition and mutual support with radical groups if they are able to transcend their anti-gay and male chauvinist patterns. We support radical and militant demands when they arise. e.g. Moratorium, People's Park; but only as a group; we can't compromise or soft-peddle our gay identity.

Problems: because radicals are doing somebody else's thing, they tend to avoid issues which affect them directly, and see us as jeopardizing their 'work' with other groups (workers, blacks). Some years ago a dignitary of SDS on a community organization project announced at an initial staff meeting that there would be no homosexuality (or dope) on the project. And recently in New York, a movement group which had a coffee-house get-together after a political rally told the gays to leave when they started dancing together. (It's interesting to note that in this case, the only two groups which supported us were Women's Liberation and the Crazies.)

Perhaps most fruitful would be to broach with radicals their stifled homosexuality and the issues which arise from challenging sexual roles.

5. *Hip and street people*: a major dynamic of rising gay lib sentiment is the hip revolution within the gay community. Emphasis on love, dropping out, being honest, expressing yourself through hair and clothes, and smoking dope are all attributes of this. The gays who are the least vulnerable to attack by the establishment have been the freest to express themselves on gay liberation.

We can make a direct appeal to young people, who are not so up-tight about homosexuality. One kid, after having his first sex with a male, said "I don't know what all the fuss is about, making it with a girl just isn't that different."

The hip/street culture has led people into a lot of freeing activities: encounter/sensitivity, the quest for reality, freeing territory for the people, ecological consciousness, communes. These are real points of agreement and probably will make it easier for them to get their heads straight about homosexuality, too.

6. *Homophile groups*: 1) reformist or pokey as they sometimes are, they are our brothers. They'll grow as we have grown and grow. Do not attack then in straight or mixed company; 2) ignore their attack on us; 3) cooperate where cooperation is possible without essential compromise of our identity.

Conclusion: An Outline of Imperatives for Gay Liberation

1. Free ourselves: come out everywhere; initiate self defense and political activity; initiate counter community institutions.

2. Turn other gay people on: talk all the time; understand, forgive, accept.

3. Free the homosexual in everyone: we'll be getting a good bit of shit from threatened latents: be gentle, and keep talking & acting free.

4. We've been playing an act for a long time, so we're consummate actors. Now we can begin *to be*, and it'll be a good show!

COMMENTS ON CARL WITTMAN'S "A GAY MANIFESTO"

(1970)

The Red Butterfly

Carl Wittman's "A Gay Manifesto" represents an important step forward for our movement. Gay Liberation is struggling for a self-understanding which would probe deeply enough into the causes of our oppression to give us a clear vision of the forms and directions our struggle must take. Wittman has provided an analysis of homosexual oppression in America which links the individual-psychological experiences of oppression to the social and economic facts which are at once the causes and effects of this situation. He has spelled out the various aspects of gay oppression from his own vantage point, with self-acknowledged limitations.

Most importantly, Wittman's "Manifesto" provides a clear statement of Gay Liberation's goal: to free ourselves as gays and to free straight society in as much as it represses its own homosexual aspects. What is noteworthy in Wittman's approach is his insistence that we must change our own consciousness to be free to change the institutions which shape our lives. Liberation of the head can never be more than a half-step, a transitional move, until fundamental changes are made in the institutions and cultural forms which create gay oppression. By making this connection so explicitly, Carl Wittman is able to go on to link our struggle to those of the other oppressed groups in this society, thus widening the viewpoint of the movement as a whole.

Our criticisms are intended as friendly amendments to Wittman's "Manifesto". As Wittman says, "we are only at the beginning". Hopefully these comments of ours will foster discussion and new thinking throughout the movement

We feel that two aspects of the "Manifesto" invite further clarification and development. They are difficult issues central to the entire movement. The first is the notion of "coming out" and the importance it ought to have within our movement. The second is the question Wittman raises in section VIII of the "Manifesto": the kind of social and economic viewpoint most conducive to our liberation as gays.

On the matter of "coming out", we agree that the phrase is a description of our movement's overall process, that it both describes what we are about and what we are working for. However, concealed within this idea is an important tension which ought to be unpacked and examined. It is the same tension which Wittman develops throughout the pamphlet: the polarity between personal head-freeing and the need for collective, social action to change institutions. This is no simple issue and it cannot be solved by simple slogans or catchwords. As in any process which has to unite two distinct and in some ways opposed actions, problems result from overemphasis on either of the poles.

Emphasis on personal liberation, the experience of feeling free, which is the meaning often given to "coming out", can and often does lead to a kind of escapism or regression, to detachment from the actual conditions confronting us. It can also lead to real personal problems for people who act unthinkingly; they end up "free" in their heads but cut off in fact from access to means for changing social conditions. This problem is especially acute for our movement since so much of our oppression consists precisely in being forced to choose between a personal life in a gay ghetto or a de-personalized life in straight society—usually to the detriment of individual growth, no matter which option is taken.

Emphasis on effective action, pushed to excess, leads to similar immobility, but in the opposite direction. The homosexual who hides his identity for the sake of the political movement, the good of his family or whatever, is likely to run into the dilemma of all "boring from within"; the inability to effect change because he is not recognized for what he is or has actually forgotten who he is himself. This is not to say that sisters and brothers may not be entirely correct to go incognito at least for a time and in certain parts of their lives. However, the danger here of copping out is real, and if this strategy were applied by everyone there would obviously be no Gay Liberation movement.

The second issue, the social and economic perspective most conducive for Gay Liberation, is also very basic. On this question Red Butterfly takes a socialist perspective. We assert that human liberation in all its forms, including Gay Liberation, requires effective self-determination, i.e., democracy, in all spheres of social life affecting the lives of people as a whole. This means particularly economic and political democracy: common ownership and decision-making with regard to economic and social matters by society as a whole. We believe that economic and social democracy are the necessary conditions for liberation. In Marxist language, we assert that a democratic socialism is the necessary basis for building a classless society, i.e., communism.

To facilitate discussion of this issue we propose the following scheme for judging a social and economic system which can make a free society possible: Given the material and technological resources of American society, how well can the system in question provide:

1) ecological well-being for the nation and the planet as a whole.
2) the basic economic and social necessities: adequate income, housing, medical care; meaningful employment and democratic civil rights for all participants in the society.
3) protection for minority groups, such as homosexuals; equal opportunities for education, leisure, and personal development for all participants.
4) cooperation with world-wide social and economic development and the self-determination of peoples.
5) effective political power for all, the ability of all social groups to resist exploitation and to determine their own destinies.

This question is basic to our movement, since the answers we give to it will determine the concrete political alignments we make and, ultimately, the success or failure of our struggle for liberation—which in the long run is a political struggle.

TODAY THE FIGHT FOR EROS, THE FIGHT FOR LIFE, IS THE POLITICAL FIGHT.
—H. Marcuse

Although her piece shares the same title as Frank Kameny's in Part III and only a year separates them, Martha Shelley's statement is worlds away from Kameny's. While Kameny earnestly seeks to assure his audience that gay is "as good as" straight, Shelley instead attacks the roles and homophobia that bind heterosexual men and women. She also describes the frustration with liberalism felt by so many in 1970. Using an argument reminiscent of Martin Luther King's in his *Letter from Birmingham Jail*, Shelley explains that liberals who profess to believe in equality but do nothing to actually remove oppression are no allies at all. She makes understandable the radical reaction to the deficiencies of liberalism; saying "it's too late for liberalism," she does not reject the liberal ideals of equality and freedom, but the liberal approach—safe, cautious, ultimately ineffective.

MARTHA SHELLEY

GAY IS GOOD

(1970)

Martha Shelley

Look out, straights. Here comes the Gay Liberation Front, springing up like warts all over the bland face of Amerika, causing shudders of indigestion in the delicately balanced bowels of the movement. Here come the gays, marching with six-foot banners to Washington and embarrassing the liberals, taking over Mayor Alioto's office, staining the good names of War Resister's League and Women's Liberation by refusing to pass for straight anymore.

We've got chapters in New York, San Francisco, San Jose, Los Angeles, Minneapolis, Philadelphia, Wisconsin, Detroit and I hear maybe even in Dallas. We're gonna make our own revolution because we're sick of revolutionary posters which depict straight he-man types and earth mothers, with guns and babies. We're sick of the Panthers lumping us together with the capitalists in their term of universal contempt—"faggot."

And I am personally sick of liberals who say they don't care who sleeps with whom, it's what you do outside of bed that counts. This is what homosexuals have been trying to get straights to understand for years. Well, it's too late for liberalism. Because what I do outside of bed may have nothing to do with what I do inside—but my consciousness is branded, is permeated with homosexuality. For years I have been branded with your label for me. The result is that when I am among gays or in bed with another woman, I am a person, not a lesbian. When I am observable to the straight world, I become gay. You are my litmus paper.

We want something more now, something more than the tolerance you never gave us. But to understand that, you must understand who we are.

We are the extrusions of your unconscious mind—your worst fears made flesh. From the beautiful boys at Cherry Grove to the aging queens in the uptown bars, the taxi-driving dykes to the lesbian fashion models, the hookers (male and female) on 42nd Street, the leather lovers ... and the very ordinary very un-lurid gays ... we are the sort of people everyone was taught to despise—and now we are shaking off the chains of self-hatred and marching on your citadels of repression.

Liberalism isn't good enough for us. And we are just beginning to discover it. Your friendly smile of acceptance—from the safe position of heterosexuality—isn't enough. As long as you cherish that secret belief that you are a little bit better because you sleep with the opposite sex, you are still asleep in your cradle and we will be the nightmare that awakens you.

We are women and men who, from the time of our earliest memories, have been in revolt against the sex-role structure and nuclear family structure. The roles we have played amongst ourselves, the self-deceit, the compromises and the subterfuges—these have never totally obscured the fact that we exist outside the traditional structure—and our existence threatens it.

Understand this—that the worst part of being a homosexual is having to keep it secret. Not the occasional murders by police or teenage queer-beaters, not the loss of jobs or expulsion from schools or dishonorable discharges—but the daily knowledge that what you are is so awful that it cannot be revealed. The violence against us is sporadic. Most of us are not affected. But the internal violence of being made to carry—or choosing to carry—the load of your straight society's unconscious guilt—this is what tears us apart, what makes us want to stand up in the offices, in the factories and schools and shout out our true identities.

We were rebels from our earliest days—somewhere, maybe just about the time we started to go to school, we rejected straight society—unconsciously. Then, later, society rejected us, as we came into full bloom. The homosexuals who hide, who play it straight or pretend that the issue of homosexuality is unimportant, are only hiding the truth from themselves. They are trying to become part of a society that they rejected instinctively when they were five years old, to pretend that it is the result of heredity, or a bad mother, or anything but a gut reaction of nausea against the roles forced on us.

If you are homosexual, and you get tired of waiting around for the liberals to repeal the sodomy laws, and begin to dig yourself—and get angry—you are on your way to being a radical. Get in touch with the reasons that made you reject straight society as a kid (remembering my own revulsion against the vacant women drifting in and out of supermarkets, vowing never to live like them) and realize that you were right. Straight roles stink.

And you straights—look down the street, at the person whose sex is not readily apparent. Are you uneasy? Or are you made more uneasy by the stereotype gay, the flaming faggot or diesel dyke? Or most uneasy by the friend you thought was straight—and isn't? We want you to be uneasy, be a little less comfortable in your straight roles. And to make you uneasy, we behave outrageously—even though we pay a heavy price for it—and our outrageous behavior comes out of our rage.

But what is strange to you is natural to us. Let me illustrate. The Gay Liberation Front (GLF) "liberates" a gay bar for the evening. We come in. The people already there are seated quietly at the bar. Two or three couples are dancing. It's a down place. And the GLF takes over. Men dance with men, women with women, men with women, everyone in circles. No roles. You ever see that at a straight party? Not men with men—this is particularly verboten. No, and you're not likely to, while the gays in the movement are still passing for straight in order to keep up the good names of their organizations or to keep up the pretense that they are acceptable—and to have to get out of the organization they worked so hard for.

True, some gays play the same role-games among themselves that straights do. Isn't every minority group fucked over by the values of the majority culture? But the really important thing about being gay is that you are forced to notice how much sex-role differentiation is pure artifice, is nothing but a game.

Once I dressed up for an American Civil Liberties Union benefit. I wore a black lace dress, heels, elaborate hairdo and makeup. And felt like—a drag queen. Not like a woman—I am a woman every day of my life—but like the ultimate in artifice, a woman posing as a drag queen.

The roles are beginning to wear thin. The makeup is cracking. The roles—breadwinner, little wife, screaming fag, bulldyke, James Bond—are the cardboard characters we are always trying to fit into, as if being human and spontaneous were so horrible that we each have to pick on a character out of a third-rate novel and try to cut ourselves down to its size. And you cut off your homosexuality—and we cut off our heterosexuality.

Back to the main difference between us. We gays are separate from you—we are alien. You have managed to drive your own homosexuality down under the skin of your mind—and to drive us down and out into the gutter of self-contempt. We, ever since we became aware of being gay, have each day been forced to internalize the labels: "I am a pervert, a dyke, a fag, etc." And the days pass, until we look at you out of our homosexual bodies, bodies that have become synonymous and consubstantial with homosexuality, bodies that are no longer bodies but labels; and sometimes we wish we were like you, sometimes we wonder how you can stand yourselves.

It's difficult for me to understand how you can dig each other as human beings—in a man-woman relationship—how you can relate to each other in spite of your sex roles. It must be awfully difficult to talk to each other, when the woman is trained to repress what the man is trained to express, and vice-versa. Do straight men and women talk to each other? Or does the man talk and the woman nod approvingly? Is love possible between heterosexuals; or is it all a case of women posing as nymphs, earth-mothers, sex-objects, what-have-you; and men writing the poetry of romantic illusions to these walking stereotypes?

I tell you, the function of a homosexual is to make you uneasy.

And now I will tell you what we want, we radical homosexuals: not for you to tolerate us, or to accept us, but to understand us. And this you can do only by becoming one of us. We want to reach the homosexuals entombed in you, to liberate our brothers and sisters, locked in the prisons of your skulls.

We want you to understand what it is to be our kind of outcast—but also to understand our kind of love, to hunger for your own sex. Because unless you understand this, you will continue to look at us with uncomprehending eyes, fake liberal smiles; you will be incapable of loving us.

We will never go straight until you go gay. As long as you divide yourselves, we will be divided from you—separated by a mirror trick of your mind. We will no longer allow you to drop us—or the homosexuals in yourselves—into the reject bin; labelled sick, childish or perverted. And because we will not wait, your awakening may be a rude and bloody one. It's your choice. You will never be rid of us, because we reproduce ourselves out of your bodies—and out of your minds. We are one with you.

As gay liberation swept across the nation, the medical profession becamethe first target of many activists. While the homophile movement never seriously challenged the conception of homosexuality as an illness, by 1970 the opposition was loud and clear. The annual meetings of the American Medical Association and the American Psychiatric Association were disrupted by gay and lesbian activities. The activists' main point was that the medical profession, through its classification and treatment of homosexuality as an illness, fostered the oppression of lesbian and gay people. Further, the goal of American psychiatry—"adjustment" of the individual to society—was an oppressive ideal, denying healthy difference and the role of social structures in mental illness.

The activism succeeded. In 1974 the American Psychiatric Association removed homosexuality from its list of disorders in its Diagnostic and Statistical Manual—the notorious DSM–III. While many doctors expressed outrage at the "political" intervention into their "scientific" proceedings, these incidents revealed the interrelationships between science and politics, as well as the possibility of transforming social judgment and structure through concerted action.

A LEAFLET FOR THE AMERICAN MEDICAL ASSOCIATION
(1970)

Chicago Gay Liberation Front

The establishment school of psychiatry is based on the premise that people who are hurting should solve their problems by "adjusting" to the situation. For the homosexual, this means becoming adept at straight-fronting, learning how to survive in a hostile world, how to settle for housing in the gay ghetto, how to be satisfied with a profession in which homosexuals are tolerated, and how to live with low self-esteem.

The adjustment school places the burden on each individual homosexual to learn to bear his torment. But the "problem" of homosexuality is never solved under this scheme; the anti-homosexualist attitude of society, which is the cause of the homosexual's trouble, goes unchallenged. And there's always another paying patient on the psychiatrist's couch.

Dr. Socarides claims, "A human being is sick when he fails to function in his appropriate gender identity, which is appropriate to his anatomy." Who determined "appropriateness"? The psychiatrist as moralist? Certainly there is no scientific basis for defining "appropriate" sexual behavior. In a study of homosexuality in other species and other cultures, Ford and Beach in *Patterns of Sexual Behavior* conclude, "Human homosexuality is not a product of hormonal imbalance or 'perverted heredity.' It is the product of the fundamental mammalian heritage of general sexual responsiveness as modified under the impact of experience."

Other than invoking moral standards, Dr. Socarides claims that homosexuality is an emotional illness because of the guilt and anxieties in homosexual life. Would he also consider Judaism an emotional illness because of the paranoia which Jews experienced in Nazi Germany?

We homosexuals of gay liberation believe that the adjustment school of therapy is not a valid approach to society.

We refuse to adjust to our oppression, and believe that the key to our mental health, and to the mental health of all oppressed peoples in a racist, sexist, capitalist society, is a radical change in the structure and accompanying attitudes of the entire social system.

Mental health for women does not mean therapy for women—it means the elimination of male supremacy. Not therapy for blacks, but an end to racism. The poor don't need psychiatrists (what a joke at 25 bucks a throw!)—they need democratic distribution of wealth. OFF THE COUCHES, INTO THE STREETS!

We see political organizing and collective action as the strategy for effecting this social change. We declare that we are healthy homosexuals in a sexist society, and that homosexuality is at least on a par with heterosexuality as a way for people to relate to each other (know any men that don't dominate women?).

Since the prevalent notion in society is that homosexuality is wrong, all those who recognize that this attitude is damaging to people, and that it must be corrected, have to raise their voices in opposition to anti-homosexualism. Not to do so is to permit the myth of homosexual pathology to continue and to comply in the homosexual's continued suffering from senseless stigmatization.

A psychiatrist who allows a homosexual patient—who has been subject to a barrage of anti-homosexual sentiments his whole life—to continue in the belief that heterosexuality is superior to homosexuality, is the greatest obstacle to his patient's health and well-being.

We furthermore urge psychiatrists to refer their homosexual patients to gay liberation (and other patients who are victims of oppression to relevant liberation movements). Once relieved of patients whose guilt is not deserved but imposed, psychiatrists will be able to devote all their effort to the rich—who do earn their guilt but not their wealth, and can best afford to pay psychiatrists' fees.

We are convinced that a picket and a dance will do more for the vast majority of homosexuals than two years on the couch. We call on the medical profession to repudiate the adjustment approach as a solution to homosexual oppression and instead to further homosexual liberation by working in a variety of political ways (re-educating the public, supporting pickets, attending rallies, promoting social events, etc.) to change the situation of homosexuals in this society.

Join us in the struggle for a world in which all human beings are free to love without fear or shame.

RADICALESBIANS "The Woman-Identified Woman" first appeared as a flyer at the second Congress to Unite Women, held in May 1970. Radicalesbians, the group that wrote the statement, took over the conference and forced discussion of the issue of lesbianism in the women's movement.

"The Woman-Identified Woman" is perhaps the definitive manifesto of lesbian-feminism. The distinctive feature of lesbian-feminism is its theoretical connection of the oppression of lesbians with that of women, and the argument that the oppression of women is the most basic, the earliest, and most enduring oppression. In this statement, Radicalesbians urge their readers to think of lesbianism less as a sexual choice and more as a political one. Lesbianism is presented here as a feminist act, as a rebellion against the female role and the self-hatred that has been part of that role. This rejection of medical descriptions of lesbian identity led to the new identification and self-identification as lesbian of many women who had previously lived and/or had sex with men.

THE WOMAN-IDENTIFIED WOMAN

(1970)

Radicalesbians

What is a lesbian? A lesbian is the rage of all women condensed to the point of explosion. She is the woman who, often beginning at an extremely early age, acts in accordance with her inner compulsion to be a more complete and freer human being than her society—perhaps then, but certainly later—cares to allow her. These needs and actions, over a period of years, bring her into painful conflict with people, situations, the accepted ways of thinking, feeling and behaving, until she is in a state of continual war with everything around her, and usually with herself. She may not be fully conscious of the political implications of what for her began as personal necessity, but on some level she has not been able to accept the limitations and oppression laid on her by the most basic role of her society—the female role. The turmoil she experiences tends to induce guilt proportional to the degree to which she feels she is not meeting social expectations, and/or eventually drives her to question and analyse what the rest of her society, more or less accepts. She is forced to evolve her own life pattern, often living much of her life alone, learning usually much earlier than her 'straight' (heterosexual) sisters about the essential aloneness of life (which the myth of marriage obscures) and about the reality of illusions. To the extent that she cannot expel the heavy socialization that goes with being female, she can never truly find peace with herself. For she is caught somewhere between accepting society's view of her—in which case she cannot accept herself—and coming to understand what this sexist society has done to her and why it is functional and necessary for it to do so. Those of us who work that through find ourselves on the other side of a tortuous journey through a night that may have been decades long. The perspective gained from that journey, the liberation of self, the inner peace, the real love of self and of all women, is something to be shared with all women—because we are all women.

It should first be understood that lesbianism, like male homosexuality, is a category of behavior possible only in a sexist society characterized by rigid sex roles and dominated by male supremacy. Those sex roles dehumanize women by defining us as a supportive/serving caste in relation to the master caste of men, and emotionally cripple men by demanding that they be alienated from their own bodies and emotions in order to perform their economic/political/military functions effectively. Homosexuality is a by-product of a particular way of setting up roles (or approved patterns of behavior) on the basis of sex; as such it is an inauthentic (not consonant with 'reality') category. In a society in which men do not oppress women, and sexual expression is allowed to follow feelings, the categories of homosexuality and heterosexuality would disappear.

But lesbianism is also different from male homosexuality, and serves a different function in the society. 'Dyke' is a different kind of put-down from 'faggot,' although both imply you are not playing your socially assigned sex role—are not therefore a 'real woman' or a 'real man.' The grudging admiration felt for the tomboy and the queasiness felt around a sissy boy point to the same thing: the contempt in which women—or those who play a female role—are held. And the investment in keeping women in that contemptuous role is very great. Lesbian is the word, the label, the condition that holds women in line. When a woman hears this word tossed her way, she knows she is stepping out of line. She knows that she has crossed the terrible boundary of her sex role. She recoils, she protests, she reshapes her actions to gain approval. Lesbian is a label invented by the man to throw at any woman who dares to be his equal, who dares to challenge his prerogatives (including that of all woman as part of the exchange medium among men), who dares to assert the primacy of her own needs. To have the label applied to people active in women's liberation is just the most recent instance of a long history; other women will recall that not so long ago, any woman who was successful, independent, not orienting her whole life about a man, would hear this word. For in this sexist society, for a woman to be independent means she can't be a woman—she must be a dyke. That in itself should tell us where women are at. It says as clearly as can be said: woman and person are contradictory terms. For a lesbian is not considered a 'real woman.' And yet, in popular thinking, there is really only one essential difference between a lesbian and other women: that of sexual orientation—which is to say, when you strip off all the packaging, you must finally realize that the essence of being a 'woman' is to get fucked by men.

'Lesbian' is one of the sexual categories by which men have divided up humanity. While all women are dehumanized as sex objects, as the objects of men, they are given certain compensations: identification with his power, his ego, his status, his protection (from other males), feeling like a 'real woman,' finding social acceptance by adhering to her role, etc. Should a woman confront herself by confronting another woman, there are fewer rationalizations, fewer buffers by which to avoid the stark horror of her dehumanized condition. Herein we find the overriding fear of many women towards exploring intimate relationships with other women: the fear of her being used as a sexual object by a woman, which not only will bring no male-connected compensations, but also will reveal the void which is woman's real situation. This dehumanization is expressed when a straight woman learns that a sister is a lesbian; she begins to relate to her lesbian sister as her potential sex object, laying a surrogate male role on the lesbian. This reveals her heterosexual conditioning to make herself into an object when sex is potentially involved in a relationship, and it denies the lesbian her full humanity. For women, especially those in the movement, to perceive their lesbian sisters through this male grid of role definitions is to accept this male cultural conditioning and to oppress their sisters much as they themselves have been oppressed by men. Are we going to continue the male classification system of defining all females in sexual relation to some other category of people? Affixing the label lesbian not only to a woman who aspires to be a person, but also to any situation of real love, real solidarity, real primacy among women is a primary form of divisiveness among women: it is the condition which keeps women within the confines of the feminine role, and it is the debunking/scare term that keeps women from forming any primary attachments, groups, or associations among ourselves.

Women in the movement have in most cases gone to great lengths to avoid discussion and confrontation with the issue of lesbianism. It puts people up-tight. They are hostile, evasive, or try to incorporate it into some 'broader issue.' They would rather not talk about it. If they have to, they try to dismiss it as a 'lavender herring.' But it is no side issue. It is absolutely essential to the success and fulfillment of the women's liberation movement that this issue be dealt with. As long as the label 'dyke' can be used to frighten women into a less militant stand, keep her separate from her sisters, keep her from giving primacy to anything other than men and family—then to that extent she is controlled by the male culture. Until women see in each other the possibility of primal commitment which includes sexual love, they will be denying themselves the love and value they readily accord to men, thus affirming their second-class status. As long as male acceptability is primary—both to individual women and to the movement as a whole—the term lesbian will be used effectively against women. Insofar as women want only more privileges within the system, they do not want to antagonize male power. They instead seek acceptability for women's liberation, and the most crucial aspect of the acceptability is to deny lesbianism—i.e., deny any fundamental challenge to the basis of the female role.

It should also be said that some younger, more radical women have honestly begun to discuss lesbianism, but so far it has been primarily as a sexual 'alternative' to men. This, however, is still giving primacy to men, both because the idea of relating more completely to women occurs as a negative reaction to men, and because the lesbian relationship is being characterized simply by sex, which is divisive and sexist. On one level, which is both personal and political, women may withdraw emotional and sexual energies from men, and work out various alternatives for those energies in their own lives. On a different political/psychological level, it must be understood that what is crucial is that women begin disengaging from male-defined response patterns. In the privacy of our own psyches, we must cut those cords to the core. For irrespective of where our love and sexual energies flow, if we are male-identified in our heads, we cannot realize our autonomy as human beings.

But why is it that women have related to and through men? By virtue of having been brought up in a male society, we have internalized the male culture's definition of ourselves. That definition views us as relative beings who exist not for ourselves, but for the servicing, maintenance and comfort of men. That definition consigns us to sexual and family functions, and excludes us from defining and shaping the terms of our lives. In exchange for our psychic servicing and for performing society's non-profit-making functions, the man confers on us just one thing: the slave status which makes us legitimate in the eyes of the society in which we live. This is called 'femininity' or 'being a real woman' in our cultural lingo. We are authentic, legitimate, real to the extent that we are the property of some man whose name we bear. To be a woman who belongs to no man is to be invisible, pathetic, unauthentic, unreal. He confirms his image of us—of what we have to be in order to be—as he defines it, in relation to him—but cannot confirm our personhood, our own selves as absolutes. As long as we are dependent on the male culture for this definition, for this approval, we cannot be free.

The consequence of internalizing this role is an enormous reservoir of self-hate. This is not to say the self-hate is recognized or accepted as such; indeed most women would deny it. It may be experienced as discomfort with her role, as feeling empty, as numbness, as restlessness, a paralyzing anxiety at the center. Alternatively, it may be expressed in shrill defensiveness of the glory and destiny of her role. But it does exist, often beneath the edge of her consciousness, poisoning her existence, keeping her alienated from herself, her own needs, and rendering her a stranger to other women. Women hate both themselves and other women. They try to escape by identifying with the oppressor, living through him, gaining status and identity from his ego, his power, his accomplishments. And by not identifying with other 'empty vessels' like themselves, women resist relating on all levels to other women who will reflect their own oppression, their own secondary status, their own self-hate. For to confront another woman is finally to confront one's self—the self we have gone to such lengths to avoid. And in that mirror we know we cannot really respect and love that which we have been made to be.

As the source of self-hate and the lack of real self are rooted in our male-given identity, we must create a new sense of self. As long as we cling to the idea of 'being a woman,' we will sense some conflict with that incipient self, that sense of I, that sense of a whole person. It is very difficult to realize and accept that being 'feminine' and being a whole person are irreconcilable. Only women can give each other a new sense of self. That identity we have to develop with reference to ourselves, and not in relation to men. This consciousness is the revolutionary force from which all else will follow, for ours is an organic revolution. For this we must be available and supportive to one another, give our commitment and our love, give the emotional support necessary to sustain this movement. Our energies must flow toward our sisters not backwards towards our oppressors. As long as women's liberation tries to free women without facing the basic heterosexual structure that binds us in one-to-one relationship with a man, how to get better sex, how to turn his head around—into trying to make the 'new man' out of him, in the delusion that this will allow us to be the 'new woman.' This obviously splits our energies and commitments, leaving us unable to be committed to the construction of the new patterns which will liberate us.

It is the primacy of women relating to women, of women creating a new consciousness of and with each other which is at the heart of women's liberation, and the basis for the cultural revolution. Together we must find, reinforce and validate our authentic selves. As we do this, we confirm in each other that struggling incipient sense of pride and strength, the divisive barriers begin to melt, we feel this growing solidarity with our sisters. We see ourselves as prime, find our centers inside of ourselves. We find receding the sense of alienation, of being cut off, of being behind a locked window, of being unable to get out what we know is inside. We feel a realness, feel at last we are coinciding with ourselves. With that real self, with that consciousness, we begin a revolution to end the imposition of all coercive identifications, and to achieve maximum autonomy in human expression.

THIRD WORLD GAY
REVOLUTION

Throughout early gay liberation, the relation between gay liberation and other liberation movements was a major issue. As
Wittman's *Manifesto* notes, politically "revolutionary" movements have often been sexually conservative. Lesbians and
gays of color have had to fight for equality within national liberation movements and
anti-racist struggles. This fight has not, by and large, led to abandonment of racial
solidarity, simply because the weight of racism is an inescapable reality in the lives
of people of color. Unlike for white middle-class gays and lesbians, struggle against
racism is not a luxury. Thus many of the most complex and thoughtful writing of the
past twenty-five years has come from gays and lesbians of color. The next several
selections document some of that thinking and writing.

The following statement was issued by Third World Gay Revolution, a group of New
York Black and Latino homosexual men. It specifically challenges heterosexual men
of color to confront their fears and transform their sense of masculinity in order to
challenge homophobia.

THE OPPRESSED SHALL NOT BECOME THE OPPRESSOR

(1970)

Third World Gay Revolution

Sisters and Brothers of the Third World, you who call yourselves "revolutionaries" have failed
to deal with your sexist attitudes. Instead you cling to male-supremacy and therefore to the
conditioned role of oppressors. Brothers still fight for the privileged position of
man-on-the-top. Sisters quickly fall in line behind-their-men. By your counterrevolutionary
struggle to maintain and to force heterosexuality and the nuclear family, you perpetuate outmoded remnants of Capitalism. By your anti-homosexual stance you have used the weapons
of the oppressor thereby becoming the agent of the oppressor.

It is up to Third World males to realistically define masculinity because it is you, who
throughout your lives have struggled to gain the unrealistic roles of "men". Third World men
have always tried to reach this precarious position by climbing on the backs of women and
homosexuals. "Masculinity" has been defined by white society as the amount of possessions
(including women) a man collects, and the amount of physical power gained over other
men. Third World men have been denied even these false standards of "masculinity".
Therefore stop perpetuating in yourselves and your community the white-supremacists'
notions which are basic to your own oppression.

We, as Third World gay people suffer a triple oppression:

1) We are oppressed as people because our humanity is routinely devoured by the car-
nivorous system of Capitalism.

2) We are oppressed as Third World people by the economically inherent racism of
white Amerikan society.

3) We are oppressed by the sexism of the white society and the verbal and physical abuse
of masculinity—deprived Third World males.

The right of self-determination over dominion of one's own body is a human right and this right must be defended with one's body being put on the line.

By the actions you have taken against your gay brothers and sisters of the Third World you who throughout your lives have suffered the torments of social oppression and sexual repression, have now placed yourselves in the role of oppressor.

Anti-homosexuality fosters sexual repression, male-supremacy, weakness in revolutionary drive, and results in an inaccurate non-objective political perspective.

LOS OPRIMIDOS NO SE CONVERTIRAN EN OPRESORES

Hermanas y hermanos del 3er Mundo: Uds., que se llaman reolucionarios, no se han enfrentado a sus actitudes sexis tas. En cambio, se han aferrado al machismo y en consecuencia al papel de opresor. Aún Uds. luchan por la posición privilegiada del machismo, y cada una de Uds., hermanas, sigue detrás de los "hombres".

Por vuestra lucha contrarrevolucionaria para mantener (y forzar) la heterosexualidad y el núcleo familiar, Uds. perpetúan las viejas ideas remanentes del capitalismo.

Por vuestra posición anti-homosexualhan usado las armas del opresor, en consecuencia convirtiéndose en agente del mismo.

Está en Uds., hombres del 3er mundo,—definir la masculinidad de un modo más realista, Porque son Uds. quienes a través de sus vidas han luchado para alcanzar esta posición precaria poniéndosepor encima de las mujeres y los homosexuales, en consecuencia perpetuando en Uds. mismos y en la comunidad las nociones capitalistas blancas del machismo, las cuáles se encuentran básicamente en vuestra propia opresión.

Nosotros, gente homosexual del 3er Mundo, sufrimos una triple opresión:

1) Estamos oprimidos como personas, pues nuestra humanidad esta sistemáticamente devorada por el sistema carnívoro capitalista.

2) Estamos oprimidos como gente del 3er Mundo por el racismo derivado del sistemas económico de la sociedad americana-blanca.

3) Estamos oprimidos por el sexismo de—esta misma sociedad blanca y a menudo ma noseados verbal y físicamente por el machismo de los hombres del 3er mundo. El derecho de autodeterminación sobre el propio cuerpo es un derecho humano y este derecho será defendido con la vida.

A consecuencia de las acciones que Uds. han tomado contra sus hermanos y hermanas homosexuales del 3er mundo, Us., que a traves de sus vidada sufrieron los tormentos de la opresión social y la represión sexual, se han puesto ahora en el papel de opresor.

Antihomosexualidad alienta y promueve represión sexual, machismo, debilidad en el empuje revolucionario, y una inexacta no-objetiva perspectiva política.

REVOLUTIONARY PEOPLE'S
CONSTITUTIONAL
CONVENTION

In the U.S. during the late nineteen sixties, the anti-Vietnam war and student movements, the Black movement for desegregation and full equality for African-Americans, the Puerto-Rican, American Indian, and other nationalist movements, and the feminist movement developed. Members of Radical Lesbians and the Gay Liberation Front declared their support of the Black Panthers, the leading militant African-American organization, and criticized white gays and lesbians on their racism, specifically on the willingness to criticize the sexism of black but not white men, and condemned classism within gay and lesbian organizations.

At the Panther-sponsored Revolutionary People's Constitution Convention held September 5-7, 1970, gay men and lesbians separately drafted and presented the following statements.

STATEMENT OF THE MALE HOMOSEXUAL WORKSHOP
(1970)

Revolutionary People's Constitutional Convention

All power to the people!

The revolution will not be complete until all men are free to express their love for one another sexually. We affirm the sexuality of our love. The social institution which prevents us all from expressing or total revolutionary love we define as sexism. Sexism is a belief or practice that the sex or sexual orientation of human beings gives to some the right to certain privileges, powers, or roles, while denying to others their full potential. Within the context of our society, sexism is primarily manifested through male supremacy and heterosexual chauvinism. Since in the short run sexism benefits certain persons or groups, in the long run it cannot serve all the people, and prevents the forming of complete social consciousness among straight men.

Sexism is irrational, unjust and counter-revolutionary. Sexism prevents the revolutionary solidarity of the people.

We demand that the struggle against sexism be acknowledged as an essential part of the revolutionary struggle. We demand that all revolutionaries deal individually with their own sexism.

We recognize as a vanguard revolutionary action the Huey P. Newton statement on gay liberation. We recognize the Black Panther Party as being the vanguard of the people's revolution in Amerikkka.

No revolution without us!

An army of lovers cannot lose!

WE DEMAND:

1. The right to be gay, any time, any place.
2. The right to free physiological change and modification of sex upon demand.
3. The right of free dress and adornment.

4. That all modes of human sexual self-expression deserve protection of the law, and social sanction.
5. Every child's right to develop in a non-sexist, non-possessive atmosphere, which is the responsibility of all people to create.
6. That a free educational system present the entire range of human sexuality, without advocating any one form or style; that sex roles and sex-determined skills not be fostered by the schools.
7. That language be modified so that no gender take priority.
8. The judicial system be run by the people through people's courts; that all people be tried by members of their peer group.
9. That gays be represented in all governmental and community institutions.
10. That organized religions be condemned for aiding in the genocide of gay people, and enjoined from teaching hatred and superstition.
11. That psychiatry and psychology be enjoined from advocating a preference for any form of sexuality, and the enforcement of that preference by shock treatment, brainwashing, imprisonment, etc.
12. The abolition of the nuclear family because it perpetuates the false categories of homosexuality and heterosexuality.
13. The immediate release of and reparations for gay and other political prisoners from prisons and mental institutions; the support of gay political prisoners by all other political prisoners.
14. That gays determine the destiny of their own communities.
15. That all people share equally the labor and products of society, regardless of sex or sexual orientation.
16. That technology be used to liberate all peoples of the world from drudgery.
17. The full participation of gays in the people's revolutionary army.
18. Finally, the end of domination of one person by another.

Gay power to gay people!
All power to the people!
Seize the time!

DEMANDS OF THE LESBIAN WORKSHOP

(1970)

Revolutionary People's Constitutional Convention

1. Sexual autonomy:
Prohibit sexual role programming of children.
2. Destruction of the Nuclear Family:
The nuclear family is a microcosm of the fascist state, where the women and children

are owned by, and their fates determined by, the needs of men in a man's world.

3. Communal care of children.

Children should be allowed to grow, in a society of their peers, cared for by adults whose aim is not to perpetrate any male-female role programming. It is advised that these adults be under the direction of woman-identified women.

4. Reparations:

(a) Women are a dispersed minority and we demand that amount of control of all production and industry that would ensure one hundred percent over our own destinies. This control includes commerce, industry, health facilities, education, transportation, military, etc.

(b) Because women have been systematically denied information and knowledge and the opportunities for acquiring these, we demand open enrollment of all schools to all women, financial support to any woman who needs it, on the job training with pay for all women attending technical schools and under apprenticeship.

(c) Women demand the time and support to research, compile and report our history and our identity.

(d) The power and technology of defense are invested in men. Since these powers are used to intimidate women, we demand the training in self-defense and the use of defense machinery. A Women's Militia would be organized to defend the demands, rights and interests of women struggling towards an unoppressive social system.

HUEY NEWTON

Huey Newton, leader of the Black Panthers, published a letter in the party's newspaper, *The Black Panther,* on August 21, 1970, which stands as the first statement by a nationally-known heterosexual leader to recognize gay and lesbian equality. While some militant gays and lesbians of this time recognized the Panthers as the "vanguard" movement of all oppressed peoples in the U.S. and demanded inclusion *as* gays and lesbians, others saw Black and gay/lesbian oppression as distinct but necessitating coalitions to be overcome.

A LETTER FROM HUEY TO THE REVOLUTIONARY BROTHERS AND SISTERS ABOUT THE WOMEN'S LIBERATION AND GAY LIBERATION MOVEMENTS

(1970)

Huey Newton

During the past few years, strong movements have developed among women and among homosexuals seeking their liberation. There has been some uncertainty about how to relate to these movements.

Whatever your personal opinions and your insecurities about homosexuality and the various liberation movements among homosexuals and women (and I speak of the homosexuals and women as oppressed groups), we should try to unite with them in a revolutionary fashion. I say "whatever your insecurities are" because, as we very well know sometimes our first instinct is to want to hit a homosexual in the mouth and want a woman to be quiet. We want to hit the homosexual in the mouth because we're afraid we might be homosexual; and we want to hit the woman or shut her up because we're afraid that she might castrate us, or take the nuts that we might not have to start with.

We must gain security in ourselves and therefore have respect and feelings for all oppressed people. We must not use the racist type attitude like the White racists use against people because they are Black and poor. Many times the poorest White person is the most racist, because he's afraid that he might lose something, or discover something that he doesn't have; you're some kind of threat to him. This kind of psychology is in operation when we view oppressed people and we're angry with them because of their particular kind of behavior, or their particular kind of deviation from the established norm.

Remember, we haven't established a revolutionary value system; we're only in the process of establishing it. I don't remember us ever constituting any value that said that a revolutionary must say offensive things towards homosexuals, or that a revolutionary should make sure that women do not speak out about their own particular kind of oppression. Matter of fact it's just the opposite: we say that we recognize the women's right to be free. We haven't said much about the homosexual at all, and we must relate to the homosexual movement because it's a real thing. And I know through reading and through my life experience, my observations, that homosexuals are not given freedom and liberty by anyone in the society. Maybe they might be the most oppressed people in the society.

And what made them homosexual? Perhaps it's a whole phenomenon that I don't understand entirely. Some people say that it's the decadence of capitalism. I don't know whether this is the case; I rather doubt it. But whatever the case is, we know that homosexuality is a fact that exists, and we must understand it in its purest form: That is, a person should have freedom to use his body in whatever way he wants to. That's not endorsing things in homosexuality that we wouldn't view as revolutionary. But there's nothing to say that a homosexual cannot also be a revolutionary. And maybe I'm now injecting some of my prejudice by saying that "even a homosexual can be a revolutionary." Quite on the contrary, maybe a homosexual could be the most revolutionary.

When we have revolutionary conferences, rallies and demonstrations there should be full participation of the gay liberation movement and the women's liberation movement. Some groups might be more revolutionary than other. We shouldn't use the actions of a few to say that they're all reactionary or counterrevolutionary, because they're not.

We should deal with the factions just as we deal with any other group or party that claims to be revolutionary. We should try to judge somehow, whether they're operating sincerely, in a revolutionary fashion, from a really oppressed situation. (And we'll grant that if they're women, they're probably oppressed.) If they do things that are un-revolutionary or counter-revolutionary, then criticize that action. If we feel that the group in spirit means to be revolutionary in practice, but they make mistakes in interpretation of the revolutionary philosophy, or they don't understand the dialectics of the social forces in operation, we should criticize that and not criticize them because they're women trying to be free. And the same is true for homosexuals. We should never say a whole movement is dishonest, when in fact they're trying to be honest, they're just making honest mistakes. Friends are allowed to make mistakes. The enemy is not allowed to make mistakes because his whole existence is a mistake, and we suffer from it. But the women's liberation front and gay liberation front are our friends, they are potential allies, and we need as many allies as possible.

We should be willing to discuss the insecurities that many people have about homosexuality. When I say "insecurities," I mean the fear that they're some kind of threat to our manhood. I can understand this fear. Because of the long conditioning process which builds insecurity in the American male, homosexuality might produce certain hangups in us. I have hangups myself about male homosexuality. Where, on the other hand, I have no hangup about female homosexuality. And that's phenomena in itself. I think it's probably because male homosexuality is a threat to me, maybe, and the females are no threat.

We should be careful about using those terms that might turn our friends off. The terms "faggot" and "punk" should be deleted from our vocabulary, and especially we should not attach names normally designed for homosexuals to men who are enemies of the people, such as Nixon or Mitchell. Homosexuals are not enemies of the people.

We should try to form a working coalition with the gay liberation and women's liberation groups. We must always handle social forces in the most appropriate manner. And this is really a significant part of the population, both women, and the growing number of homosexuals, that we have to deal with.

ALL POWER TO THE PEOPLE!

Huey P. Newton,
SUPREME COMMANDER
Black Panther Party

CUBA

Many of those who became members of Gay Liberation began in the New Left. The message of free speech and anti-imperialism blended easily with their desire to be free and open. The New Left valorization of Cuba, however, collided with the homophobia of the Cuban regime and society. As Allen Young described his journey, the official policy of the Cuban government made gay leftists unwelcome. Stalin had reinstated harsh penalties for sodomy after the decriminalization of the earlier Soviet Union, and his puritanism was shared widely throughout the communist parties of the world. While U.S. conservatives linked homosexuals to Communism, Communists labeled homosexuality a "bourgeois deviation," evidence of the decadence of capitalism. In short, queers are everyone's others.

The Venceremos Brigades were international groups of workers begun in 1969 who came to Cuba to help with the sugar cane harvest. These workers were Marxist-oriented, accustomed to notions of party unity through discipline. They also supported the Cuban government's policies under the rubric of anti-imperialism. The Cuban policy, and its support in the U.S., led many newly "out" gay liberationists to cut their ties with Marxism or with the left. Others, however, retained their independent analysis and commitment to socialism. The Gay Revolutionary Party, a U.S.-based group of gay and lesbian leftists, and the Gay Committee of Returned Brigandistas printed a condemnation of the Cuban policy in *Fag Rag*. The following documents show us that gays and lesbians are not "naturally" aligned with anyone.

LETTER FROM CUBAN GAY PEOPLE TO THE NORTH AMERICAN GAY LIBERATION MOVEMENT

(1970)

Sisters and Brothers:

By chance, we got a copy of your publication with the statement of Third World Gay Revolution (*Gay Flames* pamphlet No. 7).

We believe it is our duty to inform you of our situation as homosexuals in Cuba, as people who experience discrimination in a country which presumably is involved in a revolution and is committed to the creation of the "new man." This revolution is struggling against the traditional injustices that all Cubans have suffered as a result of economic exploitation and a class society. The vestiges of this class society still bring us suffering. We wish to inform you, however, of a series of events which fundamentally deny the postulates of the social and political movement in Cuba. In fact, our country is in a state of increasingly greater crisis, quite in contradiction with the success stories told abroad.

If in a consumption society, run by capitalists and oligarchs, like the one you are living in, homosexuals experience suffering and limitations, in our society, labeled Marxist and revolutionary, it is worse. Since its beginning—first in veiled ways, later without scruples or rationalizations—the Cuban revolutionary government has persecuted homosexuals. The methods range from the most common sort of physical attack to attempts to impose psychic and moral disintegration upon gay people. In theory, at least, the Cuban revolution holds that homosexuality is not compatible with the development of a society whose goal is communism.

Here, the homosexual is attacked in such a way that he or she becomes the victim of a series of formulas to make invisible what the authorities judge to be an aberration, a repudiable fault. One formula is for homosexuals to marry and pretend to live a "normal" life. Another has been the confinement of homosexuals on farms where they are brutally treated. This happened with the concentration camps of the UMAP, which, for the uninformed, were simply "military units to increase production," a place where people did farm work and youths received military training, the sort of thing that might take place in any civilized country. This situation provoked an international scandal, and subsequently the UMAP camps were eliminated as a branch of obligatory military service—but there still are prison farms exclusively for homosexuals.

On the street we suffer persecution, aggression, and a constant abuse of authority. We are asked to produce I.D. cards. We are arrested for wearing certain clothes or using certain hair styles, or for simple get-togethers. This is a violation of freedoms guaranteed by the Declaration of Human Rights, freedoms which, contradictorily, are more respected in societies that are called fascist than in ours—though Cuban society has been seen as a model for the solution of the problems of individual and collective freedom.

Methods of psychological repression, social isolation, control by districts, neighborhoods, work places and schools, always with the aim of negating us, are commonly used by this regime. It can be said that there are many homosexuals, some of them intellectuals, some not, who live apart from this situation. In the first place, they are very few in number. To the extent that such persons exist, they know that they cannot cross the limits of behavior that have been outlined for them, and that in the case of opposition, there is only the risk of exile or the response of a dictatorial system which can lead to the worst consequences.

It is not possible to advocate freedom, respect and justice for homosexuals throughout the world without taking into consideration the situation of thousands of individuals in our country. There must also be protests for the treatment they are given, and the search for an effective solution, not a theoretical one, to such problems.

We hope in future communications to give plenty of details and to shed light on many situations which you do not know about in this uncertain and chaotic pseudo-socialist system.

(Note: to protect ourselves, we have given a false return address.)

DECLARATION

from *GRANMA*, daily organ of the Communist Party of Cuba
(May 1971)
with responses from the Gay Revolutionary Party and the Gay Committee of
Returned Brigadistas

Cuban First National Congress on Education and Culture

The social pathological character of homosexual deviations was recognized. It was resolved that all manifestations of homosexual deviations are to be firmly rejected and prevented from spreading. It was pointed out, however, that a study, investigation, and analysis of this complex problem should always determine the measures to be adopted.

It was decided that homosexuality should not be considered a central problem or a fundamental one in our society, but rather its attention and solution are necessary.

A study was made of the origin and evolution of this phenomenon and of its present-day scope and antisocial character. An in-depth analysis was made of the preventive and educational measures that are to be put into effect against existing focuses, including the control and relocation of isolated cases and degrees of deterioration.

On the basis of these considerations, it was resolved that it would be convenient to adopt the following measures:

a) Extension of the coeducational system: recognition of its importance in the formation of children and the young.

b) Appropriate sexual education for parents, teachers and pupils. This work must not be treated as a special subject but as one falling into the general teaching syllabus, such as biology, physiology, etc.

c) Stimulation of proper approach to sex. A campaign of information should be put into effect among adolescents and young people which would contribute to the acquisition of a scientific knowledge of sex and the eradication of prejudices and doubts which in some cases result in the placing of too much importance on sex.

d) Promotion of discussion among the youth in those cases where it becomes necessary to delve into the human aspect of sex relations.

It was resolved that for notorious homosexuals to have influence in the formation of our youth is not to be tolerated on the basis of their "artistic merits."

Consequently, a study is called for to determine how best to tackle the problems of the presence of homosexuals, in the various institutions of our cultural sector.

It was proposed that a study should be made to find a way of applying measures with a view to transferring to other organizations those who, as homosexuals, should not have any direct influence on our youth through artistic and cultural activities.

It was resolved that those whose morals do not correspond to the prestige of our revolution should be barred from any group of performers representing our country abroad.

Finally, it was agreed to demand that severe penalties be applied to those who corrupt the morals of minors, depraved repeat offenders and irredeemable antisocial elements.

Cultural institutions cannot serve as a platform for false intellectuals who try to make snobbery, extravagant conduct, homosexuality and other social aberrations into expressions of revolutionary spirit and art, isolated from the masses and the spirit of the revolution.

RESPONSES

1. Gay Revolution Party

The statement on homosexuality issued in Cuba by the First National Congress on Education and Culture, which was attended and endorsed by the leaders of the Cuban government, is openly reactionary. It is a threat to the lives and freedom of gay people because of the "severe penalties" demanded for "repeat offenders" and also because it encourages individual physical violence against homosexuals. It is also a threat to gay people throughout the world because of Cuba's reputation as a revolutionary nation.

We, the Gay Revolution Party, condemn the statement of the First National Congress on Education and Culture. We demand of revolutionaries everywhere that they join us in this move initially by the printing of this statement or their own comments.

The fight of the Cuban and other Third World peoples against the imperialism of the U.S. and its lackeys cannot be won by maintaining the attitudes of cultural and sexo-economic systems which support and are nurtured by sexism, male individualism, capitalism, and imperialism. It is necessary that cultural as well as political and economic revolution occur, and that this revolution destroy the sexist roots of exploitation.

As long as anti-gay attitudes persist, not only will gay people suffer, but the exploitation of women by men will be normal, competition among males will be the rule, and true communism will be impossible. We are socialists. We have come to understand that the destruction of straight social patterns (i.e., those modeled on power-based, role-playing heterosexuality) and the creation of gayness (i.e., mutuality and equality of human relationships based on the model of free homosexuality) are inherent to the development of a true socialist society. Thus, the only way to ensure a straight Cuba is to re-establish capitalism. A people struggling toward socialism can, due to an incorrect ideological superstructure, kill, relocate, or isolate individual gay people, but they cannot help but create conditions favorable to gayness.

Gay people are not one more group struggling for liberation. We are, and have always been, considered the scum of the earth, but we are you; we are everyone. The gay revolution is basic because it will destroy the sexual and social roles which are at the bottom of *all* exploitation, establishing mutuality of relationship between all people.

We do not call upon any straight male government to change its policy or reform its laws, whether it is in Cuba, the United States, or the Soviet Union. We call instead upon all people who seek freedom and an end to domination' to examine straight relationships and to realize with us that it is the roles and attitudes inherent to the maintenance of these relationships that prevent revolutionary change.

Cuba's reactionary policy cannot defeat us. It will only strengthen our resolution to fight collectively until the gay liberation of all people.

Turn it out!

Gay Revolution Party

(Note: translated into the straight idiom for the benefit of those not yet gay)

2. Gay Committee of Returned Brigadistas

We, as gay North Americans who have identified with and supported the Cuban revolution and our gay sisters and brothers in Cuba through our participation in the Venceremos Brigade, denounce the anti-homosexual policy formulated at the recent Conference on Education and Culture and endorsed by the Cuban government.

We have seen the struggle of all Cuban people and gay people all over the world as a common struggle; we have supported the progressive economic policies of the revolution and have been excited and encouraged at the indications of a developing cultural revolution toward the liberation of women in all areas of life.

Inherent to socialism and socialist practice is the equalization of power among all people. People cannot seize control of their own lives unless they see themselves historically and analyze critically the culture and institutions which have formulated them. Centuries of sexist attitudes inculcated by all the institutions of "western civilization," especially the church, have served to solidify today's sexist superstructure which places straight men at the top—defining their masculinity by the amount of power they have over gay people, women, and other men. It is each person's revolutionary responsibility to be critical, to be critical of the racist and sexist institutions which perpetuate divisions among us. There can be no real revolution, no truly socialist society until we remove the walls of self-hatred that separate us from ourselves and other people.

Gay people owe allegiance to no nation. The anti-homosexual policy of the Cuban government does not simply fail to include gay people in the revolutionary process—it specifically excludes them from participation in that process and the right to self-determination. We have been told that it is reactionary for us to criticize and condemn our oppressors when they call themselves "revolutionary" or "socialist." A policy of ruthless and incessant persecution of gay people is contradictory to the needs of all people, and such a policy is reactionary and fascist. All sexist policies and practices are counterrevolutionary and evidence the efforts of a ruling class to crush the people's cultural revolution when it threatens the ruling class (or caste) position of privilege.

Also, we denounce the national committee of the Venceremos Brigade as the agents of a sexist hierarchy. They, in their liberalism, have not engaged in critical relationship with either the Cuban people or with revolutionaries here.

We call upon all progressive people to join in our protests against this reactionary policy and to make their feelings known by writing to the Cuban Prime Minister and First Secretary of the Communist Party in Havana.

Turn it out!

Venceremos!

Gay Committee of Returned Brigadistas

POLICY ON GAY RECRUITMENT

(January 1972)

Venceremos Brigade

Through many discussions in the past few months by the National Committee and the Regionals, we have formulated a policy concerning recruitment to the BV [Brigada Venceremos] of gay North Americans. The BV is not pretending to analyze the potential or the validity of the gay liberation movement in the United States. (The potential or validity of any sector in the U.S. will be determined by their practice within the context of the struggle carried out inside the U.S.) Our policy is based on practical considerations of the Brigade in Cuba: Cuba's position toward homosexuality, the Political Objectives of the BV, our purpose in Cuba, thus our position toward Cuban policies, and the past practice of gay North Americans on the Brigade.

The Cuban people, as a whole, do not accept homosexuality. There is no material base for the oppression of homosexuals in Cuba. They are not repressed in work camps or anything of the sort. But it should be clear that Cuba does not encourage homosexuality.

The first Congress on Education and Culture, a congress of three years of work and hundreds of thousands of participants, published a report of major importance in the creation of a Cuban culture, a culture which in the past had been robbed, denied, and infiltrated by U.S. imperialist domination.

Concerning homosexuality, this congress took the position that homosexuality is a social pathology which reflects left-over bourgeois decadence and has no place in the formation of the New Man which Cuba is building.

This position was formulated by the Cuban people for the Cuban people. It was not formulated for the U.S., or any other country. Cuba is for Cubans, and while progressive and revolutionary people are always welcome in Cuba, the Cuban culture is not created for them in particular.

As to the BV, the past activities of gay North Americans have generally been destructive. A list of specific activities would include "re-educating the Cubans" (assuming that the situation in Cuban must be the same as in the U.S.), outright attacks and denunciations of the Cuban Revolution, imposing North American gay culture on the Cubans (for example, parading in drag in a Cuban town, acting in an overtly sexual manner at parties). Also, some gay North Americans have shown a greater interest in finding out about Cuban homosexuals than in finding out about the Cuban culture. And it has demonstrated a lack of understanding of the position of Brigadistas in Cuba as guests of the Cuban Revolution—to affirm the Cuban peoples' right to self-determination. While this does not mean that we deny the importance of dialogue, we are not in Cuba to carry out confrontations over our disagreements. The BV involves activity within the Cuban setting. As guests of the Cuban Revolution, we must realize that internal questions concerning Cuba's development can only be answered by the Cuban people; answers cannot be imposed from the outside. Only the Cuban people have all of the essential elements to analyze and solve their problems correctly.

The attitudes and actions described above are particularly dangerous at this time because they join a cultural imperialist offensive against the Cuban Revolution, carried out by U.S. imperialism in an attempt to discredit the Revolution and alienate North Americans from it.

There are gay North Americans who share the objectives of the BV. Our policy is not meant to exclude them. However, given the gay North American position, the Cuban position on homosexuality, and the problems that have arisen from this situation, we will require of gay North Americans a clear understanding of revolutionary anti-imperialist priorities and total identification with the Political Objectives of the BV. It must be understood that going to Cuba means respecting Cuban culture.

GUY HOCQUENGHEM

Guy Hocquenghem was a founder of Front Homosexuelle d'Action Revolutionaire, the leading gay organization of France during the 1970s. A participant in the French radical movement of 1968, his ideas are shaped by two of its major theorists, Gilles Deleuze and Felix Guattari, who blended Marxian and Freudian thought into a critique of the power relations that inhere in "everyday life" and a theory of how they can be transformed.

This selection is from Hocquenghem's book *Homosexual Desire*, published in 1972, which had a profound effect on the ideology of the European gay movement. In it, he analyzes the social construction of heterosexual desire through the patriarchal public power of the phallus as compared with the privatization of the anus; its liberation, through gay male sexuality, undermines patriarchal social relations and their reproduction through the Oedipus complex. He explains homosexual panic among heterosexuals as a loss of the identity established through patriarchy. Similarly, the closet is an attempt by homosexuals repressed by society to integrate their sexuality into existing social relations on the basis of the public/private split of phallus/anus; the same is true for "assimilationist" gay people. Gay liberation, for Hocquenghem, involves a transformation of social structure that can be foreseen through the new kinds of relationships created through gay male sexuality, but such transformation cannot be mapped ahead of time.

Guy Hocquenghem went on to win some of France's highest literary awards; he died of complications from AIDS in 1988.

CAPITALISM, THE FAMILY, AND THE ANUS
From *Homosexual Desire* (1972)

Guy Hocquenghem
trans. Daniella Dangoor

The chief ideological modes of thinking about homosexuality date back to the turn of the century; they are thus connected, though not mechanically so, with the advance of Western capitalism. They are a perverse re-territorialisation, in a world which is tending towards de-territorialisation. The purpose of these reconstituted axiomatic modes of thinking is to replace the failing codes. We have escaped from hellfire into psychological hell. Capitalist ideology's strongest weapon is its transformation of the Oedipus complex into a social characteristic, an internalisation of oppression which is left free to develop, whatever the political conditions. The anti-capitalist movement can often be pro-family, and indeed anti-homosexual. The apologetic type of homosexual literature generally deals with homosexuality by way of judicious reference to the Greeks, and this return to phantasmatical origins is suited to the perversity of re-territorialisation: in such literature we find no hint of a society in which there might be free expression of a homosexual desire that could be opposed to our present society . . .

The place of the family is now less in the institutions and more in the mind. The family is the place where sexual pleasure is legal, though no longer in the sense that everybody has to marry in order to take their pleasure within the law; far from putting an end to the exclusive function of reproductive heterosexuality, the actual dissolution by capitalism of the functions of the family has turned the family into the rule inhabiting every individual under free competition. This individual does not replace the family, he prolongs its farcical games. The decoding of the fluxes of pleasure is accompanied by their axiomatisation, just as the disappearance of the journeyman's apprenticeship and the discovery of labour as value go hand in hand with private ownership of the means of production.

Here we find the solution to the apparent contradiction that this society appears to be increasingly sexualised yet is more deep-seatedly repressive than any other: its sexualisation, and homosexuality in particular, is placed under the sign of guilt or transgression. The more is expected from desire, the less it is allowed to express itself, nor has it ever before been associated with so many images. The advertising media flood us with the images of naked young *ephebi*; the meaning, however, is: "What we desire has already been translated into a marketable transgression." Countless discussions daily restore the family meanings and induce artificial guilt even among young people who live at the margins of society. Freud's dubious success among young revolutionaries is indicative of the guilt-inducing power of the Oedipus complex.

We have been speaking alternately about "homosexual desire" and the perverse situation of homosexuality. The social manifestation of "homosexual desire" is perverse, while that same desire is at the same time an expression of the unformulated nature of the libido. If our society really is experiencing what Marcuse believes to be a growing homosexualisation, then that is because it is becoming perverted, because liberation is immediately re-territorialised. The emergence of unformulated desire is too destructive to be allowed to become more than a fleeting phenomenon which is immediately surrendered to a recuperative interpretation. Capitalism turns its homosexuals into failed "normal people," just as it turns its working class into an imitation of the middle class. This imitation middle class provides the best illustration of bourgeois values (the proletarian family); failed "normal people" emphasise the normality whose values they assume (fidelity, love, psychology, etc.).

Homosexual desire has two aspects: one is desire, the other is homosexuality. There can only be "growing homosexualisation," in Marcuse's words, if there is also a more thorough enclosure of desire within a play of images. It is also true that our world of social relationships is largely built on the sublimation of homosexuality. The social world exploits homosexual desire more than it exploits any other kind, by converting libidinal energy into a system of representation. If one wants to attack the representations and to rid the libidinal energy of its moral cloak where homosexuality is concerned, then one must first reveal the confrontation between the social ideology and the strength of a desire which, as in the case of Charlus and Jupien, is so tightly welded as not to leave the slightest crack for interpretation to enter.

There are thus two sides to what we mean by the term "homosexual desire": an ascent towards sublimation, the superego and social anxiety, and a descent towards the abyss of non-personalised and uncodified desire . . .

This leads us to desire as the plugging in of organs subject to no rule or law.

The Phallic Signifier and the Sublimated Anus

The world of Oedipal sexuality is deprived of a free plugging in of organs, of the relations of direct pleasure. There is just one organ—a purely sexual organ—at the centre of the Oedipal triangulation, the "One" which determines the position of the three elements of the triangle. This is the organ which constructs absence; it is the "despotic signifier," in relation to which the situations of the whole person are created. It is the detached, complete object which plays the same role in our society's sexuality as money does in the capitalist economy: the fetish, the true universal reference-point for all activity. It is responsible for the allocation of both absence and presence: the little girl's penis-envy, the little boy's castration anxiety.

Ours is a phallic society, and the quantity of possible pleasure is determined in relation to the phallus. All sexual acts have an "aim" which gives them their meaning; they are organised into preliminary caresses which will eventually crystallise in the necessary ejaculation, the touchstone of pleasure . . .

Our society is so phallic that the sexual act without ejaculation is felt to be a failure. After all, what do men care if—as is often the case—the woman remains frigid and feels no pleasure? Phallic pleasure is the raison d'être of heterosexuality, whichever sex is involved.

Ours is a phallocratic society, inasmuch as social relationships as a whole are constructed according to a hierarchy which reveals the transcendence of the great signifier. . .

Whereas the phallus is essentially social, the anus is essentially private. If phallic transcendence and the organisation of society around the great signifier are to be possible, the anus must be privatised in individualised and Oedipalised persons:

"The first organ to be privatised, to be excluded from the social field, was the anus. It gave privatisation its model, just as money was expressing the new abstract status of the fluxes."

The anus has no social position except sublimation. The functions of this organ are truly private; they are the site of the formation of the person. The anus expresses privatisation itself. The analytic case-history (and we cannot help seeing "anal" in "analytic") presupposes that the anal stage is transcended so that the genital stage may be reached. But the anal stage is necessary if detachment from the phallus is to take place. In fact sublimation is exercised on the anus as on no other organ, in the sense that the anus is made to progress from the lowest to the highest point: anality is the very movement of sublimation itself.

Freud sees the anal stage as the stage of formation of the person. The anus has no social desiring function left, because all its functions have become excremental: that is to say, chiefly private. The great act of capitalist decoding is accompanied by the constitution of the individual; money, which must be privately owned in order to circulate, is indeed connected with the anus, in so far as the anus is the most private part of the individual. The constitution of the private, individual, "proper" person is "of the anus"; the constitution of the public person is "of the phallus."

The anus does not enjoy the same ambivalence as the phallus, i.e. its duality as penis and Phallus. Of course, to expose one's penis is a shameful act, but it is also a glorious one, inasmuch as it displays some connection with the Great Social Phallus. Every man possesses a phallus which guarantees him a social role; every man has an anus which is truly his own, in the most secret depths of his own person. The anus does not exist in a social relation, since it forms precisely the individual and therefore enables the division between society and the individual to be made . . .

Your excrement is yours and yours alone: what you do with it is your own business. Among the organs, the anus plays the kind of role that narcissism plays in relation to the constitution of the individual: it is the source of energy giving rise to the social sexual system and the oppression which this system imposes upon desire.

Homosexuality and the Anus

. . . Homosexual desire challenges anality-sublimation because it restores the desiring use of the anus. Schreber forgets how to shit at the point when his resistance to his own homosexual libido is partly breaking down. Homosexuality primarily means anal homosexuality, sodomy.

At the end of his article "The Nosology of Male Homosexuality," Ferenczi makes a statement of great significance:

"The reason why every kind of affection between men is proscribed is not clear. It is thinkable that the sense of cleanliness which has been so specially reinforced in the past few centuries, i.e. the repression of anal erotism, has provided the strongest motive in this direction; for homoerotism, even the most sublimated, stands in a more or less unconscious associative connection with paederastia, i.e. an anal erotic activity."

There is a certain "kind of affection"—or rather a desiring relation as opposed to its sublimated form, friendship—which anal cleanliness does not permit, "anal cleanliness" being the formation in the child of the small responsible person; and there is a relation between "private cleanliness" and "private ownership" [propreté privée and propriété privée] which is not merely an association of words but something inevitable. Ferenczi also wrote a paper on "Stimulation of the Anal Erotogenic Zone as a Precipitating Factor in Paranoia" (1911). The patient was a forty-five-year-old peasant whose social activity was notable for its extraordinary zeal: he displayed a great interest in parish affairs, in which he took an active part. After an operation for an anal fistula, he took no further part in the village affairs and fell victim to persecutory paranoia. For Ferenczi, the relationship between paranoia and homosexuality involved the following line of reasoning:

"The necessity for manipulation of his rectum by males (physicians) might have stimulated the patient's hitherto latent or sublimated homosexual tendencies."

The paranoia sprang from the resurgence of the homosexual libido, which until then had been successfully sublimated in friendship for the village men and in the patient's important public role. Ferenczi inferred from this that the disappearance of the patient's anal fixation would lead to his recovery; in other words, "the patient might recover his capacity for sublimation (for intellectualised homosexuality in a community sense)." It follows that the anal homosexual drive only has the right to emerge sublimated. The repression of the desiring function of the anus, in Schreber's case as in that of Ferenczi's peasant, is the precondition for their playing an important public role, for preserving their "goods" (in the legal sense), their property, their individuality and their anal cleanliness. Control of the anus is the precondition of taking responsibility for property. The ability to "hold back" or to evacuate the faeces is the necessary moment of the constitution of the self. "To forget oneself" is the most ridiculous and distressing kind of social accident there is, the ultimate outrage to the human person. In contemporary society, total degradation is to live in one's own waste, which only prison or the concentration camp can force us to do. "To forget oneself" is to risk joining up, through the flux of excrement, with the non-differentiation of desire. Homosexuality is connected with the anus, and anality with our civilisation. Albert Moll, a disciple of Krafft-Ebing, wrote in 1891:

"Men with homosexual tendencies have generally masturbated since their earliest age, only instead of rubbing their penis, they introduce any sort of object into their anus."

Note the words "any sort." Certainly he regards whatever the object is as a substitute phallus. But we also find here an acknowledgement that there is an independent anal orgasm, unrelated to ejaculation. This anal orgasm has only brief moments of social existence, on those occasions where it is able to take advantage of a temporary disappearance of guilt-inducing repression.

The anus is so well hidden that it forms the subsoil of the individual, his "fundamental" core . . . Your anus is so totally yours that you must not use it: keep it to yourself. The phallus is to be found everywhere, the popularisation of psychoanalysis having made it the common signifier of all social images . . .

Homosexuality and the Loss of Identity

Sex is the first digit in the French national identity card number. Neurosis consists first of all in the impossibility of knowing (which is not the same thing as innocent ignorance) whether one is male or female, parent or child. And hysteria, too, is the impossibility of knowing whether one is male or female. All homosexuals are more or less hysterical, in fact they share with women a deep identity disorder; or, to be more accurate, they have a confused identity.

Only the phallus dispenses identity; any social use of the anus, apart from its sublimated use, creates the risk of a loss of identity. Seen from behind we are all women; the anus does not practise sexual discrimination. The relation between homosexuality and sexual identity is discussed by Ralph R. Greenson, who starts by recording the fact (which he apparently finds surprising) that when homosexuality comes into the conversation, "patients react then with a feeling of anxiety and generally behave as though I had told them they were homosexual!" We already know that it is impossible to speak innocently of homosexuality, and the patient's neurosis therefore begins in the doctor's paranoia. But what is even more striking is that the "patient" (a word which clearly refers to his supposed passivity) should feel this idea to be incriminating and terrifying:

"If we then proceed with the analysis, the patient will soon describe the feeling of losing a part of himself, some essential though established part, something to do with his sexual identity, with his own answer to the question: who am I? One of my patients expressed this very concisely by saying: 'I have the feeling that you are going to tell me I am neither a man nor a woman, but some kind of monster.'"

The writer distinguishes three stages in the child's "progress" to adulthood:

"I am myself, John
I am myself, John, a boy
I am myself, John a boy, now with the desire to have sexual activity with girls."

The difference in the sexes and the attraction exercised by one sex upon the other are the preconditions of sexual identity:

"The least sexual attraction (of the patient) to a man could throw him into a state of deep panic and endanger his sexual identity."

Let us set aside for the moment the question of the relation between sexual drive and sexual object. The fact remains that the basic precondition of one's sexual identity is the dual certainty of similarity and difference, of narcissism and heterosexuality.

The phallic stage is the identity stage. If you are a boy, you will have relationships with girls. As for your anus, keep it strictly to yourself. Sexual identity is either the certainty of belonging to the master race or the fear of being excluded from it . . .

All homosexuality is concerned with anal eroticism, whatever the differentiations and perverse re-territorialisations to which the Oedipus complex subsequently subjects it. The anus is not a substitute for the vagina: women have one as well as men. The phallus's signifying-discerning function is established at the very same moment that the anus-organ breaks away from its imposed privatisation, in order to take part in the desire race. To reinvest the anus collectively and libidinally would involve a proportional weakening of the great phallic signifier, which dominates us constantly both in the small-scale hierarchies of the family and in the great social hierarchies. The least acceptable desiring operation (precisely because it is the most desublimating one) is that which is directed at the anus.

The Competitive Society and the Rule of the Phallus

Ours is a competitive society: competition between males, between phallus bearers. The anus is excluded from the social field, and the individuals created by the rule of the bourgeoisie believe that everything revolves around the possession of the phallus, the seizure of other people's phalluses or the fear of losing one's own. Freud's reconstruction merely translates and internalises this pitiless rule of the competitive hierarchy. You build better by castrating others; you can only ascend to genitality by trampling over other phallus bearers on the way. You are a phallus bearer only if you are recognised as such by others. Your phallus is constantly threatened: you are in constant fear of losing a phallus which was difficult to win in the first place. No one ever threatens to take away your anus. There is more of a threat in someone disclosing that you too have an anus, that it can be used . . .

The relation of man the phallus bearer to other men can only take place under the rule of competition for a single possible object of sexual activity, woman. Competition "begins" in the family, with the father and the brothers. It "continues" throughout the social process, as it ascends the hierarchy. To own or not to own, to possess a woman or not to possess her; that is the problem which the world around us poses, the "apparent" problem which conceals desiring production . . .

Persecutory delusion is the reconstruction of an imaginary that will enable the subject to defend himself against the emergence of homosexual desire. "We know that with the paranoiac it is precisely the most loved person of his own sex that becomes his persecutor." The jealousy-competition system is opposed to the system of non-exclusive desire, and puts up an increasing number of defensive barriers against it. With regard to relations among men, "the behaviour towards men in general of a man who sees in other men potential love-objects must be different from that of a man who looks upon other men in the first instance as rivals in regard to women." The jealousy-competition system is primitively opposed to the polyvocal system of desire. Homosexual desire also has something of this opposition, but its social use takes the sublimated form of a devotion to "men in general" and the public interest, to use Freud's language. Thus the sublimation of homosexuality can be seen as a public utility. The ambiguity arises with the vagueness of Freud's terms, "social instinctual impulses . . . devotion to the interests of the community," etc. This alleged social sense constitutes precisely the exploitation of homosexual desire and its transformation into a force for social cohesion, the component and necessary counterpart of a jealousy-competition system which, if pushed to its limit, would be an absolute law of the jungle.

Homosexual sublimation provides the solid ideological basis for a constantly threatened social unity. Capitalist society can only organise its relationships around the jealousy-competition system by means of the dual action of repression and sublimation of homosexuality; one underwrites the competitive rule of the phallus, the other the hypocrisy of human relationships. The phallocratic competitive society is based on the repression of desires directed at the anus; the repression of homosexuality is directly related to the jealousy paranoia that constitutes the daily fabric of society, and to the ideology of an integral social whole, the "human community" we live in . . .

. . . If men are in competition with each other, then the sexual relation between men (and here, of course, he forgets to specify that this is repressed and exclusively imaginary) is a relation between phalluses, a comparative and hierarchical relation. Homosexuality thus becomes phallic, in exchange for permitting the repression of desires directed at the anus and thus enabling the phallus to triumph. The release of homosexual desire from the system of the imaginary in which it is exploited has therefore become essential to the destruction of the jealousy-competition system.

Oedipal Reproduction and Homosexuality

Homosexual desire is related in particular to the pre-personal state of desire. To this is linked the fear of loss of identity, as it is state of desire. To this is linked the fear of identity, as it is experienced by the imaginary in the repressed state. The direct manifestation of homosexual desire stands in contrast to the relations of identity, the necessary roles imposed by the Oedipus complex in order to ensure the reproduction of society. Reproductive sexuality is also the reproduction of the Oedipus complex; family heterosexuality guarantees not only the production of children but also (and chiefly) Oedipal reproduction, with its differentiation between parents and children. . .

By becoming a father in turn, the former child hands the Oedipus complex down to his own descendants like the torch of civilisation, and takes his place in the great lineage of Humanity. The absolute need for the Oedipus complex to be reproduced—and not produced—explains why childhood conflicts with the father image are finally resolved by the son's stepping into his father's shoes and founding a new family: "indeed, the whole progress of society rests on the opposition between successive generations." This is how the game of taboo and transgression is historically transmitted. However, Freud adds:

"On the other hand, there is a class of neurotics whose condition is recognisably determined by their having failed in this task."

Their state is conditioned: they must be fully conscious of having failed the historical task assigned to them, so that the social significance of that task may not be weakened. To reduce the revolt of the young to the level of a "generation gap" means to impose a choice dictated by the rule of the double-bind: do as your parents did, or be neurotic. The May 1968 movement in France, for example, was plagued by the need to make a choice imposed by the dominant ideology: either be a responsible politician, or a neurotic individual.

Homosexual neurosis is the backlash to the threat which homosexual desire poses for Oedipal reproduction. Homosexual desire is the ungenerating-ungenerated terror of the family, because it produces itself without reproducing. Every homosexual must thus see himself as the end of the species, the termination of a process for which he is not responsible and which must stop at himself . . .

Homosexual production takes place according to a mode of nonlimitative horizontal relations, heterosexual reproduction according to one of hierarchical succession. In the Oedipal system, every individual knows that it will one day be his turn to occupy the place

already determined by the triangle; according to Freud, this is one of the preconditions of society's progress. Deleuze and Guattari explain that alongside the male-female disjunction which is the constant outcome of filiation, male homosexuality, far from being a product of the Oedipus complex, constitutes a totally different mode of social relation; they are therefore demonstrating that besides the Freudian myth which derives everything from filiation, there is another possible social relation which is not vertical but horizontal.

On the one hand, in so far as he represents the possibility of that repressed relation, the non-sublimated homosexual is a social misfit in the heterosexual family society; Adler (in the above-mentioned work) writes that "the homosexual does not seek a peaceful and harmonious adjustment to society, and his effusive inclination . . . leads him along a path of ceaseless struggle . . . In short, the homosexual has not developed into a partner of human society." Here, "human society" means of course the Freudian model, in which homosexuality can only find a place according to the sublimated Oedipal mode.

On the other hand, the homosexual points the way to another possible form of relationship which we hardly dare call "society". . .

Homosexual Grouping

If the direct expression of homosexual desire were to take a social direction, it would certainly not be in this society, which is based on the domination of anti-homosexual paranoia and sublimation in the form of the heterosexual family system.

The desires directed towards the anus, which are closely connected with homosexual desire, constitute what we shall call a "group" mode of relations as opposed to the usual "social" mode. The anus undergoes the movement of privatisation; the publicising or, to be more precise, the desiring "grouping" [*groupalisation*] of the anus, would cause the collapse of both the sublimating phallic hierarchy and the individual/society double-bind.

Deleuze and Guattari explain that no individual phantasy can be opposed to the collective phantasy, or in other words that the individual himself is a kind of collective phantasy, the fruit of a collectivity based on Oedipal oppression. To deal with homosexuality as an individual problem, as the individual problem, is the surest way to subject it to the Oedipus complex. Homosexual desire is a group desire; it groups the anus by restoring its functions as a desiring bond, and by collectively reinvesting it against a society which has reduced it to the state of a shameful little secret. "Practising" homosexuals are, in a sense, people who have failed their sublimation; they are "incapable of fully assuming the demands which nature and culture may impose on individuals."

To fail one's sublimation is in fact merely to conceive social relations in a different way. Possibly, when the anus recovers its desiring function and the plugging in of organs takes place subject to no rule or law, the group can then take its pleasure in an immediate relation where the sacrosanct difference between public and private, between the individual and the social, will be out of place. We can find traces of this state of primary sexual communism in some of the institutions of the homosexual ghetto, despite all the repressions and guilty reconstructions which these undergo: in Turkish baths, for example, where homosexual desires are plugged in anonymously, in spite of ever-present fears that the police may be present. The grouping of the anus is not open to sublimation, it offers not the slightest crack for the guilty conscience to infiltrate . . .

Homosexual desire becomes homosexuality and falls into the trap of the Oedipus complex because the anal "group" is a threat to the Oedipal "social". The Oedipus myth enables us to understand the need to distinguish between homosexual desire, a primary homosexuality which reveals the lack of differentiation of desire, and a perverse Oedipal homosexuality, all of whose energy goes into reinforcing the Law . . .

CHARLOTTE BUNCH

Charlotte Bunch was a member of The Furies, a lesbian feminist separatist group formed in 1971 that published a journal under that name. The following essay appeared in the first issue of *The Furies*.

Bunch's central argument is classically lesbian-feminist: sexism, the oppression of women by men, is the root of all other oppressions. This oppression is maintained through enforced female dependence and self-hatred. Lesbians challenge these, as they must support themselves and choose those like themselves. She argues that lesbianism is a political choice, because "relationships between men and women are essentially political," specifically relationships of dominance and subordination. "Sexual" lesbianism, however, is not enough. Lesbians manifest their fullest potential when they consciously withdraw from men. "Equality" for lesbians is insufficient to challenge this system; overthrow of heterosexuality is essential for female liberation.

Bunch was one of the first theorists of lesbian feminism. Though she is no longer a separatist, she remains a strong voice for women's activism. She currently teaches Women's Studies at Rutgers University.

LESBIANS IN REVOLT

(1972)

Charlotte Bunch

The development of lesbian-feminist politics as the basis for the liberation of women is our top priority; this article outlines our present ideas. In our society, which defines all people and institutions for the benefit of the rich, white male, the lesbian is in revolt. In revolt because she defines herself in terms of women and rejects the male definitions of how she should feel, act, look, and live. To be a lesbian is to love oneself, woman, in a culture that denigrates and despises women. The lesbian rejects male sexual/political domination; she defies his world, his social organization, his ideology, and his definition of her as inferior. Lesbianism puts women first while the society declares the male supreme. Lesbianism threatens male supremacy at its core. When politically conscious and organized, it is central to destroying our sexist, racist, capitalist, imperialist system.

Lesbianism is a Political Choice

Male society defines lesbianism as a sexual act, which reflects men's limited view of women: they think of us only in terms of sex. They also say lesbians are not real women, so a real woman is one who gets fucked by men. We say that a lesbian is a woman whose sense of self and energies, including sexual energies, center around women—she is woman-identified. The woman-identified-woman commits herself to other women for political, emotional, physical, and economic support. Women are important to her. She is important to herself. Our society demands that commitment from women be reserved for men.

The lesbian, woman-identified-woman, commits herself to women not only as an alternative to oppressive male/female relationships but primarily because she loves women. Whether consciously or not, by her actions, the lesbian has recognized that giving support and love to men over women perpetuates the system that oppresses her. If women do not make a commitment to each other, which includes sexual love, we deny ourselves the love and value traditionally given to men. We accept our second-class status. When women do give primary energies to other women, then it is possible to concentrate fully on building a movement for our liberation.

Woman-identified lesbianism is, then, more than a sexual preference; it is a political choice. It is political because relationships between men and women are essentially political: they involve power and dominance. Since the lesbian actively rejects that relationship and chooses women, she defies the established political system.

Lesbianism, by Itself, is Not Enough

Of course, not all lesbians are consciously woman-identified, nor are all committed to finding common solutions to the oppression they suffer as women and lesbians. Being a lesbian is part of challenging male supremacy, but not the end. For the lesbian or heterosexual woman, there is no individual solution to oppression.

The lesbian may think that she is free since she escapes the personal oppression of the individual male/female relationship. But to the society she is still a woman, or worse, a visible lesbian. On the street, at the job, in the schools, she is treated as an inferior and is at the mercy of men's power and whims. (I've never heard of a rapist who stopped because his victim was a lesbian.) This society hates women who love women, and so, the lesbian, who escapes male dominance in her private home, receives it doubly at the hands of male society; she is harassed, outcast, and shuttled to the bottom. Lesbians must become feminists and fight against woman oppression, just as feminists must become lesbians if they hope to end male supremacy.

U.S. society encourages individual solutions, apolitical attitudes, and reformism to keep us from political revolt and out of power. Men who rule, and male leftists who seek to rule, try to depoliticize sex and the relations between men and women in order to prevent us from acting to end our oppression and challenging their power. As the question of homosexuality has become public, reformists define it as a private question of whom you sleep with in order to sidetrack our understanding of the politics of sex. For the lesbian-feminist, it is not private; it is a political matter of oppression, domination, and power. Reformists offer solutions that make no basic changes in the system that oppresses us, solutions that keep power in the hands of the oppressor. The only way oppressed people end their oppression is by seizing power: people whose rule depends on the subordination of others do not voluntarily stop oppressing others. Our subordination is the basis of male power.

Sexism is the Root of All Oppression

The first division of labor, in prehistory, was based on sex: men hunted, women built the villages, took care of children, and farmed. Women collectively controlled the land, language, culture, and the communities. Men were able to conquer women with the weapons that they developed for hunting when it became clear that women were leading a more stable, peaceful, and desirable existence. We do not know exactly how this conquest took place, but it is clear that the original imperialism was male over female: the male claiming the female body and her service as his territory (or property).

Having secured the domination of women, men continued this pattern of suppressing people, now on the basis of tribe, race, and class. Although there have been numerous battles over class, race, and nation during the past three thousand years, none has brought the liberation of women. While these other forms of oppression must be ended, there is no reason to believe that our liberation will come with the smashing of capitalism, racism, or imperialism today. Women will be free only when we concentrate on fighting male supremacy.

Our war against male supremacy does, however, involve attacking the latter-day dominations based on class, race, and nation. As lesbians who are outcasts from every group, it would be suicidal to perpetuate these man-made divisions among ourselves. We have no heterosexual privileges, and when we publicly assert our Lesbianism, those of us who had them lose many of our class and race privileges. Most of our privileges as women are granted to us by our relationships to men (fathers, husbands, boyfriends) whom we now reject. This does not mean that there is no racism or class chauvinism within us, but we must destroy these divisive remnants of privileged behavior among ourselves as the first step toward their destruction in the society. Race, class, and national oppressions come from men, serve ruling-class white male interests, and have no place in a woman-identified revolution.

Lesbianism is the Basic Threat to Male Supremacy

Lesbianism is a threat to the ideological, political, personal, and economic basis of male supremacy. The lesbian threatens the ideology of male supremacy by destroying the lie about female inferiority, weakness, passivity, and by denying women's "innate" need for men. Lesbians literally do not need men, even for procreation.

The lesbian's independence and refusal to support one man undermines the personal power that men exercise over women. Our rejection of heterosexual sex challenges male domination in its most individual and common form. We offer all women something better than submission to personal oppression. We offer the beginning of the end of collective and individual male supremacy. Since men of all races and classes depend on female support and submission for practical tasks and feeling superior, our refusal to submit will force some to examine their sexist behavior, to break down their own destructive privileges over other humans, and to fight against those privileges in other men. They will have to build new selves that do not depend on oppressing women and learn to live in social structures that do not give them power over anyone.

Heterosexuality separates women from each other; it makes women define themselves through men; it forces women to compete against each other for men and the privilege that comes through men and their social standing. Heterosexual society offers women a few privileges as compensation if they give up their freedom: for example, mothers are "honored," wives or lovers are socially accepted and given some economic and emotional security, a woman gets physical protection on the street when she stays with her man, etc. The privileges give heterosexual women a personal and political stake in maintaining the status quo.

The lesbian receives none of these heterosexual privileges or compensations since she does not accept the male demands on her. She has little vested interest in maintaining the present political system since all of its institutions—church, state, media, health, schools—work to keep her down. If she understands her oppression, she has nothing to gain by supporting white rich male America and much to gain from fighting to change it. She is less prone to accept reformist solutions to women's oppression.

Economics is a crucial part of woman oppression, but our analysis of the relationship between capitalism and sexism is not complete. We know that Marxist economic theory does not sufficiently consider the role of women or lesbians, and we are presently working on this area.

However, as a beginning, some of the ways that lesbians threaten the economic system are clear: in this country, women work for men in order to survive, on the job and in the home. The lesbian rejects this division of labor at its roots; she refuses to be a man's property, to submit to the unpaid labor system of housework and child care. She rejects the nuclear family as the basic unit of production and consumption in capitalist society.

The lesbian is also a threat on the job because she is not the passive/part-time woman worker that capitalism counts on to do boring work and be part of a surplus labor pool. Her identity and economic support do not come through men, so her job is crucial and she cares about job conditions, wages, promotion, and status. Capitalism cannot absorb large numbers of women demanding stable employment, decent salaries, and refusing to accept their traditional job exploitation. We do not understand yet the total effect that this increased job dissatisfaction will have. It is, however, clear that as women become more intent upon taking control of their lives, they will seek more control over their jobs, thus increasing the strains on capitalism and enhancing the power of women to change the economic system.

Lesbians Must Form Our Own Movement to Fight Male Supremacy

Feminist-lesbianism, as the most basic threat to male supremacy, picks up part of the women's liberation analysis of sexism and gives it force and direction. Women's liberation lacks direction now because it has failed to understand the importance of heterosexuality in maintaining male supremacy, and because it has failed to face class and race as real differences in women's behavior and political needs. As long as straight women see lesbianism as a bedroom issue, they hold back the development of politics and strategies that would put an end to male supremacy and they give men an excuse for not dealing with their sexism.

Being a lesbian means ending identification with, allegiance to, dependence on, and support of heterosexuality. It means ending your personal stake in the male world so that you join women, individually and collectively, in the struggle to end your oppression. Lesbianism is the key to liberation and only women who cut their ties to male privilege can be trusted to remain serious in the struggle against male dominance. Those who remain tied to men, individually or in political theory, cannot always put women first. It is not that heterosexual women are evil or do not care about women. It is because the very essense, definition, and nature of heterosexuality is men first. Every woman has experienced that desolation when her sister puts her man first in the final crunch: heterosexuality demands that she do so. As long as women still benefit from heterosexuality, receive its privileges and security, they will at some point have to betray their sisters, especially lesbian sisters who do not receive those benefits.

Women in women's liberation have understood the importance of having meetings and other events for women only. It has been clear that dealing with men divides us and saps our energies, and that it is not the job of the oppressed to explain our oppression to the oppressor. Women also have seen that collectively, men will not deal with their sexism until they are forced to do so. Yet, many of these same women continue to have primary relationships with men individually and do not understand why lesbians find this oppressive. Lesbians cannot grow politically or personally in a situation which denies the basis of our politics: that lesbianism is political, that heterosexuality is crucial to maintaining male supremacy.

Lesbians must form our own political movement in order to grow. Changes that will have more than token effects on our lives will be led by woman-identified lesbians who understand the nature of our oppression and are therefore in a position to end it.

ROBIN MORGAN

By 1973 lesbian politics had proliferated with a vengeance. In the manner of many radical movements, lesbians were divided among themselves between separatists and non-separatists, those who worked with men and those who did not, those who saw lesbian liberation as bound to other issues of social justice and those who wanted to focus on lesbianism alone.

Los Angeles was the site for a 1973 conference hosting fifteen hundred lesbians from across the U.S. The conference promised harmony and political movement, but instead became a site of conflict and anger. Robin Morgan has suggested that the conference was orchestrated by members of the Socialist Workers Party, which had decided to infiltrate gay and lesbian organizations and align them with the SWP. Though the conference voted to bar men, a preoperative transsexual man was allowed to perform for the conference. The only resolution passed was a resolution that no resolutions be passed in the name of the conference.

Robin Morgan was the keynote speaker at the conference, and her position was another source of controversy. Morgan was married and a mother, and many felt that she was therefore not a lesbian and should not be speaking. Morgan rejected that argument, and in the following speech she articulates the lesbian-feminist anger at the gay movement and heterosexual feminists. She does not call for a lesbian vanguard, however, but urges us to understand the need for a unified feminist movement that overcomes the splits that continually strike radical movements. This document is important both for the arguments that Morgan presents and for its portrait of the relationship and controversies between lesbians, heterosexual women, the heterosexual male left, and gay men in the early 1970s.

LESBIANISM AND FEMINISM: SYNONYMS OR CONTRADICTIONS?

(1973)

Robin Morgan

Very Dear Sisters:

It seems important to begin by affirming who, how, and why, we are. We all know the male mass media stereotype of the Women's Movement: "If you've seen one Women's Libber, you've seen 'em all—they each have two heads, a pair of horns, and are fire-spouting, man-hating, neurotic, crazy, frigid, castrating-bitch, aggressive, Lesbian, broom-riding Witches." So I want to start by saying that this shocking stereotype is absolutely *true*. The days of women asking politely for a crumb of human dignity are over. Most men say, "But you've become so *hostile*," to which one good retort is a quote from a nineteenth-century Feminist who said, "First men put us in chains, and then, when we writhe in agony, they deplore our not behaving prettily." Well, enough of that. We are the women that men have warned us about.

That settled, I want to talk about a number of difficult and dangerous themes relating to what others have variously called "The Lesbian-Straight Split," "Lesbian Separatism from Straight Women," and even "The Lesbian-Feminist Split." This is the first speech, talk, what-have-you, that I have ever written down and then *read*—and it may be the last. I have done so because the content can so easily be misunderstood or willfully distorted, because misquoting is a common occurrence, because the risks I will take today are too vital for me to chance such misrepresentation. If there are disagreements with what I have to say, at least let them be based on what I *do say*, and not on some people's out-of-context mis-memory of what they thought I meant. So, for the record, one copy of this talk is lodged at the offices of *The Lesbian Tide*, another with sisters from *Amazon Quarterly*, and still another in a secret safe-deposit box guarded night and day by the spirits of Stanton and Anthony, Joan and Haiviette, and a full collective of Labyris-wielding Amazons. I also want to add that the lack of a question-discussion scene when I finish was decided upon not by me but by the Conference organizers, for lack of time and in light of the necessity to get on with the Agenda.

Before I go any further, I feel it is also necessary to deal with who, how, and why *I* am here. As far back as a month ago, I began hearing a few rumbles of confusion or criticism about my "keynoting" this conference—all from predictable people, and none, of course, expressed directly to my face. "Is she or isn't she?" was their main thrust. "Know anyone who's been to bed with her lately? Well, if we can't *prove* she's a Lesbian, then what right has she to address a Lesbian-Feminist Conference?" Now, such charges hardly devastate me, having been straight-baited before. So. It is credential time once again.

I am a woman. I am a Feminist, a radical Feminist, yea, a militant Feminist. I am a Witch. I identify as a Lesbian because I love the People of Women and certain individual women with my life's blood. Yes, I live with a man—as does my sister Kate Millett. Yes, I am a Mother—as is my sister Del Martin. The man is a Faggot-Effeminist, and we are together the biological as well as the nurturant parents of our child. This confuses a lot of people—it not infrequently confuses us. But there it is. Most of all, I am a Monster—and I am proud.

Now all of the above credentials qualify me, I feel, to speak from concrete experience on: Feminism, Lesbianism, Motherhood, "Gay Male Movements" *versus* Faggot-Effeminist consciousness about women, Tactics for the Women's Revolution, and a Vision of the Female Cosmos. I am an expert with the scars to prove it, having been, in my time, not only straight-baited, but also dyke-baited, red-baited, violence-baited, mother-baited, and artist-baited. As you can see, the above credentials further qualify me for being an excellent target, available not only to the male rulers but also to any women just dying to practice—even on a sister.

But, finally, to the subject. In order to talk intelligently about the so-called "Split," it is necessary to recap history a little. In the early days of the current Women's Movement, many of us were a bit schizoid. The very first consciousness-raising session I ever went to, for example, gave me the warning. We were talking about sexuality, and I described myself as a bisexual (this was even before the birth of the first Gay Liberation Front, and long before bisexual became a naughty or cop-out word—besides, it did seem an accurate way of describing my situation). Every woman in the room moved, almost imperceptibly, an inch or so away from me. Wow, I thought. It was not the last time I was to have such an articulate reaction.

Later, with the creation of GLF, a few of us Jewish Mother types spent a lot of time running back and forth between the two movements, telling the straight women that the Lesbians weren't ogres and telling the Lesbians that the straight women weren't creeps. Simultaneously, the intense misogyny coming against Lesbians from gay men drove many women out of the "gay movement" and into the Women's Movement. There was a brief and glorious sisterhood-glazed honeymoon period among all women in our Movement. Then, those contradictions began. For example, a personal one: I had announced my Lesbian identification in *The New York Times* (which is a fairly public place, after all) in 1968, before the first GLF had been founded. Then, in 1970, one group of Radicalesbians in New York said to me, "Don't you dare call yourself a Lesbian—you live with a man and you have a child." Now, while I might (defensively) argue the low-consciousness logic of this, since statistically most Lesbians are married to men and have children, I had nonetheless learned one important thing from all my previous years in the Left: *guilt*. So all my knee-jerk reflexes went into action, and I obeyed. Six months later, another group of Radicalesbians confronted me. "We notice you've stopped calling yourself a Lesbian," they said. "What's the matter—you gone back in the closet? You afraid?" Meanwhile, the monosexual straight women were still inching away from my presence. Wow, I thought, repeatedly.

The lines began to be drawn, thick, heavy. Friedan trained her cannon on "the Lesbian Menace." (In a show of consistent terror and hatred of Lesbians, and indeed of women, one might say, she only recently announced in *The New York Times* that the Lesbians and radical feminists in the Movement were CIA infiltrators. We met her attack with a firm *political* counter-attack in the press, never descending to a level of personal vilification or giving the media the cat-fight which they were trying to foment.) In 1970, backlash began, starting in NOW and infecting radical feminist groups as well. The bigotry was intense and wore many faces: outright hatred and revulsion of Lesbian women; "experimentation"—using a Lesbian for an interesting experiment and then dumping her afterward; curiosity about the freaks; dismissal of another woman's particular pain if it did not fall within the "common" experience, and many other examples.

Meanwhile, Lesbians, reeling from the hatred expressed by the gay male movement and the fear expressed by the Women's Liberation Movement, began to organize separately. Of course, a great many Lesbians had been in the Women's Movement since its beginning—a great many had, in fact, begun it. These included some women who were active in Daughters of Bilitis under other names, not only to keep jobs and homes and custody of their children, but also so as not to "embarrass" NOW, which they had built. In addition, a great many formerly heterosexual or asexual women were declaring themselves Lesbians, as they found the support to "Come Out" of their kitchens and communes as well as their closets. Some women *were* pressured, not necessarily, although certainly sometimes, by Lesbians. The pressure came mostly from confusion, contradictions, pulls in different directions, paths which each might have led to a united Feminism but which the Man exploited into warring factions; he was aided, of course, by the internecine hostility of any oppressed people—tearing at each other is painful, but it is after all safer than tearing at the real enemy. Oh, people *did* struggle sincerely, hour upon hour of struggle to understand and relate—but the flaw still widened to a crack and then to a split, created by our collective false consciousness. We are now teetering on the brink of an abyss, but one very different from what we have been led to expect.

At present, there are supposedly two factions. On one side, those labeled heterosexual, bisexual, asexual, and celibate women. On the other, those labeled Lesbians. Not that the latter group is monolithic—far from it, although monosexual straight women can, in their fear, try to hide their bigotry behind such a belief. No, there are some Lesbians who work politically with gay men; some work politically with straight men; some work politically with other Lesbians; some work politically only with *certain* other Lesbians (age, race, class distinctions); some work politically with *all* Feminists—(Lesbians, heterosexuals, etc.); and some, of course, don't work politically at all. As Laurel has pointed out in an incisive and witty article in the current *Amazon Quarterly*, there are sub-sub-sub-divisions, between gay women, Lesbians, Lesbian-Feminists, dykes, dyke-feminists, dyke-separatists, Old Dykes, butch dykes, bar dykes, and killer dykes. In New York, there were divisions between Political Lesbians and Real Lesbians and Nouveau Lesbians. Hera help a woman who is unaware of these fine political distinctions and who wanders into a meeting for the first time, thinking she maybe has a right to be there because she likes women.

Still, the same energy which created *The Ladder* almost twenty years ago (and we mourn its demise last year and we all hope for its resurrection this summer)—that same energy is now evident in the dynamism of *The Lesbian Tide*, the dedication to the fine points of struggle and contradiction in *Ain't I A Woman?*, in the analytical attempts of *The Furies*, and in the aesthetic excellence and serious political probings of the new *Amazon Quarterly*, to name only a few such publications. That energy, contorted into hiding and working under false pretenses for so long, has exploded in the beautiful and organized anger of groups like Lesbian Mothers (begun in San Francisco and now spreading across the country), to defend and protect the rights of the Lesbian and her children, and, by extension, to stand as guardian for all women who, the moment we embrace our own strength, rage, and politics, face the danger of having our children seized from us physically by the patriarchy which daily attempts to kidnap their minds and souls. The development of this consciousness, so tied in with ancient Mother-Right, is, I think, of profound importance to Lesbian Mothers, all Mothers, indeed all women—it is one of the basic building blocks in our creation of a Feminist Revolution. And again, that energy, which drove my sister Ivy Bottini to almost single-handedly keep the New York NOW chapter afloat for several years (despite the ministrations of Betty Friedan) has now impelled her and other sisters to create Wollstonecraft, Inc., here in Los Angeles, the first major overground national women's publishing house. And again, that energy, in Shameless Hussy Press, Diana Press, Momma, and other small radical Lesbian-Feminist presses. That woman-loving-woman energy, freed into open expression and in fact into totally new forms of relationship *by the existence of the Feminist Movement*, has exploded in marches and demonstrations and dances and films and theater groups and crisis centers and so on and on—a whole affirmative new world within the world of women.

And yet.

A funny thing happened to me on the way to the Feminist Revolution: both Betty Friedan and Rita Mae Brown condemned me for being a "man-hater." Both *Ms.* magazine and *The Furies* began to call for alliances with men, *The Furies* at one point implying that Lesbians should band together with gay *and* straight males (preferably working-class) in a coalition against the enemy: straight women. Indeed, in one by now infamous statement, Rita Mae declared that Lesbians were the only women capable of really loving men. Now of course this did come as a shock to many a Lesbian who was obviously under the misguided impression that one had become a Lesbian because she in fact loved *women*, and was indifferent-to-enraged on the subject of men. But now that the "correct line" had fallen from heaven, one was supposed to penitently dismiss such counter-revolutionary attitudes, learning to look at them *and* other women who still clung to them with contempt. One was also supposed to place issues such as the Vietnam War, political coalition with men, warmed-over Marxian class analyses, life-style differences, and other such un-lavender herrings in the path, in order to divide and polarize women. While doing all this, one was further supposed to hoist the new banner of the vanguard. You know, the vanguard—Lenin leading the shlemiels.

Before we get into vanguarditis, we have to backtrack a little, take some Dramamine for our nausea, and talk about men—and male influence, and male attempts to destroy the united Women's Movement. This is such an old subject that it bores and depresses me to once more have to wade through it. I feel that "man-hating" is an honorable and viable *political* act, that the oppressed have a right to a class-hatred against the class that is oppressing them. And although there are exceptions (as in everything), i.e., men who are trying to be traitors to their own male class, most men cheerfully affirm their deadly class privileges and power.

And I *hate* that *class*. I wrote my "Goodbye To All That" to the male Left in 1970—and thought I was done with it. Del Martin wrote her now classic article "If That's All There Is" as a farewell to the male gay movement soon after—and said it all again. We were both touchingly naive if we thought that sufficient.

Because there is now upon us yet another massive wave of male interference, and it is coming, this time, from *both* gay men *and* their straight brothers. Boys will be boys, the old saying goes—and boys *will* indulge in that little thing called male bonding—and all boys in a patriarchal culture have more options and power than do any women.

Gay men first, since they were the ones we all thought were incipient allies with women, because of their own oppression under sexism. I won't go into the facts or the manners of the male-dominated Gay Liberation Movement, since Del did all that superbly and since most women have left the "Gay Movement" a long time ago. But I will, for the sake of those sisters still locked into indentured servitude there, run through a few more recent examples of the "new changing high consciousness about male supremacy" among gay organizations and gay male heavies. Are we to forgive and forget the Gay Activist Alliance dances only a few months ago (with, as usual, a token ten percent attendance by women), at which New York GAA showed stag movies of nude men raping nude women? Are we to forgive and forget the remark of gay leader and "martyr" Jim Fouratt, who told Susan Silverwoman, a founder of New York GLF, that she could not represent GLF at a press conference because she saw herself too much as a woman, as a Feminist? Are we to forgive the editors of the gay male issue of *Motive* magazine for deliberately setting women against women, deliberately attempting to exacerbate what they see as the Lesbian-Straight Split, deliberately attempting to divide and conquer? Are we to forgive the following:

Once, when I was telling one of the Motive editors, you Roy Eddey, about the estimated nine million Wicca (witches) who were burned to death during the Middle Ages—something that appeared to be news to you—you paused for a moment, and then asked me, "But how many of those nine million women were actually lesbians?" For a moment, I missed your meaning completely as a variety of sick jokes raced through my mind: How many of the six million Jews were Zionists; how many of the napalmed Indochinese babies could be said to have lived outside the nuclear family?

Then it hit me: you had actually expressed a particle of your intense hatred for all women by asking how many of the nine million were lesbians, so that you would know how many of these victims to mourn, because YOU DIDN'T OBJECT TO WHAT WAS DONE TO THE OTHER WOMEN! This is as close as I have ever heard a man come to saying in so many words that he didn't object to men torturing and incinerating millions of women (provided only that they met his standards of burnability).

—this is a quote from the second issue of *Double–F, A Magazine of Effeminism*, in which even the faggot-effeminist *males* declare *their* Declaration of Independence from Gay Liberation and all other Male Ideologies.

Or are we, out of the compassion in which we have been positively forced to *drown* as women, are we yet again going to defend the male, supremacist, yes obscenity of male tranvestitism? How many of us will try to explain away—or permit into our organizations, even—men who deliberately *re*-emphasize gender roles, and who parody female oppression and suffering as "camp"? Maybe it seems that we, in our "liberated" combat boots and jeans aren't being mocked. No? Then is it "merely" our mothers, and *their* mothers, who had no other choice, who wore hobbling dresses and torture stiletto heels to survive, to keep jobs, or to keep husbands because *they* themselves could *get* no jobs? No, I will not call a male "she"; thirty-two years of suffering in this androcentric society, and of surviving, have earned me the name "woman"; one walk down the street by a male transvestite, five minutes of his being hassled (which *he* may enjoy), and then he dares, he *dares* to think he understands our pain? No, in our mothers' names and in our own, we must not call him sister. We know what's at work when whites wear blackface; the same thing is at work when men wear drag.

Last night, at this Conference's *first* session, women let a man divide us, pit woman against woman and, in the process, exploit the entire Lesbian Conference to become the center of attention and boost his opportunistic career.

The same man who, four years ago, tried to pressure a San Francisco Lesbian into letting him rape her; the same man who singlehandedly divided and almost destroyed the San Francisco Daughters of Bilitis Chapter; the same man who, when personally begged by women *not* to attend this Conference, replied that if he were kept out he would bring Federal suit against these women on the charges of "discrimination and criminal conspiracy to discriminate"—this is the same man some women defended last night.

Kate Millett pled for peace. What about the women who had a right to a peaceful conference for *women*, Kate, with no past *or* present male here? A true pacifist should be consistent, and preferably on the side of her own people.

The organizers of the Conference pled ignorance: that they didn't realize the issue would be "divisive" of women when they invited him! Yet they *knew* his San Francisco history. And it is too late for such ignorance. The same fine sisters who have for months worked day and night to create and organize this event, have—in one stroke, inviting this man—*directly* insulted their San Francisco sisters he previously tried to destroy, and indirectly insulted every woman here. I'm afraid they owe us a public apology on the grounds of divisiveness alone.

My point is that if even *one* woman last night felt that he should go, that should have been sufficient. Where The Man is concerned, we must not be separate fingers but one fist.

If transvestite or transsexual males are oppressed, then let them band together and organize against that oppression, instead of leeching off women who have spent entire lives *as women* in women's bodies.

And I will not name this man who claims to be a Feminist and then threatens women with Federal criminal charges; I will not give him the publicity he and his straight male theatrical manager are so greedy for, at our expense. But let him sue *me* if he dare, for *I* charge *him* as an opportunist, an infiltrator, and a destroyer—with the mentality of a rapist. And you women at this Conference know who he is. Now. You can let him into your workshops—or you can *deal* with him.

And what of the straight men, the rulers, the rapists, the right-on radicals? What of the men of the Socialist Workers' Party, for example, who a short two years ago refused membership to all homosexual people on the grounds that homosexuality was a decadent sickness, an evil of capitalism, a perversion that must be rooted out in all "correct socialist thinking"—who now, upon opportunistically seeing a large movement out there with a lot of bodies to organize like pawns into their purposes, speedily change their official line (but not their central-committee attitude on homosexuality), and send "their" women out to teach these poor sheep some real politics? Are we to forgive, forget, ignore? Or struggle endlessly through precious energy-robbing hours with these women, because they *are* after all *women, sisters*, even if they're collaborating with a politics and a party based on straight white male rule? We must save our struggle for elsewhere. But it hurts—*because* they are women.

And this is the tragedy. That the straight men, the gay men, the transvestite men, the male *politics*, the male styles, the male attitudes toward sexuality are being arrayed once more against us, and they are, in fact, making new headway this time, using women as their standard-bearers.

Every woman here knows in her gut the vast differences between her sexuality and that of any patriarchally trained male's—gay or straight. That has, in fact, always been a source of *pride* to the Lesbian community, even in its greatest suffering. That the emphasis on genital sexuality, objectification, promiscuity, non-emotional involvement, and tough invulnerability, were the male style, and that we, as women, placed greater trust in love, sensuality, humor, tenderness, strength, commitment. Then what but *male* style is happening when we accept the male transvestite who chooses to wear women's dresses and makeup, but sneer at the female who is still forced to wear them for survival? What is happening when "Street Fighting Woman," a New York all-woman bar band, dresses in black leather and motorcycle chains, and sings and plays a lot of Rolling Stones, including the high priest of sadistic cock-rock Jagger's racist, sexist song "Brown Sugar"—with lines like, "Old slaver knows he's doin' all right/hear him whip the women just about midnight/Hey, Brown Sugar, how come you taste so good?". What is happening when, in a mid-west city with a strong Lesbian-Feminist community, men raped a woman in the university dormitory, and murdered her by the repeated ramming of a broom-handle into her vagina until she died of massive internal hemorrhage—and the Lesbian activists there can't relate to taking any political action pertaining to the crime because, according to one of them, there was no evidence that the victim was a Lesbian? But the same community can, at a women's dance less than a week later, proudly play Jagger's recorded voice singing "Midnight Rambler"—a song which glorifies the Boston Strangler.

What has happened when women, in escaping the patriarchally enforced role of noxious "femininity" adopt instead the patriarch's *own* style, to get drunk and swaggering just like one of the boys, to write of tits and ass as if a sister were no more than a collection of chicken parts, to spit at the lifetime commitment of other Lesbian couples, and refer to them contemptuously as "monogs"? For the record, the anti-monogamy line originated with men, Leftist men, Weathermen in particular, in order to guilt-trip the women in their "alternative culture" into being more available victims of a dominance-based gang-rape sexuality. And from where but the male Left, male "hip" culture have we been infected with the obsession to anti-intellectualism and downward mobility? Genuinely poor people see no romanticism in their poverty; those really forced into illiteracy hardly glorify their condition. The oppressed want *out* of that condition—and it is contemptuous of real people's pain to parasitically imitate it, and hypocritical to play the more-oppressed-than-thou game instead of ordering our lives so as to try and meet our basic and just needs, so that we can get on with the more important but often forgotten business of making a Feminist Revolution.

What *about* the life-style cop-out? The one invented by two straight white young males, Jerry Rubin and Abbie Hoffman, for the benefit of other unoppressed straight white young males? What about the elite isolation, the incestuous preoccupation with one's own clique or group or commune, one's own bar/dance/tripping, which led one Lesbian to announce that the revolution has already been won, that she isn't compelled, like the rest of us, to live in a man's world anymore? As Jeanne Cordova has written in *The Lesbian Tide*, "An example of these politics is Jill Johnston's calling for tribes of women capable of sustaining themselves independent of the male species. How very beautiful! Truth, justice, and the womanly way! How very unreal." And Cordova is right in pointing out that this is the "personal solution" error—the deadly trap into which so many heterosexual women have fallen. It should be obvious how painfully much everyone wants even a little happiness, peace, joy, in her life—and should have that right. But to remain convinced that your own personal mirage is a real oasis while a sandstorm is rising in the desert is both selfish and suicidal. There is a war going on, sisters. Women are being killed. And the rapist doesn't stop to ask whether his victim is straight or Lesbian.

But the epidemic of male style among women doesn't stop there. No, it is driving its *reformist* wedge through our ranks as well: women breaking their backs working for McGovern (only to have him laugh in their faces); women in the Lesbian community especially breaking their backs to elect almost invariably *male* gay legislators, or lobbying to pass bills which will, in practice, primarily profit *men*. Myself, I have never been able to get excited over tokenism, whether it was Margaret Chase Smith in the Senate or Bernadine Dohrn in the Weather Underground, let alone a few women to give GAA a good front (which women, by the way, are finally getting wise to, and leaving), or to serve as periodic good niggers for the cheap porn reportage of *The Advocate, Gay, Gay Sunshine*, and the like.

Susan Silverwoman, a New York-based Lesbian Feminist active for years in the Women's Movement, and at one time in GLF, has written a moving and courageous paper called "Finding Allies: The Lesbian Dilemma" which is available for $.25 by writing to Labyris Books, 33 Barrow Street, New York City 10014. In it she writes, "Men have traditionally maintained power over women by keeping us separated. Gay men capitalized on the split between feminists and lesbians by suggesting and insisting that we [Lesbians] were somehow better, basically different from straight women . . . Gay men preferred to think of us not as women, but as female gay men." She goes on to say, "It is imperative that we identify with the total feminist issue . . . if we continue to define straight women as the enemy, rather than sisters . . . we rob from ourselves a movement which must be part of ourselves. We are choosing false allies when we align politically with gay men who can never understand the female experience and who, as men, have a great deal of privilege to lose by a complete liberation of women. Whether or not straight feminists come out, as potential lesbians they are far more likely to understand our experience."

Language itself is one powerful barometer of influence. More and more women use Lesbian proudly in self-description, calling on the history of that word, dating from an age and an island where women were great artists and political figures. Why do *any* of us still use "gay" to describe ourselves at all—that trivializing, male-invented, and male-defining term? If we are serious about our politics, then we must be responsible about the ways in which we communicate them to others, creating new language when necessary to express new concepts. But the sloppy thinking and lazy rhetoric of the straight and gay male movements pollutes our speech, and when Jill Johnston in one column claims Betty Friedan as a Lesbian and then, a few months later, after Friedan's attack in the *The New York Times*, calls Friedan a man—I, for one, get confused. And angry. Because the soggy sentimentality of the first statement and the rank stupidity of the second *mean nothing politically*. The point is, very regrettably, that Friedan *is* a woman. And can stand as one of many examples of the insidious and devastating effect of male *politics*.

There *is* a war going on. And people get damaged in a war, badly damaged. Our casualties are rising. To say that any woman has escaped—or can escape—damage in this day on this planet is to march under the self-satisfied flags of smug false consciousness. And get gunned down anyway for one's pains.

Personally, I detest "vanguarditis." I never liked it in the Left, and I find it especially distasteful weaseling its way into the Women's Movement. I think that if anything like a "vanguard" exists at all, it continually shifts and changes from group to group within a movement, depending on the specific strategies and contradictions that arise at given times, and on which groups are best equipped and placed to meet and deal with them—when and if called for by the movement as a *whole*. The responsibility of a vanguard, by the way, is to speak from, for, and to *all* of the people who gave it birth. Lesbian Nation cannot be the Feminist solution, much less a vanguard, when it ignores these facts. And it won't do to blame the straight women who wouldn't cooperate—after all, it is the *vanguard's* responsibility as leadership to hear messages in the silence or even hostility of all its people, and to reply creatively, no matter how lengthy or painful that dialogue is. A willingness to do this—and that to act on the message—is what *makes* the vanguard the vanguard.

I don't like more-radical-than-thou games any better than more-oppressed-than-thou games. I don't like credentials games, intimidation-between-women games, or "you are who you sleep with" games. I don't like people being judged by their class background, their sexual preference, their race, choice of religion, marital status, motherhood or rejection of it, or any other vicious standard of categorization. I hate such judgments in the male power system, and I hate them in the Women's Movement. If there must be judgments at all, let them be not on where a woman is coming *from*, but on what she is moving *toward*; let them be based on her seriousness, her level of risk, her commitment, her endurance.

And by those standards, yes, there could be a Lesbian vanguard. I think it would be women like Barbara Grier and Phyllis Lyons and Del Martin and Sten Russell, and others like them who, at the height of the fifties' McCarthyism, stood up and formed a Lesbian civil-rights movement, and whose courage, commitment, and staying power are ignored by the vulgar minds of certain younger women, newly Lesbian from two months or two years back, who presume to dismiss such brave women as "oldies" or "life-style straights" or, again, "hopeless monogs."

There is a new smell of fear in the Women's Movement. It is in the air when groups calling themselves killer-dyke-separatists trash Lesbian Feminists who work with that anathema, straight women—trash these Lesbian Feminists as "pawns, dupes, and suckers-up to the enemy." It is in the air when Peggy Allegro writes in *Amazon Quarterly* that "at a certain point, flags can begin to dominate people. For instance, women are oppressed by the flag of the freak feminist dyke. There are all kinds of rules, shoulds and shouldn'ts, in this community, that result because of the image's power. We must beware the tendency to merely impose a new hierarchy . . . a new ideal ego image to persecute people." It is in the air when ultra-egalitarianism usurps organic collectivity, or when one woman is genuinely scared to confront another about the latter's use of "chick" to describe her lover. It was in the air when I trembled to wrench the Stones' record from a phonograph at a women's dance, and when I was accused of being up-tight, a bring-down, puritanical, draggy, and, of course, doubtless, a hung-up man-hating "straight" *for doing that*. The words are familiar, but the voices used to be male. And the smell of fear was in my gut, writing this talk, and is in my nostrils now, risking the saying of these things, taking a crazy leap of faith that our own shared and potentially ecstatic womanhood will bind us across all criticism—and that a lot more Feminists in the Lesbian Movement will come out of their closets today.

Because polarization does exist. Already. And when I first thought about this talk, I wanted to call for unity. But I cannot. I am struck dumb before the dead body of a broomhandle-raped and murdered woman, and anyway, my voice wouldn't dent the rape-sound of the Rolling Stones. So instead, my purpose in this talk here today is to call for further polarization, but on different grounds.

Not the Lesbian-Straight Split, nor the Lesbian-Feminist Split, but the Feminist-Collaborator Split.

The war outside, between women and male power, is getting murderous; they are trying to kill us, literally, spiritually, infiltratively. It is time, past time, we drew new lines and knew which women were serious, which women were really committed to loving women (whether that included sexual credentials or not), and, on the other side, which women thought Feminism meant pure fun, or a chance to bring back a body count to their male Trot party leaders, or those who saw Feminist Revolution as any particular life-style, correct class line, pacifist-change-your-head-love-daisy-chain, or easy lay. We know that the personal is political. But if the political is *solely* personal, then those of us at the barricades will be in big trouble. And if a woman isn't there when the crunch comes—and it is coming—then I for one won't give a damn whether she is at home in bed with a woman, a man, or her own wise fingers. If she's in bed at all at that moment, others of us are in our coffins. I'd appreciate the polarization now instead of then.

I am talking about the rise of attempted gynocide. I am talking about survival. Susan Stein, a Lesbian-Feminist with a genius for coining aphorisms, has said, "Lesbianism is in danger of being co-opted by Lesbians." Lesbians are a minority. Women are a majority. And since it is awfully hard to be a Lesbian without being a woman first, the choice seems pretty clear to me.

There are a lot of women involved in that war out there, most of them not even active in the Women's Movement yet. They include the hundreds of thousands of housewives who created and sustained the meat boycott in the most formidable show of women's strength in recent years. Those women, Feminists or not, were moving *because* of Feminism—such a nationwide women's action would have been thought impossible five years ago. They are mostly housewives, and mothers, and heterosexuals. There are asexual and celibate women out there, too, who are tired of being told that they are sick. Because this society has said that everybody should fuck a lot, and too many people in the Women's Movement have echoed, "Yeah, fuck with women or even with men, but for god's sake *fuck* or you're *really* perverted." And there are also genuine functioning bisexuals out there. I'm not referring to people who have used the word as a coward's way to avoid dealing honestly with homosexuality, or to avoid commitment. We all know *that* ploy. I agree with Kate Millett when she says that she "believes that all people are inherently bisexual"—and I also know that to fight a system one must dare to identify with the *most* vulnerable aspect of one's oppression—and women are put in prison for being Lesbians, not bisexuals or heterosexuals *per se*. So that is why I have identified myself as I have—in the *Times* in 1968 and here today, although the Man will probably want to get *me* for hating *men* before he gets me for loving *women*.

We have enough trouble on our hands. Isn't it way past time that we stopped *settling* for blaming each other, stopped blaming heterosexual women and middle-class women and married women and Lesbian women and white women and *any* women for the structure of sexism, racism, classism, and ageism, that no woman is to blame for because we have none of us had the power to create those structures. They are patriarchal creations, not ours. And if we are collaborating with any of them for any reason, we must begin to stop. The time is short, and the self-indulgence is getting dangerous. We must stop settling for anything less than we deserve.

All women have a right to each other as women. All women have a right to our sense of ourselves as a People. All women have a right to live with and make love with *whom we choose when we choose*. We have a right to bear and raise children if we choose, and *not* to if we don't. We have a right to freedom and yes, power. Power to change our entire species into something that might for the first time approach being human. We have a right, each of us, to a Great Love.

And this is the final risk I will take here today. By the right to a great love I don't mean romanticism in the Hollywood sense, and I don't mean a cheap joke or cynical satire. *I mean a great love*—a committed, secure, nurturing, sensual, aesthetic, revolutionary, holy, ecstatic love. That need, *that right*, is at the heart of our revolution. It is in the heart of the woman stereotyped by others as being a butch bar dyke who cruises for a cute piece, however much she herself might laugh at the Lesbian couple who have lived together for decades. It is in their hearts, too. It is in the heart of the woman who jet-sets from one desperate heterosexual affair to another. It is in the heart of a woman who wants to find—or stay with—a man she can love and be loved by in what she has a right to demand are non-oppressive ways. It is in the heart of every woman here today, if we dare admit it to ourselves and *recognize* it in each other, and in *all* women. It is each her right. Let no one, female or male, of whatever sexual or political choice, dare deny that, for to deny it is to *settle*. To deny it is to speak with the words of the real enemy.

If we can open ourselves *to* ourselves and each other, as women, only then can we begin to fight for and create, in fact *reclaim*, not Lesbian Nation or Amazon Nation—let alone some false State of equality—but a real Feminist Revolution, a proud gynocratic *world* that runs on the power of women. Not in the male sense of power, but in the sense of a power plant—producing energy. And to each, that longing for, the right to, great love, filled-in reality, for all women, and children, and men and animals and trees and water and all life, an exquisite diversity in unity. That world breathed and exulted on this planet some twelve thousand years ago, before the patriarchy arose to crush it.

If we risk this task then, our pride, our history, our culture, our past, our future, all vibrate before us. Let those who will dare, begin.

In the spirit of that task, I want to end this talk in a strange and new, although time-out-of-mind-ancient manner. Earlier, I "came out" in this talk as a Witch, and I did not mean that as a solely political affiliation. I affirm the past and the present spirit of the Wicca (the Anglo-Saxon word for witch, or wise woman), affirm it not only in the smoke of our nine million martyrs, but also in the thread of *real* woman-power and *real* Goddess-worship dating back beyond Crete to the dawn of the planet. In the ruling male culture, they have degraded our ritual by beginning conferences and conventions with a black-coated male, sometimes in full priestly drag, nasally droning his stultifying pronouncements to the assemblage. Let us reclaim our own for ourselves, then, and in that process, also extend an embrace to those Lesbians who, because they go to church, are held in disrepute by counterculture Lesbians. And to those women of *whatever* sexual identification who kneel in novenas or murmur in quite moments to, oh irony, a male god for alleviation of the agony caused by male supremacy.

The short passage I am about to read is from The Charge of the Goddess, still used reverently in living Wiccan Covens, usually spoken by the High Priestess at the initiation of a new member. I ask that each woman join hands with those next to her.

I ask your respect for the oldest faith known to human beings, and for the ecstatic vision of freedom that lies hidden in each of your own precious, miraculous brains.

Listen to the words of the Great Mother. She says:

"Whenever ye have need of anything, once in the month, and better it be when the moon is full, then shall ye assemble in some secret place . . . to these I will teach things that are yet unknown. AND YE SHALL BE FREE FROM ALL SLAVERY . . . Keep pure your highest ideal; strive ever toward it. LET NAUGHT STOP YOU NOR TURN YOU ASIDE . . . Mine is the cup of the wine of life and the cauldron of Cerridwen . . . I am the Mother of all living, and my love is poured out upon the Earth . . . I am the beauty of the Green Earth, and the White Moon among the stars, and the Mystery of the Waters, AND THE DESIRE IN THE HEART

OF WOMAN ... Before my face, let thine innermost divine self be enfolded in the raptures of the Infinite ... Know the Mystery, that if that which thou seekest thou findest not within thee, thou wilt never find it without thee ... For behold, I HAVE BEEN WITH THEE FROM THE BEGINNING. And I await you now."

Dear Sisters,
As We in the Craft say, Blessed Be. ♀

THE EFFEMINIST
MANIFESTO

By claiming that gay oppression was the result of the identification of gays with women, and that therefore gay men were equally oppressed with women, some gays deliberately avoided questions of male power and privilege within "gay and lesbian" organizations. Others took feminism more seriously, analyzing their position as men as well as their oppression as gays.

Among the latter were a group of men who named themselves Effeminists. The authors of the following manifesto—Steven Dansky, John Knoebel, and Kenneth Pitchford—distanced themselves from gay liberation in terms analogous to those of lesbian feminists. They distinguish effeminate men, who pay the price for their cultural equation with women, from gays who do not otherwise challenge contemporary models of masculinity; but they note that even effeminate men have the option of participating in patriarchy, and so they refuse to claim for themselves the same oppression as women. Their radicalism is unique in the history of lesbian and gay politics. The manifesto appeared in *Double-F: a magazine of effeminism.*

THE EFFEMINIST MANIFESTO

(1973)

Steven Dansky, John Knoebel, and Kenneth Pitchford

We, the undersigned Effeminists of DOUBLE–F hereby invite all like minded men to join with us in making our Declaration of Independence from Gay Liberation & all other Male Ideologies by unalterably asserting our stand of revolutionary commitment to the following Thirteen Principles that form the quintessential substance of our politics:

Principles of Revolutionary Effeminism

On the oppression of women.

1. **SEXISM.** All women are oppressed by all men, including ourselves. This systematic oppression is called sexism.

2. **MALE SUPREMACY.** Sexism itself is the product of male supremacy, which produces all the other forms of oppression that patriarchal societies exhibit: racism, classism, ageism, economic exploitation, ecological imbalance.

3. **GYNARCHISM.** Only that revolution that strikes at the root of all oppression can end any and all of its forms. That is why we are gynarchists; that is, we are among those who believe that women will seize power from the patriarchy and, thereby, totally change life on this planet as we know it.

4. **WOMEN'S LEADERSHIP.** Exactly how women will go about seizing power is no business of ours, being men. But as effeminate men oppressed by masculinist standards, we ourselves have a stake in the destruction of the patriarchy, and thus we *must* struggle with the dilemma of being partisans—as effeminists—of a revolution opposed to us—as men. To conceal our partisanship and remain inactive for fear of offending would be despicable; to act independently of women's leadership or to tamper with questions which women will decide would be no less despicable. Therefore, we have a duty to take sides, to struggle to change ourselves—but also, necessarily, to act.

On the oppression of effeminate men.

5. **MASCULINISM.** Faggots and all effeminate men are oppressed by the patriarchy's systematic enforcement of masculinist standards, whether these standards are expressed as physical, mental, emotional, or sexual stereotypes of what is desirable in a man.

6. **EFFEMINISM.** Our purpose is to urge all such men as ourselves (whether celibate, homosexual, or heterosexual) to become traitors to the class of men by uniting in a movement of Revolutionary Effeminism so that collectively we can struggle to change ourselves from non-masculinists into anti-masculinists and begin attacking those aspects of the patriarchal system that most directly oppress us.

7. **PREVIOUS MALE IDEOLOGIES.** Three previous attempts by men to create a politics for fighting oppression have failed because of their incomplete analysis: the Male Left, Male Liberation, and Gay Liberation. These and other formulations, such as sexual libertarianism and the counter-culture, are all tactics for preserving power in men's hands by pretending to struggle for change. We specifically reject a carry-over from one or more of these earlier ideologies—the damaging combination of ultra-egalitarianism, anti-leadership, anti-technology, and downward mobility. All are based on a politics of guilt and a hypocritical attitude toward power which prevents us from developing skills urgently needed in our struggle and which confuses the competence needed for revolutionary work with the careerism of those who seek personal accommodation within the patriarchal system.

8. **COLLABORATORS AND CAMP-FOLLOWERS.** Even we effeminate men are given an option by the patriarchy: to become collaborators in the task of keeping women in their place. Faggots, especially, are offered a subculture by the patriarchy which is designed to keep us oppressed and also increase the oppression of women. This subculture includes a combination of anti-woman mimicry and self-mockery known as camp which, with its trivializing effect, would deny us any chance of awakening to our own suffering, the expression of which is called madness by the patriarchy, but which can be recognized as revolutionary sanity by the oppressed.

9. **SADO-MASCULINITY: ROLE PLAYING AND OBJECTIFICATION.** The Male Principle, as exhibited in the last ten thousand years, is chiefly characterized by an appetite for objectification, role-playing, and sadism. First, the masculine preference for thinking as opposed to feeling encourages men to regard other people as things, and to use them accordingly. Second, inflicting pain upon people and animals has come to be deemed a mark of manhood, thereby explaining the well-known proclivity for rape and torture. Finally, a lust for power-dominance is rewarded in the playing out of that ultimate role. The Man, whose rapacity is amply displayed in witch-hunts, lynchings, pogroms, and episodes

of genocide, not to mention the day-to-day (often life-long) subservience that he exacts from those closest to him.

Masculine bias, thus, appears in our behavior whenever we act out the following categories, regardless of which element in each pair we are most drawn to at any given moment: subject/object; dominant/submissive; master/slave; butch/femme. All of these false dichotomies are inherently sexist, since they express the desire to be masculine or to possess the masculine in someone else. The racism of white faggots often reveals the same set of polarities, regardless of whether they choose to act out the dominant or submissive role with black or third-world men. In all cases, only by rejecting the very terms of these categories can we become effeminists. This means explicitly rejecting, as well, the objectification of people based on such things as age; body build; color, size, or shape of facial features, eyes, hair, genitals, ethnicity or race; physical or mental handicap; life-style; sex. We must therefore strive to detect and expose every embodiment of The Male Principle, no matter how and where it may be enshrined and glorified, including those arenas of faggot objectification (baths, bars, docks, parks) where power-dominance, as it operates in the selecting of roles and objects, is known as "cruising."

10. **MASOCH-EONISM.** Among those aspects of our oppression which The Man has foisted upon us, two male heterosexual perversions, in particular, are popularly thought of as being "acceptable" behavior for effeminate men: eonism (that is, male transvestitism) and masochism. Just as sadism and masculinism, by merging into one identity, tend to become indistinguishable one from the other, so masochism and eonism are born of an identical impulse toward mock subservience in men, as a way to project intense anti-woman feelings and also to pressure women into conformity by providing those degrading stereotypes most appealing to the sado-masculinist. Certainly, sado-masoch-eonism in all its forms is the very antithesis of effeminism. Both the masochist and the eonist are particularly an insult to women since they overtly parody female oppression and pose as object lessons in servility.

11. **LIFE-STYLE: APPEARANCE AND REALITY.** We must learn to discover and value The Female Principle in men as something inherent, beyond roles or superficial decoration, and thus beyond definition by any one particular life-style (such as the recent androgyny fad, transsexuality, or other purely personal solutions). Therefore, we do not automatically support or condemn faggots or effeminists who live alone, who live together as couples, who live together in all-male collectives, who live with women, or who live in any other way—since all of these modes of living in and of themselves can be sexist but can also conceivably come to function as bases for anti-sexist struggle. Even as we learn to affirm in ourselves the cooperative impulse and to admire in each other what is tender and gentle, what is aesthetic, considerate, affectionate, lyrical, sweet, we should not confuse our own time with that post-revolutionary world when our effeminist natures will be free to express themselves openly without fear of punishment or danger of oppressing others. Above all, we must remember that it is not merely a change of appearance that we seek, but a change in reality.

12. **TACTICS.** We mean to support, defend, and promote effeminism in all men everywhere by any means except those inherently male supremacist or those in conflict with the goals of feminists intent on seizing power. We hope to find militant ways for fighting our oppression that will meet these requirements. Obviously, we do not seek the legalization of faggotry, quotas or civil-rights for faggots, or other measures designed to reform the patriarchy. Practically, we see three phases of activity: naming our enemies to start with, next confronting them, and ultimately divesting them of their power. This means both the Cock Rocker and the Drag Rocker among counter-cultist heroes, both the Radical Therapist and the Faggot-Torturer among effemiphobic psychiatrists, both the creators of beefcake

pornography and of eonistic travesties. It also means all branches of the patriarchy that institutionalize the persecution of faggots (school, church, army, prison, asylum, old-age home).

But whatever the immediate target, we would be wise to prepare for all forms of sabotage and rebellion which women might ask of us, since it is not as pacifists that we can expect to serve in the emerging worldwide anti-gender revolution. We must also constantly ask ourselves and each other for a greater measure of risk and commitment than we may have dreamt was possible yesterday. Above all, our joining in this struggle must discover in us a new respect for women, a new ability to love each other as effeminists, both of which have previously been denied us by our own misogyny and effemiphobia, so that our bonding until now has been the traditional male solidarity that is always inimical to the best interests of women and pernicious to our own sense of effeminist selfhood, as well.

13. **DRUDGERY AND CHILDCARE: RE-DEFINING GENDER.** Our first and most important step, however, must be to take upon ourselves at least our own share of the day-to-day life-sustaining drudgery that is usually consigned to women alone. To be useful in this way can release women to do other work of their own choosing and can also begin to redefine gender for the next generation. Of paramount concern here, we ask to be included in the time consuming work of raising and caring for children, as a duty, a right, and a privilege.

Attested to this twenty-seventh day of Teves and first day of January, in the year of our faltering Judeo-Christian patriarchy, 5733 and 1973,

by /s/

Steven Dansky, John Knoebel, Kenneth Pitchford

THE GAY REVOLUTIONARY PROJECT

In the liberationist tradition of Edward Carpenter and Guy Hocquenghem, Mario Mieli tries to elaborate a distinctively gay critique and theory of society, drawing also upon socialism and feminism. He states: "We have the task of reinterpreting everything from our own vantage point, with a view to enriching and transforming the revolutionary conception of history, society, and existence." His perspective, as developed in his book, *Homosexuality and Liberation: Elements of a Gay Critique* (1977), involves a separate though interrelated critique of *heterosexuality* from the vantage point of being negated homosexuality, and of *masculinity* from the vantage point of the negation of women (which gay men "unnegate" through getting fucked and through drag). Gay liberation involves communism, on a social level, realized through political transformation, and transsexuality, on an individual level, realized through interpersonal erotic relations. Gay liberation is therefore integrally connected to human liberation.

Mieli was a communist and a founder of Fuori! (Come Out), a radical Italian gay organization and magazine based in Milan beginning in 1971. He committed suicide during the 1980s.

THE GAY REVOLUTIONARY PROJECT

from *Homosexuality & Liberation: Elements of a Gay Critique* (1977)

Mario Mieli

Revolutionary criticism has shown how the ideology based on the capitalist mode of production, on the alienation of labour and the reification of the human subject, involves the absurd absolutising of contingent historical values, the hypostasis of opinions (scientific, ethico-moral, socio-political, psychological) that are in reality relative and transitory. This ideology upholds the 'naturalness' of the present system and mode of production, absolutising it in an ahistorical manner and concealing its underlying transience. What is hypostatised here by ideology as 'normal' and normative is nothing but the temporary appearance of something that is in reality changing, being transformed and developing together with the means and mode of production, with the dynamic of the contradiction between capital and the human species, with the entire movement of society. But if capital has so far withstood the revolutionary movement, and managed to repress it, in the same way its ideology has survived the upsurge and widespread progress of the theory of the proletariat, with respect to which it has sought—and often partially managed—a recuperation, without however touching the essence.

At 120 years' distance from the *Communist Manifesto*, people's heads are still filled with ideological absurdity. The ideology of wage-labour still marks the world-view of one-dimensional man, even though capital has reached the stage of real domination, in which

> it is no longer just labour, a specific and determinate aspect of human activity, that has to be subjugated and incorporated into capital, but rather the entire human life process. The embodiment (Einverleibung) process of capital, begun in the West some five centuries ago, is now complete. Today capital is the common being (Gemeinwesen) oppressing people . . . With the development of cybernetics, it becomes clear that capital appropriates and incorporates to itself the human brain; with computer technology, it creates its own language on which human language has to be remodeled, etc. At this level, it is no longer just proletarians—those who produce surplus-value—who are subjected to capital, but everyone, the greater part of people being proletarianised. This is capital's real domination over society, a domination in which all people becomes slaves of capital. [Jacques Camatte, Il Capitale Totale, 161]

This real domination is characterised by the immanent tendency to socialisation which transforms capitalism into state capitalism, while the state, as a 'committee for running the common affairs of the bourgeoisie', comes itself to bear the capitalist hallmark. This general slavery tends to present itself as participation in the management of production by the workers. These are transformed into automatons, managing and administering the very system that enslaves them. So much so that the substitution of living labour by science and technology 'becomes the universal form of material production . . . [and] circumscribes an entire culture; it projects a historical totality—a "world"' (Marcuse).

The necessary economic premises for the creation of communism are thus completely developed (and overdeveloped); capitalism itself has reduced necessary labour to a minimum. But people continue to work for capital, which now takes charge of all the activity that the proletariat performs in the factory, they continue to survive for capital's sake. This real domination so much subsumes human life, and determines people's thinking to such an extent, that even now—when it would be enough to stop the system's machinery for the species to be able to rediscover itself, its biological salvation and communist freedom—the revolution is still held up from asserting itself.

Ideology leads people to think according to the inhuman criteria of capital, and brakes the growth of a universal, communist awareness that would oppose itself once and for all to the cancerous domination of this automatic monster.

The struggle of women and the theoretical expressions of their movement have made it clear how this ideology is phallocentric, based on the subjugation of the female sex to the male at least as much as on the capitalist mode of production. And that the dominant ideology is also white and Eurocentric has literally been written in letters of fire by the struggle of black people, who, insurgent in the ghettos of America in the 1960s, and destroying the cities of capital, have reopened for the species the perspective of the communist revolution, the perspective of human emancipation.

And that 'finally' the ideology is also heterosexual, is something that we homosexuals have shown for the first time, in a forceful way, in the course of the last few years, from the founding of the New York Gay Liberation Front in summer 1969 through to today.

But through all its specific and persisting characteristics (bourgeois, male, Eurocentric, heterosexual), what we must recognise in this ideology above all today is capital itself, its real domination. Today, ideology is single, and strikes at different groups differently but in the same fashion. We have to get rid of it, in order to give life and thought back their free and human 'form' and 'essence', at present reified in the deadly cogs of the capital-machine. The 'privileges' that society cherishes today are revealed as in substance exclusively functional to perpetuating the system; the bourgeois, white, heterosexual male is also almost always an obtuse and unfortunate solipsist, the most despicable puppet of the status quo, which negates in him the woman, the black, the queen and the human being.

If ideology is single and anthropomorphic, the (in)human mask of capital, we, on the other hand, are today far too divided, and above all divided from one another, despite all being in the same underlying situation, suffocated by the weight of the system. We are divided, but it is capital that confronts and divides us.

Cultivating the deep specificities of all our individual cases of personal oppression, we can advance to the revolutionary consciousness that sees in my specific case of oppression also yours (because you, too, hetero, are a negated gay), and in your specific case, also mine (because I, too, am a negated woman), so as to recognise an 'us all' beyond all historically determinate separation and autonomy, i.e. the negated human species. Revolution cannot but come from this recognition of our common repressed being, reflected today in separate forms in society, in those who live in the first person, vis-à-vis the repression, a particular aspect of human 'nature' (being a woman, the homoerotic desire, etc.) that the system negates.

The proletariat itself, and the struggle of women, blacks and us gays, have all indicated the fundamental importance, in the perspective of human emancipation, of everyone who—in relation to the absolutised values of ideology—is considered marginal, secondary, anomolous or downright absurd. The life of the species is there. If the ruling ideology is absurd, the reality this veils can be discerned only by living what this ideology negates and relegates to a corner. Schizophrenia is a gate of access to revolutionary knowledge; and only loving a black person, knowing black people, can truly lead to understanding why communism will be black, of all colours.

A critical theory, growing as a function of a gay revolutionary project, cannot but take into account everything that is eccentric to the narrow confines of what the dominant subculture considers 'normal', permissible, rational. For us homosexuals, there is a clear alternative. Either to adapt to the established universe, and hence to marginalisation, the ghetto and derision, adopting as our own values the hypocritical morality of heterosexual idiocy that is functional to the system (even if with that inevitable and visible variant that is difficult to renounce with a cock up one's arse), and hence to opt for a *hetero*nomy; or else to oppose ourselves to the Norm, and the society of which this is the reflection, and to overturn the entire imposed morality, to specify the particular character of our existential objectives from our own standpoint of marginalisation, from our 'different' being, as lesbian, bum-boy, gay, in open contrast to the one-dimensional rule of hetero monosexuality. In other words, to opt for our 'homonomy'. As Sartre wrote about Gide:

In the fundamental conflict between sexual anomaly and accepted normality, he took sides with the former against the latter, and has gradually eaten away the rigorous principles which impeded him like an acid. In spite of a thousand relapses, he has moved forward towards his morality; he has done his utmost to invent a new Table of the Law . . . he wanted to free himself from other peoples' Good; he refused from the first to allow himself to be treated like a black sheep.

Gide's position is not essentially different from that of all of us other homosexuals. It is a question of opposing the 'normal' morality and of choosing what is good and what is bad from our own marginalised point of view. If we aspire to liberation, we must reject the existing standards. It is a question of making a choice that rejects the Norm. But a gay moralisation of life, which combats the misery, egoism and hypocrisy, the repressive character and the immorality of customary morality, cannot take place unless we root out the sense of guilt, that false guilt which still ties so many of us to the status quo, to its ideology and its death-dealing principles, preventing us from moving with gay seriousness in the direction of a totalising revolutionary project.

We know that the discovery of what is hidden by the 'anomalous' label with which the dominant ideology covers up so many expressions of life, contributes to showing the absurdity of this ideology. But the gradual accumulation of evidence against the alleged absolute value of capitalist science and morality is only a secondary result of the analysis of those questions and arguments which public opinion considers more or less taboo. Above all, it is a question of discovering what these questions disclose about our own underlying 'nature'.

A direct approach to the homosexual question shows the basic importance of the homoerotic impulse in any human being, and makes a contribution to tracing the issues inherent to its repression and its disguise. We know, in the words of Norman O. Brown, that 'it is in our unconscious repressed desires that we shall find the essence of our being, the clue to our neurosis (as long as reality is repressive), and the clue to what we might become if reality ceased to repress'.

The revolutionary gay movement is struggling to (re)conquer our mysterious underlying being. Revealing the historical-existential secret that has up till now been gleaned and preserved in our marginal position, forced as we have been for millenia and for all the most oppressed years of our individual lives to remain secret, we homosexuals, with our voice and all the expressions of our presence, are beginning to reveal what is one of the world's basic mysteries. Perhaps homosexuality is indeed the key to trans-sexuality; perhaps it does point towards something that the repressive requirements of civilisation have been keeping down for thousands of years.

The repression of homosexuality stands in direct proportion to its importance in human life and for human emancipation. If we want to escape from the massacre that has decimated us in the past, the way forward lies via a better understanding of the ancient burden of condemnation that still weighs heavily on each of us even today, a better understanding of the theatrical and ambiguous way in which this massacre is perpetuated in our own time. In this way, we shall reach a better awareness of the revolutionary force that lies within us and our desire.

With its real domination, capital seeks to take possession of even the unconscious, that 'human essence' whose manifest expressions could not but be condemned to death by the systems of repression that preceded it. It may be successful, either because it is more difficult today for the unconscious to explode in an uncontrolled fashion, give the efficiency of conditioning, or because, by way of repressive desublimation, capital enables the unconscious to 'emerge' in alienated forms, in order to subsume it, to deprive men and women of it, and to deprive women and men of themselves. The logic of money and profit that determines the liberalisation of the so-called 'perversions' is not simply an economic fact; it promotes the submission to capital of the whole of human life.

This demonstrates the very complex task of our revolutionary project, to recognise and express a humanity that transcends capital, without offering ourselves up to be devourd by it. In fact, if this should happen, then capital would simply vomit us up again in its own forms, with a view to making use of us to reproduce a new 'humanity', even more programmable, because already programmed in advance.

This is why we have to take extreme positions, not yielding a single inch on the things that really matter, nor abandoning the intransigent struggle for the liberation and conquest of every aspect of our being-in-becoming.

It is due to the awareness of this that a number of homosexuals have stressed, in the last few years, the need to forge instruments for an autonomous ('homonomous') struggle of our own, working out our own theory and deepening the critique of capitalist liberalisation. The situation of those gays who see themselves taking part in a movement (historical, rather than simply formal) differs from that of André Gide in its collective character, in that the 'system' of homosexuality provides a belonging together in which more and more people feel involved. For us, it is no longer a question of an individual project to combat the prevailing morality, but rather of a conscious intersubjective project of our own gay responsibilities and goals, with a view to involving the whole of humanity. We homosexuals must liberate ourselves from the feeling of guilt (and this is one of our immediate goals), so that homoeroticism spreads and 'catches on'. We have to make the water gush from the rock, to induce 'absolute' heterosexuals to grasp their own homosexuality, and to contribute, through the dialectical confrontation and clash between the minority and majority sexual tendencies, to the attainment of the trans-sexuality which the underlying polysexual 'nature' of desire points towards. If the prevailing form of monosexuality is heterosexuality, then a liberation of homoeroticism, this Cinderella of desire, forms an indispensable staging-post on the road to the liberation of Eros. The objective, once again, is not to obtain a greater acceptance of homoeroticism by the hetero-capitalist status quo, but rather to transform monosexuality into an Eros that is genuinely polymorphous and multiple; to translate into deeds and into enjoyment that trans-sexual polymorphism which exists in each one of us in a potential but as yet repressed form.

To conduct our struggle in a truly 'homonomous', original and originally subversive way, we lesbians and gay men have to suspend judgement on everything (ideals, theories, analyses, compartmentalised models, etc.) that has up till now both dragged us in and excluded us at the same time, as a product of the heterosexual majority. We have the task of reinterpreting everything from our own vantage point, with a view to enriching and transforming the revolutionary conception of history, society and existence.

We are fed up to the teeth with running along ready-made rails that do not take us into account, adhering to moral and theoretical systems which base their assumed reliability largely on our exclusion, on the banishment of homoeroticism (and only we ourselves can be clear about the way that this happens and why). We are tired of simply fusing our forces in with those who struggle for an ideal of the future which, even if utopian, appears to us as still too dangerously like the disgraceful present, since it does not take into account the homosexual question and its bearing on the goal of complete human emancipation.

Only we gays can know where our history is concealed, in the terrible and sublime secrets of public toilets, under the weight of the chains with which the heterosexual society has bound and subjected us to it, concealing the uniqueness of our (potential) contribution to the revolution and the creation of communism.

[Author's notes have been deleted from this excerpt—Eds.]

The 1970s were a crucial decade for U.S. gay and lesbian politics, not only in terms of liberationist and feminist thinking, but also for action. Activists extended the energy and imagination of the 1960s while confronting the coalescence of the forces that would bring Ronald Reagan to power. Assaults such as the 1992 ballot measures in Oregon and Colorado (where voters were asked to prohibit enactment of laws protecting from discrimination on the basis of sexual orientation) and their various progeny were prefigured in the 1977 battle in Dade County, Florida, in which the Right led by Anita Bryant overturned a gay rights law, and the 1978 Briggs Initiative in California, which sought to ban lesbians and gays from teaching in public schools. Then, as now, the fear of sexual difference formed one element in the reactionary agenda. Homosexuality's "threat to the family" blends with a fear of gender and racial equality as challenges to "the American way."

MARTIN DUBERMAN

Martin Duberman is professor of history and founding Director of the Center for Lesbian and Gay Studies at City University of New York. The following essay, written in 1977, examines the arguments of those opposed to equality for lesbians and gay men. The persistence of these arguments requires us to persist in our rebuttal of them, and Duberman provides invaluable assistance.

THE ANITA BRYANT BRIGADE

(1977)

Martin Duberman

Robert Hillsborough, aged 33, has been killed. A husky, gentle man, he lived in a small apartment in San Francisco's Mission District. As the newspaper accounts have it, he claimed to have had only two ambitions in life: to work as a gardener and to live quietly with someone he loved. Two years ago he got a fulltime job as a city playground gardener and called himself "the happiest man in the world." Until recently he lived with Jerry Taylor and on the night of June 21 the two had gone out to discuss resuming their relationship. They stopped off at a local Whiz-Burger. In the parking lot a group of teenage toughs baited them with taunts of "Faggots! Faggots!" (initial provocation, if any, unknown; perhaps the two had dared to hold hands, had been seen kissing in their car). To avoid a confrontation, Hillsborough drove off. Four of the teenagers followed, caught him outside his apartment and stabbed him 15 times in the chest and face. He died within minutes.

Two weeks earlier, Anita Bryant had won her spectacular victory in Dade County against the gay rights bill. She had told audience after audience that homosexuals were an abomination to the Lord. I could tell you stories about these people," she said, "that would turn your stomach." I doubt that Anita Bryant will add the story of Robert Hillsborough to her repertoire.

Simple equations between her inflammatory rhetoric and Hillsborough's murder should be avoided. Homosexuals had been beaten, tortured and burned to death for centuries before Anita Bryant began her crusade. The Christian nations of the West have, perhaps, established the outstanding record for savagery, one that until recently has been suppressed or ignored. Today scholars—gay and otherwise—are beginning to document the sick and sordid tale. Louis Crompton, professor of English at the University of Nebraska, has come away from his research convinced that "genocide"—deliberate, systematic extermination—is not too strong a word to describe the historical record.

After Greco-Roman civilization—in which same gender love and lust had been esteemed and to some extent institutionalized—gave way to Judeo-Christianity, a period of some 1500 years ensued during which those engaging in homosexual acts were ostracized, mutilated and killed. "Justification" and penalties varied through time. The sixth century Emperor Justinian blamed homosexuals for the natural disasters of plague and famine; the fourteenth century clergy linked them to sorcerers and "misbelievers"; the eighteenth century legal experts—notably Blackstone in his *Commentaries* of 1765-69—cited against them "the voice of nature and reason." The preferred form of punishment also changed; burning at the stake, an early favorite, gave way to stoning and castration. The Swiss, noted for their ingenuity, liked to cut off one limb at a time over a period of several days—a finger here, a leg there—until the lifeless trunk was eventually ready for the flames. In our own day, Hitler, that exemplar of modern technological impatience, utilized the more direct approach. In his concentration camps some over 200,000 gay people (a figure documented by the American scholar James Steakley and recently corroborated by the Austrian Lutheran Church) were put to death. Himmler, among others, publicly rejoiced in this successful "extermination of degenerates."

And the record of our own country? We came on the scene a bit late to catch the homophobic bug at epidemic height. Yet despite this—and limited population resources—the fledgling colonies managed sufficient ferocity to establish a legitimate claim to membership in the commonwealth of nations, with Virginia as early as 1624 chalking up the execution of a ship's master, and the New Haven colony prescribing the death penalty for lesbianism in 1656. Even today the United States, along with Britain, may stand in contrast to much of the world in the loathing with which the majority continues to regard same-gender sex as "always wrong," even when between consenting adults in a monogamous, longstanding relationship (that is, the kind of relationship which most closely approximates the official model of heterosexual normality). Until the last few years [mid-seventies], the "always wrong" majority hovered around 70%—the same percentage that voted against the gay rights bill in Dade County. Recent polls suggest a decided shift in attitude may be in progress, especially among the young. As early as 1973, Daniel Yankelovich found that among noncollege youths between ages 16 and 25, only 47% felt that "relations between consenting homosexuals are morally wrong" (compared with 72% in his survey of 1969). But the relatively enlightened young exert little moral authority and less political power.

Those who do control our public policies usually vary only in the degree to which they're afflicted with homophobia, though sometimes the politicians do seem to be in advance of their constituencies on the issue of gay rights. It was Dade County's elected officials who passed the original ordinance banning discrimination in jobs and housing based on sexual orientation; it was the citizenry, by a vote of more than 2 to 1, who rescinded that ordinance. This is hardly to say that our politicians can be counted on to lead and enlighten the public. During the Dade County struggle, Senator Alan Trask read *Leviticus* aloud in the state Senate, warning that "we must never pass a law that is contrary to the teachings of God." Governor Reuben Askew—he of the "liberal" reputation—went out of his way just before the climactic vote in Dade to announce publicly that he would not want a known homosexual teaching his children and that he has "never viewed the homosexual lifestyle as something that approached a constitutional right."

Sometimes when public officials do climb out on a limb, they rush to slide back down the trunk should their constituents make any move to shake it. In New York City a few years back, passage of a gay rights bill in the city council seemed assured—until pressure from the Catholic hierarchy (and to a somewhat lesser extent from Orthodox Jewish rabbis) led to the sudden reversal of several critical votes. The church did its bit in Dade as well. A letter from Archbishop Coleman Carroll urging repeal of the ordinance was read aloud in Catholic churches on the Sunday preceding the referendum.

But the Catholic vote alone could not have provided Anita Bryant with her wide margin of victory. She was heavily supported as well by Protestant fundamentalists, the Cuban community, and a coalition of right wing activists who had worked together many times previously to block measures that "threatened the American Way"—busing, ERA, the public school ban on prayers, and liberalized abortion and marijuana laws.

What assumptions and fears bind together these antigay forces? Why would people of such seemingly disparate backgrounds, status and interests—a working class Cuban, say, a Baptist farm wife, a Catholic prelate, a wealthy advertising man—find a transcending commonality in homophobia? Are their stated, public reasons for opposing civil rights legislation for gay people their real reasons? Or are these reasons buried in some tangled web of inarticulate fear and illogic, where they are hidden from everyone—their authors as well as us, their object?

It makes me angry even to formulate such questions. The homophobes have done so little to understand us—and so much to misrepresent and harm us—that to treat their insulting simplicities as legitimate arguments and to dignify their smarmy psyches with a rational probe feels like an exercise in self-hatred—a smiling curtsy to the descending ax. Habits of "rational discourse" die hard.

Not that the stuff needed for such a discourse is even available. The serious research done to date on homophobia is less than piddling—itself an index to social science priorities. Despite vaunting claims to objectivity, most social scientists share the normative values of our culture; which means they've put infinitely more effort into elaborating "explanations" and "cures" for homosexuality than for homophobia. Recently there's been some slight shift in emphasis. The most authoritative work to date [1977] is probably that done by Professor Kenneth Sherrill of Hunter College. He has concluded that those who are against human rights for gay people cluster in the "most-bigoted" category on a wide variety of other issues as well. They are deeply racist and sexist, abhor nonconformity of any kind, fiercely reject all manifestations of the "sexual revolution" (feminism, abortion, pornography, extramarital sex, etc.), are patriotic to the point of xenophobia, and in general show marked fear of all that is "other" or "different." As Sherrill puts it, "it may not matter whether the old order is sexual or political or economic. New ideas may be threatening"—and especially to those middle-aged or older, with a low level of education, living in rural areas and from authoritarian family backgrounds.

Anita Bryant and friends proudly lay claim to most of the values Sherrill describes; they insist, for example, that "women find their greatest fulfillment at home with the family." Yet the public arguments the Bryant-ites have resorted to in opposing civil rights for gay people have largely rested on other grounds. Not only have those arguments struck a deep chord in many Americans, but they seem to vibrate on an emotional frequency not susceptible to information or logic.

The official antigay argument clusters around surprisingly few points. Foremost is the issue of "immorality," the standards of judgment deriving from a literal (fundamentalist) reading of the Bible. One Baptist evangelist, echoing many others, has put the matter succinctly: "We are facing the Devil himself in these homosexuals." A state Senator, Marion Manning of Minnesota, has even managed a bizarre role reversal of victimizer and victim when he declares that gay people are a "threat to my personal rights, a threat to my religious beliefs."

The favorite citation accompanying such pronouncements is *Leviticus 18:22:* "And if a man also lie with mankind as he lieth with a woman, both of them have committed an abomination: they shall surely be put to death; their blood shall be upon them." But fundamentalist Christians seem unable to grasp the fact that interpretations of Holy Writ have, at the hands of mere mortals, undergone almost as many permutations as Supreme Court pronouncements on the Constitution—and in both cases, the most recent "truth" stands in direct contradiction to the official word that immediately preceded. As the Jesuit scholar John McNeill has recently pointed out in his book, *The Church and the Homosexual*, a number of contemporary Biblical scholars have become convinced that the "sin of Sodom" originally connoted "inhospitality," and its current equation with "homosexuality" is the accumulated result of centuries of garbled translations and corrupted texts. The point has been underscored in another recent study, *Human Sexuality: New Directions in American Catholic Thought*, commissioned by the Catholic Theological Society of America. Its five authors are all eminent Catholics (two are priests, one a nun), yet they conclude that underlying the Catholic tradition that has judged homosexual acts as "against nature and hence gravely sinful, are not only a prescientific physiology and unhistorical interpretation of Scripture but also the Stoic conviction that procreation alone justifies the enjoyment and use of sexual pleasure."

Try telling that to the fundamentalist marines. Biblical exegesis is not their strong point, nor scholarly findings among their sources of inspiration. For obvious reasons. To acknowledge recent Biblical scholarship would be tantamount to subverting their basic understanding of the Universe; Galileo, it will be remembered, was not hailed as a liberator. For people like myself, who don't derive our moral principles from the Bible, theological debate is irrelevant. But for those who do—the vast majority of our countrymen, consciously or otherwise—it's fair to insist that they at least be consistent, that they live in a manner comporting with their own literalist interpretation of biblical morality.

Yes, *Leviticus* condemns "sodomy." It also condemns swearing, covetousness, jealousy—and shaving. Adulterers, according to the same book, should be stoned to death. Fundamentalists are free to reject the view that ethics, like all spinoffs of the human mind, is subjective and changeable. They are free to insist, rather, that moral precepts are static, transcending time and culture, and free to insist that behavior conform to those precepts enunciated 2,000 years ago in the Bible. But they are not free to pick and choose among those precepts as to which ones they will follow. Not, that is, without opening themselves to the charge of hypocrisy. It is fair to expect that if biblical fundamentalists are going to follow the dictates of *Leviticus* to the literal letter, they will show equal nicety in adhering to the rest of the "original" (pre-exegetical) biblical code of behavior. Which means they will no longer break the Sabbath by attending movies or by joining bowling parties. That they will no longer accumulate worldly goods beyond providing for basic needs (one doubts if Anita Bryant's $300,000 mansion will qualify). That the men among them will grow luxuriant beards and the women silken hair on their legs. That they will no longer engage in any sexual act other than missionary intercourse—and then only when procreation is the goal. Perhaps on one matter a little hypocrisy should be tolerated; since Kinsey has shown that more than half the male population has extramarital relations, we nonfundamentalists would not demand that adulterers be stoned to death in the streets. We, too, after all, are patriots: we do not wish to see the country decimated.

When not being denounced for offending against Heaven, gay people are excoriated for the baneful influence they exert on Earth. And especially on children. Here the indictment is in two parts: we proselytize subversive ideas and we serve as invidious role models. Anita "Save Our Children" Bryant has taken out full page ads to denounce gay people as recruiters, seducers and molesters of children.

This depiction of us as child molesters has probably been the most potent weapon in the antigay arsenal—and the most impervious to factual refutation. The clinical studies and statistics about the actual nature of the sexual abuse of children have been well publicized and are incontestable. All the studies agree that the vast majority of such cases involve offenses committed by heterosexual men against young girls. Vincent De Francis' *Sexual Abuse of Children* puts the matter beyond cavil. He estimates that of the 100,000 children sexually molested each year, 92% are female and 97% of their victimizers are male—thus making it statistically impossible for more than a minuscule fraction of child molestation cases to involve same-gender assault. But for whatever reason, the Bryantites have been impervious to these truths—perhaps because Americans have grown accustomed to regarding their offspring as mere extensions of themselves, psychological surrogates for their own deepest anxieties, frustrations and repressed desires. (They're no more likely to acknowledge that possibility, of course, than they've been able to absorb the incontrovertible facts about the overwhelmingly heterosexual nature of child molestation.)

As for gay people as role models, no one knows why or how a particular sexual orientation develops, nor the extent to which, once developed, it remains fixed. Experts who have spent decades studying these matters—John Money of John Hopkins; Wardell Pomeroy, Kinsey's co-author—are far more tentative in their views than the strident advocates on either side of the nature/nurture debate.

Not that the "experts" need be automatically deferred to. The history of scientific thought on matters relating to sexuality is sobering evidence of how the opinion of "experts"—at any given moment in time trumpeted as definitive—has in fact oscillated wildly through time, conforming far more to changing social attitudes than to actual accretions of knowledge. In the late nineteenth century, most sexologists agreed that sexual orientation was biologically determined and not subject to environmental influence, familial or pedagogic. But there was sharp—and in retrospect, quaint—disagreement as to which constitutional factors were significant, with medical men authoritatively advocating alternative theories of "degenerated genes" or "embryonic malformation" or an absence of "optimal spermatozoa"—theories that have since been discredited.

Today we know far too much in some fields (cross-cultural studies, for example) and far too little in others (the barely inaugurated research in endocrinology) to indulge in the confident sophistries of the past. Currently, the nature vs. nurture debate in scientific circles is more polarized and clouded than it has been for decades. Where some of the new findings from hormonal research suggest the possible influence of prenatal factors, the accumulating data from anthropology suggest the contrary conclusion—that the incidence (and kind) of same-gender sexual contact is centrally shaped by social learning. No one with even minimal information (perhaps I mean integrity) would say—as has Mike Thompson, the "brains" behind the Save Our Children campaign in Dade County—"all the evidence indicates that homosexuals aren't born; they're made. They choose." Thompson's prescription for those who cannot or will not "choose" to change their sexual orientation is predictably merciless: They should "suppress their drive."

Perhaps more disheartening than the professional bigots, with their claims on a monopoly of truth and their narrow definitions of the permissible limits of humanness, are those professional intellectuals who disassociate themselves from the crude polemics of an Anita Bryant even as they disseminate in subtler form the basic prejudices that animate her cohorts. Intellectuals are maintaining silence (and silence, as we should have learned from what happened in Nazi Germany, is a political act) or expressing agreement—modulated and selective, to be sure—with the crusade to withhold even minimal civil rights protection from gay people.

Two such examples are George F. Will, the syndicated *Newsweek* columnist and Pulitzer Prize winner, and the political theorist Michael Novak, heterodox defender of "different-ness"—that is, when ethnic not sexual. I single out Will and Novak not because their commentaries on gay rights have been uncommonly intemperate or venomous, but precisely because they have not. Their pained thoughtfulness, their more-in-sorrow-than-in-anger tone better represents the stance thus far taken by well-educated, well-placed heterosexuals than does the outright malice of a John Simon, say, or a William Buckley. And is because of that, dangerous. Nothing persuades like "sweet reasonableness."

George Will entitled one of his *Newsweek* columns "How Far Out of the Closet?" Noting that the American Psychiatric Association had removed homosexuality from its list of mental disorders, Will questioned whether the decision had been wise. Did it not encourage a view already too prevalent that "all notions of moral normality are 'mere' conventions, or utterly idiosyncratic"? Was there not a danger that the notion would gain ground that "no form of sexuality is more natural, more *right* [his italics] than any other . . ."? Well yes, I might answer, but isn't that best viewed as a hope, not a danger—the hope that we might become a less hypocritical and conformist, a more comfortably diversified society?

Why does George Will feel otherwise? Because in his mind the prospect looms "of the repudiation of the doctrine of natural right on which Western society rests," a doctrine that allows us to know and encourage "some ways of living that are right because of the nature of man . . . more human ways of living . . ." The doctrine of natural right? The nature of man? Human ways of living? Large concepts, those. Not easy to grasp or evaluate—especially since Will provides no specific definitions, does nothing to elucidate the particular meaning he attaches to such grandly vacuous phrases. Instead, he heaps on further abstractions. Not even a liberal society, he tells us, can leave everything to chance. Certain "essential values" must be safeguarded, shored up by law. "Surely healthy sexuality is one: the family, and hence much else, depends on it."

Apparently Will equates "healthy sexuality" with "family." But instead of providing evidence and argument (a formidable task, given all we've learned of late about marital disorder and child abuse within the home), he issues papal pronouncements that do much to clarify the sources of his inspiration but nothing to authenticate them. One example: "surely homosexuality is an injury to healthy functioning, a distortion of personality." Since almost all the recent scientific literature—including the opinion of the American Psychiatric Association which Will himself cites—points to the opposite conclusion about homosexuality, it's not surprising that the sole "evidence" he offers in support of his statement is a tired stereotype: "Homosexuality often reduces sex to the physical . . . [it is a] subculture based on brief, barren assignations . . ."

One might ask George Will—since parody begets parody—if he has ever heard of the notorious "subculture" of traveling heterosexual businessmen, famed for their "brief, barren assignations"? If so, should we assume he would want to deny them access to jobs and housing, too, since they too—by his standards—threaten society's "essential values"? But then those men *do* have families, no matter the quality of their relationships, no matter the extent of deceit and oppression operative within their households. One comes away from Will's camouflaged sanctimony with a decided preference for the foot-in-mouth rantings of Anita Bryant. Both associate homosexuality with a threat to traditional sex roles and the institutions that embody them and with a "dangerously" elastic view of the permissible range of sexual pleasure. Anita uses the words. George Will, perhaps aiming at the subliminal crowd, moves his lips.

Michael Novak's language is more explicit but his attitudes no less hidebound. In a syndicated column of June 1977, he tried, for openers, to disguise his antique moralism with a few liberal platitudes: "the State should not intrude on the private lives of citizens; in the private sphere, large tolerance ought to be promoted," etc. But, he went quickly on, that does not mean society—as distinct from the state—should cease to make needed "moral discriminations." And guess who needs to be discriminated against? Right—those who follow "the homosexual way of life."

That life, you see, has "two basic deficiencies." The first is "the narcissism of one's own sex." Is Novak here defining narcissism in some special way that would not also force him to deplore deep friendships between people of the same gender? Is he aware that a statement such as his can only be based on the sexist assumption that male and female are polar opposites? We don't know. Like George Will—and most successful moralists—Novak has learned that one garners attention in direct proportion to the firmness, not the subtlety, of one's assertions.

The second deficiency Novak finds in homosexual relationships is that they are transient—"far more so than among married men and women." Perhaps. Given the latest divorce figures and the absence of research on long-standing gay relationships, one can't be sure. But even if Novak is right, he fails to ask any of the questions that could provoke a genuinely searching inquiry into the meaning of "transient." For example: Is it possible serial relationships might provide more optimal conditions for human happiness than lifetime bonding? How many of those lifetime bondings are based on emotional insecurity, lack of options, financial necessity and ingrained cultural imperatives ("the welfare of the children," etc.)—and at what cost in terms of lost affiliation with a larger community, erotic dessication, and the perpetuation of female dependence?

Novak never considers the possibility that sexual fidelity may not be the most significant gauge, let alone the equivalent, of emotional commitment. Many gay people reject the common assumption that a variety of sexual partners is incompatible with a lasting and loving primary relationship. Because gay people are less prone to overinvest in the magical expectation that one other person can fulfill all their needs, the partnerships they do form are often marked by an impressive amount of genuine independence, with both people able to cultivate the joys—so rare in our culture—of important outside relationships.

Novak concludes his article with this appalling statement: "Only a decadent society would grant them [gay people] equal status." Apparently, Novak doesn't realize that "decadence" has many definitions and is perhaps most appropriately appended to knee-jerk defenders of the injustices adherent to the status quo, rather than to those outsiders who throughout history have been responsible for initiating social amelioration and change. The concluding words in George Will's column, comparable to Novak's, make the point for me: ". . . people want a few rocks to cling to in the riptide that washes away old moral moorings. Opposition to [Dade County's pro-gay] ordinance is a way of saying 'Enough!' And it is eminently defensible."

In short: Right on, Anita! We intellectuals may differ with you on particular points, we may not speak in the same tone, use the same vocabulary or invoke the same authorities—we have, after all, different constituencies and must adjust our voices accordingly. But we *are* united on fundamentals: we view gay people as a threat to the body politic, the enemy outside the gates. They shall not pass.

Robert Hillsborough. Gentle gardener. Stabbed 15 times in the chest and face. Dead in a parking lot, age 33. "Faggot! Faggot!"

[Author's notes have been deleted—Eds.]

HARVEY MILK

Elected to the San Francisco Board of Supervisors in 1977, Harvey Milk was the most outspoken and well-known of the first generation of out gay and lesbian politicians. Like Elaine Noble, Milk never hid his sexuality. While Noble's legislative campaign was the fruit of years of activism on other issues, however, Milk's political activism grew directly out of his commitment to the gay community. Nonetheless, both realized that success would come only from reaching beyond any one issue or constituency. Milk's success came not just from the gays and lesbians in his Castro neighborhood, but also from heterosexual working people in other parts of his district who saw his commitment to improving their lives.

In 1978 Harvey Milk and George Moscone, then mayor of San Francisco, were assassinated by Dan White, a former policeman and political opponent. At the trial White's attorney offered the "twinkie defense," arguing that White suffered diminished capacity from overconsumption of junk food and was therefore not responsible for his actions. Though charged with first-degree murder, Dan White was found guilty of voluntary manslaughter on both counts. His virtual acquittal sparked riots by gays and lesbians in San Francisco and demonstrations across the country.

The following speech presents the core of Harvey Milk's message to lesbians and gays. Popularly known as "The Hope Speech," it was Milk's standard political speech. This version was delivered as the keynote address to a 1978 meeting of the gay caucus of the California Democratic Council (CDC).

THE HOPE SPEECH

(1978)

Harvey Milk

My name is Harvey Milk and I'm here to recruit you.

I've been saving this one for years. It's a political joke. I can't help it—I've got to tell it. I've never been able to talk to this many political people before, so if I tell you nothing else you may be able to go home laughing a bit.

This ocean liner was going across the ocean and it sank. And there was one little piece of wood floating and three people swam to it and they realized only one person could hold on to it. So they had a little debate about which was the person. It so happened the three people were the Pope, the President, and Mayor Daley. The Pope said he was titular head of one of the great religions of the world and he was spiritual adviser to many, many millions and he went on and pontificated and they thought it was a good argument. Then the President said he was leader of the largest and most powerful nation of the world. What takes place in this country affects the whole world and they thought that was a good argument. And Mayor Daley said he was mayor of the backbone of the United States and what took place in Chicago affected the world, and what took place in the archdiocese of Chicago affected Catholicism. And they thought that was a good argument. So they did it the democratic way and voted. And Daley won, seven to two.

About six months ago, Anita Bryant in her speaking to God said that the drought in California was because of the gay people. On November 9, the day after I got elected, it started to rain. On the day I got sworn in, we walked to City Hall and it was kinda nice, and as soon as I said the word "I do," it started to rain again. It's been raining since then and the people of San Francisco figure the only way to stop it is to do a recall petition. That's a local joke.

So much for that. Why are we here? Why are gay people here? And what's happening? What's happening to me is the antithesis of what you read about in the papers and what you hear about on the radio. You hear about and read about this movement to the right. That we must band together and fight back this movement to the right. And I'm here to go ahead and say that what you hear and read is what they want you to think because it's not happening. The major media in this country has talked about the movement to the right so much that they've got even us thinking that way. Because they want the legislators to think that there is indeed a movement to the right and that the Congress and the legislators and the city councils will start to move to the right the way the major media want them. So they keep on talking about this move to the right.

So let's look at 1977 and see if there was indeed a move to the right. In 1977, gay people had their rights taken away from them in Miami. But you must remember that in the week before Miami and the week after that, the word homosexual or gay appeared in every single newspaper in this nation in articles both pro and con. In every radio station, in every TV station and every household. For the first time in the history of the world, everybody was talking about it, good or bad. Unless you have dialogue, unless you open the walls of dialogue, you can never reach to change people's opinion. In those two weeks, more good and bad, but *more* about the word homosexual and gay was written than probably in the history of mankind. Once you have dialogue starting, you know you can break down the prejudice. In

1977 we saw a dialogue start. In 1977, we saw a gay person elected in San Francisco. In 1977 we saw the state of Mississippi decriminalize marijuana. In 1977, we saw the convention of conventions in Houston. And I want to know where the movement to the right is happening.

What that is is a record of what happened last year. What we must do is make sure that 1978 continues the movement that is really happening that the media don't want you to know about, that is the movement to the left. It's up to CDC to put the pressures on Sacramento—not to just bring flowers to Sacramento—but to break down the walls and the barriers so the movement to the left continues and progress continues in the nation. We have before us coming up several issues we must speak out on. Probably the most important issue outside the Briggs—which we will come to—but we do know what will take place this June. We know there's an issue on the ballot called Jarvis-Gann. We hear the taxpayers talk about it on both sides. But what you don't hear is that it's probably the most racist issue on the ballot in a long time. In the city and county of San Francisco, if it passes and we indeed have to lay off people, who will they be? The last in, not the first in, and who are the last in but the minorities? Jarvis-Gann is a racist issue. We must address that issue. We must not talk away from it. We must not allow them to talk about the money it's going to save, because look at who's going to save the money and who's going to get hurt.

We also have another issue that we've started in some of the north counties and I hope in some of the south counties it continues. In San Francisco elections we're asking—at least we hope to ask—that the U.S. government put pressure on the closing of the South African consulate. That must happen. There is a major difference between an embassy in Washington which is a diplomatic bureau, and a consulate in major cities. A consulate is there for one reason only—to promote business, economic gains, tourism, investment. And every time you have business going to South Africa, you're promoting a regime that's offensive.

In the city of San Francisco, if everyone of 51 percent of that city were to go to South Africa, they would be treated as second-class citizens. That is an offense to the people of San Francisco and I hope all my colleagues up there will take every step we can to close down that consulate and hope that people in other parts of the state follow us in that lead. The battles must be started some place and CDC is the greatest place to start the battles.

I know we are pressed for time so I'm going to cover just one more little point. That is to understand why it is important that gay people run for office and that gay people get elected. I know there are many people in this room who are running for central committee who are gay. I encourage you. There's a major reason why. If my non-gay friends and supporters in this room understand it, they'll probably understand why I've run so often before I finally made it. Y'see right now, there's a controversy going on in this convention about the governor. Is he speaking out enough? Is he strong enough for gay rights? And there is a controversy and for us to say it is not would be foolish. Some people are satisfied and some people are not.

You see there is a major difference—and it remains a vital difference—between a friend and a gay person, a friend in office and a gay person in office. Gay people have been slandered nationwide. We've been tarred and we've been brushed with the picture of pornography. In Dade County, we were accused of child molestation. It's not enough anymore just to have friends represent us. No matter how good that friend may be.

The black community made up its mind to that a long time ago. That the myths against blacks can only be dispelled by electing black leaders, so the black community could be judged by the leaders and not by the myths or black criminals. The Spanish community must not be judged by Latin criminals or myths. The Asian community must not be judged by Asian criminals or myths. The Italian community should not be judged by the mafia, myths. And the time has come when the gay community must not be judged by our criminals and myths.

Like every other group, we must be judged by our leaders and by those who are themselves gay, those who are visible. For invisible, we remain in limbo—a myth, a person with no parents, no brothers, no sisters, no friends who are straight, no important positions in employment. A tenth of a nation supposedly composed of stereotypes and would-be seducers of children—and no offense meant to the stereotypes. But today, the black community is not judged by its friends, but by its black legislators and leaders. And we must give people the chance to judge us by our leaders and legislators. A gay person in office can set a tone, can command respect not only from the larger community, but from the young people in our own community who need both examples and hope.

The first gay people we elect must be strong. They must not be content to sit in the back of the bus. They must not be content to accept pablum. They must be above wheeling and dealing. They must be—for the good of all of us—independent, unbought. The anger and the frustrations that some of us feel is because we are misunderstood, and friends can't feel that anger and frustration. They can sense it in us, but they can't feel it. Because a friend has never gone through what is known as coming out. I will never forget what it was like coming out and having nobody to look up toward. I remember the lack of hope—and our friends can't fulfill that.

I can't forget the looks on faces of people who've lost hope. Be they gay, be they seniors, be they blacks looking for an almost impossible job, be they Latins trying to explain their problems and aspirations in a tongue that's foreign to them. I personally will never forget that people are more important than buildings. I use the word "I" because I'm proud. I stand here tonight in front of my gay sisters, brothers and friends because I'm proud of you. I think it's time that we have many legislators who are gay and proud of that fact and do not have to remain in the closet. I think that a gay person, up-front, will not walk away from a responsibility and be afraid of being tossed out of office. After Dade County, I walked among the angry and the frustrated night after night and I looked at their faces. And in San Francisco, three days before Gay Pride Day, a person was killed just because he was gay. And that night, I walked among the sad and the frustrated at City Hall in San Francisco and later that night as they lit candles on Castro Street and stood in silence, reaching out for some symbolic thing that would give them hope. These were strong people, people whose faces I knew from the shop, the streets, meetings and people who I never saw before but I knew. They were strong, but even they needed hope.

And the young gay people in the Altoona, Pennsylvanias and the Richmond, Minnesotas who are coming out and hear Anita Bryant on television and her story. The only thing they have to look forward to is hope. And you have to give them hope. Hope for a better world, hope for a better tomorrow, hope for a better place to come to if the pressures at home are too great. Hope that all will be all right. Without hope, not only gays, but the blacks, the seniors, the handicapped, the us'es, the us'es will give up. And if you help elect to the central committee and other offices, more gay people, that gives a green light to all who feel disenfranchised, a green light to move forward. It means hope to a nation that has given up, because if a gay person makes it, the doors are open to everyone.

So if there is a message I have to give, it is that if I've found one overriding thing about my personal election, it's the fact that if a gay person can be elected, it's a green light. And you and you and you, you have to give people hope. Thank you very much.

MICHEL FOUCAULT

Michel Foucault was one of the twentieth century's most original thinkers. Holder of a chair at the College de France, author of many pathbreaking books on modern forms of power in medicine, penology, psychiatry, and sexuality, Foucault was also a gay man. Indeed, we can see his intellectual agenda as shaped by the experience of criminalization and medicalization that is so typical for lesbians and gays. His *History of Sexuality* has become a methodological manifesto for gay and lesbian studies.

In the following interview, conducted in Paris in July 1978, Foucault explains briefly his views on sexuality and pleasure. He analyses sexual practices he calls "monstrous counterfeit pleasures," thereby pointing to the constructed, transgressive, and transformative character of such practices. In so doing, he encapsulates a position with growing popularity among academic queers—the need to challenge not just the hegemony of heterosexuality, but the larger Christian frameworks of the West that tells us what practices are "natural" and "normal" and which "abominations" or "perversions."

QUESTIONS FOR MICHEL FOUCAULT

(1978)

Interview with Jean Le Bitoux and Mattias Duyves
trans. Michael West

How do you explain the fact that The History of Sexuality *has been met with such surprise?*

The surprise might be explained in part by the simplicity of some of my earlier positions. Or another possibility is that people had constructed this rather facile, boy-scout notion of the resistance to all forms of repression in my work. Things had of course changed a great deal in the past twenty years. It seemed to me that we had arrived at a situation where notions such as sexual repression had become rather worn-out or overused, and what was needed was a discussion of ways in which such notions could be operationalized as part of a struggle, a movement, or a debate. Of course it's always difficult to say whether a book has been correctly understood or not. I don't believe that an author has the right to legislate the meaning of his or her work.

How did the invention of the notion of homosexuality come about?

The notion of homosexuality dates back to the nineteenth century, as part of one region among many forms of pleasure and the complete inventory of links among sexual practices. Such is the political history of one form of pleasure or one realm of experience which was almost eliminated. The struggle to reaffirm this experience and this pleasure began in the twenty years which followed, with Magnus Hirshfeld, Oscar Wilde and André Gide, among others. It was strategically necessary to fight against this form of morality and this kind of legislation.

Has sexuality become an inadequate concept?

I'd rather say that what we need is a re-evaluation. Don't think that just because we've now got this particular concept of sexuality, which has allowed us to fight that there still aren't a number of dangers. There's still a biological aspect to sexuality that makes it accessible to doctors, psychologists, and a whole normalizing structure. There's still a whole hierarchy of doctors, educators, legislators, adults and parents who talk about sexuality! But the struggle has opened up and become stronger at the same time. It isn't enough to liberate sexuality, you have to liberate yourself from Doctor Meignant, that is, from the whole notion of sexuality itself. If a battle is always fought on the same terms, it becomes sterile, it gets stuck and finally trapped. So why not bring in other values besides the 'medical-biological-natural' approach to sexuality and escape from just one more discourse? What we need is a radical break, a change in orientation, objectives and vocabulary.

Why do you prefer to talk about 'pleasure' rather than 'desire'?

I prefer 'pleasure' in order to avoid the medical and 'natural' connotations associated with 'desire'. 'Desire' has been and can be used strategically as a tool, a sign which is easily intelligible, a standard of 'the normal': "Tell me what you desire and I'll tell you who you are,[1] whether you're normal or not, and I'll then be able to qualify or disqualify your desire." We can very easily spot this tactic, which proceeds from the Christian notion of lust to the Freudian notion of desire, going by way of the notion of sexual instinct which was formulated in the 1840s. Desire is not an event, but a permanent aspect of the subject around which an entire psychological-medical framework is constructed.

The term 'pleasure', on the other hand, is quite new and practically devoid of meaning. There is no 'pathology' of pleasure, no 'abnormal' pleasure. It's an event which is outside of the subject or at the boundaries of the subject, in something which is neither corporal nor spiritual, neither external nor internal, ultimately an unassigned and unassignable notion.

How has the science of sexuality changed, in your opinion?

I think that in the relationship of the self to the self, the science of sexuality has changed and continued to grow, at the very turning point between Christian confession and medicine. Until the fifteenth and seventeenth centuries, people were made to confess their desires, always in function of some relationship, a legal sexuality in one sense. The questions which were asked took the form of: "Are you performing your conjugal duties towards your wife? Do you screw her in the correct way, according to nature? Are you cheating on her? Do your sexual habits include bestiality?" This legal sexual relation always involved practices, intentions and desires.

Beginning in the sixteenth century with what we might call the 'colonization of childhood' and the beginnings of serious pedagogical reforms, with the periodization of a specific category called 'childhood', the question which suddenly appeared in confession manuals and spiritual guides then became: "Have you touched yourself sexually?" The masturbation taboo. Not just because a restriction has now been applied to sexuality, but because it's at this point that a particular knowledge of sexuality was born, with all its hesitations and first impressions.

We find this first problematic of sexuality in the sixteenth and seventeenth centuries in Protestantism as well as Catholicism. It ends with the famous myth at the the end of the eighteenth century which posited that the human species itself was in danger of becoming extinct if masturbation wasn't eradicated. All pedagogical practices and the whole system of relationships between parents and children were now oriented around surveillance and the threat of children masturbating. Thus the child's body became a space inhabited by watchful parents, always on guard against any kind of solitary pleasure or pleasure given by the self to the self.

How do you see the limits of public tolerance for homosexuality?

First of all, despite the strictness of Christian civilization since the sixteenth century, this civilization can only function by tolerating a certain fringe of illegality. Illegality is a part of the mechanism of legality. Thus we might be tempted to talk about sodomy, but sodomy is of course a heterosexual practice, too.

So what do people say these days about the pleasures of homosexuals among themselves? For the last few years, we've witnessed a widening of the economy of pleasure. Pleasure is poised on the brink of being recognized as indispensable, but in the end really not that important. Therefore it's tolerated. And so people say: "Pleasure passes just like youth. Why not let them have it, after all, they'll soon learn that it won't get them very far. And they'll have to pay for it in the end, and dearly at that, in terms of suffering and sadness, loneliness and break-ups, fights, hate and jealousy . . ." In the end, it has its price just like anything else, so it ends up not bothering people.

But happiness all by itself? You can't buy it at the expense of some fundamental unhappiness. An exchange economy of pleasure doesn't exist, and it's at that point that things become intolerable for certain people. Because if we have a group of people that not only experiences a form of pleasure which is denied to certain others, but publicly displays its happiness with that experience, then it becomes intolerable for the other excluded group, because there's no way to make the happy ones pay for it.

While some people might be able to tolerate the sight of two homosexuals picking each other up, very few people would be likely to forgive these same two if they were still smiling, holding hands and kissing the next day. The search for pleasure isn't unforgivable, but *finding* it is. Our powers of explanation no longer operate. They can describe pleasure, or a certain practice, but not happiness. If there's no anguish, no nightmare behind the happiness, then it can't be tolerated.

Many conceptions of male homosexuality tend to associate it with femininity or effeminacy, particularly with transvestism. What do you think about this?

I think that's a very complicated question. We tend to blur the distinction between homosexual practices and feminine appearances. The court of Henri III in France in the thirteenth century is a good example of that. But in fact the transvestite is really a construction of heterosexuality. One of the most important spaces for transvestism in the seventeenth and eighteenth centuries was the army, where a considerable number of 'women' led full lives as 'hussies' [*gourgandines*], voracious 'women' or 'whores'. Societies with a rigidly monosexual structure, like the army or the convent, attract transvestites. Cherubino is indeed a transvestite, but a heterosexual one.

When the category of homosexuality was first invented, scientific study immediately started with hermaphrodism. 'The homosexual' entered into medical annals as someone whose sexual instincts had supposedly 'split in two', making him both a man and a woman at the same time. The response to both this theory and the theory of hormonal transformation was to turn the question around: "So we're hermaphrodites? We want to be women? Sure, but even more than that!" Thus the figure of 'the queen' [*la folle*] was born. We can very easily establish a link between this kind of analysis of homosexuality as a sort of secret femininity and the queen who claims to be a woman.

Of course we can start to see quite easily the complexity of this kind of game. On the one hand here are the doctors saying, "We're dealing with hermaphrodites, thus degenerates", and certain homosexuals saying, "No, we're neither, but if we want to take hormones, it's in order to transform ourselves into women." The historical response could be found in the challenge of a similar analysis and political claim: if homosexuality represents a union of the sexes, then homosexuals have a specific sexuality. Therefore homosexuals are not wrong to insist on the notion of a specific sexuality as a basis for the struggle for their rights. This position bears careful scrutiny.

As it is, homosexuals have long found themselves labeled as feminine. It's an ambiguity at the very center of homosexuality itself. But in fact there is no basic link between homosexuality and femininity. This ambiguity laid itself open to a medical attack which demonstrated the phallocratic nature of our culture, however. It is at this point that a strategic link is opened with the feminist movements which has allowed homosexuals to show that their preference for men is not merely another form of phallocratism or 'male chauvinism'. Today, homosexuality can explain itself by presenting itself simply as a certain relationship between bodies and pleasures.

Do you think that American images of homosexuality disturb this link with femininity and point to a phallocratic impulse?

The morphologically eroticized man would be, in fact, a gay man with a moustache, at least thirty-five years old, built like a baseball player, with a lot of body hair, leather and chains. This gives a false impression of men falling back on a monosexual machismo, displaying all the signs of masculinity, remaining strictly among other men, and erecting a new iron curtain between men and women.

We have to look at it more closely, however, to realize that this display of masculinity has nothing to do with a re-evaluation of the male as male. On the contrary, in daily life, relationships between gay men are full of tenderness, with certain community practices full of life and sexuality. Sexual relationships under the sign and within the refuge of this display of masculinity quickly reveal themselves as a privileging of masochism. Practices such as fist-fucking can be considered as 'devirilized' or even de-sexualized. They are in fact monstrous counterfeit pleasures achieved only with the help of specific instruments, signs, symbols or drugs like poppers and MDA.

If such signs of masculinity exist, they do so not to return to some kind of phallocratism or machismo, but rather to permit the individual to invent himself, to turn his body into a field of production for extraordinarily polymorphous pleasure, and at the same time separate from the privileging of the genitalia and particularly of the male genitalia. It's a question of getting away from this virile form of willed pleasure known as *jouissance*, normally understood in its masculine, ejaculatory sense.

Certain homosexual lifestyles have been criticized by homosexuals themselves. What do you think of that?

You mean the kind of criticism which says things like: living with a guy labels you as bourgeois, having sex in public restrooms means you're accepting ghettoization, sex in the baths makes you just another consumer, etc. These are arguments that think they're being political when they're really only naïve. I think quite simply that it's vitally important to live in the most explicit manner possible with the person one loves, whether it's with a boy, a man or an old man. If you want to kiss a boy in public or have sex with him in the bushes, then do it.

What I find much more reprehensible politically is the economic racket that's sprung up around nearly all aspects of homosexual life, a police racket as well as an organized crime racket. Today, for example, it's impossible to open a gay bar in Paris without the police forcing you to turn to the Mafia. The police will not allow you to exist without some connection to organized crime. This is something which I think is very serious. And it's equally true for the baths.

Does the 'spectacle' which many homosexuals present strike you as somewhat incongruous?

It's true that there is a whole series of behaviors which make up what we might call 'homosexual theater'. In certain bars, for example, some men will show up only to show off their own beauty or their lover's, just out of spite, as a way of saying: "Look but don't touch", or: "How dare you stare at me when I haven't even glanced at you?" This is the case in some places, but consider Japan, for example. There are thousands of bars there, primarily in Tokyo or Kyoto. But they're tiny, with only enough room for five, maybe six men altogether. The men sit on their bar stools, they talk and get drunk. The possibility of meeting new people is quite rare, and in fact the arrival of a new face is quite an event. It's a sort of communal life organized along the same lines as the cultural imperative that a man must marry when he becomes an adult. But after dark, you drop in on your local bar, not far from the building where you live, and you meet up with a kind of faithful, slightly mobile community. Of course, on a larger scale like here [Paris], you can find the same type of relations.

So why is anonymity important to you?

Because it's the source of the intensity of pleasure. What counts is not the affirmation of identity, but rather the affirmation of non-identity. Not simply because you check your membership card, and thus your identity, at the door of the bathhouse, but also because of the multiplicity of possible configurations and re-configurations which you can find there. It's a very important experience, inventing shared pleasures together as one wants. Sometimes the result is a sort of de-sexualization, almost a kind of deep-sea dive, so complete that it leaves you with no appetite at all, without any kind of residual desire which you feel sometimes after even very satisfying sexual experiences.

What is your opinion of the sexual activity one finds in the baths?

Politically, I think it's important that sexuality be allowed to function as it does in the baths. You find people there who are much like yourself, as you are much like them: nothing else but other bodies with which combinations and creation of pleasure are made possible. You quit being held prisoner by your own face, your own past, your own identity.

It's a shame that such places don't exist for heterosexuals. Wouldn't it be wonderful for them to be able to visit such a place at any hour of the day or night and to see and experience all the comforts and possibilities one could imagine, to meet other bodies which are at the same time both present and absent? There's a wonderful potential for de-subjectifying oneself in such places, for de-subjugating oneself to a certain point, perhaps not radically but certainly significantly.

What are your thoughts on the relationships between homosexuality and political power?

The first thing required is a reform of the penal code. The easiest solution would be to say: no legislation involving sexuality. But things aren't that simple, since there is the problem of rape and the question of the age of consent. Regarding the latter, I'm inclined to favor the age of 13 to 15 years as appropriate, even though this figure seems somewhat absurd given the general sexual climate and considering what's available to any kid old enough to read these days, whether it's in books, magazines or on walls on the way to school. Legislating this kind of thing is still a very delicate matter.

In spite of this, however, the established powers are currently discovering the enormous cost associated with repression.[2] We're familiar with the work of the Trilateral [Commission] on the cost of democracy, but the opposite also deserves consideration: repression comes with a heavy cost, not only in economic terms but in institutional terms as well. Why should any establishment want to eliminate homosexuals? What would be the social advantage of punishing them? An increased birth rate? In the age of the pill? A lower incidence of sexually-transmitted diseases? But the technocrats and the governing princes know full well that this sort of thing doesn't come about as a result of repressing a specific category of the population, but rather through campaigns.

A rationalization of the use of power doesn't necessarily have to include increased repression. It would be much more advantageous for those in power to try to convince the general population to tolerate the current unemployment rate rather than to bug the shit out of them with anti-homosexual campaigns or raids on gay bars. One thing is clear now: power has its own cost, it doesn't appear as a net benefit. When someone commits an act of repression, it carries with it not only an economic cost, but a political one as well.

1. The French reads: "Dis-moi quel est ton désir et je te dirai qui tu es . . .", a paraphrase of the gastronome Brillat-Savarin's often quoted remark, "Dites-moi ce que vous mangez et je vous dirai qui vous êtes."— "Tell me what you eat and I'll tell you who you are."—Trans.

2. Foucault is referring to the moderately conservative government of Valéry Giscard d'Estaing. At the time of the interview [July 1978], Raymond Barre was the Prime Minister and had closed down all of the gay presses three months earlier.

Pedophilia has been one of the most emotional issues confronting lesbians and gays. This is so for several reasons. First, some are troubled about whether sexual relations between adults (who are almost always men) and children or youth can be consensual. Others who are less troubled by pedophilia itself are often reluctant to have it discussed because it feeds into one of the great stereotypes used by homophobes to justify second-class status for lesbians and gays. The image of the child molester has been used successfully by opponents of gay/lesbian rights despite the reality of the overwhelming abuse of female and male children by heterosexual men. Thus, discussions are sometimes aborted for fear of consequences.

NAMBLA

Organizations such as the North American Man Boy Love Association (NAMBLA) and their supporters have argued that popular understandings of pedophilia are mistaken. They appeal to the consensual nature of their relations, and distinguish their actions from child rape and abuse. While they have some supporters among both gays and lesbians, they remain embattled. In 1994 the International Lesbian and Gay Association (ILGA) removed NAMBLA from membership in order to assure their new official recognition by the United Nations. The United States government continued to block recognition, however, saying that there are other member groups of ILGA supported intergenerational sex.

The following essay appeared as an editorial in *NAMBLA News*.

THE CASE FOR ABOLISHING THE AGE OF CONSENT LAWS

editorial in *NAMBLA News* (1980)

North American Man-Boy Love Association

The Laws and their Purposes

What are age of consent laws? Generally they refer to a number of statutes which prohibit any kind of erotic or sexual contact between an adult and a person under a specified age (which varies widely from state to state) and even, in most jurisdictions, sexual contact between minors. Though the age at which the line of proscription is drawn differs from state to state, all states have "statutory rape" laws as well as related laws forbidding adult-minor contact. These include: indecent assault, intent to commit rape, unnatural acts, sexual abuse, contributing to the delinquency of a minor, etc.

Most of these laws are now thought to be vague in their wording, unclear in their intent, and overlapping in their scope. Increasingly, courts in some progressive jurisdictions overturn convictions on these laws.

Where did statutory rape laws come from? The concept goes back hundreds of years, but it hadn't become a matter of obsessional interest to the state until within the past one hundred years. Statutory rape laws evolved as a device for large property holders to have as a legal remedy to maintain chastity among their daughters prior to marrying them off. Virginity—which had more status in the past than today—was essential in property-arranged marriages. Daughters, as legal property of their fathers, had to be kept virginal. Many were literally locked away under horrible circumstances. The sexual purity of persons without property remained of no concern to the state. Propertyless persons of "loose" morals are still exempt from the "protection" extended their more chaste minor brothers and sisters. To this day, in some states in the American South, an adult male, if accused of a sex act with a minor female, can win acquittal at trial if he can demonstrate that his partner was previously sexually experienced or even if he truly believed her to be already "debauched."

What purposes are served by this growing number of laws today?

Liberals argue that the state is, by and large, a beneficent, if still imperfect, mechanism for best promoting a rational system of human interaction. Those who have been the traditional victims of this "rational system" certainly see it differently. The state, through its punitive agencies, has reserved for itself the right to determine which personal relations are to be allowed and which are to be punished. With the decline of the extended family and traditional church influence, the state has increased its investment in maintaining a preferred family structure, i.e., male-dominated, heterosexual nuclear variety. The state continues to have a vested interest in regulating and channeling sexual activity into the type it can best control. The greatest threat to this hierarchical and repressive system is presented by sexual and affectionate personal relations outside the approved mode. Specifically, this means the freedom of those over whom the state still has greatest control (minors) and those with whom these minors would create their own lives.

Though it is probably fair to assume that self-identified heterosexuals outnumber homosexuals in this society, and that heterosexual pedophile acts are more frequent than man-boy contacts, the state has reserved its special fury for gay men who develop friendships with boys. In Massachusetts, for example, there are far more gay men in jails, prisons, and at the Bridgewater Treatment Unit for statutory (non-violent) sex acts with boys than there are het males for offenses with girls.

Curiously, the state is becoming more permissive in some areas while simultaneously becoming more punitive in other related areas of sexual behavior. It's becoming more permissive in that some recent changes in laws in many states have decriminalized sex between adults and minors as long as there is no more than a few years' age difference between them. A proposed Washington D.C. law change would permit a five-year age span, allowing a 16-year-old to have contact with an 11-year-old without risking legal sanctions.

But the state is growing more intolerant in that, by rewriting the sex-offenses statutes, the state's grip over those to be targeted becomes that much more direct. Rather than doing away with the laws (which are partially undermined by the peer-peer "free-zones"), the more specifically written laws create a more precise, potential criminal class . . .

The effect of age of consent laws is to invade both the perception of one's privacy and, in many cases, the fact of one's privacy in order to punish those who would choose to relate to one another outside the narrow and strictly defined limits of state sexuality and the pattern of authority this type of repressed sexuality maintains.

It is important to keep in mind the historical context in which these recent developments have occurred. Radical critics of modern liberal democracies (like Marcuse and Wolff) have suggested the ideas of "repressive desublimation" and "repressive tolerance." Such theorizing—though generally not in favor in American social thought and certainly not regarding sexual behavior—provides a framework for understanding twin primary events in how the state adapts to changes in consciousness and behavior among the citizenry. The state—and particularly the bureaucratic kind of state which has flourished in American states and at the federal level since the New Deal—is best characterized by its attempt to promote control through accommodation. The US role as world imperial power has only concentrated these control tendencies. Discipline and conformity can be maintained through periodic purgings of those who are perceived as presenting a threat to the National Security State.

Sexuality represents the ultimate individualism—everyone's personal sexuality, their fantasies, and their erotic potential are far more idiosyncratic than are, say, their consumer choices, voting patterns, patterns of religious or social identification—and this is why sexuality is a constant fear of those who would seek to continue administered controls. Be it women's right to reproductive freedoms, homosexual activity, or youths' rights to free expression of personal sexual preference: these are the fronts on which the battles are being waged in liberal democracies in the war of personal vs. state control of our destinies.

It is no mere odd happenstance that in totalitarian and autocratic regimes, the state first seeks to establish monopoly on approved sexual behavior, usually through establishing absolute punitive legal powers and by mobilizing popular prejudice.

The Roman Church, in its periodic attempts to establish autocratic, centralized control in Europe in the last millennium, has regularly used charges of sexual deviance to wipe out threats to its power. (And developing, by the by, the most splendid form of hypocrisy—i.e. tolerating and even rewarding personal sexual hypocrisy at the highest levels *as long as outward fealty* is displayed to central control; Cardinal Spellman and Paul the Sixth are recent examples.) The liberalization of sexual mores under Lenin in the Soviet Union was targeted as soon as Stalin set a course of absolute state control: abortion rights were curbed and homosexual behavior was once again proscribed. The German Nazis targeted homosexuals immediately upon attaining power.

In recent US history, the anti-red panics of the 1940s and 1950s always had a not-so-hidden undercurrent of fag-baiting. And today, we are seeing the ascendance of The New Right and the growth of religious lobbies of the most fundamentalist stripe. Yet, their success, if that is what it is, is based on the exploitation of fragmented personalities and public hypocrisy. A man who works in a gay rights lobby in Washington, DC, has said that the offices of New Right groups are filled with closeted gay men and boy-lovers. They exploit popular prejudices for financial gain and political power while at the same time engaging in the very kind of behavior they publicly denounce.

No better example of this could be available than the recent case of US Rep. Bob Bauman, who was arrested six months after blowing a 16-year-old hustler in the Capitol. Bauman, a new-right leader and head of the American Conservative Union, regularly denounced homosexuals and those who threatened The Family while he himself would rush from the Hallowed Halls of Congress out to a boy-bar to buy some dick for his face. If there's one Bauman on Capitol Hill, there's probably another hundred.

Liberal democracies cannot play the control game the way the totalitarian countries do. Homosexuals in the Soviet Union, for example, are tolerated by the system and even promoted in the areas of their skills until it becomes convenient, for whatever internal reasons, to purge them and make an example. The recent case of Sergei Paradjanov demonstrates this.

The West, and particularly the U.S., is committed to a kind of empirical scientific method in research (with weak emphasis on theory), and this bias has made the concept of sex-science research tolerable. The US, being one of the last of the major Western democracies to develop the practice of centralized, administered governmental control, has not really established its prerogative of regulating all sexuality as of yet, though the spasms of the past few years are certainly strong indications that it has every intention of doing so.

The sex science movement in this century, and the revolution which it has fed, lacks a formal history and needs broader popular consciousness of its importance. Radical agitators and sex revolutionaries like Margaret Sanger and Alfred Kinsey lack proper appreciation in this culture.

Kinsey, who began as a typical American empirical scientist, documented, in undeniable ways, the schism between accepted sexual morality and actual sexual practice, thereby exposing the gargantuan hypocrisy that riddles our culture.

Gay liberationists in general, and boy-lovers in particular, should know Kinsey's work and hold it dear. We should recall that Kinsey's work was attacked at the time of its release. The *New York Times*, for example, refused to run ads for this breakthrough book. When it was published, liberal (and safe) paragon Lionel Trilling was called in to do a hatchet job. Sadly, Kinsey's volume on male sex behavior has been long out of print. Contemporary sex researchers seem to tilt to "counseling" rather than discovery and agitation.

But implicit in Kinsey is the struggle we fight today. Should the state be empowered to punish—on a selective basis—persons who, as part of a massive biological phenomenon, engage in sexual behavior, in consensual ways, that does not meet the approval of hypocrites and self-designated moralists who influence law-writing, and law enforcement? Within our very own lifetimes, boys "caught" masturbating—perhaps the most frequent form of male sexual release in our culture—have been sent to reformatories or assigned to punitive agencies. Extremely anti-sexual religions (like the Mormons) still today proffer devices to male adolescents to keep them from engaging in auto-erotic release. To what end? To channel, dictate, and control the ways sexual release will be allowed.

The liberal state can no longer deny sexuality, nor can it refute the importance of sexual research or deny the import of the increasing data on how we behave as sexual citizens. Yet it cannot abdicate its desire to control and its need for increasing state power over our lives. This is why it is engaging in this obsessive binge of law-rewriting in the past ten years permitting sex with age peers but prohibiting adult-minor connections. It backs off its attacks on youth sexuality but increases controls over age ghettoism—another form of control.

Simultaneously, pro-control agents step up their attacks on sexual education, discussion, public display of erotica, in order to continue the ignorance which can be mobilized for periodic assaults on those who deviate from the recommended norm.

Age and Consent

The concept of age and the concept of consent are malleable things. They change with the fashions. In the American colonies the vague concept of age of consent was legally ten—*for females only*. Since that time, the age has inched upwards, usually as the result not of any change in behavior but in reaction to moralistic crusades launched by self-aggrandizing types who use sensational issues to increase legal penalties upon a targeted group.

One of these, the great anti-white-slave campaigns of the late 19th century, did little to halt young female prostitution. They were moralists' responses to overcrowding of cities, the exploitation of labor, and the attempt to scare women into dependency relations either in a family or in employment under a boss.

The Kiddie Porno Panic of 1977 was another chimera. The objection was to kiddie porno (which I would guess less than 1% of the US population had ever seen or heard of). But charlatans and opportunists created this panic in order to cripple and set back the gay liberation movement after its phenomenal growth in the 1970s. Each panic creates a new batch of laws that give the state more power to regulate and interfere with people's private behavior. Yet the State's power—once citizens have acceded power to it—adapts itself while still maintaining control. In the 1960s a trend developed among state legislatures to lower ages of consent.

In many states, we saw sexual enlightenment—and/or criminal code revisions—which revised ages of consent in progressive moves. Curiously, the state of California, in which more sex acts take place of all types than in any other state, has an age of consent of 18, the highest in the nation.

But what we want to note is how social attitudes develop. To us it is a given that this society is anti-sex and homophobic to an enormous degree.

When it goes unchallenged that a murder is a lesser crime than sucking the cock of a 15-year-old boy—as Det. Lloyd Martin of the Los Angeles Police Department as well as several judges have stated, to no objection—then we are already in such a degenerate moral condition that trying to bring some rationality to the discussion of human sexuality may be like the lost figure on the island casting off appeals-in-bottles upon the waves. The conspiracy of silence which surrounds the injustice done those who love boys is a crime for which society's owners will one day have to answer.

In the 19th century, the absolute obsession with preventing boys from touching their cocks and masturbating resulted in the popularity of strange chastity-type belts, elaborate alarm systems that set off bells if a boy's hands reached under his bed-covers, etc. Today, it is hard for us to take such an obsession seriously, even though the battle over the right to privacy (in order to masturbate) was a long and furious one.

Youth sexuality, despite Freud, despite Kinsey, despite *overwhelming observable phenomena*, remains the diciest of topics. Yet the state—long the foe of acknowledging youth sexuality—is smart enough to co-opt progressive developments of the past 20 years. Instead of recognizing its repressive acts of the past and abdicating its role of interfering in private sexual behavior, the state reluctantly accepts youth sexuality and then creates "peer-peer" free zones where no penalty will be allowed. But adult-youth relationships remain proscribed. Increasingly, those within the women's and gay liberation movement who denounce pedophiles will reluctantly acknowledge that "children" are sexual, but instantly insist that youth only "experiment"—always their favorite word—sexually with other youth. Such thinking is characteristic of the worse ageist ghettoism that saturates our culture and stains our movement. Such distinctions—and the mentality which entertains them—are exactly those which tolerate the expanding National Security State.

Youth requires the same freedoms for personal choice in establishing relationships as adults have. This freedom for adults and minors is currently crippled by age of consent laws. Statutory rape laws serve age ghettoization and keep those who want to reach out across these artificial barriers from doing so. Statutory rape laws are the current equivalent of 19th century legal punishments for masturbation.

Consent is a much talked-about thing, be it in these matters of pedo relationships, within the bounds of marital sex (as in the recent Rideout case), or in the sexuality of our S&M brothers and sisters. Even within emerging law, consent is a "hot" issue.

Less explored is the idea of "age." One of the control mechanisms the liberal state has developed is the concept that we should be stratified by chronological age. This development is something wholly new in our cultural tradition within the past 100 years and is a function of advanced industrialism's need for specific "markets" which support a developed capitalistic culture. Admittedly, other historical cultures, ignoring such artificial age distinctions, relied on other kinds of control: class, monarchy privileges, wealth, etc. The very *fact* of age has come under control within the last century. Most US citizens can, on average, expect a life expectancy of more years than any of our ancestors. Historically, because of high infant mortality and the high number of childbirth deaths, women were put into breeding service as soon as they could conceive. Child betrothals, usually for political and/or property reasons, were not uncommon even within the modern period. Some cultures recognize pubescence as the threshold of adulthood, and this is usually a time for celebration, not punishments.

Yet in our culture, we face the odd anomaly: we are living longer, the general health of our citizens is better serviced, children—particularly those born after World War II—reach sexual maturity at younger and younger ages, overall sexual awareness is increasing through the population. But at the same time, the state seems determined to bar sexual options for this age. While the trend appears that the culture is growing more sexualized and less restrained by taboos, police and courts step up sexual surveillance and make enforcement against sexual non-conformers a high social priority.

Encouraging state control of sexuality is a particular burden to young males. The years of greatest sexual capacity and actual need are those years which the state still targets as times of denial.

The President's Commission on Pornography and Obscenity, in its numerous backup work-group reports, time and again documented that erotophobic attitudes at home and denial of sexual expression in adolescence had a high correlation with adult crime and particularly sex crimes. Denmark—often unfairly maligned by reactionaries and Rape-ideology proponents—was time and again cited in these reports. As the first Western European nation to decriminalize the sale and possession of erotic materials, Denmark noted a dramatic and *immediate* decrease in sex-related misconduct: from voyeurism, to "flashing," to rape. Cross-cultural comparisons always involve risks, but it seems both unscientific *and* inflammatory to blame gay liberationists, boy-lovers, and "pornographers" for the increase—if, in fact, any—in this nation of "sex crimes." (The quality of the commercial erotica produced for profit today is a separate matter and one we think fairly open to criticism. Current porno is by and large a function of heterosexual domination and pandering, not an outgrowth of sexual liberation movements.) We all should remember that even the commercial erotica presently produced is still made, distributed, and sold in a legally-hostile climate, with those in the business more selectively harassed, indicted and imprisoned than, say, manufacturers and retailers of commercially defective drugs, foods, and services. A disproportionately large number of gay men work in sexually-related industries—visit any porno store or theatre and you'll find gay men working there—and we should keep in mind that these guys are on the front line for official attack.

Age ghettoism is central to plans for contemporary control. The existing combination of official sex-negativity, semi-tolerance, hypocrisy and medical controls has exacted a ghastly price.

Inequality

The issue of alleged inequality between a man and a boy in a pederastic relationship is always raised by those hostile to the phenomenon. It is more apparent than real, and it is raised purely as a canard. We would challenge critics to identify just *one example of any kind* of relationship which involves two or more persons that isn't characterized by a structured or a *de facto* imbalance of power. Student-teacher; boss-employee; superstar-fan; doctor-patient; retailer-consumer, etc. Nothing could be more foolish than to advocate that approximate equality of power should exist in *every and all* human relationships. The diversity and spontaneity of the majority of voluntary associations would be instantly destroyed. Yet it is the demand of pedocritics. In fact it's more than a little ironic that it is the pro-gay pedo-advocates who are upfront about demanding legal equality *between* adults and minors—thereby removing oppressive areas of legal jeopardy.

The anti-pedo advocates don't really object to the *fact* of inequality in an adult-minor relationship. Relationships they hold dear are *full* of inequalities: husband-wife; parent-child; government-citizen. What these critics dislike about their perceived idea of inequality in man-boy affairs is that they think it exactly duplicates the *coercive* and socially-*imposed* inequality in existing heterosexual and intra-family relationships, i.e., such relationships must only occur as the result of force or the threat of force.

Behind this prejudiced view, of course, is that old classic superstition: that no one would rationally engage in homosexual activity unless corrupted, depraved, etc. Therefore, since no one would elect such behavior, the older man always uses his power (which *must* be based on the idea of force) to get the boy—who is completely depersonalized in this view, without will, desires, or ambitions—to be the "victim" of the man's sexual lusts. This view ultimately stems from that old bogey, the "homosexuality-as-contagion" school. That some people are so repressed they cannot accept the idea of homosexual sex as pleasure indicates the measure of homophobia still extant. This inequality-of-power line of attack is just a ruse to keep adult gay men scared enough to make them less available to the boys who seek them.

The idea of *equality* is a pervasive one in our society and, certainly, among progressives, held up as an ideal. Alas, the ideal is far removed from the reality of life in this land. Inequality of wealth is a scandal beyond compare. Access to services and opportunities is grossly discriminatory and getting worse. Yet suddenly, equality in sexual matters has become a foremost concern among legislators and courts in the 1970s.

Extending civil rights guarantees to everyone regardless of sex seems like a positive—if statist—solution to overt sexism. But other developments, ostensibly progressive, are of the shallowest sort, confusing a bad situation with all sorts of pop medical-legal fashions.

Here in Massachusetts, for example, an effort succeeded in 1974 to reform existing statutory rape laws. The motivating idea was to be sex-egalitarian, to provide the same extent of legal protection to boys as to girls. The *intent* seems benign. The *effect* has been to step up indictments of boy-lovers and the sentencing of them to outrageous terms in prison (including life terms in Bridgewater).

The real question is: in a time of greater rights, increasing education, and legal awareness of expanding zones of sexual and personal conduct, do "boys" need added legal protections to punish those who might engage in affairs with them? Do girls even need them? In what capacities are legislators fit to decide on such personal and private matters? Are we to be blind not only to differences in biological behavior but to socialized behavior as well? Is the banner of sex equality to march forward *by making punishments equal rather than freedoms?*

And shouldn't the notion of ending discrimination on a sex basis—so central to the feminist movement—inspire increasing freedoms rather than being perverted into setting up women as allies of the state in expanding denials *by the state* upon youth?

Inequity

Enforcement of age of consent laws has a class and status bias. All laws in this country at this time serve proprietary interests. Unlike more rigidly authoritarian nations, they are enforced through numerous, and somewhat differing, sovereign states. Yet, the law works in this country in favor of the rich and powerful and against the poor and uneducated. Dealing with pedophile relations, the law occasionally likes to snare a few higher-ups—it makes good press, wins popular approval, etc. The boy-lovers who routinely go to jail in uncelebrated cases, unpoliticized trials, and lacking contacts in the gay community, happen daily. Most never receive any attention in the straight or gay press.

When DA Garrett Byrne indicted 24 men in Boston on sex charges with teen boys, a few were well-to-do professionals; most were middle-class or working-class. The one who finally went to trial was an MD and a psychiatrist and the press followed every day of his ordeal. Such attention would never be permitted a working-class boy-lover. This gent was found guilty of four acts of blowing a 15-year-old hustler; he got probation. Another man, a NAMBLA member, went to trial in 1980, and was found guilty of one sex act with a 15-year-old boy. He got two years in prison. Another case NAMBLA has taken up, that of Richard Peluso, has a man doing life in prison after he pleaded guilty to blowing a 13-year-old boy on four different occasions.

In recent years, two Congressmen in Washington, DC have been accused of sex with teenage boys. Fred Richmond (New York) and Bob Bauman (Maryland) both faced courts on statutory sex charges. In the District of Columbia, for first offenders in such matters, a person can have charges dismissed by agreeing to attend a counseling program for six months. If age of consent laws must exist, this is a sensible way to handle these matters. *Yet we maintain that private consensual sexual conduct should not be a criminal matter.* NAMBLA hears of cases every week in which extreme penalties are handed out for simple affectionate sex acts. Yet Congressmen accused of the same thing walk out the door. . .

When the law can only justify itself as a terroristic mechanism, all its authority—on which government is supposed to be based in this country—is drained. Its legitimacy ceases and it should be abolished. Age of consent laws demonstrate this clearly.

Conclusion

In arguing in favor of abolishing all age of consent laws and for releasing all persons currently doing time for violating such laws, NAMBLA offers two primary arguments, though in this editorial we have also touched upon other important developments in social history and judicial practice which effect the way we are treated today.

Of immediate importance to us is the release of men in prison and in treatment centers who have been railroaded, or found guilty of non-violent sex offenses. It is our position that the legal and correctional treatment assigned these men is a scandal that can no longer be tolerated. The continued incarceration of these men (at least 125 in Massachusetts alone; over several thousand nationwide), and the continued abuse of their persons in the name of medical experimentation, must stop. These men have done nothing more than commit a private act of affection and/or sex with another male who happened to be beneath the age of consent in that jurisdiction. These men have been made victims to conventional statist panic over pedophilia; have been offered up by officials in the panic over homosexuality, and have been denied redress, appeals and sympathetic hearings by gay and straight bigots who would pre-

fer to banish this mammoth injustice from their minds and from public awareness at large.

Of similar importance to NAMBLA are the rights of youths. Young people in this society, who are, ostensibly, the "protectees" of these laws, often find themselves brutalized and manipulated should their private sexual behavior become an issue of the state.

Here in Boston, when we were in the midst of the "Revere Sex Ring Panic," one teenaged boy was taken from his mother and *held over one year against his will* by police and coerced into conforming with their wishes. When he showed signs of resisting state brutality, cops informed him that he would be charged with "sex crimes." So much for "child protection."

Youth are brutalized by the state in almost every capacity in which they will turn for help. Ironically, the state reserves its severest penalties for the men who love boys, to whom the boys turn for affection and support without any required obeisance. The larger issue, of course, is that by breaking down these artificial walls of fear and terror, and by allowing the natural impulse for youth and adults to connect in the myriad ways they themselves will choose and for whatever diverse pleasurable reasons, the system of erotophobia and homophobia will be diminished (and, one hopes, will collapse). NAMBLA is, truly, fighting for the future of the youth of today. We refuse to accept that they/we must be assimilated into repressed straight sexuality, that they/we must be processed into consumerist pathology, that they/we must accede to control-programming by some of the most life-denying and pleasure-hating authorities any society at any time has ever endured. Though each and every NAMBLA member accepts that we are on the front line of this battle, that each and every one of us prospectively faces life in prison, chemical castration, and our murder, we have come to the understanding that the time is now to begin a resistance. We will no longer bow to state terror. We will no longer acknowledge the ageist, heterosexist brutality of which we and our brothers have been victims for too long. *We will fight back!*

Which brings us to a central distinction between NAMBLA and other pro-pedo groups, one which has to be dealt with. These other groups—Paedophile Information Exchange in the U.K., Childhood Sensuality Circle in the U.S., and Belgium's Studiegroep Pedofilie—all fight the panic against pedophile relationships. All keep in touch with NAMBLA and, in general, we all implicitly support each other's work. Yet these other groups do not make the pivotal distinction between hetero (usually adult male-minor female) and man-boy relationships, even though, as with P.I.E. especially, they understand this. The implication is that the only issue is of age.

NAMBLA has a double duty. Not only is age an issue; we join with the rest of gay liberation in our open and positive advocacy of homosexuality. NAMBLA, after all, is an evolution from the Boston/Boise Committee which itself led the resistance to a political attack on gay boy-lovers here in the Boston area. Having emerged out of a resisting, confrontational and activist nexus, NAMBLA is dedicated to the kind of work that will affect change: keep men out of prison, free those who are there, put a check on prosecutorial and judicial homophobic and anti-BL abuse which continues to process men like us into the legal machinery, and by our example, make the issue of relationships that cross legal lines so public, so common and so accepted that we will bring a halt to the terror that exists today.

Those of us in NAMBLA today who were active in other gay liberation groups ten years ago recall the whispers and the confidences back then that, sooner or later, some persons or group would have to take on the overwhelming task of breaking down the false adult-youth dichotomy so precious to the child-haters and the sex-repressed in this culture. That time is now.

NAMBLA has emerged out front. We are not totally surprised at the venom and viciousness we see and hear in attacks on us—from reactionaries or from (usually scared) members of sexual liberationist groups. Change never comes cheap.

Implicit in men and boys loving each other is this: a commitment to a safer future through human affection, combined supportive action and constant agitation. Action aimed to benefit our brothers in prisons, boys fighting hostile families and the men daring to share affection. This is the stuff that moves mountains. As NAMBLA calls to arms (human, warm, and sexual arms—not the patriarch's cold, metallic, killing arms), the spark is ignited. No doubt there will be a price to our resistance—the oppressors do not crumble without conflict.

But we in NAMBLA are certain: despite opposition, change will come. Conditions will improve. We will triumph. Happiness and eros will out.

We are not afraid. We will not be deterred. We *shall* be free. *Every last one of us!*

NATIONAL ORGANIZATION FOR WOMEN

In the National Organization for Women, the largest mainstream feminist group in the U.S., the issue of lesbianism was difficult for many years. Over the 1970s NOW became more accepting of lesbians, but the lesbians involved brought with them a vision of feminism that frowned on many of the sexual practices that lesbians, gays, and others have engaged in. In 1980 this view was codified in a resolution adopted by NOW. The resolution caused an immediate uproar, pitting " pro-sex" feminists against lesbian opponents of pornography, sadomasochism, public sex, and pederasty. The "lesbian sex wars" of the 1980s were not a result of the resolution, but the resolution is one defining moment in their history.

RESOLUTION ON LESBIAN AND GAY RIGHTS

(1980)

National Organization for Women

Whereas, The National Organization for Women's commitment to equality, freedom, justice, and dignity for all women is singularly affirmed in NOW's advocacy of Lesbian rights; and

Whereas, NOW deines Lesbian rights issues to be those in which the issue is discrimination based on affectional/sexual preference/orientation; and

Whereas, There are other issues (i.e., pederasty, pornography, sadomasochism and public sex) which have been mistakenly correlated with Lesbian/Gay rights by some gay organizations and by opponents of Lesbian/Gay rights who seek to confuse the issue, and

Whereas, Pederasty is an issue of exploitation or violence, not affectional/sexual preference/orientation; and

Whereas, Pornography is an issue of exploitation and violence, not affectional/sexual preference/orientation; and

Whereas, Sadomasochism is an issue of violence, not affectional/sexual preference/orientation; and

Whereas, Public sex, when practiced by heterosexuals or homosexuals, is an issue of violation of the privacy rights of non-participants, not an issue of affectional/sexual preference/orientation; and

Whereas, NOW does not support the inclusion of pederasty, pornography, sadomasochism and public sex as Lesbian rights issues, since to do so would violate the feminist principles upon which this organization was founded; now therefore

Be it resolved, That the National Organization for Women adopt the preceding delineation of Lesbian rights issues and non-Lesbian rights issues as the official position of NOW; and

Be it further resolved that NOW disseminate this resolution and the resolution concept paper on Lesbian rights issues 1980 attached hereto throughout the National, State, and Local levels of the organization; and

Be it further resolved that NOW will work in cooperation with groups and organizations which advocate Lesbian Rights as issues as defined above.

Controversies about Cuba's policy toward gays and lesbians have not been limited to U.S. leftists. In 1980 three lesbian and gay organizations in Mexico—OIKABETH, a lesbian group; Grupo Lambda de Liberación (Lambda Homosexual LIberation Group) and Frente Homosexual de Acción Revolucionaria (Homosexual Revolutionary Action Front)—joined to issue the following condemnation of Cuban repression.

OIKABETH

MESSAGE FROM MEXICO: QUESTIONS FOR CUBA

(1980)

OIKABETH,
Grupo Lambda de Libberación, and Frente Homosexual de Acción Revolucionaria

A revolution not only affects the nation that carries it out but its example spreads to other nations as well. In this sense, the Cuban revolution transcends the borders of that island. On the other hand, its success depends implicitly on the solid support of other oppressed peoples of the world, among which, in the specific case of Cuba, the Latin American peoples figure prominently.

Within that framework, the Mexican people have strengthened that support against imperialism in a vital way as a political and economic mobilization and as impetus to work. Nevertheless that support has not depended on the sex or sexual preference (heterosexuality, homosexuality, bisexuality, etc.) of the thousands of individuals given dignity by the Cuban liberation toward socialism.

At present, more than twenty years after the outbreak of revolution in Cuba, the world reads and listens anxiously for news of the exodus of dissatisfied Cubans. Faced with this fact, imperialism, represented primarily by the Carter government, takes advantage of the anxiety to promote the cold war already in progress, attempting to discredit the Latin American process toward socialism. That being the case, if we really support what is revolutionary, we should not pass judgment, either for or against, on the basis of appearances only and without an intense and profound analysis.

Who is going into exile and why? As Guillermo Almeyra wrote so correctly in Uno Más Uno ("Cuba: ¿Por qué se van y por qué se quedan?", Sunday, April 20, 1980, p. 9):

If the position of the United States, that the exiles are political refugees, is completely false, that of the Cuban press is also wrong. If it is true that all the refugees are criminals, bums and homosexuals, we should wonder how it is that after twenty years of revolution and in a country that defines itself as socialist, homosexuality is persecuted as a crime to the extent of forcing those who practice it to leave in exile and how and why there could exist so many bums and criminals, particularly among the young, the children of the revolution.

Most international demonstrations of support for Cuba today reflect vestiges of a profound Stalinism when they fail to mention the sexist manipulations that Cuban state institutions continue to practice. The words of Fidel Castro in response to criticism of *machismo* reveal very clearly a conception of women as useful to men, to the family and to the state as reproductive beings; his perspective reveals an antifeminist socialist conception:

If there is to be privilege in human society, some inequality, it should be in favor of women, who are physically weaker [sic], who have to be mothers [sic], who besides their work carry the burden of motherhood. And if they tolerate the sacrifices of motherhood that these functions imply, it is only fair that in society they receive all the respect and all the consideration they deserve. And I say this clearly and frankly, because there are some men who think they have no obligation to give their seat to a pregnant woman or to an older woman or to any woman on a bus. (Fernando Morais, La Isla: Cuba y los Cubanos Hoy, Ediciones Nueva Imagen, Mexico City, pps. 68-69)

With this statement as with many others, Fidel Castro stands as a Victorian figure possessed of a heterosexist gallantry that, as Kate Millett says in *Sexual Politics*, establishes a dichotomy which "rests on the real existence of two kinds of women—wives and prostitutes—who embody sociosexual division founded on moral duplicity." (p. 119)

Or as David Cooper says, "It is a question of a means of social control, of a means of micropolitical manipulation of persons, which in an exploitative society can lead in turn only to a false reciprocity." (*La Gramática de la Vida*, Ediciones Ariel, p. 15.) Here "exploitative society" should be read not only as "capitalist society" but also, and in an important way, as "sexist society."

Nevertheless, in Cuba all of this goes beyond gallantry to develop from an economistic and biologistic view of sexuality into repression of homosexuality at a time when homosexuality, in full public view, demands recognition as having a revolutionary potential already demonstrated to a great degree.

It is necessary to stress the importance of criticizing the errors of those of us who are fighting for socialism, beginning with the supposed revolutionary marxist, criticism of whom from within the socialist movement is indispensable. Concealment of reality is inconsistent with revolution; as such it is counterrevolutionary.

We should not blind ourselves to the evidence; the way the Cuban government has classified homosexual refugees reflects a progressive bureaucratization of the revolution, reveals the problem of a lack of freedom of political dissent and bears witness to the twenty-one years of marginalization and persecution of homosexuality.

At the First National Congress on Education and Culture, which took place in Havana from the 23rd to the 30th of April, 1971, "The Year of Productivity," Fidel Castro declared in the name of the Cuban government that:

Concerning homosexual deviations their nature was defined as social pathology. The militant principle of rejecting and not admitting in any form these manifestations or the spreading of them was clearly established . . . A careful study was made of the origin and development of the phenomenon as well as its present extent, the antisocial nature of this activity and the preventive measures that should be taken. The reorientation and even the control and relocation of isolated cases, always with the goal of education and prevention was studied. There was agreement on differentiating between cases, between their degrees of deterioration and the necessarily different approaches to different cases and different degrees . . .

The commission reached the conclusion that in the treatment of aspects of homosexuality it is not permissible that known homosexuals, through "artistic qualities," attain influence which might affect the formation of our youth.

As a consequence of the above, an analysis is needed to determine how the presence of homosexuals in different agencies of the cultural front should be approached.

A study was suggested to apply measures permitting the relocation in other agencies of those who, being homosexual, should not have direct contact in the formation of our youth through artistic or cultural activities.

It should be avoided that artistic representations of our country be presented abroad by persons whose morals are not in accord with the prestige of our revolution.

Finally, it was agreed to request severe punishment in cases of corruption of minors, recurring depravities and incorrigible antisocial elements.

It is clear then that the supposed "eradication" of the "problem" of homosexuality in Cuba is a result of official terrorism and repression, not of the "social process of healing" that the Cuban state is triumphantly undertaking or of the "elimination of the open sores of rotten bourgeois society," but of the reconstruction of institutions and attitudes about sexuality, work and social organization scandalously similar to those of "rotten bourgeois society."

We raise our voices in protest before the recent events in Cuba without losing sight of the social context in which they occur. The protests of our movement must be carefully formed in the perspective of countering effectively the stigmatization and demonization of refugees who are gay men, lesbians or prostitutes. The action should be carefully suited to a situation in which refugees are being taken advantage of in an opportunistic way by U.S. imperialism, among other capitalist governments, in their assumed role as leaders of democratic freedom. And at this moment it is also important to point out that repression and persecution of homosexuals in the capitalist "liberal democracies" includes several other forms of violence.

Even the tolerance of homosexuality shown to a greater or lesser degree by "free and democratic" societies has consisted of marginalization and the obscurity of the ghetto (bars, baths, movie theaters, dark corners), the object of which is to "accept" us and silence us in clandestine affairs without permitting the removal of the heterosexist norms that maintain repressive, authoritarian and exploitative structures.

We socialist, antisexist lesbians and gay men should not lend ourselves to the antisocialist manipulations practiced by capitalist imperialism. On the contrary, at the same time that we denounce homophobia and other sexist vestiges of the Cuban government, we firmly defend and support the Cuban people in its revolutionary process.

AUDRE LORDE

Audre Lorde was one of the most powerful voices of lesbian feminism. As a Black lesbian feminist with a white partner and a male child, she crossed many of the lines that divide contemporary societies. As the author of 13 books of poetry and prose, she spoke to us of pain and of hope. Her vision of a just and loving community has inspired lesbians and gays, as well as feminists of all races and sexualities. Her death from cancer in 1992 was preceded by an international conference in her honor.

The speech that is reprinted here and was given in the early 1980s is representative of Audre Lorde's urgent call to respond to differences not by denial but by loving confrontation. She reminds her audience that homophobia and sexism serve racism when they disempower Black lesbians and prevent them from fighting for justice, and also that heterosexual women suffer from the fear of being labeled "lesbian" if they stand up to men. She urges Black heterosexuals to reach across their fears, "to begin *acting* like" they don't believe stereotypes and work with lesbians so that they can learn that their fears are unfounded.

I AM YOUR SISTER: BLACK WOMEN ORGANIZING ACROSS SEXUALITIES

(1980)

Audre Lorde

Whenever I come to Medgar Evers College I always feel a thrill of anticipation and delight because it feels like coming home, like talking to family, having a chance to speak about things that are very important to me with people who matter the most. And this is particularly true whenever I talk at the Women's Center. But, as with all families, we sometimes find it difficult to deal constructively with the genuine differences between us and to recognize that unity does not require that we be identical to each other. Black women are not one great vat of homogenized chocolate milk. We have many different faces, and we do not have to become each other in order to work together.

It is not easy for me to speak here with you as a Black Lesbian feminist, recognizing that some of the ways in which I identify myself make it difficult for you to hear me. But meeting across difference always requires mutual stretching, and until you can hear me as a Black Lesbian feminist, our strengths will not be truly available to each other as Black women.

Because I feel it is urgent that we not waste each other's resources, that we recognize each sister on her own terms so that we may better work together toward our mutual survival, I speak here about heterosexism and homophobia, two grave barriers to organizing among Black women. And so that we have a common language between us, I would like to define some of the terms I use: *Heterosexism*—a belief in the inherent superiority of one form of loving over all others and thereby the right to dominance; *Homophobia*—a terror surrounding feelings of love for members of the same sex and thereby a hatred of those feelings in others.

In the 1960s, when liberal white people decided that they didn't want to appear racist, they wore dashikis, and danced Black, and ate Black, and even married Black, but they did not want to feel Black or think Black, so they never even questioned the textures of their daily living (why should flesh-colored Band-Aids always be pink?) and then they wondered, "Why are those Black folks always taking offense so easily at the least little thing? Some of our best friends are Black . . ."

Well, it is not necessary for some of your best friends to be Lesbian, although some of them probably are, no doubt. But it is necessary for you to stop oppressing me through false judgment. I do not want you to ignore my identity, nor do I want you to make it an insurmountable barrier between our sharing of strengths.

When I say I am a Black feminist, I mean I recognize that my power as well as my primary oppressions come as a result of my Blackness as well as my womanness, and therefore my struggles on both these fronts are inseparable.

When I say I am a Black Lesbian, I mean I am a woman whose primary focus of loving, physical as well as emotional, is directed to women. It does not mean I hate men. Far from it. The harshest attacks I have ever heard against Black men come from those women who are intimately bound to them and cannot free themselves from a subservient and silent position. I would never presume to speak about Black men the way I have heard some of my straight sisters talk about the men they are attached to. And of course that concerns me, because it reflects a situation of noncommunication in the heterosexual Black community that is far more truly threatening than the existence of Black Lesbians.

What does this have to do with Black women organizing?

I have heard it said—usually behind my back—that Black Lesbians are not normal. But what is normal in this deranged society by which we are all trapped? I remember, and so do many of you, when being Black was considered *not normal,* when they talked about us in whispers, tried to paint us, lynch us, bleach us, ignore us, pretend we did not exist. We called that racism.

I have heard it said that Black Lesbians are a threat to the Black family. But when 50 percent of children born to Black women are born out of wedlock, and 30 percent of all Black families are headed by women without husbands, we need to broaden and redefine what we mean by *family.*

I have heard it said that Black Lesbians will mean the death of the race. Yet Black Lesbians bear children in exactly the same way other women bear children, and a Lesbian household is simply another kind of family. Ask my son and daughter.

The terror of Black Lesbians is buried in that deep inner place where we have been taught to fear all difference—to kill it or ignore it. Be assured: loving women is not a communicable disease. You don't catch it like the common cold. Yet the one accusation that seems to render even the most vocal straight Black woman totally silent and ineffective is the suggestion that she might be a Black Lesbian.

If someone says you're Russian and you know you're not, you don't collapse into stunned silence. Even if someone calls you a bigamist, or a childbeater, and you know you're not, you don't crumple into bits. You say it's not true and keep on printing the posters. But let anyone, particularly a Black man, accuse a straight Black woman of being a Black *Lesbian*, and right away that sister becomes immobilized, as if that is the most horrible thing she could be, and must at all costs be proven false. That is homophobia. It is a waste of woman energy, and it puts a terrible weapon into the hands of your enemies to be used against you to silence you, to keep you docile and in line. It also serves to keep us isolated and apart.

I have heard it said that Black Lesbians are not political, that we have not been and are not involved in the struggles of Black people. But when I taught Black and Puerto Rican students writing at City College in the SEEK program in the sixties I was a Black Lesbian. I was a Black Lesbian when I helped organize and fight for the Black Studies Department of John Jay College. And because I was fifteen years younger then and less sure of myself, at one crucial moment I yielded to pressures that said I should step back for a Black man even though I knew him to be a serious error of choice, and I did, and he was. But I was a Black Lesbian then.

When my girlfriends and I went out in the car one July 4th night after fireworks with cans of white spray paint and our kids asleep in the back seat, one of us staying behind to keep the motor running and watch the kids while the other two worked our way down the suburban New Jersey street, spraying white paint over the black jockey statues, and their little red jackets, too, we were Black Lesbians.

When I drove through the Mississippi delta to Jackson in 1968 with a group of Black students from Tougaloo, another car full of redneck kids trying to bump us off the road all the way back into town, I was a Black Lesbian.

When I weaned my daughter in 1963 to go to Washington in August to work in the coffee tents along with Lena Horne, making coffee for the marshalls because that was what most Black women did in the 1963 March on Washington, I was a Black Lesbian.

When I taught a poetry workshop at Tougaloo, a small Black college in Mississippi, where white rowdies shot up the edge of campus every night, and I felt the joy of seeing young Black poets find their voices and power through words in our mutual growth, I was a Black Lesbian. And there are strong Black poets today who date their growth and awareness from those workshops.

When Yoli and I cooked curried chicken and beans and rice and took our extra blankets and pillows up the hill to the striking students occupying buildings at City College in 1969, demanding open admissions and the right to an education, I was a Black Lesbian. When I walked through the midnight hallways of Lehman College that same year, carrying Midol and Kotex pads for the young Black radical women taking part in the action, and we tried to persuade them that their place in the revolution was not ten paces behind Black men, that spreading their legs to the guys on the tables in the cafeteria was not a revolutionary act no matter what the brothers said, I was a Black Lesbian. When I picketed for Welfare Mothers' Rights, and against the enforced sterilization of young Black girls, when I fought institutionalized racism in the New York City schools, I was a Black Lesbian.

But you did not know it because we did not identify ourselves, so now you can say that Black Lesbians and Gay men have nothing to do with the struggles of the Black Nation.

And I am not alone.

When you read the words of Langston Hughes you are reading the words of a Black Gay man. When you read the words of Alice Dunbar-Nelson and Angelina Weld Grimké, poets of the Harlem Renaissance, you are reading the words of Black Lesbians. When you listen to the life-affirming voices of Bessie Smith and Ma Rainey, you are hearing Black Lesbian women. When you see the plays and read the words of Lorraine Hansberry, you are reading the words of a woman who loved women deeply.

Today, Lesbians and Gay men are some of the most active and engaged members of Art Against Apartheid, a group which is making visible and immediate our cultural responsibilities against the tragedy of South Africa. We have organizations such as the National Coalition of Black Lesbians and Gays, Dykes Against Racism Everywhere, and Men of All Colors Together, all of which are committed to and engaged in antiracist activity.

Homophobia and heterosexism mean you allow yourselves to be robbed of the sisterhood and strength of Black Lesbian women because you are afraid of being called a Lesbian yourself. Yet we share so many concerns as Black women, so much work to be done. The urgency of the destruction of our Black children and the theft of young Black minds are joint urgencies. Black children shot down or doped up on the streets of our cities are priorities for all of us. The fact of Black women's blood flowing with grim regularity in the streets and living rooms of Black communities is not a Black Lesbian rumor. It is sad statistical truth. The fact that there is widening and dangerous lack of communication around our differences between Black women and men is not a Black Lesbian plot. It is a reality that is starkly clarified as we see our young people becoming more and more uncaring of each other. Young Black boys believing that they can define their manhood between a sixth-grade girl's legs, growing up believing that Black women and girls are the fitting target for their justifiable furies rather than the racist structures grinding us all into dust, these are not Black Lesbian myths. These are sad realities of Black communities today and of immediate concern to us all. We cannot afford to waste each other's energies in our common battles.

What does homophobia mean? It means that high-powered Black women are told it is not safe to attend a Conference on the Status of Women in Nairobi simply because we are Lesbians. It means that in a political action, you rob yourselves of the vital insight and energies of political women such as Betty Powell and Barbara Smith and Gwendolyn Rogers and Raymina Mays and Robin Christian and Yvonne Flowers. It means another instance of the divide-and-conquer routine.

How do we organize around our differences, neither denying them nor blowing them up out of proportion?

The first step is an effort of will on your part. Try to remember to keep certain facts in mind. Black Lesbians are not apolitical. We have been a part of every freedom struggle within this country. Black Lesbians are not a threat to the Black family. Many of us have families of our own. We are not white, and we are not a disease. We are women who love women. This does not mean we are going to assault your daughters in an alley on Nostrand Avenue. It does not mean we are about to attack you if we pay you a compliment on your dress. It does not mean we only think about sex, any more than you only think about sex.

Even if you *do* believe any of these stereotypes about Black Lesbians, begin to practice *acting* like you don't believe them. Just as racist stereotypes are the problem of the white people who believe them, so also are homophobic stereotypes the problem of the heterosexuals who believe them. In other words, those stereotypes are yours to solve, not mine, and they are a terrible and wasteful barrier to our working together. I am not your enemy. We do not have to become each other's unique experiences and insights in order to share what we have learned through our particular battles for survival as Black women . . .

There was a poster in the 1960s that was very popular: HE'S NOT BLACK, HE'S MY BROTHER! It used to infuriate me because it implied that the two were mutually exclusive—*he* couldn't be both brother and Black. Well, I do not want to be tolerated, nor misnamed. I want to be recognized.

I am a Black Lesbian, and I *am* your sister.

VICKIE M. MAYS

Lesbian-feminist communities have been largely white and middle-class. This is not due to any unique patterns among lesbians, but reflects the larger social stratification in English-speaking countries. Many women of color have found themselves overlooked within these communities because they do not participate in the same symbolic codes of dress and manner as do middle-class whites, and because the history and place of lesbianism in their home cultures is often radically different from those of European heritage. In the piece that follows, Vickie Mays discusses some of these differences and silences among lesbians. She urges African-American women to claim their lesbian heritage, both in Africa and in the Diaspora.

Vickie M. Mays is an associate professor of clinical psychology at UCLA.

I HEAR VOICES BUT SEE NO FACES: REFLECTIONS ON RACISM AND WOMAN-IDENTIFIED RELATIONSHIPS OF AFRO-AMERICAN WOMEN

(1981)

Vickie M. Mays

On campus recently I passed two young Black women walking together. Their interaction with each other carried an air of intimacy and familiarity. They interrupted their conversation long enough to exchange an acknowledging nod with me but quickly returned to their talk. I watched as one woman playfully pushed the other; they both laughed. As I walked on, I thought about our brief interaction. I began to question why I see so many more Euro-American women than Afro-American women whose lesbianism is visibly evident. Other questions began to flood my mind. Do lesbian relationships take a different form in the Black culture? What are the socio-political conditions that facilitate the "outness" of lesbians, and how do these differ for Black and white women? Why is it that the Black lesbian seems to be "invisible" in the United States? These questions began to form the basis for these notes on the impact of racism on the Afro-American lesbian.

My basic premise is that the climate created by a Euro-American world philosophy of capitalism, racism, and patriarchy has kept the Afro-American lesbian invisible. It is this Euro-American philosophy that has resulted in Afro-American lesbians being less visible in comparison to Euro-American lesbians. The Afro-American lesbian's invisibility appears to be even more deliberate when one comes to know the herstory of woman-identified marriages by African women before Euro-American colonization. This invisibility can be seen in the Afro-American lesbian's realistic fears and trepidations for her existence and safety if she openly acknowledges her lesbianism. This invisibility is manifested by the impact of the multiple oppressions of capitalism, racism, and sexism which leave the Afro-American woman with the illusion that equality, power, and privilege are possible if heterosexuality is chosen as a lifestyle. Moreover, this invisibility is perpetuated by the lack of a significant body of literature reflecting a Black feminist or Black lesbian-feminist ideology, as well as by the silencing of the herstory of woman-identified relationships in Africa. Such knowledge could guide the Afro-American lesbian in strengthening and building a visible and viable Black lesbian community. This visibility has the potential to facilitate an overall alliance in the Black community, possibly eradicating the feeling of alienation experienced by the Black lesbian.

Increasing numbers of Afro-American women are discovering a herstorical past of women-identified relationships among African women. Audre Lorde, for example, describes a tribe in West Africa, the Fon of Dahomey, in which 13 forms of marriage exist.[1] One of these is called "giving the goat to the buck." It is a marriage in which a woman of independent means marries another woman. They become co-wives. One of the co-wives may bear children by a male, but all children will be controlled by the co-wives and their heirs. While some of these marriages are entered into to allow women of means to continue to control their economic resources and jural authority, others are clearly lesbian marriages.[2]

Researchers, and often these are Euro-American women, have attempted to deny lesbianism as a possible explanation for these marriages.[3] One such researcher negates the positive choice in these woman-to-woman marriages and describes them as occurring between "women who are unable to lead satisfying lives in man-woman marriage."[4] Yet this same researcher quotes an African woman, who let it be known to her friends that she was interested in marrying a "woman of good character and a hard worker." As the African woman put it: "A man who borrows money for beer from a woman is useless as a husband-father. I could not walk into such unhappiness with my eyes wide open."[5] This woman already had two children, so clearly her decision to enter into a woman marriage was not based on her barrenness. Nor was she a woman of means. (These are the "excuses" usually given by researchers for woman-to-woman marriages.)

Woman-to-woman marriages are much more widespread than history wishes to acknowledge. This form of marriage is found in Northern Nigeria among the Yoruba. Yagoba, Akoko, Nupe, and Gana-Gana communities. It has been reported in southern Nigeria among the Iba and the Kalabari. Other tribes with woman-to-woman marriages include the Dinkas', the Barenda of the northern Transvaal, the Neurs, the Lovedu, and the Kamba in East Africa. I am sure the list will go on as we are able to uncover and write our own herstory.

The point I wish to stress here is that lesbian bonding by African women does herstorically exist. Lesbian relationships are recognized as legitimate social relationships in certain African societies. What kind of social structure and world view characterizes these particular African societies? My guess is that these societies are based on an African ideology that stresses interconnectedness and flexibility in relationships and roles.[6]

Such an orientation contrasts with the Euro-American framework in which the family has been defined as a closed nuclear unit and structured in a way that maintains patriarchy and capitalism.[7] In particular in the U.S. Black women have been used as the backbone for the building of economic growth. It is in the interests of Euro-Americans that Afro-American women should not know of their lesbian heritage. Instead, the wish is that they remain controlled and defined within a capitalist-patriarchal social structure.

Afro-American women as a group must struggle to exist in a social system in which being Black and female is defined as being powerless and inferior. As Barbara Smith so aptly points out. "Self-definition is a dangerous activity for any woman to engage in, especially a Black one."[8] There is an added danger in self-definition for the Afro-American lesbian in terms of the threat she poses for heterosexual males and females, both Black and white, and for non-Third World lesbians.

In the Black community lesbianism has traditionally been labeled as white, middle-class and bourgeois. It is viewed with distrust and contempt. Even today Black lesbians sometimes are derisively referred to as "bulldaggers." Moreover, the Afro-American lesbian who acknowledges or evidences her lesbianism may meet with a fury of violence from Black males. This abuse is qualitatively different from the abuse the Euro-American lesbian suffers at the hands of white or Black men.[9] As Marcia, a Black lesbian, describes it:

Donna and I were walking down 3rd St. holding hands. We passed a bunch of guys as we were going on our way. They turned around and followed us for about 4 blocks. There were about 5 guys. When they caught up to us, one of them grabbed Donna by the arm and asked her what did she want with me. He said she was too fine to be a stud and he had something that would make her feel good. He put her hand on his dick. I tried my best to kick his ass . . . Between he and his brothers I received a broken jaw and two broken ribs. Donna was in the hospital for two weeks with a concussion.[10]

The reaction of Black males to Black women, especially those who are woman-identified, is based on the Black male's experience of racial oppression, capitalism, and male privilege—all of which define the Black woman as a commodity. She is one of the few things the Black male can "own" and control. Toni Cade attributes the antagonism between the Black male and the Black female to an acceptance of Euro-American capitalist and misogynist definitions of manhood and womanhood.[11] When the Afro-American woman, particularly a lesbian, rejects the Euro-American definition of womanhood, she shakes the foundation of the Black male's manhood, which is often defined as controlling the Black woman and making her subservient.

The Afro-American woman has been denied power and privilege. She has been raised expecting to work, as she will need to assist in supporting her family. She will also be asked to do all she possibly can to advance the Black man and the Black race—at the cost of ignoring the oppression of sexism. Indeed, the Black woman has been taught from early childhood that one way to survive in this society is through marriage or in a male-female relationship. I agree with Barbara Smith when she writes:

Heterosexual privilege is usually the only privilege that Black women have. None of us have racial or sexual privilege, almost none of us have class privilege, maintaining 'straightness' is our last resort . . . I am convinced that it is our lack of privilege and power in every other sphere that allows so few Black women to make the leap that many white women, particularly . . . have been able to make this decade.[12]

What Black men and some Black women have failed to see is that the Afro-American woman who chooses to bond with another woman is an asset to the Black community. As Audre Lorde eloquently notes:

Black women who define ourselves and our goals beyond the sphere of a sexual relationship can bring to any endeavor the realized focus of a complete and therefore empowered individual. Black women and Black men [should] recognize that the development of their particular strengths and interests does not diminish the other . . . Black women sharing close emotional ties with each other, politically or economically, are not the enemies of Black men.[13]

Traditionally, as Lorde points out Black women have always bonded together in support of each other. Black women are very woman-oriented in their relationships. The depth of feelings, love, kinship, and bonding among Afro-American women runs very deep. One need only examine the strong grandmother-mother-daughter relationships and friendships of Afro-American women to see the quality of woman-loving in the Black community.

Yet the Black woman who openly bonds with another woman does not have the same types of support systems that are available to the Euro-American lesbian. The Afro-American lesbian who chooses to be visible often loses the support of her friends, her family, and the Black community. While the Euro-American lesbian may find support and a new family in the white lesbian community, the Afro-American lesbian loses a bond that is crucial to her vitality in her struggle as a Third World woman in a white racist patriarchal society. The Afro-American lesbian may adopt the predominantly white lesbian community as her support system, but she does so at the expense of integrating her Blackness with her lesbianism. This can leave her feeling fragmented. One need only read the excerpts of letters from Black feminists in the collection so appropriately titled: "I Am Not Meant to Be Alone and Without You Who Understands."[14] Because of her invisibility the Afro-American lesbian does not easily find her true lesbian sisters.

Yet, despite her isolation, the Black lesbian is less likely to contemplate suicide than her white counterpart.[15] The Black lesbian's attitude is one of survival. A friend of mine calls this the "make do" syndrome, while I refer to it as "there's no such thing as can't." Historically, Black women have experienced some of the most brutal and adverse conditions imaginable, and they have survived. This survival resulted from a knowledge passed on through Black culture, which taught them an ethos of "you must." One need only read the words of Toni Morrison, Zora Neale Hurston, Alice Walker, and Angela Davis to understand the characteristic survival of Black women.[16]

The Afro-American woman has rarely had the privilege to "cop out," as this would mean annihilation. I have at times heard Afro-American lesbians, in regard to relationships with Euro-American lesbians, remark about being tired of "Miss Ann" behavior in interactions with Euro-American women. Some Euro-American lesbians have not been forced to analyze their political role in the social system or come to grips with their own oppressive behaviors. This becomes a source of frustration and tension for the Afro-American lesbian. Black women have been taught from an early age that life is a series of struggles; in order to make it, there is no such thing as "can't."

By virtue of her race, the Euro-American woman has a certain power and privilege in society not available to the Afro-American woman. Family connections, education, and wealth are all resources that may facilitate the visibility of the Euro-American lesbian. For instance, from an economic standpoint, the Euro-American woman may have the *time* to generate a body of lesbian-feminist ideology, or to build a support network through volunteer activities. The Afro-American lesbian, lacking these resources, finds herself without a women's center that supports her needs and without a body of literature that tells her about her lesbian sisters. What the Euro-American lesbian community can offer is a sharing of resources so that the Afro-American lesbian can build her own community and thus become visible. All too often, however, what the Afro-American lesbian has received is an invitation to help the Euro-American community work on its racism or relieve its guilt by becoming the token Black in its group. Lorraine Bethel's poem "What Chou Mean *WE*, White Girl?" clearly portrays the racism and classism in this behavior.[17]

Racism extends beyond individual attitudes to institutional and cultural structures.

By remaining silent on this issue and failing to take an active stance, Euro-American women help to perpetuate Black women's oppression. My point here is not to "guilt-trip" Euro-American women but to energize them to use their limited privilege and economic resources to fight not only sexism but racism as well. If there is to be a cohesive lesbian-feminist movement, the Euro-American lesbian must recognize her racism and deal with her power and privilege in a manner that facilitates such a movement. The hope is for a visible and viable Black lesbian community, which will help produce the building of a united lesbian community.

This article is an edited version of a longer work which appears in Top-Ranking. A Collection of Articles on Racism and Classism in the Lesbian Community, *ed. Sara Bennett and Joan Gibbs (New York: February Third Press, 1980).*

1. Audre Lorde, "Scratching the Surface: Some Notes on Barriers to Women and Loving," Black Scholar, *Vol. 9, No. 1 (April 1978), p. 34.*

2. Melville Herskovits, who lived among the Fon, supports the existence of lesbianism. See his Dahomey, Vol. 1 *(Evanston: Northwestern University Press, 1967), pp. 320-321.*

3. Laura Bohannan, "Dahomean Marriage: A Revaluation," Africa, *Vol. 19, No. 4 (1949), pp. 273-287; Eileen Jensen Krige, "Woman-Marriage, with Special Reference to the Lovendu—Its Significance for the Definition of Marriage,"* Africa, *Vol. 44, No. 1 (1974), pp. 11-37; Christine Obbo, "Dominant Male Ideology and Female Options: Three East African Case Studies,"* Africa, *Vol. 46, No. 4 (1976), pp. 371-389.*

4. Obbo, p. 372.

5. Obbo, p. 374.

6. Wade Nobles, "Africanity: Its Role in Black Families," The Black Family, *2nd Ed., ed. Robert Staples (Belmont, Cal.: Wadsworth, 1978), pp. 19-25.*

7· Sheila Rowbotham, Woman's Consciousness, Man's World *(London: Penguin, 1973).*

8. Barbara Smith, "Toward a Black Feminist Criticism," Conditions: Two, *Vol. 1, No. 2 (1977), p. 40.*

9. This is not to negate the fact that Euro-American lesbians also experience violence, but its incidence is lower and the avenues of recourse and protection are more numerous for white women. It is not unusual for a Black woman to call the police and have them never arrive.

10. Cynthia R. Cauthern, "Nine Hundred Black Lesbians Speak." Off Our Backs, *Vol. 9, No. 6 (June 1979), p. 112.*

11. Toni Cade, "On the Issues of Roles," The Black Woman, *ed. Toni Cade (New York: New American Library, 1970), pp. 101-110.*

12. Smith, p. 40.

13. Lorde, p. 31.

14. Barbara Smith and Beverly Smith, "I Am Not Meant To Be Alone and Without You Who Understand: Letters from Black Feminists, 1972-1978." Conditions: Four, *Vol. 2, No. 1 (1979), pp. 62-77.*

15. Alan P. Bell and Martin Weinberg, Homosexualities *(New York: Simon & Schuster, 1978).*

16. Toni Morrison, The Bluest Eye *(New York: Holt, Rinehart & Winston, 1970) and* 0 *(New York: Bantam, 1973); Zora Neale Hurston,* Mules and Men *(New York: Negro Universities Press, 1935) and* Their Eyes Were Watching God *(New York: Negro Universities Press, 1937); Alice Walker,* The Third Life of Grange Copeland *(New York: Harcourt Brace Jovanovich, 1970); Angela Davis,* If They Come in the Morning *(New York: Signet, 1971) and "The Black Women's Role in the Community of Slaves,"* Black Scholar *(Dec. 1971), pp. 5-14.*

17. Lorraine Bethel, "What Chou Mean We, White Girl? OR: The Cullud Lesbian Feminist Declaration of Independence (Dedicated to the Proposition That All Women Are Not Equal. I.E., IDENTICALLY OPPRESSED)," Conditions: Five, *Vol. 2, No. 2 (1979), pp. 86-92.*

The Jewish tradition of fighting for social justice has put many Jewish lesbians at the forefront of lesbian feminist politics. That has not, however, led to an elimination of anti-Semitism among non-Jewish lesbians. While racism has been accepted as a crucial point of struggle, anti-Semitism has too often been ignored by both lesbians and gays.

IRENA KLEPFISZ

Irena Klepfisz's article began as a letter to *Womanews* about the paper's silence surrounding anti-Semitism in the U.S. While the paper responded with an issue devoted to Jewish women and anti-Semitism, they also responded with an argument, quoted by Klepfisz, that reveals the daily operation of privilege. They isolated and privatized both their omissions and Klepfisz's anger, refusing to see them as moments within a larger structure of oppression. Klepfisz responds to this privatization, and provides a list of questions for Jewish lesbians to examine their internalized anti-Semitism. The list is helpful for all of us to reflect on the specific operations of anti-Semitism in lesbian and gay communities, and for seeing the similarities and differences between forms of oppression.

Other writers represented here, such as Larry Kramer and Leo Ebreo, have used examples from Jewish history to inform our movement and have criticized homophobia among Jews.

ANTI-SEMITISM IN THE LESBIAN/FEMINIST MOVEMENT

(1981)

Irena Klepfisz

In *Prisoner Without A Name, Cell Without A Number*, the Argentinian Jew Jacobo Timerman answers the question "whether a Holocaust is conceivable" in his country, in this way:

Well, that depends on what is meant by Holocaust, though no one would have been able to answer such a question affirmatively in 1937 in Germany. What you can say is that recent events in Argentina have demonstrated that if an anti-Semitic scenario unfolds, the discussion on what constitutes anti-Semitism and persecution and what does not will occupy more time than the battle itself against anti-Semitism.

Timerman's statement can easily be applied to the situation here in the United States where, I believe, an "anti-Semitic scenario" is on the verge of developing. And like so many other issues of the "mainstream," this one is being mirrored in the lesbian/feminist movement. Repeatedly, I find that I am preoccupied not with countering anti-Semitism, but with trying to prove that anti-Semitism exists, that it is serious, and that, as lesbian/feminists, we should be paying attention to it both inside and outside of the movement.

My experience with this is much like shadowboxing, for the anti-Semitism with which I am immediately concerned, and which I find most threatening, does not take the form of the overt, undeniably inexcusable painted swastika on a Jewish gravestone or on a synagogue wall. Instead, it is elusive and difficult to pinpoint, for it is the anti-Semitism either of omission or one which trivializes the Jewish experience and Jewish oppression.

Even when confronted with these attitudes, the lesbian/feminist response is most likely to be an evasion, a refusal to acknowledge their implications. This was the case when I wrote to *Womanews* over its repeated silence on anti-Semitism. Though conceding previous omissions the collective typically resisted a deeper analysis: "Your anger is understandable, but the tone of your letter is puzzling. *An oversight, considerable as it is, is not necessarily a sign of insensitivity much less intentional silence*" (italics mine). In a movement that has focused on the meanings of oversights, silences, and absences and that has rigorously examined how they are functions of oppression *no matter what the intent*, this type of defense and excuse is very difficult for me to absorb, much less accept.

I am aware that there are many Jewish women actively participating in the lesbian/feminist movement and that makes the situation even more painful and dangerous. For it is clear that what I am confronting here is not just anti-Semitism of non-Jews, but of Jews as well.

I recently heard a Jewish woman complain about what she perceived to be a lack of pride among Jewish lesbian/feminists. Though in agreement with her observation, I felt angry with her complaint. For what philosophy, emerging out of this movement, I asked, has encouraged the development and sustaining of such pride? What strategies evolved against the growing oppression in this country have included the strategy for countering anti-Semitism, a strategy that would enable Jewish women to feel some self worth? What theory of oppression, formulated by either Jews or non-Jews, has incorporated an analysis of the history of anti-Semitism outside of the movement and within it, a theory that would reflect a caring for the fate of Jews? And how often have Jewish lesbian/feminists heard anyone declare: "I am committed to this struggle not only because I am a lesbian, but also because I am a Jew"?

The truth is that the issue of anti-Semitism has been ignored, has been treated as either non-existent or unimportant. And, therefore, I am not surprised that pride is low among Jewish lesbian/feminists. For that kind of evasion, that kind of stubborn refusal to focus can only breed low self-esteem, can only increase defensiveness about drawing attention to oneself, can only encourage apologies for distracting others from "more important" issues, can only instill gnawing doubt about whether anti-Semitism exists at all.

Yet clearly the opportunities to connect anti-Semitism with other oppressions have been with us for as long as we have been concerned with the rise of fascist activity in this country. On each occasion in which outrage has been expressed over the ideologies and goals of the Ku Klux Klan, of the American Nazi Party, of the accelerating Christian movement—on each of these occasions there was an opportunity to bring up the issue of anti-Semitism, for each of these has been and continues to be unequivocally anti-Semitic. Yet such interconnections have not been made. And Jewish women have not been insisting that they be made.

There have been a few who have sensed that something is wrong about this, but even they have been hesitant to bring it up, as if by doing so they would be just causing trouble. How is such hesitancy possible among women who have passionately devoted themselves to fighting *every* form of oppression? How can anyone, given our goals and ideals, even doubt the correctness of challenging anti-Semitism?

I believe that Jewish lesbian/feminists have internalized much of the subtle anti-Semitism of this society. They have been told that Jews are too pushy, too aggressive; and so they have been silent about their Jewishness, have not protested against what threatens them. They have been told that they control everything; and so when they are in the spotlight, they have been afraid to draw attention to their Jewishness. For these women, the number of Jews active in the movement is not a source of pride, but rather a source of embarrassment, something to be played down, something to be minimized.

For these women, it is enough that their names are Jewish. Their Jewishness never extends any further. Their theories and viewpoints are never informed by Jewish traditions and culture, or by Jewish political history and analysis, or even by Jewish oppression. In short, there is nothing about them that is visibly Jewish except their names—and that is simply a form of identification, of labelling. No, Jewish women have not been visible in this movement as Jews. They have been good, very good. They have not drawn attention to themselves. And I, a lesbian/feminist proud of her Jewishness, am as sick of it, as I am sick about it.

I think it is time that Jewish and non-Jewish women focused on this issue and got it into perspective. I think it is time for all of us in this movement, Jews and non-Jews alike, to examine our silence on this subject, to examine its source. And Jews especially need to consider their feelings about their Jewishness, for any self-consciousness, any desire to draw attention away from one's Jewishness is an internalization of anti-Semitism. And if we want others to deal with this issue, then we ourselves must start to develop a sense of pride and a sense that our survival *as Jews* is important.

If someone were to ask me did I think a Jewish Holocaust was possible in this country, I would answer immediately: "Of course." Has not America had other Holocausts? Has not America proven what it is capable of? Has not America exterminated others, those it deemed undesirable or those in its way? Are there not Holocausts going on right now in this country? Why should I believe it will forever remain benevolent towards the non-Christian who is the source of all its troubles, the thief of all its wealth, the commie betrayer of its secrets, the hidden juggler of its power, the killer of its god? Why should I believe that given the right circumstances America will prove kind to the Jew? That given enough power to the fascists, the Jew will remain untouched?

There are many, and Jews are among them, who do not accept my view. But I am firm in my belief. Not out of panic. Not out of paranoia. I believe it because of what I know of American history and of what I know of Jewish history in Christian cultures.

I am a lesbian/feminist threatened in this country. I am also a European-born Jew, born during the Second World War, a survivor of the Jewish Holocaust. That historical event, so publicized and commercialized in the mass media, so depleted of meaning, has been a source of infinite lessons to me, lessons which I value.

Fact: It took four years before the Jews of the Warsaw Ghetto could learn to trust each other and overcome their hostilities toward their divergent political philosophies; it took four years before they could pool their energies and resist the Nazis in what has become known as the Warsaw Ghetto Uprising. And before that, while the Zionists would not speak to the Socialists, and while the Socialists would not speak to the Communists, the Nazis were creating more and more efficient death camps and more and more Jews were being exterminated.

Fact: When the Jews finally staged the uprising in April, 1943, the Polish underground refused them almost every form of assistance. Even though they were facing the same enemy, even though their country was occupied, the Poles could not overcome their anti-Semitism and join the Jews in the struggle for the freedom of both groups, and instead chose to stage a *separate* Polish uprising more than a year later.

These two facts concerning this event in Jewish history are permanently etched on my consciousness. (1) The oppressed group divided against itself, incapacitated, paralyzed, unable to pull together while the enemy grows stronger and more efficient. (2) Two oppressed groups facing a common enemy unable to overcome ancient hatreds, struggling separately.

And I think about these two facts whenever I hear about a completely Jewish demonstration against the American Nazi Party in the midwest and then hear about a completely Black demonstration against the same American Nazi Party, this time on the east coast.

And I think about these two facts also in terms of this movement, the lesbian/feminist movement, consisting of diverse groups with diverse needs and diverse experiences of oppression.

I want the issue of anti-Semitism to be incorporated into our overall struggle because there are lesbian/feminists among us who are threatened in this country not only as lesbians, but also as Jews. If that incorporation simply takes the form of adding us on to the already existing list of problems, then it will be merely tokenism and lip service. But if it includes self-examination, analysis of the Jew in America, and dialogues between Jews and non-Jews, then I think this movement will have made a real attempt to deal with the issue.

The following are some questions that I think both Jewish and non-Jewish women might consider asking in trying to identify in themselves sources of shame, conflict, doubt, and anti-Semitism. They should keep in mind that the questions are designed to reveal the degree to which they have internalized the anti-Semitism around them. I hope that by examining their own anti-Semitism, Jewish women will conclude that anti-Semitism, *like any other ideology of oppression*, must never be tolerated, must *never* be hushed up, must *never* be ignored, and that, instead, it must *always* be exposed and resisted.

1) Do I have to check with other Jewish women in order to verify whether something is anti-Semitic? Do I distrust my own judgment on this issue?
2) When I am certain, am I afraid to speak out?
3) Am I afraid that by focusing on anti-Semitism I am being divisive?
4) Do I feel that by asking other women to deal with anti-Semitism I am draining the movement of precious energy that would be better used elsewhere?
5) Do I feel that anti-Semitism has been discussed too much already and feel embarrassed to bring it up?
6) Do I feel that the commercial presses and the media are covering the issue of anti-Semitism adequately and that it is unnecessary to bring it up also in the movement? Am I embarrassed by the way anti-Semitism/the Holocaust is presented in the media? Why?
7) Do I have strong disagreements with and/or am I ashamed of Israeli policies and, as a result, don't feel that I can defend Jews whole-heartedly against anti-Semitism? Is it possible for me to disagree with Israeli policy and still oppose anti-Semitism?
8) Do I feel guilty and/or ashamed of Jewish racism in this country and, as a result, feel I can't defend Jews whole-heartedly against anti-Semitism? Is is possible for me to acknowledge Jewish racism, struggle against it, and still feel Jewish pride? And still oppose anti-Semitism?
9) Do I feel that Jews have done well in this country and, therefore, should not complain?
10) Do I feel that historically, sociologically and/or psychologically, anti-Semitism is "justified" or "understandable," and that I am, therefore, willing to tolerate it?
11) Do I feel that anti-Semitism exists but it is "not so bad" or "not so important"? Why?
12) Do I believe that by focusing on the problem of anti-Semitism I will make it worse? Why?
13) Do I feel that Jews draw too much attention to themselves? How?
14) Do I associate the struggle against anti-Semitism with conservatism? Why?
15) What Jewish stereotypes am I afraid of being identified with? What do I repress in myself in order to prevent such identification?

The implications of homosexuality have always been a matter for debate. Among psychiatrists in the middle of this century, homosexual behavior and desire were evidence of a deeper psychological disorder. For those fighting such beliefs, the most popular argument has been that sexual desire and behavior are irrelevant to one's more general "adjustment" or "maturity." Among defenders, as we have seen, there has been disagreement as to whether those with such desire and behavior are "different" from those without it. In short, we may be "as good as," but does that (have to) mean we are the same as heterosexuals?

The political implications of one answer are traced here by Michael Denneny, a founder of *Christopher Street* magazine and now a senior editor at St. Martin's Press, where he has published a large proportion of contemporary gay and lesbian writing. He distinguishes homosexual behavior from gay identity, and argues that gays are in fact different and opposed to most heterosexuals. Nonetheless, he believes that the "complex, subtle, everyday transformation of values" effected by gays has a role in a larger transformation of society. Because he admits that it is not clear whether his points apply to lesbians, he invites readers to ask whether they do, and whether the two groups are and should be working toward the same transformations or different ones.

MICHAEL DENNENY

GAY POLITICS: SIXTEEN PROPOSITIONS

(1981)

Michael Denneny

> crackers are born with the right to be alive
> i'm making ours up right here in yr face
> —Ntozake Shange

Political reflection must begin with and remain loyal to our primary experience of ourselves and the world or it degenerates into nonsense, the making of idle theory of which there is no end (and consequently, no seriousness). These thoughts begin with the fact—somewhat startling when I think about it—that I find my identity as a gay man as basic as any other identity I can lay to claim to. Being gay is a more elemental aspect of who I am than my profession, my class, or my race. This is new but not unheard of. It corresponds to what Isherwood was getting at in *Christopher and His Kind*, when he frankly confesses his loyalty to his "tribe" in contrast to his desertion of his class and his troubling realization that he had less in common with his countrymen than with his German lover who had been drafted to fight against them in the Second World War. Obviously being gay was not Isherwood's sole claim to identity. Nor is it mine, but it *is* of enormous significance to how I find and feel myself in the world. Those who do not find this to be the case with themselves will probably find these reflections pointless. And since they are based on the experiences of a gay man, it is unclear how much of this discussion would be relevant to lesbians, if indeed any.

Proposition 1

Homosexuality and gay are not

the same thing; gay is when you
decide to make an issue of it.

Homosexual is properly an adjective; it describes something you do. *Gay* is a noun; it names something you are. Gore Vidal, who prefers the adjectively intensified word *homosexualist*, insists on this distinction tirelessly; one assumes he is right in his own case. For him, being homosexual is not a central part of his identity; it merely describes some of his behavior, in which case the adjective homosexualist is probably more precise, if inelegant.

Whether or not being gay is a central part of one's identity—one's felt sense of self in everyday life, who I am—*is not a theoretical question.* It is a fact and can be ascertained by fairly elemental self-reflection. There are Jews for whom that fact is an accident of birth and nothing more; blacks for whom the most monstrous aspect of racism is its bewildering irrelevance to who they are. But there are also gays, Jews, and blacks who know themselves as this particular gay man, this particular Jew, this particular black. Such people experience their humanness *through* being gay, Jewish, or black; they do not experience their humanity apart from its concrete manifestation in the world. The following analogy can illustrate, not prove, this position: one can be an athlete *through* being a pole-vaulter, football player, or swimmer; one cannot be simply an athlete without taking part in some sport.

One can argue about whether one *should* gain a significant part of one's identity in this way; whether one actually does, however, is a fact. Facts, of course, can change. Eight years ago I did not experience myself *primarily* as a gay man; today, if I spend more than four days in a totally straight environment, I feel like climbing the walls. I experience myself as a fish out of water, as a "homosexual alien," in the words of the Immigration Service.

Proposition 2

Gays insofar as they are gay are ipso facto
different from straights.

Merle Miller entitled his courageous pamphlet *On Being Different*, which was both accurate and apt. The liberal line that gays are no different from anyone else is less to the point than Richard Goldstein's observation that gays are different from other people in every way *except* in bed. Liberals assert that we are *essentially* the same as them and therefore our oppression is unjust. This passes for tolerance. However, tolerance can only be tolerance of real diversity and difference. The liberal position is not really tolerant—although it is subtle—because it denies that we are different, which at bottom is another way of denying that we exist *as gays.* This position is absurd—if we are not different, why all this fuss in the first place?

By relegating homosexuality to the realm of privacy—that which is not spoken about or seen and is therefore unimportant politically (consequently "no different")—liberal "tolerance" becomes a perfect example of what Herbert Marcuse called "repressive tolerance" (a concept that seemed to me idiotic as applied in the sixties). The way liberals have of not noticing that one is gay or, if forced to notice, of not wanting to hear about it or, if forced to hear about it, of asserting that "that's your private life and no concern of mine or of anyone else" is an extremely insidious tactic that in practice boils down to "let's all act straight and what you do in the bedroom is your own business."

This is the source of the liberals' famous lament: why *must* you flaunt your homosexuality? (Flaunt is the antigay buzzword as *shrill* and *strident* were the antifeminist buzzwords.) This position is identical to that of Anita Bryant, who repeatedly made it clear that she was no dummy, she knew that many of those "bachelors" and "spinsters" in the schools were gay, and she was not advocating a McCarthy-like witch hunt to have them rooted out and fired; all she wanted was that gay teachers not hold hands and kiss in public, that gay adults not "recruit" impressionable youngsters for the "gay life-style." In other words, get back in the closet and we won't bother you. Anita Bryant was not your traditional bigot; she was something new, a direct response to the emergence of gay liberation. As such, we can expect more of her ilk.

When you point out that this is also the essence of the liberals' position, for all its tolerance, they sometimes get infuriated. They have an odd animus against the very idea of gay oppression. People who are otherwise perfectly sensible get uncomfortable and sometimes hostile when you suggest that even *they* might have internalized some of the pervasive anti-gay hostility and prejudice of the larger society. It is hard to know how to respond when they act like you have insulted their honor, but I suspect the best answer is Curtis Thornton's simple observation about white people: "I understand why they don't want us to think they are prejudiced. But if most of them were not prejudiced, it wouldn't be a prejudiced country" (in John Gwaltney's marvelous book *Drylongso).*

Liberals in general tend to get upset if one tries to make an issue of being gay or if one says that being gay is an important and central part of one's life and identity. One feels like asking them whether their own heterosexuality is not an important part of *their* lives. But, of course, they do not talk about heterosexuality, they talk about sexuality. Which is the whole point.

Proposition 3

The central issue of gay politics is sexuality.

It is sexuality that makes us homosexuals; it is the affirmation of ourselves as homosexuals that makes us gay. Sexuality is not the same as love. Homosexuality is not the same as "men loving men," though it sounds good as a slogan to make us respectable in the eyes of the straight world. Even at our most chauvinistic it is absurd to imply that the straight world is unfamiliar with or unfriendly to the concept of men loving men. They have developed a multiplicity of forms for male bonding, some of which they even regard as noble, some of which even we can regard as noble. What drives them nuts is not love between men but sex between men. It is one of the many virtues of Martin Sherman's play *Bent* that he keeps this steadily in mind. In the face of the implacable hostility of society and the deeply insidious homophobia we have internalized, even most gay authors falter and sublimate homosexuality into homosentimentality. Sherman is unusual in being aware of the quite obvious fact that the Nazis did not throw men into concentration camps for *loving* other men but for *fucking* with other men. The theatrically and theoretically brilliant climax of the play is not the noble expression of yet another doomed love but the simultaneous orgasm of the two lovers as they face the audience—a moment that truly shocks the public, including gays.

If the central issue of homosexuality is sexuality, by definition—theirs *and* ours—it should come as no surprise that we are obsessed with sex. Indeed we are and rightly so. What else would we be obsessed by? Straights throw this at us as an accusation. What they would like—at least the liberals among them—are homosexuals not "obsessed" with sex, i.e., self-denying, repressed, closeted homosexuals, whom they have always been willing to put up with (except for a few real nut cases like Irving Bieber). The only thing wrong with being obsessed with sex is that this obsession sometimes leads to the paltry results we see in too many gay bars. There is nothing wrong with gay bars, but there is a lot wrong with bad gay bars.

Proposition 4

Society does not hate us because
we hate ourselves; we hate

ourselves because we grew up
and live in a society that hates us.

"The problem is not so much homosexual desire as the fear of homosexuality," as Guy Hocquenghem states in the first sentence of his book *Homosexual Desire*.

Many straights—and unfortunately even some gays—have the irritating habit of pointing to one of the more bizarre, extreme, confused, or self-lacerating (but rarely self-destructive) manifestations of homosexuality as the reason for their general repugnance and intolerance. But they have it ass-backward. These evasions of self, confusions of sex, and manifestations of despair are the *result* of the implacable hostility of society—"the havoc wrought in the souls of people who aren't supposed to exist" (Ntozake Shange). There is a savage hypocrisy here that reminds one of Bieber's assertion that homosexuals were neurotic because they were, among other things, "injustice collectors."

Internalized self-hatred is deep and pervasive in the gay world and the havoc it can work should not be underestimated, but to compound it by assuming guilt for the sometimes deplorable effects of society's hostility toward us is foolish and self-defeating. It leads to a miasma of depression when what is called for is anger.

The relative absence of clearly directed and cleansing anger in the gay world is surprising and worthy of note; it is probably a bad sign.

Proposition 5

The appalling violence—
physical, psychological, social,
and intellectual—unleashed
against gays by Western society
in modern times is a clear attempt
at cultural genocide.

Most gay men I know will feel uncomfortable with this assertion, which is nevertheless an unavoidable conclusion. The implied parallel with the suffering of American blacks, the Jews, the Vietnamese, and other colonized or persecuted peoples makes us sharply aware of the peculiarities influence, and a tenuous security that have historically been our options. But the point is not to claim an equality of suffering—pain, physical or psychological, is almost impossible to measure in any case, and attempts to compute or compare it reek of vulgarity—still less to assume that a preoccupation with one's own hurt somehow slights or diminishes someone else's. The point is to establish precisely what has been done and to delineate the peculiarities of our own oppression, which are grounded in the peculiarities of our situation.

American racists have inflicted extraordinary suffering on American blacks but they have not tried to pretend that the black hero, Crispus Attucks, the first casualty of the American Revolutionary War, was white. The Nazi lunatics sought to systematically exterminate Jews, yet opened perverse "museums" of "decadent" Jewish art (which, ironically, were very popular). The astonishingly systematic yet spontaneous attempts to *expunge* our very existence from the historical record—through silence, deliberate distortion, and mendacious interpretation—have very few precise parallels: one thinks of some of Stalin's more bizarre attempts at rewriting history or the nearly successful extermination of the Albigensians, even in memory. Even the cynical will be startled by the catalogue of lies briefly reviewed by John Boswell in his brilliant and seminal work, *Christianity, Social Tolerance and Homosexuality*. To quote one of the more amusing instances: "Sometimes their anxiety to reinterpret or disguise accounts of homosexuality has induced translators to inject wholly new concepts into texts, as when the translators of a Hittite law apparently regulating homosexual marriage insert words which completely alter its meaning or when Graves 'translates' a nonexistent clause in Suetonius to suggest that a law prohibits homosexual acts."

When one reflects that the Stalinist scholars worked under the threat of totalitarian terror, that the Albigensian Crusades were fueled by a wave of popular hysteria that was transitory, if devastating, and contrasts these to the calm, systematic, uncoerced, uncoordinated, utterly pervasive, enduring, and relentless attempt to destroy, falsify, and denigrate gay history, paranoia seems a sane response. What are we to do with people who will go to such lengths as to doctor the records of a Hittite civilization that flourished three-and-a-half thousand years ago?

The attempt to reclaim gay history, so ably argued and exemplified by Robert K. Martin (on Hart Crane) and Simon Karlinsky (on Diaghilev) recently in the pages of *Christopher Street*, will be accomplished only in the teeth of intense resistance by the straight scholarly establishment. Any ground won will be bitterly contested; we can expect them to get truly vicious as inroads are made. This struggle to get our history back is enormously important, for the past brings us possibility, and possibility gives us the psychological space that can prevent our suffocation in the present oppression.

In this regard it is important to note that violence *can* destroy the past along with the spirit. Force *can* destroy culture, as Simone Weil pointed out. The past can be distorted, even obliterated; it has no force of its own to preserve itself. The truth will not out in any automatic way. It is foolish in the extreme to believe that gay liberation will *inevitably* triumph.

Proposition 6

All gays are born into a
straight world and socialized
to be straight; consequently,
we have internalized the enemy,
and all political struggle must be
simultaneously a self-criticism
and self-invention.

Corollary:

Self-criticism does not mean criticism by gays of other gays who are perceived to be different, as Steve Wolf seemed to assume in a recent *Christopher Street* Guestword called "The New Gay Party Line."

The controversy kicked up by *Bent* over whether in fact the Nazis assigned the Jews or the gays to a lower circle of hell was mostly beside the point. It would be important to know exactly how the Nazis treated gays and how this compared and contrasted with the treatment of other groups—although it is morally tacky for any group to try to lay claims to preeminence in suffering in the face of the Holocaust. Sherman's dramatic point was quite different: all gays had been raised as straights; in terms of the play, every queer had internalized a Nazi within and therefore had a spiritual fifth column that could become a collaborator. When Max denies his gay self, denies his "friend" Rudy, fucks the dead twelve-year-old girl to prove he's straight, he has collaborated with the Nazis in his own spiritual extermination, the point Horst eventually teaches him. For Horst, spiritual extermination is worse than physical extermination.

To the Jew the Nazi is other, an external, if insanely malevolent, agent of destruction. To the "bent" the straight can never be so totally external.

Proposition 7

> The elemental gay emotional
> experience is the question:
> "Am I the only one?"
> The feeling of being "different,"
> and our response to it,
> dominates our inner lives.

The gradual or sudden but always unnerving awareness that one is "different" leads to the fear of being the only one. Gays emerge *as gay* in this trauma. One suspects that it haunts gay life in countless subtle ways that we have not begun to trace. One wonders if the extraordinary fear of rejection that dominates the social interactions in gay bars—and that appears so senseless, since we have all been rejected many times and know from experience that it is certainly not devastating—is nothing more than a replay of adolescent psychological scenarios, when natural sexual desire threatened to expose one as "different" and invited the devastating possibility of total rejection, even *and especially* by those "best friends" to whom one was most attracted. This undermining of sexual and affectional preference, putting into question what one *knows* with immediacy and certainty, traumatizes a person's integrity to the point of making one feel that one's very being is somehow "wrong."

This assault on the integrity of the self, which every gay experiences should never be underestimated. It is the basic tactic our weirdly homophobic culture uses to destroy us—first isolate, then terrorize, then make disappear by *self*-denial.

As our archetypal emotional donnybrook, it also helps to explain many things in the gay world—gay pornography, for instance, is by and large positive fantasy fulfillment that counteracts the nightmarish fears of our adolescent years and, as such, is politically progressive.

Proposition 8

> "Only within the framework
> of a people can a man
> live as a man without exhausting
> himself." (Hannah Arendt)

If society tries to destroy us by first isolating us, it follows that what is necessary to fight back is not only defiance but the acknowledgment of a community and the construction of a world. Individual defiance may lead to heroism—as we can see in the cases of Quentin Crisp and Jean Genet—but, while we should honor our heroes, the cost is too high. Few individuals have the integrity or the energy to sustain the violence to the soul and the consequent psychological deformations that heroism entails.

The further construction and consolidation of the gay ghetto is an immediate and necessary political objective. The singularity of the gay situation makes this "ghetto" unique, generating perplexities we have barely begun to address and rendering parallels to the experience of other groups dubious at best. But this should not obscure the fact that ghetto is another word for *world* and that *coming out* means asserting our right to appear in the world as who we are. As Walter Lippmann observed (if not practiced): "Man must be at peace with the sources of his life. If he is ashamed of them, if he is at war with them, they will haunt him forever. They will rob him of the basis of assurance, will leave him an interloper in the world."

From the blacks and the colonized we can learn much about the pain of being interlopers in the world, "invisible men," but we should also learn that if we want to live in the world and not in the closet, we must create that world ourselves on every level. It will not be handed to us on a silver platter. We need to create networks of friendships, love relationships, public places and institutions, neighborhoods, art, and literature. A gay culture is a political necessity for our survival.

Proposition 9

Gay politics (using politics in
its narrow meaning) is a
politics of pure principle.

For us there is no "social question." We are not asking for a bigger slice of the pie but for justice. We do not require social programs, jobs, day-care centers, educational and professional quotas, or any of the other legitimate demands of previously exploited minority groups. Our demands will not cost the body politic one cent. We demand only the freedom to be who we are. The fact that this demand, which takes away nothing from anyone else, is met with such obstinate resistance is a noteworthy indication of how deep-seated is the hostility against us.

On the other hand, we could expect that gay politics has its best chance in countries that are constitutional republics, where the belief that justice is the ultimate source of authority and legitimacy for the government gives us a powerful lever against the prejudice of society. It seems to me no accident that gay politics and gay culture have arisen first and most strongly in the United States. This is the only "nation" I know of that was brought into being by dissidents; whatever revisionist history may teach us are the facts of the case, the enormous authority the image of the Pilgrims and the Founding Fathers has for this country should not be underestimated. It often seems that non-American observers simply cannot understand our feeling that *as Americans* it is our *right* to be faggots if we choose—or as historian and lesbian novelist Noretta Koertge puts it: "Being American means being able to paint my mailbox purple if I want." Invoking the ultimate principles—if not realities—of this country is one of our most promising tactics, and should be explored and emphasized.

Proposition 10

We have *no natural allies*
and therefore cannot rely on
the assistance of any group.

We have only tactical allies—people who do not want barbarous things done to us because they fear the same things may someday be done to them. Tactical allies come into being when there is a perceived convergence of self-interest between two groups. One can accomplish much in politics with tactical allies, as witness the long alliance between blacks and Jews, but there are limits that emerge when the group-interests diverge, as witness the split between blacks and Jews over school decentralization in New York City.

A natural ally would be someone who is happy we are here, rather than someone who is unhappy at the way we are being treated. It would seem that the most we can expect, at least in the immediate future, is a tolerance based on decency. No one, no matter how decent, seems glad that gays exist, even when they may be enjoying works inspired by our sensibility. As far as I can see, even our best straight friends will never be thankful that we are gay in the way we ourselves (in our better moments) are thankful we are gay. This is nothing to get maudlin over. It does, however, sometimes seem to limit communication—the sharing that is the essence of friendship—with straights. It is a rare straight friend to whom one can say, "I'm so glad I'm gay because otherwise I never would have gotten the chance to love Ernie," and not draw a blank, if not bewildered and uncomfortable, reaction. It is understandable that they do not see it as something to celebrate—but we should.

On the personal level, it is generally unlikely that one's straight family or friends will easily learn genuine acceptance; luckily it would appear that they can, notwithstanding, often learn love. For our part, the paranoia that this situation tends naturally to generate should be rigorously controlled.

Proposition 11

Our political enemies are
of two kinds:
those who want us not to exist
and those who want us not to appear.

Those who want us not to exist are the well-known, old-fashioned bigots, who would stamp us out, apply shock therapy or terroristic behavior modification, cordon us off and separate us from society, and ultimately try to kill us as the Nazis did. Fortunately these bigots are also a threat to many other segments of society and a number of tactical allies can be mobilized in the fight against them. Bigots are essentially bullies, and this bullying impulse seems to be exacerbated to the point of massacre by the lack of resistance. This suggests that the best response to them is probably a violent one: unchecked aggression seems to feed on itself and simply pick up velocity, like one of Lear's rages. I suspect that when epithets are hurled at one in the street, it is best to shout epithets back; trying to ignore them with dignity or responding with overt fear seems only to intensify the hostility. Although I am open to correction on this, I have the feeling that the *safest* response to physical assault is fighting back; the bruises one may incur seem to me preferable to the corrosive rage that follows from helplessness, and I suspect they might avoid a truly dangerous stomping. In short, bullies become worse bullies when they are unchecked and the cost of resistance is probably worth it in the long run.

Those who want us not to appear are more subtle and probably more dangerous, since it is harder to mobilize tactical allies against them. This seemed to me the most significant aspect of the Anita Bryant phenomenon. By carefully explaining that she was only against overt gay behavior—the "flaunting" of our life-style and the consequent "recruitment"—she managed to seem reasonable to a large segment of the public; by disavowing any McCarthy-type witch hunt, she managed to avoid tripping the wire that would have sent large parts of the Jewish community of Miami onto red alert. The difficulty of countering these people successfully is rooted in the fact that we *can* pass, a characteristic that distinguishes us from other minority groups, and is further compounded by the fact that when you come right down to it *everyone* would be more comfortable if we remained in the closet except ourselves.

These matters require much more consideration than we have yet given them. We cannot rely forever on the stupidity of our opponents—for instance, in the overreaching language of the Briggs Initiative in California, which led to its rejection for First Amendment reasons that were so obvious they even penetrated the mind of the public. It is urgent to give tactical and strategic thought to these matters—always keeping in mind the fact that in their heart of hearts the overwhelming majority of the American people would prefer us back in the closet. Our only hope is to make it clear that that would be so costly that they will not be willing to pay the price.

Proposition 12

"The only remedy
for powerlessness is power."
(Charles Ortleb)

Economic exploitation, one of the great nineteenth-century themes of political discourse, has largely been replaced in our own day by the discussion of oppression. Exploitation means basically that someone is stealing from you; oppression is essentially a matter of invisibility, of feeling weightless and insubstantial, without voice or impact in the world. Blacks, the colonized, women, and gays all share this experience of being a ghost in their own country, the disorienting alienation of feeling they are not actually there. This psychological experience is the subjective correlate to the objective fact of powerlessness.

It is odd that the desire for power has for many an unpleasant aura about it, for powerlessness is a true crime against the human spirit and undercuts the possibility of justice among people. In his *Inquiry Concerning the Principles of Morals*, David Hume lays this out quite clearly, albeit without being aware of it, when he speculates that "were there a species intermingled with men which, though rational, were possessed of such inferior strength, both of body and mind, that they were incapable of all resistance and could never, upon the highest provocation, make us feel the effects of their resentment, the necessary consequence, I think, is that we. . . should not, properly speaking, lie under any restraint of justice with regard to them . . . Our intercourse with them could not be called society, which supposes a degree of equality, but absolute command on the one side, and servile obedience on the other . . . Our permission is the only tenure by which they hold their possessions, our compassion and kindness the only check by which they [sic] curb our lawless will . . . the restraints of justice . . . would never have place in so unequal a confederacy."

Well, we know there are such "creatures intermingled with men"—women first of all, and the colonized races, as well as homosexuals, Jews, and mental patients. It is truly strange that this philosopher, who seems to think he is idly speculating, was quite clearly laying out the premises of the power structure that at that very moment was subjugating so many groups of people. And with two centuries of hindsight, it should be clear to all of us just how effective their "compassion and kindness" is as a check against their "lawless will." If we have to rely on "the laws of humanity" to convince them "to give gentle usage to these creatures," we will stay precisely where we have been, under their heel being stomped on.

I do not pretend to understand the origin and mechanics of this strange social system in which we live. But it seems to me it should be abundantly clear to even the dimmest wit that without power you will not get justice. How anybody could rely on "compassion and kindness" after looking around at the world we live in is beyond me. "Moderate" gays who think we can achieve tolerance by respectability seem to me willfully ignorant of our own history, as well as the history of other oppressed groups. They are the court Jews of our time, however good their subjective intentions.

Straights who object to our daily increasing visibility are basically objecting to the assertion of power implicit in that phenomenon. They would prefer that we continue to rely on their "compassion and kindness" and correctly sense that our refusal to do so directly insults them. With their record on the matter it is hard to imagine why they are surprised. In fact, our extraordinary explosion into visibility, the spontaneous and visible assertion of our sexual identity that constitutes the clone look is politically valuable. Not only are we more visible to each other, we are more visible to them. Of course, one would naturally expect a backlash at this point; it is virtually unknown in history for any group to give up power over any other without a struggle.

Proposition 13

> Gay life is an issue only for gays;
> whenever straights address the
> question, they are attacking us.

The quality of gay life is obviously an issue for us. There are many aspects of the gay world, many peculiarities of gay life that are disturbing; we should face them and, keeping an open mind, try to understand and evaluate them as possibilities for ourselves. (This does not mean attacking gays who choose to live differently than we do; it means deciding how we want to live, not how other people should.) But this discussion is totally off limits to straights.

Whenever straights, usually posing as friendly but concerned liberals, address the "issue" of gay life, they are actually raising the question of whether we should exist. Curiously enough, the answer is *inevitably* no. This question is not raised about blacks and Jews, at least not in polite company, because its murderous implications are at once evident. For instance, in Midge Decter's recent hilarious attack on us in *Commentary* ("The Boys on the Beach," September 1980), one finds the following: *"Know them as a group.* No doubt this will in itself seem to many of the uninitiated a bigoted formulation. Yet one cannot even begin to get at the *truth about homosexuals* [my italics] without this kind of generalization." To see what is being said here, simply substitute "the truth about Jews" or "the truth about blacks" and reread.

Straights who raise homosexuality *as an issue* are attacking us—about this we should not be confused. From Joseph Epstein's infamous article in *Harper's*—in which this man, a father himself, decides that he would rather see his son *dead* than homosexual—to Paul Cowan's shamefully bigoted review of *States of Desire* in the *New York Times Sunday Book Review*, the position is always the same. Straights who earn their living as cultural commentators, who try to set out terms for public discussion, display an unholy fear of being peripheralized by us. Perhaps more clearly (not more basically) than any other minority group or culture gays threaten their cultural power, which is based on preserving and policing a cultural power, which is based on preserving and policing a cultural uniformity. To acknowledge diversity or plurality seems to threaten the very existence of their own values. This is sick. We may be bent, but these people are truly twisted. Nevertheless they are dangerous; they control the organs of cultural definition in this country, and they have the power to confuse us with their disguised fanaticism.

Proposition 14

> It is absurd to believe that
> after coming out we are no longer
> conditioned by the virulent hatred
> of gays apparently endemic
> to this culture. Homophobia is an
> ever-present threat and pressure,
> both externally and internally.

I suspect that by now I will have lost many readers who will feel that these comments are too militant, overblown, or emotional. One of the problems peculiar to this subject matter is that it is often hard actually to believe in the reality of gay oppression. The hatred of gays makes so little *sense* to us, seems so uncalled for and pointless, so extremely neurotic and so easily avoided (by "passing") that we tend to dismiss it from our perception of reality. How very dangerous this can be is apparent to any student of Nazism. In the thirties most Germans *and* Jews refused to take seriously Hitler's quite explicit and well-known intentions toward the Jews because it was too much of an outrage to common sense. "It's only rhetoric, no one could be that mad." Even during the war, Bruno Bettelheim and other survivors have reported people refusing to believe their first-hand accounts of the concentration camps, to the point where they themselves doubted the reality of the experiences they had so harrowingly survived.

Something similar happens when one steps back to reflect on the clearly documented evidence of homophobia—let us not take the melodramatic examples of shock treatment and forcible sexual reprogramming but the purely prosaic refusal of the City Council of New York, one of the country's liberal strongholds, repeatedly, year after year, to vote civil rights for gays. I suggest that not to give this simple fact its due weight is willfully to blind ourselves to the reality of the situation in which we live.

It is even more painful when this happens in our immediate private life. Often a chance remark or a passingly uncomfortable comment by a good friend turns out to have such devastating implications that we prefer not to think about it. And if we do think it through, the results are so harsh we do not know what to do with them. To dwell on it seems willfully fanatic, slightly hysterical, or "oversensitive," as straight friends are fond of saying. It is less painful to let it go, to go along, to accommodate ourselves to these people in spite of their quirks because we value their company and friendship.

The willing suspension of belief in the reality of gay oppression, however, has serious and destructive consequences. Chief among them is the widespread predisposition to believe that once we have accomplished the psychological ordeal known as coming out, we are suddenly and magically free of the negative conditioning of our homophobic society. This is obviously absurd. Nevertheless we tend to consider our problems—from alcoholism and unfulfilling sexual obsession to workaholism, inability to handle emotional intimacy, cynicism, the self-destructive negativism of attitude, and on and on—as simply our own fault. At most, we will trace them to our inability "to accept ourselves." The point of the matter is *no one starts off with an inability to accept himself;* this emerges *only* after we find other people unable or unwilling to accept us. The conditioning of our homophobic society runs deep and is not easily eradicated; unless explicitly acknowledged and dealt with, it will continue to distort our psyches and our lives. We urgently need to understand the ways these destructive influences continue to pervade our immediate existence, to trace their impact on our behavior in bars and in baths, in the office and in bed, carefully and *without preconceptions* distinguishing what is useful for survival, if not admirable in an ideal society, from what can only demoralize us further. In this connection, I suspect we have, by and large, seriously underestimated the help gay novelists have offered us in books like *Dancer from the Dance, Faggots,* and *Rushes.*

Proposition 15

The cultural, legal, and
psychological assault on gays
so weirdly characteristic of our
society has not ceased, and there
is no reason to believe it will cease
in the immediate future.

Theoretical analyses have absolutely no impact on any social reality. Even the understanding of our concrete situation in the world that they hopefully engender will not of itself change the situation.

A black friend of mine said recently, "If writing a book exposing racism would end it, we would have ended it ourselves a long time ago." All the understanding of homophobia in the world will not make it disappear. We are not omnipotent; neither as individuals nor as a group do we control reality, which is something we share with all those with whom we share the globe. No psychological, interpersonal, intellectual, or spiritual achievements on our part alone will eradicate homophobia, for the problem does not rest only with us— "the problem is not so much homosexual desire as the fear of homosexuality."

What we *can* do is face up to the reality of the situation and begin to change it in our own case. In the sixties there was much talk of "making the revolution"; many people seemed to think that somehow this one apocalyptic event would result in the transfiguration of human society. But the revolution never came. The gay "revolution"—if that term should even be used—can only be made in the daily lives of each one of us. What could gay liberation possibly be but a change in the quality of our actual lives? For better or worse, we create the face of gay liberation in every sexual encounter and love affair we have. With every circle of loyal gay friends established we are manifesting the gay world (the achievements we have been making in this area are documented in Ed White's *States of Desire: Travels in Gay America*). As we individually come to terms with our straight friends and help them to come to terms with us, we help to dissolve homophobia. While this prospect is not as dramatic or as emotionally satisfying as a "revolution," it does have the enormous advantage of being realistic. We are *already* in the midst of changing our lives and our world, but it will not happen automatically or without our individual participation.

Proposition 16

"We gay people are the alchemists,
the magicians, of our time.
We take the toxins of a poisonous
age, the nihilism that is given us,
and turn it into a balm that heals.
We heal ourselves and in that
we are an object-lesson
for the others"
(declared by a lesbian divinity student).

In the modern tradition, radical political theory has always assumed that society would be transformed by some group within that society which "carried" the revolutionary impulse. When Archimedes discovered the mathematical laws of leverage, he boasted that given a place to stand, he could move the entire earth. When modern political theorists thought they had discovered the laws of society, they assumed that with the proper lever the world could be transformed. The most persuasive scenario asserted that the proletariat, a class totally alienated—that is, outside the society—with "nothing to lose but its chains," would be the lever that would move the earth. But this theory forgot what Archimedes knew, that there was no such "Archimedian point" on which to stand; the voting of war credits by the German Social Democratic party in 1914 proved once and for all that the proletariat did not stand outside society; they were as jingoistic as any other group. The truly great vision of political transformation that had animated the West since the French Revolution died with that act.

But as always the debris of broken dreams lived on to confuse the minds of men. There is a constant tendency on the part of people involved in the struggle of their own group for liberation—blacks, feminists, the colonized, gays—to assume that their group is marked by history to be the liberators of all humanity, the class that carries the revolutionary impulse. It is an understandable error: since no group can be liberated unless the entire society is liberated (because of the simple fact that it is always the *others* who oppress the oppressed, therefore oppression will not cease until the oppressors cease being oppressive), it is easy enough to reverse the argument and say that the liberation of the oppressed group will liberate society. Unfortunately reality does not make such logical errors. Bertrand Russell's witty explanation of Bolshevism—since the proletariat has throughout history always been oppressed by other classes, it is only fair that they now have the chance to oppress everyone else—seems more to the point, as we can see in the unpleasant instance of the Vietnamese actions in Cambodia.

At this point in time, it would be silly and tedious for gays to make the same erroneous assertions. Gay liberation has no chance in hell of liberating society sexually. (The reverse argument is, of course, valid, if tautological; the sexual liberation of society would indeed entail the liberation of gays. The problem is only: what will cause the sexual liberation of society, who will bring this about? You see how one could fall into thinking about the agent or carrier of historical change.) Gay liberation will not be the carrier of the revolutionary idea if for no other reason than the fact that by "revolutionary idea" is meant the revaluation of all values, and values are not "things" that can be "carried" like shoulder bags or diseases. A discussion of the nature of value, however, would take us too far afield.

If gay liberation is not going to liberate society, has it any meaning beyond that of promoting the self-interests of the individuals who make up this particular group? (I hasten to add that defending and promoting the self-interest of any oppressed group is in itself totally justifiable.) I think the answer is affirmative, if somewhat speculative at this point.

It has been known for well over a century now that something is drastically wrong with our culture; our values seem to be working in reverse. Western civilization looks more and more like the sorcerer's apprentice: it has unleashed powers that threaten to overwhelm it. Nihilism is the name usually applied to this phenomenon. Our values have turned against us and threaten devastation if not extinction. This sounds rhetorical. It is not. It is a simple description of the current state of affairs, as a moment's uncomfortable reflection on the Holocaust, the threat of nuclear annihilation, the consequences of pollution and irreversible ecological intervention, genetic engineering, or a dozen other phenomena reported daily in the papers, makes quite clear. We need a revaluation of all our values, but how can this be accomplished if there is no Archimedian point on which to stand? If the salt has lost its savor, wherewith shall it be salted?

I suggest that the complex, subtle, everyday transformation of values that we gays have been engaged in for the last ten years, the self-renewal that constitutes gay liberation, is a creative response to the viciously negative values of our culture. As such, it would be a *part* of that urgently necessary revaluation of all values and could serve not as a historical catalyst that will save anybody else but as an example of what is necessary and as a welcome ally to those already engaged by this challenge. In the struggle for gay liberation we come home to ourselves and our world and take our place among the ranks of decent and responsible people everywhere who stand together at this decisive moment in humanity's career on the planet.

No doubt other propositions regarding the contemporary gay situation might be added to the sixteen I have sketched. My purpose, however, is not to be exhaustive but to give examples of the type of matters we must think about if we are to grasp the dynamics of our own lives. These are things which directly affect all gay men; what may seem at times overly theoretical or abstract is nonetheless an attempt to come to grips with the dilemmas that structure our sexual experience shape our patterns of socializing, and all too often distort our psyches and blight our loves while simultaneously bringing us a reckless joy at being alive. These are matters that our writers and artists think about, as well as philosophers and gays on the street whether they know it or not. They are important. For if we do not measure up to the unprecedented novelty of our current situation. We will pass away our lives in the confusion and evasions of a darkened epoch.

FLASHPOINTS: MARILYN FRYE AND JOHN PRESTON

The relation between gay men and lesbians has rarely been free of conflict. The rise of contemporary feminism heightened that conflict by giving women a language to describe and understand their frustration with men. Male denial that lesbian concerns were distinct from those of gays and their bafflement when lesbians do not show up at "gay and lesbian" events or projects may be symptoms of the male supremacy that is taught to both straights and gays.

On the other hand, lesbian feminists have been critical of the erotic practices of gay men and have questioned the relation of lesbian sexual practices to feminist politics. Lesbian-feminists have remained skeptical of the idea that freedom to do anything that we desire is true liberation, and they have engaged in extensive critique of the notion of "consent." Issues of pornography, sadomasochism, pedophilia, and public sex (to name a few) divided these groups in the 1970s and 1980s, and continue to do so today.

As we have seen, in 1980 the National Organization for Women passed a resolution on lesbian and gay rights that caused an immediate uproar. Sponsored by lesbian-feminists, the resolution stated that pederasty and pornography are "issue[s] of exploitation or violence," that sadomasochism is an "issue of violence," and that public sex by anyone is "an issue of violation of the privacy rights of non-participants, not an issue of affectional/sexual preference/orientation." This resolution gave form and shape to the developing gap between lesbian-feminists and those, both gay men and lesbians, who engaged in or defended the "outlawed" practices.

The following two pieces describe and enact the gap between gay liberation and lesbian-feminism. Marilyn Frye, a professor of philosophy at Michigan State University, argues that it is a mistake to see gays and lesbians as a natural community, for in fact the differences of gender are greater than the shared rejection of exclusive heterosexuality. Presented in 1981, when gay liberation had begun to recede in favor of more mainstream gay politics, the essay points to problems that continue today. In the next piece John Preston (who died of AIDS-related illness in 1994), past editor of *The Advocate* and writer of gay fiction and non-fiction, outlines his objections to lesbian feminism, based on an account of the experience of the gay everyman of that time, the "clone." His anger is more useful than the simple denial or defensiveness of many gay men, in that it delineates a terrain for debate and engages those with whom he disagrees. His essay is a useful counterpoint to Frye, and describes a battle that continues in many communities today.

LESBIAN FEMINISM AND THE GAY RIGHTS MOVEMENT: ANOTHER VIEW OF MALE SUPREMACY, ANOTHER SEPARATISM

(1981)

Marilyn Frye

Many gay men and some lesbians and feminists assume that it is reasonable to expect lesbian and feminist support for, or participation in, gay political and cultural organizations and projects, and many people think it is reasonable to expect that gay men will understand and support feminist and lesbian causes. But both of these expectations are, in general, conspicuously not satisfied.

With a few exceptions, lesbians—and in particular, feminist lesbians—have not seen gay rights as a compelling cause nor found association with gay organizations rewarding enough to hold more than temporary interest. With perhaps even fewer exceptions, gay men do not find feminist or lesbian concerns to be close enough to their own to compel either supportive political action or serious and attentive thought. Gay political and cultural organizations which ostensibly welcome and act in behalf of both gay men and gay women generally have few if any lesbian members, and lesbian and feminist political and cultural organizations, whether or not they seek or accept male membership, have little if any gay male support.

All of us deviants suffer from the fact that the dominant culture is, at least publicly, intolerant of deviations from what might be called "missionary sexuality": sexuality organized around male-dominant, female-subordinate genital intercourse. Lesbians and gay men both are subject to derision and ostracism, abuse and terror, in both cases for reasons that flow somehow out of social and political structures of sex and gender. Popular images of the lesbian and the gay man are images of people who do not fit the patterns of gender imposed on the sexes. She is seen as a female who is not feminine and he as a male who is not masculine. In many states and locales lesbians and gay men find themselves joined under a common political necessity when they must battle a Proposition This-or-That which would legally sanction their civil injury, or are under assault by such groups as the Moral Majority or the Ku Klux Klan. Gay men seem to many women to be less sexist than straight men, presumably because gay men are not interested in women sexually. And the feminist commitment to individual sexual self-determination includes, for most feminists, a commitment to gay rights.

Such things might lead one to suppose that there is, in fact, a cultural and political affinity between gay men on the one hand and women—lesbians and/or feminists—on the other, and then to assume that the absence of any firm and general alliance here must be explained by there being some sort of hitch or barrier, some accidental factor of style, language or misinformation, which obscures the common interests or makes cooperation difficult. I do not share this supposition and assumption.

A culture hostile to any but missionary sexuality is also hostile to women—the culture is a sexist, a misogynist, a male-supremacist culture. Because of this cultural reality, the worlds of what the clinicians would call "homosexual" women and men are very different: we deviate from very different norms; our deviations are situated very differently in the male-supremacist world view and political structure; we are not objects of the same phobias and loathings. If some of us feel some threads of sympathy connecting us and therefore would want to be friends to each other's causes, the first thing we should do is seek a just understanding of the differences which separate us. But these differences turn out to be so profound as to cast doubt on the assumption that there is any basic cultural or political affinity here at all upon which alliances could be built.

A look at some of the principles and values of male-supremacist society and culture suggests immediately that the male gay rights movement and gay male culture, as they can be known in their public manifestations, are in many central points considerably more congruent than discrepant with this phallocracy, which in turn is so hostile to women and to the woman-loving to which lesbians are committed. Among the most fundamental of those principles and values are the following:

1. The presumption of male citizenship.
2. Worship of the penis.
3. Male homoeroticism, or man-loving.
4. Contempt for women, or woman-hating.
5. Compulsory male heterosexuality.
6. The presumption of general phallic access.

As one explores the meaning of these principles and values, gay and straight male cultures begin to look so alike that it becomes something of a puzzle why straight men do not recognize their gay brothers, as they certainly do not, much to the physical and psychological expense of the latter.

1. The presumption of male citizenship is the principle that if, and only if, someone is male, he has a prima facie claim to a certain array of rights, such as the rights to ownership and disposition of property, to physical integrity and freedom of movement, to having a wife and to paternity, to access to resources for making a living, and so forth.* Though dominant men accept among themselves certain sorts of justifications for abridging or denying such rights of men (e.g., the necessity of raising an army), the presumption is on the side of their having these rights. If others deny a man these rights arbitrarily, that is, apparently without recognizing that such denial requires certain sorts of justification, then the implication arises that he is not really or fully a man or male. If he accepts the burden of proof, this too would suggest that he is not really or fully a man or male. Thus, what is called "discrimination"—the arbitrary abridgment of men's rights, abridgement not accompanied by certain sorts of justification—is felt as "emasculating," and those whose rights are abridged are inclined to respond by asserting their manhood.

Civil rights movements of various sorts in this country, under male leadership, have tended to take this approach which obviously does not question, but relies on, the underlying presumption of male citizenship. A civil-rights feminism, even one which means to be moderate, is pushed toward challenging this presumption, hence toward a more radical challenge to the prevailing order, by the fact that its constituency is women.** Women's only alternative to the more radical challenge is that of claiming the manhood of women, which has been tried and is not in my estimation as absurd at as it may sound; but that claim is not

*Obviously, what is considered a right of citizenship varies from nation to nation, and within nations men have among themselves more than one class of citizenship.

**There are good political reasons why it took 72 years from the first public demand for woman suffrage to the ratification of the suffrage amendment, and why the Equal Rights Amendment, which was first taken up by Congress in 1920 has not yet, 64 years later, become law. The principle of male (and not female) citizenship is very basic to phallocratic society.

easy to explain or to incorporate in persuasive political rhetoric.

Since the constituency of the male gay rights movement is very overtly and definitively classified and degraded as "womanish" or "effeminate," it might seem that a logical and proud gay political strategy would be to demand citizenship as "women"—the strategy of challenging the presumption of male citizenship. Some individual gay men lean toward this, and thus to political kinship with women, but the gay rights movement generally has taken the course of claiming the manhood of its constituents, supposing that the presumption of gay men's rights will follow upon acknowledgement of this. In so doing, they acquiesce in and support the reservation of full citizenship to males and thus align themselves with the political adversaries of feminism.

It is indeed true that gay men, generally speaking, are really men and thus by the logic of phallocratic thinking really ought to be included under the presumption of male citizenship. In fact, as some gay men have understood (even if the popular mind has not), gay men generally are in significant ways, perhaps in all important ways, only more loyal to masculinity and male-supremacy than other men.[*]

2. In phallocratic culture, the penis is deified, fetishized, mystified and worshipped. Male literature proves with convincing redundancy that straight men identify with their penises and are simultaneously strangely alienated from them.[**] The culture is one in which men are not commonly found laughable when they characterize the female as a castrated male. It is a culture in which an identification of the penis with power, presence and creativity is found plausible—not the brain, the eyes, the mouth or the hand, but the penis. In that culture, any object or image which at all resembles or suggests the proportions of an erect penis will be imbued with or assumed to have special mythic, semantic, psychological or supernatural powers. There is nothing in gay male culture or politics as they appear on the street, in bars, in gay media, which challenges this belief in the magic of the penis. In the straight culture, worship of the penis in symbolic representations is overt and common, but men's love of penises in the flesh tends to be something of a closet affair, expressed privately or covertly, or disguised by humor or rough housing. Gay men generally are only much more straightforward about it: less ambivalent, less restrained, more overt.

If worship of the phallus is central to phallocratic culture, then gay men, by and large, are more like ardent priests than infidels, and the gay rights movement may be the fundamentalism of the global religion which is Patriarchy. In this matter, the congruence of gay male culture with straight male culture and the chasm between these and women's cultures are great indeed.

Women generally have good experiential reason to associate negative values and feelings with penises, since penises are connected to a great extent with their degradation, terror and pain. The fear or dread this can generate might be a close relative of worship, but there is also the not-so-uncommon experience of boredom, frustration and alienation in the sorts of encounters with penises which are advertised as offering excitement, fulfillment and transcendence. So far as living with the threat of rape permits, many women's attitudes toward penises tend to vacillate between indifference and contempt, attitudes which are contraries of worship. Lesbians and feminists, who may know more securely the dispensibility of penis-

---

[*]*The homoeroticism celebrated in Plato's Symposium and applauded in some contemporary gay circles is clearly both generally elitist and specifically male-supremacist.*

[**]*As C. Shafer pointed out to me, according to this use of "identify with," the identification presupposes the alienation since one can only identify with something that is other than oneself.*

es to women's physical gratification and to their identity and authority, may be even more prone than most women to these unworshipful attitudes. It is among women, especially feminists and lesbians, that the unbelievers are to be found. We and gay men are on opposite sides of this part of phallophilic orthodoxy.

Let me interject that though I derogate and mock the worship of the penis, I do not despise its enjoyment. I suspect that if penises were enjoyed a good deal more and worshipped a great deal less, everyone's understanding of both male and female sexuality, of power and of love, would change beyond recognition and much for the better. But I do not read gay male culture as that radical a culture of enjoyment, in spite of its hedonistic rhetoric and the number of good cooks it produces. There are suggestions of this heresy at its outer margins only, and I will return to that matter later.

3. The third principle of male-supremacy I listed above is the principle of male homoeroticism. I am not speaking of some sort of "repressed" homosexuality to which the intense heterosexuality of so many men is said to be a reaction. I speak here not of homosexuality but of homoeroticism, and I think it is not in the least repressed.

In the dominant straight male language and world view, "sex" equals what I have called "missionary sex." In spite of the variety of things people actually do with and to each other in private under the rubrics of "having sex" or "being sexual," cultural images of sex and "sexual acts" refer and pertain overwhelmingly to male-dominant, female-subordinate genital intercourse, that is, to fucking. As has often been documented, most men claim, indeed insist, that there is no essential connection between sex (that is, fucking) and love, affection, emotional connection, admiration, honor or any of the other passions of desire and attachment. To say that straight men are heterosexual is only to say that they engage in sex (fucking) exclusively with (or upon or to) the other sex, i.e., women.[*] All or almost all of that which pertains to love, most straight men reserve exclusively for other men. The people whom they admire, respect, adore, revere, honor, whom they imitate, idolize, and form profound attachments to, whom they are willing to teach and from whom they are willing to learn, and whose respect, admiration, recognition, honor, reverence and love they desire . . . those are, overwhelmingly, other men. In their relations with women, what passes for respect is kindness, generosity or paternalism; what passes for honor is removal to the pedestal. From women they want devotion, service and sex.

Heterosexual male culture is homoerotic; it is man-loving. This is perfectly consistent with its being hetero-sex-ual, since in this scheme sex and love have nothing essential, and very little that is accidental, to do with each other.

Gay male culture is also homoerotic. There is almost nothing of it which suggests any extension of love to women, and all of the elements of passion and attachment, including all kinds of sensual pleasure and desire, are overtly involved in its male-male relations. Man-loving is, if anything, simply more transparent to the lovers and more complete for gay men than for straight men.

Lesbian and lesbian-feminist culture is also, of course, generally homoerotic. Lesbians/feminists tend to reserve passion, attachment and desire for women, and to want them from women. We tend to be relatively indifferent, erotically, to men, so far as socialization and survival in male-supremacist culture permit. Not to love men is, in male-supremacist culture, possibly the single most execrable sin. It is indicative of this, I think, that lesbians' or feminists' indifference to men is identified directly as man-hating.

When a man who considers himself firmly heterosexual fucks a boy or another man, generally he considers the other to be a woman or to be made a woman by this act.

Not to love men is so vile in this scheme of values that it cannot be conceived as the merely negative thing it is, as a simple absence of interest, but must be seen as positive enmity.

If man-loving is the rule of phallocratic culture, as I think it is, and if, therefore, male homoeroticism is compulsory, then gay men should be numbered among the faithful, or the loyal and law-abiding citizens, and lesbians feminists are sinners and criminals, or, if perceived politically, insurgents and traitors.

4. Given the sharpness of the male/female and masculine/feminine dualism of phallocratic thought, woman-hating is an obvious corollary of man-loving.

Contempt for women is such a common thing in this culture that it is sometimes hard to see. It is expressed in a great deal of what passes for humor, and in most popular entertainment. Its presence also in high culture and scholarship has been documented exhaustively by feminist scholars in every field. It is promoted by the advertising and fashion industries. All heterosexual pornography, including man-made so-called "lesbian" pornography for male audiences, exhibits absolutely uncompromising woman-hating.[1] Athletics coaches and military drill sergeants express their disgust when their charges perform inadequately by calling them "women," "ladies," "girls" and other more derogatory names for females.

Woman-hating is a major part of what supports male-supremacy; its functions in phallocratic society are many. Among other things, it supports male solidarity by setting women both apart from and below men. It helps to maintain a clear and definitive boundary between the male "us" and its corresponding "them," and it helps to sustain the illusion of superiority which motivates loyalty. Men not uncommonly act out contempt for women ritually to express and thereby reconfirm for themselves and each other their manhood, that is, their loyal partisanship of the male "us" and their rights to the privileges of membership. This is one of the functions of the exchanges of "conquest" stories, of casual derogation, gang rape, and other such small and large atrocities.[2]

In a woman-hating culture, one of the very nasty things that can happen to a man is his being treated or seen as a woman, or womanlike. This degradation makes him a proper object of rape and derision, and reverses for him the presumption of civil rights. This dreadful fate befalls gay men. In the society at large, if it is known that a man is gay, he is subject to being pegged at the level of sexual status, personal authority and civil rights which are presumptive for women. This is, of course, really quite unfair, for most gay men are quite as fully *men* as any men: being gay is not at all inconsistent with being loyal to masculinity and committed to contempt for women. Some of the very things which lead straight people to doubt gay men's manhood are, in fact, proofs of it.

One of the things which persuades the straight world that gay men are not really men is the effeminacy of style of some gay men and the gay institution of the impersonation of women, both of which are associated in the popular mind with male homosexuality. But as I read it, gay men's effeminacy and donning of feminine apparel displays no love of or identification with women or the womanly.

For the most part, this femininity is affected and is characterized by theatrical exaggeration. It is a casual and cynical mockery of women, for whom femininity is the trappings of oppression, but it is also a kind of play, a toying with that which is taboo. It is a naughtiness indulged in, I suspect, more by those who believe in their immunity to contamination than by those with any doubts or fears. Cocky lads who are sure of their immortality are the ones who do acrobatics on the ledge five stories above the pavement. What gay male affectation of femininity seems to me to be is a kind of serious sport in which men may exercise their power and control over the feminine, much as in other sports one exercises physical power and control over elements of the physical universe. Some gay men achieve, indeed, prodigious mastery of the feminine, and they are often treated by those in the know with the respect due to heroes.* But the mastery of the feminine is not feminine. It is masculine. It is not a manifestation of woman-loving but of woman-hating. Someone with such mastery may have the very first claim to manhood.

All this suggests that there is more than a little truth in the common claim that homophobia belongs most to those least secure in their masculinity. Blatant and flagrant gay male effeminacy ridicules straight men's anxious and superstitious avoidance of the feminine.[3] And there are gay men who are inclined to cheer this account, to feel smug and delighted at an analysis like this which suggests that they are superior to other men, that is, superior in their masculinity. They clearly reveal thereby that they do indeed pass the Contempt-for-Women test of manhood.[4]

(There is a gentler politic which lies behind some gay men's affectation of the feminine. It can be a kind of fun which involves mockery not of women or of straight men but of the whole institution of gender—a deliberately irreverent fooling around with one of the most sacred foolishnesses of phallocratic culture. This may be the necessarily lighthearted political action of a gender rebel rather than an exercise of masculinity. Certain kinds of light-heartedness in connection with what is, after all, the paraphernalia of women's oppression can become a rather bad joke. But when the silliness stays put as a good joke on patriarchy it betrays a potentially revolutionary levity about the serious matter of manhood and thus may express a politics more congenial to feminism than most gay politics.)

One might have hoped that since gay men themselves can be, in a way, victims of woman-hating, they might have come to an unusual identification with women and hence to political alliance with them. This is a political possibility which is in some degree actualized by some gay men, but for most, such identification is really impossible. They know, even if not articulately, that their classification with women is based on a profound misunderstanding. Like most other men who for one reason or another get a taste of what it's like to be a woman in a woman-hating culture, they are inclined to protest, not the injustice of anyone ever being treated so shabbily, but the injustice of their being treated so when they are not women. The straight culture's identification of gay men with women usually only serves to intensify gay men's investment in their difference and distinction from the female other. What results is not alliance with women but strategies designed to demonstrate publicly gay men's identification with men, as over and against women. Such strategies must involve one form or another of public acting out of male-dominance and female-subordination.

It is not easy to find ways to stage public actions and appearances which present simultaneously the gayness of gay men and their correct male-supremacist contempt for women. Affected effeminacy does display this, but it is popularly misunderstood. It would be perfect if some of the many gay men who are married would appear with their wives on talk shows where the men would talk animatedly about the joys of loving men and their wives would smile and be suitably supportive, saying they only want their husbands to be happy. But there will not be many volunteers for this work. Who then are the women who will appear slightly to the side of and slightly behind gay men, representing the female other in the proper relation and contrast to their manhood? Lesbians, of course. Gay men can credibly present themselves as men, that is, as beings defined by superiority to women, if there are lesbians in the gay rights movement—given only that males are always or almost always in the

---

Female-impersonators are a staple in the entertainment provided at gay bars and clubs, and they play to a very appreciative audience. Their skill is recognized and admired. The best of them travel around, like other entertainers, and their stage names are well known all over the country. They are idols of a sort.

visible position of leadership. By having females around, visible but in subordinate positions, gay men can publicly demonstrate their separation and distinction from women and their "appropriate" attitude toward women, which is, at bottom, woman-hating.[5]

Gay male culture and the male gay rights movement, in their publicly visible manifestations, seem to conform quite nicely to the fundamental male-supremacist principle of woman-hating. Anyone who has hung around a gay bar would expect as much: gay men, like other men, commonly, casually and cheerfully make jokes which denigrate and vilify women, women's bodies, women's genitals.[6] Indeed, in some circles, contempt for women and physical disgust with female bodies are overtly accepted as just the other side of the coin of gay men's attraction to men.

5. The fifth of the principles of male-supremacy which I listed was the principle of compulsory heterosexuality. It is a rule about having sex, that is, about "missionary" fucking. This activity is generally compulsory for males in this culture. Fucking is a large part of how females are kept subordinated to males. It is a ritual enactment of that subordination which constantly reaffirms the fact of subordination and habituates both men and women to it, both in body and in imagination. It is also one of the components of the system of behavior and values which constitutes compulsory motherhood for women. A great deal of fucking is also presumed to preserve and maintain women's belief in their own essential heterosexuality, which in turn (for women as not for men) connects with and reinforces female hetero-eroticism, that is, man-loving in women. It is very important to the maintenance of male-supremacy that men fuck women, a lot. So it is required; it is compulsory. Doing it is both doing one's duty and an expression of solidarity. A man who does not or will not fuck women is not pulling his share of the load. He is not a loyal and dependable member of the team.

Some gay men certainly are deviants in this respect, and would lobby for tolerance of their deviance without the penalties now attached to it. They would break a rule of phallocracy, but in many cases they are loathe to do their duty only because they have learned all too well their lessons in woman-hating. Their reluctance to play out this part of manhood is due only to an imbalance, where the requisite woman-hating has taken a form and reached an intensity which puts it in tension with this other requirement of manhood. Such divergence of gay life from male-supremacist culture clearly is not a turning from fundamental male-supremacist values, so much as it is a manifestation of the tensions internal to those values.

The unwillingness of some gay men to engage in fucking women seems not to be central to male homosexuality, to "gayness," as it is presented and defended by the male gay rights movement. The latter seems for the most part tolerant of the requirement of heterosexuality; its spokesmen seem to demand merely that men not be limited to heterosexuality, that is, that genital contact and intercourse be permitted as part of their homoerotic relations with other men. They point out that a great many gay men are married, and that many men who engage in what is called homosexuality also do fuck women—that is, they are "normal" and dutiful men. They point out how many gay men are fathers. I do not pretend to know the demographics here: how many gay men do fuck women or have impregnated women, nor even how many are committed to this line of persuasion in their roles as gay rights activists. But this *is* one of the themes in gay rights rhetoric. Men who take such a line are, again, no particular political allies of women. They maintain their solidarity with other men in respect of this aspect of keeping the system going, and only want credit for it in spite of some of their other activities and proclivities.

6. We now come to the only one of the fundamental principles of male-supremacist culture and society where there really is an interesting divergence between it and the values and

principles of what it labels male homosexuality. Even here, the situation is ambiguous, for the male gay rights movement only wants too much of something that is really already very dear to straight men.

Men in general in this culture consider themselves, in virtue of their genital maleness, to have a right to access to whatever they want. The kinds of limitations they recognize to this general accessibility of the universe to them are limitations imposed by other men through such things as systems of private property, the existence of the state, and the rules and rituals of limitations of violence among men. In their identification with Mankind, they recognize no limitations whatsoever on their access to anything else in the universe, with the possible exception of those imposed by the physical requirements of Mankind's own survival, and they may even ignore or scoff at those out of some strange belief in Mankind as immortal and eternal. The translation of this cosmic male arrogance to the level of the individual male body is the individual's presumption of the almost universal right to fuck—to assert his individual male dominance over all that is not himself by using it for his phallic gratification or self-assertion at either a physical or a symbolic level. Any physical object can be urinated on or in, or ejaculated on or in, or penetrated by his penis, as can any nonhuman animal or any woman, subject only to limitations imposed by property rights and local social mores—and even those are far from inviolable by the erect penis which, they say, has no conscience. The one general and nearly inviolable limitation on male phallic access is that males are not supposed to fuck other males, especially adult human males of their own class, tribe, race, etc. This is the one important rule of phallocratic culture that most gay men do violate, and this violation is central to what is defended and promoted by the male gay rights movement.

But note the form of this deviation from the rules of the male-supremacist game. It is refusing a limitation on phallic access; it is a refusal to restrain the male self. It is an excess of phallic arrogance. The fundamental principle is that of universal phallic access. What is in dispute is only a qualification of it. Gay male culture does not deny or shun the principle; it embraces it.

A large part of what maintains male-supremacy is the constant cultivation of masculinity in genital males. Masculinity involves the belief that, as a man, one is the center of a universe which is designed to feed and sustain one and to be ruled by one, as well as the belief that anything which does not conform to one's will may be, perhaps *should* be, brought into line by violence. Thus far, there really would not be room in the universe for more than one masculine being. There must be a balancing factor, something to protect the masculine beings from each other. Sure enough, there is a sort of "incest taboo" built in to standard masculinity: a properly masculine being does not prey upon or consume other masculine beings in his kin group.* It is a moderating theme like the rule of honor among thieves.

Within the kin group, masculine beings may compete in various well-defined and ritualistic ways, but they identify with each other in such a way that they cannot see each other as the "Other," that is, as raw material for the gratification of the appetites. This blending into a herd with certain other masculine beings, which they sometimes call "male bonding," is what would guarantee masculine beings some crucial bit of security among masculine beings who in infantile solipsistic arrogance would otherwise blindly annihilate each other. The proscription against male-male fucking is the lid on masculinity, the limiting principle which keeps masculinity from being simply an endless firestorm of undifferentiated self. As such, that proscription is necessarily always in tension with the rest of masculinity. This ten-

---

*I use the term "kin" here in a special sense. The group in question may be defined more or less broadly by class, race, age, religious affiliation, ethnic origin, language, etc., and may be a street gang, a Mafia "family," a corporation, students at a particular school, a political machine, etc.

sion gives masculinity its structure, but it is also forever problematic. As long as males are socialized constantly to masculinity, the spectre of their running amok is always present. The straight male's phobic reaction to male homosexuality can then be seen as a fear of an unrestricted, unlimited, un*governed* masculinity. It is, of course, more than this and more complicated; but is this, among other things.

To assuage this fear, what the rhetoric and ideology of the male gay rights movement has tried to do is to convince straight men that male-male ass-fucking and fellatio are not after all a violation of the rule against men preying upon or consuming other men, but are, on the contrary, expressions of male bonding. I do not pretend to know whether, or how often, male-male ass-fucking or fellatio is basically rape or basically bonding, or how basically it is either, so I will not offer to settle that question. What I want to note is just this: if it is the claim of gay men and their movement that male-male fucking is really a form of male bonding, an intensification and completion of the male homoeroticism which is basic to male-supremacy, then they themselves are arguing that their culture and practices are, after all, perfectly congruent with the culture, practices and principles of male-supremacy.

According to the general picture that has emerged here, male homosexuality is congruent with and a logical extension of straight male-supremacist culture. It seems that straight men just don't understand the congruency and are frightened by the "logical extension." In response, the male gay rights movement attempts to educate and encourage straight men to an appreciation of the normalcy and harmlessness of gay men. It does not challenge the principles of male-supremacist culture.

In contrast, any politics which concerns itself with the dignity and welfare of women cannot fail to challenge these principles, and lesbian feminism in particular is totally at odds with them. The feminist lesbian's style, activities, desire and values are obviously and profoundly noncongruent with the principles of male-supremacist culture. She does not love men; she does not preserve all passion and significant exchange for men. She does not hate women. She presupposes the equality of the female and male bodies, or even the superiority or normativeness of the female body. She has no interest in penises beyond some reasonable concern about how men use them against women. She claims civil rights for women without arguing that women are really men with different plumbing. She does not live as the complement to the rule of heterosexuality for men. She is not accessible to the penis; she does not view herself as a natural object of fucking and denies that men have either the right or the duty to fuck her.

Our existence as females not owned by males and not penis-accessible, our values and our attention, our experience of the erotic and the direction of our passion, places us directly in opposition to male-supremacist culture in all respects, so much so that our existence is almost unthinkable within the world view of that culture.[7]

Far from there being a natural affinity between feminist lesbians and the gay civil rights movement, I see their politics as being, in most respects, directly antithetical to each other. The general direction of gay male politics is to claim maleness and male privilege for gay men and to promote the enlargement of the range of presumption of phallic access to the point where it is, in fact, absolutely unlimited. The general direction of lesbian feminist politics is the dismantling of male privilege, the erasure of masculinity, and the reversal of the rule of phallic access, replacing the rule that access is permitted unless specifically forbidden with the rule that it is forbidden unless specifically permitted.

There are other possibilities. Gay men, at least those who are not of the upper economic classes and/or are not white, do experience the hatred and fear and contempt of straight men,* do experience ostracism and abridgment of rights, or live with the threat thereof. Gay men are terrorized and victimized significantly more than other men of their class and race by the bullies, muggers and religious zealots of the world. They do tolerate, as do women, legal and nonlegal harassment and insult no self-respecting person should ever tolerate. Out of this marginalization and victimization there could and should come something more constructive, progressive—indeed revolutionary—than a politics of assimilation which consists mainly of claims to manhood and pleas for understanding.

However a man comes to perceive himself as "different" with respect to his relation to the gender categories, in his sensual desires, in his passions, he comes so to perceive himself in a cultural context which offers him the duality masculine/feminine to box himself into. On the one hand, he is "offered" the dominant sexist and heterosexist culture which will label him feminine and castigate him, and on the other hand, he is "offered" a very misogynist and hypermasculine gay male subculture; he is invited to join a basically masculist gay rights movement mediating the two, trying to build bridges of understanding between them. If he has the aesthetic and political good taste to find all of the above repugnant, he can only do what lesbian feminists have been doing: *invent*. He has to move off, as we have, in previously indescribable directions. He has to invent what maleness is when it is not shaped and hardened into straight masculinity, gay hypermasculinity or effeminacy. For a man even to begin to think such invention is worthwhile or necessary is to be disloyal to phallocracy. For a gay man, it is to *be* the traitor to masculinity that the straight men always thought he was.

Any man who would be a friend to women must come to understand the values and principles of phallocratic culture and how his own life is interwoven with them, and must reject them and become disloyal to masculinity. Any man who would do this has to reinvent what being a man is. The initial intuition which many of us have had that gay men may be more prone than straight men to being friends to women has, perhaps, this much truth in it: for gay men, more than for straight men, the seeds both of some motive and of some resources for taking this radical turn are built into their cultural and political situation in the world. The gay man's difference can be the source of the friction which might mother invention and may provide resources for that invention.

One of the privileges of being normal and ordinary is a certain unconsciousness. When one is that which is taken as the norm in one's social environment, one does not have to think about it. Often, in discussions about prejudice and discrimination I hear statements like these: "I don't think of myself as heterosexual"; "I don't think of myself as white"; "I don't think of myself as a man"; "I'm just a person, I just think of myself as a person." If one is the norm, one does not have to know what one is.[8] If one is marginal, one does not have the privilege of not noticing what one is.

This absence of privilege is a presence of knowledge. As such, it can be a great resource, given only that the marginal person does not scorn the knowledge and lust for inclusion in the mainstream, for the unconsciousness of normalcy. I do not say this casually or callously; I know the longing for normalcy and the burden of knowledge. But the knowledge, and the marginality, can be embraced. The alternative to embracing them is erasing the meaning of one's own experience in order to blend in as normal—pretending that one's difference is nothing, really, nothing more significant than a preference for foreign cars, bourbon or western-cut clothes. Gay men and lesbians, all, are sexual deviants: our bodies move in this world on very different paths and encounter other bodies in very different ways and different places than do the bodies of the heterosexual majority. Nothing could be more fundamental. The

---

*And women, too, including some lesbians. But women's negative attitudes toward any group of men are not really as consequential as men's.

difference is not "mere," not unimportant. Whatever there is in us that longs for integrity has to go with the knowledge, not with the desire to lose consciousness in normalcy.

I cannot tell another person how the knowledge of her or his marginality will ramify through lifelong experience to more knowledge, but I think it is safe to say that since our marginality has so centrally to do with our bodies and our bodies' nonconformance with the bodily and behavioral categories of the dominant cultures, we have access to knowledge of bodies which is lost and/or hidden in the dominant cultures. In particular, both gay men and lesbians may have access to knowledge of bodily, sensory, sensuous pleasure that is almost totally blocked out in heterosexual male-supremacist cultures, especially in the streams most dominated by white, Christian, commercial and militaristic styles and values. To the extent that gay male culture cultivates and explores and expands its tendencies to the pursuit of simple bodily pleasure, as opposed to its tendencies to fetishism, fantasy and alienation, it seems that it could nurture very radical, hitherto unthinkable new conceptions of what it can be to live as a male body.

The phallocratic orthodoxy about the male body's pleasure seems to be that strenuous muscular exertion and the orgasm associated with fucking are its highest and greatest forms. This doctrine suits the purposes of a society which requires both intensive fucking and a population of males who imagine themselves as warriors. But what bodily pleasures there are in the acts which express male supremacy and physical dominance are surely not the paradigms, nor the span nor the height nor depth, of the pleasure available to one living as a male body. There is some intuition of this in gay male culture, and the guardians of male-supremacism do not want it known. A direct and enthusiastic pursuit of the pleasures of the male body will not, I suspect, lead men to masculinity, will not direct men to a life of preying on others and conquering nature, any more than pursuit of bodily pleasure leads women to monogamous heterosexuality and femininity. I can only recommend that men set themselves to discovering and inventing what it *would* lead to.

Another general thing that can safely be said about the resources provided by marginality is that marginality opens the possibility of seeing structures of the dominant culture which are invisible from within it. It is a peculiar blessing both of gay men and of lesbians that in many ways we are both Citizen and Exile, member of the family and stranger. Most of us were raised straight; many have been straight, and many of us can and do pass as straight much of the time. Most of us know that straight world from the inside *and,* if we only will, from its outer edge. We can look at it with the accuracy and depth provided by binocular vision. With the knowledge available to us from our different perches at the margins of things, we can base our inventions of ourselves, inventions of what a woman is and of what a man is, on a really remarkable understanding of humans and human society as they have been constructed and misconstructed before. If only we will. The will is a most necessary element.

It has been the political policy of lesbian feminists to present ourselves publicly as persons who have chosen lesbian patterns of desire and sensuality. Whether as individuals we feel ourselves to have been born lesbians or to be lesbians by decision, we claim as morally and politically conscious agents a positive choice to go with it: to claim our lesbianism, to take full advantage of its advantages. This is central to our feminism: that women can know their own bodies and desires, interpret their own erotic currents, create and choose environments which encourage chosen changes in all these; and that a female eroticism that is independent of males and of masculinity *is* possible and *can* be chosen. We claim these things and fight in the world for all women's liberty to live them without punishment and terror, believing also that if the world permits self-determined female eroticism, it will be a wholly different world. It has generally been the political policy of the male-dominated gay rights movement to *deny* that homosexuality is chosen, or worthy of choice. In the public arena that movement's primary stance has been: "We would be straight if we had a choice, but we don't have a choice" supplemented by "We're really just human, just like you." The implication is that it is only human to want to be straight, and only too human to have flaws and hang-ups. While apologizing for difference by excusing it as something over which one has no control, this combination of themes seeks to drown that same difference in a sentimental wash of common humanity.

For the benefits of marginality to be reaped, marginality must in some sense be chosen. Even if, in one's own individual history, one experiences one's patterns of desire as given and not chosen, one may deny, resist, tolerate or embrace them. One can choose a way of life which is devoted to changing them, disguising oneself or escaping the consequences of difference, or a way of life which takes on one's difference as integral to one's stance and location in the world. If one takes the route of denial and avoidance, one cannot take difference as a resource. One cannot see what is to be seen from one's particular vantage point or know what can be known to a body so located if one is preoccupied with wishing one were not there, denying the peculiarity of one's position, disowning oneself.

The power available to those who choose, who decide in favor of deviance from heterosexual norms, can be very great. The choosing, the deciding, challenges doctrines of genetic determinism which obscure the fact that heterosexuality is part of a politics. The choosing challenges the value placed on heterosexual normalcy. And the choosing places the choosing agent in a position to create and explore a different vision.

Many gay men, including many of those in positions of leadership in the gay rights movement, have not wanted this kind of power. They have not *wanted* any fundamental change of politics and society or any radical new knowledge, but rather have only wanted their proper (usually, white male) share of the booty. But others have begun to understand the potentially healing and revelatory power of difference and are beginning to commit themselves to the project of reinventing maleness from a positive and chosen position at the outer edge of the structures of masculinity and male supremacism.

If there is hope for a coordination of the efforts and insights of lesbian feminists and gay men, it is here at the edges that we may find it, when we are working from chosen foundations in our different differences.

1. See Pornography: Men Possessing Women, *by Andrea Dworkin (Perigee Books, Putnam, 1981). And "Sadomasochism: Eroticized Violence, Eroticized Powerlessness," in* Against Sadomasochism: A Radical Feminist Analysis, *edited by Robin Ruth Linden, Darlene R. Pagano, Diana E.H. Russell and Susan Leigh Star (Frog In The Well, 430 Oakdale Road, East Palo Alto, California 94302, 1982), p. 125 ff.*

2. See Woman Hating, *Andrea Dworkin (E.P. Dutton, 1974), and* Gyn/Ecology: The Metaethics of Radical Feminism, *by Mary Daly (Beacon Press, Boston, 1978), especially the First and Second Passages, for full discussion of the symptoms and functions of woman-hating.*

3. Thanks to C.S. for the realization that gay effeminacy has so little to do with women that it is not even primarily the mockery of women I had thought it was.

4. This observation due to C.S.

5. This point due to John Stoltenberg. See "Toward Gender Justice," WIN Magazine, *March 20, 1975, pp. 6f9.*

6. See "Sexist Slang and the Gay Community: Are You One, Too?" by Julia P. Stanley and Susan W. Robbins, The Michigan Occasional Papers Series, *Number XIV (Michigan Occasional Papers in Women's Studies, University of Michigan, 354 Lorch Hall, Ann Arbor, Michigan 48109).*

7. For explanation and elaboration of this claim, see "To Be And Be Seen: The Politics of Reality," in The Politics of Reality, *Marilyn Frye (Freedom, CA: Crossing, 1984).*

8. That this kind of unconsciousness is one of the privileges of dominance was first made clear to me by Regi Teasley, long before (to my knowledge) other feminists had understood it.

GOODBYE TO SALLY GERHART

(1981)

John Preston

The issue of pornography can be boiled down to a very sharp dichotomy:

To women:
The experience and fear of unleashed male sexuality in the form of rape is the most naked expression of women's domination by men. Freedom from rape is the first, necessary step toward women's liberation. Anything that glorifies, encourages, or forgives rape—actually or symbolically—is intolerable. To women, pornography is precisely such a symbolic act of rape.

To gay men:
The fear of one's own sexuality, especially in the form of internalized self-hatred and self-disgust, is the most pernicious expression of sexism in our society. The first step toward personal and communal liberation is unlearning those lessons of socialization which made our cocks and asses dirty. The acceptance of our bodies, the unhindered celebration of our sexuality, and the act of loving other men spiritually, romantically, and physically *is the necessary first step toward liberation. Anything that helps to free our repressed selves—including pornography—has a positive value.*

Those two statements contain a profound basis for opposition. But the recent feminist turn toward a stance of puritanical guardianship of sexual morality has short-circuited any possible explorations of the important implications of this opposition for both the gay and women's movements.

There is less and less doubt that the women's movement is perfectly willing to bully gay men over issues of male sexual expression. Recent conferences, including the last National Organization for Women (NOW) national convention, have laid down the law: you gay men must be respectable if you want to stand with us. That message provokes an automatic negative response in gay men. Just as rape is a "tape" for women, just as it produces intolerably painful associations with their sense of powerlessness, so does any injunction to be respectable activate insufferably painful tapes for us. The specific association involves the haunting memories of the desperate hope that gay men would be accepted if only . . . if only you get rid of the drag queens . . . if only you wouldn't flaunt your sexuality . . . if only you wouldn't talk about it so much . . . if only you wore decent clothes . . . if only we didn't know what you did . . . then we would accept you. The problem is that if we did do all those things and excluded all those people, we would no longer be gay.

NOW and its sister organizations have simply escalated the "if onlys." If only gay men wouldn't indulge in promiscuous sex, would give up explorations of sadomasochism, would cease any exploration of intergenerational sex, then we would be okay.

But men who define themselves as members of the gay community don't seem willing to give in to these demands any longer. For one thing, the source of liberation is increasingly seen as coming from within our own community. Relationships with the rest of society are based less often on a search for acceptance by others and more often assumed to be contentious. This, really, is the primary reason for the ghettos of gay America and the ascendance of the clone, probably the most unfairly demeaned political activist in the short history of the gay movement. It is the clone and his personal decision to wear the uniform of the ghetto that are finally quantifying gay existence to an unimagined degree. No matter how much scorn and ridicule are heaped on him, it is the clone who will spontaneously erupt in rage in San Francisco, march on Washington without his leaders telling him to do so, memorialize murder victims in New York, and call them brother.

The clone—the gay everyman—is vitally concerned with sexual expression. He does not discuss the power issues of sadomasochism in workshops; he experiences it as an often positive force which can break through his inhibitions. He is not a pedophile in the classic sense of the word, but he is certainly attracted to situations in which an age discrepancy heightens erotic appeal between men whom he sees as peers. He very probably does seek emotional attachments and worries greatly about his and other men's abilities to construct meaningful relations, but sex for him is play. Heterosexual marriage and its assumed mandate for monogamy are *not* only not accepted as models; they are undesirable. He has also produced a remarkable cultural revolution. The very uniform he wears—be it denim, leather, or Lacoste—is the externalization of a total redirection of gay sexual attraction. Theorists can search forever for its roots in the traditional American images of masculinity, but the reality is that the clone is not going after some longed-for heterosexual image. The uniform is a signal which announces a gay man's attraction to, identification with, and desire for other gay men. That often maligned look—the flannel shirts in Manhattan, the leather jackets in California, the collegiate style in Chicago—are the first widespread, visible signals that gay men exist in great numbers. They're not attempts to idolize straight men; they're announcements of *gayness,* perfectly obvious to both the wearer and the onlooker.

People who attempt to direct the gay political movement without taking into account the revolution of the clone are doomed to lead a soldierless army. The hope of overcoming divisiveness between gay men and lesbians must be rejected if the only basis upon which the breach can be mended is the acquiescence of gay men to the antimale sexual demands of feminists.

The power of the clone ghetto, however, is very limited. Even where it exists in its most mature forms in New York and San Francisco and in resort communities such as Provincetown and Key West, it exists under constant threat of very real physical violence. Only the most foolish gay man believes himself free from the danger of assault by bigots. Gay men who live outside larger ghettos are all the more open to assault—physically and politically—and are all the more aware of the danger they are in.

Gay men *are* remarkably vulnerable. It is actually quite amazing that such large numbers have risked career, family, and privilege for the sake of the exploration that is involved in being gay today. Some women's organizations have evidently perceived the vincibility of the rights and dignity of gay men. When it becomes apparent that gay men are not all united in blind obedience to a mythical, feminist truth or when it becomes apparent that a feminist goal can be most easily achieved by overriding gay concerns, there are few groups that won't take advantage of the situation.

It is almost a truism that we live in an antisexual society. The very presence of gay men and our acknowledged erotic nature is judged an ipso facto obscenity by the majority of the nation. But there is another point here: homosexuality is, after all, the most complete expression of male sexuality possible. It is very clear that the *maleness* of gay men presents an image that many feminists find repulsive. It also should be very clear to gay men that we cannot afford to give up the victory which is the celebration of that maleness. This unwillingness to accede to the feminist prohibition against male sexuality is cited by many women as an example of the gay man's powerful privilege. Gay men cannot make that illogical connection.

One of the great myths of the women's movement is the absolute law that any man is more powerful than any woman. It follows, then, in a perverse form of Aristotelian logic that any gay man must be more powerful than any woman. With increasing frequency, certain feminists are using this tight progression of reasoning to pronounce gay men the enemy. The reaction from most gay men, though, is utter incredulity. Gay men have almost no sense of power. We have all too vivid perceptions, in fact, of our own powerlessness. Nowhere is the discrepancy between self-concept and feminist accusation more apparent than in the current battle over pornography. Gay men are actively denounced for lechery, sexual self-indulgence, promiscuity, and love of erotica. Gay men's response is a great confusion.

After all, we are accustomed to prompt agreement with feminist mandates. But with this issue, there is an instinctual reaction of protest. They are wrong this time, and we know it. Yet that response is accompanied by another: gay men feel betrayed by women.

No other single group of men in this society has been willing to do so much with the women's movement as gays. None. Gay periodicals, for the most part, reflexively used non-sexist terminology as soon as it was promoted as a tool of equality. Those gay organizations which have not given up the hope of gender coalition are by far the most willing of all political groups in this country to have women in positions of key leadership; they have traditionally opted for equal gender representation on boards committees, speakers' platforms, and the like. Countless gay organizations have paralyzed themselves when they heard the shout "Sexist." Nowhere—nowhere at all—has there been as much feminist consciousness-raising among men as in the gay men's community, both inside and outside the organizations. But now gay men are the enemy. Without doubt, one reason is that we are perceived as the easiest target. It is always easy to attack male homosexuals. Anita Bryant knew that; her sisters in the movement have learned her lessons well.

Sally Gerhart's infamous election letter condemning gay male lifestyles in San Francisco and calling for the dissociation of gay male and feminist political groups is noteworthy in this context because of its honesty. The ways in which women's organizations have been willing to trade on fag-hating are seldom so forthright.

Take Back the Night (TBTN) is one of the most visible feminist organizations here in Portland, Maine. It is self-described as a coalition, a confederation of women's groups brought together to combat sexism in general and pornography and sexual harassment in particular. TBTN shares many qualities with other feminist organizations. For one thing, it has remarkable access to the media. Portland's television, radio, and print news offices do not differ from their counterparts elsewhere. The women's movement is news. Female reporters are emerging in dramatically increasing numbers—as well they should be. They and their male co-workers automatically cover whatever events women activists announce as important.

But TBTN does not passively count on such spontaneous reactions. Its leadership has proven itself virtuoso in providing that special dramatic touch that gives the media their payoff: when TBTN holds an action, it is careful to make sure that the activity justifies front-page, lead-story coverage.

The most recent TBTN event was a tour of Portland's adult bookstores. Women were given guided expeditions through the half-dozen or so sexual emporiums that exist in this city, whose metropolitan population of 200,000 makes it the largest urban area in the tristate northern New England region. Certainly similar tours have been conducted in New York, Boston, and other much larger cities. But still, the timing of this particular event was suspect, to say the least.

Adult bookstores in Portland are a joke by big-city standards. Even such relatively tame publications as the *Advocate* are stapled shut or wrapped in cellophane. Until recently, the stores were limited to Congress Street, the main thoroughfare of the downtown area. Almost all of them, in fact, were in the same two-block stretch as the city's two "adult" movie theaters. This neighborhood, Portland's red-light district, is so inconspicuous in comparison to its peers that most New Yorkers would walk right through it without recognizing its function. Most Bostonians would prefer it to untold numbers of retail blocks in their city. There are a few drunks, a bit of prostitution, and even a little hustling, and it does justify the city's concern for it as a center of what crime does exist here, but believe me, it's not Times Square, and it's no combat zone.

While adult bookstores were limited to this area, TBTN made some protests, but nothing like the current campaign of headlines, tours, speeches, and calls for eradication. The change in attitude cannot be isolated from another event: the opening of Portland's first *gay* adult bookstore.

The existence of homosexually oriented erotica was not new. But the shop, the Blueboy, broke two rules when it opened its doors. For one, it stocked *only* homoerotic material. Second, it was located in the Old Port, the city's gentrified residential and retail shopping area. While the site certainly produced some honestly motivated objections from residents who simply did not want any adult bookstores in their neighborhood, it is perfectly clear that the vast majority of complaints were not similarly motivated. The people who were making the most noise did not give a damn about the Blueboy's Old Port address. They just did not want faggots to be visible anywhere. TBTN must have loved it.

The issue was actually fairly humorous at first. Hysterical debates on the true function of glory-holes between the coin-operated movie booths took place in one of the daily newspapers. "For ventilation," insisted the proprietor. "If you don't know, I won't say," insisted the chief of police. Actually, the city council and the owner settled the dispute fairly quickly. The shop was licensed, *sans* glory-holes. There the matter might have died. But the issue of pornography in Portland was now hot, heated by its equation with homosexuality in the public mind.

One reason feminists have focused on the issue of pornography is because it is apparently the issue of radical concern that strikes the most responsive chord in the general community. While abortion, affirmative action, and lesbian concerns all seem to carry the threat of backlash because of the repugnance of some religious and ethnic groups, pornography is safe. It is a sanitary rallying point. Like most other excursions into moral politics, however, it produces some strange alliances.

A Baptist minister recently threatened a referendum drive to close all the adult sex enterprises in Portland. The goals of the referendum were strikingly similar to those of TBTN, and there was press speculation that the fundamentalists would form an alliance with the feminists. I don't know whether or not that would have happened. Qualifying a referendum for the ballot here is a formidable task. (Voters must sign petitions at City Hall between the hours of nine and five weekdays; the petitions cannot be circulated freely.) In any event, the petition drive failed. But I see no reason to believe that the women's organizations would not have supported that vote. The closure of the adult bookstores has become a well-advertised priority on their political agenda. In any event, none of them publicly spoke about the one area in which TBTN and the local quasi-Moral Majority differed: the proposed referendum not only called for the end of sales of adult erotica; it would also have closed the only gay bars that operate on a year-round basis in the entire state.

In this context, the idea that women, when they are compared to gay men, are a powerless group is an absurdity. TBTN is only one of a growing number of women's organizations in Portland. While it is clear that women have had a bitterly difficult struggle promoting their cause, it is also true that they have constructed a power base incomparably greater than gay men's. They have access to the media, where they are almost always treated with respect. They have to fight for academic appointments, but they do get them. Politics have opened to them in ways that gay men can only dream about. (Portland recently joined those American cities headed by a woman mayor.) And, with obvious, painful difficulties and not without harsh infighting and an onerous burden of needing to determine personal priorities, lesbians have been able to take advantage of this situation and assume positions of influence and leadership. Gay men have no comparable situation in their lives.

Even with the heavy economic stake in Ogunquit and the much less visible (though certainly significant) economic investment in the Old Port, gay men exist here without any discernible power. That powerlessness is not abstract. Omnipresent vulnerability to physical attack on the beaches of a gay resort like Ogunquit does not need any sophisticated analysis to be labeled as impotence.

What gay rights exist in Maine exist at the sufferance of a few liberal groups. A pattern of police harassment in Portland was broken by the Maine Civil Liberties Union a few years ago. (No one, though, has moved against an even more severe pattern in Orono, site of the University of Maine campus. A single bar in that town becomes a "private club" one day a week. Gays from the university and from neighboring Bangor, the second-largest city in the state, are routinely stopped, identified, and questioned by local police as they leave the club's parking lot.) Such liberal alliances are well known for their lack of commitment to any profound sense of gay liberation. When I recently surveyed the candidates for election to the Maine Civil Liberties Union (MCLU) Board of Directors, asking why gay issues were not mentioned as a priority in any of their position statements, I received only a single reply, from the editor of the "liberal" weekly *Maine Times*, who affirmed that gay rights was not a cause that the organization should take on as a priority. He asserted that the MCLU should act on the rights of gay people only insofar as they involved rights of privacy.

But credit where credit is due: it is amazing that Maine came closer than any other state to enacting a gay rights bill. The bill to add gays to the already-existing civil rights legislation was defeated by a narrow 16ƒ13 vote in the senate after a strong campaign by Democratic Majority Leader Gerard Conley, a prominent Roman Catholic layman whose activities should be the model for our expectations of elected officials. His attitude toward issues of "validating gay life-styles" or "passing approval on homosexuality" is especially noteworthy. When I asked him how he dealt with those objections, he gruffly responded: "When these people have jobs, can rent apartments, and can walk the streets of their hometowns without fear of being attacked by hoodlums, then I'll indulge in the luxury of commenting on the morality of their private lives. Until then, this is simply, purely, and absolutely a pressing, unjust denial of civil rights in our state. That lack of rights is the only issue I will allow myself to address."

The men who testified in favor of the gay rights bill in the hearings in Augusta, the state capital, were not middle-class professionals seeking memberships in elite organizations or media mavens seeking stardom. They were mill workers who had lost minimum-wage jobs so desperately vital for survival in this, one of the poorest of the United States. They were not men who found an abstract oppression in the news priorities of the national television networks. One man spoke of leaving his machinist position in a shoe factory—the only employer in his small town. Other workers had expressed their rage at the fact of his very existence among them by continually sabotaging the machinery with which he worked. Going to his job began to mean risking his life.

When any people of privilege made public announcements of gayness during the Augusta hearings, they were women holding managerial positions in women's organizations.

Still, even in Maine, gay men have been supportive of women's organizations. The only active, year-round gay group in the state is the Gay People's Alliance (GPA) headquartered on the Portland campus of the University of Southern Maine. (Another group exists during the academic year in Orono; there is a Dignity chapter with a Lewiston address; a primarily social organization exists in the bilingual northern extreme of the state, Northern Lambda Nord.) The GPA is a gender-mixed group with little contact with the year-round community of Portland and even less with the summer colony of Ogunquit, the two centers of gay life in Maine. It is not surprising that GPA members are the most active group of men attached to a male auxiliary to TBTN. They report little problem with total support for the women's position on rape. They understand fully the impact of sexual harassment on the job and in public places, as well they should, since such torment is not a hypothetical issue for gay men either, it's a question of sincere importance; especially for those men who understand that verbal abuse can easily escalate to fag-bashing. (Fag-bashing is a real problem in Maine, most severely in Ogunquit, where many incidents have been reported during the last few summers. Only a dullard would fail to make the connection between those beatings and the fact that when seniors in Wells High School—the regional secondary school for Ogunquit and other neighboring communities—were asked to name in their yearbook the things they hated most, the plurality wrote, "Faggots.") But the GPA men do have a problem with the issue of pornography. It is not an easy issue for them to resolve. Feminists are not responsive to the depth of the dilemmas posed by this issue for gay men.

The issues of the Blueboy bookstore and the exploitation of its infamy were not ignored by other members of the Portland gay community. While GPA members share with other gay organizations an exasperation over the seeming unwillingness of gay men to join in their activities, in reality, I witnessed a number of conversations between men which shared a common theme, a theme whose importance would be recognized by the clone if not the politico: Is this where we have to do something? Were the city, the police, the media coming down so hard on the Blueboy that it had become an issue of self-defense to support it? The final consensus was no. A primary interference was the fact that the Blueboy was owned by a straight man. That so many businesses directed toward gay men are so often owned by nongays is itself an oft repeated symbol of gay impotence.

Why, then, would an unorganized population of men consisting of Portland's own version of clones have even considered defending an adult bookstore against the forces of police, mayor, and media—and later the intrusive tours of TBTN?

Without question, the adult bookstores in small-city America are the only conduits for national gay media. The *Advocate* and *Christopher Street* are not available for retail sale anywhere else in the entire city of Portland. Not one bookstore has a gay section (all have women's sections). No matter how lacking in desirability these places are, they—and especially the Blueboy—served a real communication function. (There is also no reason to deny that many of us use erotica as a masturbatory aid or as a source of pleasure in and of itself.)

Gay men do not find delight in discovering a need to defend others for homosexual activities in public places. We do not delight in needing to go to sleazy bookstores to purchase our reading matter. We do not delight in the knowledge that most often our social contacts with one another must be made in substandard bars. But we know that this is the reality we must begin to work with, and we know that even if we individually do not indulge in what others call promiscuous sex, we are just as vulnerable to attack by a population that will always identify us with those men who do so indulge. One amazing lack of perception by feminists as they look at the entire issue of pornography retail stores has been their inability or unwillingness to deal with one of the functions of such operations: they are places of homosexual assignation.

There is a fairly universal pattern to the extraordinary gay male process of coming out. Life begins in a heterosexual family, sexual identity is self-discovered, it is hidden, some level of self-acceptance is attempted, an integration of sexuality and social existence is formulated.

This last step—the integration of sexuality and social existence—takes many forms. Often the time and place of coming out determine major elements of the result. (It should not be a surprise, for instance, that there appear to be many more gay fathers in Maine than in New York City; the rural setting provides pressures for a much earlier marriage than the urban.)

It is easy to lose touch with the enormousness of the gay revolution, which has created the clone, the ghetto, the movement, and the literature that combine to offer so many options for gay men today. Only ten years ago—certainly twenty years ago—the majority of men whose counterparts are contemporary clones chose a closeted life, mutually oppressed with those heterosexual women who often became their wives. There was a time, not so long past, when men who did take this option were considered traitors by the rest of us. Now they are pitied. They have lost out, not able to take advantage of the excitement that the rest of us now consider part of being gay. Few of those men have been able to survive without a homosexual outlet. There are no baths in a city like Portland; the bars are the turf of the clones here. Deering Oaks Park and the adult bookstores and movie houses—certainly not only the Blueboy—are the only outlets open to those left behind, those men living in need of homosexuality without the joy of gayness.

Feminists insist on perceiving adult bookstores as pandering to the most sexist, base, dangerous men. Their stock is considered fodder for the fire that will flame into violent rape. Gay men see those same bookstores as the territory of the walking wounded, those men (who once upon a time included ourselves) now cut off from communal support and identification.

So, in the end, the gay men here in Portland see the incursions into the adult stores as cruel, unfair assaults on a delicate and even poignant space for men whom we see less and less as enemies and more and more as victims. Their assailants are bullies, difficult to differentiate from the adolescents who beat up strays on the beach of Ogunquit or on the paths of Deering Oaks Park. Here, in this populist estrangement from women, is the specific example of the repercussions of feminist attempts at intimidation.

One major effect of that estrangement is contempt for the cowardice of it all. I know of no better example of that pusillanimity than the outrageous assault upon Giovanni's Room, a gay and lesbian bookstore in Philadelphia, that took place about two years ago. Certainly there were ways in which Giovanni's Room fell short of the purity that radicals of all persuasions demand of their organizations. For instance, the store, a privately owned, for-profit operation, solicited volunteer labor from the community. But the real point of contention came over the stocking of a single book: the heterosexually sadomasochistic novel *The Story of O.*

The novel, one of the first above-ground explorations of S and M, was sought by many gays as a source. But a coalition of women's groups demanded that the book be removed from the store. The owners—a gay man and a lesbian—declined. In the ensuing brouhaha picket lines were formed, editorials were written, there was even a televised debate on the entire issue, which was actually more of an ambush of the owners by their opponents. Giovanni's Room stuck to what it deemed a question of principle in resisting censorship.

The store has actually prospered and now claims to be the largest mail-order retailer of gay and lesbian books in the country. The real point is, what kind of perverse, poltroonish priorities would lead to such a massive assault against what was then a marginal operation, when nothing close to the magnitude of dissent has ever been addressed to the B. Dalton and Waldenbooks chains, whose *daily* sales of overtly sexist—and homophobic—books are measured in multiples of the *annual* revenues of even the largest gay bookstores? Why are adult bookstores in Portland, Maine, the target of a coalition as powerful as TBTN?

Cowardice.

Women seem unwilling to wage any battle that they are going to lose hands down. To gay men, who so seldom have an honest expectation of success in their continuing battles against the government, the churches, the media, and other centers of true power in our society, the choices of some women's priorities are not just questions of bad judgment, but often proof of malice. Rather than deal with the hard core that is so willing to counterattack, women have all too often chosen to feed off the vulnerable residues of guilt and the sincere desire for sexual equality that exist in gay men. How much easier it is to righteously attack us for purchasing *Drummer* than it is to tell the A&P to stop selling *Playboy.*

Another part of that cowardice is an apparent insistence that we gay men should divest ourselves of any hint of power in situations in which women perceive themselves to be less privileged than they say we are. Recently in Portland, an absurd situation developed that demonstrated this demand that gay men express a depraved solidarity with lesbians. As in most small cities, Portland's bars cater to both genders. Apparently, the lesbian community cannot support its own bars. Women in the gay nightspots demanded—and, for a brief moment this summer, won—an injunction against men taking off their shirts on the dance floor. If lesbians could not bare their breasts, then neither should gay men display their pectorals.

But the issue really was not the right of women to take off their blouses. The cowardice that is often displayed by women organizationally very often covers a more fundamental contempt for gay men than they are willing to own up to. The preposterous situation described here carries with it a rudimentary point which gay men simply can no longer overlook. The issue was clearly not just a quid pro quo insistence on equality of mistreatment. That was a transparent rationalization for the real function of the protest: women hated seeing male-mating divested of any of its disguises.

The expression of gay male sexuality is evidently experienced by women as the expression of the same male sexuality which leads to rape. *That misconception is not our problem.* If women cannot distinguish among the elemental components of gay male sexuality—a force attempting to make men equals, a process dependent upon consent, a celebration of the male body which is not dependent upon the denigration of the female body—*it is their perception that is at fault, not our behavior.* If the viewing of gay male lust—the manifestation of a primary form of gay liberation—is repulsive to women because they cannot separate it from the lust of heterosexual males whose goal is the subjugation of women, *it is not our responsibility to erase that view; it is women's responsibility to deal with the fears that entrap them.*

The goal of gay men is to release ourselves from the closet and to become pro-active forces in our own lives. *It is an intolerable expectation to think that gay men will resume the most dreaded forms of behavior for the sake of women's sensibility.*

The most important repercussion for gay men has been the deflection of our own focus as we have been reactive to the increasingly divergent priorities of feminists and ourselves. The clone has actually served a purpose here by his insistence that the actions of sexual liberation be addressed. His uniform, his willingness to spend time and money in his pursuit of sexual fulfillment, and his anxious investigation of different forms of sexuality and relationship forces us to pay attention to those areas in which he demonstrates such interest. Witness the number of articles on promiscuity and sadomasochism that have appeared in *Christopher Street* and the *Advocate* in the last year—even in such a righteously correct political publication as Boston's *Gay Community News.*

Yet too often these investigations have only been elite attempts to understand what the populace is thinking. Seldom—very seldom indeed—have they been expressions of the participants' experiences, rather they tend to be interviews with others or commentaries on another tribe's behavior. Lost in all this has been any serious pro-active investigation of what role pornography does—or can—perform in gay men's lives.

It is clear that erotic writings and photographs are very dear to gay men. Whenever a company has printed an attempt at a serious magazine and also a consciously sexual magazine, the sexually oriented publication has outsold its partner, regardless of promotion or organizational expectation. Thus, *Honcho* outsells *Mandate*; *Numbers* overshadows *Blueboy*; *Drummer* must provide the funds to support the *Alternate*. No one involved in any of these projects expected that outcome. It is simply true that the supposedly limited market for erotica is greater than anticipated and that the expected market for what is self-defined by publishers as "quality" nonfiction and fiction falls short of its goal.

Even the pretensions of the *Advocate* are not exempt. Years ago, when I was editor, we had planned to drop those nasty classifieds to make the paper more acceptable to large national advertisers and, we thought, to attract more bourgeois subscribers. The slightest bit of market research proved that any such move would have been a disaster. Too many people of every class and level of sophistication were buying the *Advocate* only for that nastiness. The segregation of sexual ads into a "pink section" was the compromise. At least some people could throw away that section—which just happens to generate the richest advertising revenues in gay publishing.

Marketing is not the only factor here. Many of the men regarded as the best gay writers also turn their talents toward exploring sexuality and relationships in ways that are most compatible with the editorial requirements of sexual magazines. Artists whose work can be seen in the better New York galleries seem to have little personal or professional problem in selling their work to publications like Honcho. These writers and artists are following an honorable tradition in American gay life. People who have published their work in erotic magazines have played many important roles in our liberation.

A seemingly universal and persistent oppression among gay men is the feeling we had when we first came out: that we existed alone, without friends, without anyone who was like us. During my own initiation into gay life in the sixties, I learned not only that I was a member of a group—potentially a community—by reading the gay periodicals that were sold only in adult bookstores, I learned much more. I read about the importance of integrity in gay life in Joseph Hansen's pseudonymous novels. Samuel Steward was the writer who, in his Phil Andros books, let me know how utterly fascinating my future was going to be. Tom of Finland's drawings promised me that that future was going to be *fun*. It was not a radical who instructed me about the political facts of my life; it was Jim French who used the name Rip Colt when he drew the first poster that would electrify me with the phrase "Gay Power."

The reality is that the erotic is recognized as an important area for gay men to explore. At first, I thought my own excursions into writing pornography were only a way to earn money. Two events changed that. First, after I had produced a certain body of work, I found consistent, nearly subconscious themes being exposed, themes of personal liberation through sexual liberation. Other chords sounded warnings about sexual danger. Here I unknowingly wandered into the tradition of Phil Andros by marking boundaries and limits of trust, realistic expectation, and danger in gay life. But second, I was forced to acknowledge that even the least impressive, least well written stories were having a tremendous impact on readers. Pornography, be it vanilla in *Mandate* or S and M in *Drummer*, is not read only by sad, lonely old men who sleep alone in hotel rooms. It is carefully read, sincerely analyzed by the clone.

We do a great disservice to ourselves and to any hope of community if we dismiss the sincerity of this gay everyman. At one time, I was certainly guilty of doing this by throwing away early opportunities to communicate with him through my fiction. I learned quickly how much he still wanted to learn about himself and his personal options by reading about others' experiences. But pornography is the vehicle that is accessible to him, not quasi-scientific articles or distanced interviews with people who do not resonate as being his peers.

Those readers are not the sexually obsessed, unconscious mass that many gay leaders insist their nonfollowers are. They were not blind to issues of liberation that were presented to them in forms that related realistically to their lives. Above all, the message of gay pornography is the affirmation of the male's love for other men. It is the most pure elevation of male beauty and male sensuality. It is for this reason that the women's movement has so much trouble accepting it. But what is male homosexuality if not the love of men? Are we supposed to deny it?

There are important parallels to this process of "cleansing" negation in gay community organizing and political activity. The purpose of leadership is not to educate the constituency on points that the constituency cannot readily identify as important so much as it is to enunciate the constituency's priorities and to identify ways to achieve them with maximal integrity.

The usual impulse of gay leadership has been one of astonishing elitism. We accepted an ideology based on feminism, attempted to synthesize it with a passive conception of homosexuality, and insisted that people buy this ideology as a revealed truth, as holy as that of the women's movement. Membership in gay organizations has been treated as a reward bestowed only on those who sign a pledge. Members have not been expected to influence the platform, they have been expected to wholeheartedly subscribe to it.

It has been as easy for gay leadership to dismiss the Nautilus-bodied man on *Christopher Street* or the leather bedecked stud on Folsom Street as it was for me to dismiss readers of *Blueboy*. The point is that neither group deserves such treatment. When they receive it, they react against it. More profoundly, we indulge in a self-destructive self-deception whenever we attempt to disassociate ourselves from those who are, after all, our fellows. I may want to think of myself with certain labels: writer, New Englander, intellectual. But I place myself in mortal danger if I forget for one moment the essential fact of my homosexuality. I may try to ignore the truth that I am a clone, but this society and its nascent forces of repression will never forget it.

Here lies the tragic fault of the lesbians in the women's movement as the clone sees it: they believe they have the power to alter their identification with us. They expect the general population will eliminate its own equation of male and female homosexuality. They have been seduced into believing that feminism equates an absence of homophobia. Gay men listen to Andrea Dworkin and wonder how she cannot be mortally terrified of Betty Friedan.

Is the clone really so apolitical? Is he really so trapped in bourgeois hedonism that it is a foregone conclusion that he will never be active in a gay movement?

To dismiss the clone, to devalue his experience, or to judge his life-style as frivolous is to ignore the central fact of gay liberation: to publicly acknowledge oneself as homosexual in this society is an act of profound political import.

The clone has not made his decision to advertise his existence lightly. It is a decision with conscious repercussions. The Portland GPA wonders why it has so few members while the men in the city's bars articulate their real concern that they may have to take a stand, alone, against the combined forces of political power in this city. The synthetic, abstract lambda was decreed the symbol of the gay movement, but the clone who converges on New York and San Francisco for an annual march of resistance wears the pink triangle of the Nazi concentration camp. To deprecate the inherent defiance which is the elemental engagement of the clone's life is to devalue the very essence of what it means to be gay in America.

It is not the rarefied theorist who is the fundamental building block of our movement, it is the gay everyman. When our aspiring leaders go to him to organize, to attempt a true understanding of our present and future, they will have to be prepared to do so through praxis, not habitus, and they will have to grasp how this population views the recent activities of the women's movement.

Women's organizations have covertly—and, in some instances, overtly—allied themselves with forces of moral repression whose priorities are not a hypothetical threat, but an integral part of the social and political forces which would actually eliminate gay men. Women's organizations are calling for the gay everyman to return to a time when he saw himself as filthy, perverse, and undesirable. But the lifework of every gay man has been the transformation of the loathed into the loved. He is not likely to give up this magic. Gay leadership—be it political, literary, or community-based—must begin its work not by pledging itself to an increasingly irrelevant feminist ideology but by making a covenant with its population that is based not only on what we might become but that also celebrates who we already are. What is homophobia if it isn't the insistence on seeing filth in the fact of homosexuality? What is gay liberation for men if it isn't an affirmation of the beauty of men?

PAT CALIFIA

While lesbian feminism produced a powerful analysis of lesbian oppression, that analysis also served through the 1970s to constrict many women whose experience and desires did not fit within some lesbian-feminists' model of "woman-identified" love. Lesbian feminists generally understood butch/femme roles to be an imitation of patriarchal heterosexuality, and advocated androgyny as a necessary element of women's liberation.

By the late 1970s many women were growing restless with that orthodoxy. With the 1980s, that vague discontent grew into what were known as "the sex wars," battles between those who felt comfortable and affirmed within lesbian-feminist communities and adhered to "orthodox" lesbian-feminist theory and those who felt silenced, shamed, or rejected.

The tension between the two sides exploded at the 1982 Feminist and the Scholar conference at Barnard College. This conference became the site of direct opposition between the "antipornography" feminists and the sex radicals. Upon hearing that many sex radicals had been invited, anti-pornography activists urged Barnard College to cancel the conference. When the conference went forward, it was picketed by women who felt that it was a forum for antifeminist views. While the participants felt otherwise, these speeches do share a common challenge to feminism as it had been articulated in lesbian communities. Pat Califia's anger at feminists for what she sees as social repression and forced orthodoxy, and her allegiance to sadomasochists (whether heterosexual or homosexual) and to gay men indeed provide some ammunition to those who would call her non- or even antifeminist. Califia considers herself a feminist, and she undeniably challenges us to examine the politics of sex within lesbian-feminism. Pat Califia is the author of *Sapphistry, Macho Sluts,* and, more recently, *Public Sex: The Culture of Radical Sex.*

FEMINISM AND SADOMASOCHISM
(1981)

Pat Califia

I hope you only do those things in leather bars. If I ever saw women doing S/M in a lesbian bar, it would make me so angry I'd want to beat them up.

—Anonymous gratuitous comment

Three years ago, I decided to stop ignoring my sexual fantasies. Since the age of two, I had been constructing a private world of dominance, submission, punishment, and pain. Abstinence, consciousness-raising, and therapy had not blighted the charm of these frightful reveries. I could not tolerate any more guilt, anxiety, or frustration, so I cautiously began to experiment with real sadomasochism. I did not lose my soul in the process. But in those three years, I lost a lover, several friends, a publisher, my apartment, and my good name because of the hostility and fear evoked by my openness about my true sexuality.

Writing this article is painful because it brings back the outrage and hurt I felt at being ostracized from the lesbian feminist community. I've been a feminist since I was 13 and a lesbian since I was 17. I didn't lose just a ghetto or a subculture—lesbian feminism was the matrix I used to become an adult. Fortunately for my sanity and happiness, I managed to construct a new social network. My friends and lovers are bisexual women (some of whom do S/M professionally), gay and bisexual men, and other outlaw lesbians. If I were isolated, I would not be strong enough to speak out about something that makes me this vulnerable.

I describe my feelings about this issue because sadomasochism is usually dealt with in an abstract, self-righteous way by feminist theorists who believe it is the epitome of misogyny, sexism, and violence. In this article I shall examine sadomasochism in a theoretical way, and attempt a rapprochement between feminism and S/M. But I am motivated by my concern for the people who are frightened or ashamed of their erotic response to sadomasochistic fantasies. I don't want to hear any more tragic stories from women who have repressed their own sexuality because they think that's the only politically acceptable way to deal with a yearning for helplessness or sexual control. I don't believe that any more than I believe homosexuals should be celibate so they can continue to be good Catholics. The women's movement has become a moralistic force, and it can contribute to the self-loathing and misery experienced by sexual minorities. Because sexual dissenters are already being trampled on by monolithic, prudish institutions, I think it is time the women's movement started taking more radical positions on sexual issues.

It is difficult to discuss sadomasochism in feminist terms because some of the slang S/M people use to talk about our sexuality has been appropriated by feminist propagandists. Terms like "roles," "masochism," "bondage," "dominance," and "submission" have become buzzwords. Their meanings in a feminist context differ sharply from their significance to S/M people. The discussion is rendered even more difficult because feminist theorists do not do their homework on human sexuality before pronouncing judgment on a sexual variation. Like Victorian missionaries in Polynesia, they insist on interpreting the sexual behavior of other people according to their own value systems. A perfect example of this is the "debate" over transsexuality. In its present form, feminism is not necessarily the best theoretical framework for understanding sexual deviation, just as unmodified Marxism is an inadequate system for analyzing the oppression of women.

Since the label "feminist" has become debased coinage, let me explain why I call myself a feminist. I believe that the society I live in is a patriarchy, with power concentrated in the hands of men, and that this patriarchy actively prevents women from becoming complete and independent human beings. Women are oppressed by being denied access to economic resources, political power, and control over their own reproduction. This oppression is managed by several institutions, chiefly the family, religion, and the state. An essential part of the oppression of women is control over sexual ideology, mythology, and behavior. This social control affects the sexual nonconformist as well as the conformist. Because our training in conventional sexuality begins the minute we are born and because the penalties for rebellion are so high, no individual or group is completely free from erotic tyranny.

I am not a separatist. I believe that men can be committed to the destruction of the patriarchy. After all, the rewards of male dominance are given only to men who perpetuate and cooperate with the system. I am not "woman-identified"—i.e., I do not believe that women have more insight, intuition, virtue, identification with the earth, or love in their genes than men. Consequently, I cannot support everything women do, and I believe the women's movement could learn a lot from politicized or deviant men. On the other hand, I do not find it easy to work with men, partly because male feminist theory is pitifully underdeveloped. I do not think separatism is worthless or bankrupt. It can be useful as an organizing strategy and teaches women valuable survival skills. The taste of autonomy that separatism provides is intoxicating, and can be a powerful incentive to struggle for real freedom.

I think it is imperative that feminists dismantle the institutions that foster the exploitation and abuse of women. The family, conventional sexuality, and gender are at the top of my hit list. These institutions control the emotional, intimate lives of every one of us, and they have done incalculable damage to women. I cannot imagine how such drastic change can be accomplished without armed struggle, the appropriation and reallocation of wealth, and a change in the ownership of the means of production. When women are liberated, women will probably cease to exist, since our whole structure of sex and gender must undergo a complete transformation.

The term "sadomasochism" has also been debased, primarily by the mass media, clinical psychology, and the anti-pornography movement. After all, homophobia is not the only form of sexual prejudice. Every minority sexual behavior has been mythologized and distorted. There is a paucity of accurate, explicit, nonjudgmental information about sex in modern America. This is one way sexual behavior is controlled. If people don't know a particular technique or lifestyle exists, they aren't likely to try it. If the only images they have of a certain sexual act are ugly, disgusting, or threatening, they will either not engage in that act or be furtive about enjoying it.

Since there is so much confusion about what S/M is, I want to describe my own sexual specialties and the sadomasochistic subculture. I am basically a sadist. About 10% of the time, I take the other role (bottom, slave, masochist). This makes me atypical, since the majority of women and men involved in S/M prefer to play bottom. I enjoy leathersex, bondage, various forms of erotic torture, flagellation (whipping), verbal humiliation, fistfucking, and watersports (playing with enemas and piss). I do not enjoy oral sex unless I am receiving it as a form of sexual service, which means my partner must be on her knees, on her back, or at least in a collar. I have non-S/M sex rarely, mostly for old times' sake, with vanilla friends* I want to stay close to. My primary relationship is with a woman who enjoys being my slave. We enjoy tricking with other people and telling each other the best parts afterward.

Because sadomasochism is usually portrayed as a violent, dangerous activity, most people do not think there is a great deal of difference between a rapist and a bondage enthusiast. Sadomasochism is not a form of sexual assault. It is a consensual activity that involves polarized roles and intense sensations. An S/M scene is always preceded by a negotiation in which the top and bottom decide whether or not they will play, what activities are likely to occur, what activities will not occur, and about how long the scene will last. The bottom is usually given a "safe word" or "code action" she can use to stop the scene. This safe word allows the bottom to enjoy a fantasy that the scene is not consensual, and to protest verbally or resist physically without halting stimulation.

The key word to understanding S/M is *fantasy.* The roles, dialogue, fetish costumes, and sexual activity are part of a drama or ritual. The participants are enhancing their sexual pleasure, not damaging or imprisoning one another. A sadomasochist is well aware that a role adopted during a scene is not appropriate during other interactions and that a fantasy role is not the sum total of her being.

S/M relationships are usually egalitarian. Very few bottoms want a full-time mistress. In fact, the stubbornness and aggressiveness of the masochist is a byword in the S/M community. Tops often make nervous jokes about being slaves to the whims of their bottoms. After all, the top's pleasure is dependent on the bottom's willingness to play. This gives most sadists a mild-to-severe case of performance anxiety.

The S/M subculture is a theater in which sexual dramas can be acted out and appreciated. It also serves as a vehicle for passing on new fantasies, new equipment, warnings about police harassment, introductions to potential sex partners and friends, and safety information. Safety is a major concern of sadomasochists. A major part of the sadist's turn-on consists of deliberately altering the emotional or physical state of the bottom. Even a minor accident like a rope burn can upset the top enough to mar the scene. And, of course, a bottom can't relax and enjoy the sex if she doesn't completely trust her top. The S/M community makes some attempt to regulate itself by warning newcomers away from individuals who are inconsiderate, insensitive, prone to playing when they are intoxicated, or unsafe for other reasons. The suppression of S/M isolates novice sadists and masochists from this body of information, which can make playing more rewarding and minimize danger.

For some people, the fact that S/M is consensual makes it acceptable. They may not understand why people enjoy it, but they begin to see that S/M people are not inhumane monsters. For other people, including many feminists, the fact that it is consensual makes it even more appalling. A woman who deliberately seeks out a sexual situation in which she can be helpless is a traitor in their eyes. Hasn't the women's movement been trying to persuade people for years that women are not naturally masochistic?

Originally, this slogan meant that women do not create their own second-class status, do not enjoy it, and are the victims of socially constructed discrimination, not biology. A sexual masochist probably doesn't want to be raped, battered, discriminated against on her job, or kept down by the system. Her desire to act out a specific sexual fantasy is very different from the pseudopsychiatric dictum that a woman's world is bound by housework, intercourse, and childbirth.

Some feminists object to the description of S/M as consensual. They believe that our society has conditioned all of us to accept inequities in power and hierarchical relationships. Therefore, S/M is simply a manifestation of the same system that dresses girls in pink and boys in blue, allows surplus value to accumulate in the coffers of capitalists and gives workers a minimum wage, and sends cops out to keep the disfranchised down.

It is true, as I stated before, that society shapes sexuality. We can make any decision about our sexual behavior we like, but our imagination and ability to carry out those decisions are limited by the surrounding culture. But I do not believe that sadomasochism is the result of institutionalized injustice to a greater extent than heterosexual marriage, lesbian bars, or gay male bathhouses. The system is unjust because it assigns privileges based on race, gender, and social class. During an S/M encounter, the participants select a particular role because it best expresses their sexual needs, how they feel about a particular partner, or which outfit is clean and ready to wear. The most significant reward for being a top or a bottom is sexual pleasure. If you don't like being a top or a bottom, you switch your keys. Try doing that with your biological sex or your race or your socioeconomic status. The S/M subculture is affected by sexism, racism, and other fallout from the system, but the dynamic between a top and a bottom is quite different from the dynamic between men and women, whites and Blacks, or upper- and working-class people. The roles are acquired and used in very different ways.

Some feminists still find S/M roles disturbing, because they believe they are derived from genuinely oppressive situations. They accuse sadomasochism of being fascistic because of the symbolism employed to create an S/M ambiance. And some S/M people do enjoy fantasies that are more elaborate than a simple structure of top versus bottom. An S/M scene can be played out using the personae of guard and prisoner, cop and suspect, Nazi and Jew, white and Black, straight man and queer, parent and child, priest and penitent, teacher and student, whore and client, etc.

However, no symbol has a single meaning. Its meaning is derived from the context in which it is used. Not everyone who wears a swastika is a Nazi, not everyone who has a pair of handcuffs on his belt is a cop, and not everyone who wears a nun's habit is a Catholic. S/M is more a parody of the hidden sexual nature of fascism than it is a worship of or acquiescence to it. How many real Nazis, cops, priests, or teachers would be involved in a kinky sexual scene? It is also a mistake to assume that the historical oppressor is always the top in an S/M encounter. The child may be chastising the parent, the prisoner may have turned the tables on the cop, and the queer may be forcing the straight man to confront his sexual response to other men. The dialogue in some S/M scenes may sound sexist or homophobic from the outside, but its real meaning is probably neither. A top can call his bottom a cocksucker to give him an instruction (i.e., indicate that the top wants oral stimulation), encourage him to lose his inhibitions and perform an act he may be afraid of, or simply acknowledge shame and guilt and use it to enhance the sex act rather than prevent it.

S/M eroticism focuses on whatever feelings or actions are forbidden, and searches for a way to obtain pleasure from the forbidden. It is the quintessence of nonreproductive sex. Those feminists who accuse sadomasochists of mocking the oppressed by playing with dominance and submission forget that *we* are oppressed. We suffer police harassment, violence in the street, discrimination in housing and in employment. We are not treated the way our system treats its collaborators and supporters.

The issue of pain is probably as difficult for feminists to understand as polarized roles. We tend to associate pain with illness or self-destruction. First of all, S/M does not necessarily involve pain. The exchange of power is more essential to S/M than intense sensation, punishment, or discipline. Second, pain is a subjective experience. Depending on the context, a certain sensation may frighten you, make you angry, urge you on, or get you hot. People choose to endure pain or discomfort if the goal they are striving for makes it worthwhile. Long-distance runners are not generally thought of as sex perverts, nor is St. Theresa. The fact that masochism is disapproved of when stressful athletic activity and religious martyrdom are not is an interesting example of the way sex is made a special case in our society. We seem to be incapable of using the same reason and compassion we apply to nonsexual issues to formulate our positions on sexual issues.

S/M violates a taboo that preserves the mysticism of romantic sex. Any pain involved is deliberate. Aroused human beings do not see, smell, hear, taste, or perceive pain as acutely as the nonaroused individual. Lots of people find bruises or scratches the morning after an exhilarating session of lovemaking and can't remember exactly how or when they got them. The sensations involved in S/M are not that different. But we're supposed to fall into bed and do it with our eyes closed. Good, enthusiastic sex is supposed to happen automatically between people who love each other. If the sex is less than stunning, we tend to blame the quality of our partner's feelings for us. Planning a sexual encounter and using toys or equipment to produce specific feelings seems antithetical to romance.

What looks painful to an observer is probably being perceived as pleasure, heat, pressure, or a mixture of all these by the masochist. A good top builds sensation slowly, alternates pain with pleasure, rewards endurance with more pleasure, and teaches the bottom to transcend her own limits. With enough preparation, care, and encouragement, people are capable of doing wonderful things. There is a special pride which results from doing something unique and extraordinary for your lover. The sadomasochist has a passion for making use of the entire body, every nerve fiber, and every wayward thought.

Recently, I have heard feminists use the term "fetishistic" as an epithet and a synonym for "objectifying." Sadomasochists are often accused of substituting things for people, of loving the leather or rubber or spike heels more than the person who is wearing them. Objectification originally referred to the use of images of stereotypically feminine women to sell products like automobiles and cigarettes. It also referred to the sexual harassment of women and the notion that we should be available to provide men with sexual gratification without receiving pleasure in return and without the right to refuse to engage in sex. A concept which was originally used to attack the marketing campaigns of international corporations and the sexual repression of women is now being used to attack a sexual minority.

Fetish costumes are worn privately or at S/M gatherings. They are as unacceptable to employers and advertising executives as a woman wearing overalls and smoking a cigar. Rather than being part of the sexual repression of women, fetish costumes can provide the women who wear them with sexual pleasure and power. Even when a fetish costume exaggerates the masculine or feminine attributes of the wearer, it cannot properly be called sexist. Our society strives to make masculinity in men and femininity in women appear natural and biologically determined. Fetish costumes violate this rule by being too theatrical and deliberate. Since fetish costumes may also be used to transform the gender of the wearer, they are a further violation of sexist standards for sex-specific dress and conduct.

The world is not divided into people who have sexual fetishes and people who don't. There is a continuum of response to certain objects, substances, and parts of the body. Very few people are able to enjoy sex with anyone, regardless of their appearance. Much fetishism probably passes as "normal" sexuality because the required cues are so common and easy to obtain that no one notices how necessary they are.

Human sexuality is a complicated phenomenon. A cursory examination will not yield the entire significance of a sexual act. Fetishes have several qualities which make them erotically stimulating and unacceptable to the majority culture. Wearing leather, rubber, or a silk kimono distributes feeling over the entire skin. The isolated object may become a source of arousal. This challenges the identification of sex with the genitals. Fetishes draw all the senses into the sexual experience, especially the sense of smell and touch. Since they are often anachronistic or draw attention to erogenous zones, fetish costumes cannot be worn on the street. Fetishes are reserved for sexual use only, yet they are drawn from realms not traditionally associated with sexuality. Fetishism is the product of imagination and technology.

Sadomasochism is also accused of being a hostile or angry kind of sex, as opposed to the gentle and loving kind of sex that feminists should strive for. The women's movement has become increasingly pro-romantic love in the last decade. Lesbians are especially prone to this sentimental trend. Rather than being critical of the idea that one can find enough fulfillment in a relationship to justify one's existence, feminists are seeking membership in a perfect, egalitarian couple. I question the value of this.

There is no concrete evidence that the childhoods of sadomasochists contained any more corporal punishment, puritanism, or abuse than the childhoods of other people. There is also no evidence that we secretly fear and hate our partners. S/M relationships vary from no relationship at all (the S/M is experienced during fantasy or masturbation) to casual sex with many partners to monogamous couples, and include all shades in between. There are many different ways to express affection or sexual interest. Vanilla people send flowers, poetry, or candy, or they exchange rings. S/M people do all that, and may also lick boots, wear a locked collar, or build their loved one a rack in the basement. There is little objective difference between a feminist who is offended by the fact that my lover kneels to me in public and suburbanites calling the cops because the gay boys next door are sunbathing in the nude. My sexual semiotics differ from the mainstream. So what? I didn't join the feminist movement to live inside a Hallmark greeting card.

Is there a single controversial sexual issue that the women's movement has not reacted to with a conservative, feminine horror of the outrageous and the rebellious? A movement that started out saying biology is *not* destiny is trashing transsexuals and celebrating women's "natural" connection to the earth and living things. A movement that spawned children's liberation is trashing boy-lovers and supporting the passage of draconian sex laws that assign heavier sentences for having sex with a minor than you'd get for armed robbery. A movement that developed an analysis of housework as unpaid labor and acknowledged that women usually trade sex for what they want because that's all they've got is joining the vice squad to get prostitutes off the street. A movement whose early literature was often called obscene and banned from circulation is campaigning to get rid of pornography. The only sex perverts this movement stands behind are lesbian mothers, and I suspect that's because of the current propaganda about women being the nurturing, healing force that will save the world from destructive male energy.

Lesbianism is being desexualized as fast as movement dykes can apply the whitewash. We are no longer demanding that feminist organizations acknowledge their lesbian membership. We are pretending that the words "feminist" and "woman" are synonyms for "lesbian."

The anti-pornography movement is the best of the worst of the women's movement, and it must take responsibility for much of the bigotry circulating in the feminist community. This movement has consistently refused to take strong public positions supporting sex education, consenting-adult legislation, the right to privacy, the decriminalization of prostitution, children's and adolescents' rights to sexual information and freedom, and the First Amendment. It has encouraged violence against sexual minorities, especially sadomasochists, by slandering sexual deviation as violence against women. Their view of S/M is derived from one genre of commercial pornography (male-dominant and female-submissive) and makes Krafft-Ebing look like a liberal.

Commercial pornography distorts all forms of sexual behavior. There are several reasons for this. One is that it is designed to make money, not to educate people or be aesthetically pleasing. The other is that it is quasi-legal, and thus must be produced as quickly and surreptitiously as possible. Another reason is that erotic material is intended to gratify fantasy, not serve as a model for actual behavior.

S/M pornography can be divided into several types, each designed for a different segment of the S/M subculture. Most of it represents women dominating and disciplining men, since the largest market for S/M porn is heterosexual submissive males. Very little S/M porn shows any actual physical damage or even implies that damage is occurring. Most of it depicts bondage, or tops dressed in fetish costumes and assuming threatening poses.

Very little S/M porn is well produced or informative. But eliminating it will have the effect of further impoverishing S/M culture and isolating sadomasochists from one another, since many of us make contact via personal ads carried in pornographic magazines. The excuse for banning "violent" porn is that this will end violence against women. The causal connection is dubious. It is indisputably true that very few people who consume pornography ever assault or rape another person. When a rape or assault is committed, it usually occurs after some forethought and planning. But legally, a free society must distinguish between the fantasy or thought of committing a crime and the actual crime. It is not a felony to fantasize committing an illegal act, and it should not be, unless we want our morals regulated by the Brain Police. Banning S/M porn is the equivalent of making fantasy a criminal act. Violence against women will not be reduced by increasing sexual repression. People desperately need better information about sex; more humanistic and attractive erotica; more readily available birth control, abortion, and sex therapy; and more models for nontraditional, nonexploitative relationships.

I am often asked if sadomasochism will survive the revolution. I think all the labels and categories we currently use to describe ourselves will change dramatically in the next 100 years, even if the revolution does not occur. My fantasy is that kinkiness and sexual variation will multiply, not disappear, if terrible penalties are no longer meted out for being sexually adventurous.

There is an assumption behind the question that bothers me. The assumption that sadomasochists are part of the system rather than part of the rebellion has already been dealt with in this article. But there is another assumption—that we must enjoy being oppressed and mistreated. We like to wear uniforms? Then we must get off on having cops bust up our bars. We like to play with whips and nipple clamps and hot wax? Then it must turn us on when gangs of kids hunt us down, harass and beat us. We're not really human. We're just a bunch of leather jackets and spike heels, a bunch of post office boxes at the bottom of sex ads.

We make you uncomfortable, partly because we're different, partly because we're sexual, and partly because we're not so different. I'd like to know when you're going to quit blaming us, the victims of sexual repression, for the oppression of women. I'd like to know when you're going to quit objectifying us.

---

*Vanilla is to S/M what straight is to gay. I don't use the term as a pejorative, but because I believe sexual preferences are more like flavor preferences than like moral political alliances.

Although lesbians and gays have been defined and have defined themselves primarily in terms of sexual choice, the role of sexuality in our lives has never been a subject of consensus. Many feel that their sexuality is a very private issue, a matter for the bedroom. Others, such as Dennis Altman, argue that the revolutionary element of gay sex is not simply with whom one has sex, but of our whole attitude toward sex and its place in our common life. Writing in the early 1980s, Altman suggests that the right's fear of sex is matched by many lesbians and gays who seek to contain it within private spaces and narrow channels. He argues that public sex is central to gay culture and deserves defense as such. He also sees opponents of sadomasochism and pedophilia as not just homophobic but also sex-phobic, unwitting collaborators in the right's agenda.

Altman's essay, originally published in the *Socialist Review*, generated a firestorm of letters. Opponents ranged from the predictably nervous heterosexual male to gays and lesbians who saw Altman as insufficiently critical of existing gay sexuality. Supporters viewed the article as a necessary corrective to a general anti-sex moralism on the part of the left.

DENNIS ALTMAN

SEX: THE NEW FRONT LINE FOR GAY POLITICS

(1982)

Dennis Altman

If there is a common element to the attacks of the Moral Majority on the social changes of the past decade it is a fear and loathing of sex itself. During the seventies there was a major movement to redefine the sexual values of this society in ways that divorced sex from procreation, and increasingly from emotional commitment. Not surprisingly, such changes had their casualties as we discovered that the new rules were not necessarily easier to live with than the old. On the whole, however, the changes were positive—above all for homosexuals, who benefited from a growing acceptance of the right to diversify in sexual lifestyles.

Now these changes are under siege. Attacks on homosexuals have escalated to an alarming extent. Whether these be direct attacks by the state (as in the February 1981 raids on Toronto's bathhouses, where more than three hundred men were arrested) or by private vigilantes and murderers (as in the shootings at a New York bar, the Ramrod, in November 1980, and increased street attacks reported in a number of cities) or by the forces of the Moral Majority (such as the Rev. Zone's announced campaign to "clean up" San Francisco), they all add up to a major outbreak of homophobia that leads some to speak darkly of a return to the repressions of the fifties.

So far the attacks have been largely directed against gay men, and have concentrated on our alleged sexual excesses in a way that, whether deliberate or not, is creating real divisions between gay women and men. It is not surprising that many lesbians, most of whom do not go to bathhouses or the Ramrod or cruise in Central Park, do not see these attacks as aimed against them. Yet the present wave of anti-gay violence cannot be seen in isolation. The failure of the ERA, the current campaign against abortion, the moves to "clean up" schools and public libraries, are all part of a larger movement directed towards the restoration of what is perceived as traditional order and morality.

In the eyes of the Moral Majority and their liberal outriders the most unforgivable characteristic of homosexuals is our assertion of sexuality as something to be enjoyed for itself. Perhaps the most unforgivable sin of homosexuals, women as much as men, is that our sexuality cannot be justified as leading to procreation; its only justification is pleasure. That homosexual sex can be as much an expression of love as can heterosexual sex does not alter this condemnation; the traditional Christian answer, of which the present pope is an ardent exponent, is to advocate sublimation. It is sex, not love, that most bothers homophobes, who like to imagine homosexuals as unhappy, frustrated and, preferably, suicidal. It is little wonder then that the literary establishment far prefers Anthony Burgess's portrayal of homosexual life in *Earthly Powers* to more authentic accounts.

Newly visible homosexuals, such as those who congregate on the streets of Greenwich Village, provoke a gut reaction among straight observers that far exceeds any objective assessment. Thus the hysteria so easily generated by allegations of homosexual molestation of "boys" despite evidence that the great bulk of child molestation involves heterosexual men and young girls, and where it does occur, "man/boy" love is more likely to be initiated by the boys themselves. (Few gay men have not experienced being cruised quite blatantly by teenage boys; my reaction is usually one of some embarrassment.)

At a time when sexual norms are so clearly in flux, conservatives need a scapegoat on which to focus their frustrations, and male homosexuals provide the almost perfect target. So far there has been much less concern about lesbians, in part because women are not perceived as sexual in the same way as men, in part because lesbians themselves have by and large not asserted their sexuality in the same way. As one woman complained at a recent gay conference: "When I was a lesbian separatist we never talked about sex."

It is comparatively easy for the Moral Majority to define gay men as sexual monsters who, having broken one taboo, can be expected to break all others and to destroy the very fabric of society itself. No matter that most homosexuals reveal a distressing eagerness to prove their Americanness and are busy developing a range of institutions that at times seem like parodies of the Horatio Alger story. (Few places sport more American flags than gay leather bars.) In the eyes of our opponents, whether fundamentalist rightists or tolerant liberals, all this fades away before what Eliot Fremont Smith called "erotic license without judgment." (I think—but with a writer of such obscurity who can be sure—he means fucking around.)

Perhaps it would be easier if we did, in fact, behave like heterosexuals: the far higher amount of rape, child abuse, domestic violence and enforced prostitution in the straight world does not arouse half the titillation and moral indignation directed against consensual fist-fucking. In the early days of the gay movement we argued that it was our oppression that led us to having sex in the bushes, the trucks, the baths. The implication was that if society would allow us we would all settle down as happily monogamous couples, perhaps raising Pekinese rather than children, but basically a homosexual version of the TV-dinner couple. Despite the enormous success of *La Cage aux Folles*, which *does* depict this model, few of us live this way.

Too much of the rhetoric of gay leaders has ignored the reality: most gay men do not behave sexually, *and do not want* to behave sexually, according to the dominant norms of this society. Increasingly I have come to see this as a virtue, and one we should be prepared to defend. Gay men are developing new forms of sexual relationships that make it possible to reconcile our needs for commitment and stability with the desire for sexual adventure and experimentation.

Lesbians too are concerned with new forms of relationships: the idea that all lesbians live as devoted monogamous (often asexual) couples never looking at other women is as big a myth as the idea that all gay men only have sex with strangers in dark corners. Thus far, how-ever, the development of lesbian culture and lifestyles has not meant the sort of visible asser-tion of sexuality common among gay men. The explanation for this is not immediately apparent. Women themselves seem divided between those who argue that the apparent con-ventionality of lesbian life is a product of the deep repression of female sexuality, and those who see it as evidence of the basic difference between women and men. That this is more than a theoretical question was made clear when the National Organization for Women adopted a resolution re-affirming support for lesbian and gay rights but condemning pederasty, pornography, sado-masochism and public sex as matters of "exploitation," "violence" or "invasion of privacy" and not issues of "sexual/affectional preference/orientation."

I doubt if many of the lesbians who supported this resolution—and it was put forward by the lesbian caucus of NOW—realized the extent to which it would be received as homo-phobic and oppressive by most gay men. The lines are not, of course, as simple as this: some gay women have opposed the resolution, some gay men endorsed it. But the debate all too quickly became perceived in male female terms.

The women who introduced the NOW resolution, and the men who support them, often argue that such issues are peripheral to our central concerns as homosexuals and only make our acceptance that much more difficult. This is the same impulse as would exclude trans-vestites from Gay Pride marches—forgetting that Stonewall was essentially a riot led by street transvestites—and would debar "manboy lovers"—ignoring the fact that hundreds of "men" go to jail for having sex with "boys" only several years younger than they.

In recent years there has been considerable debate over the ethics and politics of ped-erasty, pornography and sado-masochism. What strikes me about the critics of these phe-nomena is the sheer emotionalism with which they speak: pornography is equated with rape, man/boy love with child molestation, the wearing of leather with fascism. Too often there is a confusion between the symbolic and the real (pornography is *not* rape, and to say one causes the other is equivalent to arguing that marijuana leads to heroin), or the eleva-tion of a partial analysis to a universal precept (men often do take advantage of children sex-ually, but not all sex between "children" and "adults" is inherently exploitative; in some cases these may well be the least exploitative of child/adult relationships).

Most confusing of all is public sex, if only because the term is becoming a code word for a whole range of attitudes and behavior central to the experience of large numbers of gay men. Most public sex is, of course, nothing of the sort; the chances of actually seeing men fuck on Christopher Street in Greenwich Village are somewhat less than the chances of being shot, and given the choice most of us would opt for the former. In fact, public sex is used to describe a whole range of behavior associated with two interrelated but separate acts: sex outside the framework of an ongoing relationship and sex that takes place in other than a private home or hotel. Thus the term raises all those images of "promiscuous," "imperson-al," "anonymous" sex that have long been used to condemn gay men and that are being recy-cled through films like *Cruising* and the CBS documentary *Gay Power, Gay Politics*.

When heterosexuals indulge in similar behavior the term used is "recreational sex," and it should be noted that this is far more likely to involve prostitution; gay men go to bath-houses and cruise each other, straight men go to massage parlors and buy women. Women, on the whole, and whether straight or gay, have neither option, a fact that raises the most basic questions about the links between biology and culture in the organization of sexuali-ty. This distinction is beginning to break down with the growth of singles' bars and swingers' clubs, in which one sees the odd phenomenon of the straight world acting out those images of the gay world they have long condemned.

The NOW resolution thus introduced a moralism that is very similar to that of Jerry Falwell et al., the only difference being that it recognizes the legitimacy of homosexuality *insofar as* sex takes place within the confines of a traditional emotional relationship. It is a feature of gay male culture that it rejects this, that it recognizes sex partners, friends, and lovers as distinct, if often overlapping, categories.

One example: I am taken out to dinner by a couple, lovers of six years, both of whom work in upper-echelon white-collar jobs. We eat in the sort of restaurant to which one would take one's mother (a cuckoo clock; flowers, even in the bathrooms), then walk up the West Side to the meat district and the Mineshaft, America's most famous backroom bar. There I make out with one of the two to the slight amusement of the other; we separate and take part in sexual play with yet others; we leave on good terms.

Public versus Private

"Public sex" is not just a matter of taste, it is important precisely because it questions one of the basic assumptions that is used to control our sexuality, namely that it should remain totally private. When homosexuality was decriminalized in Britain in 1967, great stress was placed on the protection of privacy—the result being that threesomes, even in a private home, remain illegal. Pierre Trudeau earned *his* reputation for liberalism—remember *that?*—with his statement that the government had no business in the bedrooms of the nation. The conservative wing of the gay movement wants to use the concept to the right to privacy as the basic argument against the current backlash.

This argument has its tactical uses (it clearly will be very significant in future Supreme Court cases) but sex is not merely a private matter: assumptions about sex and sexual behavior underlie a great deal of state activity and regulation. When conservatives say that they recognize our right to be left alone in private they are really arguing that we should become, once again, invisible. Arresting men for taking part in "public sex," which for the most part goes on in places such as the Toronto bathhouses, is part of a more general intention, namely to a desire to restrict and repress all sexuality that cannot be contained by traditional forms.

Without necessarily accepting the romantic view of "outlaw" sex espoused by writers such as John Rechy and Guy Hocquenghem, it can be argued that public sex is a central part of gay male culture, and should be defended as such. The Meat Rack at Fire Island, the Rambles in Central Park, the piers at the end of Christopher Street, are part of our space and we have as much right to demand that they be protected as Irish-Americans have to close Fifth Avenue to traffic for the St. Patrick's Day Parade. Too often, liberals' tolerance for homosexuality extends only to the point where we behave like them, or, more accurately, like an idealized version of how they think they should behave.

Increasingly, so-called public sex takes place in commercial institutions (baths, bars, movie houses), which have proliferated and become much more luxurious over the past few years. About such places I admit to a certain ambivalence. On the one hand they offer areas in which there is the possibility for a whole range of experimentation and sexual play. On the other they represent a cooptation of sexuality, not just because of their admission prices but more importantly because they reinforce the idea that sex should only occur in specialized venues, rather than wherever the opportunity arises. Yet these places—ranging from the high tech of the Saint to the grubby toilets of Forty-second Street cinemas—are a real part of our space. To their critics, whether gay or straight, such places represent failure—our inability to form relationships, a need to objectify others, a preoccupation with genital sex, and acting out of self-hatred. What such critics fail to see is that such sex coexists with rather than replaces love and affection. Many of the men lying in cubicles at St. Mark's Baths have a whole tissue of emotional relationships in their lives; many long-lasting relationships begin at precisely these places. Of my four major affairs, two began at the baths and one in a park (the fourth I met through gay politics). Neither the language of heterosexual experience nor that of feminist analysis is adequate to describe the role of public sex in gay male lives.

I do not think it too fanciful to see in our preoccupation with public sex both an affirmation of sexuality *and* a yearning for community, which may be one of the healthier ways we can devise for coming to terms with a violent and severely disturbed society. The institutions of public sex are the beginnings of a community of lovers, just as gay women have built their networks of coffee shops, newspapers, bookshops, communes and music festivals. Of course much of the world of public sex is overlaid with features of the broader society that we need to criticize and struggle against, but we need better bathhouses rather than no bathhouses. The erotic bonding in such places is surely far preferable to the repressed homoeroticism found in armies and police forces, and very much less damaging to the society. There is less alienation and anger and hate at, say, a gay beach or bathhouse than there is in most of the respectable institutions in this society, and I would rather expose a child to even the most hardcore S and M bar than to most New York City subway stations at night.

Sex as the Battleground

Although it is difficult to be optimistic in Reagan's America, I suspect that we shall achieve most of our basic civil rights in the next decade. Those states that maintain anti-sodomy statutes will probably get rid of them (most probably via court decisions as in New York), for they are an anomaly that is embarrassing to uphold. It is even likely that certain crude forms of discrimination against homosexuals will continue to be outlawed, largely because as more of us come out such discrimination is too difficult to maintain. But this will only mean a redrawing of the lines around which the basic conflict will be fought. Just as the black movement discovered that economic equality could not be won through civil rights, important as these were, so gays are discovering that sexual liberation does not necessarily follow legal equality, though this is a necessary prerequisite.

It is my hunch that the two crucial areas around which we shall need to fight involve public sex and the alleged corruption of children, and the latter will increasingly be used to justify campaigns against the former. One of the horror stories in the CBS documentary was the girl who had seen men fucking in Buena Vista Park. Yet we need to ask why, in a society where children routinely see murder and carnage on the nightly television, this is so particularly shocking. In a healthy society sex would certainly rank well below lead poisoning as a hazard from which to protect children, and if that particular girl has been sexually traumatized one suspects it has far more to do with the fuss made by CBS than with the incident itself.

In the present political climate it is difficult to argue intelligently about sex. I can understand the impulses of those who would depict us as respectable, just as I can understand why many gays, and particularly gay women, do not want to go to the barricades over the rights of men to fellate each other in pornographic bookstores (recently a hot issue in San Francisco). I would argue that in a truly liberated society the need for such bookstores would disappear. But under present conditions even those of us who do not wish to take part in such sex have an interest in protecting it, in the same way as lesbians accept an involvement in the battle for rights to abortion. As Scott Tucker wrote: "Our right to privacy will never be secure until the public world is truly free."

There are of course ethical questions we need to ask about a whole variety of sexual behavior. While I would only proscribe that which is clearly and unambiguously exploitative (that is, sexual assault), this does not mean I feel unable to make moral and aesthetic judgments. None of us are doing so well in sorting out our emotional and sexual lives that we can afford to dispense with the experience and ideas of others. But such questions are not resolved by creating categories (eg, pederasts, sado-masochists) and condemning those people who can be so identified. It is not merely that ultimately our opponents do not make these distinctions, in the eyes of the Jerry Falwell there is little difference between Billy Jean King and the Fistfuckers of America. It is also that there is a mutual learning that can only take place if the gay men at the Mineshaft and the gay women in rural communes, the women committed to monogamous partners and the man/boy lovers, recognize that none of us have a monopoly on moral virtues.

The great ethical and political questions about sex today lie in the relationship between sex and violence, not the so-called violence of sado-masochism (which in the gay world is largely ritualized theater) but the real violence of prison camps, torture, and executions. It is not, I think, an accident that the most repressive regimes, from Nazi Germany to Maoist China, from contemporary Argentina and Chile to the Ayatollah Khomeini's Iran, are also the most oppressive of homosexuals. Some feminists argue, quite rightly, that in this connection between sex and violence lies the major psychocultural dynamics of our society. The common ground between such feminists and gay men, who increasingly risk being beaten up as a result of these dynamics, is often obscured by mutual misunderstanding. Feminists, particularly those who supported the NOW resolution, have unwittingly accepted the crudest homophobic stereotypes that see in man/boy love, gay S and M, and public sex the sort of violence and exploitation represented by snuff movies and the rape of young girls.

If the gay movement is to move beyond a search for respectability, which increasing numbers of homosexuals reject in their everyday lives, it will have to accept a radical sexual politics that effectively denies the claim of many gay spokespeople that there is nothing inherently radical in our demands. This may not seem the best time for the gay movement, besieged by the newly invigorated forces of the right, to defend publicly what not only the Moral Majority but also many liberals regard as degenerate and decadent forms of behavior. Not to do so, however, dooms the gay movement to speaking only for those homosexuals who accept uncritically the dominant sexual rules, and divorces it from the large numbers of men, and significant, if smaller, numbers of women who are developing new possibilities of managing our sexual and emotional lives.

The larger society can only benefit from such a radical sexual politics. For if the gay movement stands for anything beyond civil rights it stands for a breaking down of the sexual repressions and fears that fuel so much of the violence and paranoia of modern life. Just as the women's movement is ultimately about the liberation of *both* women and men from the limits of socially defined gender roles, so the gay movement is ultimately about a freer view of sexuality, one in which kids will not find it necessary to resolve their ambivalence about sexuality by beating us up in the streets, and the Rev. Jerry Falwell will be seen for the pathetic charlatan he really is.

When lesbian sadomasochists began to "come out" and insist on public acceptance within lesbian-feminist communities, they met with strong opposition. Critics such as Audre Lord, Adrienne Rich, and Kathleen Barry argued that sadomasochism is an embrace of violence and power that is antithetical to feminist goals. Their criticism was met with the challenge that lesbian-feminists were anti-sex and conservative, enforcing a narrow band of acceptable behavior. S/M proponents argued that such prescription was hypocritical from those who demanded respect for their sexual orientation. In the piece that follows Sarah Hoagland meets this challenge by arguing that love between women is not equivalent to a power relationship that she characterizes as addictive, both in its pattern of escalation and in its symptomatic nature. Countering charges of "moralism," she argues for the necessity of making judgments as part of a healthy community.

SARAH LUCIA
HOAGLAND

Sarah Hoagland is professor of philosophy at Northeastern Illinois State University. She is the author of *Lesbian Ethics* and coeditor with Julia Penelope of *For Lesbians Only*, a separatist reader.

SADISM, MASOCHISM, AND LESBIAN-FEMINISM

(1982)

Sarah Lucia Hoagland

For over a year now I have been ambivalent about writing a paper on Lesbian sadism and Lesbian masochism, and the claim that they are theoretically consistent with Lesbian-feminism.[1] It is so obvious to me that they are inconsistent with Lesbian-feminism that I have found myself on several occasions essentially speechless. If you have on a pair of socks and cannot see that they do not match, what can I say? I can test your eyes for color blindness and I can check to see you understand what the word "match" means. But if your vision is fine and your understanding of English good, then beyond pointing out the mismatch to you, is meaningful dialogue possible?

Still, I find myself trying once again to speak, though my speaking is not directed toward those wimmin whose goals are simply to be obnoxious and offensive. It is others to whom my speaking is directed. In a related vein, I have heard it argued that Lesbian sadomasochism is the ultimate rebellion, that sadomasochists are reinventing the outlaw and challenging the coerciveness of Lesbian-feminist political correctness. Certainly it is true that political correctness has been used coercively among Lesbian-feminists, deeply and inexcusably hurting many wimmin. Nevertheless, although embracing the values of the rule of the fathers may be a slap in the face to Lesbian-feminists, it is hardly a rebellion within the context of this society. Besides, my primary interest concerns the claim that Lesbian sadism and masochism are *consistent* with Lesbian-feminism.

I also want to say by way of preliminary remarks that all branches of masculinism have followers who attempt to co-opt feminism. So when Lesbian sadomasochists complain that wimmin in the anti-pornography movement who accept money from the right and otherwise align themselves with reactionary interests are collaborating in the cooptation of feminism, they are correct. We face a decade when it will be increasingly difficult to keep our clarity and focus. Just as we must not back off from radical feminist principles when they appear to the undiscerning eye to be consistent with the right, so must we never forget that all masculinists have their own agendas. We must keep our focus distinct. Clarity in these days is difficult and complex. But it is possible.

Possibly one of the most compelling arguments for some Lesbian-feminists regarding the Lesbian sadomasochism debate is that to refuse to print avowedly sadomasochistic scenarios in Lesbian-feminist publications or to challenge the practice of sadomasochism in a community, particularly when it is advocated in the name of Lesbian-feminism, is to encourage the type of censorship and repression exercised against Lesbians in the 1950s. And at a time when we are apparently moving right into another age of McCarthyism, this is a pressing argument. I believe this claim has most deeply divided us.

The issue of censorship is terrifying to many of us. We have been silenced and the reality of our lives has been distorted for so long. But on the other hand, Lesbian-feminist publications do not exist to print anything and everything anyone might wish to publish. Our publications do not print speeches and papers by nazis. We do not print essays advocating a return to slavery, or essays justifying white or male supremacy. We would not run such material even if it were written by a Lesbian and she claimed she was a feminist. Thus the issue that divides us does not really concern the feasibility of censorship. The simple fact that we have set up Lesbian-feminist newspapers, journals, magazines, research newsletters, presses, publishing houses and bookstores in and of itself is a declaration that there are limits, that we have a set of values, and that we want to explore ideas within these values.

The question of coercion or repression within a Lesbian community is also important. We all have wounds and as we work through them we must have our own time schedule, our own pace. For example, wimmin who are alcoholics need time and space as well as support to heal those wounds. And we need a context and analysis in which to understand that alcoholism may well be an attempt at survival in a society that wishes Lesbians dead and conceptually nonexistent. Nevertheless, if someone suddenly were to begin arguing that the solution to alcoholism is to drink, or more significantly, that embracing alcoholism is consistent with Lesbian-feminism, she would be challenged. While I am not interested in making life miserable for those who practice Lesbian sadomasochism, the claim that sadomasochism is consistent with Lesbian-feminism cannot go unchallenged.

I will say this, I am not willing to see a Lesbian-feminist party line established against which each woman is measured and scored according to her adherence to party politics. Such efforts are deadening as they are based not on growth but rather on control, a male approach to power. My efforts involve clarifying the boundaries of Lesbian-feminism. For example, racism and anti-Semitism are not consistent with Lesbian-feminism, nor are heterosexism or sexism. Nor is sadomasochism. I work to create a world in which not only are lynching, pogroms, rape and sissy-beating not practiced, they are inconceivable; I work for a world in which dominance and submission are inconceivable. And when we use force and control among each other, tools imbued with the dominance/submission ideology of the fathers, we use tools which proscribe such ends. Nevertheless, while I am not interested in controlling any individual woman's choices, I am interested in being clear on the values we affirm in making particular choices.

Two other, unspoken but seemingly compelling ideas are intimated by Lesbian sadists and masochists: first, that we do not have to question or examine any of our impulses or urges because if a womon is a Lesbian anything she does is OK, and second, that we should explore all possible expressions of our eroticism. I certainly agree that exploring our eroticism is vital. Our sensitivity to pleasure and pain changes with sensual interactions and sexual orgasm as sadomasochists have recognized. We need to learn more about this. We need to explore the different degrees of sexual appetite among us. We need to examine and explore the place of fantasy in our sexuality. And most significantly, we need to explore and develop a new language for naming and describing our sexual feelings and experiences. All we really have is male-oriented and sadomasochistic language to give conceptual and poetic life to our experiences. For instance, in sociobiology E.O. Wilson equates female receptivity with female submission. He bases his claim that overall, males dominate females in the animal world, on the fact that males sexually penetrate (most) females. For Wilson, and for many others, male penetration equals male domination.[2] We need a radical break from this paradigm. There is much to be explored.

However as for the non-evaluative exploration of our urges, it is ridiculous to assume that *any* of us has not been infected erotically, and in all other areas, by the patriarchal ideology of authority, of dominance and submission. Further, the idea that we should explore all possible areas of eroticism is incredible. Eroticism, like appetite, is malleable (as evidenced by the fact that some Lesbian sadists and masochists can no longer enjoy "vanilla" sex when once they did). And while repression, sexual and otherwise, can shape our erotic response, so can dominance or submission. Have we forgotten or failed to inform ourselves that some Nazi men found the torture of Jews highly erotic? Have we forgotten or failed to inform ourselves that some Nazi men experienced orgasm while watching Jews being beaten, tortured, mutilated, gassed, destroyed? It is just not true that all areas of eroticism should be explored by Lesbian-feminists or anyone else.

What I've found quite jolting in several communities is the impulse to silence and ostracize Lesbian batterers while at the same time providing a forum for Lesbian sadists. This is significant because most batterers do not think that beating and humiliating another Lesbian is a positive thing to do, while sadists not only think it is alright but advocate it in the name of feminism, sisterhood and trust. Advocating sadomasochism does not help the Lesbian batterer channel her very powerful energy and rage elsewhere. Instead it tells her that hitting another womon may be OK especially if the other "asks for it." Add to this the fact that masochists practice saying "no" when they mean "yes" and it must be very confusing for all involved in Lesbian battering, especially those trying to work their way out of it.

Yes, yes, I hear it: the crucial difference between Lesbian battering and Lesbian sadomasochism is consent. Assuming for the moment this is true, I want to ask: if a womon consents to her own humiliation, is it OK? Significantly we have not fully addressed this question in the feminist community because until now it would have introduced the problem of blaming the victim. Masculinists imply that battered wives, victims of daughter rape and other victims of the rule of the fathers consent to their victimization. In response we have developed sophisticated analyses explaining why consent is not the issue and suggesting other areas to explore for understanding the reactions of victims—survivors—ourselves and others. More importantly, rather than focusing on victims, we have indicated that the behavior of oppressors must be analyzed.[3]

So while we haven't yet addressed the question of whether it is alright for a womon to consent to her own humiliation, or whether if she has these tendencies she should explore and develop them rather than try to overcome them as she would try to overcome racist and anti-Semitic tendencies (no matter who she is), I will address it now. Particularly in light of patriarchal ideology which is premised on the subordination, the humiliation and degradation of wimmin, it is not OK for a womon to consent to her own humiliation. The erasure of our autonomy, integrity and humor is the essence of patriarchal rule, and to willingly participate in that erasure is to affirm the values of the fathers.

The only possibility of any real debate on the issue of consenting to humiliation is in the area of sacrificing oneself for a political end. One might argue that sacrificing oneself for the feminist struggle is feasible and that under certain conditions, say of capture or imprisonment, consenting to humiliation—choosing not to resist—is acceptable. Nevertheless, while this debate is very complex, its resolution is not essential to a discussion of masochism since the debate over political sacrifice is one of strategy, one of means, and does not imply that consent to humiliation is valuable in itself.

Actually, I have heard an argument in favor of Lesbian masochism that comes close to a political means argument from a white, gentile Lesbian attending one of my talks on Lesbian ethics. She argued that to be a Lesbian-feminist in the fullest sense one must engage in masochism because physically and emotionally submitting to another woman in this way is the ultimate act of trust and commitment to sisterhood. If one accepts this line of reasoning, one might as well argue that turning over the entire direction of one's life to another womon is an even greater act of "trust." (One might as well argue that autonomy is irrelevant to wimmin's liberation.) The problem with this idea is the rhetorical equation of trust with submission. Such an equation does not challenge but rather embraces patriarchal ideology.

The rhetorical equation of submission with trust or commitment or cooperation enjoys a context larger than explicit sadomasochistic ideology. Wimmin who choose to interpret their cooperative interaction with other wimmin in terms of dominance and submission, in terms of one woman being the leader and dominant and the other being cooperative by submitting, are embracing an ideology no more consistent with feminism than is sadomasochism. Cooperation is no more a matter of submission than is trust.[4] It is crucial that we begin to be truly creative about revaluing our interactions. Patriarchal logic is so pervasive that at every turn, even in a separatist space, we are liable to snap back into it. And as long as we view cooperating as "giving up" or trusting as "giving in," we will further entrench the ideology we have grown up with that fosters oppression.

Aside from entrapment in patriarchal logic, the idea that trusting means submitting suggests we have not yet taken ourselves seriously enough. I do not find Blacks as a political group claiming that engaging in masochism (or sadism) is consistent with Black liberation. Nor do I find Jews as a group claiming the political right or necessity of engaging in masochism (or sadism) in the name of Jewish liberation. I do not mean by this that no Blacks or Jews engage in sadomasochism. My point is that I see no one attempting to argue from within those political communities that submitting to (or dominating) another in the community is consistent with liberation.[5] The fact that some Lesbian-feminists think submitting to another Lesbian (or dominating another Lesbian) is a way to liberation suggests that as individuals within a community, we have not yet taken female autonomy seriously. Significantly, however, while I have heard all sorts of scenarios named by Lesbian sadists and Lesbian masochists—Nazi/Jew, priest/penitent, white/Black, straight man/queer and so on, I have not yet heard a male/female scenario suggested by Lesbians. Is it too close to home? Or is our political sensitivity to sexism and heterosexism as it affects wimmin so numbed that no masochist (or sadist) has yet thought to create a male/female parody?

And this brings me to the parody claim. I have read that sadists and masochists parody oppressive institutions and relationships, and thereby rebel against them. Yet Jean Genet made it painfully clear that while those parodying authoritarianism may expose it for what it really is, they are hardly able thereby to release themselves from it and so are not rebels in the sense either of resisting or of striving for change.[6]

The argument suggesting that sadists and masochists rebel against patriarchal rule examines the *behavior* of the fathers in relation to sadists or masochists, but it does not examine the *ideology* and *theory* of the fathers in comparison with sadomasochism. Sadists and masochists argue that they are persecuted by the fathers as are transsexuals and transvestites, for example, and that this persecution is *ipso facto* proof that they must be rebelling against them.

Certainly the practice of overt sadomasochism exposes the lies of the patriarchs. It shows, for instance, that protection is really predation, that paternalism is really dominance, and so on. In maintaining oppression without being blatant and using direct force, the patriarchs need a system in which oppression can establish a life of its own in the name of what is "natural" and "normal." They are threatened by exposés from the fringe such as sadists and masochists as well as Lesbian-feminists present since the exposés interfere with patriarchal subtlety and respectability. By targeting and persecuting the fringe, the patriarchs attempt to reclaim at least respectability. But such targeting is not itself proof that the targets rebel against patriarchal ideology any more than drug trafficking, although both fringe and persecuted, is thereby a rebellion against, or in any way a challenge to, the ideology of the medical establishment. The distinction between drug pushers and patriarchal doctors is legal and not ideological.

Thus the fact that one is fringe and persecuted is not itself proof of rebellion against the persecutors. One must also challenge their ideology. And (must I say this?) in challenging the persecution/fringe argument of sadomasochists, I am neither trying to minimize the persecution nor am I making a point about Lesbian-feminist assimilation or respectability. I am making a point about change.

A year ago at a panel in Chicago on sadomasochism, I described the historical and material context of sadomasochism and argued that the appeal to Nazi/Jew or master/slave ideology in sadomasochistic scenes was the ultimate insult to Jews and Blacks. During the discussion one Jewish woman, after claiming history had nothing to do with her exclaimed, "Darkies and masters, how exciting." She, of course, was simply trying to be obnoxious and offensive. And she succeeded. However there are those who seriously believe such parodies erode patriarchal ideology.

The idea that Nazi/Jew, master/slave scenes parody the Holocaust and slavery and therefore do not contribute to the context which allows such institutions to flourish, indicates a failure to understand a fundamental principle of separatism: to parody an institution is nevertheless to reinforce its world view (its *Weltanschauung*) and hence to validate it. To parody Nazis may take some of the pompousness out of their ceremony, but the parody still validates Nazism by perpetuating the language game, the conceptual framework, and thereby allows those who work with deadly earnest and intelligence toward fascism and slavery to exist in an ideological framework necessary for their growth and development. It holds their foundation intact, feeds it. And, in fact, some of the parodies I've seen appear more like emulation. Sadomasochism is no more capable of calling the foundation of patriarchy into question than is androgyny: any ideology which *presupposes* the context of dominance and submission (masculinity and femininity, master and slave) is hardly capable of breaking free of it.

In a sense, the parody thesis is distantly related to the healing thesis, a thesis Lesbian therapists and healers seem especially compelled by. I have heard it claimed that engaging in Lesbian masochism (and possibly Lesbian sadism) is a way of healing deep-seated, internalized wounds, a way of working "emotional sadomasochism" out of our systems. The womon who put forth this claim was a white Lesbian who has done much for other Lesbians. Nevertheless I find error in this line of argument. Certainly we have a lot to work out of our systems; the survival strategies of the oppressed are varied and strong. However in my experience, it is simply not true that Lesbian masochists (or sadists) are less manipulative and coercive than Lesbians who do not practice masochism or sadism. In fact, I've found the opposite to be the case. More significantly, associating orgasm with a desire to beat, humiliate or dominate, or a desire to be beaten, humiliated or dominated is hardly a way to exorcise those desires. Given sexual appetite and given the bit of conditioning theory that is accurate, it should be obvious that associating orgasm with such desires will only embed them more deeply.

I have also heard it claimed that sadomasochistic scenarios can provide a safe way for alleviating our everyday frustrations. At the same panel on sadomasochism mentioned above, a sadist claimed that we need a safe place to deal with pain and pleasure when we have been out facing all the shit at work. The speaker was a Native American Lesbian-feminist who has been an activist and on the front lines for the last ten years. She explained that engaging in sadism at home was her way of neutralizing the effects of her combat wounds.

In the first place, reenacting the agenda of the rule of the fathers is never safe. More significantly, turning our rage on each other when we are not the cause, even under carefully controlled circumstances, may relieve tension and frustration, making us feel good, or at least better, for the moment. And certainly we need to relieve tension. But it is important we remember that to simply relieve tension is not to address the cause of our anger. Thus, once relieved, the tension will build again and again. When relief of tension is then associated with orgasm, the recurrent building of tension and the need for release will not be perceived as a result of being unable to address, or of failing to address, the cause of anger and oppression. Instead it will seem to be part of the natural recurrence of sexual appetite. The process will thereby be embraced in the name of sexual pleasure while those questioning the process will be labeled anti-sex and puritanical.

This brings me to the claim that sadomasochism, or possibly just masochism, provides catharsis. While the above method of channeling tension and frustration offers temporary relief, the recurrent pattern ultimately leads to emotional numbing[7] since there is no change or growth. (That there is also sexual numbing is suggested by sadists and masochists who can no longer enjoy gentle, affectional sex.) What is purged in this catharsis is one's *sensitivity* to oppression, to domination and humiliation, not one's internalization of it.

I want to end with consideration of one final point. Repeatedly I see the claim that Lesbian sadomasochism involves an exchange of power. What does this *mean*? It means we get to play at having power over each other. Some masochists, for instance, insist they know the difference between rape or battering (which they call violent) and sadism (which they call non-violent because it is consensual) since they have experienced both. Of course there is a difference. But the difference is not a matter of consent so much as it is a matter of playing at power. Or, possibly, that is all consent means in this context.[8] (Those who believe that sadists or masochists really are exchanging power rather than playing at it would also have to believe sadists and masochists really are creating Nazi/Jew or master/slave situations, rather than parodying them.) Lesbian sadomasochism means you get to play at dominating me or I at dominating you. It means I comfort you by letting you play at being powerful momentarily. But to play at having power or to parody power is not to have power. Hence no real power is exchanged. Isn't it time we stopped playing at power and especially time we stopped playing with the power of the rule of the fathers? Surely it is time we begin to empower each other so we can become a force capable of successfully *resisting* domination.

Masculinists embrace a certain set of values. Lesbian-feminists have chosen a different set of values. We are outcasts from patriarchal social structure as much by our choice as through their design. We chose to become feminists through a series of value judgments which we call feminist process and which involves a steady saying "no" to patriarchal designs as we recognize and understand them (reactive). Out of this no-saying we have been evolving our own set of values (active). And these values are incompatible with patriarchal values.

The feminist rejection of patriarchal values cannot be half-hearted, it must be complete. Those wimmin who believe, erroneously, that it is possible to assimilate feminist values into a patriarchal social structure are trapped in a contradiction. On the one hand they would embrace a feminist value system and on the other hand they attempt to assimilate it into, and thus retain, a system which negates that feminist value system. Likewise, those wimmin, such as Lesbian sadomasochists, who would assimilate patriarchal values into a nascent feminist social structure are also trapped. Patriarchal values can no more be assimilated into a feminist social structure than feminist values can be assimilated into a patriarchal structure. As feminists make our choices, whether reactive or active, thereby exercising our autonomy, we are also affirming our right to create our culture through those choices. In this way we can begin truly to empower each other.

1. Hugs and kisses to Sidney Spinster who listened to a draft of this paper at one a.m. in Noyes Hall and made helpful comments, and to Ann Jones, Robin Ruth Linden and Julia Penelope who helped pull me out of density. Thanks also to Eleanor Harris for her insights. None of these wimmin, of course, are responsible for the content of this paper.

2. Sarah Lucia Hoagland, "Androcentric Rhetoric in Sociobiology," Women's Studies International Quarterly, Spring, 1980, reprinted in The Voices and Words of Women and Men, ed. Cheris Kramarae (London: Pergamon Press, 1980).

3. See, for example, Kathleen Barry, Female Sexual Slavery (Englewood Cliffs, NJ: Prentice-Hall, 1979).

4. In one sense, though, submitting can be cooperating. The idea is expressed in the slogan, "If you're not part of the solution you're part of the problem." And the point of the slogan is the existential thesis that no one is impartial, no one, in a certain sense, fails to choose: refusal to choose is itself a choice. Thus one is cooperating or collaborating with the enemy if one does not choose to resist the enemy. Nevertheless, the point I am trying to make is that if two feminists engage in a collective endeavor, they are not really acting cooperatively if one "cooperates" with the other by simply not resisting her.

5. Actually, this is not entirely true. From within both political communities comes tremendous pressure on wimmin to submit to men through the institution of heterosexuality in order to gain liberation for the community. Within the Black community, for example, one hears the argument that Black wimmin must stand behind Black men in order to combat racism. Within both communities there is pressure on wimmin to create families and produce children, yet Lesbian motherhood is not considered viable. My point is not concerned with wimmin who choose to provide homes for men and raise children as their way of combating racism or anti-Semitism. My point concerns wimmin who make other choices, but who are expected to submit themselves to male domination in the name of liberation.

So there are arguments within Black and Jewish political communities to the effect that dominance and submission are consistent with liberation. And the extent to which these are used is the extent to which these communities do not take female autonomy seriously. (Or, in some cases, they do take it seriously and work against it.) Nevertheless, one does not see an argument that a Jew qua Jew should submit to another Jew, or that a Black qua Black should submit to another Black. (The argument I just discussed is that a Jew qua female should submit to a Jew qua male, or that a Black qua female should submit to a Black qua male.) And in this respect Jewish and Black liberation are taken seriously within their respective political communities.

6. See Kate Millett's discussion of Genet in Sexual Politics (New York: Doubleday, 1969).

7. This point was suggested to me by Judy Seale during a discussion of Susan Griffin's book, Pornography and Silence: Culture's Revenge Against Nature (New York: Harper and Row, 1981).

8. A related point was first brought to my attention by Kate Burke.

JOAN NESTLE

Butch/femme identities and practices have a long history among lesbians. Rita Laporte's 1971 article in the *Ladder*, reprinted here in Section III, was one of the last statements on behalf of butches and femmes before lesbian-feminism forced them into hiding. Although butches (and implicitly, the femmes who were drawn to them) were rejected by the Daughters of Bilitis, the grounds of rejection by the two groups was quite different. The Daughters of Bilitis feared that butches would reinforce heterosexual stereotypes and justify continued persecution. Lesbian-feminists, on the other hand, argued that butches and femmes reproduced patriarchy. Butches were said to want to be men, and femmes were castigated for being too traditional. The lesbian-feminist ideal of equality became one of sameness, in which everyone dressed alike and shared all skills equally.

Joan Nestle is a co-founder of the Lesbian Herstory Archives in New York City and author and editor of several books. Her lesbianism predated the contemporary women's movement, and she has written powerfully of the freedoms and constraints that the movement has produced. As a self-identified fem in a movement that denigrated femininity as victimization, she has become a major figure in the reshaping of lesbian desire.

In the following essay, delivered at the Scholar and Feminist conference at Barnard in 1982, Nestle outlines her identity as a fem and her problems with 1970s lesbian feminism.

THE FEM QUESTION

(1982)

Joan Nestle

For many years now, I have been trying to figure out how to explain the special nature of butch-fem relationships to feminists and lesbian feminists who consider butch-fem a reproduction of heterosexual models, and therefore dismiss both lesbian communities of the past and of the present that assert this style. Before I continue, my editor wants me to define the term butch-fem, and I am overwhelmed at the complexity of the task. Living a butch-fem life was not an intellectual exercise; it was not a set of theories. Deep in my gut I know what being a fem has meant to me, but it is very hard to articulate this identity in a way that does justice to its fullest nature and yet answers the questions of a curious reader. In the most basic terms, butch-fem means a way of looking, loving, and living that can be expressed by individuals, couples or a community. In the past, the butch has been labeled too simplistically the masculine partner and the fem her feminine counterpart. This labeling forgets two women who have developed their styles for specific erotic, emotional, and social reasons. Butch-fem relationships, as I experienced them, were complex erotic and social statements, not phony heterosexual replicas. They were filled with a deeply lesbian language of stance, dress, gesture, love, courage, and autonomy. In the 1950s particularly, butch-fem couples were the front-line warriors against sexual bigotry. Because they were so visibly obvious, they suffered the brunt of street violence. The irony of social change has made a radical, sexual, political statement of the 1950s appear today as a reactionary, non-feminist experience. My own roots lie deep in the earth of this lesbian custom and what follows is one lesbian's understanding of her own experience.[1]

I am a fem and have been for over twenty-five years. I know the reaction this statement gets now: many lesbians dismiss me as a victim, a woman who could do nothing else
because she didn't know any better, but the truth of my life tells a different story. We fems
helped hold our lesbian world together in an unsafe time. We poured out more love and
wetness on our barstools and in our homes than women were supposed to have. I have no
theories to explain how the love came, why the crushes on the lean dark women exploded
in my guts, made me so shy that all I could do was look so hard that they had to move
away. But I wasn't a piece of fluff and neither were the other fems I knew. We knew what
we wanted and that was no mean feat for young women of the 1950s, a time when the
need for conformity, marriage and babies was being trumpeted at us by the government's
policy makers. Oh, we had our styles—our outfits, our perfumes, our performances—and
we could lose ourselves under the chins of our dancing partners who held us close enough
to make the world safe; but we walked the night streets to get to our bars, and we came out
bleary-eyed into the deserted early morning, facing a long week of dreary passing at the
office or the beauty parlor or the telephone company. I always knew our lives were a bewildering combination of romance and realism. I could tell you stories . . . about the
twenty-year-old fem who carried her favorite dildo in a pink satin purse to the bar every
Saturday night so her partner for the evening would understand exactly what she wanted
. . . or how at seventeen I hung out at Pam Pam's on Sixth Avenue and Eighth Street in
Greenwich Village with all the other fems who were too young to get into the bars and too
inexperienced to know how to forge an ID. We used this bare, tired coffee shop as a training ground, a meeting place to plan the night's forays. Not just fems—young butches were
there too, from all the boroughs, taking time to comb their hair just the right way in the
mirror beside the doorway . . . or how I finally entered my world, a bar on Abingdon
Square, where I learned that women had been finding each other for years, and how as
young fems we took on the Vice Squad, the plainclothes police women, the bathroom line
with its allotted amount of toilet paper, the Johns trying to hustle a woman for the night
and the staring straights who saw us as entertaining freaks. My passion had taken me
home and not all the hating voices of the McCarthy 1950s could keep me away from my
community.

Every time I speak at a lesbian-feminist gathering, I introduce myself as a fem who came
out in the 1950s. I do this, because it is the truth and therefore allows me to pay historical
homage to my lesbian time and place, to the women who have slipped away, yet whose voices I still hear and whose V-necked sweaters and shiny loafers I still see. I do it to call up the
women I would see shopping with their lovers in the Lower East Side supermarkets, the fem
partners of the butch women who worked as waiters in the Club 82. I remember how
unflinchingly the fem absorbed the stares of the other customers as she gently held onto the
arm of her partner. Butches were known by their appearances, fems by their choices. I do it
in the name of the wives of passing women[2] whose faces look up at me from old newspaper
clippings, the women whom reporters described as the deceived ones and yet whose histories suggest much more complicated choices. And if fems seemed to be "wives" of passing
women, the feminine protectors of the couple's propriety, it was so easy to lose curiosity
about what made them sexual heretics, because they looked like women. Thus fems became
the victims of a double dismissal: in the past they did not appear culturally different enough
from heterosexual women to be seen as breaking gender taboos and today they do not
appear feminist enough, even in their historical context, to merit attention or respect for
being ground-breaking women.

If we are to piece together a profound feminist and lesbian history,[3] we must begin asking questions about the lives of these women that we have not asked before, and to do this we will have to elevate curiosity to a much more exalted position than concepts of politically correct sexuality would ever allow us to do.[4] Politically correct sexuality is a paradoxical concept. One of the most deeply held opinions in feminism is that women should be autonomous and self-directed in defining their sexual desire, yet when a woman says, "This is my desire," feminists rush in to say, "No, no, it is the prick in your head; women should not desire that act." But we do not yet know enough at all about what women—any women—desire. The real problem here is that we stopped asking questions so early in the lesbian and feminist movement, that we rushed to erect what appeared to be answers into the formidable and rigid edifice that it is now. Our contemporary lack of curiosity also affects our view of the past. We don't ask butch-fem women who they are; we tell them. We don't explore the social life of working-class lesbian bars in the 1940s and 1950s; we simply assert that all those women were victims.[5] Our supposed answers closed our ears and stopped our analysis. Questions and answers about lesbian lives that deviate from the feminist model of the 1970s strike like a shock wave against the movement's foundation, yet this new wave of questioning is an authentic one, coming from women who have helped create the feminist and lesbian movement that they are now challenging into the new growth. If we close down exploration, we will be forcing some women once again to live their sexual lives in a land of shame and guilt; only this time they will be haunted by the realization that it was not the patriarchal code they have failed, but the creed of their own sisters who said they came in love. Curiosity builds bridges between women and between the present and the past; judgment builds the power of some over others. Curiosity is not trivial; it is the respect one life pays to another. It is a largeness of mind and heart that refuses to be bounded by decorum or by desperation. It is hardest to keep alive in the times it is most needed, the times of hatred, of instability, of attack. Surely these are such times.

When I stand before a new generation of lesbians and use this word "fem," I sometimes feel very old, like a relic from a long-buried past that has burst through the earth, shaken the dust off its mouth and started to speak. The first reaction is usually shock and then laughter and then confusion, when my audience must confront their stereotyped understanding of this word and yet face the fact that I am a powerful woman who has done some good in this brave new world of lesbian feminism. But the audience is not the only one who is going through waves of reactions. I too wonder how will I be perceived through these layers of history. A 1980s lesbian activist who defines herself as a fem poses the problem of our plight as an oppressed people in a most vivid way.

Colonization and the battle against it always poses a contradiction between appearances and deeper survivals.[6] There is a need to reflect the colonizer's image back at him yet at the same time to keep alive what is a deep part of one's culture, even if it can be misunderstood by the oppressor, who omnipotently thinks he knows what he is seeing. Butch-fem carries all this cultural warfare with it. It appears to incorporate elements of the heterosexual culture in power; it is disowned by some who want to make a statement against the pervasiveness of this power, yet it is a valid style, matured in years of struggle and harboring some of our bravest women. The colonizer's power enforces not only a daily cultural devaluing but also sets up a memory trap, forcing us to devalue what was resistance in the past in a desperate battle to be different from what they say we are.[7]

Both butches and fems have a history of ingenuity in the creation of personal style,[8] but since the elements of this style—the clothing, the stance—come from the heterosexually defined culture, it is easy to confuse an innovative or resisting style with a mere replica of the prevailing custom. But a butch lesbian wearing men's clothes in the 1950s was not a man wearing men's clothes; she was a woman who created an original style to signal to other women what she was capable of doing—taking erotic responsibility. In the feminist decades, the fem is the lesbian who poses this problem of misinterpreted choice in the deepest way. If we dress to please ourselves and the other women to whom we want to announce our desire, we are called traitors by many of our own community, because we seem to be wearing the clothes of the enemy. Make-up, high heels, skirts, revealing clothes, even certain ways of holding the body are read as capitulation to patriarchal control of women's bodies. An accurate critique, if a woman feels uncomfortable or forced to present herself this way, but this is not what I am doing when I feel sexually powerful and want to share it with other women. Fems are women who have made choices, but we need to be able to read between the cultural lines to appreciate their strength. Lesbians should be mistresses of discrepancies, knowing that resistance lies in the change of context.

The message of fems throughout the 1970s was that we were the Uncle Toms of the movement. If I wore the acceptable movement clothes of sturdy shoes, dungarees, work shirt and back pack, then I was to be trusted, but that is not always how I feel strongest. If I wear these clothes, because I am afraid of the judgment of my own people, then I am different kind of traitor, this time to my own fem sense of personal style, since this style represents what I have chosen to do with my womanness. I cannot hide it or exchange it without losing my passion or my strength. The saddest irony of all behind this misjudgment of fems is that for many of us it has been a life-long journey to take pleasure in our bodies. Butch lovers, reassuring and kind, passionate and taking, were for many of us a bridge back to acceptance of what the society around us told us to scorn: big-hipped, wide-assed women's bodies. My idiosyncratic sexual history leads me to express my feminist victories in my own way; other women, straight or gay, carry these victories of personal style within, hesitant to publicly display them, because they fear the judgment of the women's community. Our understanding of resistance is thus deeply diminished.

In the 1970s and 1980s, the fem is also charged with the crime of passing, of trying to disassociate herself from the androgynous lesbian. In the earlier decades, many fems used their appearance to secure jobs that would allow their butch lovers to dress and live the way they both wanted her to. Her fem appearance allowed her to pass over into enemy lines to make economic survival possible. But when butches and fems of this style went out together, no one could accuse the fem of passing. In fact, the more extremely fem she was, the more obvious was their lesbianism and the more street danger they faced. Now lesbian style occurs in the context of a more and more androgynous appearing society, and fem dress becomes even more problematic. A fem is often seen as a lesbian acting like a straight woman who is not a feminist—a terrible misreading of self-presentation which turns a language of liberated desire into the silence of collaboration. An erotic conversation between two women is completely unheard, not by men this time but by other women, many in the name of lesbian-feminism.

When one carries the fem identity into the arena of political activism, the layers of confusion grow. In the Spring of 1982, Deborah, my lover, and I did the Lesbian Herstory Archives slide show at the Stony Brook campus of SUNY.[9] We were speaking to fifty women health workers, four of whom identified themselves as lesbians. I wore a long lavender dress that made my body feel good and high, black boots that made me feel powerful. Deb was dressed in pants, shirt, vest and leather jacket. I led a two-hour discussion working with the women's honest expressions of homophobia, their fears of seeing their own bodies sexually, and the different forms of tyranny they faced as women. Finally one of the straight women said how much easier it was to talk to me rather than to Deb, who was sitting at the side of the room. "I look more like you," she said pointing to me. She too was wearing a long dress and boots. Here my appearance, which was really an erotic conversation between Deb and myself, was transformed into a boundary line between us. I walked over to Deb, put my arm around her and drew her head into my breasts. "Yes," I said, "but it is two of us together that make everything perfectly clear," Then I returned to the center of the room and lied. "I wore this dress so you would listen to me but our real freedom is the day when I can wear a three-piece suit and tie and you will still hear my words." I found myself faced with the paradox of having to fight for one freedom at the price of another. The audience felt more comfortable with me because I could pass, yet their misunderstanding of my femness was betraying its deepest meaning.

Because I am on the defensive many times in raising these issues, it is tempting to gloss over the difficulties that did exist in the past and do now. Being a fem was never a simple experience, not in the old lesbian bars of the 1950s and not now. Fems were deeply cherished and yet devalued as well. There were always fem put-down jokes going around the bar, while at the same time tremendous energy and caring was spent courting the fem women. We were not always trusted and often seen as the more flighty members of the lesbian world, a contradiction to our actual lives where we all knew fems who had stood by their butch lovers through years of struggle. We were mysterious and practical, made homes and broke them up, were glamorous and boring all at the same time. Butches and fems had an internal dialogue to work out, but when the police invaded our bars, when we were threatened with physical violence, when taunts and jeers followed us down the streets, this more subtle discussion was transformed into a monolithic front where both butch and fem struggled fiercely to protect each other against the attackers. Feminists need to know much more about how fems perceived themselves and how they were seen by those who loved them. Certainly the erotic clarity that was for me and many other fems at the heart of our style has never been clearly understood by sexologists or by feminists.

Since the butch-fem tradition is one of the oldest in lesbian culture, it came under investigation along with everything else when the sexologists began their study of sexual deviance. The feminine invert, as fems were called then, was viewed as the imperfect deviant. The sexology literature from 1909 stated that the "pure female invert feels like a man."[10] A few years later, the fem is described as an "effeminate tribadist."[11] In the 1950s, our pathology was explained this way:

The feminine type of Lesbian is one who seeks mother love, who enjoys being a recipient of much attention and affection. She is often preoccupied with personal beauty and is somewhat narcissistic . . . . She is the clinging vine type who is often thought and spoken of by her elders as a little fool without any realization of the warped sexuality which is prompting her actions.[12]

And then the doctor adds the final blow: "She is more apt to be bisexual and also apt to respond favorably to treatment." Here the fem lesbian is stripped of all power, made into a foolish woman who can easily be beckoned over into the right camp. Historically, we have been left disinherited, seen neither as true inverts nor as grown women.

An example from early twentieth-century lesbian literature also shows the complexity of the fem tradition. In *The Well of Loneliness*, published in 1928, two major fem characters embody some of the mythic characteristics of fems.[13] One is an unhappy wife who seduces Stephen Gordon, the butch heroine, but then betrays her, choosing the security of a safe life. The other is Beth, the lover Stephen turns over to a future husband at the end of the novel so she may have a chance at a "normal" life, thus enabling the author to make a plea for greater understanding of the deviant's plight. The reality of the author's life, however, gives a different portrait of a fem woman. Lady Una Troubridge, the partner of Radclyffe Hall, who saw herself as Hall's wife, was a major force in getting *The Well of Loneliness* published, even though she knew it would open their lives to turmoil and worse.

she [Radclyffe Hall] came to me, telling me that in her view the time was ripe, and that although the publication of such a book might mean the shipwreck of her whole career, she was fully prepared to make any sacrifice except—the sacrifice of my peace of mind.

She pointed out that in view of our union and of all the years that we had shared a home, what affected her must also affect me and that I would be included in any condemnation. Therefore she placed the decision in my hands and would write or refrain as I should decide. I am glad to remember that my reply was made without so much as an instant's hesitation: I told her to write what was in her heart, that so far an any effect upon myself was concerned, I was sick to death of ambiguities, and only wished to be known for what I was and to dwell with her in the palace of truth.[14]

Why Radclyffe Hall with this steadfast fem woman by her side could not portray the same type of woman in her lesbian novel is a topic that needs further exploration. Troubridge's cry, "I am sick of ambiguities," could become a fem's motto.

What this very brief examination of examples from sexology and literature point out, I hope, is how much more we need to know, to question, to explore. Fems have been seen as a problem through the decades both by those who never pretended to be our friends and now by those who say they are our comrades. The outcry over the inclusion of a discussion of butch-fem relationships in the Barnard sexuality conference was a shock to me; I had waited for over ten years for this part of my life to be taken seriously by a feminist gathering. I marched, demonstrated, conferenced, leafleted, CRed my way through the 1970s, carrying this past and the women who had lived it deep within me, believing that when we had some safe territory, we could begin to explore what our lives had really meant. Yet even raising the issue, even entertaining the possibility that we were not complete victims but had some sense of what we were doing, was enough to encourage a call for silence by feminists who feared our voices. Those of us who want to begin talking again are not the reactionary backlash against feminism, as some would call us. We are an outgrowth of the best of feminism in a new time, trying to ask questions about taboo territories, trying to understand how women in the past and now have had the strength and the courage to express desire and resistance. We ask these questions in the service of the belief that women's lives are our deepest text, even the life of a fem.

1. For more discussion of the butch-fem experience, see the following sources: Rita LaPorte, "The Butch/Femme Question", Ladder, vol. 15, June-July 1971, pp. 4f11; Victoria Brounworth, "Butch Femme—Myth or Reality or More of the Same", WICCE, Summer 1975, p. 7; Merril Mushroom, "How to Engage in Courting Rituals 1950 Butch Style in the Bar: An Essay", Common Lives/Lesbian Lives, no. 4, Summer 1982, pp. 6-10; Lee Lynch, "Swashbuckler", Sinister Wisdom, vol. 24, Fall 1983, and Toothpick House, Tallahassee, Fl., Naiad, 1983; Amber Hollibaugh and Cherrie Moraga, "What We're Rollin Around in Bed With: Sexual Silences in Feminism—A Conversation", Heresies Sex Issue #12, vol. 3, no. 4, 1981, pp. 58-62; "An Old Dyke's Tale: An Interview with Doris Lunden", Conditions, vol. 6, 1980, pp. 26-44; Joan Nestle, "Butch-Fem Relationships: Sexual Courage in the Fifties", Heresies Sex Issue #12, vol. 3, no. 4, 1981, pp. 21-4; "The Bathroom Line", Gay Community News, October 4, 1980; "Stone Butch, Drag Butch, Baby Butch" (poem), Big Apple Dyke News, August 1981; and "Esther's Story", Common Lives/Lesbian Lives, vol. 1, Fall 1981, pp. 5-9. Two books that are now in progress will be important new resources: the work by Liz Kennedy and Madeline Davis based on the oral histories of the pre-1970 Buffalo lesbian community and a proposed anthology by Amber Hollibaugh and Esther Newton. For a more detailed bibliography, please write to the Lesbian Herstory Educational Foundation/Lesbian Herstory Archives, P. O. Box 1258, New York, New York 10116.

2. The word "passing" is used here for lesbians who looked like men to the straight world. They wore men's clothes, took men's names and worked at jobs that were then considered men's occupations such as driving taxis and clerking in stock rooms. An excellent slide show on the historical passing women of San Francisco called "She Drank, She Swore, She Courted Girls . . . She Even Chewed Tobacco" has been prepared by the San Francisco Lesbian and Gay Men's History Project. It is available from Iris Films, Box 5353, Berkeley, California 94705. Passing women are not just an historical phenomenon; they are still very much a part of lesbian life, but they are seldom part of the organized lesbian-feminist community. They have received very little encouragement to be so.

3. For more resources on lesbian history, see Judith Schwarz (ed.), Frontiers: A Journal of Women's Studies, vol. 4, no. 3, Fall 1979, which contains a bibliography on "Lesbianism and American History" by Lisa Duggan. An updated version of this bibliography can be obtained from the Lesbian Herstory Archives. The works of John D'Emilio and Jonathan Katz are also vital sources in this field. See John D'Emilio, Sexual Politics, Sexual Communities: The Making of a Homosexual Minority in the United States, 1940-1970, Chicago, University of Chicago Press, 1983 and Jonathan Katz, Gay American History: Lesbians and Gay Men in the USA, New York, Crowell, 1976 and Gay/Lesbian Almanac: A New Documentary, New York, Harper & Row, 1983.

4. See Muriel Dimen, "Politically Correct? Politically Uncorrect?", pp. 138-48 for a discussion of the origin and development of standards of political correctness and incorrectness, particularly in regard to sexuality.

5. The work of Madeline Davis and Liz Kennedy documenting the Buffalo lesbian community pre-1970 will be a major breakthrough in ending this silence.

6. Albert Memmi's The Colonizer and the Colonized, New York, Orion, 1965, is an especially helpful text in clarifying cultural struggle in a pre-revolutionary period.

7. This is analogous to blacks not eating fried chicken (because that is what whites think all blacks do) when one loves eating it, both for the taste and the memories of home it evokes. One way of resisting this forced disinheritance is to make the cultural activity an in-house affair, where only members of the family share the pleasure. Many butch-fem individuals and communities have adopted this form of resistance. They exist on the edges of the women's and lesbian-feminist movement, or some members of the community cross over, helping to build organizations and feminist projects, but return at night to butch-fem relationships.

8. I want to make clear that butch-fem style differed from community to community and over time. I have written elsewhere of butch-fem couples who appeared similar both with short hair and in trousers; see Heresies Sex Issue # 12. Photographs of this style can be seen on many Ladder covers. The way straight people viewed these couples walking hand in hand in the 1950s was often hostile, with the added taunt of "which one of you is the man" for the less visibly defined couple. I think any of us from that time would be able to distinguish the butch from the fem by subtle differences in walk, how the shoulders were held, or how the heads bent during conversation.

9. Two slide shows have been developed by the Lesbian Herstory Archives, the first showing the concept and history of the Archives and the second illustrating lesbian life of the 1950s.

10. Katherine Bement Davis, Factors in the Sex Life of Twenty-Two Hundred Women, New York, Harper & Brothers, 1929. Davis here is citing August Forel, The Sexual Question, New York, Rebman, 1908.

11. Frank Caprio, MD, Female Homosexuality, New York, Grove, 1954, p. 18.

12. Ibid., p. 19. Caprio supports his characterization by a quotation from Dr Winifred Richmond. The Adolescent Girl, New York, Macmillan, 1925.

13. Radclyffe Hall, The Well of Loneliness, London, Jonathan Cape, 1928.

14. Lady Una Troubridge, The Life and Death of Radclyffe Hall, London, Hammond & Hammond, 1961, pp. 81-2.

Both lesbian and gay communities have had to struggle with racism. Although early liberationists and lesbian-feminists often wrote as though race would not be an issue between men or between women, especially those with a vision of a better society, that has not been the case. Racism takes many forms, from active hostility, to romanticization or objectification of people of color, to refusal to acknowledge any differences and address them.

J.R.G. De Marco details the patterns of racism in the Philadelphia community. He notes the hurdles faced by Black gays trying to gain access to bars, the stereotyping of Black men as hypersexual, and the financial inequalities between Blacks and whites that work against equality in personal relationships. He suggests that individual acts of good will are not enough and offers a program for community transformation.

J.R.G.DeMARCO

GAY RACISM

(1982)

J. R. G. DeMarco

There is a situation that's happened to me every time I've gone out. White men will approach me. They assume I don't know anything. They assume I'm uneducated and stupid," remarks Jimmy J. "They don't expect me to be able to carry on a conversation. But, when they find that I can converse and I do know something, then they're not interested. They walk away. They want *their* images."

Jimmy is 27, well-educated, a salesperson, and a Black man. He is a victim of the vicious stereotypes which all Black people must confront every day.

Negative assumptions, images and stereotypes are at the heart of the matter; they are what racism is built upon and continues to feed on. Such negative beliefs are what people use to bludgeon each other in quiet and simple ways, but the violence inherent in this type of racism is every bit as real as the lynching, burning and maiming that went on in the post-Civil War South. People are scared psychologically by racism and, because we all participate in this, we are all ruined.

The Philadelphia gay male community has never really come to grips with the problem of racism in its midst. This article attempts to uncover the problem, long buried by uncaring, uninformed and unrealistic attitudes. "They don't want to deal with racism because they don't think it affects them. They don't really dislike Blacks; they just don't think about Black people," comments Charles B., a 32-year-old artist. Charles' observation touches on another facet of racism: what writer Ralph Ellison called the invisibility of Blacks. People disregard what does not immediately concern them. In this way, many problems lose visibility until they impinge upon the world of the non-thinker.

This two-edged, racist sword is evident in the gay male community as well as in America at large. On the one hand, Black gays are largely an invisible minority. They are invisible, that is, until they attempt to mix with the White gay community. Then, all the negative stereotypes leap to the minds of the people involved.

Surprise is not uncommon among Black gay men when they find White gays to be racist. "I was surprised. Yes, in a way I was. I thought, 'Here's this group of people, a subculture sharing common interests, looking out for each other.' But it wasn't the case at all," remembers Van, a 33-year-old office worker. His experience is similar to Charles'. As Charles says, "I originally saw gays as a breed unto themselves. I assumed there would be a bond among all gay people. I was naive. Then I realized that the prejudices of society bled into the gay world."

Many Black gays did not have this preconceived notion about gays being more open. Ricardo D., 24, an office manager, declares, "I knew they were racist. People are people, whether they're gay or straight. They will have the same feelings and idiosyncracies." Far more of the men I interviewed echoed Ricardo's thoughts. Racism was no surprise, but it did hurt.

How does gay racism work?

Racism is put into practice through a variety of discriminatory techniques aimed at keeping minority group members from participating fully in society. The most visible form of discrimination in the gay community is at the bars—our most public and popular gathering places.

Carding is the practice of demanding a Liquor Control Board (LCB) card at the door of a bar before entrance is permitted.

This routine is meant to keep those people under the age of 21 out of the bars. But, as it is most frequently used, the LCB card is a means of keeping Black gays out of White gay bars—because only Black patrons are asked to produce their cards. It has gone on (or is going on) at almost every major gay bar in the city of Philadelphia.

Just going out becomes a real ordeal. "Your heart is in your throat. A block before you come to the bar, you get this awful feeling in your stomach. You wonder what will happen at the door. It makes you feel like trash. You can't even feel like an equal," remembers Stan A., a 27-year-old music student. In reliving the experience he seems almost out of breath.

"It happened to me early this summer at Odyssey II," relates Herb J., a hospital administrator. "We went to the door and were asked for IDs. We are not young looking. I showed my driver's license. The doorman said it was unacceptable." Herb takes a long deep breath—he's obviously trying to control his emotions. "Then, right in front of me, young, White gays were let into the bar. So I asked again if we could go in. We were refused. I would have called the police, but my friends didn't want to press charges."

Almost every bar in town was mentioned by one interviewee or another. There is no set policy—none set down so that you could see it, that is. The only real guide is money. Money talks. Bar owners listen to their patrons and their White patrons do not want to rub elbows with Black customers.

Two bars in town, the Smart Place and the now-defunct Letters, opened with the express purpose of being places where discrimination would not happen. In a short time, both bars became all-Black establishments, due to the refusal of most White gay men to patronize the bars on equal terms with Black gays. As Ed, the White former owner of Letters said some time before his bar closed, "White customers came to me several times and told me, 'It's getting too dark in here. If it doesn't stop, we're not coming back.' I told them that Letters was a bar for everyone."

Robin S., a graduate student in American culture and a Black activist as well as a gay activist, has his own ideas about Black acceptance in White gay bars. "One of the problems that Whites have with Blacks in bars is that they (the Whites) feel overwhelmed by the Blacks. Black men tend to be more social than middle-class, non-ethnic Whites. Also, the music in bars is music derived from Black music. It's okay to listen to Black women singing, but when it comes to having Black folk near you, they can't have it. It's a ripoff of Black culture. They take only what they like from it."

Getting past the door is only the beginning of a racist journey for some Black gays. Once inside, they are subjected to an array of racist emotions and reactions.

The racist ordeal

"Just to walk across the floor of the bar can be an ordeal. The expressions on some people's faces. The questioning looks, the 'why are you here?' expressions are all frightening. It can be mentally challenging, sometimes even physically challenging depending on the people and how hostile they are," according to Alan C., a 24-year old development researcher. Alan shifts uncomfortably in his seat as he talks about his experiences. With a sense of indignation he adds, "It's a very natural part of being a Black person. People have preconceptions. In a gay bar the preconception is: 'You shouldn't be here.' The response I must have is: 'I have every right to be here.' Dealing with this takes a lot of energy."

Like Alan, everyone has developed his own way of dealing with being in a White gay bar. Charles "will not go into a White gay bar alone." He feels strongly that "there are more important places to fight for civil rights."

But David, 32, a government worker, girds himself with feelings of self-worth and plunges ahead. "I don't go into any bar with the feeling that I may encounter discrimination. I've learned that racism is a White problem, not mine. So I go into bars and clubs with that attitude. If they don't respond to me that's their problem. I don't care how they feel or what they think. I can't let that affect my life to the point where I will become withdrawn."

Once over the initial hostile feelings, Black gay men are usually in for a variety of other experiences, all rooted in racist assumptions.

Like Jimmy, Alan has had men walk away because he did not fit their images. "I've had people talk to me, but when they find out you have some brains, they're not interested."

Herb remembers an acquaintance coming up to him in a bar and telling him, "You're too preppy. Where's your ski cap and blue jeans?" He uneasily recalls the incident and the hurt it caused him. "I thought that maybe I wasn't dressing right. I didn't know what to think. But then I decided that I'd dress the way I wanted."

Stan walked into Equus one evening and saw a person he thought was a friend. This "friend," a well-known gay activist, did not notice who Stan was from across the room. The activist did notice, however, that Stan was wearing a Lacoste shirt. Then in a loud voice the activist told the people he was with, "Well, those clothes are sure popular, even the *niggers* (emphasis added) are wearing them." Stan was shocked. "I couldn't believe it. He wasn't joking either. I've never spoken to him since. I thought he was a friend."

Another common occurrence for Black men in bars is described by John. "I'll be standing there and some White man will come up to me and, without saying a word, not even one word, he'll grab me in the crotch and look me in the eye. In front of everyone. I guess I'm expected to follow immediately. I usually tell them what will happen to their arms if they don't move." Wayne A., a college freshman with a similar experience, says, "They assume that Black men have big dicks, and that's all they're interested in. They're size queens, that's all."

Sexual stereotypes

Sexual stereotypes are common and burdensome to Black men, who feel that they are expected to behave in certain ways or meet other arbitrarily imposed standards. Charles thinks for a moment before dealing with the question: "Basically Black people are pictured as being sexually uninhibited and passionate. White men may want to receive this passion and fervor without having to give anything in return."

"They just want their fantasies," Dean interjects bluntly. "They want to be dominated by this dark man with this humongous dick and wonderfully passionate nature."

Surprisingly, with all the resentment this treatment can cause, Jimmy has room to be introspective and philosophical. He tries to cast a positive light on the matter. "I think a lot of White men are attracted to Black men because of the strength we have—not physical strength, but a spiritual strength which comes from putting up with a lot of bullshit." He is aware that this, too, is an image in some men's minds. "We ingest images that allow us to sexually objectify people, consume them, and discard them. It naturally follows that it can be done to Black men."

Sexual stereotyping is rampant, and again, the only reality is the imagery existing in the minds of those possessed of these stereotypes. Alan's anger flashes through his words: "If you don't fit their stereotypes, they become very cold. They don't bother to contact you or to communicate in any way."

Novelist James Baldwin sums up the matter in *A Rap on Race*: "They come to you for the most part, as though you're some extraordinary phallic symbol . . . As if you're nothing but a walking phallus . . . no head, no arms, no nothing . . . actually the act of love becomes an act of murder in which you are also committing suicide."

Donald has experienced another typical approach that some White men have toward Black men. "I will see White men in bars who want nothing to do with me. They're with their White Friends and don't want to show their true feelings. They don't even seem to notice me. But, later in the evening, our paths will cross again at the baths. Now they're alone. Their friends are not around to see what they do and who they do it with. They try like hell to get me into bed when no one is around to see. I remind them that they were not interested in me at the bar, and now, I'm not interested in them. If you won't deal with me in the light, you won't get me at night." He smiles as he says this.

Bathhouses also present situations for racism to occur on a variety of levels. The most obvious, of course, is discrimination at the door.

Several years ago, it was rumored that a popular bathhouse would not permit Black men in. A weekly gay newspaper no longer published in Philadelphia, *The Weekly Gayzette*, decided to test the case. Two people were sent, one White, one Black. The White person had a membership, the Black man was seeking one. At the door, the White man said he wanted to sponsor his Black friend. The clerk on duty announced, "I'm sorry, but our membership is full right now. We aren't accepting any more people. But take this card, fill it out and we'll contact you in two weeks." The bathhouse never made contact. . .

Inside the baths there are areas which are poorly lit or not lighted at all, places where the most anonymous sex happens. But even here racism finds a way. White patrons will be in these areas when someone comes along—someone they attempt to initiate sexual contact with. They reach out trying to connect. The two men will then come together for sexual contact, but on many occasions Victor B. says the following has happened: "The guy will feel me all over, then he'll reach up and feel my hair. As soon as he does that he figures out that I'm Black and loses all interest. He pushes me away." Victor was not alone in mentioning this phenomenon.

Negative assumptions

The negative assumptions do not stop at the bars and the baths, but follow people into the confines of the bedroom, where one's inhibitions are supposed to be much lower. Jimmy bristles with sexual memories: "I've gone home with White men who are always certain I'm going to steal something. If I say I have to go to the bathroom, I get escorted from the bed to the bathroom and then back again." Herb agrees: "If you meet someone, they're usually afraid to go home with you because they think it won't be safe in your neighborhood. They are also frightened to take you home because they think you'll steal half the house. They walk around the house with you and they check if you're clean."

Others, like John, have experienced relationships in which they are only sex objects. "Once I got to his apartment, I was treated like a toy. I had to do this or that. He wanted to do whatever he wanted, without considering my feelings at all."

Some see racist patterns in the interracial couples they know or observe. Charles says he has noticed "a plantation mentality in the interracial couples I've seen. The Black man is expected to be docile, timid, and often financially dependent on the White man. I maintain that when one man has to degrade himself in order to keep another, I can't see how either will benefit."

Donald sees many of the same features among the interracial couples he knows. "The White man is usually more financially well-to-do than the Black man. This perpetuates many of the stereotypes."

But Alan, who has a White lover, disagrees, "Despite the fact that one may appear dominant, this doesn't mean that this is in fact true. It is easier for them to act this way when the couple is out. A Black man gets a lot more negative attention when he chauffeurs a White man around, buys a drink for a White man, or buys clothes for a White man. You don't always want to deal with that attention. It's a defense."

Dean is quick to point out that interracial couples are subjected to another subtle form of racism built on the assumption that the White man is in control. "In restaurants, the maitre d' will talk to the White man. The waiters always give the check to the White man. Or they assume that the credit card belongs to the White man."

The instances pile up over and over again. The sense of outrage and resentment grows geometrically. Solutions seem unavailable and hope for better relations has never been more elusive. What can be done to change things? If not the world at large, what can be done to make the gay community less racist?

Almost everyone interviewed feels the same way about solving the problem of racism. "Since racism and discrimination are functions of White attitudes and White actions," concludes Robin, "it is White people who have to deal with it." Dale agrees wholeheartedly: "Blacks should stop taking the responsibility for solving the problem of racism. After all, it's not really *our* problem. We, unfortunately, reap the effects of it, though."

From this starting point—White responsibility—people had all manner of suggestions for solving the problem. They ranged from Dale's exhortation for people to "be willing to be wrong because that's where learning starts," to Jimmy who says that White gay men should try to understand what it means to be Black. "It's not fully possible, but there's a way. I ask White gay men to completely 'own' their own gayness and display it constantly, every day as I do my Blackness. This way they can see how pervasive the oppression is out there."

"They've got to acknowledge there is a problem," Robin insists, "and then acknowledge that it should be changed. This doesn't go on. Racism and discrimination exist in bars because they exist on a personal basis. It's not just the carding: it's the White people who see the carding and do nothing about it. They do *nothing*. That perpetuates it. White gays allow it to continue. That's the only way it *can* continue. Racism exists because the majority of White male gays support it."

Can Black gays help?

Not everyone felt that Whites should have to go the distance on their own. Charles, along with others, feels that, although Whites must do the majority of the work in battling racism, Blacks can help.

"There are three ways Black people can react to White racism: a) they can accept the programming and feel inferior; b) they can resent it and respond with hatred; c) they can feel compassion for Whites and work with them and help them. The last way is obviously the most constructive way."

"It's everybody's problem," declares Van animatedly. "If there's a White person who recognizes discrimination or a racist attitude, he or she should say something about it. By the same token, if the incident happens to a Black person, they should say something. It's very difficult for a person to take action if he thinks he's all alone. That's part of the problem. Part of the solution is to let people know that if they feel or think that racism is wrong, then they're not alone."

Alone or not, the problem must be dealt with. The question is: How? Charles Silberman in *Crisis in Black and White*, writes ". . . it is up to Whites to lead the way; the guilt and responsibility are theirs." Again the question is: How?

Unquestionably, a sensible, careful program is needed to begin dealing with racism in the gay male community. The following is a proposal, based on discussion with others, for a program to start with. It must be remembered that these are only suggestions and that these suggestions are merely a starting point. If every facet of this program is followed, racism will still exist and will still present a problem. This program only suggests a starting place. The only certainty is that a start must be made.

One crucial element must be worked at on all levels. Brian, a city planner, hit on this point: "You cannot turn people around unless you first convince them that the change is in their own best interest." The task is ours to work out.

Step One: Recognition and Discussion of the Problem

To deal with the problems of the gay male community they must be recognized and fully explored. Gay men have never really explored themselves or their feelings as have our lesbian sisters. In order to accomplish this, a series of all-male town meetings are required.

Because racism is the foremost problem in our community this should be the topic of, at least, the first of these meetings. Such meetings could consist of:

a) a panel of Black and White men openly and truthfully discussing the problem of racism and methods for ending it; b) a psychodrama concerning racism (perhaps provided by Plays for Living) and a discussion following; c) subsequent meetings to deal with racism through role playing, expert lecturers, and problem-solving sessions.

Step Two: Action to End Discrimination and Racism

Led by various community groups (the gay religious groups, the Philadelphia Lesbian and Gay Task Force, Black and White Men Together, Philadelphia Black Gays) a plan of action should be formulated to put a stop to discrimination at all public gathering places for gays:

a) open access to bars and baths should be insisted upon. The use of LCB cards to discriminate against Blacks should be stopped; b) a meeting of bar owners/managers with the leaders of this anti-racist coalition of community groups should be held to discuss the problem of racism and the role bars play in it; c) a vigilance committee should be set up to ensure that such discrimination does not continue.

This same coalition of groups should set up another vigilance committee to watch gay publications. Robin points out that "positive images of Blacks are necessary to ending racism. The truth must be told about the part that Blacks have played in history. For example, the Black people that were involved in the Stonewall Riots of 1969 which started the modern gay movement."

Step Three: Continuing Communication

In order for racism to be eradicated, anti-racist activity must be continual. Our community must also begin to cooperate with the Black community and support its causes and concerns. As Charles said, "When people show up on picket lines set up by Black people for Black causes, then I'll know they're concerned." To this end, various courses of action can be taken:

a) the anti-racist coalition of groups can meet with groups from the Black community and offer help; b) a series of rap groups can be set up and run by PBG or BWMT or some other outside agency so that the rap group will have a program and a set procedure; c) consciousness-raising sessions on the topic of racism should be held at the Gay and Lesbian Community Center and perhaps even in some bars; d) support groups for those interested in continuing the fight against racism should be set up and managed; e) cultural sharing sessions to be held at the Community Center could explore Black and White cultures in a positive way, with an emphasis on sharing.

Step Four: Strengthening the Bonds

Gay men have not begun to explore the concept and the comfort of Brotherhood. Our lesbian sisters have long known the joys of Sisterhood. They have, for a long time, drawn on the strengths and supports inherent in Sisterhood.

Gay men have yet to begin the journey on the long road to Brotherhood. Our common bonds as men as well as our strengths, weaknesses, and concerns are still to be explored and exploited.

To this end, a series of Brotherhood meetings should be tried, utilizing the Community Center and all of our community groups. Our community can only gain from such exploration.

Gay and lesbian religious organizations of many denominations have attracted huge numbers of participants since the 1970s. Members of these groups have tried to maintain their spiritual teachings and sense of community in an environment that nurtures their homosexuality. In turn, these institutions offer the personal and organizational support needed for political mobilization. The following piece shows how the Black gay church has played this role in the United States. James Tinney taught political science at Howard University in Washington D.C. until his death from AIDS in 1988.

JAMES S. TINNEY, Ph.D.

WHY A BLACK GAY CHURCH?

(1986)

James S. Tinney, Ph.D.

The new phenomenon of predominantly-Black gay churches being formed nationwide (with congregations already in Chicago, New York City, and Washington, prompted numerous inquiries from many interested individuals. Everywhere there seems to be unusual interest in this new development even among those who pose questions concerning it.

Sometimes the inquiries are from non-Blacks who would like to benefit from worshipping with Black gay Christians, yet who want some assurance, before attending, that they will also be welcome. At other times questions are raised by Black lesbians and gays themselves. Why should a gay-identified church be created when many Black congregations are already predominantly gay in their membership? Or why should Black Christians attend a gay church, when their sexual preference is nobody's business—and when, in fact, no one in their church confronts them about gayness even when they suspect them to be gay? Is not religion, like sexuality, a personal thing between individuals and God?

These are legitimate questions that deserve a reasoned response. Listed here are some pertinent reasons why Black lesbian and gay churches are being created, and why these new congregations should have—and are getting—the support of lesbian and gay persons in the Black community.

The Support of History: Black gay churches exist for the same reasons that separate Black churches and separate mostly white gay churches exist. Historically, the Christian church has often been fluid and dynamic enough to include many different types of congregations and denominations, many of which appeal to certain needs that are not met in other churches. In fact, sociologists know that denominations themselves reflect certain economic class characteristics—reflected in differences in liturgy and beliefs—even among persons of the same race. Among whites, for instance, the Episcopal church is a church of the upper classes (even though it has some middle-class congregations), while the Primitive Baptist church is a church of the mostly-rural poor.

On the other hand, other churches have come into existence precisely because the Christian church was not fluid and dynamic enough to be comfortable with pluralism. Black churches as a whole were created because white churches excluded Blacks from equal participation and leadership. Early in American history, Christianity officially taught that Black people were created without souls and could not be saved. In fact, the baptism of slaves was finally permitted only after Christian slave-holders became convinced that baptism would not legally alter the slaves' inferior socio-political status. (The word "Christian" is being used here to mean "formal, structural and institutional Christianity" rather than "genuine conversion or faithfulness to the truth as taught by Christ.")

The first independent Black denomination—the African Methodist Episcopal Church—came into being because even free Blacks, who were not slaves, were not permitted to kneel at the altar and receive Holy Communion at the same time whites did. Even after independent Black Baptist and Methodist churches originated, white laws did not permit Black churches to own their own property or to even worship in Black churches (in the

South) unless a white person was present.

Even today, Black denominations have been reluctant to merge with white ones, and separate Black caucuses exist in every major white denomination, and new Black congregations are being formed even under white denominations, because white churches still do not permit Black Christians the freedom to worship using Afro-American traditions in liturgy, and do not permit access to governing positions of authority over whites, and do not encourage Black liberation theology to be taught or proclaimed from the pulpit, and do not even understand or recognize the special gifts—as well as special needs—that Black Christians possess.

White gay churches have, within the past 10 years or more, come into existence under circumstances related to the oppression of sexual identity that parallel the circumstances related to oppression of Black identity. Unfortunately, however, many Black lesbians and gays find the same racial oppressiveness in these white gay churches that Blacks generally experience in predominantly white churches of whatever label.

Black gay churches should be supported because, on the one hand, they represent the pluralism that America and American Christianity are supposed to represent; and on the other hand, they represent the same desire for freedom, access, encouragement, understanding, and recognition that Blacks find impossible in most white churches, and that white gays find impossible in most "straight" churches.

The Development of Community: Black gay churches are being created spontaneously as a result of the search for, and the formation of, a sense of community. Since the sixties, there has been a growing emphasis on the wholeness and self-determination of the Black community wherever it is located. This has meant a visibly increased sense of loyalty to Black institutions and Black social cohesiveness. Similarly, since the seventies, there has been a growing emphasis on the existence of the gay community in whatever city it is found. This has meant growing support for lesbian and gay institutions.

Yet Black lesbians and gays have often found themselves "caught in the middle" (so to speak) since the "two-ness" of identity (to use a term of W. E. B. DuBois) reflected in being both Black and gay was not wholly approved in either the Black or gay communities. To maintain comfortability in the Black community, particularly in those places that cultivate Black culture and Black solidarity, many have felt a need to downplay their homosexuality. As the Rev. Renee McCoy, pastor of the Black gay Harlem Metropolitan Community Church, has said, "If Black lesbians and gay men are willing to check their sexuality at the door of the church, and come bearing gifts of talent, there are relatively few problems." And in order to maintain comfortability in the gay community, others have felt a need to downplay their Blackness.

This should not be. But the facts remain; and the pressures coming from both sides have necessitated the formation of a distinctly Black and gay community. Even without those pressures, an identifiable Black gay community would undoubtedly have still come into existence, simply because of the uniqueness in talents, gifts, sensitivity, experience, dress and behavior that is inherently a part of being both Black and gay—both as a manifestation of God's creation and our own creation.

The Black gay community—and the Black gay church which is an integral part of that community and that culture (as all churches are inseparable from some community and some culture)—are therefore not the result of some conspiratorial "invasion" of the Black community by white gays, or even the result of some "separatist" invasion of the gay community by Black extremists. Black gay churches are part and parcel of the newly-emerging

Black gay culture which is so inevitable.

Furthermore, Black gay churches are reflections of a valid and vital sense of growing commonality and unity and community among Black gay Christians. They both exhibit and promote a sense of fellowship and mission. Non-gay Black Christians should support them because they are reaching out with the message of Christ to a gay community that has been alienated from Christ and from "straight" churches. White gay Christians should support them because they are countering the many anti-gay myths in the Black community— and in the Black Christian community—that white gays cannot possibly reach.

The Possibility of Mutuality: Black gay churches are a necessary step before there can be mutuality, equality and reciprocal relationships between gay and non-gay Black Christians, and between Black and white gay Christians. Since patterns of mutuality in relationships— acting lovingly and consentingly with each other even as we desire to be treated ourselves— are at the center of the "new commandment" given by Jesus to replace all other command- ments, the creation of Black gay churches makes possible the fulfillment of Jesus' law of love. (Love is best defined as "mutuality" because it places emphasis in actions rather than senti- ments, and because it includes the element of reciprocal relations or "doing unto others as we would have them do unto us.")

Love or mutuality is possible only between equals. Otherwise, love becomes mere sen- timentality or beneficence that causes the powerful to feel good when they do something that pacifies the powerless, who are seen as "unfortunates." (Usually this sentimentality or beneficence is described as "doing something good for" or "helping" the powerless.) Similarly, it is impossible for the powerful to "give" power to the powerless, or to "give" them their rights. As Frederick Douglass said, "Power concedes nothing without a demand." Because of their vested interests, which define even their outlook, the power-holders are never able to give up their privilege, position, principles, preferences, or prerogatives. This is only natural and should be expected. The empowerment of those who are under, outside, and without, comes only as these very ones seize power for themselves.

Because this is true, all invitations on the part of the powerful represent their terms rather than the truest needs and best interests of the powerless. White churches themselves are never prone to adopt any strategy or program that really represents Black people's total concerns. Nor can they set the agenda for Black Christians. Neither can non-gay churches do this for gay Christians. Black gay Christians must do this alone. All efforts at "pluralism," "integration," "human/race relations," and "inclusiveness" on the part of whites toward Blacks, and non-gays toward gays, and white gay Christians toward Black gay Christians, are inherently deficient. True pluralism and inclusiveness is possible only when the powerless (in this case, Black gay Christians) self-assume and self-assert power, and self-define and self- determine agendas, and self-initiate and self-invite cooperation on the part of others. Only between equals can true mutuality or reciprocal relationships develop.

The formation and evolvement of Black gay churches is thus, in a real sense, a represen- tation of Black gay Christians getting their act together" among themselves so that they can then negotiate with non-gay Black Christians and with white gay Christians from a position of strength rather than weakness. Is there a role for non-gays and whites in this process? Yes, if Black gay Christians say so—and Black gay Christians have never excluded anyone from joining the struggle. But are Black gay churches only a temporary step—a preliminary stage— along a path that will eventually lead to full integration? Only if Black gay Christians decide that this should be so, and only as they (rather than others) define what is meant by "inte- gration." Will there ever come a day when Black gay churches will no longer be necessary?

Probably not, since human social and political transformation, as well as spiritual existential transformation, in this life will always be incomplete. Yet, here and there, either individually or institutionally, there will occur some shining examples of new creation—meaning, in the simplest way, there will be some non-gay Blacks and some gay whites (and other racial/sexual combinations) who will be willing to work in and for and with Black gay churches; and there some truly inter-racial and trans-sexual churches will evolve (though likely out of Black gay churches rather than out of "straight" Black churches or gay white churches).

The Realization of Authenticity: The development of Black gay churches will make it possible for Black gay Christians, for the first time, to hear the gospel in their own "language of the Spirit," respond to the gospel in their own ways, and reinterpret the gospel in their own cultural context—taking into account both race and sexual orientation at every step in this process. In a socio-political sense, this is called contextualization; in a psychological and existential sense, this is called authenticity; and in a biblical sense, this is called conversion.

Whatever it is called, however, it refers to the full liberation of the total Black gay Christian. Such liberation cannot possibly occur when the sights and sounds and symbols of faith are all derived from either "straight" Black churches or white gay churches. Neither can this total liberation when the creed and code and cultus (ritual) are all derived from non-gay Black churches or white gay churches. Particularly those elements which impinge upon race and sexual orientation will have to be—and will inevitably be—re-evaluated, redefined, and reinterpreted. This is also the work of the Spirit: creating and calling into existence "new being," doing and redoing theology and scriptural interpretation in the view of what it means to be both Black and gay. And this is also putting into practice what the Christian faith is all about (being "catholic" by making the faith universal enough to include Black gay Christians; being "reformed" by making Black gay Christians themselves participate in the priesthood of all believers; and being "evangelical" enough to sound like good news to Black lesbians and gays who have been outside the church). Of course, in this process, the new Black gay churches will at the same time ensure that the ultimate and distinctive realities of faith, particularly as these relate to Jesus Christ our savior and liberator, are preserved so that Black gay Christians remain truly and unquestionably Christian.

There will, of course, be those who question the right of Black gay churches to do all this. In some cases it will be true that "we have found the enemy and it is us." This will be necessarily so, because all of us are products of our environments; all of us bring to bear upon the task of realizing authenticity our own presumptions, biases, and fears; and all of us have to some degree been "brainwashed" by the powerful. As Frantz Fanon put it, we have all internalized our oppression to some degree. Conversion (or "conscienticization" as described by Kwame Nkrumah is a painful and difficult process. Therefore many Black gay Christians—even as many white gay Christians—will find the guilt too embedded in their inner souls, and the alienation (from God, from their bodies, from their own truest selves) too extensive to ever "leave the land of bondage" and "come out of Babylon" and into "canaan"—our own Black gay churches.

There will be others, though, for whom the price of the past and the pity of the pain are seen for what they really are. Both Black and white, both homosexual and heterosexual and pansexual, these "who walk by faith and not by sight" will count all as worthless except for the prospect of the promise.

Black gay churches represent that promise.

V

THE GAY AND LESBIAN POLITICS OF AIDS

I am optimistic that we're approaching a major breakthrough on AIDS.
—NYC Health Commissioner David J. Sencer, January 31, 1983.

My guess is that within 12–18 months, we will be able to arrest the disease at whatever stage it's at, except for people who are extremely sick. Also by that time, we will be able to begin to restore immune function back to normal...this is what I and my colleagues are talking about privately.
— Dr. Bernard Bihari, quoted in *The Body Positive*, February 1988.

One thing we do know for sure: There is indeed light shining at the end of the tunnel. In a recent meeting in Washington, the normally staid top officials of the National Institutes of Health AIDS program were practically jumping up and down in their chairs in excitement over the progress that has been made and the advances that are on the horizon.
— Martin Delaney of Project Inform, February 1989.

Which is it? (choose one): 1) There is no cure. there won't be one. AIDS has become "cancerized." AIDS activists are dead, burnt-out or bored. Families and friends have convinced themselves of their own helplessness, feeding the hopelessness felt by people with AIDS. AIDS groups are marked by dissent and despair. Too much of the fight against AIDS is driven by greed, ego and power. 2) People with AIDS are living longer and healthier lives. More treatments are available today. A vaccine is around the corner. New treatments are coming on-line soon. AIDS researchers work selflessly for long hours. AIDS activism has helped drive the campaign for reform of the healthcare system. Astounding individual stories of courage, compassion and commitment abound. 3) A lot of both.
— Sean O. Strub, editorial statement for inaugural issue of *POZ*, a magazine for "anyone impacted by AIDS," 1994.

These quotes are emblematic of the false hopes, despair, and will to survive of gay men (and later lesbians) during the AIDS epidemic, the beginnings of which were declared by the U.S. Centers for Disease Control in October 1981. In this chapter we document the emergence of a politics of AIDS through four "moments" that are chronologically overlapping but analytically distinct. They include:

1) Identifying AIDS — what it is, who has it, and why it is happening;
2) AIDS activism — originating in, drawing support from, and often in conflict with gay and lesbian activism;
3) Living with AIDS as an individual and social condition, based upon its transformation into a chronic disease, its "cancerization;"
4) The "deconstruction" of AIDS through a critique of the political economy of AIDS science and its institutionalization through academic research and biomedical technologies, as well as of clinical practice.

In spite of these four dimensions of the politics of AIDS, we have kept to a chronological format to demonstrate, genealogically, how politics unfolds over time. This chronology continues at the time we go to press in late 1996 with discoveries of natural immunity factors against HIV as well as drug treatment regimens that drastically reduce HIV in the human body. Even if health can be restored and AIDS biomedically prevented, the politics of AIDS will continue, because who will benefit from these developments is a function of the global political economy of health care.

In this chapter we document the politics of AIDS only within gay and lesbian communities. This documentation is centered on New York City and San Francisco. With NYC and San Francisco as epicenters of the AIDS epidemic, we chose to profile the "politics of AIDS" in situations where that politics was able to build from preexisting gay and lesbian communities.

During the 1960s to 1980s venues for casual male homosexual sex burgeoned. These venues included backroom bars, bathhouses, sex clubs, and porn theatres, as well as the perennial highway rest stops and other isolated areas ("meat-racks") and men's rooms (tea rooms). With the increased availability of sexual partners, sexually transmitted disease incidence increased among gay men, including amoebas, syphilis, gonorrhea, hepatitis, venereal warts, cytomegalovirus (CMV), herpes, and others. Thus, when gay men were reported to be dying from unknown causes in 1981, and STDs were already widespread, much analysis focused upon the possibility of finding the cause of these deaths in gay male sexuality. One of the most comprehensive and earliest statements of this position, by Michael Callen (founder of the People With AIDS Coalition) and others, is reprinted here.

In late 1982, when the following article was published in the *New York Native*, a gay and lesbian newspaper, little was known about AIDS transmission. Indeed, the acronym AIDS had only recently been coined, after the use of other acronyms, including of GRID (Gay-Related Immune Deficiency), ACIDS (Acquired Community Immune Deficiency Syndrome), and CAIDS (Community Acquired Immune Deficiency Syndrome). The article expresses the "lifestyle hypothesis" of transmission then current within the gay community of New York. A viral theory is here posited as politically reactionary—the idea that any minority group could carry a deadly virus is considered unconscionable bigotry toward that community. Rather, an "accumulation of risk" through reinfection with common viruses is predicated, resulting in a consequent overload of the immune system. Notable here is the confluence of medical arguments and political arguments from the very outset of the epidemic, the policy consequences (closure of venues for "promiscuity" or education within them), and the beginning of gay "ownership" of the epidemic raging in that community: "we must initiate and control this process ourselves. Be assured that if we aren't willing to conduct it [a reevaluation of our lifestyle as a medical problem] others will do it for us." The authors also wrote and published in 1983 "How to Have Sex in an Epidemic," the first safe sex manual from which we also include a brief section.

from

WE KNOW WHO WE ARE:
TWO GAY MEN DECLARE WAR ON PROMISCUITY

from the *New York Native* (1982)

Richard Berkowitz and Michael Callen with Richard Dworkin

Those of us who have lived a life of excessive promiscuity on the urban gay circuit of bathhouses, backrooms, balconies, sex clubs, meat racks, and tearooms know who we are. We could continue to deny overwhelming evidence that the present health crisis is a direct result of the unprecedented promiscuity that has occurred since Stonewall, but such denial is killing us. Denial will continue to kill us until we begin the difficult task of changing the ways in which we have sex.

What do we mean by "excessive promiscuity?" Though it has not been reported in the national or gay press, the National Cancer Institute, using figures provided by the Centers for Disease Control, stated in March 1982:

The median number of lifetime male sexual partners for homosexual male patients [with AIDS] is 1160 . . .

Few have been willing to say it so clearly, but the single greatest risk factor for contracting AIDS is a history of multiple sexual contacts with partners who are having multiple sexual contacts—that is, sex on the circuit. We know who we are.

Those of us who have been promiscuous have sat on the sidelines throughout this epidemic and by our silence have tacitly encouraged wild speculation about a new, mutant, Andromeda-strain virus. We have remained silent because we have been unable or unwilling to accept responsibility for the role that our own excessiveness has played in our present health crisis. But, deep down, we know who we are and we know why we're sick.

Do the gay communities of New York, San Francisco, and Los Angeles realize that promiscuity has become such a narcotic for some that we know of men who have been diagnosed with AIDS and Kaposi's sarcoma and who, even in the face of imminent death, are at this very moment "moderating" their sexual habits at the baths and backrooms? What does it mean that there are hustlers with AIDS and KS who are still hustling to pay their medical bills? Would those who were offended by the scene in *Taxi Zum Klo* in which the literally jaundiced protagonist cabs to the local tearoom be more shocked to recognize this behavior in their own community—perhaps even in themselves?

What has been missing so far in the investigation of the health crisis has been the informed opinions of those of us who have created it. Can researchers really comprehend the dynamics of urban gay male promiscuity? Can they understand the health implications for a 27-year-old who has had 2,000 sexual partners? Or 1,000? Or even 500?

We are the gay men who are becoming the victims of AIDS.

We, the authors, have concluded that there is no mutant virus and there will be no vaccine. We veterans of the circuit must accept that we have overloaded our immune systems with *common* viruses and other sexually transmitted infections. Our lifestyle has created the present epidemic of AIDS among gay men. But in the end, whichever theory you choose to believe, the obvious and immediate solution to the present crisis is the end of urban gay male promiscuity as we know it today.

We have developed the following questions and answers from our own personal experiences as AIDS victims, from consultations with various researchers and physicians, from participation in support groups for AIDS victims, from meetings with health crisis groups in New York City and San Francisco, and from our own reading in both the medical and the lay press.

How do you explain the present epidemic of AIDS among gay men?

We believe that it is the *accumulation of risk* through leading a promiscuous gay urban lifestyle which has led to the breakdown of immune responses that we are seeing now. Most published medical reports indicate that continued re-exposure and reinfection with common viruses (most notably cytomegalovirus), in conjunction with other common venereal infections and perhaps other factors, have led to the present health crisis among urban gay promiscuous men.

"Continued re-exposure and reinfection with common infections" means bathhouse/backroom sexual activity. Every sexually active gay man knows that he is much more likely to pick up any of a variety of sexually transmitted diseases today than he was five years ago. Five years ago, who'd ever heard of amoebas? Herpes now makes the cover of *Time.* In retrospect, these epidemics were signalling the coming of a major health crisis.

The gay men who are developing AIDS have long histories of many sexually transmitted diseases. These include amebiasis; hepatitis A, B, and non-A-non-B; venereal warts; penile, anal, and oral gonorrhea; syphilis; herpes simplex types 1 and 2; nonspecific urethritis and proctitis. It appears that we have been defining venereal disease too narrowly. We are discovering that many viruses can and have been transmitted during sex and must now add cytomegalovirus (CMV) and Epstein-Barr, among others, to the list of sexually transmitted diseases which urban gay males have been trading at an unprecedented rate over the last decade.

Why would CMV be particularly important?

In one study published in the *New England Journal of Medicine,* 94 percent of sexually active gay men tested showed evidence of CMV infection, and 14 percent were actively contagious for CMV at the time of testing. We believe that the prevalence of CMV on the circuit is the major link in the process of developing AIDS among gay men.

Many CMV infections are asymptomatic, which means that an individual may have CMV and be immunosuppressed without even knowing it. He may not realize that it is not safe for him to go to the baths, for example, because he is at a high risk for picking up the many bacterial, fungal, amoebic, and particularly viral infections in such settings. If he is contagious, he puts his sexual partners at risk, too. In a setting like the baths, it would be possible for such an individual to unknowingly infect many people with CMV during one visit.

One can be reinfected with CMV. No one knows for certain what the immunological results of reinfection are, but since a single infection with CMV can be immunosuppressive, it is easy to imagine what the cumulative effects of re-exposure to CMV and other infections might be.

I still don't understand how a promiscuous gay man would get AIDS.

Simply stated, if you live in or frequent New York, San Francisco, Los Angeles, or any of several other metropolitan areas, it is likely that you will be having sex with men who are sick. If you have sex with sick men, you may get sick too—not with any new diseases, but again and again with CMV and other common infections. Sooner or later, you simply will not recover.

Other factors may contribute to the development of AIDS in promiscuous gay men, including stress, diet, intravenous or other drug usage, the possible immunosuppressive consequences of sperm and seminal fluid, and excessive exposure to ultraviolet light. However, none of these contributing factors would be sufficient alone to cause AIDS; it is the widespread, repeated re-exposure and reinfection with common viruses—which life on the circuit makes inevitable—that has set the stage for the epidemic of AIDS that we are now witnessing.

Isn't there a theory that a new, mutant, particularly strong strain of some virus is causing all this?

There certainly has been a lot of speculation about a new or mutant virus. But no evidence supports this theory. AIDS is not "spreading" the way one would expect a single-viral epidemic to spread. As the National Cancer Institute has pointed out:

Taking all of the apparent epidemiological observations together, a growing accumulation of risk factors is suggested rather than spread in the classic sense of contagion. . . . The syndrome is occurring mainly in a particular subset of the homosexual male population, possibly but not exclusively defined by the number of sexual partners.

However, speculation regarding a single, new virus continues because:
—There are rumors that a small percentage of gay AIDS victims claim to have had a low

number of sexual partners.

—The Centers for Disease Control has found a cluster of nine gay men who apparently had sex with each other over a five-year period and each developed Kaposi's sarcoma.

—Many researchers persist in the notion that the same agent is causing the AIDS that is occurring in four very different groups: male homosexuals, Haitians, intravenous drug abusers, and hemophiliacs.

We'll refute these three arguments one at a time.

The so-called non-promiscuous AIDS victims. Many people dismiss the theory of accumulation of risk because of claims that there are "sexually celibate" or non-promiscuous gay men who have AIDS. In our review of medical journals and of literature published by the Centers for Disease Control, we have encountered no evidence that non-promiscuous gay men are contracting AIDS. Further, in our conversations with AIDS victims and with their doctors, we have yet to encounter one individual with AIDS who has not been promiscuous for a significant period.

Even assuming that there are individuals with AIDS who claim to have been non-promiscuous, an individual's estimate of the extent of his own promiscuity tends to be extremely unreliable.

The frequency of incidence of sexually transmitted diseases is perhaps a more accurate index of promiscuity. Examination of the clinical histories of individuals with AIDS who claim to have had few sexual partners could be one way of objectively verifying such claims. Analysis of the individuals' blood for evidence of antibodies to diseases common among promiscuous gay men might be another indicator.

It is entirely possible that the individual himself may have had few sexual partners, but that those few sexual partners have been highly diseased. If one partner in a couple is monogamous and the other is not, the effect of disease transmission will be similar for both partners.

The Los Angeles "Cluster." The Centers for Disease Control reasoned that it was extremely unusual for nine men to have had sex with one another over a five-year period and to have each developed KS. The CDC deduced that a single-virus causative agent must be the most likely explanation for this phenomenon.

A single causative agent may be the most attractive explanation for this cluster, but it is certainly not the only explanation. It seems quite likely that this cluster of men shared the same sexual habits, went to the same baths and bars, shared the same sexual partners, used the same drugs, and accumulated risk in a similar fashion. Indeed, in a footnote to its discussion of this cluster, the CDC noted that these nine men "tended to report having more sexual partners in the year before onset of symptoms (median = 50)" than did homosexual males without AIDS being studied.

AIDS in Haitians, intravenous drug abusers, hemophiliacs, and urban promiscuous gay men. However much one might like to think that these four discrete groups have more in common than a collapsed immune system, to date there has been no evidence of any other link.

Instead of assuming that all four groups are immunosuppressed for the same reason (as must those who believe in the single-agent or the new virus theory), it is easy to construct *different* logical explanations for each group's incidence of immunosuppression from already existing data. For example:

—Diseases associated with profoundly depressed immune responses have been noted in IV drug abusers for years. (See, for example, McDonough RJ, Madden JJ, *et al.; J. Immunol.* 125:2539–43, 1980; Brown, SM, B. Stimmel, *et al.; Arch Int. Med:* 134:1001.; Geller, S.A., and B. Stimmel, 1973; *Am. Intern. Med.* 78: 703.) By sharing unsterilized needles, they frequently expose themselves to common viruses from others' blood. By injecting these viruses directly into the bloodstream, they bypass the body's front-line defenses. Obviously, it does not help that these abusers often ingest narcotics which are further immunosuppressive. Re-exposure and reinfection might easily explain the AIDS occurring in IV drug abusers.

—Hemophiliacs periodically receive blood transfusions. Because this blood, from many different donors, may carry many common viruses, continual re-exposure and reinfection with these viruses might lead to the AIDS that has been occurring in hemophiliacs.

—Due to the generally poor sanitary conditions prevalent in Haiti, Haitians are frequently exposed and reinfected with a variety of tropical viruses endemic to the region. Once again, reinfection with common viruses could explain AIDS among Haitians.

Some single-virus speculation has verged on the insidious. To propose without supporting evidence that *any* minority group might be carrying a potentially fatal new, mutant virus is unconscionable. But to go even further and imply that "we" got "it" from the Haitians is a particularly ugly example of the Western tradition of blaming calamity on the Third World. And it's bad science. The suggestion that American gay men vacationing in Haiti brought this "new virus" back to the U.S. must be based on either of two unfounded assumptions: that AIDS is new among Haitians; or that gay men have traveled to Haiti only in the last three years (unless a theory is proposed that the "virus" is only three years old).

What promiscuous urban gay men, intravenous drug abusers, hemophiliacs, and Haitians all have in common is a pattern of accumulation of risk through reinfection with *common viruses.*

But if there is no new agent, why is AIDS only showing up in these groups now?

One cannot presume that this is the first epidemic of AIDS in history. Since the ability of medical science to detect indicators of immunosuppression is relatively recent, one must ask: (1) how long have there been individuals with collapsed immune systems; and (2) how long have such individuals been recognized and observed in classic epidemiologic terms?

It is possible that immunosuppression has existed for as long as there have been viruses; admittedly, there is no way to verify this hypothesis. However, review of autopsy reports in the United States going back thirty years has indicated the possibility that AIDS may have existed in a limited fashion as early as 1950 (*The Lancet,* 1960, 2:951–5, Williams *et al.;* The *New England Journal of Medicine,* April 15, 1982, 934–5, P. Nichols). Similar autopsy review in Denmark indicates the possibility of AIDS at least since 1963 (*The Lancet,* May 1, 1982, Jensen *et al.; cf. The Lancet,* July 3, 1982, Clemmensen letter).

Empirical verification of these reports as evidence of AIDS is impossible since the tests which detect immune deficiency have only recently come into use. However, the above cases bear such striking resemblance to AIDS—which some are claiming is a new phenomenon— that it now seems quite likely that AIDS has occurred in the United States and other countries before, but has only recently been recognized.

The heroic hunt for mutant viruses has been a response in previous epidemics when the ministrations of doctors remained ineffective. In the winter of 1978–79, an outbreak of fatal respiratory infections among children in Naples, Italy was initially believed to have been caused by some new, mutant virus. Eventually, the mystery was solved: "Naples disease" proved to be the result of immunological abnormalities caused by "socioeconomic factors, such as malnutrition and family size, and a transitory immunosuppression due to vaccination." (*The Lancet,* February 2, 1980; F. Aiuti, R. D'Amerlio, *et al.* at page 226.)

In our view, the present epidemic of AIDS among promiscuous urban gay males is occurring because of the unprecedented promiscuity of the last ten to fifteen years. The commercialization of promiscuity and the explosion of establishments such as bathhouses, bookstores, and backrooms is unique in western history. It has been mass participation in this lifestyle that has led to the creation of an increasingly disease-polluted pool of sexual partners—which has in turn very likely led to the present epidemic of AIDS.

Isn't it possible that there's a new mutant virus to which we are continually being re-exposed? Or must these two theories be mutually exclusive?

Anything is possible. Any researchers who wish to pursue a search for a new, mutant virus should certainly be free to do so; however, we reiterate that there has been no evidence to justify such a search and we point out that sufficient evidence exists to support the view that common viruses epidemic among the sexually active gay community can explain AIDS.

The determination of the correct explanation for AIDS among gay men has important ramifications for treatment and prevention. If AIDS is caused by continual re-exposure to common infections, eliminating these assaults might permit the immune system to return to normal. In the case of renal transplant patients (who are intentionally chemically immunosuppressed to receive organ or tissue transplants), the immune response eventually returns to normal when immunosuppressive medication is discontinued. Kaposi's sarcoma in renal transplant patients often runs a benign course without chemotherapy when the immunosuppressive drugs are discontinued, provided that the tumors are not life-threatening. In the case of AIDS among gay men, removing the cause of the immunosuppression—promiscuity—might allow the body to heal itself and return to a normal state of immune defense, if the immune suppression has not progressed to the point of being self-sustaining. Certainly no one on any treatment will recover from AIDS if he continues to be promiscuous.

Whichever theory you accept, promiscuity is the way AIDS is being spread among gay men. Some seem to prefer the single-virus theory because it appears to take the blame away from promiscuity and raises the hope—unrealistic, we think—that someday AIDS can be controlled with a vaccine or drug. However, by subscribing to this theory a number of physicians have opened themselves to an astounding ethical contradiction. They have advised mere "moderation" of promiscuity—without defining either moderation or promiscuity. Those who believe that there is a new, single, cancer-causing virus should be the first to insist that their patients eliminate risk by *ending* promiscuous exposure—not merely diminishing risk through moderation. If going to the baths is really a game of Russian roulette, then the advice must be to throw the gun away, not merely to play less often.

Why can't I just go to the baths less often, like smoking less or switching to lower-tar and nicotine cigarettes? Why isn't moderation enough?

The new kid in town, stepping off that proverbial plane from Iowa, might conceivably enjoy a couple of years on the circuit before he accumulates sufficient risk to develop AIDS, but for those of us who have been "pigging out" over the last decade, mere moderation is not enough. It can take months to recover from a single immunosuppressive viral infection, and the pool of promiscuous partners is still too highly polluted with disease for us to risk sexual "moderation."

Attempts by the Centers for Disease Control and other researchers to compare apparently healthy promiscuous gay men with those patients who have been diagnosed with AIDS have led to the disturbing discovery that many of these "healthy" homosexuals are actually already immunosuppressed but asymptomatic. This has led the National Cancer Institute to predict:

Tens of thousands of homosexual men may have the acquired immune dysfunction and be at risk for development of the clinical syndrome. Indeed, we very probably have seen only the tip of the iceberg.

In our discussion, we have encountered many individuals, gay and straight, who are incapable of comprehending the amount of sex which takes place in settings such as the baths and backrooms. They believe us to be saying that there is something inherently wrong with having a large number of sexual contacts. To reiterate, the risk for developing AIDS comes not from the number of different sexual contacts but instead from the number of different sexual contacts *who are diseased.* There would be no particularly adverse physiological consequences from having sex with 1,160 healthy individuals, but having sex with 1,160 diseased individuals would obviously be quite a different matter. As we all know, our chances of getting one of the many sexually transmitted diseases from an encounter at the baths are much greater today than they were a decade ago. In these settings, disease spreads exponentially. If on a typical night at the baths any one individual has sex with five people, each of whom is having sex with five people, each of whom in turn is having sex with five people, it is not difficult to comprehend the disease explosion that we have been seeing in recent years.

Some physicians have publicly suggested that we limit our sexual contacts to healthy partners while failing to define either "limitation" or "healthy"—yet while publishing data which indicates that a percentage of promiscuous gay men are both *asymptomatic* and *contagious* for cytomegalovirus. Hidden in the recommendation that we seek only "healthy" sexual partners is the implication that if we learn that a potential sexual partner goes to the baths or is otherwise promiscuous, then that individual is probably not healthy.

These physicians need to commit themselves to a clearer, less confused, position on the dangers of promiscuity.

You sound so anti-sexual. Even if promiscuity is a risk, you can't legislate it out of existence.

We are not suggesting legislating an end to promiscuity. Ultimately, it may be more important to let people die in the pursuit of their own happiness than to limit personal freedom by regulating risk. The tradition of allowing an individual the right to choose his own slow death (through cigarettes, alcohol, and other means) is firmly established in this country; but there is also another American tradition represented by the Federal Trade Commission and the Food and Drug Administration, which warns people clearly about the risks of certain products and behaviors.

It would be preferable to avoid further governmental intervention of the sort represented by the presence in the AIDS investigations of the Centers for Disease Control. The gay community must take the responsibility of providing its members with clear and unequivocal warnings about the health risks of promiscuity.

Even if you're right, promiscuity would be next to impossible to give up. If I wanted to, how could I begin to change my lifestyle?

Just because something is difficult doesn't mean it isn't necessary, especially when we're talking about life and death. If our promiscuous lifestyles are potentially fatal, shall we suffer the Pyrrhic victory of proving its joys while killing ourselves?

We, the authors of this article, can say from our own experience that changing from an obsessively promiscuous lifestyle is extremely difficult. Even believing as strongly as we do about the risks of promiscuity, we have been tempted to return to the circuit. Old habits die hard. But once one has looked death in the face and seen *pneumocystis carinii* pneumonia patients in isolation and witnessed the suffering of Kaposi's sarcoma victims, change becomes easier.

This isn't a game. People are dying—very real, horrible, and unnecessary deaths. Sure, the baths are fun; but the risks have simply become too great. A year ago, new cases of AIDS were being reported at the rate of one a day; today, the rate is three times that.

We need to support each other's search for sexual alternatives. Certainly the future holds more options than phone sex! The epidemic of AIDS need not result in abstinence or even monogamy for everyone. Perhaps the concept of "fuck buddies" can be modified to become circles of healthy individuals who can be trusted to limit their sexual contacts to members of that closed group.

We need to form support groups. Some will want to consider group or individual therapy or other means of smoothing an admittedly difficult transition.

Isn't discussion of promiscuity politically dangerous? The Moral Majority would love nothing more than to be able to say that our promiscuous lifestyle has caused cancer.

We are aware of the potential political ramifications of relating promiscuity to the current epidemic of AIDS. Unfortunately, those who would say that promiscuity is related to the incidence of AIDS would appear to be correct. This is a statement of scientific fact, not moralistic bluster.

Those who fear linking promiscuity with the present epidemic should consider the far more dangerous implication already circulating in the national media: that gay men are carrying and spreading a fatal, cancer-causing virus.

Is there anything besides ceasing promiscuity that I can do to avoid AIDS?

Educate yourself about how your body works—particularly the immune response. Read about health, and in particular read about the present epidemic of AIDS. Rely on no single source for your information: not your doctor, not this newspaper, not the Gay Men's Health Crisis, not the Centers for Disease Control. Can an opinion that's being propounded be supported by the evidence? Are there any other theories? Verify what you read and what is said to you.

Educate yourself now so that if and when the time comes, you can make informed medical decisions about treatment—and your life.

Whether we know it or not, an entire generation of gay men for whom gay life is synonymous with promiscuity is about to undertake the difficult transition to new, medically safe lifestyles. This transition is sure to have profound personal, social, and economic ramifications and will no doubt be painful, difficult, and politically volatile.

Disease has changed the definition of promiscuity. What ten years ago was viewed as a healthy reaction to a sex-negative culture now threatens to destroy the very fabric of urban gay male life. What we have in the 1980s is a positive political force tied to a dangerous lifestyle. We must recognize the self-hating short-sightedness involved in knowingly or half-knowingly infecting our sexual partners with disease, only to have that disease return to us in exponential form.

No one, including the authors, is naive enough to believe that providing a clear warning about the dangers of promiscuity will bring about its end. While a fatally disorganized gay leadership scrambles for a way to present promiscuity in a manner palatable to a generally unsophisticated heterosexist world (and an understandably defensive gay community), gay men are dying unnecessarily. Promiscuity has spawned an industry which has a stake in keeping us promiscuous, even if it kills us. Where is the money that we've spent on pleasure over the last thirteen years, now that we need it for our survival? Will bathhouses willingly post warnings and risk hurting business? In short, is the bathhouse/backroom industry going to prove itself so different from the tobacco lobby?

We can no longer tolerate knee-jerk defensiveness to any discussion of promiscuity as a medical issue. Not everyone who wishes to discuss alternatives to promiscuity is sex-negative or a sexual fascist. To date there has been little rational discussion about the impact of promiscuity on gay male culture; the present health crisis provides the unique opportunity for such a dialogue to begin.

As individuals, we must care enough about ourselves to begin this re-evaluation: gay men are dying. As a community, we must initiate and control this process ourselves. Be assured that if we aren't willing to conduct it, others will do it for us. The federal government, through the Centers for Disease Control, is already taking a long, hard look at our behavior.

The motto of promiscuous gay men has been "So many men, so little time." In the '70s we worried about so many men; in the '80s we will have to worry about so little time. For us, the party that was the '70s is over. For some, perhaps, homosexuality will always mean promiscuity. They may very well die for that belief.

The 13 years since Stonewall have demonstrated tremendous change. So must the next 13 years.

---

from

HOW TO HAVE SEX IN AN EPIDEMIC

(1983)

Richard Berkowitz and Michael Callen

Should AIDS Patients Have Sex?

This is quite a controversial issue, but regardless of what one feels, the fact is that some men who have been diagnosed with AIDS are continuing to have sex. Of course, for some AIDS patients, sex is the furthest thing from their minds. But for other AIDS patients, sexual desire remains. Some are limiting the sexual contacts they have to other AIDS patients. Others are having sex only with their lovers. And some AIDS patients are continuing to have multiple sexual contacts.

AIDS patients are human beings and need affection and human contact. AIDS patients object to being treated like lepers and some end up taking this anger and frustration out to the baths and backrooms.

The issue of AIDS patients having sex must be viewed from two perspectives: the risk to the patient and the potential risk to his partner.

The one thing AIDS patients know for sure is that they are immune suppressed. This means they are more vulnerable to infections. In addition, if they *do* develop an infection, they know that they will have a more difficult time recovering. It is possible that sex is more of a danger to the AIDS patient than to his partner. Considering the risks to the patients themselves, multiple sexual contacts, particularly in settings such as the baths and back-rooms where disease is rampant, is extremely unwise.

In terms of the risk to the partners of AIDS patients, we believe that the primary danger is the transmission of CMV. Of course, if you believe that there is a new virus which is the cause of AIDS, having sex with an AIDS patient might transmit such a new virus.

The decision of whether and how AIDS patients should have sex and the decisions of whether and how partners should have sex with AIDS patients are difficult ones to make. Each person must weigh the evidence, determine his own risk, and act accordingly. However, WE BELIEVE THAT AIDS PATIENTS HAVE AN ETHICAL OBLIGATION TO ADVISE POTENTIAL PARTNERS OF THEIR HEALTH STATUS.

We believe that AIDS patients must allow their partners to make the their own choice. There *are* gay men who are willing to take the necessary precautions designed to protect both partners' health. Obviously we believe that lovers of AIDS patients can continue having sex with AIDS patients if they exercise the precautions outlined in this paper. There are AIDS patients who are continuing to have "safe sex" and who are recovering from their immune suppression. And there are lovers who have continued to have sex safely with AIDS patients who are not showing signs of immune deficiency and who are not contracting CMV.

But apart from the issue of sex, the absence of firm evidence that AIDS can be transmitted by casual, non-sexual intimacy, we see no reason why hugging and affections should be discouraged or withheld.

Guilt, Morality and Sex Negativity

The AIDS crisis has forced many gay men to examine their lifestyles. It has also produced a lot of recommendations which are really misplaced morality masquerading as medical advice.

Gay men have always been criticized for having "too much sex" with "too many" different partners. Because the development of AIDS in gay men is obviously somehow connected with the amount and kind of sex we have, a lot of advice has focused on "reducing" the "number of different partners". Wherever we turn we are reminded of the joy of romance and dating by those who claim they are only concerned with our health.

In this age of AIDS, the advice most often given is that we should try to "cut down" on the number of different partners we have sex with and try to limit those partners we do have sex with to "healthy" men. This advice confuses many gay men. What is meant by "cut down"? Is it going to the baths once a month instead of one a week? Is it having two partners a night instead of four? And how can we determine whether or not a potential partner is "healthy" when there are many infections which don't have obvious symptoms? While having less sex will definitely reduce our chances for all STDs, it will certainly not eliminate them

Advice which focuses only on *numbers* and which ignores ways to interrupt disease transmission is incomplete. For example, a gay man who is concerned with protecting his health may decide to "cut down" on the amount of sex he has by limiting himself to one different partner a month. At the end of the year, he will have had sex with 12 different partners. Few gay men would consider having 12 sex partners a year being "promiscuous," but this example illustrates the point that the issue isn't sex, it's disease. Since one out of every four of his 12 sexual partners was probably contagious for CMV (despite his best efforts to guess who was "healthy"), he will have been exposed to CMV 3 times that year—unless he limited which sexual acts he performed to ones which interrupt disease transmission.

If a concerned gay man makes the tremendous effort to change his sexual behavior by reducing the number of different partners, yet fails to modify what he does, chances are high that he will still often get sick. This has to be demoralizing. He may even feel that all his efforts have been useless and go back to his old patterns. Or he may respond by giving up sex completely.

But deciding to stop having sex because sex may lead to AIDS is not the same as deciding to stop smoking because smoking can cause cancer. Smoking is a habit, a luxury "vice." Sex is a natural and important human need. Although every individual will ultimately have to balance need and risk himself to do so will require that he have the information necessary to make informed changes.

And while we're on the subject, what's all this talk about "anonymous" sex being dangerous. Anonymity in itself has nothing to do with disease transmission.

If your partner introduces himself, he is no longer an anonymous partner. But if he is contagious for syphilis, you'll get syphilis. It's as simple as that.

A lot of this talk about "anonymous" sex being "bad" smacks of misplaced morality. This issue is disease—not sex.

One reason why anonymity can be dangerous is that when you don't know your partners, you may not be as cautious in protecting him from disease. We need a more precise vocabulary to talk about the various lifestyles we lead. When you are receiving advice about sex, it's very important to make sure that the advice is based on sound, scientific understanding of how diseases are transmitted. Don't be fooled just because the source of advice seems authoritative. Verify what you are told by talking to physicians and consulting other sources of information.

If we are to celebrate our gayness and get on with gay liberation, we must stay healthy. To stay healthy, we must realize that the issue isn't gayness or sex; the issue is simply disease.

Love

It came as quite a shock to us to find that we had written almost 40 pages on sex without mentioning the word "love" once. Truly, we have been revealed as products of the '70s.

It has become unfashionable to refer to sex a "lovemaking." Why might this be so?

If the sexual revolution that began in the '60's confirmed one thing it was that sex and affection—sex and love—are not necessarily the same thing. The concept of "recreational sex" has gained widespread acceptance.

At the same time, as the rising epidemics of STDs have demonstrated, there are certain unfortunate (and unforeseen?) side effects when love and affection become so separated from sex.

Without affection, it is less likely that you will care as much if you give your partners disease. During the '70s fantasy was encouraged. Sex with partners you did not know—and did not want to know—was justified as being personally meaningful even if it wasn't interpersonally so. Put another way, did gay male culture of the '70's encourage us to substitute the *fantasy* of the man we were holding for his reality?

Gay men are socialized as men first; our gay socialization comes later. From the day we are born we are trained as men to compete with other men. The challenge facing gay men in America is to figure out how to love someone you've been trained to "destroy."

The goal of gay male liberation must be to find ways in which love becomes possible despite continuing and often overwhelming pressure to compete and adopt adversary relationships with other men.

Gay male politics have historically suffered from fractionalism. Might this be a symptom of the competitiveness between males? And why has it been so difficult to involve gay men politically? Is it possible that all the great sex we've been having for the last decade has siphoned off our collective anger which might otherwise have been translated into social and political action?

The commercialization of urban gay male culture today offers us places to go and get sick and places to go and get treated. Too many gay men get together for only two reasons: to exploit each other and to be exploited.

Sex and "promiscuity" have become the dogma of gay male liberation. Have we modified the belief that we could dance our way to liberation into the belief that we could somehow fuck our way there? If sex is liberating, is more sex necessarily more liberating?

It has certainly become easier to fuck each other. But has it become any easier to love each other? Men *loving* men was the basis of gay male liberation, but we have now created "cultural institutions" in which love or even affection can be totally avoided.

If you love the person you are fucking with—*even for one night*—you will not want to make them sick.

Maybe affection is our best protection.

Hard questions for hard times. But what happened to our great gay imaginations?

LAWRENCE MASS, M.D.
Lawrence Mass, M.D., was the medical writer for the *New York Native* during the early years of the epidemic. He was an employee of the NYC Health Department who was threatened with being fired for speaking out publicly about the epidemic. This article marks the beginning of transition in perception from the "lifestyle" to the "viral" hypothesis of AIDS transmission, based upon its incidence among Haitian immigrants. Also significant is the attempt to de-link AIDS as a medical problem from its existence as a political problem in the context of arguing that gay male health care is inextricably connected to the sexual freedom developed through the 1970s, a problematic that will continue through the early years of the epidemic.

from

BLOOD AND POLITICS: AN AIDS NOTEBOOK

from the *New York Native* (1983)

Lawrence Mass, M.D.

Bless Ginny Apuzzo, Roger Enlow, Larry Kramer and Ron Vachon for their strong leadership in the ongoing blood-policy controversy. As everyone has by now heard, the National Hemophilia Foundation nearly upset months of careful strategizing by publicly asking that all gay men be removed from the blood-donor pool. "Serious efforts should be made," the foundation's statement reads, "to exclude donors that might transmit AIDS. These should include: 1. identification by direct questioning of individuals who belong to groups at high risk of transmitting AIDS, specifically male homosexuals; intravenous drug users, and those who have recently resided in Haiti" (from the National Hemophilia Foundation Medical and Scientific Advisory Council. 1/14/83).

Early last summer, Apuzzo became the first representative of the gay community to publicly express concern about the political implications of tainting any minority with "bad blood." At that time, she was head of the Fund for Human Dignity. As the recently appointed executive director of the National Gay Task Force, she has placed our gay men's health crisis where it is likely to remain for some time to come: among the top priorities of our community's political agenda. Does this contradict the essential truth, often stated by Kramer and Apuzzo, that acquired immune deficiency syndrome is not a political but a medical issue? I don't think so, but it is ironic in this context that the gay community is having to repoliticize itself around AIDS in order to depoliticize this disease in society at large.

Working closely with Enlow, Kramer, Vachon, and other members of the New York City AIDS Network (which is made up of representatives from such organizations as NGTF, the National Gay Health Education Foundation, the Gay Men's Health Crisis, the American Association of Physicians for Human Rights and New York Physicians for Human Rights, as well as the New York City Department of Health; the AIDS Network meets Thursdays at 8 a.m. at the St. Mark's Clinic, ninth floor, 88 University Place), Apuzzo read an official, widely endorsed response to the National Hemophilia Foundation at a New York press conference on January 27. The NGTF statement—which has been endorsed in principle by many blood industry representatives and organizations and by many lesbian and gay organizations—admonished the Hemophilia Foundation for its simplistic, hasty, and alarmist press release: "As the NHF [itself] noted, the issues surrounding AIDS remain complex; there are no simple answers. Unfortunately, the NHF wasn't successful in following its own advice.

In agreement with the recommendations of other blood industry and AIDS observers, the NGTF statement urges the following:

1) Every effort be made by the blood industry to test blood and blood products for agents which indicate a current or past infection, e.g., Hepatitis B, which may also indicate a high risk for AIDS.
2) Funds be made available to government agencies, medical institutions, and voluntary community groups, to research the cause(s), effects, and cure of AIDS—which remain unknown—as well as to offer patient services to those suffering from this disorder.
3) All individual blood donors screen themselves, recognizing that in giving the "gift of life," there is the responsibility to give the safest gift possible.
4) The medical and scientific community acknowledge what has been known for many years: that the direct or indirect questioning of donors is an inadequate safeguard to the quality of blood; moreover, a policy to exclude any group from blood donation, whether mandated or voluntary, would be both ineffective and inappropriate.
5) Above all, it is incumbent upon the blood industry and the government agencies that regulate blood donor policy to refrain from suggestion or implementation of a blood donor screening program which, by whatever means or under whatever name, amounts to a political solution to a medical problem. Pitting victim against victim will serve only to divert attention from the vital medical and ethical concerns that lie at the heart of this health crisis.

A disturbing indicator of the spread of punitive medical approaches to the control of sexually transmitted diseases (STDs) appeared in the November 18 issue of the *New England*

Journal of Medicine. In a letter to the editor, "Against Free Care for STDs," Robert Carlen (presumably a physician) complained that since the "entire cost" of "free clinics" is borne by the public, "they foster dependency and irresponsibility. It's shockingly unfair, too, that taxpayers who get sick or injured through no fault of their own must pay for their own care and pay as well for those who have irresponsible sex.

Since most lesbian and gay community health facilities, like the St. Mark's Clinic here in Manhattan, remain almost entirely dependent on voluntary donations and services, it was not surprising to read Carlen's letter courteously described as "outrageous" in the December 1982 official newsletter of the National Coalition of Gay STD Services (NCGSTDS).

Despite considerable promotion of the new hepatitis B vaccine in the gay community, observes NCGSTDS Chairperson Mark Behar in the same issue of that newsletter, "Community response to the vaccine can be summarized in one word: underwhelming." Why? "Is it the expense?" [approximately $150], Behar asks, "or the lengthy period required for administering the three-dose vaccine? Is hepatitis B just being overshadowed by AIDS? Are gay men uninterested in their own health or inadequately informed about the dangers of hepatitis and the value of vaccination?"

In attempting to answer these brave and serious questions, Behar explores the tenuous commitment between gay politics and gay health. "There are many gay health workers," he concludes, "who have worked long and hard for their communities with little acknowledgment, commendation, or public expression of gratitude. Annual local and leadership conventions are encouraged to recognize and commend those individuals for their services. Gay health care should not take back seats to gay politics or religion."

"Will AIDS Close the Baths?" redux. In an editorial in *Homosexual Health Report* (vol.1:3), "AIDS Risk Reduction Guidelines—Process & Problems." Doctors Robert Bolan and David Ostrow cite the viewpoint expressed by Michael Callen and Richard Berkowitz in *Native* 50, "If going to the baths is really Russian roulette, then the advice must be to throw the gun away, not merely to play less often."

"These are tough times," Bolan and Ostrow conclude, "and tough questions must be asked and tough decisions made. To question the healthiness of specific forms of sexual expression is not homophobic. Also, let us not be hamstrung by our scientific method—it is slow and cannot accurately detect trends until much time and data have accrued; let us not be blind to common sense and let us say what is obvious, even if controversial."

My own thinking against closing the baths (*Native* 55) similar to that of New York City Health Commissioner Dr. David Sencer (*Native* 56) stresses several points.

- Nonvoluntary behavioral approaches to the control of infectious and sexually transmitted diseases have a terrible track record. They may work for some individuals, but, in the long run, they just don't work for large populations.
- How could one define exactly what establishments should be labeled unsafe? Would they include baths in low-risk cities or baths which cater to orthodox Jews, to bisexuals, or to heterosexuals who may be suspected of being bi-sexual or gay?
- Why not work with bathhouse personnel to devise ways of making bath-houses less fraught with health risk and of making health information more accessible to patrons?
- The issues of sexual freedom and civil liberties must not be compromised during this period of reactionary political instability, when more effective, less punitive alternatives can probably be devised.

That we still know little about risk factors in native and immigrant Haitians with AIDS is one of the conclusions of a recently published study, "Acquired Immune Deficiency in Haitians" (*New England Journal of Medicine*, 1/20/83). The report describes 10 cases of acquired immune deficiency syndrome in previously healthy heterosexual men who had no history of intravenous drug use or of receiving blood or blood products by transfusion. In their discussion of these cases, the authors acknowledge the possibility that the immune deficiency in this group of Haitians may have a different origin from that observed in gay men. On the other hand, they suggest that "a single transmissible agent such as a virus" may induce the basic immunological defect—the expression of which may be influenced by such variables as "nutritional status, other infections or chronic illnesses, environmental agents, or genetic predisposition."

Exploring the single-agent hypothesis, the authors speculate that such an agent, similar in characteristics of transmissibility to hepatitis B virus, might have been brought to the U. S. by homosexuals vacationing in Haiti and may have been introduced into the addict population by homosexual drug addicts. To substantiate any hypothesis about the origin(s) of AIDS, they conclude, "We will need to learn more about the Haitian lifestyle in both the U.S. and Haiti. The assumption that heterosexual Haitians and homosexual Americans have little in common may prove erroneous when epidemiologic and anthropologic surveys are completed."

What might these two patient populations have in common? One theory, not found in the *Journal* but recently expressed on a television interview by the *Journal* study's principal author, Dr. Jeffrey Vieira of Downstate Medical Center in Brooklyn, proposes that Haitian voodoo practices involving animal blood are the source of a new (AIDS-associated or causing) infectious agent in human beings. The reason this theory was not in the *Journal* report is that, without more solid evidence, it still qualifies as the wildest kind of speculation. It should not have been on television or in the newspapers. More surprising is the connection that is made in the *Journal* report between the Haitians and gay drug addicts. Only a small number of the latter have been identified. Unless there is concrete evidence linking one of these patients to Haitian victims of AIDS, such an association would seem to be similarly unqualified for print. Meanwhile, most observers feel that there may be a sexual connection between the cases of AIDS that have been observed in Haitians and those in gay men who were known to have vacationed in Haiti.

Larry Kramer, novelist, playwright, and a founder of both Gay Men's Health Crisis (GMHC) and AIDS Coalition to Unleash Power (ACT-UP), is one of the great polemicists of AIDS activism. In this first of several of his writings we include, he suggests the agenda for the gay movement with respect to the epidemic. Widely reprinted and distributed at the time of its publication in early 1983, its exemplary analysis and rhetoric catalyzed gay men around the U.S. to view AIDS as a political issue and act accordingly. In the words of the late journalist Randy Shilts: "[W]ith those words, Kramer threw a hand grenade into the foxhole of denial where most gay men in the United States had been sitting out the epidemic . . . Inarguably one of the most influential works of advocacy journalism of the decade, [it] was Kramer's end run around all the gay leaders and GMHC organizers worried about not panicking the homosexuals and not inciting homophobia . . . [and] swiftly crystalized the epidemic into a political movement."

LARRY KRAMER

from

1,112 AND COUNTING

from the *New York Native* (March, 1983)

Larry Kramer

If this article doesn't scare the shit out of you, we're in real trouble. If this article does-n't rouse you to anger, fury, rage, and action, gay men may have no future on this earth. Our continued existence depends on just how angry you can get.

I am writing this as Larry Kramer, and I am speaking for myself, and my views are not to be attributed to Gay Men's Health Crisis.

I repeat: Our continued existence as gay men upon the face of this earth is at stake. Unless we fight for our lives, we shall die. In all the history of homosexuality we have never before been so close to death and extinction. Many of us are dying or already dead.

Before I tell you what we must do, let me tell you what is happening to us.

There are now 1,112 cases of serious Acquired Immune Deficiency Syndrome. When we first became worried, there were only 41. In only twenty-eight days, from January 13th to February 9th [1983], there were 164 new cases—and 73 more dead. The total death tally is now 418. Twenty percent of all cases were registered this January alone. There have been 195 dead in New York City from among 526 victims. Of all serious AIDS cases, 47.3 percent are in the New York metropolitan area.

These are the serious cases of AIDS, which means Kaposi's sarcoma, *Pneumocystis carinii* pneumonia, and other deadly infections. These numbers do not include the thousands of us walking around with what is also being called AIDS: various forms of swollen lymph glands and fatigues that doctors don't know what to label or what they might portend.

The rise in these numbers is terrifying. Whatever is spreading is now spreading faster as more and more people come down with AIDS.

And, for the first time in this epidemic, leading doctors and researchers are finally admitting they don't know what's going on. I find this terrifying too—as terrifying as the alarming rise in numbers. For the first time, doctors are saying out loud and up front, "I don't know."

For two years they weren't talking like this. For two years we've heard a different theory every few weeks. We grasped at the straws of possible cause: promiscuity, poppers, back rooms, the baths, rimming, fisting, anal intercourse, urine, semen, shit, saliva, sweat, blood, blacks, a single virus, a new virus, repeated exposure to a virus, amoebas carrying a virus, drugs, Haiti, voodoo, Flagyl, constant bouts of amebiasis, hepatitis A and B, syphilis, gonorrhea.

I have talked with the leading doctors treating us. One said to me, "If I knew in 1981 what I know now, I would never have become involved with this disease." Another said, "The thing that upsets me the most in all of this is that at any given moment one of my patients is in the hospital and something is going on with him that I don't understand. And it's destroying me because there's some craziness going on in him that's destroying him." A third said to me, "I'm very depressed. A doctor's job is to make patients well. And I can't. Too many of my patients die."

After almost two years of an epidemic, there are still no answers. After almost two years of an epidemic, the cause of AIDS remains unknown. After almost two years of an epidemic, there is no cure.

Hospitals are now so filled with AIDS patients that there is often a waiting period of up to a month before admission, no matter how sick you are. And, once in, patients are now more and more being treated like lepers as hospital staffs become increasingly worried that AIDS is infectious.

Suicides are now being reported of men who would rather die than face such medical uncertainty, such uncertain therapies, such hospital treatment, and the appalling statistics that 86 percent of all serious AIDS cases die after three years' time.

If all of this had been happening to any other community for two long years, there would have been, long ago, such an outcry from that community and all its members that the government of this city and this country would not know what had hit them.

Why isn't every gay man in this city so scared shitless that he is screaming for action? Does every gay man in New York *want* to die?

Let's talk about a few things specifically.

• Let's talk about which gay men get AIDS.

No matter what you've heard, there is no single profile for all AIDS victims. There are drug users and non-drug users. There are the truly promiscuous and the almost monogamous. There are reported cases of single-contact infection.

All it seems to take is the one wrong fuck. That's not promiscuity—that's bad luck.

• Let's talk about AIDS happening in straight people.

We have been hearing from the beginning of this epidemic that it was only a question of time before the straight community came down with AIDS, and that when that happened AIDS would suddenly be high on all agendas for funding and research and then we would finally be looked after and all would then be well.

I myself thought, when AIDS occurred in the first baby, that would be the breakthrough point. It was. For one day the media paid an enormous amount of attention. And that was it, kids.

There have been no confirmed cases of AIDS in straight, white, non-intravenous-drug-using, middle-class Americans. The only confirmed straights struck down by AIDS are members of groups just as disenfranchised as gay men: intravenous drug users, Haitians, eleven hemophiliacs (up from eight), black and Hispanic babies, and wives or partners of IV drug users and bisexual men.

If there have been—and there may have been—any cases in straight, white, non-intravenous-drug-using, middle-class Americans, the Centers for Disease Control isn't telling anyone about them. When pressed, the CDC says there are "a number of cases that don't fall into any of the other categories." The CDC says it's impossible to fully investigate most of these "other category" cases; most of them are dead. The CDC also tends not to believe living, white, middle-class male victims when they say they're straight, or female victims when they say their husbands are straight and don't take drugs.

Why isn't AIDS happening to more straights? Maybe it's because gay men don't have sex with them.

Of all serious AIDS cases, 72.4 percent are in gay and bisexual men.

• Let's talk about "surveillance."

The Centers for Disease Control is charged by our government to fully monitor all epidemics and unusual diseases.

To learn something from an epidemic, you have to keep records and statistics. Statistics come from interviewing victims and getting as much information from them as you can.

Before they die. To get the best information, you have to ask the right questions.

There have been so many AIDS victims that the CDC is no longer able to get to them fast enough. It has given up. (The CDC also had been using a questionnaire that was fairly insensitive to the lives of gay men, and thus the data collected from its early study of us have been disputed by gay epidemiologists. The National Institutes of Health is also fielding a very naïve questionnaire.)

Important, vital case histories are now being lost because of this cessation of CDC interviewing. This is a woeful waste with as terrifying implications for us as the alarming rise in case numbers and doctors finally admitting they don't know what's going on. As each man dies, as one or both sets of men who had interacted with each other come down with AIDS, yet more information that might reveal patterns of transmissibility is not being monitored and collected and studied. We are being denied perhaps the easiest and fastest research tool available at this moment.

It will require at least $200,000 to prepare a new questionnaire to study the next important question that must be answered: *How* is AIDS being transmitted? (In which bodily fluids, by which sexual behaviours, in what social environments?)

For months the CDC has been asked to begin such preparations for continued surveillance. The CDC is stretched to its limits and is dreadfully underfunded for what it's being asked, in all areas, to do.

• Let's talk about various forms of treatment.

It is very difficult for a patient to find out which hospital to go to or which doctor to go to or which mode of treatment to attempt.

Hospitals and doctors are reluctant to reveal how well they're doing with each type of treatment. They may, if you press them, give you a general idea. Most will not show you their precise number of how many patients are doing well on what and how many failed to respond adequately.

Because of the ludicrous requirements of the medical journals, doctors are prohibited from revealing publicly the specific data they are gathering from their treatments of our bodies. Doctors and hospitals need money for research, and this money (from the National Institutes of Health, from cancer research funding organizations, from rich patrons) comes based on the performance of their work (i.e., their tabulations of their results of their treatment of our bodies); this performance is written up as "papers" that must be submitted to and accepted by such "distinguished" medical publications as the *New England Journal of Medicine*. Most of these "distinguished" publications, however, will not publish anything that has been spoken of, leaked, announced, or intimated publicly in advance. Even after acceptance, the doctors must hold their tongues until the article is actually published. Dr. Bijan Safai of Sloan-Kettering has been waiting over six months for the *New England Journal*, which has accepted his interferon study, to publish it. Until that happens, he is only permitted to speak in the most general terms of how interferon is or is not working.

Priorities in this area appear to be peculiarly out of kilter at this moment of life or death.

• Let's talk about hospitals.

Everybody's full up, fellows. No room in the inn.

Part of this is simply overcrowding. Part of this is cruel. Sloan-Kettering still enforces a regulation from pre-AIDS days that only one dermatology patient per week can be admitted to that hospital. (Karposi's sarcoma falls under dermatology at Sloan-Kettering.) But Sloan-Kettering is also the second-largest treatment center for AIDS patients in New York. You can be near death and still not get into Sloan-Kettering.

Additionally, Sloan-Kettering (and the Food and Drug Administration) require patients to receive their initial shots of interferon while they are hospitalized. A lot of men want to try interferon at Sloan-Kettering before they try chemotherapy elsewhere.

It's not had to see why there is such a waiting list to get into Sloan-Kettering.

Most hospital staffs are still so badly educated about AIDS that they don't know much about it, except that they've heard it's infectious. (There still have been no cases in hospital staff or among the very doctors who have been treating AIDS victims for two years.) Hence, as I said earlier, AIDS patients are often treated like lepers.

For various reasons, I would not like to be a patient at the Veterans Administration Hospital on East 24th Street or at New York Hospital. (Incidents involving AIDS patients at these two hospitals have been reported in news stories in the *Native*.)

I believe it falls to this city's Department of Health, under Commissioner David Spencer, and the Health and Hospitals Corporation, under Commissioner Stanley Brezenoff, to educate this city, its citizens, and its hospital workers about all areas of a public health emergency. Well, they have done an appalling job of educating our citizens, our hospital workers, and even, in some instances, our doctors. Almost everything this city knows about AIDS has come to it, in one way or another, through Gay Men's Health Crisis. and that includes television programs, magazine articles, radio commercials, newsletters, health-recommendation brochures, open forums, and sending speakers everywhere, including—when asked—into hospitals. If three out of four AIDS cases were occurring in straight men instead of gay men, you can bet all hospitals and staff would know what was happening. And it would be this city's Health Department and Health and Hospitals Corporation who would be telling them.

• Let's talk about what gay tax dollars are buying for gay men.

Now we're arriving at the truly scandalous.

For over a year and a half the National Institutes of Health has been "reviewing" which from among some $55 million worth of grant applications for AIDS research money it will eventually fund.

It's not even a question of NIH having to ask Congress for money. It's already there. Waiting. NIH has almost $8 million already appropriated that it has yet to release into usefulness.

There is no question that if this epidemic was happening to the straight, white, non-intravenous-drug-using middle class, that money would have been put into use almost two years ago, when the first alarming signs of this epidemic were noticed by Dr. Alvin Friedman-Kien and Dr. Linda Laubenstein at New York University Hospital.

During the first *two weeks* of the Tylenol scare, the United States Government spent $10 million to find out what was happening.

Every hospital in New York that's involved in AIDS research has used up every bit of the money it could find for researching AIDS while waiting for NIH grants to come through. These hospitals have been working on AIDS for up to two years and are now desperate for replenishing funds. Important studies that began last year, such as Dr. Michael Lange's at St. Luke's-Roosevelt, are now going under for lack of money. Important leads that were and are developing cannot be pursued. (For instance, few hospitals can afford plasmapheresis machines, and few patients can afford this experimental treatment either, since few insurance policies will cover the $16,600 bill.) New York University Hospital, the largest treatment center for AIDS patients in the world, has had its grant application pending at NIH for a year and a half. Even if the application is successful, the earliest time that NYU could receive any money would be late summer.

The NIH would probably reply that it's foolish just to throw money away, that that hasn't worked before. And, NIH would say, if nobody knows what's happening, what's to study?

Any good administrator with half a brain could survey the entire AIDS mess and come up with twenty leads that merit further investigation. I could do so myself. In any research, in any investigation, you have to start somewhere. You can't just not start anywhere at all.

But then, AIDS is happening mostly to gay men, isn't it?

All of this is indeed ironic. For within AIDS, as most researchers have been trying to convey to the NIH, perhaps may reside the answer to the question of what it is that causes cancer itself. It straights had more brains, or were less bigoted against gays, they would see that, as with hepatitis B, gay men are again doing their suffering for them, revealing this disease to them. They can use us as guinea pigs to discover the cure for AIDS before it hits them, which most medical authorities are still convinced will be happening shortly in increasing numbers.

(As if it had not been malevolent enough, the NIH is now, for unspecified reasons, also turning away AIDS patients from its hospital in Bethesda, Maryland. The hospital, which had been treating anyone and everyone with AIDS free of charge, now will only take AIDS patients if they fit into their current investigating protocol. Whatever that is. The NIH publishes "papers," too.)

Gay men pay taxes just like everyone else. NIH money should be paying for our research just like everyone else's. We desperately need something from our government to save our lives, and we're not getting it.

• Let's talk about health insurance and welfare problems.

Many of the ways of treating AIDS are experimental, and many health insurance policies do not cover most of them. Blue Cross is particularly bad about accepting anything unusual.

Many serious victims of AIDS have been unable to qualify for increasing numbers of men unable to work and unable to claim welfare because AIDS is not on the list of qualifying disability illnesses. (Immune deficiency is an acceptable determining factor for welfare among children, but not adults. Figure that one out.) There are also increasing number of men unable to pay their rent, men thrown out on the street with nowhere to live and no money to live with, and men who have been asked by roommates to leave because of their illnesses. And men with serious AIDS are being fired from certain jobs.

The horror stories in this area, of those suddenly found destitute, of those facing this illness with insufficient insurance, continue to mount. (One man who'd had no success on other therapies was forced to beg from his friends the $16,600 he needed to try, as a last resort, plasmapheresis.)

• Finally, let's talk about our mayor, Ed Koch.

Our mayor, Ed Koch, appears to have chosen, for whatever reason, not to allow himself to be perceived by the non-gay world as visibly helping us in this emergency.

Repeated requests to meet with him have been denied us. Repeated attempts to have him make a very necessary public announcement about this crisis and public health emergency have been refused by his staff . . .

On October 28th, 1982, Mayor Koch was implored to make a public announcement about our emergency. If he had done so then, and if he was only to do so now, the following would be put into action:

> 1. The community at large would be alerted (you would be amazed at how many people, including gay men, still don't know enough about the AIDS danger).
> 2. Hospital staffs and public assistance offices would also be alerted and their education commenced.
> 3. The country, President Reagan, and the National Institutes of Health, as well as

Congress, would be alerted, and these constitute the most important ears of all.

If the mayor doesn't think it's important enough to talk up AIDS, none of these people is going to, either.

The Mayor of New York has an enormous amount of power—when he wants to use it. When he wants to help his people. With the failure yet again of our civil rights bill, I'd guess our mayor doesn't want to use his power to help us.

With his silence on AIDS, the Mayor of New York is helping to kill us.

I am sick of our electing officials who in no way represent us. I am sick of our stupidity in believing candidates who promise us everything for our support and promptly forget us and insult us after we have given them our votes. Koch is the prime example, but not the only one. [Senator] Daniel Patrick Moynihan isn't looking very good at this moment, either. Moynihan was requested by gay leaders to publicly ask Margaret Heckler at her confirmation hearing for Secretary of Health and Human Services is she could be fair to gays in view of her voting record of definite anti-gay bias. (Among other horrors, she voted to retain the sodomy law in Washington, D.C., at Jerry Falwell's request.) Moynihan refused to ask this question, as he has refused to meet with us about AIDS, despite our repeated requests. Margaret Heckler will have important jurisdiction over the CDC, over the NIH, over the Public Health Service, over the Food and Drug Administration—indeed, over all areas of AIDS concerns. Thank you, Daniel Patrick Moynihan. I am sick of our not realizing we have enough votes to defeat these people, and I am sick of our not electing our own openly gay officials in the first place. Moynihan doesn't even have an openly gay person on his staff, and he represents the city with the largest gay population in America.

I am sick of closeted gay doctors who won't come out to help us fight to rectify any of what I'm writing about. Doctors—the very letters "M.D."—have enormous clout, particularly when they fight in groups. Can you imagine what gay doctors could accomplish, banded together in a network, petitioning local and federal governments, straight colleagues, and the American Medical Association. I am sick of the passivity or nonparticipation or halfhearted protestation of all the gay medical associations (American Physicians for Human Rights, Bay Area Physicians for Human Rights, Gay Psychiatrists of New York, etc., etc.), and particularly our own New York Physicians for Human Rights, a group of 175 of our gay doctors who have, as a group, done *nothing*. You can count on one hand the number of our doctors who have really worked for us.

I am sick of the *Advocate*, one of this country's largest gay publications, which has yet to quite acknowledge that there's anything going on. That newspaper's recent AIDS issue was so innocuous you'd have thought all we were going through was little worse than a rage of the latest designer flu. And their own associate editor, Brent Harris, died from AIDS. Figure that one out.

With the exception of the *New York Native* and a few, very few, other gay publications, the gay press has been useless. If we can't get our own papers and magazines to tell us what's really happening to us, and this negligence is added to the negligent non-interest of the straight press (*The New York Times* took a leisurely year and a half between its major pieces, and the *Village Voice* took a year and a half to write anything at all), how are we going to get the word around that we're dying? Gay men in smaller towns and cities everywhere must be educated, too. Has the *Times* or the *Advocate* told you that twenty-nine cases have been reported from Paris?

I am sick of gay men who won't support gay charities. Go give your bucks to straight charities, fellows, while we die. Gay Men's Health Crisis is going crazy trying to accomplish everything it does—printing and distributing hundreds of thousands of educational items, taking care of several hundred AIDS victims (some of them straight) in and out of hospitals, arranging community forums and speakers all over this country, getting media attention, fighting bad hospital care, on and on and on, fighting for you and us in two thousand ways, *and* trying to sell 17,600 circus tickets, too. Is the Red Cross doing this for you? Is the American Cancer Society? Your college alumni fund? The United Jewish Appeal? Catholic Charities? The United Way? The Lenox Hill Neighborhood Association, or any of the other fancy straight charities for which faggots put on black ties and dance at the Plaza? The National Gay Task Force—our only hope for national leadership, with its new and splendid leader, Virginia Apuzzo—which is spending more and more time fighting for the AIDS issue, is broke. Senior Action in a Gay Environment and Gay Men's Health Crisis are, within a few months, going to be without office space they can afford, and thus will be out on the street. The St. Mark's Clinic, held together by some of the few devoted gay doctors in this city who aren't interested in becoming rich, lives in constant terror of even higher rent and eviction. This community is desperate for the services these organizations are providing for it. And these organizations are all desperate for money, which is certainly not coming from straight people or President Reagan or Mayor Koch. (If every gay man within a 250-mile radius of Manhattan isn't in Madison Square Garden on the night of April 30th to help Gay Men's Health Crisis make enough money to get through the next horrible year of fighting against AIDS, I shall lose all hope that we have any future whatsoever.)

I am sick of closeted gays. It's 1983 already, guys, when are you going to come out? By 1984 you could be dead. Every gay man who is unable to come forward now and fight to save his own life is truly helping to kill the rest of us. There is only one thing that's going to save some of us, and this is *numbers* and pressure and our being perceived as united and a threat. As more and more of my friends die, I have less and less sympathy for men who are afraid their mommies will find out or afraid their bosses will find out or afraid their fellow doctors or professional associates will find out. Unless we can generate, visibly, numbers, masses, we are going to die.

I am sick of everyone in this community who tells me to stop creating a panic. How many of us have to die before *you* get scared off your ass and into action? Aren't 195 dead New Yorkers enough? Every straight person who is knowledgeable about the AIDS epidemic can't understand why gay men aren't marching on the White House. Over and over again I hear from them, "Why aren't you guys doing anything?" Every politician I have spoken to has said to me confidentially, "You guys aren't making enough noise. Bureaucracy only responds to pressure."

I am sick of people who say "it's no worse than statistics for smokers and lung cancer" or "considering how many homosexuals there are in the United States, AIDS is really statistically affecting only a very few." That would wash if there weren't 164 cases in twenty-eight days. That would wash if case numbers hadn't jumped from 41 to 1,112 in eighteen months. That would wash if cases in one city—New York—hadn't jumped to cases in fifteen countries and thirty-five states (up from thirty-four last week). That would wash if cases weren't coming in at more than four a day nationally and over two a day locally. That would wash if the mortality rate didn't start at 38 percent the first year of diagnosis and climb to a grotesque 86 percent after three years. Get your stupid heads out of the sand, you turkeys!

I am sick of guys who moan that giving up careless sex until this blows over is worse than death. How can they value life so little and cocks and asses so much? Come with me, guys, while I visit a few of our friends in Intensive Care at NYU. Notice the looks in their eyes, guys. They'd give up sex forever if you could promise them life.

I am sick of guys who think that all being gay means is sex in the first place. I am sick of guys who can only think with their cocks.

I am sick of "men" who say, "We've got to keep quiet or *they* will do such and such." *They* usually means the straight majority, the "Moral" Majority, or similarly perceived representatives of *them*. Okay, you "men"—be my guests: You can march off now to the gas chambers; just get right in line.

We shall always have enemies. Nothing we can ever do will remove them. Southern newspapers and Jerry Falwell's publications are already printing editorials proclaiming AIDS as God's deserved punishments on homosexuals. So what? Nasty words make poor little sissy pansy wilt and die?

And I am very sick and saddened by every gay man who does not get behind this issue totally and with commitment—to fight for his life.

I don't want to die. I can only assume you don't want to die. Can we fight together?

For the past few weeks, about fifty community leaders and organization representatives have been meeting at Beth Simchat Torah, the gay synagogue, to prepare action. We call ourselves the AIDS Network. We come from all areas of health concern: doctors, social workers, psychologists, psychiatrists, nurses; we come from Gay Men's Health Crisis, from the National Gay Health Education Foundation, from New York Physicians for Human Rights, the St. Mark's Clinic, the Gay Men's Health Project; we come from the gay synagogue, the Gay Men's Chorus, from the Greater Gotham Business Council, SAGE, Lambda Legal Defense, Gay Fathers, the Christopher Street Festival Committee, Dignity, Integrity; we are lawyers, actors, dancers, architects, writers, citizens; we come from many component organizations of the Gay and Lesbian Community Council.

We have a leader. Indeed, for the first time our community appears to have a true leader. Her name is Virginia Apuzzo, she is head of the National Gay Task Force, and, as I have said, so far she has proved to be magnificent.

The AIDS Network has sent a letter to Mayor Koch. It contains twelve points that are urged for his consideration and action.

This letter to Mayor Koch also contains the following paragraph:

It must be stated at the outset that the gay community is growing increasingly aroused and concerned and angry. Should our avenues to the mayor of our city and the members of the Board of Estimate not be available, it is our feeling that the level of frustration is such that it will manifest itself in a manner heretofore not associated with this community and the gay population at large. It should be stated, too, at the outset that as of February 25th, there were 526 cases of serious AIDS in New York's metropolitan area and 195 deaths (and 1,112 cases nationally and 418 deaths) and it is the sad and sorry fact that most gay men in our city now have close friends and lovers who have either been stricken with or died from this disease. It is against this background that this letter is addressed. It is this issue that has, ironically, united our community in a way not heretofore thought possible.

Further, a number of AIDS Network members have been studying civil disobedience with one of the experts from Dr. Martin Luther King's old team. We are learning how. Gay men are the strongest, toughest people I know. We are perhaps shortly to get an opportunity to show it.

I'm sick of hearing that Mayor Koch doesn't respond to pressures and threats from the disenfranchised, that he walks away from confrontations. Maybe he does. But we have *tried* to make contact with him, we are *dying*, so what other choice but confrontation has he left us?

I hope we don't have to conduct sit-ins or tie up traffic or get arrested. I hope our city and our country will start to do something to help start saving us. But it is time for us to be perceived for what we truly are: an angry community and a strong community, and therefore *a threat*. Such are the realities of politics. Nationally we are 24 million strong, which is more than there are Jews or blacks or Hispanics in this country.

I want to make a point about what happens if we *don't* get angry about AIDS. There are the obvious losses, of course: Little of what I've written about here is likely to be rectified with the speed necessary to help the growing number of victims. But something worse will happen, and is already happening. Increasingly, we are being *blamed* for AIDS, for this epidemic; we are being called its perpetrators, through our blood, through our "promiscuity," through just being the gay men so much of the rest of the world has learned to hate. We can point out until we are blue in the face that we are not the cause of AIDS but its victims, that AIDS has landed among us first, as it could have landed among them first. But other frightened populations are going to drown out these truths by playing on the worst bigoted fears of the straight world, and send the status of gays right back to the Dark Ages. Not all Jews are blamed for Meyer Lansky, Rabbis Bergman and Kahane, or for money-lending. All Chinese aren't blamed for the recent Seattle slaughters. But all gays are blamed for John Gacy, the North American Man/Boy Love Association, and AIDS.

Enough. I am told this is one of the longest articles the *Native* has ever run. I hope I have not been guilty of saying ineffectively in five thousand words what I could have said in five: we must fight to live.

I am angry and frustrated almost beyond the bound my skin and bones and body and brain can encompass. My sleep is tormented by nightmares and visions of lost friends, and my days are flooded by the tears of funerals and memorial services and seeing my sick friends. How many of us must die before *all* of us living fight back?

I know that unless I fight with every ounce of my energy I will hate myself. I hope, I pray, I implore you to feel the same.

I am going to close by doing what Dr. Ron Grossman did at GMHC's second Open Forum last November at Julia Richman High School. He listed the names of the patients he had lost to AIDS. Here is a list of twenty dead men I knew:

Nick Rock, Rick Wellikoff, Jack Nau, Shelly, Donald Krintzman, Jerry Green, Michael Maletta, Paul Graham, Toby, Harry Blumenthal, Stephen Sperry, Brian O'Hara, Barry, David, Jeffrey Croland, Z., David Jackson, Tony Rappa, Robert Christian, Ron Doud.

And one more, who will be dead by the time these words appear in print.

If we don't act immediately, then we face our approaching doom.

Volunteers Needed for Civil Disobedience

It is necessary that we have a pool of at least three thousand people who are prepared to participate in demonstrations of civil disobedience. Such demonstrations might include sit-ins or traffic tie-ups. All participants must be prepared to be arrested. I am asking every gay person and every gay organization to canvass all friends and members and make a count of the total number of people you can provide toward this pool of three thousand.

Let me know how many people you can be counted on providing. Just include the number of people; you don't have to send actual names—you keep that list yourself. And include your own phone numbers. *Start these lists now.*

GMHC organized two mammoth benefits during 1983 to raise money and morale for the fight against AIDS. Both were in Madison Square Garden, a large arena in New York; the first was a circus performance, the second a rodeo. The article reprinted here was originally published in Boston's *Gay Community News,* and was reprinted and distributed by GMHC in its program for the rodeo benefit of October 1, 1983. Note the belief, common throughout the 1980s, that lesbians were "immune" to AIDS. That belief was challenged as lesbians joined AIDS activism; not only could lesbians get AIDS, many who were at low risk chose solidarity with gay men as a response to the increased homophobia of the 1980s.

GAY MEN'S HEALTH
CRISIS

AIDS AND THE GAY MEN'S HEALTH CRISIS OF NEW YORK

from *Gay Community News* (1983)

Peg Byron

> *The homosexual is not told like the Black that he (sic) is stupid. He is not told like the Jew that he is mercenary. The invariable expression of disdain for homosexuals is that they are neurotic, "sick" . . .*

—George Weinberg,
Society and the Healthy Homosexual

The line written for women is that they have asked for it—and the hatred common to all of these invectives is now being rained upon gay men, whose response to a real health crisis is both militant and generous. In ugly contrast, the general public is dredging up all the fear and loathing it ever felt toward "the sick homosexuals," making life for those with AIDS more painful and giving the gay community at large a political jolt. Gay men are being told that they are paying for their "liberated" (read "deviant") sex lives. Many are being denied equal services, threatened with (or *de facto* forced into) quarantine. Meanwhile, in spite of much noise in state and national legislatures, research has barely begun and the National Institutes of Health (NIH) so far has no coordinating strategy for AIDS research. The message on AIDS continues bluntly to be that the government and the general public will not stand in the way if a troublesome minority group begins to drop dead or to suffer from inadequate social services. AIDS is acting as an awful social leveler on gay men, exposing them to the kinds of medical and social abuses women, Jews, IV drug users, Haitians and other people of color have long experienced. And faced with a major epidemic, the system is not simply callous, it is murderous.

This message has not been lost on what had heretofore been the least political segment of the gay community, the white middle class. One of the most dramatic examples of their political awakening is a volunteer organization in New York called Gay Men's Health Crisis (GHMC), the likes of which gay politics has not seen before. In less than two years, GMHC has grown from a vague circle of six men who hammered at their friends about a bizarre-sounding disease, to a highly structured organization with more than a thousand volunteers pouring their all into support programs, fundraising and advocacy for AIDS victims. The only previous networking done by many GMHC members may have been sharing summer houses on Fire Island or The Pines; now, they say, their work is changing their lives in many ways. "We've had to grow up fast," is a typical comment from the gay men who are now helping their peers face incurable disease. Their effective, even passionate efforts are improving the future for the gay community as a whole, not just for those with AIDS, although some of those effects are just emerging. Increasingly, GMHC is sharing political connections and even some of its treasury with other organizations for AIDS and with other lesbian and gay causes. One of its best contributions is the highly visible model it provides as a constructive gay organization.

Some AIDS activists do not like GMHC's heavy hierarchical style or its aversion to political analysis and criticism of specific public officials. But even GMHC critics recognize it for shaping information and policy nationally and for directly serving anyone with AIDS.

The support GMHC gets from the middle and upper classes of gay men plays one part in its organizational success. GMHC's weekly bank deposit resembles a more typical gay or lesbian organization's total balance. Almost $1,000 in unsolicited donations alone arrive by mail daily, and the organization's net worth is on the respectable side of half a million, most raised in the past six months. With its corporate structure and corporate efficiency, GMHC has set up a number of psycho-social programs that have kept pace with the more than doubling of the number of AIDS patients since last fall. The organization took a gamble and rented the Ringling Brothers-Barnum & Bailey Circus at Madison Square Garden on April 30 and sold out the house, raising $250,000. New York State awarded GMHC a $200,000 grant with the promise of more, and private fundraisers often net more than ten G for the group. Overall, it is accepted among congressional committees, the media (including the tight-assed *New York Times*), and with hospitals and public agencies as *the* expert of AIDS patients' needs.

With all of this, GMHC is not just another legitimate, well-greased corporation. The money and the membership are there because, as one volunteer from GMHC's more modest-sized days of last summer says, "We started out just to find out who was supposed to be dealing with these problems [of AIDS victims]. Then we realized no one was; it would have to be us."

The Acquired Immune Deficiency Syndrome, whose acronym has become a household word, is claiming five to six new victims daily. Stubbornly, it has stayed within the original high-risk groups: about half of AIDS victims are New Yorkers, 71 percent are gay men, 17 percent are non-gay IV drug users, five percent are Haitians, and less than one percent are hemophiliacs who don't fall into the other categories. That leaves just under six percent who do not belong to the apparent risk groups (or at least do not admit to belonging to them), according to the Centers for Disease Control (CDC) statistics circulated by the National Gay Task Force.

Since mid-spring, the horror stories for AIDS patients have been multiplying. A common one involves public officials and health service employees who refuse to do their jobs if their clients are AIDS patients. City and state correctional officers' fears have been well publicized (although prison conditions and the treatment given incarcerated gays and AIDS patients are not). New York State had to threaten to revoke the licenses of morticians who began refusing to embalm the remains of some AIDS victims. Those afflicted with AIDS are also facing loss of employment and housing, desertion by families and friends, and, if they are Haitians, deportation.

"Now gay men are seeing that we're second-class citizens, and that it may mean the difference between life and death," Paul Popham, president of GMHC's board of directors, says of the political impact of AIDS. In addition to government inertia in funding research, Popham can describe endless barriers those with AIDS face in getting care. He had to meet with Human Resources Administration supervisors in the Bronx "to protest people refusing to do paperwork for an AIDS patient—and they are being backed up by their union." Other incidents have ranged from a protest in a Queens neighborhood against school attendance by the children of a bisexual with AIDS and sanitation workers' refusal to collect his trash, to the attempt by a Texan group, Doctors Against AIDS, to use the issue to revive the state's sodomy law. AIDS has also been the excuse for attempts to obtain a court order against New York's gay pride march and suggestions, even from lesbians and gay men, that gathering places like bars and baths be closed. The *New York Post* has published barely disguised calls for laws quarantining gays. And many lesbians are finding that the public does not always consider them any less dangerous as AIDS carriers.

The media, first electronic and then print, have given some attention to government inaction and public fears about AIDS. Suddenly, after years of silence about the lesbian and gay community, the words "AIDS" and "Homosexual" can be found in *New York Times* headlines on a daily basis. The newspaper of record even ran an in-depth series on New York's "homosexual community," although like the rest of the mainstream media at its best, it emphasized the tragedy of AIDS, portraying gays as at times noble, but always broken, isolated people who have been trapped by their lifestyles.

There is, in fact, a heightened feeling of community among some lesbians and gay men in New York, where, politically, we have never been stronger. In the face of a deadly epidemic, it may seem callous to count the political profits, but that is the currency burying survival for gay men, for Haitians and for IV drug users, and even for the AIDS-immune lesbian populations. As a political trigger, AIDS is aptly compared to Anita Bryant's hate campaign and John Briggs' initiative to restrict lesbian and gay employment in California—attacks which provoked organizing and cohesiveness with the lesbian and gay communities in the '70s.

In this case, both the issue and the response are unprecedented. Lovers and friends are dying, and the numbers of potential new victims doubled in five months since last fall. (The New York City Health Commission and CDC report that the rate of increase is slowing, with, notes the city's commissioner, "a hopeful sign that promiscuous sexual lifestyles among homosexuals have changed.") At meetings of the New York AIDS Network, a coalition of AIDS-concerned organizations, the body count is revised every week, like a more personal version of the televised war in Viet Nam. By the end of June, 1831 AIDS cases had been reported nation-wide and 684 of the victims had died. Among them 789 cases were in New York, with 301 of the victims dead. The CDC warns that these statistics are conservative, including only those with an otherwise rare cancer, Kaposi's sarcoma, or *pneumocystis carinii* pneumonia, or some other major opportunistic infection.

Not surprisingly, GMHC Executive Director Mel Rosen explains the membership and growth of GMHC as emotionally based. "Political issues do not impinge upon the lives of middle-class folks, and so of course there is more of a response to something that might affect you . . . The issue of life and death and disease—it's much more charismatic than politics."

Ken Wein, director of patient services at GMHC, provides an eloquent example of the response to the crisis. "I was not very political in terms of being involved with gay organizations in the city. I definitely wouldn't have put myself on the line before." Wein, a psychologist, was fired from Booth Memorial Medical Center in Queens shortly after he gave a presentation on AIDS to his staff. The director of psychiatry, a frequent source of anti-gay comments, demanded Wein explain his activities and the soon-to-be unemployed doctor took the opportunity to tell the man off.

"I've really grown a lot," Wein says. "I've seen such examples of role models in this organization [GMHC]. I've never seen a more totally professional group of warm, nurturing, loving people in my life. I'm proud of this organization and I'm proud that I'm gay."

Wein is now responsible for services that include an information hotline, a "buddies" program providing volunteers who regularly visit and help AIDS patients at home, and crisis counseling and support group programs. GMHC has been especially devoted to emotional support services and has groups to accommodate people with different kinds of AIDS symptoms. Those in acute or less advanced stages, those with Kaposi's sarcoma (the cancer that emerges with large, bruise-like lesions), and those with other kinds of manifestations, can have very different needs. There are also support groups for lovers and for the families of patients.

About 200 people with AIDS are using GMHC's counseling services, for which there is an almost equal number of counselors, all volunteer professionals. The ration sounds off-balance, but the coordinator of the Crisis Intervention Counseling program, Diego Lopez, expects the summer to continue bringing more patients to GMHC. The month of May alone saw a one-third increase, and Lopez, himself a psychotherapist, adds that the counselors should not take on too heavy a case load.

"This is burn-out work" he says. "You have to look mortality smack in the face. This is working with people dying who are not a lot older and not a lot younger—your peers."

As the size of the program he runs is forced to grow, Lopez is finding "things are beginning to feel out of control. It's having a personal effect on me and with each patient I wonder if I'll be next . . . All the counselors do."

AIDS in combination with homophobia makes it unlike any other crisis situation. "Usually a crisis has a middle and an end. With AIDS, instead of an end, there is another hazardous situation—losing your job, having to come out to your family," Lopez explains.

The crisis counselors who go to the hospitals find their patients receive extremely uneven treatment. Says Lopez, "The hospitals, the V.A. Hospital, they are not wonderful."

"I went to the hospital once and found one of my patients lying in his own excrement, no one taking care of him. I went berserk." He adds that he has altered his style for GMHC and now advises his staff to "make friends with the day and evening nurses, use the hospital social workers. I came to that after doing battle with the nursing stations." Otherwise, says Lopez, "the step I would take after that—I would have taken them to the courts.

"I'm Puerto Rican, I've been political for years . . . and I have to be careful because I'm also GMHC."

Lopez sees his staff's work as successful, however. "People aren't dying alone now. They know there's a group who cares, their own peers . . . try us," he says in the calm, sincere voice you often hear from GMHC members. "You won't wear us down."

As for the politicizing side of AIDS, Lopez answers that gay men are welcoming this involvement. "Men have been looking for something—the bars, the baths haven't been just for sex. What is it?" he laughs, "Sublimating for politics?"

The volunteers drawn to GMHC, however, do not reflect the demographics of those being affected by the epidemic. Over 27 percent of those with AIDS symptoms *reported* to the CDC are black, 14.5 percent are Hispanic.

Outreach within the gay community is a problem, one GMHC is only beginning to address. "This will take time," acknowledges Lopez. "Third World folks haven't been welcome for the good times; it is taking a little time and effort to get together for the bad times.

We are as racist and bigoted and, in some ways, as homophobic as the rest of society."

The fact that GMHC's membership is nearly all white and professional may explain why just a couple dozen people with AIDS have taken advantage of its financial aid services and only a few have needed housing.

The organization's outreach and public education efforts are mixing some low-cost basics and large-scale programs. Federico Gonzalez, director of education and program development, says GMHC is setting up tables around the city with information and sample letters to congress. With $97,000 of the state's money, GMHC members will travel by van to colleges and cities in other parts of the state. Another $250,000 has been requested from CDC for an education program for all of the Northeast, helping different communities set up their own AIDS support organizations. GMHC's most ambitious patient program will be for recreation, to the tune of $75,000. Popham and Wein both point out that many AIDS patients can become seriously isolated and this program will be an important support project, to be run by GMHC members who themselves have AIDS.

In addition to their work in direct patient services, GMHC members are building support from government mental and medical agencies. This strategy is methodically tapping a gay boys' network, the well-connected of the gay community who have become more inclined to help out.

GMHC's entree to agency heads, for example, has helped it address some service personnel problems, although directives from management can have only limited effect. This "top-down" approach has been more successful for funding and regulation changes, often negotiated with help from NGTF and Lambda Legal Defense Fund. It remains to be seen what strings are being pulled in the private sector, but New York State has been extremely cooperative: working closely with these major gay organizations, it came out ahead of the federal government in adjusting Social Security regulation for disability benefits; it recently appropriated $5.25 million for research and the creation of an AIDS Institute within the New York State Department of Health; $600,000 will go to community-based outreach and service organizations—to the credit of local "homocrats" such as Peter Vogel of NYAN and GMHC efforts.

U.S. Representative Ted Weiss of Manhattan marched with the GMHC banner at the June 26 Lesbian and Gay Pride demonstration. In a telephone interview, he labeled GMHC "the principle player in calling attention to this problem." Weiss began sponsoring gay rights legislation a dozen years ago. As the chair of the House subcommittee with jurisdiction over Health and Human Services, he says he is close to using a subpoena to obtain information from the CDC and NIH, which are loath to divulge their national AIDS research plans.

"GMHC is an unusual group. They've done a magnificent job at a time when hardly anyone in our society at large understood the significance of AIDS, and [they] mobilized the gay community," Weiss says, listing the help GMHC has given him and its effects on the medical community and the media.

"The Government's reticence to react more quickly to AIDS is part of the whole syndrome of its refusal to grant human rights."

GMHC's mixture of grassroots, direct services and diplomatic, high-level advocacy has been potent, although it does not address the fast growing phobias of the general public. "We're chartered to provide support, education and research, not to develop community understanding." Popham explains, "How much of that we can do is being reviewed, our lawyers are looking into it. The law is very vague."

Popham is talking about tax law of course—the old 501C(3). It is one reason why Rosen, who is slated to be replaced on August 1, emphasized GMHC's image "as a pure force in terms of social services." That caution is understandable but it will not be the secret of GMHC's success. Nuclear disarmament and abortion have also been life and death rallying points of a sort, but when crumbs were won, single-issue organizations lost momentum. Most feminists could warn GMHC that crumbs can also be lost.

Of course Rosen, Popham and others will readily admit that if the AIDS crisis were not political, GMHC would not be necessary. That is why it has steadily been joining coalitions, working in its typically generous and influential style.

Its local arm for political action is the New York AIDS Network, whose members include NGTF and Lambda Legal Defense Fund, and also gay city liaisons, health professionals, and anyone the Network decides would be helpful at its Thursday, 8 a.m. clearinghouse-type meetings. Much of New York's policies or legislative recommendations are established here, or more accurately, reported out of committees and unofficial political liaisons. In contrast to GMHC, but more typical of lesbian and gay politics in New York, it is loosely structured and its discussions can be laborious or picayune. Instead of a chief officer, it has a "convey-or," who until he was hired for a national AIDS federation project, was Ron Vachon. He sees the Network and other AIDS-related organizing as "not just around AIDS, but around the guts of the issue, the underlying homophobia and the health care system."

GMHC's growing concern with broader health care problems can be seen in its response to discussion with the Haitian community. GMHC extended an open-handed offer of financial and technical support for independent health care organizing by that community.

In a more active role with local lesbian and gay organizations, GMHC is helping to buy a city-owned building on West 13th Street. GMHC itself is desperate for office space, although Rosen admits this is not the easiest way to get it. As an "AIDS-identified" organization, however, GMHC has already been turned down by several landlords, as has the Community Health Project (formerly the gay and lesbian St. Mark's Health Clinic). Both groups will soon be joining current tenants, including the Metropolitan Community Church and Senior Action in a Gay Environment in the 200,000 square foot ex-Food and Maritime Trades High School.

Mixing with even more of the country, GMHC has become a central part of the National AIDS Federation (unofficial name, they say) at a conference of lesbian and gay health activists in Denver in early June. Popham is on its interim board of directors as the NYAN representative and he is emphasizing the Federation's research lobby function. So is another important member, Ginny Apuzzo of NGTF. The Federation's first year will cost $200,000, an unusual start for a lesbian and gay organization, but indicative of the new wave of gay money for the AIDS cause. GMHC donated $40,000, the highest figure among the Federation's 38 member groups, which also includes the Gay Rights National Lobby. A jointly sponsored lobbyist and staff will relieve GRNL of some of its tasks in Washington, where Executive Director Steve Endean said AIDS issues were consuming much of its time.

NGTF's relationship to GMHC has already been productive and the Federation will add to their coordinated activities. John Boring of NGTF notes GMHC's help in training NGTF hotline staff and the close work between the organizations to change Social Security regulations. Boring said NGTF sets its political agenda using GMHC-supplied information; on the other hand, NGTF often brings statistics and lobby reports back to the AIDS organization.

There is a basic respect between the two groups. GMHC's meteoric growth period coincided with a renaissance at NGTF with the appointment of Virginia Apuzzo as executive director. She personally gave the young organization an award at NGTF's recent 10th anniversary dinner, and as one GMHC coordinator exalts, "Ginny Apuzzo is the first gay politician that ever shook me up."

When asked how NGTF can channel the power of GMHC's overflowing membership, Apuzzo talks legislative reforms, just as both groups prefer to stress the lobby function of the AIDS federation.

Herself very much a Democrat, Apuzzo is less specific about public education strategies against homophobia, both internal and external, and about relating lesbian concerns. The appropriation of research funding is crucial, but is small comfort to the AIDS patient who, fired from his job without insurance, joins poor women and other disenfranchised people on the stingy welfare rolls.

This crisis, as Apuzzo succinctly states, "takes us back to the fundamental time to ask this question of the gay movement: what is the power for?"

Some of the previous documents employed the phrase "AIDS victims," which is rarely used any more. This began to change in 1983 with the adoption and promulgation of the "Denver Principles" at the founding meeting of the National Association of People with AIDS. In the words of Max Navarre, a founder of the PWA Coalition in New York: "as a person with AIDS, I can attest to the sense of diminishment at seeing and hearing myself constantly referred to as an AIDS victim, an AIDS sufferer, an AIDS case—as anything but what I am, a person with AIDS. I am a person with a condition. I am not that condition." As such, the Denver Principles are an act of self-empowerment of people living with AIDS, one that will be reasserted throughout the epidemic.

These principles were followed by, for example, the formation of the PWA Coalition in 1985 and its Community Research Initiative on AIDS. The latter is a PWA community-based group that uses the facilities of local physicians to give people access to treatments for AIDS-related infections and to prod the government to approve promising treatments. This was the beginning of such efforts on the part of PWAs themselves as political actors; others included Body Positive (for seropositive individuals), AIDS Treatment Registry, Project Inform, the PWA Health Group, various holistic AIDS treatment groups, and ACT-UP.

THE DENVER PRINCIPLES

THE DENVER PRINCIPLES
Founding Statement (1983)

People With AIDS/ARC

We condemn attempts to label us as "victims," which implies defeat, and we are only occasionally "patients," which implies passivity, helplessness, and dependence upon the care of others. We are "people with AIDS."

We recommend that health care professionals
  1. Who are gay, come out, especially to their patients who have AIDS.
  2. Always clearly identify and discuss the theory they favor as to the cause of AIDS, since this bias affects the treatment and advice they give.

3. Get in touch with their feelings (fears, anxieties, hopes, etc.) about AIDS, and not simply deal with AIDS intellectually.
4. Take a thorough personal inventory and identify and examine their own agendas around AIDS.
5. Treat people with AIDS as whole people and address psychosocial issues as well as biophysical ones.
6. Address the question of sexuality in people with AIDS specifically, sensitively, and with information about gay male sexuality in general and the sexuality of people with AIDS in particular.

We recommend that all people
1. Support us in our struggle against those who would fire us from our jobs, evict us from our homes, refuse to touch us, separate us from our loved ones, our community, or our peers, since there is no evidence that AIDS can be spread by casual social contact.
2. Do not scapegoat people with AIDS, blame us for the epidemic, or generalize about our lifestyles.

We recommend that people with AIDS
1. Form caucuses to choose their own representatives, to deal with the media, to choose their own agenda, and to plan their own strategies.
2. Be involved at every level of AIDS decision making and specifically serve on the boards of directors of provider organizations.
3. Be included in all AIDS forums with equal credibility as other participants, to share their own experiences and knowledge.
4. Substitute low-risk sexual behaviors for those that could endanger themselves or their partners, and we feel that people with AIDS have an ethical responsibility to inform their potential sexual partners of their health status.

People with AIDS have the right
1. To as full and satisfying sexual and emotional lives as anyone else.
2. To quality medical treatment and quality social service provision, without discrimination in any form, including sexual orientation, gender diagnosis, economic status, age or race.
3. To full explanations of all medical procedures and risks, to choose or refuse their treatment modalities, to refuse to participate in research without jeopardizing their treatment, and to make informed decisions about their lives.
4. To privacy, to confidentiality of medical records, to human respect, and to choose who their significant others are.
5. To die and *live* in dignity.

During the early years of the epidemic, at least in the U.S., a moral panic developed that was fueled by two issues. The first was the uncertainty of the cause of the disease syndrome. Epidemiology revealed increasing numbers of cases among Haitian immigrants to the U.S., among hemophiliacs, among intravenous drug users, and among African heterosexuals. This led to a revision of etiology toward a viral hypothesis. This hypothesis was articulated when, in April 1984, the U.S. government announced the "discovery" of the viral cause of AIDS, HTLV-3, by one of its own employees, Robert Gallo (a discovery contested by the French) and later named HIV, Human Immunodeficiency Virus. This made possible a test for antibodies, hence proof of exposure to and infection with the virus.

This shift from the lifestyle to the viral hypothesis resulted in uncertainty about routes of its transmission, and this uncertainty was the second cause of panic. As the possibility of "casual transmission" emerged, people were afraid to donate blood, hemophiliac children who had been exposed to the virus, such as Ryan White, were banned from school and brutally harassed, and police, court officers, and others dealing with suspected AIDS carriers wore rubber gloves.

The panic was whipped up by the rhetoric of those such as newspaper columnist Patrick Buchanan, who stated in 1983 that homosexuals "have declared war on nature, and now nature is exacting an awful retribution" and warned of the viral dangers posed by homosexual food handlers, teachers, doctors, and dentists, and writer William F. Buckley, who in the *The New York Times* advocated tattooing (on the buttocks or upper arm) of those who test positive for the virus to protect the uninfected. A distinction between "guilty" and "innocent" victims of AIDS began to develop. The death of Rock Hudson, the first mainstream public figure to admittedly die of complications from AIDS, emblematized fear of disclosure of HIV status and uncertainty about who was "at risk."

This generalized moral panic, as well as the health crisis among gay men, contextualizes the following documents. The Coalition for Sexual Responsibility was organized to preserve sexual freedom while protecting health through personal responsibility. It's efforts at self-enforcement of safer sex within sexual institutions—largely private business—of the gay community ultimately failed due to lack of cooperation by the owners of those enterprises, an attitude of denial by their patrons, and due to increased pressure brought to bear upon public health officials to close them. (For example, bathhouses were closed in both New York and San Francisco in 1985.) Alternatively, GMHC attempted to institutionalize safer sex through the creation of new venues, workshops and parties, as well as through established ones such as gay bars and media. The political philosophy that emerges here focuses on the survival of our people and the preservation of a way of life, or ethos, of sexual freedom. Safer sex, as a political issue, then, was institutionalized by GMHC through such workshops and private parties, and safer sex education is a form of political education undertaken there, and throughout the community.

INTERIM REPORT

with Appendix AA (1985)

Coalition for Sexual Responsibility

Since December of 1984 the Coalition for Sexual Responsibility (CSR) has been working to lessen the spread and risk of AIDS in New York City establishments where on-site sexual activities occur. Following is a summary of our efforts to date.

CSR: Who We Are

The Coalition for Sexual Responsibility (CSR) was formed in December of 1984 by a group of gay men interested in engaging establishments where on-site sex occurred in AIDS education/prevention efforts (see appendix A). The members of the coalition represented a wide spectrum of views (see appendix AA 1-3), ranging from closing all establishments with on-premise sexual activity to making minor changes in how these businesses operated.

The men attending initial meetings attended as individuals and not as representatives of organizations. But all participants were involved directly in many of the community's most active organizations including: People with AIDS (PWA); Gay Men's Health Crisis (GMHC); Lambda Legal Defense; National Gay Task Force; Safer Sex Committee; Community Health Project; Wipe Out AIDS; and Gay and Lesbian Health Advocacy. We did not ask any group to take any direct or official position on any of CSR's decisions.

CSR: Objectives

The primary objectives of CSR include:
- encourage commercial establishments whose primary purpose is to permit high risk site sexual activities to occur on their premises to provide an environment where safer sex is encouraged and promoted.
- encouraging these same establishments to help educate the community about AIDS and safer sex.

These businesses include: gay bathhouses (see appendix I), gay bars with "back rooms," gay movie houses, and selected gay bookstores where on-premise sex occurs.

CSR: The Next Step

Specifically, the committee looked at these four general options:
1. How best to address the unsafe aspects of the environments of these establishments.
2. How best to get safer sex information to the clientele.
3. How and whether to regulate on-site sexual behavior (i.e., prohibiting certain kinds of sexual activities).
4. Whether to recommend if appropriate, closure of establishments if they did not comply with a list of our suggested guidelines.

The committee chose to focus on the first two points. CSR, recognizing that our community is in the midst of a most devastating health crisis, decided to draft some minimum requirements as the first step in meeting our objectives. These initial 19 bathhouse recommendations (see appendix B) provided the foundation for our volunteer effort to work with the bathhouse owners as well as further educating the community.

The coalition stopped short of calling for actual behavior modification. Instead we chose to base our recommendations on education, hygiene and structural improvements (see appendix B). These guidelines were put into inspection sheet form (see appendix C) which our volunteers used to inspect the bathhouses.

Before finalizing our recommendations one of our members, Steven Caiazza, MD, resigned because of his strong belief that the bathhouses should be closed. He felt that any changes CSR would convince the bathhouses to make would be too little, too late (see appendix D).

After finalizing our recommendations we then invited the bathhouses to a February 11 meeting with selected CSR members (see appendix E). This meeting and subsequent ones were facilitated by the Directors of Lambda Legal Defense and National Gay Task Force.

Again, no organizational endorsement was implied.

One of the primary motivating factors for NGTF and Lambda Legal Defense involvement was that if the government decided to regulate (including closure) baths, then restaurants and other places frequented by gays where no on-premise sex occurs could become vulnerable to governmental regulation.

On the other hand, several members felt if the establishments whose cooperation we sought failed to comply with our modest recommendations then they would be inviting government intervention by their non-action.

Most of the bathhouse owners who attended the initial February meeting indicated a willingness to cooperate by implementing our recommendations. We asked for letters from each establishment indicating their willingness to cooperate. Seven out of ten agreed in writing (see appendix H). Another meeting was held to work out some details and then volunteers were then [sic] recruited for the first round of unannounced inspections of the ten bathhouses (see appendix I) beginning in May.

After corresponding with the New York City administration we received support from both Patricia Mahr, AIDS Education Coordinator, and Ron Vachon, Director of the Office and Gay and Lesbian Affairs (see appendix F & G).

CSR: The Results

Considering the fact that New York City is in the midst of the AIDS crisis, the response of the bathhouses has been woefully inadequate. The first inspections began in May 1985 and were completed a month later. The first round of inspections demonstrated that most of the bathhouses virtually ignored the recommendations of the CSR (see appendix J & N). NOTE: all three inspections' results can be found at the end of the appendices.

After the first round of inspections a letter was sent out on June 4, 1985 by CSR telling them of the poor results and requesting that they take immediate remedial action (see appendix K). Another meeting was held on June 13 with seven of the ten bathhouse owners. This meeting was held to clear up any questions about our guidelines and our procedures. A follow-up letter to the June 13 meeting was sent to all owners to underscore our desire to have the bathhouses in full compliance as soon as possible (see appendix L).

The second round of inspections occurred in late June and July on 1985. While the results were somewhat better with some of the establishments there were still no establishments in full compliance. One establishment declined to participate at all (the Barracks). The Barracks was not inspected the second or third time.

During this same period meetings were held with GMHC (Gay Men's Health Crisis) education staff members about participating in our effort. GMHC agreed by convincing several bathhouses to allow GMHC to set up education tables in the bathhouses and to educate patrons about safe sex. Six bathhouses agreed initially (see appendix M). One interesting observation by the coordinator of his GMHC effort was that "almost 50% of the those approaching us (at the education table) did not know how AIDS was spread.

After the second round of inspections were completed, CSR saw slight improvements but the results were still very disappointing (see appendix O). Another meeting was held in August to determine if we should proceed with the inspections or consider more direct action. It was determined to have one more round of inspections and then to share our findings with concerned members of the community, public health officials, and media.

The third and latest round of inspections took place in October of this year. Once again, while we saw some improvement, there was only full compliance with two of the ten bathhouses in the city—a full ten months later (see last section of all three inspection results).

What's Ahead

Despite the effort from within the community to reach these establishments and have them make minimal efforts to respond to this health crisis, eight out of ten have continued to fall short of full compliance.

Currently there are discussions about the possibility of closing and/or tightly restricting the bathhouse's operations. In early October the State AIDS Institute Advisory Board recommended that the CSR's guidelines be adopted immediately. If they are not followed the board recommended the non-complying establishments be closed. The minority report, made up of three physicians scientists on the bathhouse subcommittee and the only physician on full Board, voted for immediate closure.

Both the New York Governor and New York City Mayor have said it is now time to look at this issue from a health perspective as well as from a legal perspective. CSR had been promoting this position for almost a year.

The gay community has made its effort to work from within without unnecessary State intervention. But the response from the bathhouses has been, for the most part, irresponsible and disappointing.

There are not current plans to inspect the bathhouses further but efforts have begun to reach other establishments where high-risk multiple-partner sex occurs on the premises. The next group we have approached are "back rooms" where high-risk multiple-partner sex is allowed.

Back Rooms

CSR sent out on July 31, 1985, by certified mail, our initial request to meet with the eleven back rooms on August 16, 1985 (see appendix P). Seven of the bars received the certified letter. Followup calls were made to the establishments. Only one establishment (The Mineshaft) showed up for the meeting. Clearly, these establishments had no current interest to work within the gay community on issues surrounding AIDS education and prevention.

In light of the recent negative bathhouse publicity, three of the back rooms are now willing to meet with the committee. Others may follow.

The coalition feels that under our current guidelines set for the baths that the traditional back rooms, which are almost totally dark, must become a thing of the past. Other requirements dealing with educational materials and environmental changes will, in effect, make the "back rooms" obsolete.

Plans for future dealings with these establishments have not been finalized.

Appendix AA
Initial Issues Facing CSR

CSR: Getting Started

In formulating the initial list of 17 recommendations, there was a great deal of discussion as to how to get the AIDS education message while garnering the support of the bathhouses. A number of issues were raised by CSR ranging from keeping the status quo to calling for closure. Issues we discussed included:

- "government promises NEVER to close baths"—early in 1985 assurances came from both New York City and State health officials that they would never close the bathhouses. Some argue that this took away the incentive for the bathhouse owners to alter "business as usual" during this health crisis.
- "education is the best alternative"—some argue that the bathhouses and other estab-

lishments, if cooperative, where on-site sex activity occurs are the best place to reach people who are sexually active. These places are easy to identify and have the ability to distribute much needed education/prevention information on AIDS.

- "homophobia"—some argue that any move on gay sex affirmative institutions (bathhouses, back rooms in bars, movie houses and bookstores where anonymous multiple sex is permitted) are an attack on gays and their lifestyle. They argue that the effort to limit the spread of AIDS is consistent with government policy to further limit the rights of gay people. Others argue the State is already involved through subsidizing health care and housing for AIDS patients.
- "civil rights"—others argue that the government should not intervene in determining business activity. They argue that the civil rights of the owners as well as the patrons would be seriously eroded if any restrictions, let alone closure, were implemented. They argue that there will never be a legitimate health rationale that will override the civil liberties issues (free choice, no government intervention, etc.).
- "free choice"—some activists argue that people who go to the baths were doing so by "free choice." The assumption is that "everyone knows about AIDS and how it is spread" and bathhouse patrons are choosing to go to unsafe environments and have unsafe sex. Our evidence based on samples within the baths demonstrated the opposite. During recent GMHC education efforts in some bathhouses (volunteers staffing tables with AIDS information) nearly 50% of those who approached the tables said they did not know how AIDS is spread. Further, thousands of people who visit NYC from all over the world every month are not always well educated about AIDS.
- "bathhouses are a tangential issue"—some argue that by discussing the on-site sex premises issue publicly, even in the gay press, the public's attention will be directed toward these establishments. They fear the issue would be misunderstood and people would react negatively. This may harm efforts to garner attention and funding from more important programs for housing, services and anti-discrimination measures. Others argue that inaction could produce the same kind of negative public reaction.
- "floodgates"—some argue that if the government is allowed to close the baths without any resistance then they will quickly move to close gay bars, gay restaurants and other places where gays congregate—ultimately rounding up gays in the streets.
- "what's good for gay business is good for all gays"—some feel it is important for gay bathhouse owners to survive in their businesses. There is a sense by others in the community that these same owners who expect support for their businesses should reciprocate by demonstrating concern for their customers.
- "confusion about 'cause' of AIDS"—as has been true throughout the AIDS health crisis no one will speak unequivocally about the cause of AIDS or absolutely how AIDS is spread. Instead one hears how it is likely that HTLV-III is the AIDS virus and that it is highly unlikely that AIDS is spread through causal contact. Some charge people exploit this uncertainty to perpetuate "business as usual." Some claim that until there is absolutely no doubt about the cause and spread of this disease, nothing should be done to restrict any business in any way.
- "political influence"—many concerned with this issue are well connected in both the gay and the straight political communities. They have been somewhat successful in convincing the existing powers that they can do more good by keeping their businesses open.
- "what about other gay on-site sex establishments"—some ask about what is being done in back rooms, bookstores and movie houses where multiple-partner, anonymous,

high-risk, sex occurs. The response is that the CSR decided to start with the bathhouses because:

> • they provide more opportunity to reach more people
> • there are traditionally several sex contacts per visit to bathhouses
> •we felt this group would be highly cooperative and initial success would make subsequent negotiations with back rooms and others easier.

- "what about straight sex establishments"—these should also be regulated and/or closed if they do not meet specified health requirements.
- "it's an election year"—the issue of election year maneuvering cut both ways. Some argue that this was a good time to pressure all officials running for office to address this among a number of other important AIDS issues (housing, services, discrimination). On the other hand others argue that the raising of the gay sex establishments issue could backfire and consequently hurt the move for greater services and rights for our community—especially if people thought that we were not doing enough ourselves to curb the spread of the disease. Others feel inaction ignores the reality of the AIDS epidemic and does nothing to educate those at risk or the public-at-large.
- "gay leaders should not be seen disagreeing publicly"—public dissent about this issue among gay leaders would show the gay community not being unified in its fight against AIDS and further hamper overall AIDS efforts. This is, in part, the same rationale that kept the gay community from agreeing on any educational efforts in the early years of the health crisis.

THE EMERGENCE OF AIDS ACTIVISM

By early 1987 when there were several national AIDS organizations and celebrities and when public figures began to take up AIDS as a political issue. In addition, there had been annual international scientific conferences on AIDS since 1985 (US President Reagan managed to give a speech at one and not even mention the word "AIDS") and the year would see the launching of a Presidential Commission on the HIV Epidemic, "balanced" between members who saw science and government fighting a disease, not people, and members who were publicly homophobic and in favor of mandatory testing and physical restriction of seropositives.

During this period, also, lesbian and gay activism distinct from AIDS continued. One New York-based direct action group, the Lavender Hill Mob, demonstrated against the US Supreme Court's *Bowers vs. Hardwick* decision that upheld criminalization of homosexuality, "zapped" NY's St. Patrick's Cathedral in protest of Cardinal O' Connor's endorsement of a Vatican document widely believed to explicitly condone anti-gay and -lesbian violence, and occupied the office of a NY Senator for not speaking out about gay/lesbian and AIDS issues. Another collective of politicized graphic artists designed, printed, and posted throughout New York City, posters framing an inverted pink triangle and reading:

Silence = Death. Why is Reagan silent about AIDS? What is really going on at the Center for Disease Control, the Federal Drug Administration, and Vatican? Gays and lesbians are not expendable . . . Use your power . . . Vote . . . Defend yourselves . . . Turn anger, fear, grief into action.

This is the context within which ACT UP, the AIDS Coalition to Unleash Power, was formed in New York City in March 1987, the first of what would become close to one hundred chapters throughout the world.

In January 1987, Larry Kramer published in the *New York Native* the following scathing critique of Gay Men's Health Crisis (GMHC) as an open letter to its then Executive Director, the late Richard Dunne. Expelled earlier from the organization's board for his criticism of both the board and the city government, Kramer believed that while founded as a political actor in the face of social hostility and political indifference, GMHC had become at best merely a social service agency for the privatization of welfare, at worst, a burial society for gay men. The political results of the letter were an institutional commitment to: an advocacy division within GMHC (on parity with client services) to lobby the government and build coalitions with other organizations; more public relations work including education about and positions on AIDS issues before the public via mass media; reconstituting and reconceptualizing the board of directors to make it more accountable to the community it serves and make it more politically activist; and a return to mass fund-raisers (rather than expensive elitist ones) to strengthen the morale of the besieged community. However, immediately after the letter was publicly responded to, Kramer was asked to substitute for a cancellation in the Lesbian and Gay Community Services Center's twice-monthly speaker's series. When word got out that he would speak, activists from around the city showed up for a meeting that turned out to be the beginning of ACT UP. Kramer's speech is also reprinted below.

AN OPEN LETTER TO RICHARD DUNNE AND THE GAY MEN'S HEALTH CRISIS

from the *New York Native* (1987)

Larry Kramer

Dear Richard,

The doomsday Scenario that many have feared for so long comes closer. Next week, 274 people will die from AIDS. Next, 374 more will become infected with the killer virus. In four years' time, 270,000 people will have AIDS. Of these, 179,000 will have died. Around the globe, many millions already are infected. As many as 50 percent of these millions will die.

Two out of three AIDS cases in America are still happening to gay men.

For all the worthy Patient Services and Education that have been provided, the rate of infection and death continues unabated.

As presently construed, organized, and managed, Gay Men's Health Crisis, Inc., of which you are Executive Director, is simply not equipped or prepared or able to deal with an emergency of this magnitude.

This letter is an urgent plea to you and your Board of Directors to wake up, look coldly and harshly at the realities you have been ignoring for so long, and reconstitute yourselves so that at last you perform the actions you were established to perform in the first place: to fight for gay men—that we may go on living.

For the past five years I have painfully watched as GMHC has attempted to be all things to all people, in so doing losing complete sight of the larger picture, of what is happening, of what you should be doing and are not doing.

I call for nothing less than a total reassessment of your goals and a rethinking of what you are there for, what we need you there for, and what you must accomplish for us.

This letter has been in my mind for some time. I have not written it before because I kept hoping someone up there would come to his or her senses. This has not happened, and the action that finally prompted this letter is this:

In *The New York Times* of January 10th, you are quoted (concerning the release by ICN Pharmaceuticals of its most promising ribavirin data at a press conference) as follows: "We cannot understand why they chose to raise the hopes of so many people by releasing their clinical trial information through a press conference instead of a more responsible manner such as an appropriate medical journal."

I prayed that you did not say this. I prayed that the Executive Director of the organization that is meant to fight for the rights of gay men—men and rights that have been constantly, continuously denied, with a disregard for us bordering on the murderous—did not say this to a newspaper and to a world filled with heterosexual connivance, bordering on collusion at the least and conspiracy at the most—ignoring us, treating us like so much offal fit to die in agony while tests, trials, delays, ignorance, inhumane uncaring, lying, and ass-dragging characterize the daily activities of just about everyone and everything in sight, particularly the "appropriate medical journals."

I do not give a flying fuck what the *New England Journal of Medicine* reports about AIDS, or *Science* or *Lancet* or the *Journal of the American Medical Association*. From the very beginning of this epidemic they have shown scant humane concern for us, for our rights, for our continued healthy survival on this planet. Indeed, one of the main reasons this epidemic became an epidemic was that the *New England Journal of Medicine*—that "responsible . . . appropriate medical journal"—would not accept papers of warning from leading doctors observing a new phenomenon that they wished to warn the world about quickly, when they had little clinical data or test results, only observation. For an entire year, doctors at New York University and UCLA Medical Centers could not get the *New England Journal of Medicine*—that "responsible . . . appropriate medical journal"—to publish their frightening observations. And, of course, during that year, that crucial first year, an epidemic that could have been controlled and contained got woefully out of hand. These "responsible . . . appropriate medical journals" have scarcely been better since. How dare you be so trusting and naive—you who are head of Gay Men's Health Crisis!

Why could you not applaud them? The ribavirin data is promising, as Dr. Mathilde Krim had the good sense to remark in the *Times*, "but not conclusive" (which no one is stating it is). From such encouragement can come swifter action at the FDA level, can come swifter and further tests, can come the release and availability of this drug to a wider market—can come all the things those who are dying so desperately pray for: PROGRESS.

But what does Auntie GMHC say and sound like? You sound like my old great-uncle Herschel—whom we loved very much, but who was nevertheless an unimaginative, whining, superior, dried-up old stuffed shirt, who was smelly and had been around too long. We used to call my great-uncle Herschel "the old fart."

I speak metaphorically of course, of the attitude that you represent and the philosophy GMHC has come to represent. I cannot for the life of me understand how the organization I helped to form has become such a bastion of conservatism and such a bureaucratic mess. The bigger you get, the more cowardly you become; the more money you receive, the more self satisfied you are. No longer do you fight for the living; you have become a funeral home. You and your huge assortment of caretakers perform miraculous talks helping the dying to die. I do not cast aspersions on these activities, but I ask you to realize how exceedingly negative this concentration of your energy is. Your words to *The New York Times* only confirm this negativism yet again.

I think it must now come as a big surprise to you and your Board of Directors that Gay Men's Health Crisis was not founded to help those who are ill. It was founded to protect the living, to help the living go on living, to help those who are still healthy to stay healthy, to help gay men stay alive. Mercifully, there are still far more of us who are yet alive. Patient Services were added almost as an afterthought. I do not deny the importance of some of these services, though in most cases think it inappropriate for you to be providing them. (More on this below.) GMHC was founded to utilize any strength it might be fortunate enough to acquire along the way: to bargain with, to fight with, to negotiate with—to use this strength to confront our enemies, to *make* them help us. This is what political strength is all about. It is *all*.

In this city, our enemies include our mayor and our Department of Health. In this country, our enemies include our President, our Department of Health and Human Services, the Hitlerian Centers for Disease Control, the US Food and Drug Administration, the Public Health Service, and the self-satisfied, iron-fisted, controlling, scientific frankensteinian monsters who are in charge of research at the National Institutes of Health and who, with their stranglehold grip of death, prevent any research or thinking that does not coincide with the games their narrow minds are playing. If, after six years of this epidemic and the years you have been in charge at GMHC, you can view any of these entities or personages as anything other than our enemies, then you are perversely unsuited for your job and should be replaced immediately.

These are a lot of enemies. It would appear to represent the entire "Outside World." I did not believe in 1981 that by 1987 I would sound paranoid; I consider myself to be blessed with hard-nosed, cold sanity, which becomes more objective and realistic day by day.

Most of GMHC's efforts are devoted to providing services the city should be providing and would probably be forced to provide if GMHC were not in existence. This is not to say you are not providing them better than the city would; you are, but in taking our money, you are, in essence, asking us to pay twice for what you are doing—once in our contributions to you, and once in our taxes to this city. Thus you should be providing for us additional services our city will never provide—gay services, gay leadership. You don't. You have become simply another city social service agency, and at the rate one hears about your inner squabbling, the rapidly declining quality of the staff you are hiring, and the increasing unhappiness of those who work for you, it will not be long before you are indistinguishable from any of the city departments—Health, Police, Parking Violations—that serve our city so tepidly.

1. AIDS patients in New York still receive care far inferior to that in San Francisco, Los Angeles, Houston, Boston, and Paris (to name only a few cities that come to mind). I would not like to get sick with AIDS in New York and be forced to deal with the lack of decent treatment facilities, particularly if I had no adequate health insurance. How have you let this happen? First rate health care should be your highest priority. Houston has an entire new and gleaming hospital dedicated solely to AIDS patients. San Francisco, from the very beginning, had entire divisions of hospitals put aside for us. How dare you, your executive staff, and your Board not be the leaders in fighting for these decent treatment centers?

The mayor has seen to it that GMHC has been given just enough money to shut you up. But in buying your silence, this city has lost: coordinated AIDS care, decent hospital care, home care, housing, systematic public education programs, extensive risk-reduction education programs. Through no fault of your own, you are actually perpetuating misery.

2. Your role in demanding better city education has been lackluster at best. You may congratulate yourselves on the many brochures and pamphlets you have distributed, but as you well know, this is like throwing crumbs to only the few hungry birds. Why have you not

pressured government, city, state, and federal, to educate more widely? It is appalling that, consistently, year after year, this is overlooked. And it is fully in your province to expedite it. The governments of England, France, Germany, and Norway are mailing to EVERY SINGLE PERSON IN THOSE COUNTRIES full educational information, pamphlets with specific do's and don'ts. It is simply puerile and futile to believe that you can educate an entire city and an entire world yourselves with pamphlets and brochures. You can't. It is a gigantic and enormous task. That you do not fight for the education of everyone is a shocking waste of both your energies and an ignoble denial of your charter. How dare you?

3. And just who is it you are attempting to educate? You seem to go at it in such scattershot fashion. You are given a great deal of money to educate everyone, but you overlook with amazing aplomb the vast majority of women, blacks, outer-borough and inner-city residents, children—almost everyone except gay men. It is hard to defend you against charges of racism and sexism. If you are going to cater mainly to gay, white, middle-class males, then you should say so and accept only a percentage of your city and state grants. (Your recent sad and sorry attempt to provide an educational forum for women was a total embarrassment from beginning to end. Much of the best AIDS work in this city and country has been developed by women. Why were so many of them actually forbidden input?)

4. Why have you not been in the forefront of demanding the immediate availability of drugs on a "compassionate usage" basis to those who are in the throes of dying anyway? Even putting aside the (I think untenable) notion that false hope is being provided, the availability of these drugs could provide invaluable efficacy tests. I know few PWA's who are not begging somehow to be on some kind of drug protocol somewhere, anywhere, but who are turned away at every door. How dare you not use your strength and muscle to further these ends? Why, in fact, are you not fighting for those who would administer drug trials? There are now many treatment modalities that are promising. You continue to pooh-pooh them all—a negativism beyond comprehension to those of us who have seen so many die. You possess the biggest captive pool of people with AIDS in the world. Such studies would be far more valuable than most of the studies you *do*. Why was it left to Dr. Mathilde Krim to crusade courageously for the release of AZT? How dare you not have supported her in this cause? And where are you now, when the government and Burroughs Wellcome have gone back on their word to release the drug widely, embarrassing Dr. Krim, who had been promised more than she was given? Why is it that whenever there is a fight for something substantive and controversial (in an epidemic where *everything* is controversial), GMHC is rarely to be heard?

Why aren't you pioneering the availability and use of antivirals as prophylactic treatment for those now carrying the virus? There is enough medical evidence that this will prove helpful, and each day that a virus carrier goes unattended is a day his T-cells can be declining. Studies in this area are desperately important—truly life-saving evidence may lie in their results, but they are overlooked and ignored by the NIH, by the CDC, by the FDA, and hence by hospitals and pharmaceutical companies who don't wish to finance them themselves. How can you be so retrograde and inhumane in this most important field?

And why isn't GMHC providing drugs that are unavailable, actually selling them to the needy at cost? Why must sufferers fly to San Diego, rent a car, drive to Mexico, and sneak drugs back over the border like common criminals, at a cost in money and energy they can ill afford? Ribavirin once cost three dollars for a box of twelve in Mexico; now it costs thirty dollars a box. It will undoubtedly increase now that Mexico knows its true value. Compassionate doctors in Texas and elsewhere are now buying the drug directly from the manufacturer at cost, picking it up in Mexico, and selling it to their patients at cost. Why aren't you providing services like this? So what if this is circumventing the law? A lawsuit brought by the government against you would be the best thing that could happen to underline the horror of how the FDA is attending to AIDS. When *People* magazine ran a story on the one courageous New York gay doctor, Dr. Barry Gingell, who brought back ribavirin from Mexico illegally, the FDA was roundly criticized. Confrontation helps! Why are you such sissies!

It is now reported that AZT is going to cost each patient $10,000 a year when it becomes available. What are you doing to confront this abhorrent future in which few patients will be able to afford the very drug that might save them?

How dare you ignore issues like these? These are the things you should be doing.

5. Why do you not ride hard on Research—leaving it to others—like the *Native*—to cry out in alarm when obvious false trials are championed and legitimate avenues are ignored? Why have you not pushed for an Office of AIDS Coordination in Washington? Where is the systematic Master Plan promised by Dr. Edward Brandt years ago, when he was head of the Department of Health and Human Services, and promised as well by Reagan, Cuomo, and Koch? How can you be so infernally silent on this top priority?

6. Why are you spending so much of your time, energy, and money on these interminable "Safe Sex" pageants? I find it ironic to find myself asking this. My initial fights with the GMHC Board, which resulted in my being brutally exiled from your organization, had to do with my insistence, and your refusal, to say anything about sex at all. Now you appear to have gone to the other extreme—as if GMHC were a sort of sex clinic to compete with Masters and Johnson and the hateful Dr. Helen Singer Kaplan.

It simply isn't cost-effective to teach eight hundred men how to play with their pee-pees when millions infected are playing with theirs.

7. What has happened to your presence in Washington? There once was a network of AIDS organizations—of which GMHC was and is the richest and most powerful—that hired a lonely lobbyist—though you could afford many more. He's gone, and I hear nothing about his solitary replacement. Of all the areas that demand your strong attention and support, and our money, at the very top of the list is the necessity of establishing a power base in Washington. I have said time and again until I am blue in the face that it is appalling that some 254 million men and women have no lobbying presence in Washington to speak of. How do we expect to achieve anything at all? The smallest unions, the tiniest of organizations, have staffs of lobbyists, and that is how small-interest groups, minorities, accomplish things. That is how the National Rifle Association is so powerful and achieves results that are anathema to so many. They organize and fight and lobby. They let Washington know they are there. You have the money for this. How dare you not use it?

Again I state what may come as a surprise to you, your Board, and readers, that GMHC WAS FOUNDED TO FIGHT. How dare you not have some sort of political wing, some sort of spin-off that would see to it that lobbying is done by experienced hands? (Three years ago GMHC Board member Bob Diario was supposed to be preparing such a plan. What happened to it? Why is it taking so long?) Every successful charity works this way, finds legal ways to fight, pressure, lobby. You cannot tell me that the Catholic church is not one of the most politically savvy organizations around, as is the Salvation Army, the American Cancer Society, Sloan-Kettering, you name it. Hiding behind a tax-exempt status (your constant excuse for being so cowardly every time you have to stand up and be counted on any controversial issue—in an epidemic where just about everything is controversial!) is simply no longer tolerable. Cardinal O' Connor's got one of the biggest mouths around. And he uses it. Just like Ed Koch. Where's your big mouth? If you haven't got one—get one! How can you justify having sixty case workers on staff and not one lobbyist?

8. Since I left GMHC, your image, your sense of public relations savvy, your visibility, to put it impolitely, sucks.

There is not a better way to increase your power than through press visibility. Article after article appears, and there is no mention of GMHC. Story after story, and no longer is it centered, as it should be, on GMHC. Human-interest stories must be created by talented and imaginative public-relations people and press coordinators and planted in the media. It is not a job for one person; it is a job for a number of people. The papers should have GMHC in every single AIDS story, every single day. That is how you become stronger; that is how you get more money from donations and from grants and foundations; that is how you gain respect and acquire the power necessary to negotiate. That is how you make the mayor provide adequate treatment for everyone in this city. That is how you get the release of drugs to dying patients. That is how you get educational materials provided to everyone, in the mail, on TV. That is how you get TV stations to broadcast condom ads. How dare you not use adult methods to run an adult organization? How dare you not use the rudimentary tools of modern communications to bolster the power you have inherently been handed by the gay community, your constituents. In the past months there has been another burst of AIDS media attention, with many cover stories, many TV documentaries. In former times, GMHC was front and center. I am saddened to see how rarely you are even mentioned now.

You have more than enough money to hire these people. I don't think it's an accident that your public profile has declined. I think this comes from specific Board instructions. It is an appalling choice.

9. Yes, GMHC was founded to fight, to spread information to gay men, and to fight for them. It was *not* founded, believe it or not, to provide Patient Services of any sort. This came later—and it has come to dominate you. It has provided you with the excuse to be cowards. It has provided you with a cover so that you can say, anytime something controversial requires attention: "We are too busy taking care of patients."

The time has come to rethink this devotion. As cases increase so horrendously day by day, there is no way on this earth that you can continue to provide Patient Services to the whole world. Already the quality of that service you are providing is suffering—how could it be otherwise? Soon you will drown and be totally useless.

If you were the fighting organization, negotiating from the strength that our numbers and our contributions have provided you with, you would use these numbers, this strength, this money to force the system to provide these services. It is no mystery why San Francisco has services paid for by the city. GMHC was founded to fight for these services. Instead, like some hurt little boy, it has cowered in fear, avoided the fight to get them, and decided that "we'll take care of our own, ourselves." Well, now there are too many to take care of, and you must demand help.

It is no secret that the gay community in New York is not strong. The gay community in New York is invisible and weak. The gay community in New York is, I believe, in the worst shape it has ever been in politically for as long as I have been in New York, ironically just as the Gay Rights Bill has finally passed.

Since we appear to be a community that is incapable of organizing itself with strength, cohesion, unity, or networking, but only one that is capable of dealing with each other in combat, backbiting, and mistrust (I am no exception to this), the services GMHC was founded to provide are more essential than ever. You have had millions of our dollars. You have a mailing list of over sixty thousand—by far the largest mailing list any gay organization has ever had.

You are the strongest organization we have, and our only hope.

Numbers and dollars equal power. How are you able, day by day, week by week, month by month, year by year, to deny this power, to ignore the fact that you have it, and to continually hide from it, as a sissy runs away from a fight? I have in the recent past referred in print to your Board of Directors as "a bunch of nerds." Any issue that is remotely controversial is certain to be turned away from your Board's table. I am ashamed of the whole lot of you. I did not spend two years of my life fighting for your birth to see you turn into a bunch of cowards. I did not spend two years of my life fighting to establish Gay Men's Health Crisis to see it turn into the organization it now is.

Get off your fucking self-satisfied asses and fight! That is what you were put there for! That is what people give you money for!

10. You continue to deny the political realities of this epidemic. THERE IS NOTHING IN THIS WHOLE AIDS MESS THAT IS NOT POLITICAL! How can you continue to deny this fact and assert that your role must remain unpolitical?

You have shut out every dissenting voice. You have effectively cut yourselves off from much of the gay community. If anyone doesn't agree with you, he or she is ignored. The list of your victims is endless—strong voices that, were they a part of your organization, would give you more strength and additional power. Because you would not harbor them, splinter groups were forced to take their issues and start their own homes—a splintering that only weakens, only makes everyone less strong. AIDS Resource Center, the PWA Coalition, AmFar, the once powerful and most useful AIDS Network (so sadly missed, now more necessary than ever as you continue to shilly-shally)—these and innumerable individuals are unwelcome at GMHC. Year after year, I wonder when someone up there will be man enough to offer peace—will try to heal the wounds—if only in the name of efficacy.

11. The world needs to know who dies from AIDS. This is essential if we are to underline the horror of what is happening. When Perry Ellis, Roy Cohn, Terry Dolan dies from AIDS, we must not allow this to be hidden or denied. (In the case of Perry Ellis, not only should we not allow the conglomerate that controls his company to put out lies to the press, but we should encourage a boycott of Perry Ellis products to rebel against the shame of their acts, just as we should not fly Delta Airlines now that it has ruled that a gay man's life is not as valuable as a straight man's.)

Why are you not fighting constantly with the Obituary Department of *The New York Times* to see that AIDS is listed as the cause of death, when it is? (The *Washington Post* reported Terry Dolan's death as from AIDS, as did *Newsweek*; the *Times* and *Time* magazine were the liars. Why did you not set the record straight?) And to insist that lovers be identified as lovers—not as one of the battery of stupid euphemisms they come up with. It has been proved that the *Times* will eventually respond to pressure. You are never there to pressure. Every time you keep your mouth shut, you tacitly claim the shame.

12. GMHC is what its Board of Directors wants it to be. Therefore, if any major changes are to be made, they will have to emanate from that holy table.

But GMHC has also placed itself in thrall to forces other than its Board. Somewhere along the line, the organization was completely taken over by Professional Custodians—social workers, psychologists, psychiatrists, therapists, teachers—all of whom have vested interests in the Sick, in the Dying, in establishing and perpetuating the Funereal. You help people to the grave, to face death. GMHC was founded to fight for life. But the fighters have been shut out, banished, as I have outlined above. Why is it not possible to do both!

Now—what can we do?

1. The fighters must be allowed to return. A branch of GMHC devoted to political fighting, to advocacy (if you must find a nice word to satisfy your tax-exemption excuses), must be established immediately and money poured into it. Your mailing list must be used for fighting. Congresspersons respond to the number of letters they receive, as do mayors. Your volunteers must be utilized for their outreach activities. They, too, must cease hiding behind their nurses' pinafores.

Professor Philip Kayal has done excellent research that has uncovered the fact that your volunteers identify their motives in working for you as more humanitarian than political. They must be made to realize that these two are intertwined, that we will have no future for them to be humanitarians in if they are not political. You have more volunteers than any gay organization has ever had. You have so many you cannot process them efficiently. Many are turned away because they do not have social service or welfare skills. You would have hundreds upon hundreds more if there was an arm of GMHC that allowed for advocates and their tactics. How dare you delay this any longer?

2. You must commence a complete rethinking of your goals and cease in your futile attempts to be *THE* AIDS SERVICE AND EDUCATION FOUNDATION. You are uncomfortable providing services to anyone other than gay men; perhaps you should concentrate your services just upon gay men. You have become weaker mainly as you have tried to take care of everyone. The addict population is the fastest-growing AIDS category, and you are simply out to lunch in this area. There is nothing wrong in becoming a special-interest group. Indeed, that is what you were first established to be.

3. Weed out the wimps on your Board of Directors and among your staff. Replace them with fighters, with men and women who are unafraid, who have connections in high places they are not afraid to use. I am constantly appalled that at least two members of your Board are on close personal terms with the mayor, and that this has produced absolutely zilch in tangible results for GMHC.

4. Begin the healing process. Draw back to yourselves the splinter AIDS organizations dealing with gay men. Draw back to yourselves the many in our community that you have alienated and exiled. Educate your staff on the history of GMHC, who founded it and what they fought for and went through to make it the organization you inherited.

5. I call upon your hundreds of volunteers to mobilize and discuss what I am writing about. I hear so many stories of volunteer discontent. Now is your chance to make your voices heard. You are, in essence, GMHC's slaves—the oil for the Board's machinery—you do what they allow you to do. But, as with all forms of slavery, the masters could not exist without you.

6. As for everyone reading this:

We are all exceptionally tired. We are all AIDSed out. In our exhaustion we allow the tendency to Let Someone Else Do It. In our exhaustion we foster our continued ignorance: We don't keep up with what is going on; we don't want to know. We should read the *Native*; we should read every article on AIDS. In this ignorance and exhaustion is our destruction. There is no one to do anything but ourselves, each individual one of us. If the Board of GMHC has been cowardly, we have allowed it to become so. If GMHC is on the wrong course, we have allowed it to drift. If Reagan has not uttered the word AIDS, we have abetted this. We have given much money to GMHC with the hope that they would leave us alone, with the notion They Would Take Care of Everything for Us. But it does not work that way. Yes, they need our money, and will need it now more than ever. But they also need to be told you agree with what I am writing about.

To sum up:

GMHC cannot hope to provide Patient Services for the dying at the rate they are dying, or preventive education for the potentially infected at the rate they are becoming infected. The only way to force the system to provide these services across the board is by political pressure.

Our only salvation lies in aggressive scientific research. This will come only from political pressure. Every dime for research that we've had has come only from hard political fighting.

Thus all our solutions can only be achieved through political action. All the kindness in the world will not stem this epidemic. Only political action can change the course of events.

I challenge you and your Board to lead us. I challenge you and your Board to initiate the process that will bring about your metamorphosis into the organization that will fight for us in all the areas I have outlined above. It is a major challenge and I fear for our continued survival if you fail and we let you fail. GMHC is the only organization strong enough and rich enough and potentially powerful enough. There is no one else. You can no longer shirk your responsibilities, and we cannot let you. I pray that all those reading this will register their support either by writing to the *Native* or to Richard Dunne. I pray that many will agree, that you will not remain silent. I pray that GMHC will respond to this challenge. I am prepared to sit down so that jointly a list of community leaders can be formulated and agenda drawn so that we can once again attempt to form a united stand against this horrific threat.

The worst years of the AIDS pandemic lie ahead of us. We are woefully unprepared. There are millions of us yet to die. Please etch this thought on your consciousness: THERE ARE MILLIONS OF US YET TO DIE. Three out of four AIDS cases are still occurring in gay men. Many millions of people carry the virus. Three out of four AIDS cases are gay men. THERE ARE MILLIONS OF US YET TO DIE.

THE BEGINNING OF ACTING UP
(1987)

Larry Kramer

On March 14th, 1983, almost four years ago to this date, I wrote an article in the *New York Native.* There were at that time 1,112 cases of AIDS nationwide. My article was entitled "1,112 and Counting," and through the courtesy of *Native* publisher Chuck Ortleb, it was reprinted in seventeen additional gay newspapers across the country. Here are a few of the opening sentences from this article:

"If this article doesn't scare the shit out of you, we're in real trouble. If this article doesn't rouse you to anger, fury, rage, and action, gay men may have no future on this earth. Our continued existence depends on just how angry you can get. . . . I repeat: Our continued existence as gay men upon the face of this earth is at stake. Unless we fight for our lives, we shall die. In all the history of homosexuality we have never before been so close to death and extinction."

When I wrote that, four years ago, there were 1,112 cases of AIDS nationwide. There are now officially—and we all know how officials count—32,000 with 10,000 of these in New York.

We have not yet even begun to live through the true horror. As it has been explained to me, the people who have become ill so far got ill early; the average incubation period is now thought to be five and one-half years, and the real tidal wave is yet to come: people who got infected starting in 1981. You had sex in 1981. I did, too. And after.

Last week, I had seven friends who were diagnosed. In one week. That's the most in the shortest period that's happened to me.

I would like everyone from this right-hand side aisle, all the way to the left-hand side of the room—would you stand up for a minute, please? [They do so.] At the rate we are going, you could be dead in less than five years. Two-thirds of this room could be dead in less than five years. Please sit down.

Let me rephrase my *Native* article of 1983. If my speech tonight doesn't scare the shit out of you, we're in real trouble. If what you're hearing doesn't rouse you to anger, fury, rage, and action, gay men will have no future here on earth. How long does it take before you get angry and fight back?

I sometimes think we have a death wish. I think we must want to die. I have never been able to understand why for six long years we have sat back and let ourselves literally be knocked off man by man-without fighting back. I have heard of denial, but this is more than denial; it *is* a death wish.

I don't want to die. I cannot believe that you *want* to die.

But what are we doing, *really*, to save our own lives?

Two-thirds of you—I should say of *us,* because I am in this, too—could be dead within five years. Two-thirds of this room could be dead within five years.

What does it take for us to take responsibility for our own lives? Because we are *not*—we are not taking responsibility for our own lives.

I want to talk about a few specific things.

I've just come back from Houston. My play *The Normal Heart* was done at the Alley Theatre, there. I did not want to go to see it, but a very insistent woman who works with AIDS patients there would not take no for an answer. Thus I had the opportunity and the great privilege to visit our country's first AIDS hospital, which is called the Institute for Immunological Disorders. I've finally discovered the place I want to go if I get sick.

You know how the topic of conversation in New York always turns to: Where would you go if you got sick? What hospital? Which doctor? Quite frankly, I don't want to go to *any* hospital in New York. And I don't want to go to most of the doctors. They pooh-pooh everything new that comes along; they don't know anything about any new drug or treatment. They don't want to know. They throw you into the hospital, give you a grotesquely expensive workup, pump you full of some drug that they've heard about from another doctor, and your insurance company pays for it, if you're lucky enough to have insurance. These doctors won't fight for anything, they won't go up against the FDA, they don't want to hear about any theories or ideas. Why are they always so negative about everything? These doctors are making a fucking fortune out of us. They ridicule anything new that comes along, without trying it. The horror stories emanating from almost every hospital in this city, with the possible exception of NYU, are grotesque—all the way from an attempted murder of an AIDS patient at a New York hospital to a friend of mine who lay in the emergency room at St. Vincent's for seventeen hours just last week, before anyone looked at him. No, I don't want to go to any hospital or any doctor in New York.

The Institute for Immunological Disorders is run by Peter Mansell, who is one of the top AIDS doctors in America. It has space for 150 patients. There are only sixteen patients there. This most wonderful AIDS hospital in the world—you probably don't even know about it; some of you are hearing about it for the first time. How can it happen that it only has sixteen patients? Only in America.

I'm going to tell you—it's not explicitly germane to us, but it is interesting—Texas is the only state in this country where if you don't have insurance, where if you're indigent, the state will not reimburse you or a hospital for the cost of your care. Most of those with AIDS in Houston don't have insurance. They can't afford to go to Dr. Mansell's hospital. Dr. Mansell treats 150 patients every week, as outpatients, free. Dr. Mansell's hospital, which is owned by a for-profit corporation, is losing a great deal of money. This hospital must not be allowed to die.

Dr. Mansell has found out some very interesting things. He has found out that 90 percent of all AIDS problems are better treated at home, and this includes home treatment for PCP. He has found that he can treat patients for two-thirds less than it costs anywhere else—an average of $11,000 vs. $33,000. He has found that the average length of hospital stay of his patients is ten days, versus thirty days anywhere else. The hitch, of course, is that no insurance policy covers outpatient care. The very insurance companies that are threatening to take away our insurance because we cost them too much won't pay for cheaper treatment. That doesn't make much sense, does it?

But the real horror stories that Dr. Mansell told me have to do with drugs and the FDA. Dr. Mansell has five drugs waiting to be tested. I never heard of four of them. He tells me that each has been shown to prove as promising as AZT was when it was approved. Each has passed what are called Phase One Safety Trials, which show them to lack noticeable side effects. The drugs are called Ampligen, Glucan, DTC, AS 101, and MTP-PE (for KS). He cannot get near the FDA. When one of the top AIDS doctors in the United States can't get protocols through the FDA, we're in big trouble. He showed me the protocols that he submits, and he showed me how they're sent back—the FDA asking for one sentence rewritten, three words revised—nothing substantial—each change causing a delay of six to eight months. Ampligen is a drug that has been around for a long time. Concerned citizens of Houston have formed a foundation and bought $250,000 worth of Ampligen, so neither the hospital nor the government had to pay for it—and the drug remains unused and untested because of FDA quibbling.

You know—each step of this horror story that we live through, we come up against an even bigger brick wall. First it was the city, then the state, then the CDC, then the NIH. Now it's the FDA. Ann Fettner wrote last week in the *Village Voice* about the FDA: "It is a bureaucratic mess, they aren't even computerized, things 'are likely to get stuck in the mailroom,' says Duke University economist Henry Grabowski—which means that much of our pharmaceutical talent diddles with refinements of approved drugs while many that are desperately needed are put on hold." A new drug can easily take ten years to satisfy FDA approval. Ten years! Two-thirds of us could be dead in less than five years.

In 1980 the then head of the FDA said, "Ribavirin is probably the most important product discovered during the intensive search for antiviral agents." It's 1987 and we still can't get it. Fettner says, "It's astonishing that ribavirin wasn't chosen before AZT." Leading researchers I have talked to explain this one way: The FDA doesn't like the difficult, obstreperous head of ICN Pharmaceuticals, which manufactures ribavirin, while Burroughs Wellcome, which makes AZT, is smooth, polite, savvy, with strong PR people. The fast introduction of AZT was described to me in one word by a leading doctor: "Greed." He thinks little of AZT, refers to it as "Yesterday's drug, that Burroughs Wellcome is trying to make their fortune out of before it's too late. I have too many patients on it, who are becoming transfusion-dependent." I have a few friends who seem to be doing well on it. I have some who aren't. It's certainly not our savior.

AL 721 isn't even a drug—it's a food! How dare the FDA refuse to get it into fast circulation when it has proved promising in Israel at their famous Weizmann Institute? Indeed, Praxis Pharmaceuticals, which holds the American rights to it, could put it out as a food; but they apparently are gambling for big bucks by waiting for FDA approval to put it out as a drug, which is going to take forever, because Praxis doesn't appear to have much experience in putting out drugs at all. Rumor has it, also, that Praxis has forbidden the Weizmann Institute and Israeli doctors from giving AL 721 to any non-Israelis who go to Israel to get it.

What's going on here? To quote Dr. Mansell: "The FDA makes me froth at the mouth." We have reached a brick wall. There is a fortune being tossed at AIDS, but it's not buying anything. To quote Dr. Mansell: "A lot of money, a lot of energy—and very little to show for it." He runs one of the NIH-designated AIDS treatment centers and he has a hospital with sixteen patients! And we have ten thousand cases in New York City. He has an empty hospital, and he is one of the smartest men in this epidemic. How can this country be so wasteful!

Another researcher: "The NIH is too slow and too determined to maintain central control. It is hugely bureaucratic, much like your own GMHC and other AIDS organizations have become." Not my words. Dr. Mansell again: "Many of the drugs that the NIH is testing have already proved useless and ineffective somewhere else. Why do they insist on testing them? Why do they refuse to test any of these new drugs that are brought to their attention?"

Let's talk about double-blind studies that we're forced to endure. Did you know that double-blind studies were not created originally for terminal illnesses? I never knew that. Did you know that? How dare they, then, make us endure double-blind studies? They are ludicrously inhumane when two-thirds of this room could be dead in less than five years.

Double-blind studies are also exceptionally foolish, because PWAs lie to get the drugs. I'd lie. Wouldn't you? If they told me what to say to get a promising treatment, I'd say it, whether it was true or not. I have friends who have forged their medical records, who have gone to medical libraries to learn the correct terminology to fill in the blanks. So all the results from all these double-blind studies aren't going to tell anyone a thing. We're willing to be guinea pigs, all of us. Give us the fucking drugs! Especially if Dr. Mansell has five drugs that he says may have fewer side effects than AZT.

Almost one billion dollars will be thrown at AIDS, and it's not buying anything that will save two-thirds of the people in this room. I just heard about a college on Long Island that's been awarded a $600,000 grant from the Centers for Disease Control—an organization I have come to loathe—to study AIDS stress on college students. I can tell them right now and save the government $600,000. I know what it's like to be stressed. So do you.

I called up the offices of our elected officials and asked them to send someone here tonight. Cuomo, D'Amato, Moynihan, Koch. Every single one of them treated me as if I was ungrateful. "We have been on the front line of getting you your money," each one of them said. "Leave us alone. You got your money. What else do you want?" That was from Moynihan's office: "What else do you want? We got you your money." When I try to tell them that this money isn't working right, isn't buying us anything, isn't properly supervised—once again, they don't want to know. I find the offices of Moynihan and D'Amato particularly insensitive to gay issues. Our only friend in Congress, and he's getting real tired, is Ted Weiss. And, of course, from Los Angeles, Henry Waxman.

So what are we going to do? Time and time again I have said—no one is going to do it for us but ourselves.

We have always been a particularly divisive community. We fight with each other too much, we're disorganized, we simply cannot get together. We've all insulted each other. I'm as much at fault in this as anyone.

I came back from Houston and I called people I haven't spoken to in many years. I called Paul Popham. Those of you who are familiar with the history of GMHC and with *The Normal Heart* will know of the fights that he and I had and the estrangement of what had once been an exceptionally close friendship. Paul is very ill now. He and I spoke for over an hour. It was as if it were the early days GMHC again, and we were planning strategy of what had to be done. We talked not about the hurts that each had caused the other. He supported me in everything that I am saying to you tonight, and that I have been writing about in the *Native* in recent issues. He would be here tonight, except that he had chemotherapy today. He asked me to say some things to you. "Tell them we have to make gay people all over the country cooperate. Tell them we have to establish some way to cut through all the red tape. We have to find a way to make GMHC, the AIDS Action Council, and the other AIDS organizations stronger and more political."

We talked a lot about GMHC, the organization that represents so much of our joint lives. As you know, I have been very critical of GMHC recently, and wrote a rather stinging attack on them. Paul and I both feel that GMHC is the only AIDS game in town in this country, and, like it or not, they have to be made to act stronger in the areas of lobbying and advocacy. There are no other organizations with as much clout, with as much money, with as much staff. San Francisco's AIDS organizations still have not even put their pledged contributions into the AIDS Action Council, our joint lobbying effort in Washington, which is an appalling act on the part of San Francisco's gay community. "We have to shame them into their contributions," Paul said.

The people administering GMHC are running what amounts to a big corporation. We cannot fault them for running such a sound ship, such a fiscally sound ship.

But we desperately need leadership in this crisis. We desperately need a central voice and a central organization to which everything else can plug in and be coordinated through. There isn't anyone else. And in this area of centralized leadership, of vision, of seeing the larger picture and acting upon it, GMHC is tragically weak. It seems to have lost the sense of mission and urgency upon which it was founded—which Paul and I fought so hard to give it.

In my recent article attacking them, I asked GMHC for very specific things: lobbying; an advocacy division; more public-relations people to get the word out; a change of their tax-exempt status to allow for increased political activities; fighting for drugs; more strong members put on their Board. I was promised everything. I couldn't believe it; it was too good to be true.

Two months later, precious little has been done. The tax-exempt status has been changed. A lobbyist has been identified for Albany. A *part-time* PR person is about to be hired. When I asked why they were not hiring a full-time PR person, six full-time PR persons, the excuse I was given was "We don't have a desk." Two-thirds of us are going to be dead in five years, and this rich organization is not hiring people to get the work out because they haven't got room for a desk. [Cries from the audience of "Shame, shame!"]

No advocacy plan has emerged from GMHC, despite the fact that we have been promised one for six months. Paul Popham himself told me that the "Mission Statement" that was prepared by GMHC's executives is one that he never would have accepted when he was president of the Board.

Today's front page of *The New York Times* has an article about two thousand Catholics marching through the halls of Albany today. On the front page of the *Times*. With their six bishops (including one whom we know to be gay). Two thousand Catholics and their bishops marching through the halls of government. That's advocacy! That's what GMHC has to plan and facilitate and encourage. That's what all of us have to do. Southern Methodist University gets on national television protesting something about their football team. Black people marched on Mayor Koch's apartment only days after Howard Beach. Why are we so invisible, constantly and forever! What does it take to get a few thousand people to stage a march!

Did you notice what got the most attention at the recent CDC conference in Atlanta? It was a bunch called the Lavender Hill Mob. The got more attention than anything else at the meeting. They protested. They yelled and screamed and demanded and were blissfully rude to all those arrogant epidemiologists who are ruining our lives.

We can no longer afford to operate in separate and individual cocoons. There cannot be a Lavender Hill Mob protesting without a GLAAD mobilizing the media, without a National Gay and Lesbian Task Force and AIDS Action Council lobbying in Washington, without a Human Rights Campaign Fund raising money, and without GMHC and its leaders leading us. That's coordination. Without every organization working together, networking, we will get nowhere.

We must immediately rethink the structure of our community, and that is why I have invited you here tonight: to seek your input and advice, in the hope that we can come out of tonight with some definite and active ideas. Do we want to reactivate the old AIDS Network? Do we want to start a new organization devoted solely to political action?

I want to talk to you about power. We are all in awe of power, of those who have it, and we always bemoan the fact that we don't have it. Power is little pieces of paper on the floor. No one picks them up. Ten people walk by and no one picks up the piece of paper on the floor. The eleventh person walks by and is tired of looking at it, and so he bends down and picks it up. The next day he does the same thing. And soon he's in charge of picking up the paper. And he's got a lot of pieces of paper that he's picked up. Now—think of those pieces of paper as standing for responsibility. This man or woman who is picking up the pieces of paper is, by being responsible, acquiring more and more power. He doesn't necessarily want it, but he's tired of seeing the floor littered. All power is the willingness to accept responsibility. But we live in a city and a country where no one is willing to pick up pieces of paper. Where no one wants any responsibility.

It's easy to criticize GMHC. It's easier to criticize, period. It's harder to do things. Everyone of us here is capable of doing something. Of doing something strong. We have to go after the FDA—fast. That means coordinated protest, pickets, arrest. Are you ashamed to be arrested? I would like to acknowledge one of the most courageous men in this country, who is with us here tonight. He is so concerned about the proliferation of nuclear weapons that he gets arrested at the expense of his own career. He uses his name and his fame to help make this world a better place. Martin Sheen. Stand up, Martin. The best man at Martin's wedding, his oldest friend, died today, from AIDS.

Look at this article from the *San Francisco Chronicle*, written by openly gay journalist Randy Shilts (just about the only reporter and the only newspaper in this entire country covering AIDS with proper thoroughness and compassion). Look who is our friend: the Surgeon General, C. Everett Koop. A fundamentalist is our friend. Koop said, "We have to embarrass the administration into bringing the resources that are necessary to deal with this epidemic forcefully." He said a meeting has been arranged with the President several times, and several times this meeting has been canceled. His own Surgeon General is telling us that we have to embarrass the President to get some attention to AIDS. Why didn't any other paper across this country pick up this story? You sure didn't see it in *The New York Times.*

It's our fault, boys and girls. It's our fault. Two thousand Catholics can walk through the corridors of Albany. The American Foundation for AIDS Research has on its board Elizabeth Taylor, Warren Beatty, Leonard Bernstein, Woody Allen, Barbra Streisand, Michael Sovern (the president of Columbia University) a veritable *Who's Who*; why can't they get a meeting with the President—their former acting buddy? Why don't we think like that?

Well, until we all bend over and pick up all those little pieces of paper, I don't have to tell you what's going to happen.

TREATMENT ACTIVISM

Although ACT UP was founded by PWAs, HIV-positives, their advocates, and gays and lesbians to agitate for the development of drug therapies and treatment regimens, it was founded primarily as a new organization devoted solely to political action. During the mid-nineteen eighties, a treatment activist movement emerged focusing both on making experimental drugs, such as AZT, available to PWAs on a "compassionate use" basis while being tested to achieve government approval, and once approved for sale, on keeping drugs from being prohibitively expensive for PWAs. Since 1985, a new organization had been growing in San Francisco called Project Inform. Led by Martin Delaney and Joseph Brewer, its mission, as quoted in *The Advocate* in 1988, was three-fold. First, it aimed at "educating people on the need for early diagnosis and treatment . . . HIV infection is a manageable chronic illness if it's diagnosed and treated early enough." This includes the mandate to advocate learning your HIV antibody status through antibody testing; in San Francisco, Project Inform was the first gay group to advocate this. This mandate was reflected in a fundraising appeal sent out by the group in early 1989; on the outside of the envelope an imperative to govern much future treatment activism elliptically and succinctly was announced: "There are two ways to find out—1) Get tested, or 2) Get sick. Project Inform's second mission was "getting out information on the best-proven treatments in simple, easy-to-understand language;" to do so, a toll-free telephone hot line was opened. Third was political activism around studying, testing, and gaining access to treatments. In relation to the federal government, Delaney said: They persist in studying and testing drugs in precisely the same ways that they always have . . . that's fine in peacetime. In wartime you have doctors on the battlefield with a whole new set of guidelines [who], as a consequence, save far more lives than they would have if they were operating under peacetime rules. That's what has got to happen with AIDS: crash programs to test more drugs more quickly."

Here we present a document marking the beginning of what later came to be called "the cancerization of AIDS." Larry Kramer frames this development and the societal indifference within which it has occurred more warily, as "*managing* the crisis, turning the crisis into a condition, something that is a part of the way things are, something that happens like a flood or hurricanes or poverty—to be managed, thus creating new bureaucracies." The document here is an excerpt from an overall statement of this perspective by Martin Delaney within a framework of the belief that "the personal is the political."

We follow Delaney's article with excerpts from *Positively Healthy News* of London. While many groups at the time accepted the view that HIV is the causative agent in AIDS, Positively Healthy did not. This skepticism carries different implications for one's relationship to the medical profession and government regulatory bodies and for what treatments one deems appropriate, even though their goals are the same as Delaney's. This statement is from the first issue of *Positively Healthy News*, edited by Cass Mann, Stuart Marshall, and Andrew Christian, and funded by British gay rock singers Jimmy Somerville and Richard Coles.

STAYING ALIVE: MAKING THE ULTIMATE POLITICAL STATEMENT
NEW REASONS TO CONSIDER TAKING THE ANTIBODY TEST

from *The Advocate* (1989)

Martin Delaney

Entering into a conversation about HIV testing is certainly no one's idea of a good time. Our community is rapidly splitting into two divergent groups: those who have already taken the test and are acting on its implications and those who haven't and are sick of hearing about it. If this second group includes you, I urge you to keep on reading as if your life depended on it. It may.

Most of us have heard the arguments for and against testing ad nauseum. For every good reason to take the test, someone can raise a seemingly good reason not to. Even well-meaning AIDS service organizations have fueled the confusion with ads showing scales in balance — "on the one hand, and on the other hand" — leading many to conclude that testing is simply a matter of personal preference.

That just isn't so. Not anymore. There are profoundly important medical reasons why you must learn your antibody status as soon as possible: If you don't you may needlessly die. Two important facts lead to this conclusion:

1. The most common and most deadly killer with AIDS—*Pneumocystis carinii* pneumonia (PCP)—has become a controllable disease. People who are at short-term risk of getting this infection can now use safe, effective treatment to prevent it. The catch: They must first know they are at risk, a process that begins with taking the test. The alternative is to wait for the infection to announce itself and to deal with the consequences—including the AIDS diagnosis that comes with it.

2. There is a growing belief among many physicians, researchers, and patients that the best time to begin treating HIV infection is as soon as possible. There is considerable evidence that available medicine, when used early enough and properly, can dramatically slow or stall the progression of HIV infection towards AIDS, with fewer side effects than when such medicines are used later.

PCP prevention alone is a sufficient reason to warrant wide-scale voluntary and anonymous testing. Nearly 65% of all AIDS patients receive their diagnosis as a result of PCP, and an equal percentage die of it. Using available blood tests, physicians are finding it possible to predict who is in imminent danger of contracting PCP; using available medicine, physicians are finding it possible to prevent PCP.

The Second Closet

This is wonderful, hopeful news. But a great many people haven't heard it; they are still in the "second closet," hiding their HIV status from themselves and their doctors. Even some who have heard the news resist, arguing we do not know how many seropositives will get sick, so there is no point in stirring everyone up. On the contrary, we do know how many people will become sick *if left untreated*: most, if not all, of them. Although researchers disagree on the exact numbers, every long-term study points in the same upward direction, with virtually all the studies concluding that the majority of those infected are progressing toward illness, if not AIDS itself. One of the most often-cited studies has reported that 78% of HIV-infected people developed immune-related disorders within seven years after infection: roughly 35% with full AIDS, 42% with lesser symptoms. Other studies have suggested that it may take, on the average, 11 years to develop full AIDS. Although debate continues on the precise figures, only outright denial and very rosy glasses could lead HIV seropositives to expect a free pass.

The same studies state that the greatest rate of infection in "ground zero" communities—San Francisco, Los Angeles, and New York—occurred between 1978 and 1982. After that, safer sex and raised consciousness drove the rate of new infection drastically downward.

This has profound implications. Assuming an average infection point somewhere between 1978 and 1982, one can predict that 1989 through 1993 will be critical years: A great number of those walking around today in blissful ignorance of their HIV status are going to get sick.

There are only two ways to find out if this includes you: *Take the test*, voluntarily and anonymously; or *wait until you get sick*.

If you take the test, you can get the results on a day you choose, at a time when you have lined up the appropriate support and have obtained any needed information, and when you still have the best possible medical options in front of you.

If you learn by waiting for an opportunistic infection, you're likely to get the news by surprise, at a time when you least expect it, when you are unprepared to hear it, and when your future medical options may have already been diminished.

Far too many gay men continue to take the second option, usually acting on the assumption that they will have minor symptoms or warning signals before a serious infection like PCP sets in. Were it only the case. While some people do have symptoms, others go directly from seemingly good health to hospitalization with PCP, sometimes in as little as a month.

Predicting the short-term risk of PCP requires only a simple blood test, available from any doctor: the T cell subset test, which yields the T4 count, a number typically between zero and 1,500. While not a perfect predictor, the T4 count is far more accurate than playing wait and see. Information that will soon be released from a National Institutes of Health study concludes that, on the average, people risk coming down with PCP when their T4 count falls below 200. Thus, the T4 test tells when it is time to begin using preventive treatment against PCP. When such treatment is employed, PCP can be held at bay for many months or perhaps indefinitely.

Civil Liberties, Psychological Concerns

What, then, of the civil rights and psychological concerns about testing? Since these issues are raised so frequently elsewhere, I will only briefly mention them here. (Oddly enough, it is the medical argument in favor of testing that is underreported in the media.)

Civil liberties concerns demand that testing be *anonymous* (using a code number or at least not a real name) and *voluntary* (done freely at a time you choose). When a person waits for illness to announce the infection, civil rights concerns almost always go out the window, since in virtually all states an AIDS diagnosis must be reported.

The psychological concerns—that a positive test result could create emotional burdens or even drive someone to depression or suicide—are also real but sometimes overstated. Depression and suicide seem most likely when testing is not accompanied by proper support services. With help and after a week or two of confusion, righteous anger, and scrambling for information, most reasonably well-balanced people pick themselves up and get on with their lives.

The lack of any counseling services means that a person is in the wrong place to get tested.

Is testing, then, the right answer for everyone? Whatever the general recommendation, there will always be exceptions. People who are emotionally incompetent probably have little to gain from knowledge of their antibody status, although their doctors may have good reason to know. Someone in a temporarily fragile emotional state should wait for a more secure moment. The better question might not be whether to test but rather, When is the appropriate moment?

Taking Action Now

Five general categories of intervention are currently available: general health maintenance, holistic or complementary therapies, antiviral medicine, immunemodulating medicine, and preventive medicine against opportunistic infections.

The biggest mistake we can make in exploring these approaches is to assume that we must choose one, as if it were an election campaign. No singular method of intervention is sufficient on its own. Unfortunately, some advocates ask people to religiously adhere to one approach and reject all others. A good rule of thumb: When someone makes an intervention a matter of dogma or faith, suggesting that it is the only answer and discouraging use of any others, it's time to look elsewhere . . .

Where We Stand Now

Despite the rapidly changing debate over early intervention, there are several points that most researchers and physicians seem to agree on:

- The need for PCP prevention, starting when a person has around 200 T cells (and always after an initial bout of PCP or any other serious opportunistic infection, regardless of T cell count). Some argument remains as to which treatment to use: the expensive, safe, but inconvenient aerosol pentamidine or the inexpensive, convenient, and sometimes more problematic oral drugs.
- Beginning treatment when serious symptoms indicate immediate danger or when blood markers reach the levels described in the original FDA approval of AZT (under 200 T4 cells).
- The use of acyclovir whenever any of the herpes-related viruses are present.
- Monitoring a patient's use of unapproved but promising drugs currently under study, such as dextran sulfate.

The treatment debate is increasingly focused on deciding when the imaginary line is crossed that calls for intervention. Is it at 200 T cells, 400 T cells plus some symptoms, or simply seropositivity and declining T cells? Does waiting until serious symptoms occur let the disease go so far that the patient may never recover full immune response? The answer, for the moment, must be one of personal choice. Highly respected researchers and physicians admit that treatment strategies are clearly shifting toward earlier intervention. Perhaps a year from now, there will be no debate.

One thing we do know for sure: There is indeed light shining at the end of the tunnel. In a recent meeting in Washington, the normally staid top officials of the National Institutes of Health AIDS program were practically jumping up and down in their chairs in excitement over the progress that has been made and the advances that are on the horizon.

Now, more than ever, the challenge is to use all that is at our command to hang on. We are very, very close, and some reputable sources believe we are already there for those who begin treatment sufficiently early.

POSITIVELY HEALTHY

from *Positively Healthy News* (1989)

Respectable . . . We ain't ever gonna be respectable . . .
—*Mel & Kim, 1987*

PH was born out of our anger at the passive acceptance of the extraordinarily garbled and contradictory science which launched HIV as being the sole cause of AIDS and the resulting research being based solely on this hypothesis. We were well aware of the multifactorial theory of AIDS and the fact that HIV could not be isolated in a significant percentage of PLAs (over 20 percent according to the UK Health Minister in 1988). Our suspicion deepened when our open questioning of the various issues involved invoked reactions from many doctors varying from rage to derision, and mainly elicited indifference and a 'so what' attitude from the existing AIDS organisations.

We soon become aware that we stood alone in challenging the very epidemiology and etiology of AIDS—what it is, how it originated, how it was being mismanaged and why the treatments for it were limited to high-tech profit-dominated commercially lucrative medications. Cass Mann and Simon Martin already knew from their extensive researches into cancer and its massive mismanagement and profitability, that more people were making a living from cancer than dying from it; and that we were witnessing the very same scenario unfolding in the case of AIDS. It seems that within a suspiciously short amount of time AIDS organisations sprang up which were little more than mouthpieces for various government and pharmaceutical interests and who made no inroads into questioning what lay behind the information and what the hidden agendas were.

The ridiculous advertising campaign launched by the UK Government 'AIDS—Don't Die of Ignorance' misspent twenty million pounds and thoroughly confused the vast majority of the people who received it. It's basic message was "There is no cure. It (HIV) kills". HIV is continually referred to as the 'AIDS virus" and the insistently repeated message is ". . . they (HIV AB+ people) become ill and die from illnesses they can not fight off."

We in PH suggest that a significant cause of disease in PLAs is the effect of believing misinformation such as this which programmes people to a 'certain death' following a diagnosis of being HIV AB+. The very same death-oriented agenda is emphasised by Burroughs Wellcome along with the British Medical Association in their joint booklet issued in 1988 "AIDS And You' in their statement "AIDS kills everyone who gets it." PH learned to hear the underlying message behind these ghastly proclamations and heard that when it was stated "There is no known cure" what was really being said "There is no known PHARMACEUTI-CAL cure" viz a new drug which can be launched in order to obtain a patent and massive profits for the shareholders of our pharmaceutical multinationals. . .

The greatest tragedy we discovered with the management of AIDS was that the clinicians in charge of it were venereologists with little or no experience in working with people who were now beginning to seriously question their drug regimes and therapies as the result of doing their own researches. Venereologists had never previously had to confront very young people presenting with an 'incurable disease'. Difficulties arose in counselling 'patients' about the fact that they had no answer or 'magic bullet' and that the current prognosis was 'invariably' death within a variable but short period of time. This was based on their lack of success using the severely limited drugs they had available.

'Patients' who questioned any aspects of their treatments were often told that the doctor was unable to discuss the matter as the 'patient' had not had six years of medical training and was not a qualified clinician in the field. When PH advised our members to suggest to their doctors that in that case, the only way to equalise the relationship was for the doctor to develop HIV antibodies or AIDS—we found the suggestion was not taken up!

The persistence of inequality in the doctor/patient relationship is perhaps the most serious factor in depriving people of control over their disease and relegates them to a passive spectator role in its management. A long-term study undertaken by Michael Callen, one of the founders of the PWA Coalition in New York, found that of the many people who had lived successfully with AIDS for many years, every one had been a 'difficult patient' and almost every single one had shopped around for a doctor who would accept them as active partners in the joint effort to stay healthy and in the treatment of any opportunistic infections if they arose. Doctors who refused were, very simply, fired! Regrettably, in the UK people are rather passive in their relationship to the medical profession as they are in dealing with most autocratic bodies. It is PH's major function to destroy this passivity and to create a group of AIDS rebels and radicals who will then rewrite the rules of the game whereby they can occupy centre-stage and starring roles instead of being bit players in a script where the ending has been written with no consultation with them.

The following quote from Dr. Paul Volberding MD, Chief of the AIDS Activities Division at San Francisco General Hospital clarifies PH's stand on drug therapies in AIDS treatments: "Despite the development of efficacious treatments to control the opportunistic infections and cancers that result from AIDS, their impact on AIDS-related mortality will be minimal UNTIL THE UNDERLYING IMMUNE DEFICIENCY CAN BE CORRECTED' (Our capitals and our viewpoint as well). AIDS Principles Practices and Politics" Edited by Drs. Corless and Pittman-Lineman 1988. We were alarmed that 100 percent of the news being released about AIDS was negative and destructive as well as profoundly disempowering for PLAs for whom these were the only sources of information. The fact that people were managing to live successfully with AIDS was never reported. Therapies which existed and were being used successfully were being ignored and dismissed, often by the very same doctors who refused to even examine their data or research them.

It is criminally insane to assume that less than three years into treating AIDS we can state that we already know enough about it in order to make definitive ex-cathedra proclamations and draw conclusions about it. The science surrounding it is in constant flux and the leading players no longer make the ironclad announcements about it they originally did.

Dr. Robert Gallo, who co-discovered HIV with Dr. Luc Montagnier, always maintained that HIV was the sole cause of AIDS and derided any alternative theory as utter madness. However, in the October 1988 issue of Scientific American, Gallo stated, "(although) a LARGE enough dose of the RIGHT strain of HIV can cause AIDS on its own, cofactors can clearly influence the progression of the disease. Interactions with other pathogens may also increase the likelihood that AIDS will develop. Specifically a herpes virus named HBLV (Human B-cell Lymphotropic virus) or HHV6 (Human Herpes Virus 6 discovered in Gallo's laboratory) can interact with HIV in a way that may increase the severity of the HIV infection. One of the main hosts of HHV6 is a white blood cell called the B-cell (and) the virus can also infect T4 lymphocytes. If the T-cell is simultaneously infected with HIV, HHV6 can activate (HIV) further impairing the immune system and worsening the cycle" (our capitals).

The only organisation to constantly propagate this state of-the-art update on AIDS is PH and we are highly suspicious when the others do not make this their priority as well . . .

PH does not create any dependencies on itself and designs its work to empower each individual to become self-referencing and radical in their relationship with AIDS and with the self proclaimed 'experts' who mislead people as to its management. We are amply supported by the more radical doctors, nurses and health-care professionals within the NHS and recognise their courage in contradicting the bad science and therapies which pass for current AIDS information today. PH categorically states that the only people who will survive AIDS will be the very same people who survive the misinformation surrounding AIDS.

We issue an invitation to all AIDS organisations to take up a questioning and critical attitude alongside us in the areas we are addressing and to help up destroy the assumption that the information which is propagated about AIDS is uniformly accurate and unquestioningly accepted, because it is neither. If our organisations worked in support of this fiercely questioning approach, we could change the face of AIDS overnight. Our emphasis MUST be that of radical and aggressive unbelievers. The soft option is obviously NOT working. This is why you are now holding the first issue of Positively Healthy News in your hands.

INFORMATION IS POWER.

POWER IS IN YOUR HANDS.

At Last Eight Principles of Power

The Aims and Objectives of Positively Healthy News:

To present a forum for informed debate and dialogue concerning the context, content and circumstance of AIDS.

To present a forum for radical dialogue between scientists, physicians and clients with differing views on AIDS etiology, epidemiology and treatment.

To network with and present state-of-the-art information from leading sources worldwide.

To examine disease in the individual in relation to its social, economic, historical, cultural and ecological context.

To examine the multifactorial hypothesis of AIDS and the role of co-factors acting with HIV to produce clinical disease.

To harmonise complementary and orthodox AIDS treatment for the sole benefit of the client.

To transform and equalise the relationship between clients and physicians.

To present options, not answers.

ACT UP marked the watershed of what has since come to be called "AIDS activism" as distinct from, and sometimes in conflict with (as we shall see) lesbian and gay activism. In its wake, new groups were formed and existing ones revitalized. Some of these included: Housing Works (for homeless PWAs); AIDS Treatment Registry (for information on drug trials); Treatment Action Group (TAG, treatment development through collaboration with pharmaceutical companies and government research and approval institutions); Queer Nation (direct action around lesbian and gay visibility); Lesbian Avengers (lesbian visibility, health, and other issues) to name but a few. While it would be an overstatement to attribute the workings of these groups to ACT UP Chapters, the latter was central to the networking in New York and other cities through which many of these groups either came into existence or sustained themselves.

ACT UP NY's definition of itself, states: "ACT UP is a diverse, non-partisan group united in anger and committed to direct action to end the AIDS crisis. We meet with government and public health officials; we research and distribute the latest medical information. *We protest and demonstrate; we are not silent.*" Weekly meetings facilitated by one or more individuals were conducted as participatory democracy; whoever wanted an issue addressed or an action taken would raise it and have it discussed and voted on by "the floor." The organization became a combination of public education, political action, and networking (and, of course, cruising.) Its actions were directed at: local, state, and federal governments; pharmaceutical, insurance, and other health-related businesses; the annual international AIDS conferences; private individuals (for example, for positions taken in the media or government); the "general public" for consciousness-raising; and religious organizations. For each action, which often involved civil disobedience, debate at the regular meetings was informed by the compilation of fact, issue, and position booklets distributed to participants; the action itself was planned and executed by the general membership but the civil disobedience by means of "affinity groups," assisted by lawyers to monitor and navigate through the legal system. Mass media were deliberately cultivated for educating the public about the politics of AIDS, supplemented by graphic art evocative of other moments in the history of political art, such as socialist realism. Afterwards at the weekly meeting, actions would be dissected and criticized for improvement next time.

We document here only one action and supply several other documents produced by members of NY's ACT UP. The action documented was one of the most spectacular and controversial, the civil disobedience within NY's St. Patrick's Cathedral on December 10, 1989. "Stop the Church" was occasioned by the increasing homophobic stridency of Cardinal O'Connor, his hypocrisy in showing "mercy" for PWAs when they were dying while opposing prevention measures in schools and public funding for such measures anywhere else, and the church's opposition to abortion, which enabled ACT UP to form coalitions with women's groups, in particular, the Women's Health Action and Mobilization (WHAM) which coordinated the demonstration with ACT UP. While thousands demonstrated peacefully outside the cathedral during a Sunday morning mass, 111 were arrested inside for nonviolent symbolic statements of opposition, ranging from handcuffing oneself with one's lover to a pew to symbolize the church's treatment of partnerships, to laying down in the aisle to symbolize deaths from AIDS, to the most widely publicized, a gay catholic young man crumbling the communion host and throwing it to the ground. Documents included here are an internal ACT UP informational flier distributed to members before the action, an open letter distributed to St. Patrick's parishioners the Sunday before the action, ACT UP's position statement and the statements of other groups after the action, as well as statements of dissidents. Civil disobedience within a house of worship was an act intended to demonstrate the magnitude of organized religion's deliberate invasion, through intimidation of government officials, into the lives of gay men and all women. At the Monday night meeting immediately following the action, critics asked "the floor" whether ACT UP would be upset if homophobic Catholics did civil disobedience at an ACT UP meeting. Catholic members of ACT UP responded that their own dissent was heard at ACT UP meetings, but not within the church by its hierarchy. Some of the statements passed out during that meeting are included here.

Documentation of "Stop the Church" is followed by statements showing the increasing diversity within ACT UP: those of the Majority Action Committee, the Latino/a Caucus, and the Caucus of Asian & Pacific Islander AIDS Activists. Other documents here include one by a member of the ACT UP/New York Women and AIDS Book Group. It is evidence of the ascendance of lesbians giving voice to the concerns of women with AIDS—many of whom were people of color—within an organization founded overwhelmingly by white gay men. The book, *Women, AIDS, and Activism*, begun in 1989 and published in 1990, includes essays on how the definition of AIDS-related illness needed to be expanded to include those afflicting HIV-positive and immune-suppressed women; this will figure later in the critique of the HIV-AIDS hypothesis by those who view the expansion of the definition as logically undermining what AIDS is conceived to be. The selection presented here is by a member of the group who is a veteran labor, feminist, lesbian, then AIDS activist and later Queer National, Maxine Wolfe, and concerns how AIDS activism has transformed lesbian and gay activism. Next, a mainstay of ACT UP/New York's Treatment and Data Committee explains how AIDS activists' direct action tactics have transformed the federal medical bureaucracy. Significantly, the author (with Peter Staley, to whom reference is made in the next selection), was later a founder of an ACT UP offshoot, Treatment Action Group, to continue the same work separate from the participatory democracy that was becoming the treatment activists' stumbling block in their dealings with government policy makers, research institutions, and pharmaceutical companies. Finally, we present an article reflecting upon these "limits" of ACT UP, written by a lesbian who is described as regularly attending ACT UP/New York meeting but, in her words, "she has not voted in the group since she began writing about ACT UP two years ago." ACT UP continues; for example, at the time of this writing, 1994, it is educating the public about the consequences of and protesting the New York Mayor's proposed dismantling of the City's Department of AIDS Services as a way of cutting the municipal budget.

STOP THE CHURCH

ACTION UPDATE,
LETTER TO PARISHIONERS OF ST. PATRICK'S CATHEDRAL,
POST-ACTION POSITION STATEMENT, and MEDIA REPORT

(1989)

ACT UP and WHAM

STOP THE CHURCH
Action Update

STOP THE CHURCH is an action co-sponsored by the AIDS Coalition to Unleash Power (ACT UP) and the Women's Health Action and Mobilization (WHAM). It will take place on Sunday, December 10, at 9:30 a.m., at St. Patrick's Cathedral, Fifth Avenue and Fiftieth Street, New York City.

OUR TARGETS are John Cardinal O'Connor and the Catholic church hierarchy.

OUR FRONTLINE ISSUES are safer sex education, condoms and needles, abortion, homophobia, and violence against gays and lesbians. Our underlying issues are freedom of choice, the right to control our own bodies, and the separation of church and state.

OUR MEANS are to use direct action to draw attention to the political activities and lethal policies of the cardinal and the church, to drive a wedge between the hierarchy and lay

Catholics, and to generate a debate of the issues in the media.

OUR GOALS are to stop the interference of the cardinal and the church in politics and our lives and thereby TO SAVE LIVES.

PROPOSED SCENARIO FOR THE DEMONSTRATION

At 9:30 a.m. demonstrators will gather in "mass" in front of St. Patrick's Cathedral for a legal picket. As our numbers grow the picket will attempt to encircle the square block area of the cathedral, culminating in a combined group action—a "mass" die-in on the streets and sidewalks surrounding the cathedral. The objective is to stop all action around the cathedral, thus isolating the target of the action and sending a powerful message to O'Connor, the church, and the public at large.

AFFINITY GROUPS

It is recommended that affinity groups that wish to participate in civil disobedience inside the cathedral consider all the political ramifications of such an action as well as the legal situation around the cathedral. Affinity groups may wish to time their actions to coincide with the homily of the mass—the time when O'Connor gives his sermon. This will help to isolate O'Connor as the target of the action, as opposed to the people gathered for worship that day. All participants in this action will be advised of the legal situation and other risks involved.

VIDEO

Video coverage at the demonstration will be an important means of helping to ensure our protection from violence and of documenting our history. Participants are encouraged to form video affinity groups to cover the demonstration. ACT UP already has one video collective, DIVA TV.

MEDIA

There will be a press conference held prior to the action for the purpose of stating our issues, positions, and demands.

OUTREACH

We are currently doing outreach through wheatpasting, tabling, mailings to various gay/lesbian/pro-choice groups, and advertisements in the Village Voice, the City Sun, and various college newspapers. We need volunteers for help with leafleting at the Center and at gay/lesbian events. Leafleting on car windshields, leafleting at bars and churches, putting up posters at shops and restaurants, posting listings on computer bulletin boards, and stencilling. We will send speakers to any groups that are interested.

The cultural dimension of this action is enormous. It is vital that the focus of the action remain on the target—O'Conner and the church's political activities.

Dear Parishioners of Saint Patrick's Cathedral:

Next Sunday, there will be a demonstration outside of your church. It has been called by WHAM! (Women's Health Action Mobilization) and ACT UP (AIDS Coalition to Unleash Power). We are activist groups concerned about the rights of women, lesbian and gay people, and people with AIDS. We are also concerned about education and healthcare as they pertain to all people. HIV and AIDS prevention are paramount to the work that we do. The right of all women to choose when and when not to have children is also of key importance to us.

You may be wondering why we have chosen Saint Patrick's Cathedral as our focal point. It is, after all, your place of worship. We are aware of this and yet, we ask for your understanding and participation.

We are worried. On Sunday, October 1st, Cardinal O'Connor told this congregation of his wish to join Operation "Rescue," the radical group that blockades women's health facilities and harasses their clientele. He encouraged all Catholics to join them. In fact, he said, "all good Catholics."

Every year in New York City, there is a Gay Pride March. Because so many people from our communities have died of AIDS, we've built two minutes of silence into this event. Churches throughout the city pay respect to our moment of remembrance and ring their bells in unison. Missing from that polyphony are the bells of Saint Patrick's.

And so, we continue to worry. At the Vatican Conference on AIDS a few weeks ago, the Cardinal scoffed at the use of condoms to stop the spread of HIV, the virus believed to cause AIDS. His solution: "good morality is good medicine."

The moral beliefs of the Catholic Church pertain only to its members. The doctrine of any one religion cannot be made into law without undermining our entire system of government. Religious freedom is dependent on a separation of church and state.

Nonetheless, Cardinal O'Connor has been active in city politics for years. He openly lobbied against the passage of the New York City Gay Rights Bill. Two weeks ago, he proposed that there be an order of nuns dedicated solely to the legal, medical and political opposition to abortion and euthanasia. He continues to oppose safer-sex education in AIDS healthcare facilities and in our schools.

And then there is the question of excommunication. The Cardinal has spoken of excommunicating Governor Cuomo for his pro-choice stance on abortion. We oppose the punishment of Catholic people for having political beliefs that differ from those of the church hierarchy.

SEPARATION OF CHURCH AND STATE
IS IN ALL OF OUR BEST INTERESTS

Join us, December 10th at 9:30 AM
ACT UP, AIDS Coalition To Unleash Power
WHAM!, Women's Health Action and Mobilization

POSITION STATEMENT

In the days following the massive demonstration at St. Patrick's Cathedral, Cardinal O'Connor has portrayed himself as an innocent victim of the demonstrators who interrupted his sermon. ACT UP stresses that we do not apologize for the actions of the 5,000 people who came on Sunday to protest Church actions that limit the rights of all Americans to make personal decisions in their own lives.

We respect the Cardinal's right to believe what he chooses and to preach to any Catholics who choose to follow him. But we are alarmed at church leaders' oppressive public policies that infringe upon the rights of all Americans. The right of teenagers in public schools to have complete sex and AIDS education, and the right of women to decide about their own bodies.

We went to the church on Sunday to tell America that the Cardinal and Church leaders are using their immense political clout to push public policies that are dangerous for all Americans, not just for Catholics. For instance:

Cardinal O'Connor's knowledge of AIDS prevention or treatment methods is limited to the foolishly simplistic view "morality is good medicine," yet he sits on the Presidential AIDS Policy Panel, telling our President what to do about AIDS. AIDS is not a religious issue. The Cardinal's attempts to push Church moralizing as public health policy show a disrespect for those dead from AIDS and a profane lack of compassion for those who remain at grave risk of contracting this disease.

The Cardinal's representatives sit on the Board of Education's AIDS Curriculum Task Force and have prevented teenagers of all religious faiths from obtaining lifesaving AIDS information in their public schools. Americans did not elect the Cardinal. This kind of political bullying is a clear violation of the constitutional separation of church and state—in fact, this issue is currently on trial in the courts.

Homeless teenagers who turn to prostitution or drug use are at greatest AIDS risk. But the Church's policy at Covenant House, which is touted as New York's best hope for runaway kids, is to prohibit distribution of any AIDS prevention literature. Worse, when some young residents brought in such flyers given by ACT UP and WHAM!, the kids were promptly expelled—thrown out in the street. Is this what the Cardinal means when he boasts about merciful, charitable response to the AIDS crisis?

Individual ACT UP and WHAM members who chose to enter the church—a number of them Catholics and People With AIDS—were not trying to deny parishioners' right to worship. Instead, these demonstrators felt so strongly about the issues that they needed to make this peaceful, non-violent political statement—some silently, some vocally—in the place where Cardinal O'Connor himself has made so many dangerous and misguided political statements. They entered peacefully, as members of the congregation, and were greeted by a sea of uniformed police officers.

The real victims today are not the Cardinal and his followers whose service was interrupted for a half hour on Sunday. The real victims are the hundreds of thousands of people in New York City and across the USA with HIV and AIDS, who might have been spared from this terrible disease if it weren't for the Church's ongoing distortion of the AIDS crisis to further its own moralistic and political goals.

As long as the epidemic rages and the Church fights in direct opposition to the policies recommended by responsible doctors, scientists and public health officials, ACT UP will never be silent—not in the streets, not in the capital, and not even in the Church itself.

MEDIA REPORT: "Stop the Church"

"Stop the Church," our biggest demo to date, got us the most coverage yet. We were the top story on TV news at 6 pm. News radio reported live at least hourly during the demo. We were the cover story on 3 of the 4 daily papers Monday, and again on 2 of them Tuesday. And the columnists went wild—notably Dennis Hamill (*Newsday*) and the odious Ray Kerrison

(*Post*), later echoed by equally awful Patrick Buchanan (syndicated, *Post*).

But, coverage of the demonstration was unfavorable. More importantly, the issues we tried to present were largely ignored or distorted, and the Archdiocese did a very good job of diverting the discussion and presenting the church as the victim. There were many problems with the reporting.

- Actions inside the church got the bulk of the coverage, completely overshadowing the much larger demonstration outside.
- TV coverage vastly undercounted the number of demonstrators, saying there were 1000; papers got it right at 4500 (Even the cops said 2000.)
- In some cases, those interviewed as "people in the street" were parishioners or Operation Rescue people—NOT identified as such—whereas ACT UP and WHAM! protesters were always identified that way.
- Demonstrators were frequently called "gay activists," ignoring the AIDS and pro-choice focus of the action.

There were also, though, a few good points:

- Some of the broadcast coverage of the demo was directly followed by the story of the first gay Episcopal priest.
- DIVA-TV did fantastic work and got a rough-cut tape out Sunday night,
- Nationally syndicated "USA Tonight" was not only concise but humorous: they showed protesters carted off in a bus that said "Showtime in the city" on the side, and used DIVA-TV footage (above).
- WBAI (naturally) had two hours of live coverage during the demo, and then a one-hour interview with ACT UP and WHAM! people that night.
- Channel 2 on Sunday night said this was the largest protest of its kind; they did cover the issues and showed scenes from both inside and outside; also interviewed 3 church dissenters.

The Archdiocese unleashed a powerful, sophisticated PR blitz Monday. The second-day coverage was virtually all the church's side of the story—no opportunity for demonstrators to rebut or to discuss the issues. (We also didn't have Mayor Koch or soon-to-be-Mayor Dinkins on our side.)

To try to rebut this, Media Committee held a press conference Wednesday, Dec. 13, at the Simon Watson Gallery. EVERYONE was there, both broadcast and print media. Tim Powers, Gerri Wells, and Vincent Gagliosto spoke from ACT UP; Maryann Stanishevski and Stacey Mink spoke from WHAM! The press conference was heated, but did get coverage.

STATEMENT

Coalition for Lesbian and Gay Rights

John Cardinal O'Connor is a religious bigot whose pronouncements on homosexuality and AIDS deserve condemnation. His statement that we have only to stop "abberational sex" in order to end the AIDS crisis is not only insulting but dangerous to the millions of people who engage in sexual acts not condemned by O'Connor but just as likely to transmit HIV. His virulent opposition to the use of condoms as protection from HIV will lead, according to the New York City Health Commissioner, to "an increase in deaths from AIDS in New York."

The Catholic Church in New York is a powerful religious and political force. We in the gay and lesbian community cannot, however, shy away from attacking its leaders when they promote misinformation and bigotry. That is why the Coalition for Lesbian and Gay Rights endorsed and participated in the massive demonstration sponsored by ACT UP and WHAM on Sunday, December 10, 1989 outside St. Patrick's Cathedral.

The actions of a few demonstrators inside the church—some of whom lay down silently in protest, others who shouted in rage and frustration at this sanctimonious right-wing fanatic in clerical garb, and one of whom refused Communion by letting a host fall to the floor—are totally understandable in light of the Cardinal's relentless campaign of attack on the gay and lesbian community and the Constitutional rights of all women to safe abortions. In fact, it was precisely the response that the Cardinal wanted. Indeed, he cynically prepared for the event and is glorying in his role as martyr.

While it deeply pains us at a time of crisis to publicly differ with a group dedicated to the same cause, we reject this *tactic* as divisive and distracting from our common goal—to end O'Connor's influence in civic affairs. We affirm the civil right of all to worship free of interference, even when a congregation is led by someone as abusive of his pulpit as the Cardinal. This right springs from the same Bill of Rights to which we appeal for protection as we assemble, protest, petition, and, indeed, conduct our private lives. Unlike the Cardinal, who supports physically blocking women from entering family planning clinics, we do not support blocking access to worship.

The late gay African-American civil rights leader Bayard Rustin used to say, "Don't waste your time on the 10% of the people who will never agree with you—concentrate on the 90% who are potential allies." Upwards of 80% of American Catholics support gay and lesbian rights according to a recent poll in *U. S. Catholic* magazine. Tactics such as that employed at St. Patrick's can only lessen that percentage.

This is not a call to make peace with the Cardinal or to condone the many in his church whose silence in the face of bigotry could be construed as giving consent to it. It is a call to escalate our tactics against the many governmental officials who have formed unholy alliances with him and who refuse to dissociate themselves from his bigotry. We must isolate O'Connor the politician and demand from our representatives that they free public health policy from his moralistic (and immoral) influence.

We call for an end to public financing of religiously affiliated institutions as a gross violation of the separation of church and state. We call for an end to the tax-exempt status of those religions that directly inject themselves into partisan politics (as the Catholic Church has repeatedly, especially on abortion). The Cardinal has *paid* lobbyists in Albany using moneys from his tax-exempt collections. We demand that political leaders speak out against the anti-gay and anti-lesbian and anti-woman bigotry of the Cardinal as strongly as they have spoken out against the actions of a few demonstrators on Sunday.

These goals are high, but realizable. We must keep our eyes on the prize and, as strong as it is, not let our anger distract us into counter-productive tactics. It is good to show our fierce anger in the face of this injustice. It is bad to let it lead us into actions that give comfort to the enemy.

We do not pretend to command the troops of ACT UP. We look to ACT UP for leadership. We hope that future actions will build broader coalitions to hasten the end of the AIDS crisis uniting not just the lesbian and gay community, but all New Yorkers concerned with ending bigotry and promoting health.

STATEMENT ON ACTION AT ST. PATRICK'S CATHEDRAL

Gay Men's Health Crisis

We are in complete sympathy with the rage and pain that motivated the protesters, and feel that the need for direct action has never been more urgent than now. This is a complex battle requiring multiple strategies. However, the action shifted public attention from the real issues raised by Cardinal O'Connor's damaging positions and actions on AIDS. For that reason alone we feel that the action by ACT UP and WHAM inside St. Patrick's Cathedral was a mistake. The only winner was the Cardinal, who no doubt is enjoying this divisive discussion within the AIDS community while his destructive role in the battles to prevent AIDS and empower women is buried.

Cardinal O'Conner disputes the well-documented fact that condoms prevent the transmission of HIV. This position endangers human lives. If the Cardinal cannot accept scientific facts about AIDS, he should stay out of the debate. And if he makes political statements, he must expect a political response. The Cardinal's compassion must extend to people without HIV whose lives might be saved through the use of condoms, and to people with HIV who might avoid reinfection by using condoms. The Cardinal's concern about the epidemic could be better expressed by a trip to City Hall, Albany or Washington to push for funding; by promoting life-saving education; by condemning bigotry; and by educating himself thoroughly about the facts on HIV transmission.

SUPPORT YOUR CHURCH!!

Courage
(distributed outside the cathedral during the action)

Stop militant anti-Catholic bigotry & suppression!
Protect Catholics' Freedom of Speech & Religion!

... A Message From Local Catholics and Friends:

1. On the Church "Imposing Views on Others":
   - Abortion is a human rights issue, not a Catholic issue. Pro-life laws would restore protection to the unborn, educate the public to respect life, and modify destructive behavior over time.
   - Church leaders have the freedom of speech and religion to teach clearly on the moral & public policy dimensions of all human life issues.
   - Pro-"choice" (abortion) advocates are determined to maintain abortion funding (at taxpayers', i.e, Catholics, and others' expense) and abortion on demand for the full nine months! They "impose their views" on society by denying the child's right to life, forcing us to pay for killing the child and eliminating both a husband's right to stop the killing of his child, and grandparents' right to protect their unborn grandchildren.
   - Who criticizes the Cardinal for speaking out on Nicaragua, El Salvador, housing, hunger, homelessness, tax structures, etc.? Doesn't the Church "impose its views" on these issues? Why the censure only when it comes to the killing of unborn children?

2. On Operation Rescue:
   - Over 3000,000 people nationwide have participated in Operation Rescue events and over 50,000 have been arrested attempting to stop child-killing by peacefully intervening at abortion killing centers.
   - U. S. citizens, including bishops, priests, rabbis, ministers, nuns and laity have joined in Rescues with love and sacrifice as witnesses to the tragedy of abortion and have helped save over 400 babies to date.
   - Cardinal O'Conner's verbal support for Rescue is legal, welcome and praiseworthy. He supports all peaceful, constructive action which champions the defenseless unborn, and the church provides free services to any pregnant woman in need.

3. On the Right of Bishops & Priests to Refuse Communion to Catholics
   - Catholic members of the U.S. House of Representatives, Senate & local governments who vote pro-abortion are in direct conflict with moral law, and oppose their Church's teaching flagrantly.
   - Our bishops and priests are morally justified in refusing communion to public sinners who cause public scandal with their support for legalized child-killing in America.
   - We support a more morally consistent role of the Bishops to impose Church sanctions against those who defy Church teaching on abortion. No Catholic can responsibly take a "pro-choice" stand.
   - The Roman Catholic Church reserves the right to establish its own Church rules, regulations, laws and policies without outside interference from the State. Freedom of Religion is law!

4. On Homosexuality, Homosexual Activity and "Gay Rights" Issues
   - We support the "Letter to the Bishops of the Catholic Church on the Pastoral Care of Homosexual Persons" from the Congregation for the Doctrine of the Faith (which is responsible for the preservation of Catholic teaching), October, 1986. (For a copy, try the Daughters of St. Paul Book Shop.)
   - The Congregation:
     1. States that homosexual orientation is not sinful in itself, but an objective disorder;
     2. Deplores "homosexual bashers";
     3. Calls all Christians including homosexuals to a chaste life.
   - We support Church opposition to expanding "Gay Rights" because laws protecting the "human right" to practice homosexual behavior could have a severely damaging effect on

society at large, adversely affecting marriage and family life. "Gay Rights" advocates impose their own "Religion of Civil Rights" on society.

To support Pro-Life Abortion Alternatives of the Archdiocese of New York, the New York Office of Courage (the Church-approved, pro-chastity group for homosexuals), and to provide volunteer support of financial help to AIDS patients, contact:

Catholic Home Bureau, 1011 First Avenue, New York, NY 10022

Courage, St. Michael's Rectory, 424 West 34 Street, New York, NY 10001

St. Caire's Hospital & Health Center, 426 West 52nd Street, New York, NY 10019

STOP THE CHURCH

from *Piss + Vinegar* (an ACT-UP/NY member's newsletter) distributed at the December 18, 1989 meeting

I am disappointed but not surprised at the editorials of the major N.Y. daily newspapers condemning ACTUP and WHAM's protest at St. Patrick's cathedral last Sunday as being sacrilegious and disgraceful behavior.

What is indeed sacrilegious and a disgrace is the fact that tens of thousands of young men and women have died and are dying horrible deaths while in the prime of their lives for the past ten years and this society just plain doesn't give a damn! And that especially includes the religious community, or so called moral leaders. It's because this materialistic society has absolutely no sanctity for life whatsoever but only a reverence for money and power that this sad state of affairs has come to being. AIDS is still largely perceived as being a gay disease and since homosexuals are considered "intrinsically evil" by the church, we are simply an expendable segment of the population.

I say it's too bad that Cardinal O'Connor had his feathers ruffled because we disrupted his sermon of hate and bigotry last Sunday. It was long overdue! And if he's offended by our actions Sunday, we are offended by his spearheading the Church's campaign of condemnation of our very existence! Who is Cardinal O'Connor and the Catholic Church to judge anyone with their bloody 2000 year history of violent repression, censorship, bigotry, hypocrisy, racism, torture and murder? (One historian calculated over 100 million human beings met with violent deaths directly because of this Church over the centuries—the 400 year Inquisition, the Crusades, the burning of witches, etc., etc.). The Catholic Church was the single biggest obstacle to the development of scientific knowledge in the history of western civilization, a tradition it continues in the subject of sexuality. It has effectively reduced its membership to the status of superstitious primitive savages. How dare this vile institution preach morality to anyone with the incredible amount of human suffering that can be laid at its doorstep? How many unwanted, unloved and economically-deprived children have been born into this world because of the Church's idiotic stand on birth control and abortion? Wherever you find the Catholic Church entrenched you'll find ignorance and poverty in the surrounding communities. The first amendment provides for the separation of

Church and State as the foundation of our democracy. The Catholic Church makes a mockery of this provision—despite the generous tax exempt status it enjoys upon its prolific wealth—which we as taxpayers are subsidizing.

The media laments about how we attacked freedom of religion—I'm much more concerned with freedom FROM religion. It has consistently intruded its morbid and guilt-ridden moral teachings in our lives because it enjoys so much power in influencing the public, our politicians and the media. Where were the editorials of outrage when O'Connor publicly stated that he wanted to get arrested with Operation Rescue, an organization that violates the law by blocking entrances to abortion clinics thus interfering with women's health care, not to mention the violent verbal abuse these women are subjected to by these fanatics. What about the thirty plus abortion clinics that were bombed because of the hate campaign engineered by the Church? We have the right to prevent his monstrous organization from continuing to interfere with our lives. Demagogues like O'Connor have made substantial contributions to creating an atmosphere of intolerance and hatred toward gays in general and therefore the resulting "we-don't-care" attitude of society towards people dying of AIDS. We lost sympathy by this demonstration? We never had any sympathy by society at any time. We still have to buy drugs from the underground to help prolong our lives because the Federal Government, the NIH, the FDA and the pharmaceutical companies select drug testing based upon profit potential, not saving human lives. What should we do? Throw flowers at the Church and thank them for persecuting us so thoroughly for 2000 years? For once we stood up to the Church and now it hides behind its robes and rituals and feigns injury.

Peaceful demonstrations are lost against our oppressors. The only real gains we have enjoyed have come from less than polite confrontations as we enter the second decade of the AIDS genocide. If nothing else we communicated our outrage at society's indifference to this epidemic by going into a very major source of hatred and ignorance against gays—the Church. As far as I'm concerned, disrupting a Catholic Church Mass is like disrupting a Nazi rally. Their stupidity and sourness has killed and is continuing to kill our community. O'Connor served on the President's Commission on AIDS for a full year. He knows what's going on. He commands the media like no one I know. Has he ever spoken out once on the criminal lack of testing of drugs for AIDS? No, he hasn't! But he incessantly rambles on about how gays are moral degenerates (even though homosexuality is rampant among the church's clergy). The Catholic Church doesn't show any respect toward us as human beings—why shouldn't we return the favor, as we did last Sunday? When their policies and dogma result in gay and straight people dying, then we should continue to disrupt their organization—whatever form it takes.

According to Christian mythology, Jesus Christ walked into the temple of God with a whip and drove the money-changers out! I think we did something comparable last Sunday when we entered and protested at the Cathedral last Sunday. ACTUP is becoming increasingly isolated from society as our voices grow louder and our tactics escalate in intensity. But there can be no doubt of the righteousness of our cause. I'm proud of ACTUP's involvement last Sunday at St. Patrick's and I salute the courageous activists that got arrested there that day. We will not die quietly!

—Tom Shultz

RE: CATHEDRAL PROTEST

In the recent media coverage concerning the protest sponsored by ACT UP and WHAM at St. Patrick's Cathedral, a number of points and facts concerning the action were omitted.

In attempting to influence and legislate public policy under the pretext of morality, Cardinal O'Connor and the Catholic Church hierarchy have for years been interfering with the rights of individuals to control their bodies and their lives.

There is a long history, in this city, of the Cardinal and the Catholic Church hierarchy continually abrogating the separation of church and state.

Four years ago, prior to the passage of the ordinance to protect all New Yorkers from discrimination in housing, employment and in all public places, on the basis of sexual orientation (heterosexual, homosexual or bisexual) Cardinal O'Connor was the bill's most outspoken opponent, and in addressing the media on this issue, contended that council members who voted in favor of this bill had their careers at stake.

More recently the Cardinal stated "I wish I could join Operation Rescue" and urged all good catholics to block access to women's health clinics. In doing so, the Cardinal has advocated that people break the law and violate an amendment that still remains protected under the constitution. How ironic it is, then, that the Cardinal feigns shock and anger when his own tactics are used by others in expressing outrage at an institution that for many represents the epitome of hypocrisy, not to mention the complete distortion of biblical teaching and interpretation. Cardinal O'Connor has recently proposed an order of nuns dedicated to full time legal, medical and political opposition to a woman's right to choose termination of pregnancy.

In addition O'Connor openly opposes education about safer sex, contraception, the usage of condoms, discussion of AIDS and the distribution of clean needles to substance abusers in the public and parochial schools. It is not surprising than, that the fastest growing population infected with HIV illness are teenagers.

As a result of this direct interference in public policy there is a complete lack of access to information and interventions that could be saving peoples lives.

In lobbying our elected officials on civil legislation, it is Cardinal O'Connor who violates fundamental concepts of our constitution. The infringement of peoples' rights, including First Amendment rights started long before the protest last Sunday. The church has been infringing on peoples' right to control their bodies and lives for hundreds of years and continues today, and now the church in a desperate attempt to divert attention away from the issues behind the protest, is trying to deceitfully present itself as the victimized and oppressed recipient of out of control and militant protesters.

Cardinal O'Connor 5,000 people stood in unison on Sunday, to send you a very loud and clear message. An overwhelming majority of Americans disagree with Catholic Church teachings and policy on these issues, including catholics. People are tired of the Church hierarchy and the Cardinal telling them what they can, cannot and should not do with their lives and bodies. Interference in public policy, our lives and our bodies will no longer be tolerated. The double standard is over. Advocating "good Catholics" to deny women their right to choose, will only see our presence at your church over and over again. We are not going away, nor will we be silenced or rendered invisible on any of these issues.

On a final note, some segments of the media have been more than enthusiastic on confusing, and trying to distort the intention of the protest, by focusing on a single action within the cathedral by one individual. Obviously, some people are far more concerned with the symbolism that is attached to a wafer, than people who are actually dying as a result of

Catholic Church policy, that promotes, sexism, racism and violence towards various groups of people in society. Revoke tax exempt status for the Church, NOW!

—*Neil M. Broome*

THE MAJORITY ACTION COMMITTEE

We are the Majority Action Committee of ACT-UP (AIDS Coalition To Unleash Power). We address issues of all communities affected by the AIDS crisis. In response to the lack of action by minority leaders and the federal government in this crisis, the Majority Action Committee has mobilized with other AIDS-related organizations to address the issue of AIDS in all of our minority communities. We believe the time has come to SOUND A CALL OF ACTION to ALL minority communities. We need to take a stand against AIDS in our communities without isolating people in the community who suffer from HIV infection.

- To date, adequate studies have yet to be done on the effects of AIDS on minority communities. Our communities are experiencing a holocaust, yet we have not seen the kind of leadership come from our communities in fighting the AIDS epidemic that we have seen in past struggles throughout history—leadership that goes into the streets, informing our people about AIDS prevention and treatment.
- Many AIDS organizations in our communities don't suffer from lack of funding, THEY SUFFER FROM NO FUNDING AT ALL!

In response to this unforgivable situation, the Majority Action Committee urges timely and consistent DIRECT ACTION BY:

- Participating in AIDS educational forums within our communities.
- Distributing information on "clean works" and other issues pertaining to IV drug use.
- Distributing explicit safe sex information on the streets of our communities.
- Initiating a petition to members of the Black and the Hispanic Caucuses representing other minority groups to demand a hearing concerning AIDS and our communities.
- Demanding a national program for dealing with AIDS in all minority communities as well as demanding leadership from our elected officials.
- Fighting for the participation of minorities, women, and IV drug users in the drug protocols to be administered by doctors we can trust.
- Monitoring the situation of children with AIDS in hospitals and stopping the inhumane experiments upon them.

THE MAJORITY ACTION COMMITTEE WAS FORMED TO EDUCATE AND INFORM ALL MINORITY COMMUNITIES IN THE AIDS CRISIS. WE CALL FOR NATIONAL ACTION AGAINST THE HOLOCAUST, WHICH IS CAUSED NOT ONLY BY ILLNESS BUT BY HOMOPHOBIA, RACISM, SEXISM, INDIFFERENCE AND PROFITEERING AT THE EXPENSE OF THE DYING!

MAJORITY ACTION COMMITTEE

SILENCE=DEATH

Latina/o AIDS Activists of ACT UP

WHO ARE WE?

We are a group of Latinas/os in ACT UP dedicated to ending the AIDS epidemic.

WHAT IS ACT UP?

The AIDS Coalition To Unleash Power is a diverse organization of groups and individuals committed to direct action.

WHAT IS DIRECT ACTION?

Identifying the flaws in the system that perpetuate the AIDS epidemic. Bringing those flaws to the public eye and directly confronting them through protest and education.

WHY WE DO IT?

Because the government does not care about the lives of people with AIDS/HIV; and because after 11 years of deadly negligence, we must take matters into our own hands.

WHY ARE WE HERE?

For the past eleven years, AIDS has been killing the Latino Communities of New York City. We are now seeing the results of a government and medical establishment that do not care about our lives. Our communities are still living in ignorance, not knowing how HIV is transmitted and how it can be prevented. People living with AIDS/HIV in our communities do not know where to go for treatments/medications. The Public Health System is not equipped to help. It discriminates against Latinos, African Americans, Asians, Native Americans, Pacific Islanders, Gays and Lesbians and others by not giving us the health care we are entitled to.

As of December 1990, New York City accounted for 30,169 cumulative reported AIDS cases. Of this number:

- Latinas/os represent 27% of cumulative adult cases.
- Latino men account for 26% of the total cumulative male cases.
- Latina women account for 33% of the total cumulative female cases.
- Latino children represent 38% of the total cumulative Pediatric AIDS cases.
- In New York City AIDS is the leading cause of death among Latino men and women between the ages of 25-44.

WHAT IS THE GOVERNMENT DOING TO END THE AIDS EPIDEMIC?

Right now we find this government spending 1 billion dollars a day to fight a war for oil companies. In the meantime, Bush, Cuomo, and Dinkins tell us that there is no money for AIDS, Housing, Education, Jobs, Drug Treatment, and other social programs. The war is killing people of color just like AIDS is. People of Color are represented disproportionately in both the war in the Middle East and the AIDS war. The war is here!

WHAT ARE THE BLACK AND LATINO POLITICIANS DOING TO RESOLVE THE AIDS PROBLEM?

The total absence of leadership shown by the elected officials, including the Black and Latino politicians, is the primary reason why our communities find themselves in poverty, lack of education, horrible health conditions, high unemployment, drug addiction, crime and other social ills. In order to cope with New York State fiscal problems, Governor Cuomo is attempting to balance his budget with people's lives. What happened to his five-year AIDS plan? Budgets must be balanced, but not at the cost of thousands of New Yorkers' lives. You are the Black and Latino legislators of the AIDS capital of the world. Your "family of New York" is dying. Where is the leadership New York needs to weather this storm? MANDATE RELIEF = DEATH. Health Care must not be subjected to any budgetary cuts. Last year Cuomo allocated 964 million dollars for the State Department of Health. Half of those funds were reappropriated, 455 million dollars. Why wasn't this money spent last year and where is this money today?

"If we keep delaying, if we keep penny-pinching, if we keep trying to save money in this sector (AIDS), we won't. We'll just kill more people." Dr. David Rogers, Chairman of the State AIDS Advisory Council.

MANIFESTO
CAUCUS OF ASIAN & PACIFIC ISLANDER AIDS ACTIVISTS

WE ARE

People descended from Bangladesh, Bhutan, Borneo, Burma, Cambodia, China, Guam, Hong Kong, India, Indonesia, Japan, Korea, Laos, Malaysia, Mongolia, Nepal, Pakistan, Philippines, Polynesia, Singapore, Sri Lanka, Taiwan, Thailand, Tibet, Vietnam, and countries and territories in the Polynesian, Micronesian, and Melanesian Islands.

WE ARE CULTURALLY DIVERSE, MULTILINGUAL, AND WE ARE ALL LIVING WITH HIV, THE VIRUS THAT CAUSES AIDS.

WE ARE HERE BECAUSE

The U.S. Immigration policy mandates all immigrants applying for residency to be tested for HIV. If testing positive, the applicant will be subject to deportation. Under such status, he/she will not be eligible for any public assistance or health care, especially HIV/AIDS treatments that are only available in the U.S.

IN THE PAST EIGHT YEARS, DURING THE HEIGHT OF THE AIDS CRISIS, ASIANS AND PACIFIC ISLANDERS WERE THE LARGEST IMMIGRANT GROUP ENTERING THE UNITED STATES.

In 1988, the CDC (Federal Center for Disease Control) finally gave Asians and Pacific Islanders our own category in its AIDS statistics. However, due to our relatively small number, in New York City's statistics (as of October 1990), we are still grouped together with Native Americans and Alaskan Natives. In New York State's epidemiological studies, we are still classified as "Others".

FUNDING FOR ASIAN AND PACIFIC ISLANDER SPECIFIC HIV PREVENTION MATERIALS AND SERVICES WAS DENIED BY THE CDC ON THE BASIS OF INSUFFICIENT STATISTICS AND THEREFORE INSUFFICIENT NEEDS.

Well into the 11th year of the AIDS crisis, due to the lack of funding, there are still no ASIAN/HIV specific advocacy and social service agency in New York. As the result, neither New York City nor New York State has any culturally relevant HIV prevention materials in

Asian and Pacific Islander languages, and no outreach efforts into the communities.

ACCORDING TO CDC, ASIANS AND PACIFIC ISLANDERS ARE THE FASTEST GROWING "MINORITY GROUP" DIAGNOSED WITH FULL BLOWN AIDS CASES IN THE U.S.

Confronted with language and cultural barriers, the fear of deportation, lack of affordable health care and drug treatment, no guarantee of anonymity, and no information about AIDS, Asians and Pacific Islanders infected with HIV do not seek help and are not counted. When we do, help is often not available.

THERE IS ONLY ONE COMMUNITY-BASED CLINIC TARGETED TOWARDS ASIANS AND PACIFIC ISLANDERS, LOCATED IN CHINATOWN IN NYC, AND THERE IS ONLY ONE CHINESE SPEAKER ON THE NYC AIDS HOT LINE.

WE DEMAND

- That the United States government abolish its racist and AIDSphobic mandatory HIV testing policy imposed on immigrants.
- That the U.S. government fund the production and distribution of HIV prevention information, including safer sex and safe IV-drug use information which is culturally relevant and in languages specific to the Asian and Pacific Islander communities.
- That specific materials be created targeting the special needs of teenagers, women, IV-drug users, sex workers, gay men, and lesbians within our communities, and that these materials be supportive and non-judgmental in their approaches.
- That the U.S. Government fund and establish community-based advocacy and service provider agencies for Asians and Pacific Islanders living with HIV, and that these organizations be created with active involvements of Asian and Pacific islanders with HIV diseases and our advocates.
- That community-based health care and drug treatment clinics be instituted. That health care and drug treatment be provided regardless of ability to pay and/or legal status, and that anonymity be assured.
- That the United States government conduct accurate and specific epidemiological studies with regard to HIV transmission in Asians and Pacific Islanders, and that these studies be sensitive to confidentiality and follow up by providing counseling and health care services.

WE ARE COMMITTED TO DIRECT ACTION TO MAKE THE U.S. GOVERNMENT RESPONSIVE TO THE NEEDS OF OUR COMMUNITIES. WE ARE COMMITTED TO DISSEMINATE HIV PREVENTION AND TREATMENT INFORMATION TO OUR NATIVE COUNTRIES. WE WILL NOT BE SACRIFICED IN THE NAME OF "INSUFFICIENT NEED."

FIGHT RACISM, FIGHT SEXISM, FIGHT HOMOPHOBIA, FIGHT GOVERNMENT NEGLECT, FIGHT INVISIBILITY, FIGHT AIDS.

JOIN US.

AIDS AND POLITICS:
TRANSFORMATIONS OF OUR MOVEMENT

Speech given at the National Gay and Lesbian Task Force Town Meeting
for the Gay Community (1989)

Maxine Wolfe

Over most of the 30 years of my political activism I was somehow always on the "periphery of the periphery", as my friend Sarah described it the night she hung out at one of the early meetings of the ACT UP women's caucus at a local bar. The question I want to address tonight, then, is: how could a nice Jewish girl from Brooklyn, who once described herself as a bisexual, Trotskyist, anarchist, Reichian, lesbian-feminist, end up in an organization people continually describe as white, male, bourgeois (worse yet, upper-middle-class), single-issue, not gay-identified, arrogant, resource-rich and every other thing that people who describe themselves as "progressive" don't like? The second question is why have I stayed in it? And, the last one is what will happen next?

I came to AIDS activism and to NY ACT UP out of a queer consciousness, a consciousness forced on me by the sexism and homophobia of the male-identified left in this country and by the homophobia of the women's movement. I came to ACT UP because of the inability of lesbians to organize around or even figure out what their issues were and because of the dead-end of the "identity" politics of the early 1980's.

1981, the year that the first article about what would eventually be called AIDS appeared, was also the year that the Family Protection Act was introduced into the U.S. Congress—the social agenda for Reagan America which, by the way, contained the original wording of the Helms Amendment about AIDS educational materials. Where was I? I had nothing to do with the mainstream lesbian and gay movement in N.Y. which had spent most of its time trying to get the Gay Rights Bill passed (16 years, in fact). On the other hand, I wasn't in the center of the lesbian-feminist movement either, women who were mostly working on anti-violence issues or were active in the Women's Pentagon Action. I was on the "periphery of the periphery," working in what was then called the reproductive rights movement and I was also working with the lesbian and gay left in N.Y., what little there was of it.

I had joined the reproductive rights movement three years earlier to organize around the elimination of medicaid funding for abortion, after I had left the Trotskyist group whose periphery I had been on for several years. I had left the Trotskyist group because my concerns fell under what they still called "the woman question", because of their alternating condescension and romanticization of the working class from which I came, because they never mentioned gays or lesbians, because they operated on a Marxist-Leninist model of the party with a hierarchy and an absolute set of politics with no room for individual experience to be discussed. Everything was abstract and happening to someone else. They were pure. The rigidity and superficiality of their ideology and practice was suffocating me and, after trying long enough I finally had to admit that they weren't about to change. They disparagingly called the reproductive rights group which I joined "feminist", which it was on the surface, but I said I would rather argue for my Marxist politics in a feminist group than for my feminist politics in a Marxist group. I was wrong. Five years later, in 1984, I decided I'd rather do neither. And, by that time I had decided I didn't want to work with straight feminists from the left, I didn't want to be in a lesbian-feminist group and I didn't want to be in a lesbian and gay left group. What had happened?

By 1982 I had been forced out of the reproductive rights group for daring to suggest that lesbian sexuality as well as lesbian motherhood should fit somewhere in our politics. I was called an "unconscious lesbian separatist"—that was to rationalize the fact that I worked with gay men in a mixed-left coalition. The national network I had helped form in 1979, and of which it was a part, folded two years later, with racism and homophobia central to its demise. The six of us on the steering committee, all lesbians—3 white, 2 Black and 1 Latina, were told we were "vanguardist" for asking straight white women to put their actions where their words were. The white straight women accused me of "having lost my political judgment" for supporting the women of color and the women of color didn't think I supported them enough. In terms of homophobia, I can remember having a discussion with a straight white feminist who I respected quite a lot in which I kept asking her to explain why the only time men appeared on our leaflets was in connection with the lesbians—as in "lesbian and gay rights." I remember saying to her: "the lesbians in this group want to be women but you can only see us as queer." The lesbians of color went off to form their own group, found out what their differences were, and then formed several separate groups.

The lesbian and gay, multi-racial left coalition I had been part of also died, as its odd assortment of independent groups, independent people and people from left parties got mired in the question of "who were we anyway?" Each of the groups had their own agenda and the independent people wanted this to be their group and what was the point anyway since we couldn't get any support from the lesbian and gay community who didn't seem to care about the Family Protection Act or about how the Gay Pride March was run?

Some of the things these groups had in common was an outdated concept of organizing, an unwillingness to reach outside their known constituencies, and a rigid set of politics around which everyone had to agree and then you couldn't question anything or you were suspect.

The lesbian community in N.Y. wasn't in any better shape. The lesbian-feminist group I helped form in 1982 collapsed with the collapse of the reproductive rights network of which it also became a part. Without being part of a larger women's movement, many of the lesbians couldn't figure out what to do. Although we printed a button that said "Lesbian Visibility Means Lesbian Survival", somehow all other women's issues seemed like something you could act on but what kinds of actions could you do about lesbians? And, without a common enemy we found out we had lots of differences, especially brought out in the pro- and anti-sex debates. For example, there were women who wouldn't talk to me because I agreed to talk in support of the North American Man-Boy Love Association when they were being hounded by the FBI. Then NAMBLA tried to use me as a stand-in for their tirade against the National Organization for Women.

"Identity politics" had gotten to the point where, apparently, the only woman I was supposed to feel comfortable talking to was another working-class, Jewish lesbian mother of two children from the left who was neither vanilla nor chocolate. Everybody was in their own separate box and I didn't have a box to fit into.

By 1984, I was severely depressed. All of the groups I had worked with since 1979 no longer existed. I was forced to re-evaluate every political perspective and value I ever had. I started going to every meeting I could find, including lesbian and gay democrats. I decided I had to clear out my head of previous indoctrination, really listen to what people said and really look at what they were doing.

When an article appeared asking for volunteers to work at the Lesbian Herstory Archives, I began my still-weekly treks to the upper-west side. The Archives has remained, for me, a nurturing place, the only remaining women-only space in N.Y. and a place where rigid ideology fades as a truly diverse group of lesbians work together committed to preserving the full range of lesbian experience and life. There are no boxes there. But, it was not enough for my activist bones.

I did a range of different things between 1984 and 1987 but two events stand out. First, going to the first public meeting of the Gay and Lesbian Alliance Against Defamation and seeing that at least 400 gay men and a few lesbians wanted to do activist work around homophobia and AIDS. I didn't join, however, because their operating style was the familiar "progressive" model. In addition, in response to my questions about what they were about, the answer they gave me was that they were neither for or against the closing of the bath-houses. That turned me off. I was against the closing of the bath-houses. The second significant event (or rather, events) were the Hardwick demos, both the spontaneous sit-in of hundreds that night in Sheridan Square and the several thousand who, four days later on July 4th, marched into the throngs of tourists at the Statue of Liberty Centennial—against the desires of the self-appointed "gay leadership", who thought it would "look bad" if we disrupted the party. I realized that the community was ahead of its so-called "leadership" and willing to put their bodies on the line at the right moment. This gave me hope.

Almost 1 year later, a week before the Lesbian and Gay Pride March in 1987, a friend of mine told me about an AIDS activist group. I decided to go to their next meeting the day after the march. As if by fate, at the march I saw this guy selling "Silence=Death" T-shirts. I went over to him and said "Are there women in your group?" "Sure", he said. So the next evening I found myself at the Lesbian and Gay Community Center in a group of a couple of hundred men who I didn't know and about 4 visible women, two of whom turned out to be straight. I had assumed it was a lesbian- and gay-identified group. I was wrong again.

Why did I stay when, in terms of political perspective, many things about this group should have told me to leave? For example, people didn't want to be called lesbian and gay activists; they wanted to be called AIDS activists. They seemed to believe in the health-care system, even if it had gone awry. But everything was run democratically and people got up and said what they thought. I could get up and say what I thought. They wanted to end the AIDS crisis, period, and if you had a good idea they would listen. No one spouted rhetoric; there was no party line. They had great ideas for actions without any pre-set idea of the right way to do things. They thought tabling was a new idea. They had a great sense of the visual and they used the media but they didn't cater to it. No one quibbled over words on a flyer. If you wanted to do an action you proposed it. Most likely people would do it. In fact, they did more actions in a week then I'd ever thought possible. And *they* have made more of an impact, both conceptually and in terms of saving people's lives, than any group I've ever been part of. These were people organizing not from some abstract concept but to save their lives and the lives of people they cared about. And, they were pro-sex at a time when sex was being connected to death.

But I am a realist and not a romantic. I don't think ACT UP is the be-all and end-all. There are and have been problems. You can ask me all about them. I stayed in ACT UP because it is a place where I can be a lesbian, a woman and an activist working on an issue that is real to me and that brings together so many of my political concerns. I stayed in ACT UP because I have seen people *develop* a political perspective, including myself. I have changed and learned or I wouldn't still be there. It is also the first real organizing I feel I've ever done. I have seen men who wanted to hide being gay behind their AIDS activism do a teach-in on lesbian and gay history, become more and more openly gay and develop a gay liberation and not a gay rights perspective. I have seen the issues expand—a year ago no one talked about nationalized health care; now we have a national health care committee and are talking to unions about doing an action together. ACT UP is a true coalition. Everyone puts up with what my mother would call, everyone else's "mischagas"—craziness. I have come to appreciate what each person can and will contribute because they have a shared commitment to the saving of lives. In a way, it is very similar to the Archives.

I am not on the periphery of the periphery. For the first time, rather than feeling that I am reacting to exclusion and responding from the margins, I feel I am acting from my center but not from the mainstream. I feel I'm helping to build a movement that is mine rather than trying to fit into someone else's.

I don't know where ACT UP will go. Your guess is as good as mine. As for our movement, the lesbian and gay and AIDS movement, I believe that in order to take advantage of the momentum for the future, especially older lesbians and lesbians and gay men who identify with progressive movements need to seriously check out our own homophobia and our rigid rules for evaluating political movements. For example, there are two questions I am always asked by lesbians who look down on AIDS work and by lesbian and gay men working in other progressive movements. One is: "Would gay men have done the same thing for lesbians if the situation had been reversed?" The first thing I say is "I am not in this movement for gay men; I am in this movement for myself." And then I ask them: "What have straight women and straight men done for us? What have the anti-nuclear and anti-intervention movements done for us?" I am not saying that people shouldn't work in these movements. I am saying "Check out the homophobia in your question." The second question I am asked is: "If a cure for AIDS happened tomorrow, wouldn't all those gay men go home and not care about access issues"? Probably a lot would, I answer, just like all the women who went home after *Roe v. Wade* and who only come out again when *Roe v. Wade* is threatened, for e.g. the Webster case. The fact is that poor women, and because of institutional racism in this country, Black and Latin women who are disproportionately among the poor, and young women and rural women have not had access to abortion for many, many years. Where were these women in 1977 when the Hyde Amendment, cutting off federal medicaid funding for abortion, was passed? Gay men, as a group, are no better and no worse than anyone else. We have to get past this mentality.

In that respect, one of the most important roles that ACT UP plays is that it is a place where many younger gay men and lesbians have come to understand that what we want is the right to exist—not the right to privacy; the right to a life, not to a life-style; and a life that is as important as anyone else's but not any more important that anyone else's. This is the basis for any kind of work outside of the lesbian and gay community and it is why ACT UP has been managing to do some of that work.

Many younger lesbians in ACT UP see themselves as "queer" and both their political and social life is tied to that of gay men. While I have made good gay male and lesbian friends in ACT UP, many of whom will remain my friends for a long time, ACT UP does not satisfy my social needs. But I am not into coupledom or monogamy in my political life any more than in my social life. ACT UP is my political home for now. And, I can honestly say that while in 1979 there were only a handful of gay men in New York I could work with politically, after ACT UP, there will be more. That's not bad.

LET MY PEOPLE IN

from *Outweek* (1990)

Mark Harrington

We cannot sweep under the rug the criticisms received in the last year. We are scientists, and science is based on skepticism.

> —Larry Corey, ACTG Executive Committee chair, to the Ninth AIDS Clinical Trials Group (ACTG) meeting June 11, 1990

Science thrives on doubt, and you are bringing doubt into the system.

> —Dan Hoth, NIAID Division of AIDS, to ACT UP members, June 12, 1990

I want we, and not others, to be our severest critics.

> —Anthony Faud to the Ninth ACTG, June 11, 1990

I have long wondered why AIDS activists seem to make more headway within the realm of science than in, say, local and state politics. Is it a difference in facts or in the susceptibility of targets? Unlike most politicians, bureaucrats and journalists, many scientists are actually capable of rational discourse, and sometimes they even change their minds. There is another difference too: While most politicians, bureaucrats and journalists would rather not deal with AIDS (they wish that it would go away, so they help make us go away), the scientists in question have actually chosen to work on AIDS (and they are the exception, not the rule). Basic scientists have never had a rebellion on the part of their laboratory mice; clinical scientists have often labored under the illusion that controlled trials in humans are merely lab-rat studies on a larger scale. This is no longer so. For all the threats that if activists did not shut up, scientists would leave the field, it is hard to imagine eminent virologists who have invested ten years in their AIDS work suddenly reverting to the days before the war, treating little old ladies with shingles. Their only other option was to admit us into the system—and now, after a year-long struggle, they have.

No more secret meetings. The Ninth AIDS Clinical Trials Group (ACTG) meeting was the first in which people with AIDS and activists were allowed to attend most sessions of official registrants, without bureaucratic resistance or impediment. Even the press was allowed in for the first time. The meeting was characterized by an unprecedented degree of openness, and many scientists, both from NIH and from academic centers, seemed to have undergone a good deal of soul-searching over the past few months.

It was a far cry from the hostility with which ACT UP members were received in November 1989, when they first barged into the closed counsels of AIDS science, and equally unlike the patronizing and patriarchal greeting extended to a few carefully selected community representatives when they first met the entire ACTG Executive Committee in March of this year.

AIDS activist groups and others will be permitted to send observers to all future ACTG meetings, which will be held at a larger hotel in downtown Washington. The National Institute of Allergy and Infectious Diseases (NIAID), which oversees the ACTG and conducts much other AIDS research, will open its related conferences, such as the National Cooperative Drug Discovery Groups (NCDDGs) to community representatives.

This does not mean that activists have won an unqualified victory, or that the tasks before us are not as daunting as they ever were. But at least we will not have to skirmish over access to those who set research priorities, select drugs and design and carry out clinical trials.

Participation in decision making. By November, members of the ACTG Patient Constituency Working Group, which includes AIDS activists, people with AIDS, representatives from diverse community groups and even a community-based AIDS clinician will have voting membership on all the ACTG's research committees, including two members on the all-powerful Executive Committee.

Redesigning the system. In 1991, the entire ACTG system will be revamped, as the five-year cooperative agreements between NIAID and the 49 academic sites are up for renewal. Division of AIDS Director Hoth has promised that ACT UP and other activist groups will have input into the redesign.

A conflict-of-interest policy. NIAID is not going to wait for NIH to put forth new guidelines regulating conflicts of interest among investigators receiving both federal and corporate funds. It is going to implement its own rules calling for full disclosure of all corporate equity holdings and consultancies held by NIAID-sponsored investigators. This is in line with ACT UP's demands in May.

Involvement at local AIDS Clinical Trials Units (ACTU) sites. Each local ACTU site will be required to establish a Community Advisory Panel, to assist with trial design, enrollment and dissemination of results.

Openness to new trial designs. The ACTG Statistical Working Group, led by chief NIAID biostatistician, Susan Ellenberg, spent its July meeting fleshing out the implications of ACT UP's 1990 Treatment Agenda, including the design of a quick screening program for testing new anti-HIV drugs against each other in under three months, before deciding which ones should go on to larger, longer comparative trials.

Recognition of the need to study more new treatments. NIAID Director Fauci said repeatedly that either the ACTG must devise an initiative to conduct small pilot studies of new treatments (such as the 99 that ACT UP listed in its *Treatment Agenda* at the San Francisco AIDS conference), or NIAID will have to begin a separate initiative to do so.

Recognition of the need to study drugs used in the community. Another unmet need recognized by Fauci is a program to quickly test drugs which catch on in the community, either inside or outside the ACTG. This might spare thousands of PWAs the expense and disappointment of wasting money, time and hope on useless substances such as AL-721, oral dextran sulfate or (more recently) oral alpha interferon.

More emphasis on opportunistic infections. This year, for the first time, the ACTG plans to open trials for all five major opportunistic infection groups: PCP, CMV, toxoplasmosis, fungal infections and MAI. Trials are slated as well to improve treatments for the most common HIV-related cancers, Kaposi's sarcoma and the various lymphomas.

More emphasis on women and HIV. More resources will be given to the Obstetrical and Gynecological Subcommittee of the Pediatric Committee, enabling it to expand its focus from pregnant women to all women with HIV.

In a way, the new openness at the ACTG amounts to calling the community's bluff. We said that we wanted input and access: What will we do now that we have it?

As a start, we must become more conversant with the real problems at local research sites. We cannot focus all our attention on the center and the hierarchy and ignore the realities of research work. It is time to get our hands dirty, learning about the complex realities of AIDS research in the diverse settings where it is conducted.

We must not abandon our criticism of the systemic flaws which continue to afflict the ACTG. Research priorities are not yet in balance. There are no options for people who are still asymptomatic but for whom AZT has worn out its usefulness. Too few anti-HIV alternatives to AZT-like drugs are being studied. The ddI protocols are going too slowly and use unrealistic entry criteria. Opportunistic-infection studies are not implemented enthusiastically. The expertise of the pharmacologists, neurologists, research nurses and data managers is, all too often, ignored by the ACTG hierarchy. A few investigators are waging a last-ditch effort to kill parallel track in its infancy. These and other problems remain, but at least we will be able to bring our concerns and our demands directly to those responsible.

None of this could have happened without the efforts of thousands of people with AIDS over the last ten years and those of the hundreds of activists who stormed the NIH on May 21.

ACT UP AT A CROSSROADS

from the *Village Voice* (1990)

Donna Minkowitz

Like many sometime anarchists, funky-minded leftists, and radical democrats, I lost my heart at my first ACT UP meeting. For years I'd resigned myself to working in progressive political groups whose structure had all too little to do with their vision of a freer society. Suddenly the AIDS crisis had generated a group that recognized organizational structure as *political*: there were 400 people in the room and most of them voiced their opinions to the other 399 at some time during the meeting. The entire group decided on every action to be done in ACT UP's name. For people born in a country where political passivity is imbibed along with mother's milk, this degree of participation was like eating political spinach. No wonder the federal health bureaucracy quaked when this massive empowerment-machine rolled toward it.

Other organizations say they function democratically but they don't mean this: a passionate determination to avoid even an informal hierarchy. In this spirit, each ACT UP member was allowed no more than a minute and a half to speak on any given topic: the charismatic, mediagenic, or politically adept were not specially favored. Meetings, therefore, were cacophonous but almost never nasty: ACT UP might shout Ed Koch or Stephen Joseph down, but shouting down fellow ACT UP members was considered a blow against the brave attempt each week to build community in that dingy room.

Now that the group has emerged as a model for activism in the 90's ACT UP is torn between its present course and two other directions: centralization and schism. New pressures and opportunities stemming from ACT Up's surge in size and media attention have left this group—so brilliant at incorporating differences—struggling to contain its political divisions

ACT UP/NEW YORK, the first of what would eventually be 50 chapters around the country, was founded in 1987 by white middle class gay men who were forced to confront their despised status when AIDS decimated their numbers while the government did nothing. The fledgling group was soon joined by Black and Latin gay men, lesbians, straight women, and even a few straight men, inspired by ACT Up's radical demands and moved by the struggle to focus attention on AIDS. On any given Monday night, when ACT UP packs a ground floor meeting space at the city's Lesbian and Gay Community Services Center, women constitute about a quarter of their 500 to 600 attendees, and people of color represent about a sixth.

This unusual coalition has enabled ACT UP to address the AIDS crisis in all its manifestations: picketing *Cosmopolitan* for giving women incorrect information on AIDS transmission; campaigning for needle distribution to IV-drug users; fighting the attempt to place homeless people with AIDS in city shelters; and demonstrating against sodomy laws. In 1989, the group sent several buses to the prochoice march in Washington. At ACT UP's third anniversary action in Albany last March, the three main banners proclaimed: HEALTH CARE IS A RIGHT. DRUG TREATMENT NOW. AIDS HOUSING NOW"

This coalition is by no means without its strains. A powerful minority of the group's white men believes that ACT UP should concentrate on getting AIDS drugs approved by the federal bureaucracy—an issue that affects even the healthy AIDS patient while subordinating other struggles, such as obtaining services for indigent PWA's or providing counseling and treatment to IV-drug users. There are continual disputes about the extent to which the group should work for gay and lesbian liberation, as well as the end of AIDS. Yet ACT UP has evolved into a structure that seeks to incorporate political differences without tearing apart the whole.

Doing both isn't easy: on the one hand, the entire membership must concur on all decisions; at the same time, anything an individual wants to do at a protest is acceptable as long as it doesn't involve violence. When one protester crushed a communion wafer after at the St. Patrick's Cathedral demo against Cardinal O'Connor, he was never censured by ACT UP. A plethora of caucuses, committees, and affinity groups (see box, "An ACT UP Glossary") are places where the like-minded can undertake actions with or without the entire groups approval; an organizational nod is needed only if a subgroup is invoking ACT Up's name or using its funds. Rhetoric intoned at the beginning of every meeting describes the group as "a diverse, nonpartisan group of individuals, united in anger and committed to direct action to end the AIDS crisis."

At my first meeting back in 1988, facilitators charged with not allowing personal opinions to influence their direction of discussions helped the room focus on specific, agreed-upon topics, but there was also much laughter, spontaneous burst of chanting, kissing. And weeping: when friends died, no one gave a thought to keeping a stiff upper lip. Activists planning a demonstration actually discussed the need to provide emotional support to fellow ACT UP members who might get upset or scared when they were arrested. (No one with whom I worked politically had ever mentioned emotional support.) Later, at a demonstration ACT UP took over the street, marching 15 abreast, linking arms street corner to street corner. "which one of you is the leader?" the police captain asked. " We're all the leader. None of us is the leader." Came the reply. "If you want to talk, you have to talk to all of us."

Though power in ACT UP is widely dispersed, and often spontaneously claimed, there are a few officers. Usually electing them is the most uneventful part of ACT UP meetings; how many people would compete to be the unpaid full-time administrator who must answer the phones and open the mail, with almost no power make decisions for the group? But last month, all this changed. On April 30, not only was more than one person running for administrator, but the two candidates were strongly identified with different political currents in ACT UP.

Victor Mendolia had the backing of Larry Kramer and Peter Staley, two of ACT Up's best known members, men who have met with government officials on the group's behalf and who are frequently interviewed by the news media. In his campaign speech, Mendolia said it was time for a change in the way ACT UP is run, if elected he would share the job with others in an "administrative committee" of his choosing. This idea was similar to one Staley and Kramer had advanced in separate interviews with me as one of a series of steps to increase the group's efficiency. The committee as they envisioned it, would eventually make some decisions of an administrative nature without the floor's approval.

Those most strenuously backing Mendolia were the faction that wants ACT UP to focus its energies on speedy drug approval, abandoning what Staley has called "left-wing" tendencies. Terming ACT UP'S situation under incumbent administrator Tom Cunningham "a mess," this group called for professionalizing the group's office and "streamlining" the organization's chain of command.

Cunningham, for his part, stressed his work organizing the group's first team to translate leaflets into Spanish, and in increasing ACT UP's accessibility to the disabled. (Cunningham has AIDS: like Staley, who has ARC, he lives on disability.) Cunningham emphasized his strong support for keeping ACT Up decentralized—"a coalition not a corporation"—and inclusive of women and people of color. Cunningham had the backing of the group's black and Latin members, who are generally suspicious of the move to "professionlize" ACT UP.

Though the vote occurred after 10 p.m., hundreds of members remained in the cramped room to participate. In the end Cunningham won by a large margin, but not before an unprecedented bitterness had engulfed ACT UP. Venomous letters appearing on the literature table questioned the commitment of fellow activists. *Tell it to ACT UP*, an internally circulated newsletter whose contents are determined by suggestion box, began publishing anonymous personal attacks on members. (Rollerna, the beloved activist who makes his rounds in a gown and roller skates, was condemned for spending "several of our precious minutes telling us that she is the Belle of Three Counties.")

Staley, a former Wall Street bond trader who has worked hard on fundraising for ACT UP, traded verbal barbs with Cunningham. If Mendolia didn't win, Staley told fellow activists, he would start a separate AIDS activist organization. Now, several weeks after the election, he says he has no immediate plans to leave the group, but adds that he is not optimistic about ACT UP's current course and might soon reach the level of "desperation" that would induce him to fund another group in the offing. Members of an ACT UP affinity group known as Queer Nation, which specializes in actions against homophobia (as opposed to AIDS), recently started a strike force for gay and lesbian liberation. So far, Queer Nation has made its presence felt by invading singles bars and zapping a book-signing by Greg Louganis. Its de facto nature is part of an effort to avoid becoming "bureaucratized like ACT UP." ACT UPpers in the new group say they plan to work in both organizations. Yet they are driven by nostalgia for the sense of community and participation that ACT UP has lost in the past several months as meetings became overcrowded with hundreds of new members.

One of the new group's founders is Maxine Wolfe, a professor of environmental psychology who has been a persuasive proponent of decentralization. Wolfe, a veteran of many movements, believes that ACT UP has now gotten too large to be democratic and favors its dissolution into smaller, local chapters (e.g., Brooklyn ACT UP, East Village ACT UP, etc.)

Wolfe and her co-nationals fear that ACT UP will lose its affiliation with gay and lesbian liberation. This is an ongoing anxiety within the group: even a recent decision to move meetings from the Gay Center to a larger space has been fraught with ideological conflict. Says Wolfe: "Heterosexuals in ACT UP have to confront their homophobia at each meeting just by walking through those doors."

In recent weeks, ACT UP has been occupied with preparations for a massive demonstration at the National Institutes of Health. But now that the protest has passed, the group is likely to confront its internal divisions over structure and scope. The membership is drawn in three distinct directions: to professionalize and moderate its edge, banking on a gain in efficiency; to stay the leftward course, maintaining the current freewheeling structure, and focus on issues affecting communities of color, or to remain decentralized but also "stay gay", even as the AIDS crisis takes on a more diverse character.

In the midst of this tug of war—and pulling hard on one end—is Larry Kramer, "IT IS TIME TO ORGANIZE ACT UP INTO A LEAN AND MEAN FIGHTING ORGANIZATION THAT WORKS." Kramer thundered in an open letter to the group last January. "NOT EVERY ONCE IN A WHILE, BUT EVERY DAY OF THE WEEK."

Kramer was reacting to a climactic series of events last winter that made him and others in the group perceive a dramatic discrepancy between ACT UP's current performance and its potential. On December 3, ACT UP had its biggest-ever fund-raiser, an art auction that raised over $330,000, a staggering amount for a group whose first year budget tallied a few thousand. A week later, ACT UP had its largest action to date, the 6000-strong demonstration against the Catholic church hierarchy, which brought negative mentions on almost every editorial page—and hundreds of new activists into ACT UP meetings.

Yet a few weeks later, David Dinkins appointed Woodrow Myers as New York City health commissioner, over ACT UP's strenuous objections. "We have suffered a cruel and humiliating defeat," Kramer wrote is his open letter. "I hope you realize that this organization is not, currently, in the trim and fighting shape it requires to wage all-out war . . . This organization is not currently in the shape [to] capitalize on the power it has acquired."

Kramer proposed that the standing committees form a Security Council, which could approve expenditures up to $5000 on its own and engage in "brainstorming and long range planning" for the group. The council could select a Secretary General who will in essence speak for the Security Council and also for the organization if necessary. "No one would be allowed to vote on the floor unless they were a member "in good standing" of an ACT UP committee. New members would be given a month to affiliate. ("It's called responsibility," Kramer explained.) Kramer also called on the group to elect a permanent facilitator who would not permit "everybody's laundry list of pet grievances" to be aired. "Conversely," Kramer objected to facilitators who "cut people off in mid sentence because your time is up." (In the past, Kramer himself has wrangled with facilitators who asked him to adhere to the time limits.)

Kramer's plan was never raised as a formal proposal, but it has galvanized the group around structural questions. Setting the agenda or speaking for longer that 90 seconds may not seem like important issues, but for ACT UP they suggested the imposition of dreaded hierarchy. Up till now, anything somebody wanted on the agenda would be on it, with order hinging primarily on timeliness. Under a proposal supported by Kramer and Staley, the Coordinating Committee—which heretofore had only the power to approve small expenditures and written materials—would set a preliminary agenda. It could be altered by the floor, but in the Monday night crush for time that would be difficult. The new system was approved for a month-long trial period, but recently voted down after heated debate.

Staley and others began considering alternative approaches, such as impaneling new committees to make all fundraising and administrative decisions for ACT UP independent of the Monday night meeting. "As the agenda grows, there's simply too much of it for a four-hour meeting." Says Staley. "We need more time for discussions on policy decisions." But aren't administrative and fundraising decisions also policy? (In one hotly contested fundraising debate, for example, the floor voted to hold benefits only at those clubs without selective admissions, since black and Latin gays and lesbians have long charged that such door policies are used to exclude them.)

Kramer, Staley, and their allies remain a crucial element in the ACT UP mix. They are the group's main liaisons with federal agencies, and they have ready access to the media. But their very visibility has become a bone of contention in the group since the media, unaccustomed to dealing with grassroots activism, takes spokespersons for leaders. Kramer's views, in particular, are often conflated with those of ACT UP. When a *Wall Street Journal* reporter asked Kramer about protests at the International AIDS Conference next month, he replied: "It hurts me to say I think the time for violence has now arrived." The reporter got a comment from ACT UP's media committee disavowing violence, but not every journalist is so scrupulous.

Implicit in the clash of classes and personalities is the larger issue of centralizing ACT UP. That would certainly present some practical advantages. A group of 500 to 1000 cannot take action swiftly; an anarchic coalition cannot always present a unified voice to the press and public, but equally practical considerations argue for retention of ACT UP'S freewheeling structure. The exhilaration of working in a participatory democracy has been one of ACT UP's greatest attractions, and it is doubtful that a centralized cadre could draw the same large numbers. Without its shock troops—without a mass movement—would ACT UP be able to force more changes on the government?

There's another practical reason for ACT UP to stay as it is. FBI and police infiltration and manipulation did much to destroy radical movements of the '60's yet top-down organizations are much more easily damaged in this way than bottom-up ones. "One of the strengths of being an amorphous democracy is that infiltration has a much more limited effect," says Mike Spiegel, once national secretary of Students for a Democratic Society and currently an ACT UP member. Michael Wiggins, an organizer of an ACT UP antiracist affinity group called WAR, puts it another way: "No one can infiltrate chaos. People can only manipulate order".

AN ACT-UP GLOSSARY:
DIVERSITY = STRENGTH

The work of ACT UP is largely done by a series of committees that bring the fruits of their research to the floor. Each *working committee* has a vote on the coordinating committee, with the approval of the floor, working groups that don't desire such certification can either be *subcommittees*, which have a loose affiliation to established committees; *caucuses*, which combine individuals with similar characteristics or concerns; or *groups*, which have an even more amorphous description. *Affinity groups* provide mutual support for civil disobedience, and plan and undertake actions that need to be secret. *Art collectives* decide what visual materials to produce in ACT UP's name, but the floor votes on whether to officially endorse these works.

In fact, the floor must vote on virtually everything bearing ACT UP's name. Demonstrations are called to a halt so the participants can decide what to do next, and even in which direction to march.

What follows is a breakdown of grouping within ACT UP, subject, of course, to sudden (and democratic) change:

- **Action Tours.** An affinity group that dresses up as tourists, visiting landmarks and parades, and, at an appropriate moment, revealing their true colors.
- **Administrator.** Maintains the ACT UP "workspace' (progressive for "office" Unpaid, elected.
- **Alternative and Holistic Treatments.** A subcommittee of the Treatment and Data Committee fights attempts to suppress information about holistic treatments.
- **Art Positive.** Fights art censorship à la Helms [conservative U.S. Senator who blocked funding for gay arts—Eds.] This is an organization in its own right, but also an affiliate of ACT UP.
- **At-large Representatives.** Two people who represent all ACT UPers who choose not to be on any committee: they also orient new members. Elected positions.
- **Awning Leapers.** An affinity group that loves to afix banners in prominent places.
- **City Action Committee.** Originally formed around the 1989 City Hall demonstration, then revived after the Myers affair. Deals with the mayor and the Department of Health.
- **Coordinating Committee.** Has voting representatives from ACT UP working committees; the administrator and the two elected at-large representatives also vote. Anyone can attend meetings.
- **Costas.** A left-leaning and abundantly queer affinity group named in memory of Costa Pappas, an ACT UP videographer who died of AIDS.
- **Cuomophobes.** An affinity group. Self explanatory. [Mario Cuomo was then governor of New York—Eds.]
- **DIVA TV.** Stands for Damned Interfering Video Activists. Takes pictures at demos in order to deter police violence; also makes militant, stylish videos about ACT UP.
- **Facilitators.** Four people with great self control. They call on people at Monday night meetings and count votes. Elected positions.
- **Foreign National Caucus.** Used to be called "Aliens From Mars".
- **Fundraising Committee.** Self-explanatory.
- **Gran Fury.** Started before ACT UP did; an art collective that has made some of ACT UP's most well-known graphics, such as Silence = Death.
- **Housing Committee.** Fights HRA [Human Resources Administration] and the mayor's office to secure humane housing for homeless people with HIV.
- **INS Action Group.** Challenges U.S. policy on immigrants with AIDS.
- **Insurance and Access Committee.** Agitates against insurance companies' AIDS discrimination, and for a national health plan.
- **InterACT.** A caucus for the purpose of exchanging information with other AIDS activist groups.
- **Jailbait.** An affinity group about prison issues.
- **Latino/Latina AIDS Activist Caucus.** Recently formed.
- **Lawyers.** Indispensable.
- **Lesbian Caucus.** Used to be the Women's Caucus.
- **Majority Action Committee.** Works on AIDS issues affecting people of color, soon to be the majority of AIDS cases in New York; open to all.
- **Media Committee.** Gets the press to demos.
- **Needle Exchange Committee.** Joins with John Parker's National AIDS Brigade in distributing clean needles to IV-drug users; hopes to provoke a court challenge to the state law against needle distribution.

- **New Jersey ACT UP.** Does actions across the border.
- **Outreach committee.** More like advertising, comes up with the snazzy posters for demonstrations.
- **NIH Working Group.** An ad hoc committee organizing (and cleaning up after) the May 21 demonstration at the National Institutes of Health.
- **PISD Caucus.** People with Immune Systems Disorders, including AIDS, RC, HIV, lupus, and chronic fatigue, among others. An affinity group.
- **Power Tools.** An affinity group that once bedeviled Burroughs Wellcome by walling themselves inside B.W offices; also, stock exchange actions that involve chains and welding.
- **Rats.** Radical Art Truth Squad, an art collective
- **San Francisco Ad Hoc Committee.** For the June international AIDS conference that ACT UP, unlike almost all other progressive health entities, is not boycotting.
- **Spanish Translation and Communications Committee.** New; translates ACT UP literature.
- **Speakers Bureau.** Talks to college classes and others. A subcommittee of Outreach.
- **Treasurer.** Elected.
- **Treatment and Data Committee.** One of ACT UP's oldest committees; collects information on new AIDS drugs, lobbies federal agencies for speedy and humane drug approval.
- **Wave Three.** The oldest ACT UP affinity group in existence. Takes its name from the "wave" in which civil disobedience was planned at the 1988 Wall Street action.
- **WAR.** An affinity group; Wipe out AIDS and Racism.
- **Women's Action Committee.** Open to all; works on women and AIDS. Often branches out as an affinity group during demos.
- **Youth Brigade.** Not composed of youths, but for them; a caucus that hounds the Board of Education and hands out condoms and info at high schools.

AIDS AND THE GAY/ LESBIAN MOVEMENT

Donna Minkowitz's article, reproduced above, is one angle, specific to ACT UP, of a critique of AIDS organizations and of the institutionalization of AIDS as a chronic disease. This critique runs in parallel and sometimes overlaps with a "deconstruction of AIDS" to which we shall return. For Minkowitz, the tension was between participatory democracy and the need for expertise and regularized leadership in order to affect government decision-making bodies. At around the same time, Darrell Yates Rist, who died from AIDS complications in 1993, wrote an article titled "The Deadly Cost of an Obsession" for *The Nation*, a left-liberal weekly that, by the article's publication in 1989, had paid scant attention to the eight-year-old epidemic. Rist argued that too much of the lesbian and gay community's resources had been devoted to AIDS at the expense of other issues, for example of anti-gay and anti-lesbian violence and lesbian/gay youth. The article was followed by an avalanche of letters to the editor both for and against his position.

In one of the writings presented here, Eric Rofes reflects upon the "de-gaying" of AIDS organizations. He writes from personal experience as director of the San Francisco Bay area's Shanti Project, a death and dying organization founded in the 1970s that became primarily an AIDS organization in the 1980s. He analyzes the extent to which AIDS organizations should represent issues of the lesbian and (especially) gay male movement, or put them on the back burner or in the closet for efficacy in representing AIDS as an issue distinct in itself to a public wider than lesbians and gay men. He sees this as the political effect of the practical reality that, as the "face" of the epidemic has changed as a result of prevention efforts and deaths among gay men, the caseload of such organizations is increasingly heterosexual—including women, intravenous drug users (IVDUs), and children—as well as bisexuals who do not identify with the lesbian and gay movement.

In New York City, a similar argument was made in 1991 by white gay men who founded AIDS activism and still formed the largest caseload, but who were being ignored in the decision-making processes of some activist organizations and even perceived themselves as being "bashed" by them. Writing about how AIDS activism abandoned gay men, late ACT UP member Robin Hardy stated, in the *Village Voice*'s gay pride issue:

It's obvious that despite an eagerness to adopt—or impose—the goals of other minorities, no hoards of righteous straights cram the meetings, nor do people of color stream south from Harlem or the Bronx on Monday nights "united in anger." The promise of a grand coalition has proven empty, and gay men in ACT UP are left to fight battles for women, IVDUs, African-Americans, Hispanics, prisoners, the homeless, even children with AIDS. The vital interests of gay men are left by the wayside . . . The "greatest obstacle to conscious and visible gay and lesbian ownership of the AIDS issue is our deep-rooted fear of repeating the injustices done to us by excluding the other communities affected by AIDS." [Hardy, citing another author] . . . But . . . an authentic ally never demands that you cease to be yourself in order to include them.

Obviously, many gay men are Hispanic, African-American, prisoners, IVDUs, and homeless, but he continues:

In the ACT UP newsletter, a lesbian asks: "Why do men exist," apparently unaware that existence is problematic for most of the men with whom she sits through meetings . . . When a flyer states that 11,000 "women, children, and men died of AIDS this year, the ranking seems reminiscent of degrees of putative innocence . . . Said one person leaving [an ACT UP meeting]: "As a gay man I didn't feel safe in there."

The Rofes argument is generalized and placed on a more theoretical level by Daniel Defert. When his lover, Michel Foucault died from AIDS-related causes in 1984, Defert in his mourning and resolve founded what became France's largest AIDS organization, AID$_E$S; he now teaches sociology and advises the World Health Organization on AIDS throughout the world. In his article originally published in the now-defunct French gay magazine, *Le Gai Pied* he calls for a renewal of activism around an analysis of the relationship between homosexuality and the disease: the interrelation of seropositives and seronegatives in a shared way of life, including open discussion of sexual practices within those relationships and the creation of a distinctive homosexual politics that incorporates AIDS but is not defined by it.

GAY LIB VS. AIDS:
AVERTING CIVIL WAR IN THE 1990s

from *Out/Look* (1990)

Eric E. Rofes

A conflict is deepening that threatens to wrench apart the gay and lesbian community in the United States. Unseen, denied, or hushed through the shame of "political correctness," a growing rift between AIDS-focused organizations and progressive gay and lesbian groups appears to be pushing our community toward civil war.

Those in the trenches or community organizing heard the early rumblings by the mid-1980s. Key AIDS groups, conceived within local gay and lesbian communities, rapidly became million-dollar agencies and enjoyed the "goodies" that accompany media limelight. Parallel groups with a specific focus on gay and lesbian health concerns struggled to maintain paid staff and keep doors open. The two quietly began facing off, like boxers entering the ring. Tensions over a perceived shift in community resources have deepened over the past five years because of conflicts over political issues, openness about gay and lesbian participation, sexual liberation, and organizational culture.

AIDS leaders can no longer avoid confronting some critical questions: Are we a part of the gay and lesbian movement, or do we stand outside of it? If we expect the gay and lesbian community to support us, does it have a right to expect anything in return beyond the provision of HIV-related services? If we become multicultural organizations, do we need to relinquish any commitment to a gay and lesbian agenda? In an increasingly homophobic United States in 1990, there is no neutral position. Which side are we on?

The Imbalance of Resources

Gay and lesbian organizers have been critical of AIDS advocates, but primarily behind closed doors, where they'll complain that "all the money is going to AIDS," or that "the community's entire agenda has been swallowed up by AIDS." When I left my job at a gay and lesbian service center to work for an exclusively AIDS-focused organization, I repeatedly heard one version or another of "Yet another gay organizer sells out to the AIDS bureaucracy." I questioned my motives too and worried that directing an AIDS service organization would mean opting out of the gay and lesbian liberation movement.

Throughout most of the 1980s few gay and lesbian groups felt comfortable articulating these concerns overtly. Instead, they plugged away, responding to the perceived shift in resources by adding AIDS components to existing programs—sometimes in a true and appropriate desire to serve, and sometimes primarily to enhance their fundraising appeals.

Meanwhile, AIDS organizers developed their own criticism of gay and lesbian groups, arguing that "they lack professionalism and stability" or that they're "made up of a bunch of bitchy queens and politically correct dykes who spend hours 'processing' but don't do any work."

Some representatives of AIDS groups competing for funding with gay and lesbian projects warned funders that their colleagues were "well intentioned" but "unpredictable and radical"—a true funding risk. When gay and lesbian groups issued direct-mail appeals focused on their HIV-related components, some AIDS organizers scoffed at the "exaggerated" level of work the groups claimed to do in the AIDS area and derided their desperate attempt to "latch on" to the AIDS funding bandwagon.

As the decade drew to a close, the situation escalated from behind-the-scenes rumblings to public confrontations. Direct-action AIDS activists found themselves attacked in community newspapers for maintaining a narrow focus and failing to make homophobia as much of a priority as AIDS-related discrimination. Community activists began attacking AIDS service groups for trying to capture additional public support by "sanitizing" or "de-gaying" their agenda. Angry that almost a decade of lesbian leadership and caregiving in the AIDS arena has seen little substantive response from gay men on women's issues, some lesbians confronted gay men on unkept promises and continued self-centered agendas.

Many believe that these escalating conflicts are based solely on economic disparity, the drain of community resources into HIV-related efforts at the expense of other gay and lesbian issues.[*] For progressive activists, however, the real issues underlying this concern about resources have to do with the *politics* of AIDS organizations—and these issues intensify as AIDS organizations diversify and share power with other constituencies.

The Deliberate De-Gaying of AIDS

While some explicitly activist and lobbying groups such as ACT UP and the AIDS Action Council define themselves and their issues as political, most service and education groups labor under the belief that their work is "non-political." They embrace a self-concept as "social-service agencies" or "healthcare providers" and often insist that their mission is simply to care for sick or needy people. Supporters of this view, reading Larry Kramer's angry open letters to Gay Men's Health Crisis in which he demands that the organization move to a higher level of political militancy, wonder if he's asking for too much. After all, do people with leukemia expect the Leukemia Society to be political?

Yet gay and lesbian movement activists look to AIDS groups and wonder how they can deny the profound impact of politics on their work and their "client" base. They see AIDS organizations' failure to articulate a clear and concise position on their relationship to the gay and lesbian community as the most troubling example of this lack of awareness.

About five years ago a key decision was made by AIDS leaders to put forward the message that "AIDS is not a gay disease." The intent of this strategy apparently was to win increased public support and funding, and to alert all sectors of the population about AIDS prevention. Since that time many AIDS groups have downplayed gay and lesbian participation, denied they are "gay organizations," and attempted to appeal to the "general public" by expunging gay references and sanitizing gay culture.

At other times AIDS groups do acknowledge our bases in the gay and lesbian community, particularly when seeking support for fundraising events or trying to draw in new volunteers. This schizophrenia on the part of AIDS organizations sets off movement activists who have struggled for years to bring gay and lesbian issues out of the closet. Since Stonewall, gay liberationists persistently have demanded that "the G word" and "the L word" be said, arguing that the overt articulation of our identities as gay men or lesbians must be at the top of the movement's agenda to end homophobia. Others believe that the gay and lesbian community deserves credit for mobilizing the massive numbers of volunteers and for pioneering new service-delivery models that have emerged in response to AIDS.

The majority of people working to improve public support for AIDS are gay and lesbian people, yet the mainstream media chooses as our public heroes only heterosexuals (Mathilde Krim, Everett Koop, Dionne Warwick, Liz Taylor). AIDS organizers can spend their work lives running up against this kind of institutionalized homophobia and directing a great deal of energy toward changing the system. For example, at the August 1988 Center for Disease Control (CDC) conference on AIDS in the people-of-color communities, gay men and lesbians of color confronted the homophobia of the government hosts and non-gay people-of-color health providers who attempted to make gay and lesbian issues invisible.

It is one thing, though, for organizers to grapple with homophobia and de-gaying from traditional systems and institutions, and quite another to confront it when we come "home" to our AIDS projects—especially those founded by and based in the gay and lesbian community:

- At AIDS Project Los Angeles' 1986 Walkathon, the overwhelming majority of participants were gay men and lesbians. Throughout the opening ceremony no explicit acknowledgment was given to this community, though speakers mentioned other key populations.
- Boston's AIDS Action Committee hosted what they termed a "Pride Dance" during Lesbian and Gay Price Weekend in 1988. The flyers distributed for the event failed to include any direct reference to the gay and lesbian community.
- Our nation's most explicitly gay-identified AIDS organization, New York Gay Men's Health Crisis, entered the 1990s keeping "the G word" in its title, though encouraging the public to identify with the organization's initials rather than its name. The sign in front of its building simply reads "GMHC," and the group has run advertisements in gay publications utilizing only the initials. The group's logo consists of the initials with the "H" underlined, emphasizing "Health," rather than the "G".

AIDS service providers often find these concerns petty or obsessive. Why focus on logos? Why care if "the G word" is stated? Everyone knows gay men get AIDS. Why does the community need recognition and acknowledgment? If our own aim is to serve people with AIDS (PWA), aren't we justified if we can win increased funding and provide better services by de-emphasizing our gay participation?

When they hear this argument, activists rooted in the gay and lesbian movement wonder whether AIDS workers wear blinders. Have they no memory of years spent meeting with public officials, journalists, religious leaders, educators, and lawyers to force them to simply say the words "gay" and lesbian"? Are they unaware that we still struggle to force publications to allow individuals to be identified as gay, phone directories to include specifically gay and lesbian listings, and obituary writers to name lovers as lovers, rather than as "friends" or "companions"? De-gaying AIDS might bring more funding, but isn't the cost too high?

In the hearts of movement activists, the failure by AIDS groups to say "gay" goes deeper, and strikes at our culture's tendency to discount, minimize, or deny participation by upfront lesbians and gay men. This appeared to be the core of the community debate over the display of the Names Project AIDS Quilt in Washington, DC, in 1988. One letter writer summarized his experience that weekend:

> Arriving on the Ellipse early Saturday morning, I purchase my directory of names and found on the cover not an obviously gay family but instead a photograph of a mother and children. Looking inside the directory I could find no direct editorial mention of the lesbian and gay community from any of the three principals writing for the project. At the time I dismissed these as mere oversights on someone's part.
>
> That evening the candlelight march was led by invited parents of people with AIDS as thousands of mostly gay people marched behind them in the silent sea of candles. While this gesture towards parents was certainly

admirable and appropriate, it was unforgivable for the project not to show the same level of respect for the partners of people who had died of AIDS. Surely it is not too much to expect an overwhelmingly gay-run organization to strive to recognize gay relationships in a more sensitive manner than society has shown.

When the candle-bearers stood in silence around the reflecting pool listening to five very carefully selected speakers deliver their eloquent messages, not one word was uttered about the lesbian and gay community. It was now unmistakably clear that someone had decided to package the Quilt without recognizing that the vast majority of names that make up the fabric of this beautiful memorial belong to gay men. . . .

—*Keith Griffith,* San Francisco Sentinel, *November 4, 1988*

As the debate played itself out on the letters pages of community papers nationwide, Cleve Jones and Michael Smith of the Names Project responded, saying in part:

The Names Project Quilt is a memorial to all people who have died of AIDS—regardless of who they were or how they got it. It is true that we do not often use the words "gay" and "lesbian." We also do not use words like "drug abuser," "black," or "Hispanic."

Our critics who insist on such labels cause great harm. They strip away the individuality of each life and once again reduce the epidemic to categories and statistics. They also negate the humanity of others in the quilt who are not gay (or IV drug users or hemophiliacs, etc.), but whose battle with AIDS was no less difficult and whose loss was not less painful to their families and friends. . . .

—Bay Area Reporter, *November 24, 1988*

The anger that erupted in discussions with community activists during this period reflected a profound sense of betrayal. Individuals were willing to wipe out the entire quilt experience—discount its impressive power as an educational tool, its central function as a force for grief and healing, its key role in impacting public policy—simply because the gay and lesbian community went unacknowledged from the stage.

Some focused their fury on Names Project founder Cleve Jones, a veteran grassroots activist who, to their minds, had turned his back on his movement's past in de-gaying the quilt's display. Boston's gay paper *Bay Windows* editorialized:

Should the Names Project have insisted that a gay man speak? We think so. Although Names Project Executive Director Cleve Jones is correct when he says that nobody could walk around the Quilt and not be struck by the gay community's losses, that doesn't mean that the current trend among AIDS organizations to put gay men at the bottom of the outreach heap is right. (December 1, 1988)

When the San Francisco AIDS Foundation applauded four worthy honorees at its "Leadership Recognition Dinner" in May 1989, it chose four heterosexually identified individuals, in a city where 92 percent of documented AIDS cases are gay and bisexual men. Reasonable organizers might say, Yes, honor the heterosexuals—but also honor our community.

The AIDS Civil Rights Project of National Gay Rights Advocates gave a posthumous "Life Achievement" award to Michael Bennett, a public figure who would not publicly acknowledge either his gay identity or his AIDS diagnosis. This from the organization that sponsors National Coming Out Day. Some gay and lesbian activists might excuse Bennett's self-closeting by insisting on his "right to privacy," but should this man receive acclaim and honors from our community?

The fury of movement activists about all these kinds of decisions by AIDS organizations was stated by Michael Callen in the March 1989 issue of *PWA Coalition Newsline* (New York):

> *AIDS IS A GAY DISEASE! There. I said it. And I believe it. If I hear one more time that AIDS is not a gay disease, I shall vomit. AIDS is a gay disease because a lot of gay men get AIDS. Nationally, gay and bisexual men still account for more than half of all AIDS cases. More important, most of what has been noble about America's response to AIDS has been the direct result of the lesbian and gay community. All this AIDS-is-not-a-gay disease hysteria is an insulting attempt to downplay the contributions of lesbians and gay men.*

At work I often confront issues that set me at odds with my own history of movement activism. A staff member calls me after receiving a copy of Shanti's newsletter and insists that for future issues I screen out any photos that show men in drag. A volunteer calls me to express concern about a line in my monthly column in the newsletter: "Providing services to gay men—including gay men of color—will continue to be a priority at Shanti." He insists this makes it appear as if we are only serving gay men (despite my very conscious wording—*a* priority, rather than *the* priority—a compromise I had made and already begun to feel guilty about).

The Lack of a Broad Political Agenda

Disaffection with AIDS organizations' absent or narrowly defined politics goes beyond de-gaying. Many of these groups have developed within the community, are composed primarily of gay men and lesbians, and proudly call themselves "community-based organizations." Yet they appear unaware of critical battlefronts in gay liberation, operating without the analytical context provided by the movement's history.

AIDS organizations' relationship to electoral politics provides a key example of this tension. At the height of community furor over Massachusetts governor Michael Dukakis's implementation of state policy that excludes lesbians and gay men from becoming foster parents, the governor was invited to speak at the opening ceremony of the AIDS Action Committee's fundraising walk. AIDS workers argued that the governor had taken leadership on AIDS funding and that his participation at the kickoff would shore up future support, while grassroots lesbian and gay activists were horrified that someone who had institutionalized his personal homophobia into public policy would be an honored guest at an AIDS event.

The Lobby for Individual Freedom and Equality in California—which has taken the lead in pressing both for positive AIDS policies and gay and lesbian issues in Sacramento—takes as a logo for its AIDS lobby a design comprising geometric figures (circles, squares, triangles) that appear to symbolize a man, a woman, and a child—the image of a nuclear family. During the 1987 March on Washington the head of a national AIDS lobbying group wanted the "Wedding" (the celebration of gay and lesbian relationships in front of the Internal Revenue Service) canceled, fearing such a public event would "harm AIDS lobbying efforts." And the rising tension between AIDS service groups and direct-action networks like ACT UP is often about the discomfort of service-providers' lobbyists with ACT UP's appearance as a group of up-front queers engaging in political tactics rooted in early gay lib zaps.

Some would explain these differing perspectives as AIDS groups opting for a short-term gain over the long-term agenda, or pragmatism over idealism. But movement activists question how much AIDS groups will give up in the context of their efforts to woo elected officials or mainstream their image.

Another source of conflict between AIDS organizations and gay and lesbian groups is their marked differences in organizational structure and culture, especially around issues of gender parity, affirmative action, decision-making processes, and economic accessibility. Hierarchical structures and corporate cultures are an unchallenged norm in AIDS organizations. Women and people of color are routinely absent from leadership positions, though accepted as caregivers. AIDS administrators interpret these differences as gay groups opting for "political correctness" over efficiency. Gay and lesbian activists observe these differences and conclude that AIDS organizations lack political consciousness.

Ten years ago few would have imagined a group with strong gay and lesbian community involvement called "God's Love We Deliver." Fewer still would have believed that a corporation funding anti-gay political activity (Coors) would be welcomed as the lead sponsor of a fundraising event for this group. Movement activists wonder why so few AIDS organizations have supported women's right to choose abortion—especially when an increasing client caseload of HIV-positive women and women with AIDS faces some risk during pregnancy. And with the Catholic Church expelling Dignity chapters throughout the nation, they question why gay-based HIV groups cooperated with church-based service providers such as Catholic Charities, Mother Theresa's hospices, and church-affiliated hospitals.

Sex-Positive Public Policy

Another key part of progressive organizers' sense of betrayal by AIDS organizations lies in their failure to maintain a gay liberation politic surrounding sex issues in both public-policy debate and the creation of prevention materials. During the 1980s, a decade of increasing political repression (Reagan, AIDS, the Meese Commission, vice squads), many gay and lesbian activists adopted a revisionist history of gay male sex culture of the 1970s and of the early movement's relationship to sexual freedom. Without an analysis of sexual politics, they paint the period as a time of mindless, drug-induced, compulsive promiscuity.

Sexual liberation in the 1970s, however, was as much about politics as about pleasure. It took place within a context that resisted the oppression of the nuclear family, strove to free men and women from constrictive gender roles, and developed bonding between adults based on playfulness, passion, and erotic exploration, rather than ownership (which was how marriage or monogamy was seen in those days). Many contemporary AIDS educators remain unaware that self-help models of HIV prevention and treatment advocacy are rooted directly in both the women's health movement and early gay liberation's efforts to prevent sexually transmitted diseases and promote a sex-positive gay culture.

To activists who weren't present for the movement's pre-AIDS sex debates, concerns about this history often appear absurd. Veteran activists, however, are outraged at the inability of AIDS organizations to address sex issues without aping the traditionalism of contemporary mainstream culture. AIDS groups throughout the nation are challenged by government officials about the language and content of AIDS prevention materials. While some of these organizations responded by seeking independent funding and producing materials that eroticize diverse gay safe-sex practices and use explicit language, others have accepted regulation by the state and produced materials in line with conservative fantasies of gay male behavior.

In these materials men are instructed to "limit themselves to one faithful partner," despite consensus since 1985 that acts, not the number of partners, put an individual at greatest risk. They present lists that exclude controversial yet practiced behavior (S/M, water sports, fisting, rimming), and almost all ignore the existence of lesbian sexuality. They distribute homophobic materials such as the CDC's "America Responds to AIDS" brochures, which fully ignore gay men, the group most at risk for HIV exposure in the United States, and Red Cross brochures, which ingenuously urge the reader to avoid sexual activity with HIV-positive people or people at risk for infection—leaving gay men nowhere.

The most visible internal community battles during the mid-1980s focused on health officials' often successful attempts to close or crack down on places of communal sexual activity: bathhouses, sex clubs, theaters, and outdoor cruise areas. Mainstream lesbian and gay community activists considered these spaces embarrassments, obstacles to their attempts to assimilate, win civil rights, and prove that "gays are no different than straights." When public sentiment supported closure of the clubs and bathhouses, they were relieved. Other organizers—particularly men who retained a gay liberation agenda, and anti-censorship feminist women—have been dismayed to find that, in the age of AIDS, speaking on behalf of "public" sex spaces, controversial sex acts, or "promiscuity" makes one an outcast.

Five years ago some AIDS leaders still advocated defining gay male sexuality outside traditional heterosexual constrictions. Today it is almost impossible to find a leader of an AIDS organization speaking on the record on behalf of keeping baths open, protecting cruise areas, or defending group sex clubs. AIDS prevention organizations will target gay men in their prevention campaigns but hesitate to jump into public-policy debate on government regulation of sex spaces. Gay-based AIDS groups throughout the nation, such as the San Francisco AIDS Foundation, Gay Men's Health Crisis, and Black and White Men Together, create critically important workshops and promote them as efforts to "eroticize safer sex." They hold support groups for individuals who have multiple partners and "kinky" sex, or who bring their erotic life into parks and sex clubs. Yet it's rare in 1990 for any organization to articulate public-policy positions that defend these actions.

My own roots as an activist supporting sexual liberation and my current position managing an AIDS service organization lead me into similar conflicts. In my professional role managing a large organization, I fully understand the need to have personnel policies setting limits on sexual relations between staff members and clients, or managers and staff. As an advocate for sex-positive attitudes and policies, these rules can strike me as repressive, sex-negative, and at odds with gay male culture. I allow my professional self to win out over the liberationist in me, and I wonder if I've sold out.

As a single gay male who holds a position with some visibility and stature in my local community, I wrestle with the appropriate way to navigate through the social and sexual scenes of San Francisco. On the one hand, I want to define my own sexuality and be true to my erotic interests and identity. I also want to model a type of community leadership that is not de-sexed. I'd like to conduct myself as a healthy sexual being who enjoys particular aspects of gay male culture. Yet I won't visit sex clubs, jerkoff groups, or orgy parties, because I don't want to deal with running into staff members, volunteers, or clients. Am I being sex-negative, or operating with appropriate boundaries, or both?

Perhaps the most difficult struggle for me is finding the courage to be true to my ideals on sex issues in discussions with public officials, journalists, and people within my organization. I find myself doing a lot of self-censoring. If I think I would be voicing a minority opinion about the closing of bathhouses at a dinner party discussion, I say nothing. My fear is less that people won't like me than that they'll be horrified at my organization. Maybe I don't give them enough credit. I took my current position heading an AIDS service organization the same week I was the convener of the Leather Institute at the National Lesbian and Gay Health Conference. Several donors and staff members voiced concern at this connection. To this day, when I'm asked to give a speech or a workshop on a topic related to sexual liberation, my initial reaction is to say no. Then my activist self kicks in and I detach from my fears and internalized shame.

A Call for Integrity

I know I am not alone in the conflicts I feel in my work life. My desire for more integration is shared by others, as is my belief that effective and healthy AIDS organizations could work in consort with a progressive political movement. What we need today, in 1990, is for dialogue and debate to take place within the AIDS system, so that both gay groups and AIDS groups can be clear on reasonable expectations of one another.

Progressive activists working in the AIDS arena have failed to explicitly articulate how to keep our work from running afoul of a movement agenda. We can do better than running at cross purposes or maintaining what we imagine to be political neutrality. Our AIDS work, to be truly effective, can and should further gay and lesbian liberation. There are countless heroic examples where our major AIDS groups and leaders have acted with integrity toward our movement. We can do more than care for the dying and fight for the living—we can ensure that the community most impacted by HIV makes full and creative use of the opportunities the epidemic presents for advancing a gay and lesbian liberation agenda.

*This was the focus of Darrell Yates Rist's landmark piece in The Nation, "The Deadly Costs of an Obsession" (February 13, 1989).

THE HOMOSEXUALIZATION OF AIDS
from *Gai-Pied Hebdo* (1990)

Daniel Defert

For the past three years the World Health Organization has designated December 1st as World AIDS Day. This year that day is dedicated to women. The new directors of the Global Programme on AIDS in Geneva estimate that the number of HIV carriers worldwide has reached between eight and ten million people, of whom a third are women. They repeat that the most common form of sexual transmission is heterosexual. Do these figures and pronouncements point to a de-homosexualization of AIDS today?

Concurrent with these announcements we have witnessed a stagnation of preventive measures in the gay world. In France, the use of condoms has fallen off; sexually transmitted diseases are on the rise; the decrease in the number of sexual partners that had been observed beginning in 1987 has reversed itself since 1988. Michael Pollak recently reported at an international conference that we seem to be arriving at the end of a cycle of change. In San Francisco, epidemiologists have been alarmed at the rejection of safer sex practices among young people who are just starting to become sexually active, and there are fears of a second wave of AIDS among the gay population between 1993 and 1995.

These results are certainly not due to any lack of information about the risks of transmission of the disease. There are probably a certain number of psychological factors related to this blockage that deserve some consideration. I would like to suggest a few hypotheses as to these psychological factors and call for a debate on the subject.

The violent history of the relationships between homosexuals and AIDS is complex. It has become an essential element in both the individual and collective experience of gays. It has taken an enormous toll on the representations and strategies that have contributed to the social construction of the disease. Beginning in 1981, we have witnessed three very different and successive forms of the homosexualization of AIDS.

First was the announcement in July 1981 in the famous *New York Times* article by Lawrence Altman of a phenomenon that had been observed by the Centers for Disease Control in Atlanta beginning in February of that year: forty-one cases of a new disease among gay men. The bombshell impact of that article has been well documented in an excellent film describing ten years of the epidemic, *Longtime Companion*, currently showing in France. Until it was discovered that the disease could also be transmitted through blood transfusions, the most irrational hypotheses had sprung up around possible links between the disease and homosexual behavior. The notion of a "gay cancer" circulating so quickly seemed to threaten gays collectively, while the exact nature of the threat remained misunderstood. The sheer irrationality of these hypotheses suggested some kind of fantasy on the part of the "Moral Majority," or at least some kind of social attack that would threaten gays until a rational scientific explanation of the infection as caused by a virus could be found.

Epidemiology, then, discovered the disease within the gay community. But in this observation, two major elements are obscured:

1) If gays had not started coming out in great numbers beginning in the 1970s, it would not have been possible to identify the disease with them. Ten to fifteen years earlier, it would not have been possible to identify the disease with the gay male population.

2) Part of the coming-out process includes the notion of gay-specific health care. Gays manage clinics for the treatment of sexually transmitted diseases; gay physicians have organized themselves to treat gay patients. All of this has contributed to the identification of the disease with the gay community.

Thus it was observed afterwards that intravenous drug users in New York began to show at the same time symptoms of this new disease and an increased rate of mortality. However, being less integrated into society and less cared for medically, they were not immediately associated with the disease. Therefore the immediate association of the disease with homosexuality and AIDS (which still did not have a name at that point) conflated two distinct realities: an epidemiological event and a recent social phenomenon, the visibility of gay behavior.

The second phase of the homosexualization of AIDS was quite different. First of all, it concerned only a minority of gays themselves, and only rarely those who had any leadership in the gay liberation movement. It has been this mobilization of gays themselves to provide mutual assistance for those infected which has provoked fear and caution within the gay community, specifically the creation in January 1982 of Gay Men's Health Crisis in New

York. But of course this was only possible for a community which has been both profoundly affected by the epidemic and deeply conscious of its own identity as a community. In France, for example, this kind of community identity is much more problematic, first of all because France in general does not have a tradition of pluralistic communities; rather, it is a nation of assimilation of individuals. This relatively recent gay community-building behavior emerged with more difficulty in France around 1978 with the opening in Paris around Les Halles of bars that were open to the street, open during the day, and whose prices were competitive with those of other bars. It was these commercial establishments that served to organize the community: a gay press, gay restaurants and bars, but no places for community activism or services such as have been established in San Francisco and Amsterdam. Likewise, there have been no gay leaders in public opinion. People began to talk about "homosociability" as evidenced in certain styles of fashion, consumption and forms of affection, but not as a phenomenon establishing itself within the fabric of urban life such as we have seen in San Francisco, with the exception of the gay Parisian business world. The gay business world of France could not afford to identify itself with the disease because such an identification would threaten its commercial interests and thus its very existence. A collective consciousness of the epidemic did not begin in France until 1984 and the mobilization of the gay community as such consisted—except for the efforts of a handful of volunteers— of the mobilization of gay businesses essentially around the dissemination of information about the risks of contamination through certain unprotected sexual practices. The internationalization of the gay movement to combat AIDS helped legitimize this mobilization. In constituting a collective reality and a new style of sexual relationships, prevention has a chance to succeed, and we have witnessed in retrospect, beginning in France in 1986, that the epidemic has started to slow down in the gay population. I think it is necessary to emphasize that this particular form of the homosexualization of AIDS has had two major effects which have marked the entire social response since them:

1) Homosexuals have managed to convince first of all the medical establishment and secondly the general public that one cannot treat a patient as a symptom or a body and reject that same patient as an individual. They have demonstrated that one cannot at the same time cure and pass judgment on someone, nor can one tell a patient that he or she has contracted a potentially fatal disease without disclosing the most current information about treatments. One must treat a patient holistically. The medical establishment carries with it its own peculiar form of violence which tends to alienate those who need it most.

2) Homosexuals have proposed their own form of prevention by inventing the notion of "safe" or "safer" sex. This notion has had several consequences. It allows a community that has openly ordered itself around sexuality to protect itself (even though heterosexuals perform the same sort of ordering based on sexuality without being conscious of it), and it also allows the gay community to keep those who are infected within the bounds of community life and community pleasures. This is probably the first time that a group has been concerned not only with protecting those who are not infected but also with the pleasures and desires of those who are infected. There has truly been a secularization of the public representation of the infected in our society. Society feels compassion for the sick because they are suffering: religion has always inscribed the image of Christ on the afflicted. Now, however, even though one might be ill or infected, one is not barred from sexual pleasure at the same time.

Far too often even gay literature has made homosexuals acceptable through figures of suffering. There has been a real struggle to defend the right to pleasure, to protect it socially and biologically, which has effectively perpetuated the struggles for equal rights begun in the 1970s. This collective affirmation of prevention and solidarity surrounding AIDS has allowed the movements of the 1970s to survive the onslaughts of homophobia. It has allowed for both a collective and an individual expression: by volunteering for various organizations and making charitable contributions, by affirming one's own personal commitment to the fight against AIDS, many people in fact end up coming out. Thus there has been a gradual confusion, both individual and collective, between homosexual identity and AIDS, as if it were somehow easier now to participate in an AIDS demonstration than to announce one's own homosexuality. I believe we are currently entering a third phase of the homosexualization of AIDS.

What characterizes this third phase in which we find ourselves today? It is first of all a collective experience of the personal cost of the epidemic in our own lives, in our sexual lives, in our friendships, in the disappearance of so many people we have known and loved. Currently, if heterosexuals are beginning to share in this consciousness surrounding AIDS, they still do not have this collective experience of the sheer weight of grief or seropositivity. It has become an international experience for those who travel extensively to seek out those they have known. It is a limiting experience for those who attempt to create long-term relationships, one that disrupts the lives of couples who have different HIV status when one partner is positive and the other negative, or on rare occasions where it intensifies the relationship of a couple who share the same HIV status, uniting them fiercely until the end of their lives.

This new situation has, I think, three major consequences that also explain perhaps why campaigns targeting safer sexual practices have started to stagnate and wear out.

1) This consciousness of a collective loss has created a defense mechanism that resembles a state of depression. Characteristically, the only group of people within the French gay community who have managed to display collective strength has been the participants in the national convention Living with HIV and AIDS. For a long time many people have avoided being tested for fear of losing their insurance or their job—both very well founded fears, incidentally. Along with the lack of a medical support system, all of this has contributed to the feeling that many Americans expressed for a while back in 1985 that "no test is best." It has taken the development of treatments such as aerosolized pentamidine and the prescription of AZT to asymptomatic infected people, along with the establishment of a support network of people with AIDS, to convince people of the advantages of being tested. But for a long time many people preferred to act as though they were already infected without trying to find out for certain, telling themselves: "whether you're positive or negative, it doesn't matter; no penetration without prevention". This had the effect of assuming a general seropositivity, unconsciously blending two different identities, homosexuality and AIDS, and denying the very real differences between seropositivity and seronegativity for everyone. We know, however, that while denial may have some short-term benefits, the long-term results are eventually detrimental.

2) Those who are HIV-negative are beginning to feel a very uneasy integration into the general community, best expressed as the "survivor syndrome" which has been identified and studied in conjunction with those who live through major accidents or catastrophes. Perhaps this feeling is not yet very widespread in France, but I can attest to having felt it myself following the death of my lover. In a wish to identify oneself with a lost loved one, and out of a sense of guilt one feels as a survivor, one wants to expose oneself as a way of overcoming depression and guilt. Just two days ago I was talking to someone outside of Paris about this who told me, "Yes, you feel much stronger somehow if you're able to announce that you're HIV-positive." In a number of studies conducted in San Francisco, in particular one by Walt Odets, this "survivor syndrome" and accompanying feelings of guilt have been making

progress within the HIV-negative gay and bisexual communities. It has been noted as well that many people who were always unable to reveal their sexuality to family and coworkers will often rush to announce their seropositivity as soon as they learn it, as if were more acceptable to communicate biological information than to announce one's sexual choice.

3) It has been said everywhere, in France and internationally, that gays showed responsibility very quickly and took charge of prevention and solidarity before anyone else. Safer sex has become our official passport which we must not let expire. We might even say that a kind of legend has arisen surrounding the gay community's collective ability to protect itself. Still, one must admit that living a life of safer sex day after day ultimately becomes very difficult, and that many people's reactions take the form of sexual dysfunction: a loss of desire or a denial of anguish. If people refuse to debate the difficulties of establishing new sexual relationships and a new homosociability and refuse to debate issues that are specifically homosexual and not related generally to AIDS, we risk seeing the fight against AIDS become a cover or decoy, to which everyone pays lip service without really believing in, like making a contribution in church without actually believing in virtues such as hope and charity.

We must realize that both unprotected sex and safer sex are not merely individual behaviors but essentially social relations. For example, when two men start living together as a couple, they often get tested to find out whether they can live without practicing safer sex, because they believe intimacy to be founded upon unprotected sex. If our relations with each other are no longer the subject of debate, a debate such as the one that was at the center of the struggles of the 1970s, those relations will again become a kind of cover or decoy. Safer sex also is a form of sexuality; outside of the gay community safer sex is too often considered *asexuality*. To announce one's seropositivity often appears to those outside the gay community as a declaration of an asexual life. There is a danger in making "safer sex" an official ideology instead of an opportunity to discuss our actual sexual practices and the status of homosexual relationships in society (such as the relationship between HIV-positive and –negative partners in a couple). If we transform safer sex into empty and doctrinaire cant, we risk imposing a new silence on the truth of sexuality and homosexuality that will have unfortunate consequences.

I think that there has been, therefore, a "bad" homosexualization of AIDS, one which consists of completely identifying a homosexual way of life, which is still difficult to accept psychologically and socially, with AIDS, which has become better accepted because it is less sexual. Volunteerism has always had its limits. My biggest surprise in creating AIDES has been the discovery of just how little has been won in terms of rights and lifestyles by the homosexual movements of the 1970s. Very quickly, it became apparent that issues such as "domestic partnership" have turned into objects of contention, and there still remains much progress to be made in terms of social tolerance. If today I am convinced that the organization of responses to the epidemic and solidarity is effectively an important instrument in the individual and collective recognition of homosexual reality, I also believe that homosexuals cannot reduce all their efforts into the creation of an image of being masters of the disease. If this image ultimately turns out to be false, it will cost them tremendously not only in terms of lives but also in terms of the reaction of society.

SOUTHEAST ASIA   By 1991 there was alarm in the international AIDS activist community about a projected explosion of cases in Southern Asia. Here we present two brief perspectives on gay and lesbian politics within the context of AIDS from Asia.

The first page of the inaugural issue of *Bombay Dost* (Dost = Friend) states its purpose as a platform for people with "alternative sexuality" rather than those who are "gay" or "lesbian." However, a third page editorial states "if you are 'gay', which means that you consciously enjoy male-male or female-female sex, then this newsletter is for you . . . This newsletter is primarily for health purposes. It will try to tell you what is 'safe' and what is 'unsafe.' Please understand that it is a matter of life and death." This perspective reflects organizing on the basis of same-sex sexuality where it is not conceived in Euro-American terms.

Our second selection if from *GayaKeris*, a semimonthly publication of Pink Triangle Malaysia. (The keris is a Malaysian symbol for courage and strength, "a blade that is never straight, that curves gracefully, that is always bent.") The report on World AIDS Day (1992) demonstrates, in their words, "courage and strength to persuade others that in a caring society there is a place in the sun for everyone. These are the same qualities we need in our fight against ignorance and negligence of AIDS issues."

THE CHARTER & EDITORIAL

from *Bombay Dost* (1990)

The Charter

To provide a platform for people interested in an alternate sexuality and all its implications.

To provide a framework whereby all such peoples, both males and females, from the Indian sub-continent can come together and support each other so as to show solidarity and a sense of community of such persons who have this identify of an alternate sexuality.

To encourage self-awareness, self-confidence and self-esteem in the practice of such an alternate sexuality and to seek legal remedies to prevent harassment to such persons by the executive and judicial arms of the state.

To provide counseling, information and advice in all such areas which are of interest to this alternate sexuality and its safe practice.

To reach out into all sectors of the Indian sub-continent regardless of creed, caste, class and colour and link up with those who feel isolated in the practice of such alternate sexuality; to provide authentic information shorn of value judgments, informed by the latest research on sexuality and without moral issues clouding the advice given thereof.

To act as an information cell and to collect all such information deemed as research so that a resource base is created for students interested in alternate sexuality and its practice.

To network with south Asian groups, organizations and individuals who will support such an alternate sexuality whether in the Indian sub-continent or abroad.

To act as an agent of progress and liberalism, to fight for it wherever it threatens the heterogeneity of an alternate sexuality or its practice and to discourage the idea that sexual identity separates one from the larger cultural heritage of humankind.

Editorial—Think It Over

It has taken the team-work of a whole lot of people to start *Bombay Dost*. So it's impossible to thank anybody and everybody. But here's a sincere thanks to all who helped. There have been touching little incidents. Thank you 'R' for sending that money order for Rs.150 as a token of your happiness. We're keeping it and will send you five copies in gratitude. Now first things, first! Read the charter and tell us whether you agree or not. If you don't tell us clearly why and what can or should be done about it. Suggest Indian terms in English or any of the recognized scheduled languages of India (check your bank note to know what are scheduled languages).

This newsletter is primarily for health purposes. It will try its best to tell you what is 'safe' and what is 'unsafe'. Please understand that it is matter of life and death. As you are our *dosts*, please understand you are special to *Bombay Dost*.

A few small points. If you are 'gay', which means that you consciously enjoy male-male or female-female sex, then this newsletter is for you. There is no forwarding address in the first issue for several reasons. But please don't think this is deliberate. It's because everything has been moving too fast. Wait for another few issues and we'll be more organized.

The International Lesbian and Gay Association has sent out a newsletter and appeal to all groups in the Indian sub-continent asking for contacts. If you need help, information and networking then write to: Information Secretariat, C/o RFSL, Box 350, S-101 24 Stockholm, Sweden. Register there to show your presence in the world. You will be part of a worldwide community and thus able to help more people when needed.

Each well-wisher of *Bombay Dost* might as well ask the inevitable question: "Why now?" Yes! what is so propitious about the times now that we need a newsletter like *Dost*? The times are tragic. Friends are dying, many more don't seem to have even heard of safe sex. There are layers upon layers of cultural and social problems that obstruct even the most basic of sexual education.

Of course, we need to be united. To be united means solidarity and solidarity is strength, which is what we need now most of all.

Surely, someone must make a beginning somewhere? If this sounds a bit too pompous, then please don't get upset. There is enough room in *Dost* columns for fun and entertainment. We are also looking for erotic poetry, anecdotes from the press, little non-sexist jokes, snippets about local happenings that are relevant to our form of alternate sexuality. In fact, anything that you think should be shared.

To share means sharing the brighter events in life with all your *dosts*. It means taking life not so seriously that you can't laugh to see it rain on your parade.

Eventually, we want this newsletter to be a platform for a non-prejudiced readership: which hopes to know everything there is to know about alternate sexuality.

The main thrust of this newsletter's editorial policy will be to expose the hypocrisy of the patriarchal strains within the cultures of South Asia. It would be great to know more about our matrilineal and matriarchal traditions.

Let me end with a small anecdote. A recent column by Khushwant Singh mentions that India's top nuclear scientist, Dr. Homi Bhabha, was a homosexual. Now it so happens that Bhabha, Nehru and Krishna Menon, the three men who modernised India; were very close friends. There is more than meets the eye in Menon's private life too. All three, it is now observed, were wearing masks.

We are all wearing masks. And if we're so afraid of ripping them off, learn to peel off the edges to let your friends know the real you. But to all those who wish to take a stand, rip off your mask—NOW!

SEVEN DAYS AND FIVE NIGHTS IN KUALA LUMPUR

from *Gayakeris* of Pink Triangle, Malaysia (1993)

Julain Jayaseelan

Seven days at Central Market

For the last four years Pink Triangle Malaysia has had a public AIDS campaign at Central Market—a popular cultural cum shopping complex—to mark World AIDS Day. For 1992 the event was billed as an AIDS awareness week. Central Market was selected as the venue for such a campaign as the intention was to reach a wide cross section of the Kuala Lumpur population.

The main objective of the AIDS Awareness week was to promote the AIDS message as effectively as possible to enable people to make informed decisions about protecting themselves.

The government sponsored AIDS information campaigns in the media had us worried. Although the message that "AIDS Kills" was very clear it did not deal with self protection and very often gave the impression that promiscuous sex or an "unhealthy lifestyle" (whatever that means) could lead to AIDS.

It was therefore necessary in Pink Triangle's Central Market campaigns to provide accurate user friendly information; deal with the practice of safe sex; and familiarize the public with condoms and lube.

The activities encompassed an international poster exhibition, which dealt with transmission and prevention, women and AIDS, condom usage, gay sex, and needle cleaning. Videos with an AIDS/HIV theme were screened including videos on the quilt project.

In evaluating the calls received on our counseling lines we identified a crucial need for women to be informed about AIDS. A "Women and AIDS" program was developed which consisted of posters, T-shirts and pamphlets plus a photographic exhibition entitled "Women let's talk AIDS" which was frank, humorous and very Malaysian.

In line with the belief that the AIDS message is most effective when it is personalized, tables were available where members of the public could sit and talk with the counselors and pick up relevant information. Daily workshops targeting youth and women were held allowing members of the public to hold discussions with their peers. It was also the first time in a public campaign that the PLWH/A perspective was evident.

The support we received was very promising. A number of singers, actors and television personalities came forward to make a community commitment during one of the shows. Corporate sponsors were quite willing to provide necessary equipment and fund some of the projects.

The deputy health minister, Dato Farid Ariffin, who has always been supportive of our efforts agreed to launch the week. During the launch a former beauty queen and a national body building champion came forward to make public commitments to AIDS prevention work. The next day almost every local newspaper carried photographs of the minister handing out condoms to a bemused public, or the celebrities fooling around with the condoms. "10,000 condoms being distributed in Central Market" cried some newspapers. In parliament YB Dato Farid was questioned on the distribution of condoms and whether he was encouraging promiscuous sex.

The next few days the papers focused on the explicitness of the exhibition and the distribution of condoms. For many the open display of condoms being distributed was upsetting and too much to handle. We had crossed the line—a line that is rapidly being blurred by the industrialization and modernization of our society. This contradiction was evident in the newspaper reports. One daily, calling the event a condom exhibition, asked if the wrong impression of sex was being provided to teenagers. The young women who were interviewed on how they felt about the "Women lets talk AIDS" photographic exhibition said that the exhibition was educational, brave, open, discussed AIDS in a clear and non-confrontational manner, and that they could relate to it and yet when probed further they felt that it was not very appropriate for young people!

Commenting on a set of photographs taken during AIDS Awareness week, which showed a group of schoolgirls giggling as they dared each other to buy a box of condoms, the former deputy director of the education ministry said that although it could not be denied that more and more youth including school children were getting involved in unhealthy activities such as having "promiscuous and free sex" the safe sex message should be delivered in a way that does not appear to encourage such sexual and criminal activities!

The editorial of a more daily newspaper felt that although it was hypocritical to take the view that our society would not be exposed to AIDS simply because of Malaysians' religious and eastern values, the distribution of condoms to young people in a happy atmosphere and in an open space was not appropriate to our culture and values!

One journalist, while interviewing a Pink Triangle representative was visibly upset over a poster on how to use a condom because it portrayed an erect penis. "I lose my dignity as a man when I see that poster," he gasped.

Remarks from members of the public including our Prime Minister in the comments book were more than encouraging. The support for forthright non-judgmental AIDS prevention work is increasing. From the Ministry of Health to the entertainment industry, individuals are coming forward to strengthen AIDS prevention work in the country. Although we felt justified in desensitizing the public toward condoms and to present condom use as a method of self protection, we were surprised at just how far we had managed to push the 'line' dealing with the issue of sex in a frank and honest manner, dispelling the misinformation surrounding AIDS and providing the required information in a way that members of the public could relate to.

Five Nights at Blue Boy

Developing models for safe sex education in a Malaysian context needs to take into consideration the cultural, social, economic and psychological position of the groups that are being reached out to. This has been difficult for safe sex campaigners with the gay community as there is no ready frame-work that can be utilized given that the gay community is only just developing a sense of identity.

The issues of language, class and sexual identity need to be constantly discussed and debated before any such campaign can be implemented. However difficult and unproductive this may seem, it is a necessary part of the process for working with newly emerging gay communities.

Safe sex programs are comparatively easier to implement with the more visible sector of the gay community in Kuala Lumpur. Blue Boy—the only exclusive gay bar in Kuala Lumpur—has been the only place where AIDS awareness programs for the gay community have been carried out. The most recent being the marathon "5 nights at Blue Boy" safe sex campaign which was launched in conjunction with World AIDS Day 1992.

The five nights, stretching from the first till the fifth of December, were similar to other safe sex shows that had been carried out over the last four years. They included condom distribution, flyers which carried information on safe sexual practices and condom usage, information on services offered by Pink Triangle together with messages about the significance of World AIDS Day, awareness of a community commitment and reasons for wearing the red ribbon, the main draw card for those evenings were undoubtedly the Safe Sex variety shows—something that Pink Triangle has become identified with and which has popularized the organization. The shows took on issues such as self-protection and safe sex negotiation, and coming out and being gay in Malaysia. The success of these shows can be attributed to the fact that the men at Blue Boy had strong gay identification and could identify with the awareness messages that were presented appropriate to this gay cultural context.

Not only was the crowd responsive to the shows, but it was interesting to note that the guys seemed less embarrassed about safe sex. A year ago many would refuse to take condoms, saying "I don't fuck". Now many were asking for more, had questions about the condoms being distributed or admitted to carrying condoms of their own.

One part of the show had the MC speaking to individuals in the audience. The guys were asked questions on what they did in bed and were checked to see if they were prepared with condoms. It was encouraging to see how candidly they spoke about personalized safe sex guidelines and gave impressive demonstrations of how to put on a condom.

The development of this awareness campaign to raise safe sex consciousness has been facilitated by the constant work that Pink Triangle has done with the Blue Boy crowd and the fact that the volunteers identify or are part of that particular community. The shows have also been important in forging a good working relationship with the management of Blue Boy.

However, Blue Boy symbolizes the more visible part of the gay community. Do the messages transmitted from Blue Boy reach other segments of this community especially when many homosexual men do not identify as gay? It is necessary for us to identify the different needs of the community to enable the effective implementation of out-reach programs. Three months ago Pink Triangle began a needs assessment study of the gay community with the goal of developing outreach programs which would cater to other sectors of the community.

LESBIANS AND AIDS

By the 1990s, the belief that "lesbians don't get AIDS" was slowly eroding. At GMHC, a growing number of cases involved lesbians. In 1993, Amber Hollibaugh, a longtime feminist lesbian activist, became coordinator of the GMHC Lesbian AIDS project. Her article here is an analysis of common beliefs about lesbians and AIDS. She notes lesbians' long record of activism as well as the ways in which lines of class, race, and sexual practice divide lesbians from one another. The relative reticence of lesbians about their sexual practices and desires makes it harder to provide safe-sex information and support, but she finds room for hope in younger lesbians' greater willingness to acknowledge HIV in their lives.

from

LESBIAN LEADERSHIP AND LESBIAN DENIAL IN THE AIDS EPIDEMIC: BRAVERY AND FEAR IN THE CONSTRUCTION OF A LESBIAN GEOGRAPHY OF RISK

(1993)

Amber Hollibaugh

WANTED: ATTRACTIVE FEMININE WOMAN FOR ROMANCE. PLEASURE AND POS-SIBLE LONG-TERM RELATIONSHIP. NO HIV+S NEED APPLY.

LOOKING FOR SERIOUS RELATIONSHIP WITH WOMYN-LOVING-WOMYN—NO BUTCHES, DRUGGIES, DRINKERS OR HIV'S

LESBIAN LOOKING FOR LESBIAN LOVE. HOT SEX. GOOD TIMES. GREAT PARTNER . . . COULD BE PERMANENT! FEMMES, FATTIES, HIV+S DON'T BOTHER.

These are all current personal ads running in lesbian newspapers around the country. I found them in lesbian papers published in San Francisco, Los Angeles, New York, Illinois and Michigan. These magazines ran the gamut from lesbian-separatist newspapers to sex-positive lesbian mags like *On Our Backs*. And while they contain many descriptions that are awful, each contain one identical and terrifying disqualifier: no HIV+ lesbians wanted here.

How can lesbians' risk for HIV/AIDS still be debatable thirteen years into the epidemic? How can some lesbians still not know any lesbians with HIV? Yet the debate continues. I spend an incredible amount of my time as the director of a lesbian AIDS project disagreeing with other lesbians who are still repeating the dyke mantra "real lesbians don't get AIDS," while listening to the numerically spiraling voices of lesbians who are HIV+ or have AIDS (or talking to their friends and lovers). In between the two groups of women are a third chorus of female voices full of panicky questions about risk, about who to believe and how to think when they look at their own behavior as lesbians.

Lesbian Leadership In The AIDS Movement

Lesbians have been leaders in the AIDS movement since its earliest breath. We have influenced and shaped the discussions, outreach programs, demonstration, services and prevention drives since the earliest moments of this crisis. Working early on with gay men, we were often the first women to see how broadly different communities were being impacted on by HIV and to use our political histories as organizers and health, feminist, civil rights and left activists to inform the creation and responses of this new movement. It is hard to write this history to show our powerful role and at the same time credit the broad leadership of so many and varied men and women fighting against HIV.

Many of us doing this work, together with the HIV+ lesbians we were beginning to meet, first began to talk amongst ourselves about the risks lesbians were facing the epidemic. But for many years it was a quiet discussion between lesbians doing AIDS work and HIV+ lesbians, each of us coming up against the growing numbers of HIV+ dykes we were meeting every day. This was happening at the same time we were being told that "lesbians are not at risk for HIV." We would meet in small groups together to repair ourselves from hard parts of doing AIDS work or to get away from the sexism or racism of this new movement but we would quickly move into talking about how many lesbians, how many women-who-sleep-with-other-women, we were seeing who were HIV+. We would compare notes and shake our heads. It did not add up. We would talk late into the night, trying to unravel the keys to our risk at the same time we remained completely invisible as a community at risk for AIDS.

My Own History, Coming Home

I have been organizing and writing about sexuality for fifteen or twenty years, and doing work around HIV for nearly ten. I have been a part of the large contingent of lesbians who, from the early days of the epidemic, began to do AIDS work and became AIDS activists. And through those years I have talked to lesbians about what compelled us to get involved. For some of us it was the shared *gay* identity we felt with gay men which brought us forward early in the epidemic: for some of us it was the dramatic increase in the already devastating daily occurrences of homophobia and gay bashing which occurred because of the government's misrepresentation of AIDS (or GRID—Gay related immune deficiency disease, as it was known then) as a gay disease. In that increased violence, "all gay people, both gay men and lesbian, looked alike." For many gay women and men of color, the devastation in their communities and the need for their engagement and activism was urgent and obvious to them; for many progressive lesbians, the communities most under siege were exactly the communities we were committed to working within (women and men in prisons, poor people, communities of color, young people, women etc.) and many of us were losing friends every week, every month, more each year. Our reasons as lesbians were numerous, varied and passionate.

The aforementioned reasons all applied to me, and one other I have only seen clearly in the last year or so and which I speak of much less openly. I was deeply disillusioned and bitter at the horrific fights about sex which had erupted so viciously twelve years ago in the feminist, lesbian-feminist and antipornography movements of the early eighties, the fights that have now been called "the sex wars" in the feminist movement. I come from a poor-white-trash working-class background and I am a high-femme dyke passionately committed to butch and femme lives. The sexualities which I defended in those bitter fights and the sexualities I wanted to continue to explore were drawn from all the ways women (and men) feel desire. But I was particularity driven to explore a woman-identified sexuality which was risky, smart, dangerous, often secretive and often capable of encompassing great variation and erotic need between women who sleep with women. And I wanted sex to have a right to its own history without forcing some women to hide or reinterpret their past (or on-going) desires through a constantly shifting lesbian ideology. I was also tired of trying to say that the political lesbian community was only the smallest tip of the lesbian iceberg, with the vast majority of lesbians still uncharted, vastly different set of groupings of desires, identities, contradictions and sexual dynamics. Many brave feminist women spoke against the right-wing drift of the sex wars and the porn fights, but we were a minority in a feminist and lesbian movement already beleaguered by Reaganomics Christian fundamentalism and fight to keep open women's ability to control our own reproduction. The times were hard.

The Women I Come From

Finally, I wanted to return, go home again to the women I came from. I longed to build a *new* revolution, made up of lesbians who had mostly been left out of the current feminist explosion: working-class women, women in prisons, reform schools and juvie halls, women locked down in mental institutions for being too queer, women of color, women in the military and in the bars, women surviving in "straight" marriages and dead-end jobs who longed each day to touch another woman, women who were peep show girls—sex workers—carnival strippers, women who shot drugs and women in recovery from those drugs and the streets. Women in trailers, small towns and cities across America, women who filled the floors of the factories, fast-food restaurants and auto plants of this country, women whose lives were situated in PTA's, shopping malls and teamsters unions: these were the women I came from and they were the women I longed to build a movement with. It was here, with these women, that I hoped for the possibility of a new political dialogue about sex and desire and power. They were also, I quickly realized, the women most immediately at risk for HIV.

The struggle against AIDS brought (and brings) all my worlds together, instead of being barely tolerated because of my sex politics and my sense of urgency about the meaning and power of erotic desires (*was that really political?*). Here, in this movement, I was welcomed. In those early years when the government refused to take on the leadership of this battle (we still have to wait and see about Clinton), it forced us to create a movement based on grassroots organizing, word of mouth and long range goals. Each day we had to bite back our urgency and despair at how to get the messages out quickly enough. It was a movement which understood the critical need to talk about the uncomfortable or ragged edges of our sexualities and desires and which wasn't fooled by what we each called ourselves: as though these identity words would explain what we did in bed (or who we do it with), or who we were on the streets or in our jobs.

My first paid job doing AIDS work was as a HIV pre- and post-test counselor and hotline worker in New York. It was a revelation, to talk to people on a phone often frees them up to tell you more honestly what they're afraid of what their risks were. You couldn't see anybody's face on a phone. Couldn't trace them after the conversation. It radically shaped what I understood about the epidemic. About how enormous the groups of people affected were and gaps between peoples' perception of what constituted their individual risks and their understanding of how that translated to their personal lives. Each day I listened to voices and stories and each day I took people by their numbers, into a small room to reveal to them their test results. The pain and shattering of peoples' hopes (often regardless of the results) I heard and saw on that phone or in that room and the bravery, changed me like I hadn't been changed since the early civil rights movement.

My second job was with the AIDS Discrimination Division of the NYC Human Rights Commission. The work was to intercede against the fear and stigma that had arisen so violently around HIV. The work relied on, demanded, a sharp understanding of class and race in this country to know where to pay attention for the most vulnerable amongst us to HIV. And as an educator and filmmaker for the AIDS Discrimination Unit, I was organizing as a filmmaker at a community level around my passion to bring forward the voices and stories of the women (and men) who lived in long overlooked communities: letting them and their stories finally stand center stage where they belong.

When I wasn't at a paid job, I was an AIDS activist. And in spite of the difficulties that are always a part of building an imperfect movement, of the sexism that was often there and in the face of the governments locked tight doors, in spite of the times there was racism or fear of us as women and a refusal to understand or support women and men whose risks were different than the ones generally understood as gay. Still, it was work where everything remained to be done and anyone willing to confront those obstacles could join.

And my heart was breaking from the deaths of those I loved. I could tick it off on my fingers: life and death amongst my friends and in my communities, the urgency of people struggling to live with HIV.

As time went on there was one other reason that moved inside me. At some time in my life (and into the present), I had engaged in every one of the behaviors that I know put lesbians at risk. I heard my own personal and often secret, unspoken narrative in the stories and histories of the lesbians I met who had AIDS or who were at risk for HIV. I was lesbian and I had been one for twenty-seven years. Through all those years I had engaged, frequently, in every risky activity associated with AIDS, regardless of what I called myself at the time I was doing them. If that was true for me as a lesbian political organizer and activist, what was really happening for the vast majority of lesbians, bisexual women, young lesbians, transgendered lesbians, lesbians who were "coming out," passing women and women-who-partnered-with-other-women? What about the hundreds and thousands of women who used none of these words as they loved and desired another woman? What was happening to them? What, finally, about the huge unseen *us* which resides primarily outside the confines of our political networks: that vast geography of women building their lives against or with their desire for another woman and which runs like a underground river beneath the "straight" female landscape of America?

Creating the Lesbian AIDS Project at GMHC has been a major part of that answer for me; it is my own history coming home. And because I see the issues of HIV for lesbians as totally intertwined with the issues of sexuality, class, race gender and erotic desires which I have spent much of my political life working on, it has both combined and thrust me back into a level of organizing I haven't been involved in since the early civil rights and anti-war movements of the 1960's and 70's. It is an organizing project which engages me with a breadth, depth and diversity of women-who-sleep-with-women which is powerful and engaging. Going back to this work with my history as an organizer committed to a politics of inclusion; returning as a forty-six-year-old lesbian who has been doing this political work since I was seventeen, allows the richness of my own life-history to illuminate the gigantic map of our actual lesbian world, a map with sharp relief and global scope and a map which I see as needing, at its base, to grasp and then chart the wildly disparate universes of queer female lives and communities in order to understand our survival.

LAP [the Lesbian AIDS Project-GMHC] is an organizing project with two core ideas: lesbian HIV visibility and lesbian sexuality. Lesbians at risk or with HIV have been "the disappeared" lesbians in our communities for too long. Wrong class, wrong color, wrong desires, wrong histories, but these are the women who need to become the center of the lesbian movement, not just the AIDS movement, and their stories, struggles and issues have to be integrated throughout our understanding of which women are lesbians, who we count when we ask that question and which women will have voice and power to determine our overall political direction. And sex, our sexuality in all it's variety and contradiction, needs to be opened up, aired and considered as a major component of the unique political understanding we bring to all other social change movements.

Who Is the "We" in Our Sisterhood?

But the lines of the map linking our communities of women-who-partner-with-women are very faint. The terrains through which most lesbians can openly travel are very restricted. It is a geography rigorously determined by our backgrounds, our class and color, by rural landscape or city street, by whether we are politically active or spiritually inclined, by the narrow confines of age and health and physical ability, by the marks on the map which identify us as lesbians from the bars, the trade union, the military, from gay studies programs or as art history majors, by how we each came out and with whom, by the shape of our desires and our willingness (or ability) to risk it all on our love for a woman, by our status as mothers or our decision not to have kids, by the nature of our dreams and aspirations, by our very ability to nurture and sustain hope for our futures.

As lesbians in this culture we suffer from the same lack of power and resources common to all women. Within that oppression we must also navigate our health, sexuality and social existence in an environment committed to imagining all women as heterosexual. In a universe without voice or presence, lesbians and our particular risks for HIV have remained submerged inside a "straight" female landscape, keeping us ignorant and uninformed about our own risks for HIV. We are a specific population of women with high numbers of HIV+ members but no official recognition or accounting.

In the midst of this blank space, the "secret" of lesbian risk and lesbian death due to HIV spirals. This spiral magnifies the confusion amongst us, leading the entire community into doubt and anger. Some lesbians deny all vulnerability to HIV, making the question of risky behaviors, from shooting drugs and sex with men to safe sex between women appear negligible or unrealistic and unknowable. This guarantees that lesbians who are HIV+ or have AIDS will fall through this crack of fear and denial and be marked outside the status of "real" lesbians. Our openness about our histories as women engaged in these activities and behaviors works to disown us as an integral part of the big lesbian landscape.

And it is here that race and class background becomes a particularly vicious component of our risks and our understanding about HIV. For working class women without any buffers, the picture is immediately fragile: our need for our communities of birth are accentuated if we are women of color, women whose first language is not English or we are poor or working class women who are responsible for and committed to the survival of our extended families. In this already contested setting, HIV/AIDS is often devastating, while our resources remain scarce. We are often forced to lie and hide our sexual desire for other women so that we can access the health care of social services we need. We also hide in order to guarantee the commitment and support of our biological families, our jobs, our neighborhoods, our children, our language and our access to valued cultural institutions. Medically, socially, and economically, the less room we have to turn around, the more problematic our crisis becomes as we balance precariously between the women we desire and the help and support we need.

It has also become clear to me that the process of "coming out," one of the most celebrated aspects of lesbian myth and queer story-telling, is often a "high risk activity." I meet too many lesbians from lesbian/gay/bisexual student unions on their campuses who have become HIV-infected during the period they were "coming out." Or women who have struggled to leave small towns and come to cities have moved in and out of many social networks before finding community or identity. Think of it: this is often the time when confusion and silence about desire for another woman is the most terrifying to come to terms with. It is often a time of lots of sexual experimentation, often for women sleeping with other women their partners are gay men and that is often combined with drug use and drinking. It is a period when we fall between communities and identities and it can often be a time of isolation or shame from former friends, our families and the figures of authority or support in our lives. For middle-class lesbians the margins of their privilege from birth can slip away quickly when (or if) it becomes known that they are sleeping with another woman. For whatever age, "coming out" is a highly charged and often dangerous path each of us walk. HIV magnifies that risk a thousand times over.

Whose Voice, Whose Leadership, Whose Movement?

HIV makes a mockery of pretend unity and false sisterhood. Though the women now affected cross all classes and races, the majority of lesbians right now who are HIV+ are predominantly lesbians of color or poor white women, usually struggling with long histories of shooting drugs or fucking men for the money to get those drugs. These are not the women usually identified as the primary voices feminism or the lesbian movement most value and try to organize to create a progressive political agenda. The HIV+ lesbians who continue to come forward as leaders in the lesbian AIDS movement have histories and lives lived in neighborhoods most gay studies courses rarely identify as lesbian, let alone use as the bases of understanding queer females' lives and experiences.

The question of HIV, of race and class, becomes a question of whose movement and whose leadership. Will lesbians who shoot drugs or are in recovery be the women turned to to speak for the movement? Will categories that depend on the construction of "real" lesbians disappear and reveal instead the incredible numbers of women who hold another woman in their arms, regardless of what each woman calls herself when she does this, no matter who else she may be fucking? Will histories of low paying jobs, the revolving door of prisons, the military and bar life, the sound of kids playing while the lesbian group convene, become common and ordinary occurrences within our movement? Will the power of being butch or femme, the stories of life as a lesbian mom or a runaway teenage street dyke predominate? When will femmes with long nails and sharp-assed attitude be the voice heard leading Gay Pride Day marches? Whose movement, whose voice, whose stories, whose hope for transformation and change? Whose? These are the questions I see in front of me every day.

Some Complications On Our Way To Understanding Lesbian HIV

The crisis for lesbians struggling to understand the impact of HIV in our communities is compounded by the general lack of decent, nonjudgmental information about lesbian sexuality. Because it remains unacceptable to love and desire other women sexually, we are also left with little substantial information about what we do in bed with each other, including what might put us at risk sexually. STD's (sexually transmitted diseases) of all kinds are little understood or discussed between women partners and the fear and ignorance surrounding HIV compounds the already existing blank space silencing this discussion in our communities. Homophobia, like all silences and prejudices, hurts us profoundly, leaving us unarmed and unprotected, as though forbidding the word (*lesbian*) of our existence can stop the act of our love. It doesn't of course, it just leaves us vulnerable and uniformed. Our communities' confusion about whether AIDS is really a lesbian issue reflects this oppression.

The denial about our risk for HIV is often supported by a circumscribed lesbian sexual border we have constructed which refuses to acknowledge or accept that we sleep with each other in many, many different ways. We are butch/femme women, we are queer or androgynous, we are lesbian-feminist, we don't believe in labels: we practice S/M, we use our hands, our mouths, our bodies, sex toys to pleasure and please each other and we may also sleep with men, whether we call that "bisexuality," "coming out," "economic necessity" or we don't dare talk about it.

For a small though growing number of HIV-positive lesbians, their only (or primary) risk for HIV was that their female partner was HIV-positive when they became lovers. When these lesbian couples looked for good information about female to female transmission they were rarely successful. And when they went to other lesbians to try and discuss it (if they dared) few other lesbians could help. Like so many other people before them, the lack of adequate and specific information to help them assess their risks was unavailable. This third group of lesbians, though by far the smallest subset of HIV+ lesbians, is growing each year. But like all the other risks in our communities, female to female sexual transmission remains scientifically undocumented or reliably researched. This combines dangerously with the denial of HIV in our communities and with the crisis of our drug use and the alcoholism which continues throughout our communities. This crisis about our risks is compounded by our invisibility and our lack of political clout.

All of these activities and identities are components of our communities' sexual and social lives. While we have taken an extraordinary risk in daring to love another woman, this has not guaranteed our judgments against each other's erotic or drug choices won't be as cruel as the general culture's judgments against us. Our understanding of the reasons many of us shoot or snort drugs, drink 'til it harms us, experiment with substances which can kill us are stories that we have not let surface enough inside our communities, hoping that by not telling aloud those pieces of our lives we will not be hit any harder by social condemnation than we already are. It's as though we think that by disavowing a set of activities (and the women we stereotype as doing them) we can protect ourselves from even more homophobia.

We also carry those historical silences into our sexual judgments as well, thinking that if we don't enjoy a particular sexual activity ourselves, no other lesbian could either. If another woman *wants* differently she is in danger of having her credibility as a "normal" lesbian questioned. Yet the irony is that we remain women who are sexual outlaws, originators and social inventors, leaping across the sexual and emotional silences surrounding womens' desires for other women, daring to touch and possess each other sexually, daring to claim our right to be sexual, to love and want another woman.

So the Voice on My Phone Machine Said, "What's Your Problem Anyway?"

One of the first things I did when we created the Lesbian AIDS Project was develop a sex survey. The survey is very explicit and was done to try and determine how we are really having sex with each other, how often in what combinations and with who else and what we think of ourselves as we do it. This was not a survey primarily about relationships. It appeared in the *1992 Lesbian and Gay Pride Guide* of which 60,000 copies were produced for the June Gay/Lesbian March and which is picked up and used as a resource book by a wide variety of lesbians, including women who don't necessarily hook into the gay bookstores and lesbian political organizations in New York City. When the survey appeared my answering machine was suddenly full of "anonymous" messages from "normal dykes" suggesting that what I really needed was to go "fuck a man." Sometimes the messages were from "regular" lesbians telling me how sick they considered some of the categories and activities were that I had included on the survey. Usually those messages ended with a free swinging interpretation of what they imagined "I was into." These anonymous messages always hurt. They made clear to me again how problematic the real world of female sexuality is for all of us and what an added minefield being a lesbian could be when it was thrown into the mix. Sex in our community remains our smoking gun and the fight for whose hand is on the trigger continues.

Still, many women were thrilled by the survey and over 1,600 women filled them out and sent them back. These numbers were very high. Women wrote their opinions in the margins and on Post-its stuck over the sections they loved or despised. Lesbians said, "Congratulations, I've waited a long time for someone to care enough about our survival to finally ask us what we do sexually." Women who answered used exclamation marks and red pens to write their ideas and express their opinions. "I didn't even know lesbians could do this!" " I love these questions. My girlfriend and I are going to try them all before we finish the survey." "Hot survey! Getting steamy just answering it." But other women wrote, "I didn't even know that lesbians could get AIDS."

The Lesbian Construction of Magical Thinking

In one of the surveys, I found this note attached, it said: " I am glad you're doing this survey for those lesbians that can use it, but my lover and I don't really have any use for these questions. *We are both women and because of that we understand each other's bodies and desires.* Maybe women that are more fucked up don't understand this, but for us it's really just natural. Thanks anyway".

In anthropology, this is called magical thinking and this magical thinking is rife throughout the communities I have to speak with every day. It is the most common idea I hear across the wide groups of lesbians I talk to. The notion that because we are women touching other women, we automatically understand and empathize so totally that we know intrinsically how to caress each other, how much pressure to use when we suck or lick each others bodies, how to stroke or fuck each other to climax, is very dangerous and very widespread. It is hard to imagine, if that's where we're beginning, how to start discussing safer sex, negotiating up front and directly with a lover, to talk openly about HIV and STD protection methods, or discuss our drug or sex work or sex histories.

Magical thinking also leads a lot of women I talk with to assert that they don't think we can transmit sexual diseases (or yeast infections) between each other. And it leads to other dangerous and incorrect sexual notions. One of the most common is that if STD's are transmitted between women partners it's probable due to a lesbian sleeping with a "bisexual" woman. In this lesbian worldview, men are dirty, women who sleep with them are contaminated, and only lesbians who sleep with other "real" lesbians can remain safe. I hear these stories and watch us say these things as yeast infections spread back and forth sexually between us and STD's remain out of control in our communities and are still not discussed regularly. How can safer sex ever be a regular part of our lives, when we are literally forced to risk our right to community in order to tell the truth about what we do and who we do it with? The legacy of being women in this culture, of being denied decent non-judgmental information about our bodies and our desires is multiplied for lesbian women.

HIV+ Lesbians and Young Lesbians Lead the Way

Still, in the face of this culturally imposed ignorance, I see women who love other women trying to carve out an erotic terrain of our own which claims and encourages all of us to explore and reckon with our desires for each other. It assumes that there are thousands of complex ways we each feel desire and passion. Especially in younger lesbians, I have seen a much more matter-of-fact acceptance of HIV risk for lesbians. These are women who have grown up sexually in the first decade of AIDS and they are much less resistant to the idea of lesbian risk and HIV safety. And in lesbian communities already hard hit by HIV, the question of safer sex, regardless of presumed mode of transmission, is also different and more open. It is there, in working class lesbian political and social organizations that I see the most innovative and least judgmental struggle to integrate HIV knowledge into daily lesbian life. These are often communities of lesbians which have had the tragic example of numbers and the powerful voices of HIV+ lesbians to reckon with and to lead the discussion. There, HIV is no stranger. In these communities, HIV+ lesbians are lovers, mothers, sisters, best friends.

Growing numbers of HIV+ lesbians are regularly speaking out. More than anything else, it has been their bravery and their insistence to tell the truth of their own lives (and histories) that have cracked the silence and denial in the larger lesbian communities. Like the role that HIV has played in other settings, AIDS transmission always exposes the gap between who we want to believe ourselves to be and what we really do in our regular lives. The leadership of lesbians who are infected of affected by HIV is a powerful and original model for the building of a new, more inclusive movement of women-who-partner-with-other-women. It brings into one dialogue the lives of all of us throughout our evolution as lesbians. The work being done by these lesbians in AIDS organizations, women's outpatient health clinics, detox centers, youth programs for runaway lesbians, prisons and recovery programs and in neighborhood organizations is rarely documented but it is some of the most powerful lesbian activism happening. And it is building a new foundation and a different class base for a larger lesbian political movement.

Claiming the Power of Our Lives

Our right to be sexual with each other and to struggle with the issues of our daily lives, like our drug use and the sex we have with men, are all pieces of the lesbian puzzle. Whether or not the larger culture acknowledges us, we must recognize each other and our different struggles. The lesbian map is very large, our numbers are significant, and we must pick up this fight to protect ourselves and each other while we fight to be seen and respected. We can't wait for other people to see what is right in front of our noses: that we are an integral part of this world, not outside it, and so is a potentially life threatening virus, HIV. Our community is not immune and lesbianism is not a condom for AIDS. Like everyone else, we are vulnerable and must take the steps necessary to learn how to protect each other's lives. No one else will do it for us, and no one will do it as well. We have been taking risks to love each other for millennia. Now we need to expand our understanding of who we are and what we do in order to understand the many ways we need to go forward. Our communities are fabulously sexual and inventive, our lives and histories varied and full of meaning. We can support each other in taking the step each of us needs to be safe, erotic, and powerful. And we can build a movement, starting here, that refuses to privilege rigid ideological categories over the truths of our lives and to finally build a lesbian movement which bases its theories on a more complicated and irreducible map of lesbian desire and lesbian voice.

RETHINKING AIDS

Controversy over the cause of AIDS, what infections "count" as being part of AIDS, and the epidemiology that constitute AIDS as a global pandemic has existed virtually since the epidemic was declared by the Centers for Disease Control in 1981. A detailed overview of the controversies has yet to be written, but some examples can be given here. Michael Callen's doctor, Joseph Sonnabend, argued as early as 1983 for a multifactorial and immune-overload theory of causation, challenging the idea that a new microbe was responsible. Other early arguments against the viral theory pointed to the use of recreational drugs, especially poppers by gay men. This argument was picked up in 1987 by Peter Duesberg, a Berkeley molecular biologist who tried to show epidemiologically that AIDS was not a single disease and that there was not a single agent that caused it. Then, in 1987 to 1989, criticism of AZT therapy began; this criticism ranged from the argument that the trials were hasty or even fraudulent, that AZT was the cause of immune system deterioration, and that gay men who didn't take it stayed healthier and lived longer than those who did, to the most recent criticism based on the 1993 European Concorde Study that seriously questioned *any* efficacy of the drug. Beginning in 1988, a British film documentary company, Meditel, both criticized AZT therapy as well as questioned whether there even was an AIDS epidemic in Africa—the latter based upon inaccurate "false positives" in HIV testing, and that now, those individuals with diseases that have been prevalent in Africa for a long time (such as wasting syndrome and malaria) are diagnosed with AIDS. This latter argument was later taken up by the *Sunday Times* of London. In 1989, Pulitzer prize-winning journalist John Crewdson published a long investigative article as a special supplement to the *Chicago Tribune*. In it he charged scientific fraud in the laboratory of HIV co-discoverer Robert Gallo; the article led to Congressional hearings and an investigation of misconduct that was eventually dropped, although Gallo was not cleared.

The Group for the Scientific Reappraisal of the HIV/AIDS Hypothesis was founded in 1992, "in order to get the following four sentence letter published in a number of prominent scientific journals. All have refused to do so. *'It is widely believed by the general public that a retrovirus called HIV causes the group of diseases called AIDS. Many biomedical scientists now question this hypothesis. We propose that a thorough reappraisal of the existing evidence for and against this hypothesis be conducted by a suitable independent group. We further propose that critical epidemiological studies be devised and undertaken.'"* [The argument here is based upon a tautology that arises from incorporating the HIV hypothesis of causation into the definition of AIDS: when people get sick and HIV is present or thought to be present, the disease is AIDS, when HIV is not present, it is called something else, not AIDS.] Over a hundred scientists and several hundred others signed the letter and the group publishes an international newsletter, *Rethinking AIDS*, that is excerpted below.

Such dissent also moves one step beyond critique of the HIV hypothesis both to criticize the vested interests in the institutionalization of AIDS as a chronic disease and to challenge the very definition of AIDS itself. In this view, there are enough anomalies to "deconstruct" the hypothesis of AIDS as a single syndrome of immune deficiency caused by HIV that then allows opportunistic infections to kill the host. Instead, medicine should simply treat such individual infections as such; attempts to find a single cause of overall immune deficiency have been misguided. In the next excerpt from *The AIDS War*, John Lauritsen, a longtime gay activist and critic of the HIV hypothesis and of AZT, questions not only the entity "AIDS" but also the activities of AIDS organizations. While the argument against AIDS organizations has already been seized upon by homophobes to decrease funding and blame gay men for perpetuating the epidemic, the dimensions of the debate need to be discussed openly so that gay people can begin to set its terms, as they have struggled to do throughout the politics of AIDS.

The third statement below is from the founder and publisher of the *New York Native*, a newspaper that has monitored and proposed alternative interpretations of the AIDS epidemic from the beginning. The editorial position of the *Native* has been controversial. For example, in 1989, ACT-UP, led by Peter Staley, called for a boycott of the newspaper for advising its readers to be wary of taking AZT because of its side effects. Writing in 1993, Charles Ortleb presents an alternative explanation of what AIDS is that connects it to Chronic Immune Deficiency Syndrome and the political economy of scientific research.

When the readings in this volume were collected in 1994, AIDS research around arresting HIV had seemingly reached a standstill. Then in 1996, announcements of the discovery of drug therapy regimens aroused considerable hope at the International AIDS Conference in Vancouver. These regimens, using a new class of drugs called "protease inhibitors," were able to reduce HIV in some human hosts to an undetectable level. Discourse about "the cure" arose simultaneously with cautionary discourse about premature speculation, dire side effects, and the economic costs of such therapy (raising questions about unequal access to health care that have arisen in the politics of AIDS from its outset). As seems evident from the quotes at the beginning of this chapter as well as from the growing pandemic in the developing world, hope may need to be tempered through our historical perspective and with critical analysis of the global political economy of AIDS.

IT'S TIME TO RE-EVALUATE THE HIV-AIDS HYPOTHESIS

from *Rethinking AIDS* (1992)

The Editors

In April 1984, U.S. Health and Human Services Secretary Margaret Heckler announced to the world at a press conference that an American government scientist had discovered the cause of AIDS. This claim, made in the absence of the usual scrutiny and debate that is provided by refereed publication, was nonetheless received as fact by the general scientific community, and without further investigation a vast research program was launched. Based on the proposition that a newly identified retrovirus, termed HIV, is responsible for the apparently irreversible destruction of T-helper cells characteristic of AIDS patients, this program has until now been unsuccessful at providing either a vaccine or a cure, and has resulted in public health policies that are of questionable value in preventing the spread of AIDS.

Since 1987, data contradicting a single-virus etiology of AIDS have been accumulating. As a result, a loosely affiliated worldwide network of scientists—The Group for the Scientific Reappraisal of the HIV-AIDS Hypothesis—was formed in an attempt to bring about an impartial investigation of the question that was inadequately considered in 1984: Is HIV really the cause of AIDS?

As an explanation for the origin of AIDS, the HIV *hypothesis* is implausible because:

1. It contradicts a number of established principles of virology and immunology:

—Retroviruses do not typically kill their host cells. On the contrary, they depend on continued replication of the host for their own survival (Weiss et al., Mol. Biol. of RNA Tumor Viruses, 1985, Cold Spring Harbor Press, NY). It is therefore improbable that a retrovirus would have evolved that kills its only natural host with an efficiency close to 100%, and yet is horizontally transmitted as inefficiently as HIV. It is even more unlikely that two such viruses (HIV-1 and HIV-2), which differ by almost 50% in their nucleotide sequence (GeneBank), would have simultaneously evolved.

—Pathogenic viruses typically cause disease as a consequence of infecting, replicating in, and killing more cells than blood mononuclear cells (in both asymptomatic and symptomatic persons), and HIV RNA is detected in 1 in 10,000 to 1 in 100,000 such cells (Simmonds et al., J. Virol. 64:864, 1990). Yet 5% of the body's T-cells are regenerated in the two days it takes HIV to establish an infection (Guyton, Textbook of Medical Physiology, 1987, WB Saunders, Phil.).

—Viruses typically cause disease shortly after infection, before the immune systems of their hosts can respond. There is no other example of a viral pathogen which causes primary disease only after long and unpredictable latent periods, only in the presence of neutralizing antibodies, and in the virtual absence of gene expression, as HIV is said to do.

2. It is at variance with a growing body of empirical observations:

—Antiviral immunity to HIV is sufficient to keep infectious virions in cell-free serum below the limits of detection until the final stages of AIDS when B-cell immunity is lost and HIV (along with all other chronically latent viruses) is sometimes reactivated (Ho et al., NEJM 321:1621, 1989).

—Extensive studies of HIV gene structure and function have neither identified any specific determinants of pathogenicity, nor shown it to be significantly different from many other retroviruses, which are not said to cause degenerative diseases (Duesberg, PNAS 86:755, 1989).

—Many chimpanzees have been successfully infected with HIV, yet all have remained disease-free until now, up to 7 years later (Weiss and Jaffe, Nature 345: 659, 1990).

—HIV is said to be a sexually transmitted virus, yet it is barely detectable in the semen of AIDS patients (Van Voorhis et al., Fertil, and Steril. 55:588, 1991).

—The number of HIV carriers in the U.S. has remained constant at one million since 1985, when widespread antibody testing was introduced (Institute of Medicine, Confronting AIDS, 1986, Nat. Acad. Press, Wash. DC, and Vermund, J. NIH Res. 3:77, 1991), yet new viruses spread exponentially in a susceptible population (Freeman, Burrows Textbook of Microbiology, 1979, WB Saunders, Phil.).

—AIDS has remained confined to the same risk groups since it was first identified as a new disease syndrome, and there are many fewer cases than predicted. Forecasts of the spread of AIDS continue to be falsified, with one notable exception, that is the model published by Bregman and Langmuir—Farr's Law Applied to AIDS Projections (JAMA, 263:1522, 1990). This model predicted a crest in the AIDS epidemic in 1988–1989, with a subsequent decline to an epidemic level. Data from the July, 1991 public domain diskette compiled by the Centers for Disease Control tends to confirm such a crest in 1989–1990.

—Approximately 75% of American hemophiliacs have been infected with HIV for more than 7 years (Confronting AIDS, op. cit.). according to the HIV hypothesis at least 50% should have died of AIDS by now, yet mortality among hemophiliacs has not increased (Koerper, In: AIDS Pathogenesis and Treatment, Levy (Ed.), 1989, Marcel Dekker, NY) and only 2% of HIV-positive hemophiliacs develop AIDS indicator-diseases annually (CDC, HIV/AIDS Surveillance, 1986-1991, US Dept. of Health and Human Services, Atlanta, GA).

—The same diseases are found in similar frequencies in HIV positive and HIV negative intravenous drug users, and the overall mortality in the two groups is the same (Stoneburner et al., Science 242:916,1988).

Despite these and many other inconsistencies, the HIV-AIDS hypothesis remains the sole basis for public health policies that are aimed at controlling the spread of AIDS by advocating (1) "safe-sex" practices, (2) the use of "clean" needles to inject toxic, unsterile drugs, and (3) the long-term administration of potent metabolic poisons, like AZT, which are claimed to prolong the lives of HIV-infected persons; and for research programs directed almost exclusively at developing pharmaceuticals designed to interfere with HIV replication.

It is in the interests of formulating an approach to the prevention and cure of AIDS consistent with what we really know that we call for a re-evaluation of the evidence for and against the HIV-AIDS hypothesis. It is the obligation of scientists to ask the most unpleasant and difficult questions of even the most cherished theories, especially when the answers may prevent possibly needless suffering and loss of life.

---

from

THE AIDS WAR

(1993)

John Lauritsen

CHAPTER XXXII
The Incidence Quagmire[1]

You cannot track a non-existent entity

From the very beginning I realized that something was very wrong with the basic concept of "AIDS", but it is one thing to sense something and quite another to understand it analytically. Several AIDS-critics were influential in clarifying my thinking on the core problem of AIDS: whether it actually exists in any rationally definable way.

Harry Rubin, Professor of Molecular Biology at Berkeley, the man who virtually created the science of retrovirology, gave a talk in Washington, DC in 1988, in which he expressed skepticism regarding the simplistic notion that the 20 (at the time) AIDS diseases constituted a single entity caused by a single virus. This he referred to as "Cartesian reductionism"—the tendency to reduce complex phenomena to a single cause. Rubin's comments not only cast doubt upon the HIV-AIDS hypothesis, but upon the very existence of "AIDS" as well.[2]

Peter Duesberg, also Professor of Molecular Biology at Berkeley, has consistently ridiculed the Centers for Disease Control (CDC) definitions of "AIDS", expressed by the formula: **Indicator Disease + HIV = AIDS**. The first part of the equation is absurd because of the extreme heterogeneity of the official AIDS-indicator diseases or conditions (about which more below). The second part of the equation is also absurd, because the HIV requirement can be satisfied in so many different ways: a positive result on the highly inaccurate HIV-antibody tests; a positive result on the Polymerase Chain Reaction (PCR) test; actually cultivating the virus from a patient's blood plasma[3], or, as is done in about half of the "AIDS" diagnoses, simply "presuming" that HIV is present. As Duesberg mischievously points out,

dementia + HIV = AIDS, but **dementia − HIV = stupid.**

Kawi Schneider in Berlin has vigorously polemicized for years against the core mythology of "AIDS". In a 1989 article he wrote "AIDS" is a fraudulent diagnostic label that, in conjunction with statistical patchwork, has created an epidemiological castle in the air, which can be considered the first freely invented pseudo-epidemic.[4] In a recent letter to me he commented:

Even from the orthodox standpoint, "AIDS" is not the name of a disease, but rather the name of a coincidence, interpreted as causation, of lab parameters (antibodies and T-cell counts) and at least one item from the list of 30 conventional diseases known as "AIDS-indicator diseases"... I never write or say "person with AIDS", but "person with an AIDS-diagnosis", never "spread of AIDS" but "spread of AIDS-diagnoses"... never "HIV-infection" but "antibody presence indicated by a test". (29 March 1993)

The 29 AIDS-Indicator Diseases

Last January the CDC expanded the surveillance definition of "AIDS" still another time. Since I wanted to know exactly what and how many the indicator diseases were, I called the CDC, where I spoke to Press Officer Kent Taylor. My request turned out to be more difficult than I had imagined it would be. The CDC had never thought to compile a simple list of the indicator diseases, let alone a *numbered* list. But Taylor was resourceful, and got back to me in a couple of hours with the raw material from which I myself have made a numbered list.[5]

The following list is taken from a table, "AIDS-Indicator diseases diagnosed in patients reported in 1991, by age group—United States", which appeared in the CDC's *HIV/AIDS Surveillance Report* of January 1992:

1. Bacterial infections, multiple or recurrent (applies only to children)
2. Candidiasis of bronchi, trachea, or lungs
3. Candidiasis of esophagus (either a "definitive diagnosis" or a "presumptive diagnosis")
4. Coccidioidomycosis, disseminated or extrapulmonary
5. Cryptococcosis, extrapulmonary
6. Cryptococcosis, chronic intestinal
7. Cytomegalovirus disease other than retinitis
8. Cytomegalovirus retinitis (either a "definitive diagnosis" or a "presumptive diagnosis")
9. HIV encephalopathy (dementia)
10. Herpes simplex, with esophagitis, pneumonia, or chronic mucocutaneous ulcers
11. Histoplasmosis, disseminated or extrapulmonary
12. Isosporiasis, chronic intestinal
13. Kaposi's sarcoma (either a "definitive diagnosis" or a "presumptive diagnosis")
14. Lymphoid interstitial pneumonia and/or pulmonary lymphoid hyperplasia (either a "definitive diagnosis" or a "presumptive diagnosis")
15. Lymphoma, Burkitt's (or equivalent term)
16. Lymphoma, immunoblastic (or equivalent term)
17. Lymphoma, primary in brain
18. *Mycobacterium avium* or *M. kansasii*, disseminated or extrapulmonary (either a "definitive diagnosis" or a "presumptive diagnosis")
19. *M. tuberculosis*, disseminated or extrapulmonary (either a "definitive diagnosis" or a "presumptive diagnosis")
20. Mycobacterial diseases, other, disseminated or extrapulmonary (either a "definitive diagnosis" or a "presumptive diagnosis")

21. *Pneumocystis carinii* pneumonia (either a "definitive diagnosis" or a "presumptive diagnosis")
22. Progressive multifocal leukoencephalopathy
23. Salmonella septicemia, recurrent
24. Toxoplasmosis of brain (either a "definitive diagnosis" or a "presumptive diagnosis")
25. HIV wasting syndrome

On 8 December 1992 a letter was mailed by the CDC to State Health Officers, informing them: "On January 1, 1993, an expanded surveillance definition for AIDS will be effective." The following AIDS-indicator conditions were added to the list:

26. A CD4+ T-lymphocyte count <200 cells/uL (or a CD4 percent <14)
27. Pulmonary tuberculosis
28. Recurrent pneumonia (within a 12-month period)
29. Invasive cervical cancer

To my knowledge, I am the first writer to compile a numbered list of the official AIDS-indicator diseases or conditions. It is a very mixed bag. Many of the diseases are caused by funguses, for example, candidiasis, coccidioidomycosis, cryptococcosis, histoplasmosis, and *pneumocystis carinii*. Others are caused by bacteria, like salmonella. Others, by mycobacteria, like tuberculosis. Still others, by viruses, like cytomegalovirus or herpes. And still others, like the various cancers and neoplasms, including lymphoma and Kaposi's sarcoma, have no established etiology. And still others, like dementia or wasting, are poorly defined and can have many different causes.

Dementia is presented on the list as "HIV encephalopathy", but it is difficult to imagine how a retrovirus, like HIV, could cause encephalopathy. Retroviruses, by their very nature, can only infect cells that are capable of undergoing cell division. Brain cells do not divide. Therefore, HIV does not and cannot infect brain cells.

Some of the indicator diseases/conditions can be diagnosed presumptively. This is a charming situation. Not only can HIV be diagnosed presumptively, but some of the indicator diseases as well. This means that a physician, following the CDC's rules, would be able to diagnose someone who behaved eccentrically, or had difficulty swallowing, or had a bad cough, or just seemed in poor health, as having "AIDS" on the basis of a *presumptive* diagnosis of HIV infection coupled with a *presumptive* diagnosis of toxoplasmosis of the brain, or candidiasis of esophagus, or *pneumocystis carinii* pneumonia, or a mycobacterial infection, or whatever.

One also notices that two items on the list are known and expected consequences of AZT therapy: lymphoma and wasting. I'll have more to say about this below . . .

CHAPTER XXXIII
AIDS Organizations

The bitter reality is that, in the AIDS War, the mainstream AIDS organizations are in the camp of the enemy. On the whole, it would have been better if not a single AIDS organization had ever come into existence. Many good people have died horribly because of lies promulgated by the AIDS Establishment, which very much includes the leading AIDS organizations.

It is important, however, to make a distinction between the organizations themselves and the many thousands of people who have worked in those organizations, as volunteers or lower-level salaried employees. The latter includes kind and courageous individuals who came to the aid of those in need. The volunteers bought groceries, ran errands, cleaned up messes, and did all kinds of chores for very sick people who had been diagnosed as having

"AIDS". They acted selflessly. Nothing I will say about the mainstream AIDS organizations should reflect upon the basic goodness and decency of these people . . .

The Indictment

When I use the word "lies", I do not wish to imply that all, or even most, of the people in leading AIDS organizations were deliberately engaged in promulgating falsehoods. It is possible that most of them believed the falsehoods that were disseminated in the literature of their organizations. Nevertheless, falsehoods they were.

The ethical indictment to be issued against the leaders of the mainstream AIDS organizations is not that they made mistakes—not that they were stupid and gullible, though this is nothing to be proud of. Rather, their blame consists of having suppressed dialogue. The AIDS organizations were rigidly and ruthlessly totalitarian in censoring any viewpoint that did not fit the orthodox dogmas of the moment. They inspired sufficient fear among their employees that none, while still employed, publicly expressed a doubt about the HIV-AIDS hypothesis or the benefits of AZT therapy—though some did so after resigning or being fired.

In criminal cases it makes a difference whether an act be committed deliberately or unintentionally. But even an unintentional misdeed is not free from culpability. If someone drives his automobile carelessly, causes an accident, and kills someone, he is held responsible for his actions. The same principle ought to apply to the top people in AIDS organizations. Whether intentionally or not, they have spread lies which defiled the principles of science, which squandered public resources, and which brought suffering and death to many people. Ethically and intellectually, if not necessarily criminally, they are to blame.

Lies about etiology:

The AIDS organizations were not just passive dupes of the Public Health Service. They actively collaborated in creating the AIDS mythologies. They themselves not only endorsed, but refined and elaborated on the prevailing paradigm: that "AIDS" is a new, single disease entity, which is caused by the newly discovered retrovirus, HIV-1.

This is not the place to repeat the arguments against the rococo-idiocies of the HIV-AIDS hypothesis. Suffice it to say that from the very beginning there were critics of the hypothesis, and that our voices were silenced. While a scientific controversy over the causes of AIDS was raging all over the world, the AIDS organizations never admitted in their literature that anyone had ever doubted HIV was the cause. Never, indeed, did they admit that the HIV-AIDS hypothesis was just that, a *hypothesis*. The sole exception was Project Inform, which on occasion acted as an attack pit bull for the AIDS Establishment, viciously misrepresenting the arguments and motivations of AIDS-critics.

Lies about risk-reduction:

The mainstream AIDS organizations have put forward risk-reduction guidelines which have consistently been, not merely wrong, but dangerous. The basic premise underlying all of the guidelines is that "AIDS" is an infectious disease though the relevant evidence, from survey research to molecular biology, solidly indicates that the syndrome is not infectious. The guidelines have intransigently neglected the one truly germane issue, *toxicology*.

In Chapter XIX I argued: "In the great majority of cases, AIDS illnesses have resulted from the toxic effects of chemicals, including both medical and 'recreational' drugs." If this is the case, and the evidence is very powerful that it is, then risk-reduction efforts ought to have been directed towards warning members of the two main risk groups, intravenous drug users (IVDUs) and gay men, in the strongest possible terms, to avoid drugs. The AIDS organizations did just the opposite.

Through such lame-brained schemes as the BleachMan campaign, IVDUs have been given the message that it is all right to inject drugs, so long as the needles are clean. Indeed, the thrust of needle cleaning advice from a superhero type like BleachMan is that injecting drugs is a *good* thing to do. Now, I am in complete agreement that using dirty needles is dangerous; no one in his right mind would do that. At the same time, it is equally true that no one in his right mind would inject "recreational" drugs. Heroin, cocaine amphetamines, *etc.* really are dangerous, no matter how cleanly they are injected into the blood stream.

Risk-reduction advice directed at gay men has concentrated almost entirely on "safer sex", with an obsessional touting of condoms. Almost the only caution regarding drugs has been along the line that they might cloud the judgment, thus causing a lapse into "unsafe sex". *Don't get too high, or you might forget about condoms!* In reality, there is not an iota of evidence that even a single case of "AIDS" has ever been transmitted either homosexually or heterosexually. There have been innumerable assertions to this effect, and many myths, but no convincing evidence.

Risk-reduction advice, based on theological notions of what is sinful, rather than upon rational evaluations of what is physically harmful, has consistently portrayed sex as more dangerous than drugs . . .

Partnership in pharmacogenocide:

By pharmacogenocide I mean the destruction of groups of people through therapy with any of the drugs known as nucleoside analogues, which include AZT, ddI, ddC, and d4T. These drugs are lethal by their very nature they attack the basic molecule of life, DNA. These drugs do not and could not have benefits of any kind. They are sufficiently toxic as to be "incompatible with life".

I have already described how GMHC in New York City and Terence Higgins Trust in London colluded with Wellcome, the manufacturer of AZT, in a scam to get healthy, HIV-positive individuals to take AZT as "early medical intervention? They were not alone. With very few exceptions, which will be mentioned at the end of this chapter, the AIDS organizations went along with the "Living With HIV"/early intervention campaign.

I am not condemning these organizations for disagreeing with me on the benefits and toxicities of AZT. I condemn them for withholding crucial information from the people they advised. In advocating "early medical intervention" for healthy HIV positive individuals, none of the AIDS organizations adequately described the toxicities of AZT. Not one of them came right out and said that AZT is a carcinogen.

Careerism:

Many people have experienced hardship as a result of the "health crisis", and many more have voluntarily made sacrifices in order to help out. But for others, the health crisis has been a bonanza. Quite a few of the leading "AIDS experts" are *nouveau* millionaires, who made their fortunes in the eight years since the HIV-AIDS hypothesis, and the commodities it spawned, were put on the market—examples being Robert Gallo, Luc Montagnier, William Haseltine, and Max Essex. Some of the leading AIDS-doctors, who are now worth millions, were second-rate "clap doctors" back in the 70s.

There are *nouveaux riches* in the AIDS movement also, from bribes, drug-smuggling operations, and so on. More important than graft, however, is the phenomenon of *careerism*. For hundreds of individuals, the AIDS organizations have provided an opportunity for personal gain. People of modest educational backgrounds and negligible work experience, who would normally be unable to obtain any but the most menial jobs in the business world, have abruptly become executives, with fabulous salaries, fabulous benefits, and fabulous expense accounts. I know of several executives in AIDS organizations, who had never before held a job in their lives. One "editor" of a leading newsletter, who has refused to disclose his age, educational background, or previous work experience, is unable to write even minimally literate English.

In Chapter XIX I argued that "AIDS" is a phoney construct, and that for the most part the AIDS-indicator illnesses are caused by toxins. I believe that the so-called health crisis would come to an end soon, if the truth were told. But for the AIDS-careerists, it must go on forever. If the crisis were to end next month, and the world were to learn that the whole thing has been an enormous hoax, what would happen to their pensions? Who would employ them? How would they pay their fabulous rents? . . .

CHAPTER XXXV
What Next?

Discredited AIDS expert

For a decade, Robert Gallo of the National Cancer Institute was promoted as the world's foremost expert on "AIDS". It was a serious blow to the AIDS Establishment when, in December 1992, he was found guilty of "scientific misconduct" by the Public Health Service's Office of Research Integrity (ORI). The ORI called for increased oversight of Gallo's laboratory for a three-year period, with a copy of its report placed in his personnel file.

Although the sanctions may seem slight, a National Institutes of Health official, who asked not to be named, said they are "devastating": "To be found guilty of misconduct in the scientific world is a major thing. Science is based on trust."[1]

Gallo's misconduct consisted of having told lies, and perhaps fudged data, in order to establish himself as the discoverer, or at least co-discoverer, of HIV, in which capacity he has illegitimately received many hundreds of thousands of dollars in royalties from the HIV-antibody tests. (In a way, this is rather trivial, considering that HIV is not the cause of AIDS. As Michael Verney-Elliott of Meditel put it: "Who cares who stole the fake jewel?")

Even before Gallo's personal downfall, three of his closest associates—men who had written scientific papers with him and played important roles in his laboratory—had either been found guilty of, or placed under indictment for, felonies.

Discredited AZT

On 12 February 1992, Channel 4 Television in London broadcast a 45-minute documentary, "AZT: Cause For Concern". Produced by Meditel, it explained, with great clarity, the shortcomings of AZT research and the terrible toxicities of the drug. Millions of viewers saw exactly how AZT attacks DNA, the basic molecule of life, and how the drug can actually *cause* many of the symptoms of "AIDS". At this time the Wellcome Foundation chose to divest itself of most of its stock in Wellcome Pharmaceuticals, the parent company of Burroughs Wellcome, the manufacturer of AZT.

In the *Lancet* of 3 April 1993 appeared a letter announcing the preliminary results of the Concorde trial, which for four years had studied the effects of AZT therapy for healthy individuals with HIV-antibodies. The researchers concluded:

Concorde has not shown any significant benefit from the immediate use of zidovudine [AZT] compared with deferred therapy in symptom-free individuals in terms of survival or disease progression, irrespective of their initial CD4 count.[2]

The Concorde findings invalidated those of the two NIAID studies, Protocols 016 and

019, which had provided the rationale for giving AZT to asymptomatic, HIV-positive people.[3] In every way the Concorde trial was superior research: it had many times more subjects, it ran four times as long, and, perhaps most importantly, it was independent of the drug manufacturer.

Since CD4 counts have been used to claim benefits for AZT, and actually formed the basis for the approval of ddI, the Concorde findings regarding CD4 counts are especially troublesome. According to Ian Weller, of Britain's Medical Research Council:

The study does bring into question the place of this degree of changes in CD4s in accessing anti-virals . . . The other issue that goes along with that is the wisdom of using this degree of change as a basis for licensing anti-viral drugs, in case we might cause more harm than good in long term, from the point of view of side effects.[4]

What should be done?

Research should be done to determine why people became sick with AIDS-indicator illnesses. It is mandatory that no one even remotely connected with the Public Health Service or the AIDS Establishment should be allowed to participate in this research, for they would certainly sabotage it.

A large, true, random-probability, national serological survey should be conducted to establish benchmarks on various blood cell counts; incidences of various microbes and microbial antibodies, according to all standard tests; and so on. Research should done on treatments for the opportunistic infections, as opposed to "AIDS".

The Public Health Service, modern medicine, and the United States generally are in very bad shape, and I don't know of an easy solution. Somehow we must return to older and better standards. This means a return to the authority of intellect and ethics, as opposed to the authority of money and power.

Fiat justitia et pereat mundus

Let there be justice, though the world perish! An obsession with injustice can be harmful, and, as Nietzsche observed, we should be distrustful of anyone motivated by a strong desire to punish. But the slave philosophy of turning the other cheek is even more harmful.

The Crimes Against Humanity committed in the AIDS War rank with any in history. It takes awhile for the enormity of the situation to sink in: that at this very moment, a quarter of a million people are being murdered by nucleoside analogue therapy. This catastrophe is not just the product of honest mistakes and blunders. In the AIDS War, there is a vast army of fools: venal fools and non-venal fools, crooked fools and honest fools, malevolent fools and charitable fools. At the same time, there are also those in the AIDS Establishment who know exactly what they are doing, and are profiting thereby.

If there were justice in the world, the AIDS-criminals would be brought to justice, given fair trials, and executed. I doubt this will happen, especially to those who are rich or well-connected politically. My only consolation is knowing that these people will be destroyed from within. According to an old Latin saying, NEMO MALUS FALIX. No evil person is happy.

The important thing now is to get out the truth. We must save lives, stop the squandering of our national resources, and rescue the good name of Science.

Chapter XXXII

1. This chapter has not been published before.

2. John Lauritsen, Chapter XII: "Kangaroo Court Etiology", Poison by Prescription: The AZT Story, New York 1990.

3. *This is almost never done. When attempts are made, it is impossible to cultivate HIV from the plasma of at least 50% of "AIDS patients".*

4. *"'AIDS'—die neue Religion" ["'AIDS': the New Religion"], raum&zeit June/July 1989. Schneider's views and those of other AIDS-critics can be found in the special issue of* raum&zeit #4, *"'AIDS'—Die Krankheit, die es gar nicht gibt" ["'AIDS': the Disease that Doesn't Even Exist"], Ehlers Verlag, Sauerlach, 1992. His critique of the media, "AIDS:Medicine, Moral und die Medien. Von der Virus-Theorie befallen" ["AIDS-Medicine: Morality and the Media. Infected with the Virus-Theory"], appeared in* Wochenzeitung, Zürich, 19 June 1992.)

5. *All of the information in this section is taken from a fax sent to me on 10 January 1993 by CDC Press Officer Kent Taylor.*

Chapter XXXV

1. *Paul Reger, "Gallo Investigation", Associated Press, 30 December 1992.*

2. *Jean-Pierre Aboulker and Ann Marie Swart, (letter) "Preliminary analysis of the Concorde trial",* Lancet, *3 April 1993.*

3. *See Chapters XIV and XVII.*

4. *Cynthia Johnson, "Study Casts Doubts on Best Measure of AIDS Drug Efficacy",* Reuters, *2 April 1993.*

WHY AIDS IS REALLY AIDSGATE

(1993)

Charles Ortleb

I am writing this as someone who has observed the AIDS epidemic for the entire ten years of its devastation, as the publisher of a national gay newspaper, the *New York Native*.

The *Native* is credited with being the first newspaper to break the story on the epidemic when AIDS was only a rumor of a strange pneumonia showing up in several gay men. We ran a story about that rumor in May of 1981, two months before the first reports broke in the mainstream media.

As a result of our exhaustive and critical coverage of the epidemic, the *Native* has become one of the most controversial gay publications in America. We have taken a major publishing risk by continually suggesting that we don't believe what government scientists have been telling the world about the AIDS epidemic. In fact, what we have been publishing has been so provocative that the mainstream media has refused to even acknowledge that New York's oldest and largest circulation gay newspaper has reported for years that the government is lying about the epidemic.

Some scientists who are now researching AIDS were still undergraduates when the *Native* was reporting on the epidemic. The *Native* is considered an important primary historical source for graduate students writing on various aspects of the epidemic.

From the vantage point of a decade of writing and publishing on AIDS, here are some of the controversial and unsettling conclusions I have come to about the real nature of the epidemic.

1. "AIDS" is part of a larger epidemic which could more accurately be called Chronic

Immune Dysfunction Syndrome. Heard about the weird, vague epidemic called "Yuppie Flu" or "Chronic Fatigue Syndrome"? Our reporting has led us to believe that it is actually the breakout of "AIDS" in the heterosexual population. How come reporters haven't looked more deeply into the discrepancy between the epidemic in Africa and the epidemic here? If they did they would find that we have a major heterosexual epidemic here too. It's just that we have another name for AIDS when it occurs in white heterosexuals. We call it Chronic Fatigue Syndrome.

2. Human Immunodeficiency Virus (HIV), which has been officially declared the cause of "AIDS," is only that—"officially declared." It has really not been shown to be the cause of "AIDS." Some people develop "AIDS," its symptoms, or its hallmark immunodeficiencies, without being positive for that virus. Many people who test positive for antibodies to that virus don't develop "AIDS." The distinguished scientist who first suggested that HIV is not the cause of AIDS has been punished for his belief. His name is Dr. Peter Duesberg and he lost his funding from the National Institutes of Health because he has voiced his dissent with the conventional wisdom on AIDS. He was recently joined by thirty-five other scientists who agree with him. If AIDS is such a threat and such a big story, where are the investigative pieces on Duesberg and the growing list of scientists who believe that the fundamental ideas about the epidemic are mistaken? Some reporters keep reassuring the public that they are not really in danger of getting AIDS because they don't test positive for HIV. Unfortunately, HIV is not the cause of the syndrome, so all bets are off. Even Luc Montagnier, the French researcher who discovered "HIV," now has doubts about its role in "AIDS."

3. Our reporting has led us to the conclusion that the cause of "AIDS" is most likely a virus called Human Herpes Virus-6. That virus causes more direct damage to the immune system than HIV. Scientists have to come up with all kinds of convoluted explanations to justify their belief that HIV is the cause of "AIDS." The *Native* has done many stories on this new virus. It was discovered after "HIV." All anyone has to do is read the scientific literature and it becomes clear that it is the most likely cause of AIDS. Even the so-called discoverer of HIV, Dr. Robert C. Gallo of the National Cancer Institute has suggested that this virus might be responsible for much of the damage to the immune system in AIDS. Many people are now infected with this virus. I'll bet that you never even heard of it or that most Americans are infected with it, or that it's the possible cause of AIDS. Federal officials want people to think that because it is now so widespread, it always has been, and it therefore is essentially harmless.

4. Human Herpes Virus-6 is also the likely cause of Chronic Fatigue Syndrome. People who are seriously infected with Human Herpes Virus-6 develop immune system problems very similar to "AIDS." Some doctors already refer to Chronic Fatigue Syndrome as "AIDS Minor." Any papers that have bothered to give any ink to the Chronic Fatigue Epidemic have merely aired the debate about whether the syndrome is real or not. None dares mention the obvious: that it's a form of AIDS. Entire middle-class families have been stricken with the syndrome. That would mean that the real AIDS epidemic is unbelievably worse than any newspaper has yet reported. There are estimates that as many as thirteen million Americans now have Chronic Fatigue Syndrome. And it's clearly very contagious. If we're correct that it is a form of AIDS, it's kind of a big story, isn't it?

5. Further complicating this matter is the probability that Human Herpes Virus-6 is not exactly what scientists have described. From a long series of reports in the *Native*, we have suggested that it is actually a virus called African Swine Fever Virus, which causes an AIDS-like illness in pigs. The scientist who has probably mislabeled this virus is Gallo himself. Gallo has been under investigation for the last few years for allegedly mislabeling the so-

called AIDS virus. The *Native* was the first newspaper to call for an investigation of Gallo. The only other paper to give any real coverage to his outrageous behavior has been the *Chicago Tribune*. Both the *Washington Post* and the *Times* have looked the other way. The *Washington Post* approached the story by investigating the *Tribune*'s John Crewdson, the reporter who has stayed on the Gallo story for the last few years. The best way to avoid digging into the story is to pull the rug out from under the reporter who has. The *Native* has done everything possible to bring Crewdson's reporting on fraud in AIDS research to our readership's attention. I'm proud to say that as a result of our uncompromising reporting we are the only newspaper—gay or straight—in America that is currently the object of a boycott by Act-Up, the national AIDS activist group.

6. Most people are not aware that there is currently an AIDS-like illness in pigs all over the world. It has received very little media coverage, even though it is affecting pigs internationally. The disease is called, tentatively, Swine Mystery Disease. The earliest reports of the epidemic date back to 1981, around the time that AIDS and Chronic Fatigue Syndrome were being noticed in people. I think it is certainly not unreasonable to suggest that the AIDS-like Swine Mystery Disease epidemic is connected to the AIDS and AIDS-like Chronic Fatigue Syndrome epidemics in people. Yes, I'm actually telling you that the next time you bite into a ham sandwich you may be getting a mouthful of immune-compromised pig. All you have to do is read the *Native*'s coverage and you won't feel the same way about pork for a while. Even though many in the media know that the *Native* has been screaming that there is a link between AIDS and a pig disease, no one has seen fit to report the curious fact that there is an AIDS-like disease in pigs now, something we basically predicted and warned about.

7. Probably no stand the *Native* has taken has been more controversial than our position on the government's official treatment for AIDS. Reporter John Lauritson has written one devastating critique after another about how fraudulent the research that went into the licensing of AZT is. The treatment itself causes AIDS. Recently the New York State Department had to begin a propaganda campaign to convince the Black Community that it's not a deliberate plot to kill them. The intuitions of the Black Community are more on the money then most people realize.

These seven points sum up ten years of the *Native*'s investigative reporting on this international crisis. It shouldn't come as any surprise to many Americans that either through stupidity or malfeasance, government scientists may have brought about one of the greatest tragedies of our time. Do reporters somehow think that AIDS would be immune from the kinds of human folly that were uncovered during Vietnam, Watergate, the Savings and Loan crisis, Irangate, Iraqgate and the October Surprise?

I believe that the AIDS/CFS epidemic will turn out to be the mother of all cover-ups and that one day we will look back on our reporting with a great deal of pride.

Our final selections in this chapter are personal voices. Jeffrey Schmalz, the *New York Times* beat reporter on AIDS, states his own frustration after years of dashed hopes. He died just before this article was published. Herbert Daniel was an AIDS activist in Brazil until his death in 1993, as his article was in press. His statement shows the difficulty of fighting to live with AIDS in the context of its incidence among the economically disadvantaged under an authoritarian political regime. Finally, Robert E. Penn, a novelist, poet, and outreach worker at GMHC, wrote specifically for this volume. An earlier version of the essay appeared in *Essence* as an appeal for recognition of gay and HIV-positive members of the African-American community.

PERSONAL VOICES

from

WHATEVER HAPPENED TO AIDS?

from *The New York Times Magazine* (1993)

Jeffrey Schmalz

I have come to the realization that I will almost certainly die of AIDS. I have wavered on that point. When the disease was first diagnosed in early 1991, I was sure I would die—and soon. I was facing brain surgery; the surgeons discovered an infection often fatal in four months. I would shortly develop pneumonia, then blood clots. I was hospitalized four times over five months. But by the end of that year, I thought differently. My health rebounded, almost certainly because of AZT. I was doing so well; I really might beat it.

Now it is clear I will not. You can beat the statistics only so long. My T-cell count, which was only 2 when I got my diagnosis, has never gone above 30—a dangerously low level. I have lived longer than the median survival time by 10 months. The treatments simply are not there. They are not even in the pipeline. A miracle is possible, of course. And for a long time, I thought one would happen. But let's face it, a miracle isn't going to happen. One day soon I will simply become one of the 90 people in America to die that day of AIDS. It's like knowing I will be killed by a speeding car, but not knowing when or where.

I used to be the exception in my HIV support group, the only one of its eight members who was not merely infected with the virus but who had advanced to full-blown AIDS. Now, just a year and a half later, the exception in my group is the one person who does not have AIDS. All the rest of us have deteriorated with the hallmarks of the disease—a seizure, Kaposi's sarcoma, pneumonia. Our weekly meetings simmer with desperation: We are getting sicker. *I* am getting sicker. Time is running out.

Once AIDS was a hot topic in America—promising treatments on the horizon, intense media interest, a political battlefield. Now, 12 years after it was first recognized as a new disease, AIDS has become normalized, part of the landscape. It is at once everywhere and nowhere, the leading cause of death among young men nationwide, but little threat to the core of American political power, the white heterosexual suburbanite. No cure or vaccine is in sight. And what small treatment advances had been won are now crumbling. The world is moving on, uncaring, frustrated and bored, leaving by the roadside those of us who are infected and who can't help but wonder: Whatever happened to AIDS? As a journalist who has written about this disease for five years, and as a patient who has had it for nearly as long, *I* went out looking for answers.

The Disease and the Doctors

Dr. Anthony S. Fauci speaks with a hint of a Brooklyn accent, which is out of sync with the elegance of his appearance—well tailored, tidy, trim. At 52, he is scientist-cum-celebrity, ridiculed by Larry Kramer in the play "The Destiny of Me," lionized by George Bush in the 1988 Presidential debate as a hero.

Being the Government's point man on AIDS has made Tony Fauci (rhymes with OUCH-EE) famous. He professes to be solely the scientist. But in fact, he is very much the star and the politician, one year defending modest Reagan-Bush AIDS budget proposals as adequate, the next defending generous Clinton proposals as necessary. He is the activist's enemy— "Murderer!" Kramer once called him in an essay published in *The Village Voice*. He is the activist's friend, a comrade in arms, showing up last October at the opening of the Kramer play wearing a red AIDS ribbon.

Fauci's starring AIDS role comes from the many hats he wears—among them director of the National institute of Allergy and Infectious Diseases and director of the National Institutes of Health's Office of AIDS Research.

"Fauci deserves a lot of the blame for where we are on AIDS," said Peter Staley of TAG, the activist Treatment Action Group. But others say that is not fair. "You can't blame any one person," said Gregg Gonsalves, who wrote TAG's report on the status of AIDS research. "We've gotten to the edge of a scientific cliff."

Whatever Fauci's faults, I have never doubted his commitment. Still, he is the face of the AIDS scientific community, and 12 years into the disease there are only temporary treatments that work for a few years at most. AIDS remains a fatal illness. Approximately a million Americans are believed to be infected with the human immunodeficiency virus, the key component of AIDS, and virtually all of them are expected to develop the disease eventually. Close to half a million Americans are expected to have full-blown AIDS by the end of next year; more than 2,000,000 have already died. Roughly 350,000 will have died by the end of 1994. The World Health Organization puts the number infected worldwide at more than 13 million adults and an additional 1 million or more children.

So far, the only treatments are nucleoside analogues, drugs like AZT, DDC and DDI. A fourth nucleoside analogue, D4T, is expected to be approved by the spring. Fauci has focused national research efforts on these analogues, which slow the virus by fooling it with a decoy of genetic material it needs to reproduce. But the analogues were of limited use, but the horrible surprise was just *how* limited. A report issued just before the meeting—the Concorde Study, conducted in England. France and Ireland—found that, contrary to the recommendations of the United Stated Government, use of AZT before the onset of AIDS symptoms did not necessarily prolong life. (In an extraordinary action, a United States Government panel has since pulled back the earlier recommendation. AZT is still recommended for those with full-blown AIDS. But the panel left if for patients and their doctors to decide on earlier use.)

A subsequent Australian study, published in July, found that AZT, used early did prolong life. I have always felt that it has prolonged mine. Still, what makes the fuss over AZT so stunning is not just that the drug has shortcomings—almost everyone knew that from the start. It is that AZT, flawed as it was, had become the Gold Standard of treatment, against which other therapies were being measured. The chilling message of the AZT dispute is this:

Things are not just failing to get better; they are getting worse. We are losing ground.

"The fallout from Berlin has been devastating," said Martin Delaney, founding director of Project Inform, an AIDS treatment information and lobbying group. "There were no surprises. But the risk now is that AIDS gets put up on the shelf along with a lot of other long-term unresolved problems. We lose the urgency for money and the scientific momentum." The bad news has left drug companies scrambling. Last spring things were so desperate that a group of 15 announced they would pool research data. Many scientists—and activists—are fed up with the drug companies, which seem hell-bent on pursuing more nucleoside analogues when the real future of AIDS treatment probably lies with gene therapy. The idea is to alter the genetic structure of cells to make them inhospitable to HIV. But the problem is, no one knows how to translate the occasional test-tube success into a workable treatment. In addition, most of the gene therapies are being developed by small biotechnology companies that will take years to get into full production.

So was all the time and money spent on the nucleoside analogues wasted? Fauci, who obviously has an investment in the answer, was emphatic that it wasn't. "People say the Berlin meeting was so depressing, nothing's happening," Fauci said in his office overlooking the N.I.H. campus in Bethesda, Md. "I say that's not the way science works. There are little steps, building blocks. What's important is whether you're going in the right direction, and I am convinced that we are.

"Was it grossly inappropriate to do the extensive studies of AZT and DDI?" he continued. "No. Should we have done more with other drugs? If we had them, one could say, yes.

"Let's say a year and a half from now, nevirapine isn't working," Fauci said of an experimental drug undergoing trials in combination with the nucleoside analogues. "Somebody's going to say, 'Why did you waste all that time with it?' but you don't know it doesn't work until you test it."

If Fauci is defensive, it may be because he is still smarting from a political bruising. His Office of AIDS Research has been reorganized by the Clinton Administration and he has been, in effect, ousted—done in by the AIDS activists through their Democratic friends in Congress. And while some of his time is being divert to playing politics, in his own laboratory research he has now returned to basics—Square 1—where many AIDS researchers are working. Fauci is studying the pathogenesis of the disease, its route through the body.

I asked him the obvious: 12 years into the disease—shouldn't we know that already? "More effort looking at pathogenesis might have been appropriate in retrospect," Fauci responded. "But we were constantly being diverted—by the activists, by congress. It was: 'What can you give me right now? Get those drugs out there as quickly as you can.'"

Not so long ago we believed that if we just could find enough money, we could make the disease manageable, like diabetes. But in a further sign of how little hope exists these days in the scientific community, money isn't seen as the main issue anymore.

"Certainly, there are more scientific opportunities than there are resources to fulfill them," Fauci said, echoing the views of other scientists. "But should we dump billions into AIDS research now? I think we'd reach a point of diminishing returns."

Fauci presents a front of optimism, at least for me. After all, there is no cure for any virus, only vaccines to prevent them—measles is an example. By the year 2000, he predicted, "we'll be into vaccine trials that show a vaccine is much more feasible than we thought, though we may not have the best vaccine then."

Other scientists are unconvinced. They point out that the rapid mutation of the AIDS virus and its many strains make development of a vaccine difficult.

"The public is frustrated; it says, 'You've been working on this for 10 years,'" said Dr.

Irvin S. Y. Chen, director of the AIDS Institute at the University of California at Los Angeles. Chen bemoaned the lack of money for biomedical research in general, which he said was discouraging the best and brightest from entering the field.

"We're in that in-between state," said Dr. Merle A. Sand, an AIDS expert at the University of California at San Francisco; he was head of the Government panel of AZT use. "We know a lot about the virus, but we just don't seem able to translate that knowledge into significant treatment advances. It's incredibly frustrating."

Still, the frustration of the public and the scientists is nothing compared with the frustration of those of us living with AIDS or HIV. Will people still be dying of AIDS in the year 2000? Fauci didn't hesitate for a second before replying, "I don't think there's any question that will be the case."

The Activists and the Government

Tim Bailey was one of the Marys, and that's as close to ACT UP royalty as anybody can get.

The Marys are a subgroup of ACT UP, the group involved in the more radical demonstrations, like disruption services at St. Patrick's Cathedral. When Bailey died in June at 35, stipulating that he wanted a political funeral in Washington, ACT UP was obliged to comply.

So on a drizzly Thursday at 7 A.M., two buses filled with ACT UP members set out from New York. They were to rendezvous with the body in Washington, then carry the open coffin through the streets from the Capitol to the White House. They would show Bill Clinton the urgency of AIDS, they would bring one of its carcasses to his doorstep.

But it was not to be. The police would not let them march, and the day turned into a sodden fiasco, as the police and activists quarreled over the body, shoving the coffin in and out of a van parked in front of the Capitol. The rage was there, but the organization was not. And when the police said no, whom did ACT UP members run to for help but the White House, the very target of their protest, getting Bob Hartoy, a White House staff member with AIDS, to intervene. In the end, ACT UP members gave up and went home, taking the body with them.

It was a perfect metaphor for the site of AIDS activism—raging in desperate but unfocused anger, one foot on the inside, one on the outside.

The AIDS movement was built on grass-roots efforts. Now those efforts are in disarray. Many ACT UP leaders have died, the group's very existence was based on the belief that AIDS could be cured quickly if only enough money and effort were thrown at it—something that now seems increasingly in doubt. Besides, it is hard to maintain attacks against a government that is seeking big increases in AIDS spending. Much of the cream of ACT UP has fled, forming groups like TAG and joining mainstream AIDS organizations like the Gay Men's Health Crisis and the American Foundation for AIDS Research.

Those left behind are ACT UP's hard core. ACT UP was always part theater, part group therapy. Now, sadly, ACT UP is increasingly reduced to burying its dead.

To say all that is not to belittle the accomplishments of the group. One reason for ACT UP's decline is that it has got so much of what it wanted. ACT UP forced AIDS into the Presidential race, dogging candidates. Because of ACT UP the price of AZT is lower. Drugs are approved more quickly. Today it is a given that the communities affected by a disease have a voice, and must be consulted. To a great extent, ACT UP deserves much of the credit for the increasing political power of the entire gay rights movement. But now even the gay movement has pushed AIDS to the sidelines.

Anyone questioning how AIDS ranks as an issue among gay groups need only look to the march on Washington on April 25. Six years earlier, in 1987, a similar gay march had on overriding theme: AIDS. If there was a dominant theme last April, it was homosexuals in the military. To be sure, AIDS was an element of the march but *just* an element. Speaker after speaker ignored it.

"It's like they are waiting for us to die so they can get on with their agenda," said Dr. Nicholas A. Rango, the director of New York State's AIDS Institute, a gay man who himself has AIDS and watched the march on C-Span from his Manhattan hospital bed. [He died on Nov. 10.]

Torie Osborn, formerly executive director of the National Gay and Lesbian Task Force, argued that the shift was inevitable with the election of a Democratic President, renewed attacks from the right wing and just plain burnout. Increasingly, many homosexuals, especially those who test negative for HIV, do not want a disease to be what defines their community. "There is a deep yearning to broaden the agenda beyond AIDS," she said. "There's a natural need for human beings who are in deep grieving to reach for a future beyond their grieving.

"It's one thing to be fighting for treatment, believing you're going to get a cure that will have everyone survive," continued Osborn, who recently buried three friends who had died of AIDS. "But it's an incredibly depressing truth that AIDS has become part of the backdrop of gay life."

What is to some a broadening of the gay agenda, however, is to others desertion. "It's one thing for the politicians to abandon AIDS," Kevin Frost, a TAG member, said "but for our own community to abandon the issue . . . Who brought this issue of gays in the military out in the open? A couple of flashy queers with checkbooks. Well, what about AIDS?"

What *about* AIDS? Perhaps the greatest development affecting ACT UP, the activist community and the entire AIDS care world is the changing face of the disease. Homosexual sex still accounts for the majority of cases, 57 percent. But that number is dropping, down from 61 percent in 1989. Meanwhile, the percentage of cases tied to intravenous drug use is beginning to climb. It is now at 23 percent, up from 21 percent in 1989.

Black and Hispanic groups are clamoring for a greater role in running AIDS care organizations. Their intentions seem genuine—what do gay groups know of inner-city drug use?—but also seem driven in part by a desire for money and power. In an age of government cutbacks, AIDS is where the money is—"today's equivalent of the Great Society programs of the 60's," as Rango put it.

In Washington and Houston, gay groups and black and Hispanic groups are bickering over who should control the money and programs. In New York, the largest AIDS care organization, the Gay Men's Health Crisis, is trying valiantly to be all things to all constituencies—it contributed $25,000 to the lobbying effort to allow homosexuals in the military even as it was helping to expand legal services in Harlem. Inevitably, focus is lost.

G.M.H.C. has recently changed executive directors, as have many of the more than 3,500 AIDS organizations in the United States. The average executive director of an AIDS service group lasts less than two years, burned out by depression and exhausted by the bickering among AIDS constituencies.

"We should be fighting the virus, not each other," said Dan Bross, the executive director of the AIDS Action Council. "We're eating our young."

Mary Fisher, who addressed the Republican National Convention in Houston as a woman infected with HIV, whom I interviewed at the time and who has since become a friend, also believes the AIDS movement is adrift. She was sitting at lunch in Manhattan with Larry Kramer, both of them bemoaning the state of AIDS activism.

"We need to agree on the goals," Fisher said.

"That's just rhetoric," Kramer shot back "the goal is to find a cure."

Fisher sees AIDS entering a dangerous never-never land, with the day fast approaching when *no one* will be carrying the AIDS banner.

"The gay community is going to stop screaming," she said, "it is already stopping."

"I'm very despondent," Kramer said. "You don't know where to yell or who to yell at. Clinton says all the right things, then doesn't do anything."

Indeed, the Clinton administration does say all the right things, at times coming close to being patronizing about it.

"I have a real understanding that the people who feel the strongest about this, they don't have time," Carol H. Rasco, the President's top- domestic policy adviser said in defense of the zealotry of ACT UP. "When a bomb is ticking inside you, you have to keep pushing."

Where once Washington doors were closed to AIDS activists, they are now open, indeed, perhaps the single biggest AIDS change in Washington under the Clinton Administration has been one of tone. AIDS sufferers are no longer treated as immoral lepers. David Barr, director of treatment education and advocacy for the Gay Men's Health Crisis, recalled a May meeting with Donna E. Shalala, the Secretary of Health and Human Services.

"She agreed to everything we wanted," Barr said. "I was amazed. We're so used to doing battle. But is it a ploy?"

Certainly Bill Clinton is a vast improvement over George Bush. The president proposed a major increase in spending on AIDS research, about 20 percent, coming up with an additional $227 million. That would raise the total N.I.H. spending on AIDS research to $1.3 billion. In aid for outpatient care, the White House proposed a giant increase in what is known as Ryan White money, named for the Midwestern teen-ager who died of AIDS in April 1990. The current appropriation is $348 million, which the Administration proposed to nearly double by adding $310 million. The House didn't add the entire amount, just a $200 million increase, but it still brought the total to $548 million. The Senate was slightly more generous, and the final appropriation was $579 million.

But is more money enough? AIDS activists say they want leadership, but they are not sure anymore what that means.

"It was much easier," said Torie Osborn, "when we could hate George Bush and Ronald Reagan, when we thought we had evil genocidal Republican Presidents who weren't doing what needed to be done to get a cure."

Still, as is so often the case with Bill Clinton, he is a victim of his own lofty campaign rhetoric. He spoke eloquently about AIDS in his pitches for the gay vote. He insisted that people infected with the AIDS virus, Bob Hattoy and Elizabeth Glaser, speak at the Democratic National Convention. On Election Night, he mentioned AIDS high in his victory speech. It all seemed so promising. David B. Mixner, a Clinton friend who helped rally the gay vote, exclaimed in the flush of a Clinton victory, "I believe thousands of my friends who wouldn't make it, who would die of AIDS, might make it now because Bill Clinton is President."

There it is: the man from Arkansas was to be not just President but savior. He's not. Bogged down early on in a battle over homosexuals in the military Clinton has grown wary of anything that the public might perceive as a gay issue. He delayed fulfilling his campaign pledge to name an AIDS czar, finally naming her five months into his term—and only when the National Commission on AIDS was about to attack him for not providing leadership on the epidemic.

More than anything else, what the AIDS community wants from Bill Clinton is a sense of urgency. Carol Rasco maintains that Clinton is committed. "Health-care reform and AIDS are the only thing I've worked on every day since I got here," said the domestic policy adviser. But others, even in the Administration, think Clinton is doing little to help.

"Other than myself, who lives with AIDS every day, there's no one at the White House for whom this is their first-tier issue," said Bob Hattoy, who, after serving six months as a White House aide often critical of the Administration's AIDS policies, was shifted to the Interior Department. He praised the President and Mrs. Clinton for having "a profoundly sensitive awareness about AIDS," but at the staff level, he said "AIDS is not on the radar screens at the White House every day." And the political advisers? Hattoy scoffed. "I don't think they'll address AIDS until the Perot voters start getting it."

The Czar and the Press

There was a time when it was thought that the solution to the AIDS crisis could be found in two words: AIDS czar. One omnipotent public figure with the power to marshal funds, direct research, cut through the bureaucracy—in short, to lead a Manhattan Project-size effort to force a cure for AIDS. Kristine M. Gebbie doesn't look like a czar, and she doesn't think of herself as one, either . . .

Now, she is the AIDS czar—a far cry from the stellar names that AIDS activists had fantasized about: H. Norman Schwarzkopf, Jimmy Carter, C. Everett Koop.

"We wanted 'Jurassic Park,' and we got 'Snow White,'" Larry Kramer likes to say.

"The activists wanted a war on AIDS," Gebbie said, shaking her head. "I am not one of the big names. I am someone who has struggled with systems around this epidemic since the beginning. I think I have a feel for what it takes to bring people together . . ."

And what happened to the eagerly awaited Manhattan Project? "Manhattan Project?" Gebbie said. "I don't know what that means. Both the Manhattan project and the Man-on-the-moon project involved, I think, a much more targeted goal. We know where we'd like to go—fix AIDS—but I'm not sure we can conceptualize what it would take to do that. On the other hand, if what 'Manhattan Project' conveys is: 'The Government if behind you,' well, if I do my job right, we will target and have energy and direction. What we won't have is somebody in general's stripes who can walk around and order people, 'Drop what you're doing and work on HIV.'"

"There's this contradiction," said Dr. Mark D. Smith, a San Francisco AIDS expert who discussed the job with the Administration but eventually withdrew, "between the public perception of great responsibility and the reality of no real organizational authority . . ."

To be fair, on that sunny Friday in the Rose Garden when he announced the appointment of Gebbie, the President sounded like the old Bill Clinton, the one in the campaign. He finally did what the activists wanted—he spoke out on AIDS as President. He labeled the virus "one of the most dreaded and mysterious diseases humanity has ever known" and "an epidemic that has already claimed too many of our brothers and sisters, our parents and children, our friends and colleagues."

But the trouble was, no one was listening. Newspapers and the networks, reported the naming of Gebbie, but few carried the President's comments on AIDS. Newsweek magazine, in a week-in-the-life-of-the-President piece, didn't even mention the Gebbie announcement. At the news conference, there was only one question on AIDS, and that was directed to Gebbie about her qualifications. Reporters were eager to move on to the real news, like the budget and homosexuals in the military.

AIDS, it seems had become old news.

"In the early days of AIDS, when knowledge was expanding, there were lots of very compelling thing to write about," said Marlene Cimons, who covers AIDS and Federal health policy out of the Washington Bureau of *The Los Angeles Times*. "We were in the infant stages of making policy decisions about AIDS that had unique social and political ramifications. Now it's become harder to find angles. We've written to death most aspects of the disease. AIDS in the classroom. AIDS in the workplace. Testing. They filled the front pages. Now there's a vacuum."

Stuart Shear, a reporter for "The MacNeil/Lehrer Newshour" who covers AIDS, said the conflicts that had made for good stories—the fights between Republican Administrations and AIDS advocates—were gone.

"It's become a pure science story," he said. "When it gets down to the clinical nitty-gritty, that's not what we look at. It's hard to get people to come on and complain about an Administrations that's increasing funding."

The Patient and the Journalist

In my interviews for this article and others, I always ask people with AIDS if they expect to die of the disease. One reason for that is a genuine reporter's curiosity; the answer is part of the profile of who they are. But I am also searching for hope for myself. Increasingly, the answers coming back are the same, even from the most optimistic of ACT UP zealots: Yes, we will die of AIDS.

I thought about that the other day in the emergency room at Lenox Hill Hospital. I had taken my boyfriend there for a blood transfusion to offset the anemia caused by the chemotherapy for his Kaposi's sarcoma. I realized on that Sunday morning in the emergency room that the moment of crisis wasn't coming tomorrow or the next day for my boyfriend. It was here today. And it will soon be here today for me, too.

Does that make me angry? Yes. I had such hope when I interviewed Bill Clinton about AIDS and gay issues for this magazine in August 1992. He spoke so eloquently on AIDS. I really did see him as a white knight who might save me. How naive I was to think that one man could make that big a difference. At its core, the problem isn't a government; it's a virus.

Still, in interviews with researchers and Administration officials, it was clear that we are talking from different planets. I need help now, not five years from now. Yet the urgency just wasn't there. Compassion and concern, yes; even sympathy, but urgency, no. I felt alone, abandoned, cheated.

I asked Gebbie what she says to someone with AIDS—in other words, what she says to me. And for one brief moment, there was a glimmer of realization that delay means death.

"I say, 'I hear you and I appreciate the frustration and the sorrow and the loneliness,'" she said. "That can sound trite, but it is genuine. It's inappropriate for me to hold out a false promise to you. It would be easy to say: 'There, there. It will be better soon.' That's a disservice, so I have to be honest with you. We don't have quick answers. I can't tell you when we're going to have a cure."

I am on the cutting edge of drug testing, in a trial at New York Hospital for a new combination therapy: AZT, DDI, and nevirapine. That is the combination that drew so much publicity last February when researchers in Boston declared that they had found the combination was effective inhibiting the virus. But at the Berlin conference, the formulator of the concept, Yung-Kang Chow, a Harvard medical student, reported a flaw in part of the original study. Other researchers challenged the findings after they were unable to confirm the results.

I was surprised at how jealous many of my fellow members of the support group were when I got into the trial—1 of only 25 people accepted out of more than 400 applicants. The group members felt that I had used influence. I had not. Yet admission to these trials is not purely luck either—a point driven home when a number of leading researchers called, offering to get me into one of the nevirapine trials. I did not take them up on it. If my doctors used influence to get me in, it was not with my knowledge. But I am grateful if they did. The ship is beginning to sink; the water is lapping onto the deck. I am eager for any lifeboat, however leaky.

The letters pour in from readers who know I have AIDS, which I wrote about in this newspaper last December. A Florida woman wrote detailing her son's agonizing death from AIDS. Halfway through the letter, she caught herself, suddenly blurting out, "I don't know why I am writing this to you." Like so many of the letters, it was really not so much for me as for the writer, and excuse to open up her heart and let out the pain. She ended with a line I think of often, a line as much for dead son, also named Jeffrey, as for me. "I intend this letter," she wrote, " as a mother's hug."

Hardly a day goes by without my getting a letter or call from someone who has the cure for AIDS. Many are crackpots. But others, I'm not so sure. Perhaps I will soon be desperate enough to pursue them.

More and more of the letters are nasty, even cruel. They are still the minority, but they make clear how deep the resentment runs against the attention given AIDS.

"As an average American," a man from Brooklyn wrote in a letter to the editor that made its way to me, "I cannot feel compassion for those who contracted AIDS through the pleasures of homosexuality, promiscuity or drug injection. The advent of AIDS sickness in the world breaks my heart—but only for those who contracted it from blood transfusion, medical skin pricks or birth. The insipid news stories and other media accounts of AIDS pain, pneumonias and cancers attempt to reach me, but they only turn me off. And I, in turn, turn them off, as I suppose that millions of your readers do. Let's permit these pleasure seekers of the flesh to live out their years in hospices or homes at minimal cost and then die."

Am I bitter? Increasingly, yes. At the ACT UP funeral for Bailey in Washington, I thought of how much the anger of the activists mirrored my own. I, too, wanted to shout—at no one really, just to vent the rage. I am dying. Why doesn't someone help us?

I didn't shout. I couldn't. All I could think about on that rainy Thursday afternoon was that a political funeral is not for me. It is at once very noble and very tacky.

What, then, is for me? I usually say that my epitaph is not a phrase but the body of my work. I am writing it with each article, including this one. But actually, there is a phrase that I want shouted at my funeral and written on the memorial cards, a phrase that captures the mix of cynicism and despair that I feel right now and that I will almost certainly take to my grave: *Whatever happened to AIDS?*

from

ABOVE ALL, LIFE

from *Sexuality, Politics and AIDS in Brazil* (1993)

Herbert Daniel

I burst at times just because I am alive . . .
　　　　—*Gilberto Gil*

I know that I have AIDS. I know what this means for me. I try not have any illusions about it. Only I don't know what other people mean when they say that I have 'AIDS'. Most of the time they mean 'you are going to die' (but who isn't?). Other times, the more prejudicial say, 'you are already dead' (my daily experience refutes that). Sometimes they sum it up by saying, 'you've lost your resistance' (not yet! Not yet . . . I indignantly resist). In the end, what AIDS is this?

The concept of AIDS was constructed in the last decade, in a world of political and ideological battle. The source of the problem lies in medical definition of what is called, incorrectly, the AIDS epidemic. In fact, the epidemic was caused by several retroviruses called HIV (Human Immunodeficiency Virus), which were transmitted either sexually through blood, or vertically (from mother fetus or baby). Meanwhile, world consciousness adopted the acronym AIDS (or SIDA) a fact based on, and transcending, technical and medical definition. Many different meanings nebulously criss-crossed in the dance of words that sought to define the new disease—or if not really new, at least new to contemporary minds and certainly a novelty as a worldwide epidemic.

From a medical stand point the definition of AIDS was pure fiction. The acronym very primitively referred to a set of signs and symptoms. (A syndrome, in medical terminology) which resulted from a deficiency in the body's immune system. This immunodeficiency was denominated 'acquired' to distinguish it from similar congenital conditions. However, similar 'acquired' immunodeficiencies were also seen in radiation victims, in patients who had undergone certain types of chemotherapy (in preparation for transplants, for example, to avoid refection of the transplanted tissue), in certain leukemia cases, etc. The terms which composed the acronym were still few and incomplete.

Even this lay person's analysis of the acronym shows that if derived from the systematization of some early generic observations about the disease. If critically examined, the acronym reveals how little was known about the disease at that time. Lack of knowledge is less than it was ten years ago but it still exist today. Meanwhile, that acronym has stuck, the problem is to define that to which it refers, considering the complex circumstances surrounding individual or collective infection by HIV.

The expression 'acquired immunodeficiency syndrome' is as pompous as it is vague. Solemn words that try to say too much say nothing in the end. Surely we have here a formidable display of medical rhetoric. We all know how this rhetoric rushes to cover up, with resoundingly erudite words, the gaping hole of its own ignorance. Where doubt and uncertainty exist, arrogant jargon soothes with an expression that tries to stand for truth. A word, fragile veil of uncertainty, becomes a truth in itself, an ether filling the emptiness that totalitarian knowledge so abhors.

Because it did not refer to anything in particular, the word 'AIDS' began to slide over available significants, thereby producing a signifier for social fissures which previously had no exact expression. AIDS became the syndrome of our days.

It is important to remember that at the time of its first discovery the disease was called GRID—Gay Related Immunodeficiency. It was extraordinary that medical jargon should have come up with the expression 'gay plague' or 'gay cancer'. Which later became so widespread. Even more notable was the use of the word 'gay' rather than the term 'homosexual', a clear indication of profound changes at the time in the medical view of homosexuality—no doubt as a result of the gay movement's political effects especially in the United States. A new age was blowing in the wind. Medicine no longer saw homosexuality as an illness, but, instead, subtly began to consider it a source of illness: no longer a pathology, it has become a pathogenic condition.

Medical discourse, replete with generalizing definitions that take on the airs of definite truths, has drawn upon established taboos to generate the idea that AIDS is either a fatality or a fatal mystery. Yet while much about the disease remains unknown, accumulated knowledge does allow the assertion that at least AIDS is not mystery it is a challenge, but there is nothing magical or fantastic about it. In the end AIDS is an illness like other illness. But because medical science knows no more about the disease than the classification of the sexuality of those who have it—understanding nothing of homosexualities—this only results in the fueling of existing prejudices. The infectiousness of AIDS, signaled by the ambiguity of the word 'acquired' conceptually linked to taboos of homosexuality, making the disease a scandal, a terror and a fascination. And because medical science cannot admit, on ideological principle, the idea of death, an intrinsic incurability was invented for the disease. Medical incompetence became AIDS' own destiny, as if its incurability was of a sacred nature laden with ulterior motives.

At present public discussion of the disease has focused on three aspects: its infectiousness, its incurability, and its fatality. In fact, three myths engender the most distorted and distorting views of the epidemic. Along with the viruses identified as causal agents of the epidemic, an ideological virus has spread in a more generalized and unrestrained manner.

Without resorting to the use of metaphor, it can be said that our society is sick with AIDS—sick with panic, disinformation, prejudice and immobility before the real disease. Effective measurses against the HIV epidemic must begin with concrete steps to combat the ideological virus. This means the provision of correct information, effective action, the demystification of fear, the removal of prejudice and the permanent exercise of social solidarity.

For the person who has AIDS or is HIV positive, living with the consequences of the mythologies produced by the ideological virus can be tragic, since objectively mystification kills as much a or more than cellular immunodeficiency. Some dramatic consequences of mystification include the inability to fight against infection, failure to get treatment, the resort to 'miracle' cures and charlatanism, and increased violence against people with AIDS and HIV. Two other consequences are the solitude and secrecy with which people with AIDS often feel forced to survive. At the root of the mystifications about AIDS is a series of half-truths based on apparently 'objective' facts, resulting from 'scientific' observations. The 'fact' that the disease is infectious, incurable and fatal has become, thanks to simplification, part of the minimum operational definition society uses to deal symbolically with the disease. Profound prejudices directed against already marginalized groups (principally male homosexuals) re-emerge and are reinforced.Worst of all, the person with AIDS or HIV is declared dead while still alive. Before his or her biological death, he or she suffers civil death, which is the worst form of ostracism that a human being is forced to bear.

There are other problems with the definitions of AIDS which reveal the operation of distinctive types of prejudice. The disease's original definition stemmed from North American and European epidemiological research. The fundamental 'model' of the epidemic derived from first world experience, and third world models were the 'exceptions to the rule'. The 'African model' (where transmission is basically heterosexual) thereby serves as a contrast rather than a starting point for understanding the global dimensions of the pandemic. The racism of this ethnocentric view has had devastating effect.

In Brazil, where studies about the disease are still insufficient, Ministry of Health bureaucrats have been fascinated by these 'chic models'. All too often they tried to demonstrate that a 'North American pattern' would apply in Brazil. This has two consequences: (1) to disseminate the idea that HIV/AIDS is an elite disease, coming to our privileged classes from the 'developed world' (an idea which those who work with the disease have proven untrue); (2) to camouflage characteristics of the disease that are unique to Brazil, such as the question of transmission through contaminated blood transfusion (blood continues to be a scandalous issue in our country—genocide is being committed against people with hemophilia and others who need blood transfusion).

In Brazil the disease will affect predominantly poor people because the majority of the population is poor, and any epidemic affects all people in a real country. AIDS is not a foreign disease. The virus is here among us; it is 'ours'. It does not distinguish on the basis of sexual orientation, gender, race, color, creed, class or nationality.

The epidemic will develop among us according to our specific cultural characteristics—our sexual culture, our material and symbolic resources for dealing with health and disease, and our prejudices and capacity to exercise solidarity. AIDS inscribes itself upon each culture in a different way. Each culture constructs it own particular kind of AIDS as well as its own answers to the disease. Today these answers depend largely on civil society's capacity to mobilize itself against AIDS and to force the Brazilian government to accept its responsibilities. The current government is still not aware of the epidemic's importance. This government is only a death rattle, ridiculous in its mediocrity, of the authoritarian system which predated it. There is little that looks like a national program to control and prevent the HIV epidemic. As a result, AIDS in Brazil will bear the scars of the government incompetence.

I know I have AIDS. I know what it means for me to have it in this country. I don't have any illusions about it, even though I am a person with privileges. I am watching many people die as a result of government negligence; I too am dying because of it. We will all die because of it. I know very well what so many living dead mean, know that I want to shout with them: 'We are alive.' In the end what AIDS is this which has diseased this (which?) country?. . .

The disease surreptitiously created a mythology so complex that people who have it are seen as special beings, called 'aidetics', in Brazil. Consequently, many people have told me that I have accepted or 'assumed' my AIDS. I find it funny, this business of 'assuming'—an act of will which implies admitting that something exists. What I have done is to assume my place at the door of the world, in order to say: I'm alive; all this talk about my death is an outright lie. People with AIDS must come forward to destroy the misunderstandings created by a corrosive ideology of condemnation followed by pity which has created a melodrama wherein a tragedy is taking place. Undeniably, AIDS is a modern tragedy. It has quickly dismantled the medical and moral assumptions of bourgeois rationality. It reminds us all that pain, suffering and death—as well as pleasure—are integral parts of the world and that no pleasure survives far from the shadow of death. The world of melodramas, which extinguishes the conflict of tragedy to impose a false egalitarianism in the face of death, can only offer counsel, consolation or consumption: the counsel of a pacification-by-passivity before death; the consolation of forgiveness, only possible if the sinner admits his guilt; and the consumption of soothing therapies that render fat profits to laboratories and other charlatans. The dead—above all, those who have suffered civil death—may no longer be. But they are not entirely unprofitable.

For years I lived undercover in Brazil, while fighting against the dictatorship. At the time I kept my sexuality a secret. They were hard times then. Because I fought for freedom, I was persecuted by the police force. During the fight I thought that being a guerrilla was incompatible with being homosexual. Later I learned that one cannot fight for half-baked liberties, and that there is no freedom without sexual freedom. Many years ago I came to understand that my sexuality openly meant demanding citizenship for everyone, not just those who are, or are said to be, homosexual.

To this day, even in large cities and in the most liberal circles, homosexuality is lived either in complete or partial secrecy. AIDS revealed the most tragic aspect of this living in the shadows. For many, the worst thing is not the disease; it is having to reveal that one is gay, since the person with AIDS is forced to reveal how he was infected. The diagnosis is transformed into denunciation, so much so that people who do not get AIDS though sexual contact feel compelled repeatedly and permanently to 'differentiate' themselves, so as not to be confused with those who have the very same illness!

I know many people with AIDS. Homosexual or not, their greatest suffering comes from prejudice. It comes from not being allowed to be sick, but having instead to bear the stigmata of being an 'aidetic'. It means feeling fear due to frequent, yet invisible, social pressures (the worst prejudices are not always necessarily direct discrimination). It means panic at the thought that their sexual and emotional lives be over. It means the constant presence of those who seem to be waiting to carry your coffin. It means the invisible web of oppression created by family members, sometimes doctors, priests and even friends.

In the face of all this, the most frequent choice is to go undercover—a way of fleeing in order to die, since death is the only kind of life that society seems to offer the sick person. The issue here is not finding better conditions for the sick to die in peace, but finding better conditions for living. Concealment is proof of society's inability to deal with this particular disease. It is a testimony to its bankruptcy.

Many people live with AIDS secretly in Brazil, from those who die without knowing they have the disease to those who are killed by discrimination. Sick people who remain anonymous are not able to resist the forces that seek to strip our citizenship from us.

To satisfy this spoliation, tinged by the morbidity of a distorted curiosity, people with AIDS are shown in the shadows, their faces darkened, principally on TV. This is not a way to preserve the sick person's privacy—which is an essential right. It is instead a way of depicting a depersonalized destiny, of fumbling in a region where we all live, unknowingly—it is a darkness that tests our civil rights.

The person with AIDS has become someone without a name or a history. We must take him out of the darkness of concealment so that he can say, in the light of day: 'This is my name, this is my story.' Much more than 'assuming' a 'state of being' or a 'condition', this action will be a collective way for us to write, more democratically, our history . . .

SPIRITUALITY AND HIV: REALITY AND HEALING

(1994)

Robert E. Penn

Donald Woods died in June of 1992. Early in his career, he had worked as an administrator of the Brooklyn Children's Museum. After the AIDS epidemic started, he brought his expertise to the position of Executive Director of AIDS Films, a non-profit media organization that produces AIDS prevention materials. He was instrumental in the founding and/or maintaining of several New York gay organizations and participated on the national level in the struggle for gay rights and particularly Black lesbian and gay rights. His poetry, some of it homoerotic, appears in a number of anthologies. Donald Woods was an openly gay and proud Black man who did nothing whatsoever to hide the fact that he was living with AIDS. And yet, there was no mention of his contributions to the gay community or to his years surviving AIDS in his official eulogy.

During the funeral, I felt as if the man whom I and so many others at the service had known, was not dead . . . in fact, had never existed. It was an extraordinarily disappointing and disheartening event, until Yves Lubin, a.k.a. Assotto Saint took the rostrum and spoke of Donald as the openly gay activist his family had either not known or chosen not to acknowledge. Only after that extemporaneous contribution to the service could I begin to mourn Donald's death.

Since Donald Woods' funeral, I have taken steps to ensure that if I die a young man my affairs will be handled proudly. I have spoken many times to my mother about my death. She gets depressed when I bring up the subject. I wonder how she thinks I feel about it: after all it's my death we're talking about.

She asks me questions like: Why do I have to announce to the world that it was AIDS if that's what you die from? Why do I have to tell everybody if you died of AIDS the only way you could have gotten HIV was through sex with another man? Why do I have to put our business in the street?

Because, I tell her: I am not a skeleton in a closet. I am an example. I must be the best example of a proud, Black, gay, HIV+ man that I can be so that people in general recognize that any one of the above categories cannot stop me from being a productive, loving human being. And more importantly, so that my young sister or brother who senses that he or she is homosexual will see from my example that living the life of an openly gay man has up sides, too. My openly gay peers and I are getting a lot done that will hopefully make living better for those of us who accept our homosexuality in this puritanical, heterosexist nation.

But she doesn't get it. Not yet, anyway. She still thinks silence will protect her. I won't give up on her. She bore me and I want to bring her the recognition of my mortality and set her free of the fear. I may, however, need to disengage, detach, distance, divorce. She still feels she is somehow responsible. Still thinks that if I had told her earlier she could have helped. Still thinks that if she had done something differently I would have turned out "all right"—her words for heterosexual and happily married, well at least, married with children. Magical thinking doesn't work with sexual orientation either. I assure her that she could have raised me 50,000 different ways and I still would be homosexual because that is just part of who I am.

She argues that homosexuality is not condoned by the Bible. I counter that (Judeo-

Christian) God didn't write the Bible, men did and ask her if she has consulted other writings on homosexuality. She admits she hasn't. I point out that if she read supremacist arguments which allege the Bible decrees that Blacks are genetically inferior to Whites, she would be highly motivated to seek out other opinions. That she would find a wide range of theories on racial equality or inequality. And that she would make her informed decision after reviewing several of the alternatives. Why can't she do the same regarding same-sex orientation? Why can't she call Parents and Friends of Lesbians and Gays (P-FLAG) for some recommended reading?

She does not feel comfortable enough yet to do that.

"I may be dead by the time you feel comfortable."

"Yes, you may," she admits.

Her words slap me in the face and I tell her so just before I hang up the phone.

Mother, this is for you:

I agree that differences of opinion do not diminish the love between us. I know I can't compel you to do anything. Nor can you compel me. I cannot judge you. Nor you me. The only thing I owe you is to love you. My only responsibility is to tell you what I need; know that I won't always get what I ask and become willing to reduce or eliminate communication with you if I believe contact with you becomes detrimental to me.

I want you to be comfortable before you call P-FLAG but I am not sure that I have a lot of time for you to become willing to get comfortable.

What you seem insensitive to is the fact that I don't have a lot of time to dilly-dally around with theories of morality. I must deal in reality. I have huge doctor bills: $750 every three months just for basic doctor visits and blood tests, plus acupuncture, physical therapy, chiropractic and grief and bereavement therapy totaling another $900 per month and pharmaceutical, vitamin and herb therapy that costs about $300 per month. The total in 1992 ran about $17,500.

The insurance company refuses to pay for vitamins, herb therapy, some of the blood work and some lab fees so I don't get reimbursed for many of these expenses. Fortunately, most of my doctors will accept the assignment that my insurance company offers, so I don't have to pay all the bills up front. Insurers drag their feet in making reimbursements, and have tried to reject payments of T-cell blood tests which are considered to be medically essential for people living with HIV.

We who are infected did not invent this virus nor did we go out seeking it in some self-destructive behavior. We just got infected with it like a person gets infected with any other blood-borne or sexually transmitted disease. Insurers do not refuse payment of blood tests for syphilis, gonorrhea or the much more common herpes and NSU (non-specific urethritis), all sexually transmitted and at epidemic levels among heterosexuals as well as all other sexually active Americans. Insurance companies discriminate against HIV related medical expenses and in so doing perpetuate the stigma associated with AIDS.

There is no cure for AIDS yet, and you seem to think that I am trying to get attention, that I am just joking about being infected with HIV.

Being infected with HIV is incredibly stressful. I am a young man, at my prime, and instead of having the chance to focus all of my energy on my contribution to humanity, I must put considerable effort into just staying alive. So you can perhaps under-stand how thoughtless it was for you to speak so off-handedly about my being dead before you are comfortable enough to call P-FLAG or deal with the reality rather than the so-called morality of homosexuality.

What you don't seem to understand is that I blamed myself for being gay many, many times and for many, many years. As a child and adolescent, I thought everything that went wrong in our household was because of my secret sexual attraction to other boys and to men. I asked the God of my childhood to tell me what I had done wrong, what penance I could make so that I would be "normal." I asked Him, "Why me?"

And the answer I got to each question was: Nothing. When today, just to be sure, I ask these questions again, each answer is still: Nothing. I hadn't awakened one morning and selfishly decided to be gay so that I wouldn't have to raise children or assume the other responsibilities of adulthood. I hadn't taken the easy or evil way out. I wasn't trying to hurt my family. I had done nothing wrong so there was no reparation possi-ble or needed. I could do nothing to change. This is me as God/dess created me.

I have also thought many times that I am HIV-infected because of a mistake that I made. No one ever taught us to use condoms. No one ever talked about sex and birth control, not to us boys anyway. But I thought I should have known better. And since I hadn't figured things out, I deserved this: it served me right for being sexually active with other men. I should never have had sex with men. But I have not once felt or been told I should not have had sex with a woman. And, who knows, I may have been infected by a woman, because prior to learning about HIV transmission and the pre-vention thereof, I had sex with a number of women without using a condom.

If you want to blame, blame the virus—human immunodeficiency virus. It is a human parasite which thrives in symbiosis with a specimen of species homo sapiens but it is too stupid to recognize that when it grows aggressively, it kills its host and loses its nurturing environment.

I'm not in the hospital and I intend to keep it that way. I believe that unconditional support from my friends and family helps. I also believe that conditional love kills. I don't want people around me who think, "Too bad he chose the life of a homosexual. He would be well now if he hadn't," or "Such a waste of a good man." Those thoughts, no matter how well people think they conceal them, slip out and are noticeable, espe-cially to small children, the very old, and the ill. I would rather let go of people who only offer conditional love than die as a result of accepting their restrictions.

Are you going to wait until I'm dead to face reality? I humbly request that you not wait, that you risk a little discomfort this time for my sake because I am not afraid of dying, I will not die as your outcast.

Mother, that is all for now.

I will not wave my mother off like some disinterested bystander or the malicious HIV-negative gay men who won't date those of us who are HIV-positive. After all she is my flesh. HIV and AIDS affect her world, too. But I will stay away from her if it is in my best interest. And this life-affirming action is difficult to conceive of and implement because I am so accustomed to obeying her in spite of my needs. I am in the habit of acting the way she and other heterosexual people assume all people act. For them, the behaviors come spontaneously. For me, it is a matter of adapting my natural instincts in order to appear as if I automatically behave straight.

I have devoted a great deal of time and concentration pretending to be on the outside the way my Black heterosexual sisters and brothers are on the inside. I have spent equal energy, along with many of my upwardly mobile Black brothers and sisters, assimilating into the White mainstream culture, taking actions, making decisions, working until all hours of the night, giving two-hundred percent in order to survive in this homophobic, AIDSphobic and racist environment known as the land of the free. But alas, no matter what I do, no matter how I present myself as straight or as "someone who just happens to be Black," the fact remains no matter how much I do I will never be assimilated. Both because some American oppressors—heterosexist and/or white—will change the rules or proclaim me an exception as soon as my mutation is nearly complete and, more importantly, because, as a self-loving and self-respected, God/dess-created being, I can never assimilate into something I am not even when others may be willing to pretend that I pass.

I am not, don't need to be and, even if I wanted it with all my heart, could never be what many people of all races believe to be that to which every American must ever strive: White, heterosexual and male. And because I won't aspire thusly, this country in general remains hostile to me and other self-accepting lesbians and gays. How do I go on? I am a Black homosexual male living in the racism-denying, misogynist, homo-hating, illness and death fearing, token-seeking American culture of the late twentieth century. So why do I even try? It is beautifully simple: God/dess made me a Black gay man living with HIV so that the universe would be a better place in which to live, a more complete place in which to live.

I don't remember my father telling me to grow into a race man but I got the message: each Black man is asked to, no, must be a Black Hercules: strong, untiring and above reproach, so that the race might advance against all the odds. And I thank my ancestors for the power. I am standing on their shoulders and asking for the esteem due each and every one of us—*in the warmth of daylight*—to be myself: to be Black among White gays, to be gay among Blacks. To be a proud Black, gay, HIV+ man: me. Where ever, whenever.

Yes, I am a "race man." And among "race" people, my sexual orientation is sometimes denied, ignored, suppressed or oppressed because so many Blacks, my former self included, believe in scarcity: that there is only room in the American "big house" for the Whites first and maybe one minority. Blacks who believe in scarcity think there is neither room for other minorities nor for homosexuals. They are wrong! There is space to include everyone.

I must, therefore, be an "out" gay man. I am an "out race" man. I work hard and persevere, doing what is needed to uphold lesbian and gay people of color, especially those who are also HIV+. I openly accept, no embrace, my race and my sexual and health groups that many would rather not acknowledge. Because if I am not proud of my gender, sexual orientation, race, HIV status, and so on, how can I expect anyone else to uphold my rights? I make every effort to be beyond reproach so that, when things are equal, I must be accepted and listened to, in a word: respected. I insist upon respect.

And with that in mind, I wrote my mother demanding that she desist in telling me "that God don't like homosexuals" according to a Bible that was written by men, prejudiced men raised to fear God and to believe that He only had love enough for a chosen few. That she accept my reality.

Well, the letter to my mother worked, though I had not written it with the expectation that it would. I wrote the letter for my sanity. Change usually takes a lot of time and I was not sure that my mother was ready. My letter was blunt solely to describe as effectively as I could the lengths to which I was prepared to go in order to achieve that respect and acceptance that any person deserves, regardless of race, religion, gender, national origin, color, sexual orientation, size, shape, health status, appearance, age, ability, attitude, tone of voice, and so on. I sent the letter for my sanity.

Mother surprised me with the gift of listening. She heard in the letter what I had tried to explain on the telephone several times. Why now? I don't know and I'm definitely not complaining. She surprised me with an unscheduled visit to New York. Face to face, she told me she had reached the P-FLAG switchboard in her city but the only meeting was at eight in the evening clear across town. I understood the time and place to be a real obstacle for a seventy-two year old woman who wears thick glasses. So I got her a telephone number of someone from P-FLAG in her town with whom she could personally discuss things over the telephone.

About a week after her visit, Mother gave me another gift: She wrote me that she had spoken with the P-FLAG person and enjoyed the conversation.

I thank whatever God/dess, Higher Power there is.

I congratulate my mother! It must have been very difficult for her to make that call, to listen to another point of view. At least as difficult as it was for me to take a stand. She is so brave!

I wonder now if I really needed to write such an extreme communication—the angry letter—to pull her toward me, to share my reality more fully with her. I will never know.

I do know, however, that I may have to be just as firm again in the future. It was only one step. Should she slide back or sink into her fears again, I must be persistent, even vigilant. I insist upon respect from all who cross my path.

I must speak out. We, lesbians and gays, HIV+ and people living with AIDS must speak out. We did not choose our orientation or health status anymore than we elected our gender. We, women, lesbians, gays, Latino/as, Asians, Native Americans, Europeans, Pacific Islanders, Africans, HIV-infected, HIV-affected must speak out. We did not pick our condition anymore than we selected our species. We have to inform both adversaries and friends alike whom they are dealing with so that we are taken whole: as fully integrated individuals. We are not "as good as anybody else." We are exactly as we are meant to be.

VI

THE
PRESENT MOMENT
AND THE FUTURE
OF DESIRE

Contemporary lesbian and gay politics is both like and unlike its earlier manifestations. It is similar in that the issues addressed by earlier writers and movements—social stigma and invisibility, sexism, racism, political inequality—remain. It is different because these factors, while still present, have been drastically reduced and reshaped by the efforts of generations of activists.

One of the major changes that marks the current movement is the effect of AIDS. As we have seen, AIDS incited a major debate among gay men about their sexuality, about their unequal social status regardless of their class or race, and about the nature of their relationship to governmental authorities, especially those concerned with health care. It also, however, changed the landscape for lesbians. Lesbian-feminists have seen little or no common cause with men, gay or straight. Gay men were seen as the opposite of lesbians: where lesbians were seen as gentle, non-genitally focused, and communally oriented, gay men were viewed as predatory and sex-obsessed. As a countercultural movement, lesbian-feminism also has not focused on legal issues that treated "homosexuals" as a unified group, and so there was little need to join with gay men.

That changed in the 1980s. The first reason for change was AIDS. As women saw men become vulnerable, as they saw them attacked by a virus and by a homophobic society, they moved increasingly to conceive and act upon a common cause with those men. Lesbians who had had nothing to do with men in the 1970s and early 1980s built coalitions that began with AIDS activism and extended beyond them to the range of gay and lesbian concerns.

The second change was increased political power for lesbians and gays. While far from unified or even visible, in many major cities the gay and lesbian vote began to form a bloc akin to other groups. Improved communication made possible discussion of political issues locally nationally and internationally. This trend has enabled both the election of many gay and lesbian officials to local and geographically broader-based offices and has led to an increased desire by heterosexual politicians to court our votes. In the U.S., Gay and lesbian Democratic Clubs, the Log Cabin Federation among Republicans, the Human Rights Campaign (a gay-lesbian political fundraising organization), and the Gay and Lesbian Victory Fund, founded to develop openly gay-lesbian candidacies for public office, are all part of this movement. Legal and advocacy organizations such as the National Gay and Lesbian Task Force, Lambda Legal Defense and Education Fund, the National Center for Lesbian Rights, and the ACLU's Lesbian and Gay Rights Project (the first three began in the 1970s) now work to protect and extend the rights of gay and lesbian people in the U.S.. President Clinton's promise to end the ban on gays in the military, though not fulfilled, signalled a new willingness of national politicians to be publicly identified with us.

This new political role forces us to confront questions that have long been with us: Do we want to be in the military at all? Do we want marriage, or some "equivalent"? Should we claim to be "just like everyone else," or should we insist on the value of sexual and cultural diversity? While many activists are fighting to "get inside the door," many others continue to argue that these institutions are inherently flawed and do not deserve our allegiance. Just as AIDS politics has encompassed both GMHC and ACT UP, contemporary lesbian and gay movements range from the Campaign for Military Service to Queer Nation and beyond. The street activism of Queer Nation, and some of the new coalitions being built around the term "queer" itself, are in stark contrast to the more incremental reformist politics of the larger organizations. Queers have often expressed disdain for "lesbians" and "gays" analogous to the Stonewall generation's view of homophiles.

The third major event was the continued rise of the religious right in the U.S. and fundamentalism around the world and their targeting of homosexuality as the new focus issue. In the wake of the downfall of the Soviet Union, the gay and lesbian "threat to the family" was chosen as the issue that would scare their constituencies into continued allegiance, donation and activism. While the 1970s saw antigay organizing in a few locations, in the 1990s the attack on lesbians and gays has become a major industry. Efforts to ban equal rights have appeared on the ballot across the U.S., often succeeding as their proponents misinform the public about our status. The attacks have also worked to bring together gay men and lesbian women, as the common threat overcomes any differences among us.

Running throughout these patterns has been a progressively greater sense of the cost of racism, classism, and sexism. At an earlier point many whites saw charges of racism, classism, and sexism as distractions from the main point of equal rights. Now there is an increasing, if still incomplete, understanding that we will succeed only if we build a truly inclusive movement in which everyone has something to contribute and is personally empowered by so doing. These issues are far from resolved—as we will read, not everyone has even come to agree on the principles involved—but they are now an inescapable part of our discussions and action.

These movements are present not just in the United States. The movement for equality and justice has grown around the world, with organizations in Asia, Europe, Australia, and Latin America. Africa is seeing the beginnings of such a discussion. Each country has its own issues and inflections; as we have seen, not all places have a concept of "homosexuality" like the Euro-American one, and so a politics centered around that issue will not always take shape as it has in North America and Europe. Increasingly, though, men and women around the world are resisting strictures on their sexuality and fighting for change. They are often labelled agents of Western imperialism, as gays in Cuba have been, but they have argued against this through their recovery of indigenous homoerotic conceptions, traditions, and practices.

Whatever the name and whatever the tradition, the fight for sexual freedom, social dignity and political equality for those we have called gay and lesbian will continue until it is won. The dedication of activists and the courage of every individual who chooses not to live a lie are making it increasingly impossible for heterosexuals to think they do not know a homosexual or that denial of freedom for gays is not relevant to their lives.

GLORIA ANZALDÚA

Gloria Anzaldúa has been a major voice in lesbian feminism. Through her work as an editor of two volumes of work by women of color, she has transformed the terrain of feminist theory, bridging the gap between "theory" as practiced in the academy and what she and coeditor Cherríe Moraga call "theory in the flesh," the vision and understanding of women that speaks through their lives and their political practice. As an author she has described "the new mestiza," she who bridges cultures and identities to build a new world. In the American Southwest, the mestiza is the product of the Colombian invasion, of the encounter between Native Americans and the Spanish. In *Borderlands/La Frontera*, Anzaldúa describes the consciousness that emerges from that history, and that she sees as the key to progressive change. In the speech printed here, she describes the various political possibilities open to lesbians of color. Her analysis serves to guide anyone whose social position places them with unreliable but necessary allies.

BRIDGE, DRAWBRIDGE, SANDBAR, OR ISLAND

Lesbians-of-Color Hacienda Alianzas[1](1988)

Gloria Anzaldúa

La gente hablando se entiende
(People understand each other by talking)
—Mexican proverb

Buenos dias marimachas, lesberadas, tortilleras, patlaches,[2] dykes, bulldaggers, butches, femmes, and good morning to you, too, straight women. This morning when I got up I looked in the mirror to see who I was (my identity keeps changing), and you know how hair looks when you've washed it the night before and then slept on it? Yes, that's how mine looked. Not that I slept that much. I was nervous about making this talk and I usually never get nervous until just before I'm on. I kept thinking, What am I going to tell all those women? How am I going to present and represent myself to them and who, besides myself, am I going to speak to and for? Last night lying in bed in the dorm room I got disgusted with my semiprepared talk so I wrote another one. I threw that out too. Then I skimmed several papers I was working on, looking for ideas. I realized that I couldn't use any of this material and ordered my unconscious to come up with something by morning or else. This morning I walked over here, picking lint off my shirt, feeling wrinkles, and thinking, Here I am, I'm still the poor little Chicanita from the sticks. What makes me think I have anything useful to say about alliances?

Women-of-color such as myself do have some important things to say about alliance and coalition work. The overlapping communities of struggle that a *mestiza lesbian* finds herself in allows her to play a pivotal role in alliance work. To be part of an alliance or coalition is to be active, an activist. Why do we make alliances and participate in them? We are searching for powerful, meaning-making experiences. To make our lives relevant, to gain political knowledge, to give our lives a sense of involvement, to respond to social oppression and its debilitating effects. Activists are engaged in a political quest. Activists are alienated from the dominant culture but instead of withdrawing we confront, challenge. Being active meets some basic needs: emotional catharsis, gratification, political epiphanies. But those in an alliance group also feel like a family and squabble and fight like one, complete with a favorite (good child) and a scapegoat (bad child).

The fracture: at homeness/estrangement

I look around me and I see my *carnalas*, my *hermanas*, the other half and halves, *mita' y mita'*, (as queer women are called in South Texas), and I feel a great affinity with everyone. But at the same time I feel (as I've felt at other conferences) like I am doing this alone, I feel a great isolation and separateness and differentness from everyone, even though I have many allies. Yet as soon as I have these thoughts—that I'm in this alone, that I have to stand on the ground of my own being, that I have to create my own separate space—the exact opposite thoughts come to me: that we're all in this together, *juntas*, that the ground of our being is a common ground, *la Tierra*, and that at all times we must stand together despite, or because, of the huge splits that lie between our legs, the faults among feminists are like the fractures in the earth. Earthquake country, these feminisms. Like a fracture in the Earth's crust splitting rock, like a splitting rock itself, the quakes shift different categories of women past each other so that we cease to match, and are forever disaligned—colored from white, Jewish from colored, lesbian from straight. If we indeed do not have one common ground but only shifting plots, how can we work and live and love together? Then, too, let us not forget *la mierda* between us, a mountain of *caca* that keeps us from "seeing" each other, being with each other.

Being a mestiza queer person, *una de las otras* ("of the others") is having and living in a lot of worlds, some of which overlap. One is immersed in all the worlds at the same time while also traversing from one to the other. The mestiza queer is mobile, constantly on the move, a traveler, *callejera*, a *cortacalles*. Moving at the blink of an eye, from one space, one world to another, each world within its own peculiar and distinct inhabitants, not comfortable in anyone of them, none of them "home," yet none of them "not home" either. I'm flying home to South Texas after this conference, and while I'm there, I'm going to be feeling a lot of the same things that I'm feeling here—a warm sense of being loved and of being at home, accompanied by a simultaneous and uncomfortable feeling of no longer fitting, of having lost my home, of being an outsider. My mother, and my sister and my brothers, are going to continue to challenge me and to argue against the part of me that has community with white lesbians, that has community with feminism, that has community with other *mujeres-de-color*, that has a political community. Because I no longer share their world view, I have become a stranger and an exile in my own home. "When are you coming home again, *Prieta*," my mother asks at the end of my visit, of every visit. "Never, Momma."[3] After I first left home and became acquainted with other worlds, the *Prieta* that returned was different, thus "home" was different too. It could not completely accommodate the new *Prieta*, and I could barely tolerate it. Though I continue to go home, I no longer fool myself into believing that I am truly "home."

A few days ago in Montreal at the Third International Feminist Book Fair (June 1988), I felt a great kinship with women writers and publishers from all over the world. I felt both at home and homeless in that foreign yet familiar terrain because of its strangeness (strange because I had never been there). At the conference, and most especially at the lesbian reading, I felt very close to some white lesbian separatist friends. Then they would make exclusionary or racist remarks and I would feel my body heating up, I would feel the space between us widening. Though white lesbians say their oppression in a heterosexist, homophobic society is similar to the suffering of racism that people-of-color experience, they *can* escape from the more overt oppressions by hiding from being gay (just as I can). But what I can't hide from is being Chicana—my colors and features give me away. Yes, when I go home I have to put up with a lot of heterosexist bullshit from my family and community, from the whole Chicano nation who want to exclude my feminism, my lesbianism. This I have in common with women-of-all-colors. But what really hurts, however, is to be with people that I love, with you *mujeres-de-todos-colores*, and to *still* feel, after all our dialogues and struggles, that my cultural identity is *still* being pushed off to the side, being minimized by some of my so-called allies who unconsciously rank racism a lesser oppression than sexism. Women-of-color feel especially frustrated and depressed when these "allies" participate in alliances dealing with issues of racism or when the theme of the conference we are attending is racism. It is then that white feminists feel they have "dealt" with the issue and can go on to other "more important" matters.

At the Montreal Conference I also felt an empathy with heterosexual women-of-color and with the few men who were there, only to be saddened that they needed to be educated about women-only space. It also made me sad, too, that white lesbians have not accepted the fact that women-of-color have affinities with men in their cultures. White lesbians were unconsciously asking women-of-color to choose between women and men, failing to see that there is more than one way to be oppressed. Not all women experience sexism in that way, and for women-of-color sexism is not the only oppression. White lesbians forget that they too have felt excluded, that they too have interrupted women-of-color-only space, bringing in their agenda in their hunger to belong, pushed ours to the side.

Alliance work is the attempt to shift positions, change positions, reposition ourselves regarding our individual and collective identities. In alliance we are confronted with the problem of how we share or don't share space, how we can position ourselves with individual groups who are different from and at odds with each other, how we reconcile one's love for diverse groups when members of these groups do not love each other, cannot relate to each other, and don't know how to work together.

The activist y la tare de alianzas

Alliance-coalition work is marked or signaled by framing metacommunication, "This is alliance work."[4] It occurs in bounded specific contexts defined by the rules and boundaries of that time and space and group. While it professes to do its "work" in the community its basis is both experiential and theoretical. It has a discourse, a theory guides it. It stands both inside (the community one is doing the work for) and outside ordinary life (the meeting place, the conference). Ideally one takes alliance work home.

In alliance-coalition work there is an element of role playing, as if one were someone else. Activists possess an unspoken, untalked about ability to recognize the unreality and game-playing quality of their work.[5] We very seriously act/perform as well as play at being an ally. We adopt a role model or self-image and behave as if one *were* that model, the person one is trying to be. Activists picture themselves in a scenario: a female hero venturing out and engaging in nonviolent battles against the corrupt dominant world with the help of their trusted *comadronas*. There are various narratives about working at coalition, about making commitments, setting goals and achieving those goals. An activist possesses, in lesser or greater degree, a self-conscious awareness of her "role" and the nature of alliance work. She is aware that not only is the alliance-coalition group struggling to make specific changes in certain institutions (health care, immigration laws, etc.) but in doing so the group often engages in fighting cultural paradigms[6]—the entire baggage of beliefs, values and techniques shared by the community. But in spite of all cultural inscriptions to the contrary, the activist with her preconceived self-image, her narrative, and self-reflectivity resists society's "inscribing" cultural forms, practices, and paradigms on her. She elects to be the one "inscribing" herself and her culture. Activists are agents.

In collusion, in coalition, in collision

For now we women-of-color are doing more solidarity work with each other. Because we occupy the same or similarly oppressed cultural, economic space(s) or share similar oppressions, we can create a solidarity based on a "minority" coalition. We can build alliances around differences, even in groups which are homogenous. Because people-of-color are treated generically by the dominant culture—their seeing and treating us as parts of a whole, rather than just as individuals—this forces us to experience ourselves collectively. I have been held accountable by some white people for Richard Rodriguez's views and have been asked to justify Cesar Chavez's political strategies. In classes and conferences I am often called to speak on issues of race and am thereafter responsible for the whole Chicano/Mexicano race. Yet, were I to hold a white woman responsible for Ronald Reagan's acts, she would be shocked because to herself she is an individual (nor is her being white named because it is taken for granted as the norm).

I think we people-of-color can turn this fusion or confusion of individual/collectivity around and use it as a tool for collective strength and not as an oppressive representation. We can subvert it and use it. It could serve as one based for intimate connection between personal and collective in solidarity work and in alliances across differences. For us the issue of alliances affects every aspect of our lives—personal growth, not just social. We are always working with white women or other groups unlike ourselves toward common and specific goals for the time the work of coalition is in process. Lesbians-of-color have always done this. Judith Moschkovitz wrote: "Alliances are made between people who are different."[7] I would add between people who are different but who have a similar conscience that impels them toward certain actions. Alliances are made between persons whose vague unconscious angers, hopes, guilts and fears grow out of direct experiences of being either perpetrators or victims of racism and sexism.

Feelings of anger, guilt, and fear rose up nine years ago at Storrs, Connecticut, at the 1981 NWSA Women Respond to Racism Conference, when issues of alliances and racism exploded into the open. Along with many women-of-color I had aspirations, hopes, and visions for multiracial *comunidades*, for communities (in the plural) and among all women, of *mundos surdos* (left-handed worlds). Cherrí Moraga and I came bringing an offering, *This Bridge Called My Back: Radical Writings By Radical Women Of Color*; it made its debut at that conference. Some of my aspirations were naive, but without them, I would not have been there nor would I be here now. This vision of *communidad* is still the carrot that I, the donkey, hunger for and seek at conferences such as this one.

At the 1981 conference we laid bare the splits between whitewomen and women-of-color, white lesbians and lesbians-of-color, separatists and nonseparatists. We risked exposing our true feelings. Anger[8] was the strongest in/visible current at that conference, as it is at this one, though many of us repressed it then and are still repressing it now. Race, was the big issue then, as it is now for us. Race, the big difference. When asked what I am, I never say I'm a woman. I say I am a Chicana, a mestiza, a *mexicana*, or I am a women-of-color—which is different from "woman" (woman always means whitewoman). Monique Wittig claims that a lesbian is not a woman because woman exists only in relation to men; woman is part of the category of sex (man and woman) which is a heterosexual construct.[9] Similarly, for me a women-of-color is not just a "woman"; she carries the markings of her race, she is a gendered racial being—not just a gendered being. However, nonintellectual, working-class women-of-color do not have the luxury of thinking of such semantic and theoretical nuances, much less exempting themselves from the category "woman." So though I myself see the distinction, I do not push it.

A large part of my identity is cultural. Despite changes in awareness since the early eighties, racism in the form of, "Your commitment has to be to feminism, forget about your race and its struggles, struggle with us not them" is still the biggest deterrent to coalition work between whitewomen and women-of-color. Some white feminists, displacing race and class and highlighting gender, are still trying to force us to choose between being colored or female, only now they've gone underground and use unconscious covert pressures. It's all very subtle. Our white allies or colleagues get a hurt look in their eyes when we bring up their racism in their interactions with us and quickly change the subject. Tired of our own "theme song" (Why aren't you dealing with race and class in your conference, classroom, organization?) and not wanting to hurt them and in retaliation have them turn against us, we drop the subject and, in effect, turn the other cheek. Women-of-color need these and other manipulations named so that we can make our own articulations. Colored and whitewomen doing coalition work together will continue to reflect the dominated/dominator dichotomy UNLESS whitewomen have or are dealing with issues of racial domination in a "real" way. It is up to them *how* they will do this.

Estranged strangers: a forced bonding

Alliance stirs up intimacy issues, issues of trust, relapse of trust, intensely emotional issues. "We seem to be more together organizationally and estranged individually."[10] There is always some, no matter how minimal, unease or discomfort between most women-of-color and most whitewomen. Because they can't ignore our ethnicity, getting our approval and acceptance is their way to try to make themselves more comfortable and lessen their unease. It is a great temptation for us to make whitewomen comfortable. (In the past our lives may have depended on not offending a white person.) Some of us get seduced into making a whitewoman an honorary woman-of-color, when she wants it so badly. But it makes us fidget, it positions us in a relationship founded on false assumptions. A reversed dependency of them upon us emerges, one that is as unhealthy as our previous reliance on them. There is something parasitic about both of these kinds of dependencies. We need to examine bondings of this sort and to "see through" them to the unconscious motivations. Both white and colored need to look at the history of betrayal, the lies, the secrets and misinformation both have internalized and continue to propagate. We need to ask, Do women-of-color want only patronage from white women? Do white feminists only need and expect acceptance and acknowledgment from women-of-color? Yet there is an inherent potential for achieving results in both personal and political cross-racial alliances. We could stick to each other like velcro, whose two different sides together form a great bond—the teeth of one fasten onto the fabric of the other half and hold with a strength greater than either half alone.

Though the deepest connections colored dykes have is to their native culture, we also have strong links with other races, including whites. Though right now there is a strong return to nationalist feeling, colored lesbian feminists in our everyday interactions are truly more citizens of the planet. "To be a lesbian is to have a world vision."[11] In a certain sense I share this vision. If we are to create a lesbian culture, it must be a mestiza lesbian culture, one that partakes of all cultures, one that is not just white in style, theory, or direction, that is not just

Chicana, not just Black. We each have a choice as to what people, what cultures, and what issues we want to live with and live in and the roles we want to play. The danger is that white lesbians will "claim" us and our culture as their own in the creation of "our" new space.

"Chusando" movidas/*a choice of moves*

There are many roles, or ways of being, of acting, and of interacting in the world. For me they boil down to four basic ones: being a bridge, drawbridge, sandbar, and island. Being a bridge means being a mediator between yourself and your community and white people—lesbians, feminists, white men. You select, consciously or unconsciously, which group to bridge with—or they choose you. Often, the you that's the mediator gets lost in the dichotomies, dualities, or contradictions you're mediating. You have to be flexible yet maintain your ground, or the pull in different directions will dismember you. It's a tough job, not many people can keep the bridge up.

Being a drawbridge means having the option to take two courses of action. The first is being "up," i.e., withdrawing, pulling back from physically connecting with white people (there can never be a complete disconnection because white culture and its perspectives are inseparable on us/into us). You may choose to pull up the drawbridge or retreat to an island in order to be with your colored *hermanas* in a sort of temporary cultural separatism. Many of us choose to "draw up our own bridges" for short periods of time in order to regroup, recharge our energies, and nourish ourselves before wading back into the frontlines. This is also true for whitewomen. The other option is being "down"—that is, being a bridge. Being "down" may mean a partial loss of self. Being "there" for people *all the time, mediating all the time* means risking being "walked" on, being "used." I and my publishing credentials are often "used" to "colorize" white women's grant proposals, projects, lecture series, and conferences. If I don't cooperate I am letting the whole feminist movement down.

Being an island means there are no causeways, no bridges, maybe no ferries, either, between you and whites. I think that some women-of-color are, in these reactionary times, in these very racist times, choosing to be islands for a little while. These race separatists, small in number, are disgusted not only with patriarchal culture, but also with white feminism and the white lesbian community. To be an island, you have to reject certain people. Yet being an island cannot be a way of life—there are no life-long islands because no one is totally self-sufficient. Each person depends on others for the food she eats, the clothing on her back, the books she reads, and though these "goods" may be gotten from within the island, sequestering oneself to some private paradise is not an option for poor people, for most people-of-color.

At this point in time, the infrastructures of bridge and drawbridge feel too man-made and steel-like for me. Still liking the drawbridge concept, I sought and found the sandbar, a submerged or partly exposed ridge of sand built by waves offshore from a beach. To me the sandbar feels like a more "natural" bridge (though nature too, some argue, is a cultural construction). There is a particular type of sandbar that connects an island to a mainland—I forget what it is called. For me the important thing is how we shift from bridge to drawbridge to sandbar to island. Being a sandbar means getting a breather from being a perpetual bridge without having to withdraw completely. The high tides and low tides of your life are factors which help decide whether or where you're a sandbar today, tomorrow. It means that your functioning as a "bridge" may be partially underwater, invisible to others, and that you can somehow choose who to allow to "see" your bridge, who you'll allow to walk on your "bridge," that is, who you'll make connections with. A sandbar is more fluid and shifts locations, allowing for more mobility and more freedom. Of course there are sandbars called shoals, where boats run amuck. Each option comes with its own dangers.

So what do we, lesbians-of-color, choose to be? Do we continue to function as bridges? Do we opt to be drawbridges or sandbars? Do we isolate ourselves as islands? We may choose different options for different stages of our process. While I have been a persistent bridge, I have often been forced to "draw the bridge," or have been driven to be an island. Now I find myself slowly turning into a sandbar—the thing is that I have a fear of drowning.

Mujeres-de-color, mujeres blancas, ask yourselves what are you now, and is this something that you want to be for the next year or five years or ten? Ask yourself if you want to do alliance-coalition work and if so what kind and with whom. The fact that we are so estranged from whitewomen and other women-of-color makes alliance work that much more imperative. It is sad that though conferences allow for short-term alliances, the potential for achieving some feminists' goals are short-circuited by politically correct "performances" by participants instead of more "real" and honest engagement. Choosing to be a bridge, a drawbridge, and a sandbar allows us to connect, heart to heart, *con corazones abiertos*. Even islands come to NWSA conferences—perhaps they come to find other islands.

Terms of engagement

Mujeres-of-color, there are some points to keep in mind when doing coalition work with whitewomen. One is to not be lulled into forgetting that *coalition work attempts to balance power relations and undermine and subvert the system of domination-subordination* that affects even our most unconscious thoughts. We live in a world where whites dominate colored and we participate in such a system every minute of our lives—the subordination/domination dynamic is that insidious. We, too, operate in a racist system whether we are rebelling against it or are colluding with it. The strategies of defense we use against the dominant culture we also knowingly and unknowingly use on each other.[12] Whites of whatever class always have certain privileges over colored people of whatever class, and class oppression operates among us women-of-color as pervasively as among whites.

Keep in mind that if members of coalitions play at the deadly serious and difficult game of making alliances work we have to set up some ground rules and define the terms we use to name the issues. We need to "see through" some common assumptions. One is that there is no such thing as a common ground. As groups and individuals, we all stand on different plots. Sisterhood in the singular was a utopia fantasy invented by whitewomen, one in which we women of color were represented by whitewomen, one in which they continued to marginalize us, strip us of *our* individuality. (One must possess a sense of personhood before one can develop a sense of sisterhood.) It seems to me that through extensive coalitions, various "*hermanidades*" may be a created—not one sisterhood but many. We don't all need to come together, *juntas* (total unity may be another utopian myth). Some of us can gather in affinity groups, small grassroots circles and others. All parties involved in coalitions need to recognize the necessity that women-of-color and lesbians define the terms of engagement: that we be listened to, that we articulate who we are, where we have come from (racial past), how we understand oppression to work, how we think we can get out from under, and what strategies we can use in accomplishing the particular tasks we have chosen to perform. When we don't collectively define ourselves and locations, the group will automatically operate under white assumptions, white definitions, white strategies. Formulating a working definition, preferably one subject to change, of alliance/coalition, racism and internalized racism will clear the floor of patriarchal, white, and other kinds of debris and make a clean (well, sort of clean) space for us to work in. I've given you my definitions for alliance and coalition. Racism is the subjugation of a cultural group by another for the purpose of gaining economic advantage, of mastering and having power over that group—the result being harm done, consciously or unconsciously, to its members. We need to defy ethnocentrism, the attitude that the whole culture is superior to all others. Ethnocentrism condones racism. Racism is a theory, it is an ideology, it is a violence perpetuated against colored ethnic cultures.

The intensity of the violence may range from hidden, indirect forms of discrimination (housing) through overt forms of ethnocidal practices (enforced schooling, religious harassment) to forms of physical and direct violence culminating in genocide (holocaust) . . . It becomes structurally institutionalized as the basis of hegemony, it turns into systematic racism.[13]

Internalized racism means the introjecting, from the dominant culture, negative images and prejudice against outsider groups such as people-of-color and the projection of prejudice by an oppressed person upon another oppressed person or upon her/himself. It is a type of "dumping."[14] On the phone the other day I was telling my mother that I'd confronted my neighbor—a Black man who "parties" everyday, from morning til night, with a dozen beer-drinking buddies—and demanded that he not intrude on my space with his noise. She said, "No, don't tell them anything, Black men kill. They'll rape you." This is an example of internalized racism, it is not racism. Chicanos as a group do not have the power to subjugate Black people or any other people. Where did my mother learn about Blacks? There are very few Black people in the Rio Grande Valley of South Texas. My mother has internalized racism from the white dominant culture, from watching television and from our own culture which defers to and prefers light-skinned *gueros* and denies the Black blood in our *mestisaje*—which may be both a race and class prejudice, as darker means being more *indio* or *india*, means poorer. Whites are conditioned to be racist, colored are prone to internalize racism and, for both groups, racism and internalized racism appear to be the given, "the way things are." Prejudice is a "stabilized deception of perception."[15] I call this "deception" "selective reality"—the narrow spectrum of reality that human beings choose to perceive and/or what their culture "selects" for them to "see."[16] That which is outside of the range of consensus (white) perception is "blanked-out." Color, race, sexual preferences, and other threatening differences are "unseen" by some whites, certain voices not heard. Such "editing" of reality maintains race, class, and gender oppressions.

Another point to keep in mind is that feminists-of-color threaten the order, coherence, authority, and the concept of white superiority and this makes some white feminists uncomfortable and assimilated colored women uneasy. Feminists of color, in turn, are made uncomfortable by the knowledge that, by virtue of their color, white feminists have privilege and white feminists often focus on gender issues to the exclusion of racial ones. After centuries of colonization, some whitewomen and women-of-color, when interacting with each other, fall into old and familiar patterns: the former will be inclined to patronize and to "instruct"; the latter to fall into subservience consciously or unconsciously, model herself after the whitewoman. The woman-of-color might seek white approval or take on gradations of stances, from meek to hostile, which get her locked into passive-aggressive to violently reactive states.

But how are you to recognize your *aliada*, your ally in a roomful of people? Coalition work is not a sport where members of a particular team go bare-chested or wear T-shirts that say AMIGA (which stands for an actual organization in Texas). It can get confusing unless you can distinguish each other. And once you identify each other, how will you work together?

When calling a foul, do you harangue the other person in a loud voice? Do you take on a *matador* defense—neglect to guard opposing player in favor of taking the limelight to inflate your ego? Will your organization be a collective or a hierarchy? Should your *modus operandi* be hands on or hands off? Will your offensive strategies consist of nudges, bumps, shoves or bombs? You may have to accept that there may be no solutions, resolutions or even agreement *ever*. The terms *solution*, *resolution*, and *progressing* and *moving forward* are Western dominant cultural concepts. Irresolution and disagreement may be more common in life than resolutions and agreements. Coalition work does not thrive on "figurehead" leaders, on grandstanding, "leadership always makes you master and the other slaves."[17] Instead, coalition work succeeds through collective efforts and individual voices being heard. Once we focus on coalition/alliance we come to the questions, how long should we stay together? Should we form temporary *carnalaship* of extended family which leads to strong familial and tribal affiliations but which work against larger coalitions?

If you would be my ally

Ideally as allies (all lies), we can have no major lies among us, and we would lay our secrets on the conference table—the ones we've internalized and the ones we propagate. In looking at the motivations of those we are in solidarity with (women-of-color) and those who want to make alliances with us (whitewomen), we not only need to look at who they are, the space(s) they occupy, and how they enter our space and maneuver in it, *but* we have to look at our own motivations. Some issues to ponder and questions to ask ourselves: If all political action is founded on subconscious irresolutions and personal conflicts, then we must first look at that baggage we carry with us before sorting through other folks' dirty laundry. Having examined our own motives we can then inquire into the motivations of those who want to be our allies: Do they want us to be like them? Do they want us to hide the parts of ourselves that make them uneasy, i.e., our color, class, and racial identities? If we were to ask white lesbians to leave their whiteness at home, they would be shocked, having assumed that they have deconditioned the negative aspects of being white out of themselves by virtue of being feminist or lesbians. But I see that whiteness bleeds through all the baggage they port around with them and that it even seeps into their bones. Do they want to "take over" and impose their values in order to have power over us? I've had white and colored friends tell me I shouldn't give my energy to male friends, that I shouldn't go to horror movies because of the violence against women in them, that I should only write from the perspective of female characters, that I shouldn't eat meat. I respect women whose values and politics are different from mine, but they do not respect me or give me credit for self-determining my life when they impose trendy politically correct attitudes on me. The assumption they are making in imposing their "political correctness" on me is that I, a woman, a Chicana, a lesbian should go to an "outside" authority rather than my own for how to run my life.

When I am asked to leave parts of myself out of the room, out of the kitchen, out of the bed, these people are not getting a whole person. They are only getting a little piece of me. As feminists and lesbians, we need all of us together, *tlan* (from the Nahuatl meaning close together), and each one of us needs all the different aspects and pieces of ourselves to be present and totally engaged in order to survive life in the late twentieth century.

Do they only want those parts of us that they can live with, that are similar to theirs, not different from them? The issue of differences continues to come up over and over again. Are we asked to sit at the table, or be invited to bed, because we bring some color to and look good behind the sheets? Are we there because those who would be our allies happen to have ancestors that were our oppressors and are operating out of a sense of guilt? Does this whitewoman or woman-of-color or man-of-color want to be our ally in order to atone for racial guilt or personal guilt? Does this person want to be "seen" and recognized by us? According to Lacan, every human action, even the most altruistic, comes from a desire for recognition by the Other and from a desire for self-recognition in some form.[18] For some, love is the highest and most intense recognition.

Maria Lugones, a Latina philosopher, a woman who is at this conference, wrote a paper with a whitewoman, Vicky Spelman, "Have We Got a Theory For You: Feminist Theory, Cultural Imperialism, and the Demand for the Woman's Voice,"[19] in which they posit that the only motivation for alliance work is love and friendship. Nothing else. I have friends that I totally disagree with politically, friends that are not even from the same class, the same race, the same anything, but something keeps us together, keeps us working things out. Perhaps Lugones and Spelman are right. Love and friendship can provide a good basis for alliance work, but there are too many

tensions in alliance groups to dismiss with a light comment that bonds are based on love and friendship. This reminds me of Dill's critique of sisterhood being based on common (white) interests and alikeness.[20]

What may be "saving" the colored and white feminist movement may be a combination of all these factors. Certainly the tensions between opposing theories and political stances vitalize the feminist dialogue. But it may only be combined with respect, partial under-standing, love, and friendship that keeps us together in the long run. So *mujeres* think about the *carnalas* you want to be in your space, those spaces you want to have overlapping yours.

Ritualizing coalition and alliance building

Speaking and communicating lay the ground work, but there is a point beyond too much talk that abstracts the experience. What is needed is a symbolic behavior performance made concrete by involving body and emotions with political theories and strategies, rituals that will connect the conscious with the unconscious. Through ritual we can make some deep level changes.

Ritual consecrates the alliance. Breaking bread together, and other group activities that physically and psychically represent these ideals, goals, and attitudes promote a quickening, thickening between us.

Allies, remember that the foreign woman, "the alien," is *nonacayocapo* which in Nahuatl means one who possesses body (flesh) and blood like me. *Aliadas, recuerda que la mujer ajena tambien es nonacayocapo, la que tiene cuerpo y sangre como yo.* Remember that our hearts are full of compassion, not empty. And the spirit dwells strong within. Remember also that the great emptiness, hollowness within the psyches of whitewomen propels them to coalition with colored. Oh, white sister, where is your soul, your spirit? It has run off in shock, *susto*, and you lack shamans and *curanderas* to call it back. *Sin alma no te puedes ani-marte pa'nada.* Remember that an equally empty and hollow place within us allows that con-nection, even needs that linkage.

It is important that whitewomen go out on limbs and fight for women-of-color in work-places, schools, and universities. It is important that women-of-color in positions of power support their disempowered sisters. The liberation of women is the private, individual, and collective responsibility of colored and white men and women. *Aliada por pactos de alianzas,* united by pacts of alliances we may make some changes—in ourselves and in our societies.

After reading this paper consider making some decisions and setting goals to work on yourself, with another, with others of your race, or with a multiracial group as a bridge, drawbridge, sandbar, island, or in a way that works for you. *En fin quiero tocarlas de cerca,* I want to be allied to some of you. I want to touch you, kinswomen, *parientas, companeras, paisanas, carnalas,* comrades, and I want you to touch me so that together, each in our separate ways, we can nourish our struggle and keep alive our visions to recuperate, validate, and transform our histories.

Rather than discussing anti-Semitism, a dialogue I choose not to take on in this paper for reasons of length, boundaries of topic, and ignorance on my part of all its subtleties though I am aware that there is a connection between racism and anti-Semitism I am not sure what it is), I've decided not to take it on nor even make a token mention of it. I realize that this is a form of "If you don't deal with my racism I won't deal with yours," and that pleading ignorance is no excuse.

1. This is an elaboration and reworking of a speech given at the Lesbian Plenary Session, "Lesbian Alliances: Combatting Heterosexism in the 80's," NWSA, June, 1988. Quiero darles las gracias a, I want to thank Lynet Uttal for her generous critical reading of this text. I also want to thank Jaime Lee Evans, Helen Moglen, Joan Pinkvoss, Lisa Albrecht, Audrey Berlowitz, Rosalinda Ramirez, and Claire Riccardi for the various ways they encouraged and helped my writing of this paper.

2. The words marimachas and tortilleras are derogatory terms that mujeres who are lesbians are called. Patlache is the Nauhtl term for women who bond and have sex with other women. Lesberadas is a term I coined, prompted by the word desperado.

3. Gloria Anzaldúa, "Never, Momma," a poem published in Third Woman, Fall, 1983.

4. The concept of framing metacommunication was articulated by Gregory Bateson in Steps to an Ecology of Mind. *New York: Ballantine, 1972.*

5. Ibid.

6. For a definition of cultural paradigms see: Kuhn, T.S., 1970. The Structure of Scientific Revolutions. *Chicago: University of Chicago Press.*

7. Judith Moschkovich.

8. This was documented by Chela Sandoval, "Women Respond to Racism," A Report on the National Women's Studies Association Conference held in Storrs, Connecticut, 1981 in Making Face, Making Soul/Haciendo caras: Creative and Critical Perspectives by Feminists-Of-Color, *ed. Gloria Anzaldúa (San Francisco: Spinsters/Aunt Lute, 1990. See also Audre Lorde, "The Uses of Anger: Women Responding to Racism," in* Sister Outsider: Essays and Speeches *(Trumansburg, NY: The Crossing Press, 1984, 145-175).*

9. Monique Wittig. 1981, "One is Not Born A Woman," Feminist Issues, *Vol. 1, no. 2, Winter.*

10. Lynet Uttal, from commentary notes of her reading of this text, February 1990.

11. Elana Dykewomon. Talk given in June, 1988, in Montreal at the Third International Feminist Book Fair for a panel on Lesbian Separatism.

12. See Anzaldúa's, "En Rapot, In Opposition: Cobrando cuentas a las nuestras." In Making Face, Making Soul/Haciendo curas: Creative and Critical Perspectives by Feminists-Of-Color, *ed. Gloria Anzaldúa (San Francisco: Spinsters/Aunt Lute, 1990.) The essay first appeared in* Sinister Wisdom *33, Fall 1987.*

13. Minority Literature in North America: Contemporary Perspectives, *ed. Wolfgang Karrer and Hartmut Lutz, unpublished manuscript.*

14. Gail Pheterson defines internalized domination as "the incorporation and acceptance by individuals within a dominant group of prejudices against others." "Alliances Between Women: Overcoming Internalized Oppression and Internalized Domination," in this collection.

15. Alexander Mitscherlich's definition of prejudice in Minority Literature America: Contemporary Perspectives, *ed. Wolfgang Karrer and Hartmut Lutz.*

16. See my introduction to Making Face, Making Soul/Haciendo caras *cited above as rationale for hyphenating women-of-color, capitalizing Racism, and making whitewoman one word is in this introduction.*

17. Maria Lucia. 1986. Santaella, "On Passion as (?)Phanevou (maybe on phenomenology of passion)." Third Woman: Texas and More, *Vol. III, Nos. 1 and 2, p. 107.*

18. Lacan, Jacques. 1977. Ecrits, A Selection, *trans. Alan Sheridan. New York: Norton.*

19. Maria Lugones and Elizabeth V. Spelman. 1983. "Have We Got a Theory for You! Feminist Theory, Cultural Imperialism and the Demand for "The Woman's Voice'." Women's Studies Int. Forum, *Vol. 6, No. 6, pp. 573–81. Reprinted in* Making Face, Making Soul/Haciendo caras: Creative and Critical Perspectives by Feminists-of-Color, *ed. Gloria Anzaldúa (San Francisco: Spinsters/Aunt Lute, 1990).*

20. Lynet Uttal, from commentary notes of her reading of this text, February 1990. Uttal refers to Bonnie Thornton Dill, 1983 "Race, Class, and Gender: Prospects for an All Inclusive Sisterhood." Feminist Studies *9:131–48.*

The United States is not the only site of contemporary anti-gay reaction. In the 1980s Great Britain was ruled by Margaret Thatcher's Conservative Party, and the results were similar to those in the U.S. In 1988 the British Parliament passed the Local Government Bill, which included a clause—"Clause 28"—that reads as follows:

WAGES DUE LESBIANS

2A - 1) A local authority shall not—
(a) intentionally promote homosexuality or publish material with the intention of promoting homosexuality:
(b) promote the teaching in any maintained school of the acceptability of homosexuality as a pretended family relationship.
2) Nothing in subsection 1) above shall be taken to prohibit the doing of anything for the purpose of treating or preventing the spread of disease.
3) In any proceedings in connection with the application of this section a court shall draw such inferences as to the intention of the local authority as may reasonably be drawn from the evidence before it.

Initially the clause included the following: "(c) give financial assistance to any person for either of the purposes referred to in paragraphs (a) and (b) above." Upon protest this section was removed.

The following discussion of Clause 28 is by Wages Due Lesbians, an international network formed in 1975 as part of the Wages for Housework movement. They connect the sexual oppression of Clause 28 with economic exploitation and women's poverty, and argue that fiscal conservatism and social conservatism are tightly linked. Their analysis stands in marked contrast to the increasingly mainstream views of U.S. gays and lesbians, reflecting larger differences between the political cultures of the two countries.

from

OUT OF THE CLAUSE, INTO THE WORKHOUSE:
A LESBIAN WOMEN'S VIEW OF WHAT CLAUSE 28 INTENDS, PRETENDS AND PROMOTES, AND WHAT WE INTEND TO PROMOTE AGAINST IT

from *Policing the Bedroom* (1988)

Wages Due Lesbians

Abseiling into history

On 24 May 1988, the Local Government Bill became law. After all the Tory justifications for Clause 28 of the Bill, moralizing about how modern education force-feeds children with homosexuality, and how it was vital to "stop the rot," it has now become clear that schools were not its target. The week following its passage the press reported an Environment Department circular which spelled out that Section 28 of the Local Government Act would *not* apply to sex education in schools: local authorities no longer control the teaching of sex education—teachers and school governors do. This could not have been news to the government, since it introduced this change in 1986. So what has the introduction of Clause 28 been about? The government has wide objectives.

First, Clause 28 is being used as a political litmus test—to find out how strong the movement is, how well we can defend ourselves against such repression, and whether the famous and prestigious, so many of whom are lesbian and gay, will speak out on our/their own behalf. In the advertising industry, the operative phrase used to be "Let's run up the flag and see who salutes." Before it fully commits itself in law to the repression which Clause 28 was supposed to unleash, the government is testing what it is likely to get away with. The campaign against the Clause has begun to provide the same information to those it seeks to repress.

On the one hand, some people have refused to allow the implementation of this repression, instead coming out and looking for others whom they can organize with. On the other hand, some groups and individuals have retreated into censoring themselves and/or others, accepting and feeding the existing divisions between us.

If the government expected that Clause 28 would put homosexuality back in the closet, they must be very disappointed . . .

The Clause has helped to bring to the surface a massive movement of lesbian and gay people. Many others have joined us, attracted by our obvious determination, and aware of what time it is in Britain, when a threat to our sexual choices is bound to be a threat to everyone's.

Although we have been told that Clause 28 as a law cannot be enforced in schools by local authorities, this does not mean that it will not be used as a precedent and an example, both in and out of schools. It would be self-defeating for the lesbian and gay movements to accept this, and suicidal to assume that if Clause 28 is not legally effective, there is no need to fight on.

What we say below presumes that the movement should now be moving to resist the implementation of Clause 28 which will be used to create the climate for witch-hunts, cuts in funding, harassment, raids and other persecutions—and to turn up the soil for planting the seeds of future legislation which would do what Clause 28 can't do. In December 1987, Clause 28 was suddenly added, during the Committee stage (i.e., very late in its life), to the Local Government Bill—a Bill which imposes more central government control over local government. The period from then till 16 June 1988 [when we first went to press] has been a trial run not only for the government but for the movement. We aim here to put down what we have been learning so we can concentrate on cleaning up our own act and ultimately the political climate which the government's Act expresses, promotes and imposes.

In all the furious debates, little has been said about lesbian women specifically. When lesbian women abseiled down from the public gallery onto the floor of the House of Lords during the Third Reading of the Bill on 31 January 1988, women's visibility in the campaign against the Clause increased. But Clause 28's particular implications for lesbian and other women have not been spelled out often enough, if at all, and opposition to the Clause is partial and weaker because these implications and lesbian women ourselves remain hidden.

Coming out in millions

As women we have less economic and social power (no wages/lower wages) than men, including gay men. As lesbian women, we have less access to men's (higher) wages which, like non-lesbian women, we've fought not to be dependent on. Because women have less money, especially if we are Black, immigrant or Third World, often have children to support, and therefore have less possibility of living independently of families, it is much harder for lesbian women to come out than for gay men. This is why even in a place like San Francisco, "they gay capital of the world", gay men are so much more visible than lesbian women. In fact we have no idea how many women are lesbian or how many men are gay. We do know that in metropolitan countries, where there are more financial options—waged employment outside the home, higher wages, State welfare and social services—women have much more chance of coming out and the lesbian movement is much more visible.

But people don't usually connect sexual and social choice with economic possibilities. Women who can least afford to come out are often put down as lacking courage or consciousness, not cash. Such an attack on those who have least resources inevitably reinforces racist stereotypes and class prejudices: that Black/Third World/working class women are not interested in sexual choices, or are more submissive to men, or that Black/Third World/working class men are more sexist. The fact is that in every country, greater economic possibilities for women definitely help overcome the barriers to being lesbian, promoting lesbian visibility and discouraging sexism. But possibilities are not certainties. Increasing cuts and unemployment make it much harder to come out.

And even if we can find the money and other resources, other obstacles may tie us down. Immigration laws can mean deportation if women leave men on whom their right to residence depends. Many married women who have children are trapped in that closet by the terrifying prospect of losing custody. Thus, despite the breakthrough of many lesbian women being out, many more millions all over the world are still living hidden lesbian lives, and the lesbian movement appears to be smaller and therefore feels weaker than it really is.

Lesbian mothers and our children

The past decade has seen an explosion of lesbian motherhood. Since the mid-70s when for the first time in Britain a known lesbian mother won custody of her children in the courts, lesbian mothers have fought against hostility and prejudice and for recognition of our existence both in society and within the lesbian and women's movements. While the number of single mothers is constantly rising, women have also made accessible artificial insemination by donor—which opens the possibility of having children without relating to a man. This breakthrough, largely independent of the medical establishment, cheap, easy to do and undetectable, has opened a range of possibilities for women to have children which many of us would not otherwise have.

Neither we nor the State know how widely it's used, and as other women take advantage of what lesbian women pioneered, no-one knows what the consequences will be for motherhood generally. What we do know is that the State is most concerned about the level of discipline in families, about the "standard" of workers being produced, and that lesbian mothers are part of a far-reaching refusal by mothers to produce the kind of docile disciplined workforce it demands. Children growing up in lesbian or other woman-headed households can at least see for themselves that there are possibilities for living outside marriage, mortgage and a 40-hour week plus overtime.

For this and other reasons, the State treats lesbian mothers as a threat, and has used loss of custody to punish women, trying to prevent us from stepping out of line. Now that lesbian mothers and our children have officially been branded as "pretended family relationships" [Section 2A 1(b)], we are in even more danger of losing our children, either to the custody of individual fathers/husbands backed by the courts and social services, or to Local Authorities [local governments-Eds.] through the direct intervention of social workers, male and female. Where gay men are bringing up children (this is much rarer), they face the same sort of threat. Gay men have not on the whole been involved in lesbian women's battles for child custody, many of which have ended in tragic loss.

What happens to lesbian women affects all women. The "unfit mother" label, routinely used against lesbian mothers, is a classic example. It is also used against mothers who are poor, Black, or have convictions for prostitution, shoplifting, etc., or are accused of being feminists, "mentally ill," "political," "bad housewives," living at Greenham Common Women's Peace-Camp [A camp established next to a U.S. nuclear installation to protest militarism and nuclear weapons-Eds.] or any combination of these. Since the Clause reinforces the "unfit mother" label, the weapon with which the State can rob the children of lesbian mothers, many more non-lesbian women can be robbed behind the same label.

Targeting any group of women as "unfit mothers" is bound to act as a precedent for increased powers against other groups. The March 1987 legal decision to sterilize "Jeanette," a young woman with a learning disability, opened the way for a stream of officially backed sterilizations of women with disabilities and had wide implications for the autonomy of women with both learning and physical disabilities, and for our right to custody.

This is especially true with the change in recent years from courts almost automatically giving custody to mothers, to courts punishing women by awarding custody to fathers, even when the father is known to have been violent to the mother and/or the children. This is done in the name of "equality": the mother—the parent who actually does most or all of the work, first of bearing and then of day-to-day caring, even in the "liberated" household—has no more right to custody than the father. Yet few women have equal money/status/prestige with men; and we are also more likely to be the parent who "doesn't work," i.e., doesn't do waged work. So that if courts award custody to the parent who can provide more material resources without reference to the contribution of love and care, mothers are almost always bound to lose out. Until mothers' poverty is ended, or at least the burden of mothers' work acknowledged as a social contribution, "equality" between parents can only be one more weapon against the mother, which Clause 28 will exploit against lesbian mothers.

On top of physically caring for children, mothers do the work of helping them learn how to protect themselves and survive in a hierarchical, competitive and exploitative—capitalist—society. For those of us who are Black, this includes the work of challenging and coping with the consequences of racism, which adds another dimension to every other injustice. If those of us who are white are not challenging racism, we are inevitably inflicting it—being lesbian doesn't put white women above being racist!

In such a society, lesbian mothers face the constant work and worry of coping with the pressures, hostility and prejudices which children are bound to face as part of a lesbian-headed family. We have to weigh up when and whether it is best for them, and for our relationship with them, to be open about our lesbianism and to confront what society may think of us and do to them as our children. If we decide not to come out to them we have to be constantly on our guard against discovery; if we do come out we may not want anyone else to know and then they too have to be on guard against discovery. At the same time, we want to encourage our children to make their own sexual choices by ensuring that they have possibilities which we may not have had.

Describing lesbian mothers and our families as "pretended" gives the power structures another excuse to dismiss all the work we contribute to society, another excuse to ignore all women's unwaged work.

Clause 28 will increase lesbian mothers' unwaged emotional housework: more hiding and lying in all our dealings with schools, doctors, other parents, the police, neighbours, children's friends; more fear and worry about the ways our every word and gesture, as well as whatever happens to our children, can be misinterpreted, taken down and used in evidence against us; how even childhood illnesses and accidents like measles or scraped knees can be given sinister connotations (are we beating them, or neglecting them in some way, as "real mothers" would not?); how, in other words, the work of mothering is made even tougher because lesbian women's mothering is under constant suspicion and scrutiny.

All this puts great strain on the relationship between mothers and children. It is also a strain on partners/non-biological mothers whose mothering and other contributions to the family are usually invisible: hidden behind "She's just a friend." We all know women who have been forced by social services, the courts or ex-husbands to choose between their lovers and their children. Dismissed as "pretended," our greater emotional housework as lesbian mothers is driven further into invisibility and we are denied resources and facilities which should be ours as of right, as mothers doing mothering work.

Nor do we know what might next be described as a "pretended" family. The number of woman-headed households worldwide is estimated by the United Nations to range from 20% to 40% of all families. Will the "pretended" family label apply to all the families in Britain which are headed by women? or are extended families? or where the parents are separated, divorced, remarried, or just living in poverty or "in sin"? Among nuclear families which qualify as "real," how many husbands and fathers rape and/or batter their wives and children? These are the "real" (Victorian) family values Clause 28 promotes.

Clause 28 in the classroom

Clause 28 intends to reverse the victories of many years of organizing, demonstrating, lobbying and other campaigning by the lesbian and gay movements, which also drew power from other movements. One victory of the 80s, along with much else, was initiatives in schools which begin—and only begin—to counter the stereotypes children imbibe about homosexuality, and to replace them with more realistic (not "pretended") images of lesbian women and gay men. Such images combined with the erosion of stereotypes and the fear of being identified by them, let young people know that there were many possibilities to choose from of how they may want to live and who they may want to know. They need not be confined to the ghetto of marriage, mortgage and 2.2 children. But the State doesn't want them to be aware there are other options. Clause 28 makes homophobia mandatory, once again dividing people and, by censoring basic information, deprives young people in particular of the raw material with which to invent their own lives.

Along with the National Curriculum, opting out, and media distortion of the Burnage Report to say that anti-racism, not racism, is what's wrong with the schools, Clause 28 is an attempt to privatize, cut or shut down the school system—to Black people, women, lesbian and gay people, people with disabilities, everyone demanding access, resources, accountability and an end to miseducation policies which "promote the teaching of . . . the acceptability of" racism, homophobia and discrimination and injustice of all kinds.

Clause 28 promotes a new reign of terror in schools by:

—formally ordering teachers to indoctrinate children with standards which divide families into those which are "pretended" as opposed to "real", "deviant" as opposed to "normal". If a child's home life doesn't match the State photofit, other children will be trained to treat that child as an outcast.

—preventing discussion of any aspect of the home life of the children of lesbian or gay parents, except in the context of an attack on their parent(s). Such children from the earliest age will sense that their mothers and fathers are a liability, and that it's safer and more socially acceptable to distance themselves from and even disown and inform on them. Already working hard in order to survive in a hostile society, children will be under increased pressure to hide and deceive, for fear of endangering themselves and those they love and are dependent on.

—giving a green light to censorship, intimidation, coercion and other violence against children and their lesbian/gay parents, especially if the children in their own right are also daring to challenge the status quo.

—criminalizing teachers who try to encourage children to understand and accept differences among them, among all of us, without condemning and punishing. Teachers who are lesbian or gay will be even more likely to be sacked: since "promoting" can easily become "not condemning", their very presence in school can be interpreted as "promoting homosexuality."

Lesbian women and waged work

Clause 28 is one more attack on protection against discrimination in waged jobs. There are already signs of increased pressure against employing lesbian/gay people in any job working with young children, for example, in children's homes or other institutions—the kind of job women traditionally do and which many lesbian women living outside the family have traditionally depended on to support an independent life. We say *increased* pressure because in this area, lesbian/gay people have always worked under threat of slanderous accusations, whispering campaigns and instant dismissal.

Although high unemployment has undermined everyone's choices during the past nine years, the introduction of equal opportunity employment policies by many councils has opened some jobs for lesbian women and other people who are discriminated against (often disparagingly referred to as "minorities"). As councils feel the pressure of Clause 28, equal opportunities policies are likely to go. Lesbian women will be among the first to lose waged work in councils and in the public sector generally.

Faced with this wagelessness—in which lesbian women will be joining other unwaged workers of the world in the international trend of increasing unemployment—our economic power to survive and/or come out as lesbian women will hinge on a few alternatives:

—claiming welfare in whatever form from the State—a limited/non-existent option in Third World countries;

—marriage with men while having sexual relations with someone;

—prostitution and other "crimes of poverty," rapidly increasing throughout Third World and industrialized countries;

—migration to where there are either more waged jobs, welfare or other economic possibilities;

—joining religious orders and institutions—which for women in both Third World and industrialized countries serve as a base for charity, the refusal of sexual relations with men and different forms of liberation theology;

—and, last but not least, the dismantling of the international military-industrial complex so that the wealth which women's waged and unwaged work has produced, but which has been stolen from us, limiting our sexual and all other choices, is finally returned.

Censorship and repression

Clause 28 makes lesbian and gay people a new target for "Neighbourhood Watch": local residents who, in the name of safety, monitor an area—including their neighbours' movements—and pass this information to the police. Neighbours who are lesbian or gay will be among the first to be monitored and reported on.

Cuts increase competition among working class people for scarce resources, which in turn foments racism and prejudice of every kind. Escalating police powers enforce this scarcity and protect the Establishment which profits from it.

Clause 28, by helping to create a climate of active State disapproval on the streets where we live, makes lesbian-headed families convenient scapegoats for people frustrated and infuriated by losing what it took working class people years to win. Because it is easier to bash those lower down the pecking order than to challenge the higher-ups with real power, Clause 28 will inevitably increase not only social discrimination but also physical violence, which for women also means more rape and sexual assault.

The government has already used AIDS to witch-hunt lesbian and gay people. Clause 28 promotes its own witch-hunt.

The Clause is already being used to censor not only literary and other artistic creations by or about lesbian women/gay men but any material which challenges the status quo. Among the effects will be to disorganize and destroy grassroots information networks which have taken years to build; to deny access to information and ideas which widen understanding; to cut generations off from each other, hiding the history of the movement from young people especially; to isolate lesbian and gay people; and to further terrorize everyone into staying in, or retreating back into, the closet.

Even before Clause 28 became law, the London borough of Haringey, where lesbian and gay groups had spearheaded the drive for "positive images" in schools, faced Tory moves to cut funding to lesbian and gay groups and to a local bookshop, *Reading Matters*; to impose censorship in schools; and to remove homosexuality from the Council's equal opportunities policy, all of which amounted to implementation of the Clause. At a council meeting on 25 April 1988, picketed by about 500 women and men, Haringey Council threw out this proposal by 33 votes to 13. The unrestrained fervour of Haringey's Tories foreshadows the reaction Clause 28 will strengthen and inspire in the Tory shires. Right-wing politicians and other hooligans had to retreat as the lesbian and gay movements advanced; now Clause 28 is signaling that it's safe for them to come out.

Clause 28 could mean that lesbian and gay groups, clubs, meeting places, centres, pubs would be forced to shut down, either because they are "intentionally promoting homosexuality," or because of AIDS panic and scapegoating, or because of police raids and/or vigilante attacks, or because they just won't have the money and other resources to continue when fear causes attendance to drop, or because of a combination of all of these.

The first to go will be hard-won lesbian spaces. Some of us remember the 60s and early 70s when, although there were gay men's clubs, some of which tolerated women, there were hardly any lesbian clubs, partly because women did not spend enough to finance them. Lesbian clubs became financially viable when, because of the strength of the lesbian/women's movements, the numbers swelled of lesbian women which they attracted. Straight women were also attracted to women-only spaces and felt confident enough not to be intimidated by guilt by association. This is what Clause 28 could destroy, throwing us back to underground parties and meetings in private homes which neighbours can monitor and complain to the authorities about.

Because lesbian spaces and funding may be cut, any autonomous women's space is insecure. Where men alone (men-only) are not only taken for granted, but applauded as the height of masculinity, women alone (women-only)—women's sports teams, for example—appear to be threatening and are often attacked for being lesbian. In fact any women-only gathering has always been susceptible to the charge of lesbianism, as hard to prove as to disprove, and the Clause could be used against other women-only venues such as women's centres whose funding/activities may be attacked. Here again, if lesbian women are under threat, all women are threatened.

We must also remember that what the lesbian/gay/women's movements have won in cities like London, Manchester or Edinburgh, is not felt as strongly in smaller cities, towns, villages, suburbs, or local neighbourhoods, where pressure to conform is more intense, and individual lesbian/gay people don't have the power of numbers to withstand it nor the crowd in which to be anonymous. Given this great disparity in levels of power between "the big city" and the town/village/neighbourhood, Clause 28 will make local life even more narrowminded and repressive, finally eradicating any allowance for the "eccentric" who may traditionally have been tolerated.

Social support networks and information about where to go, what to read and how to get help, all of which it has taken a movement to put together, are less likely to survive outside of the big centres. Women in particular, whose movements are usually more monitored, and who are in any case less mobile, will find it harder to get out or come out. More lesbian and gay people will be forced to emigrate to the "big city," on the one hand hoping to escape with their sanity and dignity intact, but on the other hand facing the prospect of being jobless and homeless when they arrive.

Labour Party cop-out

The Labour Party's initial front bench support for Clause 28—support later withdrawn under pressure—and the fact that Labour did not impose a whip in the Lords (i.e., tell Labour Lords to vote against it), reflect their politics of being generally terrified of, and therefore led by, the Tories. Desperate to shed the "loony left" label which the media manufactured to describe some Labour councils' equal opportunities policies for women and Black and lesbian/gay people, the Labour leadership are clearly determined to jettison all principles and witch-hunt anyone who dents their new respectable, moderate, Yuppie image . . .

Labour's half-hearted opposition to Clause 28 is grounded in excluding sexual politics from what it defines as class politics. For John Cunningham, Shadow spokesman on the environment, it seems, sexual choice is not a working class concern—and if it is, it shouldn't be! ["Shadows" are opposition members who 'shadow' government ministers of a particular minority or department—Eds.] In the same way, it has taken years for trade unions even to begin to acknowledge child benefit, rape, racial and sexual harassment, abortion and forced sterilization, and childcare, as working class issues. According to traditional Labour Party (and some other Left) definitions, the working class is white, male, straight, ablebodied, over 20, under 50, has 2.2 children, loves football [soccer], the police and nuclear power (dear also to Cunningham's heart), and lives on a council estate [i.e. housing project—Eds.]. The cream of the working class belongs to a (white dominated) trade union and to an all-white or white-dominated tenants' association. Anyone who doesn't conform to this stereotype is other than working class, and could be an "outside agitator," whose rights need not be defended, in fact who need not have rights.

Yet to the degree that Labour fails to support so-called "outsiders" and "minorities," to that degree they fail to oppose the military budget, nuclear weapons and nuclear power, the government's refusal to impose sanctions on South Africa, increasing police powers, attacks on strikers—the list is as long as the Tories make it.

But for real (not Labour Party pretended) working class people, the issue is how we get ourselves moving and working together and building autonomous working class movements—of Black people, women, lesbian and gay people, people with disabilities . . .

Sexual politics versus class politics, separatism versus autonomy

It is not only the Labour Party hierarchy which separates "sexual politics" from "class politics." The same separatism has undermined the lesbian and gay movements and been a major weakness in mobilizing against Clause 28.

We agree of course that being lesbian/gay is a "sexual choice." But it is not as if whatever choice we make about what we want to do in bed can be made in isolation from other choices and necessities. Because we are pulled by choices and by necessities in such opposite directions, it's a constant struggle to choose to be lesbian/gay and to live it, despite this or any government with the power to control, repress and divide us.

Before we described ourselves as lesbian, and even if we believe we have always been, we struggled as little girls, and maybe also as wives, mothers and lovers of men, for the power to discover and then act on our sexual desires. We drew and continue to draw understanding and power from all of these battles and confrontations, our own and other people's, redefining our possibilities and raising our standards as we find out more about who we can be.

Sexual choice is not an issue only for a "minority"; it is inseparable from all the other issues where we fight for the power to have every other choice. Putting forward any particular sexual choice as the only revolutionary strategy for everyone, can in fact find accommodation with the status quo by denigrating and undercutting all other working class people whose struggles and goals for change are different. The classic point of view of lesbian separatism—that if we all only went to live in self-sufficient (there is no self-sufficiency in today's global capitalist economy) lesbian communities and had no dealings with men (who they assume are "the enemy"), we change the world—is an example of such accommodation to the status quo, that is, pretended revolution.

Separating sexual choice from the politics of sex, race, class, age, nation, disability, etc., not only separates lesbian and gay people from others; it throws us together in an artificial and defensive way, veiling the many issues and individual and social distinctions which divide us, even on the issue of sexual choice. We can only consider ourselves to be "all in the same boat" if we define homosexuality as a sexual choice without reference to who else we are and what else we do. The sexual choice of being lesbian/gay means living quite different lives in different situations, depending on our sex, race, class, income, disability, occupation, country and so on. And there are wide disagreements among lesbian and gay people about safe sex, S&M sex, cottaging, cruising, marriage, coming out, about the direction and accountability of the lesbian and gay movements, about what strategy and tactics we use, and much more.

The debate over whether opposing Clause 28 should be nothing more than a single issue campaign which narrowly defines the effects of the Clause, or whether the campaign should connect with other issues, reflects the deep divisions among us which the single issue campaign has on the whole hidden. It is always tempting to believe what our enemies tell us, that only if we stick to one issue and define it narrowly, do we have a chance of winning.

The tendency to separate sexual politics from the rest of class politics is much stronger when people are under attack and are rushing to their ghettoes and closets for cover, locking the doors behind them. Thus police entrapment of gay men is separated from police racism in St Paul's or Moss-Side or police illegality against prostitute women in King's Cross or police violence against strikers at Orgreave or Wapping; lesbian-bashing is disconnected from the legality of rape in marriage; homophobia is completely "different," a "separate oppression" from ageism or disability racism, etc.

Separating our needs and priorities from the needs and priorities of others, inevitably results in sexism and racism against those "outside"—but also within—the movement. For example, the organizing against Clause 28 rarely acknowledges that much of what the Clause aims to launch against lesbian women and gay men is already happening to Black people, whether or not those of us who are Black are also lesbian/gay, and that those of us who are Black and who are most exposed and most vulnerable, must be given the support we need, not as a charity but for the sake of the movement as a whole. The speed with which the National Front background of anti-Clause 28 organizer in Manchester was glossed over recently, has reinforced divisions between Black and white in the lesbian and gay movements, and does not augur well for the future. [The National Front is an anti-immigrant, racist fascist political organization—Eds.]

The Left is often unwilling to see how the situation of lesbian and gay people is unique and specific. But the lesbian and gay movements can't deal with that kind of attack by refusing to see our situation is similar to, and interconnected with, others. We build our autonomy on the need to voice and fight for our unique and specific case. We also build on the power which comes from unity among ourselves and with others. By not considering other people's needs, and by not appealing to our mutual interests, we make enemies of potential allies before we even know who they are. And when we are not aware of the power against our enemies which the struggles of others provide for us, we act out of weakness. If other struggles are not seen as inseparable from our own, ultimately—and usually soon—we demean and dismiss other people's needs and priorities, in order to protect and promote our own, as if they are incompatible we choose our interest over others' instead of working out how and where our interests coincide with and reinforce the interests of others so wherever possible we can choose both and strengthen both.

The State within the movement

Making these connections between the interests of different sectors of people is not often the guiding principle of any movement. Many times the lesbian and gay movements have been divided internally about whether we should all be trying to be respectable, whether if only we were less flagrant/loud/militant/aggressive—in a word, less working class, less "out"—we would be more acceptable to the tabloid press, and could convince the powers-that-be to give us our rights (they've never given us anything). In fact, the tabloid press which misrepresents and demeans us are not just making a mistake about lesbian and gay people; they distort who we are and what we want because that is their job.

The lesbian and gay movements have been divided about whether all we ever wanted as lesbian/gay people was simply to be accepted as "normal," "just like everyone else," retaining—but moving up in—whatever hierarchy of privilege and power we're already part of; whether we wanted "equal rights" with others as though everyone else had rights, or if they had them, that they were enough; or whether being lesbian/gay is a challenge to the whole social hierarchy and all its power relations.

Whether or not these battles were called that, they have been battles over which class interests the lesbian and gay movements would serve. For example, should the lesbian/gay movement promote "pink capitalism"—gay businesses—as the pinnacle of achievement? Is the Black working class lesbian mother really in the same boat as a gay white male company director? Lesbian women have had to work overtime for the gay movement not to remain an arena dominated by the traditional power of the social hierarchy—white-dominated, male-dominated, with one foot in the Establishment. And just as lesbian women, Black and white, had to take autonomy from gay men because of their sexism, Black lesbian women had to take autonomy from both white lesbian women and gay men because of their racism.

Being lesbian or gay is not necessarily a challenge to the status quo. It can mean being best placed to manage other people, including lesbian/gay people, on behalf of the State. Take ex-Lambeth Council Leader Linda Bellos, described in a media profile (*The Guardian* 11 May 1987) as "the perfect choice—hard Left, a woman, Black, a lesbian and Jewish." Of Bello's actions, implementing cuts in Lambeth is perhaps the most far reaching in its impact on women and those most vulnerable in the community. We recall Bellos's feminist days when she attacked Greenham women by writing that the enemy is not cruise missiles and the "anonymous, overwhelming militaristic threat," but "the man next door"—whoever he is.

During an April 1987 picket of Lambeth Town Hall over the Council's allocations policy towards an older woman wheelchair user who had been raped, WinVisible, Women Against Rape, Black Women for Wages for Housework and supporters won a demand to see Council Leader Linda Bellos, the person with overall responsibility. She accused Black and white women protesters, including four wheelchair users and other women with disabilities, of racism for making demands about women's safety on her as a Black woman. Faced with criticism for doing virtually nothing for the woman concerned, who was picketing, she walked away, saying "Do you pay me?" and "I serve a quarter of a million women in Lambeth!" Evidently she did not consider the women, or others who would benefit from a change in policy, to be among that number. When lack of accountability to those with least access to resources is the price of wielding political power/getting a job, then the sex, race, class or sexual orientation of the person who fills the vacancy becomes either irrelevant or even a power against us.

All these divisions among us, uncertainty about how to handle them, and whether to face them at all, have been played out in many different ways since the birth of the present movement in the 60s. One expression of uncertainty today is lack of effective resistance to pressure from the Yuppie wing of the movement that we not "protest too much" about Clause 28. But if the movement responds to this life-endangering attack as if we and the government were gentlemen agreeing to differ, we are likely to be defeated on this issue and the movement can get its throat cut: no one will know, or care, what happens to us—if we as a movement don't protest, why should others?

That's why the lesbian and gay movements must not respond to these attacks with more self-repression and self-policing, with people getting crushed in the stampede to show that we are "sensible" and don't really want to rock the boat. Our job as a movement is to rock "the ship of State," most fundamentally by showing how an attack on us is an attack on all working class people.

It shouldn't come as a surprise that the more powerful people in the movement are shying away from taking a stand with the less powerful. We are shaped by a society which assumes that this is the only practical behaviour. It's a lot of work to connect your own situation with the situation of those with less power. It's a battle all the time to get men, including gay men, not to refuse the work of connecting their situation with women's, including lesbian women's. Such connections lead to confronting, and even breaking with, friends, family, lovers, and ultimate the Establishment: it's a lot of work to face the fact that the perpetrators of Clause 28, the defenders of queer-bashing, are also the defenders of rapists, racists, nuclear weapons, etc., and to admit to oneself that the enemy we have to take on and defeat is powerful and pervasive. It's less work and a rosier prospect of less work if there's only one thing wrong: the government hates queers. But that isn't true—or rather, that is only a small part of the truth which, if it is allowed to pass for the whole truth, is a lie.

On the other hand, the enemy has understood very well the power we gain by connecting. Long before the parliamentary hooligans launched Clause 28 to disconnect us, graffiti was daubed on our Women's Center door proclaiming "Paki lesbos out," signed "NF" (National Front), explicitly attacking the connections being made at our Centre. It is not accidental that it is precisely those of us who have understood that we are both lesbian/gay and women/Black/working class, etc., who have been singled out for attack from the hooligans in and out of government. Our crime is that we "widen the issue" by not hiding any of our interests and refusing to choose between our right fist and our left. Unless the issue is widened, we ourselves are narrowed, our reality amputated to fit a definition of ourselves which leaves most of us out, as individuals, as groups, as movements.

And when we are under pressure, as with Clause 28, we feel the implications of such grave weaknesses not "eventually" but immediately: we could wake up to find a movement heading away from supporting all lesbian women under attack, and heading towards defending only the women who meet the "right-on" standard imposed by those with more social power in society generally; social power to impose what is in effect a Clause 28 within the movement: dividing lesbian women between "real" and "pretended." And you can be sure that the most vulnerable will be labeled the most "pretended."

Additionally, grassroots lesbian women have had to confront careerism within the lesbian movement. As the power of the movement has grown, so has the heterosexism industry, in much the same way as the gender and race relations industries have flourished off the backs of, and often at the expense of, survival struggles of women and Black people. When Ken Livingstone became leader of the Greater London Council (GLC) he began funding lesbian/gay projects at a previously unimaginable rate, and some other Labour-controlled councils followed suit. "Jobs for the girls" became relatively plentiful, both in local government and in the voluntary sector. Heterosexism awareness programmes became the rage and money was to be made. (Of course groups such as WDL, which were critical of the social/political friendship networks of the money lenders, never got a penny.)

To gain the confidence to be able to face the divisions and power relations which are the real "enemy within" the movement, it is important to be fully aware of what we've won which the State is trying to clause back: precisely a taste of the power which comes from breaking these divisions and destroying these power relations.

Monetarism and moralism

. . . Separating ourselves as lesbian/gay from ourselves as working class, disarms us both against the State and against those in the movement who identify more with the "non-political" homosexuality of the powers-that-be, than with a struggle to determine our own lives, sexually and otherwise.

Clause 28 is integral to the government's double-edged economic strategy: removing access to wages through unemployment on the one hand, and on the other, lowering the social wage through cuts in welfare benefits, health care, housing, social services, the National Health Service, etc. To succeed, this strategy must be accompanied by an attack on our rights to self-determination and to information/education about ourselves and each other—in other words, an attack on our power to organize with all kinds of people against exploitation and repression. Monetarism—government by market forces—needs moralism—government by police forces, in the bedroom, in the classroom and on the street.

The entire Local Government Bill, orchestrated by a malignant media, is a backlash against a major working class victory of the 1980s: wresting some degrees of accessibility and accountability from Labour local councils.

Ensuring that the political climate in local councils is oppressive, narrowminded, racist, sexist, ageist, homophobic, ableist—through cuts in choices and money, such as with Clause 28—is one key to undermining and silencing resistance to other major attacks such as workfare, the poll tax, and outlawing strikes. Defeating this strategy is dependent on making the connection between these issues, and between people directly affected by these issues. A movement which is determined to win has to be prepared to work at making those connections as if its life depends on them—because it does!

The women's movement has won greater possibilities for millions of women on the basis of greater social/legal/financial independence than previous generations. As a result, women in many situations are less tied to families we don't want, less coerced into living up to expectations we reject. All of us are convinced, in varying degrees, that we have or should have rights over our own bodies.

It certainly seems that considering whether or not to have an intimate social and sexual life with your own sex is now widespread in the population, especially among the younger generation in industrialized countries. But in order for "considering" to become "choosing" on any serious scale, people—and particularly women, who are the poorest and work the hardest in any community—must have or at least see the possibility of having financial independence.

Clause 28 seeks to reverse the breakdown of, which has made and continues massively to make inroads into the repressive patterns of people's lives and relationships. Clause 28 intends to make sure that we are only comfortable in a very straight jacket, and extremely uptight if we open ourselves to new sexual and social possibilities.

This connection between accessing new sexual and social possibilities and the shutting off of access to financial support lies at the heart of the recent Thatcherite major restructuring of the welfare system. Not only has the general level of benefits been cut for everyone, young people will now lose money from their Supplementary Benefit if they choose not to live with parents. On the one hand we are to be frightened off from sexual choices; on the other hand, we are to be cut off from the financial power to explore and pursue them.

The ferocity of this twin attack can give us some idea of how subversive the widespread desire for sexual choice can be. The movement of the 60s which won many of the victories we build on, was so massive and so pervasive that what the State proclaims it is threatened by, we now take for granted: how can my going to a gay bar and sleeping with my girlfriend be threatening to the State? you can hear people say.

But such a social life presumes the public rejection by many millions of people of the repressive family and the training and discipline it is supposed to instill: that we should be prepared to spend our lives having to do work we hate, waged work and unwaged work, or even having to do all the time work we sometimes like to do. This rejection may not bring on utopia, but it does help shake up all robotic intellectual, physical and social responses to the assumptions we have been force-fed and will be force-fed again if Clause 28 and measures which could follow are allowed to operate unchallenged.

We must confront these financial cuts together with the sexual and social "cut" of Clause 28, as the twin enemy, because both attack our sexual choices and both attack our economic choices and we need both sexual and economic choices, not only to hold onto what the lesbian and gay movements have won so far but to begin to absorb and act on what the present times are teaching us.

16 June 1988
12th Anniversary of the 1976 Soweto Uprising

HUNTER MADSEN AND
MARSHALL KIRK

As a result of the activism of the 1970's and 1980's, more and more lesbians and gays have come out. As they have, there has been a revival of "mainstream" gay politics and writing. This politics is of the Mattachine variety in its claims for equality rather than celebration of gay culture. These more conservative writers are impatient with other movements for liberation and hope that a narrower agenda will advance the cause of gay and lesbian equality. This perspective is also characterized by a rejection of "fringe" elements that make us look different, such as leather people, drag queens, and pedophiles.

Hunter Madsen and Marshall Kirk exemplify this perspective. They are convinced that their sexuality is not a source of major difference between themselves and their heterosexual friends. In their book *After the Ball,* they recommend a public-relations campaign aimed at convincing heterosexuals that we are just like them. The following selection describes their campaign and is followed by their "Self-Policing Social Code," which they hope will win acceptance and improve relations between "gays."

STRATEGY: PERSUASION, NOT INVASION

Chapter 3 of *After the Ball* (1989)

Hunter Madsen and Marshall Kirk

Groups are subject to the truly magical power of words.
—Sigmund Freud

Good Propaganda: The Idea behind 'Waging Peace'

Gay life in America is hard, and promises little improvement unless something is done, and promptly, to transform society's antigay attitudes. If this isn't clear by now, you must be reading our book from the wrong end: we closed Chapter 1 with a daunting checklist of the myths and injustices which grow out of homohatred learned in childhood.

What's to be done about this checklist? Many solutions could be proposed, ranging from the idealistic and fanciful to the necessary but insufficient. Such solutions will be noted (and castigated) briefly below. But from here on, this book is devoted to the one scheme that would, if correctly administered, radically hasten and broaden the spread of tolerance for gays in straight society.

We have in mind a strategy as calculated and powerful as that which gays are *accused* of pursuing by their enemies—or, if you prefer, a plan as manipulative as that which our enemies themselves employ. It's time to learn from Madison Avenue, to roll out the big guns. *Gays must launch a large-scale campaign—we've called it the Waging Peace campaign—to reach straights through the mainstream media.* We're talking about propaganda.

To most people, the word 'propaganda' has the worst connotations. Propaganda is supposed to be what Communists and Fascists (and certain TV weathermen) are up to—gross distortion and fraud perpetrated for evil ends. This is a misconception. *The term 'propaganda' applies to any deliberate attempt to persuade the masses via public communications media.* Such communication is everywhere, of course, being a mainstay of modern societies. Its function is not to perpetrate, but to *propagate*; that is, to spread new ideas and feelings (or reinforce old ones) which may themselves be either evil or good depending on their purpose and effect. The purpose and effect of progay propaganda is to promote a climate of increased tolerance for homosexuals. And that, we say, is good.

Three characteristics distinguish propaganda from other modes of communications and contribute to its sinister reputation. First, propaganda relies more upon emotional manipulation than upon logic, since its goal is, in fact, to bring about a change in the public's feelings. Bertrand Russell once asked, "Why is propaganda so much more successful when it stirs up hatred than when it tries to stir up friendly feelings?" The answer is that the public is more eager to hate than to love, especially where outgroups are concerned; and that, knowing this, propagandists have seldom attempted to elicit friendly feelings or dampen hatred. This time, however, we gays will attempt precisely that. And we'll be more successful than before because we can base our efforts on techniques (desensitization, jamming, and conversion) derived directly from a solid understanding of the psychology of homohatred.

The second sinister characteristic of propaganda is its frequent use of outright lies, a tactic we neither need nor condone. In the long run, big fat lies work only for propagandists of totalitarian states, who can make them stick by exercising almost complete control over public information. But in pluralistic societies, such as ours, chronic liars on controversial subjects are invariably found out and discredited in the press by their opponents. (There is, alas, an exception: certain lies become hallowed public myths, persisting for as long as the public *chooses* to believe them. Need we mention the Big Lie?)

Third, even when it sticks to the facts, propaganda can be unabashedly subjective and one-sided. There is nothing necessarily wrong with this. Propaganda tells its own side of the story as movingly (and credibly) as possible, since it can count on its enemies to tell the other side with a vengeance. In the battle for hearts and minds, effective propaganda knows enough to put its best foot forward. This is what out own media campaign must do.

When, in a 1985 *Christopher Street* article, we presented a blueprint for a national propaganda effort, doubters derided the proposal as irrelevant or impotent, the methods as demeaning and fraudulent, and our intent as reactionary. In February 1988, however, a "war conference" of 175 leading gay activists, representing organizations from across the land, convened in Warrenton, Virginia, to establish a four-point agenda for the gay movement. The conference gave first priority to "a nation-wide media campaign to promote a positive image of gays and lesbians," and its final statement concluded:

We must consider the media in every project we undertake. We must, in addition, take every advantage we can to include public service announcements and paid advertisements, and to cultivate reporters and editors of newspapers, radio, and television. To help facilitate this we need national media workshops to train our leaders . . . Our media efforts are fundamental to the full acceptance of us in American life.

Since the war conference, local gay advertising efforts have sprung up across the nation—in California, Ohio, Virginia, and other states—and GLAAD and the Fund for Human Dignity for a time, even co-sponsored the beginnings of a national "Positive Images Campaign." Clearly, something is afoot. Recognition is dawning that antigay discrimination begins, like war, in the minds of men, and must be stopped there with the help of propaganda. Recognition is likewise dawning that certain other strategy, touted in earlier days by idealistic activists, cannot accomplish the task on their own. Several of these strategies deserve mention.

Outreach Strategies Of The Past: Why Only A Media Campaign Will Do

Those oft are stratagems which errors seem.
—*Alexander Pope, 1738*
Pope's got it backwards.
—*Erastes Pill, 1989*

First Strategy: Come Thou, Mountain, To Mohammed.

As discussed earlier, some gays believe we shouldn't reach out at all to heterosexuals in order to dispel discrimination. Some stalwart revolutionaries feel strongly that appealing for acceptance bespeaks groveling capitulation and conformitarianism. Instead, the radicals demand that straights simply accept us entirely on our own terms, or not at all. They point out that gays have spent their lives trying to force-fit themselves into a straight mold, so now it is the straights' turn to adjust.

In this scenario, it is the public's job to disburden itself magically, on its own, of its massive sexual hang-ups; the homosexual's only duty is to 'learn how to love' himself or herself. Who needs respect from others when he has self-respect? If 'they' don't like homosexuality, they can just lump it; 'liberated' gays will form their own proud nation—imagined as a sort of urban Navaho reservation—and ignore the larger world. Sooner or later, straights will be impressed by our gay pride, and come around.

As you might guess by now, we think this radical argument is rubbish (which has been sitting rankly on the sidewalk ever since the early '70s, waiting for someone to haul it away). There can be no reservation-like enclave, no sailing off on the good ship Sodom to colonize new lands of our own. We are Americans, going nowhere, living cheek-by-jowl with our persecutors.

In this unyielding predicament, to gain straight tolerance and acceptance is not just a legitimate goal of gay activism, it must be the *principal* goal. Certainly, helping gays to see themselves more positively is important too, but this in no way suffices. It's just as preposterous to argue, as one of our critics did recently, that "gay pride makes [straight] acceptance," as it is to pretend that gays could safely turn their backs on the straight world. The heterosexual majority's hostility is real, brutal, and largely indifferent in whether its victims have gay pride or not. Bigotry mauls gays, so our aim must be to muzzle and tame it. There's no point pretending to be Mohammed and waiting for straights to come around: left to itself, the mountain won't budge an inch.

Second Strategy: I'd Like To Teach The World To Sing.

Why not simply appeal to straights and gays to learn to love one another and give peace a chance; to be nice, for a change, on their own recognizance? After all, people are really good inside; one need only appeal to that universal goodness, and hard feelings will peel away like a dried old husk. Every man a saint, and a world of Leo Buscaglias!

There is, in fact, much to be said for efforts at self-improvement. Some social reform, like charity, does begin at home. Straights who have read this far will wish hereafter to challenge their own bigoted feelings, and those of their society, with renewed determination, while they reassess their stereotypic beliefs about gays.

Gays, on the other hand—particularly the men—can take greater responsibility, and refuse to live down to the gay stereotype. As the authors will argue strenuously in Chapter 6 (so strenuously, in fact, that everyone is guaranteed a sharp pain in the neck before we leave off), we gays can establish for ourselves a studies code of ethics stressing maturity in love relationships, moderation in the pursuit of sex and other entertainments, sincerity and loving-kindness—that venerable Old Testament notion toward all our fellows, and restraint in our public deportment. In sum, we can and should assert more control over our own actions, rather that let ourselves be shoved back and forth as abused playthings between the puerile dictates of our own undisciplined impulses, on the on hand, and society's unreasonable demands for mindless conformity on the other. Self mastery is freedom. Fidelity to an ethical code of one's own construction is independence, not conformity. Gays must know what they will live by and then live by it. Period.

If gays could, further, agree upon the general outlines of a code and begin to regulate themselves *as a community*, this would be better still. To date, our movement has been so fixed upon the attainment of what the philosopher Isaiah Berlin calls "negative liberty"—being left alone—that it has utterly failed to appreciate the value of "positive liberty"—being encouraged and helped by one's companions to achieve the good.

Admittedly, our campaign espouses, in part, this idealistic strategy for transforming social relations through self-conscious effort. *We'd* like to teach the world to sing, too; who wouldn't? But that strategy will be most effective for improving relations *within* the gay community, and only secondarily in reaching bigoted straights. After all, most heterosexuals dislike homosexuals on fundamentally emotional, not intellectual, grounds, and are, therefore, unwilling and unable to abolish their own prejudices through a change of principles and beliefs. Nor would the miraculous transformation of the gay *demimonde* into a province of virtue—though plenty nice for its own members—automatically wing over straights, since their hostility is guided more by caricatures in their head than by the gay reality that unfolds right under their noses.

Third Strategy: Come Out, Come Out, Wherever You Are.

This is another scheme we heartily recommend but have faint hope of implementing until more fundamental changes have first occurred: *wherever possible, come out.* Naturally, coming out is a grave and dangerous step for anyone. Only a few will proclaim their sexuality all at once to everybody they know; most prefer to be more selective, to inform intimates one by one over time, on a 'need-to-know' basis. It's like the difference between ripping a bandage off all at once or bit by bit. But whatever the approach, coming out makes an enormous contribution to fight against homohatred, since it generally provides an ideal opportunity to activate the psychological mechanisms we have called desensitization, jamming, and conversion. Here's how it works:

First, coming out helps desensitize straights. As more and more gays emerge into everyday life, *gays as a group* will begin to seem more familiar and unexceptional to straights, hence less alarming and objectionable. (Remember that most *gays are* otherwise unexceptional—or else straights would recognize them.) The more gays come out, the more the Big Lie will crumble, and with it the irrational foundation for moral condemnation and mistreatment.

Second, coming out allows more jamming of the reward system of homohatred. Jamming, you'll recall, means interrupting the smooth workings of bigotry by inducing inconsistent feelings in the bigot. One jams, for example, by displacing with shame and guilt satisfying sense of social approval and self-righteousness that a homohater would otherwise feel when he attacks homosexuals. As gays come out, they and their friends will be free to play a more vigorous role in jamming, openly showing their disapproval of homohatred. Jamming can work, even if open gays merely stand around homohaters without saying a work: in their presence, extreme bigots become less confident that their incitements will generate applause, and are further inhibited by the majority of "mild" bigots, who now become uneasy that a fag slur might provoke an unpleasant scene. Once these dynamics get going, displays of homohatred suddenly become off-color and boorish. Thus, when gays come out, they help transform the social climate from on that supports prejudice to one that shuts homohaters up. And when bigots fall silent, they cannot as easily pass their social disease on to the next generation.

Third, coming out is a critical catalyst for the all-important 'conversion' process, as well. Conversion is more than merely desensitizing straights or jamming their homohatred: it entails making them actually like and accept homosexuals as a group, enabling straights to *identify* with them. This becomes possible when a heterosexual learns that someone he already likes and admires, such as a friend or family member, is homosexual. The discovery leads to an internal showdown between the straight's personal affection on the one hand and his bigotry on the other. When the gunsmoke finally clears—and it can take years to do so—the stronger sentiment emerges more or less victorious. If it is the stronger, affection for the friend wins out and subdues bigotry, the straight's concept of gays is modified for the better, and a favorable conversion takes place. Imagine: all that, just because you decided to come out.

Finally, in addition to making desensitization, jamming, and conversion possible, coming out is the key to sociopolitical empowerment, the ability of the gay community to control its own destiny. The more gay individuals who stand up to be counted, the more voting and spending power the gay community will be recognized to have. As an inevitable result, politics and business will woo us, the press will publicize our concerns and report our news, and our community will enjoy enhance prestige.

If coming out does such positive things to combat bigotry, why even bother with a national media campaign? Why not just wait for everyone to come out? Because *gay America is coming out too slowly*. The way things are going—and there are no firm statistics on this, only impressions—no more than a fraction of the gay population is likely to come out over the next thirty years, and that's not sufficient to transform public attitudes at a satisfactory pace. (Perhaps others have the patience of Job, but the authors least, are unwilling to be worried still in the year 2020 about receiving their basic civil rights, at an age when they should be worrying instead about receiving their first social security check and hair transplants.)

The percentage of gays who are out remains low because many still feel, with some justification, that any benefits of coming out that might redound to themselves or to the gay movement do not outweigh the personal penalties of self-exposure. Indeed with AIDS reinforcing their pariah status, it appears that gays who might otherwise have come out completely—particularly among the younger generation—are now electing to dangle no more than a hand or a foot outside the closet. Because these gays go unrecognized, their homo-hating straight acquaintances may never be desensitized, jammed or converted.

All this means that the long-term strategy of Everyone Comes Out must be supplemented and prepped by a media campaign which will help in several ways. For starters, it will go some distance in compensating for the public's lack of direct personal contact with openly homosexual Americans. After 'meeting' enough likable gays on television, Jane Doe may begin to feel she knows gays as a group, even if no has ever introduced himself to her personally. Although it operates less quickly and effectively to thwart bigotry than does a personal confrontation with a gay loved one, familiarization with gays through the media nonetheless prepares the public for the gradual desensitization, jamming and conversion that will take place during our community's slow motion coming-out party.

Furthermore, carefully crafted, repeatedly displayed mass-media images of gays could conceivably do even more to reverse negative stereotypes than could the incremental coming-out of one person to another. One of the peculiarities of bigotry is that it's carriers have a tendency to exceptionalize the few minority friends they have, retaining their dislike of the minority group as a whole. They accomplish this neat mental contortion by perceiving their minority friends as somehow different from, unrepresentative of, the rest. ('Ah, yes, Herr Himmler—Rosenbloom's *nose* is all Jew, but his *heart* is pure Aryan!') Homohatred would find it harder to get away with such selective prejudice if a media campaign were to expose them to an unending series of 'positive' gay images.

Indeed, the wide range of favorably sanitized images that might be shown in the media could eventually have a more positive impact on the homosexual stereotype than could exposure to gay friends, since straights will otherwise generalize a suboptimal impression of gays from the idiosyncratic admixture of good and bad traits possessed by their one or two gay acquaintances. (One of the special advantages of a media campaign is that it can—and should—portray only the most *favorable* side of gays, thereby counterbalancing the already unfairly negative stereotype in the public's mind. When this is done, the picture labeled 'queer' is aggressively painted over; prior images of dirty drag queens or coarsened dykes are overlaid with pleasing new images of all-American and Miss American types.)

Lastly, the media campaign will work in tandem with the Everyone Comes Out strategy because *it is actually a catalyst to coming out.* As mass-media advertising legitimizes homosexuality, enhancing public receptiveness and sensitivity, the balance between the costs and benefits of coming out will shift decisively toward the latter, prompting more and more gays to declare themselves. A media campaign, then, becomes an iron pickax driving at a widening crack in the dam of gay secrecy until, sooner or later, everybody comes rushing forth. The sooner, the better.

Fourth Strategy: Political Conspiracies.

As most activists see it, there are two different avenues to gay liberation: Education (i.e., propaganda) and Politics. The dissemination of propaganda is enormously expensive and difficult, however, so little has been done to date. Instead, activists have concentrated their efforts on politics, meaning efforts to secure gay rights by conspiring with liberal elite's within the legal and legislative systems.

Gay activists first tried to manipulate the American judicial system via the Bill of Rights but, as noted in an earlier chapter, most courts have provided cold comfort, especially recently. Many activists turned, therefore, to the tactic of urgent whispering into the ears of liberal and moderate public servants at all levels of government. Given the generally conservative climate of recent years, our lobbyists have worked extra hard to present themselves as terribly polite, dignified, and respectful ladies and gentlemen; they have had to cut their suit to fit the available political cloth—a suit that is tailored with the utmost discretion and dressed to the right. The goal here has been to forge a little *entente* or conspiracy with the power elite, to jump ahead of public sentiment or ignore it altogether.

Sometimes the tactic works: many executive orders (which side-step the democratic process) and ordinances passed by city councils now protect certain limited civil rights for gays in selected cities. Many of these victories constitute political payoffs by elected officials whose candidacy the organized gay community has supported, and demonstrate both our electoral muscle and savvy back room politicking.

Yet the scheme to build elite conspiracies often proves impractical in the short run and imprudent if the long run. In the short run, politicians must be responsive to public sentiment of sensational issues if they value their careers. A sympathetic straight politico can be a co-conspirator, perhaps, but only up to a point, after which he is unreliable and immobilized: one of his feet is nailed to the floor. (No wonder gays find themselves being danced around in circles.)

In the long run, even if a conspiracy is formed and some legislative deal is struck, the agreement is built on beach sand so long as the public is left out of the bargain. Time and again, religious conservatives have washed away our gains with a frothy tide of public out-cry and backlash. The classic example was cited in Chapter 1: after their mayor had, in 1984, slipped a clause protecting gay government employees into the city's antidiscrimination ordinance, a referendum was called and Houston's more reactionary citizens were mobilized to defeat the clause by a four-to-one margin. (This lopsided plebiscite didn't necessarily reflect the general public's attitudes: the conservative fringe mobbed the voting booths, while many moderates stayed home. But this often happens in politics, especially on the gay issue where, as Yeats would say, "the best lack all conviction, while the worst are full of pas-sionate intensity.")

The solution is not for activists to abandon Politics for Education, of course. All things considered, legal and political efforts have come along slowly but surely—at least until AIDS threw the brakes. Yet, with the first gust of direct opposition, elite conspiracies blow apart like a house of cards, unless fortified by a significant shift in public attitudes. Like the other partial solutions discussed above, our political success could be greatly advanced by a media campaign conducted prior to, or simultaneously with, political initiatives.

The Strategy Of 'Waging Peace': Eight Practical Principles For The Persuasion Of Straights

Those who have supreme skill use strategy to bend others without coming to conflict.
—Sun Tzu, The Art of War

After gleefully pitching stones at other strategies (always an invigorating aerobic exer-cise), it's time to examine the recommended alternative in detail. Any effective media cam-paign to 'educate' straights must be guided by what we now know about the origins and workings of homohatred.

Generally speaking, the most effective propaganda for our cause must succeed in doing three things at once.

- Employ images that desensitize, jam, and/or convert bigots on an emotional level. This is, by far, the most important task.
- Challenge homohating beliefs and actions on a (not too) intellectual level. Remember, the rational message serves to camouflage our underlying emotional appeal, even as it pares away the surrounding latticework of beliefs that rationalize bigotry.
- Gain access to the kinds of public media that would automatically confer legitimacy upon these messages and, therefore, upon their gay sponsors. To be accepted by the most prestigious media, such as network TV, our messages themselves will have to be—at least initially—both subtle in purpose and crafty in construction.

Guided by these several objectives, we offer eight practical principles for the persuasion of straights via the mass media.

Principle 1. Don't Just Express Yourself: Communicate!

Although gay activists regularly confuse the two, self-expression and communication are different process motivated by different objectives. The first can be done in isolation, like singing in the shower—*sans* audience—whereas the second cannot. Self-expression is usu-ally its own reward, but communication is not rewarding unless one has 'reached' (i.e., per-suaded or moved) the listener.

To date, most public acts by the gay community have accomplished self-expression without communication (at least, without communication to the general public). These acts, ranging from modes of dress to mass demonstrations, have typically been enacted for the sake of self-affirmation, an effort to cast off shame by standing tall in the crowd and crowing, 'I gotta be me: either accept me as I am, or to hell with you.' (To say this in a spectacular way, as you know, certain gay men who would not otherwise be caught dead out of doors without their Brooks Brothers sack suits, metamorphose into bespangled drag queens one day each year and sashay through town in gay pride marches.) It may be psychologically liberating and therefore healthy for some *individuals* to do things of this sort. But, you must always remember, what is healthy for the individual isn't necessarily healthy for his community. Don't mistake these acts of self-expression for public outreach.

Genuine pubic outreach requires careful communication. If it helps, think of yourself as an explorer cautiously approaching a spear-wielding tribe of suspicious, belligerent natives in New Guinea. Suddenly you're caught in a deadly game of sheer strategy, in which, as political economist Thomas Schelling defines it, "the best course of action for each player depends on what the other players do." The natives are debating whether to treat you as a dinner guest or as a dinner. Somehow, you must win them over—*quickly*. This is no time to burst out singing 'I gotta be me.' Each word, each gesture, is watched, stereotyped, interpreted by them *in native terms*. You must help them relate to you and your humanity, to recognize that you and they share many good things in common, and that they can like and accept you on their own terms. (Rest assured, they won't go to the trouble of accepting you on your terms.) To win them over will require your finest skills at communication.

Communication, then, not self-expression, is the basis of a mass media campaign. To achieve it, every public message in the campaign should be the direct result of gays having put themselves in the public's binding high-button shoes and asked: if I were straight and felt the hostility most straights feel toward gays, *what would it take to get me to change my antigay feelings?* In other words, don't start by deciding what you most ardently want to tell straights: start by determining what they most *need* to hear from you.

An essential corollary of this communication rule is that *straights must be helped to believe that you and they speak the same language.* They must become convinced that, despite a key difference—sexual orientation—you and they nevertheless share enough ideas and values so that dialogue can proceed in a meaningful and fruitful way. Straights won't even stop to listen to your message unless reassured by certain obvious surface cues—dressing and speaking like them, for example—that you and they transmit on the same wavelength.

Principle 2. Seek Ye Not The Saved Nor The Damned: Appeal To The Skeptics

Once gays are ready and willing to communicate, the next question is: with whom? Our media strategists must know their target audiences; know which are ripe for persuasion, which not. On gay rights, the public is of several minds. There are, in this sense, several different publics to consider, each comprising, very roughly, one third of the populace.

As noted during our field trip to straight America, at one end of the spectrum there is already a wing—perhaps 25-30% of the public (including most gays)—that tells pollsters it doesn't seriously disapprove of homosexuality per se and is ready to defend equal treatment of gays. At the other extreme prowl the denizens of bigotry's darkest realm—say, 30-35% of the citizenry—so vehemently opposed to homosexuality that they would not permit one of its adherents to utter a single word in their community. Between our professed friends and our implacable foes—between the saved and the damned (or damnable)—are found the ambivalent remainder (35-45%), those who are basically skeptical about homosexuality but unwilling to nail gays to the wall.

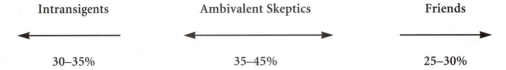

Intransigents	Ambivalent Skeptics	Friends
30–35%	35–45%	25–30%

Toward which audience, then, should gay media efforts be directed? Should we seek to protect ourselves by going after our most dangerous persecutors and taming them? Or should we merely preach to our own choir of supporters, as political advertising textbooks recommend, on the promise that you can only inflame the opinions people already hold, not change those opinions?

In our view, the campaign shouldn't set out to do either. It would make little headway against Intrasigents, for whom homohatred serves essential emotional functions. Some Intransigents fight desperately to suppress their own homosexual proclivities; others, for complicated reasons, feel compelled to adhere rigidly to an authoritarian belief structure (e.g., an orthodox religion) that condemns homosexuality. Our primary objective regarding diehard homohaters of this sort is to cow and *silence* them as far as possible, not to convert or even desensitize them.

As for our handful of Friends, they must be agitated and mobilized for our cause. But this should not be the primary goal of a national media campaign, for two reasons. First, such a minority can accomplish little while it remains steadfastly opposed by three fourths of the citizenry. Second, our supporters will receive ample encouragement and reinforcement from *whatever* campaign we might undertake to reach the rest of the nation.

We conclude, therefore, that Ambivalent Skeptics are our most promising target. If we can win them over, produce a major realignment solidly in favor of gay rights, the Intransigents (like the racists twenty years ago) will eventually be effectively silenced by both law and polite society. Our Friends, on the other hand, will be emboldened to support our interests more aggressively.

Now, Ambivalent Skeptics are, themselves, anything but homogeneous. They number, on the one hand, those more or *less passively negative* about homosexuality, who display automatic, unthinking opposition without getting very worked up over the subject. They also include citizens more *ambivalently positive*, who have strong convictions in favor of civil fights for all, but a weak stomach when it comes to the issue of homosexuality (rather like gourmets who profess a love of shellfish but cannot bear the look of oysters).

Every Skeptic is a candidate for desensitization. It may turn out however, that passive negatives can be reached *only* by desensitization (further debating those who already don't care much either way); whereas ambivalent-positives (those already emotionally torn) may respond more favorably to jamming and conversion techniques, in addition to desensitization. If this reasoning is correct, then we can assign different propaganda objectives to specific target segments of the population. Mind you, all these objectives could be achieved by a campaign focused on Ambivalent Skeptics:

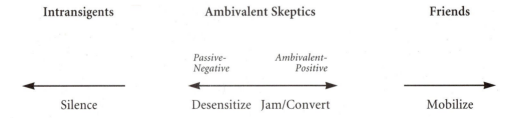

Intransigents	Ambivalent Skeptics		Friends
	Passive-Negative	*Ambivalent-Positive*	
Silence	Desensitize	Jam/Convert	Mobilize

Principle 3. Keep Talking

The mind of the bigot is like the pupil of the eye:
the more light you pour on it, the more it will contract.
—O.W. Holmes, Jr.

The third principle is our recipe for desensitizing Ambivalent Skeptics; that is, for helping straights view homosexuality with neutrality rather than keen hostility. At least at the outset, we seek desensitization *and nothing more*. You can forget about trying right up front to persuade folks that homosexuality is a *good* thing. But if you can get them to think it is just *another* thing—meriting no more than a shrug of the shoulders—then your battle for legal and social rights is virtually won.

Application of the keep talking principle can get people to the shoulder-shrug stage. The free and frequent discussion of gay rights by a variety of persons in a variety of places give the impression that homosexuality is commonplace. That impression is essential, because, as noted in the previous chapter, the acceptability of any new behavior ultimately hinges on the proportion of one's fellows accepting or doing it. One may be offended by its novelty at first. Many, in decades past, were initially scandalized by goldfish swallowing, high hemlines, premarital sex, and "streaking." But as long as the behavior remains popular and Joe Sixpack feels neither physically nor financially threatened by it (and the gay lifestyle posed little threat in either regard until AIDS came along), he soon gets used to it, and life goes on. The conservative may still shake his head and think, "People are crazy these days," but in time his objections will become more reflective, more philosophical, less emotional.

The fastest way to convince straights that homosexuality is commonplace is to get a lot of people talking about the subject in a neutral supportive way. Open, frank talk makes gayness seem less furtive, alien, and sinful more aboveboard. Constant talk builds the impression that public opinion is at least divided on the subject, and that a sizable block—the most modern, up-to-date citizens—accept or even practice homosexuality. Though risky (because it can keenly arouse, and thereby reinforce, the homohatred ingrained in listeners), even serious debate between opponents and defenders can serve the purpose of desensitization so long as appealing gays are front and center to make their own pitch. The main thing is to *talk about gayness until the issue becomes thoroughly tiresome.*

And when we say *talk* about homosexuality, we mean just that. In the early stages of the campaign, the public should not be shocked and repelled by premature exposure to homosexual behavior itself. Instead, the imagery of sex per se should be down played, and issues of gay rights reduced, as far as possible, to an abstract social question. As it happens, the AIDS epidemic—ever a curse and boon for the gay movement—provides ample opportunity to emphasize the civil rights/discrimination side of things, but unfortunately it also permits our enemies to draw attention to gay sex habits that provoke public revulsion.

Would a campaign of open, sustained talk about gay issues be enough? Could talk alone, for example, quell the religious heebie-jeebies felt by many Ambivalent Skeptics and played upon by Intransigents? Not completely, and this remains a grave tactical difficulty. While public opinion is one important source of mainstream values, religious training in childhood is another. Yet two things *can* be done to confound the homohatred of the moderated religious.

First, gays can use talk to muddy the moral waters, that is, to undercut the rationalizations that 'justify' religious bigotry and to jam some of its psychic rewards. This entails publicizing support by moderate churches and raising serious theological objectionable conservative biblical teachings. It also means exposing the inconsistency and hatred underlying antigay doctrines. Conservative churches, which pay as much lip service to Christian charity as anybody else, are rendered particularly vulnerable by their callous hypocrisy regarding AIDS sufferers.

Second, gays can undermine the moral authority of homohating churches over less fervent adherents by portraying such institutions as antiquated backwaters, badly out of step with the times and with the latest findings of psychology. Against the atavistic tug of Old Time Religion one must set the mightier pull of Science and Public Opinion (the shield and sword of that cursed "secular humanism"). Such an "unholy" alliance has already worked well in America against churches, on such topics as divorce and abortion. With enough open talk about the prevalence and acceptability of homosexuality, that alliance can work for gays.

Where we talk is critical. We'll discuss specific media tactics shortly. It suffices here to recall that the visual media—television, films, magazines—are the most powerful image makers in Western civilization. For example, in the average American household, the TV screen radiates its embracing bluish glow for more than fifty hours every week, bringing films, sitcoms, talk shows, and news reports right into the living room. These hours are a gateway into the private world of straights, through which a Trojan horse might be passed. For once, Marshall McLuhan is right: where desensitization is concerned, the medium *is* the message . . . of normalcy.

Principle 4. Keep The Message Focused: You're A Homosexual, Not A Whale

If desensitization is to work, it mustn't be weakened by admixture with superfluous issues that might further upset or distract ordinary Americans. So when we say "talk about homosexuality," we mean talk about gay rights issues and nothing more: be single-minded. The gay community must explode a multitude of nasty stereotypes of itself, and must accomplish this Augean task with a painfully limited fund of dollars and credibility. We literally cannot afford to introduce additional prejudices into the picture by allying our movement with that of every other righteous cause in the political universe.

Yet this is exactly what our leaders have long done. Those drawn to gay activism seem inclined to regard themselves less as hard-boiled lobbyists for a particular interest group than as philosophical crusaders for a grand panoptic program to inaugurate the Age of Aquarius—with harmony and understanding for all. In this, the American gay movement shows its 1969 vintage and its predilection for wishful thinking all too plainly. (Or perhaps its schemes for radical social reform trace their inspiration back to the lesbian dual agenda, mixing gay rights with desiderata for the root-and-branch transformation of our male chauvinist society.)

Typically, Wayne Olson exhorts fellow activists, in a 1986 *Christopher Street* article, with the following bad advice:

Show throughout [public debates on gay rights] that you identify with all those who are persecuted unjustly, that you advocate rights for all human beings, not just homosexuals. Talk about racism, sexism, militarism, poverty, and all the conditions that oppress the unempowered. A victory for any oppressed group is a victory for all.

Because of such thinking, any and all fellow outcasts are embraced as political partners, and the gay community has filled its dance card with a 'rainbow coalition' of society's underdogs and benevolent but offbeat causes. Our activists have waltzed from one political issue to the next, publicly committing our movement to solidarity with the Sandinistas, animal protection leagues, migrant farm worker, Trotskyite revolutionaries, the Fat Person Liberation Front, the anti-apartheid movement, the antinuclear movement, and the Greenpeace Save-the-Whales campaign, to name a few. They speak at our rallies, we speak at their rallies (though less frequently), and everyone has a delightfully militant time.

While some of these causes may indeed be noble, not one of them is directly concerned with the issue of homosexuality. Not one of them is even a "natural ally" of gays, if by that term you meant "someone who is happy we [gays] are here, rather than someone who is unhappy at the way we are being treated." As Michael Denneny has rightly perceived, "We have no natural allies and therefore cannot rely on the assistance of any group. We have only tactical allies—people who do not want barbarous things done to us because they fear the same thing may someday be done to them".

Not surprisingly, our motley little crew of foul-weather friends appreciates our support but is generally restrained in reciprocation on behalf of the gay cause. In any case, none of them has much clout or good will with the American public. On the contrary, even though gays constitute a far larger and broader constituency than any of these, association with other marginal groups only reinforces the mainstream's suspicion that gays are another microfaction on the lunatic fringe.

How can straights be expected to take gay rights seriously when gay activists seem just as passionately devoted to a bulging grab-bag of utterly extraneous causes as they are to their own? What are straights to make of the following cobbled together chants, all shouted vigorously during the 1988 Gay Pride March in New York City? "Cruise men, not missiles"; "The people fight back from Stonewall to South Africa"; "Gays yes, Contras no"; "Gay lib through atheist lib"; "End Racism, sexism, and war/Money for aids/ We won't take no more"; "First dogs and monkeys too/Next time they'll cut into you." From what we could see, straight on-lookers at the march were curiously bewildered, bemused, or annoyed by these *non sequitur* protests. One of them reacted with eloquent simplicity: "I don't get it." Clearly, while it might be comforting and kind to link arms with the wider losers' circle in American society, we do little thereby to advance our cause.

As a practical rule of thumb, then, gay organizations (and their media strategists) are advised to think twice about public association with any group that is:
- generally unpopular;
- smaller than the gay community; and /or
- concerned with issues remote from, and more ephemeral than, those that must permanently concern the gay community.

Because our movement must first grow stronger before it can help its still weaker friends, we recommend a rule for public alliance that is tough and selfish. But that rule doesn't favor insularity: the movement should eagerly ally itself with large, mainstream groups that can actually advance our interests (e.g., the Democratic party, the National Organization for Women, or the Presbyterian Church). But even then, we should demand to see some major public demonstration of their commitment to our cause before we rush to commit to theirs.

Unless and until such bold alliances materialize, however, the bottom line remains: be *focused* in your efforts to reach the public via mass media. In the minds of straights, we must be gay people, not leftists or whales. So talk, talk, talk about gay rights, and leave it at that. (Feel free to agitate for any other cause you like, of course, but do so while wearing another hat.) And downplay any support from outgroups whose very names are likely to arouse suspicion and antipathy. Otherwise, desensitization will be all the harder to achieve.

Principle 5. Portray Gays As Victims Of Circumstance And Oppression, Not As Aggressive Challengers

In any campaign to win over the public, gays must be portrayed as victims in need of protection so that straights will be inclined by reflex to adopt the role of protector. If gays present themselves instead, as a strong and arrogant tribe promoting a defiantly non-conformist lifestyle, they are more likely to be seen as a public menace that warrants resistance and oppression. For that reason we must forego the temptation to strut our gay pride publicly to such an extent that we undermine our victim image. And we must walk the fine line between impressing straights with our great numbers, on the one hand, and igniting their hostile paranoia—they're all around us!—on the other.

The purpose of victim imagery is to make straights feel very uncomfortable; that is, to jam with shame the self-righteous pride that would ordinarily accompany and reward their antigay belligerence, and to lay groundwork for the process of conversion by helping straights identify with gays and sympathize with their underdog status.

To this end, an effective media campaign would make use of symbols and spokespersons that reduce the straight majority's sense of threat and induce it to lower its guard. Mr. And Mrs. Public must be given no extra excuses to say, "They are not like us (so they deserve to be punished)." Persons featured in the media campaign should be wholesome and admirable by straight standards, and completely unexceptional in appearance; in a word they should be indistinguishable form the straights we'd like to reach.

In practical terms, this means that cocky mustachioed leather men, drag queens, and bull dykes would not appear in gay commercials and other public presentations. Conventional young people, middle-aged women, and older folks of all races would be featured, not to mention the parents and straight friends of gays.

One could also argue that lesbians should be featured more prominently than gay men in the early stages of the media campaign. Straights generally have fewer and cloudy preconceptions about lesbians and may feel less hostile toward them. And *as women* (generally seen as less threatening and more vulnerable than men), lesbians may be more credible objects of sympathy.

It cannot go without saying, incidentally, that groups on the farthest margins of acceptability, such as NAMBLA, must play no part at all in such a campaign. Suspected child molesters will never look like victims.

Now, two different messages about the Gay Victim are worth communicating. First, the public should be persuaded that gays are *victims of circumstance*, that they no more chose their sexual orientation than they did, say, their height, skin color, talents, or limitations. (We argue that, for all practical purposes, gays should be considered to have been *born gay*—even though sexual orientation, for most humans, seems to be the product of a complex interaction between innate predisposition's and environmental factors during childhood and early adolescence.) To suggest in public that homosexuality might be *chosen* is to open the can of worms labeled "moral choice and sin" and give the religious intransigents a stick to beat us with. Straights must be taught that it is as natural for some persons to be homosexual as it is for others to be heterosexual: wickedness and seduction have nothing to do with it. *And since no choice is involved, gayness can be no more blameworthy than straightness.* In fact, it is simply a matter of the odds—one in ten—as to who turns out gay, and straight. Each heterosexual must be led to realize that he might easily have been born homosexual himself.

Second, gays should be portrayed as *victims of prejudice*. Straights don't fully realize the suffering they bring upon gays, and must be shown: graphic pictures of brutalized gays, dramatizations of job and housing insecurity, loss of child custody, public humiliation, etc. (For the complete and dismal list, see our Agenda for Change at the end of Chapter 1.)

Bear in mind that these arguments are no more than an appeal to rationality and as such would scarcely make a dent in an emotional condition like homohatred. What arguments can do, however, is suspend the straight viewer's rush to judgment just long enough to slip in front of her visual images that either arouse shame over her homohatred or else build favorable emotions toward gays.

More than any other single element of our blueprint for a media campaign, this principle of Victim Imagery has been criticized by the gay community. Few have questioned whether it will have the desired effect on straights; we are convinced it will. But some are offended, even so, by the proposition that gays should be be portrayed as victims. They fear that this will make our community look weak, miserable, and self-hating, equating homosexuals with some dreadful disease that strikes fated "victims." If gays point out that they never chose to be gay, it is claimed, this implies they would rather not be gay, and so suggests that gays themselves view homosexuality as a bad thing. All very negative in the community's self-image.

We can only reply that gays indisputably *are* victims of circumstance, regardless of whether their leaders pretend otherwise. A victim of circumstance is someone thrust by events into a tough spot—like a black child who happens upon a gang of racists. This child has every reason to be proud of his identity but also has good cause to remind his persecutors that there is no sense of justice in condemning him for his skin color. The campaign can and should make this distinction clear.

It's nonsense to claim as some do, that a person who acknowledges himself in any way a victim thereby accepts that condition and *becomes* a victim; such is merely magical thinking. Nor is it true that straights will look down on gays more than they already do, simply because we have managed to arouse in them feelings of shame for past bigotry and a new protectiveness toward the gay community. This has not happened to the Jews, who have effectively leveraged widespread sympathy for themselves as past victims of circumstance. The plain fact is that the gay community like the Jewish, is a permanent minority: it is weak and must deploy the special powers of the weak, including the play for sympathy and tolerance. The arousal of protective instincts doesn't require that homosexuality be cast in a negative light.

Others worry that, by our techniques, gays will gain the world but lose their souls. They fear that victim imagery will mean that homosexuals, who have struggled so long to get beyond guilt and self-hatred, must now forego self-affirmation and smother their gay pride. After all, gay pride parades can be wonderfully positive exercises for their participants, even if their excesses disturb straight onlookers.

We recommend a compromise: *march, if you must, but don't parade.* Drop the Mardi Gras foolishness and assemble yourselves into a proud, dedicated legion of freedom fighters, like the civil rights marchers of the '60's. Such marches would certainly enable gay self-affirmation yet would be taken more seriously by straights. Don't expect too much, though.

For some critics, it isn't so much the idea of victim imagery that offends, but *whom* we will present as victims: all-American types so starchily conformist in appearance that they can barely bend their knees. Let alone stoop to fellatio. Some fear that a media campaign featuring only 'ordinary-looking' gays would disdainfully disenfranchise drag queens, bull dykes, and other exotic elements of the gay community. This is not our goal, and it is painful to think that such people might begin to feel like second-class members of their own outgroup.

Our ultimate objective is to expand straight tolerance so much that even gays who look unconventional can feel safe and accepted. But like it or not, by the very nature of the psychological mechanism, desensitization works gradually or not at all. For the moment, therefore, unconventional-looking gays are encouraged to live their lives as usual, but out of the limelight. Drag queens must understand that the gay stereotype is already heavily skewed in their direction, and that more balance should be achieved by leaning in the opposite direction for a while. In time, as hostilities subside and stereotypes weaken, we see no reason why more and more diversity should not be introduced into the projected image. This would be healthy for society as well as for gays.

Principle 6. Give Potential Protectors A Just Cause

The Waging Peace media campaign will reach straights on an emotional level, casting gays as society's victims and inviting straights to be their protectors. For this to work, however, we must make it easier for responsive straights to assert and explain their new protective feeling. Few straight women, and fewer straight men, will be bold enough to defend homosexuality per se. Most would rather attach their awakened protective impulse to some principle of justice or law, some general desire for consistent and fair treatment in society.

Thus, our campaign should not demand explicit support for homo*sexual* practices, but should instead take *antidiscrimination as* its theme. Fundamental freedoms, constitutional rights, due process and equal protection of laws, basic fairness and decency toward all of humanity—these should be the concerns brought to mind by our campaign.

It's especially important for the gay movement to hitch its cause to pre-existing standards of law and justice, because its straight supporters must have at hand a cogent reply to the moralistic arguments of it enemies. Homohaters cloak their emotional revulsion in the daunting robes of religious dogma, so defenders of gay rights must be ready to counter dogma with principle. Thrice armed is he who hath his quarrel just.

Principle 7. Make Gays Look Good

In order to make a Gay Victim sympathetic to straights, you have to portray him as Everyman. But an additional theme of the campaign will be more aggressive and upbeat. To confound bigoted stereotypes and hasten the conversion of straights, strongly favorable images of gays must be set before the public. The campaign should paint gay men and lesbians as *superior*—veritable pillars of society. Yes, yes, we know, this trick is so old it creaks. Other minorities have used it often, in ads that proudly exclaim, "Did you know that this Great Man was Thuringian (or whatever)?" But the message is vital for all those straights who still picture gays as "queer" losers—shadowy, lonesome, frail, drunken, suicidal, child-snatching misfits.

The honor roll of prominent gay or bisexual men and women is truly eye-popping. From Socrates to Eleanor Roosevelt, Tchaikovsky to Bessie Smith, Alexander the Great to Alexander Hamilton, and Leonardo da Vinci to Walt Whitman, the list of suspected 'inverts' is old hat to us but surprising news to heterosexual America. Famous historical figures are especially useful to us for two reasons: first, they are invariably dead as a doornail, hence in no position to deny the truth and sue for libel. Second, and more serious, the virtues and accomplishments that make these historic gay figures admirable cannot be gainsaid or dismissed by the public, since high school history textbooks have already set them in incontrovertible cement. By casting its violet spotlight on such revered heroes, in no time a skillful media campaign could have the gay community looking like the veritable fairy godmother to Western civilization.

Along the same line, our campaign should not overlook the Celebrity Endorsement. The celebrities in question can, of course, be either straight or gay (and alive, for a change), but must always be well liked and respected by the public. If homosexual, the celebrity jams homohatred by presenting a favorable gay image at odds with the stereotype. If straight, the spokesperson (who deserves the Medal of Valor) provides the public with an impressive role model of social tolerance to emulate. In either case, the psychological response among straight is the same, and lays the groundwork for conversion:

> *I like and admire Mr. Celeb;*
> *Mr. Celeb is queer and/or respects queers;*
> *so either I must stop liking and admiring Mr. Celeb, or else*
> *it must be all right for me to respect queers.*

Principle 8. Make Victimizers Look Bad

The real target here is not victimizers themselves but the homohatred that impels them. Understand this point clearly: while it will be a sheer delight to besmirch our tormentors, we cannot waste resources or media access on revenge alone (indeed the media will not *allow* us to do so). The objective is to make homohating beliefs and actions look so nasty that average Americans will want to dissociate themselves from them. This, of course is a variant on the process of jamming. We also intend, by the tactic, to make the very expression of homohatred so discreditable that even Intransigents will eventually be silenced in public much as rabid racists and anti-Semites are today.

The best way to make homohatred look bad is to vilify those who victimize gays. The public should be shown images of taunting homohaters whose associated traits and attitudes appall and anger Middle America. The images might include:

- Klansmen demanding that gays be slaughtered or castrated;
- Hysterical backwoods preachers, drooling with hate to a degree that looks both comical and deranged;
- menacing punks, thugs, and convicts who speak coolly about the 'fags' they have bashed or would like to bash;
- a tour of Nazi concentration camps where homosexuals were tortured and gassed.

In TV and print, images of victimizers can be combined with those of their gay victims by a method propagandists call the 'bracket technique'. For example, for several seconds an unctuous beady-eyed Southern preacher is shown pounding the pulpit in rage against 'those perverted, abominable creatures.' While his tirade continues over the soundtrack, the picture switches to heart-rending photos of badly beaten persons, or of gays who look decent, harmless, and likable; and then we cut back to the poisonous face of the preacher. The contrast speaks for itself. The effect is devastating.

The viewer will ordinarily recoil from these images of victimizers, thinking automatically: 'I don't like those maniacs, don't want to be like them, and would be ashamed if others thought I was like them. Surely I'm more compassionate and sophisticated, because I don't share their irrational hatred of gays.' Every time a viewer runs through this comparative self-appraisal, he reinforces a self-definition that consciously reflects homohatred and validated sympathy for gay victims. Exactly what we want.

A campaign to vilify victimizers will only enrage our most fervid enemies, of course. Yet the shoe surely fits, and we should make them try it on for size, with all America watching. Gay media strategists must, however, try to slide the slipper on very gradually. At least at the beginning, the broadcast media—which have not yet permitted gays even to say nice things about themselves on the air—certainly will not allow any direct attacks on archconservatives. On the other hand, they just might permit some mention of Nazi atrocities, the pink triangle as a symbol of victimization, and so forth. If so, the Nazi story alone will be a sufficient opening wedge into the vilification of our enemies. After all, who on earth would choose to be associated with the Nazis? (Argentina doesn't count.)

Summary: Strategic Principles For The Persuasion Of Straights

We have reviewed the range of public-outreach strategy commonly touted by gays. Like zealous prosecutors, we've rounded up all the usual suspects, studied their trial records, and concluded with disappointment that none of the most popular strategies can be promptly, effectively executed.

So, instead we propose our own strategy for a large-scale media campaign, whose objectives and reasoning are expressed in terms of eight practical principles for persuading straights:

1. Don't just express yourself: communicate!
2. Appeal to the Ambivalent Skeptics.
3. Keep talking about gayness.
4. Keep your message focused: the issue is homosexuality.
5. Portray gays as victims, not as aggressive challengers.
6. Give potential projectors a just cause.
7. Make gays look good.
8. Make victimizers look bad.

Do these strategic principles seem straightforward, even a bit bland? Perhaps, but just try—as we do in the next chapter—to develop p.r. events and TV commercials that obey all the rules and you'll see what a challenge they present. Any ten-year-old can balance a spinning plate on her finger; it takes a preternaturally clever Chinese acrobat to balance eight of them at once.

A SELF-POLICING SOCIAL CODE

Rules for Relations with Straights

I won't have sex in public places.
I won't make passes at straight acquaintances, or at strangers who might not be gay.
Wherever possible and sensible, I will come out—gracefully.
I will make an effort, when among straights, not to live down to gay stereotypes.
I won't talk gay sex and gay raunch in public.
If I'm a transvestite however glamorous I'll graciously decline invitations to model lingerie for "Oprah" or "Donahue."

Rules for Relations with Other Gays

I won't cheat on my lover—or with someone else's.
I'll encourage other gays to come out, but never expose them against their will.
Tested or otherwise, I'll practice safe sex.
I'll contribute money in meaningful amounts to the gay cause.
I will not speak scornfully or cruelly of another's age, looks, clothing, or social class in bars or elsewhere, lest I reveal my own insecurities.
When forced to reject a suitor, I will do so firmly but kindly.
I'll drop my search for Mr. Right and settle for what's realistic.
I won't reenact straight oppression by name-calling and shouting down gays whose opinions don't square with mine.

Rules for Relations with Yourself

I'll stop trying to be eighteen forever and act my age; I won't punish myself for being what I am.
I won't have more than two alcoholic drinks a day; I won't use street drugs at all.

I'll get a stable, productive job and become a member of the wider community
    beyond the gay ghetto.
I'll live for something meaningful beyond myself.
When confronted by real problems. I'll listen to common sense, not emotion.
I will not condone sexual practices I think harmful to individuals or to the community
    just because they're homosexual.
I'll start making some value judgments.

One of the most basic and intractable questions in lesbian and gay politics is that of what our differences from heterosexuals should mean for our political goals. Those who believe that we are "just like" heterosexuals except for what we do in private (and this group believes sex should be done in private) argue that we should strive for the same rights and benefits accorded to heterosexuals. Those who think that our sexual difference has produced distinctively different cultures or practices (and that this is a positive difference) paraphrase the feminist adage that "women who want to be equal to men lack ambition." This debate encompasses a range of issues, but it is perhaps most acute concerning the right to marry and the right or duty to serve in the military. The 1992 election, in which Bill Clinton promised to lift the ban on gays and lesbians in the military (a promise he did not keep), temporarily silenced debate on the military issue as people fought for a clear measure of equality. The failure of that struggle ironically reopens space for the debate to begin again. The marriage debate remains wide open.

The following articles present the debate over marriage. The promarriage piece is by Thomas B. Stoddard, an attorney who has been Executive Director of the Lambda Legal Defense and Education Fund and headed the Campaign for Military Service in 1993. The argument against marriage is presented by Paula Ettelbrick, an attorney and director of public policy for the National Center for Lesbian Rights.

GAY MARRIAGE

WHY GAY PEOPLE SHOULD SEEK THE RIGHT TO MARRY

from *Out/Look* (1989)

Thomas B. Stoddard

Even though, these days, few lesbians and gay men enter into marriages recognized by law, absolutely every gay person has an opinion on marriage as an "institution." (The word "institution" brings to mind, perhaps appropriately, museums.) After all, we all know quite a bit about the subject. Most of us grew up in marital households. Virtually all of us, regardless of race, creed, gender, and culture, have received lectures on the propriety, if not the sanctity, of marriage—which usually suggests that those who choose not to marry are both unhappy and unhealthy. We all have been witnesses, willing or not, to a lifelong parade of other people's marriages, from Uncle Harry and Aunt Bernice to the Prince and Princess of Wales. And at one point or another, some nosy relative has inevitably inquired of every gay person when he or she will finally "tie the knot" (an intriguing and probably apt cliché).

I must confess at the outset that I am no fan of the "institution" of marriage as currently constructed and practiced. I may simply be unlucky, but I have seen preciously few marriages over the course of my forty years that invite admiration and emulation. All too often, marriage appears to petrify rather than satisfy and enrich, even for couples in their twenties and thirties who have had a chance to learn the lessons of feminism. Almost inevitably, the partners seem to fall into a "husband" role and a "wife" role, with such latter-day modifications as the wife who works in addition to raising the children and managing the household.

Let me be blunt: in its traditional form, marriage has been oppressive, especially (although not entirely) to women. Indeed, until the middle of the last century, marriage was, at its legal and social essence, an extension of the husband and his paternal family. Under the English common law, wives were among the husband's "chattel"—personal property—and could not, among other things, hold property in their own names. The common law crime of adultery demonstrates the unequal treatment accorded to husbands and wives: while a woman who slept with a man who wasn't her husband committed adultery, a man who slept with a woman not his wife committed fornication. A man was legally incapable of committing adultery, except as an accomplice to an errant wife. The underlying offense of adultery was not the sexual betrayal of one partner by the other, but the wife's engaging in conduct capable of tainting the husband's bloodlines. (I swear on my *Black's Law Dictionary* that I have not made this up!)

Nevertheless, despite the oppressive nature of marriage historically, and in spite of the general absence of edifying examples of modern heterosexual marriage, I believe very strongly that every lesbian and gay man should have the right to marry the same-sex partner of his or her choice, and that the gay rights movement should aggressively seek full legal recognition for same-sex marriages. To those who might not agree, I respectfully offer three explanations, one practical, one political, and one philosophical.

The Practical Explanation

The legal status of marriage rewards the two individuals who travel to the altar (or its secular equivalent) with substantial economic and practical advantages. Married couples may reduce their tax liability by filing a joint return. They are entitled to special government benefits, such as those given surviving spouses and dependents through the Social Security program. They can inherit from one another even when there is no will. They are immune from subpoenas requiring testimony against the other spouse. And marriage to an American citizen gives a foreigner a right to residency in the United States.

Other advantages have arisen not by law but by custom. Most employers offer health insurance to their employees, and many will include an employee's spouse in the benefits package, usually at the employer's expense. Virtually no employer will include a partner who is not married to an employee, whether of the same sex or not. Indeed, very few insurance companies even offer the possibility of a group health plan covering "domestic partners" who are not married to one another. Two years ago, I tried to find such a policy for Lambda, and discovered that not one insurance company authorized to do business in New York—the second-largest state in the country with more than 17 million residents—would accommodate us. (Lambda has tried to make do by paying for individual insurance policies for the same-sex partners of its employees who otherwise would go uninsured but these individual policies are usually narrower in scope than group policies, often require applicants to furnish individual medical information not required under most group plans, and are typically much more expensive per person.)

In short, the law generally presumes in favor of every marital relationship, and acts to preserve and foster it, and to enhance the rights of the individuals who enter into it. It is usually possible, with enough money and the right advice, to replicate some of the benefits conferred by the legal status of marriage through the use of documents like wills and power of attorney forms, but that protection will inevitably, under current circumstances, be incomplete.

The law (as I suspect will come as no surprise to the readers of this journal) still looks upon lesbians and gay men with suspicion, and this suspicion casts a shadow over the documents they execute in recognition of a same-sex relationship. If a lesbian leaves property to her lover, her will may be invalidated on the grounds that it was executed under the "undue influence" of the would-be beneficiary. A property agreement may be denied validity because the underlying relationship is "meretricious"—akin to prostitution. (Astonishingly, until the mid-seventies, the law throughout the United States deemed "meretricious" virtually *any* formal economic arrangement between two people not married to one another, on the theory that an exchange of property between them was probably payment for sexual services; the Supreme Court of California helped unravel this quaint legal fantasy in its 1976 ruling in the first famous "palimony" case, *Marvin v. Marvin.*) The law has progressed considerably beyond the uniformly oppressive state of affairs before 1969, but it is still far from enthusiastic about gay people and their relationships—to put it mildly.

Moreover, there are some barriers one simply cannot transcend outside of a formal marriage. When the Internal Revenue Code or the Immigration and Naturalization Act say "married," they mean "married" by definition of state statute. When the employer's group health plan says "spouse," it means "spouse" in the eyes of the law, not the eyes of the loving couple.

But there is another drawback. Couples seeking to protect their relationship through wills and other documents need knowledge, determination and—most importantly—money. No money, no lawyer. And no lawyer, no protection. Those who lack the sophistication or the wherewithal to retain a lawyer are simply stuck in most circumstances. Extending the right to marry to gay couples would assure that those at the bottom of the economic ladder have a chance to secure their relationship rights, too.

The Political Explanation

The claim that gay couples ought to be able to marry is not a new one. In the seventies, same-sex couples in three states—Minnesota, Kentucky and Washington—brought constitutional challenges to the marriage statutes, and in all three instances they failed. In each of the three, the court offered two basic justifications for limiting marriage to male-female couples: history and procreation. Witness this passage from the Supreme Court of Minnesota's 1971 opinion in *Baker v. Nelson:* "The institution of marriage as a union of man and woman, uniquely involving the procreation and rearing of children within a family, is as old as the book of Genesis.... This historic institution manifestly is more deeply founded than the asserted contemporary concept of marriage and societal interests for which petitioners contend."

Today no American jurisdiction recognizes the right of two women or two men to marry one another, although several nations in Northern Europe do. Even more telling, until earlier this year, there was little discussion within the gay rights movement about whether such a right should exist. As far as I can tell, no gay organization of any size, local or national, has yet declared the right to marry as one of its goals.

With all due respect to my colleagues and friends who take a different view, I believe it is time to renew the effort to overturn the existing marriage laws, and to do so in earnest, with a commitment of money and energy, through both the courts and the state legislatures. I am not naive about the likelihood of imminent victory. There is none. Nonetheless—and here I will not mince words—I would like to see the issue rise to the top of the agenda of every gay organization, including my own (although that judgment is hardly mine alone).

Why give it such prominence? Why devote resources to such a distant goal? Because marriage is, I believe, the political issue that most fully tests the dedication of people who are *not* gay to full equality for gay people, and also the issue most likely to lead ultimately to a world free from discrimination against lesbians and gay men.

Marriage is much more than a relationship sanctioned by law. It is the centerpiece of our entire social structure, the core of the traditional notion of "family." Even in its present tarnished state, the marital relationship inspires sentiments suggesting that it is something almost suprahuman. The Supreme Court, in striking down an anti-contraception statute in 1965, called marriage "noble" and "intimate to the degree of being sacred." The Roman Catholic Church and the Moral Majority would go—and have gone—considerably further.

Lesbians and gay men are now denied entry to this "noble" and "sacred" institution. The implicit message is this: two men or two women are incapable of achieving such an exalted domestic state. Gay relationships are somehow less significant, less valuable. Such relationships may, from time to time and from couple to couple, give the appearance of a marriage, but they can never be of the same quality or importance.

I resent—indeed, I loathe—that conception of same-sex relationships. And I am convinced that ultimately the only way to overturn it is to remove the barrier to marriage that now limits the freedom of every gay man and lesbian.

That is not to deny the value of "domestic partnership" ordinances, statutes that prohibit discrimination based on "marital status," and other legal advances that can enhance the rights (as well as the dignity) of gay couples. Without question, such advances move us further along the path to equality. But their value can only be partial. (The recently enacted San Francisco "domestic partnership" ordinance, for example, will have practical value only for gay people who happen to be employed by the City of San Francisco and want to include their non-marital spouses in part of the city's fringe benefit package; the vast majority of gay San Franciscans—those employed by someone other than the city—have only a symbolic victory to savor.) Measures of this kind can never assure full equality. Gay relationships will continue to be accorded a subsidiary status until the day that gay couples have *exactly* the same rights as their heterosexual counterparts. To my mind, that means either that the right to marry be extended to us, or that marriage be abolished in its present form for all couples, presumably to be replaced by some new legal entity—an unlikely alternative.

The Philosophical Explanation

I confessed at the outset that I personally found marriage in its present avatar rather, well, unattractive. Nonetheless, even from a philosophical perspective, I believe the right to marry should become a stated goal of the gay rights movement.

First, and most basically, the issue is not the desirability of marriage, but rather the desirability of the *right* to marry. That I think two lesbians or two gay men should be entitled to a marriage license does not mean that I think all gay people should find appropriate partners and exercise the right, should it eventually exist. I actually rather doubt that I, myself, would want to marry, even though I share a household with another man who is exceedingly dear to me. There are others who feel differently, for economic, symbolic, or romantic reasons. They should, to my mind, unquestionably have the opportunity to marry if they wish and otherwise meet the requirements of the state (like being old enough).

Furthermore, marriage may be unattractive and even oppressive as it is currently structured and practiced, but enlarging the concept to embrace same-sex couples would necessarily transform it into something new. If two women can marry, or two men, marriage—even for heterosexuals—need not be a union of a "husband" and a "wife." Extending the right to marry to gay people—that is, abolishing the traditional gender requirements of marriage—can be one of the means, perhaps the principal one, through which the institution divests itself of the sexist trappings of the past.

Some of my colleagues disagree with me. I welcome their thoughts and the debates and discussions our different perspectives will trigger. The movement for equality for lesbians and gay men can only be enriched through this collective exploration of the question of marriage. But I do believe many thousands of gay people want the right to marry. And I think, too, they will earn that right for themselves sooner than most of us imagine.

SINCE WHEN IS MARRIAGE A PATH TO LIBERATION?
from *Out/Look* (1989)

Paula L. Ettelbrick

"Marriage is a great institution . . . if you like living in institutions," according to a bit of T-shirt philosophy I saw recently. Certainly, marriage is an institution. It is one of the most venerable, impenetrable institutions in modern society. Marriage provides the ultimate form of acceptance for personal intimate relationships in our society, and gives those who marry an insider status of the most powerful kind.

Steeped in a patriarchal system that looks to ownership, property, and dominance of men over women as its basis, the institution of marriage long has been the focus of radical feminist revulsion. Marriage defines certain relationships as more valid than all others. Lesbian and gay relationships, being neither legally sanctioned or commingled by blood, are always at the bottom of the heap of social acceptance and importance.

Given the imprimatur of social and personal approval which marriage provides, it is not surprising that some lesbians and gay men among us would look to legal marriage for self-affirmation. After all, those who marry can be instantaneously transformed from "outsiders" to "insiders," and we have a desperate need to become insiders.

It could make us feel OK about ourselves, perhaps even relieve some of the internalized homophobia that we all know so well. Society will then celebrate the birth of our children and mourn the death of our spouses. It would be easier to get health insurance for our spouses, family memberships to the local museum, and a right to inherit our spouse's cherished collection of lesbian mystery novels even if she failed to draft a will. Never again would we have to go to a family reunion and debate about the correct term for introducing our lover/partner/significant other to Aunt Flora. Everything would be quite easy and very nice.

So why does this unlikely event so deeply disturb me? For two major reasons. First, marriage will not liberate us as lesbians and gay men. In fact, it will constrain us, make us more invisible, force our assimilation into the mainstream, and undermine the goals of gay liberation. Second, attaining the right to marry will not transform our society from one that makes narrow, but dramatic, distinctions between those who are married and those who are not married to one that respects and encourages choice of relationships and family diversity. Marriage runs contrary to two of the primary goals of the lesbian and gay movement: the affirmation of gay identity and culture; and the validation of many forms of relationships.

When analyzed from the standpoint of civil rights, certainly lesbians and gay men should have a right to marry. But obtaining a right does not always result in justice. White male firefighters in Birmingham, Alabama have been fighting for their "rights" to retain their jobs by overturning the city's affirmative action guidelines. If their "rights" prevail, the courts will have failed in rendering justice. The "right" fought for by the white male firefighters, as well as those who advocate strongly for the "rights" to legal marriage for gay people, will result, at best, in limited or narrowed "justice" for those closest to power at the expense of those who have been historically marginalized.

The fight for justice has as its goal the realignment of power imbalances among individuals and classes of people in society. A pure "rights" analysis often fails to incorporate a broader understanding of the underlying inequities that operate to deny justice to a fuller range of people and groups. In setting our priorities as a community, we must combine the concept of both rights and justice. At this point in time, making legal marriage for lesbian and gay couples a priority would set an agenda of gaining rights for a few, but would do nothing to correct the power imbalances between those who are married (whether gay of straight) and those who are not. Thus, justice would not be gained.

Justice for gay men and lesbians will be achieved only when we are accepted and supported in this society *despite* our differences from the dominant culture and the choices we make regarding our relationships. Being queer is more than setting up house, sleeping with a person of the same gender, and seeking state approval for doing so. It is an identity, a culture with many variations. It is a way of dealing with the world by diminishing the constraints of gender roles which have for so long kept women and gay people oppressed and invisible. Being queer means pushing the parameters of sex, sexuality, and family, and in the process transforming the very fabric of society. Gay liberation is inexorably linked to women's liberation. Each is essential to the other.

The moment we argue, as some among us insist on doing, that we should be treated as equals because we are really just like married couples and hold the same values to be true, we undermine the very purpose of our movement and begin the dangerous process of silencing our different voices. As a lesbian, I am fundamentally different from non-lesbian women. That's the point. Marriage, as it exists today, is antithetical to my liberation as a lesbian and as a woman because it mainstreams my life and voice. I do not want to be known as "Mrs. Attached-To-Somebody-Else." Nor do I want to give the state the power to regulate my primary relationship.

Yet, the concept of equality in our legal system does not support differences, it only supports sameness. The very standard for equal protection is that people who are similarly situated must be treated equally. To make an argument for equal protection, we will be required to claim that gay and lesbian relationships are the same as straight relationships. To gain the right, we must compare ourselves to married couples. The law looks to the insiders as the norm, regardless of how flawed or unjust their institutions, and requires that those seeking the law's equal protection situate themselves in a similar posture to those who are already protected. In arguing for the right to legal marriage, lesbians and gay men would be forced to claim that we are just like heterosexual couples, have the same goals and purposes, and vow to structure our lives similarly. The law provides no room to argue that we are different, but are nonetheless entitled to equal protection.

The thought of emphasizing our sameness to married heterosexuals in order to obtain this "right" terrifies me. It rips away the very heart and soul of what I believe it is to be a lesbian in this world. It robs me of the opportunity to make a difference. We end up mimicking all that is bad about the institution of marriage in our effort to appear to be the same as straight couples.

By looking to our sameness and deemphasizing our differences, we don't even place ourselves in a position of power that would allow us to transform marriage from an institution that emphasizes property and state regulation of relationships to an institution which recognizes one of many types of valid and respected relationships. Until the constitution is interpreted to respect and encourage differences, pursuing the legalization of same-sex marriage would be leading our movement into a trap; we would be demanding access to the very institution which, in its current form, would undermine *our* movement to recognize many different kinds of relationships. We would be perpetuating the elevation of married relationships and of "couples" in general, and further eclipsing other relationships of choice.

Ironically, gay marriage, instead of liberating gay sex and sexuality, would further outlaw all gay and lesbian sex which is not performed in a marital context. Just as sexually active non-married women face stigma and double standards around sex and sexual activity, so too would non-married gay people. The only legitimate gay sex would be that which is cloaked in and regulated by marriage. Its legitimacy would stem not from an acceptance of gay sexuality, but because the Supreme Court and society in general fiercely protect the privacy of marital relationships. Lesbians and gay men who do not seek the state's stamp of approval would clearly face increased sexual oppression.

Undoubtedly, whether we admit it or not, we all need to be accepted by the broader society. That motivation fuels our work to eliminate discrimination in the workplace and elsewhere, fight for custody of our children, create our own families, and so on. The growing discussion about the right to marry may be explained in part by this need for acceptance. Those closer to the norm or to power in this country are more likely to see marriage as a principle of freedom and equality. Those who are more acceptable to the mainstream because of race, gender, and economic status are more likely to want the right to marry. It is the final acceptance, the ultimate affirmation of identity.

On the other hand, more marginal members of the lesbian and gay community (women, people of color, working class and poor) are less likely to see marriage as having relevance to our struggles for survival. After all, what good is the affirmation of our relationships (that is, marital relationships) if we are rejected as women, black, or working class?

The path to acceptance is much more complicated for many of us. For instance, if we choose legal marriage, we may enjoy the right to add our spouse to our health insurance policy at work, since most employment policies are defined by one's marital status, not family relationship. However, that choice assumes that we have a job *and* that our employer provides us with health benefits. For women, particularly women of color who tend to occupy the low-paying jobs that do not provide healthcare benefits at all, it will not matter one bit if they are able to marry their woman partners. The opportunity to marry will neither get them the health benefits nor transform them from outsider to insider.

Of course, a white man who marries another white man who has a full-time job with benefits will certainly be able to share in those benefits and overcome the only obstacle left to full societal assimilation—the goal of many in his class. In other words, gay marriage will not topple the system that allows only the privileged few to obtain decent health care. Nor will it close the privilege gap between those who are married and those who are not.

Marriage creates a two-tier system that allows the state to regulate relationships. It has become a facile mechanism for employers to dole out benefits, for businesses to provide special deals and incentives, and for the law to make distinctions in distributing meager public funds. None of these entities bothers to consider the relationship among people; the love, respect, and need to protect that exists among all kinds of family members. Rather, a simple certificate of the state, regardless of whether the spouses love, respect, or even see each other on a regular basis, dominates and is supported. None of this dynamic will change if gay men and lesbians are given the option of marriage.

Gay marriage will not help us address the systemic abuses inherent in a society that does not provide decent health care to all of its citizens, a right that should not depend on whether the individual 1) has sufficient resources to afford health care or health insurance, 2) is working and receives health insurance as part of compensation, or 3) is married to a partner who is working and has health coverage which is extended to spouses. It will not address the underlying unfairness that allows businesses to provide discounted services or goods to families and couples—who are defined to include straight, married people and their children, but not domestic partners.

Nor will it address the pain and anguish of the unmarried lesbian who receives word of her partner's accident, rushes to the hospital and is prohibited from entering the intensive care unit or obtaining information about her condition solely because she is not a spouse or family member. Likewise, marriage will not help the gay victim of domestic violence who, because he chose not to marry, finds no protection under the law to keep his violent lover away.

If the laws change tomorrow and lesbians and gay men were allowed to marry, where would we find the incentive to continue the progressive movement we have started that is pushing for societal and legal recognition of all kinds of family relationships? To create other options and alternatives? To find a place in the law for the elderly couple who, for companionship and economic reasons, live together but do not marry? To recognize the right of a long-time, but unmarried, gay partner to stay in his rent-controlled apartment after the death of his lover, the only named tenant on the lease? To recognize the family relationship of the lesbian couple and the two gay men who are jointly sharing child-raising responsibilities? To get the law to acknowledge that we may have more than one relationship worthy of legal protection?

Marriage for lesbians and gay men still will not provide a real choice unless we continue the work our community has begun to spread the privilege around to other relationships. We must first break the tradition of piling benefits and privileges on to those who are married, while ignoring the real life needs of those who are not. Only when we de-institutionalize marriage and bridge the economic and privilege gap between the married and the unmarried will each of us have a true choice. Otherwise, our choice not to marry will continue to lack legal protection and societal respect.

The lesbian and gay community has laid the groundwork for revolutionizing society's views of family. The domestic partnership movement has been an important part of this progress insofar as it validates non-marital relationships. Because it is not limited to sexual or romantic relationships, domestic partnership provides an important opportunity for many who are not related by blood or marriage to claim certain minimal protections.

It is crucial, though, that we avoid the pitfall of framing the push for legal recognition of domestic partners (those who share a primary residence and financial responsibilities for each other) as a stepping stone to marriage. We must keep our eyes on the goals of providing true alternatives to marriage and of radically reordering society's view of family.

The goals of lesbian and gay liberation must simply be broader than the right to marry. Gay and lesbian marriages may minimally transform the institution of marriage by diluting its traditional patriarchal dynamic, but they will not transform society. They will not demolish the two-tier system of the "haves" and the "have nots." We must not fool ourselves into believing that marriage will make it acceptable to be gay or lesbian. We will be liberated only when we are respected and accepted for our differences and the diversity we provide to this society. Marriage is not a path to that liberation.

Simon Nkoli (1959–) is a black gay activist in South Africa. This interview was conducted by Mark Chestnut for the former gay NY weekly *Outweek* and made during Nkoli's visit to the United States in 1989.

SIMON NKOLI

As we go to press, the democratic changes in South Africa have resulted in the drafting of a new constitution that, if adopted, will be the first in the world to guarantee civil rights for gays and lesbians. The relevent clauses state:

Chapter 3: Fundamental Rights / Equality
8. (1) Every person shall have the right to equality before the law and to equal protection of the law
(2) No person shall be unfairly discriminated against, directly or indirectly, and, without derogating from the generality of this provision, on one or more of the following grounds in particular: race, gender, sex, ethnic or social origin, colour, sexual orientation, age, disability, religion, conscience, belief, culture or language.
(3) (a) This section shall not preclude measures designed to achieve the adequate protection and advancement of persons or groups or categories of persons disadvantaged by unfair discrimination, in order to enable their full and equal enjoyment of all rights and freedoms.

OUT OF SOUTH AFRICA
ENDING A U.S. TOUR, GAY ANTI-APARTHEID ACTIVIST SIMON NKOLI VISITS NEW YORK

from *Outweek* (1989)

Interviewed by Mark Chesnut

Growing Up in South Africa

MC: Where were you born?
SN: I was born in Soweto in 1959 and I grew up in a small town in Orange Free State. I

left the Orange Free State when I was eleven to go to the Township.

MC: How would you describe your childhood?

SN: My growing up years were not really so good, in terms of I being a child of many children my age. You know, my parents were not allowed to live in [Bopeelone] Township. They had to have a temporary permit to be allowed to live there and until maybe after 13 years, they could be considered residents of the Township. So when I moved to them, life was not so easy for me because of the raids the police used to do on people living there without being residents. So my parents were part of those people.

MC: They would have to hide from the police?

SN: I think they did. If you had money they would not arrest you, but if you didn't, they *would* arrest you, so you would have to appear in court, or otherwise you would have to be released at the police station.

MC: What sort of housing did you have then?

SN: At that time, we were in a squatter camp. Until 1976, when my parents found a house of their own, and even those houses, they're not proper houses, you should see, the township houses are what we call a "box of matches." They're small, tiny little things, four-roomed things, and we were six at home, my mother, my stepfather and the four children. We were very crowded. But some other people live in those little houses, being eight to twelve members of a family.

MC: What during your formative years influenced you to become involved in activism?

SN: I grew up seeing conditions that Black people live in in our township, experiencing the hardship. I mean, if police come to the township and arrest you for a pass law and they arrest your father for a pass law, we used to see them not coming home. We used to see our mothers going from one police station to another looking for our fathers. When I was at high school, I saw a lot of these things in practice, especially in our schools where the students were subjected to wear school uniforms, and because the parents could not afford to buy school uniforms, could not afford to buy textbooks, lots of schoolchildren were expelled from school. And I became involved in dealing with those issues practically, because I didn't really believe, if one child was brilliant, wanted to have an education for her or his future, he should not have to leave school because he did not have those school uniforms. It was then that I really decided that the government should have put more money to Black education.

MC: So was that what really pushed you to become involved in improving conditions for Black South Africans?

SN: Well, there are lots of other things, Mark. If I have to mention every particular thing, I'll really spend a long time talking about it. Things started very early. I started experiencing racial discrimination on the farm when I was a little boy. When I was eight years to eleven, I experienced it. I was one of the children who were working for nothing in the white man's field. I was one of those kids who would wake up early in the morning at about 5:00 and take the sheep and cattle to the fields. And I would see these white people chasing Black men and whipping them. Things like that make me very angry because at that time I was too small to react. And some Black people had accepted the situation like that as part of life.

Coming Out

MC: When did you first identify yourself as gay?

SN: In 1978, I suspected that I was gay.

MC: And what response did you get when you came out? What view does the Black culture in South Africa have regarding homosexuality?

SN: The Black population doesn't accept homosexuality and they don't really think it is there, it is existing in the Black community. And if they happened to know that there is a homosexual man in society, they really fear that this person is either bewitched, or this person is insane, abnormal or something. And they try all the possible means to take that person to witch doctors or psychologists or whatever. And they try to convert that person, to make that person straight. And it's also very difficult according to our own cultural background and traditions. We live in the Black community that we, as children, our parents want us to grow up like they did. And I as a man, they were very disappointed because all they need to do is for me to get our family name going. So I have to have children, I have to have a son.

MC: So there was a lot of pressure from your family?

SN: Yeah.

MC: Do some Black South Africans think that homosexuality was brought by whites?

SN: That is true. Lots of people believe so. My mother, for example, regretted sending me to Catholic school, which was dominated by whites. I had just finished at school when I came out. I went to Catholic school for two years. It was a boys-only school, I think there were about 400 boys and only 24 of us were Black.

MC: It was predominantly white?

SN: Yeah, it was a private school. Private schools are very expensive. I was lucky.

MC: What was the reaction at school about you being gay?

SN: My mother told my priest about me being gay, and my priest wanted to talk to me. And I was really depressed at the time when I was coming out. Especially because in the beginning I didn't really accept it myself. I found it very difficult to cope with it. But when I had learned to accept it, I didn't think I was doing anything wrong. I was not even involved in practical things at that time.

MC: What influence does religion have on South African attitudes about homosexuality?

SN: The Christian religion doesn't favor it at all, they condemn it. The priest condemned my lover. He told me that man must be possessed and his evil spirit is coming into me. So there is no church that supports homosexuality. But there are a few priests who are in the closet and coming out now and then.

MC: Homosexuality is illegal according to white South African law, isn't it?

SN: Well, they don't mention it in the book of law. They mention sodomy and immorality. Whenever gay people have been arrested, it's been for sodomy, and anybody that's been arrested for sodomy has been gay people, gay men. It's very difficult. They cannot arrest you for being gay.

MC: Do they use other charges as an excuse for arresting gay people?

SN: Well, they can use other things as an excuse. A lot of gay people have been arrested for child molestation, for loitering, for soliciting. Many gay people who go to parks and stations to pick up people, they're being arrested under soliciting.

MC: How did being involved in the anti-apartheid movement affect your coming out? Did it make you more aware of the struggle for gay rights?

SN: Yeah, it did. That's why when I came out, I decided not to waste time, and really think of gay rights. Because in the beginning, I thought I was the only one. And as time went on, I realized that I could not be the only one. There must be other people going through the same crisis that I went. And those people, if there is no one there to help them, who will help them? So I decided that it's high time, that we needed a gay support organization. And that's why I joined the Gay Association of South Africa (GASA).

MC: Did you help to found that group?

SN: No, I didn't. The papers are very wrong to say that I had.

MC: I won't say that, then. But were you involved with anti-apartheid groups while you were involved with GASA?

SN: I was a member of a support committee then.

MC: And what sort of response did you get when you came out in the group?

SN: I did come out to some of my anti-apartheid people, and some of them accepted me, and some found it very difficult to communicate with me. But the general response is that people responded really well to me. They never discriminated against me. And I did not hide the fact that I was gay. I did not talk about it very much in anti-apartheid organizations. I didn't really need to talk about it, because nobody had ever talked about his own sexuality. So the most important thing was for me to be accepted. So if people asked me, I would tell them . . .

AIDS and Racism in Gay South Africa

MC: I understand there is not a lot of education about AIDS in the black community.

SN: No, there is not. Part of my travelling now is to raise awareness and funds for the Township AIDS Project that GLOW [the Gay and Lesbian Organization of the Wiwatersrand] has helped to found.

MC: Is that the Zulu AIDS Project?

SN: The Zulu AIDS Project is helping us. That's the name the New York people gave it.

MC: Is there any other AIDS education program in the Black community besides the Township AIDS Project?

SN: No, not in the Black community. The white community is well-organized around the whole issue of AIDS. They can't come to our townships and share with us their knowledge, or educate us on AIDS. The leaflets that they have been sending, they're written in only one language, and that is English, and the majority of the Black people speak very different languages. So GLOW is hoping, together with Township AIDS Project, to publish more information in a language that people are able to read.

MC: Is GLOW a multi-racial organization?

SN: We prefer to call ourselves a non-racial organization.

MC: So you have a mixed membership?

SN: Yes. We are actually mixed both racially and as far as sex is concerned, men and women.

MC: Most of the people we hear about in the gay rights movement in South Africa are men. To what extent are women involved?

SN: There is OLGA (the Organizations for Lesbian and Gay Activists) in Cape Town, and their leadership is women. Sheila Lapinsky and Julia Nicol.

MC: What are the attitudes of the Black community regarding AIDS? Do they see it as a threat?

SN: No, they actually ignore it. They think it's a white gay man's disease. Just the same that they think being gay is a western thing. They think AIDS is from the western countries.

MC: How hard has AIDS actually hit the Black community?

SN: Well, at the moment we don't have statistics of AIDS in the Black community, we only have it in the white community.

Lesbian and Gay Spaces

MC: How much do different races interact within the lesbian and gay community?

SN: We all have the same problems of wanting to be accepted in our society, but the difference is that we come from different backgrounds. I mean, the white people, at least now, they've got more tolerance to homosexuality than Black people. And then of course the white community has more resources. It's easy for white people to live comfortably as gays and lesbians. At the age of 18, the white young people can move out of their parents' place and live by themselves. While we who are Black have to live with our parents until we can afford to move out, and normally, we don't until we get married. In the Black community, we don't even have privacies. The same applies to the place of socializing. In the town, they've got lots of gay bars, gay and lesbian restaurants, etc. In the [Black] township, nothing. Until last year, GLOW founded the GLOW Bar in Soweto.

MC: What sort of reception did the opening of the bar receive?

SN: We really had a good reception. We were surprised to have that good a turnout because we had advertised our thing even in the commercial press, and we thought "oh my gosh, now we're going to be gay-bashed." But there was really nothing. There were lots of people who were curious to see "these queers who were going to open their own bar next door to our places," etc. It's quite popular now.

MC: What about the gay establishments in the cities—can anyone go into one?

SN: Well, now anybody can go, at least in Johannesburg, anybody can go anywhere. But there are still attitudes, if you get what I mean.

MC: You still might encounter racism from individuals.

SN: Yeah, from individual gay people. But anyway, the bar that we all like in Johannesburg is called Skyline. It's at least 20 percent Black.

The Gay and Straight of South African Politics

MC: What do you think is the significance of the loss of seats by the National Party in the recent elections?

SN: Well, I'm not optimistic, and sometimes I really prefer not to talk about it. I mean, I'm not optimistic until the Black people are allowed also to vote.

MC: Do you think there is any chance of this with deKlerk? How does he compare to Botha?

SN: Mark, I'll tell you that I'm going back to South Africa, and some of the questions I really have to be careful when I answer them. I really don't know who is going to have your publication here. I think one is followed all the time and that's why I'm avoiding the conventional press.

MC: Do any of the political parties address gay rights?

SN: Not as far as I know. All I remember, before I left South Africa, the Democratic Party had called on gay people to discuss with them, but by gay people, they meant white gay people.

MC: That was one of the problems with the GASA. They were mainly interested in looking for gay power within the current racist political structure. You broke away from the GASA, right?

SN: When I was in prison, yeah. They were not supportive of me, but that was not the only reason. The other reason was that they did not do anything to improve the life of people in our country. They didn't say anything against apartheid. It was a social organization mainly aimed at white members. I was a Black member of that organization and I had encountered difficulty with them. That's why the Saturday Group was formed, because they didn't do much for the Black gay community.

MC: Was that one of the reasons you helped to start GLOW last year?

SN: That was one of the reasons GLOW was founded. GLOW was founded last year, after I came out of prison.

MC: What about the Congress of Pink Democrats?

SN: The Congress of Pink Democrats was supposed to be a national organization, an umbrella for gay and lesbian organizations in South Africa, but it is now defunct.

MC: Is there any sort of organization trying to take its place?

SN: No, not at the moment, because GLOW and OLGA have the same thinking, that we have to organize our local organizations first, build them up to be strong organizations, before we can concentrate on national organization.

MC: How many cities have local organizations?

SN: Johannesburg has got lots of local organizations, and Cape Town, Port Elizabeth, Durban, Bloemfontein, Pretoria; several cities.

MC: What kind of support do gay organizations get from other institutions?

SN: So far, we don't really get any.

MC: Where to you meet?

SN: GLOW was meeting in people's homes. At least now, we're meeting at the GLOW bar. And of course we meet at the offices of the South African Institute of Race Relations where I used to work. They've got a community hall. We have to hire it, we have to pay it.

The Visit Abroad

MC: When did you first get the idea to make this tour to Europe and North America?

SN: The Canadian people, the ones from Toronto, they phoned me three days after I was acquitted and asked me whether I would like to do a tour in Canada, and I said, "Yes I will." I didn't know that I would have a problem obtaining my passport, because as far as I'm concerned, I'm acquitted and I'm out, a free person. And then I went to holiday in Cape Town and when I got back, I applied for a passport and I never got it. That was for 18 weeks. And at the end I managed to get it. And it was only because I had to involve lots of people.

MC: Is this your first time in the United States?

SN: It is my first time anywhere. I haven't travelled.

MC: Where else did this tour bring you?

SN: I went to London—I spent more than 13 days in Canada. I went to Vienna.

MC: You were at the International Conference there. What did you do there?

SN: I've been really harassed by the press people, I want to say. It's not an exciting thing. I attended some workshops. I had so many interviews from everybody. It was so tiring. It was just like it was in San Francisco. And I'm not going to allow that to happen anymore.

MC: What happened in San Francisco?

SN: I never had time for myself. I really don't know how people think of *me*, I know they want to interview me, but as a person. I want to be treated like any other person, not just to be interviewed and have big receptions and things like that.

MC: What are your impressions of North America and its lesbian and gay community?

SN: Well, I love them. I found the gay and lesbian community here very much privileged. More than our gay and lesbian community in South Africa. I mean, here at least gay people, they don't seem to be struggling to get venues to meet, and in South Africa we do. And anyway in South Africa, white gay people, the majority of those gay people are out. They don't even think that it is important to pursue gay rights. Here, what impresses me is the way the gay community in these countries I have been in are doing so much work on AIDS. And I think we also need to do the same thing.

MC: What do you think will be the result of your visit abroad, what do you hope to have accomplished when you go home?

SN: Well, firstly I would have shared my experience that the gay and lesbian community share and elsewhere I have been. And I would have also made contact for our gay and lesbian organization in South Africa. And I would have, for example, raised enough funds for the Township AIDS Project, and for GLOW as well. And I would have gained a lot of knowledge, especially on the field that I want to concentrate on, being an AIDS educator.

OUTING

In the 1990s, a new, but not historically unprecedented, debate has raged in the lesbian and gay community. The focus has been a practice now known as "outing," in which journalists or others acknowledge the homosexuality of public figures who are gay or lesbian. The debate began when Michelangelo Signorile, a regular columnist for *Outweek*, published an article detailing Malcolm Forbes' relationships with men. Outing was soon was condemned by many, including gay journalist Randy Shilts, as a violation of privacy. Signorile responds that this is no more a violation than revelations about heterosexual activity, and that collusion in hiding the sexuality of gays and lesbians amounts to reinforcement of the belief that our sexuality is shameful. We reprint here two examples of the debate between Shilts and Signorile.

Michelangelo Signorile is the author of *Queer in America*. Randy Shilts was the author of several books on modern lesbian and gay history, including *The Band Played On: People, Politics, and AIDS* and *Conduct Unbecoming*, on gays and lesbians in the U.S. military. He died of complications due to AIDS in 1993.

IS "OUTING" GAYS ETHICAL?

The New York Times op-ed page, April 12, 1990

Randy Shilts

In more polite times, gay organizers and journalists generally agreed that homosexuals in the closet had a right to stay there if they didn't choose to publicly acknowledge their sexuality. It was an unspoken rule.

With the AIDS epidemic now causing a significant depopulation of gay men in major urban areas, however, the times have become less congenial for covert homosexuals. Both gay newspapers and militant AIDS activists have launched a campaign of "outing": publicly revealing the sexual orientation of people who'd rather keep it quiet.

The controversy over outing recently erupted in force when the sexual activities of a famous, deceased millionaire were documented in a New York City gay newspaper. Over the past year, various AIDS groups have also circulated fliers announcing that several national and local politicians were gay. They did this after the officials took actions that the activists considered inimical to the fight against AIDS.

For journalists and gay leaders themselves, these tactics present a panoply of ethical quandaries.

Most mainstream daily newspapers have refused to name those exposed in gay newspapers and AIDS protests. In most cases, this has made sense. The outings of politicians, for example, were based on nothing more than gossip and did not contain the factual substantiation that would warrant reporting in a legitimate news story.

Moreover, none of the politicians thus far exposed by outings have engaged in rabidly anti-gay politicking. By the standards of most journalists, such hypocrisy would warrant a public outing, because the politicians themselves would have already asserted that homosexuality was an issue that demanded intense public scrutiny.

The outing of the dead presents a different dilemma. There are no privacy issues here: under American law, the dead have no right to privacy. That's how it should be.

Some newspaper editors maintain that they would not reveal even a deceased person's homosexuality because they always refrain from discussing sex lives. But that just isn't so. In the most recent case, the late millionaire's heterosexual affairs with some of the world's most celebrated women were the stuff of news coverage for more than a decade. Many newspapers included the information in their obituaries.

It seems then that the refusal of newspapers to reveal a person's homosexuality has less to do with ethical considerations of privacy than with an editor's homophobia. In my experience, many editors really believe that being gay is so distasteful that talk of it should be avoided unless absolutely necessary.

This has left us with newspapers that often are more invested in protecting certain people than in telling the truth to readers. In Hollywood and New York, hundreds of publicists make their living by planting items in entertainment columns about whom this or that celebrity is dating. Many of these items are patently false and intended only to cover up the celebrity's homosexuality.

Moreover, many newspaper writers and editors know full well that this is the case and merrily participate in the deceptions. Editors who would never reveal a public figure was gay are routinely lying to their readers by implying the same person is straight.

It is in rage against this hypocrisy—and in desperation over the ravages of AIDS—that the trend of outing was born. In major urban areas across the country, the homosexual community must watch helplessly as AIDS decimates the gay male population. Meanwhile, just about every eminent body studying the Government's response to the AIDS crisis has agreed that it is woefully inadequate.

Just about everyone also agrees that the response to the epidemic is so pathetic because gay men comprise the largest population struck by AIDS—and gay men are largely viewed as degenerate reprobates. In truth, of course, lesbians and gay men are to be found among the most respected public figures in every field of American society.

Gay organizers hope that if more Americans knew this, the nation might see a better response to the AIDS epidemic. Fewer people might die. That's a major reason why outing started. That's also why it will become more pronounced, as more people die and frustration among AIDS activists grows.

At the same time, outing presents gays with their own moral quandaries. In outing politicians, gay activists often have acted more from vindictiveness over a particular vote than from a genuine desire to enlighten the public. Outing threats are political blackmail. And what happens if religious conservatives threaten to reveal a politician's homosexuality if he or she doesn't vote a certain party line? Outing is a powerful political weapon that can cut both ways.

Gay activists counter that young gay people have a right to role models of successful gay adults. That's true, but someone who is only public because he or she has been hauled from the closet is certainly no paragon of psychological integration.

As a journalist, I cannot imagine any situation in which I would reveal the homosexuality of a living person who was not a public official engaged in voracious hypocrisy.

Yet, as someone who has chosen to be open about being gay, I have nothing but disdain for the celebrated and powerful homosexuals who remain comfortably closeted while so many are dying. Most of these people have nothing to lose by stepping forward and they could do much to instruct society about the contributions gays daily make to America.

As I watch my friends die all around me, a certain part of me hopes against all hope that the outing stories now appearing in the press may do something to stop the avalanche of death around me.

WHO SHOULD OPEN THE CLOSET DOOR?

Michelangelo Signorile

Whenever so-called "gay leaders" discuss outing—revealing a public figure's homosexuality without his or her consent—they rarely address the mainstream media's double standard regarding reportage about the private lives of homosexuals. Instead, they conjure up the most archaic of gay movement principals[sic]—the right to privacy—and stand by it firmly. But a new generation of young, vocal gays is insisting that there is no right to the closet.

In March of 1990, I wrote a cover story about Malcolm Forbes for the now-defunct New York lesbian and gay weekly, *OutWeek*. The article sent shock waves throughout the media. Forbes was gay. And that fact, I felt, should have been reported, if only for the sake of correcting the historical record.

Publications from *The New York Times* and *USA Today* to *Playboy* and *Screw* soon zeroed in on what *Time* magazine termed, "outing." In editorials and commentaries, many of them came down hard on it. According to quite a few, this was "fascism" and an "invasion of privacy." Of course, none of these seasoned journalists think twice about their own day-to-day descriptions of the sex lives of *heterosexuals*—from Gary Hart and Donald Trump to Liz Taylor and Warren Beatty to, more recently, Arkansas Governor Bill Clinton. Somehow, that's right to do. It's considered "reportage," while what I do is an invasion of people's privacy.

I smell homophobia. It seems that the American media don't report about the lives of famous lesbians and gay men simply because they see homosexuality as the most disgusting thing imaginable—worse than extramarital affairs, abortions, boozing, divorces and out-of-wedlock babies, all of which are fodder for the press.

But if we are going to become a society in which homosexuals are treated equally, then the media have got to normalize the discussion of homosexuality to that of heterosexuality. Whenever it's pertinent—and certainly if a subject is out-and-out lying—a public figure's homosexuality should be discussed. This should be true *only* for public figures—famous and powerful individuals who've made a deal with the public: In return for the millions of dollars they earn, or the political power they wield, their lives are open for dissection by the media. If the media are going to report on public figures' heterosexual love affairs—whether that is right or not—it is simply homophobic of them to refuse to report on homosexual ones. By not doing so, the message the media send is clear: homosexuality is so utterly grotesque that it should never be discussed, while straight sexual encounters, whether the subject wants them reported or not, are acceptable, titillating grist for the mill.

The new generation of gay activists wasn't around during the blacklisting era of the 1950s. We've enjoyed the first few benefits of gay liberation of the sixties and seventies. And we simply don't see why we can't speak freely about who's gay.

Indeed, we're challenging the very notion of "privacy." Is being a gay man or a lesbian a "private" issue in this country, in 1992 when so many millions of younger, more liberated Americans see their homosexuality as no different from such "public" issues as their race, gender or ethnicity? If, as we've said all along, being gay is not about what we do in our bedrooms but is rather a much larger issue regarding our identities and our specific culture and community, then how can the mere fact of being gay be private? The fact of being *straight* is not private. Sex is private. But we're not discussing anyone's sex life. We're only saying that they're gay.

GAY CONSERVATISM

In the 1980s, more and more people began to come out. As they did, myths about the political or economic or cultural unity of gays and lesbians have been exploded. We saw that lesbians and gays come in all stripes, and that their sense of the relation between their sexuality and their politics is anything but monolithic.

One of the most dramatic examples of this variety is the following "coming-out" letter. In 1990 Marvin Liebman, a long-time conservative activist, came out in the pages of *National Review*, the conservative magazine edited by his close personal friend William F. Buckley, Jr. In this letter Liebman describes his sense of the difference between "old" and "new" conservatism, and his fear that homophobia is becoming the center of the conservative agenda. Buckley's brief response, not reprinted here, combines personal generosity toward a friend with the refusal to "repeal . . . convictions that are more, much more, than mere accretions of bigotry."

In 1995, Liebman made a further step when he wrote in the *Advocate* that he can no longer call himself a Republican or a conservative. In the face of the antigay hatred that is central to contemporary Republican conservatism, Liebman abandoned the party and the label that he fought under for fifty years.

LETTER TO WILLIAM F. BUCKLEY, JR.

from the *National Review*, July 9, 1990

Marvin Liebman

Dear Bill:
I have given long and careful thought to what follows. It is something I feel I have to do.

I urge you to give it sympathetic and immediate consideration. I send it to you 1) because you are my best friend; and 2) because *NR* is the logical publication for this statement.

It has been nearly four years since *NR* published "John Woolman's" missive, "A Conservative Speaks Out for Gay Rights." It may not surprise you to know that I have kept a clipping of that article all this time. It sits in a file which although not titled may as well be called my file on Conservatives of Courage on the Issue of Homosexuality. It is a very thin file. You were courageous to run John Woolman's letter as a prominent article, and to allow him, 18 months later, to publish his "AIDS and Right Wing Hysteria." Your doing so brought a feeling of genuine admiration in this old friend.

We've known each other for almost 35 years now, and ten years ago you served as my godfather when I entered the Catholic Church. Though the subject never arose, you and Pat, among my oldest friends, must have known that I'm gay. It never seemed to matter.

But it does matter to many "movement" conservatives—this question of who is, who is not gay; and they wonder whether homosexuals are a menace to society. Just as, too often, there has been an undercurrent of anti-Semitism among even some mainstream conservatives, there has always been an element of homophobia among us. In many years of service to The Cause, I've sat in rooms where people we both know—brilliant, thoughtful, kind people—have said, without any sense of shame, vulgar and cruel things about people who through no fault of their own happen to be different in their sexuality.

Anti-Semitism is something that, happily for the history of the last three decades, *National Review* helped to banish at least from the public behavior of conservatives. *National Review* lifted conservatism to a more enlightened plane, away from a tendency to engage in the manipulation of base motives, prejudices, and desires: activity which in my view tended to be a major base of conservatism's natural constituency back then. Political gay bashing, racism, and anti-Semitism survive even in this golden period of conservatism's great triumphs: but they are for the most part hidden in the closet. I think they are waiting to be let out once again. I worry that the right wing, having won the cold war and, for all intents and purposes, the battle over economic policy, will return to the fever swamps. I see evidence of this. It disturbs me greatly. It is for this reason that I write.

I am almost 67 years old. For more than half of my lifetime I have been engaged in, and indeed helped to organize and maintain, the conservative and anti-Communist cause. The names of some of the enterprises we helped launch may bring a nostalgic tug. I name some of them to establish my bona fides as someone who has toiled on behalf of the movement.

Among the more obscure committees I was involved with were the American Committee for Aid to the Katanga Freedom-Fighters; the American Emergency Committee for Tibetan Refugees; the Emergency Committee on the Panama Canal; the Aid to Refugee Chinese Intellectuals. Among the better known, of course, are the Committee of One Million, Young Americans for Freedom, the American Conservative Union, the Conservative Party of New York, and the Goldwater and Reagan campaigns. All the time I labored in the conservative vineyard, I was gay.

This was not my choice: the term "sexual preference" is deceptive. It is how I was born; how God decreed that I should be. As with most gay men of my generation, I kept it secret. It was probably not a secret to those who knew me well—my beloved friends and family—but no one Spoke Its Name. I now regret all those years of compliant silence.

Why have I chosen this moment to go public with that part of my life that had been so private for all these years? Because I feel that our cause might sink back into the ooze in which so much of it rested in pre-*NR* days. In that dark age the American Right was heavily, perhaps dominantly, made up of bigots: anti-Semites, anti-Catholics, the KKK, red-necks,

Know Nothings, a sorry lot of public hucksters and religious medicine men. I think there is general agreement that it wasn't until the founding of this publication that the modern American conservative movement was granted light and form.

I was privileged to be a part of the enterprise from its earliest days, together with such great men as Whittaker Chambers, Frank Meyer, James Burnham, Russell Kirk, Brent Bozell—all of them. This effort, combined with the groups we founded, resulted in the eight-year reign of Ronald Reagan.

Now times are changing. There is no longer the anti-Communist cement to hold the edifice together. The great enterprise, in which so much time has been invested, is in danger of sinking back to an aggregation of bigotries.

Too many of our friends have recently used homophobia to sell their newsletter, or to raise money through direct mail for their causes and themselves. This letter isn't designed to settle scores, but rather to give warning to the movement from someone who's been a part of it for three and a half decades.

I've watched as some of our conservative brethren, employing the direct-mail medium I helped pioneer, use Robert Mapplethorpe's bad taste and the NEA's poor judgment to rile small donors, provoking them with a vision of a homosexual vanguard intent on forcing sadomasochistic images into every schoolroom . . . I have been appalled to read in newsletters by conservative leaders that George Bush, by inviting a gay leader to a White House ceremony, is caving in to "the homosexual lobby." . . . I was outraged to see a spokesman for one of the more prominent conservative foundations quoted as saying that the cost of treating AIDS patients "could be the greatest impetus for euthanasia we've ever seen."

I worry about those allegedly Christian televangelists preaching hatred and fear of gays. These are men who would deny to more than twenty million Americans even the joy of peaceful union with their own families . . . None of this seems to me to be the purpose of the cause I joined, along with you, 35 years ago.

A personal note is in order. I am both gay and conservative and don't find a contradiction. There shouldn't be any "shame" in being gay. Moreover, the conservative view, based as it is on the inherent rights of the individual over the state, is the logical political home of gay men and women. The conservative movement must reject the bigots and the hypocrites and provide a base for gays as well as others. The politics of inclusion is the model by which what we achieved with Ronald Reagan can continue and flourish without the anti-Communist and the anti-tax movements as sustaining elements. Conservatives need to remind themselves that gay men and women, almost always residing in the closet, were among those who helped in the founding, nurturing, and maintaining of the movement. They should be welcomed based on common beliefs, and without regard to our response to different sexual stimuli. One's sexuality should not be factored into acceptance in a cause that is based on beliefs, no more than color, or ethnic origin: because sexuality isn't a belief, it's a factor of birth.

One day the conservative movement will recognize that there are gays among us who have advanced our cause. They should not be victims of small-mindedness, prejudice, fear, or cynicism. That day may be a long way off, and I sometimes think the trend is in the opposite direction. *National Review* could have an important role here, once again guiding conservatives toward the more enlightened path. I pray that it will.

As ever, your friend,
Marvin Liebman

In the early 1990s a new generation of radicals began to challenge what had become the "establishment" of gay and lesbian politics. This establishment is represented by organizations such as the National Gay and Lesbian Task Force, the Gay and Lesbian Alliance Against Defamation, and Lambda Legal Defense and Education Fund. Such groups have worked through legal and educational strategies to reduce the oppression of lesbians and gays in the U.S. They have, as a consequence, become more willing to accommodate themselves within existing structures of power than groups that are more focused on cultural issues. While too "radical" for most Americans, such groups are the old guard among lesbians and gays.

Frustration with the old guard has included increasing contest over identities. The drive of some gays and lesbians to ally themselves with other "sexual minorities," and the resistance of others to this, has produced a new identity—the queer. While for some, "queer" is simply another name for gay and lesbian, others have adopted it to signify all those who do not live by the heterosexual, monogamous, patriarchal model. In either case, queers have reinvigorated the terrain we persist in calling "gay and lesbian" through direct action, in-your-face writing, and expanded theory.

The following pieces are defining moments of queer politics. Originally distributed as leaflets, they have been passed on across the U.S. (and perhaps beyond). They capture the anger and the hope of people who refuse to accommodate themselves to socio-cultural structures that they view as the source of their oppression.

QUEERS READ THIS; I HATE STRAIGHTS
(1990)

Published Anonymously by Queers

How can I tell you. How can I convince you, brother, sister that your life is in danger: That everyday you wake up alive, relatively happy, and a functioning human being, you are committing a rebellious act. You as an alive and functioning queer are a revolutionary. There is nothing on this planet that validates, protects or encourages your existence. It is a miracle you are standing here reading these words. You should by all rights be dead.

Don't be fooled, straight people own the world and the only reason you have been spared is you're smart, lucky or a fighter. Straight people have a privilege that allows them to do whatever they please and fuck without fear: But not only do they live a life free of fear; they flaunt their freedom in my face. Their images are on my TV, in the magazine I bought, in the restaurant I want to eat in, and on the street where I live. I want there to be a moratorium on straight marriage, on babies, on public displays of affections among the opposite sex and media images that promote heterosexuality. Until I can enjoy the same freedom of movement and sexuality, as straights, their privilege must stop and it must be given over to me and my queer sisters and brothers.

Straight people will not do this voluntarily and so they must be forced into it. Straights must be frightened into it. Terrorized into it. Fear is the most powerful motivator. No one will give us what we deserve. Rights are not given they are taken, by force if necessary.

It is easier to fight when you know who your enemy is. Straight people are your enemy.

They are your enemy when they don't acknowledge your invisibility and continue to live in and contribute to a culture that kills you.

Every day one of us is taken by the enemy. Whether it's an AIDS death due to homophobic government inaction or a lesbian bashing in an all-night diner (in a supposedly lesbian neighborhood), we are being systematically picked off and we will continue to be wiped out unless we realize that if they take one of us they must take all of us.

An Army of Lovers Cannot Lose

Being queer is not about a right to privacy; it is about the freedom to be public, to just be who we are. It means everyday fighting oppression; homophobia, racism, misogyny, the bigotry of religious hypocrites and our own self-hatred. (We have been carefully taught to hate ourselves.) And now of course it means fighting a virus as well, and all those homo-haters who are using AIDS to wipe us off the face of the earth.

Being queer means leading a different sort of life. It's not about the mainstream, profit-margins, patriotism, patriarchy or being assimilated. It's not about executive director, privilege and elitism. It's about being on the margins, defining ourselves; it's about gender-fuck and secrets, what's beneath the belt and deep inside the heart; it's about the night. Being queer is "grass roots" because we know that everyone of us, every body, every cunt, every heart and ass and dick is a world of pleasure waiting to be explored. Everyone of us is a world of infinite possibility.

We are an army because we have to be. We are an army because we are so powerful. (We have so much to fight for; we are the most precious of endangered species.) And we are an army of lovers because it is we who know what love is. Desire and lust, too. We invented them. We come out of the closet, face the rejection of society, face firing squads, just to love each other! Every time we fuck, we win.

We must fight for ourselves (no one else is going to do it) and if in that process we bring greater freedom to the world at large then great. (We've given so much to that world: democracy, all the arts, the concepts of love, philosophy and the soul, to name just a few gifts from our ancient Greek Dykes, Fags.) Let's make every space a Lesbian and Gay space. Every street a part of our sexual geography. A city of yearning and then total satisfaction. A city and a country where we can be safe and free and more. We must look at our lives and see what's best in them, see what is queer and what is straight and let that straight chaff fall away! Remember there is so, so little time. And I want to be a lover of each and every one of you. Next year, we march naked.

THE STRONG SISTERS TOLD THE BROTHERS THAT THERE WERE TWO IMPORTANT THINGS TO REMEMBER ABOUT THE COMING REVOLUTIONS. THE FIRST IS THAT WE WILL GET OUR ASSES KICKED. THE SECOND IS THAT WE WILL WIN.

1. I'm angry. I'm angry for being condemned to death by strangers saying, "You deserve to die" and "AIDS is the cure." Fury erupts when a Republican woman wearing thousands of dollars of garments and jewelry minces by the police lines shaking her head, chuckling, and wagging her finger at us like we are recalcitrant children making absurd demands and throwing a temper tantrum when they aren't met. Angry while Joseph agonizes over $8000 a year for AZT which might keep him alive a little longer and which does make him look sicker than the disease he is diagnosed with. Angry as I listen to a man tell me that after changing his will five times he's running out of people to leave things to. All of his best friends are dead. Angry when I stand in a sea of quilt panels, or go to a candlelight march or attend yet another memorial service. I will not march silently with a fucking candle and I want to take that goddamned quilt and wrap myself in it and furiously rend it and my hair and curse every god religion ever created. I refuse to accept a creation that cuts people down in the

third decade of their life. It is cruel and vile and meaningless and everything I have in me rails against the absurdity and I raise my face to the clouds and a ragged laugh that sounds more demonic than joyous erupts from my throat and tears stream down my face and if this disease doesn't kill me, I may just die of frustration. My feet pound the streets and Peter's hands are chained to a pharmaceutical company's reception desk while the receptionist looks on in horror and Eric's body lies rotting in a Brooklyn cemetery and I'll never hear his flute resounding off the walls of the meeting house again. And I see the old people in Tompkins Square Park huddled in their long wool coats in June to keep out the cold they perceive is there and to cling to whatever little life has left to offer them, and I think, ah, they understand. And I'm reminded of the people who strip and stand before a mirror each night before they go to bed and search their bodies for any mark that might not have been there yesterday. A mark that this scourge has visited them. And I'm angry when the newspapers call us "victims" and sound alarms that "it" might soon spread to the "general population." And I want to scream "Who the fuck am I?" And I want to scream at New York Hospital with its yellow plastic bags marked "isolation linen/ropa infecciosa" and its orderlies in latex gloves and surgical masks skirt the bed as if its occupant will suddenly leap out and douse them with blood and semen giving them too the plague. And I'm angry at straight people who sit smugly wrapped in their self-protective coat of monogamy and heterosexuality confident that this disease has nothing to do with them because "it" only happens to "them." And the teenage boys who upon spotting my Silence=Death button begin chanting "Faggots gonna die" and I wonder, who taught them this? Enveloped in fury and fear, I remain silent while my button mocks me every step of the way. And the anger I feel when a television program on the quilt gives profiles of the dead and the list begins with a baby, a teenage girl who got a blood transfusion, an elderly baptist (sic) minister and his wife and when they finally show a gay man, he's described as someone who knowingly infected teenage male prostitutes with the virus. What else can you expect from a faggot? I'm angry.

2. Since time began, the world has been inspired by the work of queer artists. In exchange, there has been suffering, there has been pain, there has been violence. Throughout history society has struck a bargain with its queer citizens: they may pursue creative careers, if they do it discreetly. Through the arts queers are productive, lucrative, entertaining and even uplifting. These are the clear-cut and useful by-products of what is otherwise considered anti-social behavior. In cultured circles, queers may quietly coexist with an otherwise disapproving power elite.

At the forefront of the most recent campaign to bash queer artists is Jesse Helms, arbiter of all that is decent, moral, christian (sic) and amerikan. For Helms, queer art is quite simply a threat to the world. In his imaginings, heterosexual culture is too fragile to bear up to the admission of human or sexual diversity. Quite simply, the structure of power in the Judeo-Christian world has made procreation its cornerstone. Families having children assures consumers for the nation's products and a work force to produce them, as well as a built-in family system to care for its ill, reducing the expense of public healthcare systems. ALL NON-PROCREATIVE BEHAVIOR IS CONSIDERED A THREAT, from homosexuality to birth control to abortion as an option. It is not enough, according to the religious right, to consistently advertise procreation and heterosexuality . . . it is also necessary to destroy any alternatives. It is not art Helms is after . . . IT IS OUR LIVES! Art is the last safe place for lesbians and gay men to thrive. Helms knows this, and has developed a program to purge queers from the one arena they have been permitted to contribute to our shared culture.

Helms is advocating a world free from diversity or dissent. It is easy to imagine why that might feel more comfortable to those in charge of such a world. It is also easy to envision an amerikan landscape flattened by such power. Helms should just ask for what he is hinting at: State sponsored art, art of totalitarianism, art that speaks only in christian terms, art which supports the goals of those in power, art that matches the sofas in the Oval Office. Ask for what you want, Jesse, so that men and women of conscience can mobilize against it, as we do against the human rights violations of other countries, and fight to free our own country's dissidents.

3. IF YOU'RE QUEER, SHOUT IT!

Queers are under siege.

Queers are being attacked on all fronts and I'm afraid it's ok with us.

In 1969, Queers were attacked. It wasn't ok. Queers fought back, took the streets, SHOUTED.

In 1990, there were 50 "Queer Bashings" in the month of May alone. Violent attacks. 3720 men, women and children died of AIDS in the same month, caused by a more violent attack—government inaction, rooted in society's growing homophobia. This is institutionalized violence, perhaps more dangerous to the existence of queers because the attackers are faceless. We allow these attacks by our own continued lack of action against them. AIDS has affected the straight world and now they're blaming us for AIDS and using it as a way to justify their violence against us. They don't want us anymore. They will beat us, rape us and kill us before they will continue to live with us. What will it take for this not to be ok? Feel some rage. If rage doesn't empower you, try fear. If that doesn't work, try panic.

Be proud. Do whatever you need to do to tear yourself away from your customary state of acceptance. Be free. Shout.

In 1969, Queers fought back. In 1990, Queers say ok.

Next year, will we be here?

4. I hate Jesse Helms. I hate Jesse Helms so much I'd rejoice if he dropped down dead. If someone killed him I'd consider it his own fault.

I hate Ronald Reagan too, because he mass-murdered my people for eight years. But to be honest, I hate him even more for eulogizing Ryan White without first admitting his guilt, without begging forgiveness for Ryan's death and for the deaths of tens of thousands of other PWA's—most of them queer. I hate him for making a mockery of our grief.

I hate the fucking Pope, and I hate John fucking Cardinal fucking O'Connor, and I hate the whole fucking Catholic Church. The same goes for the Military, and especially for Amerika's Law Enforcement Officials—the cops—state sanctioned sadists who brutalize street transvestites, prostitutes and queer prisoners. I also hate the medical and mental health establishments, particularly the psychiatrist who convinced me not to have sex with men for three years until we (meaning he) could make me bisexual rather than queer. I also hate the education profession, for its share in driving thousands of queer teens to suicide every year. I hate the "respectable" art world; and the entertainment industry, and the mainstream media, especially the *New York Times*. In fact, I hate every sector of the straight establishment in this country—the worst of whom actively want all queers dead, the best of whom never stick their necks out to keep us alive.

I hate straight people who think they have anything intelligent to say about "outing." I hate straight people who think stories about themselves are "universal" but stories about us are only about homosexuality. I hate straight recording artists who make their off [sic] of queer people, then attack us, then act hurt when we get angry and then deny having wronged us rather than apologize for it. I hate straight people who say, "I don't see why you feel the need to wear those buttons and t-shirts. I don't go around telling the whole world I'm straight."

I hate that in twelve years of public education I was never taught about queer people. I hate that I grew up thinking I was the only queer in the world, and I hate even more that most queer kids still grow up the same way. I hate that I was tormented by other kids for being a faggot, but more that I was taught to feel ashamed for being the object of their cruelty, taught to feel it was my fault. I hate that the Supreme Court of this country says it's okay to criminalize me because of how I make love. I hate that so many straight people are so concerned about my goddamned sex life. I hate that so many twisted straight people become parents, while I have to fight like hell to be allowed to be a father. I hate straights.

5. WHERE ARE YOU SISTERS?

Invisibility is our Responsibility.

I wear my pink triangle everywhere. I do not lower my voice in public when talking about lesbian love or sex. I always tell people I'm a lesbian. I don't wait to be asked about my "boyfriend." I don't say it's "no one's business."

I don't do this for straight people. Most of them don't know what the pink triangle even means. Most of them couldn't care less that my girlfriend and I are totally in love or having a fight on the street. Most of them don't notice us no matter what we do. I do what I do to reach other lesbians. I do what I do because I don't want lesbians to assume I'm a straight girl. I am out all the time, everywhere, because I WANT TO REACH YOU. Maybe you'll notice me, maybe we'll start talking, maybe we'll exchange numbers, maybe we'll become friends. Maybe we won't say a word but our eyes will meet and I will imagine you naked, sweating, openmouthed, your back arched as I am fucking you. And we'll be happy to know we aren't the only ones in the world. We'll be happy because we found each other, without saying a word, maybe just for a moment.

But no.

You won't wear a pink triangle on that linen lapel. You won't meet my eyes if I flirt with you on the street. You avoid me on the job because I'm "too" out. You chastise me in bars because I'm "too political." You ignore me in public because I bring "too much" attention to "my" lesbianism. But then you want me to be your lover, you want me to be your friend, you want me to love you, support you, fight for "OUR" right to exist.

WHERE ARE YOU?

You talk; talk, talk about invisibility and then retreat to your homes to nest with your lovers or carouse in a bar with pals and stumble home in a cab or sit silently and politely by while your family, your boss, your neighbors, your public servants distort and disfigure us, deride us and punish us. Then home again and you feel like screaming. Then you pad your anger with a relationship or a career or a party with other dykes like you and still you wonder why we can't find each other, why you feel lonely, angry, alienated.

GET UP, WAKE UP SISTERS!!

Your life is in your hands.

When I risk it all to be out, I risk it for both of us. When I risk it all and it works (which it often does if you would try it), I benefit and so do you. When it doesn't work, I suffer and you do not.

But girl you can't wait for other dykes to make the world safe for you. STOP waiting for a better more lesbian future! The revolution could be here if we started it.

Where are you sisters?

I'm trying to find you, I'm trying to find you.

How come I only see you on Gay Pride Day?

We're OUT. Where the fuck are YOU?

6. WHEN ANYONE ASSAULTS YOU FOR BEING QUEER, IT IS QUEER BASHING. Right?

A crowd of 50 people exit a gay bar as it closes. Across the street, some straight boys are shouting "Faggots" and throwing beer bottles at the gathering, which outnumbers then 10 to 1. Three queers make a move to respond, getting no support from the group. Why did a group this size allow themselves to be sitting ducks?

Tompkins Square Park, Labor Day. At an annual outdoor concert/drag show, a group of gay men were harassed by teens carrying sticks. In the midst of thousands of gay men and lesbians, these straight boys beat two gay men to the ground, then stood around tri-umphantly laughing amongst themselves. The emcee was alerted and warned the crowd from the stage: "You girls be careful. When you dress up it drives the boys crazy," as if it were a practical joke inspired by what the victims were wearing rather than a pointed attack on anyone and everyone at that event.

What would it have taken for that crowd to stand up to its attackers?

After James Zappalorti, an openly gay man, was murdered in cold blood on Staten Island this winter, a single demonstration was held in protest. Only one hundred people came. When Yuseuf Hawkins, a black youth, was shot to death for being on "white turf" in Bensonhurst, African Americans marched through that neighborhood in large numbers again and again. A black person was killed BECAUSE HE WAS BLACK, and people of color throughout the city recognized it and acted on it. The bullet that hit Hawkins was meant for a black man, ANY black man. Do most gays and lesbians think that the knife that punctured Zappalorti's heart was meant only for him?

The straight world has us so convinced that we are helpless and deserving victims of the violence against us, that queers are immobilized when faced with a threat. BE OUTRAGED! These attacks must not be tolerated. DO SOMETHING. Recognize that any act of aggres-sion against any member of our community is an attack on every member of the commu-nity. The more we allow homophobes to inflict violence, terror and fear on our lives, the more frequently and ferociously we will be the object of their hatred. Your body cannot be an open target for violence. Your body is worth protecting. You have a right to defend it. No matter what they tell you, your queerness must be defended and respected. You'd better learn that your life is immeasurably valuable, because unless you start believing that, it can easily be taken from you. If you know how to gently and efficiently immobilize your attacker, then by all means, do it. If you lack those skills, then think about gouging out his fucking eyes, slamming his nose back into his brain, slashing his throat with a broken bottle, do whatev-er you can, whatever you have to, to save your life!

7. WHY QUEER

Queer!

Ah, do we really have to use that word? It's trouble. Every gay person has his or her own take on it. For some it means strange and eccentric and kind of mysterious. That's okay; we like that. But some gay girls and boys don't. They think they're more normal than strange. And for others "queer" conjures up those awful memories of adolescent suffering. Queer. It's forcibly bittersweet and quaint at best—weakening and painful at worst. Couldn't we just use "gay" instead? It's a much brighter word. And isn't it synonymous with "happy"? When will you militants grow up and get over the novelty of being different?

Well, yes, "gay" is great. It has its place. But when a lot of lesbians and gay men wake up in the morning we feel angry and disgusted, not gay. So we've chosen to call ourselves queer. Using "queer" is a way of reminding us how we are perceived by the rest of the world. It's a way of telling ourselves we don't have to be witty and charming people who keep our lives discreet and marginalized in the straight world. We use queer as gay men loving lesbians and lesbians loving being queer. Queer, unlike GAY, doesn't mean MALE.

And when spoken to other gays and lesbians it's a way of suggesting we close ranks, and forget (temporarily) our individual differences because we face a more insidious common enemy. Yeah, QUEER can be a rough word but it is also a sly and ironic weapon we can steal from the homophobe's hands and use against him.

NO SEX POLICE

8. For anyone to say that coming out is not part of the revolution is missing the point. Positive sexual images and what they manifest saves lives because they affirm those lives and make it possible for people to attempt to live as self-loving instead of self-loathing. As the famous "Black is beautiful" slogan changed many lives so does "Read my lips" affirm queerness in the face of hatred and invisibility as displayed in a recent governmental study of suicides that states that at least 1/3 of all teen suicides are Queer kids. This is further exemplified by the rise in HIV transmission among those under 21.

We are most hated as queers for our sexualness, that is, our physical contact with the same sex. Our sexuality and sexual expression are what makes us most susceptible to physical violence. Our difference, our otherness, our uniqueness can either paralyze us or politicize us. Hopefully, the majority of us will not let it kill us.

9. Why in the world do we let heteros into queer clubs? Who gives a fuck if they like us because we "really know how to party?" WE HAVE TO IN ORDER TO BLOW OFF THE STEAM THEY MAKE US FEEL ALL THE TIME! They make out wherever they please, and take up too much room on the dance floor doing ostentatious couples dances. They wear their heterosexuality like a "Keep Out" sign, or like a deed of ownership.

Why the fuck do we tolerate them when they invade our space like it's their right? Why do we let them shove heterosexuality—a weapon their world wields against us—right in our faces in the few public spots where we can be sexy with each other and not fear attack?

It's time to stop letting the straight people make all the rules. Let's start by posting this sign outside every queer club and bar:

RULES OF CONDUCT FOR STRAIGHT PEOPLE

1) Keep your displays of affection (kissing, handholding, embracing) to a minimum. Your sexuality is unwanted and offensive to many here.
2) If you must slow dance, be as inconspicuous as possible.
3) Do not gawk or stare at lesbians or gay men, especially bull dykes or drag queens. We are not your entertainment.
4) If you cannot comfortably deal with someone of the same sex making a pass at you, get out.
5) Do not flaunt your heterosexuality. Be Discreet. Risk being mistaken for a lezzie or a homo.
6) If you feel these rules are unfair, go fight homophobia in straight clubs, or
7) Go Fuck Yourself.

I HATE STRAIGHTS

I have friends. Some of them are straight.

Year after year, I see my straight friends. I want to see them, to see how they are doing, to add newness to our long and complicated histories, to experience some continuity.

Year after year I continue to realize that the facts of my life are irrelevant to them and that I am only half listened to, that I am an appendage to the doings of a greater world, a world of power and privilege, of the laws of installation, a world of exclusion. "That's not true," argue my straight friends. There is the one certainty in the politics of power: those left out of it beg for inclusion, while the insiders claim that they already are. Men do it to women, whites do it to blacks, and everyone does it to queers.

The main dividing line, both conscious and unconscious, is procreation . . . and that magic word—Family. Frequently, the ones we are born into disown us when the find out who we really are, and to make matters worse, we are prevented from having our own. We are punished, insulted, cut off, and treated like seditionaries in terms of child rearing, both damned if we try and damned if we abstain. It's as if the propagation of the species is such a fragile directive that without enforcing it as if it were an agenda, humankind would melt back into the primeval ooze.

I hate having to convince straight people that lesbians and gays live in a war zone, that we're surrounded by bomb blasts only we seem to hear, that our bodies and souls are heaped high, dead from fright or bashed or raped, dying of grief or disease, stripped of our personhood.

I hate straight people who can't listen to queer anger without saying "hey, all straight people aren't like that. I'm straight too, you know." as if their egos don't get enough stroking or protection in this arrogant, heterosexist world. Why must we take care of them, in the midst of our just anger brought on by their fucked up society?! Why add the reassurance of "Of course, I don't mean you. You don't act that way." Let them figure out for themselves whether they deserve to be included in our anger.

But of course that would mean listening to our anger, which they almost never do. They deflect it, by saying "I'm not like that" or "now look who's generalizing" or "You'll catch more flies with honey . . ." or "If you focus on the negative you just give out more power" or "you're not the only one in the world who's suffering." They say "Don't yell at me, I'm on your side" or "I think you're overreacting" or "BOY, YOU'RE BITTER."

They've taught us that good queers don't get mad. They've taught us so well that we not only hide our anger from them, we hide it from each other. WE EVEN HIDE IT FROM OURSELVES. We hide it with substance abuse and suicide and overachieving in the hope of proving our worth. They bash us and stab us and shoot us and bomb us in ever increasing numbers and still we freak out when angry queers carry banners or signs that say BASH BACK. For the last decade they let us die in droves and still we thank President Bush for planting a fucking tree, applaud him for likening PWAs to car accident victims who refuse to wear seatbelts. LET YOURSELF BE ANGRY. Let yourself be angry that the price of our visibility is the constant threat of violence, anti-queerviolence to which practically every segment of this society contributes. Let yourself feel angry that THERE IS NO PLACE IN THIS COUNTRY WHERE WE ARE SAFE, no place where we are not targeted for hatred and attack, the self-hatred, the suicide—of the closet. The next time some straight person comes down on you for being angry, tell them that until things change, you don't need any more evidence that the world turns at your expense. You don't need to see only hetero couple grocery shopping on your TV . . . You don't want any more baby pictures shoved in your face until you can have or keep your own. No more weddings, showers, anniversaries, please, unless they are our own brothers and sisters celebrating. And tell them not to dismiss you by saying "You have rights," "You have privileges," "You're overreacting," or "You have a victim's mentality." Tell them "GO AWAY FROM ME, until YOU can change." Go away and try on a world without the brave, strong queers that are its backbone, that are its guts and brains and souls. Go tell them go away until they have spent a month walking hand in hand in public with someone of the same sex. After they survive that, then you'll hear what they have to say about queer anger. Otherwise, tell them to shut up and listen.

While lesbian separatism came under fire in the 1980s, it is far from extinct. Most "lesbian" events must deal with the question of who will be welcome, and how to screen out those who are not. For instance, the National Lesbian Conference in 1991 faced intense controversy over whether male-to-female transgendered persons were welcome. The Michigan Womyn's Music Festival has struggled for years over the question of male children of lesbians, as well as transgendered or transsexual people.

In the following article, first published in 1990, Julia Penelope invites lesbians to rethink the issue of separate space. She urges us to think of women-only or lesbian-only events and spaces as "containers," places removed from the patriarchy in which only those who choose to abide by the rules are welcome. On the basis of a lesbian feminist analysis of the antagonism between men (including gays) and women, she argues that those who do not or will not respect the wishes of separatists at these events are breaking trust and harming lesbians.

Julia Penelope has authored and coedited numerous volumes on lesbian lives and literature. She has been a powerful voice for lesbian separatism for two decades.

JULIA PENELOPE

WIMMIN- AND LESBIAN-ONLY SPACES: THOUGHT INTO ACTION

(1990)

Julia Penelope

There are women and Lesbians who take wimmin-and Lesbian-only spaces[1] for granted, perceiving them as efforts that aren't difficult or dangerous to maintain, on a par with sneaking beer into a movie theater. But such spaces are always endangered and vulnerable to trespass and infiltration. Attempts to discredit, disrupt, and destroy Lesbian- and wimmin-only spaces have persisted since Lesbians began establishing spaces and insisting upon our right to them. This isn't new information. We have learned that those who take the risks to create wimmin- and Lesbian-only spaces cannot assume that other Lesbians and wimmin will respect them. Unless we find a way to maintain male-free spaces, the intrusions typical of the 1970s and 1980s will persist through yet another decade.

- In June, 1987, Sisterfire[2] coordinators ignored male assaults on two Separatists and told them they didn't belong at the festival and "had no right" to deny men access to their booth.
- In 1989, Lesbian mothers brought at least four male children to the first East Coast Lesbian Festival even though the festival brochure said specifically: "Lesbians and Girl Children Welcome."
- A gayman, Bob Kavin, threatened to file a complaint against Crones' Harvest, then a new wimmin's bookstore in Jamaica Plain, Massachusetts, for advertising "wimmin-only" events in Gay Community News. He characterized such male-free events as "divisive" and said the ad "pissed him off."
- Also in 1990, Rex Wockner, a syndicated gay columnist, made Mountain Moving Coffeehouse, a wimmin-only space in Chicago, the center of a controversy in its fifteenth year of existence.

- A woman describing herself as "strayt" occupied a full page in a 1990 issue of *Dykes, Disability & Stuff* and promised (!) to send more "stuff."
- Two men have crashed into an issue of the Women's Braille Press newsletter.

In spite of their apparent dissimilarity, these events have several common features. Each violation is an attempt to force *normalization*[3] on Lesbians and wimmin who are consciously encouraging and cherishing attitudes, values, and behaviors devalued by the majority culture—what heteropatriarchal society labels "abnormal" and "unnatural": wimmin loving and attending to one another. These people insist that Lesbians and wimmin respect and condone the heteropatriarchal values they bring with them. In the heteropatriarchy, it is *normal* and *natural*, not deviant, for men to have unchallenged access to women. The gaymen trying to destroy Crones' Harvest and Mountain Moving Coffeehouse and the Sisterfire coordinators insist that men retain their privilege to invade and occupy wimmin's spaces. Men justify their intrusions by asserting that the privileges they have in the heteropatriarchy are their "natural right."

The claim of "natural right" is also used by a few mothers of male children who insist on bringing their sons with them into wimmin- and Lesbian-only spaces. Most mothers of sons support and respect our spaces, either by arranging to leave their male children at home or, for financial reasons, stay at home themselves. Why, then, do a few mothers *insist* that we tolerate their sons? For one thing, they have millenia of heteropatriarchal dogma behind their demands: Because breeding is considered "normal" and "natural," those mothers *expect* to take their offspring wherever they wish. When denied access for their male children, they protest as though their privilege were an "inalienable right." Some Lesbian mothers persist in demanding that we allow them to bring male children to wimmin- and Lesbian-only events. Their insistence on giving males access to wimmin- and Lesbian-only spaces reaffirms the breeders' privilege they enjoy in the heteropatriarchy.[4]

There is no space on this planet that men do not claim as theirs "by right." However much space they dominate, it never seems to be "enough" for them. Wimmin- and Lesbian-only spaces challenge the male "right" to occupy and control territory. In this culture, "it's a man's world." Whatever is "public" space is theirs. Men assume they have the right to occupy any "public" space because it's *their* world. Women's lives have been confined to the "private" sphere. But men control the private as well as the public sphere. As Catherine MacKinnon has pointed out,[5] men's laws operate only in the public sphere; they cease to operate in the private sphere, because that is where men "exercise" their freedom and do whatever they want to women and children. If Lesbians want to raise males, they should be teaching them that wimmin have the right to establish our own spaces; that no man has any right to be where we don't want him; that "No" doesn't mean "Yes."

When we create a space we label Lesbian- or wimmin-only, we mean what we say. This isn't something that's open to interpretation! Yet, a few women and Lesbians feel compelled, year after year, to defend and insist upon men's "right" to unlimited access to other wimmin and Lesbians. By demanding that we admit them with their male children, these individuals make it clear that they value men more than they value wimmin and/or Lesbians *and* the desire we make explicit by creating these spaces. Each intrusion devalues wimmin-only space, negating it by introducing male presence, male values and male behaviors, sometimes all three. In every case, the Lesbians trying to establish and maintain wimmin-only space are trivialized and attacked, and the mothers of sons and their supporters justify their attacks by the tactic of reversal: they cast themselves as the "victims" of Lesbians who reject the claims of men and Lesbian mothers of male children. The violators attempt to coerce and intimidate other Lesbians and wimmin into supporting men and condoning their values and behaviors by describing themselves as an "oppressed minority."

In each case I've cited, some type of "discrimination" is alleged in order to deny our right to control the spaces we create: at Sisterfire, the two Lesbians were accused of racism and "provoking" a man's physical assault by telling him they didn't want him to enter their booth; Lesbian mothers of males portray themselves as taking "risks" to raise male children, as "pioneering" radical ways of parenting. They describe Lesbians who won't support them as their "oppressors." Men who resort to their legal system to redress the "wrong" done to them when wimmin or Lesbians create wimmin-only events claim that they are the "victims" of "sexist" oppression.

For some reason I don't understand, some Lesbians, women, and men either don't grasp the principles involved in wimmin- and Lesbian-only space, or they pretend not to understand. I don't understand why they don't understand. I've thought the ideas were easily grasped and the labels we use to describe them were literally interpreted: "wimmin-only" space means *wimmin only*; "Lesbian-only" space means *Lesbians only*. There is no ambiguity in either phrase. Sons are, by definition, inherently *male*; otherwise, they would be daughters. Where, then, is the problem? Why is the concept of "female-only" space so difficult to entertain and so frequently challenged?

I've been thinking about how we think about Lesbian-/wimmin-only space and trying to understand why there are conflicts when we stake out some area as our "own." What do we *imagine* we're doing when we say we're "creating" Lesbian-/wimmin-only space? Our thinking is based on the CONTAINER metaphor[6]: we imagine that we create a container (or draw a circle) that has an inside and an outside. *Inside*, within our circle, we say we want only wimmin or only Lesbians; individuals who aren't wimmin or Lesbians we expect to remain *outside* our circle. We *include* all other wimmin or Lesbians and we *exclude*, by default, anyone who doesn't identify as woman or Lesbian, and those women and Lesbians who prefer male company. There is, or should be, a process of self-selection: anyone who doesn't like Lesbian- or wimmin-only spaces needn't come.

Where do we imagine we "draw" our imaginary circles? Where do we think we've created our wimmin- or Lesbian-only space *in relation to* patriarchal space? Do we imagine our "space" to be "inside" or "outside" of male-dominated space? I, for one, have imagined Lesbian-/wimmin-only space as being "outside" or "beyond" patriarchal social space in a metaphorical sense. I know that I've thought of it that way in the past: Standing naked "downtown" at the Michigan Womyn's Music Festival, I have thought of myself as "inside" and of the patriarchal world as "out there" somewhere beyond the borders of the womyn-owned land. While I'm at the Festival, I rarely remind myself that the two worlds are connected by the public road that lies just outside the gates of the Festival. The spaces we create for ourselves may have physical boundaries, but, more importantly, they're an idea we nourish in our minds.

Whatever spaces we temporarily carve out for ourselves from the world of men and label wimmin- or Lesbian-only space are just that: temporary. Using the CONTAINER metaphor to think about wimmin- and Lesbian-only spaces tricks us into thinking of them as "insides" that have "outsides," but this isn't true. We are always *in* heteropatriarchy, never *outside* of it. For this reason, our spaces cannot be defended against intrusion. In spite of their vulnerability, we have been able so far to at least curtail men's access to wimmin- and Lesbian-only spaces. What we seem unable to discourage or halt are the persistent attempts of a few women and Lesbians to breach the spaces we claim as Lesbian- or wimmin-only. Such encroachments are more insidious than male intrusion. I don't *expect* men to respect wimmin-only spaces; nonetheless, some do. I *expect* other wimmin and Lesbians to respect such spaces; some don't.

For example, when Lisa Vogel and Barbara Price discovered that some workers had brought men's music to listen to at the Michigan Womyn's Music Festival, they were shocked that those workers failed to perceive their actions as contradictory or invasive, and were dismayed that the propriety of listening to male voices in that context could be an "issue." Why isn't it clear that the sound of male voices at a *womyn's* music festival introduces men's ideas, values, and behaviors? What some or many of us assume are self-evident labels—*wimmin's music*, *wimmin-only* dance, *Lesbian-only* workshop—are apparently labels that others feel compelled to violate.

More dangerously, such violations are often gradual or clandestine. For example, it was not "enough" when the Michigan coordinators responded to the protests of the mothers of boys by establishing the Brother Sun Camp for boys up to the age of ten. For the past two years, a special area has been set aside *at the center of the Festival* for mothers with children under three.[7] It is common knowledge among festie-goers that mothers of sons, apparently not satisfied by their successful encroachment into the "wimmin-only" space of the Michigan Festival, have deliberately proceeded to violate the essential idea of wimmin-/Lesbian-only space by disguising their male children as girls and sneaking them onto the land! Such purposeful disregard for the implied rights of other wimmin and Lesbians to define and control our spaces violates our trust as well as our declared boundaries.

Why are a few mothers of sons so determined to violate the spaces some of us cherish and work so hard to create? I don't think they even understand what all the fuss is about; I don't think they perceive their actions as betrayals or violations because they don't think of wimmin- or Lesbian-only spaces as *containers*. In their minds, they haven't yet distinguished between "the male world *out there*" and the world we create and think of as *in here*. To them, our spaces are the same as the rest of the world: males have and, thanks to the intervention of a few mothers of sons, *do* have access to both. We will continue to repeat this conflict until, or unless, these few perceive wimmin- and Lesbian-only spaces as we do, and come to think of them in terms of the CONTAINER metaphor.

How are we to deal with such women and Lesbians? Can we deal honorably and honestly with those who refuse to be honorable or honest with us? Since *some* mothers of male children seem utterly uninterested in or incapable of respecting the boundaries and definitions other wimmin and Lesbians have said we want them to honor, our options are limited. Some Lesbians think it is a contradiction to "exclude" wimmin and Lesbians from wimmin- and Lesbian-only spaces even though they have violated the boundaries we have said we wish to maintain when they sneak in their male children. For example, when I was explaining what I thought "Lesbian-only" space meant from the stage at the East Coast Lesbian Festival in 1989, someone in the audience screamed out, "The mothers are Lesbians, too!" But this is a diversionary tactic. The issue isn't whether the mothers of male children are or are not Lesbians. The issue is their demand that we accept their male children *as a corollary* to accepting them. An 18-month-old male child is *not* a Lesbian. About that there is no question. Yet, their reasoning seems to go something like this:

I am a Lesbian. Therefore I have a right to be in Lesbian-only space. (So far, so good.) I have a son. Because I am a Lesbian, I have the right to bring my son (or exceptional man) with me.

Having identified themselves as Lesbian, they proceed to use that identity as an umbrella of immunity for any male *they* feel safe with. (But many of us have been raped and/or assaulted by boys and men that other females felt "safe" with.)

All of the examples I've mentioned represent *violations* of the boundaries of other Lesbians and wimmin and betrayals of our trust in their integrity and values. Those who insist upon their "right" to bring men into wimmin- or Lesbian-only space cannot seem to distinguish between the heteropatriarchal culture in which we all live and the small, temporary spaces we attempt to claim as our own for hours, days or weeks. Their demands force us to compromise and ignore our own values and priorities. Lesbian- and wimmin-only spaces give us many joys and opportunities we can't get anywhere else in this world:

- they provide us with some respite from the dangers and anxieties of our lives in heteropatriarchy;
- the atmosphere and joy we experience reenergizes us and enables us to go on surviving and working for change;
- in them, we can creatively explore and develop Lesbian values and ways of relating to each other;
- we can talk, roam, play, and sleep undisturbed by male intrusiveness and interruptions;
- we don't have to listen to men or the sound of their voices;
- such spaces are the only ones in which girl children can run free without fearing male predation and violence.

For all these reasons (and more), these spaces are important to many of us. They are one of the greatest and most lasting gifts we can give to girl children. *We have a right to them* and, as well, *the right to expect that others will respect them.*

If we are to maintain these spaces, what are we to do with women and Lesbians who demand access for their men and male children to them and *believe* that their demands and surreptitious violations have the weight of moral righteousness behind them? We have been explaining to them *for years* why we want them to respect our spaces, and they seem unwilling to understand their own hypocrisy in the situation. They fail to perceive how bringing their sons into Lesbian- and wimmin-only events violates the very spirit and intent of such spaces, when their ostensible reason for coming is to enjoy their unique qualities with the rest of us. They cannot have things both ways.

What is involved here is a choice that they must make, one they have, so far, refused to consider: Either they figure out how to leave their sons at home or they voluntarily exclude themselves. And, in so doing, they have to take responsibility for their choice. Their claim—that we "exclude" them when we exclude their sons—is false (unless we agree with the heteropatriarchal notion that mothers become indissolubly *merged* with their children), and most mothers of sons reject this claim by their ability to choose.

It's long past time to stop trying to reason with them and to acknowledge that our explanations are just not sufficient for them. One would think that the simple statement about what we want for ourselves would be enough to dissuade these few from continuing to violate our spaces. Judging from their behavior and what they say, this doesn't seem to be the case. Their persistent encroachments require an unsavory vigilance and a constant drain on our energies to defend the spaces we claim. If we continue to give in to these demands and ignore the tremendous toll these violations exact, we will no longer be able to enjoy even those few, isolated and extremely vulnerable wimmin- or Lesbian-only spaces we establish.

Again and again, a few women violate our spaces without any apparent regard for us. What are our options for dealing with Lesbians and women who prioritize men and male values over the expressed desires of other wimmin and Lesbians? Obviously, naming our events "Lesbian-" or "wimmin-only" has failed; they refuse to honor them. Explanations of the political and personal reasons for having wimmin- and Lesbian-only spaces have consistently failed us, but the alternatives to explanation are unappealing. We could think of these spaces as "wimmin-only-sort of" or "Lesbian-only-sort of," which seems to be the approach already in use. A space is wimmin- or Lesbian-only except for when it's not. Or, we could establish "strip searches" at festival registrations and have every mother with a child open its diapers or pants to prove that it's a girl child. Such a solution is repugnant. Yet, we cannot, it seems, trust each other, or, at least, not *all* of us. If we can't trust each other to respect our expressed wishes, whom can we trust? If some women and Lesbians who value men over the rest of us persist in their refusal to respect us, I don't know how we can continue to honor an illusory respect or trust that isn't mutual.

I do know that some of us will continue to create, participate in, and enjoy Lesbian- and wimmin-only spaces, and we will continue to repulse the intrusions of gaymen and sons of mothers: We will refuse to admit gaymen to such events and ask mothers to leave their male children at home or accept responsibility for their decision to exclude themselves.

1. *I realize that my repetition of* wimmin- and Lesbian-only *will seem cumbersome to readers; for this, I apologize. I want to acknowledge that heterosexual wimmin as well as Lesbians support and enjoy male-free spaces. But I also want to represent a distinction that's important to me. In my own experience, both kinds of space are different in a number of ways: they establish very different frameworks, contexts, and expectations. What is talked about in an all-women context differs from the subjects Lesbians choose to talk about; the life-experiences discussed and validated are dissimilar; the perspectives with which participants approach each context reflect different values and assumptions. These differences became clear to me one night when I watched a tape of a female comedian who has taken women-only space mainstream and is performing to sell-out,* women-only *crowds! While I laughed out loud at some of her jokes, I found most of them either distasteful or boring because she focused almost entirely on men and women's feelings about and relationships with them. I have no quarrel with what she's doing; the women who attended her show seemed to be enjoying themselves and that's enough reason to support what the comedian is doing. But Lesbian-only space is something altogether different and more pleasing to me: It is the only space in this world where Lesbians focus exclusively on each other, on our ideas, on our desires, on our relations with each other. And, for most of us, it provides us with a much-needed respite from having to deal with men and women who focus their entire beings on men.*

2. *Sisterfire was an annual music festival organized and produced by Roadworks, a Washington, D.C. collective; it was the only wimmin's music festival that attempted an explicitly multiracial, multi-ethnic focus that reflected the cultural diversity of our communities. Two years after the fiasco I discuss here, the Sisterfire festival ceased to exist.*

3. *For a thorough discussion of the many ways Lesbian motherhood co-opts Lesbian values and spaces, see* Dykes-Loving-Dykes *by Bev Jo, Linda Strega, and Ruston (Oakland: Battleaxe, 1990), esp. pp. 212–234. Kate Moran, in a conversation, described the process discussed here as "normalization," and I'm indebted to her for our many talks about this issue and how it affects Lesbians.*

4. *Many mothers expect privileges and certain behaviors from others. I meet them everywhere I go. They expect strangers to smile approvingly at them; they expect others to allow them to cut into long lines; they expect others to put up with their childrens' screeches and squalls in restaurants, theaters, and other public places. I don't know why. There are already too many people in the world. Once, I boarded a plane, expecting my reserved seat to be available. Instead, there sat a breeder with her baby spread out in what was supposed to have been my seat! As I approached and began checking the numbers of the seats to be sure I hadn't made a mistake, she smiled at me confidently. I asked, "Who do you think you are? Do you think that, because you're a breeder, you have the right to take over my seat?" The stewardess came rushing down the aisle, saying "Oh, I'm so sorry. I thought it would be all right." Why would someone assume that I wouldn't mind having my seat taken away from me?*

5. *In* Feminism Unmodified: Discourses on Life and Law *(1987) MacKinnon elaborates how the liberal concept of the "private sphere" is "an ideological division that lies about women's shared experience and that mystifies the unity among the spheres of women's violation" (102), with respect to abortion (100–102) and pornography (155 and 211).*

6. *Michael Reddy first identified the "Container Metaphor" in "The Conduit Metaphor—A Case of Frame Conflict,"* Metaphor and Thought, *ed. Andrew Ortony (Cambridge: Cambridge University Press, 1979), 284–324. Readers interested in other ways the Container Metaphor structures how we think about other aspects of our daily lives will find a more detailed explanation in* Speaking Freely: Unlearning the Lies of the Fathers' Tongues *(Pergamon, 1990), in which I discuss the function of that metaphor in heteropatriarchal thinking, and illustrate how it shapes our understanding of language, writing, and ourselves as females as well.*

7. *When a Michigan festie-goer complained about the creation of the toddler camping area, where mothers can have male sons up to the age of three, Lisa Vogel explained that she and Barbara Price established the new area because too many mothers dropped off their infants and small children, and then apparently "forgot" the children and failed to return for them. Announcements, asking mothers to return to the daycare area for their abandoned children, have been a too common feature of the nightstage at Michigan. Understandably, Michigan workers are reluctant to accept responsibility for very young children and to bear the brunt of their mothers' neglect.*

Craig Harris was a community health organizer at the time of his
death from AIDS in 1991 at the age of 33. His keynote address
to CARE, Black Gays and Lesbians United Against AIDS delivered
on June 23, 1990 is important as a manifestation of political
inspiration and rhetorical art. It is a Black gay man with AIDS talking about his collective history with other African American gays and lesbians, the sharing of information
that has not often been included within lesbian and gay history books—information that
can be used for organizing today, and a charge to the audience to build upon the
accomplishments of their forerunners to "speak out" and to become activists.

CRAIG HARRIS

CELEBRATING AFRICAN-AMERICAN LESBIAN AND GAY HISTORY: FINDING OUR WAY TO THE FUTURE

keynote address to the CARE, Black Gays and Lesbians United Against AIDS Conference
Denver, Colorado (1990)

Craig G. Harris

We have joined together this eve of Gay Pride Day under a theme which is of utmost importance to the survival of the African-American community . . . the entire African-American
community. The theme "Celebrating Our History, Creating Our Future . . ." reminds me of
the title of a novel by a West African Gay writer named Yulissa Amadou Maddy. The novel,
entitled *No Past, No Present, No Future*, is the rather grim story of the life of a young man
who grows up in a West African village, is granted a scholarship to study in London, and
while in London grapples with the contradictions between his desires for men, for a better
life, and greater exposure to a more global perspective, and the values, traditions and expectations of his family and village kinspeople. Maddy's main character lives a life of internal
and social struggle . . . not understanding his own feelings, not being understood by his
friends and peers, and never reaching his full potential for professional growth, romantic
satisfaction, and personal development.

The story is a sad one, indeed; one which I would love to deny exists in the real world.
I am afraid, however, that this story is all too common, and my denial will do nothing to better the situation of other African-American Lesbians and Gay men. Similarly, your denial
will do nothing to empower the African-American Lesbian and Gay community.

My belief is that the main character of Maddy's novel suffers from a very common
affliction in our community. It is the belief that as the title suggests, we do not have a legitimate history, that our present is not built upon an honorable legacy, and that our future will
not be a bright one. On the contrary, we have a history of being some of the most valuable
contributors to the African-American community. We are currently involved on the front
lines of progressive movements, and we are destined for a future of survival.

The demise of Maddy's main character was not the result of his questioning and opposing the values and customs of his people, nor of living an immoral lifestyle. His demise came
about because he had no one to instill in him a belief that he was not alone, not a freak, not
even particularly unusual. His demise was the result of his lack of connection to his history

and to others who felt and experienced what he was feeling and experiencing. His isolation and alienation prohibited him from having any hope for a better future.

My goal this evening is to share a bit of our collective history as well as some personal histories, with the hope that you will be inspired to do all you can individually and as a group to create a brighter future for the entire African-American community; a future in which we will all live safely, in good health, and in communion with our brothers and sisters. It could not be more appropriate that I have the opportunity to do this on the eve of the celebration of the anniversary of the event which marks the beginning of the modern Lesbian and Gay movement.

During this weekend, twenty-one years ago, New York City vice police raided a bar in Sheridan Square in the Greenwich Village section of Manhattan. The name of the bar was the Stonewall Inn. It was a Gay bar, one frequented by predominantly African-American and Latino transpersons and cross-dressers. The raid on this bar was not unusual. Gay bars were frequently raided during the 1950s and 1960s. African Americans and Latinos have consistently been the recipients of police brutality. Nothing new, right? Well, let us remember the era of which we are speaking. It is 1969. Dr. Martin Luther King, Jr. has just been assassinated a year earlier. The nonviolent Civil Rights Movement is a memory which has been replaced by the Black Power Movement—a movement which embraced the words of Malcolm X: ". . . by any means necessary." Students' Democratic Society are raising hell on American college campuses in protest of the Vietnam War and the inability of the American government to maintain peace abroad and at home. The women's movement is underway with bra-burnings and demands for access to equal employment with equal pay. Social protest is the rage.

So, in the midst of all this civil unrest, the New York City vice squad—probably not realizing they represented the greatest ill of our society in the form of a paramilitary, patriarchal, racist, sexist and homophobic symbol of authority—decided to enter the Stonewall Inn this weekend, twenty-one years ago, and interrupt the partying that was taking place inside by denying patrons the ability to commune with other lesbians and gay men over cocktails.

Well, it was the wrong group of African-American and Latino queens to mess with on that evening, 'cause there was a considerable amount of blood shed. Yes, there was more than a little stained taffeta and chiffon, but there were equal amounts of bloodstained blue serge uniforms and a number of busted police heads. That's what I call a revolution! . . . a revolution started by the very "drag queens" which we, as a community are all too quick to ignore, chastise, and attack more vehemently than would heterosexuals.

Let's go further back in time . . . way back. For those who would assert that homosexuality in the African-American community is a fad, a newfound side effect of assimilation, a product of African-Americans buying into the white man's corrupted sexual ideas and ideals, I'm going to take you back to the days of slavery . . . 1646 to be exact. In that year, *The Calendar of Dutch Historical Manuscripts* reports a court case which was heard on Manhattan Island, then called New Netherland Colony. The court proceedings from June 25, 1646 (exactly three hundred and forty-four years ago, come Monday[1990-Eds.]) cite the case of the *Fiscal* [public prosecutor] *vs. Jan Creoli,* a Negro. Said Negro was accused of "sodomy; second offense; this crime being condemned of God (Genesis 19; Leviticus, 18:22–29) as an abomination, prisoner is sentenced to be conveyed to the place of public execution, and there choked to death, and then burnt to ashes."[1] We have been around for quite a while as you see. You will also note, I trust, that our right to love has been challenged for just as long.

Let's move beyond the days of slavery—if we believe that the institution of slavery was, in fact, abolished. Let's move on to the year 1893, when a white heterosexual physician by the name of Dr. Charles H. Hughes of St. Louis, MO, wrote briefly about African-American male transvestites in an American medical journal, saying:

"I am credibly informed that there is, in the city of Washington D.C. an annual convocation of [N]egro men called the drag dance, which is an orgie of lascivious debauchery beyond pen power of description. I am likewise informed that a similar organization was lately suppressed by the police of New York city.

"In this sable performance of sexual perversion, all of these men are lasciviously dressed in womanly attire, short sleeves, low-necked dresses and the usual ball-room decorations and ornaments of women, feathered and ribboned head-dresses, garters, frills, flowers, etc., and deport themselves as women. Standing or seated on a pedestal, but accessible to all the rest is the necked queen (a male), whose phallic member, decorated with a ribbon, is subject to the gaze and osculations in turn of all the members of this lecherous gang of sexual perverts and phallic fornicators.

"among those who annually assemble in this strange libidinous display are cooks, barbers, waiters and other employees of Washington families, some even higher in the social scale—some being employed as subordinates in the government departments."2

The lack of empirical objectivity in Dr. Hughes's report, written ninety-seven years ago, is obvious. I ask you, how many times can one use the word "lascivious" in three paragraphs? I detect an ever so slight bias—one which seems to have caused the author, whose goal was to observe and report, to become side-tracked into editorializing the behaviors of these men. Notice also, Hughes' not so subtly expressed disdain for women. One is left to infer that Dr. Hughes believes that the role of women is to be displayed on a pedestal and admired as the sexual objects of men. We must always remember that the prejudice and oppression which has and continues to subjugate gay men, is rooted in the prejudice and oppression of women and in the arrogant assumption of women's inferiority. Our history of struggle as gay men is inextricably linked to the struggle of Lesbians, and indeed all women.

Let us look at another important period in American history. Let us move into the 1920s—the period we refer to as the Harlem Renaissance. During this period, African-American arts, particularly literature, thrived. If any one individual could be viewed as being responsible for creating the African-American literary movement of that time, it would be Alain Locke, author of *The New Negro*, and professor of English at Howard University. Locke, who taught many writers of the Harlem Renaissance, was also the inspiration for a short-lived literary journal entitled *Fire!* which was first published in 1927. This publication contained a short story by Richard Bruce Nugent, entitled: "Smoke, Lillies, and Jade." It was the first piece of Gay fiction focusing on the life of an African-American Gay male to be published in this country. I would venture to say that this story would not have been published, in fact, it would probably not have been written, had it not been for the support, advice, and collaborative efforts of other African-American lesbian and gay writers, such as Wallace Thurman (the editor of *Fire!*) Zora Neale Hurston, Countee Cullen, Alice Dunbar-Nelson, Angelina Weld Grimké, and Langston Hughes to name a few.

Let us now jump to the 1960s. Let's look at some of the experiences of the late Bayard Rustin, a strategist for the Civil Rights Movement and friend and advisor to the late Rev. Dr. Martin Luther King, Jr. Looking back at his life and his working relationship with Dr. King, Rustin stated:

"It is difficult for me to know what Dr. King felt about gayness except to say that I'm sure he would have been sympathetic and would not have had the prejudicial view . . . My being gay was not a problem for Dr. King but a problem for the movement. He finally came to the decision that he needed to talk with some people in his organization. Reverend Thomas Kilgore, a good friend of mine and pastor of Friendship Baptist Church, was a man Dr. King turned to. Rev. Kilgore asked Martin to set up a committee to advise him. the committee finally came to the decision that my sex life was a burden to Dr. King . . . they advised him that he should ask me to leave."3

It was mainly the issue of Rustin's homosexuality which caused Dr. King to appoint A. Philip Randolph to be director of the 1963 March on Washington. Randolph, knowing Rustin's expertise was necessary to pull off the largest national civil rights march which the country had ever seen, sought approval to name Rustin as his deputy director. His wish was granted. However, it was met with noticeable objections from Roy Wilkins, the director of the National Association for the Advancement of Colored People.4

The story reminds me of another account of the 1963 March on Washington. It is the account of African-American Lesbian feminist author Audre Lorde. Lorde's recollection of the event is one of standing beside Lena Horne staffing a concession stand, making coffee for the menfolk because as she put it, "That was what most Black women did in the 1963 March on Washington . . ."5 Thank God we've come a long way, baby. But we have a lot further to go!

The year 1980 witnessed the vice presidential candidacy of the first openly gay African-American to throw his hat into the ring. At the 1980 National Democratic Convention held in New York City, a Dartmouth- and Yale-educated, Washington, D.C. resident named Melvin Boozer schmoozed delegates to get his name on the ballot. While we all know Boozer did not manage to get his name on the party ticket, his achievements were nonetheless quite laudable. By lobbying delegates, holding press conferences, and distributing campaign literature, Boozer was able to bring to the floor of the National Democratic Convention issues such as the ailing social conditions of the African-American community as well as the lack of civil rights for lesbian and gay Americans. In an address to delegates, Boozer explained, "I know what it means to be called a nigger, and I know what it means to be called a faggot, and I can sum up the difference in one word: none."6

In the late 1970s and 1980s, African-American lesbians and gay men undertook the task of creating a strong, vibrant and most importantly visible community. In 1975 a collective of New York-based lesbians founded Salsa Soul Sisters (now called African-American Wimmin United for Societal Change) as a support group for lesbians of color. In 1979, the National Coalition for Black Lesbians and Gays was formed to lobby government officials and provide technical assistance to smaller groups of lesbians and gay men. In 1986, Gay Men of African Descent was created as a sociopolitical network for African-American men in New York City.

During the 1980s, we experienced the increasing visibility of African-American writers and artists. Barbara Smith founded Kitchen Table: Women of Color Press in order to publish the work of lesbians and feminists of color. The Blackheart Collective and Other Countries published literary journals by African-American gay men, and the late Joseph Beam edited *In The Life*, the first anthology of African-American Gay male writing. Poet Essex Hemphill was granted a fellowship from the National Endowment for the Arts. Filmmakers Michelle Parkerson, Isaac Julien, and Marlon Riggs broke new ground with the films: "Stormé: A Life in the Jewel Box," "Looking for Langston," and "Tongues Untied."

In just the last twelve months, we have seen ground-breaking achievements for African-American lesbians and gay men. In New York City, Mayor David Dinkins has appointed Dr.

Marjorie Hill to head the City's Office of Lesbian and Gay Affairs. In Albany, New York, Keith St. John was made Alderman, giving him the honor and distinction of being the first openly Gay African-American elected official in this country. Also in New York City, Dr. Billy E. Jones, an openly Gay psychiatrist was appointed Commissioner of Mental Health. If that does not sound like much to you, please realize that it was not until 1973 that the American Psychiatric Association voted to remove homosexuality from its list of mental illnesses.

Now I dare anyone in this room to tell me that we have not come this far by faith. And I mean to tell you that there is no stopping us now. Each of the individuals and groups I've spoken about have been able to advance their work because they have had a strong knowledge of their history. There is an old Yoruba proverb which says: we stand on the shoulders of our ancestors. This proverb means simply that we build on the experiences and accomplishments of the generations which have come before us in order to attain more and to reach a higher level of consciousness.

We cannot do this if we are not visible. In the words of Audre Lorde, "Your silence will not protect you."[7] We must all become zealous activists speaking out against the injustices we suffer. We must speak out against sexist, homophobic, and racially motivated bias in our homes, in our work places, in our churches, schools, community centers, and our courtrooms. Our ancestors expect it of us. Our survival demands it of us!

It is customary to close a keynote address by leaving the audience with a charge. I could not, myself, compose a mandate which would be half as powerful or eloquent as the words of Pat Parker, an African-American lesbian feminist poet who died of cancer a year ago this month. [in 1989-Eds.] Parker's query as to what contributions we will make to ourselves, to our community, and to our movement is entitled: "Where Will You Be?":

Boots are being polished/Trumpeters clean their horns/Chains and locks forged/The Crusade has begun. Once again flags of Christ/are unfurled in the dawn/and cries of soul saviors/sing apocalyptic on air waves. Citizens, good citizens all/parade into voting booths/and in self-righteous sanctity/X away our right to life. I do not believe as some/that the vote is an end,/I fear even more/It is just a beginning. So I must make assessment/Look to you and ask:/Where will you be/when they come? They will not come/a mob rolling/through the streets,/but quickly and quietly/ move into our homes/and remove the evil,/the queerness,/the faggotry,/the perverseness/ from their midst./They will not come/clothed in brown,/and swastikas, or bearing chest heavy with/gleaming crosses./The time and need/for ruses are over./They will come/in business suits/to buy your homes/and bring bodies to/fill your jobs./They will come in robes/to rehabilitate/and white coats/to subjugate/and where will you be/when they come? Where will we all be when they come?/And they will come—they will come/because we are/defined as opposite—/perverse/and we are perverse. Every time we watched/a queer hassled in the/streets and said nothing—/It was an act of perversion. Everytime we lied about/the boyfriend or girlfriend/at coffee break—/It was an act of perversion. Everytime we heard,/ "I don't mind gays/but why must they/be blatant?" and said nothing—/It was an act of perversion. Everytime we let a lesbian mother/lose her child and did not fill/the courtrooms—/It was act of perversion. Everytime we let straights/make out in our bars while/we couldn't touch because/of laws—/It was an act of perversion. Everytime we put on the proper/clothes to go to a family/wedding and left our lovers/at home—/It was an act of perversion. Everytime we heard/ "Who I go to bed with/is my personal choice—/It's personal not political"/and said nothing—/It was an act of perversion. Everytime we let straight relatives/bury our dead and push our/lovers away—/It was an act of perversion. And they will come./They will come for/the perverts & it won't matter/if you're/homosexual, not a faggot/lesbian, not a dyke/gay, not queer/It won't matter/if you/own your business/have a good job/or are on S.S.I./It won't matter/if you're Black/Chicano/Native American/Asian/or White It won't matter/if you're from/New York/or Los Angeles/Galveston/or Sioux Falls/It won't matter/if you're Butch, or Fem/Not into roles/Monogamous/Non Monogamous/It won't matter/if you're Catholic/Baptist/Atheist/Jewish/or M.C.C. They will come/They will come/to the cities/and to the land/to your front rooms/and in your closets. They will come for/the perverts/and where will/you be/When they come?[8]

1. O'Callaghan, Edmund O., ed. Calendar of Historical Manuscripts in the Office of the Secretary of State, Albany, N.Y. Albany:Weed, Parsons, 1865.

2. Hughes, Charles H., "Erotopathia.—Morbid Eroticism," Alienist and Neurologist, St. Louis, MO., Vol. 14, no. 4, October 1893, pp. 531–578.

3. Jeanmarie, Redvers, "An Interview With Bayard Rustin," Other Countries: Black Gay Voices, New York, NY, Vol. 1, Spring 1988, p. 5.

4. Ibid. p. 6.

5. Lorde, Audre, "I Am Your Sister: Black Women Organizing Across Sexualities," A Burst of Light, Firebrand Books, Ithaca, NY, 1988, p. 23.

6. Pearson, Richard, "Homosexual Rights Activist Melvin Boozer Dies at 41," The Washington Post, Washington, DC, March 10, 1987, p.B6.

7. Lorde, Audre, "The Transformation of Silence into Language and Action," Sister Outsider, The Crossing Press, Freedom CA, 1984, p.41.

8. Parker, Pat, "Where Will You Be?" Movement in Black, (Diana Press, 1978/The Crossing Press, 1983) Firebrand Books, Ithaca, NY, 1980, pp. 73–78.

CARLA TRUJILLO

Feminists within Chicano/a communities in the U.S. have repeatedly been baited by charges that their demands for equality divide movements for racial equality or autonomy. One of the forms of this attack is the charge of lesbianism. As everyone's "other," lesbians and gays are disavowed by heterosexual cultures and associated with the "enemy." Many Chicanas are told that lesbianism is treason, that it is a white thing that threatens the continuity and strength of Chicana/o communities. In the last fifteen years, however, a growing number of Chicana lesbians are speaking out. They do not all agree on their position in their communities of birth; some see themselves as outcast, others reject it by choice, but most remain, insisting on their position in a reshaped culture that welcomes them.

Carla Trujillo, a teacher and administrator at the University of California at Berkeley, is the editor of *Chicana Lesbians: The Girls Our Mothers Warned Us About.* In the following essay she describes the obstacles to sexual freedom for Chicanas and the potential for alliances across sexuality. She rejects the idea that lesbians are *vendidas,* but argues that "Chicana lesbians pose a threat to the Chicano community" because they challenge it to become more egalitarian and sex-positive.

CHICANA LESBIANS: FEAR AND LOATHING IN THE CHICANO COMMUNITY

(1990)

Carla Trujillo

The vast majority of Chicano heterosexuals perceive Chicana lesbians as a threat to the community. Homophobia, that is, irrational fear of gay or lesbian people and/or behaviors, accounts, in part, for the heterosexist response to the lesbian community. However, I argue that Chicana lesbians are perceived as a greater threat to the Chicano community because their existence disrupts the established order of male dominance, and raises the consciousness of many Chicana women regarding their own independence and control. Some writers have addressed these topics,[1] however an analysis of the complexities of lesbian existence alongside this perceived threat has not been undertaken. While this essay is by no means complete, it attempts to elucidate the underlying basis of these fears which, in the very act of the lesbian existence, disrupt the established norm of patriarchal oppression.

Sexuality

As lesbians, our sexuality becomes the focal issue of dissent. The majority of Chicanas, both lesbian and heterosexual, are taught that our sexuality must conform to certain modes of behavior. Our culture voices shame upon us if we go beyond the criteria of passivity and repression, or doubts in our virtue if we refuse.[2] We, as women, are taught to suppress our sexual desires and needs by conceding all pleasure to the male. As Chicanas, we are commonly led to believe that even talking about our participation and satisfaction in sex is taboo. Moreover, we (as well as most women in the United States) learn to hate our bodies, and usually possess little knowledge of them. Lourdes Arguelles did a survey on the sexuality of 373 immigrant Latina women and found that over half of the women possessed little knowledge of their reproductive systems or their own physiology. Most remarked they "just didn't look down there."[3]

Not loving our bodies affects how we perceive ourselves as sexual beings. As lesbians, however, we have no choice but to confront our sexuality before we can confront our lesbianism. Thus the commonly held viewpoint among heterosexuals that we are "defined by our sexuality" is, in a way, partially true. If we did not bring our sexuality into consciousness, we would not be able to confront ourselves and come out.

After confronting and then acknowledging our attraction, we must, in turn, learn to reclaim that what we're told is bad, wrong, dirty, and taboo—namely our bodies, and our freedom to express ourselves in them. Too often we internalize the homophobia and sexism of the larger society, as well as that of our own culture, which attempts to keep us from loving ourselves. As Norma Alarchat said we are "definana lesbians [and] must act to negate the negation."[4] A Chicana lesbian must learn to love herself, both as a woman and a sexual being, before she can love another. Loving another woman not only validates one's own sexuality, but also that of the other woman, by the very act of loving. Understanding this, a student in a workshop Cherríe Moraga and I conducted on lesbian sexuality stated, "Now I get it. Not only do you have to learn to love your own vagina, but someone else's too."[5] It is only then that the subsequent experiences of love and commitment, passion and remorse can also become our dilemmas, much like those of everyone else. The effort to consciously reclaim our sexual selves forces Chicanas to either confront their own sexuality or, in refusing, castigate lesbians as *vendidas* to the race, blasphemers to the church, atrocities against nature, or some combination.

Identification

For many Chicanas, our identification as women, that is, as complete women, comes from the belief that we need to be connected to a man.[6] Ridding ourselves of this parasitic identification is not always easy, for we grow up, as my Chicana students have pointed out, defined in a male context: daddy's girl, some guy's girlfriend, wife, or mother. Vying for a man's attention compromises our own personal and intellectual development. We exist in a patriarchal society that undervalues women.[7] We are socialized to undervalue ourselves, as well as anything associated with the concept of self. Our voice is considered less significant, our needs and desires secondary. As the Chicanas in the MALCS [*Mujeres Activas en Letras y Cambio Social*] workshop indicated,[8] our toleration of unjust behavior from men, the church, the established order, is considered an attribute. How much pain can we bear in the here-and-now so that we may be better served in the afterlife? Martyrdom, the cloth of denial, transposes itself into a gown of cultural beauty.

Yet, an alliance with a man grants a woman heterosexual privileges, many of which are reified by the law, the church, our families and, of course, "la causa." Women who partake in the privileges of male sexual alliance may often do so at the cost of their own sense of self, since they must often subvert their needs, voice, intellect, and personal development in these alliances. These are the conditional contradictions commonly prescribed for women by the patriarchy in our culture and in the larger society. Historically, women have been viewed as property.[9] Though some laws may have changed, ideologically little else has. Upon marriage, a father feels he can relenquish "ownership" and "responsibility" of his daughter to her husband. The Chicana feminist who confronts this subversion, and critiques the sexism of the Chicano community, will be called *vendida* if she finds the "male defined and often anti-feminist" values of the community difficult to accept.[10]

The behaviors necessary in the "act of pursuing a man" often generate competition among women, leading to betrayal of one another.[11] When a woman's sense of identity is tied to that of a man, she is dependent on this relationship for her own self-worth. Thus, she must compete with other women for his attention. When the attention is then acknowledged and returned, she must work to ensure that it is maintained. Ensuring the protection of this precious commodity generates suspicion among women, particularly single, unattached women. Since we're all taught to vie for a man's attention, we become, in a sense, sexual suspects to one another. The responsibility is placed entirely upon the woman with little thought given to the suspected infidelity of the man.

We should ask what role the man places himself in regarding his support of these behaviors. After all, the woman is commonly viewed as his possession. Hence, in the typical heterosexual relationship both parties are abetting the other, each in a quest that does not improve the status of the woman (nor, in my view, that of the man), nor the consciousness of either of them.

How does the Chicana lesbian fit into this picture? Realistically, she doesn't. As a lesbian she does many things simultaneously: she rejects "compulsory heterosexuality";[12] she refuses to partake in the "game" of competition for men; she confronts her own sexuality; and she challenges the norms placed upon her by culture and society, whose desire is to subvert her

into proper roles and places. This is done, whether consciously or unconsciously, by the very aspect of her existence. In the course of conducting many workshops on lesbian sexuality, Chicana heterosexuals have often indicated to me that they do not associate with lesbians, since it could be assumed that either (1) they too, must be lesbians, or (2) if they're not, they must be selling out to Anglo culture, since it is implied that Chicana lesbians do and thus any association with lesbians implicates them as well. This equivocation of sexual practice and cultural alliance is a retrograde ideology, quite possibly originating from the point of view that the only way to uplift the species is to propagate it. Thus, homosexuality is seen as "counter-revolutionary."

Heterosexual Chicanas need not be passive victims of the cultural onslaught of social control. If anything, Chicanas are usually the backbone of every *familia*, for it is their strength and self-sacrifice which often keeps the family going. While heterosexual Chicanas have a choice about how they want to live their lives (read: how they choose to form their identities[13]), Chicana lesbians have very little choice, because their quest for self-identification comes with the territory. This is why "coming out" can be a major source of pain for Chicana lesbians, since the basic fear of rejection by family and community is paramount. For our own survival, Chicana lesbians must continually embark on the creation or modification of our own *familia*, since this institution, as traditionally constructed, may be non-supportive of the Chicana lesbian existence.[15]

Motherhood

The point of view that we are not complete human beings unless we are attached to a male is further promoted by the attitude that we are incomplete as women unless we become mothers. Many Chicanas are socialized to believe that our chief purpose in life is raising children.[16] Not denying the fact that motherhood can be a beautiful experience, it becomes rather, one of the few experiences not only supported, but expected in a traditional Chicano community. Historically, in dual-headed households, Chicanas (as well as other women) were relegated to the tasks of home care and child rearing, while the men took on the task of earning the family's income.[17] Economic need, rather than feminist consciousness, has been the primary reason for the change to two-income households. Nevertheless, for many Chicanas, motherhood is still seen by our culture as the final act in establishing our "womanhood."

Motherhood among Chicana lesbians does exist. Many lesbians are mothers as by-products of divorce, earlier liaisons with men, or through artificial insemination. Anecdotal evidence I have obtained from many Chicana lesbians in the community indicates that lesbians who choose to become mothers in our culture are seen as aberrations of the traditional concept of motherhood, which stresses male-female partnership. Choosing to become a mother via alternative methods of insemination, or even adopting children, radically departs from society's view that lesbians and gay men cannot "successfully" raise children. Therefore, this poses another threat to the Chicano community, since Chicana lesbians are perceived as failing to partake in one of their chief obligations in life.

Religion

Religion, based on the tradition of patriarchal control and sexual, emotional, and psychological repression, has historically been a dual means of hope for a better afterlife and social control in the present one. Personified by the Virgen de Guadalupe, the concept of motherhood and martyrdom go hand in hand in the Catholic religion. Nevertheless, as we are all aware, religion powerfully affects our belief systems concerning life and living. Since the Pope does not advocate a homosexual lifestyle,[18] lesbians and gay men are not given sanction by the largely Catholic Chicano community—hence, fulfilling our final threat to the established order. Chicana lesbians who confront their homosexuality must, in turn, confront (for those raised in religious households) religion, bringing to resolution some compromise of religious doctrine and personal lifestyle. Many choose to alter, modify, or abandon religion, since it is difficult to advocate something which condemns our existence. This exacerbates a sense of alienation for Chicana lesbians who feel they cannot wholly participate in a traditional religion.

In sum, Chicana lesbians pose a threat to the Chicano community for a variety of reasons, primarily because they threaten the established social hierarchy of patriarchal control. In order to "come-out," Chicana lesbians must confront their sexuality, therefore bringing a taboo subject to consciousness. By necessity, they must learn to love their bodies, for it is also another woman's body which becomes the object of love. Their identities as people alter and become independent of men, hence there is no need to submit to, or perform the necessary behaviors that cater to wooing the male ego. Lesbians (and other feminist women) would expect to treat and be treated by men as equals. Men who have traditionally interacted with women on the basis of their gender (read femininity) first, and their brains second, are commonly left confused when the lesbian (or feminist) fails to respond to the established pecking order.

Motherhood, seen as exemplifying the final act of our existence as women, is practiced by lesbians, but usually without societal or cultural permission. Not only is it believed that lesbians cannot become mothers (hence, not fulfilling our established purpose as women), but if we do, we morally threaten the concept of motherhood as a sanctified entity, since lesbianism doesn't fit into its religious or cultural confines. Lastly, religion, which does not support the homosexual lifestyle, seeks to repudiate us as sinners if we are "practicing," and only tolerable if not. For her personal and psychological survival, the Chicana lesbian must confront and bring to resolution these established cultural and societal conflicts. These "confrontations" go against many of the values of the Chicano community, since they pose a threat to the established order of male control. Our very existence challenges this order, and in some cases challenges the oftentimes ideologically oppressive attitudes toward women.

It is widely assumed that lesbians and heterosexual women are in two completely different enclaves in regard to the type and manner of the oppression they must contend with. As illustrated earlier in this essay, this indeed, may be true. There do exist, however, different levels of patriarchal oppression which affect all of us as women, and when combined inhibit our collective liberation. If we, as lesbian and heterosexual Chicana women, can open our eyes and look at all that we share as women, we might find commonalities even among our differences. First and foremost among them is the status of *woman*. Uttered under any breath, it implies subservience; cast to a lower position not only in society, but in our own culture as well.

Secondly, the universal of the body. We are all female and subject to the same violations as any woman in society. We must contend with the daily threat of rape, molestation, and harassment—violations which affect all of us as women, lesbian or not.

As indicated earlier, our sexuality is suppressed by our culture—relegated to secrecy or embarrassment, implicating us as wrongful women if we profess to fulfill ourselves sexually. Most of us still grow up inculcated with the dichotomy of the "good girl-bad girl" syndrome. With virtue considered as the most admirable quality, it's easy to understand which we choose to partake. This generates a cloud of secrecy around any sexual activity, and leads, I am convinced, to our extremely high teenage pregnancy rate, simply because our families refuse to acknowledge the possibility that young women may be sexually active before marriage.

We are taught to undervalue our needs and voices. Our opinions, viewpoints, and expertise are considered secondary to those of males—even if we are more highly trained. Time and again, I have seen otherwise sensible men insult the character of a woman when they are unable to belittle her intellectual capacities.[19] Character assassinations are commonly disguised in the familiar "*vendida* to the race" format. Common it seems, because it functions as the ultimate insult to any conscientious *politica*. Because many of us are taught that our opinions matter little, we have difficulty at times, raising them. We don't trust what we think, or believe in our merits. Unless we are encouraged to do so, we have difficulty thinking independently of male opinion. Chicanas must be constantly encouraged to speak up, to voice their opinions, particularly in areas where no encouragement has ever been provided.

As Chicanas (and Chicanos), most of us are subject to the effects of growing up in a culture besieged by poverty and all the consequences of it: lack of education, insufficient political power and health care, disease and drugs. We are all subject to the effects of a society that is racist, classist and homophobic, as well as sexist, and patriarchally dominant. Colonization has imposed itself and affected the disbursement of status and the collective rights of us as individuals. Chicana women are placed in this order at a lower position, ensconced within a tight boundary which limits our voices, our bodies, and our brains. In classic dissonant fashion, many of us become complicit in this (since our survival often depends on it) and end up rationalizing our very own limitations.

The collective liberation of people begins with the collective liberation of half its constituency—namely women. The view that our hierarchical society places Chicanos at a lower point, and they in turn must place Chicanas lower still, is outmoded and politically destructive. Women can no longer be relegated to supporting roles. Assuaging delicate male egos as a means of establishing our identities is retrograde and subversive to our own identities as women. Chicanas, both lesbian and heterosexual, have a dual purpose ahead of us. We must fight for our own voices as women, since this will ultimately serve to uplift us as a people.

1. Cherríe Moraga, Loving in the War Years: Lo que nunca paso por sus labios *(Boston: South End Press, 1983), 103, 105, 111, 112, 117.*

2. See Ana Castillo's essay on sexuality in this issue, "La Macha: Toward a New Whole Self". Also see The Sexuality of Latinas, *Third Woman 4 (1989).*

3. Lourdes Arguelles, "A Survey of Latina Immigrant Sexuality," presented at the National Association for Chicano Studies Conference, Albuquerque, New Mexico, March 29–April 1, 1990.

4. Norma Alarcón, personal communication, MALCS (Mujeres Activas en Letras Y Cambio Social) Summer Research Institute, University of California, Los Angeles, August 3–6, 1990.

5. Chicana Leadership Conference, Workshop on Chicana lesbians, University of California, Berkeley, Feb. 8–10, 1990.

6. This was spoken of in great detail in a workshop on Chicana Empowerment and Oppression by Yvette Flores Ortiz at the MALCS, 1990.

7. There are multitudes of feminist books and periodicals which attest to the subordinate position of women in society. Listing them is beyond the scope of this essay.

8. Yvette Flores Ortiz, MALCS, 1990.

9. Peggy R. Sanday, "Female Status in the Public Domain," in Women, Culture & Society, *eds. Michelle Rosaldo and Louise Lamphere (Stanford: Stanford University Press, 1974), 189–206.*

10. Loving in the War Years, *113.*

11. See Ana Castillo's "La Macha: Toward a Beautiful Whole Self" in this issue. See also Loving in the War Years, *136.*

12. Adrienne Rich, "Compulsory Heterosexuality and Lesbian Existence," in Women: Sex and Sexuality, *eds. Catharine R. Stimpson and Ethel Spector Person (Chicago: University of Chicago Press, 1980), 62–91.*

13. As Moraga states, "only the woman intent on the approval can be affected by the disapproval", Loving in the War Years, *103.*

14. Rejection by family and community is also an issue for gay men, however, their situation is muddied by the concomitant loss of power.

15. Cherríe Moraga attests to the necessity of Chicanas needing to "make familia from scratch," in Giving Up the Ghost (Los Angeles: West End Press, 1986), 58.

16. Loving in the War Years, 113.

17. Karen Sacks, "Engels Revisited: Women, the Organization of Production and Private Property" in Women, Culture & Society, 207–222.

18. Joseph Cardinal Ratzinger, Prefect, and Alberto Bouone, Titular Archbishop of Caesarea in Numedia, Secretary, "Letter to the Bishops of the Catholic Church in the Pastoral Care of Homosexual Persons", October 1, 1986. Approved by Pope John Paul II, adopted in an ordinary session of the Congregation for the Doctrine of Faith and ordered published. Reprinted in The Vatican and Homosexuality, eds. Jeannine Gramick and Pat Furey (New York: Crossroad Publishing Co., 1988), 1–10. 19. This occurred often to the women McChA (Movimiento Estudiantil Chicano de Aztlán) leaders who were on the Berkeley campus between 1985–1989. It also occurred to a Chicana panel member during a 1990 National Association for Chicano Studies presentation, when a Chicano discussant disagreed with the recommendations based on her research.

URVASHI VAID

The National Lesbian Conference held in Atlanta in April 1991 brought together three thousand lesbians from across the U.S. The conference combined workshops, plenary sessions, and caucusing to bring lesbians together and form a "national agenda." While no such agenda emerged from the conference, most who attended came away excited and encouraged by the presence of active lesbians.

Some were less thrilled. Carmen Vazquez, the coordinator for lesbian and gay health services in San Francisco, spoke strongly about her concern that lesbians are better at addressing symbolic or surface manifestations of problems than at attacking their substance. In her speech reprinted here, Urvashi Vaid, past executive director of the National Gay and Lesbian Task Force, challenged the participants to rethink their activism. She suggests that, in spite of the gains of the last decades, beyond the centers of feminist culture such as bookstores and festivals, lesbian life remains much as it was in the 1950s. She links this to lesbians' failure to support national organizations and more "mainstream" legal and political efforts, and our tendency to criticize one another to exhaustion rather than fight the greater enemy. In short, Vaid argues that lesbians are killing ourselves with our insistence on a certain sort of "feminist" politics and process. As the right's power grows, her words deserve serious consideration.

LET'S PUT OUR OWN HOUSE IN ORDER
Speech to the National Lesbian Conference, Atlanta, Georgia (1991)

Urvashi Vaid

Good Evening. Thank you. I was asked to speak tonight on what the national lesbian agenda is; on where it is at; and what the obstacles are to its implementation. I hope to do that—but I want to begin very simply by asking us all to remember *why* we are here at this conference asking this question?

We are here at the National Lesbian Conference because of the passion, love, excitement and desire we feel for women.

We are here because spectacular forces of evil and prejudice threaten our very existence as lesbians.

It is this evil present in Judge Campbell's decision denying Karen Thompson guardianship of Sharon Kowalski.

It is this evil that murdered Rebecca Wight, and wounded her lover, Claudia Brenner as they were camping in the mountains of Pennsylvania.

It is this evil found in the cowardly silence of all politicians who will not stand up to defend lesbians, will not pass laws to end the daily, massive relentless mountain of prejudice we face.

What brings us together tonight are the realities of discrimination we face us as lesbians and our commitment to changing these realities.

Let us never forget the social context we gather in:

- To be lesbian today means to face loss of our jobs, loss of housing, denial of public accommodation, loss of custody, loss of visitation simply because of our sexual orientation.
- To be lesbian today means to face violence as a queer and violence as a woman.
- To be lesbian today means to have no safety for the families we have created, to face the loss of our children and our loved ones, to have no status for our committed relationships.
- To be lesbian means to be invisible, as Kate Clinton says, like the stealth bomber, low-flying, undetectable—to be a stealth lesbian, hidden from a world whose sight is monochromatic and patriarchal; hidden even when we are out and powerful, by a world that is obsessed with the relationships between men.
- To be lesbian means to work in social change movements, in gay and lesbian organizations, in civil rights and feminist organizations that still ghettoize the multiple issues of discrimination that we face and that still tokenize us or put our concerns and voices on the back burner.
- To be lesbian is to have, until very recently, absolutely no images in mainstream culture of out, proud, powerful, strong, independent women.
- To be lesbian today is to live in a society that identifies and defines us only through our relation (or lack thereof) to men—lesbians are masculine, man-haters, the sexual fantasies of straight men.
- To be lesbian today is to face multiple systems of oppression—to face homophobia, sexism, racism, ageism, ableism, economic injustice—to face a variety of systems of oppression *all at once*, with the type of oppression changing depending on who we are, but the fact of oppression remaining constant.

We gather here at this conference in Atlanta in *1991*, not 1951, not 1971, not 1981, but today. And the context of this time is ominous. The world in which we strive to live as openly lesbian has taken off its ugly white hood to show its sexist, anti-gay, racist, and capitalist face as never before.

- When a Ku Klux Klansman can run for the U.S. Senate and get 44% of the vote—the hood is off.
- When the President of the United States is elected on the heels of an orchestrated racist campaign—the hood is off.
- When he campaigns for Helms in North Carolina, when he vetoes the Civil Rights Act of 1990, when he introduces a Crime Bill that will strip our civil liberties, when he speaks in strong support of the anti-choice, anti-woman, anti-abortion movement, when he opposes

equal rights for women, when he lets our brothers and sisters with HIV and AIDS die from negligence, when he engineers a war to win re-election—the hood of evil is off.

A second piece of the context in which we gather is more hopeful:

- We meet at this lesbian conference at an historic moment in the lesbian and gay movement's history. Today tens of thousands of lesbians are actively engaged in the movement for lesbian liberation. At the workshops and caucuses I have attended it is clear that the two thousand of us at this conference are deeply and intimately involved in our movement for freedom.
- Today, we are a truly *mixed* movement through the involvement of lesbians. And through our involvement, we are changing the face, the politics, and the content of our gay and lesbian organizations.

There is a revolution underway in the lesbian and gay liberation movement. The fact that organizations are developing multicultural plans and dealing with racism on their staffs, boards and in their programs is a direct result of lesbian-feminist organizing and politics. The fact that the gay and lesbian movement has begun to be multi-issue, that it is prochoice, that it dares to speak out on the broad social issues of the day (like the war) is a direct result of lesbian leadership. The fact that the feminist health agenda of the 1970's—the agenda of disability rights, insurance reform, health care access for all, welfare reform, etc.—the fact that these issues are now on the central burner of the gay and lesbian movement is in part a function of the painful experience of the AIDS crisis—and in part a result of lesbian-feminist analysis and organizing.

The parallel contexts of great danger and great change frame our meeting together tonight as lesbians.

And as we have seen in this week together, the work we must do, our *agenda for action,* is large and quite specific!

There are two big pieces to our national lesbian agenda: one is movement building; and the second is public policy. Put another way, I believe that our lesbian agenda for the 1990s is about: organizing and power; it is about taking and making as Audre Lorde said "Power out of hatred and destruction."

These are not easy agenda items to move.

Movement Building

The experience of this conference suggests to me that we do not in fact have a national lesbian movement. We have a vital cultural movement, we have a huge amount of talent, we have a lot of grassroots leadership, we have lesbians active in a million projects, but the locus of lesbian community in our cities and towns today remains the same as it was in the 1950s, it remains the bar, augmented by women's cultural events, the Festival network and local feminist and lesbian bookstores.

We have no national movement, no national newspaper, no national annual gathering place for lesbian activists to meet and talk politics, we have one annual state conference I am aware of—in Texas—and for all the talk of a national lesbian organization let me remind everyone that we have a national lesbian organization that struggles for its daily existence—the National Center for Lesbian Rights. How many of us here support this ten-year old pillar of lesbian advocacy?

The centerpiece of our national lesbian agenda must be the recreation of a lively, open, organized and unafraid lesbian movement. It existed once.

The challenges to the recreation of this lesbian movement are manifest throughout this, our National Lesbian Conference. The NLC is a mirror to the current state of the movement. And the mirror shows us several harsh truths:

1) Truth: That we are not one lesbian community but a series of very splintered communities who have in fact not been working with each other at home or at this conference.

2) Truth: In this conference we have demonstrated that we do not trust each other at all; that we refuse to claim the cloak of "leadership" even when we have it—perhaps because we rightly fear the backlash or ostracism all lesbians who dare say the word leadership fear; we have shown that we do not understand that diversity politics is not about kneejerk or paying lip service but about action and internalizing the message, not about making sure that we have one of each, but learning and accepting that we have each in one, that we respect and carry the commitment to act in ourselves.

3) Truth: In this conference two thousand have gathered. I have met so many fierce, powerful, seasoned, interesting lesbians, and it pains me that any of us might leave this place feeling dejected and hurt, angry and excluded. Let us not do that. Remember—we will never feel included entirely, because the big social context is what excludes us completely.

4) Truth: That developing alternative decision-making processes are wonderful and radical, but that all processes must be accountable and take responsibility for their actions.

5) Truth: That we can get so intense and focused on criticizing each other and focused on ourselves that we forget that we are in this together that we are in this to change the fucked-up world outside.

We must begin in our own house to put it in order. We must begin by taking a deep collective breath and looking around at the fierce, powerful women that we are. Look around at the skills we bring and let us let go of perfectionism and a purity politics based in fear; let us proactive instead a courageous and honest politics based in lesbian pride.

It is time for lesbians like me and you to bring our energies back home into our own movement and our own communities. It is time for us to mobilize on the grassroots level *first*.

Every state must have a lesbian conference to encourage involvement by lesbians.

Every city and town should have lesbian activist networking breakfasts or potlucks to reconnect us to each other.

Let us certainly do our organizing on our particular and separate piece of the social change pie—but let us not forget that we are allies as lesbians—we are not the enemy.

Let us encourage and promote lesbianism! Let us link up across age to talk political vision. Let us not be afraid of doing the wrong thing—let us just do some thing!

Public policy/politics

On a political level, in the two years of planning for this conference, I have sat through many discussions of what is the lesbian political agenda. Lesbians have tried to define lesbian-specific issues—well, that is not my vision of my lesbian movement's political agenda.

My vision is to claim quite simply the fact that the lesbian agenda is (as it has always been) radical social change.

It is the reconstruction of family, it is the reimagining and claiming of power, it is the reorganization of the economic system, it the reinforcement of civil rights for all peoples. It is the enactment of laws and the creation of a society that affirms choice. It is the end to the oppression of women, the end to racism, the end to sexism, ableism, homophobia, the protection of our environment.

I have no problem claiming all these issues as the lesbian agenda for social change, because that is the truth. Lesbians have a radical social vision: we are the bearers of a truly new world order, not the stench of the same old world odor.

This large agenda does not overwhelm me, it tells me how far I must go until we all win. It tells me who my allies really are.

How do we enact our agenda? We enact it by continuing to do what we are doing in each of our communities. We enact it by involving more of our sisters, the thousands of lesbians who do not interact with us or with our movement for social change.

We enact our lesbian agenda by building a movement for *power*. What are we afraid of? Why are we afraid of power? We surely will not make things more fucked up than they already are.

I am not suggesting that all of us drop the work we are doing to focus on this new exclusively lesbian thing called lesbian agenda; I am suggesting that we continue to do what we are doing, but that we do it as *out* lesbians. That we claim our work as lesbian work, that we be out about who and why we are how we are.

I proudly claim our unique multi-issue perspective. I am proud of my lesbian community's politics of inclusion. I am engaged in my people's liberation. Let us just do it.

LISA ORLANDO

The "bisexuality debates" of the 1980s and 1990s were fundamentally different from earlier discussions. Feminist debates of the 1970s had largely portrayed sexual choice as voluntary on a deep level; one could, if one tried, change the direction of one's desire. Bisexual women were thus women who refused to eliminate their alliance with men. While this view has not died, the terms of the debate have shifted. In an era in which lesbians are making common cause with gay men, older ideas of sexuality as innate, genetic, or unchangeable have made a comeback. Bisexuals do not necessarily win in this new world, however; as Lisa Orlando's article describes, bisexuals are still vilified as "confused" or untrustworthy. She links this reaction to the larger cultural fear of "messiness" and the desire for neat and exclusive categories. Orlando's article also exemplifies the new "gay 90s" sensibility, in which many women—bisexual and exclusively lesbian alike—identify as "gay" rather than as "lesbian" or as "feminist."

Lisa Orlando is an activist and writer currently living in San Francisco.

from

LOVING WHOM WE CHOOSE

(1991)

Lisa Orlando

The struggles of "sexual minorities" within the lesbian and gay and feminist movements have recently revived interest in issues of sexual freedom. Within our movements such interests seemed, over the years since Stonewall, to have become increasingly confined to our radical margins. Now, however, S/M, man—boy love, butch and femme role-playing, sex workers, cross-dressing, and other sexual behavior are widely discussed in our publications and community meetings, with the result that a renaissance of our early "sex radicalism" seems to be occurring. However, in the midst of all this talk of sex, one sexual practice—bisexuality—is rarely discussed. If we really want a sexually liberating renaissance, we must discuss and rethink bisexuality in the same way that we have other forms of gay "deviance."

In the early days of our movement, many gay liberationists agreed that both homosexual and heterosexual potentials existed in all human beings. They believed that heterosexual culture so vigorously oppresses those who insist on expressing homosexual desire because, as Martha Shelley, one of the first post-Stonewall theorists, wrote, we are heterosexuals' "own worst fears made flesh."[1] Even later separatist lesbian-feminists like the Furies collective affirmed the inherent bisexuality of human nature.[2] If the feminist and gay liberation movements succeeded, they thought, the gay and straight dichotomy would disappear. Although, as Dennis Altman pointed out, many people would still not practice bisexuality, we would nevertheless achieve the "end of the homosexual" as a meaningful category.[3]

Belief in bisexuality as a utopian potential has not always coincided, as it has for Altman, with support for and acceptance of bisexuals. Nevertheless, bisexuals who were active in the earliest days of the gay liberation movement seem to have had little trouble being accepted as gay. But times change. Few gay activists now claim to be striving for a bisexual paradise or to regard bisexuality as a repressed human potential. And while many nonbisexual gays have, as individuals, supported us and encouraged our attempts to organize, the lesbian and gay community abounds with negative images of bisexuals as fence-sitters, traitors, cop-outs, closet cases, people whose primary goal in life is to retain "heterosexual privilege," power-hungry seducers who use and discard their same-sex lovers like so many Kleenex . . .

These stereotypes result from the ambiguous position of bisexuals, poised as we are between what currently appear as two mutually exclusive sexual cultures, one with the power to exercise violent repression against the other. Others grow out of the popular assumption, contrary to that of early gay liberation, that homosexual and heterosexual *desires* exclude each other. Still others result from lesbian-feminism,[4] which argues that lesbianism is a political choice having little to do with sexual desire *per se*. From this point of view, a bisexual woman "still define[s] herself in terms of male needs"[5] rather than, as she herself might argue, in terms of her own desires. Since lesbian-feminism equates meeting male needs with supporting male supremacy, it considers bisexual women traitors by definition.

Other factors may have played a role in shifting attitudes toward bisexuals in the lesbian and gay community: the growth of lesbian and gay "lifestyles" and ghettoes; the boundaries produced by constructing gay people as a "minority;" the development of sexual identity as a political concept; and even, as Cindy Patton has argued, the brief heyday of media-created "bisexual chic" . . . that trivialized bisexuality as just another fashion.[6]

But these stereotypes also resonate with some people's personal experience and with the gay subculture lore developed out of collective experience. Most stereotypes reflect some small aspects of reality which they then serve to reinforce. Some bisexuals do act in stereotypical ways, often because we have internalized our social image. And because nonbisexuals view this behavior through the lens of the stereotype, they perceive it as evidence of the truth of the stereotype rather than as an individual action. As more bisexuals refuse to hide our sexuality, as we organize within the gay community, we can better challenge these negative images and demonstrate that they are, like other stereotypes, essentially false. Other gay people will be forced to recognize that as a group bisexuals are no more "promiscuous" or incapable of commitment than anyone else (like many stereotypes of bisexuals, this also runs rampant in the straight world). "Heterosexual privilege" doesn't prevent us from being queerbashed on our way home from the bars or having our children taken away when we come out. We look just like other queers; i.e., we range from blatant to indistinguishable from straights. And many of us not only involve ourselves in lesbian and gay struggles but also identify ourselves primarily with the gay community.

As we challenge people on their more easily disproved beliefs, they may also begin to question whether they perceive their personal experiences with bisexuals in a distorted way. For example, I think we might better explain at least some of the stories about bisexuals who leave their same-sex lovers for heterosexual relationships in the same ways we explain being left, period, rather than as some special form of desertion and betrayal. And if gay people examine the problems we have had with bisexual lovers whose primary relationships are heterosexual, they resemble quite closely the problems we have had in similar "secondary" relationships with homosexuals.

Since most bisexuals are acutely aware of the differences between heterosexual and homosexual relationships, some probably do "settle" for heterosexual relationships, at whatever emotional cost, and for all the reasons one might imagine. I find it as difficult to condemn them as to condemn homosexuals who seek therapy to "become" heterosexual —oppression is ugly and we all want out, whether we seek individual or collective solutions. Other gay people rarely notice, however, that most bisexuals continue to have homosexual relationships *despite* the weight of heterosexist[7] oppression. This can only testify to the fact that heterosexual relationships generate their own problems—and that the power of desire often overcomes that of oppression. Many homosexuals resent the fact that the thoughtless pleasures of a heterosexual relationship always exist as an option for bisexuals and fear that, as homophobia intensifies, more bisexuals will take that option. But "option" seems a strange expression to describe repressing an entire aspect of one's sexuality, and the closet exists as an "option" for *all* queers.

We all suffer oppression when we choose to express homosexual desire. We may suffer even more when we force ourselves to repress it. And although the experiences differ, we suffer whether, as with bisexuals, our desire might take other paths or whether, as with homosexuals, the only path is total repression. In each of these cases, our suffering results from the power of a homophobic society. We *all* share an interest in assuring that bisexuals make their choices, conscious or not, on the basis of desire rather than oppression. And gay liberation offers the only guarantee that this will happen.

Those who view bisexuals as untrustworthy because of our "options" at least acknowledge that we exist. Others insist that we are closet cases temporarily stuck in a transitional stage in the coming-out process. I hope that as bisexuals begin to speak for ourselves, we will weaken this notion since many of us have identified as such for years—and lifetimes. I wonder, however, if the power of this belief might not resist such evidence. While I would argue that gay identity is essentially political—something we construct to promote solidarity and oppose our oppression—for many people, gay identity seems to imply that we all naturally possess a *sexual* identity and that this identity just as naturally fits into one of two categories.

Why do so many people who oppose the other forms of madness created and perpetuated by the psychiatric and medical establishment so wholeheartedly embrace the notion of a strict division between heterosexuality and homosexuality, a notion which originated alongside that of homosexuality as disease? As much gay historical research has shown, "homosexuality" as we understand it in the West didn't exist until, with the advent of capitalism, religious ideology began to lose ground and medical ideology took its place. What Christianity saw as a sinful potential in everyone, psychiatry reconceptualized as a sickness which permeated one's being, displacing heterosexual desire.[8] But if we reject the psychiatric definition of homosexuality, why do we cling to the notion of homosexual desire as exclusive? That we do testifies, I think, to the incredible power of our need to fit things into neat dichotomies.

Human beings tend to use dual classification when we think about our world—pairs such as up and down and hot and cold as well as pairs such as human and animal and man and woman, where more value is placed on one term—possibly because such oppositions structure the human mind itself. Many anthropologists believe that when some aspect of a culture gains particular prominence or importance people feel an even stronger need to fit it into such a scheme and will become uneasy in the face of ambiguities. The "disorder" resulting from central features of our lives which we cannot fit into dichotomies with sharp boundaries disturbs us deeply.[9] I suspect that the homosexual and heterosexual dichotomy gained acceptance as both sexuality and "personal identity" became central to our culture. Whether or not this is true, most of us feel threatened when the categories we believe in are challenged, especially if they shape our sense of who we are. Not only do bisexuals contradict a primary set of cultural categories—our culture calls us "decadent" because we refuse to play by the rules, thereby undermining the social "order"—but we challenge many people's personal sense of what constitutes sexual identity. Whether we threaten by introducing a third category or by undermining the notion of categories altogether, we cause enough discomfort that many people deny our existence.

If we wish to develop liberating politics, we must ask, as early gay liberation did, whether our need to classify simultaneously violates the truths of at least some people's desires and plays into heterosexism. Obviously we will never stop classifying; we couldn't speak or even think if we did. But we must be wary of both our obsession with order, with getting rid of "dirt,"[10] and our tendency to see the categories we use as natural or simply given rather than as the social and political constructions they are. This is particularly true with those categories which bear the most political weight. But the historically specific categories we adopt in order to think about our world, including ourselves, do more than merely describe, or violate the truths of, our desires. They also shape and even create them. We must question as well the whole notion of an essential sexual truth which somehow resides in each of us.

I don't think anyone knows what desire is, where it comes from, or why it takes the general and specific forms it does. I'm inclined to believe that some kind of interaction between a more or less shapeless biological "drive" and a combination of individual experiences and larger social forces creates each of our unique sexualities. But the way we as "modern" people experience them, the mere fact that we experience something we call "sexual identity," is peculiar to our particular culture and historical period. Much current historical research argues that all our talk about "identity crisis" and "finding ourselves," even our very notion of sexuality, would mean nothing to people from another time and place.[11] If both the way we view our selves and the categories into which we fit them are modern social constructions, not timeless truths, I can't view my own sense, however subjectively powerful, that I am "really" *anything* with less than suspicion. The human mind too easily interprets—and reinterprets—anything and everything to fit its current beliefs.

But we still have no better way of describing our experience than by saying that we have discovered what we "really" are. In using the term "really," we acknowledge the experience many people have either of having "always known" or of coming to a place where they finally feel at home. I, too, believe, seventeen years after "discovering" my bisexuality and ten years after relinquishing my lesbian identity, that I am "really" bisexual . . .

Many exclusive homosexuals *do* experience bisexuality as a stage (as indeed do some heterosexuals). This obviously bolsters the belief that "real" bisexuality doesn't exist. People who have had this experience tend to look back at their old selves with condescension and embarrassment. I suspect that the word "bisexual" triggers unpleasant feelings in many of them which they project on anyone claiming a bisexual identity.

While most self-defined homosexuals and heterosexuals may be correct in seeing their own bisexuality as just a stage, inevitably some people who see themselves as exclusively homosexual or heterosexual will have repressed rather than "grown out of" bisexuality. As some lesbians in the fifties who were neither butch nor femme felt forced to choose,[12] so do some bisexuals. Both sides often exert so much pressure to "make up your mind" and direct so much contempt at people who are unwilling to do so—and most of us are so unaware of bisexuality as a legitimate possibility—that a simple need for acceptance and community often forces people (particularly, and often most painfully, young people) to repress one aspect of their desire. Just as closet queers (also perhaps bisexual) often lead the pack in homophobic attacks, so may closet bisexuals be the most intensely biphobic. I think this is particularly true among women who came out via lesbian-feminism.

Many women, in fact, who now identify as bisexual, experienced *lesbianism* as a stage. I identified as bisexual before the women's movement, but as happened with many women, consciousness-raising and traumatic experiences fueled an acute anger and disgust with men that led me to lesbianism. Some women became lesbians because "feminism is the theory and lesbianism is the practice."[13] Or they may simply have succumbed to peer pressure (even some heterosexual women "became" lesbians for these reasons). Over the years, many of us, often because of working in political coalitions, have reconnected with the world outside the "women's community" and have discovered our heterosexual desires. We are now attacked for having "gone back into the closet," as traitors, and as self-deceiving fools.

The theoretical and emotional need to keep alive both the notion that all true feminists are lesbians and the belief that no rapprochement with men is possible fuels lesbian-feminist hatred of bisexuals. Many lesbians who oppose other forms of separatism, who work with men politically and have male friends, still see *sexual* separatism as an eternal given. But as political separatism falls into disrepute, sexual separatism also loses its rationale. As many lesbians recognize that class, race, age, etc. may be as powerful sources of oppression as gender and sexual orientation, they also recognize the futility of separatism as more than a stage. Few people—and fewer sexual radicals—really want a movement which forbids us to relate sexually to people whose race, sex, class, physical abilities, age, looks, etc. aren't exactly the same as ours. And many of us also refuse to have our desires and sexual practices dictated by anyone else's idea of "political correctness."

Many bisexuals, like many homosexuals, have never identified with gay politics. But some of us, including many women who have rejected lesbian-feminism, *have* committed ourselves to gay liberation. We see gay identity and solidarity as crucial, since heterosexism oppresses all gay people, whether homosexual or bisexual, and we can only struggle against it as a self-conscious group. The ambiguous nature of our sexuality needn't imply any ambiguity in our politics. By choosing gay identity we acknowledge that sexuality dominates our identity in a heterosexist world while recognizing that in a nonoppressive society no one would care who we wanted or who our sexual partners were, and sexuality would no longer be so central to our sense of who we are.

Unfortunately, political movements and embattled subcultures have particular difficulty acknowledging ambiguities of any kind,[14] and the current plethora of "ex-lesbians" . . . haunts the political unconscious of the lesbian and gay movement. Clearly, the rest of the gay community ignores or ostracizes us at its peril; embattled as we all are, we need all the forces we can muster. Bisexuals often encounter unusual opportunities to confront and contradict homophobia and, if we have been encouraged to develop a gay consciousness, we will act powerfully and efficiently in such situations.

But if it rejects us, the gay movement loses more than numbers and strategic force. It also loses another opportunity, similar to that offered by other "sexual minorities," to re-examine its commitment to sexual freedom rather than to mere interest-group politics. What would it mean for the gay movement to acknowledge that some people experience their sexuality as a lifelong constant, others as a series of stages, some as a choice, and many as a constant flux? It would certainly mean a drastic reworking of the standard categories which have grounded gay politics over the last decade. And it might mean a renewed commitment to the revolutionary impulse of gay liberation, which, believing that homosexual desire is a potential in everyone, insisted that "gay" is a potentially universal class, since sexual freedom for all people is the ultimate goal of our struggle.

1. *Quoted in Dennis Altman,* Homosexual: Oppression and Liberation, *Avon Books, 1971, p. 69.*

2. *Loretta Ulmschneider for the Furies, "Bisexuality," in* Lesbianism in the Women's Movement, *ed. Nancy Myron and Charlotte Bunch, Diana Press, 1975, p. 88.*

3. *Altman,* Homosexual, *especially chapter 7, "The End of the Homosexual?"*

4. *Throughout this article I use "lesbian-feminism" to refer to the ideology explicated in the text. It does not refer here to the belief that women's and gay liberation requires each other (a belief to which I subscribe) nor to the belief that lesbian and gay oppression is merely a by-product of women's oppression (lesbian-feminists share this belief with many feminists and gay activists who otherwise disagree with them). Nor am I using the term simply to designate all women who are both lesbians and feminists. One of the earliest and most comprehensive explications of lesbian-feminist doctrine can be found in Myron and Bunch, eds.,* Lesbianism in the Women's Movement.

5. *Ulmschneider, p. 86.*

6. *Quoted in Arthur Kroeber, "Bisexuality: Towards a New Understanding of Men, Women, and Their Feelings,"* Boston Globe, *October 10, 1983, p. 53.*

7. *"Heterosexism" designates the ideology that posits heterosexuality as the "natural," "normal," and "superior" sexual orientation and condemns deviations from this norm. As with other oppressive ideologies, heterosexism is supported by law and custom and reinforced by socially condoned violence.*

8. *For historical writings on the "homosexual" as a modern construction, see Michel Foucault,* The History of Sexuality, Vol. 1, An Introduction, *trans. Robert Hurley, Pantheon, 1978; Jeffrey Weeks,* Coming Out: Homosexual Politics in Britain, *Quartet Books, 1977; John d'Emilio, "Capitalism and Gay Identity," in* Powers of Desire: The Politics of Sexuality, *ed. Ann Snitow, Christine Stansell, and Sharon Thompson, Monthly Review Press, 1983, pp. 100–113; and Robert Padgug, "Sexual Matters: On Conceptualizing Sexuality in History,"* Radical History Review *20 (1979): 3–23. See also Mary MacIntosh, "The Homosexual Role,"* Social Problems *16 (1968): 182–192.*

9. *The above argument draws primarily on Barry Schwartz,* Vertical Classification: A Study in Structuralism and the Sociology of Knowledge, *University of Chicago Press, 1981. See also Mary Douglas,* Purity and Danger: An Analysis of the Concepts of Pollution and Taboo, *Routledge & Kegan Paul, 1966.*

10. *Douglas, ibid., defines "dirt" as a "residual category rejected from our normal scheme of classification" (p. 36). I think the point I am making here would have been stronger if, rather than drawing on the notion of "vertical classification" in the above passage, I had discussed Douglas's arguments about boundaries and margins, ambiguities and anomalies. The point that bisexuals transgress boundaries which, in our culture, are intimately related to notions of pollution and contagion hardly needs to be belabored, especially considering the current hysteria over AIDS. Nevertheless, it seemed a more difficult argument to make from the perspective of the margins themselves.*

11. *Foucault, Weeks, d'Emilio, Padgug, op. cit. Here I refer particularly to the work of Michel Foucault on the "technologies of the self," especially his comparison of the ancient Greek notion of the self as an aesthetic creation to our notion of the self as something "discovered." See, for example, Paul Rabinow and Hubert L. Dreyfus, "How We Behave: An Interview with Michel Foucault,"* Vanity Fair, *November 1983, pp. 60–69.*

12. *For a discussion of the pressures in lesbian subcultures in the 1950s, see Elly Bulkin, "An Old Dyke's Tale: An Interview with Doris Lundin,"* Conditions *6 (1980): 36–48. The degree of pressure that existed in the 1950s is a topic of debate in the contemporary lesbian community. For other viewpoints, see Joan Nestle, "Butch-Femme Relationships: Sexual Courage in the 1950s,"* Heresies *12: 22; and Merrill Mushroom, "Confessions of a Butch Dyke,"* Common Lives/Lesbian Lives *9 (1983): 40.*

13. *The slogan originated with a heterosexual feminist, Ti-Grace Atkinson, who first used it in a speech before the New*

York chapter of the Daughters of Bilitis, an early homophile organization, in late June 1970. Toby Marotta, *The Politics of Homosexuality,* Houghton Mifflin, 1981, p. 258.

14. Douglas, op. cit., p. 124.

TRANSSEXUALS

The relation between homosexuals and other sexual/gendered minorities has never been an easy one. While almost half of male-to-female transsexuals are lesbians, their status has been contested. In 1979 Janice Raymond wrote *The Transsexual Empire,* a radical feminist analysis of transsexual medical practices. Following her lead, many lesbian-feminists have seen male-to-female transsexuals as invaders, men masquerading as women and demanding entrance into lesbian communities. Their argument is that women and men are formed by their social experiences, including male privilege and female subordination, and that male privilege cannot be erased or changed through surgery. As a consequence, they have urged that male-to-female transsexuals be barred from "women-only" events. Transsexuals have responded that they were not raised as other men because their inner gender never corresponded to the lessons they were being taught. This dissonance, indeed, is the reason for their decision to change their anatomy. Upon the completion of such changes, they argue, they live as other women and should be welcomed as women. In the following articles, the group Lesbians for Justice offer an argument for the recognition and inclusion of transsexual lesbians in lesbian communities and organizations.

This issue has shifted ground somewhat as the category of "transsexuals" has metamorphosed into "transgendered people." Increasing numbers of people who feel themselves to be "in the wrong body" are choosing to stay in those bodies and confront dominant assumptions of masculinity and femininity, views shared by lesbians and gays. As they do so, they challenge us to think through the relation between sex and gender and sexuality. What exactly is the dividing line between a very masculine woman and a man? Are sex organs, or hormones, or chromosomes a proof of identity? What is the relation between that identity and the politics of an individual? The arguments and their rebuttals continue to divide many lesbian communities.

RESOLUTION CONDEMNING DISCRIMINATION AGAINST AND EXCLUSION OF TRANSSEXUAL LESBIANS WITHIN THE GAY AND LESBIAN COMMUNITY

(1992)

Lesbians for Justice

WHEREAS approximately one half of all male-to-female transsexuals define themselves as lesbian, either exclusively or primarily, and

WHEREAS there are already several thousand transsexual lesbians in the United States alone, and

WHEREAS the population of transsexual lesbians is continually growing, and can be expected to continue to grow, and

WHEREAS transsexuality is a universal phenomenon which has appeared in all cultures throughout history, and

WHEREAS the etiology of transsexuality can not be precisely determined, and

WHEREAS transsexuality *per se* is not indicative of any character disorder, delusional state or other pathological condition, and

WHEREAS emotional, psychological and spiritual factors are more significant determinants of an individual's sexuality than are biology and environment, and

WHEREAS attempts to change the sexual identity of transsexuals have proven to be universally unsuccessful, and are regard by transsexuals as violations of the integrity of their core identities, and

WHEREAS the only treatment for transsexuality which has demonstrated a significant rate of success is sex reassignment surgery, and

WHEREAS transsexuals are an oppressed sexual minority, as are lesbians and gay men, and

WHEREAS transsexual lesbians who have completed a medical and legal process of changing their sex from male to female are legally recognized as women, and

WHEREAS transsexual lesbians live and function in society entirely as women, and

WHEREAS transsexual lesbians are affected by all of the same issues and concerns of other lesbians, and

WHEREAS transsexual lesbians experience the same oppression as other women, as well as forms of oppression unique to their nation, and

WHEREAS transsexual lesbians have rejected patriarchal conditioning, values and privileges, at great personal expense to themselves, by the act of changing their anatomical sex to correspond with their inner gender, and

WHEREAS transsexual lesbians share the same values and goals as other lesbians, and

WHEREAS transsexual lesbians are able to make valuable contributions to the larger lesbian community, and

WHEREAS there are transsexual lesbians who are actively involved in the struggle for gay and lesbian rights, or are otherwise involved in various ways within the larger gay and lesbian community, and

WHEREAS the majority of the larger lesbian community does not have a problem with accepting transsexual lesbians as women and as lesbian sisters, and

WHEREAS many transsexual lesbians are the lovers of non-transsexual lesbians, and

WHEREAS transsexual lesbians still experience discrimination from other other lesbians, and exclusion from some segments of the larger lesbian community, and

WHEREAS such discrimination and exclusion tends to force transsexual lesbians back "into the closet," and

WHEREAS the issue of transsexual lesbians is one that cannot be ignored by the larger gay and lesbian community,

THEREFORE BE IT RESOLVED that any form of discrimination against transsexual lesbians within the larger gay and/or lesbian community, or any form of exclusion of transsexual lesbians from any aspect or segment of the larger gay and/or lesbian community is in fundamental contradiction to the principles of tolerance for diversity of lifestyle and of gay and lesbian solidarity, and that any such discrimination against transsexual lesbians or exclusion of transsexual lesbians from any aspect or segment of the larger gay and lesbian community by other gays or lesbians is entirely equivalent to the discrimination which lesbians and gay men experience from the heterosexual population, and that such discrimination and/or exclusion is in conflict with the best interests of the larger gay and lesbian community.

AN OPEN LETTER TO THE ORGANIZERS OF THE MICHIGAN WOMYN'S MUSIC FESTIVAL
(1992)

Lesbians for Justice

Dear Ms. Vogel & Ms. Price,

Lesbians for Justice is a group of lesbians and allies who, recognizing that all forms of oppression are interrelated, are committed to working toward the elimination of all forms of oppression. As such, we would like to express our disapproval of the expulsion of Nancy Jean Burkholder from the Sixteenth Annual Michigan Womyn's Music Festival in August of 1991, as well as the manner in which it was conducted, and the manner in which you have failed to adequately respond to the issues raised by the incident. It is also our intention to express our disapproval of your policy of excluding post-operative male-to-female transsexuals from attendance at this festival, as well as the absence of adequate due process available to all women in attendance at the festival in any potential dispute regarding festival policy. We feel that the action taken against Ms. Burkholder was arbitrary, unethical and anti-feminist in nature, particularly since this exclusionary policy was not explicitly stated in your festival literature. However, it is also our position that the issue in this situation is not merely whether or not such exclusionary policy was explicitly stated, but that such a policy lacks sufficient justification, and that there is simply no rational basis for the existence of this policy.

We feel that the exclusion of postoperative male-to-female transsexuals from the Michigan Womyn's Music Festival not only lacks justification, but it is likewise contrary to expressed ideals of tolerance and respect for diversity, concern for the safety of attendees, universal sisterhood, and feminist values which you claim the festival is intended to represent, for the following reasons:

1.) It is impossible to enforce this policy in a fair and equitable manner, as decisions as to who is and who is not a transsexual ultimately must rely on the discretion of security staff, thus also threatens the safety and security of women of ambiguous gender appearance who are not transsexuals.

2.) Such exclusionary policy is necessarily elitist in nature in that it excludes some women while claiming to be a festival for all women.

3.) Such exclusionary policy, as well as the manner in which it was enforced, are reminiscent of exclusionary laws, customs, policies and practices based on concepts rooted in patriarchal values of racism, sexism and heterosexism.

4.) Such exclusionary policy reflects patriarchal attitudes and values based on assumptions of biological determinism, which have been used to oppress women, gay men and lesbians for centuries and is therefore inherently anti-feminist in nature.

5.) Such exclusionary policy exists to address concerns based in ignorance and bigotry held by a very small minority within the lesbian community, and does not reflect the feelings and opinions of the vast majority of the lesbian community, without whom the existence of the Michigan Womyn's Music Festival would not be possible.

6.) Transsexual women have attended the festival undetected for many years without causing any disruption or threat to the safety or security of any women in attendance at the festival.

7.) Transsexuals have been no less victimized and persecuted by patriarchal society than have been women in general, and in most cases have been so to an even greater degree.

8.) Such exclusionary policy unduly and unfairly stigmatizes and marginalizes transsexual women, many of whom are actively involved in, and making valuable contributions to their respective lesbian and feminist communities, in which they are generally overwhelmingly accepted.

9.) Any objective criterion utilized to distinguish between post-operative transsexual women and non-transsexual women other than comparison of their respective medical histories would necessarily exclude some non-transsexual women and/or include some transsexual women. This demonstrates that there is no real substantive difference between the two groups according to any relevant criteria, thus such exclusionary policy is necessarily arbitrary in nature.

10.) Festival organizers have demonstrated an unwillingness to engage in open and honest debate regarding the issue of transsexual exclusion.

In recognition of the fact that the marginalization and ostracization of transsexual women provides a mirror in which the oppressive elements of the feminist and lesbian communities can see how they perpetuate some of the very social evils and stereotypes that they fight against in the dominant culture. Lesbians for Justice therefore appeals to the organizers of the Michigan Womyn's Music Festival to nullify its "womyn-born womyn" only policy; and to allow the attendance of postoperative male-to-female transsexuals at all future festivals.

In addition, Lesbians for Justice is very concerned regarding the lack of due process available to all festival participants, as this is a matter which transcends the issue of transsexual exclusion, and represents a threat to the safety, security and dignity of all women in attendance at the festival. We therefore appeal to festival organizers to establish procedures to ensure adequate due process for all women in attendance at the festival in a fair and democratic manner, addressing not merely the opinions and feelings of festival organizers, but likewise addressing the concerns of festival participants . . .

ARNIE KANTROWITZ

In the last two hundred years, the struggles for sexual freedom have been fought under many banners and in many venues. Through poetry, fiction, critical analysis, and theory; through mass demonstrations and insider politics; through separatist, revolutionary, reformist, and assimilationist strategies; and simply by showing up, the people we now call lesbian, gay or queer have adapted to promises of quality and liberty to demand the freedom to love whom we choose. The history of these movements is not that of simple linear progress, but it does manifest a trend toward greater openness to sexual difference.

In the face of social marginalization, each generation is confronted with the task of inventing identities and learning strategies for continuing the struggle. We hope that this book will contribute to that process, as we make our history more visible, and thus reduce the need to reinvent the wheel with each new generation.

Arnie Kantrowitz, a professor of English at the College of Staten Island (NY), has witnessed and participated in the last four decades of gay life in the United States. His "Letter to the Queer Generation," printed in 1992, was elicited by one of the irreverent queer "'zines" reaction to the "outing" trend by "inning" supposed gays and lesbians that the editors of the 'zine, *Bimbox* felt "defile the good name of our people." When a reader wrote to *Bimbox* protesting the "inning" of longtime gay and AIDS activist, film writer, and recently-deceased PWA Vito Russo (who was one of Kantrowitz's best friends), the *Bimbox* editors responded as follows. "Just 'cause someone has AIDS doesn't mean they're exempt from being labeled an asshole. Russo is/was/and will remain one of the most miserable disgusting insufferable clones ever to enter the public eye. Honey, rest assured we were well aware of his medical condition at the time our inning list was together, and to be honest, we're elated he's off the planet . . . Oh sure, Vito's finally dead and we got our wish and we should just drop the whole thing, but we won't be satisfied until we dig him up and drive a stake through his filthy film queen heart.—ed"

Kantrowitz's message to the newest generation of activists touches on this and many themes reflecting cycles of political activism and the relation between generations.

LETTER TO THE QUEER GENERATION

from *NYQ* (1992)

Arnie Kantrowitz

I've never much liked the word "gay." It sounds frivolous, and though I've had my moments of fabulousness, I've never felt especially frivolous. Even though I spelled out GAY in rhinestones on the vest I wore in the 1973 Gay Pride March (with no shirt, red-lensed glasses, a shaved head and some kind of feather contraption hanging from my bare arm), I'm not the kind of guy you'd call "light in his loafers," especially considering that my idea of a fruitful evening is wallowing in Holocaust documentaries (a tribute to my happy heritage). In fact, the English professor in me blanched when I first heard "gay" used as a noun, as in, "He's a Jew, a writer and a gay" (with much argument as to whether to use a small or capital G). But the English language will go where it wants to—as it has always done.

You probably won't believe this, but one stoned night in 1975 I sat down to come up with a better word than "gay"—and after a couple of hours, I finally settled on "queer." It sounded perfectly good as a noun. (After all, I was familiar with such phrasing as "What are you, some of kind of queer?") I liked the idea that it signified otherness in a non-specific way—though I was concerned that (like "bent" vs. "straight") its pejorative connotation seemed to imply that the "norm" from which is deviated was somehow desirable. Also, whenever you encounter "queer," you have to decide whether it's being used by a friend or an enemy, and who's looking for more barriers to being understood? The dialogue quoted here is a good example of such a barrier, when she says "queer," you may read "post-gay," but what she meant is "kinky."

I remember how much hassle there was when "gay" replaced the clinical sounding "homosexual," which in turn had replaced the more discreet "homophile" in the '60s—and there wasn't much point in trying to go back to the nineteenth century when we were called "uranians" or "urnings" and nobody considered us a category of human being in the first place.

There are some people who don't believe such a category exists at all, because human experience is such a fluid, undefinable thing; since some people are only partly homoerotic, or are attracted to members of the same sex for only certain periods of their lives, why be limited by labels? Besides, aren't we all citizens of Earth anyway?

If that were all there was to it, we wouldn't need to worry about what to call ourselves, but we might have to ask ourselves why we're reading a minority magazine like this one, and exactly who it is being bashed over the head in the sullen city streets. Those who dwell in ivory towers like to sit around in circles and endlessly reconsider themselves according to the prevailing fashions of academia. (What is it about sitting a circle that makes certain people want to masturbate?) But even if we could define ourselves out of existence, that wouldn't convince our enemies to stop calling us names.

For some reason, people seem to care about names. The women in Gay Activists Alliance, whose vice president I was in 1971, always thought that "gay" signified only men, and so every organization with an ounce of intelligence after that became called "gay and lesbian," or "lesbian and gay," if they wanted to be politically correct. Later, I was a founding member of GLADD (the Gay and Lesbian Alliance Against Defamation," but QUADD doesn't seem to make as cheerful an acronym as GLAAD, don't you agree?

"Queer" seems to refer to both men and women, and we don't hear about "queer men and lesbians," perhaps because feminist rage has gone out of fashion. In the '70s, that rage meant that men in drag were being told that they were oppressive by women who were wearing men's overalls. The rest of us were advised not to wear tight jeans because it was politically incorrect to make ourselves into sex objects. (Were they kidding? After decades of hiding under a baggy academic tweed jacket, I was thrilled to be seen as a sex object. I remember wearing my clone drag—along with what seemed like a tasteful excess of rings, bracelets and necklaces—to work at the College of Staten Island, only to have one of my tweedy colleagues inform me "You may consider me pedestrian, Arnold, but frankly, I find you bizarre!" What did he know about fashion statements?) Anyway, the proliferation of '70s "clones" in tight Levi 501s shows how popular that advice was.

Queers, both male and female, dress pretty much alike these days. Sometimes I think the biggest change has been from brown leather bomber jackets to black leather motorcycle jackets (which have proliferated so fast that serious sadomasochists are showing up in sweaters—soon we'll be right back in the nasty '50s!)

The feminist idea that it was politically correct for either sex partner to be on top was even ghastlier. (If I had to choose between corrrectness and coming . . . well, you get the picture.) Unhappily, political correctness seems to be as humorless now as it was then. When they're not busy calling each other names like "pseudo-bourgeois left-liberal neo-determin-ist anti-constructionist het-imitating sons of clones," the "pomo-homo" (Newspeak for post-modern homosexuals) are busy labeling the gay generation "racist," "sexist" and god knows what else.

The truth is, the gay generation worked incredibly hard at manifesting the quality of women and embracing minority groups, like "African-Americans" (who in my time have been politically known as "colored people," "Negroes," "Afro-Americans," "blacks" and "peo-ple of color"). Each generation needs to redefine and rename itself, so even though a lot of people my age are a little upset about the term "queer" and even though I can't imagine an organization called "Nigger Nation" or "Crippled Liberation Front," I don't get too worked up about it. Most people my age seem to have forgotten the T-shirt popular among '70s politicos, which proclaimed in blue lettering across a gray chest simply: "Faggot." (Maybe the "pomo-homos" should use "queer," so they could have T-shirts that read "pomo-ques." I kind of like that; it has a certain *je ne sais quoi*.) Not to worry—"That which we call a rose by any other name would smell as sweet," as Shakespeare's Juliet said.

Call me what you will, but I do try to be a nice person: sensitive, compassionate, coop-erative, generous of spirit, wise, warm, wonderful and all the other things Bette Davis's char-acters used to be. I make an exception, however, for certain unforgivable moron pig ass-holes—which brings us to the subject of *Bimox*.

It seems that some pasty-faced word-pimp who courageously hides behind the name "Johnny Noxema," and his lover, "Rex Boy," and a brave "psychologist" who allowed his left elbow to be photographed for the *Advocate*, want to say they're at war with me and that they will join in if they see me being assaulted. It took me a while, but I think I can accept it. Even if it doesn't make me laugh, it does make me think.

But apparently that wasn't good enough for them. After nursing Vito Russo, my beloved friend of 20 years, through years of debilitating illnesses, while he struggled—under his real name—to keep encouraging other people to believe in themselves and to be angry at their real enemies, not at each other, I learned that Messrs. "Noxema" and "Boy" had called Vito an "ugly old clone" and said that they were glad he had died of AIDS. Not only do I fail to see the humor, I fail to think rationally. All I can say is that if they don't know a real hero when they see one and they want to go to war with gays, let them come to my neighborhood, where I might just forget I'm a lady and flush both of them and their so-called "zine" down the nearest toilet.

The question is: Why are they getting so much space in the American press? Even the "psychologist" half of the pair should know that they're just being bad boys so they can get some attention. Are we fresh out of real problems to deal with so that we have time and ener-gy to spend on ego-deficient brats? Have all our states repealed their sodomy laws? Can we adopt orphaned children, keep our jobs, and inherit our lovers' possessions without prob-lems? Are we allowed to serve in the military, if we're foolish enough to want to? Has Hollywood stopped ignoring and misrepresenting and defaming us? Have we stopped being murdered in the streets (even without the help of Mr. Noxema)? Has the AIDS crisis ended? Has anyone even asked about gay or queer or uranian-people among the homeless?

Mercifully, these idiots don't speak for all queers. The young people who call themselves "queer" look good to me (although I'm sad to see how many of them still feel they have to use pseudonyms when they discuss these issues in print). Their ideas are their own, even if some aren't quite as new as they may think. (Does anybody think separatism is a new con-cept? Do modern queers know that in the early '70s gay people tried to take over Alpine Country in California, moving in enough of our people to vote our own government into office? (The whole project failed miserably; the ghetto is an urban institution.)

Even as a state of mind, it seems the gay ghetto can't survive the complexity of the human spirit. I lived in a gay commune for two years, suspending contact with most of my family and straight friends. There were more than enough interesting gay people to keep me busy; I felt understood, appreciated, part of a new family without nagging parents or benighted siblings. Those years were wonderful, exciting, sexy—yet after a while I felt like I was drowning. I needed to talk about something else besides gay problems; I needed other kinds of input. Eventually, I realized that my heterosexual relatives and friends of many years loved me too, even if they didn't always understand me, and had value in my life. I came back into the world—on my own terms, as an openly (you'll pardon the expression) gay man. For all the violence and ignorance and pain that has been showered upon us, I still believe that heterophobia makes no more sense than homophobia, and our best bet is to make room for ourselves in the world that already exists.

Some of us fear that if we assimilate into the mainstream culture, we'll lose our special-ness—we won't be "queer." The romantics among us prefer to wait until the ultimate revolu-tion takes place, when everyone rises up to overthrow everything, so we can be among the founders of the new order—or lack of order, for anarchists—which will, by some metaphys-ical means, be not only totally free but politically correct. As a '60s idealist in the '70s, I still believed I might live to see total change, yet I chose to work for specific reforms in the mean-time. I thought it would take America only a few years to see the error of its ways and grant us justice. Eventually, I realized the process would take generations. As we approach the end of the century, those who are still waiting for that total revolution to suddenly change every-thing remind me of Dickens's Miss Havisham, sitting in her yellowed wedding gown, watch-ing the cobwebs accumulate on her wedding cake while she waits for her groom to arrive.

For all the accusations that have been heaped upon the "gaycrat" reformers of the '70s, it should be pointed out that all of the concrete signs of progress in our movement—repeal of sodomy statutes, changes in city and state anti-discrimination laws, bringing our faces out from behind the potted palms that used to obscure them on television shows, fairer hiring practices, the opening of public accommodations, the proliferation of a gay press, the advent of gay studies—can be attributed to gays. It took nearly 20 years to get the *New York Times* to use the word "gay" instead of "homosexual." Good luck getting them to change to "queer."

Not long ago, I went to a meeting of Queer Nation, to tune in on the present. There were only about 50 people there, but as they say, "It was a dark a stormy night." I felt as if I'd been flung back 20 years and was sitting in at an early Gay Activists Alliance meeting. The issues were the same; only the faces—and in a couple of cases, not even those—were different. The announcements were just as tedious; the hopes and ideals were just as high. Where the queers have "actions," we had "zaps." Queers have a "phone tree," the gays had a "Joseph Cohen" list, with which we alerted people at work about forthcoming zaps by leaving the message that "Joseph Cohen" had called. Queers have affinity groups; we had committees. The queers were organizing against job discrimination at Cracker Barrel restaurants; the gays had organized against job discrimination at the Board of Education. The queers were going to protest queer-bashing in Bellmore, Long Island; we had gone out to protest gay-bashing in Happauge, Long Island. Today's queers went same-sex dancing at straight clubs; gays had danced at the Rainbow Room in 1971. Because I had seen it happen in GAA and ACT UP, in the Christopher Street Liberation Day Committee (now Heritage of Pride) and in GLADD, I knew the larger QN grew, the more factionalized it would become, the more problems there would be keeping order, and the more complex and confining procedural rules would have to be enacted. I felt right at home.

We don't come from nowhere. When Larry Kramer and Vito Russo watched Vito's last Gay Pride March in 1990, thousands of ACT UP activists shouted up the balcony, "We love you, Vito!" (Take that, *Bimbox!* You'll never hear the like.) My lover, Larry Mass, heard Larry Kramer say to Vito, "These are our children." Queer Nation is the child of ACT UP, which is the stepchild of GMHC. GAA gave birth to the Gay Teachers Association, Lambda Legal Defense and Education Fund and a host of other groups; GAA in its turn was the child of its forebears, the Gay Liberation Front, the Mattachine Society, the Daughters of Bilitis, the Society for Individual Rights, even Magnus Hirschfeld's Institute for Sexual Science in pre-Nazi Germany. Queer people are not newly born, only newly named. You have a history, and you should not only be proud of it, you should learn from it.

I know that oedipal rebellion against our predecessors is an important step, as is reinventing ourselves in each generation, but reinventing the wheel as well is a waste of valuable energy and time. My gay generation rebelled against the Mattachine Society because we considered it too obsequious and against the Gay Liberation Front because we found it too doctrinaire, but we learned things from their experience, as you should learn from ours. The people who scheduled a demonstration while the nation was absorbed in the Superbowl might learn something from schedulers of the past; the Queer Nation woman who sold fund-raiser tickets to only three people might pick up some pointers from fund-raisers of the past. And those gay activists of the past owe it to the future to put away their cozy bitterness, at least long enough to pass on what they know. No one expects them to have the energy they had two decades ago, but the least they can do is share whatever wisdom they have gained—especially on the subjects of gay factionalism and empowerment.

The thing that homosexual/lesbian/gay/queer people are best at is fighting amongst ourselves. That is what *Bimbox* is trying to foster, for its own arrogant amusement, though intergenerational prejudice is every bit as stupid as every other kind. In this era when the buzzword is "empowerment," battling each other is how our power is sapped. If empowerment comes from anywhere, it comes from working together, from belonging to the something larger than yourself. Most people seem to think that "empowerment" means learning to feel good about yourself, but that is only a beginning, not an end in itself. People who imagine themselves powerful because they can hold hands on one street in one city at certain hours are fooling themselves; in terms of actual power in the world, the illusion of power is not only useless, it's destructive. People command respect in the world when they make it clear that no matter how many defeats they suffer, they will remain on the stage of history generation after generation, and they will not stop until their cause has been won. Such people are more than "empowered": they are powerful.

Reviling people who could be your allies is not empowerment; it is bullshit. If you want to feel empowered, feel the richness of your past. Learn from those who came before you and build on what they have accomplished. There are wonderful people who have come before you: strong individuals who carried forward the ages-long task of challenging the values of Western civilization, leaders like Harry Hay and Barbara Gittings and Frank Kameny and Joan Nestle and Vito Russo. You could do worse than follow their examples. Should they be dismissed because you don't like their haircuts or their clothes or the name they call themselves? Remember, there will be a generation that comes after you, with its own ideals and styles and its own new name for itself. Like all young people, they will probably have contempt for their elders, and like all older people you will probably nod your head wisely and say "They'll learn."

The "gay" generation is in the process of its mid-life crisis. After fomenting amazing changes in our culture, we suddenly find ourselves uncomfortable with more change—a sign our day is drawing to a close. It is a reminder that we are one step closer to death (as if a generation traumatized by the grim spectacle of AIDS needed any reminders.)

I thought I had come from the best era of all. I had survived the oppression of the '50s, participated in the social experiments of the '60s, and emerged from the closet into the sunlight of the '70s, managing to have a great deal of fun and fulfillment before the plague years of the '80s. Not long ago, I gave a reading at the Lesbian and Gay (or should it be retitled "Queer?") Community Services Center. I read an essay about the changes I had seen during my quarter century in Greenwich Village. When the applause was over, a gentleman who looked about 70 years old came up to me and said, "You should have been there in the 40s. That's when we really had fun!"

Good luck being queer. I hope you really have fun, and I hope you make us proud of you.

As we have seen, there is often a connection between conservative attempts to forestall feminist change and hatred of gays and lesbians. Every era of feminist activity has been met with new crackdowns on women's sexuality. While formerly communist countries were no less puritanical than capitalist ones, the position of women did in fact often improve. As these countries become "Westernized," we are also witnessing a return to older, religious-based patriarchal constrictions. This especially impacts lesbians, because economic opportunity has been crucial for lesbians' ability to live independently of men. Christina Schenck's article examines the recent history of lesbians in what was East Germany, and expresses concern that unification will roll back gains for lesbians. Her concern is already being justified by events throughout Eastern Europe.

CHRISTINA SCHENCK

LESBIANS AND THEIR EMANCIPATION IN THE FORMER GERMAN DEMOCRATIC REPUBLIC: PAST AND FUTURE

(1993)

Christina Schenck

I. Homosexuals: Outsiders in GDR Society

The ways in which a society deals with deviation from the norm, with those who are "different" and especially with homosexuality and homosexuals, develop within a historical context and take specific national forms. In the GDR the legal system was sufficiently ambiguous to be used as an instrument of repression. There were no public forums for debate, for the expression and exchange of opinion or a balance of interests. Instead there was a secret service intended to ward off "internal enemies." Yet despite the absence of basic civil liberties, since the GDR was founded in 1949 a liberalization of attitudes toward homosexuality has taken place, albeit very slowly.

At the beginning of the 1970s, gays and lesbians set up the first private gay and lesbian groups in order to make contact with each other, to work through their personal experiences, and to provide support for those who were "coming out." It was also the declared aim of these groups to draw public attention to the situation of homosexuals and to demand changes. Given that at that time homosexuality was generally portrayed not only as a pathological condition but also as a crime, and prejudice against homosexuals continued to be endemic, these activities were of great importance for the self-confidence and self-image of lesbians and gay men.

In view of the restrictive interpretation of civil law, however, public expression and self-organization were out of the question. The Socialist Unity Party of Germany (SED) had not concerned itself with the issue of homosexuality, and as a result there were no clear-cut guidelines for the organs of the state to follow. This led to uncertainty on the part of the authorities, other political parties, and mass organizations when confronted with the demands of homosexual groups. The groups' applications to register as official associations were all rejected.

When specific interests were articulated by lesbian and gay men's groups, they met with a negative response and were dismissed as demands for unjustified privileges (!) or special conditions. Until the late 1980s, calls for public debate of hitherto taboo social issues and for official recognition of gay liberation groups were seen as implicit criticisms of "socialist society" and were thus rejected outright.

For lesbians and gay men the situation remained unchanged until the late 1970s, when the Protestant church, witnessing the state's repression of dissidents, increasingly offered its protection and the use of its facilities to anyone who challenged "really existing socialism in the GDR," especially on ecology, peace, human rights, and feminist issues. The first church-based opposition groups were formed, from which the opposition movement in the GDR was later to develop. Very few members of these groups were Christians; the Protestant church imposed no such condition upon the groups seeking shelter. This was the major factor enabling an opposition movement to form on church territory in a country where almost three-quarters of the population were atheists.

In Leipzig in 1982 a group of gay men and several lesbian women founded the first (semi-) official homosexual group in the GDR. Admittedly, the official (Protestant) church viewed the establishment of this and subsequent groups with disfavor, and expressed its views with varying degrees of outspokenness; but thanks to the support of clergy and individual parishes it proved possible to set up the group. Similar groups were soon established in other cities. For the first time the groups were able to work autonomously in an atmosphere relatively free of fear. The State Security Service did subsequently attempt to infiltrate but was unable to reduce the groups' newfound effectiveness in drawing public attention to their agenda, or to hamper processes within the groups. The groups were able to make use of the church infrastructure to some extent; the church press could be used for publicity purposes, and the groups were able to raise their profile by participating in well-publicized church events such as the annual rallies, as well as organizing their own events for the public to attend.

Over the next few years, the network of gay and lesbian working groups set up under the auspices of the church continued to expand, providing a forum for self-help, counseling, social activities, and discussion for the first time, and enabling gays and lesbians to initiate campaigns to attract public attention.

The groups exchanged experiences on a fairly regular basis, coordinating their campaign. An annual members' meeting enabled lesbians and gay men from the various working groups to report on their activities and to discuss joint action and objectives. The foundation stone for a lesbian and gay liberation movement in the GDR had thus been laid.

Homosexual groups were not permitted to exist outside the church until the mid to late 1980s. These groups were founded by lesbians and gay men who did not want to enter into contact with the church on principle, or who did not consider themselves to be in "opposition" to the state. The groups were set up as "clubs for lesbians and gay men" on youth club premises, in municipal cultural centers, or under the auspices of the local "Freethinkers" associations, which had been established in 1988 in response to instructions "from above." Permission to set up these groups was conditional upon members' proving their conformity to state and system. As a result, the approach and aims of the lesbians and gay men who met in these groups differed radically from their counterparts meeting under the auspices of the Protestant church.

The political dimension of being homosexual, combined with criticism of the GDR state, formed the common basis of the church-based groups, which called for the emancipation, democratization, and restructuring of society. The purpose of the homosexual clubs, on the other hand, was to integrate homosexuals into socialist society, without questioning that society or subjecting it to any form of critical analysis. The aim was to become an invisible part of "normal" society. The clubs demanded equal treatment of homosexuals and heterosexuals by the state bureaucracy at a formal level, and expected their members to make a collective effort to conform to heterosexual standards, as by expressing disapproval of promiscuity. The strategy was to conform at all costs and to keep in the government's good graces. As a result they assiduously avoided any contact with the church-based lesbian and gay groups. They even attempted to present themselves to the state as the sole representative of the interests of lesbians and gay men. As a result, relations between the church-based groups and the homosexual clubs became considerably strained.

Despite these activities, traditional homophobia still colored public attitudes toward homosexuality, and archetypical behavior patterns continued, such as, marginalization on the part of the public and voluntary self-segregation on the part of gays themselves.

II. The Lesbian Movement in the GDR: From Female Homosexuality to a Lesbian Identity

Although women in the GDR had the financial security to adopt independent and alternative lifestyles, the model was a monogamous heterosexual relationship and parenthood. In addition, there were no women's centers, cafés, or libraries. For a long time, lesbian personal ads were either forbidden or permitted only in cryptic form in a few newspapers. There was no public recognition that lesbians existed, and absolutely no information provided. In terms of the officially promoted role model for women in the GDR, a lesbian way of life was a deviation from the norm. It was dismissed by the state as a fringe phenomenon, a social irrelevance that could safely be ignored; if taken seriously, it was treated as a potentially subversive phenomenon which had to be dealt with. Joined by the common bond of their homosexuality, lesbians and gay men began to campaign together for improvements in their situation.

The gendered patterns inherent in this situation went virtually unnoticed at first. This was due in part to the nature of the relationship between male and female, which if basically patriarchal was nonetheless less hierarchical and sexist than was the case in West Germany. It was also due to the impact of the official image promoted by the state, which ignored the difference in the situation of men and women in society or at least portrayed it as unproblematic and idealized. It took time for homosexual working groups to confront the divergent and conflicting interests of lesbians and gay men and the elements of traditional sex-role behavior that emerged, particularly in the form of nonverbal dominance and dominant speech patterns.

By its third meeting, the lesbian and gay men's working group in Berlin had already decided to split. From then on (1983) two separate working groups—one for lesbians and another for gay men—existed in Berlin. In the other church-based working groups the lesbians tended to split from the gay men much later, and they did not reject joint action when they felt this was helpful for lesbians.

The separatist trend clearly increased in the late 1980s, and when the GDR ceased to exist, there were eight autonomous lesbian groups in various towns. The close links between the groups justify the term "lesbian movement" in the case of the GDR. An important contribution was made by the lesbian newspaper "*frau anders*," founded in 1989 and published by women in Jena.

Remarkably, lesbians who joined the "clubs for homosexuals" set up independently of the churches did not establish autonomous lesbian groups. This is perhaps not surprising, given that there was a considerable degree of conformity to state and system within these groups, which made it impossible to discuss the continuing existence of the mechanism of repression, whether traditional or inherent in socialism.

III. Lesbians in Politics

The radical changes that swept GDR society in the autumn of 1989 were brought about by grass-roots movements, some of which had sprung from the church-based opposition movement, while others came into being as the peaceful revolution progressed. Although some women were prominent in these movements, they were underrepresented to a considerable degree, and there was virtually no discussion of women's issues or feminism at the time.

As a result, the Independent Women's Association (UFV) was founded at the beginning of December 1989, soon acquiring a high profile on the political landscape of the GDR. Lesbian women played an important role in setting up and working within the UFV from the start. Even at its constituent meeting, attended by women from all over the GDR, lesbian groups and lesbians from mixed groups voiced their opinions. Their demands to participate on an equal footing were accepted, without discussion, as readily as those of the other women's groups. This was unusual in itself, given that for years lesbianism had been a subject shrouded in silence.

The UFV's program states: "We aim to establish a modern society in which every women and man is free to choose the lifestyle s/he prefers, without suffering marginalization or disadvantage because of his/her gender, origin, nationality, or sexual orientation." The fundamental aims of the UFV are to ensure that all lifestyles that do not encroach on others' rights to self-determination are accepted as equally valid; and that the relationship between the sexes, based as it is upon power, is fundamentally changed. The UFV used its influence at the Round Table to ensure that a ban on discrimination on the basis of "sexual orientation" was incorporated into several fundamental draft laws, including the draft of a new constitution for the GDR (Articles 1 and 22), the Party Law (paragraph 3 [2]), the Unification Law (par. 2 [2]), and the Electoral Law (par. 8 [2]). The working groups on "Equality of Women and Men" and "Education, Upbringing, Youth" issued manifestoes stating specifically that all lifestyles, irrespective of sexual orientation, were equally valid; they also expressed the principle of "respecting the dignity of every person, irrespective of age, sex, sexual orientation, nationality, social and family origin, cultural, political, or religious identity." Yet the UFV was not represented only by lesbians in Round Table talks and its working groups. The principles expressed by the UFV in its policy regarding lifestyles were vigorously supported by the nonlesbian women in the negotiations as well. There was no sign of the "lesbian-straight conflict" that has played such a considerable role in the women's movement in the West.

In mid-1990 representatives of a number of lesbian groups and lesbians from other UFV groups met together for the first time since the political upheavals in the GDR. Their aim was to discuss possible ways of reestablishing the network of contacts that had existed prior to the peaceful revolution in the GDR, and to seek ways to raise the lesbian profile in the UFV. It was decided to issue a declaration to the other women in the UFV, stating that lesbianism was a central aspect of their activities within the women's movement, focusing on the role of lesbian women in the UFV, and urging other UFV women to lend their support to lesbian policy initiatives in the future. They also demanded that "on appropriate occasions the existence and role of lesbians in the UFV should not be ignored or 'overlooked' and that they should play a part commensurate with their numbers in the UFV in building up the association and making it effective." It was proposed that "in accordance with the scale of the problems associated with a lesbian lifestyle in a heterosexist, patriarchal society, one of the spokeswomen of the UFV could be authorized by the lesbian women in the association to speak out on the situation of lesbian women in the area of the GDR." The association accepted the declaration without debate.

The UFV has been represented by two women in the German parliament since December 1990. One of them was elected from the PDS (Partei Demokratischen Sozialismus, the renamed communist party) list, while I myself stood as a candidate for Bündnis 90/Greens (party of civil rights and ecology groups).

I am the only member of the German Bundestag who lives openly as a lesbian. My main fields of work are women's issues and lesbian politics, and—as far as this is possible—gay politics. One achievement in the current electoral term is that the words "lesbian" and "gay" may be used in motions and draft laws by the German Bundestag. Prior to this, only the term "homosexual" was permitted. It is important to use the avenues of parliamentary democracy (plenary debates, motions, draft laws) to make the public aware of these issues in order to combat general ignorance, and if laws are prepared in Parliament that discriminate against lesbians and gays, also to mobilize the lesbian and gay movement.

At the time of this writing in 1992, efforts are being made to abolish section 175 of the West German penal code, which made male homosexual acts with someone under eighteen illegal (in the GDR the age of consent had already been lowered to sixteen in 1989). But it is proposed that it be replaced with a new paragraph 182, being marketed under the name "Sexual abuse of youth." Under this proposed law punishment would be a fine or a maximum of three years' imprisonment. The proposed law makes it punishable to abuse anyone under sixteen by having sex with them or attempting to do so, by exploiting their "immaturity or sexual inexperience." This language was appropriated from the ex-GDR paragraph 149. The terms are vague, opening the door to an interrogation of the purported victim about his or her intimate life, as has often been the case for rape victims. Presumably this new law would eliminate discrimination against gay men, by making the punishment and age of consent independent of gender or sexual orientation. But the previous paragraph 182 had made the age of consent for heterosexuals and lesbians fourteen; here, it would be increased to sixteen. It would also become criminal for an adult woman to have sexual contact with either male or female youths under sixteen, while the age of consent for men would be reduced from eighteen to sixteen. It would become possible, for the first time in the

Federal Republic of Germany, to prosecute lesbians under the penal code. In practice this would provide an opportunity for that overwhelming majority of parents hostile to their daughter's or son's emerging homosexuality to control that sexuality with threats of criminal proceedings.[1]

If the real purpose of the proposed law is to prevent sexual abuse, the issue should be sexual activity that takes place "against the will" of the person, whether in or out of marriage, and independent of age, while the punishment for rape should be increased.

IV. GDR Lesbians and German Unification

For the women in the UFV and many other grass-roots activists, the peaceful revolution in autumn 1989 was a euphoric time. We felt that this was the start of the "third way" for the GDR. But issues now on the agenda in 1992 differ radically from those of that period:

—In a capitalist society on the Federal German model, in which economic pragmatism takes priority over the creation of a society in which the needs of individuals (women and men) and the preservation of the ecosphere are paramount, to what extent is it possible to challenge and change the relationship between the sexes as a social, cultural, economic, and sociopsychological problem?

—To what extent is it possible to remove all the various forms of marginalization in society, and in particular, what measures will ensure that all lifestyles are acceptable and that marriage no longer receives privileged status?

—What strategies for success are possible for women in capitalist German society?

The social transformation will be complete in a matter of years. For women, and for lesbians, who lived in the GDR, the graphic differences between the patriarchies of the Federal Republic of Germany and the GDR are becoming only too clear. Consider that:

—Today only about 36 percent of women who are able to work hold a job, in contrast to a figure of more than 80 percent in the GDR. This may change once the East German economy is consolidated, but a number of leading politicians have already made it quite clear that the "excessive level of employment of women in the GDR" should be reduced to "normal" levels. At present, women are steadily being eased out of employment.

—Women's economic independence, which is the prerequisite for an independent lifestyle, is under threat. This thrusts them back into a position of humiliating dependency and makes it particularly difficult for lesbians to find the lifestyle that suits them.

V. The Relationship of the Sexes

The current process of marginalization will lead to a radical change in the relationship between the sexes in East Germany. Society—and women themselves—will attribute a higher status to men, and women's status will decline accordingly. Men will once more be the "breadwinners" and heads of the family, with women primarily assuming responsibility for reproduction. Whereas in the GDR men were increasingly assuming domestic responsibilities, this role will be reassessed, and the main burden will be borne by women once more.

It will no longer be generally accepted, as it was in the GDR, that every woman will have a career as a matter of course, and girls' and women's expectations will therefore change. They will now focus once again on men for their economic security. These processes will make it increasingly difficult for girls and women to come out as lesbians.

The problem of sexism is compounded by the massive attempt now being undertaken by the churches to "re-Christianize" East Germany. Standards and values which became obsolete long ago (value of marriage, abortion) are being revived. As a result, the social status of women is changing dramatically, and these changes directly affect lesbian women.

The fall of the Wall brought many lesbians in East and West Germany into contact for the first time. It very quickly became clear that forty years of separate development in the two German states had resulted in very different mentalities, approaches, and political intentions. The great challenge now facing the lesbian movements in East and West Germany is to ensure that they draw strength and inspiration from their differences and do not allow their dissimilarities to drive a wedge between them. Much will depend on the newly won freedoms being used effectively to make the women's and lesbian movement in both East and West Germany a politically relevant force for the future.

1. *Studies in Hamburg have shown that 41 percent of males and 37 percent of females have sexual intercourse by the age of sixteen.* Die Tageszeitung, *February 19, 1992.*

The author of the following article founded a community-based AIDS prevention project in Manila, the Philippines. His text is an important contribution to a global understanding of homosexuality as a political issue. Fleras recalls the extermination of indigenous peoples by colonizers on the basis of their homosexuality and traces the continuity of homoerotics and cross-dressing from tribal cultures to the present. Finally, he analyzes homoerotics in the context of socioeconomic and political forces, including government promotion of sex tourism (which occurs in many other countries as well) and the implications of this for the politics of AIDS.

JOMAR   FLERAS

RECLAIMING OUR HISTORIC RIGHTS: GAYS AND LESBIANS IN THE PHILIPPINES
(1993)

Jomar Fleras

Rise up, Sisters!
This is not a moment for mourning.
The earth may rumble, the sky turn dark,
but Heaven a legacy for the brave!

Now is the time to sing
Our song of Liberation!
    —Nick Deocampo, Filipino gay poet

June 1991. The Philippines. After more than six hundred years of silence, Mount Pinatubo awakened and unleashed its pent-up, seething fury. From the bowels of hell, the angry volcano spewed tons and tons of sulphuric ash, burying the twin cities of Angeles and Olongapo, sites of two of the largest American military installations and infamous centers of the flesh trade. The doomsday moralists likened this calamity to the destruction of Sodom and Gomorrah—signs of the Armageddon—and consequently called for repentance for past sins.

In defiance of the apocalyptic warnings, the first gay Mass was celebrated in Manila. In a booming recalcitrant voice, a gay ex-priest narrated the Old Testament love story of David and Jonathan and preached the virtues of homosexual love. Witnessing the event were twenty brave Filipino gay men who dared possible excommunication by the Catholic Church and the threats of fire and brimstone. Later on, seven gay men were elected to the Board of Directors of the Metropolitan Community Church Manila, the only Christian church in the Philippines which advocates that homosexuality is not a sin.[1]

Earlier, Reachout AIDS Education Foundation held its world premiere of *Poisoned Blood,* the first documentary on the social impact of AIDS in the Philippines.[2] This video documentary analyzed the sexual make-up of the Filipino and blamed the sexual hypocrisy resulting from three hundred years of Catholic indoctrination under the Spanish colonizers as a contributor to the spread of AIDS in the country.[3] Not surprisingly, the religious right condemned the documentary as blasphemous. (This was partly because the opening sequence showed a man dancing naked with a rosary around his neck.)

In another part of the city, the organization Katlo (Third Sex) was being formed by gay men from different walks of life. Initiated by the politicized theater artists of the Philippine Educational Theater Association (PETA), Katlo dared to tackle highly sensitive issues of gay consciousness and gay pride. Another group composed mainly of young "butch" gay customers of the Library Sing-Along Bar started getting involved in issues concerning "coming out" and self-esteem.

On the other hand, the feminist movement, which had been initially preoccupied primarily with the anti-prostitution, anti-U.S. bases movement, started confronting lesbian issues. The lesbian faction of the feminist movement opposed a definition of lesbianism based primarily on sex, and reasserted that lesbian women, too, could desire and shape sexual experience. During the sixth International Women and Health Meeting in Manila, lesbianism was redefined as a form of resistance to patriarchy and male oppression.

It was amazing that all these unorchestrated "awakenings" of homosexual men and women were happening with a volcanic eruption as a dramatic background. Nick Deocampo, internationaly acclaimed alternative filmmaker and gay poet, whose gay film *Oliver* shocked the world with its Marxist dialectical exposé of a gay prostitute, used the imagery of the volcano as his poetic metaphor: "The awakening of lesbian and gay consciousness is like the awakening of a volcano. We have long been dormant. It's now about time that lesbian women and gay men come out with a bang."[4]

Homosexuality as Superstructure

The Philippines is a neocolonial, multicultural society with a population of over 60 million. About 85 percent of the population is Catholic. Philippine history may be summarized as follows: an Indo-Malayan tribal culture from A.D. 500 to the mid-sixteenth century, 333 years of Spanish colonial rule, forty-five years of American colonial rule, four years of Japanese occupation, ten years of democracy, twenty years under the dictatorship of Ferdinand Marcos, and a democratic government from 1986.

In analyzing the historical struggle of homosexuals in the Philippines for sociopolitical organization at the macro level and for personhood at the micro level, we must first realize that homosexuality is part of the socioeconomic and political superstructure of society.

Robert Padgug, an expert on sexuality and classical history writes: "The important comprehension that sexuality, class, and politics cannot easily be disengaged from one another must serve as the basis of a materialist view of sexuality in historical perspective as well.... The history of sexuality is therefore the history of a subject whose meaning and contents are in continual process of change. It is the history of social relations."[5]

In this article I will trace the evolution and metamorphosis of homosexuality in the Philippines vis-à-vis the histories of the powers that be—the economic, religious, and social realities and world developments. In order to reconstruct our homosexual past, I have extensively used not only chronicles of Filipino and Western writers but also oral accounts. In the absence of unprejudiced written materials on gay and lesbian history in the Philippines, oral history is critical in recovering our homosexual history.

The Pre-Hispanic Shamans

Before the Spanish conquistadores came, the Philippines were populated by Indo-Malayan scattered tribes known as *balangays*. At the head of the tribe was the village chieftain. But exercising more de facto power than the chieftain was the *babaylan* or *catalonan*, who was the shaman, the medicine man, the high priest, the overseer of sacred functions, and adviser to the chieftain. Power among tribal people is not perceived as political or economic, but supernatural and paranormal.

In most cases, a "man whose nature inclined toward that of a woman," called a *bayoguin*, was assigned the role of the *babaylan*.[6] The ancient tribes believed that the godhead consisted of the interaction of male and female components, and that bisexuality or androgyny represented immortality. Thus, the male priest who dressed as a female symbolized bisexuality and, therefore, immortality.[7]

A 1738 chronicle of Fray Juan Francisco de San Antonio reports that *hombres maricones* (effeminate men), who were "inclined to be like women and to all the duties of the feminine sex," were "ministers of the devil" or "served as priests to a hermaphrodite god" of the Tagalogs (a Philippine ethnic grouping) prior to the Spanish arrival.[8]

Religious transvestism was not unique to the Philippines. In fact, the practice was probably inherited from immigrants from the Indonesian empires of SriVijaya and Madjapahit.[9] Parallelisms exist with the religious transvestism of the *tadu mburake* shamans of the Toraja Pamona tribe of Central Sulawesi (Celebes), the *bisu* of the Makassarese tribe of Southern Sulawesi, and the *basir* of the Ngaju Dayak tribe of Kalimantan (Borneo).[10]

Animism was widely practiced before the Spanish came. Our ancestors worshiped a hermaphrodite god called *Bathala*, which literally means "man and woman in one."[11]

The effeminate *babaylans* were also known to have married men and to have lived with them.[12] It was considered a great honor for a family to have its young son cohabit with the elderly *babaylan*. However, the man-boy relationship would be terminated when the boy was ready to marry; after all, men were still needed to repopulate the tribe. Again, this practice of pederasty was prevalent in Indonesia tribal cultures, such as in the Minangkabau society of West Sumatra.[13] We do not have colorful accounts of sex between women during pre-Spanish times. But ethnographic accounts and folk legends record the existence of female warriors, chieftains, and shamans. The most famous of them was Queen Urduja, legendary not only for her beauty but also for her strength. It was said that she could do battle with any man.

Whether these women were lesbians was never mentioned. They could have indulged in sex with each other, or they could have merely been Amazons who were forced to do the work of men for the preservation of the tribe. With the dearth of written documents, we can only conjecture.

What we may conclude from the available documents, is that before the Westernization of the Philippines, sex between people of the same gender was considered normal. Like most ancient societies, the *balangays* did not discriminate on the basis of sexual orientation. Effeminate men and masculine women enjoyed powerful and respected positions in society. Like the berdache of the Native American tribes, they were not only accepted but revered for their ability to assume both male and female roles.

Christian Intolerance

Since the twelfth century, Christian Europe has had made illicit all sexual relations between two persons of the same gender. In the sixteenth century, Catholic reformations in Europe brought about a growing concern with legislating moral conduct and curbing heresy, an offense traditionally associated with homosexuality.[14]

Saint Thomas Aquinas' *Summa Theologiae* listed the following as lustful vices against nature: masturbation, bestiality, coitus in an unnatural position, and copulation with one's own sex.

In Spain, Gregorio Lopez' *Las Siete Partidas* (1256) decreed, "Women sinning in this way [lesbianism or what he termed "the silent sin" (*peccatum mutum*) are punished by burning according to the law of their Catholic Majesties, which orders that this crime against nature be punished with such a penalty, especially since the said law is not restricted to men, but refers to any person of whatever condition who has unnatural intercourse."[15]

When the Spanish began colonizing the Philippines in the early sixteenth century, the homophobia that was fast spreading throughout Europe was transplanted. The Spanish repressed and labeled immoral the homosexuality that Filipinos had taken so casually before then.[16]

The conquistadores did to the Philippines what they did in Central America: they tried to destroy the native culture and the old religion. In Colombia, Gonzalo de Oviedo y Valdes boasted of destroying a gold relief depicting "a man mounted upon another in that diabolic and nefarious act of Sodom."[17] In the Philippines, they destroyed the *anitos* (the gods of flora and fauna) and they stripped the transvestite shamans of their authority.

To enable the Spanish empire to strengthen its control of the colony, the Catholic faith was instituted and pagan beliefs were destroyed. The *babaylans* were persecuted not so much because of their homosexuality but, rather, because they represented the old religion. According to John Silva, "The Spanish priests were not only assiduous in writing about 'disgusting sodomites and servants of the devil'; they proceeded to crucify, burn at the stake, and savagely kill large numbers of *babaylans* who were men-lovers."[18]

Male transvestism was especially condemned because it struck at the very heart of European ideas of gender power relations. Male transvestism defied not only the moral but also the social order. Unlike the pre-Spanish tribes which had a more flexible social organization, the new feudal structure introduced by the Spanish had rigid hierarchies: men and women were assigned specific, inflexible roles.

Sodomy was also being practiced during that time. Early Spanish historians claimed that sodomy was introduced to Filipinos by the Chinese, when the Chinese started immigrating as a result of the galleon trade. Archbishop of Manila Miguel de Benavides wrote to the king of Spain, Felipe III, in 1603: "The continual sodomy which the Chinese practice in these islands is so great in extent that they communicate these to the Indians [the term for early Filipinos]."[19]

Although lesbianism was recognized as a sin, it did not receive the attention given to male homosexuality. The waste of male seed was considered a worse offense against the laws of God and nature than the misuse of female seed.[20] Lesbian sex was more tolerated than sex between men partly because of that era's perverse fetish with female chastity. In Agnolo Firenzuola's *Ragionamenti amorosi* (1548), the women argue that it would be better for them to love each other to avoid risking their chastity.

What is also ironic is that the Spanish clergy during that time was known to get enmeshed in not only heterosexual but also homosexual scandals. Friars flaunted openly their native mistresses and altar boys. Even in Spain, as early as the twelfth century, Muslim writers considered the Spanish clergy peculiarly prone to homosexuality.[21] Lesbian sex in monastic orders was also known to exist as early as A.D. 423. The councils of Paris (1212) and Rouen (1214) went to the extent of prohibiting nuns from sleeping together.[22] What is also interesting to note is that effeminate men did not completely abandon their traditional roles as priests.

They became actively involved in Church rituals. Some even went to the extent of entering the priesthood. Effeminate men and even misogamist women found refuge and immunity from persecution behind the hallowed walls of the Almighty Church; they found new freedom to express their "homosexualities" as priests and nuns. Even to this day, when parents observe that a son has pronounced effeminate traits, he is encouraged to enter the priesthood.

We do not have written accounts of homosexual practices among the laity during the Spanish era. However, we do know that passionate but chaste emotional intimacies between men and between women, patterned after classical models of *amicitia,* or friendship, were considered honorable. Pair-bonding was practiced in the all-boy and all-girl schools introduced by the clergy. Once again, we suspect that, just as in European boarding schools, homosexual love and even sex found discreet gratification in these exclusive schools.

To escape social ridicule and to conform with family pressures, many men and women who loved their own sex were forced into marriage and procreation. Still, we do have, in almost all families, the presence of maiden aunts and genteel bachelor uncles.

An historical twist proved fortunate in that when the Napoleonic Code was introduced in Europe in the early 1800s, we were under the rule of Spain, which was part of the empire of Napoleon. Thus the code, which did not fix penalties for sodomy, was adapted as part of our laws. Homosexuality was then decriminalized. In any case, during the last years of Spanish colonial rule, as more and more homosexual men and women infiltrated the clergy and religious orders, the Catholic Church became more tolerant toward gays and lesbians.

American Liberalism

Before the last century, there was no concept of the homosexual as a person; homosexuality was simply regarded as a sinful perverse behavior which anyone might choose to indulge in. The word "homosexual" was not introduced into English until 1892. The turn of the century witnessed the "invention of the homosexual," that is, "the new determination that homosexual desire was limited to certain identifiable individuals for whom it was an involuntary sexual orientation of some biological or psychological origin."[23]

Although identification not only of "deviance" but also of the "deviant" may in some ways be liberating and a legitimizing of social relations, it can also be stigmatizing. This was clearly the case in America at the turn of the century, when the seeds both of homosexual liberation and of homophobia were planted. American men and women learned to love each other in both verbal and physical forms, and attempted to locate that expression of love in tradition and social order.[24]

Freed from moralistic Victorian norms, the turn of the century witnessed the sexualization of America and its exploration of its colonial might. America focused its erotic fantasies and greed for conquest on the South Seas. "The noble savages of these exotic lands provided both sexual excitement and cultural difference." Love for the young men of the South Seas became not only the personal affection for the exotic but also a political statement: America stretching its erotic muscles and discovering its imperial and sexual hold over its colonies.[25]

At the end of the nineteenth century, America procured the Philippines as a spoil of its war with Spain. The new colonial power introduced new concepts of sexual liberalism primarily through the U.S. military, which was notorious as a haven for homosexuals.[26]

The relaxing of three centuries of sexual repression opened the proverbial floodgates. The newfound sexual freedom slowly encouraged gay men and lesbian women to express themselves. The introduction of capitalism and the subsequent industrialization of the Philippines pulled men and women from the bondage of the home and land into the marketplace and the factories. Under these conditions, men and women were given the opportunity to seek self-identity, and to discover their sexual and emotional attractions. Slowly, subcultures of gay men and, much later, of lesbian women, grew as homosexuals rediscovered themselves and each other. Gay men were the first to be liberated because they were less bounded than women by social norms; also, since industrialized centers had traditionally been male spaces, gay male life developed significantly faster than the lesbian subculture.

This era witnessed as well the rebirth of the cross-dressers. Understandably, the lower classes were the first to be sexually liberated since they were not as constrained by demands of society as the upper classes, who were expected to exhibit proper decorum in public.

According to oral accounts, lower-class transvestites working as laundry "women" inside the American military bases would service the sexual needs of the GI's. They were not particularly pretty, but the Americans claimed, "We just cover their faces with the flag and fuck their asses." Oral accounts also claim that the Americans introduced fellatio.

Upper-class gay men found their own sexual expression within exclusive schools operating on the buddy and best friend system. Later on, since there were no gay bars then, moneyed gay men began holding clandestine private parties, which turned into orgies.

Just as in America, cross-dressing was being practiced by working-class women for a variety of economic, sexual, and adventure-seeking reasons, and to rebel at the male order. These mannish lesbians drank, smoked, and worked in traditionally macho occupations.[27] On the other hand, girls belonging to the new bourgeoisie discovered the joys of lesbian sex as interns of exclusive schools for girls. They became best friends with other girls their own age, shared secrets, and developed infatuations for an older student or a teacher.

However, society rejected the personhood that homosexual men and women were discovering, and tried to quash the homosexual's struggle for self-identity by creating the stereotypes.

As early as the 1920s, gay men were being portrayed as comic screaming queen characters and lesbian women were ridiculed as mannish, offensive dykes in stage-show vaudevilles. This trend would continue in the movies and, later, on television.[28] What is interesting to note is that cross-dressing was only shown as a physical manifestation of a social deviance; the deeper sexual meaning of the phenomenon, i.e., attraction to the same sex, was never even implied. Cross-dressing (homosexuality itself was not really discussed) was also portrayed as merely a passing fancy—the effeminate hero would turn straight in the end when he found the right woman, or the butch heroine would turn into a princess, once kissed by the handsome hero.

But perhaps the worst stigmatization that homosexuals suffered during this era was the belief that it was "bad luck" for a family to have a homosexual son or daughter. In response, homosexuals strove hard to prove their worth. They excelled in school, in the creative arts, and even in athletic competitions. They made money, sent their siblings to school, and took care of their parents during their old age.

The end of World War II, the end of American occupation, and the beginning of the Republic witnessed the continuing struggle of homosexual men and women to forge their own subculture.

Neocolonial Macho Feudalism

Four centuries of white supremacy in the Philippines conceived a people enchained by a neocolonial feudal structure that, even today, dictates sexual prejudices. The deeply ingrained macho feudal structure, introduced by the Spanish and encouraged by the Americans as part of its complicity with the ruling capitalist class, molded the psychology and sexuality of homosexual men and women.

The feudal mode revolves around the myth of the macho. Men assume leadership roles while the women are subservient. Men are expected to be virile, libidinous, and even promiscuous, while women are, like the Virgin Mary, chaste, docile, and servile. The strong are idolized while the weak are held in contempt. Those who dare to contest these feudal roles are ridiculed and treated like outcasts.

Homosexual men are called *bakla*, a condescending term that connotes physical and mental weakness, indecisiveness, frailty, unreliability, impotency, and emasculation. Lesbian women are called by the more innocuous term "tomboy," which carries imagery of boyish young girls who are able to outrun their brothers.

Human sexuality is viewed as phallocentric: the penis is considered necessary in the sexual act. People regard it as normal for women to be attracted to men, and even understandable for men to be attracted to other men, but illogical for women to be attracted to women. Men do not consider lesbian women as a serious threat to their own access to women's sexual favors.

Even homosexual relations are affected by the neocolonial structure. Sexual colonialism has fostered the view of the lower class as sexual trade. These class and gender interactions have played an important role in the rise of male prostitution. Colonial fantasies have also given rise to a fixation with the huge penis and, as a result, a preference for *meztizos* (Eurasians or Amerasians) as well as for white men. According to Doreen Fernandez, "Many of the gay relationships are composed of couples of quite unequal social or intellectual standing. More frequently, one sees the patron-ward model, with one the dispenser of bounty and the other in some form of dependent role, be it social or financial."[29]

The Marcos Years

The twenty-year conjugal dictatorship of Ferdinand and Imelda Marcos (1965–1985) created a perverse culture that further reenforced macho feudalism. It was the height of decadence and conspicuous consumption set in the midst of economic deprivation.

As Deocampo has stated, "The Marcos years were characterized by the general complicity of homosexual men and women with the dictatorship. This era was the height of gay sexuality, the emergence of the homosexual subculture, and the insidious rise of prostitution."

While the Stonewall riots gave birth to gay liberation in the U.S., in the Philippines, homosexual men and women were still perpetuating the feudal stereotypes. Gay men portrayed themselves in the media as "screaming queens" who did nothing but gossip, act silly, and lust after men. Even the sexual revolution of the late 1960s did not free homosexuals but only made sure that women were available for the use of men.

To legitimize their existence, homosexual men and women came out with the concept of gender dysphoria: The gay man thought of himself as a woman trapped in a man's body while the lesbian woman envisioned herself with a trapped male soul that phallicized her. Thus, homosexuals were considered neither male nor female, but members of a "third sex."

Homosexual men were the first to create their own subculture: fashion and lifestyle, bars, cruising areas, language, and organizations. Transvestism, sex changes, hormonal injections, and silicon implants became the most convenient ways for gay men to assert their own identities.

Female impersonation became popular when a group called the Paper Dolls did the rounds not of only gay bars but of TV shows and private parties. This group was famous for its realistic impersonation of such famous stars as Liza Minnelli, Dionne Warwick, Diana Ross, and Julie Andrews.

Gay men even had their own lingua franca, popularly known as swardspeak. Gay men invented new words and new expressions as a means to communicate discreetly with one another.

Gay organizations were formed during this era. Two of the first gay organizations were Manila 500 and Sining Kayumanggi Royal Family based at Mehan Garden, a park which was transformed into a cruising area. Other gay groups that formed were primarily trade-related (fashion designers and hairdressers), religious, and social. These groups organized fashion shows, May flower festivals where transvestites would spend fortunes for their gowns, and beauty contests.

Gay bars offering diverse forms of entertainment—macho dancing, sex shows, discos, and drag shows—began sprouting in major urban centers. The earliest gay bars were Talipapa, 690, and Coco Banana.

Unfortunately, at the height of the Marcos regime, sex tourism was encouraged by the government as a means to raise the dollars needed to finance the "edifice complex" of Imelda. With the influx of tourists looking for cheap sex, male, female, and child prostitution became rampant. Men, women, and children discovered that by selling their bodies to sex-starved heterosexual men, rich gay men, and pedophiles, they would be able to buy their next meal.

Lesbian women in general were "unobtrusive." They did not scream their identities as gay men did. They did not have their own macho contests or lesbian bars. They did not even have their own organization.

Filipina author Arlene Babst writes: "There is a relieving thought that tomboys are easier to handle than boys, less socially shattering than male homosexuals, less expensive than a pregnant daughter, and easier to live with than whores. The lesbian is saved by default, by the Filipino's tendency to think of the worst and then thank God that, bad as things are, the worst has not yet befallen them."[30]

General tolerance of homosexuals increased during the Marcos regime. Gay men became the court jesters. Imelda herself was said to be very fond of gay men; after all, these gay men came out with entertaining shows and antics that, like an "opium," made society forget the bigger social realities of moral decay, poverty, and corruption.

Families even started thinking of their homosexual son or daughter as good luck, for they contributed to the family income. Gay men and women saved their families from starvation by working as hairdressers, manicurists, fashion designers, peddlers, or even as prostitutes.

However, there were homosexual men and women who dared to confront, question, and defy the status quo. We know of several of our brother and sisters who have gone up to the mountains to wage an armed revolution against the oppressive ruling class. Their battle, however, was against the whole political system and not against the sexual feudalism that still enchained gay men and lesbian women.

There were those who planted the seeds of gay and lesbian liberation. Filmmaker Lino Brocka came out with *Tubog sa Ginto (Dipped in Gold)*, his first serious gay film which tackled the sensitive issue of male prostitution. Playwrights produced serious works dealing with issues of "coming out," homosexual relationships, and human rights abuses against gay men and lesbian women.

Human Rights Abuses

Homosexuality is not illegal in the Philippines. Homosexual men and women are tolerated but not accepted; they are still very much marginalized. The general attitude is patronizing.

Leni Marin, a lesbian Filipina from the Commission on the Status of Women in California, explains, "Homophobia could range from outright bashing saying 'these people are sick and should be shot' to saying 'let's just forgive them because they're human beings, too.'"[31]

Human rights abuses against homosexuals range from fathers who beat up their gay sons, gay bashings, police entrapment, exploitation by prostitutes, inequality in the workplace, theft, and even murder. But when they do happen, people just think of them as isolated cases, believing that "they deserve it because they have been promiscuous."

One can be overtly gay as long as he is in the arts or as long as he practices stereotypical professions like hairdressing or design. No gay man is welcome in traditionally cloistered, macho-dominated business or in military service.

One executive said, "I have been told that homosexuals are easily influenced. So they should not be in security jobs or jobs involving secret or sensitive data. We are also very particular about jobs that entail cash handling." (The executive probably thought that a homosexual person would embezzle company funds to give to his or her lover.)

There are laws which protect homosexuals from discrimination but in a country where justice, if not denied, is often delayed, these laws are never really enforced. There is no systematic oppression of lesbian women and gay men. Thus, the seeming lack of systematic homophobia has resulted in the lack of a systematic homosexual response. Isn't a stereotype "systematic oppression?"

Gay Liberation and the Feminist Movement

When Ferdinand Marcos declared martial law in 1972 and imprisoned his political rivals and critics, many politicized homosexuals went into exile to America. There they became involved in the gay and lesbian liberation movement. When Marcos was ousted by the People's Power Revolution in 1986, many of these exiled homosexuals returned with fresh ideas and new concepts of gay and lesbian liberation.

Gay men and lesbians started deconstructing and breaking away from the feudal stereotype imposed upon them by society. Now, it has become acceptable for gay men to be "butch" or for lesbian women to be "feminine." Closet queens and dykes have slowly started to come out in the open. Relationships that are non-feudal and between persons of equal social status have become fashionable.

We are also witnessing the emancipation of women in general. The new woman has gotten involved in the movement to obtain equality in rights, duties, freedom, responsibilities, and employment. The new woman has become a social and a political actor. The rise of the new woman is now helping in the lesbian woman's struggle for self-identity.

Fernandez writes, "Considering the circumstances of Philippine society and the mechanism of acceptance presently existing, gay liberation in the Philippines will come with women's liberation and indeed with the liberation of society. It will come with the throwing off of the shackles of feudal thinking, in which male dominance means female subservience and relegation to nonpersons in charge of child-bearing; and not being male/macho means being somewhat less of a person, remembered mainly for a sexual orientation and not for personhood."[32]

The Specter of AIDS

The late 1980s created a new monster that is stalking the homosexual community: AIDS. Homosexual transmission officially makes up only 10 percent of the known HIV cases in the country but 49 percent of the known clinical AIDS cases are gay men. No extensive HIV testing has been done on gay men (less than 7 percent of the total of 165,514 HIV tests already done in the country). Gay men are being diagnosed only when they are confined in hospitals with AIDS symptoms.

The spread of AIDS among homosexual men is mainly due to ignorance. Many still believe that AIDS is transmissible through donating blood, sharing utensils, casual contact, mosquito bites, public toilets and swimming pools. The majority practice unprotected anal sex; few have even tried using condoms.[33]

In the event of a major epidemic in the gay community, there is a great possibility that gay men will become scapegoats of society, with the result that whatever progress has been made toward gay liberation will certainly be set back, if not undone completely.

Conclusion

The 1990s will continue to witness the emergence of politicized homosexual men and women in the Philippines. Slowly, the individual and fragmented efforts of gay men and lesbian women are being collectivized. Solidarity of gays and lesbians will catalyze the centuries of struggle for social acceptance and political power.

Plans are even under way for a Gay Pride week, which will feature an international lesbian and gay film festival, a theater festival, mardi gras, and a symposium. Soon there will be a gay press. Gay men are even now banding together to battle the spread of AIDS in the Philippines. Just as in the West, gay men here are poised to be at the forefront of the AIDS activist movement.

Gay and lesbian activism is, in practical terms, just starting. But society can no longer deny the homosexual community's right to be heard. Gay men and lesbian women will assert their personhoods. They will fight and eventually win their historic rights as leaders and as healers.[*]

[*]Jomar Fleras has produced a documentary film based on this essay.

1. Metropolitan Community Church Manila was founded in June 1991. It is a member of the Universal Fellowship of Metropolitan Community Churches, a Christian denomination with a predominantly lesbian and gay ministry founded in Los Angeles in 1968.

2. The Reachout AIDS Education Foundation is composed primarily of gay and lesbian artists, who are committed to using arts and culture in stopping the spread of AIDS in the Philippines.

3. Jomar Fleras, Poisoned Blood (June 1991).

4. Interview with Nick Deocampo, October 1991.

5. Robert Padgug, "Sexual Matters: Rethinking Sexuality in History," Hidden from History: Reclaiming the Gay and Lesbian Past (Meridian Books, 1990), pp. 55, 58.

6. Juan de Plasencia O.S.F., "Customs of the Tagalogs" (1589).

7. Justus M. van der Kroef, "Transvestism and the Religious Hermaphrodite in Indonesia," Journal of East Asiatic

Studies 3, no. 8 (April 1954): 257–58.

8. Juan Francisco de San Antonio, "The Native People and their Customs" (1738).

9. The hypothesis that the ancient Philippines were once a part of the Sri Vijayan empire (A.D. 670) was formulated by Prof. Otley Beyer of the University of the Philippines in 1921.

10. Doreen Fernandez, "The Gay," in Being Filipino (GCF Books, 1981), p. 259.

11. Ibid., p. 263.

12. Padgug, "Sexual Matters."

13. Dede Oetomo and Bruce Emond, "Homosexuality in Indonesia," unpublished paper.

14. Arlo Karlen, "The Homosexual Heresy," Chaucer Review 6, no. 1 (1971): 44–63.

15. Chronicle found in "Las siete partidas del sabio rey Don Alfonso el Nono, nuevamente glosadas por el licenciado Gregorio Lopez" (Salamanca 1829–31; reprint of 1565 ed.), 3: 178.

16. de Plasencia, "Customs of the Tagalogs."

17. Peter Webb, The Erotic Arts (Boston: New York Graphic Society, 1975), pp. 103–136.

18. John Silva, A Photograph of a Gay Ancestor (Lavender Godzilla).

19. Miguel de Benavides, "Letters from Benavides to Felipe III," in Blair and Robertson, op. cit. 12. pp. 101–126. The traditional belief that sodomy was introduced by the Chinese is reflected in the local English term "Chinese kick" for anal intercourse. (Donn V. Hart, "Homosexuality and Transvestism in the Philippines: The Cebuano Filipino Bayot and Lakin-on," Behavior Science Note [1968]: 231). This is not surprising since in Chinese Buddhism, the sublimely gentle Bodhisattva is represented as a hermaphrodite god. Documented homosexuality was being practiced in Imperial China as early as the third century B.C. in the "Chronicles of Warring States" (Vivien W. Ng, "Homosexuality and the State in Late Imperial China," in Hidden from History).

20. Judith C. Brown, "Lesbian Sexuality in Medieval and Early Modern Europe," Hidden from History, p. 71.

21. John Boswell, Christianity, Social Tolerance and Homosexuality: Gay People in Western Europe from the Beginning of the Christian Era to the Fourteenth Century (Chicago: University of Chicago Press, 1980).

22. de Benavides, "Letters from Benavides to Felipe III," in Hidden from History, p. 69.

23. George Chauncey, Jr., "Christian Brotherhood or Sexual Perversion? Homosexual Identities and the Construction of Sexual Boundaries in the World War I Era," in Hidden from History, p. 312.

24. Robert K. Martin, "Knights-Errant and Gothic Seducers," in Hidden from History, p. 170.

25. Ibid., p. 171.

26. A notorious lesbian from San Francisco, called Babe Bean, who disguised herself as Jack Garland, probably even made it to the Philippines as a lieutenant during the Spanish-American war (San Francisco Gay History Project, in Hidden from History, p. 191).

27. Esther Newton, "The Mythic Mannish Lesbian," in Hidden from History, p. 282.

28. Dolphy, a Filipino heterosexual comedian, came out in a series of "gay" films titled Facifica Falayfay and Fefita Fofonggay.

29. Fernandez, "The Gay," in Being Filipino.

30. Arlene Babst, "The Lesbian," in Being Filipino, p. 94.

31. Lani T. Montreal, "Pars & Mars," Sunday Inquirer Magazine, November 25, 1990, p. 17.

32. Fernandez, "The Gay," in Being Filipino, p. 90.

33. These findings are based on figures released by the National AIDS Prevention and Control Program dated October 1991. A Knowledge-Attitudes-Practices survey among gay men was done in 1989 by the Department of Health in collaboration with AIDSCOM.

ILGA

One of the most important recent developments in lesbian and gay politics is the foundation and strengthening of ILGA, the International Lesbian and Gay Association. Founded in 1978, it has had a significant impact for lesbians and gays on international organizations such as the U.N. and its agencies and the European Community, and on transnational human rights organizations such as Amnesty International; it has been indispensable in the formation and nurturing of local lesbian and gay organizations throughout the world, particularly the Third World. As such, ILGA's activities have included the exchange of information, networking, public education, and direct political action.

In the article presented here, written for this volume by Micha Ramakers (a Brussels-based gay human rights activist), ILGA's recent history is outlined and assessed.

THE INTERNATIONAL LESBIAN AND GAY ASSOCIATION FIVE YEARS LATER: TOWARDS A TRULY WORLDWIDE MOVEMENT?

(1994)

Micha Ramakers

In the Second ILGA Pink Book Herman Holtmaat and Rob Pistor described the structure of the International Lesbian and Gay Association and provided a history of the organization.[1]

From the 1988 article it becomes clear that the ILGA was a loose network of mainly Western European lesbian and gay organizations. Although some permanent structures existed, the organization's work was focused mostly on its Annual Conference and consisted to a very large extent of information exchange, networking and ad hoc actions.

Since 1988 there have been fundamental changes both in the structure of the organization and in its impact on the situation for lesbians and gay men around the world. This article attempts to show how the organization has changed.

Membership

The ILGA was founded in England in 1978 by seventeen European groups and from the start was a real success story in Europe. At the moment of writing the majority of its membership still consists of European organizations. The number of non-European members has however increased significantly since 1988. In early 1994 there were 176 member organizations in Europe (thirty-six in Eastern Europe and the CIS), forty-seven in North America, forty-one in Latin America, nineteen in the Asia-Pacific region and nine in Africa (which means that almost all lesbian and gay organizations in that continent are ILGA members). The ILGA offers full membership to lesbian, gay and bisexual non-profit organizations. Associate membership is available to lesbian, gay and bisexual profit making bodies, non-lesbian, gay and bisexual organizations and to individuals. The ILGA has 110 individual members. Only full members have the right to vote at ILGA conferences. Organizations from economically disadvantaged countries are granted membership at a reduced fee and, in some cases, are able to join free of charge.

Structure

Since 1988 there have been a number of important constitutional changes. At the Stockholm Annual Conference in 1990 the ILGA formally established itself as a permanent body which exists outside its Annual Conference. Up until then this had not officially been the case, although many activities were carried out outside the conference week. The Secretariats and Secretaries General had formed a de facto steering committee which met quarterly to ensure that the ILGA's activities were conducted in line with the organization's existing policies.[2]

In 1990 the Secretariats' Committee was inscribed in the Constitution. This consisted of four Secretariats (Action, Women, Finances and Information) and four Backup Secretariats, which were hosted by full member groups and had voting rights at the Secretariats' Committee meetings. The female and male Secretary General and the Information Secretary (the coordinator of the Information Secretariat and, since, 1989, a paid staff person) also had a seat on the Committee, but did not have voting rights. The Committee was made responsible for executing the policies and managing the business of the ILGA between Annual Conferences.

Another important constitutional change was the formal recognition of regional ILGA conferences, which already existed for Asia, Europe and Eastern and Southeastern Europe. These conferences were given a large degree of autonomy to set their own procedures, decide on actions in their region and make proposals to the Annual Conference. The drive towards regionalisation became a priority for the organization at the 1991 Annual Conference which was held in Acapulco. Although, following tumultuous events in Mexico, the conference was cancelled and then resurrected in a different location at two weeks' notice, and therefore did not have the full status of an ordinary Annual Conference, it proved to be an event of singular importance to the future of the ILGA. It was the first Annual Conference where representatives from the South outnumbered delegates from the Northern hemisphere. This brought out into the open the distortion of the power balance which existed in the organization. All its management bodies and most of its projects were controlled by Northern organizations and individuals. It became abundantly clear that, were the ILGA to live up to its ambition of being a worldwide federation, the structures would have to change.

After extensive consultation, the 1993 Annual Conference passed further constitutional changes, which built in part on the 1990 amendments, but in other respects potentially changed the very nature of the organization. The change was twofold, aimed at increasing regionalisation and centralisation, and has major consequences for the future operation of the organization.

First, to increase regionalisation, the conference created six new regional secretariats which would be responsible for coordinating supranational activities (protests, projects, networking, etc) in their part of the world and for contacts with the central ILGA bodies. The regional secretariats would have voting status on the Secretariats' Committee. The philosophy behind this was to improve the representativity of the ILGA and to ensure a wide geographical presence at the management level, thus empowering the currently underrepresented regions. Furthermore the change was intended to allow for more intense networking between its members, to heighten its impact on the regional level and to increase the organization's presence throughout the world. In order to allow for thorough discussion and preparation of this vital change, the conference decided to establish a regionalisation working party, with members from Africa, Asia-Pacific, Latin and North America and Europe.

This body is responsible for proposing ways of implementing the constitutional change in a manner which ensures full empowerment of all the regions. The regionalised structure will only come into effect after a report by the working party has been considered by the 1994 Annual Conference. Once this regional structure has come into effect the Backup Secretariats will be abolished.

Second, a more centralised structure was created. Until this moment, the ILGA did not have a central office, although the Information Secretariat had for many years de facto fulfilled that function. In 1993 the Information Secretariat was abolished and replaced by a central Administrative Office. This is responsible for co-ordinating information management, membership administration and Secretariats' Committee business and for preparing the programme of the Annual Conference. The activities of the office are co-ordinated by an employed Co-ordinator. Both the office and the co-ordinator are appointed by the Secretariats' Committee, whereas before the Information Secretariat was elected by the conference and the Information Secretary was appointed by the Information Secretariat. Thus the ILGA's main administrative entity was depoliticised and charged with clearly defined tasks and responsibilities. This new structure ensures that the elected Secretariats' Committee can be held accountable for its policies at the Annual Conference without a possible vote of no confidence having the disastrous effect of destroying all administrative continuity.

These constitutional changes came into effect immediately following the Annual Conference in Barcelona. The constitutional position of the Secretaries General remained unchanged. These moves have brought the ILGA more into line with conventional NGO structures and should allow for more effective internal and external communication.

Activities

In 1988 the ILGA's main activities were subdivided by Holtmaat and Pistor into three areas: conferences, actions and projects, and information exchange through the *Bulletin*, the *Pink Book* and information pools (topical and regional).[3] Much of this formal subdivision remains valid. However, the contents have over the past five years changed substantially.

Conferences

Since its inception the ILGA has held 15 Annual Conferences. Three of these have been held outside Europe (Washington DC 1982, Toronto 1985, Acapulco 1991). The 1994 Annual Conference will be held in New York and the 1995 Annual Conference will be held in Rio de Janeiro. These conferences remain the ILGA's supreme decision making body and are still to a large extent run in the same way as described by Holtmaat and Pistor, but efforts have been made towards a more structured, inclusive and accessible format.[4] In 1993 for the first time the programme was subdivided into thematic tracks, and panel discussions were held on the situation in the different regions which are present in the ILGA. In 1994 for the first time the Annual Conference will be preceded by three pre-conference institutes, for disabled people, people of color and women.

There are also a number of regional conferences. To date six Asian Regional Conferences, six Eastern and Southeastern European Regional Conferences, one Latin American Regional Conference and sixteen European Regional Conferences have taken place. These conferences are self-organizing and have considerable power over business pertaining to their region (see supra). Following the most recent constitutional changes the regional conferences are also responsible for electing their regional secretariat and have the power to create other regional bodies as they see fit. There are currently plans for further conferences in all the aforementioned regions. There are no plans for a North American or an African regional conference.

Actions

Through its Action Secretariat, the ILGA has for more than a decade initiated a very large number of protests against the often vicious oppression with which lesbians and gays are confronted. The basic precondition for initiating an action is a request from an ILGA member group based in the country with which the action is concerned. This basic rule ensures that actions are called with the support of the local movements and cannot be perceived as an "imperialist" act from a foreign entity.

As the ILGA on average calls for three or four new actions per month, it is impossible to give a full list here. However, its actions are mainly concerned with direct violations of basic human rights and cover a wide range of specific cases. Many of these ad hoc actions have in the past led to positive changes, e.g. the deletion on January 1, 1993, by the World Health Organization of homosexuality from its codex of illnesses. ILGA actions are coordinated by the Action Secretariat, which has been held by the San Francisco-based International Gay and Lesbian Human Rights Commission for the last two years. Actions are publicised as joint ILGA-IGLHRC initiatives, and are distributed through the ILGA Bulletin, the IGLHRC Emergency Response Network, press releases and computer bulletin boards. This joint effort has ensured that ILGA actions are researched and co-ordinated in a professional way.

Projects

Over the last five years, the ILGA has established a number of long-term projects which have led to significant results. In the following paragraphs I will briefly describe the work of three such projects; the United Nations Working Party, the Amnesty International Project and the AIDS Working Party. There are, however, more ILGA projects than the ones discussed below. Some of these have also led to significant improvements in the situation of lesbians and gay men (e.g. the Europe Working Party, which focuses on the Council of Europe, the Conference on Security and Co-operation in Europe, and the European Union).

The United Nations Working Party was set up in 1988 in New York, and now functions in the three cities where the UN has offices; New York, Geneva, and Vienna. Through the Working Party's efforts the ILGA succeeded in 1993 in obtaining Non-Governmental status with the United Nations' Economic and Social Council. This was an historic achievement as the ILGA was the first ever lesbian and gay organization to obtain such recognition in an international forum, and as it happened despite harsh opposition from a number of member states. ILGA's Roster Status, the most limited form of NGO status, allows it to bring written presentations to the attention of ECOSOC meetings and ECOSOC subgroups such as the Human Rights Commission in Geneva. In order to be able to make oral presentations during ECOSOC meetings, the ILGA has formed alliances with NGOs which have speaking rights. Prior to obtaining the NGO status, the ILGA had already become involved in UN work. It had made presentations at the 1992 and 1993 sessions of the Human Rights Commission in Geneva, participated in the regional preparatory meetings for the UN World Conference on Human Rights in Vienna in June 1993, and participated in the conference itself. The documents and presentations it brought to that meeting were widely seen as being of high quality. The ILGA participation in the World Conference meant that for the first time the human rights of lesbians and gay men were discussed widely in the international human rights community. In preparation of the 1995 UN World Conference for Women, a project has been initiated in 1993 to ensure visible lesbian participation.

The ILGA Amnesty International Project was active throughout the eighties, was then coordinated from Stockholm, and is now based in New York. It was the driving force behind a worldwide campaign, which actively involved many ILGA members from the South and the North, designed to convince Amnesty of the need to widen its mandate to include, as eligible for recognition as prisoners of conscience, people detained because of their sexual orientation. After much internal debate and external pressure, in 1991 Amnesty International changed its mandate at a meeting in Yokohama. Through a Japanese ILGA member, OCCUR, the ILGA ensured a visible presence at the AI meeting. Since the change, the AI Project has continued to lobby AI to ensure that good guidelines for national sections would be developed, and to bring AIs attention to cases which were considered to be of interest to that organization's work. As a result, AI has adopted a number of gay men as prisoners of conscience and has repeatedly spoken out against discrimination of lesbians and gay men.

The ILGA AIDS Working Party was set up to defend the rights of people with HIV, and to ensure attention for the needs of gay men and lesbians with HIV and AIDS. The working party is composed of groups from Africa, Asia, Latin and North America and Europe. As a result of its activities, the ILGA now holds observer status with the World Health Organization's Global Programme on AIDS. It has organized a number of conferences in collaboration with the WHO, and participates in a large number of international non-governmental AIDS initiatives and conferences. For example, in early 1994 the ILGA cosponsored a European consultation on collaboration between lesbian and gay community organizations and governmental or statutory agencies convened by the UK Health Education Authority. Furthermore ad hoc actions against HIV/AIDS related human rights violations are undertaken through the Action Secretariat.

Information Exchange

From the beginning of the ILGA, information exchange has been one of the most important aspects of its work and an information Secretariat was established at the founding meeting. In 1990 this secretariat moved to Brussels, where it was hosted by the Federatie Werkgroepen Homoseksualiteit and Tels Quels/Antenne Rose. Due to the increasing demands made upon the organization, the ILGA had in 1989 started employing the then-Information Secretary, David Murphy, for one day per week. When the secretariat moved to Brussels I took over the post, which was then expanded to twenty hours per week. In 1993 the Information Secretariat was replaced by a central Administrative Office, which has absorbed its functions into a wider range of service activities.

The *ILGA Bulletin*, published five times per year, was made more attractive and accessible by improvements to the layout and enhanced editing. The ILGA also aimed to increase its public profile by publishing more press releases on its actions and projects. This resulted in increased journalistic interest and over the last few years the organization has become a resource for many working both in the lesbian and gay and in the mainstream media.

Another product of ILGA's attention to information sharing is the *Pink Book*. A new edition was published in 1993 by Prometheus Books in the USA. The *Third Pink Book* contains a large selection of background articles about the situation around the world, and an updated country-by-country survey of the legal and social position of lesbians and gay men. As the book is only published every five years, plans exist to make an updated survey available every year in the form of a brochure. The first update should be available by mid-1994.

Conclusion

The International Lesbian and Gay Association has changed significantly over the last five years. It has widened its membership base outside Europe, although in this respect much work remains to be done to ensure full and equal participation from the South. At this moment, the Female Secretary General is Rebeca Sevilla, a Peruvian lesbian. The Women's Backup Secretariat is hosted by CLA of Chile and the Action Backup Secretariat is hosted by GLOW of South Africa. The other elected posts remain within North America and Europe, and therefore the power imbalance remains—even though it was reduced at the elections held during the 1993 Annual Conference in Barcelona. It is likely that the regionalisation plan as approved by the 1993 Annual Conference will soon lead to increased presence of groups from the South in ILGAs management and, thus, to greater representation of Southern groups and issues in the international organization as a whole.

The position of women in the organization has improved considerably. In general, participation of women in conferences stands around forty per cent—in one case, at the 1993 Regional Conference for Eastern and Southeastern Europe, gender parity was attained. Conferences are run by a Chairing Pool which has gender parity. Women have autonomy to make decisions on issues specifically relevant to women. Many ILGA projects and secretariats are led by women and their share in the leadership of the organization continues to increase.

ILGA projects and actions have been instrumental in improving the situation for lesbians and gay men around the world. Significant progress has been made towards the recognition of the rights of lesbians and gay men as human rights. The entry into the UN is an illustration of this progress. A further sign was the fact that several governments mentioned these rights in official statements made at the 1993 UN World Conference on Human Rights However, this increased visibility has also led to attacks on both the ILGA and the rights it defends. At the grassroots level, one can point towards the strong emergence of lesbian and gay groups in most countries of Eastern and Central Europe as a direct result of a very significant effort by the ILGA, sustained throughout the eighties and to this date, to encourage and support—both morally, logistically and materially—the development of a lesbian and gay movement in that part of the world.

An enormous problem for the ILGA remains its lack of funding. The organization operates on a minimal yearly budget of less than a hundred thousand US dollars and finds it difficult to raise funds. Because of this permanent financial crisis situation, its scope for action is limited and it can only afford to employ one part-time staff member, the coordinator of its central administrative office. It is therefore a huge challenge for the ILGA to dramatically increase its funding. This will be the key to its future success, both internally and externally. If regionalisation is to be achieved and power is to be shared more effectively, and if ILGA's campaigning efforts are to be increased, a large amount of money will have to be made available. In this respect it is a minor miracle that the organization, which started as a loose network merely fifteen years ago, has achieved so much over the last years.

1. Herman Holtmaat and Rob Pistor, *Ten Years of International Gay and Lesbian Solidarity: Ten Years of ILGA, in Second ILGA Pink Book. A Global View of Lesbian and Gay Liberation and Oppression, pp. 33–45, Utrecht, Interfacultaire Werkgroep Homostudies, Rijksuniversiteit Utrecht, 1988.*

2. *Op. cit., p. 37.*

3. *id., p. 35.*

4. *ibid., pp. 35–36*

STONEWALL 25

In the twenty-five years since the Stonewall riots, the movements of lesbians and gays for justice, civil rights, and social transformation have changed the map of politics around the world. In 1994 ILGA was on the verge of recognition as a non-governmental organization by the United Nations, until the United States objected. Violence against gays and lesbians (both individual and state-sponsored) is now recognized as an international human rights problem by Amnesty International, and oppression based on sexual orientation is becoming recognized as a basis for asylum in some countries. As part of the celebrations of Stonewall's twenty-fifth anniversary, the following charge was given to the United Nations. We find it a fitting close to a book that continues to be written in the streets, in the legislatures, in print and broadcast media, and in the hearts and minds of people around the world.

STATEMENT FROM THE INTERNATIONAL MARCH ON THE UNITED NATIONS TO AFFIRM THE HUMAN RIGHTS OF LESBIAN AND GAY PEOPLE

(1994)

Stonewall 25

We call upon the United Nations, its agencies, its member states and its affiliated non-governmental organizations to take all necessary action to assure that:

1. The promises of the Universal Declaration of Human Rights not be denied to lesbian, gay and bisexual people;

2. The rights and freedoms of the Universal Declaration of Human Rights be fulfilled to all people, including lesbian, gay and bisexual people, without distinction of any kind, such as race, gender, sexual orientation, religion, ethnicity, language, age, disability, socio-economic status and national or social origin;

3. The agencies of the United Nations and non-governmental organizations affiliated with the UN undertake to report on violations of the Universal Declaration of Human Rights affecting lesbian, gay and bisexual people;

4. The promises of the Universal Declaration of Human Rights not be denied to people who have AIDS or are HIV positive;

5. The promises of the Universal Declaration of Human Rights with regard to the right to health care not be denied to people with HIV/AIDS, not to lesbian, gay and bisexual people who desire to engage in reproduction;

6. The global effort to combat HIV/AIDS be intensified;

7. The Member States of the United Nations adopt a protocol to the Convention on the Prevention and Punishment of the Crime of Genocide to define as a crime of genocide the intended destruction of any of the targets of the Holocaust, including lesbian, gay, and bisexual people, and the intentional destruction of any population group based on that group's race, gender, sexual orientation, religion, ethnici-

ty, language, age, disability, socio-economic status and national or social origin;

8. The agencies of the UN not deny non-governmental organizations recognition or consultative status on the basis of their support for lesbian, gay and bisexual people, or people who have AIDS or are HIV positive;

9. The General Assembly of the UN proclaim an International Year of Lesbian and Gay People (possibly 1999);

10. The UN and its agencies not discriminate against lesbian, gay and bisexual people in matters of contracting, hiring, employment conditions and termination;

11. The member states increase the funding of the human rights agencies of the UN to accelerate the progress toward realizing the promises of the Universal Declaration of Human Rights;

12. The right of lesbian, gay and bisexual people to create families be recognized and protected, and that our family relationships with each other and our children be celebrated in 1994, The International Year of the Family.

We call upon the United Nations and the people of the world to join us in affirming the dignity and legitimacy of lesbian, gay and bisexual people as participants in the rich mosaic that constitutes the diversity of the human family.

COPYRIGHT INFORMATION

PART I: Baron de Montesquieu, *The Spirit of the Laws*. Reprinted with the permission of Hafner Press, an imprint of Macmillan Publishing Company, from *The Spirit of the Laws* by Baron de Montesquieu, translated by Thomas Nugent. Copyright 1949 by Macmillan Publishing Company. ¶ Cesare Beccaria, *On Crimes and Punishments*, trans. David Young, 1986, Hackett Publishing Company, Inc., all rights reserved. ¶ Marquis de Sade, *Philosophy in the Bedroom*, copyright 1965 by Richard Seaver and Austryn Wainhouse, used by permission of Grove/Atlantic, Inc. PART II: Karl Heinrich Ulrichs, "Critische Pfeile/Critical Arrow," trans. Hubert Kennedy pp. 196-98 in his *Ulrichs: The Life and Work of Karl Heinrigh Ulrichs*, Alyson Publications, 1988. Reprinted by permission of the author and publisher. ¶ Karoly Maria Benkert, "Open Letter to the Prussian Minister of Justice" translated by Michael Lombardi-Nash. Copyright by Urania Manuscripts, 1982, reprinted by permission. ¶ Anna Rueling "What Interest Does the Women's Movement have in the Homosexual Question?" originally published in *Lesbians in Germany: 1890s-1920s*, ed. Lillian Faderman and Brigitte Eriksson, Niaid Press 1990. Reprinted by permission of the publisher. ¶ Benedict Friedlander, "Memoir for the Friends and Contributors of the Scientific Humanitarian Committee in the Name of the Secession of the Scientific Humanitarian Committee" and "Seven Propositions," Adolf Brand, "What We Want" from *Homosexuality & Male Bonding in Pre-Nazi Germany* trans. Harry Oosterhuis and Hubert Kennedy. Copyright by the Haworth Press, Inc. All rights reserved. Reprinted with permission. ¶ Natalie Barney, "Predestined for Free Choice." Originally published in Natalie Barney, *A Perilous Advantage*, ed. and trans. Anna Livia, New Victoria Press, 1992, used with permission. ¶ V.V. Rosanov "People of the Moonlight." Originally published in *Four Faces of Rosanov*, Philosophical Library, 1978, used with permission. ¶ Robert Duncan, "The Homosexual in Society," originally published in *Politics* in August 1944. Reprinted with permission of the estate of Robert Duncan. ¶ James Baldwin, "Preservation of Innocence," was originally published in *Zero*. Summer, 1949, Vol. 1., No. 2, Tangiers, Morocco. Reprinted here by permission of the James A. Baldwin estate. PART III: Donald Webster Cory, *The Homosexual in America*. ¶ Selections from *Mattachine Review* reprinted with permission from Ayer Co. Publishers. ¶ Selections from *ONE Magazine* reprinted with permission of W. Dorr Legg, ONE, Inc. ¶ Selections from *The Ladder* reprinted with permission of Barbara Grier, Naiad Press. Frank Kameny, Chapter 10. ¶ Pg., 129-145 "Gay is Good" as found in *The Same Sex* ed. Ralph W. Weltge, copyright 1969 The Pilgrim Press. PART IV: Carl Wittman's "A Gay Manifesto," Martha Shelley's "Gay is Good," "Letter from the Cuban Gay People to the North American Gay Liberation Movement," "Responses, Gay Revolutionary Party and Gay Committee of Returned Brigandists" are reprinted from *Out of the Closets: Voices of Gay Liberation*, edited by Karla Jay and Allen Young. 1972; rpt. 1992 New York University Press. Copyright 1972 by Carl Wittman; Martha Shelley copyright 1970 by *Rat*. Reprinted by permission of Karla Jay and Allen Young. ¶ Red Butterfly pamphlet reprinted by permission of John Lauritsen for Red Butterfly Collective. ¶ Huey Newton's "Letter to the Revolutionary Brothers & Sisters" reprinted from Donn Teal, *The Gay Militants*, 1971; rpt. 1995 St. Martin's Press. Reprinted by permission of Donn Teal. ¶ "Venceremos Brigade Policy on Gay Recruitment" originally published in *Gays Under the Cuba Revolution* by Allen Young. Reprinted by permission of Allen Young. ¶ Guy Hocquenghem, "Capitalism, the Family, and the Anus" originally appeared as chapter 4 of *Homosexual Desire* trans. Daniella Dongoor. Copyright Alyson & Busby, London, 1978. Reprinted with permission of the estate of Guy Hocquenghem. ¶ Charlotte Bunch, "Lesbians in Revolt" is reprinted by permission of the author. ¶ "Lesbianism and Feminism: Synonyms or Contradictions?" from *Going Too Far: The Personal Chronicle of a Feminist* by Robin Morgan. Copyright 1968, 1970, 1973, 1975, 1977 by Robin Morgan. By permission of Edite Kroll Literary Agency. ¶ Mario Mieli, "The Gay Revolutionary Project," pp. 114-121 of *Homosexuality and Liberation: Elements of a Gay Critique*, trans. David Fernbach, copyright 1980 Gay Men's Press London. Reprinted with permission of David Fernbach. ¶ "The Anita Bryant Brigade," "The Gay Movement: From Radicalism to Reformism," from *About Time: Exploring the Gay Past*, revised Ed. by Martin Duberman. Copyright 1991 by Martin Duberman. Used by permission of Dutton Signet, a division of Penguin Books USA Inc. ¶ Harvey Milk's "The Hope Speech" was originally published in Randy Shilts, *The Mayor of Castro Street: The Life and Times of Harvey Milk*, St. Martin's Press, 1982. Reprinted by permission of the publisher. ¶ "Questions for Michel Foucault" excerpts an interview conducted by Mattias Duyves and originally published in *Interviews met Michel Foucault*, Boskoop/Utrecht 1982. Reprinted with the permission of Mattias Duyves and the publisher. ¶ "The Case for Abolishing the Age of Consent Laws" was first published in *NAMBLA News* 4 (December 1980), reprinted by permission of the Steering Committee of NAMBLA. ¶ OIKABETH's "Message from Mexico: Questions for Cuba," trans. David Morris, first published in *Gay Community News*, July 26, 1980. Reprinted by permission of *Gay Community News*. ¶ Irena Klepfisz, "Anti-Semitism in the Lesbian/Feminist Movement" from *Nice Jewish Girls: A Lesbian Anthology* by Evelyn T. Beck. Copyright ©1982, 1989 by Evelyn Torton Beck. Reprinted by permission of Beacon Press. ¶ Michael Denneny, "Sixteen Propositions," reprinted by permission of the author. ¶ Marilyn Frye, "Lesbian Feminism and the Gay Rights Movement" from *The Politics of Reality*, The Crossing Press 1983. Reprinted by permission of the publisher. ¶ John Preston, "Goodbye to Sally Gearhart" reprinted by permission of the author. ¶ Pat Califa, "Feminism and Sadomasochism" first appeared in *Heresies* 12 (1980). Reprinted by permission of the author. ¶ Dennis Altman, "Sex: The New Front Line for Gay Politics" was originally published in *Socialist Review* 65 (1982). Reprinted by permission of the author. ¶ Sara Lucia Hoagland, "Sadism, Masochism, and Lesbian-Feminism" first appeared in *Against Sadomasochism*, ed. Darlene Pagano et al. Reprinted by permission of the author. ¶ Joan Nestle, "The Fem Question" was first published in *Pleasure and Danger*, ed. Carole Vance, Routledge, copyright 1992 Joan Nestle. ¶ Vickie

Mays, "I Hear Voices but See No Faces," Joe DeMarco, "Gay Racism" originally appeared in *Black Men, White Men* ed. Michael J. Smith, copyright Gay Sunshine Press. Reprinted by permission of the author and publisher. ¶ "I Am Your Sister: Black Women Organizing Across Sexualities" from *A Burst of Light* by Audre Lorde, Firebrand Books, Ithaca, New York. Copyright ©1988 by Audre Lorde. Reprinted by permission of the publisher. ¶ "Bridge, Drawbridge, Sandbar or Island" first appeared in *Bridges of Power* by Gloria Anzaldua, New Society Publishers. Reprinted by permission of the publisher. **PART V:** Michael Callen and Richard Berkowitz (with Richard Dworkin), "We Know Who We Are," *New York Native* 50 (November 8-21, 1982) reprinted with permission of Richard Berkowitz and the Michael Callen estate. ¶ Michael Callen and Richard Berkowitz, *How to Have Sex in an Epidemic*," News From the Front Publications, 1983, reprinted with permission of Richard Berkowitz and the Michael Callen estate. ¶ Lawrence Mass, "Blood and Politics," *New York Native* (February 14-20, 1983), reprinted with permission of the author. ¶ Larry Kramer, "1,112 and Counting," "An Open Letter to Richard Dunne and Gay Men's Health Crisis," and "The Beginning of ACTing-UP," from *Reports from the Holocaust: The Making of an AIDS Activist*, St. Martin's Press, 1989. Copyright 1983 and 1987 by Larry Kramer, reprinted by permission. ¶ Peg Byron, "AIDS and the Gay Men's Health Crisis of New York," *Gay Community News* (August 6, 1983), reprinted by permission of the author. ¶ Martin Delaney, "Staying Alive: Making the Ultimate Political Statement," *The Advocate* (February 28, 1989), reprinted by permission of the author. ¶ "Respectable, We Ain't Never Gonna be Respectable" and "8 Principles of Power," *Positively Healthy News* No. 1, January 1989, reprinted by permission of Wayne Moore, Chair. ¶ Maxine Wolfe, "AIDS and Politics: Transformation of Our Movement," reprinted by permission of the author. ¶ Mark Harrington, "Let My People In," *Outweek* (August 8, 1990), reprinted by permission of the author. ¶ Donna Minkowitz, "ACT-UP at a Crossroads," *The Village Voice* (June 5, 1990), reprinted by permission of the author and *The Village Voice*. ¶ Eric Rofes, "Gay Lib vs. AIDS: Averting Civil War," *Outlook* No. 8 (Spring 1990), reprinted by permission of the author. ¶ Daniel Defert, "The Homosexualization of AIDS," originally published in *Gai-Pied Hebdo*, No., 446 (November 29, 1990), revised and reprinted by permission of the author. ¶ "The Charter" and "Editorial: Think it Over," *Bombay Dost*, reprinted by permission of the editor. ¶ Julian Jayaseelan, "Seven Days and Five Nights" originally published in *Gaya Keris: The Voice of Our Community*, 1993, reprinted by permission of the author and Pink Triangle Malaysia. ¶ Amber Hollibaugh, "Lesbian Leadership and Lesbian Denial in the AIDS Epidemic," Lesbian AIDS Project of Gay Men's Health Crisis, reprinted by permission of the author. ¶ "It's Time to Re-Evaluate the HIV-AIDS Hypothesis," *Rethinking AIDS*, Vol. 1, No. 1 (June 1992), reprinted by permission of the publisher. ¶ John Lauritsen, *The AIDS War*, Askleios/Pagan Press, 1993, reprinted by permission of the author. ¶ Charles Ortleb, "Why AIDS is really AIDSGate," reprinted by permission of the author. ¶ Jeffrey Schmalz, "Whatever Happened to AIDS?" *The New York Times Magazine* (November 28, 1993), copyright 1993 by the New York Times company. Reprinted by permission. ¶ Herbert Daniel, "Above All, Life," originally published in Richard Parker and Herbert Daniel, eds., *Sexuality, Politics and AIDS in Brazil*, Falmer Press, Taylor & Francis: London, 1993, reprinted by permission of the estate of Herbert Daniel and Falmer Press. ¶ Robert E. Penn, "Spirituality and HIV: Reality and Healing," by permission of the author. **PART VI:** "Out of the Clause and Into the Workhouse" originally appeared as pp. 9-42 of *Policing the Bedroom*, Crossroads Books. Reprinted by permission of Wages Due Lesbians. ¶ *After the Ball* by Marshall Kirk and Hunter Madsen, pp. 161-190, from *After the Ball* by Marshall Kirk and Hunter Madsen. Copyright 1989 by Marshall Kirk and Hunter Madsen Used by permission of Doubleday, a division of Bantam Doubleday Dell Publishing Group, Inc. ¶ Tom Stoddard, "Why Gay People Should Seek the Right to Marry" first appeared in *Out/Look* (1989). Reprinted by permission of the author. ¶ "Out of South Africa: Interview with Simon Nkoli" originally appeared in *Outweek*, Sept. 24, 1989. Reprinted by permission of Mark Chesnut. ¶ Randy Shilts, "Is Outing Gays Ethical?" originally appeared in the *New York Times*. ¶ Michelangelo Signorile's "Correcting Journalism's Double Standard" originally appeared in a different form as "Who Should Open the Closet Door?" in the *Washington Times*, March 15, 1992. Reprinted by permission of the author. ¶ Marvin Liebman's letter to William F. Buckley was originally published as an appendix to *Coming Out Conservative*, Chronicle Books, 1990. Reprinted by permission of Marvin Liebman. ¶ "Wimmin- and Lesbian-Only Spaces: Thought into Action" from *Call Me Lesbian*, copyright 1992 by Julia Penelope, publisher: The Crossing Press. ¶ Craig G. Harris, "Celebrating African-American Lesbian and Gay History, Finding Our Way to the Future" reprinted by permission of Thelma M. Harris. ¶ Carla Trujillo, "Chicana Lesbians: Fear and Loathing in the Chicano Community" was originally published in *Chicana Lesbians: The Girls Our Mothers Warned Us About*, ed. Carla Trujillo, Third Woman Press. Reprinted by permission of the author. ¶ Urvashi Vaid, "Let's Put Our Own House In Order" first appeared in *Out/look* 14 (1991). Reprinted by permission of the author. ¶ Lisa Orlando, "Loving Whom We Choose" was originally published in *Bi any Other Name: Bisexual People Speak Out* ed. Loraine Hutchins and Lani Kaahumanu, Alyson Publications. Reprinted by permission of the author. ¶ Arnie Kantrowitz, "Letter to the Queer Generation" was originally published in *NYO*. Reprinted by permission of the author. ¶ Juan Mendez, "SM = DV" originally published in *Newslink: GMSMA Newsletter* (Spring 1994). Reprinted by permission of the author. ¶ Christina Schenk, "Lesbians and Their Emancipation in the former GDR" originally appeared in *Gender Politics and Post-Communism*. Reprinted by permission of the author. ¶ Jomar Fleras, "Reclaiming Our Historic Rights: Gays and Lesbians in the Philippines" originally published in *The Third Pink Book: A Global View of Lesbian and Gay Liberation and Oppression* ed. Aart Kendriks, Rob Tielman, and Evert van der Veen, copyright Prometheus Press. Reprinted by permission of the publisher. ¶ Micha Ramakers, "The International Lesbian and Gay Association" was written for this volume.